Visit class...om and get connected

Online resources for students and parents

ClassZone resources provide instruction, practice, and learning support.

eEdition Plus ONLINE

This interactive version of the text encourages students to explore algebra.

Interactive Review Games

Engaging games help students review vocabulary and key concepts.

Problems and Quizzes

Self-scoring questions offer comprehension checks and test practice.

More Help

Extra examples, practice, and keystroke tips provide at-home support.

State Test Practice

Online practice prepares students for success on state tests.

Now it all clicks!™

CLASSZONE.COM

McDougal Littell

ALGEBRA 1

Ron Larson
Laurie Boswell
Timothy D. Kanold
Lee Stiff

McDougal Littell
A HOUGHTON MIFFLIN COMPANY
Evanston, Illinois • Boston • Dallas

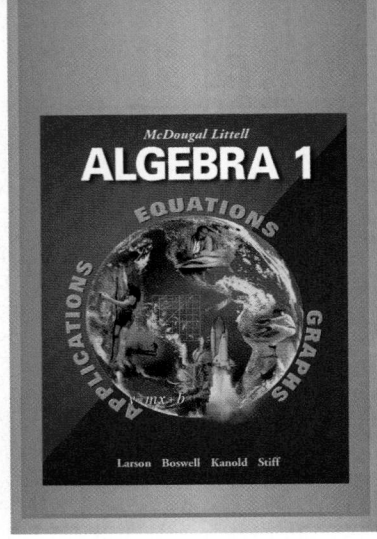

About the Cover

Algebra 1 brings math to life with many real-life applications. The cover illustrates some of the applications used in this book. Examples of mathematics in baseball, space exploration, mountain climbing, and graphic design are shown on pages 8, 66, 158, 175, 184, 304, 318, 501, and 695. Circling the globe are three key aspects of Algebra 1—the *equations, graphs,* and *applications* that you will use in this course will help you understand how mathematics relates to the world. As you explore the applications presented in the book, try to make connections between mathematics and the world around you!

ISBN: 0-618-25018-2   89–DWO–07 06

Internet Web Site: http://www.classzone.com

About the Authors

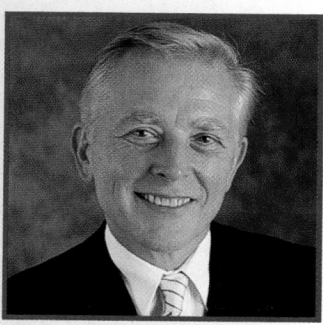

▶ **Ron Larson** is a professor of mathematics at Penn State University at Erie. He is the author of a broad range of mathematics textbooks for middle school, high school, and college students. He is one of the pioneers in the use of multimedia and the Internet to enhance the learning of mathematics. Dr. Larson is a member of the National Council of Teachers of Mathematics and is a frequent speaker at NCTM and other national and regional mathematics meetings.

▶ **Laurie Boswell** is a mathematics teacher at Profile Junior-Senior High School in Bethlehem, New Hampshire. She is active in NCTM and local mathematics organizations. A recipient of the 1986 Presidential Award for Excellence in Mathematics Teaching, she is also the 1992 Tandy Technology Scholar and the 1991 recipient of the Richard Balomenos Mathematics Education Service Award presented by the New Hampshire Association of Teachers of Mathematics.

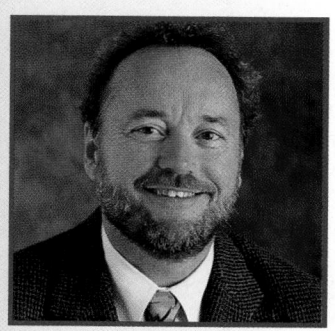

▶ **Timothy D. Kanold** is Director of Mathematics and a teacher at Adlai E. Stevenson High School in Lincolnshire, IL. In 1995 he received the Award of Excellence from the Illinois State Board of Education for outstanding contributions to education. He served on NCTM's Professional Standards for Teaching Mathematics Commission. A 1986 recipient of the Presidential Award for Excellence in Mathematics Teaching, he served as president of the Council of Presidential Awardees of Mathematics.

▶ **Lee Stiff** is a professor of mathematics education in the College of Education and Psychology of North Carolina State University at Raleigh and has taught mathematics at the high school and middle school levels. He served on the NCTM Board of Directors and was elected President of NCTM for the years 2000–2002. He is the 1992 recipient of the W. W. Rankin Award for Excellence in Mathematics Education presented by the North Carolina Council of Teachers of Mathematics.

▶ REVIEWERS

Kay S. Cassidy
Mathematics Facilitator
Cactus High School
Glendale, AZ

José Castro
Mathematics Teacher
Liberty High School
Bakersfield, CA

Tammy Parker Davis
Mathematics Teacher
Valdosta High School
Valdosta, GA

Edna Horton Flores
Mathematics Department Chair
Kenwood Academy
Chicago, IL

Doyt M. Jones
Mathematics Department Head
John Bartram High School
Philadelphia, PA

Warren Zarrell
Mathematics Department Chair
James Monroe High School
North Hills, CA

▶ CALIFORNIA TEACHER PANEL

Courteney Dawe
Mathematics Teacher
Placerita Junior High School
Valencia, CA

Dave Dempster
Mathematics Teacher
Temecula Valley High School
Temecula, CA

Pauline Embree
Mathematics Department Chair
Rancho San Joaquin Middle School
Irvine, CA

Tom Griffith
Mathematics Teacher
Scripps Ranch High School
San Diego, CA

Diego Gutierrez
Mathematics Teacher
Crawford High School
San Diego, CA

Roger Hitchcock
Mathematics Teacher
Buchanan High School
Clovis, CA

Joseph Jacobs
Mathematics Teacher
Luther Burbank High School
Sacramento, CA

Louise McComas
Mathematics Teacher
Fremont High School
Sunnyvale, CA

Viola Okoro
Mathematics Teacher
Laguna Creek High School
Elk Grove, CA

Jon Simon
Mathematics Department Chair
Casa Grande High School
Petaluma, CA

▶ CLEVELAND TEACHER PANEL

Laura Anfang
University Supervisor, Teacher of
    Secondary Math Methods
John Carroll University
University Heights, OH

Patricia Benedict
Mathematics Department Liaison
Cleveland Heights High School
Cleveland Heights, OH

Carol Caroff
Mathematics Department
    Chair/Teacher
Solon High School
Solon, OH

Fred Dillon
Mathematics Teacher
Strongsville High School
Strongsville, OH

Bill Hunt
Past President, Ohio Council
    of Teachers of Mathematics
Strongsville, OH

Dr. Margie Raub Hunt
Executive Director, Ohio Council
    of Teachers of Mathematics
Strongsville, OH

Robert Jones
Mathematics Supervisor (K–12)
Cleveland City School District
Cleveland, OH

Andrea Kopco
Mathematics Teacher
Midpark High School
Cleveland, OH

Sandy Sikorski
Mathematics Teacher
Berea High School
Berea, OH

Gil Stevens
Mathematics Teacher
Brunswick High School
Brunswick, OH

▶ KANSAS TEACHER PANEL

Rosemary Arb
Mathematics Department Chair
North Kansas City High School
Kansas City, MO

Jerry Belshe
Mathematics Teacher
Indian Woods Middle School
Overland Park, KS

Carol Edwards
Mathematics Teacher
Belton High School
Belton, MO

Robert Franks
Mathematics Teacher
Park Hill High School
Kansas City, MO

Cynthia Hardy
Mathematics Teacher
Oxford Middle School
Overland Park, KS

Julie Knittle
Secondary Mathematics Resource Specialist
Shawnee Mission District Office
Shawnee Mission, KS

Glenda Morrison
Mathematics Teacher
Central High School
Kansas City, MO

Mitch Shea
Mathematics Teacher
Leavenworth High School
Leavenworth, KS

Ginny Taylor
Mathematics Department Chair
Santa Fe Trail Junior High School
Olathe, KS

▶ STUDENT REVIEW PANEL

Luke Aguirre
Lincoln Middle School
Illinois

R-Jay Albano
James Lick High School
California

Fred Anthony III
Longfellow Junior High School
Michigan

Curtis Antoine
Springfield Central High School
Massachusetts

Yuri Awanohara
Tilden Middle School
Maryland

Gill Beck
Milton High School
Georgia

Kevin Berghamer
John W. North High School
California

Jared W. Billings
Meadow Park Middle School
Oregon

James Bottigliero
Jonathan Law High School
Connecticut

Lindsay Chapman
Strongsville High School
Ohio

Alison Davis
Hinsdale Middle School
Illinois

Emily Dougherty
Huron High School
Michigan

Roxanne Ilano
Gahr High School
California

Brad Larsen
Thomas Jefferson Junior High School
Utah

Wendy Mathis
Carlsbad High School
New Mexico

Agnes Mazurek
Streamwood High School
Illinois

Calvin Medious
Jim Hill High School
Mississippi

Megan Ann Merrifield
Douglas County Comprehensive High School
Georgia

Julie Nguyen
Lincoln High School
California

Omar Ramos
University High School
New Jersey

Natalie Rock
Les Bois Junior High School
Idaho

Elizabeth Sabol
Park Forest Middle School
Pennsylvania

Divino S. San Pedro, Jr.
Laguna Creek High School
California

Kristen Sands
Taunton High School
Massachusetts

Chris Sarabia
Buchanan High School
California

Jonathan Tin
Woodinville High School
Washington

Virginia Thao Tran
Fountain Valley High School
California

Jenny Waxler
Parkway North High School
Missouri

Amy E. Williams
Brookhaven High School
Ohio

Stephanie Williams
Cholla High Magnet School
Arizona

Connections to Algebra

CHAPTER
2

Properties of Real Numbers

CHAPTER 3

Solving Linear Equations

Graphing Linear Equations and Functions

Writing Linear Equations

CHAPTER 6

Solving and Graphing Linear Inequalities

CHAPTER
7

Systems of Linear Equations and Inequalities

CHAPTER

8

Exponents and Exponential Functions

CHAPTER

9

Quadratic Equations and Functions

Polynomials and Factoring

CHAPTER
11

Rational Equations and Functions

CHAPTER

12

Radicals and Connections to Geometry

▶ Student Resources

▶ Who Uses Mathematics in Real Life?

Here are some careers that use the mathematics you will study in Algebra 1.

REAL LIFE

SURVEYOR *p. 231*
Surveying land is the responsibility of surveyors, survey technicians, and mapping scientists. They measure distances, angles between points, and elevations.

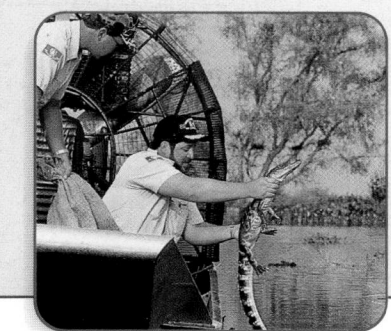

ZOOLOGIST *p. 236*
Zoologists are biologists who study animals in natural and controlled surroundings.

LANDSCAPE DESIGNER *p. 606*
Landscape designers plan and map out the appearance of outdoor spaces like parks, gardens, golf courses, and other recreational areas.

WEBMASTER *p. 400*
Webmasters build Web sites for clients. They often update their technical skills to meet the demands for first-class Web sites.

NURSE *p. 252*
Registered nurses are often responsible for measuring vital signs and giving correct doses of medication.

STUDENT HELP

YOUR BUILT-IN LEARNING SUPPORT

▶ *Your textbook contains* many special elements to help you learn. It provides several study helps that may be new to you. For example, every chapter begins with a Study Guide.

Chapter Preview The Study Guide starts with a short description of what you will be learning.

Key Vocabulary This list highlights important new terms that will be introduced in the chapter as well as reviewing terms that you already know.

Skill Review These exercises review key skills that you'll apply in the chapter. They will help you identify any topics that you need to review.

Study Strategy The study strategies suggest ideas to help you better understand the math you are learning as well as help you prepare for tests.

CHAPTER 1

Study Guide

PREVIEW

What's the chapter about?

Chapter 1 is an **introduction to algebra**. In Chapter 1 you'll learn to

- write and evaluate expressions.
- check solutions to equations and inequalities and use mental math.
- use verbal and algebraic models to represent real-life situations.
- organize data and represent functions.

KEY VOCABULARY

▶ New
- variable expression, p. 3
- unit analysis, p. 5
- verbal model, p. 5
- power, p. 9
- exponent, p. 9
- base of a power, p. 9
- order of operations, p. 16
- equation, p. 24
- solution of an equation, p. 24
- inequality, p. 26
- function, p. 46
- input-output table, p. 46
- domain, p. 47
- range, p. 47

PREPARE

Are you ready for the chapter?

SKILL REVIEW Do these exercises to review key skills that you'll apply in this chapter. See the given **reference page** if there is something you don't understand.

STUDENT HELP

▶ **Study Tip**
"Student Help" boxes throughout the chapter give you study tips and tell you where to look for extra help in this book and on the Internet.

Write the percent as a decimal and as a fraction or a mixed number in lowest terms. (Skills Review, pp. 784–785)

1. 60%   **2.** 33%   **3.** 0.08%   **4.** 150%

Complete the statement using > or <. (Skills Review, pp. 779–780)

5. 899 _?_ 901   **6.** 64.1 _?_ 64.03   **7.** 2050 _?_ 2005   **8.** 0.099 _?_ 0.01

Find the area and perimeter of the figure. (Skills Review, pp. 790–791)

9. 3.5 cm   **10.** 5 ft, 4 ft, 3 ft   **11.** 1.6 mi, 5.2 mi

STUDY STRATEGY

Here's a study strategy!

Keeping a Math Notebook

- Keep a notebook of math notes about each chapter, separate from your homework exercises. This will help you remember new concepts and skills.
- Review your notes each day before you start your next homework assignment.

Also, in every lesson you will find a variety of Student Help notes.

STUDENT HELP

 In the Book

Study Tip The study tips will help you avoid common errors.

Skills Review Here you can find where to review skills you've studied in earlier math classes.

Look Back Here are references to material in earlier lessons that may help you understand the lesson.

Extra Practice Your book contains more exercises to practice the skills you are learning.

Homework Help Here you can find suggestions about which Examples may help you solve Exercises.

 On the Internet

Homework Help: *Extra Examples* These are places where you can find additional examples on the Web site.

Homework Help: *Problem Solving Help* Here you can find additional suggestions for solving an exercise.

Keystroke Help These provide the exact keystroke sequences for many different kinds of calculators.

THE LEFT-TO-RIGHT RULE Operations that have the same priority, such as multiplication and division *or* addition and subtraction, are performed using the *left-to-right rule*, as shown in Example 2.

EXAMPLE 2 *Using the Left-to-Right Rule*

a. $24 - 8 - 6 = (24 - 8) - 6$ Work from left to right.

$= 16 - 6$

$= 10$

b. $15 \cdot 2 \div 6 = (15 \cdot 2) \div 6$ Work from left to right.

$= 30 \div 6$

$= 5$

c. $16 + 4 \div 2 - 3 = 16 + (4 \div 2) - 3$ Divide first.

$= 16 + 2 - 3$

$= (16 + 2) - 3$ Work from left to right.

$= 18 - 3$

$= 15$

> **STUDENT HELP**
> ► **Study Tip**
> In part (c) of Example 2, you do not perform the operations from left to right because division has a higher priority than addition and subtraction.

ORDER OF OPERATIONS

1. First do operations that occur within grouping symbols.
2. Then evaluate powers.
3. Then do multiplications and divisions from left to right.
4. Finally, do additions and subtractions from left to right.

A fraction bar can act as a grouping symbol: $(1 + 2) \div (4 - 1) = \dfrac{1 + 2}{4 - 1}$

> **STUDENT HELP**
> **HOMEWORK HELP**
> Visit our Web site www.mcdougallittell.com for extra examples.
> ► **Skills Review**
> For help with writing fractions in lowest terms, see pp. 781–783.

EXAMPLE 3 *Using a Fraction Bar*

$\dfrac{7 \cdot 4}{8 + 7^2 - 1} = \dfrac{7 \cdot 4}{8 + 49 - 1}$ Evaluate power.

$= \dfrac{28}{8 + 49 - 1}$ Simplify the numerator.

$= \dfrac{28}{57 - 1}$ Work from left to right.

$= \dfrac{28}{56}$ Subtract.

$= \dfrac{1}{2}$ Simplify.

1.3 *Order of Operations*   **17**

PRACTICE AND APPLICATIONS

> **STUDENT HELP**
> ► **Extra Practice**
> to help you master skills is on p. 800.

USING GRAPHS TO FIND INTERCEPTS Use the graph to find the *x*-intercept and the *y*-intercept of the line.

14.   **15.**   **16.**

FINDING *X*-INTERCEPTS Find the *x*-intercept of the graph of the equation.

17. $x + 3y = 5$ **18.** $x - 2y = 6$ **19.** $2x + 2y = -10$

20. $3x + 4y = 12$ **21.** $5x - y = 45$ **22.** $-x + 3y = 27$

23. $-7x - 3y = 42$ **24.** $2x + 6y = -24$ **25.** $-12x - 20y = 60$

FINDING *Y*-INTERCEPTS Find the *y*-intercept of the graph of the equation.

26. $y = -2x + 5$ **27.** $y = 3x - 4$ **28.** $y = 8x + 27$

29. $y = 7x - 15$ **30.** $4x - 5y = -35$ **31.** $6x - 9y = 72$

32. $3x + 12y = -84$ **33.** $-x + 1.7y = 5.1$ **34.** $2x - 6y = -18$

USING INTERCEPTS Graph the line that has the given intercepts.

35. *x*-intercept: -2 **36.** *x*-intercept: 4   **37.** *x*-intercept: -7
     y-intercept: 5   *y*-intercept: 6   *y*-intercept: -3

> **STUDENT HELP**
> ► **HOMEWORK HELP**
> **Example 1:** Exs. 17–34
> **Example 2:** Exs. 35–55
> **Example 3:** Exs. 44–55
> **Example 4:** Exs. 60–63

38. *x*-intercept: -3 **39.** *x*-intercept: -12 **40.** *x*-intercept: -7
     y-intercept: -7 *y*-intercept: -8 *y*-intercept: 15

4.3 *Quick Graphs Using Intercepts*   **221**

CONNECTIONS TO ALGEBRA

▶ *How does water pressure affect a scuba diver?*

APPLICATION: Scuba Diving

On the surface of Earth only the atmosphere is pressing on you. When you dive under the water, the weight of the water also presses on you. The volume of air in your lungs gets squeezed by these forces.

To design equipment for a dive, people need to know what the variables are, such as the depth of a dive and the dive time. You'll learn to write mathematical models for such real-life problems in Chapter 1.

Think & Discuss

The table shows that for every 10 feet a diver descends, the weight of the water on the diver increases by about 4.45 pounds per square inch.

Depth (feet)	Additional Pressure (pounds per square inch)
10	4.45
20	4.45 × 2
30	4.45 × 3
40	4.45 × 4

1. You are diving at a depth of 40 feet. What is the pressure of the water on you?

2. Use the pattern in the table to predict the pressure of the water on a diver at 100 feet.

Learn More About It

You will learn more about diving and water pressure in Example 3 on page 48.

 APPLICATION LINK Visit www.mcdougallittell.com for more information about scuba diving.

Study Guide

PREVIEW

What's the chapter about?

Chapter 1 is an **introduction to algebra**. In Chapter 1 you'll learn to

- write and evaluate expressions.
- check solutions to equations and inequalities and use mental math.
- use verbal and algebraic models to represent real-life situations.
- organize data and represent functions.

KEY VOCABULARY

▶ **New**
- variable expression, p. 3
- unit analysis, p. 5
- verbal model, p. 5
- power, p. 9

- exponent, p. 9
- base of a power, p. 9
- order of operations, p. 16
- equation, p. 24
- solution of an equation, p. 24

- inequality, p. 26
- function, p. 46
- input-output table, p. 46
- domain, p. 47
- range, p. 47

PREPARE

Are you ready for the chapter?

SKILL REVIEW Do these exercises to review key skills that you'll apply in this chapter. See the given **reference page** if there is something you don't understand.

STUDENT HELP

▶ **Study Tip**
"Student Help" boxes throughout the chapter give you study tips and tell you where to look for extra help in this book and on the Internet.

Write the percent as a decimal and as a fraction or a mixed number in lowest terms. (Skills Review, pp. 784–785)

1. 60%   **2.** 33%   **3.** 0.08%   **4.** 150%

Complete the statement using > or <. (Skills Review, pp. 779–780)

5. 899 _?_ 901   **6.** 64.1 _?_ 64.03   **7.** 2050 _?_ 2005   **8.** 0.099 _?_ 0.01

Find the area and perimeter of the figure. (Skills Review, pp. 790–791)

9.

10.

5 ft   4 ft

3 ft

11.

1.6 mi

5.2 mi

3.5 cm

STUDY STRATEGY

Here's a study strategy!

Keeping a Math Notebook

- Keep a notebook of math notes about each chapter, separate from your homework exercises. This will help you remember new concepts and skills.
- Review your notes each day before you start your next homework assignment.

1.1

Variables in Algebra

What you should learn

GOAL 1 Evaluate a variable expression.

GOAL 2 Write a variable expression that models a **real-life** situation, as in the hiking problem in **Example 5**.

Why you should learn it

▼ To express **real-life** number relationships, such as pitching speed in **Exs. 48 and 49**.

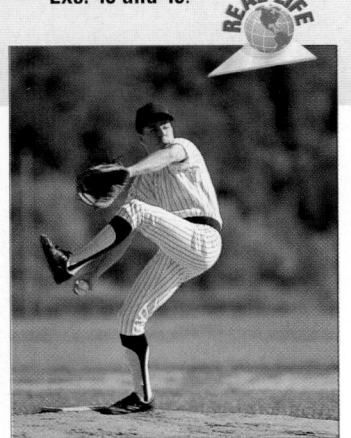

GOAL 1 EVALUATING VARIABLE EXPRESSIONS

A **variable** is a letter that is used to represent one or more numbers. The numbers are the **values** of the variable. A **variable expression** is a collection of numbers, variables, and operations. Here are some examples.

VARIABLE EXPRESSION	MEANING	OPERATION
$8y$ $8 \cdot y$ $8(y)$	8 times y	Multiplication
$\dfrac{16}{b}$ $16 \div b$	16 divided by b	Division
$4 + s$	4 plus s	Addition
$9 - x$	9 minus x	Subtraction

The expression $8y$ is usually not written as $8 \times y$ because of possible confusion with the variable x. Replacing each variable in an expression by a number is called **evaluating the expression**. The resulting number is the value of the expression.

Write the variable expression.	→	Substitute values for variables.	→	Simplify the numerical expression.

EXAMPLE 1 *Evaluating a Variable Expression*

Evaluate the expression when $y = 2$.

   a. $8y$ **b.** $\dfrac{10}{y}$ **c.** $y + 3$ **d.** $14 - y$

SOLUTION

   a. $8y = 8(2)$ Substitute 2 for *y*.

        $= 16$ Simplify.

   b. $\dfrac{10}{y} = \dfrac{10}{2}$ Substitute 2 for *y*.

        $= 5$ Simplify.

   c. $y + 3 = 2 + 3$ Substitute 2 for *y*.

        $= 5$ Simplify.

   d. $14 - y = 14 - 2$ Substitute 2 for *y*.

        $= 12$ Simplify.

Travel

EXAMPLE 2 *Evaluating a Real-Life Expression*

Average speed is given by the following formula.

$$\text{Average speed} = \frac{\text{Distance}}{\text{Time}} = \frac{d}{t}$$

Find the average speed (in miles per hour) of a car that traveled 180 miles from Boise, Idaho, to the Minidoka National Wildlife Refuge in 3 hours.

SOLUTION

$$\text{Average speed} = \frac{d}{t} \qquad \text{Write expression.}$$

$$= \frac{180}{3} \qquad \text{Substitute 180 for } d \text{ and 3 for } t.$$

$$= 60 \qquad \text{Simplify.}$$

▶ The average speed was 60 miles per hour.

EXAMPLE 3 *Evaluating a Geometric Expression*

GEOMETRY CONNECTION The perimeter of a triangle is equal to the sum of the lengths of its sides: $a + b + c$.

Find the perimeter of the triangle. The dimensions are in feet.

$c = 17$

$a = 8$

$b = 15$

SOLUTION

$$\text{Perimeter} = a + b + c \qquad \text{Write expression.}$$

$$= 8 + 15 + 17 \qquad \text{Substitute values.}$$

$$= 40 \qquad \text{Simplify.}$$

▶ The triangle has a perimeter of 40 feet.

Interest

EXAMPLE 4 *Evaluating Simple Interest*

The simple interest earned by money P (called the *principal*) at an annual interest rate r for t years is given by Prt. You deposit $650 at a rate of 8% per year. How much simple interest will you earn after one half of a year?

SOLUTION

$$\text{Simple interest} = Prt \qquad \text{Write expression.}$$

$$= (650)(0.08)(0.5) \qquad \text{Substitute 650 for } P, 0.08 \text{ for } r, \text{ and 0.5 for } t.$$

$$= 26 \qquad \text{Simplify.}$$

▶ After one half of a year, you will have $26 of simple interest.

STUDENT HELP

▶ **Skills Review**
For help with writing percents as decimals, see pp. 784–785.

COASTAL REDWOODS, found in California and Oregon, are the tallest trees on Earth. Only 4% of original redwood forests remains. The tallest living redwood is 370 feet high.

FOCUS ON APPLICATIONS

GOAL 2 MODELING A REAL-LIFE SITUATION

Writing the units of each variable in a real-life problem helps you determine the units for the answer. This is called **unit analysis** and it is often used in problem solving in science. When the same units of measure occur in the numerator and the denominator of an expression, you can cancel the units.

In real-life problems, you may need to translate words into mathematics. One way to do this is to use the **verbal model** shown in Example 5.

EXAMPLE 5 *Finding Time*

HIKING AMONG REDWOODS You plan to go hiking in the Jedediah Smith Redwoods State Park in California. You estimate you'll hike at a rate of 2 miles per hour on a steep trail. How long will it take you to hike from Howland Hill Road along the Boy Scout Tree Trail and back?

Round Trip Distances	
Boy Scout Tree Trail	7.4 miles
Little Bald Hills Trail	9 miles

———— Redwood National Park Boundary
- - - - - Trail
———— Paved Road

▶ Source: Redwood National and State Parks

SOLUTION

The map shows that the round-trip distance is about 7.4 miles.

PROBLEM SOLVING STRATEGY

VERBAL MODEL $\text{Time} = \dfrac{\text{Distance}}{\text{Rate}}$

LABELS   Time = t (hours)

Distance = **7.4**   (miles)

Rate = **2**   (miles per hour)

ALGEBRAIC MODEL $t = \dfrac{7.4}{2}$ **Write algebraic model.**

$= 3.7$ **Simplify.**

▶ It should take you about 3.7 hours to hike the Boy Scout Tree Trail.

UNIT ANALYSIS Use unit analysis to check that *hours* are the units of the solution.

$$\text{Time} = \frac{\text{Distance}}{\text{Rate}} = \frac{\text{mi}}{\text{mi/h}} = \cancel{\text{mi}} \cdot \frac{\text{h}}{\cancel{\text{mi}}} = \text{h}$$

1.1 *Variables in Algebra*   **5**

GUIDED PRACTICE

Vocabulary Check ✔

1. Explain what it means to *evaluate a variable expression.*

Concept Check ✔

2. What operation is indicated by the expression?

    a. $4y$ **b.** $\dfrac{7}{d}$ **c.** $t + 8$ **d.** $3 - t$

3. Write a variable expression for "5 divided by r."

4. How is unit analysis helpful in solving real-life problems?

Skill Check ✔

Evaluate the expression when $y = 6$.

  5. $5y$ **6.** $\dfrac{24}{y}$ **7.** $y + 19$ **8.** $y - 2$

  9. $y \div 3$ **10.** $27 - y$ **11.** $2.5y$ **12.** $3.2 + y$

Simplify the real-life expression and show unit analysis.

13. time $= \dfrac{15 \text{ mi}}{5 \text{ mi/h}}$ **14.** perimeter $= 3 \text{ cm} + 4 \text{ cm} + 5 \text{ cm}$

15. distance $= (60 \text{ mi/h})(2.3 \text{ h})$ **16.** simple interest $= (\$100)\left(\dfrac{0.05}{\text{year}}\right)(2.5 \text{ years})$

🌐 **HIKING** **In Exercises 17 and 18, you want to hike a round-trip distance of 10 miles from the Hiouchi Information Center along the Little Bald Hills Trail and back. Calculate how long it will take if you hike at a rate of 1.25 miles per hour.**

17. Write a verbal model, provide labels, and write an algebraic model.

18. Show unit analysis.

PRACTICE AND APPLICATIONS

STUDENT HELP

▶ **Extra Practice**
to help you master
skills is on p. 797.

EVALUATING EXPRESSIONS Evaluate the expression for the given value of the variable.

19. $12x$ when $x = 5$ **20.** $b - 7$ when $b = 24$ **21.** $0.5d$ when $d = 0.5$

22. $9 + p$ when $p = 11$ **23.** $r(10)$ when $r = 8.2$ **24.** $3.67a$ when $a = 2$

25. $\dfrac{6.3}{x}$ when $x = 3$ **26.** $\dfrac{2}{3} \cdot x$ when $x = \dfrac{1}{3}$ **27.** $\dfrac{d}{12}$ when $d = 60$

28. $\dfrac{18}{t}$ when $t = 3$ **29.** $\dfrac{5}{8} - p$ when $p = \dfrac{3}{16}$ **30.** $\dfrac{1}{2} + t$ when $t = \dfrac{1}{2}$

STUDENT HELP

▶ **HOMEWORK HELP**
Example 1: Exs. 19–30
Example 2: Exs. 35–38
Example 3: Ex. 32
Example 4: Exs. 31, 33, 34
Example 5: Ex. 39

31. 🌐 **INTEREST EARNED** You invest \$80 at a simple annual interest rate of 2%. How much simple interest would you earn in 1.5 years? Use unit analysis to check the units in your response.

32. **GEOMETRY** ▶ **CONNECTION** The perimeter of a square is equal to $4s$, where s is the length of one side. Find the perimeter of the square at the right. Show unit analysis.

7 ft

ERROR ANALYSIS In Exercises 33 and 34, Samantha deposits $300 in an account that earns an annual interest rate of 2.5%. After 9 months, she computes the simple interest.

33. What mistake did Samantha make?

$$(\$300)\left(\frac{2.5}{\text{year}}\right)(0.75 \text{ year}) = \$562.50$$

34. What is the correct amount of simple interest earned after 9 months?

STUDENT HELP

HOMEWORK HELP
Visit our Web site
www.mcdougallittell.com
for help with Exs. 35–39.

🌎 **CALCULATING AVERAGE SPEEDS** In Exercises 35–38, find the average speed for the given distance and time. Show unit analysis to check units.

35. A train travels 75 miles in 55 minutes.

36. In 5 seconds, an athlete runs 40 feet.

37. A horse gallops 4 kilometers in 30 minutes.

38. Dick Rutan and Jeana Yeager flew nonstop around the world, a distance of 24,986.73 miles, in 216.06 hours. ▶ Source: National Air and Space Museum

39. 🌎 **DRIVING TIME** If you are driving at a constant speed of 96 kilometers per hour, how long will it take you to travel 288 kilometers?

🌎 **CALORIES BURNED** In Exercises 40–42, use the following information. The number of calories burned while doing an activity can be expressed by rm, where r is the rate of calories burned and m is the number of minutes spent doing the activity.
▶ Source: *Home & Garden* Bulletin No. 72, U.S. Government Printing Office

40. A 120-pound student playing volleyball burns 2.7 calories per minute. If the student plays for 30 minutes, how many calories does the student burn?

41. An in-line skater, who is the same weight as the student in Exercise 40, burns 387 calories in 90 minutes. How many calories does the in-line skater burn per minute?

42. Which activity burns more calories per minute, volleyball or in-line skating?

43. 🌎 **MOUNTAIN CLIMBING** Heidi Zimmer plans to climb the highest peak in each continent. She has already climbed summits in North America, Europe, Africa, and South America. Copy and complete the table. Convert h, the height in meters, to the height in feet by dividing each given value of h by 0.3048. The last column shows how much shorter each mountain is than Mt. Everest, which is 29,029 feet high.

FOCUS ON
PEOPLE

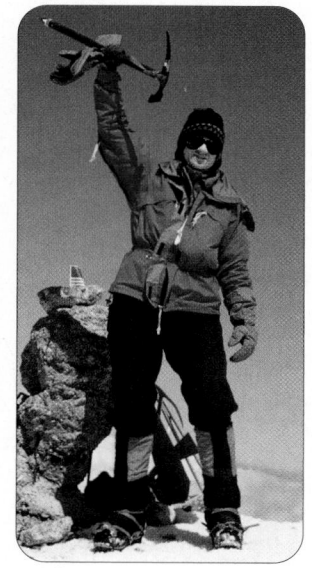

🌎 **HEIDI ZIMMER** is the first deaf woman to climb Mt. McKinley. It took her 18 days to reach the top of Mt. McKinley.

APPLICATION LINK
www.mcdougallittell.com

Mountain, Continent	h	$\dfrac{h}{0.3048}$	$29{,}029 - \dfrac{h}{0.3048}$
Mt. McKinley, North America	6194	?	?
Mt. Elbrus, Europe	5633	?	?
Mt. Kilimanjaro, Africa	5963	?	?
Mt. Aconcagua, South America	6959	?	?

▶ Source: Peakware™ World Mountain Encyclopedia

44. **BATTING AVERAGE** A baseball player's batting average is found by dividing the number of hits h by the official times at bat b. During the 1998 baseball season, Alex Rodriguez of the Seattle Mariners had 686 official times at bat and made 213 hits. Use a verbal model to find his batting average. Round your answer to the nearest thousandth.

Test Preparation

45. **MULTIPLE CHOICE** You drove 200 miles in 3 hours 20 minutes. Which expression represents your average speed if d represents distance and t represents time?

    A dt **B** $\dfrac{d}{t}$ **C** $\dfrac{t}{d}$ **D** $d + t$

46. **MULTIPLE CHOICE** You invest $300 at a simple annual interest rate of 4.5%. How much simple interest will you earn in 10 years?

    A $115   **B** $120   **C** $135   **D** $150

47. **MULTIPLE CHOICE** A rectangular computer screen measures 28 centimeters by 21 centimeters. What is the perimeter of the screen?

    A 49 cm   **B** 98 cm   **C** 294 cm   **D** 588 cm

★ **Challenge**

PITCHING SPEED In baseball the pitcher's mound is 60.5 feet from home plate. The strike zone, or distance across the plate, is 17 inches. The time it takes for a baseball to reach home plate can be determined by dividing the distance the ball travels by the speed at which the pitcher throws the baseball.

48. If a pitcher throws a baseball at 90 miles per hour, how many seconds does it take for the baseball to reach home plate?

EXTRA CHALLENGE

www.mcdougallittell.com

49. For Exercise 48, how long is the ball in the strike zone?

MIXED REVIEW

FRACTIONS Perform the indicated operation. Simplify your answer, if possible. (Skills Review, pp. 781–783)

50. $1\dfrac{7}{8} + \dfrac{3}{4}$ **51.** $\dfrac{2}{5} - \dfrac{1}{10}$ **52.** $5\dfrac{3}{4} \cdot \dfrac{1}{3}$ **53.** $2\dfrac{1}{5} \div \dfrac{4}{5}$

54. $3\dfrac{2}{3} \cdot 3$ **55.** $\dfrac{6}{5} \div \dfrac{3}{10}$ **56.** $4\dfrac{5}{9} - \dfrac{1}{5}$ **57.** $8\dfrac{9}{10} + 1\dfrac{1}{5}$

GEOMETRY **CONNECTION** Find the area of the rectangle. (Skills Review, p. 791)

58.

4 cm

8 cm

59.

10 in.

7 in.

60.

6 m

28 m

EXPRESSIONS Evaluate the expression when $x = 2$. (Review 1.1 for Lesson 1.2)

61. $2x$ **62.** $(x)(x)$ **63.** $3x$ **64.** $(x)(x)(x)$

65. $4x$ **66.** $(x)(x)(x)(x)$ **67.** $5x$ **68.** $(x)(x)(x)(x)(x)$

1.2 Exponents and Powers

What you should learn

GOAL 1 Evaluate expressions containing exponents.

GOAL 2 Use exponents in **real-life** problems such as finding the volume of an aquarium in **Example 6**.

Why you should learn it

▼ To solve **real-life** problems, such as finding the volume of a glass cube in **Ex. 64**.

GOAL 1 EXPRESSIONS CONTAINING EXPONENTS

An expression like 4^6 is called a **power**. The **exponent** 6 represents the number of times the **base** 4 is used as a factor.

$$\text{base} \longrightarrow \underbrace{4^6}_{\text{power}} = \underbrace{4 \cdot 4 \cdot 4 \cdot 4 \cdot 4 \cdot 4}_{\text{6 factors of 4}}$$

exponent

EXAMPLE 1   *Reading and Writing Powers*

Express the meaning of the power in words and then with numbers or variables.

SOLUTION

EXPONENTIAL FORM	WORDS	MEANING
a. 10^1	ten to the first power	10
b. 4^2	four to the second power, or four squared	$4 \cdot 4$
c. 5^3	five to the third power, or five cubed	$5 \cdot 5 \cdot 5$
d. 7^6	seven to the sixth power	$7 \cdot 7 \cdot 7 \cdot 7 \cdot 7 \cdot 7$
e. x^n	x to the nth power	$x \cdot x \cdot x \cdot x \cdot \ldots \cdot x$

and so on

For a number raised to the first power, you usually do not write the exponent 1. For instance, you write 5^1 simply as 5.

EXAMPLE 2   *Evaluating Powers*

Evaluate the expression x^3 when $x = 5$.

SOLUTION

$$x^3 = 5^3 \qquad \text{Substitute 5 for } x.$$
$$= 5 \cdot 5 \cdot 5 \qquad \text{Write factors.}$$
$$= 125 \qquad \text{Multiply.}$$

▶ The value of the expression is 125.

GROUPING SYMBOLS For problems that have more than one operation, it is important to know which operation to do first. **Grouping symbols,** such as parentheses ( ) or brackets [ ], indicate the order in which the operations should be performed. Operations within the innermost set of grouping symbols are done first. For instance, the value of the expression $(3 \cdot 4) + 7$ is not the same as the value of the expression $3 \cdot (4 + 7)$.

Multiply. Then add.	**Add. Then multiply.**
$(3 \cdot 4) + 7 = 12 + 7 = 19$	$3 \cdot (4 + 7) = 3 \cdot 11 = 33$

EXAMPLE 3 *Evaluating an Exponential Expression*

STUDENT HELP

HOMEWORK HELP
Visit our Web site
www.mcdougallittell.com
for extra examples.

Evaluate the expression when $a = 1$ and $b = 2$.

a. $(a + b)^2$ **b.** $(a^2) + (b^2)$

SOLUTION

a. $(a + b)^2 = (1 + 2)^2$	Substitute 1 for *a* and 2 for *b*.
$= 3^2$	Add within parentheses.
$= 3 \cdot 3$	Write factors.
$= 9$	Multiply.

b. $(a^2) + (b^2) = (1^2) + (2^2)$	Substitute 1 for *a* and 2 for *b*.
$= 1 + 4$	Evaluate power.
$= 5$	Add.

. . . .

An exponent applies only to the number, variable, or expression immediately to its left. In the expression $2x^3$, the base is x, not $2x$. In the expression $(2x)^3$, the base is $2x$, as indicated by the parentheses.

EXAMPLE 4 *Exponents and Grouping Symbols*

Evaluate the expression when $x = 4$.

a. $2x^3$ **b.** $(2x)^3$

SOLUTION

a. $2x^3 = 2(4^3)$	Substitute 4 for *x*.
$= 2(64)$	Evaluate power.
$= 128$	Multiply.

b. $(2x)^3 = (2 \cdot 4)^3$	Substitute 4 for *x*.
$= 8^3$	Multiply within parentheses.
$= 512$	Evaluate power.

GOAL 2 REAL-LIFE APPLICATIONS OF EXPONENTS

Exponents often are used in the formulas for area and volume. In fact, the words *squared* and *cubed* come from the formula for the area of a square, $A = s^2$, and the formula for the volume of a cube, $V = s^3$.

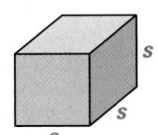

Area of Square: $A = s^2$ **Volume of Cube: $V = s^3$**

Units of area, such as square feet, ft^2, can be written using a second power. Units of volume, such as cubic centimeters, cm^3, can be written using a third power.

EXAMPLE 5 *Making a Table*

You can find the volume of cubes that have edge lengths of 1 inch, 2 inches, 3 inches, 4 inches, and 5 inches by using the formula $V = s^3$.

Edge, s	1	2	3	4	5
s^3	1^3	2^3	3^3	4^3	5^3
Volume, V	1 in.^{3}	8 in.^{3}	27 in.^{3}	64 in.^{3}	125 in.^{3}

EXAMPLE 6 *Finding Volume*

Aquarium

The aquarium has the shape of a cube. Each edge is 2.5 feet long.

  a. Find the volume in cubic feet.

  b. How many gallons of water will the cubic aquarium hold? Convert to liquid volume, where one cubic foot holds 7.48 gallons.

SOLUTION

  a. $V = s^3$ **Write formula for volume.**

        $= 2.5^3$ **Substitute 2.5 for s.**

        $= 15.625$ **Evaluate power.**

  ▶ The volume of the aquarium is 15.625 ft^3.

  b. $V = 15.625 \text{ ft}^3 \left(7.48 \text{ gal}/1 \text{ ft}^3\right)$ **Write conversion factor.**

        $= 116.875 \text{ gal}$ **Multiply.**

  ▶ A 15.625 cubic foot aquarium will hold 116.875 gallons of water.

STUDENT HELP

↳ **KEYSTROKE HELP**

Your calculator may have a y^x key or a $\wedge$ key that you can use to evaluate powers.

1.2 *Exponents and Powers*   **11**

GUIDED PRACTICE

Vocabulary Check ✓   **1.** In the expression 15^3, what is 15 called? What is 3 called? What is the expression called?

Concept Check ✓   **2.** The expressions $3x^2$ and $(3x)^2$ do not have the same meaning. Explain the difference.

3. Evaluate the expressions $3x^2$ and $(3x)^2$ when $x = 4$.

Skill Check ✓   **Match the power with the words that describe it.**

     A. five to the sixth power   **B.** two to the fifth power

     C. five squared   **D.** five cubed

     4. 5^2 **5.** 5^3 **6.** 2^5 **7.** 5^6

Evaluate the expression when $x = 3$.

     8. x^2 **9.** $(x + 1)^3$ **10.** $2x^2$ **11.** $(2x)^3$

     12. $(x - 1)^4$ **13.** 5^x **14.** $(3x)^4$ **15.** 10^x

16. 🌐 **STEREO SPEAKERS** A cubical stereo speaker measures 35 centimeters along each edge. The expression for finding the surface area of a cube is $6s^2$, where s is the length of each edge. Find the surface area of the stereo speaker.

PRACTICE AND APPLICATIONS

STUDENT HELP

▸ **Extra Practice**
to help you master
skills is on p. 797.

EXPONENTIAL FORM **Write the expression in exponential form.**

17. two cubed   **18.** p squared   **19.** nine to the yth power

20. b to the eighth power   **21.** $3 \cdot 3 \cdot 3 \cdot 3 \cdot y$ **22.** $t \cdot t$

23. $c \cdot c \cdot c \cdot c \cdot c \cdot c$ **24.** $5 \cdot x \cdot x \cdot x \cdot x \cdot x$ **25.** $4x \cdot 4x \cdot 4x$

EVALUATING POWERS **Evaluate the power.**

26. 10^2 **27.** 5^2 **28.** 8^2

29. 6^4 **30.** 10^5 **31.** 7^4

32. 4^6 **33.** 9^3 **34.** 2^5

EVALUATING EXPRESSIONS **Evaluate the expression for the given value of the variable.**

35. 4^n when $n = 5$ **36.** b^4 when $b = 9$ **37.** x^6 when $x = 10$

38. c^6 when $c = 2$ **39.** w^3 when $w = 13$ **40.** p^2 when $p = 2.5$

STUDENT HELP

▸ HOMEWORK HELP
Example 1: Exs. 17–25
Example 2: Exs. 26–40
Example 3: Exs. 41–46
Example 4: Exs. 55–60
Example 5: Ex. 61
Example 6: Exs. 63–66

EXPONENTIAL EXPRESSIONS **Evaluate the expression for the given values of the variables.**

41. $(x + y)^2$ when $x = 5$ and $y = 3$ **42.** $m - n^2$ when $m = 25$ and $n = 4$

43. $(a - b)^4$ when $a = 4$ and $b = 2$ **44.** $c^3 + d$ when $c = 4$ and $d = 16$

45. $(d - 3)^2$ when $d = 13$ **46.** $16 + x^3$ when $x = 2$

EVALUATING POWERS Use a calculator to evaluate the power. For keystroke help see Student Help box on page 11.

47. 9^5 **48.** 2^{10} **49.** 5^9 **50.** 3^{11}

51. 8^6 **52.** 12^7 **53.** 6^8 **54.** 13^5

EXPONENTIAL EXPRESSIONS Evaluate the expression for the given value of the variable.

55. $(5w)^3$ when $w = 5$ **56.** $6t^4$ when $t = 3$ **57.** $7b^2$ when $b = 7$

58. $2x^2$ when $x = 15$ **59.** $(8x)^3$ when $x = 2$ **60.** $5y^5$ when $y = 2$

61. USING A TABLE The area of a square is s^2. Show the relationship between the side length of a square and its area by copying and completing the following table.

Side length, s	1	2	3	4	5
Area, s^2	?	?	?	?	?

62. CRITICAL THINKING Copy and complete the table. What pattern do you see?

Power	10^2	100^2	1000^2	$10,000^2$
Evaluate	100	?	?	?

63. 🌎 **INTERIOR DESIGN** One room in Jean's apartment is a square measuring 12.2 feet along the base of each wall. How many square feet of wall-to-wall carpet does Jean need to carpet the room?

64. **ART** **CONNECTION** In 1997 the artist Jon Kuhn of North Carolina created a cubic sculpture called Crystal Victory, shown at the left. Each edge of the solid glass cube is 9.5 inches in length. How much liquid glass did Kuhn need to make the cube?

65. 🌎 **VOLUME OF A SAFE** Each dimension of the cubical storage space inside a fireproof safe is 12 inches. What is the volume of the storage space?

66. 🌎 **SWIMMING POOL** A swimming pool is 50 meters long, 19.5 meters wide, and 3 meters deep. Use the formula for the volume of a rectangular prism to find the volume of water in the pool. The formula is the length times the width times the height.

67. 🌎 **RAIN FOREST PYRAMID**
The formula for the volume of a pyramid is $\frac{1}{3}$ times the height times the area of the base.
The Rain Forest Pyramid in Moody Gardens near Galveston, Texas, is 100 feet high and 200 feet along each side of its square base. What is the volume of space inside the Rain Forest Pyramid?
▶Source: Morris Architects

68. MULTI-STEP PROBLEM You are making candles to sell at your school's art festival. You melt paraffin wax in a cubic container. Each edge of the container is 6 inches in length. The container is one half full.

a. What is the volume of the wax in the container?

b. Which of the candle molds could hold all of the melted wax?

Ⓐ 5 in. 5 in. 5 in.

Ⓑ 3 in. 3 in. 3 in.

Ⓒ 4.5 in. 4.5 in. 4.5 in.

c. *Writing* Design a cubic candle mold different from those given that will hold all of the melted wax. Draw a diagram of the mold. Explain why your mold will hold all of the melted wax.

★ **Challenge**

FINDING A PATTERN **Copy the table.**

Power	9^1	9^2	9^3	9^4	9^5	9^6	9^7	9^8
Evaluate	?	?	?	?	?	?	?	?

69. Evaluate the powers of 9 in the table. What pattern do you see for the last digit of each product?

70. Make a table like the one shown for powers of 8. Describe any patterns.

71. Make a table for powers of 7. Describe any patterns.

MIXED REVIEW

GEOMETRY CONNECTION **Find the perimeter of the figure when $x = 1.7$.**
(Skills Review, pp. 790–791)

72.

73.

74.

FRACTIONS, DECIMALS, AND PERCENTS **Write the fraction as a decimal and as a percent.** **(Skills Review, pp. 784–785)**

75. $\frac{5}{8}$

76. $\frac{3}{4}$

77. $\frac{11}{20}$

78. $\frac{4}{25}$

EVALUATING VARIABLE EXPRESSIONS **Evaluate the expression for the given value of the variable.** **(Review 1.1 for 1.3)**

79. $7x$ when $x = 3$

80. $y + 2$ when $y = 10$

81. $\frac{a}{2}$ when $a = 8$

82. $m - 5$ when $m = 17$

83. $\frac{9}{b}$ when $b = 4$

84. $9b$ when $b = 4$

ACTIVITY 1.2

Using Technology

Making a Table

Using a graphing calculator to create a table can make it easier to evaluate an expression for many different values of the variable.

▶ EXAMPLE

You are offered a two penny salary that doubles every week. How much is your salary in the 20th week? Use a graphing calculator to make the table.

Week, x	1	2	4	6	8	10	12	14	16	18	20
Salary, 2^x	2	4	16	?	?	?	?	?	?	?	?

▶ SOLUTION

① Press **Y=** and enter the expression 2^x as Y_1.

② Use the Table Setup function to choose values beginning at 6 and increasing by 2.

③ View your table. Scroll down to read the twentieth week in the table.

④ The value for the twentieth week is 1.05 E6. This means 1.05×10^6 or 1,050,000.

▶ EXERCISES

EVALUATING EXPRESSIONS Use the table feature on a graphing calculator to evaluate the exponential expression for the given values of x.

1. 2^x for $x = 25, 50, 75, 100$

2. 3^x for $x = 5, 7, 9, 11, 13$

3. 4^x for $x = 2, 3, 4, 5, 6$

4. 5^x for $x = 4, 8, 12, 16$

5. 6^x for $x = 2, 4, 6, 8, 10$

6. 10^x for $x = 4, 7, 10, 13, 16$

1.3

Order of Operations

What you should learn

GOAL 1 Use the order of operations to evaluate algebraic expressions.

GOAL 2 Use a calculator to evaluate **real-life** expressions, such as calculating sales tax in **Example 5**.

Why you should learn it

▼ To solve **real-life** problems, such as calculating the cost of admission for a family to a state fair in **Exs. 50** and **51**.

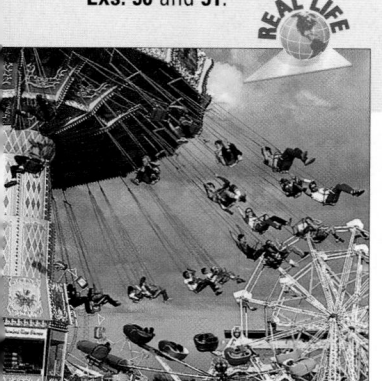

GOAL 1 USING THE ORDER OF OPERATIONS

Mathematicians have established an **order of operations** to evaluate an expression involving more than one operation. Start with operations within grouping symbols. Then evaluate powers. Then do multiplications and divisions from left to right. Finally, do additions and subtractions from left to right.

EXAMPLE 1 *Evaluating Without Grouping Symbols*

Evaluate the expression when $x = 4$.

a. $3x^2 + 1$ **b.** $32 \div x^2 - 1$

SOLUTION

a. $3x^2 + 1 = 3 \cdot 4^2 + 1$ Substitute 4 for *x*.

            $= 3 \cdot 16 + 1$ Evaluate power.

            $= 48 + 1$ Evaluate product.

            $= 49$ Evaluate sum.

b. $32 \div x^2 - 1 = 32 \div 4^2 - 1$ Substitute 4 for *x*.

                  $= 32 \div 16 - 1$ Evaluate power.

                  $= 2 - 1$ Evaluate quotient.

                  $= 1$ Evaluate difference.

· · · · · · · · · ·

When you want to change the established order of operations for an expression, you *must* use parentheses or other grouping symbols.

▶ ACTIVITY

Developing Concepts

Investigating Grouping Symbols

Without grouping symbols, the expression $3 \cdot 4^2 + 8 \div 4$ has a value of 50. You can insert grouping symbols to produce a different value. For example:

$$3 \cdot (4^2 + 8) \div 4 = 3 \cdot (16 + 8) \div 4 = 3 \cdot 24 \div 4 = 72 \div 4 = 18$$

Insert grouping symbols in the expression $3 \cdot 4^2 + 8 \div 4$ to produce the indicated values.

1. 146   **2.** 54   **3.** 38

THE LEFT-TO-RIGHT RULE Operations that have the same priority, such as multiplication and division *or* addition and subtraction, are performed using the *left-to-right rule*, as shown in Example 2.

EXAMPLE 2 *Using the Left-to-Right Rule*

a. $24 - 8 - 6 = (24 - 8) - 6$ **Work from left to right.**

$$= 16 - 6$$

$$= 10$$

b. $15 \cdot 2 \div 6 = (15 \cdot 2) \div 6$ **Work from left to right.**

$$= 30 \div 6$$

$$= 5$$

c. $16 + 4 \div 2 - 3 = 16 + (4 \div 2) - 3$ **Divide first.**

$$= 16 + 2 - 3$$

$$= (16 + 2) - 3$$ **Work from left to right.**

$$= 18 - 3$$

$$= 15$$

STUDENT HELP

Study Tip
In part (c) of Example 2, you do not perform the operations from left to right because division has a higher priority than addition and subtraction.

ORDER OF OPERATIONS

1. First do operations that occur within grouping symbols.
2. Then evaluate powers.
3. Then do multiplications and divisions from left to right.
4. Finally, do additions and subtractions from left to right.

A fraction bar can act as a grouping symbol: $(1 + 2) \div (4 - 1) = \dfrac{1 + 2}{4 - 1}$

STUDENT HELP

HOMEWORK HELP
Visit our Web site www.mcdougallittell.com for extra examples.

Skills Review
For help with writing fractions in lowest terms, see pp. 781–783.

EXAMPLE 3 *Using a Fraction Bar*

$$\frac{7 \cdot 4}{8 + 7^2 - 1} = \frac{7 \cdot 4}{8 + 49 - 1}$$ **Evaluate power.**

$$= \frac{28}{8 + 49 - 1}$$ **Simplify the numerator.**

$$= \frac{28}{57 - 1}$$ **Work from left to right.**

$$= \frac{28}{56}$$ **Subtract.**

$$= \frac{1}{2}$$ **Simplify.**

GOAL 2 EVALUATING EXPRESSIONS WITH A CALCULATOR

Many calculators use the established order of operations, but some do not. See if your calculator follows the established order of operations in Example 4. If your calculator does not follow the order of operations, you must enter the operations in the correct order.

EXAMPLE 4 Using a Calculator

When you enter the following in your calculator, does the calculator display 6.1 or 0.6?

10.5 ⊟ 6.3 ÷ 2.1 ⊟ 1.4 [ENTER]

SOLUTION

a. If your calculator uses order of operations, it will display 6.1.
$$10.5 - 6.3 \div 2.1 - 1.4 = 10.5 - (6.3 \div 2.1) - 1.4$$
$$= 10.5 - 3 - 1.4$$
$$= 6.1$$

b. If it displays 0.6, it performs the operations as they are entered.
$$[(10.5 - 6.3) \div 2.1] - 1.4 = (4.2 \div 2.1) - 1.4$$
$$= 2 - 1.4$$
$$= 0.6$$

Retail Sales

EXAMPLE 5 Calculating Sales Tax

Suppose you live in a state that charges no sales tax on essentials, such as clothes or food, but charges 6% sales tax on nonessentials, such as CDs or games. You decide to buy a sweatshirt for $24 and a video game for $39. Your calculator follows the established order of operations. Which of the following keystroke sequences will show the correct amount you owe? Explain why.

a. 24 ＋ 39 ＋ 39 × 0.06 [ENTER]

b. 39 ＋ 24 ＋ 24 × 0.06 [ENTER]

c. 39 ＋ 24 ＋ (24 ＋ 39) × 0.06 [ENTER]

SOLUTION

a. $65.34 is correct. Tax is added on the video game, but not the sweatshirt.

b. $64.44 is wrong. Tax is added on the sweatshirt, but not the video game.

c. $66.78 is wrong. Tax is added on both items.

GUIDED PRACTICE

Vocabulary Check ✓

Concept Check ✓

Skill Check ✓

1. Describe the order of operations agreed upon by mathematicians.

2. If an expression without grouping symbols includes addition and an exponent, which operation should you do first?

3. If an expression without grouping symbols includes multiplication and division, which operation should you do first?

Evaluate the expression for the given value of the variable.

4. $x^4 - 3$ when $x = 2$

5. $5 \cdot 6y$ when $y = 5$

6. $a^3 + 10a$ when $a = 3$

7. $\frac{16}{x} - 2$ when $x = 4$

8. $\frac{22}{x} \div 2 + 16$ when $x = 11$

9. $\frac{16}{n} + 2^3 - 10$ when $n = 8$

10. $(x + 5) \div 4$ when $x = 9$

11. $b + 6 \div 4$ when $b = 1.5$

12. **ERROR ANALYSIS** Julio's calculator displayed 7 when he evaluated the following expression. Did his calculator use the established order of operations? If not, how can he use grouping symbols to find the correct value?

72 [+] 12 [÷] 4 [−] 14 [ENTER]   [7]

PRACTICE AND APPLICATIONS

STUDENT HELP

▶ **Extra Practice**
to help you master skills is on p. 797.

EVALUATING VARIABLE EXPRESSIONS **Evaluate the expression for the given value of the variable.**

13. $3 + 2x^3$ when $x = 2$

14. $y^4 \div 8$ when $y = 4$

15. $6 \cdot 2p^2$ when $p = 5$

16. $t^5 - 10t$ when $t = 3$

17. $13 + 3b$ when $b = 7$

18. $3r^2 - 17$ when $r = 6$

19. $\frac{x}{7} + 16$ when $x = 14$

20. $27 - \frac{24}{b}$ when $b = 8$

21. $\frac{4}{5} \div n + 13$ when $n = \frac{1}{5}$

22. $\frac{9}{10} \cdot y - \frac{3}{10}$ when $y = \frac{1}{2}$

EVALUATING NUMERICAL EXPRESSIONS **Evaluate the expression.**

STUDENT HELP

▶ HOMEWORK HELP
Example 1: Exs. 13–22
Example 2: Exs. 23–37
Example 3: Exs. 38–40, 42
Example 4: Exs. 43–46
Example 5: Ex. 41

23. $4 + 9 - 1$

24. $3 \cdot 2 + \frac{5}{9}$

25. $6 \div 3 + 2 \cdot 7$

26. $5 + 8 \cdot 2 - 4$

27. $16 \div 8 \cdot 2^2$

28. $2 \cdot 3^2 \div 7$

29. $10 \div (3 + 2) + 9$

30. $7[(18 - 6) - 6]$

31. $[(7 - 4)^2 + 3] + 15$

32. $3(2.7 \div 0.9) - 5$

33. $6(5 - 3)^2 + 3$

34. $[10 + (5^2 \cdot 2)] \div 6$

35. $\frac{1}{3}(9 \cdot 3) + 18$

36. $\frac{1}{2} \cdot 26 - 3^2$

37. $2.5 \cdot 0.5^2 \div 5$

EXPRESSIONS WITH FRACTION BARS Evaluate the expression.

38. $\dfrac{9 \cdot 2}{4 + 3^2 - 1}$

39. $\dfrac{13 - 4}{18 - 4^2 + 1}$

40. $\dfrac{5^3 \cdot 2}{1 + 6^2 - 8}$

41. *Writing* You decide to buy two rings from an outdoor vendor. One ring costs $10.89. The other ring costs $12.48. The sales tax is 8%. The vendor uses a calculator to obtain the price including sales tax for both rings and gets $24.37. What mistake did the vendor make?

42. LOGICAL REASONING Which is correct? Explain.

A. $\dfrac{(9 - 7)^2 + 3}{5} = (9 - 7)^2 + 3 \div 5$

B. $\dfrac{(9 - 7)^2 + 3}{5} = [(9 - 7)^2 + 3] \div 5$

ORDER OF OPERATIONS In Exercises 43–46, two calculators were used to evaluate the expression. They gave different results. Which calculator used the established order of operations? Rewrite the calculator steps with grouping symbols so that both calculators give the correct result.

43. 15 [−] 6 [÷] 3 [×] 4 [ENTER] Calculator A: 12; Calculator B: 7

44. 15 [−] 9 [÷] 3 [+] 7 [ENTER] Calculator A: 19; Calculator B: 9

45. 15 [+] 10 [÷] 5 [+] 4 [ENTER] Calculator A: 21; Calculator B: 9

46. 4 [×] 3 [+] 6 [÷] 2 [ENTER] Calculator A: 9; Calculator B: 15

47. HOTEL RATES A hotel charges $49.99 per room per night for adults and $44.10 per room per night for senior citizens. The expression $2 \times \$49.99 + 3 \times \$44.10$ represents the total cost of five rooms for two adults and three senior citizens for an overnight stay. Where in the expression can you put grouping symbols to make sure it is evaluated correctly?

FOOTBALL UNIFORMS In Exercises 48 and 49, use the following information. The table shows the cost of parts of a professional football player's uniform. A sporting goods company offers a $3200 discount for orders of 30 or more complete professional football player uniforms.

48. Write an expression that represents the cost for an order of 35 complete professional football player uniforms.

49. Evaluate the expression you wrote in Exercise 48.

Part of uniform	Jersey and pants	Shoulder pads	Lower body pads	Knee pads	Cleats	Helmet
Cost	$230	$300	$50	$25	$100	$200

ADMISSION PRICES In Exercises 50 and 51, use the table below. It shows the admission prices for the California State Fair in 1998. Suppose a family of 2 adults, 1 senior, and 3 children go to the State Fair. The children's ages are 13 years, 10 years, and 18 months.

50. Write an expression that represents the admission price for the family.

51. Evaluate the expression you wrote in Exercise 50.

California State Fair Admission Prices	
Age	Admission price
General Admission (13–61 years of age)	$7.00
Seniors (62 years and above)	$5.00
Children (5–12 years)	$4.00
Children (4 years and under)	Free

▶ Source: *Sacramento Bee*

STUDENT HELP

Study Tip
The expression $b_1 + b_2$ is read "*b* sub 1 plus *b* sub 2".

52. **GEOMETRY CONNECTION** The area A of a trapezoid with parallel bases of lengths b_1 and b_2 and height h is $A = \frac{1}{2}h(b_1 + b_2)$.

Find the area of a trapezoid whose height is 2 meters and whose bases are 6 meters and 10 meters.

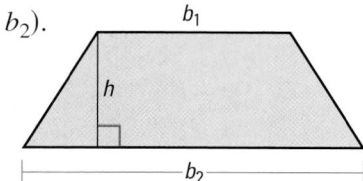

GEOMETRY CONNECTION In Exercises 53 and 54, use the following information. The surface area of a cylinder equals the lateral surface area $(2\pi r \cdot h)$ plus the area of the two bases $(2 \cdot \pi r^2)$.

53. Write the expression for the surface area of a cylinder.

54. Evaluate the expression when $h = 10.5$ centimeters and $r = 2.5$ centimeters. Use 3.14 as an approximation for π.

Test Preparation

55. **MULTI-STEP PROBLEM** You are shopping for school supplies. A store is offering a 10% discount on binders and a 20% discount on packages of paper. You want to buy 5 binders originally marked $2.50 each and 10 packages of paper originally marked $1.30 each.

    a. Write an expression that shows how much you will save after the discounts.

    b. Evaluate the expression.

    c. *Writing* If you have $25 to spend on supplies, how much money will you have left over? Explain how you arrived at your answer.

★ Challenge

56. **CRITICAL THINKING** Without grouping symbols, the expression $2 \cdot 3^3 + 4$ has a value of 58. Insert grouping symbols in the expression $2 \cdot 3^3 + 4$ to produce the indicated values.

    a. 62   **b.** 220   **c.** 4374   **d.** 279,936

57. Create a math puzzle like the one in Exercise 56 with an expression that produces different values when grouping symbols are inserted in different places.

EXTRA CHALLENGE
www.mcdougallittell.com

MIXED REVIEW

STUDENT HELP

➡ **Skills Review**
For help with fractions, see pp. 781–783.

EVALUATING EXPRESSIONS Evaluate the expression for the given value of the variable. (Review 1.1)

58. $8a$ when $a = 4$

59. $\dfrac{24}{x}$ when $x = 3$

60. $c + 15$ when $c = 12.5$

61. $\dfrac{4}{3} \cdot x$ when $x = \dfrac{1}{6}$

62. $9d$ when $d = 0.5$

63. $\dfrac{5}{16} - p$ when $p = \dfrac{3}{8}$

EVALUATING EXPONENTIAL EXPRESSIONS Evaluate the expression for the given value of the variable. (Review 1.2)

64. $(6w)^2$ when $w = 5$

65. $4(t^3)$ when $t = 3$

66. $9b^2$ when $b = 8$

67. $5x^2$ when $x = 16$

68. $(7x)^3$ when $x = 2$

69. $6y^5$ when $y = 4$

70. 🌐 **INTEREST EARNED** You deposit $120 in a savings account that pays an annual interest rate of 2.5%. How much simple interest would you earn in 2 years? (Review 1.1)

71. 🌐 **DRIVING TIME** If you are driving at a constant speed of 68 miles per hour, how long will it take you to travel 170 miles? (Review 1.1)

72. **GEOMETRY** ▶ **CONNECTION** Find the volume of the cube shown at the right and find the area of one of its sides. (Review 1.2 for 1.4)

4 cm

4 cm

4 cm

QUIZ 1

Self-Test for Lessons 1.1–1.3

Evaluate the expression when $x = 3$. (Lesson 1.1)

1. $6x$

2. $\dfrac{36}{x}$

3. $x + 29$

4. $x - 2$

5. $x \div 3$

6. $21 - x$

7. $4.5x$

8. $13.7 + x$

🌐 **TRAVEL** Find the average speed. (Lesson 1.1)

9. 120 miles in 3 hours

10. 90 miles in 1.5 hours

11. 360 miles in 6 hours

Write the expression in exponential form. (Lesson 1.2)

12. six cubed

13. $4 \cdot 4 \cdot 4 \cdot 4 \cdot 4$

14. $5y \cdot 5y \cdot 5y$

15. five squared

16. $3 \cdot 3 \cdot 3 \cdot 3 \cdot 3 \cdot 3 \cdot t$

17. $7x \cdot 7x$

Evaluate the expression when $x = 6$. (Lesson 1.2)

18. x^5

19. $2x^3$

20. $(2x)^3$

21. $x^2 - 3$

Evaluate the expression. (Lesson 1.3)

22. $\dfrac{6 \cdot 3}{7 + (2^3 - 1)}$

23. $\dfrac{2^5 - 12}{2(5^2 - 5)}$

24. $\dfrac{(3^2 - 3)}{2 \cdot 9}$

25. $\dfrac{2(17 + 2 \cdot 4)}{6^2 - 11}$

26. 🌐 **PACKING BOXES** A cubic packing box has dimensions of 1.2 feet on each side. What is the volume of the box? (Lesson 1.2)

● ACTIVITY 1.4

Developing Concepts

SET UP
Work in a small group.

MATERIALS
• graph paper
• pencil

Finding Patterns

▶ **QUESTION** How can you use algebra to describe a pattern?

▶ **EXPLORING THE CONCEPT**

❶ Copy the first four figures on graph paper. Then draw the fifth and sixth figures of the sequence.

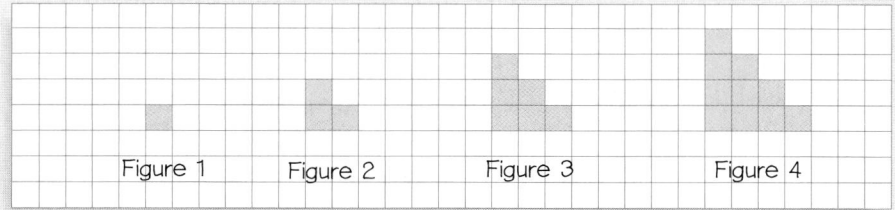

Figure 1   Figure 2   Figure 3   Figure 4

❷ The table shows the mathematical pattern for the perimeters of the first four figures. Copy and complete the table.

Figure	1	2	3	4	5	6
Perimeter	4	8	12	16	?	?
Pattern	4 • 1	4 • 2	4 • 3	4 • 4	4 • ?	4 • ?

❸ Use the pattern in the table to predict the perimeter of the 25th figure.

❹ What is the perimeter of the *n*th figure? Explain your reasoning.

▶ **DRAWING CONCLUSIONS**

1. Copy the four figures shown below on graph paper. Then draw the fifth and sixth figures for the sequence.

Figure 1   Figure 2   Figure 3   Figure 4

2. Calculate the perimeters for all six figures. Organize your results in a table.

3. What is the perimeter of the *n*th figure? Explain your reasoning.

4. Repeat Exercises 1–3 for the sequence below.

Figure 1   Figure 2   Figure 3   Figure 4

1.4 *Concept Activity*   **23**

1.4

Equations and Inequalities

What you should learn

GOAL 1 Check solutions and solve equations using mental math.

GOAL 2 Check solutions of inequalities in a **real-life** problem, such as regulating your cat's caloric intake in **Example 5**.

Why you should learn it

▼ To solve a **real-life** problem such as how long you must save money to buy a violin in **Ex. 68**.

GOAL 1 CHECKING AND SOLVING EQUATIONS

An **equation** is formed when an equal sign ($=$) is placed between two expressions creating a left and right side of the equation. An equation that contains one or more variables is an **open sentence**. Here are some examples.

$$4 - b = 3 \qquad 3x + 1 = 7 \qquad a + 3 = 3 + a$$

When the variable in a single-variable equation is replaced by a number, the resulting statement can be true or false. If the statement is true, the number is a **solution of an equation**.

Substituting a number for a variable in an equation to see whether the resulting statement is true or false is called *checking* a possible solution.

EXAMPLE 1 *Substituting to Check Possible Solutions*

Check whether the numbers 2 and 3 are solutions of the equation $3x + 1 = 7$.

SOLUTION

To check the possible solutions, substitute them into the equation. If both sides of the equation have the same value, then the number is a solution.

x	3x + 1 = 7	Result	Conclusion
2	$3(2) + 1 \stackrel{?}{=} 7$	$7 = 7$	2 is a solution
3	$3(3) + 1 \stackrel{?}{=} 7$	$10 \neq 7$	3 is not a solution

↑
is not equal to

▶ The number 2 is a solution of $3x + 1 = 7$. The number 3 is *not* a solution.

EXAMPLE 2 *Checking Possible Solutions*

Check whether the numbers 2, 3, and 4 are solutions of the equation $4x - 2 = 10$.

SOLUTION

x	4x − 2 = 10	Result	Conclusion
2	$4(2) - 2 \stackrel{?}{=} 10$	$6 \neq 10$	2 is not a solution
3	$4(3) - 2 \stackrel{?}{=} 10$	$10 = 10$	3 is a solution
4	$4(4) - 2 \stackrel{?}{=} 10$	$14 \neq 10$	4 is not a solution

▶ The number 3 is a solution, and 2 and 4 are *not* solutions of the equation.

Finding all the solutions of an equation is called **solving the equation**. Later in the book, you will study several ways to systematically solve equations.

Some equations are simple enough to solve in your head with mental math. For instance, to solve $x + 2 = 5$, ask yourself the question

> *"What number can be added to 2 to obtain 5?"*

If you can see that the answer is 3, then you have solved the equation!

⊙ **ACTIVITY**

Developing Concepts

Using Mental Math to Solve Equations

❶ Match the equation with the question that can be used to find a solution of the equation.

❷ Then use mental math to solve the equation.

EQUATION	MENTAL MATH QUESTION
1. $x + 2 = 6$	**A.** 2 times what number gives 10?
2. $x - 3 = 4$	**B.** What number divided by 3 gives 1?
3. $2x = 10$	**C.** What number minus 3 gives 4?
4. $\frac{x}{3} = 1$	**D.** What number cubed gives 8?
5. $x^3 = 8$	**E.** What number plus 2 gives 6?

Using mental math to solve equations is something that you already do in everyday life. You probably don't think of it as solving equations, but the mental math process is the same.

Grocery Shopping

EXAMPLE 3 *Using Mental Math to Solve a Real-Life Equation*

You need to buy ingredients for nachos. In the supermarket you find that a bag of tortilla chips costs $2.99, beans cost $.99, cheese costs $3.99, two tomatoes cost $1.00, and olives cost $1.49. You have a ten-dollar bill. About how much more money do you need?

SOLUTION

You can ask the question: The total cost equals 10 plus what number of dollars? Let x represent any additional money you may need. Use rounding to estimate the total cost.

$$3 + 1 + 4 + 1 + 1.5 = 10 + x$$

$$10.5 = 10 + x$$

▶ Because the total cost of the ingredients is approximately 10.5 or $10.50, you can see that you need about $.50 more to purchase all the ingredients.

GOAL 2 CHECKING SOLUTIONS OF INEQUALITIES

Another type of open sentence is an **inequality**. An inequality is formed when an inequality symbol, such as $<$, is placed between two expressions.

SYMBOL	MEANING
$<$	is less than.
$\leq$	is less than or equal to
$>$	is greater than
$\geq$	is greater than or equal to

A **solution of an inequality** is a number that produces a true statement when it is substituted for the variable in the inequality.

EXAMPLE 4 *Checking Solutions of Inequalities*

Decide whether 4 is a solution of the inequality.

a. $2x - 1 < 8$ **b.** $x + 4 > 9$ **c.** $x - 3 \geq 1$

SOLUTION

INEQUALITY	SUBSTITUTION	RESULT	CONCLUSION
a. $2x - 1 < 8$	$2(4) - 1 \overset{?}{<} 8$	$7 < 8$	4 is a solution.
b. $x + 4 > 9$	$4 + 4 \overset{?}{>} 9$	$8 \not> 9$	4 is not a solution.
c. $x - 3 \geq 1$	$4 - 3 \overset{?}{\geq} 1$	$1 \geq 1$	4 is a solution.

EXAMPLE 5 *Checking Solutions in Real Life*

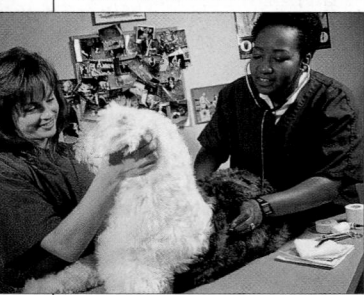

VETERINARIAN Your vet told you to restrict your cat's caloric intake to no more than 500 calories each day. Three times a day, you give your cat a serving of food containing x calories. Do the following values of x meet the vet's restriction?

a. 170 calories   **b.** 165 calories

SOLUTION

a.
$3x \leq 500$	Write original inequality.
$3(170) \leq 500$	Substitute 170 for *x*.
$510 \not\leq 500$	Simplify.

▶ No. This is too many calories per serving.

b.
$3x \leq 500$	Write original inequality.
$3(165) \leq 500$	Substitute 165 for *x*.
$495 \leq 500$	Simplify.

▶ Yes. If each serving has 165 calories, you will meet your goal.

GUIDED PRACTICE

Vocabulary Check ✓

Decide whether the following is an *expression*, an *equation*, or an *inequality*. Explain your decision.

1. $3x + 1 = 14$ **2.** $7y - 6$ **3.** $5(y^2 + 4) - 7$

4. $5x - 1 = 3 + x$ **5.** $3x + 2 \leq 8$ **6.** $5x > 20$

7. Identify the left side and the right side of the equation $8 + 3x = 5x - 9$.

Concept Check ✓

8. ERROR ANALYSIS Jan says her work shows that 6 is not a solution of $3x - 4 = 14$. What is a likely explanation for her error?

$$3 \cdot (6) - 4 = 6$$

Skill Check ✓

9. Which question could be used to find the solution of the equation $5 - x = 1$?

A. What number can 5 be subtracted from to get 1?

B. What number can be subtracted from 5 to get 1?

C. What number can 1 be subtracted from to get 5?

🌐 **ELECTIONS** The number of votes received by the new student council president is represented by *x*. Match the sentence with the equation or inequality that represents it.

A. $x = 125$ **B.** $x < 125$ **C.** $x \geq 125$ **D.** $x \leq 125$

10. She received no more than 125 votes.   **11.** She received at least 125 votes.

12. She received exactly 125 votes.   **13.** She received less than 125 votes.

PRACTICE AND APPLICATIONS

STUDENT HELP

▶ **Extra Practice**
to help you master
skills is on p. 797.

CHECKING SOLUTIONS OF EQUATIONS Check whether the given number is a solution of the equation.

14. $3b + 1 = 13; 4$ **15.** $5 + x^2 = 17; 3$ **16.** $4c + 2 = 2c + 8; 2$

17. $2y^3 + 3 = 5; 1$ **18.** $5r - 10 = 11; 5$ **19.** $4s - 4 = 30 - s; 7$

20. $6d - 5 = 20; 5$ **21.** $\frac{x}{4} - 9 = 9; 36$ **22.** $m + 4m = 60 - 2m; 10$

23. $10 + \frac{a}{7} = 12; 14$ **24.** $p^2 - 5 = 20; 6$ **25.** $4h - h = \frac{12}{h}; 3$

MENTAL MATH Write a question that could be used to solve the equation. Then use mental math to solve the equation.

STUDENT HELP

▶ **HOMEWORK HELP**
Example 1: Exs. 14–25
Example 2: Exs. 14–25
Example 3: Exs. 26–37,
65, 66
Example 4: Exs. 38–55
Example 5: Exs. 67, 68

26. $x + 3 = 8$ **27.** $n + 6 = 11$ **28.** $p - 11 = 20$

29. $3y = 12$ **30.** $\frac{x}{4} = 5$ **31.** $4p = 36$

32. $4r - 1 = 11$ **33.** $2t - 1 = 9$ **34.** $m^2 = 144$

35. $\frac{x}{7} = 3$ **36.** $5q - 2 = 3$ **37.** $y^3 = 125$

CHECKING SOLUTIONS OF INEQUALITIES Check whether the given number is a solution of the inequality.

38. $n - 2 < 6$; 3   **39.** $5 + s > 8$; 4   **40.** $5 + 5x \geq 10$; 1

41. $4p - 1 \geq 8$; 2   **42.** $3r - 15 < 0$; 5   **43.** $11x \leq x - 7$; 9

44. $6 + y \leq 8$; 3   **45.** $29 - 4b > 5$; 7   **46.** $t^2 + 6 > 40$; 6

47. $a - 7 \geq 15$; 22   **48.** $6x - 16 < 20$; 7   **49.** $y^3 - 2 \leq 8$; 2

50. $r + 2r < 30$; 9   **51.** $a(3a + 2) > 50$; 4   **52.** $\dfrac{c + 5}{3} \leq 4$; 3

53. $\dfrac{25 - d}{d} \geq 4$; 5   **54.** $x^2 - 10 > 16$; 6   **55.** $n(21 - n) < 100$; 8

EQUATIONS AND INEQUALITIES Match the verbal sentence with its mathematical representation.

56. The sum of x and 16 is less than 32.   **A.** $\dfrac{x}{16} > 32$

57. The product of 16 and x is equal to 32.   **B.** $x^4 = 16$

58. The difference of x and 16 is 32.   **C.** $x + 16 < 32$

59. The quotient of x and 16 is greater than or equal to 32.   **D.** $16 + x \leq 32$

60. The product of 16 and x is less than 32.   **E.** $16x > 32$

61. The fourth power of x is 16.   **F.** $x - 16 = 32$

62. The sum of 16 and x is less than or equal to 32.   **G.** $16x = 32$

63. The quotient of x and 16 is greater than 32.   **H.** $\dfrac{x}{16} \geq 32$

64. The product of 16 and x is greater than 32.   **I.** $16x < 32$

65. 🌐 **COMPUTER CENTER** Your school is building a new computer center. Four hundred square feet of the center will be available for computer stations. Each station requires 20 square feet. You want to find how many computer stations can be placed in the new center. You write the equation $20x = 400$ to model the situation. What do 20, x, and 400 represent? Solve the equation. Check your solution.

66. 🌐 **PLAYING A COMPUTER GAME** You are playing a new computer game. For every eight screens you complete, you receive a bonus. You want to know how many bonuses you will receive after completing 96 screens. You write the equation $8x = 96$ to model the situation. What do 8, x, and 96 represent? Solve the equation. Check your solution.

67. 🌐 **BUYING GAS** You are taking a trip by automobile with the family of a friend. You have $65 to help pay for gas. It costs $15 to fill the tank. Can you completely fill the gas tank four times? You use the inequality $15x \leq 65$ to model the situation. What do 15, x, and 65 represent?

68. 🌐 **BUYING A VIOLIN** You are budgeting money to buy a violin and bow that cost $250 including tax. If you save $5 per week, will you have enough money in a year? You write the inequality $5n \geq 250$ to model the situation. What do 5, n, and 250 represent? Solve the inequality.

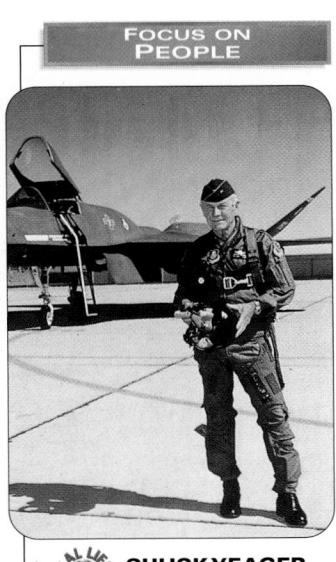

🌐 **APPLYING FORMULAS** In Exercises 69–76, match the problem with the formula needed to solve the problem. Then use the Guess, Check, and Revise strategy or another problem-solving strategy to solve the problem.

Area of a rectangle	$A = lw$	Distance	$d = rt$
Simple interest	$I = Prt$	Volume of a cube	$V = s^3$
Temperature	$C = \frac{5}{9}(F - 32)$	Surface area of a cube	$S = 6s^2$

69. What is the average speed of a runner who completes a 10,000-meter race in 25 minutes?

70. How long must $1000 be invested at an annual interest rate of 3% to earn $300 in simple interest?

71. A car travels 60 miles per hour for a distance of 300 miles. How long did the trip take?

72. Carpeting costs $20 per square yard. You carpet a room that has a width of 15 feet for $800. What is the length of the room in feet?

73. You measure the temperature of a substance in a chemistry lab at 32°F. What is the temperature in degrees Celsius?

74. A piece of cheese cut in the shape of a cube has a volume of 27 cubic inches. What is the length of each edge of the piece of cheese?

75. You want to construct a patio of 80 square feet with a length of 10 feet. What is the width of the patio?

76. A cubic storage box is made with 96 square feet of wood. What is the length of each edge?

77. 🌐 **AIRCRAFT DESIGN** In the diagram, let x represent the length of a passenger jet and let y represent the jet's wingspan.

a. What does the equation $1.212y = x$ say about the relationship between the length and the wingspan of the passenger jet?

b. Is the passenger jet longer than it is wide or wider than it is long? Explain your reasoning.

199 ft 11 in.

242 ft 4 in.

78. 🌐 **MACH NUMBERS** The *Mach number* of an aircraft is the ratio of its maximum speed to the speed of sound. Copy and complete the table. Use the equation $v = 660m$, where v is the speed (in miles per hour) of the aircraft and m is the Mach number, to find the speed of each aircraft.

Airplane type	X-15A-2	Supersonic transport	Commercial jet
Mach number, m	6.7	2.2	0.9
Speed, v	?	?	?

Test Preparation

79. MULTIPLE CHOICE You tune and restore pianos. As a piano tuner you charge $75 per tuning. The expenses for your piano restoration business are $2600 per month. Which of the following inequalities could you use to find the number of pianos p you must tune per month in order to at least meet your business expenses?

Ⓐ $75p \le 2600$ Ⓑ $75p \ge 2600$ Ⓒ $\dfrac{75}{p} \ge 2600$ Ⓓ $75p = 2600$

80. MULTIPLE CHOICE The width of a soccer field cannot be greater than 100 yards. The area cannot be greater than 13,000 square yards. Which of the following would you use to find the possible lengths of a soccer field?

Ⓐ $100x \ge 13{,}000$ Ⓑ $100x \le 13{,}000$

Ⓒ $100 + x \le 13{,}000$ Ⓓ $100x = 130{,}000$

81. MULTIPLE CHOICE For which inequality is $x = 238$ a solution?

Ⓐ $250 \ge x + 12$ Ⓑ $250 < x + 12$ Ⓒ $250 > x + 12$

★ Challenge

🌐 **BUSINESS** **You plan to start your own greeting card business. Your startup cost of buying a computer and color printer is $1400. You also want to run an ad for $50 a week for 4 weeks. You plan to sell each card for $1.79. How many cards must you sell to equal or exceed your initial costs?**

82. Write an inequality that models the situation. Solve the inequality to find the minimum number of cards you must sell.

83. *Writing* Try raising the price per card. How does the price increase change the number of cards you must sell to equal or exceed your initial costs? What are some factors you need to consider in choosing a price?

EXTRA CHALLENGE
➞ www.mcdougallittell.com

MIXED REVIEW

EVALUATING EXPRESSIONS Evaluate the expression for the given value of the variable. **(Review 1.1)**

84. $1.2n$ when $n = 4.8$

85. $\dfrac{1}{12} + x$ when $x = \dfrac{1}{6}$

86. $b - 12$ when $b = 43$

87. $\dfrac{4}{5} \cdot y$ when $y = \dfrac{1}{5}$

EXPONENTIAL FORM Write the expression in exponential form. **(Review 1.2)**

88. three cubed

89. y squared

90. $6 \cdot 6 \cdot 6 \cdot 6 \cdot 6$

91. $c \cdot c \cdot c \cdot c$

92. five to the fourth power

93. $5y \cdot 5y \cdot 5y \cdot 5y$

94. three squared

95. $9a \cdot 9a \cdot 9a \cdot 9a \cdot 9a \cdot 9a$

96. seven squared

97. one to the third power

98. $6 \cdot x \cdot x \cdot x \cdot x \cdot x \cdot x$

99. $t \cdot t \cdot t \cdot t \cdot t \cdot t$

100. 🌐 **WATER TEMPERATURE** The temperature of the water in a swimming pool is 78° Fahrenheit. What is the temperature of the water in degrees Celsius? Use the formula $C = \dfrac{5}{9}(F - 32)$, where F is the Fahrenheit temperature and C is the Celsius temperature. **(Review 1.3 for 1.5)**

◐ ACTIVITY 1.5

Developing Concepts

Exploring Problem Solving

SETUP
Work with a partner.

MATERIALS
• paper
• pencil

▶ **QUESTION** **How can problem solving strategies help you find solutions to problems?**

When solving a problem, you need to understand two things: what you are asked to find and what information you need to solve the problem. Then you can use algebra or a problem solving strategy.

▶ **EXPLORING THE CONCEPT**

1 State what you are asked to find in the following problem.

In science class you have five 100-point tests and one final 200-point test that counts as two tests. You need an average of at least 90 points to get an A. Your scores for the five 100-point tests are 88, 92, 87, 98, and 81. What is the lowest score you can get on the final test to get an A?

2 List the information you need to solve the problem.

3 Use the strategy Guess, Check, and Revise to solve the problem.

Test Average: $\dfrac{88 + 92 + 87 + 98 + 81 + ?}{7}$

Sample First Guess: $\dfrac{88 + 92 + 87 + 98 + 81 + 149}{7} = 85$ Too low

Sample Second Guess: $\dfrac{88 + 92 + 87 + 98 + 81 + 191}{7} = 91$ Too high

Your Guess: $\dfrac{88 + 92 + 87 + 98 + 81 + ?}{7} = \underline{?}$

The lowest score you can get on the final test to get an A is $\underline{?}$.

▶ **DRAWING CONCLUSIONS**

Solve the real-life problem. Explain your strategy.

1. A plumber charges a basic service fee plus a labor charge for each hour of service. A 2-hour job costs $120 and a 4-hour job costs $180. Find the plumber's basic service fee.

2. Jerry has received the following math test scores: 80, 75, 79, 86. His final exam is worth 200 points and counts as two tests. What is the lowest score he can get to keep an average of at least 80 points?

3. A Native American art museum charges $8 per visit to nonmembers. Members pay a $40 membership fee and get in for a reduced rate of $5. How many times must a person visit the museum for membership to be less expensive than paying for each visit as a nonmember?

┌─ STUDENT HELP ─┐
↳ **Skills Review**
For help with problem solving strategies, see pp. 795–796.

1.5 A Problem Solving Plan Using Models

What you should learn

GOAL ① Translate verbal phrases into algebraic expressions.

GOAL ② Use a verbal model to write an algebraic equation or inequality to solve a **real-life** problem, such as making a decision about an airplane's speed in **Example 3**.

Why you should learn it

▼ To solve **real-life** problems such as finding out how many plates of dim sum were ordered for lunch in **Example 2**.

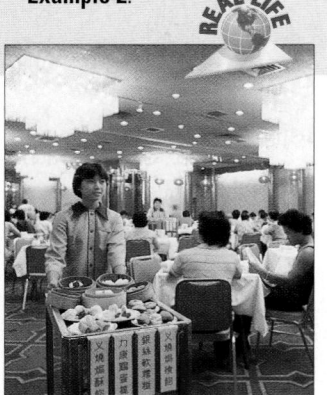

REAL LIFE

GOAL ① TRANSLATING VERBAL PHRASES

To translate verbal phrases into algebra, look for words that indicate operations.

Operation	Verbal Phrase	Expression
Addition	The *sum* of six and a number	$6 + x$
	Eight *more than* a number	$y + 8$
	A number *plus* five	$n + 5$
	A number *increased* by seven	$x + 7$
Subtraction	The *difference* of five and a number	$5 - y$
	Four *less than* a number	$x - 4$
	Seven *minus* a number	$7 - n$
	A number *decreased* by nine	$n - 9$
Multiplication	The *product* of nine and a number	$9x$
	Ten *times* a number	$10n$
	A number *multiplied* by three	$3y$
Division	The *quotient* of a number and four	$\dfrac{n}{4}$
	Seven *divided* by a number	$\dfrac{7}{x}$

Order is important for subtraction and division, but *not* for addition and multiplication. "Four less than a number" is written as $x - 4$, *not* $4 - x$. On the other hand, "the sum of six and a number" can be written as $6 + x$ or $x + 6$.

EXAMPLE 1 *Translating Verbal Phrases into Algebra*

Translate the phrase into an algebraic expression.

SOLUTION

a. Three more than the quantity five times a number n

$$5n + 3 \qquad \text{Think: 3 more than what?}$$

b. Two less than the sum of six and a number m

$$(6 + m) - 2 \qquad \text{Think: 2 less than what?}$$

c. A number x decreased by the sum of 10 and the square of a number y

$$x - (10 + y^2) \qquad \text{Think: } x \text{ decreased by what?}$$

GOAL 2 USING A VERBAL MODEL

In English there is a difference between a phrase and a sentence. Verbal phrases translate into mathematical expressions and verbal sentences translate into equations or inequalities.

Phrase	The sum of six and a number	**Expression**	$6 + x$
Sentence	The sum of six and a number is twelve.	**Equation**	$6 + x = 12$
Sentence	Seven times a number is less than fifty.	**Inequality**	$7x < 50$

Sentences that translate into equations have words that tell how one quantity relates to another. In the first sentence, the word "is" says that one quantity is equal to another. In the second sentence, the words "is less than" indicate an inequality.

Writing algebraic expressions, equations or inequalities that represent real-life situations is called **modeling**. The expression, equation or inequality is a **mathematical model** of the real-life situation. When you write a mathematical model, we suggest that you use three steps.

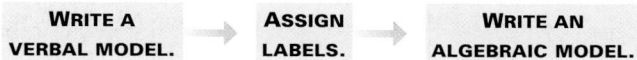

WRITE A VERBAL MODEL. → ASSIGN LABELS. → WRITE AN ALGEBRAIC MODEL.

Dining Out

EXAMPLE 2 *Writing an Algebraic Model*

You and three friends are having a dim sum lunch at a Chinese restaurant that charges $2 per plate. You order lots of plates of wontons, egg rolls, and dumplings. The waiter gives you a bill for $25.20, which includes tax of $1.20. Use mental math to solve the equation for how many plates your group ordered.

SOLUTION

Be sure that you understand the problem situation before you begin. For example, notice that the tax is added after the cost of the plates of dim sum is figured.

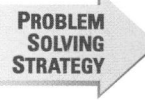
PROBLEM SOLVING STRATEGY

VERBAL MODEL

$$\boxed{\text{Cost per plate}} \cdot \boxed{\text{Number of plates}} = \boxed{\text{Bill}} - \boxed{\text{Tax}}$$

LABELS

Cost per plate = **2**   (dollars)

Number of plates = ***p***   (plates)

Amount of bill = **25.20**   (dollars)

Tax = **1.20**   (dollars)

ALGEBRAIC MODEL

$2p = 25.20 - 1.20$

$2p = 24.00$

$p = 12$

▶ Your group ordered 12 plates of food costing $24.00.

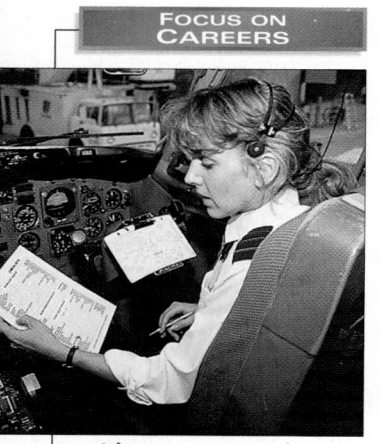
A PROBLEM SOLVING PLAN USING MODELS

VERBAL MODEL	Ask yourself what you need to know to solve the problem. Then write a verbal model that will give you what you need to know.
LABELS	Assign labels to each part of your verbal model.
ALGEBRAIC MODEL	Use the labels to write an algebraic model based on your verbal model.
SOLVE	Solve the algebraic model and answer the original question.
CHECK	Check that your answer is reasonable.

REAL LIFE **JET PILOT**
Pilots select a route, an altitude, and a speed that will provide the fastest and safest flight.

CAREER LINK
www.mcdougallittell.com

Verbal and algebraic modeling can be used as part of a general problem solving plan that includes solving and checking to see that an answer is reasonable.

EXAMPLE 3 *Using a Verbal Model*

JET PILOT A jet pilot is flying from Los Angeles, CA to Chicago, IL at a speed of 500 miles per hour. When the plane is 600 miles from Chicago, an air traffic controller tells the pilot that it will be 2 hours before the plane can get clearance to land. The pilot knows that at its present altitude the speed of the jet must be greater than 322 miles per hour or the jet will stall.

a. At what speed would the jet have to fly to arrive in Chicago in 2 hours?

b. Is it reasonable for the pilot to fly directly to Chicago at the reduced speed from part (a) or must the pilot take some other action?

SOLUTION

a. You can use the formula (rate)(time) = (distance) to write a verbal model.

PROBLEM SOLVING STRATEGY

VERBAL MODEL

$$\boxed{\text{Speed of jet}} \cdot \boxed{\text{Time}} = \boxed{\text{Distance to travel}}$$

LABELS

Speed of jet = x (miles per hour)

Time = 2 (hours)

Distance to travel = 600 (miles)

ALGEBRAIC MODEL

$2x = 600$ Write algebraic model.

$x = 300$ Solve with mental math.

▶ To arrive in 2 hours, the pilot would have to slow the jet down to a speed of 300 miles per hour.

b. It is not reasonable for the pilot to fly at 300 miles per hour, because the jet will stall. The pilot should take some other action, such as circling in a holding pattern, to use some of the time.

GUIDED PRACTICE

Vocabulary Check ✓

In Exercises 1 and 2, consider the verbal phrase: *the difference of 7 and a number n.*

1. What operation does the word *difference* indicate?

2. Translate the verbal phrase into an algebraic expression.

Concept Check ✓

3. Is order important in the expression in Exercise 2?

4. Describe how to use a verbal model to solve a problem.

Skill Check ✓

Match the verbal phrase with its corresponding algebraic expression.

5. Eleven decreased by the quantity four times a number x

6. Four increased by the quantity eleven times a number x

7. Four times the quantity of a number x minus eleven

8. Four times a number x decreased by eleven

A. $4x - 11$

B. $4(x - 11)$

C. $11 - 4x$

D. $11x + 4$

Write the verbal sentence as an equation or an inequality.

9. A number x increased by ten is 24.

10. The product of seven and a number y is 42.

11. Twenty divided by a number n is less than or equal to two.

12. Ten more than a number x is greater than fourteen.

PRACTICE AND APPLICATIONS

STUDENT HELP

▶ **Extra Practice**
to help you master
skills is on p. 797.

TRANSLATING PHRASES **Write the verbal phrase as an algebraic expression. Use x for the variable in your expression.**

13. Nine more than a number

14. One half multiplied by a number

15. Three more than half of a number

16. A number increased by seven

17. Quotient of a number and two tenths

18. Product of four and a number

19. Two cubed divided by a number

20. Difference of ten and a number

21. Five squared minus a number

22. Twenty-nine decreased by a number

TRANSLATING VERBAL SENTENCES **Write the verbal sentence as an equation or an inequality.**

23. Nine is greater than three times a number s.

24. Twenty-five is the quotient of a number y and 3.5.

25. The product of 14 and a number x is one.

26. Nine less than the product of ten and a number d is eleven.

27. Three times the quantity two less than a number x is ten.

28. Five decreased by eight is four times y.

STUDENT HELP

▶ **HOMEWORK HELP**
Example 1: Exs. 13–38
Example 2: Exs. 39–48
Example 3: Exs. 49–57

TRANSLATING VERBAL SENTENCES In Exercises 29–38, write the verbal sentence as an equation, or an inequality.

29. Twenty-three less than the difference of thirty-eight and a number n is less than eight.

30. A number t increased by the sum of seven and the square of another number s is ten.

31. Five less than the difference of twenty and a number x is greater than or equal to ten.

32. Fourteen plus the product of twelve and a number y is less than or equal to fifty.

33. Nine plus the quotient of a number b and ten is greater than or equal to eleven.

34. Seventy divided by the product of seven and a number p is equal to one.

35. A number q is equal to or greater than one hundred.

36. A number x squared plus forty-four is equal to the number x to the fourth power times three.

37. The quotient of thirty-five and a number t is less than or equal to seven.

38. Fifty multiplied by the quantity twenty divided by a number n is greater than or equal to two hundred fifty.

ALGEBRAIC MODELING In Exercises 39–48, write an equation or an inequality to model the real-life situation.

39. Ben's hourly wage b at his after school job is $1.50 less than Eileen's hourly wage e.

40. The distance s to school is $\frac{1}{5}$ mile more than the distance c to the Community Center swimming pool.

41. The length c of the Colorado River is three times the length r of the Connecticut River, plus 229 miles.

42. Pi (π) is the quotient of the circumference C and the diameter d of a circle.

43. The volume V of a cube with a side length s is less than or equal to thirty minus three.

44. The product of $25 and the number m of club memberships is greater than or equal to $500.

45. The perimeter P of a square is equal to four times the difference of a number s and two.

46. The simple interest earned on a principal of three hundred dollars at an annual interest rate of x percent is less than or equal to seventy-two dollars.

47. The area A of a trapezoid is equal to one half times the sum of seven and nine, times a number h plus seven.

48. The square of the length c of the hypotenuse of a right triangle is equal to four squared plus three squared.

FUNDRAISING In Exercises 49–53, use the following information.

The science club is selling magazine subscriptions at $15 each. The club wants to raise $315 for science equipment.

49. Write a verbal model that relates the number of subscriptions, the cost of each subscription, and the amount of money the club needs to raise.

50. Assign labels and write an algebraic model based on your verbal model.

51. Use mental math to solve the equation.

52. How many subscriptions does the science club need to sell to raise $315?

53. Check to see if your answer is reasonable.

STUDENT HELP

HOMEWORK HELP

Visit our Web site www.mcdougallittell.com for help with problem solving in Exs. 54–57.

🌐 **LAW ENFORCEMENT** In Exercises 54–57, use the following information.

Jeff lives in a state in which speeders are fined $20 for each mile per hour (mi/h) over the speed limit. Jeff was given a ticket for $260 for speeding on a road where the speed limit is 45 miles per hour. Jeff wants to know how fast he was driving.

$$\boxed{\begin{array}{c}\textbf{Fine per mi/h}\\\textbf{over speed limit}\end{array}} \cdot \boxed{\begin{array}{c}\textbf{Miles per hour}\\\textbf{over speed limit}\end{array}} = \boxed{\begin{array}{c}\textbf{Amount of}\\\textbf{ticket}\end{array}}$$

54. Assign labels to the three parts of the verbal model.

55. Use the labels to translate the verbal model into an algebraic model.

56. Use mental math to solve the equation. What does the solution represent?

57. Perform unit analysis to check that the equation is set up correctly.

58. 🌐 **CLASS ELECTION** You are running for class president. At 2:30 on election day you have 95 votes and your opponent has 120 votes. Forty-five more students will be voting. Let x represent the number of students (of the 45) who vote for you.

    a. Write an inequality that shows the values of x that will allow you to win the election.

    b. What is the smallest value of x that is a solution of the inequality?

🌐 **MOUNTAIN BIKES** In Exercises 59 and 60, use the following information.

You are shopping for a mountain bike. A store sells two different models. The model that has steel wheel rims costs $220. The model with aluminum wheel rims costs $480. You have a summer job for 12 weeks. You save $20 per week, which would allow you to buy the model with the steel wheel rims. You want to know how much more money you would have to save each week to be able to buy the model with the aluminum wheel rims.

59. Write a verbal model and an algebraic model for how much more money you would have to save each week.

60. Use mental math to solve the equation. What does the solution represent?

61. 🌐 **BASKETBALL** The girls' basketball team scored 544 points in 17 games last year. This year the coach has set a goal for the team to score at least 5 more points per game. If 18 games are scheduled for this year, write an inequality that represents the total number of points the team must equal or exceed to meet their season goal.

FOCUS ON APPLICATIONS

REAL LIFE **MOUNTAIN BIKES** More than 50% of all bicycles sold in the United States are mountain bikes.

DATA UPDATE of Bicycle Product Suppliers Association data at www.mcdougallittell.com

62. MULTIPLE CHOICE Translate the phrase "a number decreased by the quotient of three and four."

(A) $n - \dfrac{3}{4}$ (B) $\dfrac{3}{4} - n$ (C) $\dfrac{n-3}{4}$ (D) $\dfrac{3}{4-n}$

63. MULTIPLE CHOICE Give the correct algebraic translation of "Howard's hourly wage h is \$2 greater than Marla's hourly wage m."

(A) $h < m + 2$ (B) $h = m + 2$ (C) $m = h + 2$ (D) $h > m + 2$

64. MULTIPLE CHOICE A jet is flying nonstop from Baltimore, Maryland, to Jacksonville, Florida, at a speed r of 500 miles per hour. The distance d between the two cities is about 680 miles. Which equation models the number of hours t the flight will take?

(A) $t = \dfrac{680}{500}$ (B) $t = 680(500)$ (C) $680 = \dfrac{t}{500}$ (D) $t = \dfrac{500}{680}$

★ **Challenge**

🌎 **SCHOOL DANCE** **In Exercises 65 and 66, use the following information.**
You are in charge of the music for a school dance. The school's budget allows only \$300 for music, which is enough to hire a disc jockey for 4 hours. You would rather hire a live band, but the band charges \$135 per hour. Your school does not allow students to be charged an admission fee. To raise the money for a live band, you obtain permission for a voluntary contribution of \$1.25 per person.

65. How much extra money do you need to raise?

66. How many students must contribute \$1.25 to cover the cost of a live band?

MIXED REVIEW

COMPARING DECIMALS **Compare using $<$, $=$, or $>$.** (Skills Review, p. 779)

67. $0.3 \; \underline{?} \; 0.30$ **68.** $21.1 \; \underline{?} \; 20.99$ **69.** $6.7 \; \underline{?} \; 6.079$

70. $5.68 \; \underline{?} \; 5.678$ **71.** $0.333 \; \underline{?} \; 0.3333$ **72.** $18.45 \; \underline{?} \; 18.5$

73. 🌎 **EATING HABITS** The table gives the number of servings per day of fruits and vegetables consumed by adults in California. Create a bar graph of the data. (Skills Review, pp. 792–794)

Servings of Fruits and Vegetables Eaten by California Adults					
Year	1989	1991	1993	1995	1997
Servings per day	3.8	3.9	3.7	4.1	3.8

▶ Source: California Department of Health Services

74. 🌎 **PLANT GROWTH** Kudzu is a vine native to Japan. Kudzu can grow a foot per day during the summer months. Write an expression that shows how much a 20-foot kudzu vine can grow during August. (Review 1.1)

EVALUATING VARIABLE EXPRESSIONS **Evaluate the expression.** (Review 1.3)

75. $4 + 3x$ when $x = 2$ **76.** $y \div 8$ when $y = 32$

77. $5 \cdot 2p^2$ when $p = 6$ **78.** $t^4 - t$ when $t = 7$

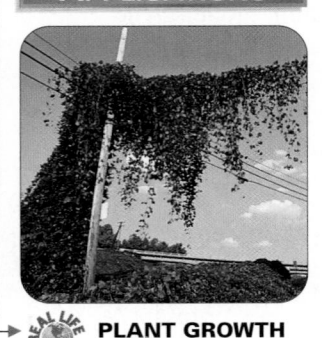

Evaluate the expression. (Lesson 1.3)

1. $12 \div (7 - 3)^2 + 2$

2. $32 - 5 \cdot (2 + 1) + 4$

3. $x^2 + 4 - x$ when $x = 6$

4. $y \div 3 + 2$ when $y = 30$

5. $\frac{r}{s} \cdot 7$ when $r = 30$ and $s = 5$

6. $5x^2 - y$ when $x = 4$ and $y = 26$

Check whether the given number is a solution of the equation or inequality.
(Lesson 1.4)

7. $2x + 6 = 18$; 9

8. $13 - 3x = 7$; 2

9. $4y + 7 = 5 + 5y$; 2

10. $2s + s = 4s$; 6

11. $3x - 4 > 0$; 2

12. $8 - 2y > 4$; 3

13. **PIZZA PARTY** You and three friends bought a pizza. You paid $2.65 for your share $\left(\frac{1}{4} \text{ of the pizza}\right)$. Write an equation that models the situation. What was the total cost of the pizza? (Lesson 1.5)

MATH & History — Problem Solving

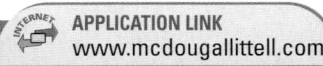

APPLICATION LINK
www.mcdougallittell.com

THEN **IN THE NINTH CENTURY**, mathematician al-Khwarizmi studied at the House of Wisdom in Baghdad. He developed and published important concepts in algebra. In the 1100s, al-Khwarizmi's text was translated from Arabic into Latin, making his ideas available to Western scholars. The step-by-step problem solving techniques invented by al-Khwarizmi are called *algorithms*—a Latinized form of al-Khwarizmi.

NOW **TODAY,** computer programmers use algorithms to write new programs. Algorithms are also an important part of every algebra course. In this chapter you learned the following algorithm.

| Write a verbal model. | → | Assign labels. | → | Write an algebraic model. |

1. Write a word problem and use the algorithm shown to solve the problem.

2. Give two more examples of step-by-step methods you have learned in your study of mathematics. Show a worked-out problem using each method.

825

Scholars study at the House of Wisdom.

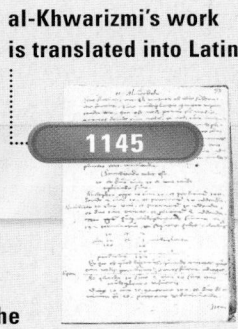

al-Khwarizmi's work is translated into Latin.

1145

1840

Ada Byron Lovelace writes the first computer program.

```
READ 1, N,
FORMAT (13
BIGA=A(1)
DO 20 I = 2
IF (BIGA-A
BIGA=A(I
CONTINUE
PRINT 2, N, BIGA
FORMAT 922H1 THE LARGEST
```

1956

John Backus develops the programming language Fortran.

Tables and Graphs

GOAL 1 USING TABLES TO ORGANIZE DATA

What you should learn

GOAL 1 Use tables to organize data.

GOAL 2 Use graphs to organize **real-life** data, such as the amounts of various foods consumed in **Example 2**.

Why you should learn it

▼ To help you see relationships among **real-life** data, such as the average cost of making a movie in **Example 3**.

Almost every day you have the chance to interpret **data** that describe real-life situations. The word *data* is plural and it means information, facts, or numbers that describe something.

A collection of data is easier to understand when the data are organized in a table or in a graph. There is no "best" way to organize data, but there are many good techniques. Often it helps to put numbers in either increasing or decreasing order. It also helps to group numbers so that patterns or trends are more apparent.

EXAMPLE 1 *Using a Table*

The data in the table were taken from a study on what people in the United States eat. The study grouped what people eat into over twenty categories. The three top categories (listed in pounds per person per year) are shown in the table.

Top Categories of Food Consumed by Americans (lb per person per year)							
Year	1970	1975	1980	1985	1990	1995	2000
Dairy	563.8	539.1	543.2	593.7	568.4	584.4	590.0
Vegetables	335.4	337.0	336.4	358.1	382.8	405.0	410.0
Fruit	237.7	252.1	262.4	269.4	273.5	285.4	290.0

DATA UPDATE of U.S. Department of Agriculture at www.mcdougallittell.com
Year 2000 data are projected by the authors.

In which 5-year period did the total consumption per person of dairy, fruit, and vegetables increase the most? When was there a decrease in total consumption?

SOLUTION

Add two more rows to the table. Enter the total consumption per person of all three categories and the amount of change from one 5-year period to the next.

Year	1970	1975	1980	1985	1990	1995	2000
Total	1136.9	1128.2	1142.0	1221.2	1224.7	1274.8	1290.0
Change	——	−8.7	13.8	79.2	3.5	50.1	15.2

▶ From the table, you can see that the greatest increase in total consumption per person occurred from 1980 to 1985. During that 5-year period, total yearly consumption of dairy, vegetables, and fruit increased by 79.2 pounds per person. The minus sign indicates a decrease of 8.7 pounds from 1970 to 1975.

GOAL 2 USING GRAPHS TO ORGANIZE DATA

One way to organize data is with a **bar graph**. The bars can be either vertical or horizontal. Example 2 shows a vertical bar graph of the data from Example 1.

Eating Habits

EXAMPLE 2 *Interpreting a Bar Graph*

The bar graph shows the total amount of dairy products, vegetables, and fruit consumed by Americans in a given year. If you glance at the graph, it appears Americans ate seven times the amount of dairy products, vegetables, and fruit in 1995 as compared with 1970. If you study the data in Example 1, you can see that the bar graph could be misleading.

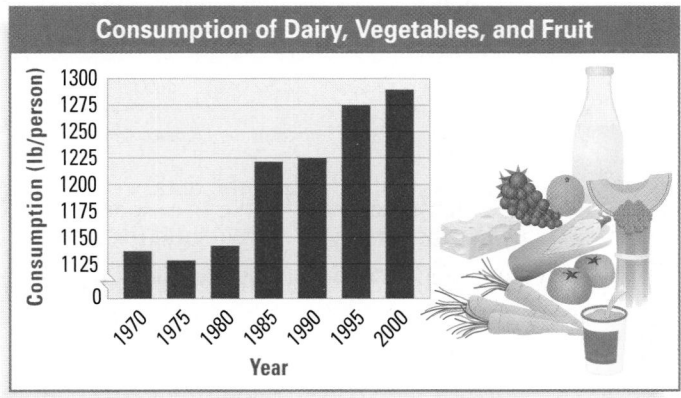

a. Explain why the graph could be misleading.

b. Draw a new bar graph that would not be misleading.

SOLUTION

a. The bar graph could be misleading because the vertical scale is not consistent. A gap exists between 0 and the first tick mark on the vertical axis. This could give the visual impression that consumption for 1970, 1975, and 1980 is much lower than for the other years.

b. To make a bar graph that would not be misleading, you must eliminate the gap and make sure that each tick mark represents the same amount.

STUDENT HELP

▶ **Skills Review**
For help with drawing bar graphs, see pp. 792–794.

STUDENT HELP

HOMEWORK HELP
Visit our Web site www.mcdougallittell.com for extra examples.

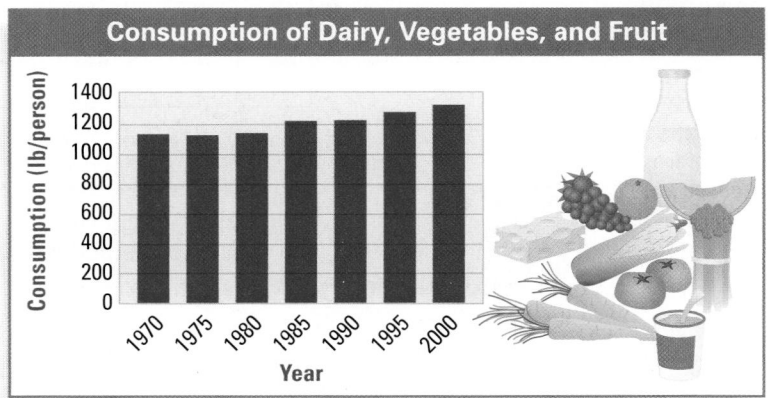

Another way to organize data is with a **line graph**. Line graphs are especially useful for showing changes in data over time.

Movie Making

EXAMPLE 3 *Making a Line Graph*

From 1983 to 1996, the average cost (in millions of dollars) of making a movie is given in the table.

Average Cost of Making a Movie (millions of dollars)							
Year	1983	1984	1985	1986	1987	1988	1989
Average cost	$11.8	$14.0	$16.7	$17.5	$20.0	$18.1	$23.3

Year	1990	1991	1992	1993	1994	1995	1996
Average cost	$26.8	$26.1	$28.9	$29.9	$34.3	$36.4	$33.6

▶ Source: *International Motion Picture Almanac*

a. Draw a line graph of the data.

b. During which three years did the average cost decrease from the prior year?

c. Which year showed the greatest decrease?

SOLUTION

a. Draw the vertical scale from 0 to 40 million dollars. Use units of 5 for the vertical axis to represent intervals of five million dollars. Draw the horizontal axis and mark the number of years starting with 1983.

For each average cost in the table, draw a point on the graph.

Draw a line from each point to the next point.

DIRECTOR OF PHOTOGRAPHY

The composition of the movie shots, type of film, and equipment used are chosen by the director of photography who works closely with the director and producer.

CAREER LINK
www.mcdougallittell.com

b. In 1988, 1991, and 1996 the average cost of making a movie decreased from the prior year.

c. The greatest decrease in the average cost of making a movie occurred in 1996.

GUIDED PRACTICE

Vocabulary Check ✓

Concept Check ✓

1. Explain what *data* are and give an example.

2. What kind of graph is useful for showing changes over time?

3. 🌐 **OLYMPIC EVENTS** For a report about the Olympic Games, you want to include the winning times for women running the 100-meter, 200-meter, 400-meter, 800-meter, 1500-meter, and 3000-meter races in 1992, 1996, and 2000. Make a table that you could use to organize the data.

Skill Check ✓

🌐 **WEATHER Based on the graph, decide whether each statement is *true* or *false*.**

4. Rainfall increased each month.

5. The amount of rainfall was about the same in May and July.

6. The greatest amount of rainfall occurred in June.

7. The amount of rainfall was the same in January and July.

Average Rainfall in Erie, PA

▶ Source: National Oceanic and Atmospheric Administration

PRACTICE AND APPLICATIONS

STUDENT HELP

▶ **Extra Practice**
to help you master
skills is on p. 797.

🌐 **SALARIES In Exercises 8–10, use the table. It shows average salaries for females of different ages with different numbers of years of education. Based on the table, decide whether each statement is *true* or *false*.**

Age (years)	9–11 years of school	High school graduate	Associate degree	Bachelor's degree
18–24	$2948	$7758	$11,804	$15,245
25–34	$9838	$15,017	$20,835	$25,800
35–44	$11,044	$15,720	$21,807	$26,831
45–54	$11,415	$16,603	$21,944	$27,716

▶ Source: U.S. Bureau of the Census

8. As the years of education increase, the average salary increases.

9. As the years of education increase, the average salary decreases.

10. As the age increases, the average salary increases.

11. 🌐 **WATER NEEDS** The table shows the number of gallons of water needed to produce one pound of some foods. Make a bar graph of the data.

Food (1 lb)	lettuce	tomatoes	melons	broccoli	corn
Water (gallons)	21	29	40	42	119

▶ Source: Water Education Foundation

STUDENT HELP

▶ **HOMEWORK HELP**
Example 1: Exs. 8–10
Example 2: Exs. 11–14
Example 3: Exs. 15–19

MUNICIPAL WASTE In Exercises 12–14, use the double bar graph, which shows the amount of different kinds of waste generated and recycled by city and town dwellers in the United States in 1995.

12. Which was the most common waste generated by city dwellers? How many millions of tons of this waste were generated?

13. Which kind of waste had the greatest amount recycled? How many millions of tons of this waste were recycled?

14. Which kind of waste had the least amount recycled? How many millions of tons of this waste were recycled?

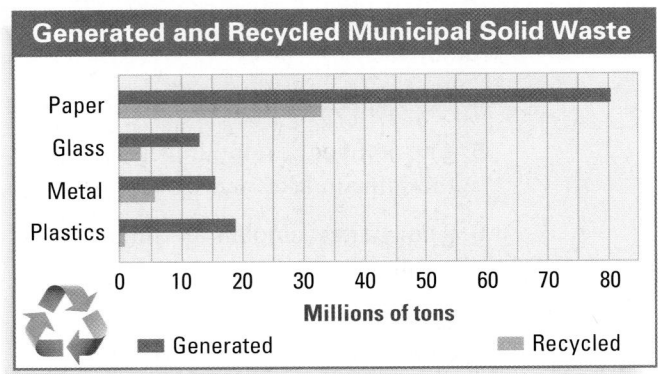

▶ Source: Franklin Associates

MINIMUM WAGE In Exercises 15–17, use the line graph, which shows the minimum wage for different years.

15. For how many years did the minimum wage remain the same?

16. What was the minimum wage during the time when it remained the same?

17. In which year did the minimum wage increase to over $4?

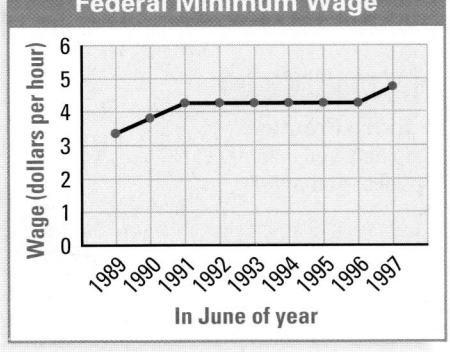

▶ Source: U.S. Bureau of Labor Statistics

18. **TELEVISION STATIONS** The table shows the number of commercial television stations for different years. Make a line graph of the data. Discuss what the line graph shows.

Year	1991	1992	1993	1994	1995	1996
Number of stations	1098	1118	1137	1145	1161	1174

▶ Source: *Television Digest*

19. **FUEL EFFICIENCY** The table shows the average fuel efficiency for passenger cars for different years. Make a line graph of the data.

Year	1980	1985	1990	1995	1996
Fuel efficiency (miles per gallon)	24.3	27.6	28.0	28.6	28.7

▶ Source: National Highway Traffic Safety Administration

20. MULTI-STEP PROBLEM Use the graphs below.

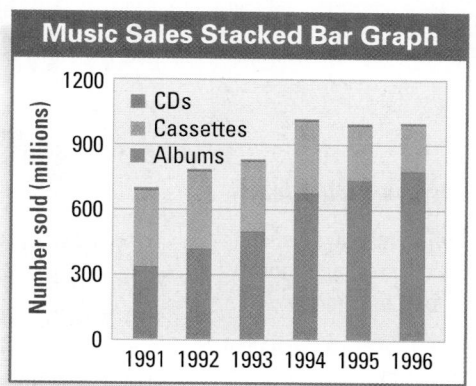

▶ Source: Recording Industry Association of America

a. From 1991 to 1996 which type of recording showed an increase in the number sold? Which showed a decrease? Which remained about the same?

b. In which two years did the total number of all types of recordings sold remain about the same?

c. CHOOSING A DATA DISPLAY Compare the usefulness of the two graphs.

★ **Challenge**

21. *Writing* The graphs show the same data. Write a statement supported by one graph but *not* the other. Could either graph be misleading? Why?

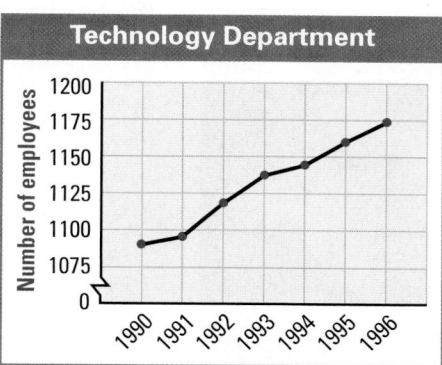

MIXED REVIEW

SOLUTIONS Is the number given a solution of the equation? (Review 1.4 for 1.7)

22. $5x + 2 = 17$; 3

23. $12 - 2y = 6$; 4

24. $3x - 4 = 12 - 5x$; 2

25. $2y + 8 = 4y - 2$; 5

TRANSLATING Translate the verbal sentence into an equation. (Review 1.5)

26. 3 more than a number is 5.

27. Twelve is the quotient of a number and 3.

28. 🌎 **STAMP COLLECTION** In your collection of 53 stamps, 37 cost less than $.25. Let y be the number of stamps that cost $.25 or more. Which equation models the situation? (Review 1.5)

A. $53 - y = 37$　　**B.** $53 + y = 37$　　**C.** $53 + 37 = y$

1.7

An Introduction to Functions

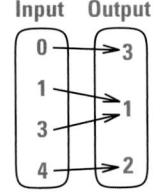

What you should learn

GOAL 1 Identify a function and make an input-output table for a function.

GOAL 2 Write an equation for a **real-life** function, such as the relationship between water pressure and depth in **Example 3**.

Why you should learn it

▼ To represent **real-life** relationships between two quantities such as time and altitude for a rising hot-air balloon in **Example 2**.

GOAL 1 INPUT-OUTPUT TABLES

A **function** is a rule that establishes a relationship between two quantities, called the **input** and the **output**. For each input, there is exactly one output. More than one input can have the same output.

Input	0	1	3	4
Output	3	1	1	2

One way to describe a function is to make an **input-output table**. This table lists the inputs and outputs shown in the diagram.

The collection of all input values is the **domain** of the function and the collection of all output values is the **range** of the function. The table shows that the domain of the function above is 0, 1, 3, 4 and the range is 1, 2, 3.

EXAMPLE 1 *Making an Input-Output Table*

GEOMETRY CONNECTION The diagram shows the first six triangular numbers, 1, 3, 6, 10, 15, 21, which continue on following the same pattern.

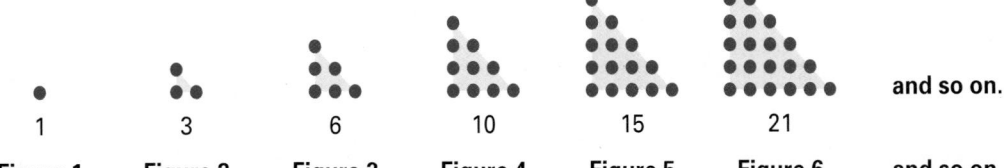

| 1 | 3 | 6 | 10 | 15 | 21 | and so on. |

| **Figure 1** | **Figure 2** | **Figure 3** | **Figure 4** | **Figure 5** | **Figure 6** | **and so on.** |

a. Make an input-output table in which the input is the Figure number n and the output is the corresponding triangular number T.

b. Does the table represent a function? Justify your answer.

c. Describe the domain and the range.

SOLUTION

a. Use the diagram to make an input-output table.

b. Yes, because for each input there is exactly one output.

c. The collection of all input values is the domain: 1, 2, 3, 4, 5, 6, ... The collection of all output values is the range: 1, 3, 6, 10, 15, 21, ...

Input n	Output T
1	1
2	3
3	6
4	10
5	15
6	21
...	...

EXAMPLE 2 *Using a Table to Graph a Function*

You are at an altitude of 250 feet in a hot-air balloon. You turn on the burner and rise at a rate of 20 feet per minute for 5 minutes. Your altitude h after you have risen for t minutes is given by the function

$h = 250 + 20t$, where $0 \le t \le 5$.

a. For several inputs t, use the function to calculate an output h.

b. Organize the data into an input-output table.

c. Graph the data in the table. Then use this graph to draw a graph of the function.

d. What is the domain of the function? What part of the domain is shown in the table?

SOLUTION

a. List an output for each of several inputs.

INPUT	FUNCTION	OUTPUT
$t = 0$	$h = 250 + 20(0)$	$h = 250$
$t = 1$	$h = 250 + 20(1)$	$h = 270$
$t = 2$	$h = 250 + 20(2)$	$h = 290$
$t = 3$	$h = 250 + 20(3)$	$h = 310$
$t = 4$	$h = 250 + 20(4)$	$h = 330$
$t = 5$	$h = 250 + 20(5)$	$h = 350$

Altitude of Balloon

b. Make an input-output table.

t	0	1	2	3	4	5
h	250	270	290	310	330	350

c. The points in blue are the graph of the table data. The black line is the graph of the function.

d. The domain of the function is all values of t such that $0 \le t \le 5$. The values of t shown in the table are 0, 1, 2, 3, 4, 5.

CONCEPT SUMMARY **DESCRIBING A FUNCTION**

Example 1 and Example 2 illustrate that functions can be described in these ways:

- Input-Output Table
- Description in Words
- Equation
- Graph

GOAL 2 WRITING EQUATIONS FOR FUNCTIONS

EXAMPLE 3 *Writing an Equation*

SCUBA DIVING As you dive deeper and deeper into the ocean, the pressure of the water on your body steadily increases. The pressure at the surface of the water is 14.7 pounds per square inch (psi). The pressure increases at a rate of 0.445 psi for each foot you descend. Represent the pressure P as a function of the depth d for every 20 feet you descend until you reach a depth of 120 feet.

a. Write an equation for the function.

b. Create an input-output table for the function.

c. Make a line graph of the function.

SOLUTION

a. To write an equation for the function, apply the problem solving strategy you learned in Lesson 1.5. Write a verbal model, assign labels, and write an algebraic model.

PROBLEM SOLVING STRATEGY

VERBAL MODEL	$\boxed{\text{Pressure at given depth}}$ = $\boxed{\text{Pressure at surface}}$ + $\boxed{\text{Rate of change in pressure}}$ · $\boxed{\text{Diving depth}}$

LABELS	Pressure at given depth = P	(psi)
	Pressure at surface = **14.7**	(psi)
	Rate of change in pressure = **0.445**	(psi per foot of depth)
	Diving depth = d	(feet)

ALGEBRAIC MODEL $P = 14.7 + 0.445\,d$ where $0 \le d \le 120$

b. Use the equation to make an input-output table for the function. For inputs, use the depths for every 20 feet you descend down to 120 feet.

Depth d	Pressure P
0	14.7
20	23.6
40	32.5
60	41.4
80	50.3
100	59.2
120	68.1

c. You can represent the data in the table with a line graph.

Underwater Pressure

GUIDED PRACTICE

Vocabulary Check ✓   **Complete the sentence.**

1. A function is a relationship between two quantities, called the ? and the ? .

2. The collection of all input values is the ? of the function. The collection of all output values is the ? of the function.

Concept Check ✓   3. Four ways to represent a function are (1) ? , (2) ? , (3) ? , and (4) ? .

For a relationship to be a function, it must be true that for each input, there is exactly one output. Does the table represent a function? Explain.

4.

Input	Output
1	3
2	4
3	5
4	6

5.

Input	Output
1	3
2	3
3	4
4	4

6.

Input	Output
1	3
1	4
2	5
3	6

Skill Check ✓   🌐 **CAR RACING The fastest winning speed in the Daytona 500 is about 178 miles per hour. Calculate the distance traveled *d* (in miles) after time *t* (in hours) using the equation *d* = 178*t*.** ▶ Source: NASCAR

7. Copy and complete the input-output table.

Time (hours)	0.25	0.50	0.75	1.00	1.25	1.50
Distance traveled (miles)	?	?	?	?	?	?

8. Describe the domain and the range of the function whose values are shown in the table.

9. Graph the data in the table. Use this graph and the fact that when $t = 0$, $d = 0$ and when $t = 2.81$, $d = 500$ to graph the function.

PRACTICE AND APPLICATIONS

STUDENT HELP

▶ **Extra Practice**
to help you master
skills is on p. 797.

CRITICAL THINKING Does the table represent a function? Explain.

10.

Input	Output
5	3
6	4
7	5
8	6

11.

Input	Output
1	3
2	6
3	11
4	18

12.

Input	Output
9	5
9	4
8	3
7	2

STUDENT HELP

▶ HOMEWORK HELP
Example 1: Exs. 10–25
Example 2: Exs. 26–32
Example 3: Exs. 33–36

INPUT-OUTPUT TABLES Make an input-output table for the function. Use 0, 1, 2, and 3 as the domain.

13. $y = 3x + 2$ 14. $y = 21 - 2x$ 15. $y = 5x$

16. $y = 6x + 1$ 17. $y = 2x + 1$ 18. $y = x + 4$

MAKING INPUT-OUTPUT TABLES Make an input-output table for the function. Use 1, 1.5, 3, 4.5, and 6 as the domain.

19. $y = 4x + 2.5$

20. $y = 32 - 3x$

21. $y = \dfrac{9}{x} + 10$

22. $y = 2 + \dfrac{x}{0.5}$

23. $y = x^2 - 0.5$

24. $y = 1.5 + x^2$

25. 🌎 **APPLE TREES** A large apple tree may absorb 360 liters of water from the soil per day. The amount of water W absorbed over a short period of time is modeled by the function $W = 360d$, where d represents the number of days. Copy and complete the table.

Input	Function	Output
$d = 1$	$W = 360 \cdot 1$	$W = 360$
$d = 2$	$W = ?$	$W = ?$
$d = 3$	$W = ?$	$W = ?$
$d = 4$	$W = ?$	$W = ?$
$d = 5$	$W = ?$	$W = ?$

🌡️ **TEMPERATURE In Exercises 26–29, use the following information.**
You use a Celsius thermometer when measuring temperature in science class. Your teacher asks you to show the relationship between Celsius temperature and Fahrenheit temperature with a graph. Use the equation $F = \dfrac{9}{5}C + 32$ to convert degrees Celsius C to degrees Fahrenheit F.

Input	Function	Output
$C = 0$	$F = \dfrac{9}{5}(0) + 32$	$F = 32$
$C = 5$	$F = ?$	$F = ?$
$C = 10$	$F = ?$	$F = ?$
$C = 15$	$F = ?$	$F = ?$
$C = 20$	$F = ?$	$F = ?$

26. Copy and complete the input-output table for the function.

Input C	0	5	10	15	20	25	30	35	40
Output F	32	?	?	?	?	?	?	?	?

27. Graph the data in the table. Label the vertical axis Temperature (°C) and the horizontal axis Temperature (°F). Use this graph to graph the function.

STUDENT HELP

▶ **Look Back**
For help with drawing line graphs, see p. 42.

28. *Writing* Explain why $F = \dfrac{9}{5}C + 32$ represents a function.

29. Describe the domain and the range of the function whose values are shown in the table.

🎬 **DRIVE-IN MOVIE In Exercises 30–32, use the following information.**
A drive-in movie theater charges $5 admission per car and $1.25 admission for each person in the car. The total cost C at the drive-in movie theater is given by $C = 5 + 1.25n$, where n represents the number of people in the car. (Assume a maximum of 7 people per car.)

30. Make an input-output table for the function.

31. Describe the domain and range of the function whose values are shown in the table.

32. Graph the data shown in the input-output table.

🌐 **ADVERTISING** In Exercises 33–36, use the following information.
You are in charge of advertising for the drama club's next performance. You can make two signs from a poster board that is 36 inches long and 24 inches wide. Each poster board costs $.75.

33. Write an equation that shows the relationship between the number of signs and the total cost of the poster board. Let n represent the number of signs and let C represent the total cost of the poster board.

34. Evaluate the equation for $n = 6$, 8, 10, and 12. Organize your results in an input-output table.

35. What do the values in the table represent?

36. Suppose you have $5 to spend on poster board. Do you have enough money to make 14 signs? If not, how much more money do you need?

🌐 **HOUSESITTING** In Exercises 37 and 38, use the following information.
As a summer job, you start a housesitting service in your neighborhood. You agree to get the mail, pick up newspapers, water plants, and feed pets for an initial fee of $5, plus $2 per day.

37. Write an equation that shows the relationship between the number of days you housesit and the amount of money you earn for each house.

38. How much money will you earn housesitting one house for one week?

Test Preparation

MULTI-STEP PROBLEM In Exercises 39–43, use the following information.
You start a portable catering business. One of your specialties is a barbecue sandwich plate that costs $.85 to prepare. Suppose you cater an auction where you sell each sandwich plate for $2.00.

39. Write a function that gives the profit you expect from catering the auction.

40. You must also spend $50 on equipment and supplies to cater the auction. Write a function that includes this cost.

41. Use your equation from Exercise 40 to find the profit you will earn if you sell 75 barbecue sandwich plates.

42. Suppose the cost of sandwich rolls increased by $.05 each. What effect do you think this will have on the profit? Write a function that includes this cost.

43. Use your equation from Exercise 42 to find how many barbecue sandwich plates you must sell to make a $100 profit.

★ **Challenge**

44. 🖩 **PERSONAL RECREATION**
The amount of money spent on personal recreation in billions of dollars M can be modeled by $M = 116.3 + 28.5t$, where t is the number of years since 1985. The bar graph shows the amount of money spent on personal recreation in 1985, 1990, and 1995.

Use a calculator to predict the amount of money spent in billions of dollars in the years 2000 and 2005.

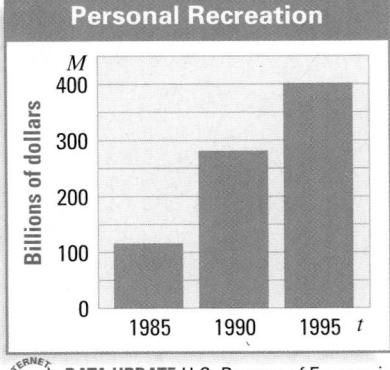

Personal Recreation

MIXED REVIEW

Write the expression in exponential form. (Review 1.2)

45. x raised to the sixth power

46. nine cubed

47. $y \cdot y \cdot y \cdot y \cdot y \cdot y \cdot y$

48. $15 \cdot 15 \cdot 15 \cdot 15$

Evaluate the expression. (Review 1.3)

49. $\dfrac{3b + 3c}{5}$ when $b = 1$ and $c = 9$

50. $6 + \dfrac{x + 2}{y}$ when $x = 7$ and $y = 3$

51. $3y^2 + w$ when $y = 8$ and $w = 27$

52. $2s^3 - 3t$ when $s = 4$ and $t = 6$

Check whether the number is a solution of the equation or the inequality.
(Review 1.4 for 2.1)

53. $7y + 2 = 4y + 8; \ 2$

54. $5x - 1 = 3x + 2; \ 4$

55. $32 - 5y > 11; \ 3$

56. $7m + 2 < 12; \ 1$

57. $s - 7 \geq 12 - s; \ 9$

58. $n + 2 \leq 2n - 2; \ 4$

59. 🌎 **SHOE SALES** A major athletic footwear company had about $3750 million in sales of athletic footwear during the year ending May 31, 1997. The company's sales fell to about $3500 million in 1998. By how much did the company's sales decrease? **(Review 1.5)**

QUIZ 3

Self-Test for Lessons 1.6 and 1.7

🌎 **ARTS ACTIVITIES** In Exercises 1 and 2, use the table which shows the percent of 18-to-24-year-olds that attended various arts activities at least once in 1997. **(Lesson 1.6)**

Arts Activities Attended by 18-to-24-year-olds				
Jazz	Musical play	Non-musical play	Art museum	Historic park
15%	26%	20%	38%	46%

▶ Source: Statistical Abstract of the United States, 1998

1. Make a bar graph of the data.

2. What conclusions can you draw from the bar graph?

3. Which equation describes the function that contains all of the data points shown in the table? **(Lesson 1.7)**

Input x	0	1	2	3	4	5
Output y	1	2	5	10	17	26

A. $y = x^2$ **B.** $y = x^2 + 1$ **C.** $y = 2x + 3$ **D.** $y = x^2 - 1$

🌎 **HOT-AIR BALLOONING** You are at an altitude of 200 feet in a hot-air balloon. You turn on the burner and rise at a rate of 25 feet per minute for 6 minutes. **(Lesson 1.7)**

4. Write an equation for your altitude as a function of time.

5. Make an input-output table for the function.

Chapter Summary

WHAT did you learn?

Evaluate and write variable expressions. (1.1)

Evaluate and write expressions containing exponents. (1.2)

Use the order of operations. (1.3)

Use mental math to solve equations. (1.4)

Check solutions of inequalities. (1.4)

Translate verbal phrases and sentences into expressions, equations, and inequalities. (1.5)

Translate verbal models into algebraic models to solve problems. (1.5)

Organize data using tables and graphs. (1.6)

Use functions to show the relationship between inputs and outputs. (1.7)

WHY did you learn it?

Estimate the time it will take you to hike the length of a trail and back. (p. 5)

Calculate the volume of water that a cubic aquarium holds. (p. 11)

Calculate sales tax on a purchase. (p. 18)

Estimate the amount you owe for groceries. (p. 25)

Check a pet's caloric intake. (p. 26)

Calculate the total number of dim sum plates ordered at a restaurant. (p. 33)

Model the decision-making of a commercial jet pilot. (p. 34)

Interpret information about eating habits in the United States. (pp. 40 and 41)

Represent the rise of a hot-air balloon as a function. (p. 47)

How does Chapter 1 fit into the BIGGER PICTURE of algebra?

In this chapter you were introduced to many of the terms and goals of algebra. Communication is a very important part of algebra, so it is important that algebraic terms become part of your vocabulary. Algebra is a language that you can use to solve real-life problems.

STUDY STRATEGY

How did you use the notes in your notebook?

The notes you made, using the **Study Strategy** on page 2, may include this one about order of operations.

Remembering Order of Operations

1. First do operations that occur within grouping symbols.

2. Then evaluate powers.

3. Then do multiplications and divisions from left to right.

4. Finally, do additions and subtractions from left to right.

Chapter Review

1.1 VARIABLES IN ALGEBRA

Examples on pp. 3–5

EXAMPLES Evaluate the expression when $y = 4$.

$$10 - y = 10 - 4 \qquad 11y = 11(4) \qquad \frac{16}{y} = \frac{16}{4} \qquad y + 9 = 4 + 9$$

$$= 6 \qquad\qquad\qquad = 44 \qquad\qquad = 4 \qquad\qquad\qquad = 13$$

Evaluate the expression for the given value of the variable.

1. $a + 14$ when $a = 23$

2. $1.8x$ when $x = 10$

3. $\dfrac{m}{1.5}$ when $m = 15$

4. $\dfrac{15}{y}$ when $y = 7.5$

5. $p - 12$ when $p = 22$

6. $b(0.5)$ when $b = 9$

7. How long will it take to walk 6 miles if you walk at a rate of 3 miles per hour?

1.2 EXPONENTS AND POWERS

Examples on pp. 9–11

EXAMPLES Evaluate the expression when $b = 3$.

$$b^2 = 3^2 \qquad (10 - b)^3 = (10 - 3)^3 \qquad 12(5^b) = 12(5^3) \qquad b^4 + 18 = 3^4 + 18$$

$$= 3 \cdot 3 \qquad\qquad = 7^3 \qquad\qquad\qquad = 12(5 \cdot 5 \cdot 5) \qquad = (3 \cdot 3 \cdot 3 \cdot 3) + 18$$

$$= 9 \qquad\qquad\qquad = 7 \cdot 7 \cdot 7 \qquad\qquad = 12(125) \qquad\qquad = 81 + 18$$

$$\qquad\qquad\qquad\qquad = 343 \qquad\qquad\qquad = 1500 \qquad\qquad\qquad = 99$$

Evaluate the expression.

8. eight to the fourth power

9. $(2 + 3)^5$

10. s^2 when $s = 1.5$

11. $6 + (b^3)$ when $b = 3$

12. $2x^4$ when $x = 2$

13. $(5x)^3$ when $x = 5$

1.3 ORDER OF OPERATIONS

Examples on pp. 16–18

EXAMPLE Evaluate $550 - 4 (3 + 5)^2$.

$$550 - 4(3 + 5)^2 = 550 - 4(8)^2 \qquad \text{Evaluate within grouping symbols.}$$
$$= 550 - 4 \cdot 64 \qquad \text{Evaluate powers.}$$
$$= 550 - 256 \qquad \text{Multiply or divide.}$$
$$= 294 \qquad \text{Add or subtract.}$$

Evaluate the expression.

14. $4 + 21 \div 3 - 3^2$ **15.** $(14 \div 7)^2 + 5$ **16.** $\dfrac{6 + 2^2}{17 - 6 \cdot 2}$ **17.** $\dfrac{x - 3y}{6}$ when $x = 15$ and $y = 2$

1.4 EQUATIONS AND INEQUALITIES

Examples on pp. 24–26

EXAMPLE You can check whether the number 4 is a solution of $5x + 3 = 18$.

4 is not a solution, because $5(4) + 3 \neq 18$.

Check whether the given number is a solution of the equation or inequality.

18. $2a - 3 = 2; 4$ **19.** $x^2 - x = 2; 2$ **20.** $9y - 3 > 24; 3$ **21.** $5x + 2 \leq 27; 5$

1.5 A PROBLEM SOLVING PLAN USING MODELS

Examples on pp. 32–34

EXAMPLE You can model problems like the following: If you can save $5.25 a week, how many weeks must you save to buy a CD that costs $15.75?

VERBAL MODEL
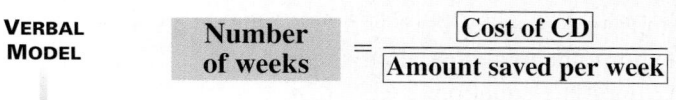
$$\boxed{\text{Number of weeks}} = \dfrac{\boxed{\text{Cost of CD}}}{\boxed{\text{Amount saved per week}}}$$

LABELS
Number of weeks = w (weeks)
Cost of CD = **15.75** (dollars)
Amount saved per week = **5.25** (dollars per week)

ALGEBRAIC MODEL
$w = \dfrac{15.75}{5.25}$ **Write algebraic model**
$w = 3$ **Solve with mental math**

▶ You must save for 3 weeks.

22. You are given $75 to buy juice for the school dance. Each bottle of juice costs $.75. Write a verbal and an algebraic model to find how many bottles of juice you can buy. Write an equation and use mental math to solve the equation.

EXAMPLES Using the bar graph you can tell the following. From the vertical axis of the graph, you can see that male and female tennis players from the United States both have won the Australian Open 14 times.

You can also see that United States men have won the French Open 10 times, while United States women have won 25 times. So United States women have won 15 more French Open titles than the United States men.

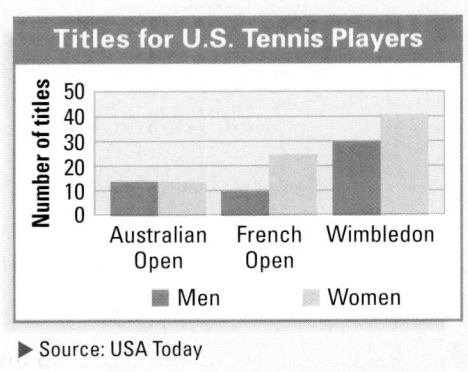

Titles for U.S. Tennis Players

▶ Source: USA Today

In Exercises 23 and 24, use the graph above.

23. Compare the number of titles won by United States women at Wimbledon with the number won by United States men.

24. Find the total number of titles won by United States men and compare with the total for women.

Use the data in the table.

25. Make a line graph of the data.

26. What can you conclude from the line graph?

Percent of Voting-Age Population That Voted in Yearly Municipal Referendum, 1976–1996						
Year	1976	1980	1984	1988	1992	1996
Percent	53.5	52.8	53.3	50.3	55.1	48.9

EXAMPLES Line for your fishing reel costs $.02 per yard. One lure costs $3.50. Make an input-output table that shows the total cost of buying one lure and 100, 200, 300, or 400 yards of fishing line. The equation is $C = .02n + 3.50$, where n is the number of yards of fishing line. To find C Substitute the given values of n.

Fishing line (yards), n	100	200	300	400
Total (dollars), C	5.50	7.50	9.50	11.50

In Exercises 27–29, you are buying rectangular picture frames that have side lengths of $2w$ and $3w$.

27. Write an equation for the perimeter, starting with a verbal model.

28. Make an input-output table that shows the perimeter of the frames when $w = 1, 2, 3, 4,$ and 5.

29. Describe the domain and range of the function whose values are shown in the table.

Chapter Test

Evaluate the expression when $y = 3$ and $x = 5$.

1. $5y + x^2$

2. $\dfrac{24}{y} - x$

3. $2y + 9x - 7$

4. $(5y + x) \div 4$

5. $2x^3 + 4y$

6. $8(x^2) \div 25$

7. $(x - y)^3$

8. $x^4 + 4(y - 2)$

In Exercises 9–11, write the expression in exponential form.

9. $5y \cdot 5y \cdot 5y \cdot 5y$

10. nine cubed

11. six to the nth power

12. Insert grouping symbols in $5 \cdot 4 + 6 \div 2$ so that the value of the expression is 25.

13. 🌎 **TRAVEL TIME** If you can travel only 35 miles per hour, is $2\frac{1}{2}$ hours enough time to get to a concert that is 85 miles away? Give the expression you used to find the answer.

Write an algebraic expression.

14. seven times a number

15. x is at least ninety

16. the quotient of m and two

In Exercises 17–22, decide whether the statement is *true* or *false*.

17. $(2 \cdot 3)^2 = 2 \cdot 3^2$

18. quotient of 3 and 12 is 4

19. $8 - 6 = 6 - 8$

20. 10% of $38 is $.38

21. $8 \leq y^2 + 3$ when $y = 3$

22. $9x > x^3$ when $x = 3$

23. The senior class is planning a trip that will cost $35 per student. If $3920 has been collected from the seniors for the trip, how many have paid for the trip?

🌎 **MARCHING BAND** **In Exercises 24 and 25 members of the marching band are making their own color-guard flags. Each rectangular flag is 1.2 yards by 0.5 yard. The material costs $1.75 per square yard.**

24. Write a function showing the relationship between the number of flags and the cost of the material.

25. How much will it cost to make 20 flags?

🌎 **SCHOOL** **In Exercises 26–29 the bar graph shows the number of students enrolled in schools in the United States in 1995 and the number of students expected to be enrolled in 2000.**

26. How many students are expected to be in kindergarten through eighth grade in 2000?

27. Describe why the K–8 category might be so much larger than 9–12 or College.

28. What group of students is expected to show the smallest change in enrollment from 1995 to 2000?

29. Is the number of students enrolled in school higher in 1995 or in the year 2000? How do you know?

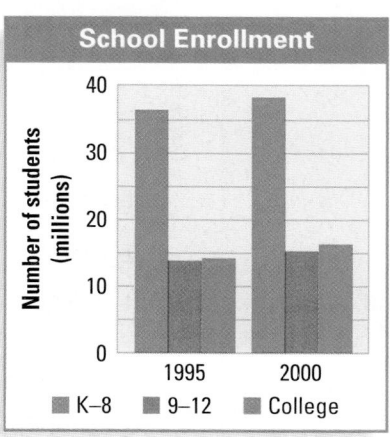

▶ Source: U.S. Bureau of the Census

Chapter Standardized Test

▶ **TEST-TAKING STRATEGY** Avoid spending too much time on one question. Skip questions that are too difficult for you, and spend no more than a few minutes on each question.

1. **MULTIPLE CHOICE** What is the average speed of a car that traveled 209.2 km in 2 hours?

    Ⓐ 20.92 km/h   Ⓑ 104.6 km/h

    Ⓒ 20.92 h/km   Ⓓ 104.6 h/km

    Ⓔ 70 mi/h

2. **MULTIPLE CHOICE** What is the perimeter of the figure?

    6.4

    Ⓐ 18.8   Ⓑ 19.2   Ⓒ 27.6

    Ⓓ 38.4   Ⓔ 192

3. **MULTIPLE CHOICE** What is the value of the expression $[(5 \cdot 9) \div x] + 6$ when $x = 3$?

    Ⓐ 5   Ⓑ 15   Ⓒ 18

    Ⓓ 21   Ⓔ 45

4. **MULTIPLE CHOICE** If $4t + 5 = 21$, then $t^2 - 3 = \underline{\ ?\ }$.

    Ⓐ 6   Ⓑ 13   Ⓒ 18

    Ⓓ 22   Ⓔ 39

5. **MULTIPLE CHOICE** In the table, what is the value of m?

b	$7b - 2$
2	12
4	26
m	47

    Ⓐ 6   Ⓑ 7   Ⓒ 8

    Ⓓ 40   Ⓔ 49

6. **MULTIPLE CHOICE** What is the value of $6 \cdot (15 + 8) - [(2 \cdot 7) - 4]^2$?

    Ⓐ −462   Ⓑ 38   Ⓒ 62

    Ⓓ 102   Ⓔ 134

QUANTITATIVE COMPARISON **In Exercises 7–9, choose the statement below that is true about the given numbers.**

Ⓐ The number in column A is greater.

Ⓑ The number in column B is greater.

Ⓒ The two numbers are equal.

Ⓓ The relationship cannot be determined from the information given.

	COLUMN A	COLUMN B
7.	$3 \cdot 5 - 4$	$3 \cdot (5 - 4)$
8.	$2x \div 5 + 7$	$2x \div (5 + 7)$
9.	$42 - (5^2 + 2)$	$42 - (5^2) + 2$

10. **MULTIPLE CHOICE** What is the area of a square with sides that are 6.3 cm in length?

    Ⓐ 3.969 m^2 Ⓑ 25.2 cm

    Ⓒ 25.2 cm^2 Ⓓ 39.69 cm

    Ⓔ 39.69 cm^2

11. **MULTIPLE CHOICE** Which of the following numbers is a solution of the equation $50 - x^2 = 1$?

    Ⓐ 5   Ⓑ 6   Ⓒ 7   Ⓓ 8   Ⓔ 9

12. **MULTIPLE CHOICE** Which of the following numbers is a solution of the inequality $20 - x \geq x + 2$?

    Ⓐ 9   Ⓑ 9.5   Ⓒ 10   Ⓓ 10.5   Ⓔ 11

13. **MULTIPLE CHOICE** What is the value of $3.4x - 2.3y$, when $x = 11$ and $y = 12$?

    Ⓐ 1.1   Ⓑ 2.1   Ⓒ 9   Ⓓ 9.8   Ⓔ 28.7

14. **MULTIPLE CHOICE** You have decided to save $6 a week to buy an electric guitar costing $150. Which expression shows how much money you still need to save after n weeks?

    Ⓐ $150 + 6n$ Ⓑ $150 - 6n$

    Ⓒ $(150 + 6)n$ Ⓓ $(150 - 6)n$

    Ⓔ $150n + 6n$

15. MULTIPLE CHOICE Which algebraic expression is a translation of "five times the difference of eight and a number x"?

(A) $5(8 - x)$ (B) $x - 5 \cdot 8$ (C) $5 \cdot 8 - x$ (D) $5 - 8x$ (E) $5x - 8$

16. MULTIPLE CHOICE The number of students on the football team is two more than three times the number of students on the basketball team. If the basketball team has y students, how many students are on the football team?

(A) $3y$ (B) $3y - 2$ (C) $6y$ (D) $2y + 3$ (E) $2 + 3y$

17. MULTIPLE CHOICE Which equation represents the function in the table?

(A) $y = x + 5$ (B) $y = 2x + 3$

(C) $y = x^2 + 5$ (D) $y = x^2 + 3$

(E) $y = 3x + 1$

Input x	Output y
0	3
1	4
2	7

18. MULTIPLE CHOICE Which of the following represents a function?

I.
Input	Output
1	4
2	4
3	6
4	6

II.
Input	Output
1	3
2	3
3	4
4	4

III.
Input	Output
1	3
1	−3
2	4
3	5

(A) All (B) I and II (C) I and III (D) II and III (E) None

MULTI-STEP PROBLEM Use the graph to compare the amount of chocolate eaten in different countries.

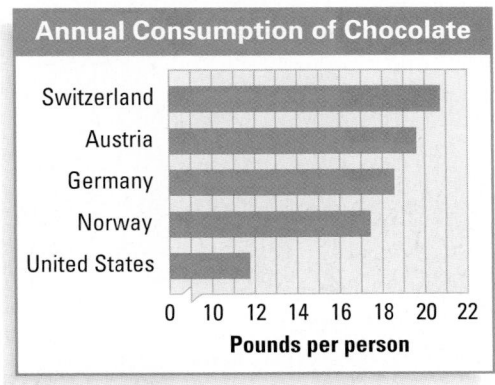

19. About how much more chocolate per person is consumed in Switzerland than in the United States?

20. About how much more chocolate per person is consumed in Norway than in the United States?

21. How could the bar graph be misleading?

22. Draw a bar graph representing the same information that would not be misleading.

▶ Source: Chocolate Manufacturers Association

MULTI-STEP PROBLEM If you place one marble in a measuring cup that contains 200 milliliters of water, the measure on the cup indicates that there is a one millimeter increase in volume. How much does the volume increase when you place from 1 to 10 marbles in the measuring cup?

23. Write an equation to represent the function.

24. Complete an input-output table for the function with domain 0, 1, 2, 3, 4, 5, 6, 7, 8, 9, 10.

25. Describe the domain and range of the function whose values are shown in the table.

26. Graph the data in the table. Use this graph to graph the function.

PROPERTIES OF
REAL NUMBERS

▶ *Why are helicopters able to take off and land without runways?*

APPLICATION: Helicopters

Helicopters are capable of vertical flight—flying straight up and straight down. Rotor blades generate an upward force (lift) as they whirl through the air.

Mathematics provides a useful way of distingushing between upward and downward motion. In this chapter we will use positive numbers to measure the velocity of upward motion and negative numbers to measure the velocity of downward motion.

Think & Discuss

1. Describe some real-life situations that you might represent with negative numbers.

2. Describe the average speed and direction of each helicopter's movement if it travels the given distance in 15 seconds.

Not drawn to scale

Learn More About It

You will find the speed and velocity of different objects in Exercises 76–78 on p. 69.

 APPLICATION LINK Visit www.mcdougallittell.com for more information about helicopters.

Study Guide

PREVIEW

What's the chapter about?

Chapter 2 is about **real numbers**. In Chapter 2 you'll learn

- how to add, subtract, multiply, and divide real numbers.
- how to determine the likelihood of an event using probability and odds.

KEY VOCABULARY

▶ **Review**
- variable, p. 3
- order of operations, p. 16
- data, p. 40
- function, p. 46

▶ **New**
- real numbers, p. 63
- integers, p. 63
- absolute value, p. 65
- counterexample, p. 66

- matrix, p. 86
- distributive property, p. 100
- reciprocal, p. 108
- probability of an event, p. 114

PREPARE

Are you ready for the chapter?

SKILL REVIEW Do these exercises to review key skills that you'll apply in this chapter. See the given **reference page** if there is something you don't understand.

STUDENT HELP

▶ **Study Tip**
"Student Help" boxes throughout the chapter give you study tips and tell you where to look for extra help in this book and on the Internet.

Put the numbers in order from least to greatest. (Skills Review, pp. 779–780)

1. 4.6, 6.1, 5.5, 5.06, 4.07, 5.46

2. $2\frac{5}{6}$, $2\frac{2}{3}$, $\frac{11}{4}$, $2\frac{5}{8}$, $\frac{25}{11}$, $2\frac{3}{5}$

Find the value of the expression. Write the answer as a fraction or mixed number in lowest terms. (Skills Review, pp. 781–782)

3. $\frac{9}{14} - \frac{3}{7}$

4. $\frac{5}{6} + \frac{2}{3}$

5. $1\frac{3}{4} + 2\frac{1}{8}$

6. $8\frac{7}{15} - 2\frac{4}{5}$

7. $\frac{5}{9} \div \frac{2}{9}$

8. $\frac{7}{9} \cdot \frac{3}{14}$

9. $6\frac{6}{7} \cdot 4\frac{1}{12}$

10. $9\frac{1}{6} \div 1\frac{3}{8}$

Evaluate the expression. (Review Example 2, p. 17)

11. $4 + 7 - 3 \cdot 2$

12. $64 \div 16 + 5 - 7$

13. $9 - 8 \div 4 + 12$

14. $16 - 9 \cdot 5 \div 3$

15. $8 \cdot 3 - 6 \cdot 4$

16. $12.8 - 7.5 \div 1.5 + 3.2$

STUDY STRATEGY

Here's a study strategy!

Studying a Lesson

- Read the goals and study tips.
- Review the examples and highlighted vocabulary.
- Be sure you understand the rules and properties given in boxes.
- Take notes. Add to your list of vocabulary, rules, and properties in your notebook.

2.1

The Real Number Line

What you should learn

GOAL 1 Graph and compare real numbers using a number line.

GOAL 2 Find the opposite and the absolute value of a number in **real-life** applications such as the speed and velocity of an elevator in **Example 8**.

Why you should learn it

▼ To help you understand negative amounts in **real life**, such as "below zero" temperature in the wind-chill table in **Exs. 79–81**.

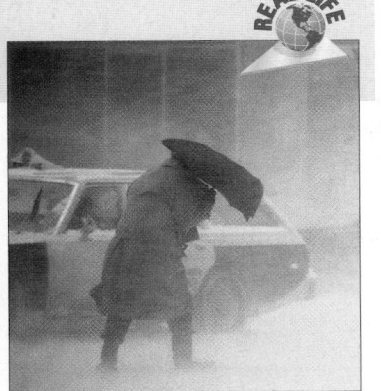

GOAL 1 GRAPHING REAL NUMBERS

The numbers used in this algebra book are **real numbers**. They can be pictured as points on a horizontal line called a **real number line**.

The point labeled 0 is the **origin**. Points to the left of zero represent **negative numbers** and points to the right of zero represent **positive numbers**. Zero is neither positive nor negative.

REAL NUMBER LINE

Negative numbers Positive numbers

-6 -5 -4 -3 -2 -1 0 1 2 3 4 5 6

The scale marks are equally spaced and represent **integers**. An integer is either negative, zero, or positive.

$$..., -3, -2, -1, \qquad 0, \qquad 1, 2, 3, ...$$

Negative integers   Zero   Positive integers

The three dots on each side in the list above indicate that the list continues in both directions without end. For instance, the integer immediately to the left of -3 is -4, read as *negative four*.

The real number line has points that represent fractions and decimals, as well as integers. The point that corresponds to a number is the **graph** of the number, and drawing the point is called graphing the number or **plotting** the point.

EXAMPLE 1 *Graphing Real Numbers*

Graph the numbers $\frac{1}{2}$ and -2.3 on a number line.

SOLUTION

The point that corresponds to $\frac{1}{2}$ is one half unit to the *right* of zero. The point that corresponds to -2.3 is 2.3 units to the *left* of zero.

EXAMPLE 2   Comparing Real Numbers

STUDENT HELP

➡ **Skills Review**
For help with comparing
and ordering numbers,
see pp. 779–780.

Graph -4 and -5 on a number line. Then write two inequalities that compare the
two numbers.

SOLUTION

On the graph, -5 is to the left of -4, so -5 is **less than** -4.

$$-5 < -4$$

On the graph, -4 is to the right of -5, so -4 is **greater than** -5.

$$-4 > -5$$

EXAMPLE 3   Ordering Real Numbers

Write the following numbers in increasing order: $-2, 4, 0, 1.5, \frac{1}{2}, -\frac{3}{2}$.

SOLUTION

Graph the numbers on a number line.

▶ From the graph, you can see that the order is $-2, -\frac{3}{2}, 0, \frac{1}{2}, 1.5, 4$.

EXAMPLE 4   Comparing Real Numbers

**FOCUS ON
APPLICATIONS**

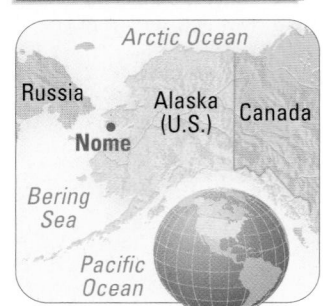

NOME, ALASKA
Around December
21, the northern hemisphere
has its shortest day and
longest night. On that day,
Nome has only 3 hours and
54 minutes of daylight.

DATA UPDATE
Visit our Web site
www.mcdougallittell.com

NOME, ALASKA The table at the right shows the
low temperatures recorded in Nome, Alaska, each
day for five days in December.

   a. Which low temperature reading was the coldest?

   b. Which dates had low temperatures above 10°F?

   c. Which dates had low temperatures below -5°F?

Date	Temp. (°F)
Dec. 18	-10°F
Dec. 19	-11°F
Dec. 20	16°F
Dec. 21	3°F
Dec. 22	2°F

SOLUTION

   a. The coldest temperature was -11°F on December 19.

   b. On December 20, the low temperature, 16°F, was above 10°F.

   c. Low temperatures were below -5°F on December 18 (-10°F)
      and December 19 (-11°F).

GOAL 2 FINDING OPPOSITES AND ABSOLUTE VALUES

Two points that are the same distance from the origin but on opposite sides of the origin are **opposites**.

EXAMPLE 5 *Finding the Opposite of a Number*

The numbers -3 and 3 are opposites because each is 3 units from the origin.

. . . .

The expression -3 can be stated as "negative 3" or "the opposite of 3." You can read the expression $-a$ as "the opposite of a." You should not assume that $-a$ is a negative number. For instance, if $a = -2$, then $-a = -(-2) = 2$.

The **absolute value** of a real number is the distance between the origin and the point representing the real number. The symbol $|a|$ represents the absolute value of a number a.

> **CONCEPT SUMMARY** THE ABSOLUTE VALUE OF A NUMBER
>
> - If a is a positive number, then $|a| = a$. Example: $|3| = 3$
> - If a is zero, then $|a| = 0$. Example: $|0| = 0$
> - If a is a negative number, then $|a| = -a$. Example: $|-3| = 3$

The absolute value of a number is *never* negative. If the number a is negative, then its absolute value, $-a$, is positive. For instance, $|-6| = -(-6) = 6$.

EXAMPLE 6 *Finding Absolute Values*

Evaluate the expression.

a. $|2.3|$ **b.** $\left|-\dfrac{1}{2}\right|$ **c.** $-|-8|$

SOLUTION

a. $|2.3| = 2.3$ If a is positive, then $|a| = a$.

b. $\left|-\dfrac{1}{2}\right| = -\left(-\dfrac{1}{2}\right) = \dfrac{1}{2}$ If a is negative, then $|a| = -a$.

c. $-|-8| = -(8)$ The absolute value of -8 is 8.

$\qquad\quad = -8$ Use definition of opposites.

EXAMPLE 7 *Solving an Absolute Value Equation*

STUDENT HELP

→ **Look Back**
For help with the solution of an equation, see p. 24.

Use mental math to solve the equation.

a. $|x| = 7$ **b.** $|x| = -5$

SOLUTION

a. Ask "what numbers are 7 units from the origin?" Both 7 and -7 are 7 units from the origin, so there are two solutions: 7 and -7.

b. The absolute value of a number is never negative, so there is no solution.

· · · · · · · · ·

Velocity indicates both speed and direction (up is positive and down is negative). The speed of an object is the absolute value of its velocity.

FOCUS ON APPLICATIONS

EXAMPLE 8 *Finding Velocity and Speed*

SPACE SHUTTLE ELEVATORS A space shuttle launch pad elevator drops at a rate of 10 feet per second. What are its velocity and speed?

SOLUTION

Velocity $= -10$ feet per second   **Motion is downward.**

Speed $= |-10| = 10$ feet per second   **Speed is positive.**

· · · · · · · · ·

In mathematics, to prove that a statement is true, you need to show that it is true for all examples. To prove that a statement is false, you need to show that it is *not* true for only one example, called a **counterexample**.

REAL LIFE SPACE SHUTTLE
The space shuttle's elevators have been designed to endure the stress of 320,000 gallons of water released at lift off to lessen heat and vibration.

APPLICATION LINK
www.mcdougallittell.com

EXAMPLE 9 *Using a Counterexample*

Decide whether the statement is *true* or *false*. If it is false, give a counterexample.

a. The opposite of a number is *always* negative.

b. The absolute value of a number is *never* negative.

c. The expression $-a$ is *never* positive.

d. The expression $-a$ is *sometimes* greater than a.

SOLUTION

a. False. Counterexample: The opposite of -5 is 5, which is positive.

b. True, by definition.

c. False. Counterexample: If $a = -2$, then $-a = -(-2) = 2$, which is positive.

d. True. For instance, if $a = -8$, then $-a = -(-8) = 8$, and $8 > -8$.

GUIDED PRACTICE

Vocabulary Check ✓

1. Write an inequality for the sentence: *Three is greater than negative five.*

Concept Check ✓

2. Copy the number line. Use it to explain why $-2.5 > -3.5$.

3. Use a counterexample to show that the following statement is false. *The opposite of a number is never positive.*

Skill Check ✓

Complete the statement using > or <.

4. $-3 \underline{\ ?\ } -5$ **5.** $-3 \underline{\ ?\ } 0$ **6.** $-2 \underline{\ ?\ } -\frac{1}{2}$ **7.** $-8 \underline{\ ?\ } 7$

Graph the numbers on a number line. Then write the numbers in increasing order.

8. $3, -5, 0$ **9.** $2, 3, -4$ **10.** $-\frac{1}{2}, -\frac{3}{4}, \frac{1}{4}$ **11.** $-0.1, -1.1, -1$

Evaluate the expression.

12. $|-12|$ **13.** $|4.1|$ **14.** $\left|-\frac{1}{5}\right|$ **15.** $|-103|$

Tell whether you would use a positive number or a negative number to represent the velocity.

16. The velocity of a rising rocket **17.** The velocity of a falling raindrop

PRACTICE AND APPLICATIONS

STUDENT HELP

▶ **Extra Practice**
to help you master
skills is on p. 798.

WRITING INEQUALITIES Graph the numbers on a number line. Then write two inequalities that compare the two numbers.

18. -6 and 4 **19.** -6.4 and -6.3 **20.** -7 and 2

21. -0.1 and -0.11 **22.** 5.7 and -4.2 **23.** -2.8 and 3.7

24. -2.7 and $\frac{3}{4}$ **25.** -0.5 and $-\frac{1}{3}$ **26.** $-1\frac{5}{6}$ and $-1\frac{7}{9}$

ORDERING NUMBERS Write the numbers in increasing order.

27. $4.66, 0.7, 4.6, -1.8, 3, -0.66$ **28.** $-0.03, 0.2, 0, 2.0, -0.2, -0.02$

29. $4.8, -2.6, 0, -3, \frac{1}{2}, -\frac{1}{2}$ **30.** $3\frac{1}{2}, 3.4, 4.1, -5, -5.1, -4\frac{1}{2}$

31. $7, -\frac{1}{2}, 2.4, -\frac{3}{4}, -5.8, \frac{1}{3}$ **32.** $6.03, -6.08, -6.1, -6.11, -6.02, 6.07$

OPPOSITES Find the opposite of the number.

33. 8 **34.** -3 **35.** 3.8 **36.** -2.5

37. $-\frac{5}{6}$ **38.** $3\frac{4}{5}$ **39.** -2.01 **40.** $-\frac{1}{9}$

STUDENT HELP

▶ **HOMEWORK HELP**
Example 1: Exs. 18–26
Example 2: Exs. 18–26
Example 3: Exs. 27–32
Example 4: Exs. 66–70
Example 5: Exs. 33–40

continued on p. 68

STUDENT HELP

→ **HOMEWORK HELP**
continued from p. 67
Example 6: Exs. 41–49
Example 7: Exs. 50–53
Example 8: Exs. 76–78
Example 9: Exs. 54–57

FINDING ABSOLUTE VALUES Evaluate the expression.

41. $|7|$

42. $|-4|$

43. $|-4.5|$

44. $\left|\dfrac{2}{3}\right|$

45. $\left|-\dfrac{4}{5}\right|$

46. $|0| + 2$

47. $|6.3| - 2$

48. $-\left|-\dfrac{8}{9}\right|$

49. $|-6.1| - 6.01$

SOLVE AN EQUATION Use mental math to solve the equation.

50. $|x| = 4$ **51.** $|x| = 0$ **52.** $x = |-3.8|$ **53.** $|-x| = 1$

COUNTEREXAMPLES Decide whether the statement is *true* or *false*. If it is false, give a counterexample.

54. The absolute value of a negative number is always negative.

55. The opposite of $-a$ is always positive.

56. The opposite of $|a|$ is never positive.

57. The value of $|-a|$ is sometimes negative.

LOGICAL REASONING Complete the statement using >, <, ≥, or ≤.

58. If $x > -4$, then -4 _?_ x.

59. If $3 \le y$, then y _?_ 3.

60. If $m \le 8$, then 8 _?_ m.

61. If $-7 \ge w$, then w _?_ -7.

🌐 **ELEVATION** In Exercises 62–65, write a positive number, a negative number, or zero to represent the elevation of the location.
Elevation is represented by comparing a location to sea level, which is given a value of zero. A location above sea level has a positive elevation, and a location below sea level has a negative elevation.

62. Granite Peak, Montana, 12,799 feet above sea level

63. New Orleans, Louisiana, 8 feet below sea level

64. Death Valley, California, 282 feet below sea level

65. Long Island Sound, Connecticut, sea level

FOCUS ON APPLICATIONS

ASTRONOMY
A star may *appear* to be dim because of its great distance from Earth. Such a star may burn brighter than another star that looks very bright because it is closer to Earth.

🌐 **ASTRONOMY** In Exercises 66–70, use the table showing the apparent magnitude of several stars.
A star's brightness as it appears to a person on Earth is measured by its *apparent magnitude*. A bright star has a lesser apparent magnitude than a dim star.

66. Which star looks the brightest?

67. Which star looks the dimmest?

68. Which stars look dimmer than Altair?

69. Which stars look brighter than Procyon?

70. Write the stars in order from dimmest to brightest.

Star	Apparent magnitude
Canopus	-0.72
Procyon	0.38
Pollux	1.14
Altair	0.77
Spica	0.98
Vega	0.03
Regulus	1.35
Sirius	-1.46
Arcturus	-0.04
Deneb	1.25

GOLF SCORES
If you complete a round of golf in 68 strokes at a course with a par of 71 strokes, you have shot "3 under par," or −3.

🌐 **GOLF** In Exercises 71–75, use the table, which lists several players and their final scores at a 1998 Ladies Professional Golf Association tournament.

In golf the total score is given as the number of strokes above or below *par*, the expected score. If you are at "even par," your score is zero. The player with the lowest score wins.

71. Which player scored closest to par?

72. Which player scored farthest from par?

73. Which players scored above par?

74. Which players scored below par?

75. One of the players listed won the tournament. Who was it?

Player	Score
Luciana Bemvenuti	+6
Liz Early	+15
Michelle Estill	−9
Hiromi Kobayashi	+1
Jenny Lidback	−4
Joan Pitcock	−11
Nancy Scranton	+4
Annika Sörenstam	−19

▶ Source: Ladies Professional Golf Association

🌐 **SPEED AND VELOCITY** Find the speed and the velocity of the object.

76. A helicopter is descending for a landing at a rate of 6 feet per second.

77. An elevator in the Washington Monument in Washington, DC, climbs about 429 feet per minute. ▶ Source: National Park Service

78. A diver plunges to the ocean floor at a rate of 3 meters per second.

🌐 **WIND CHILL** The faster the wind blows, the colder you feel. In Exercises 79–81, use the wind-chill index table to identify the combination of temperature and wind speed that feels colder.

To use the table, find the temperature in the top row. Read down until you are in the row for the appropriate wind speed. For example, when the temperature is 0°F and the wind speed is 10 mi/h, the temperature feels like −22°F.

Wind-Chill Index					
Wind speed (mi/h)	Temperature (°F)				
0	−10	−5	0	5	10
5	−15	−10	−5	0	6
10	−34	−27	−22	−15	−9
15	−45	−38	−31	−25	−18
20	−53	−46	−39	−31	−24
25	−59	−51	−44	−36	−29
30	−64	−56	−49	−41	−33

79. A temperature of 10°F with a wind speed of 25 mi/h, or a temperature of −5°F with a wind speed of 10 mi/h

80. A temperature of 5°F with a wind speed of 15 mi/h, or a temperature of −5°F with a wind speed of 5 mi/h

81. A temperature of −10°F with a wind speed of 5 mi/h, or a temperature of 10°F with a wind speed of 20 mi/h

82. *Writing* You are writing a quiz for this lesson. Write a problem to test whether students can write a set of real numbers in increasing order. Include positive and negative decimals and fractions. Show the answer to your problem on a number line.

Test Preparation

QUANTITATIVE COMPARISON **In Exercises 83–85, choose the statement that is true about the given numbers.**

(A) The number in column A is greater.

(B) The number in column B is greater.

(C) The two numbers are equal.

(D) The relationship cannot be determined from the given information.

	Column A	Column B
83.	$-\left|\dfrac{2}{3}\right|$	$\left|-\dfrac{2}{3}\right|$
84.	$x + |2|$	$x + |-2|$
85.	$|x| + 8$	$x + 8$

★ **Challenge**

86. **LOGICAL REASONING** Is the opposite of the absolute value of a number ever the same as the absolute value of the opposite of the number? In other words, is it ever true that $-|x| = |-x|$? Explain.

EXTRA CHALLENGE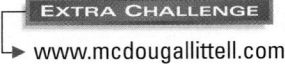
www.mcdougallittell.com

87. **LOGICAL REASONING** Is it *always, sometimes,* or *never* true that $|x| = |-x|$?

MIXED REVIEW

FRACTION OPERATIONS **Find the sum.** (Skills Review, p. 781)

88. $\dfrac{2}{4} + \dfrac{3}{8}$ **89.** $\dfrac{2}{3} + \dfrac{1}{6}$ **90.** $\dfrac{2}{5} + \dfrac{1}{4}$

91. $\dfrac{5}{8} + \dfrac{1}{3}$ **92.** $3\dfrac{2}{7} + 4\dfrac{1}{2}$ **93.** $1\dfrac{7}{9} + 4\dfrac{3}{7}$

EVALUATING EXPRESSIONS **Evaluate the expression for the given value(s) of the variable(s).** (Review 1.1)

94. $5x + 3$ when $x = 2$ **95.** $2a - 7$ when $a = 6$

96. $3y + 12$ when $y = 0$ **97.** $6b - 39 + c$ when $b = 15$ and $c = 2$

98. $\dfrac{5}{6}a - b$ when $a = 6$ and $b = 5$ **99.** $\dfrac{x}{5} - 2y$ when $x = 12$ and $y = \dfrac{4}{5}$

TRANSLATING VERBAL SENTENCES **Write the verbal sentence as an equation or an inequality.** (Review 1.5)

100. Five less than z is eight.

101. Eight more than r is seventeen.

102. Nine more than three fourths of y is less than six times w.

▶ **ACTIVITY 2.2**

Developing Concepts

Modeling Addition of Integers

▶ **QUESTION** How can you model addition of integers with algebra tiles?

GROUP ACTIVITY
Work with a partner.

MATERIALS
algebra tiles

▶ **EXPLORING THE CONCEPT**

To model addition problems involving positive and negative integers, you can use tiles labeled $+$ and $-$. Each $+$ represents positive 1, and each $-$ represents negative 1. Combining a $+$ with a $-$ gives 0. You can use algebra tiles to find the sum of -8 and 3.

1 Model negative 8 and positive 3 using algebra tiles.

2 Group pairs of positive and negative tiles. Count the remaining tiles.

Each pair has a sum of 0.

3 The remaining tiles show the sum of -8 and 3.

Complete the statement: $-8 + 3 = \underline{\ ?\ }$.

▶ **DRAWING CONCLUSIONS**

Use algebra tiles to find the sum. Sketch your solution.

1. $4 + 5$	**2.** $3 + 3$	**3.** $-4 + (-2)$
4. $-1 + (-7)$	**5.** $-3 + 2$	**6.** $5 + (-2)$
7. $-6 + 6$	**8.** $2 + (-2)$	**9.** $-6 + (-3)$

Use your results from Exercises 1–8 to help you decide whether the statement is *true* or *false*. Give an example that supports your answer.

10. The sum of a positive integer and a positive integer is always a positive integer.

11. The sum of a negative integer and a negative integer is always a positive integer.

12. The sum of a positive integer and a negative integer is sometimes a negative integer.

13. The sum of a negative integer and a negative integer is never zero.

2.2 Addition of Real Numbers

What you should learn

GOAL ① Add real numbers using a number line or addition rules.

GOAL ② Use addition of real numbers to solve **real-life** problems such as finding the profit of a business in **Example 5**.

Why you should learn it

▼ To solve **real-life** problems, such as finding the number of yards gained by a football team in **Ex. 51**.

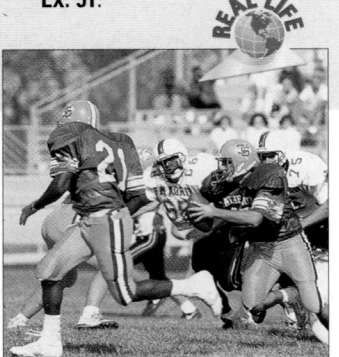

GOAL ① ADDING REAL NUMBERS

Addition can be modeled with movements on a number line.

• You add a positive number by moving to the right.

• You add a negative number by moving to the left.

EXAMPLE 1 *Adding Two Real Numbers*

Use a number line to find the sum.

a. $-2 + 5$ **b.** $2 + (-6)$

SOLUTION

a.

▶ The sum can be written as $-2 + 5 = 3$.

b.

▶ The sum can be written as $2 + (-6) = -4$.

EXAMPLE 2 *Adding Three Real Numbers*

Use a number line to find the sum: $-3 + 5 + (-6)$.

SOLUTION

▶ The sum can be written as $-3 + 5 + (-6) = -4$.

The rules of addition show how to add two real numbers without a number line.

RULES OF ADDITION

TO ADD TWO NUMBERS WITH THE *SAME SIGN*:
STEP ❶   Add their absolute values.
STEP ❷   Attach the common sign.

   Example: $-4 + (-5)$ Step 1 ▸ $|-4| + |-5| = 9$ Step 2 ▸ -9

TO ADD TWO NUMBERS WITH *OPPOSITE SIGNS*:
STEP ❶   Subtract the smaller absolute value from the larger absolute value.
STEP ❷   Attach the sign of the number with the larger absolute value.

   Example: $3 + (-9)$ Step 1 ▸ $|-9| - |3| = 6$ Step 2 ▸ -6

The above rules of addition will help you find sums of positive and negative numbers. It can be shown that these rules are a consequence of the following Properties of Addition.

PROPERTIES OF ADDITION

COMMUTATIVE PROPERTY
The order in which two numbers are added does not change the sum.
   $a + b = b + a$ **Example:** $3 + (-2) = -2 + 3$

ASSOCIATIVE PROPERTY
The way you group three numbers when adding does not change the sum.
   $(a + b) + c = a + (b + c)$ **Example:** $(-5 + 6) + 2 = -5 + (6 + 2)$

IDENTITY PROPERTY
The sum of a number and 0 is the number.
   $a + 0 = a$ **Example:** $-4 + 0 = -4$

PROPERTY OF ZERO (INVERSE PROPERTY)
The sum of a number and its opposite is 0.
   $a + (-a) = 0$ **Example:** $5 + (-5) = 0$

EXAMPLE 3   *Finding a Sum*

a. $1.4 + (-2.6) + 3.1 = 1.4 + (-2.6 + 3.1)$ **Use associative property.**

$\qquad\qquad\qquad\qquad = 1.4 + 0.5$ **Simplify.**

$\qquad\qquad\qquad\qquad = 1.9$

b. $-\dfrac{1}{2} + 3 + \dfrac{1}{2} = -\dfrac{1}{2} + \dfrac{1}{2} + 3$ **Use commutative property.**

$\qquad\qquad\qquad = \left(-\dfrac{1}{2} + \dfrac{1}{2}\right) + 3$ **Use associative property.**

$\qquad\qquad\qquad = 0 + 3 = 3$ **Use identity property and property of zero.**

STUDENT HELP

HOMEWORK HELP
Visit our Web site
www.mcdougallittell.com
for extra examples.

▶ **Look Back**
For help with fraction operations, see pp. 781–783.

CRYSTALS are often made up of ions. The attraction of positive and negative ions to each other results in a regular geometric pattern.

GOAL 2 **USING ADDITION IN REAL LIFE**

EXAMPLE 4 *Adding Real Numbers*

SCIENCE CONNECTION Atoms are composed of electrons, neutrons, and protons. Each electron has a charge of -1, each neutron has a charge of 0, and each proton has a charge of $+1$. The total charge of an atom is the sum of all the charges of its electrons, neutrons, and protons. An atom is an ion if it has a positive or negative charge. If an atom has a charge of zero, it is *not* an ion. Are the following atoms ions?

a. Aluminum: 13 electrons, 13 neutrons, 13 protons

b. Aluminum: 10 electrons, 13 neutrons, 13 protons

SOLUTION

a. The total charge is $-13 + 0 + 13 = 0$, so the atom is not an ion. In chemistry this aluminum atom is written as Al.

b. The total charge is $-10 + 0 + 13 = 3$, so the atom is an ion. In chemistry this aluminum ion is written as Al^{3+}.

· · · · · · · · · ·

PROFIT AND LOSS A company has a *profit* if its income is greater than its expenses. It has a *loss* if its income is less than its expenses. Business losses can be indicated by negative numbers.

EXAMPLE 5 *Finding the Total Profit*

A consulting company had the following monthly results after comparing income and expenses. Add the monthly profits and losses to find the overall profit or loss during the six-month period.

JANUARY	FEBRUARY	MARCH
-$13,142.50	-$6,783.16	-$4,734.86
APRIL	MAY	JUNE
$3,825.01	$7,613.17	$12,932.54

STUDENT HELP

▸ **KEYSTROKE HELP**
To enter -5 on a calculator with a +/- key, enter 5 +/- . To enter -5 on a calculator with a (−) key, enter (−) 5.

SOLUTION With this many large numbers, you may want to use a calculator.

13142.50 +/- + 6783.16 +/- + 4734.86 +/-

+ 3825.01 + 7613.17 + 12932.54 = ⬚ −289.8

▸ The display is -289.8. This means the company had a loss of $289.80.

GUIDED PRACTICE

Vocabulary Check ✔ 1. Would a business represent *profits* or *losses* with negative numbers?

Concept Check ✔ 2. Is the order in which you add two numbers important? Make a sketch to help explain your answer. What property does this illustrate?

3. Show how to model the sum of -3, 2, and -1 in two ways. Make a sketch to illustrate both ways.

Skill Check ✔ 4. Write an addition equation to represent the sum modeled on the number line.

Find the sum.

5. $-2 + 0$ 6. $4 + (-3)$ 7. $-2 + (-3)$

8. $-7 + 7$ 9. $-1 + 6$ 10. $-4 + \frac{1}{2}$

11. 🌐 **TEMPERATURE** The highest recorded temperature in Hawaii is 100°F. The highest recorded temperature in Colorado is 18°F higher than that of Hawaii. What is the highest recorded temperature in Colorado?
▶ Source: National Oceanographic and Atmospheric Administration

PRACTICE AND APPLICATIONS

STUDENT HELP

▶ **Extra Practice**
to help you master
skills is on p. 798.

NUMBER LINE SUMS Use a number line to find the sum.

12. $-8 + 12$ 13. $2 + (-5)$ 14. $-3 + (-3)$

15. $-3 + (-7)$ 16. $-4 + 5$ 17. $-10 + 4$

18. $-5 + 8 + (-2)$ 19. $2 + (-9) + 3$ 20. $-5 + 8 + \left(-3\frac{1}{2}\right)$

RULES OF ADDITION Find the sum.

21. $-4 + 6$ 22. $17 + 35$ 23. $19 + 0$

24. $0 + (-5)$ 25. $-13 + (-6)$ 26. $14 + (-11)$

27. $-5 + 10 + (-3)$ 28. $-4 + 10 + (-6)$ 29. $-11.6 + 6.4 + (-3.0)$

30. $5.7 + (-9.5) + 5.2$ 31. $6.8 + 3.3 + (-4.1)$ 32. $9.8 + (-6.3) + (-7.2)$

ADDITION PROPERTIES Name the property that makes the statement true.

33. $-8 + 0 = -8$ 34. $2 + (-3) = -3 + 2$

35. $-2 + 2 = 0$ 36. $(-4 + 3) + 1 = -4 + (3 + 1)$

STUDENT HELP

▶ **HOMEWORK HELP**
Example 1: Exs. 12–17
Example 2: Exs. 18–20
Example 3: Exs. 21–36
Example 4: Exs. 52–54
Example 5: Exs. 37–42,
55

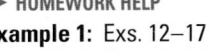 **FINDING SUMS** Find the sum. Use a calculator if you wish.

37. $-2.95 + 5.76 + (-88.6)$ 38. $10.97 + (-51.14) + (-40.97)$

39. $20.37 + 190.8 + (-85.13)$ 40. $300.3 + (-22.24) + 78.713$

41. $-1.567 + (-2.645) + 5308.34$ 42. $-7344.28 + 2997.65 + (-255.11)$

STUDENT HELP

Look Back
For help with evaluating expressions,
see p. 3.

EVALUATING EXPRESSIONS Evaluate the expression for the given value of *x*.

43. $5 + x + (-8); x = 2$

44. $4 + x + 10 + (-10); x = 3$

45. $-24 + 6 + x; x = 8$

46. $-6 + x + 4; x = -3$

47. $2 + (-5) + x + 14; x = -8$

48. $-11 + (-2) + 11 + x; x = -10$

49. $x + (-6) + (-11); x = -7$

50. $9 + x + (-8) + (-3); x = -12$

51. 🌎 **CHAMPIONSHIP GAME** In the game that decides the high school football championship, your team needs to gain 14 yards to score a touchdown and win. Your team's final four plays result in a 9-yard gain, a 5-yard loss, a 4-yard gain, and a 5-yard gain as time runs out. Use a number line to model the gains and losses. Did your team win?

SCIENCE ▸ CONNECTION In Exercises 52–54, use the information in Example 4 on page 74 and in the table below. The table shows the number of electrons and protons in atoms of sodium (Na) and fluorine (F).

52. Find the total charge of each sodium atom. Then decide whether the atom is an ion. Which atom has a symbol of Na^+?

53. Find the total charge of each fluorine atom. Then decide whether the atom is an ion. Which atom has a symbol of F^-?

Atom	Electrons	Protons
Na atom 1	10	11
Na atom 2	11	11
F atom 1	9	9
F atom 2	10	9

54. CRITICAL THINKING You do not need to know the number of neutrons in an atom to find its total charge. Explain why not. Which property of addition supports your answer?

55. 🌎 **PROFIT AND LOSS** A pest control company had a profit of $3,514.65 in April, a profit of $5,674.25 in May, a loss of $8,992.88 in June, and a loss of $1,207.03 in July. Did the company make a profit during the 4-month period? Explain.

🌎 **TIME ZONES** In Exercises 56 and 57, use the time zones map. It shows the time in different zones of the country when it is 1:00 P.M. in California.

56. A Thanksgiving Day parade in New York City is scheduled to begin at 9:00 A.M. and will be televised live. If you live in Nevada, at what time can you see the parade begin on television?

57. A New Year's Day parade in California is scheduled to begin at 8:00 A.M. and will be televised live. If you live in Illinois, at what time can you see the parade begin on television?

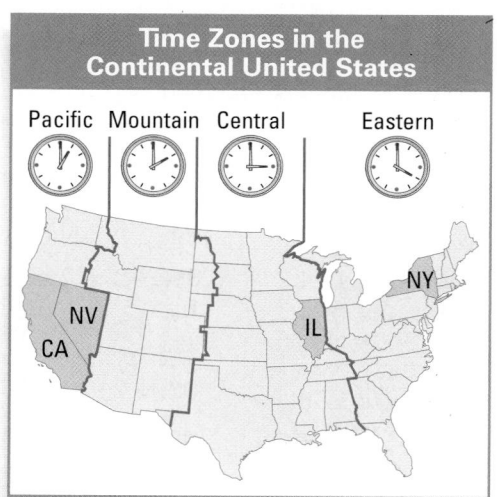

🌎 **SODIUM** is one of the two elements that make salt, NaCl. Salt, or sodium chloride, is a naturally occurring mineral mined from the ground.

MULTIPLE CHOICE In Exercises 58–60, use the table, which shows a 6-month record of a household budget used to calculate monthly savings.

58. In which month did the household save the most money?

Ⓐ January   Ⓑ March

Ⓒ May   Ⓓ June

59. In which month did the household's spending most exceed its earnings?

Ⓐ January   Ⓑ February

Ⓒ April   Ⓓ June

Month	$ Earned	$ Spent	$ Saved
Jan.	1676.05	−1427.37	?
Feb.	1554.52	−1771.89	?
Mar.	1851.89	−1556.44	?
Apr.	1567.96	−1874.72	?
May	1921.03	−1602.19	?
June	1667.67	−1989.82	?

60. How much money did the household save during the 6-month period?

Ⓐ $83.31   Ⓑ $16.69   Ⓒ $116.69   Ⓓ $183.31

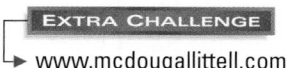
61. LOGICAL REASONING Formulate the following statement in terms of variables. Then decide whether it is *true* or *false*. *The opposite of the sum of two numbers is equal to the sum of the opposites of the numbers.* If false, give a counterexample. If true, give two examples involving negative numbers.

MIXED REVIEW

FRACTION OPERATIONS Find the difference. (Skills Review, p. 781)

62. $\frac{4}{5} - \frac{2}{5}$ **63.** $\frac{8}{9} - \frac{2}{3}$ **64.** $\frac{3}{4} - \frac{5}{12}$ **65.** $\frac{7}{8} - \frac{1}{4}$

66. $4\frac{2}{3} - 2\frac{1}{5}$ **67.** $\frac{5}{6} - \frac{1}{9}$ **68.** $7\frac{9}{10} - 5\frac{3}{7}$ **69.** $\frac{5}{12} - \frac{3}{16}$

VARIABLE EXPRESSIONS Evaluate the expression. (Review 1.3)

70. $a^4 + 8$ when $a = 10$ **71.** $79 - v^3$ when $v = 4$

72. $t^2 - 7t + 12$ when $t = 8$ **73.** $2x^2 + 8x - 5$ when $x = 3$

CHECKING SOLUTIONS Check whether the given number is a solution of the equation. (Review 1.4)

74. $x + 5 = 11$; 7   **75.** $12 - 2a = 18$; 4   **76.** $7y - 15 = 6$; 3

77. $3 + 2d = 9 + d$; 6   **78.** $3w - 7 = w + 1$; 5   **79.** $6z + 5 = 8z - 12$; 8.5

🌐 **PIZZA In Exercises 80–82, use the following information. A pizzeria charges $6.00 for a large cheese pizza, and $.85 for each additional topping. The total cost C of a large cheese pizza with n additional toppings is given by C = 6 + 0.85n. (Review 1.7)**

80. Write an input-output table that shows the total cost of a pizza with 0, 1, 2, 3, 4, and 5 additional toppings.

81. Describe the domain and range of the function.

82. Graph the data in the input-output table.

ACTIVITY 2.3

Developing Concepts

GROUP ACTIVITY
Work with a partner.

MATERIALS
algebra tiles

┌─────────────────────────┐
│ **STUDENT HELP** │
│ **Look Back** │
│ For help with using │
│ algebra tiles, see p. 71. │
└─────────────────────────┘

Modeling Subtraction of Integers

▶ **QUESTION** How can you model the subtraction of integers?

▶ **EXPLORING THE CONCEPT: MODELING $-6 - (-2)$**

You can use algebra tiles to find differences.

1 Use algebra tiles to model -6.

-6

2 Subtract -2 by taking away two -1-tiles.

$-6 - (-2)$

3 The remaining tiles show the difference of -6 and -2.

Complete the statement: $-6 - (-2) = \underline{?}$.

▶ **EXPLORING THE CONCEPT: MODELING $3 - 6$**

4 Use algebra tiles to model 3.

3

Add 3 "zero pairs"
so you can subtract 6.

5 Subtract 6 by taking away six 1-tiles.

$3 - 6$

6 The remaining tiles show the difference of 3 and 6.

Complete the statement: $3 - 6 = \underline{?}$.

▶ **DRAWING CONCLUSIONS**

Use algebra tiles to find the difference. Sketch your solution.

1. $7 - 2$ **2.** $-7 - (-3)$ **3.** $-5 - (-1)$

4. $-6 - (-6)$ **5.** $2 - 3$ **6.** $4 - 7$

7. $3 - 5$ **8.** $5 - 8$ **9.** $0 - (-5)$

In Exercises 10 and 11, decide whether the statement is *true* or *false*. Use algebra tiles to show an example that supports your answer. Sketch your example.

10. To subtract a positive integer, add the opposite of the positive integer.

11. To subtract a negative integer, add the opposite of the negative integer.

Subtraction of Real Numbers

What you should learn

GOAL 1 Subtract real numbers using the subtraction rule.

GOAL 2 Use subtraction of real numbers to solve **real-life** problems such as finding the differences in stock market prices in **Example 5**.

Why you should learn it

▼ To solve **real-life** problems such as analyzing data on visitors to a historical site in **Ex. 81**.

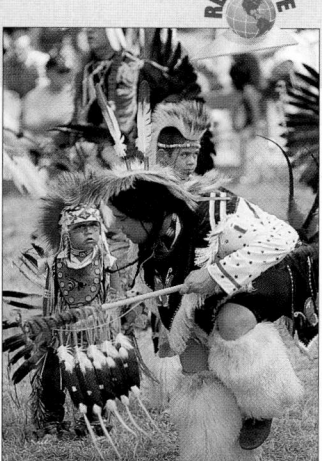

Native American dance at Nez Perce National Historical Park

GOAL 1 SUBTRACTING REAL NUMBERS

Some addition expressions can be evaluated using subtraction.

ADDITION PROBLEM	EQUIVALENT SUBTRACTION PROBLEM
$5 + (-3) = 2$	$5 - 3 = 2$
$9 + (-6) = 3$	$9 - 6 = 3$

Adding the opposite of a number is equivalent to subtracting the number.

SUBTRACTION RULE

To subtract b from a, add the opposite of b to a.

$$a - b = a + (-b) \qquad \textbf{Example: } 3 - 5 = 3 + (-5)$$

The result is the difference of a and b.

EXAMPLE 1 *Using the Subtraction Rule*

Find the difference.

a. $-4 - 3$ **b.** $10 - 11$ **c.** $11 - 10$ **d.** $-\dfrac{3}{2} - \left(-\dfrac{1}{2}\right)$

SOLUTION

a. $-4 - 3 = -4 + (-3)$	Add the opposite of 3.
$= -7$	Use rules of addition.
b. $10 - 11 = 10 + (-11)$	Add the opposite of 11.
$= -1$	Use rules of addition.
c. $11 - 10 = 11 + (-10)$	Add the opposite of 10.
$= 1$	Use rules of addition.
d. $-\dfrac{3}{2} - \left(-\dfrac{1}{2}\right) = -\dfrac{3}{2} + \dfrac{1}{2}$	Add the opposite of $-\dfrac{1}{2}$.
$= -1$	Use rules of addition.

· · · · · · · · · ·

The commutative property of addition, $a + b = b + a$, shows that the order in which two numbers are added does not affect the result. But as you may have noticed in parts (b) and (c) of Example 1, the order in which two numbers are subtracted does affect the result. Subtraction is *not* commutative.

Expressions containing more than one subtraction can also be evaluated by "adding the opposite." To do this, use the left-to-right rule for order of operations.

STUDENT HELP

HOMEWORK HELP
Visit our Web site
www.mcdougallittell.com
for extra examples.

EXAMPLE 2 *Evaluating Expressions with More than One Subtraction*

Evaluate the expression $3 - (-4) - 2 + 8$.

SOLUTION

$3 - (-4) - 2 + 8 = 3 + 4 + (-2) + 8$	Add the opposites of -4 and 2.
$= 7 + (-2) + 8$	Add 3 and 4.
$= 5 + 8$	Add 7 and -2.
$= 13$	Add 5 and 8.

. . . .

When an expression is written as a sum, the parts that are added are the **terms** of the expression. For instance, you can write the expression $5 - x$ as the sum $5 + (-x)$. The terms are 5 and $-x$. You can use the subtraction rule to find the terms of an expression.

EXAMPLE 3 *Finding the Terms of an Expression*

Find the terms of $-9 - 2x$.

SOLUTION Use the subtraction rule.

$$-9 - 2x = -9 + (-2x) \qquad \text{Rewrite the difference as a sum.}$$

▶ In this form, you can see that the terms of the expression are -9 and $-2x$.

STUDENT HELP

Look Back
For help with
functions, see p. 46.

EXAMPLE 4 *Evaluating a Function*

Evaluate the function $y = -5 - x$ for these values of x: $-2, -1, 0,$ and 1. Organize your results in a table and describe the pattern.

SOLUTION

Input	Function	Output
$x = -2$	$y = -5 - (-2)$	$y = -3$
$x = -1$	$y = -5 - (-1)$	$y = -4$
$x = 0$	$y = -5 - (0)$	$y = -5$
$x = 1$	$y = -5 - (1)$	$y = -6$

▶ From the table, you can see that each time x increases by 1, y decreases by 1.

STOCK MARKET
The Dow Jones
utilities average is an
average price of the shares
of 15 large gas and electric
companies. The average is
used to show the general
trend in the stock prices of
these types of companies.

GOAL ② **USING SUBTRACTION IN REAL LIFE**

EXAMPLE 5 *Subtracting Real Numbers*

STOCK MARKET You are writing a report about the Dow Jones utilities average.
The daily closing averages for one week are given in the table. Find the change in
the closing average since the previous day to complete the table.

Date	Feb. 9	Feb. 10	Feb. 11	Feb. 12	Feb. 13
Closing average	266.13	268.08	267.11	269.37	268.02
Change	——	?	?	?	?

▶ Source: *Wall Street Journal*

SOLUTION

Subtract each day's closing average from the closing average for the
previous day.

DATE	CLOSING AVERAGE	CHANGE
Feb. 9	266.13	——
Feb. 10	268.08	$268.08 - 266.13 = +1.95$
Feb. 11	267.11	$267.11 - 268.08 = -0.97$
Feb. 12	269.37	$269.37 - 267.11 = +2.26$
Feb. 13	268.02	$268.02 - 269.37 = -1.35$

EXAMPLE 6 *Using a Calculator*

 Use the solution from Example 5 to answer the following questions.

a. Write the changes you found in order.

b. Find the difference of the greatest number and the least number.

SOLUTION

a. Written in order from least to greatest, the numbers are as follows.
$-1.35, -0.97, 1.95, 2.26$

b. The difference of the greatest number and the least number is
$2.26 - (-1.35)$.

With a calculator, you can find the difference.

KEYSTROKES	DISPLAY
2.26 $\boxed{-}$ 1.35 $\boxed{+/-}$ $\boxed{=}$	$\boxed{3.61}$

▶ The greatest number is 3.61 more than the least number.

STUDENT HELP

KEYSTROKE HELP
Visit our Web site
www.mcdougallittell.com
to see keystrokes for
several models of
calculators.

GUIDED PRACTICE

Vocabulary Check ✓

1. Is $7x$ a term of the expression $4y^2 - 7x - 9$? Explain.

Concept Check ✓

2. Use the number line to complete: $-2 - 5 = \underline{\ ?\ }$.

3. Explain the steps you would take to evaluate the expression $5 - 7 - (-4)$.

Skill Check ✓

Use the subtraction rule to rewrite the subtraction expression as an equivalent addition expression. Then evaluate the expression.

4. $4 - 5$ **5.** $3 - (-8)$ **6.** $0 - 7$ **7.** $2 - (-3) - 6$

8. $-2.4 - 3$ **9.** $-3.6 - (-6)$ **10.** $\frac{1}{2} - \frac{1}{4}$ **11.** $\frac{2}{3} - \left(-\frac{1}{6}\right) - \frac{1}{3}$

Find the terms of the expression.

12. $12 - 5x$ **13.** $-7y^2 + 12y - 6$ **14.** $23 - 5w - 8y$

15. Evaluate the function $y = -x - 3$ for these values of x: $-2, -1, 0, 1,$ and 2. Organize your results in a table. Describe the pattern.

PRACTICE AND APPLICATIONS

STUDENT HELP

▶ **Extra Practice**
to help you master
skills is on p. 798.

DIFFERENCES **Find the difference.**

16. $4 - 9$ **17.** $6 - 13$ **18.** $8 - (-5)$ **19.** $-2 - (-7)$

20. $-11 - 8$ **21.** $24 - 39$ **22.** $137 - 355$ **23.** $-65 - (-59)$

24. $12.5 - 9.8$ **25.** $-3.2 - 1.7$ **26.** $5.4 - (-3.8)$ **27.** $-6.6 - (-16.1)$

28. $\frac{4}{3} - \frac{7}{3}$ **29.** $\frac{3}{4} - \left(-\frac{9}{4}\right)$ **30.** $-\frac{5}{8} - \frac{3}{4}$ **31.** $-\frac{9}{10} - \frac{1}{4}$

32. $6 - |-2|$ **33.** $15 - |-6|$ **34.** $|5| - 7.9$ **35.** $34.1 - |-57.2|$

EVALUATING EXPRESSIONS **Evaluate the expression.**

36. $2 - (-4) - 7$ **37.** $8 - 11 - (-6)$ **38.** $4 + (-3) - (-5)$

39. $3 - (-8) + (-9)$ **40.** $14 + (-7) - 12$ **41.** $-7 + 42 - 63$

42. $-8 - (-12) + 3$ **43.** $6 - 1 + 10 - (-8)$ **44.** $14 - 8 + 17 - (-23)$

45. $2.3 + (-9.1) - 1.2$ **46.** $1.3 + (-1.3) - 4.2$ **47.** $-8.5 - 3.9 + (-16.2)$

48. $8.4 - 5.2 - (-4.7)$ **49.** $-\frac{4}{9} - \frac{2}{3} + \left(-\frac{5}{6}\right)$ **50.** $\frac{7}{12} - \left(-\frac{3}{4}\right) + \left(-\frac{1}{8}\right)$

STUDENT HELP

▶ **HOMEWORK HELP**
Example 1: Exs. 16–35
Example 2: Exs. 36–50
Example 3: Exs. 51–58
Example 4: Exs. 59–64
Example 5: Exs. 71–75
Example 6: Exs. 65–70

FINDING TERMS **Find the terms of the expression.**

51. $-4 - y$ **52.** $-x - 7$ **53.** $-3x + 6$ **54.** $9 - 28x$

55. $-9 + 4b$ **56.** $a + 3b - 5$ **57.** $x - y - 7$ **58.** $-3x + 5 - 8y$

EVALUATING FUNCTIONS **Evaluate the function for these values of**
x: **−2, −1, 0, and 1. Organize your results in a table.**

59. $y = x - 8$ **60.** $y = 12 - x$ **61.** $y = -x + 12.1$

62. $y = -8.5 - (-x)$ **63.** $y = 27 + x$ **64.** $y = -x + 13 - x$

EVALUATING EXPRESSIONS **Evaluate the expression. Use estimation to check your answer.**

65. $5.3 - (-2.5) - 4.7$ **66.** $8.9 - (-2.1) - 7.3$

67. $-4.89 + 2.69 - (-3.74)$ **68.** $-7.85 + 5.96 - (-2.49)$

69. $-13.87 - (-13.87) + 5.8$ **70.** $-15.7 + 0.01 + (-34.44)$

71. 🌎 **SUBMARINE DEPTH** A submarine is at a depth of 725 feet below sea level. Five minutes later, it is at a depth of 450 feet below sea level. What is the change in depth of the submarine? Did it go up or down?

72. 🌎 **GASOLINE PRICES** Last month the price of gasoline was $1.19 per gallon. This month the price of gasoline is $1.13 per gallon. What was the change in the price per gallon of gasoline?

🌎 **GOLD PRICES IN LONDON** **At 9 A.M., an ounce of gold sells for $287.56. At noon, gold sells for $286.90 per ounce. At 4 P.M., the final price for the day is $287.37 per ounce.**

73. What is the change in the price per ounce of gold from 9 A.M. to noon?

74. What is the change in the price per ounce of gold from noon to 4 P.M.?

75. What is the change in the price per ounce of gold from 9 A.M. to 4 P.M.?

🌎 **HIKING** **Use the diagram for Exercises 76–78. It shows the elevation above sea level (in feet) of various points along the Mount Langdon Trail in the White Mountain National Forest in New Hampshire.**

Not drawn to scale

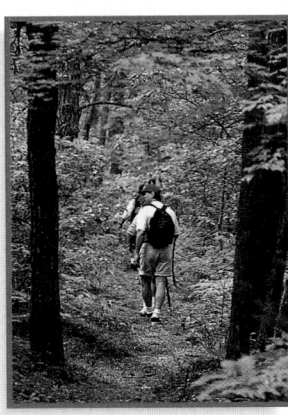
White Mountain National Forest, NH

76. How much higher is the cave than the start of the trail?

77. Determine the change in elevation from each point to the next in the diagram.

78. You hike along the trail, visit a cave, and then climb Oak Ridge. From there, you reach a trail junction and continue to the top of Mt. Parker. Find the total of these changes to determine your overall change in elevation.

SCIENCE **CONNECTION** In Exercises 79 and 80, use the diagram, which shows the journey of a water molecule from left to right.

79. Find the change in elevation from each point to the next point.

80. Write an expression using addition and subtraction that models the journey of the water molecule. Then evaluate the expression.

Test Preparation

81. **MULTI-STEP PROBLEM** Use the bar graph, which shows the number of visitors to Nez Perce National Historical Park during 1997.

 DATA UPDATE of National Park Service data at www.mcdougallittell.com

    a. Find the change in the number of visitors from each month to the next month. Organize your results in a table.

    b. What does a negative value for a monthly change represent? What does a positive value represent?

    c. *Writing* Write a paragraph describing the pattern of visitors to Nez Perce National Historical Park during the year. Use mathematically descriptive words like *most*, *least*, *increase*, and *decrease*.

★ Challenge

LOGICAL REASONING Decide whether the statement is *true* or *false*. Use the subtraction rule or a number line to support your answer.

82. If you subtract a negative number from a positive number, the result is always a positive number.

83. If you subtract a positive number from a negative number, the result is always a negative number.

MIXED REVIEW

EVALUATING NUMERIC EXPRESSIONS Evaluate the expression. (Review 1.3)

84. $89 - 8 \cdot 5 - 27$

85. $\frac{10}{3} - \frac{2}{3} \cdot 4 + 5$

86. $12 \cdot 9 \div 6 - 13.5$

87. $17 + 100 \div 25 - 5$

88. $5 \cdot \frac{8}{9} - \frac{6}{9} + 51 \div 3$

89. $13 + 11 \cdot 7 - 6 \div 3$

90. $25 - \left[\frac{3}{10}(6 \cdot 5) - 2\right]$

91. $(27 \div 9) \div (7 - 5)$

92. $[(12 \cdot 9) \div 6] - 13.5$

🌐 **SPORTS** In Exercises 93 and 94, use the table, which shows the number of male and female participants in high school sports for three years. Based on the table, decide whether the statement is *true* or *false*. (Review 1.6)

High School Sports Participants (millions)		
Year	Male	Female
1994–95	3.54	2.24
1995–96	3.63	2.37
1996–97	3.71	2.24

▶ Source: National Federation of State High School Associations

93. There were more than six million total participants during 1994–1995.

94. During the three-year period, female participation grew more than male participation.

95. 💲 **PROFIT AND LOSS** A landscaping company had a loss of $5,126.55 in March. It then had a profit of $2,943.21 in April, a profit of $4,988.97 in May, and a loss of $1,807.81 in June. Did the company make a profit during the four-month period? Explain. (Review 2.2 for 2.4)

QUIZ 1   *Self-Test for Lessons 2.1–2.3*

Write the numbers in increasing order. (Lesson 2.1)

1. $5.31, 5.04, -5.32, -6.2, 6.3, 5.3$

2. $-1.07, 1.06, 1.16, -1.6, 0.18, -0.28$

3. $7.3, -7.5, 7\frac{2}{3}, -7\frac{1}{3}, 7.5, 7\frac{1}{3}$

4. $-6\frac{2}{5}, 6.42, \frac{33}{5}, -6.3, -\frac{33}{5}, 6.05$

Evaluate the expression. (Lesson 2.1)

5. $|3.76|$

6. $|-75|$

7. $-|345|$

8. $|-27.5|$

9. $14 - |-7|$

10. $|-75| - 7.6$

Evaluate the expression. (Lessons 2.2 and 2.3)

11. $-11 + 35$

12. $29 - 501$

13. $-17 - (-14)$

14. $-8 + 12 + (-5)$

15. $-32 - (-27) - 9$

16. $35 - 0 - (-19)$

17. $12 + (-1.2) + (-7)$

18. $-143 - (-60) - 8$

19. $14.1 + (-75.2) + 60.7$

20. 🌐 **POOL DEPTH** The water in a pool is 47.3 inches deep on Monday. On Tuesday, 2.1 inches of depth is splashed out. On Wednesday, the depth decreases 11.3 inches due to a leak. On Thursday night, the leak is fixed and 12.9 inches of depth is added overnight. Write and evaluate an expression to find the depth of the water in the pool on Friday morning. (Lesson 2.3)

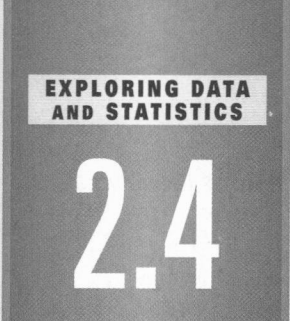

Adding and Subtracting Matrices

GOAL 1 **ORGANIZING DATA IN A MATRIX**

A **matrix** is a rectangular arrangement of numbers into horizontal rows and
vertical columns. Each number in the matrix is called an **entry** or an **element**.
(The plural of *matrix* is *matrices*.)

row →
$$\begin{bmatrix} 3 & 1 & 0 & 8 \\ -1 & 2 & 4 & -2 \\ 5 & -7 & 3 & 6 \end{bmatrix}$$

The entry in the second row
and third column is 4.

The size of a matrix is described as follows.

(the number of **rows**) × (the number of **columns**)

The matrix above is a 3 × 4 (read "3 by 4") matrix, because it has three rows
and four columns. Think of a matrix as a type of table that can be used to
organize data.

Two matrices are equal if the entries in corresponding positions are equal.

$$\begin{bmatrix} 3 & -2 \\ \frac{1}{2} & 0 \end{bmatrix} = \begin{bmatrix} 3 & -2 \\ 0.5 & 0 \end{bmatrix} \qquad \begin{bmatrix} -4 & 7 \\ 0 & -1 \end{bmatrix} \neq \begin{bmatrix} 7 & -4 \\ 0 & -1 \end{bmatrix}$$

EXAMPLE 1 *Writing a Matrix*

Write a matrix to organize the following information about your CD collection.

    Country: 4 groups, 6 solo artists, 0 collections

    Rock: 8 groups, 3 solo artists, 3 collections

    Blues: 1 group, 5 solo artists, 2 collections

SOLUTION

Country, Rock, and *Blues* can be labels for the rows or for the columns.

AS ROW LABELS:

	Group	Solo artist	Collection
Country	4	6	0
Rock	8	3	3
Blues	1	5	2

AS COLUMN LABELS:

	Country	Rock	Blues
Group	4	8	1
Solo artist	6	3	5
Collection	0	3	2

ADDING AND SUBTRACTING MATRICES

To add or subtract matrices, you add or subtract corresponding entries. Each matrix must have the same number of rows and columns. For instance, you cannot add a matrix that has three rows to a matrix that has only two rows.

EXAMPLE 2 *Adding and Subtracting Matrices*

a. $\begin{bmatrix} 4 & 2 \\ 0 & -3 \\ -5 & 1 \end{bmatrix} + \begin{bmatrix} 1 & 0 \\ 2 & -1 \\ 6 & -4 \end{bmatrix} = \begin{bmatrix} 4+1 & 2+0 \\ 0+2 & -3+(-1) \\ -5+6 & 1+(-4) \end{bmatrix}$

$= \begin{bmatrix} 5 & 2 \\ 2 & -4 \\ 1 & -3 \end{bmatrix}$

b. $\begin{bmatrix} 10 & -6 \\ 5 & 0 \end{bmatrix} - \begin{bmatrix} 4 & 5 \\ -3 & 2 \end{bmatrix} = \begin{bmatrix} 10-4 & -6-5 \\ 5-(-3) & 0-2 \end{bmatrix}$

$= \begin{bmatrix} 6 & -11 \\ 8 & -2 \end{bmatrix}$

EXAMPLE 3 *Political Composition of U.S. Congress*

CONGRESS The United States Congress is composed of the House of Representatives and the Senate. The matrices below show the number of men and women in the Senate and the House at the 1999 start of the 106th Congress. Write and label a single matrix that shows the number of men and women in Congress in 1999. **DATA UPDATE** of United States Congress data at www.mcdougallittell.com

HOUSE

	Men	Women
Democrat	172	39
Republican	206	17
Other	1	0

SENATE

	Men	Women
Democrat	39	6
Republican	52	3
Other	0	0

SOLUTION Add the two matrices. Then label the result.

$\begin{bmatrix} 172 & 39 \\ 206 & 17 \\ 1 & 0 \end{bmatrix} + \begin{bmatrix} 39 & 6 \\ 52 & 3 \\ 0 & 0 \end{bmatrix} = \begin{bmatrix} 211 & 45 \\ 258 & 20 \\ 1 & 0 \end{bmatrix}$

▶ The result can be written as follows.

CONGRESS

	Men	Women
Democrat	211	45
Republican	258	20
Other	1	0

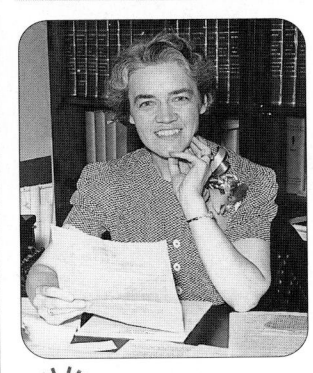

ORGANIZING DATA As you learned in Example 1, matrices are a useful way to organize and keep track of data. For example, if you have a business, it is important to keep track of revenue (or income) and expenses (or costs). You can find out how much profit has been made by subtracting expenses from revenue. If the profit is a negative number, you lost money.

Business

EXAMPLE 4 *Finding a Profit Matrix*

You own two stores that sell household appliances. The matrices below show revenue and expenses for three months at each store.

REVENUE ($)

	Store 1	Store 2
January	78,432	109,345
February	82,529	120,429
March	94,311	118,782

EXPENSES ($)

	Store 1	Store 2
January	59,426	98,459
February	64,372	104,972
March	85,456	120,833

a. Write a matrix that shows the monthly profit for each store.

b. Which store had higher overall profits during the three-month period?

c. Which store lost money? In which month?

SOLUTION

Profit is the difference of revenue and expenses.

a. To find the *profit matrix,* you can subtract the *expenses matrix* from the *revenue matrix.*

$$\begin{bmatrix} 78{,}432 & 109{,}345 \\ 82{,}529 & 120{,}429 \\ 94{,}311 & 118{,}782 \end{bmatrix} - \begin{bmatrix} 59{,}426 & 98{,}459 \\ 64{,}372 & 104{,}972 \\ 85{,}456 & 120{,}833 \end{bmatrix} = \begin{bmatrix} 19{,}006 & 10{,}886 \\ 18{,}157 & 15{,}457 \\ 8{,}855 & -2{,}051 \end{bmatrix}$$

▶ Label the matrix to identify the monthly profit at each store.

PROFIT ($)

	Store 1	Store 2
January	19,006	10,886
February	18,157	15,457
March	8,855	−2,051

b. Add the entries in each column of the profit matrix to find the total profit for each store during the three-month period.

Store 1: $19{,}006 + 18{,}157 + 8{,}855 = \$46{,}018$

Store 2: $10{,}886 + 15{,}457 + (-2{,}051) = \$24{,}292$

▶ Store 1 had higher overall profits.

c. Store 2 had a negative profit of $-2{,}051$ in March. This means the store lost $2,051 during March.

GUIDED PRACTICE

1. How many rows are there in the matrix at the right? How many columns?

$$\begin{bmatrix} 5 & -7 & 3 \\ 2 & -2 & -4 \end{bmatrix}$$

2. Is the matrix at the right a 3×2 matrix or a 2×3 matrix?

3. 🌎 **CONGRESS** Use the matrix showing the number of Democratic and Republican members of the House of Representatives from Arkansas, Delaware, and North Dakota. What is the entry in the first row and second column? What does the number represent?

$$\begin{array}{c} \\ AR \\ DE \\ ND \end{array} \begin{array}{cc} \text{Democrat} & \text{Republican} \\ \begin{bmatrix} 2 & 2 \\ 1 & 0 \\ 0 & 1 \end{bmatrix} \end{array}$$

4. 🌐 **VIDEO RENTALS** Write a matrix to organize the information about a video store's movies. Label each row and column.

    Comedy: 25 new releases, 215 regular selections

    Drama: 30 new releases, 350 regular selections

    Horror: 26 new releases, 180 regular selections

Find the sum and the difference of the matrices.

5. $\begin{bmatrix} -3 & 0 \\ -6 & 4 \\ 1 & -4 \end{bmatrix}, \begin{bmatrix} 2 & -4 \\ 1 & -3 \\ -1 & 9 \end{bmatrix}$

6. $\begin{bmatrix} 1 & 8 & -2 \\ -4 & -5 & 6 \end{bmatrix}, \begin{bmatrix} -1 & 9 & 2 \\ 3 & 3 & -5 \end{bmatrix}$

PRACTICE AND APPLICATIONS

STUDENT HELP

▶ **Extra Practice**
to help you master
skills is on p. 798.

MATRIX OPERATIONS Tell whether the matrices can be added.

7. $\begin{bmatrix} 4 & -1 \\ 7 & 5 \end{bmatrix}, \begin{bmatrix} 2 & -2 \\ 5 & -6 \end{bmatrix}$

8. $\begin{bmatrix} 3 & -2 & 0 \\ -4 & 1 & -8 \end{bmatrix}, \begin{bmatrix} -4 & 5 \\ 10 & 5 \end{bmatrix}$

9. $\begin{bmatrix} 4 & 2 \\ -6 & 3 \\ -1 & -2 \end{bmatrix}, \begin{bmatrix} 6 & 4 & -3 \\ 7 & -8 & 1 \end{bmatrix}$

10. $\begin{bmatrix} 8 & 5 & -8 \\ 4 & -1 & 2 \end{bmatrix}, \begin{bmatrix} -2 & -9 & 1 \\ -6 & 0 & 4 \end{bmatrix}$

ADDING MATRICES Find the sum of the matrices.

11. $\begin{bmatrix} 3 & -2 \\ 5 & 1 \end{bmatrix} + \begin{bmatrix} 4 & -3 \\ -8 & -2 \end{bmatrix}$

12. $\begin{bmatrix} 4 & -1 \\ -5 & -9 \end{bmatrix} + \begin{bmatrix} -6 & -3 \\ 2 & -3 \end{bmatrix}$

13. $\begin{bmatrix} 1 & -2 & 2 \\ 0 & -3 & 4 \end{bmatrix} + \begin{bmatrix} 3 & -4 & 5 \\ -8 & 1 & 6 \end{bmatrix}$

14. $\begin{bmatrix} -2.4 & 1.6 & -7.8 \\ 14.3 & 1.1 & -3.9 \end{bmatrix} + \begin{bmatrix} -2.8 & 5.4 & 2.3 \\ -1.7 & 4.2 & 5.6 \end{bmatrix}$

STUDENT HELP

▶ **HOMEWORK HELP**
Example 1: Exs. 23, 24
Example 2: Exs. 7–20
Example 3: Exs. 25, 26
Example 4: Exs. 25, 26

15. $\begin{bmatrix} 6.2 & -1.2 \\ -2.5 & -4.4 \\ 3.4 & -5.8 \end{bmatrix} + \begin{bmatrix} 1.5 & 9.2 \\ 6.6 & -2.2 \\ 5.7 & -7.1 \end{bmatrix}$

16. $\begin{bmatrix} 2 & 9 & -3 \\ 1 & 8 & -2 \\ -3 & -1 & -7 \end{bmatrix} + \begin{bmatrix} -2 & -6 & 4 \\ -1 & -2 & 5 \\ 2 & 0 & 8 \end{bmatrix}$

SUBTRACTING MATRICES Find the difference of the matrices.

17. $\begin{bmatrix} 8 & -3 \\ 4 & -1 \end{bmatrix} - \begin{bmatrix} 7 & 7 \\ -2 & -5 \end{bmatrix}$

18. $\begin{bmatrix} 4 & 3 \\ -12 & -10 \end{bmatrix} - \begin{bmatrix} -6 & 1 \\ -4 & 2 \end{bmatrix}$

19. $\begin{bmatrix} -4 & 1 \\ 0 & -13 \\ 2 & -8 \end{bmatrix} - \begin{bmatrix} -6 & 3 \\ -5 & 8 \\ 2 & -7 \end{bmatrix}$

20. $\begin{bmatrix} -5 & 11 & -2 \\ -10 & 4 & 6 \end{bmatrix} - \begin{bmatrix} -3 & 0 & 2 \\ 8 & -5 & -1 \end{bmatrix}$

MENTAL MATH Use mental math to find *a, b, c,* and *d.*

21. $\begin{bmatrix} 3a & 5b \\ c-6 & d \end{bmatrix} = \begin{bmatrix} -12 & -5 \\ 1 & -3 \end{bmatrix}$

22. $\begin{bmatrix} 4a & b+3 \\ c & d-3 \end{bmatrix} = \begin{bmatrix} 8 & -1 \\ 0 & -6 \end{bmatrix}$

WRITING A MATRIX Write and label a matrix to organize the information.

23. Music Store Inventory:

    CDs: 52 sale price titles, 3300 regular price titles

    Tapes: 28 sale price titles, 1600 regular price titles

24. Team Uniform Order:

    Shirts: 3 small, 7 medium, 10 large, 5 extra large

    Shorts: 7 small, 4 medium, 2 large, 2 extra large

DOG KENNEL The owner of a kennel keeps records of all the dogs she cares for each year. In Exercises 25 and 26, use the matrices below, which show her records for 3 breeds of dogs cared for in 1999 and 2000.

	1999 Male	Female
Beagle	36	28
Dalmatian	24	26
Bulldog	51	32

	2000 Male	Female
Beagle	40	31
Dalmatian	26	20
Bulldog	46	34

25. Find the sum of the two matrices.

26. *Writing* Explain what the data represent in the matrix you wrote in Exercise 25.

WAGES AND RAISES In Exercises 27 and 28, use the matrix, which shows employees' hourly wage rates at a grocery store. The wage rates depend on the job and the number of years of experience.

WAGE RATES

	0–1 year	2–3 years	4+ years
Service Clerk	5.50	6.50	7.00
Cashier	6.50	8.00	9.50
Deli Clerk	7.50	8.75	11.00

27. The store is giving $.20 raises to all services clerks, $.35 raises to all cashiers, and $.45 raises to all deli clerks. Write a matrix that you can add to the matrix above to find the new wage rates after raises are given.

28. Write a matrix that shows the new wage rates after raises are given.

29. **MULTI-STEP PROBLEM** Use the table, which shows the monthly average high and low temperatures in degrees Fahrenheit in three cities.

	May		June		July	
City	High	Low	High	Low	High	Low
Atlanta, GA	79.6	58.7	85.8	66.2	88.0	69.5
San Francisco, CA	66.5	49.7	70.3	52.6	71.6	53.9
Anchorage, AK	54.4	38.8	61.6	47.2	65.2	51.7

▶ Source: National Climatic Data Center

a. Write a matrix for the average high temperatures in each city during May, June, and July.

b. Write a matrix for the average low temperatures in each city during May, June, and July.

c. **CRITICAL THINKING** Explain how to find the difference of average temperatures in each city during May, June, and July. Use the matrices you wrote in parts (a) and (b). Then write a matrix for the difference of average temperatures in each city during May, June, and July.

★ **Challenge**

PROPERTIES OF MATRIX ADDITION In Exercises 30 and 31, recall the properties of addition you learned on page 73.

30. a. Does $\begin{bmatrix} 5 & -9 \\ -4 & 1 \\ -1 & 4 \end{bmatrix} + \begin{bmatrix} 2 & 8 \\ 1 & 9 \\ -3 & -1 \end{bmatrix} = \begin{bmatrix} 2 & 8 \\ 1 & 9 \\ -3 & -1 \end{bmatrix} + \begin{bmatrix} 5 & -9 \\ -4 & 1 \\ -1 & 4 \end{bmatrix}$? Explain.

b. Does the commutative property apply when adding matrices?

31. Does the associative property apply when adding matrices? Give an example to support your answer.

MIXED REVIEW

EXPONENTIAL FORM Write the expression in exponential form. (Review 1.2)

32. $2y \cdot 2y \cdot 2y$ **33.** five squared   **34.** four to the sixth power

35. $x \cdot x \cdot y \cdot y \cdot y$ **36.** two to the xth power   **37.** $3 \cdot (t \cdot t \cdot t \cdot t)$

FINDING ABSOLUTE VALUES Evaluate the expression. (Review 2.1)

38. $|-82|$ **39.** $-|43.7|$ **40.** $-|-4.5|$

41. $|-29| + 7$ **42.** $-|13 - 12.1|$ **43.** $14 + |-11| - 10$

RULES OF ADDITION Find the sum. (Review 2.2 for 2.5)

44. $-19 + (-6)$ **45.** $-12 + (-9)$ **46.** $-3 + 0 + (-29)$

47. $0 + (-5) + 2$ **48.** $-3 + (-6) + (-2)$ **49.** $-5 + (-6) + (-3)$

50. $-7 + (-8) + (-9)$ **51.** $-1 + (-1) + (-1)$ **52.** $-4 + (-4) + (-4)$

● ACTIVITY 2.4

Using Technology

Adding and Subtracting Matrices

▶ **EXAMPLE**

Use a graphing calculator to find the sum and difference of $\begin{bmatrix} -5 & 0 \\ -8 & 4 \\ 1 & 5 \end{bmatrix}$ and $\begin{bmatrix} -3 & -1 \\ 4 & 0 \\ 1 & -7 \end{bmatrix}$.

▶ **SOLUTION**

1 Follow your calculator's procedures to name the first matrix [A].

```
NAMES MATH EDIT
1:[A]
2:[B]
3:[C]
4:[D]
5:[E]
```

2 Enter the size of the matrix, and then enter each entry in the appropriate position.

```
MATRIX [A] 3X2
[-5      0       ]
[-8      4       ]
[1       5       ]

3,2=5
```

"3,2 = 5" means 5 is the entry in the 3rd row, 2nd column.

3 Name the second matrix [B]. Enter the size of the matrix and the entries.

```
MATRIX [B] 3X2
[-3      -1      ]
[4       0       ]
[1       -7      ]

3,2=-7
```

4 Enter [A] + [B] to find the sum, and [A] − [B] to find the difference.

```
[A]+[B]
        [[-8 -1]
         [-4 4 ]
         [2  -2]]
[A]-[B]
        [[-2  1 ]
         [-12 4 ]
         [0   12]]
```

▶ The sum is $\begin{bmatrix} -8 & -1 \\ -4 & 4 \\ 2 & -2 \end{bmatrix}$ and the difference is $\begin{bmatrix} -2 & 1 \\ -12 & 4 \\ 0 & 12 \end{bmatrix}$.

▶ **EXERCISES**

Use a graphing calculator to find the sum and difference of the matrices.

1. $\begin{bmatrix} 7 & -5 \\ 5 & -3 \\ -9 & -8 \end{bmatrix}, \begin{bmatrix} 0 & -1 \\ 1 & 0 \\ -1 & -6 \end{bmatrix}$

2. $\begin{bmatrix} 52 & 79 & -61 \\ -84 & 21 & -76 \end{bmatrix}, \begin{bmatrix} 10 & 45 & -62 \\ -16 & 98 & -28 \end{bmatrix}$

3. $\begin{bmatrix} 7.4 & -5.1 \\ -0.6 & -4.6 \\ 9.9 & -9.4 \\ 2.1 & -3.6 \\ -0.5 & 7.1 \end{bmatrix}, \begin{bmatrix} 3.3 & 3.2 \\ -3.2 & 2.7 \\ -8.2 & -1.7 \\ 5.1 & -4.8 \\ -3.9 & 6.1 \end{bmatrix}$

4. $\begin{bmatrix} 44 & -51 & 17 \\ 76 & 63 & 25 \\ -20 & -60 & 42 \end{bmatrix}, \begin{bmatrix} -53 & -18 & 11 \\ 29 & -27 & -62 \\ 29 & -35 & -28 \end{bmatrix}$

2.5

Multiplication of Real Numbers

What you should learn

GOAL 1 Multiply real numbers using properties of multiplication.

GOAL 2 Multiply real numbers to solve **real-life** problems like finding how much money is owed on a loan in **Exs. 64 and 65**.

Why you should learn it

To solve **real-life** problems like finding how much money a grocery store loses in **Example 5**.

GOAL 1 MULTIPLYING REAL NUMBERS

Remember that multiplication can be modeled as repeated addition. For example, $3(-2) = (-2) + (-2) + (-2) = -6$. The product of a positive number and a negative number is a negative number.

> **ACTIVITY**
> Developing Concepts
> ## Investigating Multiplication Patterns
>
> Identify and extend the patterns to complete the lists. What generalizations can you make about the sign of a product of real numbers?
>
> | FACTOR OF −3 | FACTOR OF −2 | FACTOR OF −1 |
> |---|---|---|
> | $(3)(-3) = -9$ | $(3)(-2) = -6$ | $(3)(-1) = -3$ |
> | $(2)(-3) = -6$ | $(2)(-2) = -4$ | $(2)(-1) = -2$ |
> | $(1)(-3) = -3$ | $(1)(-2) = -2$ | $(1)(-1) = -1$ |
> | $(0)(-3) = 0$ | $(0)(-2) = 0$ | $(0)(-1) = 0$ |
> | $(-1)(-3) = ?$ | $(-1)(-2) = ?$ | $(-1)(-1) = ?$ |
> | $(-2)(-3) = ?$ | $(-2)(-2) = ?$ | $(-2)(-1) = ?$ |

The results of the activity can be extended to determine the sign of a product of more than two factors.

STUDENT HELP

► **Study Tip**
- A product is negative if it has an *odd* number of negative factors.
- A product is positive if it has an *even* number of negative factors.

EXAMPLE 1   *Multiplying Real Numbers*

a. $(-3)(4)(-2) = (-12)(-2) = 24$ Two negative factors; positive product

b. $\left(-\frac{1}{2}\right)(-2)(-3) = (1)(-3) = -3$ Three negative factors; negative product

c. $(-1)^4 = (-1)(-1)(-1)(-1) = (1)(-1)(-1)$ Four negative factors;
$= (-1)(-1) = 1$ positive product

In Example 1(c), be sure you understand that $(-1)^4$ is not the same as -1^4.

MULTIPLYING REAL NUMBERS

The product of two real numbers with the same sign is the product of their absolute values. The product of two real numbers with different signs is the *opposite* of the product of their absolute values.

EXAMPLE 2 *Products with Variable Factors*

a. $(-2)(-x) = 2x$ **Two negative signs**

b. $3(-n)(-n)(-n) = -3n^3$ **Three negative signs**

c. $(-1)(-a)^2 = (-1)(-a)(-a) = -a^2$ **Three negative signs**

d. $-(y)^4 = -(y \cdot y \cdot y \cdot y) = -y^4$ **One negative sign**

CONCEPT SUMMARY   **PROPERTIES OF MULTIPLICATION**

COMMUTATIVE PROPERTY The order in which two numbers are multiplied does not change the product.

$a \cdot b = b \cdot a$ **Example:** $3 \cdot (-2) = (-2) \cdot 3$

ASSOCIATIVE PROPERTY The way you group three numbers when multiplying does not change the product.

$(a \cdot b) \cdot c = a \cdot (b \cdot c)$ **Example:** $(-6 \cdot 2) \cdot 3 = -6 \cdot (2 \cdot 3)$

IDENTITY PROPERTY The product of a number and 1 is the number.

$1 \cdot a = a$ **Example:** $(-4) \cdot 1 = -4$

PROPERTY OF ZERO The product of a number and 0 is 0.

$a \cdot 0 = 0$ **Example:** $(-2) \cdot 0 = 0$

PROPERTY OF OPPOSITES The product of a number and −1 is the opposite of the number.

$(-1) \cdot a = -a$ **Example:** $(-1) \cdot (-3) = 3$

EXAMPLE 3 *Evaluating a Variable Expression*

Evaluate the expression when $x = -5$.

a. $-4(-1)(-x)$ **b.** $(-9.7 \cdot x)(-2)$

SOLUTION You can simplify the expression first, or substitute for x first.

a. $-4(-1)(-x) = -4x$ **Simplify expression first.**

$= -4(-5)$ **Substitute −5 for x.**

$= 20$ **Product of two negatives**

b. $(-9.7 \cdot x)(-2) = [-9.7 \cdot (-5)] \cdot (-2)$ **Substitute −5 for x first.**

$= -9.7 \cdot [-5 \cdot (-2)]$ **Use associative property.**

$= -9.7 \cdot 10$ **$-5 \cdot (-2) = 10$**

$= -97.0$ **Simplify.**

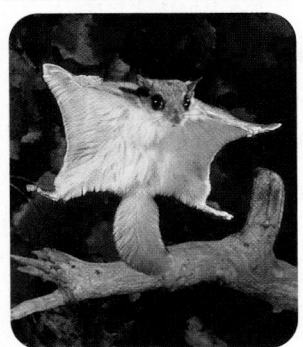

REAL LIFE FLYING SQUIRRELS can't really fly as birds do. But they can glide through the air by using "gliding membranes," flaps of loose skin that extend from wrist to ankle.

GOAL 2 USING MULTIPLICATION IN REAL LIFE

Displacement is the change in the position of an object. Unlike distance, displacement can be positive, negative, or zero.

EXAMPLE 4 Application of Products of Negatives

FLYING SQUIRRELS A flying squirrel descends from a tree with a velocity of -6 feet per second. Find its vertical displacement in 3.5 seconds.

SOLUTION

VERBAL MODEL

$$\boxed{\text{Vertical displacement}} = \boxed{\text{Velocity}} \cdot \boxed{\text{Time}}$$

LABELS

Vertical displacement $= d$ (feet)

Velocity $= -6$ (feet per second)

Time $= 3.5$ (seconds)

ALGEBRAIC MODEL

$$d = -6 \cdot 3.5$$
$$= -21$$

▶ The negative displacement indicates downward motion. The squirrel traveled a vertical displacement of -21 feet or 21 feet downward.

UNIT ANALYSIS: Check that *feet* are the units of the solution.

$$\frac{\text{feet}}{\text{second}} \cdot \text{seconds} = \text{feet}$$

Grocery Stores

EXAMPLE 5 Application of Products of Negatives

A grocery store sells pint baskets of strawberries as loss leaders, which means the store is willing to lose money selling them. The store hopes to make up the loss with additional sales to customers attracted to the store. The store loses $.17 per pint. How much will the store lose if it sells 3450 pints?

SOLUTION

Use a calculator. Multiply the number of pints sold by the loss per pint to find the total loss.

3450 [×] [.] 17 [+/-] [=]   (−586.50)

▶ The store loses $586.50 on strawberry sales.

UNIT ANALYSIS: Check that *dollars* are the units of the solution.

$$\text{pints} \cdot \frac{\text{dollars}}{\text{pint}} = \text{dollars}$$

GUIDED PRACTICE

Vocabulary Check ✓

1. Multiplying -12 by -97 produces the same result as multiplying -97 by -12. What property is this?

Concept Check ✓

2. Is the product of an odd number of factors always a negative number?

3. Is the product of an even number of factors always a positive number?

4. **ERROR ANALYSIS** Describe the error shown at the right.

$-(-5)^2 = 5^2$ 2 negative factors
         $= 25$ Simplify.

Skill Check ✓

Find the product.

5. $8 \cdot (-1)$ 6. $-3 \cdot 0$ 7. $-5 \cdot (-7)$ 8. $-7 \cdot (-5)$

9. $-12 \cdot (-6)$ 10. $-30 \cdot 8$ 11. $-5 \cdot 2 \cdot (-7)$ 12. $-(-1)^5$

Evaluate the expression.

13. $2(-6)(-x)$ when $x = 4$ 14. $5(x - 4)$ when $x = -3$

15. 🌐 **HAWKS** A hawk dives from a tree with a velocity of -10 feet per second. Find the vertical displacement in 4.7 seconds.

PRACTICE AND APPLICATIONS

STUDENT HELP

→ **Extra Practice**
to help you master
skills is on p. 798.

PRODUCTS Find the product.

16. $(-8)(3)$ 17. $(4)(-4)$ 18. $(20)(-65)$ 19. $(-1)(-5)$

20. $(-7)(-1.2)$ 21. $(-11)\left(\frac{1}{8}\right)$ 22. $(-15)\left(\frac{3}{5}\right)$ 23. $\left|(-12)(2)\right|$

24. $(-3)(-1)(-6)$ 25. $(13)(-2)(-3)$ 26. $(5)(-2)(7)$

27. $(-4)(-7)\left(\frac{3}{7}\right)$ 28. $(-3)(-1)(4)(-6)$ 29. $(-13)(-2)(-2)\left(-\frac{2}{13}\right)$

SIMPLIFYING EXPRESSIONS Simplify the variable expression.

30. $(-3)(-y)$ 31. $(7)(-x)$ 32. $5(-a)(-a)(-a)$

33. $(-4)(-x)(x)(-x)$ 34. $-(-b)^3$ 35. $-(-4)^2(y)$

36. $\left|(8)(-z)(-z)(-z)\right|$ 37. $-\left(y^4\right)(y)$ 38. $\left(-b^2\right)\left(-b^3\right)\left(-b^4\right)$

39. $-\frac{1}{2}(-2x)$ 40. $\frac{2}{3}\left(-\frac{3}{2}x\right)$ 41. $-\frac{3}{7}\left(-w^2\right)(7w)$

STUDENT HELP

→ **HOMEWORK HELP**
Example 1: Exs. 16–29
Example 2: Exs. 30–41
Example 3: Exs. 42–49
Example 4: Exs. 61–65
Example 5: Exs. 50–57,
           61–63

EVALUATING EXPRESSIONS Evaluate the expression.

42. $-8x$ when $x = 6$ 43. $y^3 - 4$ when $y = -2$

44. $3x^2 - 5x$ when $x = -2$ 45. $4a + a^2$ when $a = -7$

46. $-4\left(|y - 12|\right)$ when $y = 5$ 47. $-2\left(|x - 5|\right)$ when $x = -5$

48. $-2x^2 + 3x - 7$ when $x = 4$ 49. $9r^3 - (-2r)$ when $r = 2$

EVALUATING EXPRESSIONS Use a calculator to evaluate the expression. Round your answer to two decimal places.

50. $(-7.39)(4.41)(-2.9)$

51. $(4.67)(-8.01)(1.89)$

52. $(3.6)(-2.67)^3(-9.41)$

53. $(-6.3)^2(9.5)(4.8)$

54. $x^3 - 8.29$ when $x = -2.47$

55. $8.3 + y^3$ when $y = -4.6$

56. $4.7b - (-b^2)$ when $b = 1.99$

57. $x^2 + x - 27.2$ when $x = -7$

STUDENT HELP

▶ **Look Back**
For help with counterexamples, see p. 66.

COUNTEREXAMPLES Decide whether the statement is *true* or *false*. If it is false, give a counterexample.

58. $(-a) \cdot (-b) = (-b) \cdot (-a)$

59. The product $(-a) \cdot (-1)$ is always positive.

60. If $a > b$, then for any real number c, $a \cdot c > b \cdot c$.

🍌 **LOSS LEADERS** To promote sales, a grocery store advertises bananas for $.25 per pound. The store loses $.11 on each pound of bananas it sells.

61. Write a verbal model that you can use to find the amount of money that the store loses depending on the number of pounds of bananas it sells.

62. The store sells 2956 pounds of bananas. How much money does the store lose on banana sales?

63. The store also advertises apple juice for $1.19 per 64-ounce bottle, and loses $.08 per bottle sold. Use a verbal model to find how much the store loses on sales of 3107 bottles of apple juice.

🎸 **PAYING BACK A LOAN** Your aunt lends you $175 to buy a guitar. She will decrease the amount you owe by $25 for each day you help her by doing odd jobs.

64. Write a verbal model that you can use to find the decrease in the amount you owe your aunt depending on the number of days you help her out.

65. What is the change in the amount you owe your aunt after helping her out for 5 days? How much do you still owe her?

🌍 **VACATION TRAVEL** You and your family take a summer vacation to Ireland. You discover that the number of Americans visiting Ireland is increasing by 80,000 visitors per year. Let *x* represent the number of visitors in 1997.

66. Write an expression for the number of visitors in 2000.

67. If the number of visitors in 1997 was 700,000, how many visitors were expected in 2000? Use unit analysis to check your answer.

FOCUS ON APPLICATIONS

IRELAND More people of Irish descent live in New England (4 million) than in Ireland (3.5 million)!
▶ Source: Irish Tourist Board

EXTENSION: SCALAR MULTIPLICATION Multiply the matrix by the real number.

Sample: $-3\begin{bmatrix} 1 & -2 \\ -4 & 0 \end{bmatrix} = \begin{bmatrix} -3(1) & -3(-2) \\ -3(-4) & -3(0) \end{bmatrix} = \begin{bmatrix} -3 & 6 \\ 12 & 0 \end{bmatrix}$

68. $-8\begin{bmatrix} -4 & -7 \\ 3 & 3 \end{bmatrix}$

69. $-7\begin{bmatrix} 6 & -4 & 3 \\ -1 & 2^2 & -9 \end{bmatrix}$

70. $-5x\begin{bmatrix} 2x & -6y \\ 4b & -8a \end{bmatrix}$

71. COMPARING METHODS As parts (a) and (b) of Example 3 show, it is sometimes easier to evaluate an expression by simplifying it before substituting, and sometimes easier if you substitute for the variable first.

    a. Write an expression that is easier to evaluate if you simplify *before* substituting 12 for *x*.

    b. Write an expression that is easier to evaluate if you substitute 12 for *x* first.

Test Preparation

72. MULTIPLE CHOICE Which of the following statements is *not* true?

    A The product of any number and zero is zero.

    B The order in which two numbers are multiplied does not change the product.

    C The product of any number and -1 is a negative number.

    D The product of any number and -1 is the opposite of the number.

73. MULTIPLE CHOICE Which of the following has the least value?

    A $\left[\frac{3}{8}(8-6)+\frac{1}{4}\right]\cdot(-12)$ **B** $\frac{3}{8}\cdot 8 - 6 + \frac{1}{4}\cdot(-12)$

    C $-\frac{3}{8}\cdot 8 - 6 + \frac{1}{4}\cdot 12$ **D** $-\frac{3}{8}\cdot\left(8-6+\frac{1}{4}\right)\cdot(-12)$

★ Challenge

GROUPING SYMBOLS Evaluate the expression.

74. $\frac{3}{4}\cdot[-7\cdot(-4-6)+30]-11$ **75.** $-3\cdot\left[\left(2\frac{9}{14}-3\frac{3}{7}\right)\cdot\frac{28}{11}\right]+5\left(-9\frac{1}{5}-9\right)$

MIXED REVIEW

MENTAL MATH Write a question that can be represented by the equation. Then use mental math to solve the equation. (Review 1.4)

76. $x + 4 = 9$ **77.** $y - 7 = 3$ **78.** $6x = 18$

79. $\frac{y}{8} = 4$ **80.** $2x + 1 = 7$ **81.** $x^2 = 121$

GRAPHING NUMBERS Graph the numbers on a number line. Then write two inequalities that compare the two numbers. (Review 2.1)

82. 6 and -3 **83.** -4 and 9   **84.** $-\frac{1}{2}$ and $\frac{1}{3}$

85. -3.8 and -4.0 **86.** -2.8 and 0.5   **87.** -4.1 and -4.02

FINDING TERMS Find the terms of the expression. (Review 2.3 for 2.6)

88. $12 - z$ **89.** $-t + 5$ **90.** $4w - 11$

91. $31 - 15n$ **92.** $-7 + 4x$ **93.** $m - 2n - t^2$

94. $c^2 - 3c - 4$ **95.** $y + 6 - 8x$ **96.** $-9a^2 + 4 - 2a^3$

97. 🌐 **FEDERAL BUDGET** In 1997 the federal government reported a budget deficit of $21.9 billion. In 1998 the deficit was $10 billion. What was the change in the deficit? ▶ Source: U.S. Office of Management and Budget **(Review 2.3)**

Developing Concepts

Modeling the Distributive Property

GROUP ACTIVITY
Work with a partner.

MATERIALS
algebra tiles

► QUESTION How can you model equivalent expressions using algebra tiles?

► EXPLORING THE CONCEPT

You can use algebra tiles to model algebraic expressions.

1 **1-tile**

This 1-by-1 square tile
has an area of
1 square unit.

1 **x-tile**

This 1-by-x rectangular
tile has an area
of x square units.

1 Model $3(x + 4)$.

2 Model $3x + 12$.

The models show that $3(x + 4) = 3(x) + 3(4) = 3x + 12$. So $3(x + 4)$ and $3x + 12$ are equivalent. This is an example of the distributive property.

► DRAWING CONCLUSIONS

1. Use the algebra tiles shown below. Write the expression shown by the tiles in two ways.

Each equation illustrates the distributive property. Use algebra tiles to model the equation. Draw a sketch of your models.

2. $2(x + 6) = 2x + 12$ **3.** $4(x + 2) = 4x + 8$

4. $4(x + 4) = 4x + 16$ **5.** $3(x + 5) = 3x + 15$

ERROR ANALYSIS In Exercises 6 and 7, tell whether the equation is *true* or *false*. If false, explain the error and correct the right-hand side of the equation.

6. $4(x + 6) \stackrel{?}{=} 4x + 6$ **7.** $3(x + 5) \stackrel{?}{=} 3x + 15$

8. *Writing* Use your own words to explain the distributive property. Then use a, b, and c to represent the distributive property algebraically.

The Distributive Property

What you should learn

GOAL 1 Use the distributive property.

GOAL 2 Simplify expressions by combining like terms.

Why you should learn it

▼ To solve **real-life** problems such as finding how much you can spend on jeans in **Exs. 70 and 71**.

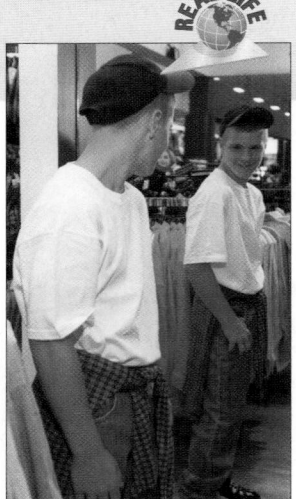

GOAL 1 USING THE DISTRIBUTIVE PROPERTY

To multiply 3(68) mentally, you could think of 3(68) as

$$3(60 + 8) = 3(60) + 3(8) = 180 + 24 = 204.$$

This is an example of the *distributive property*.

The distributive property is a very important algebraic property. Before discussing the property, study an example that suggests why the property is true.

EXAMPLE 1   *Using an Area Model*

Find the area of a rectangle whose width is 3 and whose length is $x + 2$.

SOLUTION

You can find the area in two ways.

▶ Because both ways produce the same area, the following statement is true.

$$3(x + 2) = 3(x) + 3(2)$$

Example 1 suggests the **distributive property**. In the equation above, the factor 3 is *distributed* to each term of the sum $(x + 2)$. There are four versions of the distributive property, as follows.

THE DISTRIBUTIVE PROPERTY

The product of a and $(b + c)$:

$a(b + c) = ab + ac$ **Example:** $5(x + 2) = 5x + 10$

$(b + c)a = ba + ca$ **Example:** $(x + 4)8 = 8x + 32$

The product of a and $(b - c)$:

$a(b - c) = ab - ac$ **Example:** $4(x - 7) = 4x - 28$

$(b - c)a = ba - ca$ **Example:** $(x - 5)9 = 9x - 45$

EXAMPLE 2   *Using the Distributive Property*

a. $2(x + 5) = 2(x) + 2(5) = 2x + 10$

b. $(x - 4)x = (x)x - (4)x = x^2 - 4x$

c. $(1 + 2x)8 = (1)8 + (2x)8 = 8 + 16x$

d. $y(1 - y) = y(1) - y(y) = y - y^2$

Study the next problems carefully. Remember that a factor with a negative sign must multiply *each* term of an expression. Forgetting to distribute the negative sign to each term is a common error.

EXAMPLE 3   *Using the Distributive Property*

a. $-3(x + 4) = -3(x) + (-3)(4)$	Distribute the -3.
$\quad = -3x - 12$	Simplify.
b. $(y + 5)(-4) = (y)(-4) + (5)(-4)$	Distribute the -4.
$\quad = -4y - 20$	Simplify.
c. $-(6 - 3x) = (-1)(6 - 3x)$	$-a = -1 \cdot a$
$\quad = (-1)(6) - (-1)(3x)$	Distribute the -1.
$\quad = -6 + 3x$	Simplify.
d. $(x - 1)(-9x) = (x)(-9x) - (1)(-9x)$	Distribute the $-9x$.
$\quad = -9x^2 + 9x$	Simplify.

Shopping

EXAMPLE 4   *Mental Math Calculations*

You are shopping for compact discs. You want to buy six compact discs for $11.95 each. Use the distributive property to calculate the total cost mentally.

SOLUTION
If you think of $11.95 as $12.00 − $.05, the mental math is easier.

$6(11.95) = 6(12 - 0.05)$	Write 11.95 as a difference.
$\quad = 6(12) - 6(0.05)$	Use the distributive property.
$\quad = 72 - 0.30$	Find the products mentally.
$\quad = 71.70$	Find the difference mentally.

▶ The total cost of 6 compact discs at $11.95 each is $71.70.

GOAL 2 SIMPLIFYING BY COMBINING LIKE TERMS

In a term that is the product of a number and a variable, the number is the **coefficient** of the variable.

$$-x + 3y^2$$

−1 is the coefficient of **x**.   3 is the coefficient of **y²**.

Like terms are terms in an expression that have the same variable raised to the same power. In the expression below, $5x$ and $-3x$ are like terms, but $5x$ and $-x^2$ are *not* like terms. The **constant terms** -4 and 2 are also like terms.

$$-x^2 + 5x + (-4) + (-3x) + 2$$

The distributive property allows you to *combine like terms* that have variables by adding coefficients. An expression is **simplified** if it has no grouping symbols and if all the like terms have been combined.

EXAMPLE 5 *Simplifying by Combining Like Terms*

a. $8x + 3x = (8 + 3)x$ Use the distributive property.

$\qquad\qquad = 11x$ Add coefficients.

b. $4x^2 + 2 - x^2 = 4x^2 - x^2 + 2$ Group like terms.

$\qquad\qquad\qquad = 3x^2 + 2$ Combine like terms.

c. $3 - 2(4 + x) = 3 + (-2)(4 + x)$ Rewrite as an addition expression.

$\qquad\qquad\quad = 3 + [(-2)(4) + (-2)(x)]$ Distribute the −2.

$\qquad\qquad\quad = 3 + (-8) + (-2x)$ Multiply.

$\qquad\qquad\quad = -5 + (-2x) = -5 - 2x$ Combine like terms and simplify.

BUSES Some cities offer discount fares to students who use public transportation to get to school.

EXAMPLE 6 *Using the Distributive Property to Simplify a Function*

GETTING TO SCHOOL It takes you 45 minutes to get to school. You spend t minutes walking to the bus stop, and the rest of the time riding the bus. You walk 0.06 mi/min and the bus travels 0.5 mi/min. The total distance you travel is given by the function $D = 0.06t + 0.5(45 - t)$. Simplify this function.

SOLUTION

$D = 0.06t + 0.5(45 - t)$ Write original function.

$\quad = 0.06t + 22.5 - 0.5t$ Use the distributive property.

$\quad = 0.06t - 0.5t + 22.5$ Group like terms.

$\quad = -0.44t + 22.5$ Combine like terms.

▶ The total distance you travel can be given by $D = -0.44t + 22.5$.

GUIDED PRACTICE

Vocabulary Check ✓

1. In the expression $4x^2 - 7y - 8$, what is the coefficient of the x^2-term? What is the coefficient of the y-term?

2. What are the like terms in the expression $-6 - 3x^2 + 3y + 7 - 4y + 9x^2$?

Concept Check ✓

ERROR ANALYSIS Describe the error. Then simplify the expression correctly.

3.

$$-2(6.5 - 2.1) = 13 - 4.2$$
$$= 8.8$$

4.
$$5 - 4(3 + x) = 5 - 12 + x$$
$$= -7 + x$$

Skill Check ✓

Use the distributive property to rewrite the expression without parentheses.

5. $5(w - 8)$

6. $(y + 19)7$

7. $(12 - x)y$

8. $-4(u + 2)$

9. $(b - 6)\left(-\dfrac{5}{6}\right)$

10. $-\dfrac{2}{3}(t - 24)$

Use the distributive property and mental math to simplify the expression.

11. $6(1.15) = 6(1 + 0.15)$
$= \underline{\ ?\ }$

12. $9(1.95) = 9(\underline{\ ?\ } - \underline{\ ?\ })$
$= \underline{\ ?\ }$

Simplify the expression by combining like terms if possible.

13. $9x + 2$

14. $6x^2 - 4x^2$

15. $-3y - 2x$

16. $3x^2 + 4x + 8 - 7x^2$

17. $8t^2 - 2t + 5t - 4$

18. $-6w - 12 - 3w + 2x^2$

PRACTICE AND APPLICATIONS

STUDENT HELP

▶ **Extra Practice**
to help you master
skills is on p. 798.

LOGICAL REASONING Decide whether the statement is *true* or *false*. If false, rewrite the right-hand side of the equation so the statement is true.

19. $3(2 + 7) \stackrel{?}{=} 3(2) + 7$

20. $(3 + 8)4 \stackrel{?}{=} 3(4) + 8(4)$

21. $7(15 - 6) \stackrel{?}{=} 7(15) - 7(6)$

22. $(9 - 2)13 \stackrel{?}{=} 9 - 2(13)$

23. $\dfrac{2}{9}\left(\dfrac{1}{3} - \dfrac{4}{9}\right) \stackrel{?}{=} \dfrac{2}{9}\left(\dfrac{1}{3}\right) - \dfrac{2}{9}\left(\dfrac{4}{9}\right)$

24. $-3.5(6.1 + 8.2) \stackrel{?}{=} -3.5(6.1) - 3.5(8.2)$

DISTRIBUTIVE PROPERTY Use the distributive property to rewrite the expression without parentheses.

STUDENT HELP

▶ **HOMEWORK HELP**
Example 1: Exs. 81, 82
Example 2: Exs. 19–48
Example 3: Exs. 19–48
Example 4: Exs. 83–85
Example 5: Exs. 49–69
Example 6: Exs. 72–78

25. $3(x + 4)$

26. $(w + 6)4$

27. $5(y - 2)$

28. $(7 - m)4$

29. $-(y - 9)$

30. $-3(r + 8)$

31. $-4(t - 8)$

32. $(x + 6)(-2)$

33. $x(x + 1)$

34. $(3 - y)y$

35. $-r(r - 9)$

36. $-s(7 + s)$

37. $2(3x - 1)$

38. $(4 + 3y)5$

39. $(2x - 4)(-3)$

40. $-9(a + 6)$

41. $4x(x + 8)$

42. $-2t(12 - t)$

43. $(3y - 2)5y$

44. $-2x(x - 8)$

45. $-9(-t - 3)$

46. $(6 - 3w)(-w^2)$

47. $5\left(\dfrac{1}{2}x - \dfrac{2}{3}\right)$

48. $-y(-y^2 + y)$

SIMPLIFYING EXPRESSIONS Simplify the expression by combining like terms.

49. $15x + (-4x)$ **50.** $-12y + 5y$ **51.** $-8b - 9b$

52. $5 - x + 2$ **53.** $-3 + y + 7$ **54.** $4 + a + a$

55. $1.3t - 2.1t$ **56.** $\frac{7}{9}w + \left(-\frac{2}{3}\right)w$ **57.** $107a - 208a$

58. $3x^2 + 2x^2 - 7$ **59.** $9x^3 - 4x^3 - 2$ **60.** $8b + 5 - 3b$

COMBINING LIKE TERMS Apply the distributive property. Then simplify by combining like terms.

61. $(3y + 1)(-2) + y$ **62.** $4(2 - a) - a$ **63.** $12s + (7 - s)2$

64. $(5 - 2x)(-x) + x^2$ **65.** $7x - 3x(x + 1)$ **66.** $-4(y + 2) - 6y$

67. $3t(t - 5) + 6t^2$ **68.** $-x^3 + 2x(x - x^2)$ **69.** $4w^2 - w(2w - 3)$

🌐 **BUYING JEANS** **You have $58, and you want to buy a pair of jeans and a $20 T-shirt. There is a 6% sales tax. If *x* represents the cost of the jeans, then the following inequality is a model that shows how much you can spend on the jeans.**

$$x + 20 + 0.06(x + 20) \le 58$$

70. Simplify the left side of the inequality.

71. If the jeans cost $35, can you buy both the T-shirt and the jeans?

🌐 **FREIGHT TRAINS** **A train with 150 freight cars is used to haul two types of grain. Each freight car can haul 97.3 tons of barley or 114 tons of corn. Let *n* represent the number of freight cars containing corn.**

72. Which function correctly represents the total weight the train can haul?

　　A. $W = 97.3(150 - n) + 114n$　　**B.** $W = 97.3n + 114(150 - n)$

73. If 90 freight cars contain corn, what is the total weight the train is hauling?

74. If 72 freight cars contain barley, what is the total weight the train is hauling?

🌐 **INVESTING MONEY** **You receive $5000. You decide to invest the money in a one-year bond paying 2% interest and in a one-year certificate of deposit paying 6% interest.**

75. Let *m* represent the amount of money invested in the one-year bond. Write a function that represents the total amount of money *T* that you have after one year. Simplify the function.

76. If you invest $2000 in the one-year bond, how much money do you have after one year? What if you invest $3000 in the one-year bond?

🌐 **MOVING** **The van that you are using to move can hold 16 moving boxes. Each box can hold 60 pounds of books or 15 pounds of clothes.**

77. Let *b* represent the number of boxes filled with books. Write a function that represents the total weight *w* of the boxes in the van.

78. Use the function you wrote in Exercise 77 to make an input-output table that shows the total weight of the boxes for each combination of boxes of books and clothes.

STUDENT HELP

▶ **Skills Review**
For help with perimeter and area, see p. 790.

GEOMETRY **CONNECTION** **Write and simplify an expression for the perimeter of the figure.**

79.

80.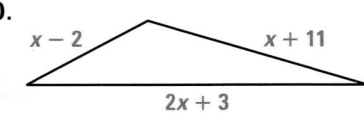

GEOMETRY **CONNECTION** **Write an expression modeling the area of the large rectangle as the product of its length and width. Then write another expression modeling this area as the sum of the areas of the two smaller rectangles. Simplify each expression.**

81.

82.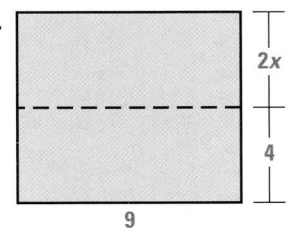

🌐 **LEAVING A TIP** **In Exercises 83–85, use the following information.**
You and a friend decide to leave a 15% tip for restaurant service. You compute the tip, T, as $T = 0.15C$, where C represents the cost of the meal. Your friend claims that an easier way to mentally compute the tip is to calculate 10% of the cost of the meal plus one half of 10% of the cost of the meal.

83. Write an equation that represents your friend's method of computing the tip.

84. Simplify the equation. What property did you use to simplify the equation?

85. Will both methods give the same results? Explain.

🌐 **PLANTING PLAN** **In Exercises 86–89, use the sketch below. You are a farmer planting corn and soybeans in a rectangular field measuring 200 yards by 300 yards. It costs $.06 per square yard to plant corn and $.05 per square yard to plant soybeans.**

86. Let x represent the width of the field you plant with corn. Write a function that represents the cost of planting the entire field. Simplify.

87. If the width of the field you plant with corn is 75 yards, what is the cost of planting the entire field?

88. If the width of the field you plant with soybeans is 125 yards, what is the cost of planting the entire field?

89. You have $3400 to plant the entire field. Do you have enough money to plant a field of soybeans that is 90 yards wide?

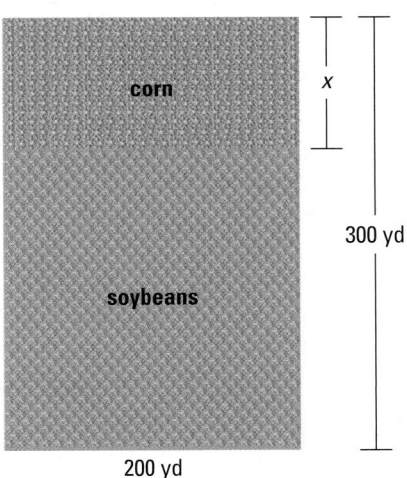

90. *Writing* Write a problem like Exercise 81 that deals with the area of a rectangle. Explain how you can use the distributive property to model the total area of a rectangle as the sum of two rectangles.

91. MULTI-STEP PROBLEM A customer of your flower shop wants to send flowers to 23 people. Each person will receive an $11.99 "sunshine basket" or a $16.99 "meadow bouquet."

a. Let *s* represent the number of people who will receive a sunshine basket. Which function can you use to find *C*, the total cost of sending flowers to all 23 people, depending on how many of each arrangement is sent?

    Ⓐ $C = 16.99(23 - s) + 11.99s$ **Ⓑ** $C = 11.99s + 16.99(23)$

b. If 8 people receive a sunshine basket, what is the total cost of the flowers?

c. If 13 people receive a meadow bouquet, what is the total cost of the flowers?

d. CRITICAL THINKING If your customer can spend only $300, what is the greatest number of people that can receive a meadow bouquet?

★ Challenge

92. LOGICAL REASONING You are tutoring a friend in algebra. After learning the distributive property, your friend attempts to apply this property to multiplication and gets $2(xy) = 2x \cdot 2y$.

Write a convincing argument to show your friend that this is incorrect.

93. LOGICAL REASONING Your friend does not understand how the product of *a* and $(b + c)$ is given by both $ab + ac$ and $ba + ca$.

Use the properties of multiplication to write a convincing argument to show your friend that both statements are correct.

EXTRA CHALLENGE
www.mcdougallittell.com

MIXED REVIEW

RECIPROCALS Find the reciprocal. (Skills Review, p. 782)

94. $\frac{2}{7}$ **95.** $\frac{6}{11}$ **96.** 7   **97.** 1

98. $\frac{1}{121}$ **99.** 435   **100.** $4\frac{1}{2}$ **101.** $3\frac{3}{8}$

EXPRESSIONS WITH FRACTION BARS Evaluate the expression. (Review 1.3)

102. $\frac{10 \cdot 8}{4^2 + 4}$ **103.** $\frac{6^2 - 12}{3^2 + 15}$ **104.** $\frac{75 - 5^2}{11 + (3 \cdot 4)}$

105. $\frac{(3 \cdot 7) + 9}{2^3 + 5 - 3}$ **106.** $\frac{(2 + 5)^2}{3^2 - 2}$ **107.** $\frac{6 + 7^2}{3^3 - 9 - 7}$

EVALUATING EXPRESSIONS Evaluate the expression. (Review 2.2, 2.3)

108. $6 - (-8) - 11$ **109.** $4 - 8 - 3$ **110.** $6 + (-13) + (-5)$

111. $-7 + 9 - 8$ **112.** $20 + (-16) + (-3)$ **113.** $12.4 - 9.7 - (-6.1)$

1. Find the sum and difference of the matrices. (Lesson 2.4)

$$\begin{bmatrix} 2 & -6 \\ -5 & 5 \\ -7 & 0 \end{bmatrix}, \begin{bmatrix} 3 & -7 \\ 1 & 4 \\ -2 & -8 \end{bmatrix}$$

Find the product. (Lesson 2.5)

2. $(-7)(9)$

3. $(3)(-7)$

4. $(-2)(-7)$

5. $(35)(-80)$

6. $(-15)\left(\dfrac{1}{5}\right)$

7. $(-1.8)(-6)$

8. $(11)(-5)(-2)$

9. $(-10)(-3)(9)$

Simplify the variable expression. (Lessons 2.5, 2.6)

10. $(-t)(-7.1)$

11. $(13)(-x)$

12. $(-5)(-b)(2b)(-b)$

13. $(-4)(-x)^3(x)\left(-\dfrac{1}{8}\right)$

14. $-28x + (-15x)$

15. $11y + (-9y)$

16. $-17t + 9t$

17. $-3(8 - b)$

18. $(-4y - 2)(-5)$

19. 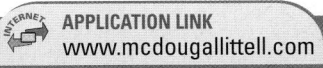 **SKYSCRAPERS**
The heights (in feet and in meters) of the three tallest buildings in the United States are shown in the table. Organize the data in a matrix. (Lesson 2.4)

Building	Height (ft)	Height (m)
Sears Tower	1454	443
Empire State Building	1250	381
Aon Center	1136	346

▶ Source: Council on Tall Buildings and Urban Habitat

MATH & History

History of Negative Numbers

APPLICATION LINK
www.mcdougallittell.com

THEN ▶ **THE 7TH CENTURY** Hindu mathematician Brahmagupta explained operations with negative numbers. As late as the 16th century, many mathematicians still considered the idea of a number with a value less than zero absurd.

1. As early as 200 B.C., negative numbers were used in China. About how many years was it between the time the Chinese displayed a concept of negative numbers and when they were used in 628 A.D. in India?

Hindu math manuscript

NOW ▶ **TODAY,** negative numbers are used in many ways, including financial statements, altitude measurements, temperature readings, golf scores, and atomic charges.

200 B.C.
The Chinese used red rods for positive quantities and black rods for negative quantities.

628 A.D.
Brahmagupta used negative numbers.

1700's
Algebraic use of the negative number became widespread.

NOW
A digital thermometer shows a negative value.

Division of Real Numbers

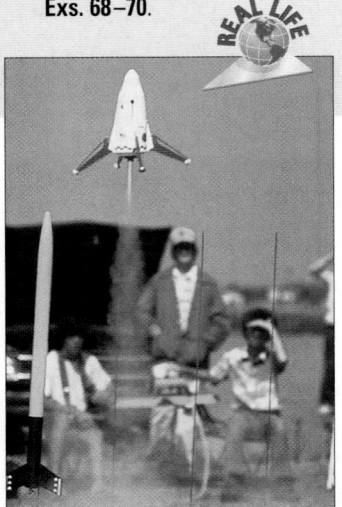

GOAL 1 **DIVIDING REAL NUMBERS**

For every real number other than zero there exists a number called its *reciprocal*. The product of a number and its **reciprocal** is 1. For instance, the product of the number -3 and its reciprocal $-\frac{1}{3}$ is 1. This property is sometimes referred to as the *inverse property of multiplication*.

- The reciprocal of a is $\frac{1}{a}$. $(a \neq 0)$ **Example:** -8 and $-\frac{1}{8}$

- The reciprocal of $\frac{a}{b}$ is $\frac{b}{a}$. $(a \neq 0, b \neq 0)$ **Example:** $-\frac{2}{5}$ and $-\frac{5}{2}$

Zero is the only real number that has no reciprocal. There is no number that when multiplied by zero gives a product of 1. Because zero does not have a reciprocal, you cannot divide by zero.

You can use a reciprocal to write a division expression as a product.

DIVISION RULE

To divide a number a by a nonzero number b, multiply a by the reciprocal of b.

$$a \div b = a \cdot \frac{1}{b}$$ **Example:** $-1 \div 3 = -1 \cdot \frac{1}{3} = -\frac{1}{3}$

The result is the quotient of a and b.

EXAMPLE 1 *Dividing Real Numbers*

Find the quotient.

a. $10 \div (-2)$ **b.** $-39 \div \left(-4\frac{1}{3}\right)$ **c.** $\dfrac{-\frac{1}{3}}{4}$ **d.** $\dfrac{1}{-\frac{3}{4}}$

SOLUTION

a. $10 \div (-2) = 10 \cdot \left(-\frac{1}{2}\right) = -5$

b. $-39 \div \left(-4\frac{1}{3}\right) = -39 \div \left(-\frac{13}{3}\right) = -39 \cdot \left(-\frac{3}{13}\right) = 9$

c. $\dfrac{-\frac{1}{3}}{4} = -\frac{1}{3} \div 4 = -\frac{1}{3} \cdot \frac{1}{4} = -\frac{1}{12}$

d. $\dfrac{1}{-\frac{3}{4}} = 1 \div \left(-\frac{3}{4}\right) = 1 \cdot \left(-\frac{4}{3}\right) = -\frac{4}{3}$

GOAL 2 WORKING WITH ALGEBRAIC EXPRESSIONS

In Example 1, notice that applying the division rule results in the following patterns for finding the sign of a quotient.

THE SIGN OF A QUOTIENT

- The quotient of two numbers with the same sign is positive.

$$-a \div (-b) = \frac{a}{b}$$ **Example:** $-20 \div (-4) = 5$

- The quotient of two numbers with opposite signs is negative.

$$-a \div b = -\frac{a}{b}$$ **Example:** $-20 \div 4 = -5$

EXAMPLE 2 *Using the Distributive Property to Simplify*

Simplify the expression $\frac{32x - 8}{4}$.

SOLUTION

$$\frac{32x - 8}{4} = (32x - 8) \div 4$$ **Rewrite fraction as division expression.**

$$= (32x - 8)\left(\frac{1}{4}\right)$$ **Multiply by reciprocal.**

$$= (32x)\left(\frac{1}{4}\right) - (8)\left(\frac{1}{4}\right)$$ **Use distributive property.**

$$= 8x - 2$$ **Simplify.**

The order of operations you learned in Chapter 1 also applies to real numbers and to algebraic expressions.

EXAMPLE 3 *Evaluating an Expression*

Evaluate the expression when $a = -2$ and $b = -3$.

a. $\frac{-2a}{a + b}$ **b.** $\frac{a^2 - 4}{b}$ **c.** $\frac{a}{3 + b}$

SOLUTION

a. $\frac{-2a}{a + b} = \frac{-2(-2)}{-2 + (-3)} = \frac{4}{-5} = -\frac{4}{5}$

b. $\frac{a^2 - 4}{b} = \frac{(-2)^2 - 4}{-3} = \frac{4 - 4}{-3} = \frac{0}{-3} = 0$

c. $\frac{a}{3 + b} = \frac{-2}{3 + (-3)} = \frac{-2}{0}$ (Undefined)

STUDENT HELP

HOMEWORK HELP
Visit our Web site
www.mcdougallittell.com
for extra examples.

STUDENT HELP

▶ **Study Tip**
Remember that 0 can be divided by any nonzero number. The result will always be zero.

Division *by* zero is undefined.

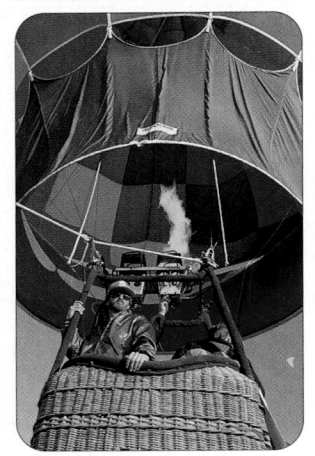

STUDENT HELP

► **Look Back**
For help with domain and
range, see p. 47.

EXAMPLE 4 *Finding a Velocity*

HOT-AIR BALLOONING You are descending in a hot-air balloon. You descend
500 feet in 40 seconds. What is your velocity?

SOLUTION

**VERBAL
MODEL**

$$\boxed{\text{Velocity}} = \frac{\boxed{\text{Displacement}}}{\boxed{\text{Time}}}$$

LABELS

$\text{Velocity} = \boxed{v}$ (ft/sec)

$\text{Displacement} = -500$ (feet)

$\text{Time} = 40$ (seconds)

**ALGEBRAIC
MODEL**

$$\boxed{v} = \frac{-500}{40}$$

$$= -12.5$$

▶ Your velocity, -12.5 ft/sec, is negative because you are descending.
· · · · · · · · · ·

When a function is defined by an equation, its domain is restricted to real
numbers for which the function can be evaluated. Division by zero is undefined,
so input values that make you divide by zero must be excluded from the domain.

For instance, the function $y = \dfrac{5}{x-2}$ does not have $x = 2$ in its domain.

EXAMPLE 5 *Finding the Domain of a Function*

Find the domain of the function $y = \dfrac{-x}{1-x}$.

SOLUTION

To find the domain of $y = \dfrac{-x}{1-x}$, you must exclude any values for which the
denominator, $1 - x$, is equal to zero. To do this, you need to solve the equation
$1 - x = 0$. Use mental math.

> You can ask: What number subtracted from 1 equals 0?
> The answer is 1, because $1 - 1 = 0$.

▶ Since $1 - x = 0$ when $x = 1$, you can see that $x = 1$ is not in the domain of
the function, because you cannot divide by zero. All other real numbers are in
the domain because there are no other values of x that will make the
denominator zero. The domain is all real numbers *except* $x = 1$.

✓ **CHECK** When $x = 1$, $y = \dfrac{-x}{1-x}$

$$= \frac{-(1)}{1-(1)}$$

$$= \frac{-1}{0} \quad \longleftarrow \quad \text{Undefined}$$

GUIDED PRACTICE

Vocabulary Check ✔

1. The product of a number and _?_ is 1.

Concept Check ✔

2. Is dividing by a number the same as multiplying by the opposite of the number? Explain your reasoning.

3. Is the reciprocal of a negative number *sometimes*, *always*, or *never* positive?

4. A friend tells you that $-\frac{a}{b} = \frac{-a}{b} = \frac{a}{-b}$. Is your friend correct? Use examples or counterexamples to support your answer.

5. Describe the error shown at the right.

Skill Check ✔ **Find the reciprocal of the number.**

6. 34   **7.** -8 **8.** $-\frac{3}{4}$ **9.** $-2\frac{1}{5}$

Find the quotient.

10. $7 \div \frac{1}{2}$ **11.** $10 \div \left(-\frac{1}{5}\right)$ **12.** $-12 \div 3$ **13.** $\dfrac{\frac{16}{-2}}{9}$

14. Find the domain of the function $y = \frac{x+1}{x+2}$.

15. 🌐 **STOCK** You own 18 shares of stock in a computer company. The total value of the shares changes by $-\$3.06$. By how much does the value of each share of stock change?

PRACTICE AND APPLICATIONS

STUDENT HELP

→ **Extra Practice**
to help you master
skills is on p. 798.

FINDING QUOTIENTS **Find the quotient.**

16. $-51 \div (-17)$ **17.** $45 \div (-9)$ **18.** $-24 \div 4$ **19.** $49 \div (-7)$

20. $64 \div (-8)$ **21.** $-99 \div 9$ **22.** $-35 \div (-70)$ **23.** $18 \div (-54)$

24. $-90 \div \left(-\frac{2}{3}\right)$ **25.** $56 \div \left(-2\frac{4}{7}\right)$ **26.** $\dfrac{-26}{-\frac{1}{2}}$ **27.** $\dfrac{36}{-\frac{5}{6}}$

28. $60 \div (-10)$ **29.** $-12.6 \div 1.8$ **30.** $-18 \div \frac{3}{8}$ **31.** $-87 \div \left(-\frac{3}{5}\right)$

SIMPLIFYING EXPRESSIONS **Simplify the expression.**

32. $42y \div \frac{1}{7}$ **33.** $6t \div \left(-\frac{1}{2}\right)$ **34.** $58z \div \left(-\frac{2}{5}\right)$ **35.** $-\frac{x}{12} \div 3$

STUDENT HELP

→ **HOMEWORK HELP**
Example 1: Exs. 16–47
Example 2: Exs. 48–51
Example 3: Exs. 52–57
Example 4: Exs. 62–64
Example 5: Exs. 58–61

36. $\frac{d}{4} \div 6$ **37.** $\frac{3y}{4} \div \frac{1}{2}$ **38.** $-\frac{2b}{7} \div \frac{7}{9}$ **39.** $33x \div \frac{3}{11}$

40. $49x \div 3\frac{1}{2}$ **41.** $8x^2 \div \left(-\frac{4}{5}\right)$ **42.** $68x \div \left(-\frac{17}{9}\right)$ **43.** $-54x^2 \div \frac{-9}{5}$

44. $\frac{42t}{-14z} \div \frac{-6}{7t}$ **45.** $8 \cdot \frac{x}{8}$ **46.** $3 \cdot \left(-\frac{y}{3}\right)$ **47.** $-7 \cdot \left(-\frac{2w}{-7}\right)$

DISTRIBUTIVE PROPERTY Simplify the expression.

48. $\dfrac{18x - 9}{3}$ **49.** $\dfrac{22x + 10}{-2}$ **50.** $\dfrac{-56 + x}{-8}$ **51.** $\dfrac{45 - 5x}{5}$

EVALUATING EXPRESSIONS Evaluate the expression for the given value(s) of the variable(s).

52. $\dfrac{x - 5}{6}$ when $x = 30$

53. $\dfrac{3r - 7}{11}$ when $r = 17$

54. $\dfrac{3a - b}{a}$ when $a = \dfrac{1}{3}$ and $b = -3$

55. $\dfrac{15x^2 + 10}{y}$ when $x = -3$ and $y = \dfrac{2}{3}$

56. $\dfrac{28 - 4x}{y}$ when $x = 2$ and $y = \dfrac{1}{2}$

57. $\dfrac{3a - 4b}{ab}$ when $a = -\dfrac{1}{3}$ and $b = \dfrac{1}{4}$

FINDING THE DOMAIN Find the domain of the function.

58. $y = \dfrac{1}{3x}$ **59.** $y = \dfrac{3}{2 - x}$ **60.** $y = \dfrac{1}{x + 2}$ **61.** $y = \dfrac{4}{x^2}$

62. 🌐 **COOKING** *Tom Kar Gai* is a soup from Thailand. You need $13\dfrac{3}{4}$ ounces of chicken broth to make one serving. If you have $82\dfrac{1}{2}$ ounces of chicken broth, how many servings can you make?

63. 🌐 **SCUBA DIVING** You are scuba diving in the ocean. You dive down 22.5 feet in 9 seconds. What is your average velocity?

64. 🌐 **BASKETBALL** Kareem Abdul-Jabbar scored 38,387 points and grabbed 17,440 rebounds in 1560 National Basketball Association games. How many points did he average per game? How many rebounds did he average per game? (Round your answers to the nearest tenth.) ▶ Source: NBA

FINDING A PATTERN In Exercises 65–67, use the table below.

Fraction	$\dfrac{x}{1}$	$\dfrac{x}{0.1}$	$\dfrac{x}{0.01}$	$\dfrac{x}{0.001}$	$\dfrac{x}{0.0001}$	$\dfrac{x}{0.00001}$
Product	$1x$	$10x$	?	?	?	?

65. Copy and complete the table by expressing the fraction as a product that has no decimal factor.

66. Describe the pattern in the products.

67. Use the pattern to simplify the expression $\dfrac{x}{0.0000001}$.

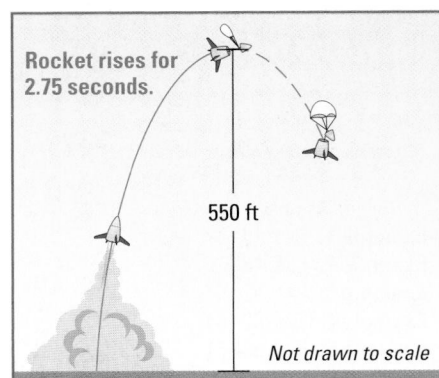

🌐 **MODEL ROCKET** You launch a model rocket that rises 550 feet in 2.75 seconds. It then opens a parachute and falls at a rate of 11 feet per second.

Rocket rises for 2.75 seconds.

550 ft

Not drawn to scale

68. What is the rocket's average velocity going up?

69. What is the rocket's velocity coming down?

70. In how many seconds after the launch will the rocket reach the ground?

71. *Writing* If a and b are positive and $a < b$, is it true that $\frac{1}{b} < \frac{1}{a}$? Explain and show an example or a counterexample.

Test Preparation

72. MULTIPLE CHOICE Which of the following expressions is equivalent to the expression $\dfrac{6x - 4}{-\frac{2}{3}}$?

(A) $2(3x - 2) \cdot \frac{3}{2}$ (B) $(6x - 4) \cdot \left(-\frac{2}{3}\right)$ (C) $-9x + 6$ (D) $9x - 6$

73. MULTIPLE CHOICE Which of the following statements is false?

(A) The reciprocal of any negative number is a negative number.

(B) Dividing by a number is the same as multiplying by the reciprocal of the number.

(C) The reciprocal of any positive number is a positive number.

(D) The reciprocal of any number is greater than zero and less than 1.

★ **Challenge**

74. EXTENSION: CLOSURE A set of numbers is *closed* under an operation if applying the operation to any two numbers in the set results in another number in the set. For instance, positive integers are closed under addition because the sum of any two positive integers is a positive integer. Decide whether the set is closed under the given operation.

EXTRA CHALLENGE
www.mcdougallittell.com

a. positive integers; subtraction   **b.** integers; addition and subtraction

c. integers; multiplication   **d.** integers; division

MIXED REVIEW

CONVERTING FRACTIONS Write the fraction as a decimal. Round to the nearest hundredth if necessary. (Skills Review, pp. 784–785)

75. $\frac{3}{4}$ **76.** $\frac{3}{5}$ **77.** $\frac{1}{10}$ **78.** $\frac{7}{25}$

79. $\frac{1}{6}$ **80.** $\frac{2}{7}$ **81.** $\frac{30}{40}$ **82.** $\frac{5}{11}$

EXPONENTIAL EXPRESSIONS Evaluate the expression for the given value of the variable. (Review 1.2, 2.5)

83. $3x^2$ when $x = 7$ **84.** $4\left(b^3\right)$ when $b = \frac{1}{2}$ **85.** $2\left(y^3\right)$ when $y = -5$

86. $5y^3$ when $y = 4$ **87.** $(6w)^4$ when $w = 2$ **88.** $12d^2$ when $d = 9$

89. $5x^2$ when $x = 0.3$ **90.** $32x^7$ when $x = -1$ **91.** $(7t)^3$ when $t = -\frac{3}{7}$

NUMERICAL EXPRESSIONS Evaluate the expression. (Review 1.3, 2.5)

92. $12 - 9 + 7$ **93.** $42 \div 6 + 8$ **94.** $2(11 - 7) \div 3$

95. $8 + (91 \div 13) \cdot \frac{4}{7}$ **96.** $\frac{3}{4} \cdot 8 - 6$ **97.** $23 - [(12 \div 3)^2 + 8]$

98. $11 \cdot (-5) + 20$ **99.** $-8 \cdot (-9) - 80$ **100.** $-16 + (-6) \cdot (-8)$

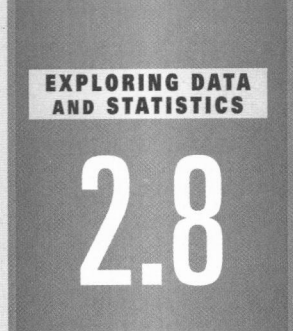

EXPLORING DATA AND STATISTICS

2.8

What you should learn

GOAL 1 Find the probability of an event.

GOAL 2 Find the odds of an event.

Why you should learn it

▼ To represent **real-life** situations, like the probability that a baby sea turtle reaches the ocean in **Ex. 22**.

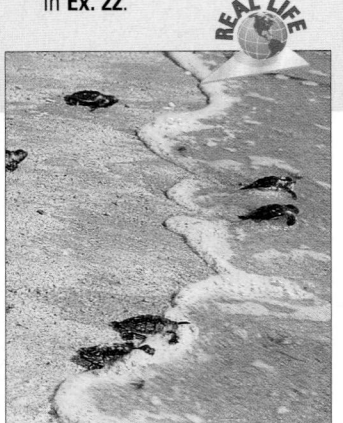

Probability and Odds

GOAL 1 FINDING THE PROBABILITY OF AN EVENT

The **probability of an event** is a measure of the likelihood that the event will occur. It is a number between 0 and 1, inclusive.

$P = 0$	$P = 0.25$	$P = 0.5$	$P = 0.75$	$P = 1$
Impossible	Unlikely	Occurs half the time	Quite likely	Certain

When you do a probability experiment, the different possible results are called **outcomes**. When an experiment has *N equally likely* outcomes, each of them occurs with probability $\frac{1}{N}$. For example, in the roll of a six-sided number cube, the possible outcomes are 1, 2, 3, 4, 5, and 6, and the probability associated with each outcome is $\frac{1}{6}$.

An **event** consists of a collection of outcomes. In the roll of a six-sided number cube, an "even roll" consists of the outcomes 2, 4, and 6. The **theoretical probability** of an even roll is $\frac{3}{6} = \frac{1}{2}$. The outcomes for an event you wish to have happen are called **favorable outcomes**, and the theoretical probability of this event is calculated by the following rule.

$$\text{Theoretical probability } P = \frac{\text{Number of favorable outcomes}}{\text{Total number of outcomes}}$$

EXAMPLE 1   *Finding the Probability of an Event*

a. You toss two coins. What is the probability P that both are heads?

b. An algebra class has 17 boys and 16 girls. One student is chosen at random from the class. What is the probability P that the student is a girl?

SOLUTION

a. There are four possible outcomes that are equally likely.

$$P = \frac{\text{Number of favorable outcomes}}{\text{Total number of outcomes}} = \frac{1}{4} = 0.25$$

favorable outcome = both heads

b. Because the student is chosen at random, it is equally likely that any of the 33 students will be chosen. Let "number of girls" be the favorable outcome. Let "number of students" be the total number of outcomes.

$$P = \frac{\text{Number of favorable outcomes}}{\text{Total number of outcomes}} = \frac{\text{Number of girls}}{\text{Number of students}} = \frac{16}{33} \approx 0.485$$

Another type of probability is **experimental probability**. This type of probability is based on repetitions of an actual experiment and is calculated by the following rule.

$$\text{Experimental probability } P = \frac{\text{Number of favorable outcomes observed}}{\text{Total number of trials}}$$

> **ACTIVITY**
> Developing Concepts
>
> ## Investigating Experimental Probability
>
> **Partner Activity** Toss three coins 20 times and record the number of heads for each of the 20 tosses.
>
> **❶** Use your results to find the experimental probability of getting three heads when three coins are tossed.
>
> **❷** Combine your results with those of all the other pairs in your class. Then use the combined results to find the experimental probability of getting three heads when three coins are tossed.
>
> **❸** Find the theoretical probability of getting three heads when three coins are tossed. How does it compare with your results from **Step 2**?

A survey is a type of experiment. Probabilities based on the outcomes of a survey can be used to make predictions.

EXAMPLE 2 *Using a Survey to Find a Probability*

SURVEYS Use the circle graph at the right showing the responses of 500 teens to a survey asking "Where would you like to live?"

If you were to ask a randomly chosen teen this question, what is the experimental probability that the teen would say "large city?"

Where Would You Like to Live?

- Large city 155
- Small town 90
- Suburbs 100
- Rural/ranch 70
- Wilderness area 85

▶ Source: *Youth Views*

FOCUS ON CAREERS

MARKET RESEARCHERS
use surveys to predict the needs and interests of their potential customers. Then they can make their products better.

CAREER LINK
www.mcdougallittell.com

SOLUTION

Let "choosing large city" be the favorable outcome. Let "number surveyed" be the total number of trials.

$$\text{Experimental probability } P = \frac{\text{Number choosing large city}}{\text{Number surveyed}}$$

$$= \frac{155}{500}$$

$$= 0.31$$

GOAL 2 FINDING THE ODDS OF AN EVENT

STUDENT HELP

▸ **Study Tip**
Odds are always read as the ratio of one quantity *to* another. For example, $\frac{4}{3}$ is read as "four *to* three," not as "four thirds."

THE ODDS OF AN EVENT

When all outcomes are equally likely, the **odds** that an event will occur are given by the formula below.

$$\text{Odds} = \frac{\text{Number of favorable outcomes}}{\text{Number of unfavorable outcomes}}$$

EXAMPLE 3 *Finding the Odds of an Event*

You randomly choose an integer from 0 through 9. What are the odds that the integer is 4 or more?

SOLUTION There are 6 favorable outcomes: 4, 5, 6, 7, 8, and 9. There are 4 unfavorable outcomes: 0, 1, 2, and 3.

$$\text{Odds} = \frac{\text{Number of favorable outcomes}}{\text{Number of unfavorable outcomes}} = \frac{6}{4} = \frac{3}{2}$$

▸ The odds that the integer is 4 or more are 3 to 2.

· · · · · · · · · ·

If you know the probability that an event will occur, then you can find the odds.

$$\text{Odds} = \frac{\text{Probability event will occur}}{\text{Probability event will not occur}} = \frac{\text{Probability event will occur}}{1 - (\text{Probability event will occur})}$$

Pets

EXAMPLE 4 *Finding Odds from Probability*

The probability that a randomly chosen household has a cat is 0.27. What are the odds that a household has a cat? ▸Source: American Veterinary Medical Association

SOLUTION

$$\text{Odds} = \frac{\text{Probability event will occur}}{1 - (\text{Probability event will occur})}$$

$$= \frac{0.27}{1 - 0.27} \qquad \textbf{Substitute for probabilities.}$$

$$= \frac{0.27}{0.73} \qquad \textbf{Simplify denominator.}$$

$$= \frac{27}{73} \qquad \textbf{Multiply numerator and denominator by 100.}$$

▸ The odds are 27 to 73 that a randomly chosen household has a cat.

GUIDED PRACTICE

Vocabulary Check

1. Using the results of a student lunch survey, you determine that the probability that a randomly chosen student likes green beans is 0.38. Is this probability theoretical or experimental?

Concept Check

2. The probability that an event will occur is 0.4. Is it more likely that the event will occur, or is it more likely that the event will *not* occur?

3. The odds that an event will occur are 3 to 4. Is it more likely that the event will occur, or is it more likely that the event will *not* occur?

Skill Check ✓

Tell whether the event is best described as *impossible, unlikely, likely to occur half the time, quite likely,* or *certain.* Explain your reasoning.

4. The probability of rain is 80%, or 0.8.

5. The odds in favor of winning a race are $\frac{1}{3}$.

6. The odds of being chosen for a committee are 1 to 1.

🌐 **TEST PLANNING Suppose it is equally likely that a teacher will chose any day from Monday, Tuesday, Wednesday, Thursday, and Friday to have the next test.**

7. What is the probability that the next test will be on a Friday?

8. What are the odds that the next test will be on a day starting with the letter T?

PRACTICE AND APPLICATIONS

STUDENT HELP

▶ **Extra Practice**
to help you master
skills is on p. 798.

PROBABILITY Find the probability of randomly choosing a red marble from the given bag of red and white marbles.

9. Number of red marbles: 16
Total number of marbles: 64

10. Number of red marbles: 8
Total number of marbles: 40

11. Number of white marbles: 7
Total number of marbles: 20

12. Number of white marbles: 24
Total number of marbles: 32

ODDS Find the odds of randomly choosing the indicated letter from a bag that contains the letters in the name of the given state.

13. S; MISSISSIPPI

14. N; PENNSYLVANIA

15. A; NEBRASKA

16. G; VIRGINIA

STUDENT HELP

▶ HOMEWORK HELP
Example 1: Exs. 9–12
Example 2: Exs. 21–24,
  26, 28, 29
Example 3: Exs. 13–16,
  25, 27, 30
Example 4: Exs. 17, 18,
  20

PROBABILITY TO ODDS Given the probability, find the odds.

17. The probability of randomly choosing a club from a deck of cards is 0.25.

18. The probability of tossing a total of 7 using two number cubes is $\frac{1}{6}$.

COIN TOSS You toss two coins.

19. What is the theoretical probability that only one is tails?

20. Use the theoretical probability to find the odds that only one is tails.

21. NUMBER CUBES You toss a six-sided number cube 20 times. For twelve of the tosses the number tossed was 3 or more.

    a. What is the experimental probability that a number tossed is 3 or more?

    b. What are the odds that a number tossed is 3 or more?

22. 🌎 **BABY SEA TURTLES** A sea turtle buries 90 eggs in the sand. From the 50 eggs that hatch, 37 turtles do not make it to the ocean. What is the probability that an egg chosen at random hatched and the baby turtle made it to the ocean?

STUDENT HELP

HOMEWORK HELP
Visit our Web site
www.mcdougallittell.com
for help with Exs. 23–27.

🌎 **PETS** In Exercises 23–25, use the graph.

23. What is the probability that a pet-owning household chosen at random owns a dog?

24. What is the probability that a pet-owning household chosen at random does *not* own a fish?

25. There are approximately 98.8 million households in the United States. If a household is chosen at random, what are the odds that the household owns a pet?

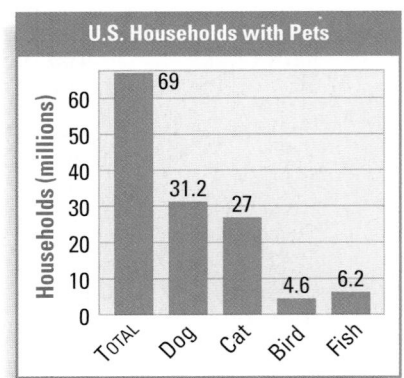

U.S. Households with Pets

Households (millions)

TOTAL: 69, Dog: 31.2, Cat: 27, Bird: 4.6, Fish: 6.2

▶ Source: American Veterinary Medical Assoc.

🌎 **MOVING** In Exercises 26 and 27, use the table, which shows the percent of citizens from various age groups who changed homes within the United States from 1995 to 1996.

26. What is the probability that a citizen from the 15–19 age group changed homes?

27. What are the odds that a citizen from the 25–29 age group moved to a home in a different state?

Percent of U.S. Citizens of Given Ages who Moved				
Age group	Total	Same county	Different county, same state	Different state
15 to 19	15	10	3	2
20 to 24	33	21	6	5
25 to 29	32	20	7	5
30 to 44	16	10	3	3

▶ Source: U.S. Bureau of the Census

FOCUS ON APPLICATIONS

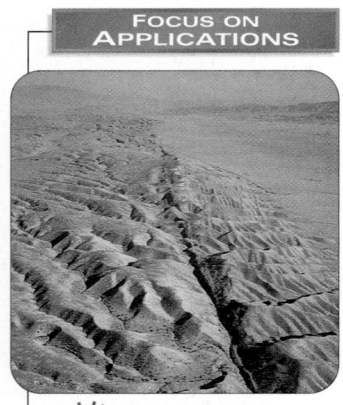

FAULT LINES
A fault line, like the one shown above, may appear in the earth's surface in a region that is prone to earthquakes.

🌎 **EARTHQUAKES** In Exercises 28–30, use the table, which shows the number of earthquakes of magnitude 4.0 or greater in the western United States since 1900. The magnitude of an earthquake indicates its severity.

28. What is the probability that the magnitude of an earthquake is from 6.0 to 6.9?

29. What is the probability that the magnitude of an earthquake is *not* from 4.0 to 4.9?

30. What are the odds that the magnitude of an earthquake is from 7.0 to 7.9?

Magnitude	Number of earthquakes
8 and higher	1
7.0–7.9	18
6.0–6.9	129
5.0–5.9	611
4.0–4.9	3171

▶ Source: U.S. Geological Survey

31. **WARDROBE** Your cousin spills spaghetti sauce on her shirt and asks to borrow a clean shirt from you for the rest of the day. You decide to let her choose from a selection of 4 sweatshirts, 1 hockey shirt, 8 T-shirts, and 3 tank tops. If it is equally likely that your cousin will choose any shirt, what are the odds that she will choose a sweatshirt?

32. *Writing* Suppose you randomly choose a marble from a bag holding 11 green, 4 blue, and 5 yellow marbles. Use probability *and* odds to express how likely it is that you choose a yellow marble. Compare the two ways of expressing how likely it is to choose a yellow marble. If you find one (probability or odds) easier to understand or more useful than the other, explain why.

Test Preparation

MULTIPLE CHOICE Use the table, which shows the number of students in each grade for three high schools and the number that get to each school by riding the bus.

3rd District High School Student Bus Riders						
	Marshall		Jordan		King	
Grade	Total	Bus riders	Total	Bus riders	Total	Bus riders
9th	247	198	326	195	265	151
10th	232	176	311	205	273	142
11th	194	141	304	196	264	139
12th	211	142	285	173	231	106

33. If you are in the tenth grade, what is the probability that you ride a bus to get to school?

Ⓐ $\frac{141}{194} \approx 0.73$ **Ⓑ** $\frac{196}{304} \approx 0.64$ **Ⓒ** $\frac{523}{816} \approx 0.64$ **Ⓓ** $\frac{139}{264} \approx 0.53$

34. If you go to Marshall High School, what are the odds that you do *not* ride the bus to get to school?

Ⓐ 657 to 227 **Ⓑ** 657 to 884 **Ⓒ** 227 to 657 **Ⓓ** 227 to 884

★ Challenge

BULL'S-EYE In Exercises 35–38, use the drawing of the dart board below, and the following information.

Assume that when a dart is thrown and hits the board, the dart is equally likely to hit any point on the board. The probability that a dart lands within the red bull's-eye circle is given by the following equation.

$$P = \frac{\text{Area of bull's-eye}}{\text{Area of board}}$$

(*Hint*: See the Table of Formulas on p. 813.)

35. What is the area of the bull's-eye?

36. What is the probability that a dart lands within the middle circle?

37. What is the probability that a dart lands between the middle and outer circles?

38. What are the odds that a dart lands on the bull's-eye?

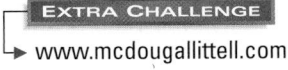

MIXED REVIEW

MENTAL MATH Write a question that can be used to solve the equation. Then use mental math to solve the equation. (Review 1.4)

39. $x + 17 = 25$ **40.** $a - 5 = 19$ **41.** $2b - 1 = 10$

42. $11t = 110$ **43.** $\dfrac{y}{15} = 8$ **44.** $3x + 15 = 24.6$

TRANSLATING VERBAL SENTENCES Translate the sentence into an equation or an inequality. (Review 1.5, 2.1)

45. 17 less than a number z is 9.

46. 8 more than a number r is less than 17.

47. -3 is the sum of a number y and -6.

48. -9 is equal to a number y decreased by 21.

EVALUATING EXPRESSIONS Evaluate the expression. (Review 2.3 for 3.1)

49. $-8 + 4 - 9$ **50.** $12 - (-8) - 5$ **51.** $20 + (-17) - 8$

52. $-17 + 25 - 34$ **53.** $-6.3 + 4.1 - 9.5$ **54.** $2 - 11 + 5 - (-16)$

55. $-29.4 - (-8) + 4$ **56.** $\dfrac{1}{2} + \left(-\dfrac{4}{5}\right) - \dfrac{2}{3}$ **57.** $-1\dfrac{3}{8} + 4\dfrac{3}{4} - 7\dfrac{1}{2}$

QUIZ 3

Self-Test for Lessons 2.7 and 2.8

Find the quotient. (Lesson 2.7)

1. $-28 \div \dfrac{4}{7}$ **2.** $\dfrac{36}{\frac{2}{3}}$ **3.** $\dfrac{32}{\frac{1}{4}}$ **4.** $48 \div (-12)$

5. $75 \div (-15)$ **6.** $-144 \div 9$ **7.** $-120 \div \dfrac{3}{8}$ **8.** $-\dfrac{13}{27} \div \left(-1\dfrac{4}{9}\right)$

In Exercises 9–16, simplify the division expression. (Lesson 2.7)

9. $42x \div (-6)$ **10.** $-56 \div (-8x)$ **11.** $9x \div \dfrac{1}{2}$ **12.** $20 \div \dfrac{4}{x}$

13. $25x \div \dfrac{5}{7}$ **14.** $15t \div \left(-\dfrac{3}{4}\right)$ **15.** $66y \div \left(-\dfrac{6}{5}\right)$ **16.** $-\dfrac{2x}{18} \div (-4)$

17. What is the probability that you randomly choose a purple marble from a bag containing 11 red, 6 green, and 8 purple marbles? (Lesson 2.8)

Tell whether the event is best described as *impossible, unlikely, likely to occur half the time, quite likely,* or *certain.* Explain your reasoning. (Lesson 2.8)

18. The probability of snow is 20%, or 0.2.

19. The probability of taking the test is 1.

20. The odds in favor of winning a car are $\dfrac{1}{30,000}$.

21. The odds of being chosen for the softball team are 15 to 6.

Chapter Summary

WHAT did you learn?

Graph and compare real numbers. **(2.1)**

Find the opposite and the absolute value of a real number. **(2.1)**

Add real numbers. **(2.2)**

Subtract real numbers. **(2.3)**

Organize data in a matrix. **(2.4)**

Add and subtract two matrices. **(2.4)**

Multiply real numbers. **(2.5)**

Use the distributive property. **(2.6)**

Combine like terms. **(2.6)**

Divide real numbers. **(2.7)**

Express the likelihood of an event as a probability or as odds. **(2.8)**

WHY did you learn it?

Find the coldest temperature recorded. **(p. 64)**

Find the speed and velocity of an elevator. **(p. 66)**

Decide whether an atom is an ion. **(p. 74)**

Find the price change of an ounce of gold. **(p. 83)**

Organize music store price data. **(p. 90)**

Find employee wage rates after a raise. **(p. 90)**

Find the vertical distance a hawk travels. **(p. 96)**

Find the total weight a train is hauling. **(p. 104)**

Simplify algebraic expressions. **(p. 102)**

Find the price change of a share of stock. **(p. 111)**

Find how likely it is that a test is given on a Friday. **(p. 117)**

How does Chapter 2 fit into the BIGGER PICTURE of algebra?

The numbers you worked with in Chapter 1 were zero or positive. In this chapter you studied rules for adding, subtracting, multiplying, and dividing with both positive and negative numbers. You are building a sense for the type of problems associated with negative numbers, such as losses, deficits, and low temperatures.

This chapter introduces some of the rules of algebra. By learning to create, simplify, and evaluate algebraic expressions and matrices, you will be able to solve many real-life problems. These skills will also prepare you for the algebra that you will study later in this course.

STUDY STRATEGY

How did you use the lessons in this chapter?

The notes you made as you studied Chapter 2, using the **Study Strategy** on page 62, may include these properties.

Lesson 2.2

Commutative Property
$$a + b = b + a \qquad -4 + 6 = 6 + (-4)$$

Associative Property
$$(a + b) + c = a + (b + c)$$
$$(-8 + 5) + 3 = -8 + (5 + 3)$$

Identity Property
$$a + 0 = a \qquad -9 + 0 = -9$$

Property of Zero
$$a + -a = 0 \qquad -7.5 + 7.5 = 0$$

Chapter Review

2.1 THE REAL NUMBER LINE

Examples on pp. 63–66

EXAMPLES You can use a number line to graph the real numbers 2, $-\frac{1}{2}$, 0.8, $-1\frac{1}{4}$, -2, and -0.8, and then put them in order from least to greatest.

In order from least to greatest, the numbers are -2, $-1\frac{1}{4}$, -0.8, $-\frac{1}{2}$, 0.8, and 2.

The *opposite* of 0.8 is -0.8. Both 2 and -2 have an *absolute value* of 2.

Graph the numbers on a number line. Then write two inequalities that compare the two numbers.

1. 7 and -6

2. -3.9 and -4.3

3. -9 and 8

4. -0.2 and -0.25

5. 13.9 and -14.9

6. $\left|-\frac{4}{7}\right|$ and $-\left|\frac{5}{11}\right|$

2.2 ADDITION OF REAL NUMBERS

Examples on pp. 72–74

EXAMPLES Find $-8 + (-6)$.

$|-8| + |-6| = 14$ **Same sign rule**
$-8 + (-6) = -14$ **Attach common sign.**

Find $4 + (-7)$.

$|-7| - |4| = 3$ **Opposite sign rule**
$4 + (-7) = -3$ **Attach sign of -7.**

Find the sum.

7. $12 + (-7)$

8. $-24 + (-16)$

9. $2.4 + (-3.1)$

10. $9 + (-10) + (-3)$

11. $-35 + 41 + (-18)$

12. $-2\frac{3}{4} + 5\frac{3}{8} + \left(-4\frac{1}{2}\right)$

SUBTRACTION OF REAL NUMBERS

Examples on pp. 79–81

EXAMPLES To subtract a real number, add its opposite.

$$3 - (-5) = 3 + 5 \quad \text{Add the opposite.} \quad -8 - 7 = -8 + (-7) \quad \text{Add the opposite.}$$
$$= 8 \quad \text{Find the sum.} \quad = -15 \quad \text{Find the sum.}$$

Evaluate the expression.

13. $-2 - 7 - (-8)$

14. $5 - 11 - (-6)$

15. $-18 - 14 - (-15)$

16. $-5.7 + 3.1 - 8.6$

17. $-\frac{7}{16} + \left(-\frac{3}{8}\right) - \frac{13}{4}$

18. $-\frac{23}{36} - \left|-\frac{4}{9}\right| + \left(-\frac{7}{12}\right)$

ADDING AND SUBTRACTING MATRICES

Examples on pp. 86–88

EXAMPLES To add or subtract matrices, add or subtract corresponding entries.

$$\begin{bmatrix} -1 & 3 \\ 2 & -2 \end{bmatrix} + \begin{bmatrix} 2 & 0 \\ -5 & 1 \end{bmatrix} = \begin{bmatrix} -1+2 & 3+0 \\ 2+(-5) & -2+1 \end{bmatrix} = \begin{bmatrix} 1 & 3 \\ -3 & -1 \end{bmatrix}$$

$$\begin{bmatrix} 6 & -6 \\ -2 & 4 \\ -2 & 1 \end{bmatrix} - \begin{bmatrix} -3 & 3 \\ -2 & 5 \\ 7 & -4 \end{bmatrix} = \begin{bmatrix} 6-(-3) & -6-3 \\ -2-(-2) & 4-5 \\ -2-7 & 1-(-4) \end{bmatrix} = \begin{bmatrix} 9 & -9 \\ 0 & -1 \\ -9 & 5 \end{bmatrix}$$

Find the sum and the difference of the matrices.

19. $\begin{bmatrix} -3 & -2 \\ 8 & 4 \end{bmatrix}, \begin{bmatrix} 4 & -2 \\ -7 & 5 \end{bmatrix}$ **20.** $\begin{bmatrix} -2 & 5 & 9 \\ -3 & 10 & 0 \end{bmatrix}, \begin{bmatrix} -1 & -6 & 11 \\ -2 & -7 & 1 \end{bmatrix}$

MULTIPLICATION OF REAL NUMBERS

Examples on pp. 93–95

EXAMPLES A product is negative if it has an odd number of negative factors. A product is positive if it has an even number of negative factors.

a. $(-4)(5) = -20$ One negative factor

b. $\left(-\frac{1}{3}\right)(-3)(2) = 2$ Two negative factors

c. $(-2)(-1)(-3) = -6$ Three negative factors

Find the product.

21. $(-3)(12)$

22. $(5)(-8)$

23. $(-40)(-15)$

24. $(-1)(9)$

25. $(-17)\left(\frac{2}{9}\right)$

26. $(-14)(-0.3)$

27. $\left|(9)(-5.5)\right|$

28. $(-3.2)(-10)(2)$

29. $(-7)(-6)(-2)$

30. $(-12)(2)(-0.5)$

31. $(-24)\left(-\frac{7}{12}\right)$

32. $(11)(-1)(-7)(-3)$

THE DISTRIBUTIVE PROPERTY

Examples on pp. 100–102

EXAMPLES You can use the distributive property to rewrite expressions without parentheses.

$$8(x + 3) = 8x + 24 \qquad a(b + c) = ab + ac \text{ or } (b + c)a = ba + ca$$

$$3(x - 6) = 3x - 18 \qquad a(b - c) = ab - ac \text{ or } (b - c)a = ba - ca$$

Use the distributive property to rewrite the expression without parentheses.

33. $5(x + 12)$ **34.** $(y + 6)9$ **35.** $5.5(b - 10)$ **36.** $(3.2 - w)2$

37. $(t + 11)(-3)$ **38.** $-2(s + 13)$ **39.** $-2.5(z - 5)$ **40.** $-x\left(\dfrac{3}{7} + y\right)$

DIVISION OF REAL NUMBERS

Examples on pp. 108–110

EXAMPLE To divide 7 by -6, multiply 7 by the reciprocal of -6.

$$7 \div (-6) = 7 \cdot \left(-\frac{1}{6}\right) = -\frac{7}{6} \qquad b \div a = b \cdot \frac{1}{a}$$

Find the quotient.

41. $48 \div (-12)$ **42.** $-34 \div 2$ **43.** $39 \div (-13)$ **44.** $-57 \div (-19)$

45. $55 \div (-1.1)$ **46.** $-63 \div 4\frac{1}{5}$ **47.** $\dfrac{48}{-\frac{3}{4}}$ **48.** $-\dfrac{-84}{\frac{7}{8}}$

PROBABILITY AND ODDS

Examples on pp. 114–116

EXAMPLES Find how likely it is that you will randomly choose a green marble from a bag with 11 green, 2 blue, and 7 red marbles.

Probability

$$P = \frac{\text{Number of favorable outcomes}}{\text{Total number of outcomes}}$$

$$P = \frac{11}{20} = 0.55$$

The probability is 0.55.

Odds

$$\text{Odds} = \frac{\text{Number of favorable outcomes}}{\text{Number of unfavorable outcomes}}$$

$$= \frac{11}{9}$$

The odds are 11 to 9.

Find the probability and the odds of randomly choosing a red marble from a bag of red and white marbles.

49. Number of red marbles: 12
Total number of marbles: 48

50. Number of red marbles: 9
Total number of marbles: 81

51. Number of white marbles: 36
Total number of marbles: 40

52. Number of white marbles: 17
Total number of marbles: 68

CHAPTER 2

Chapter Test

Find the value of the expression.

1. $|8|$

2. $|-2.7|$

3. $|-6.4| - 3.1$

4. $-(-4.5)$

5. $4 + (-9)$

6. $-4.5 + (-9.1)$

7. $-2\frac{5}{6} + 3\frac{1}{4}$

8. $9 + (-10) + 2$

Add or subtract the matrices.

9. $\begin{bmatrix} 3 & -7 \\ \frac{1}{2} & 6 \\ 0 & 2 \end{bmatrix} + \begin{bmatrix} 4 & 2 \\ \frac{1}{2} & 4 \\ 5 & \frac{1}{2} \end{bmatrix}$

10. $\begin{bmatrix} -5 & -1 \\ 5 & 8 \\ 7 & 2\frac{1}{2} \end{bmatrix} - \begin{bmatrix} 6 & 3 \\ \frac{1}{2} & -2 \\ 0 & 2 \end{bmatrix}$

11. $\begin{bmatrix} 2 & \frac{1}{2} & 4 \\ 5 & 16 & -7 \end{bmatrix} + \begin{bmatrix} 5 & \frac{1}{2} & -1 \\ -2 & 8 & 4 \end{bmatrix}$

Find the product or quotient.

12. $(-6)(4)$

13. $72 \div (-12)$

14. $-36 \div (-4)$

15. $(-8.4)(-100)$

16. $-56 \div \left(-\frac{7}{8}\right)$

17. $(-9)(8)\left(-\frac{5}{6}\right)$

18. $-3740 \div (-10)$

19. $-(-18)(-5)\left(\frac{7}{15}\right)$

20. $-\frac{3}{8} \div \frac{1}{2}$

21. $\left(1\frac{2}{7}\right)\left(1\frac{5}{9}\right)$

22. $\left(-\frac{1}{2}\right)\left(\frac{3}{5}\right)\left(-\frac{2}{3}\right)\left(\frac{5}{8}\right)$

23. $-7\frac{4}{5} \div \left(-1\frac{3}{10}\right)$

Simplify the expression.

24. $(-5)(-w)(w)(w)$

25. $(-8)^2(-x)^3$

26. $8(4 - q)$

27. $(6 + y)(-12)$

28. $(35 - 10q)\left(-\frac{2}{5}\right)$

29. $-9(y + 11)$

30. $5(3 - z) - z$

31. $14p + 2(5 - p)$

In Exercises 32–37, evaluate the expression for the given value of *x*.

32. $5 - (-8) + x$ when $x = -5$

33. $|-9| - 2x + 5$ when $x = 6$

34. $-9x + 12$ when $x = -2$

35. $1 - 2x^2$ when $x = -2$

36. $\frac{4 - x}{-3}$ when $x = -1$

37. $-4x^2 - 8x + 9$ when $x = -5$

38. 🌐 **PROFIT** A company had a first-quarter profit of $2189.70, a second-quarter profit of $1527.11, a third-quarter loss of $2502.18, and a fourth-quarter loss of $266.54. What was the company's profit or loss for the year?

39. 🌐 **EAGLES** An eagle dives from its nest with a velocity of $-8\frac{1}{3}$ feet per second. Find the vertical displacement in $4\frac{1}{2}$ seconds.

🌐 **BEVERAGE SURVEY** You do a survey asking students to identify their favorite beverage from the following categories: *soda, juice, water,* and *other.* You get the following results: 132 students choose soda, 59 choose juice, 43 choose water, and 26 choose other.

40. What is the probability that a randomly chosen student's favorite drink is juice?

41. What are the odds that a randomly chosen student's favorite drink is water?

CHAPTER 2

Chapter Standardized Test

● **TEST-TAKING STRATEGY** If you can, check an answer using a method that is different from the one you used originally, to avoid making the same mistake twice.

1. MULTIPLE CHOICE Which integer is between $-\frac{55}{4}$ and $-\frac{37}{3}$?

(A) -13 (B) -12 (C) 2

(D) $\frac{7}{3}$ (E) $-\frac{69}{5}$

2. MULTIPLE CHOICE What is the value of $|x| + |y| - 10$ when $x = -9$ and $y = 2$?

(A) 17 (B) -43 (C) -1

(D) 1 (E) 21

3. MULTIPLE CHOICE Which of the following is a counterexample that proves the statement $|x| = -x$ is *not* true?

(A) $x = -9.5$ (B) $x = -2$ (C) $x = -\frac{1}{2}$

(D) $x = 0$ (E) $x = 4.7$

4. MULTIPLE CHOICE What is the value of the expression $-9 + 3 + (-14)$?

(A) -26 (B) -20 (C) -8

(D) -2 (E) 26

QUANTITATIVE COMPARISON In Questions 5–7, choose the statement that is true about the given quantities.

(A) The quantity in column A is greater.

(B) The quantity in column B is greater.

(C) The two quantities are equal.

(D) The relationship cannot be determined from the given information.

	Column A	Column B
5.	$2 - 5 + (-3)$	$2 + (-5) - 3$
6.	$-\frac{7}{9} - \frac{1}{3}$	$-\frac{11}{12} - \frac{1}{6}$
7.	x	$-2x$

8. MULTIPLE CHOICE What is the value of the expression $-4 - 6 - (-10)$?

(A) -20 (B) -12 (C) -8

(D) 0 (E) 12

9. MULTIPLE CHOICE What is the value of the expression $9 - (-13) + (-17) + (-10)$?

(A) -41 (B) -31 (C) -5

(D) 5 (E) 15

10. MULTIPLE CHOICE Find the sum.

$$\begin{bmatrix} -5 & -4 \\ 2 & -4 \\ 1 & -3 \end{bmatrix} + \begin{bmatrix} 8 & 9 \\ -6 & 1 \\ -1 & 4 \end{bmatrix} = \underline{\ ?\ }$$

(A) $\begin{bmatrix} 3 & 5 \\ -6 & -3 \\ 0 & 1 \end{bmatrix}$ (B) $\begin{bmatrix} -3 & 5 \\ 4 & -3 \\ 0 & -1 \end{bmatrix}$

(C) $\begin{bmatrix} 3 & 5 \\ -4 & -3 \\ 0 & 1 \end{bmatrix}$ (D) $\begin{bmatrix} 3 & 5 \\ -4 & -3 \\ 0 & -1 \end{bmatrix}$

(E) None of these

11. MULTIPLE CHOICE Find the difference.

$$\begin{bmatrix} -1 & 3 \\ -6 & 4 \\ 2 & -5 \end{bmatrix} - \begin{bmatrix} -7 & 3 \\ 2 & 6 \\ 0 & -8 \end{bmatrix} = \underline{\ ?\ }$$

(A) $\begin{bmatrix} 6 & 0 \\ -8 & -2 \\ 2 & -3 \end{bmatrix}$ (B) $\begin{bmatrix} -8 & 0 \\ -8 & -2 \\ 2 & 3 \end{bmatrix}$

(C) $\begin{bmatrix} 6 & 0 \\ -8 & 2 \\ -2 & -3 \end{bmatrix}$ (D) $\begin{bmatrix} 6 & 0 \\ -8 & -2 \\ 0 & 3 \end{bmatrix}$

(E) None of these

12. MULTIPLE CHOICE $-\frac{1}{2} \cdot \frac{-2}{3} \cdot \frac{3}{-4} \cdot \frac{4}{5} = \underline{\ ?\ }$

(A) $-\frac{24}{60}$ (B) $-\frac{1}{5}$ (C) $-\frac{1}{6}$

(D) $\frac{1}{5}$ (E) $\frac{5}{6}$

13. MULTIPLE CHOICE What is the value of $-2m^6 \div 4m^3$ when $m = -2$?

    Ⓐ -32 **Ⓑ** -16 **Ⓒ** -4 **Ⓓ** 4 **Ⓔ** 16

QUANTITATIVE COMPARISON In Questions 14 and 15, choose the statement that is true about the given quantities.

    Ⓐ The quantity in column A is greater.

    Ⓑ The quantity in column B is greater.

    Ⓒ The two quantities are equal.

    Ⓓ The relationship cannot be determined from the given information.

	Column A	Column B
14.	$(-10)^4$	$(-10)^5$
15.	$-3 \cdot 24 \div (-9)$	$-12 \cdot 8 \div 6$

16. MULTIPLE CHOICE The expression $6(x + 3) - 2(4 - x)$ can be simplified to $\underline{\ ?\ }$.

    Ⓐ $5x + 5$ **Ⓑ** $8x + 10$ **Ⓒ** $5x - 5$ **Ⓓ** $8x + 1$ **Ⓔ** $4x + 10$

17. MULTIPLE CHOICE What is the value of $\dfrac{4p + 6pq}{p^2 q}$ when $p = -2$ and $q = -3$?

    Ⓐ $-\dfrac{11}{3}$ **Ⓑ** $\dfrac{28}{12}$ **Ⓒ** 2 **Ⓓ** $-\dfrac{7}{3}$ **Ⓔ** $\dfrac{11}{3}$

18. MULTIPLE CHOICE On March 1, you own 15.5 shares of mutual fund stock that are worth \$142.91. On May 1, the shares are worth \$135.16. What was the change in the price per share of stock?

    Ⓐ $-\$7.75$ **Ⓑ** $-\$.50$ **Ⓒ** $-\$.05$ **Ⓓ** $\$.05$ **Ⓔ** $\$.50$

MULTIPLE CHOICE In Questions 19 and 20, you randomly choose a marble from a bag holding 5 red, 7 blue, and 13 yellow marbles.

19. What is the probability that you choose a blue marble?

    Ⓐ 0.2 **Ⓑ** 0.07 **Ⓒ** 0.28 **Ⓓ** 0.52 **Ⓔ** 0.7

20. What are the odds that you choose a red marble?

    Ⓐ 1 to 4 **Ⓑ** 5 to 13 **Ⓒ** 7 to 13 **Ⓓ** 5 to 7 **Ⓔ** 13 to 5

21. MULTI-STEP PROBLEM The spinner at the right is evenly divided into 6 sections. Each of the players spins the spinner. Their results are added together. Player A wins if the sum is negative. Otherwise, Player B wins.

    a. List all the possible outcomes for one pair of spins.

    b. What are the odds of Player A winning?

    c. CRITICAL THINKING A game is fair when all the players have the same probability of winning. Is this a fair game? Explain your reasoning.

    d. CREATING A FAIR GAME Create your own game like the one described above. Your game should be fair. You may change the numbers on the spinner or the rules of the game. Describe your game and explain why it is fair.

SOLVING LINEAR EQUATIONS

▶ *Why do you think the bald eagle was chosen as a national symbol?*

APPLICATION: Bald Eagles

A bald eagle is featured on the Great Seal of the United States. The bald eagle is considered a symbol of power, strength, grace, and freedom. These birds, found only in North America, can fly up to 30 miles per hour and dive at speeds up to 100 miles per hour.

To solve problems involving flying rates of bald eagles, you can use equations containing variables for distance, rate, and time. In Chapter 3 you will use linear equations to describe many real-world situations.

Think & Discuss

1. Find the distance a bald eagle can travel for the given flying rate and time.

Flying Rate (miles per hour)	Time (hours)	Distance (miles)
30	1	?
30	$\frac{1}{2}$	?
30	$\frac{1}{12}$	?

2. Rewrite the flying rate in miles per minute.

Learn More About It

You will use equations to find flying and diving times of bald eagles in Exercise 57 on p. 143.

 APPLICATION LINK Visit www.mcdougallittell.com for more information about bald eagles.

Study Guide

PREVIEW

What's the chapter about?

Chapter 3 is about **solving linear equations**. In Chapter 3, you'll learn

- techniques for solving linear equations systematically.
- ways to apply ratios, rates, percents, and problem solving strategies.

KEY VOCABULARY

▶ **Review**
- solution of an equation, p. 24
- opposites, p. 65
- distributive property, p. 100
- reciprocal, p. 108

▶ **New**
- equivalent equations, p. 132
- inverse operations, p. 132
- linear equation in one variable, p. 133

- ratio of a to b, p. 140
- identity, p. 155
- formula, p. 174
- rate of a per b, p. 180

PREPARE

Are you ready for the chapter?

SKILL REVIEW Do these exercises to review key skills that you'll apply in this chapter. See the given **reference page** if there is something you don't understand.

Find the percent of the number. (Skills Review, p. 786)

1. 11% of 650   **2.** 41% of 71.5   **3.** 6% of 250   **4.** 4.2% of 60

Check whether the given number is a solution of the equation.
(Review Examples 1 and 2, p. 24)

5. $9 - x = 7; -2$ **6.** $-11 = -4y + 1; 3$ **7.** $4 - 3w + 5w = 2; -1$

Use the distributive property to rewrite the expression without parentheses. (Review Examples 2 and 3, p. 101)

8. $3(4r + 6)$ **9.** $-6(3 - 5z)$ **10.** $(-x + 7)(-3)$

Find the terms of the expression. Then simplify the expression by combining like terms. (Review Example 3, p. 80 and Example 5, p. 102)

11. $-2 + 3x - 7$ **12.** $4a + 2 - a$ **13.** $1 - 3x + 4y + 3x$

STUDENT HELP

▶ **Study Tip**
"Student Help" boxes throughout the chapter give you study tips and tell you where to look for extra help in this book and on the Internet.

STUDY STRATEGY

Here's a study strategy!

Learning to Use Formulas

Be sure you know what each variable means in a formula. To study for tests, it is helpful to write a formula on one side of a 3 × 5 card and a sample problem using that formula on the other side. There is also a helpful Table of Formulas on page 813.

▶ ACTIVITY 3.1
Developing Concepts

GROUP ACTIVITY
Work with a partner.

MATERIALS
algebra tiles

Modeling One-Step Equations

▶ **QUESTION** How can you use algebra tiles to solve one-step equations?

▶ **EXPLORING THE CONCEPT: SOLVING** $x + 5 = -2$

1 Model the equation $x + 5 = -2$. A [+] represents the unknown value x.

2 To find the value of x, get the x-tile by itself on the left side of the equation. You can undo the addition by subtracting 5. Be sure to subtract the same amount on each side of the equation, so that the two sides stay equal.

STUDENT HELP

▶ **Look Back**
For help with zero pairs, see p. 78.

First add 5 zero pairs so you can subtract 5.

3 The resulting equation shows the value of x. So, $x = \underline{?}$.

▶ **EXPLORING THE CONCEPT: SOLVING** $x - 3 = 2$

4 Model the equation $x - 3 = 2$.

5 To get the x-tile by itself, add 3 to each side to undo the subtraction.

You can model the subtraction with −1-tiles because $x - 3 = x + (-3)$.

6 Group positive and negative tiles to make zero pairs. What are the remaining tiles on each side of the equation? So, $x = \underline{?}$.

▶ **DRAWING CONCLUSIONS**

Use algebra tiles to model and solve the equation. Sketch each step you use.

1. $x + 4 = 6$	**2.** $x + 5 = 3$	**3.** $x + 6 = -1$	**4.** $x + 3 = -3$
5. $x - 1 = 5$	**6.** $x - 6 = 2$	**7.** $x - 7 = -4$	**8.** $x - 5 = -5$

9. What operation do you use to solve an addition equation? to solve a subtraction equation?

10. A student solved the equation $x + 3 = -4$ by subtracting 3 on the left side of the equation and got $x = -4$. Is this the correct solution? Explain.

3.1
Solving Equations Using Addition and Subtraction

What you should learn

GOAL 1 Solve linear equations using addition and subtraction.

GOAL 2 Use linear equations to solve **real-life** problems such as finding a record temperature change in **Example 3**.

Why you should learn it

▼ To model **real-life** situations, such as comparing the sizes of city parks in **Exs. 52 and 53**.

GOAL 1 ADDITION AND SUBTRACTION EQUATIONS

You can solve an equation by using the *transformations* below and on page 138 to isolate the variable on one side of the equation. When you rewrite an equation using these transformations, you produce an equation with the same solutions as the original equation. These equations are called **equivalent** equations. For example, $x + 3 = 5$ and $x = 2$ are equivalent because $x + 3 = 5$ can be transformed into $x = 2$ and each equation has 2 as its only solution.

To change, or *transform*, an equation into an equivalent equation, think of an equation as having two sides that are "in balance."

Original equation:
$x + 3 = 5$

Subtract 3 from both sides to isolate x on the left. Scale stays in balance.

Simplify both sides. Equivalent equation: $x = 2$

Any transformation you apply to an equation must keep the equation in balance. For instance, if you subtract 3 from one side of the equation, you must also subtract 3 from the other side of the equation. Simplifying one side of the equation does not affect the balance, so you don't have to change the other side.

TRANSFORMATIONS THAT PRODUCE EQUIVALENT EQUATIONS

	ORIGINAL EQUATION		EQUIVALENT EQUATION
• Add the same number to *each* side.	$x - 3 = 5$	Add 3.	$x = 8$
• Subtract the same number from *each* side.	$x + 6 = 10$	Subtract 6.	$x = 4$
• Simplify one or both sides.	$x = 8 - 3$	Simplify.	$x = 5$
• Interchange the sides.	$7 = x$	Interchange.	$x = 7$

Inverse operations are operations that undo each other, such as addition and subtraction. Inverse operations help you to *isolate the variable* in an equation.

EXAMPLE 1 *Adding to Each Side*

Solve $x - 5 = -13$.

SOLUTION

On the left side of the equation, 5 is subtracted from x. To isolate x, you need to undo the subtraction by applying the inverse operation of adding 5. Remember, to keep the balance you must add 5 to *each* side.

$x - 5 = -13$	Write original equation.
$x - 5 + 5 = -13 + 5$	Add 5 to each side.
$x = -8$	Simplify.

▶ The solution is -8. Check by substituting -8 for x in the original equation.

✓**CHECK**

$x - 5 = -13$	Write original equation.
$-8 - 5 \stackrel{?}{=} -13$	Substitute -8 for x.
$-13 = -13$	Solution is correct.

· · · · · · · · ·

Each time you apply a transformation to an equation, you are writing a **solution step**. Solution steps are written one below the other with the equals signs aligned.

EXAMPLE 2 *Simplifying First*

Solve $-8 = n - (-4)$.

SOLUTION

$-8 = n - (-4)$	Write original equation.
$-8 = n + 4$	Simplify.
$-8 - 4 = n + 4 - 4$	Subtract 4 from each side.
$-12 = n$	Simplify.

· · · · · · · · ·

The equations in this chapter are called *linear equations*. In a **linear equation** the variable is raised to the *first* power and does not occur in a denominator, inside a square root symbol, or inside absolute value symbols.

LINEAR EQUATION	NOT A LINEAR EQUATION
$x + 5 = 9$	$x^2 + 5 = 9$
$-4 + n = 2n - 6$	$\lvert x + 3 \rvert = 7$

In Chapter 4 you will see that *linear equations* get their name from the fact that their graphs are straight lines.

GOAL 2 **USING LINEAR EQUATIONS IN REAL-LIFE PROBLEMS**

Temperature

EXAMPLE 3 *Modeling a Real-Life Problem*

Several record temperature changes have taken place in Spearfish, South Dakota. On January 22, 1943, the temperature in Spearfish fell from 54°F at 9:00 A.M. to −4°F at 9:27 A.M. By how many degrees did the temperature fall?

SOLUTION

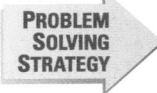

PROBLEM SOLVING STRATEGY

VERBAL MODEL

$$\boxed{\text{Temperature at 9:27 A.M.}} = \boxed{\text{Temperature at 9:00 A.M.}} - \boxed{\text{Degrees fallen}}$$

LABELS

Temperature at 9:27 A.M. $= -4$ (degrees Fahrenheit)

Temperature at 9:00 A.M. $= 54$ (degrees Fahrenheit)

Degrees fallen $= T$ (degrees Fahrenheit)

ALGEBRAIC MODEL

$-4 = 54 - T$ Write algebraic model.

$-4 - 54 = 54 - T - 54$ Subtract 54 from each side.

$-58 = -T$ Simplify.

$58 = T$ *T* is the opposite of −58.

▶ The temperature fell by 58°. Check this in the original statement of the problem.

STUDENT HELP

Study Tip
When you solve an equation, if you get a solution such as −x = 9, remember that this is the same as saying "the opposite of x is 9" or "x is the opposite of 9," which you can write as x = −9.

EXAMPLE 4 *Translating Verbal Statements*

Match the real-life problem with an equation.

$$x - 4 = 16 \qquad x + 16 = 4 \qquad 16 - x = 4$$

a. You owe $16 to your cousin. You paid x dollars back and you now owe $4. How much did you pay back?

b. The temperature was x°F. It rose 16°F and is now 4°F. What was the original temperature?

c. A telephone pole extends 4 feet below ground and 16 feet above ground. What is the total length x of the pole?

SOLUTION

a. Original amount owed (**16**) − Amount paid back (x) = Amount now owed (**4**)

b. Original temperature (x) + Degrees risen (**16**) = Temperature now (**4**)

c. Total length (x) − Length below ground (**4**) = Length above ground (**16**)

GUIDED PRACTICE

Vocabulary Check ✔

1. Two equations that have the same solutions are called _?_ equations.

Concept Check ✔

2. Show how to check the solution found in Example 3.

3. Explain each solution step for the equation $-3 - x = 1$. Use the Study Tip and Example 3 on page 134 to help.

Skill Check ✔

Solve the equation.

4. $r + 3 = 2$

5. $9 = x - 4$

6. $7 + c = -10$

7. $-3 = b - 6$

8. $8 - x = 4$

9. $r - (-2) = 5$

🌐 **SPENDING MONEY** **You started with some money in your pocket. All you spent was $4.65 on lunch. You ended up with $7.39 in your pocket.**

10. Write an equation to find how much money you started with.

11. Describe the transformation you would use to solve the equation.

12. Solve the equation. What does the solution mean?

PRACTICE AND APPLICATIONS

STUDENT HELP

▶ **Extra Practice**
to help you master
skills is on p. 799.

STATING THE INVERSE **State the inverse operation.**

13. Add 28.

14. Add 17.

15. Subtract 15.

16. Subtract 3.

17. Add -3.

18. Add -12.

19. Subtract -45.

20. Subtract $-2\frac{1}{2}$.

SOLVING EQUATIONS **Solve the equation.**

21. $x = 4 - 7$

22. $x + 5 = 10$

23. $t - 2 = 6$

24. $11 = r - 4$

25. $-9 = 2 + y$

26. $n - 5 = -9$

27. $-3 + x = 7$

28. $\frac{2}{5} = a - \frac{1}{5}$

29. $r + 3\frac{1}{4} = 2\frac{1}{2}$

30. $t - (-4) = 4$

31. $|-6| + y = 11$

32. $|-8| + x = -3$

33. $19 - (-y) = 25$

34. $|2| - (-b) = 6$

35. $x + 4 - 3 = 6 \cdot 5$

36. $-b = 8$

37. $12 - 6 = -n$

38. $3 - a = 0$

39. $4 = -b - 12$

40. $-3 = -a + (-4)$

41. $-r - (-7) = 16$

MATCHING AN EQUATION **In Exercises 42–44, match the real-life problem with an equation. Then solve the problem.**

STUDENT HELP

▶ **HOMEWORK HELP**
Example 1: Exs. 13–29
Example 2: Exs. 30–35
Example 3: Exs. 36–49
Example 4: Exs. 42–49

A. $x + 15 = 7$ **B.** $15 - x = 7$ **C.** $15 + 7 = x$ **D.** $x + 15 = -7$

42. You own 15 CDs. You buy 7 more. How many CDs do you own now?

43. There are 15 members of a high school band brass section. After graduation there are only 7 members. How many members graduated?

44. The temperature rose 15 degrees to 7°F. What was the original temperature?

SOLVING EQUATIONS Write and solve an equation to answer the question.

45. 🌎 **VIDEO PRICES** The selling price of a certain video is $7 more than the price the store paid. If the selling price is $24, find the price the store paid.

46. 🌎 **TRACK** Jackie Joyner-Kersee won a gold medal in the Olympic Heptathlon in 1988 and in 1992. Her 1992 score was 7044 points. This was 247 fewer points than her 1988 score. What was her 1988 score?

47. 🌎 **BASEBALL STADIUMS** Turner Field in Atlanta, GA, has 49,831 seats. Jacobs Field in Cleveland, OH, has 43,368 seats. How many seats would need to be added to Jacobs Field for it to have as many seats as Turner Field?

48. 🌎 **TEST SCORES** The last math test that you took had 100 regular points and 10 bonus points. You received a total score of 87, which included 9 bonus points. What would your score have been without any bonus points?

49. 🌎 **COMPUTER TIME** The average 12-to-17-year-old spends 645 minutes per month on a personal computer. This is 732 fewer minutes per month than the average 18-to-24-year-old spends. How many minutes per month does the average 18-to-24-year-old spend on a personal computer?
▶ Source: Media Matrix

GEOMETRY **CONNECTION** Find the length of the side marked *x*.

50. The perimeter is 12 feet.

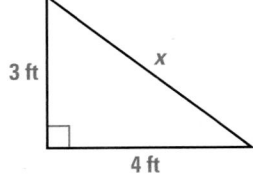

51. The perimeter is 43 centimeters.

🌎 **CITY PARKS** In Exercises 52 and 53, use the table that shows the sizes (in acres) of the largest city parks in the United States.

Park (location)	Size (in acres)
Cullen Park (Houston, TX)	?
Fairmount Park (Philadelphia, PA)	8700
Griffith Park (Los Angeles, CA)	4218
Eagle Creek Park (Indianapolis, IN)	?
Pelham Bay Park (Bronx, NY)	2764

▶ Source: The Trust for Public Land

52. You are researching United States city parks. You note that Griffith Park is only 418 acres larger than Eagle Creek Park. Write an equation that models the size of Eagle Creek Park. Solve the equation.

53. You note that the largest city park, Cullen Park, is only 248 acres smaller than the sum of the sizes of Griffith Park, Eagle Creek Park, and Pelham Bay Park. Write an equation that models the size of Cullen Park. Solve the equation. (*Hint:* Use the result of Exercise 52.)

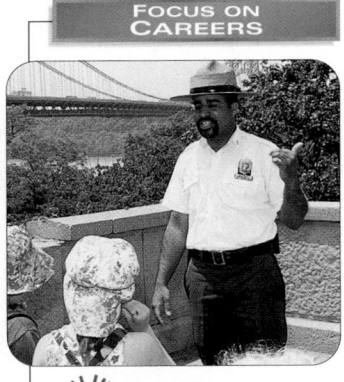

FOCUS ON CAREERS

PARK RANGER
Possible duties of a park ranger include gathering and presenting historical or scientific information, managing resources, guiding tours, and maintaining order and safety.

🌐 **CAREER LINK**
www.mcdougallittell.com

136 **Chapter 3** *Solving Linear Equations*

54. MULTI-STEP PROBLEM The table shows the number of Digital Versatile Disc (DVD) players sold in the first ten months after their release in 1997.

Month	Cumulative sales	Sales equation	Monthly sales
March	5,828	——	5,828
April	13,198	$5,828 + x = 13,198$	7,370
May	22,254	?	?
June	31,580	?	?
July	40,972	?	?
Aug.	51,401	?	?
Sept.	68,702	?	?
Oct.	83,494	?	?
Nov.	108,897	?	?
Dec.	158,068	?	?

▶ Source: INTELECT ASW

a. Copy the table. For each month, write a sales equation relating cumulative and monthly sales. Let x represent the number of players sold that month.

b. Solve your sales equations to fill in the monthly sales column.

c. *Writing* Suppose a DVD player manufacturer started an advertising campaign in September. Use your table to judge the campaign's effect on sales. Write a report explaining whether the campaign was successful.

★ **Challenge**

55. LOGICAL REASONING You decide to see if you can ride the elevator to street level (Floor 0) without pushing any buttons. The elevator takes you up 4 floors, down 6 floors, up 1 floor, down 8 floors, down 3 floors, up 1 floor, and then down 6 floors to street level. Write and solve an equation to find your starting floor.

MIXED REVIEW

TRANSLATING VERBAL SENTENCES **Write the verbal sentence as an equation.** (Review 1.5 for 3.2)

56. Five times a number is 160.

57. A number divided by 6 is 32.

58. One fourth of a number is 36.

59. A number multiplied by $\frac{2}{3}$ is 8.

SIMPLIFYING EXPRESSIONS **Simplify the expression.** (Review 2.5 and 2.7 for 3.2)

60. $8\left(\frac{x}{8}\right)$ **61.** $\frac{1}{8}y \cdot 8$ **62.** $-\frac{3}{5}\left(-\frac{5}{3}x\right)$ **63.** $-4x \div (-4)$

64. $6\left(-\frac{1}{6}x\right)$ **65.** $\frac{7}{12}y \cdot \frac{12}{7}$ **66.** $\frac{t}{-4}(-4)$ **67.** $-19a \div 19$

DISTRIBUTIVE PROPERTY **Apply the distributive property.** (Review 2.6)

68. $4(x + 2)$ **69.** $7(3 - 2y)$ **70.** $-5(-y - 7)$ **71.** $(3x + 8)(-2)$

72. $-x(x - 6)$ **73.** $-5x(y + 3)$ **74.** $2y(8 - 7y)$ **75.** $(-3x - 9y)(-6y)$

3.2 Solving Equations Using Multiplication and Division

What you should learn

GOAL 1 Solve linear equations using multiplication and division.

GOAL 2 Use multiplication and division equations to solve **real-life** and geometric problems as in **Example 4**.

Why you should learn it

▼ To model and solve **real-life** problems, such as finding how far away you are from a thunderstorm in **Exercise 54**.

GOAL 1 MULTIPLICATION AND DIVISION EQUATIONS

In this lesson you will study equations that can be solved by multiplying or dividing each side by the same nonzero number.

Remember, when you solve a linear equation your goal is to isolate the variable on one side of the equation. In the last lesson you used the fact that addition and subtraction are inverse operations to solve linear equations. In this lesson you will use the fact that multiplication and division are inverse operations.

TRANSFORMATIONS THAT PRODUCE EQUIVALENT EQUATIONS

	ORIGINAL EQUATION		EQUIVALENT EQUATION
• Multiply *each* side of the equation by the same nonzero number.	$\frac{x}{2} = 3$	Multiply by 2.	$x = 6$
• Divide *each* side of the equation by the same nonzero number.	$4x = 12$	Divide by 4.	$x = 3$

EXAMPLE 1 *Dividing Each Side of an Equation*

Solve $-4x = 1$.

SOLUTION

On the left side of the equation, x is multiplied by -4. To isolate x, you need to undo the multiplication by applying the inverse operation of dividing by -4.

$$-4x = 1 \qquad \text{Write original equation.}$$

$$\frac{-4x}{-4} = \frac{1}{-4} \qquad \text{Divide each side by } -4.$$

$$x = -\frac{1}{4} \qquad \text{Simplify.}$$

▶ The solution is $-\frac{1}{4}$. Check this in the original equation.

✓ CHECK

$$-4x = 1 \qquad \text{Write original equation.}$$

$$(-4)\left(-\frac{1}{4}\right) \stackrel{?}{=} 1 \qquad \text{Substitute } -\frac{1}{4} \text{ for } x.$$

$$1 = 1 \qquad \text{Solution is correct.}$$

EXAMPLE 2 **Multiplying Each Side of an Equation**

Solve $\frac{x}{5} = -30$.

SOLUTION

On the left side of the equation, x is divided by 5. You can isolate x by multiplying each side by 5 to undo the division.

$$\frac{x}{5} = -30 \qquad \text{Write original equation.}$$

$$5\left(\frac{x}{5}\right) = 5(-30) \qquad \text{Multiply each side by 5.}$$

$$x = -150 \qquad \text{Simplify.}$$

· · · · · · · · ·

STUDENT HELP

↳ **Look Back** For help with reciprocals, see page 108.

When you solve an equation with a fractional coefficient, such as $10 = -\frac{2}{3}m$, you can isolate the variable by multiplying by the reciprocal of the fraction.

EXAMPLE 3 **Multiplying Each Side by a Reciprocal**

Solve $10 = -\frac{2}{3}m$.

SOLUTION

$$10 = -\frac{2}{3}m \qquad \text{Write original equation.}$$

$$\left(-\frac{3}{2}\right)10 = \left(-\frac{3}{2}\right)\left(-\frac{2}{3}m\right) \qquad \text{Multiply each side by } -\frac{3}{2}.$$

$$-15 = m \qquad \text{Simplify.}$$

· · · · · · · · ·

The transformations used to isolate the variable in Lessons 3.1 and 3.2 are based on rules of algebra called **properties of equality**.

CONCEPT SUMMARY   **PROPERTIES OF EQUALITY**

ADDITION PROPERTY OF EQUALITY	If $a = b$, then $a + c = b + c$.
SUBTRACTION PROPERTY OF EQUALITY	If $a = b$, then $a - c = b - c$.
MULTIPLICATION PROPERTY OF EQUALITY	If $a = b$, then $ca = cb$.
DIVISION PROPERTY OF EQUALITY	If $a = b$ and $c \neq 0$, then $\frac{a}{c} = \frac{b}{c}$.

You have been using these properties to keep equations in balance as you solve them. For instance, in Example 2 you used the multiplication property of equality when you multiplied each side by 5.

GOAL 2 SOLVING REAL-LIFE PROBLEMS

EXAMPLE 4 Modeling a Real-Life Problem

RESTORING MOVIES A single picture on a roll of movie film is called a frame. Motion picture studios try to save some older films from decay by cleaning and restoring the film frame by frame. This process is very expensive and time-consuming.

a. The usual rate for taking and projecting professional movies is 24 frames per second. Find the total number of frames in a movie that is 90 minutes long.

b. If a worker can restore 8 frames per hour, how many hours of work are needed to restore all of the frames in a 90-minute movie?

SOLUTION

a. Let x = the total number of frames in the movie. To find the total number of seconds in the movie, multiply 90 · 60 because each minute is 60 seconds.

$$\frac{\text{Total number of frames in the movie}}{\text{Total number of seconds in the movie}} = \text{Number of frames per second}$$

$$\frac{x}{5400} = 24$$

▶ The solution is x = 129,600, so a 90-minute movie has 129,600 frames.

b. Let y = the number of hours of work and use the result from part (a).

$$\begin{array}{c}\textbf{Number of frames} \\ \textbf{restored per hour}\end{array} \cdot \begin{array}{c}\textbf{Number of} \\ \textbf{hours of work}\end{array} = \begin{array}{c}\textbf{Total number of} \\ \textbf{frames in the movie}\end{array}$$

$$8 \cdot y = 129{,}600$$

▶ The solution is y = 16,200, so 16,200 hours of work are needed.

. . . .

You can model some real-life situations with an equation that sets two *ratios* equal. If a and b are two quantities measured in the *same* units, then the **ratio of a to b** is $\frac{a}{b}$.

Two triangles are **similar triangles** if they have equal corresponding angles. It can be shown that this is equivalent to the ratios of the lengths of corresponding sides being equal. Corresponding angles are marked with the same symbol.

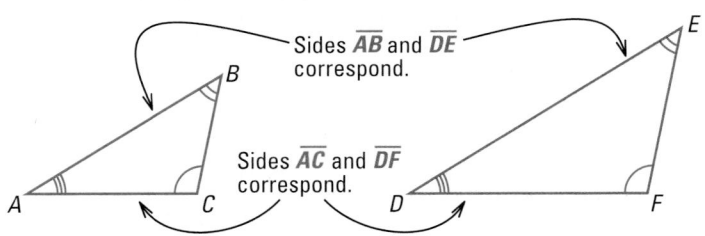

Sides $\overline{AB}$ and $\overline{DE}$ correspond.

Sides $\overline{AC}$ and $\overline{DF}$ correspond.

STUDENT HELP

▶ **Skills Review**
For help with ratios
and rates, see p. 787.

The ratio $\dfrac{\text{length of } \overline{AB}}{\text{length of } \overline{DE}}$ is equal to the ratio $\dfrac{\text{length of } \overline{AC}}{\text{length of } \overline{DF}}$.

MOVIE FRAMES
A motion picture camera takes a series of separate pictures as frames. These are projected in rapid sequence when the movie is shown.

EXAMPLE 5 *Solving Problems with Similar Triangles*

GEOMETRY CONNECTION The two triangles are similar. What is the length of side $\overline{AB}$?

SOLUTION

Set up equal ratios to find the unknown side length.

PROBLEM SOLVING STRATEGY

VERBAL MODEL

$$\frac{\boxed{\text{Length of } \overline{AB}}}{\boxed{\text{Length of } \overline{DE}}} = \frac{\boxed{\text{Length of } \overline{BC}}}{\boxed{\text{Length of } \overline{EF}}}$$

LABELS

Length of $\overline{AB} = \boxed{x}$ (inches)

Length of $\overline{DE} = \mathbf{7}$ (inches)

Length of $\overline{BC} = \mathbf{10}$ (inches)

Length of $\overline{EF} = \mathbf{5}$ (inches)

ALGEBRAIC MODEL

$$\frac{x}{7} = \frac{10}{5}$$ Write algebraic model.

$$7\left(\frac{x}{7}\right) = 7\left(\frac{10}{5}\right)$$ Multiply each side by 7.

$$x = 14$$ Simplify.

▶ The length of $\overline{AB}$ is 14 inches.

GUIDED PRACTICE

Vocabulary Check ✓

1. Name two pairs of inverse operations.

Concept Check ✓

2. Describe six ways to transform an equation into an equivalent equation.

3. What is the first step you would use to solve each equation in Exercises 4–7?

Skill Check ✓

Solve the equation.

4. $6x = 18$
5. $\dfrac{y}{4} = 8$
6. $\dfrac{r}{-5} = 20$
7. $\dfrac{5}{6}a = -10$

8. $-7b = -4$
9. $-3x = 5$
10. $-\dfrac{3}{8}t = -6$
11. $\dfrac{1}{7}x = \dfrac{5}{7}$

12. 🌎 **CAR TRIPS** Write and solve an equation to find your average speed on a trip from St. Louis to Dallas. You drove 630 miles in $10\frac{1}{2}$ hours.

13. The two triangles are similar triangles. Write and solve an equation to find the unknown side length.

PRACTICE AND APPLICATIONS

STUDENT HELP

→ **Extra Practice**
to help you master
skills is on p. 799.

STATING INVERSES State the inverse operation.

14. Divide by 6.
15. Multiply by -2.
16. Divide by -4.

17. Multiply by $\frac{2}{3}$.
18. Multiply by $-\frac{9}{4}$.
19. Divide by $-\frac{4}{3}$.

EQUIVALENT EQUATIONS Tell whether the equations are equivalent.

20. $-4x = 44$ and $x = 11$
21. $21x = 7$ and $x = 3$

22. $\frac{x}{10} = -4$ and $x = -40$
23. $\frac{2}{3}x = 24$ and $x = 16$

SOLVING EQUATIONS Solve the equation.

24. $10x = 110$
25. $-21m = 42$
26. $18 = -2a$

27. $30b = 5$
28. $-4n = -24$
29. $288 = 16t$

30. $7r = -56$
31. $8x = 3$
32. $-10x = -9$

33. $\frac{y}{7} = 12$
34. $\frac{z}{2} = -5$
35. $\frac{1}{2}x = -20$

36. $\frac{1}{3}y = 82$
37. $\frac{m}{-4} = -\frac{3}{4}$
38. $0 = \frac{4}{5}d$

39. $-\frac{4}{5}x = 72$
40. $-\frac{1}{5}y = -6$
41. $\frac{t}{-2} = \frac{1}{2}$

42. $-\frac{2}{3}t = -16$
43. $\frac{3}{4}z = -5\frac{1}{2}$
44. $\frac{1}{3}y = 5\frac{2}{3}$

45. $\frac{3}{4}t = |-15|$
46. $-\frac{1}{2}b = -|-8|$
47. $-6y = -|27|$

NEWSPAPERS
Each week the
average household reads
five pounds of newspapers.
▶ Source: Newspaper
Association of America

48. 🌐 **BUNDLING NEWSPAPERS** You are loading a large pile of newspapers onto a truck. You divide the pile into four equal-size bundles. You find that one bundle weighs 37 pounds. You want to find the weight x of the original pile. Which equation models the situation? Solve the correct equation.

A. $\frac{x}{4} = 37$ **B.** $4x = 37$

🌐 **MODELING REAL-LIFE PROBLEMS** In Exercises 49–53, write and solve an equation to answer the question.

49. Each household in the United States receives about 676 pieces of junk mail per year. About how many pieces does a household receive per week?

50. About one eighth of the population is left-handed. In what size school would you expect to find about 50 left-handed students?

51. You ate three of the eight pizza slices and you paid $3.30 as your share of the cost. How much did the whole pizza cost?

52. It takes 45 peanuts to make one ounce of peanut butter. How many peanuts will be needed to make a 12-ounce jar of peanut butter?

53. A 10,000-square-foot pizza was created on October 11, 1987. This pie was eaten by about 30,000 people. On average, how much did each person eat?

STUDENT HELP

→ HOMEWORK HELP
Example 1: Exs. 14–47
Example 2: Exs. 14–47
Example 3: Exs. 14–47
Example 4: Exs. 48–54
Example 5: Exs. 58–59

REAL LIFE **THUNDER-
STORMS** You see
a flash of lightning instantly
since light travels so rapidly
(186,000 miles/second). You
hear the thunder later since
sound takes about 5 seconds
to travel a mile near the
ground.

54. 🌐 **THUNDERSTORMS** You can tell how many miles you are from a thunderstorm by counting the seconds between seeing the lightning and hearing the thunder, and then dividing by five. How many seconds would you count for a thunderstorm nine miles away?

55. CRITICAL THINKING Look back at Example 4. For each situation, write a different model than the one shown. The solutions should stay the same.

56. 🌐 **GARDENS** A homeowner is installing a fence around the garden at the right. The garden has a perimeter of 216 feet. Write and solve an equation to find the garden's dimensions.

57. 🌐 **BALD EAGLES** On page 129 you learned that bald eagles fly up to 30 miles per hour and dive at speeds up to 100 miles per hour. Using this information, write and solve an equation to answer each question.

   a. What is the least amount of time that an eagle could take to fly 6 miles?

   b. An eagle a mile above the water spots a fish. What is the shortest time it would take the eagle to dive for the fish? Express your answer in seconds.

GEOMETRY ▸ **CONNECTION** In Exercises 58 and 59, the two triangles are similar. Write and solve an equation to find the length of the side marked *x*.

58.

59.

🌐 **COOKING** In Exercises 60 and 61, use the recipe shown below.

60. You have only 3 cups of rice, so you decrease the recipe. To find the amount of each ingredient, you can write an equation that sets two ratios equal. For the rice you can use the ratio $\frac{3 \text{ cups}}{4 \text{ cups}} = \frac{3}{4}$ that compares the reduced amount to the original amount.

Choose and solve the equation you can use to find the number of teaspoons of soy sauce.

A. $\frac{3}{4} = \frac{2}{x}$ **B.** $\frac{3}{4} = \frac{x}{2}$

FRIED RICE
1 tablespoon vegetable oil
1/2 cup chopped bamboo shoots
1/2 cup chopped mushrooms
1/4 cup chopped scallions
4 cups cooked rice
1 cup cooked diced chicken
1/2 cup chicken broth
2 teaspoons soy sauce

61. You have 5 cups of rice, so you increase the recipe. Write and solve an equation to find the amount of chicken.

62. MULTIPLE CHOICE What is the first step you would use to solve $\frac{1}{4} = -7x$?

(A) Divide by 4. **(B)** Multiply by 4.

(C) Multiply by -7. **(D)** Divide by -7.

63. MULTIPLE CHOICE Solve $-\frac{5}{7}x = -2$.

(A) $\frac{14}{5}$ **(B)** $-\frac{14}{5}$ **(C)** $\frac{10}{7}$ **(D)** $\frac{7}{5}$

64. MULTIPLE CHOICE Which of the triangles below are similar triangles?

  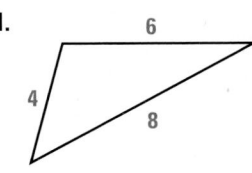

I. II. III.

(A) I and II **(B)** I and III **(C)** II and III **(D)** None

★ Challenge

65. 🌐 **ATTENDANCE** In 1997, the average home attendance at New York Yankees' baseball games was a little more than 150% of the average home attendance at Anaheim Angels' baseball games. The average home attendance at New York Yankees' baseball games was about 33,000. Write and solve an equation to estimate the average home attendance at Anaheim Angels' baseball games. ▶ Source: *ESPN 1998 Information Please® Sports Almanac*

EXTRA CHALLENGE
www.mcdougallittell.com

MIXED REVIEW

TRANSLATING VERBAL SENTENCES Write the verbal sentence as an equation. (Review 1.5 for 3.3)

66. The sum of 18 and five times a number is 108.

67. Twelve less than nine times a number is 60.

68. Five more than two thirds of a number is 11.

69. Eleven is two fifths of the quantity n decreased by thirteen.

SIMPLIFYING EXPRESSIONS Simplify the expression. (Review 2.6 for 3.3)

70. $15 - 8x + 12$ **71.** $4y - 9 + 3y$ **72.** $(x + 8)(-2) - 36$

73. $5(y + 3) + 7y$ **74.** $12x - (x - 2)(2)$ **75.** $-25y - 6(-y - 9)$

SOLVING EQUATIONS Solve the equation. (Review 3.1)

76. $4 + y = 12$ **77.** $t - 2 = 1$ **78.** $5 - (-t) = 14$

79. $x - 2 = 28$ **80.** $19 - x = 37$ **81.** $-9 - (-a) = -2$

82. 🌐 **PHOTOGRAPHY** You take 24 pictures. Seven of the pictures cannot be developed because of bad lighting. Let x represent the number of pictures that can be developed successfully. Which of the following is a correct model for the situation? Solve the correct equation. (Review 3.1)

A. $x + 7 = 24$ **B.** $x - 7 = 24$

3.3 Solving Multi-Step Equations

What you should learn

GOAL 1 Use two or more transformations to solve an equation.

GOAL 2 Use multi-step equations to solve **real-life** problems, such as finding the temperature inside the Earth in **Example 7**.

Why you should learn it

▼ To model and solve **real-life** problems, such as the fountain problem in **Exercise 58**.

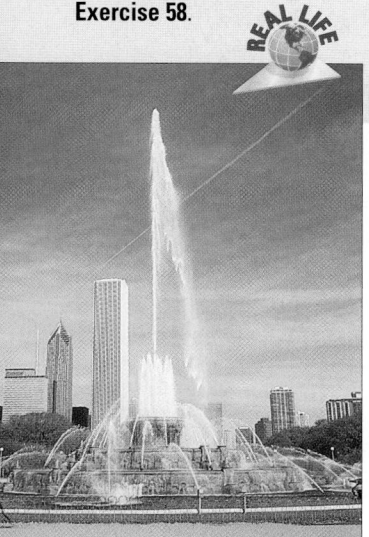

GOAL 1 USING TWO OR MORE TRANSFORMATIONS

Solving a linear equation may require two or more transformations. Here are some guidelines.

- Simplify one or both sides of the equation (if needed).
- Use inverse operations to isolate the variable.

EXAMPLE 1 Solving a Linear Equation

Solve $\frac{1}{3}x + 6 = -8$.

SOLUTION To isolate the variable, undo the addition and then the multiplication.

$\frac{1}{3}x + 6 = -8$	Write original equation.
$\frac{1}{3}x + 6 - 6 = -8 - 6$	Subtract 6 from each side.
$\frac{1}{3}x = -14$	Simplify.
$3\left(\frac{1}{3}x\right) = 3(-14)$	Multiply each side by 3.
$x = -42$	Simplify.

EXAMPLE 2 Combining Like Terms First

Solve $7x - 3x - 8 = 24$.

SOLUTION

$7x - 3x - 8 = 24$	Write original equation.
$4x - 8 = 24$	Combine like terms.
$4x - 8 + 8 = 24 + 8$	Add 8 to each side.
$4x = 32$	Simplify.
$\frac{4x}{4} = \frac{32}{4}$	Divide each side by 4.
$x = 8$	Simplify.

▶ The solution is 8. When you check the solution, substitute 8 for *each x* in the original equation.

EXAMPLE 3 *Using the Distributive Property*

Solve $5x + 3(x + 4) = 28$.

SOLUTION

STUDENT HELP

▸ **Look Back**
For help with the distributive property and combining like terms, see pp. 100–102.

Method 1 Show All Steps

$$5x + 3(x + 4) = 28$$
$$5x + 3x + 12 = 28$$
$$8x + 12 = 28$$
$$8x + 12 - 12 = 28 - 12$$
$$8x = 16$$
$$\frac{8x}{8} = \frac{16}{8}$$
$$x = 2$$

Method 2 Do Some Steps Mentally

$$5x + 3(x + 4) = 28$$
$$5x + 3x + 12 = 28$$
$$8x + 12 = 28$$
$$8x = 16$$
$$x = 2$$

EXAMPLE 4 *Distributing a Negative*

Solve $4x - 3(x - 2) = 21$.

SOLUTION

$4x - 3(x - 2) = 21$	Write original equation.
$4x - 3x + 6 = 21$	Use distributive property.
$x + 6 = 21$	Combine like terms.
$x = 15$	Subtract 6 from each side.

EXAMPLE 5 *Multiplying by a Reciprocal First*

Solve $66 = -\frac{6}{5}(x + 3)$.

SOLUTION

It is easier to solve this equation if you don't distribute $-\frac{6}{5}$.

$66 = -\frac{6}{5}(x + 3)$	Write original equation.
$\left(-\frac{5}{6}\right)(66) = \left(-\frac{5}{6}\right)\left(-\frac{6}{5}\right)(x + 3)$	Multiply by reciprocal of $-\frac{6}{5}$.
$-55 = x + 3$	Simplify.
$-58 = x$	Subtract 3 from each side.

STUDENT HELP

▸ **Study Tip**
Before you apply the distributive property, examine the equation. Although you can distribute in Example 5, multiplying by the reciprocal is easier, because it clears the equation of fractions.

Solving equations systematically is an example of deductive reasoning. Notice how each solution step is based on number properties or properties of equality.

EMERGENCY MEDICAL TECHNICIANS

EMTs quickly evaluate and respond to a patient's condition. For instance, quick treatment of hypothermia may prevent heart and breathing rates from becoming dangerously low.

 CAREER LINK
www.mcdougallittell.com

GOAL 2 **SOLVING REAL-LIFE PROBLEMS**

EXAMPLE 6 *Using a Known Formula*

CHECKING VITAL SIGNS A body temperature of 95°F or lower may indicate the medical condition called hypothermia. What temperature in the Celsius scale may indicate hypothermia?

The Fahrenheit and Celsius scales are related by the equation $F = \frac{9}{5}C + 32$.

SOLUTION Use the formula to convert 95°F to Celsius.

$F = \frac{9}{5}C + 32$	Write known formula.
$95 = \frac{9}{5}C + 32$	Substitute 95° for *F*.
$63 = \frac{9}{5}C$	Subtract 32 from each side.
$35 = C$	Multiply by $\frac{5}{9}$, the reciprocal of $\frac{9}{5}$.

▶ A temperature of 35°C or lower may indicate hypothermia.

EXAMPLE 7 *Using a Verbal Model*

SCIENCE CONNECTION The temperature within Earth's crust increases about 30° Celsius for each kilometer of depth beneath the surface. If the temperature at Earth's surface is 24°C, at what depth would you expect the temperature to be 114°C?

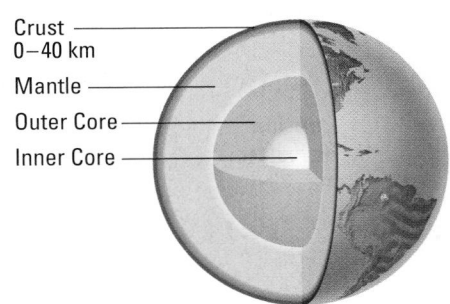

Crust
0–40 km

Mantle

Outer Core

Inner Core

SOLUTION

PROBLEM SOLVING STRATEGY

VERBAL MODEL

Temperature inside Earth	=	Temperature at Earth's surface	+	Rate of temperature increase	·	Depth below surface

LABELS

Temperature inside Earth = **114**   (degrees Celsius)

Temperature at Earth's surface = **24**   (degrees Celsius)

Rate of temperature increase = **30**   (degrees Celsius per kilometer)

Depth below surface = **d**   (kilometers)

ALGEBRAIC MODEL $114 = 24 + 30 \cdot d$

▶ The solution is *d* = 3. The temperature will be 114°C at 3 kilometers deep.

GUIDED PRACTICE

Concept Check ✓

1. **LOGICAL REASONING** Copy the solution steps shown. Then, in the right-hand column, describe the transformation that was used in each step. (Lists of types of transformations are shown on pages 132 and 138.)

Solution Steps	Explanation
$\frac{5x}{2} + 3 = 6$	Original Equation
$\frac{5x}{2} = 3$	_____?_____
$5x = 6$	_____?_____
$x = \frac{6}{5}$	_____?_____

2. For which equations in Exercises 6–8 would you use the distributive property first when solving? Explain.

Skill Check ✓

In Exercises 3–8, solve the equation. Show how to check your solution.

3. $4x + 3 = 11$

4. $\frac{1}{2}x - 9 = 11$

5. $3x - x + 15 = 41$

6. $5(x - 7) = 90$

7. $\frac{3}{4}(x + 6) = 12$

8. $6x - 4(-3x + 2) = 10$

9. 🌐 **SUMMER JOB** You have a summer job running errands for a local business. You earn $5 per day, plus $2 for each errand. Write and solve an equation to find how many errands you need to run to earn $17 in one day.

PRACTICE AND APPLICATIONS

STUDENT HELP

➔ **Extra Practice**
to help you master skills is on p. 799.

CHECKING SOLUTIONS Check whether the given number is a solution of the equation.

10. $9x - 5x - 19 = 21; -10$

11. $\frac{3}{4}x + 1 = -8; -12$

12. $6x - 4(9 - x) = 106; 7$

13. $7x - 15 = -1; -2$

14. $\frac{1}{2}x - 7 = -4; 6$

15. $\frac{x}{4} - 7 = 13; 24$

SOLVING EQUATIONS Solve the equation.

16. $2x + 7 = 15$

17. $3x - 1 = 8$

18. $\frac{x}{3} - 5 = -1$

19. $\frac{x}{2} + 13 = 20$

20. $30 = 16 + \frac{1}{5}x$

21. $6 = 14 - 2x$

STUDENT HELP

➔ **HOMEWORK HELP**
Example 1: Exs. 16–36
Example 2: Exs. 10–40
Example 3: Exs. 16–40
Example 4: Exs. 37–40
Example 5: Exs. 16–36
Example 6: Exs. 57–58
Example 7: Exs. 51–56

22. $7 + \frac{2}{3}x = -1$

23. $3 - \frac{3}{4}x = -6$

24. $22 = 18 - \frac{1}{4}x$

25. $8x - 3x = 10$

26. $-7x + 4x = 9$

27. $x + 5x - 5 = 1$

28. $3x - 7 + x = 5$

29. $3(x - 2) = 18$

30. $12(2 - x) = 6$

31. $\frac{9}{2}(x + 3) = 27$

32. $-\frac{4}{9}(2x - 4) = 48$

33. $17 = 2(3x + 1) - x$

34. $\frac{4x}{3} + 3 = 23$

35. $-10 = 4 - \frac{7x}{4}$

36. $-10 = \frac{1}{2}x + x$

SOLVING EQUATIONS Solve the equation.

37. $5m - (4m - 1) = -12$

38. $55x - 3(9x + 12) = -64$

39. $22x + 2(3x + 5) = 66$

40. $9x - 5(3x - 12) = 30$

ERROR ANALYSIS In Exercises 41–43, find and correct the error.

41.

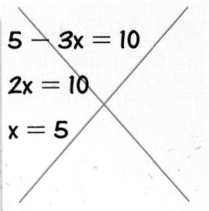

$2(x - 3) = 5$
$2x - 3 = 5$
$2x = 8$
$x = 4$

42.

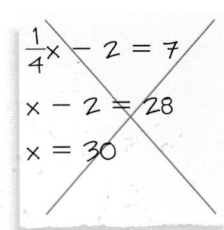

$5 - 3x = 10$
$2x = 10$
$x = 5$

43.

$\frac{1}{4}x - 2 = 7$
$x - 2 = 28$
$x = 30$

44. LOGICAL REASONING Solve the equation $-6x + 3(4x - 1) = 9$. Organize your work into two columns. In the left-hand column show the solution steps. In the right-hand column explain the transformation you used in each step.

45. *Writing* Solve the equation $\frac{1}{9}x + 1 = 4$ by following each sequence of steps described in parts (a) and (b). Which method do you prefer? Explain.

   a. Multiply and then subtract.   **b.** Subtract and then multiply.

CHOOSING A METHOD In Exercises 46–49, solve the equation two different ways as in Exercise 45. Explain which method you prefer and why.

46. $\frac{1}{8}x - 5 = 3$ **47.** $\frac{x}{3} + 6 = -2$ **48.** $-4x - 2 = 4$ **49.** $\frac{2}{3}x + 1 = \frac{1}{3}$

50. CONSECUTIVE INTEGERS *Consecutive integers* are integers that follow each other in order (for example, 5, 6, and 7). You want to find three consecutive integers whose sum is 84.

   a. Why does the equation $n + (n + 1) + (n + 2) = 84$ model the situation?

   b. Solve the equation in part (a). Then find the three consecutive integers.

51. FIND THE NUMBERS The sum of three numbers is 123. The second number is 9 less than two times the first number. The third number is 6 more than three times the first number. Find the three numbers.

52. 🌐 **FARMING PROJECT** You have a 90-pound calf you are raising for a 4-H project. You expect the calf to gain 65 pounds per month. In how many months will the animal weigh 1000 pounds?

53. 🌐 **HOURS OF LABOR** The bill (parts and labor) for the repair of a car was $458. The cost of parts was $339. The cost of labor was $34 per hour. Write and solve an equation to find the number of hours of labor.

54. `GEOMETRY` `CONNECTION` In any triangle, the sum of the measures of the angles is 180°. In triangle ABC, $\angle A$ is four times as large as $\angle B$. Angle C measures 20° less than $\angle B$. Find the measure of each angle.

55. 🌐 **STUDENT THEATER** Your school's drama club charges $4 per student for admission to *Our Town*. The club borrowed $400 from parents to pay for costumes, props, and the set. After paying back the parents, the drama club has $100. How many students attended the play?

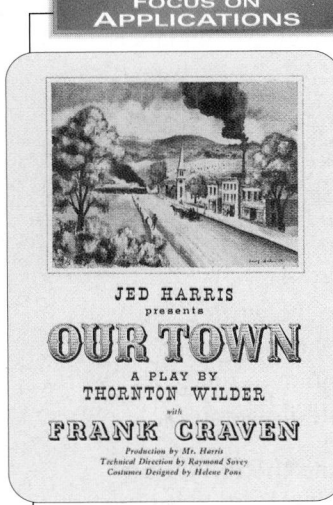

56. 🌐 **HOLIDAY PAY** You earn $9 per hour. On major holidays, such as Thanksgiving, you earn twice as much per hour. You earned a total of $405 for the week including Thanksgiving. Write and solve an equation to find how many hours you worked on Thanksgiving if you worked 35 hours during the rest of the week.

57. 🌐 **FIREFIGHTING** The formula $d = \frac{n}{2} + 26$ relates nozzle pressure n (in pounds per square inch) and the maximum distance the water reaches d (in feet) for a fire hose with a certain size nozzle. How much pressure is needed if such a hose is held 50 feet from a fire? ▶ Source: *Fire Department Hydraulics*

Distance, d

Nozzle pressure, n

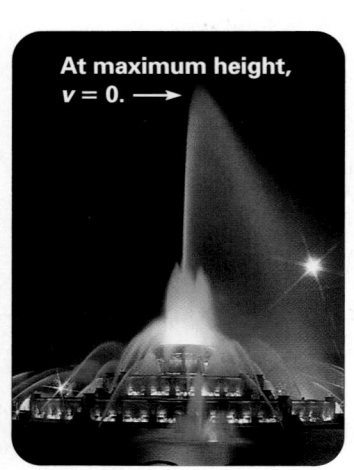

At maximum height, $v = 0$. ⟶

Ex. 58

58. 🌐 **HEIGHT OF A FOUNTAIN** Neglecting air resistance, the upward velocity of the water in the stream of a particular fountain is given by the formula $v = -32t + 28$, where t is the number of seconds after the water leaves the fountain. While going upward, the water slows down until, at the top of the stream, the water has a velocity of 0 feet per second. How long does it take a droplet of water to reach the maximum height?

59. 🌐 **PHOTOCOPYING** An office needs 20 copies of a 420-page report. One photocopier can copy 1800 pages per hour. Another copier is faster and can copy 2400 pages per hour. To find the time it would take the two copiers together to complete the project, you can use this verbal model. Assign labels to the model to form an equation. Then solve the equation.

| Rate of first machine | · | Time to complete | + | Rate of second machine | · | Time to complete | = | Total pages |

60. **CRITICAL THINKING** Explain how you can use unit analysis to check that the verbal model in Exercise 59 is correct.

61. 🌐 **DATA ENTRY** A publishing company needs to enter 910 pages it received from an author into its word processing system, so the writing can be edited and formatted. One person can type 15 pages per hour. Another person can type 20 pages per hour. Write and solve an equation to find how long it will take the two people working together to enter all of the pages.

REPRESENTING COIN PROBLEMS In Exercises 62 and 63, use the following information. A person has quarters, dimes, and nickels with a total value of 500 cents ($5.00). The number of nickels is twice the number of quarters. The number of dimes is four less than the number of quarters.

62. Explain why the expression $5(2q)$ represents the value of the nickels if q represents the number of quarters. How can you simplify the expression?

63. Write and solve an equation to find the number of each type of coin.

64. **COIN PROBLEM** There are 4 times as many nickels as dimes in a coin bank. The coins have a total value of 600 cents ($6.00). Find the number of nickels.

65. MULTI-STEP PROBLEM Two student volunteers are stuffing envelopes for a local food pantry. The mailing will be sent to 560 possible contributors. Luis can stuff 160 envelopes per hour and Mei can stuff 120 envelopes per hour.

  a. Working alone, what fraction of the job can Luis complete in one hour? in t hours? Write the fraction in lowest terms.

  b. Working alone, what fraction of the job can Mei complete in t hours?

  c. Write an expression for the fraction of the job that Luis and Mei can complete in t hours if they work together.

  d. CRITICAL THINKING To find how long it will take Luis and Mei to complete the job if they work together, you can set the expression you wrote in part (c) equal to 1 and solve for t. Explain why this will work.

  e. How long will it take Luis and Mei to complete the job if they work together? Check your solution.

★ **Challenge**

66. ODD INTEGERS Consecutive odd integers are odd integers listed in order such as 5, 7, and 9. Find three consecutive odd integers whose sum is 111. Are there three consecutive odd integers whose sum is 1111? Explain.

MIXED REVIEW

WRITING POWERS Write the expression in exponential form. (Review 1.2)

67. four squared   **68.** b cubed   **69.** $(a)(a)(a)(a)(a)(a)$

70. 10   **71.** $2 \cdot 2 \cdot 2 \cdot 2$ **72.** $3x \cdot 3x \cdot 3x \cdot 3x \cdot 3x$

EVALUATING EXPRESSIONS Evaluate the expression. (Review 1.3, 2.7)

73. $5 + 8 - 3$ **74.** $3^2 \cdot 4 + 8$ **75.** $16.9 - 1.5(1.8 + 0.2)$

76. $5 \cdot (12 - 4) + 7$ **77.** $-6 \div 3 - 4 \cdot 5$ **78.** $10 - [4.3 + 2(6.4 \div 8)]$

79. $\dfrac{-5 \cdot 4}{3 - 7^2 + 6}$ **80.** $2 - 8 \div \dfrac{-2}{3}$ **81.** $\dfrac{(3 - 6)^2 + 6}{-5}$

82. 🚲 **BICYCLING** If you ride a bicycle 5 miles per hour, how many miles will you ride in 45 minutes? (Review 1.1)

🌎 **PROFIT** In Exercises 83–85, use the following information. You open a snack stand at a fair. The income and expenses (in dollars) for selling each type of food are shown in the matrices. (Review 2.4)

	Day 1	Income	Expenses		Day 2	Income	Expenses
	Hamburgers	72	14		Hamburgers	62	10
	Hot dogs	85	18		Hot dogs	52	11
	Tacos	46	19		Tacos	72	26

83. What were your total income and expenses for selling each type of food for the two days of the fair?

84. Which type of food had the largest profit?

85. Which type of food had the smallest profit?

Solve the equation. (Lessons 3.1, 3.2, and 3.3)

1. $8 - y = -9$ **2.** $x + \dfrac{1}{2} = 5$ **3.** $\left|-14\right| + z = 12$

4. $8b = 5$ **5.** $\dfrac{3}{4}q = 24$ **6.** $\dfrac{n}{-8} = -\dfrac{3}{8}$

7. $\dfrac{x}{5} + 10 = \dfrac{4}{5}$ **8.** $\dfrac{1}{4}(y + 8) = 5$ **9.** $25x - 4(4x + 6) = -69$

10. 🌐 **HISTORY TEST** You take a history test that has 100 regular points and 8 bonus points. You receive a total score of 91, which includes 4 bonus points. Write and solve an equation to find the score you would have had without the bonus points. (Lesson 3.1)

11. 🌐 **TEMPERATURE** The temperature is 72°F. What is the temperature in degrees Celsius? $\left(\text{Use the equation } F = \dfrac{9}{5}C + 32.\right)$ (Lesson 3.3)

MATH & History

History of Stairs

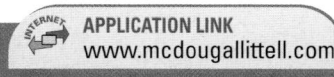
APPLICATION LINK
www.mcdougallittell.com

THEN   **IN 1675,** François Blondel, director of France's Royal Academy of Architecture, decided upon a formula for building stairs to accommodate the human gait. He came up with $2R + T = 24$ inches (25.5 in today's inches) where $R =$ riser height and $T =$ tread width.

NOW   **IN THE 1990S,** a group of building code officials adopted the "7-11" rule which states that a riser should be no taller than 7 inches and no shorter than 4 inches, with a minimum tread width of 11 inches.

In Exercises 1 and 2 you will compare a traditional staircase with an 8.25-inch riser and a 9-inch tread and a staircase built using the 7-11 rule that has a 7-inch riser and an 11-inch tread. Each of the staircases has 12 steps.

1. Sketch and label an individual stair for each staircase.

2. Sketch and label each staircase. Which staircase is steeper? Which design will require more stairs if both need to reach the same height?

First escalators installed

1900

900–1200

The pyramid *El Castillo* in Chichen Itza, Mexico

Now

Modern escalator in New York City

▶ ACTIVITY 3.4

Developing Concepts

Modeling Equations with Variables on Both Sides

GROUP ACTIVITY
Work with a partner.

MATERIALS
algebra tiles

▶ **QUESTION** How can you use algebra tiles to solve an equation with a variable on both the left side and the right side of the equation?

▶ EXPLORING THE CONCEPT

1 Use algebra tiles to model the equation $4x + 5 = 2x + 9$.

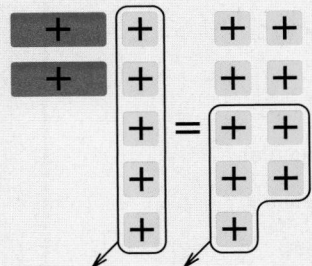

2 You want to have x-tiles on only one side of the equation, so subtract 2 x-tiles from each side. Write the new equation.

3 To isolate the x-tiles, subtract five 1-tiles from each side. Write the new equation.

4 You know the value of $2x$. To find the value of x, split the tiles on each side of the equation in half to get $x = \underline{\ ?\ }$.

▶ DRAWING CONCLUSIONS

Use algebra tiles to model and solve the equation.

1. $4x + 4 = 3x + 7$ **2.** $2x + 3 = 6 + x$

3. $6x + 5 = 3x + 14$ **4.** $5x + 2 = 10 + x$

5. $8x + 3 = 7x + 3$ **6.** $x + 9 = 1 + 3x$

7. The model at the left shows the solution of an equation. Copy the model. Write the solution step and an explanation of the step beside each part of the model.

8. Look back at **Step 2**. To get x-tiles on only one side of the equation you can subtract 4 x-tiles from each side instead of subtracting 2 x-tiles from each side. How is the result different? Which method do you prefer? Why?

3.4
Solving Equations with Variables on Both Sides

What you should learn

GOAL 1 Collect variables on one side of an equation.

GOAL 2 Use equations to solve **real-life** problems such as renting video games in **Example 5.**

Why you should learn it

▼ To solve **real-life** problems, such as deciding whether to join a rock-climbing gym in **Exercise 46.**

GOAL 1 COLLECTING VARIABLES ON ONE SIDE

Some equations have variables on both sides. To solve such equations, you may first collect the variable terms on the side with the *greater* variable coefficient.

EXAMPLE 1 *Collect Variables on Left Side*

Solve $7x + 19 = -2x + 55$.

SOLUTION Look at the coefficients of the x-terms. Since 7 is greater than -2, collect the x-terms on the left side.

$7x + 19 = -2x + 55$	Write original equation.
$7x + 19 + 2x = -2x + 55 + 2x$	Add **2x** to each side.
$9x + 19 = 55$	Simplify.
$9x + 19 - 19 = 55 - 19$	Subtract 19 from each side.
$9x = 36$	Simplify.
$\dfrac{9x}{9} = \dfrac{36}{9}$	Divide each side by 9.
$x = 4$	Simplify.

✓ **CHECK**

$7x + 19 = -2x + 55$	Write original equation.
$7(4) + 19 \stackrel{?}{=} -2(4) + 55$	Substitute 4 for each x.
$47 = 47$	Solution is correct.

EXAMPLE 2 *Collect Variables on Right Side*

Solve $80 - 9y = 6y$.

SOLUTION Look at the coefficients of the y-terms. Think of $80 - 9y$ as $80 + (-9y)$. Since 6 is greater than -9, collect the y-terms on the right side.

$80 - 9y = 6y$	Write original equation.
$80 - 9y + 9y = 6y + 9y$	Add **9y** to each side.
$80 = 15y$	Simplify.
$\dfrac{80}{15} = \dfrac{15y}{15}$	Divide each side by 15.
$\dfrac{16}{3} = y$	Simplify.

STUDENT HELP

↳ **Look Back**
For help with terms of an expression, see page 80.

Linear equations do not always have one solution. An **identity** is an equation that is true for all values of the variable. Some linear equations have no solution.

STUDENT HELP

HOMEWORK HELP
Visit our Web site
www.mcdougallittell.com
for extra examples.

EXAMPLE 3 *Many Solutions or No Solution*

Solve the equation.

a. $3(x + 2) = 3x + 6$ **b.** $x + 2 = x + 4$

SOLUTION

a. $3(x + 2) = 3x + 6$	Write original equation.
$3x + 6 = 3x + 6$	Use distributive property.
$6 = 6$	Subtract 3*x* from each side.

▶ All values of x are solutions, because $6 = 6$ is always true. The original equation is an *identity*.

b. $x + 2 = x + 4$	Write original equation.
$2 \neq 4$	Subtract *x* from each side.

▶ The original equation has no solution, because $2 \neq 4$ for any value of x.

EXAMPLE 4 *Solving More Complicated Equations*

Solve the equation.

a. $4(1 - x) + 3x = -2(x + 1)$ **b.** $\frac{1}{4}(12x + 16) = 10 - 3(x - 2)$

SOLUTION Simplify the equation before you decide whether to collect the variable terms on the right side or the left side of the equation.

a. $4(1 - x) + 3x = -2(x + 1)$	Write original equation.
$4 - 4x + 3x = -2x - 2$	Use distributive property.
$4 - x = -2x - 2$	Add like terms.
$4 + x = -2$	Add 2*x* to each side.
$x = -6$	Subtract 4 from each side.

b. $\frac{1}{4}(12x + 16) = 10 - 3(x - 2)$	Write original equation.
$3x + 4 = 10 - 3x + 6$	Use distributive property.
$3x + 4 = 16 - 3x$	Simplify.
$6x + 4 = 16$	Add 3*x* to each side.
$6x = 12$	Subtract 4 from each side.
$x = 2$	Divide each side by 6.

STUDENT HELP

▶ **Study Tip**
You can multiply by
the reciprocal first
in part (b) of Example 4,
but distributing the $\frac{1}{4}$ is
easier here. Before you
solve, look to see which
method seems easier.

3.4 *Solving Equations with Variables on Both Sides* **155**

GOAL 2 SOLVING REAL-LIFE PROBLEMS

Membership Fees

EXAMPLE 5 *Using a Verbal Model*

A video store charges $8 to rent a video game for five days. You must be a member to rent from the store, but the membership is free. A video game club in town charges only $3 to rent a game for five days, but membership in the club is $50 per year. Which rental plan is more economical?

SOLUTION

Find the number of rentals for which the two plans would cost the same.

PROBLEM SOLVING STRATEGY

VERBAL MODEL

| Store rental fee | · | Number rented | = | Club rental fee | · | Number rented | + | Club membership fee |

Video store   Video club

LABELS

Store rental fee = **8**   (dollars per game)

Number rented = **x**   (games)

Club rental fee = **3**   (dollars per game)

Club membership fee = **50**   (dollars)

ALGEBRAIC MODEL

$8 \cdot x = 3 \cdot x + 50$ Write algebraic model.

$5x = 50$ Subtract 3x from each side.

$x = 10$ Divide each side by 5.

STUDENT HELP

CAREER LINK
Visit our Web site
www.mcdougallittell.com
for information about
video game designers.

If you rent 10 video games in a year, the cost would be the same at either the store or the club. If you rent more than 10, the club is more economical. If you rent fewer than 10, the store is more economical.

UNIT ANALYSIS Check that *dollars* are the units of the solution.

$$\frac{\text{dollars}}{\text{game}} \cdot \text{games} = \frac{\text{dollars}}{\text{game}} \cdot \text{games} + \text{dollars}$$

✓**CHECK** A table can help you check the result of Example 5.

Number rented	2	4	6	8	10	12	14	16
Cost at store	$16	$32	$48	$64	$80	$96	$112	$128
Cost at club	$56	$62	$68	$74	$80	$86	$92	$98

Store is cheaper.   Club is cheaper.

GUIDED PRACTICE

Vocabulary Check ✓   **1.** Is the equation $-2(4 - x) = 2x - 8$ an identity? Explain why or why not.

Concept Check ✓   **2.** Decide if the statement is *true* or *false*. The solution of $x = 2x$ is zero.

3. Solve $9(9 - x) = 4x - 10$. Explain what you are doing at each step.

Skill Check ✓   **Solve the equation if possible. Does the equation have *one solution*, is it an *identity*, or does it have *no solution*?**

4. $2x + 3 = 7x$

5. $12 - 2a = -5a - 9$

6. $x - 2x + 3 = 3 - x$

7. $5x + 24 = 5(x - 5)$

8. $\frac{2}{3}(6c + 3) = 6(c - 3)$

9. $6y - (3y - 6) = 5y - 4$

10. 🌐 **FUNDRAISING** You are making pies to sell at a fundraiser. It costs $3 to make each pie, plus a one-time cost of $20 for a pastry blender and a rolling pin. You plan to sell the pies for $5 each. Which equation should you use to find the number of pies you need to sell to break even?

A. $3x = 20 + 5x$

B. $3x + 20 = 5x$

C. $3x - 20 = 5x$

D. $20 - 5x = 3x$

11. Find the number of pies you need to sell to break even in Exercise 10.

PRACTICE AND APPLICATIONS

STUDENT HELP

▶ **Extra Practice**
to help you master
skills is on p. 799.

WRITING Solve the equation and describe each step you use.

12. $7 - 4c = 10c$

13. $-8x + 7 = 4x - 5$

14. $x + 2 = 3x - 1$

15. $7(1 - y) = -3(y - 2)$

16. $\frac{1}{5}(10a - 15) = 3 - 2a$

17. $5(y - 2) = -2(12 - 9y) + y$

SOLVING EQUATIONS Solve the equation if possible.

18. $4x + 27 = 3x$

19. $12y + 21 = 9y$

20. $-2m = 16m - 9$

21. $4n = -28n - 3$

22. $12c - 4 = 12c$

23. $-30d + 12 = 18d$

24. $6 - (-5r) = 5r - 3$

25. $6s - 11 = -2s + 5$

26. $12p - 7 = -3p + 8$

27. $-12q + 4 = 8q - 6$

28. $-7 + 4m = 6m - 5$

29. $-7 + 11g = 9 - 5g$

30. $8 - 9t = 21t - 17$

31. $24 - 6r = 6(4 - r)$

32. $3(4 + 4x) = 12x + 12$

33. $-4(x - 3) = -x$

34. $10(-4 + y) = 2y$

35. $8a - 4(-5a - 2) = 12a$

36. $9(b - 4) - 7b = 5(3b - 2)$

37. $-2(6 - 10n) = 10(2n - 6)$

38. $-(8n - 2) = 3 + 10(1 - 3n)$

39. $\frac{1}{2}(12n - 4) = 14 - 10n$

40. $\frac{1}{4}(60 + 16s) = 15 + 4s$

41. $\frac{3}{4}(24 - 8b) = 2(5b + 1)$

STUDENT HELP

▶ **HOMEWORK HELP**
Example 1: Exs. 12–41
Example 2: Exs. 12–41
Example 3: Exs. 18–41
Example 4: Exs. 12–41
Example 5: Exs. 45, 46

3.4 *Solving Equations with Variables on Both Sides* **157**

ERROR ANALYSIS In Exercises 42 and 43, describe the errors.

42.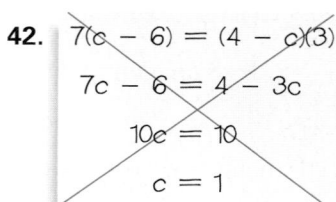
$$7(c - 6) = (4 - c)(3)$$
$$7c - 6 = 4 - 3c$$
$$10c = 10$$
$$c = 1$$

43.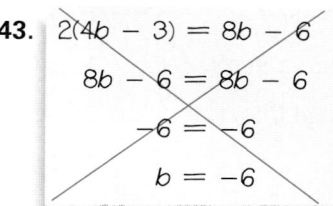
$$2(4b - 3) = 8b - 6$$
$$8b - 6 = 8b - 6$$
$$-6 = -6$$
$$b = -6$$

44. CRITICAL THINKING A student was confused by the results when solving this equation. Explain what the result means.

$$7(y - 2) = -y + 8y - 14$$
$$7y - 14 = 7y - 14$$
$$7y = 7y$$
$$y = y$$

45. 🌐 **COMPUTER TIME** A local computer center charges nonmembers $5 per session to use the media center. If you pay a membership fee of $25, you pay only $3 per session. Write an equation that can help you decide whether to become a member. Then solve the equation and interpret the solution.

46. 🌐 **ROCK CLIMBING** A rock-climbing gym charges nonmembers $16 per day to use the gym and $8 per day for equipment rental. Members pay a yearly fee of $450 for unlimited climbing and $6 per day for equipment rental. Write and solve an equation to find how many times you must use the gym to justify becoming a member.

🌐 **TALL BUILDINGS** In Exercises 47–49, use the following information.
In designing a tall building, many factors affect the height of each story. How the space will be used is important. At the Grand Gateway at Xu Hui in Shanghai, the lowest 7 stories have a combined height of about 126 feet. These stories next to a shopping mall are unusually tall. The building's other 43 stories have a more typical height. If the average height of the other stories had been used for the lowest 7 stories, then the building could have fit about $3\frac{1}{2}$ more stories.

▶ Source: Callison Architecture. (Actual dimensions have been simplified.)

$$\boxed{\begin{array}{c}\text{Combined height of}\\\text{lowest 7 stories}\end{array}} + \boxed{\begin{array}{c}\text{Number of other}\\\text{stories}\end{array}} \cdot \boxed{\begin{array}{c}\text{Average height}\\\text{of other stories}\end{array}} =$$

$$\boxed{\begin{array}{c}\text{Possible number}\\\text{of stories}\end{array}} \cdot \boxed{\begin{array}{c}\text{Average height}\\\text{of other stories}\end{array}}$$

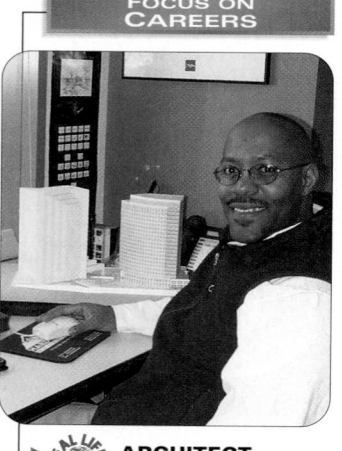
47. Explain why you would use $53\frac{1}{2}$ for the "possible number of stories" in the verbal model.

48. Let h represent the average height of the other stories. Finish assigning labels and write the algebraic model.

49. Solve the equation. Be sure to simplify the answer. About how many feet tall are the stories above the 7th floor?

penthouse {

other stories

lowest 7 stories {

Test Preparation

50. MULTIPLE CHOICE Which equations are equivalent?

    I. $7x - 9 = 7$ **II.** $-9 = 7 - 5x$ **III.** $3(2x - 3) = 7 - x$

    (A) I and III   **(B)** II and III   **(C)** All   **(D)** None

51. MULTIPLE CHOICE Which equation has more than one solution?

    (A) $18y + 13 = 12y - 25$ **(B)** $6y - (3y - 6) = -14 + 3y$

    (C) $-\frac{1}{2}(30x - 18) = 9 - 15x$ **(D)** $\frac{1}{5}(2x - 5) = 3x + 7$

52. MULTIPLE CHOICE Solve $\frac{1}{3}(7x + 5) = 3x - 5$.

    (A) 15   **(B)** -5 **(C)** 10   **(D)** $\frac{-5}{2}$

★ Challenge

SUBSCRIPTIONS **In Exercises 53 and 54, use the table. It shows monthly expenses and income of a magazine for different numbers of subscribers.**

Number of subscribers	50	100	150	200	250	300	350	400
Income	$75	$150	$225	$300	$375	$450	$525	$600
Expenses	$150	$200	$250	$300	$350	$400	$450	$500

53. EXPLAINING A PATTERN Look for patterns in the table. Write an equation that you can use to find how many subscribers the magazine needs for its income to equal its expenses.

EXTRA CHALLENGE
www.mcdougallittell.com

54. Explain how to use the table to check your answer in Exercise 53.

MIXED REVIEW

EQUIVALENTS **Write the percent as a decimal.** (Skills Review, pages 784–785)

55. 28%   **56.** 40%   **57.** 3%   **58.** 19.5%

PERCENT OF A NUMBER **Find the number.** (Skills Review, page 786)

59. 45% of 84   **60.** 7% of 28.5   **61.** 76% of 540

62. 16.3% of 132   **63.** 8% of $928.50   **64.** 5.5% of $74

UNIT ANALYSIS **Find the resulting unit of measure.** (Review 1.1 for 3.5)

65. (dollars per hour) · (hours)   **66.** (years) · (people per year)

67. (miles) ÷ (miles per hour)   **68.** (meters) · (kilometers per meter)

GEOMETRY **The two triangles are similar. Find the length of the side marked x.** (Review 3.2)

69.

70.

3.5

Linear Equations and Problem Solving

What you should learn

GOAL 1 Draw a diagram to help you understand **real-life** problems, such as planning where bicyclists should meet in **Exercise 22**.

GOAL 2 Use tables and graphs to check your answers.

Why you should learn it

▼ To solve **real-life** problems, such as designing a high school yearbook in **Example 1**.

GOAL 1 DRAWING A DIAGRAM

You have learned to use a verbal model to solve real-life problems. Verbal models can be used with other problem solving strategies, such as drawing a diagram.

EXAMPLE 1 *Visualizing a Problem*

YEARBOOK DESIGN A page of your school yearbook is $8\frac{1}{2}$ inches by 11 inches. The left margin is $\frac{3}{4}$ inch and the space to the right of the pictures is $2\frac{7}{8}$ inches. The space between pictures is $\frac{3}{16}$ inch. How wide can each picture be to fit three across the width of the page?

SOLUTION

DRAW A DIAGRAM The diagram shows that the page width is made up of the width of the left margin, the space to the right of the pictures, two spaces between pictures, and three picture widths.

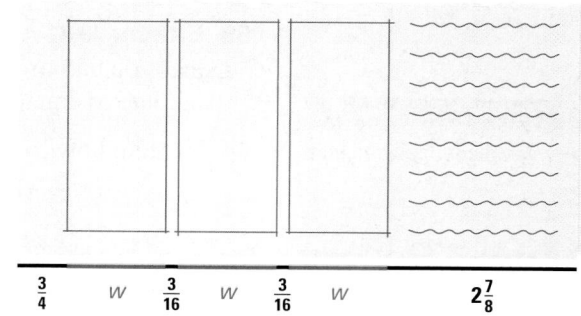

VERBAL MODEL		

$$\boxed{\text{Left margin}} + \boxed{\begin{array}{c}\text{Space to} \\ \text{right of} \\ \text{pictures}\end{array}} + 2 \cdot \boxed{\begin{array}{c}\text{Space} \\ \text{between} \\ \text{pictures}\end{array}} + 3 \cdot \boxed{\begin{array}{c}\text{Picture} \\ \text{width}\end{array}} = \boxed{\begin{array}{c}\text{Page} \\ \text{width}\end{array}}$$

LABELS

$$\text{Left margin} = \frac{3}{4} \qquad \text{(inches)}$$

$$\text{Space to right of pictures} = 2\frac{7}{8} \qquad \text{(inches)}$$

$$\text{Space between pictures} = \frac{3}{16} \qquad \text{(inches)}$$

$$\text{Picture width} = w \qquad \text{(inches)}$$

$$\text{Page width} = 8\frac{1}{2} \qquad \text{(inches)}$$

ALGEBRAIC MODEL

$$\frac{3}{4} + 2\frac{7}{8} + 2 \cdot \frac{3}{16} + 3 \cdot w = 8\frac{1}{2}$$

▶ When you solve for w, you will find that each picture can be $1\frac{1}{2}$ inches wide.

GOAL 2 USING TABLES AND GRAPHS AS CHECKS

Language Study

EXAMPLE 2 *Using a Table as a Check*

At East High School, 579 students take Spanish. This number has been increasing at a rate of about 30 students per year. The number of students taking French is 217 and has been decreasing at a rate of about 2 students per year. At these rates, when will there be three times as many students taking Spanish as taking French?

SOLUTION

First write an expression for the number of students taking each language after some number of years. Then set the expression for students taking Spanish equal to three times the expression for students taking French. Subtraction is used in the expression for students taking French, because there is a decrease.

PROBLEM
SOLVING
STRATEGY

VERBAL MODEL

$$\boxed{\text{Number taking Spanish now}} + \boxed{\text{Rate of increase for Spanish}} \cdot \boxed{\text{Number of years}} =$$

$$3 \cdot \left(\boxed{\text{Number taking French now}} - \boxed{\text{Rate of decrease for French}} \cdot \boxed{\text{Number of years}} \right)$$

LABELS

Number of students taking Spanish now = **579**   (students)

Rate of *increase* for Spanish = **30**   (students per year)

Number of years = **x**   (years)

Number of students taking French now = **217**   (students)

Rate of *decrease* for French = **2**   (students per year)

ALGEBRAIC MODEL

$579 + 30 \cdot x = 3(217 - 2 \cdot x)$ **Write algebraic model.**

$579 + 30x = 651 - 6x$ **Use distributive property.**

$579 + 36x = 651$ **Add 6x to each side.**

$36x = 72$ **Subtract 579 from each side.**

$x = 2$ **Divide each side by 36.**

▶ At these rates, the number of students taking Spanish will be three times the number of students taking French in two years.

✔**CHECK** Use the information in the original problem statement to make a table.

For example, the number of students taking Spanish in Year 1 is 579 + 30 = 609.

Year	0 (now)	1	2
Number taking Spanish	579	609	639
Number taking French	217	215	213
3 · Number taking French	651	645	639

equal

HOMEWORK HELP
Visit our Web site
www.mcdougallittell.com
for extra examples.

EXAMPLE 3 *Using a Graph as a Check*

GAZELLE AND CHEETAH A gazelle can run 73 feet per second for several minutes. A cheetah can run faster (88 feet per second) but can only sustain its top speed for about 20 seconds before it is worn out. How far away from the cheetah does the gazelle need to stay for it to be safe?

SOLUTION

You can use a diagram to picture the situation. If the gazelle is too far away for the cheetah to catch it within 20 seconds, the gazelle is probably safe.

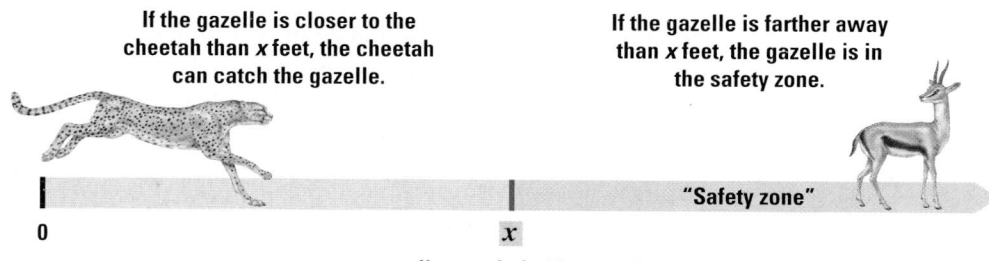

If the gazelle is closer to the cheetah than *x* feet, the cheetah can catch the gazelle.

If the gazelle is farther away than *x* feet, the gazelle is in the safety zone.

"Safety zone"

0   *x*

gazelle caught in 20 seconds

To find the "safety zone," you can first find the starting distance for which the cheetah reaches the gazelle in 20 seconds.

To find the distance each animal runs in 20 seconds, use the formula $d = rt$.

PROBLEM SOLVING STRATEGY

VERBAL MODEL	$\begin{array}{c}\textbf{Distance}\\\textbf{gazelle runs}\\\textbf{in 20 sec}\end{array}$	$+$	$\begin{array}{c}\textbf{Gazelle's}\\\textbf{starting distance}\\\textbf{from cheetah}\end{array}$	$=$	$\begin{array}{c}\textbf{Distance}\\\textbf{cheetah}\\\textbf{runs in 20 sec}\end{array}$

LABELS
Gazelle's distance = **73 · 20**   (feet)

Gazelle's starting distance from cheetah = x (feet)

Cheetah's distance = **88 · 20**   (feet)

ALGEBRAIC MODEL
$$73 \cdot 20 + \boxed{x} = 88 \cdot 20$$

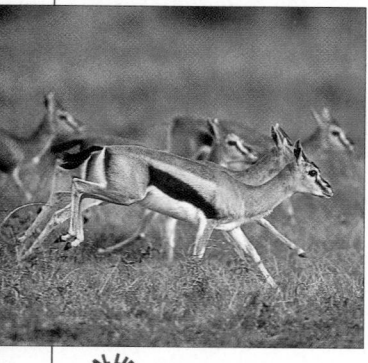

▶ You find that $x = 300$, so the gazelle needs to stay more than 300 feet away from the cheetah to be safe.

✓ **CHECK** You can use a table or a graph to check your answer. A graph helps you see the relationships. To make a graph, first make a table and then plot the points. You can just find and mark the points for every 5 seconds.

Gazelle and Cheetah

Gazelle starting at 300 feet from cheetah is caught in 20 seconds.

GAZELLES seem to have an instinct for the distance they must keep from predators. They usually will not run from a prowling cheetah until it enters their "safety zone."

APPLICATION LINK
www.mcdougallittell.com

GUIDED PRACTICE

Concept Check ✓

1. 🌐 **YEARBOOK DESIGN** In Example 1, the top and bottom margins are each $\frac{7}{8}$ inch. There are 5 rows of pictures, with $\frac{3}{16}$ inch of vertical space between pictures. Draw a diagram and label all the heights on your diagram. Then write and solve an equation to find the height of each picture.

2. Show how unit analysis can help you check the verbal model for Example 3.

Skill Check ✓

🌐 **DISTANCE PROBLEM** **In Exercises 3–5, use the following problem.**
You and your friend are each driving 379 miles from Los Angeles to San Francisco. Your friend leaves first, driving 52 miles per hour. She is 32 miles from Los Angeles when you leave, driving 60 miles per hour. How far do each of you drive before you are side by side? Use the following verbal model.

$$\boxed{\begin{array}{c}\text{Rate your}\\\text{friend is}\\\text{driving}\end{array}} \cdot \boxed{\begin{array}{c}\text{Time after}\\\text{you start}\\\text{driving}\end{array}} + \boxed{\begin{array}{c}\text{Friend's distance}\\\text{when you leave}\end{array}} = \boxed{\begin{array}{c}\text{Rate}\\\text{you are}\\\text{driving}\end{array}} \cdot \boxed{\begin{array}{c}\text{Time after}\\\text{you start}\\\text{driving}\end{array}}$$

3. Assign labels to each part of the verbal model. Use the labels to translate the verbal model into an algebraic model.

4. Solve the equation. Interpret your solution. How far do each of you drive before you are side by side?

5. Make a table or a graph to check your solution.

PRACTICE AND APPLICATIONS

> **STUDENT HELP**

▶ **Extra Practice**
to help you master
skills is on p. 799.

🌐 **PACKAGE SIZE** **In Exercises 6–8, use this U.S. postal regulation: a rectangular package can have a combined length and *girth* of 108 inches. Suppose a package that is 36 inches long and as wide as it is high just meets the regulation.**

← **Girth** is the distance around the end of the package.

6. **USING A DIAGRAM** Which diagram do you find most helpful for understanding the relationships in the problem? Explain.

A.

B.

C.

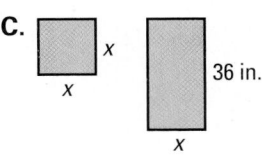

> **STUDENT HELP**

▶ **HOMEWORK HELP**
Example 1: Exs. 6–7,
14–16
Example 2: Exs. 8–12,
17–21
Example 3: Exs. 9–13,
17–21

7. **CHOOSING A MODEL** Choose the equation you would use to find the width of the package. Then find its width.

   A. $x + 36 = 108$ **B.** $2x + 36 = 108$ **C.** $4x + 36 = 108$

8. **MAKING A TABLE** Make a table showing possible dimensions, girth, and combined length and girth for a "package that is 36 inches long and as wide as it is high." Which package in your table just meets the postal regulation?

UNIT ANALYSIS **In Exercises 9–12, find the resulting unit of measure.**

9. (hours per day) • (days)　　10. (feet) ÷ (minute)

11. (inches) ÷ (inches per foot)　　12. (miles per hour) • (hours per minute)

13. **A VISUAL CHECK** Use the graph to check the answer to the problem below. Is the solution correct? Explain.

You have \$320 and save \$10 each week. Your brother has \$445 and spends his income, plus \$15 of his savings each week. When will you and your brother have the same amount in savings?

$$320 + 10t = 445 - 15t$$
$$320 = 445 - 5t$$
$$-125 = -5t$$
$$25 = t \quad \text{(in 25 weeks)}$$

Comparing Savings

Your brother

You

Dollars in savings: 460, 440, 420, 400, 380, 360, 340, 320, 300, 0

Time (weeks): 0 1 2 3 4 5 6 *t*

🌎 **COVER DESIGN** **In Exercises 14–16, you want the cover of a sports media guide to show two photos across its width. The cover is $6\frac{1}{2}$ inches wide, and the left and right margins are each $\frac{3}{4}$ inch. The space between the photos is $\frac{1}{2}$ inch. How wide should you make the photos?**

14. Draw a diagram of the cover.

15. Write an equation to model the problem. Use your diagram to help.

16. Solve the equation and answer the question.

17. 🌎 **LANGUAGE CLASSES** At Barton High School, 45 students are taking Japanese. This number has been increasing at a rate of 3 students per year. The number of students taking German is 108 and has been decreasing at a rate of 4 students per year. At these rates, when will the number of students taking Japanese equal the number taking German? Write and solve an equation to answer the question. Check your answer with a table or a graph.

BIOLOGY **CONNECTION** **In Exercises 18–21, use the following information.**

A migrating elephant herd started moving at a rate of 6 miles per hour. One elephant stood still and was left behind. Then this stray elephant sensed danger and began running at a rate of 10 miles per hour to reach the herd. The stray caught up in 5 minutes.

18. How long (in hours) did the stray run to catch up? How far did it run?

19. Find the distance that the herd traveled while the stray ran to catch up. Then write an expression for the total distance the herd traveled. Let *x* represent the distance (in miles) that the herd traveled while the stray elephant stood still.

20. Use the distances you found in Exercises 18 and 19. Write and solve an equation to find how far the herd traveled while the stray stood still.

21. Make a table or a graph to check your answer.

22. MULTI-STEP PROBLEM Two friends are 60 miles apart. They decide to ride their bicycles to meet each other. Sally starts from the college and heads east, riding at a rate of 21 miles per hour. At the same time Teresa starts from the river and heads west, riding at a rate of 15 miles per hour.

a. Draw a diagram showing the college and the river 60 miles apart and the two cyclists riding toward each other.

b. How far does each cyclist ride in *t* hours?

c. When the two cyclists meet, what must be true about the distances they have ridden? Write and solve an equation to find when they meet.

d. CHOOSING A DATA DISPLAY Would a park that is 26 miles west of the river be a good meeting place? Explain. Use a diagram, a table, or a graph to support your answer.

★ **Challenge**

🌍 **RABBIT AND COYOTE**
In Exercises 23–26, use this information. A rabbit is 30 feet from its burrow. It can run 25 feet per second. A coyote that can run 50 feet per second spots the rabbit and starts running toward it.

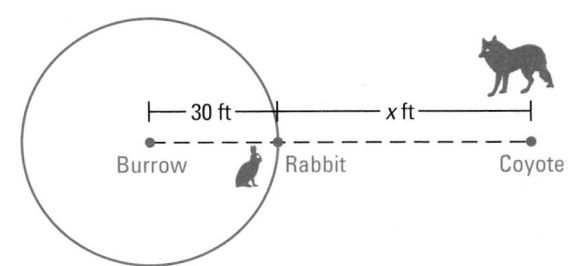

23. Write expressions for the time it will take the rabbit to get to its burrow and for the time it will take the coyote to get to the burrow.

24. Write and solve an equation that relates the two expressions in Exercise 23.

25. CRITICAL THINKING Interpret your results from Exercise 24. Include a description of what happens for different values of *x*.

EXTRA CHALLENGE
www.mcdougallittell.com

26. Use a table or a graph to check your conclusions.

MIXED REVIEW

FRACTIONS, DECIMALS, AND PERCENTS Write as a decimal rounded to the nearest hundredth. Then write as a percent. (Skills Review, pages 784–785)

27. $\frac{3}{11}$ **28.** $\frac{11}{12}$ **29.** $\frac{25}{31}$ **30.** $\frac{100}{201}$

EVALUATING EXPRESSIONS Evaluate the expression. (Review 2.5 and 2.7)

31. $\frac{-6}{q} - 2r$ when $q = 2$ and $r = 11$ **32.** $\frac{3}{5}x - y$ when $x = -25$ and $y = -10$

33. $\frac{x + y}{12}$ when $x = -24$ and $y = 6$ **34.** $\frac{ab}{3a - 10}$ when $a = 8$ and $b = 7$

SOLVING EQUATIONS Solve the equation. (Review 3.3 and 3.4 for 3.6)

35. $18 + \frac{x}{3} = 9$ **36.** $8 = -\frac{2}{3}(2x - 6)$ **37.** $4(2 - n) = 1$

38. $-3y + 14 = -5y$ **39.** $-4a - 3 = 6a + 2$ **40.** $5x - (6 - x) = 2(x - 7)$

3.6

Solving Decimal Equations

What you should learn

GOAL 1 Find exact and approximate solutions of equations that contain decimals.

GOAL 2 Solve **real-life** problems that use decimals such as calculating sales tax in **Example 5**.

Why you should learn it

▼ To solve **real-life** problems, such as finding the expansion gap for a bridge in **Exs. 56–58**.

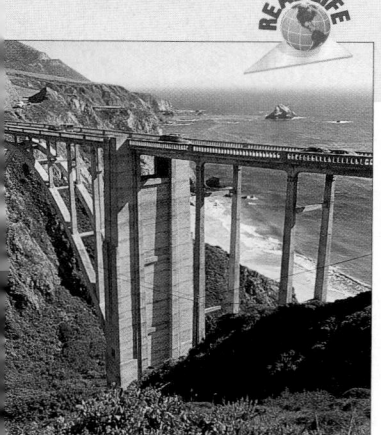

GOAL 1 **SOLVING DECIMAL EQUATIONS**

So far in this chapter you have worked with equations that have exact solutions. In real life, exact solutions are not always practical and you must use rounded solutions. Rounded solutions can lead to **round-off error**, as in Example 1.

EXAMPLE 1 *Rounding for a Practical Answer*

Three people want to share equally in the cost of a pizza. The pizza costs $12.89. You can find each person's share by solving $3x = 12.89$.

$3x = 12.89$	**Write original equation.**
$x = 4.29666. . .$	**Exact answer is a repeating decimal.**
$x \approx 4.30$	**Round to nearest cent.**

▶ The exact answer is not practical, but three times the rounded answer does not correspond to the price of the pizza. It is one cent too much due to round-off error.

EXAMPLE 2 *Rounding for the Final Answer*

Solve $-38x - 39 = 118$. Round to the nearest hundredth.

SOLUTION

$-38x - 39 = 118$	**Write original equation.**
$-38x = 157$	**Add 39 to each side.**
$x = \dfrac{157}{-38}$	**Divide each side by −38.**
$x \approx -4.131578947$	**Use a calculator.**
$x \approx -4.13$	**Round to nearest hundredth.**

▶ The solution is approximately -4.13.

✓**CHECK** When you substitute a rounded answer into the original equation, the two sides of the equation may not be exactly equal, but they should be almost equal.

$-38x - 39 = 118$	**Write original equation.**
$-38(-\mathbf{4.13}) - 39 \overset{?}{=} 118$	**Substitute −4.13 for x.**
$117.94 \approx 118$	**Rounded answer is reasonable.**

EXAMPLE 3   *Original Equation Involving Decimals*

Solve $3.58x - 37.40 = 0.23x + 8.32$. Round to the nearest hundredth.

SOLUTION

Use the same methods you learned for solving equations without decimals.

$3.58x - 37.40 = 0.23x + 8.32$	**Write original equation.**
$3.35x - 37.40 = 8.32$	**Subtract 0.23x from each side.**
$3.35x = 45.72$	**Add 37.40 to each side.**
$x = \dfrac{45.72}{3.35}$	**Divide each side by 3.35.**
$x \approx 13.64776119$	**Use a calculator.**
$x \approx 13.65$	**Round to nearest hundredth.**

▶ The solution is approximately 13.65.

✓**CHECK**

$3.58x - 37.40 = 0.23x + 8.32$	**Write original equation.**
$3.58(\mathbf{13.65}) - 37.40 \stackrel{?}{=} 0.23(\mathbf{13.65}) + 8.32$	**Substitute 13.65 for each x.**
$11.467 \approx 11.4595$	**Rounded answer is reasonable.**

· · · · · · · · · ·

An equation involving decimals can be rewritten as an equivalent equation with only integer terms and coefficients.

EXAMPLE 4   *Changing Decimal Coefficients to Integers*

Solve $4.5 - 7.2x = 3.4x - 49.5$. Round to the nearest tenth.

SOLUTION

Because the coefficients and constant terms each have only one decimal place, you can rewrite the equation without decimals by multiplying each side by 10.

$4.5 - 7.2x = 3.4x - 49.5$	**Write original equation.**
$45 - 72x = 34x - 495$	**Multiply each side by 10.**
$45 = 106x - 495$	**Add 72x to each side.**
$540 = 106x$	**Add 495 to each side.**
$\dfrac{540}{106} = x$	**Divide each side by 106.**
$5.094339623 \approx x$	**Use a calculator.**
$5.1 \approx x$	**Round to nearest tenth.**

▶ The solution is approximately 5.1. Check this in the original equation.

Retail Purchase

EXAMPLE 5 *Using a Verbal Model*

You are shopping for earrings. The sales tax is 5%. You have a total of $18.37 to spend. What is your price limit for the earrings?

SOLUTION

The total cost is your price limit plus the tax figured on the price limit.

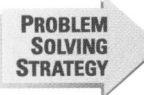

PROBLEM
SOLVING
STRATEGY

**VERBAL
MODEL**

Price limit $+$ Sales tax rate $\cdot$ Price limit $=$ Total cost

LABELS

Price limit $= x$ (dollars)

Sales tax rate $= 0.05$ (no units)

Total cost $= 18.37$ (dollars)

STUDENT HELP

▸ **Skills Review**
For help with finding a percent of a number, see p. 786.

**ALGEBRAIC
MODEL**

$x + 0.05 \cdot x = 18.37$ **Write algebraic model.**

$1.05x = 18.37$ **Combine like terms.**

$x = \dfrac{18.37}{1.05}$ **Divide each side by 1.05.**

$x \approx 17.4952381$ **Use a calculator.**

$x \approx 17.49$ **Round down.**

▸ Because you have a limited amount to spend, the answer is rounded *down* to $17.49. If you round up to $17.50, you will be a penny short because the sales tax is rounded up to $.88.

● ACTIVITY

Developing
Concepts

Investigating Round-Off Error

❶ Work with a partner. Each of you will solve the equation below in a different way.

$$18.42x - 12.75 = (5.32x - 6.81)3.46$$

Student 1: Round to the nearest hundredth in intermediate steps.

Student 2: Round to the nearest hundredth only in the last step.

❷ Compare the answers you get using both methods. Which method do you think is more accurate? Why?

When solving an equation that has decimals, you need to realize that rounding in the intermediate steps can increase the round-off error.

GUIDED PRACTICE

Vocabulary Check ✓

1. What special notation do you need to use when you are giving an approximate answer?

Concept Check ✓

2. Look back at Example 3. What number would you multiply the equation by to rewrite the equation without decimals?

🌐 **FIELD TRIP** In Exercises 3 and 4, school buses that hold 68 people will be used to transport 377 students and 65 teachers.

3. Write and solve an equation to find the number of buses needed.

4. Is the exact answer in Exercise 3 practical? Explain.

Skill Check ✓

Round to the nearest tenth.

5. 23.4459   6. 108.2135   7. -13.8953 8. 62.9788

Solve the equation. Round the result to the nearest hundredth. Check the rounded solution.

9. $2.2x = 15$

10. $14 - 9x = 37$

11. $2(3b - 14) = -9$

12. $2.69 - 3.64x = 8.37 + 23.78x$

13. 🌐 **BUYING A SWEATSHIRT** You have $35.72 to spend for a sweatshirt. The sales tax is 7%. What is your price limit for the sweatshirt?

PRACTICE AND APPLICATIONS

STUDENT HELP

▶ **Extra Practice**
to help you master
skills is on p. 799.

ROUNDING Perform any indicated operation. Round the result to the nearest tenth and then to the nearest hundredth.

14. -35.1923

15. $5.34(6.79)$

16. $-7.895 + 4.929$

17. $47.0362 - 39.7204$

18. $5.349 \div 46.597$

19. $-25.349(-1.369)$

SOLVING AND CHECKING Solve the equation. Round the result to the nearest hundredth. Check the rounded solution.

20. $13x - 7 = 27$

21. $18 - 3y = 5$

22. $-7n + 17 = -6$

23. $38 = -14 + 9a$

24. $47 = 28 - 12x$

25. $14r + 8 = 32$

26. $358 = 39c - 17$

27. $37 - 58b = 204$

28. $3(31 - 12t) = 82$

29. $4(-7y + 13) = 49$

30. $2(-5a + 7) = -a$

31. $-(d - 3) = 2(3d + 1)$

STUDENT HELP

▶ **HOMEWORK HELP**
Example 1: Exs. 14–39, 44
Example 2: Exs. 14–39
Example 3: Exs. 32–39
Example 4: Exs. 40–43
Example 5: Exs. 49–53

SOLVING EQUATIONS Solve the equation. Round the result to the nearest hundredth.

32. $12.67 + 42.35x = 5.34x + 26.58$

33. $4.65x - 4.79 = 13.57 - 6.84x$

34. $7.45x - 8.81 = 5.29 + 9.47x$

35. $39.21x + 2.65 = -31.68 + 42.03x$

36. $5.86x - 31.94 = 27.51x - 3.21$

37. $-2(4.36 - 6.92x) = 9.27x + 3.87$

38. $6.1(3.1 + 2.5x) = 15.3x - 3.9$

39. $4.21x + 5.39 = 12.07(2.01 - 4.72x)$

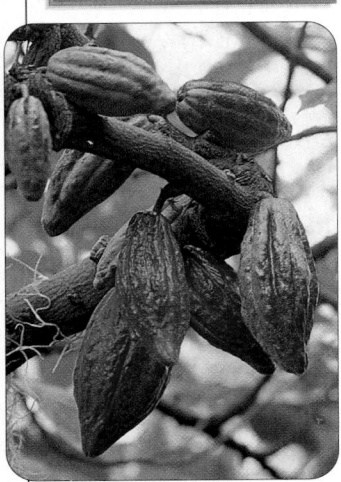
CHANGING TO INTEGER COEFFICIENTS Multiply the equation by a power of 10 to write an equivalent equation with integer coefficients.

40. $2.5x + 0.7 = 4.6 - 1.3x$

41. $-0.625y - 0.184 = 2.506y$

42. $1.67 + 2.43x = 3.29(x - 5)$

43. $4.5n - 0.375 = 0.75n + 2.0$

44. 🌎 **COCOA CONSUMPTION** The 267.9 million people in the United States consumed 639.4 million kilograms of the cocoa produced in the 1996–1997 growing year. Which choice better represents the amount of cocoa consumed per person that year? Explain. ▶ Source: International Cocoa Organization

   A. 2.38671146 kilograms   **B.** about 2.4 kilograms

CRITICAL THINKING Describe a situation where you would round as indicated.

45. to nearest whole   **46.** to nearest tenth   **47.** to nearest hundredth

48. 🖩 **COMPARING ROUNDING METHODS** At the 1998 winter Olympics, Marianne Timmer of the Netherlands won the women's 1000-meter speed skating race with a time of 76.51 seconds. Use a calculator to find Timmer's rates in parts (a)–(d) following each method below. Do the two methods give the same final result after rounding to the nearest tenth in part (d)?

Method 1 Round any decimal answers to the nearest tenth before going on.
Method 2 Use the full calculator display until you round for the final answer.

   a. speed in meters per second   **b.** speed in meters per minute

   c. speed in meters per hour   **d.** speed in kilometers per hour

49. 🌎 **BUYING DINNER** You have $8.39 to spend for dinner. You want to leave a 15% tip. What is your price limit for the dinner with tax included?

🌎 **INTERPRETING DATA** In Exercises 50–52, use the data from a survey about T-shirts. The survey found that 93 out of 100, or 0.93, of the adults responding own at least one T-shirt. The bar graph shows where those adults who own T-shirts got their oldest T-shirt.

50. Suppose the survey takers counted 186 people who own at least one T-shirt. Choose the equation you could use to find the number of people in the survey. About how many people were surveyed?

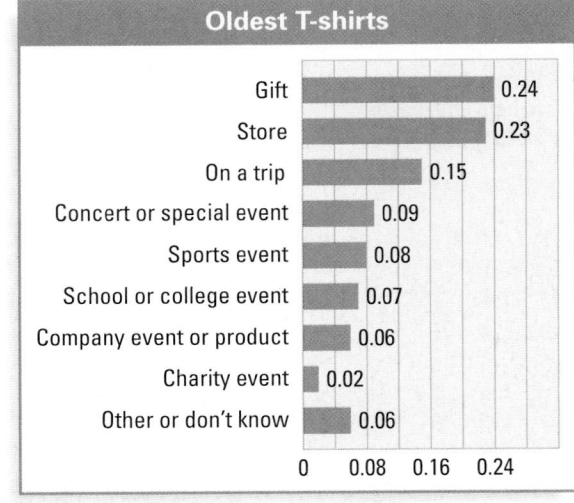

Oldest T-shirts

Gift	0.24
Store	0.23
On a trip	0.15
Concert or special event	0.09
Sports event	0.08
School or college event	0.07
Company event or product	0.06
Charity event	0.02
Other or don't know	0.06

▶ Source: Opinion Research

   A. $x + 0.93 = 186$ **B.** $0.93 \div x = 186$ **C.** $0.93x = 186$

51. **PROBABILITY** **CONNECTION**   What is the probability that an adult chosen at random from a group of adults who own at least one T-shirt received his or her oldest T-shirt as a gift?

52. Suppose a group of adults who own T-shirts includes 42 people who got their oldest T-shirt from a charity event. Estimate the total size of the group.

53. 🌐 **WHALES** A bottle-nosed whale can dive 440 feet per minute. Suppose a bottle-nosed whale is 500 feet deep and dives at this rate. Write and solve an equation to find how long it will take to reach a depth of 2975 feet. Round to the nearest whole minute.

🌐 **INTERNET SERVICE** In Exercises 54 and 55, your Internet service provider charges \$4.95 per month for the first 3 hours of service, plus \$2.50 for each additional hour. Your total charges last month were \$21.83. Let x represent the number of hours you used the service.

54. Which equation models the situation?

A. $4.95 + 2.5x - 3 = 21.83$ **B.** $4.95 + 2.5(x - 3) = 21.83$

55. Solve the equation you chose in Exercise 54 and round the result to the nearest hundredth. What does the result represent?

SCIENCE ▸ **CONNECTION** In Exercises 56–58, use the following information.

Bridge sections expand as the temperature goes up, so a small *expansion gap* is left between sections when a bridge is built. As the sections expand, the width of the gap gets smaller.

Suppose that for some bridge the expansion gap is 16.8 millimeters wide at 10°C and decreases by 0.37 millimeter for every 1°C rise in temperature.

Bridge sections

Not drawn
to scale

Width of expansion gap

56. If the temperature is 18°C, by how many degrees did the temperature rise? By how much would the width of the gap decrease? What would the new width of the gap be? Round to the nearest tenth of a millimeter.

57. The temperature rises to t°C. Write expressions for the temperature rise, the decrease in the width of the gap, and the new width of the gap.

58. Use the expressions from Exercise 57. Write and solve an equation to find the temperature at which the gap decreases to 9.4 millimeters.

59. MULTI-STEP PROBLEM You are running water into a laundry sink to get a mixture that is one-half hot water and one-half cold water. The hot water flows more slowly, at a rate of 7.8 liters per minute, so you turn it on first. Two minutes later, you also turn on the cold water which flows at a rate of 12.3 liters per minute. You want to know how long to wait before turning the two faucets off.

   a. Let t represent the number of minutes the hot water is on. Write a variable expression for the amount of time the cold water is on.

   b. Write an equation that models the situation. Then solve the equation.

   c. *Writing* Interpret your solution. If the solution is a decimal, decide what form of the number is most appropriate. Explain your choice.

60. ROUND-OFF ERROR For some decimal equations, you get almost the same solution whether you round early in the solution process or only at the end. For other equations, such as the one in the Activity on page 168, rounding early has a big effect on the solution. Write a decimal equation for which rounding early produces a significant difference in the answer.

Test 🖊
Preparation

★ Challenge

61. **INPUT-OUTPUT TABLES** Make an input-output table for the function $A = 8 + 2.5t$ when $t = 2, 3, 4, 5,$ and 6. Describe the domain and the range of the function whose values are shown in the table. **(Review 1.7 for 3.7)**

OPPOSITES **Find the opposite of the number.** **(Review 2.1)**

62. 8 **63.** -3 **64.** -4.9 **65.** 7.9

PROBABILITY **Find the probability of the event.** **(Review 2.8)**

66. Choosing the letter N from a bag that contains all 26 letters of the alphabet

67. Choosing a blue marble from a bag that contains 16 blue marbles and 14 white marbles

68. Rolling an even number using a six-sided number cube

ACCOUNT ACTIVITY **In Exercises 69–71, use the table. It shows all of the activity in a checking account during June. Deposits are positive and withdrawals are negative.** **(Review 2.2)**

Day	Activity
June 6	$-\$225.00$
June 10	$+\$310.25$
June 17	$+\$152.33$
June 25	$-\$72.45$
June 30	$-\$400.00$

69. How did the amount of money in the account change from the beginning of June through June 10?

70. Find the total amount withdrawn in June.

71. What was the total change in the account balance over the course of the month?

QUIZ 2

Self-Test for Lessons 3.4–3.6

Solve the equation if possible. **(Lesson 3.4)**

1. $3x + 1 = 5x$ **2.** $8 - 2y = 21 - 6y$ **3.** $3n = (6 - n)(-3)$

4. $\frac{1}{2}(14 + 8a) = 9a$ **5.** $7 - 6d = 3(5 - 2d)$ **6.** $-7(b + 1) = 5(b - 2)$

Solve the equation. Round the result to the nearest hundredth. **(Lesson 3.6)**

7. $15y - 8 = 4y - 3$ **8.** $2(2n + 11) = 31 - 3n$

9. $7.6x + 3.7 = 2.8 - 1.6x$ **10.** $4.9(3.7x + 1.4) = 34.7x$

11. **PET SHOW** The city is sponsoring a pet show. The number of cats, birds, and hamsters equals the number of dogs and turtles. There are 3 birds, 3 turtles, and 5 hamsters. There are twice as many dogs as cats. Let n be the number of cats. Draw a diagram to decide which equation models the situation. **(Lesson 3.5)**

A. $2n + n = 3 + 3 + 5$ **B.** $n + 3 = 2n + 3 + 5$

C. $n + 3 + 5 = 2n + 3$ **D.** $2n + 5 = 3 + 3 + n$

12. Use the results of Exercise 11 to find the number of dogs. **(Lesson 3.5)**

ACTIVITY 3.6
Using Technology

Using a Table or Spreadsheet to Solve Equations

One way to solve multi-step equations is to use a graphing calculator or spreadsheet software on a computer to generate a table of values. The table can show a value of x for which the two sides of the equation are approximately equal.

▶ **EXAMPLE**

Use a table on a graphing calculator to solve $4.29x + 3.89(8 - x) = 2.65x$. Round your answer to the nearest tenth.

▶ **SOLUTION**

1 Use the *Table Setup* function on your graphing calculator to set up a table. Choose values beginning at 0 and increasing by 1.

```
TABLE SETUP
  TblStart=0
  △Tbl=1
Indpnt:  Auto  Ask
Depend:  Auto  Ask
```

2 You want the table to show the value of the left-hand side of the equation in the second column and the value of the right-hand side of the equation in the third column.

Press **Y=**. Enter the left-hand side of the equation as Y_1 and the right-hand side of the equation as Y_2.

Enter **×** for each multiplication. It prints as *.

```
Y1=4.29*X+3.89*(8-
X)
Y2=2.65*X
Y3=
Y4=
Y5=
Y6=
```

3 View your table. The first column of the table should show values of x. Scroll down until you find values in the second and third columns that are approximately equal. The values are closest to being equal when $x = 14$, so the solution must be greater than 13 and less than 15.

```
X    Y1      Y2
12   35.92   31.8
13   36.32   34.45
14   36.72   37.1
15   37.12   39.75
16   37.52   42.4
```

4 To find the solution to the nearest tenth, go back to the table setup and change it so that x starts at 13.1 and increases by 0.1. Then view your adjusted table. The values in the second and third columns are closest to being equal when $x = 13.8$.

```
X     Y1      Y2
13.6  36.56   36.04
13.7  36.6    36.305
13.8  36.64   36.57
13.9  36.68   36.835
14    36.72   37.1
```

▶ The solution to the nearest tenth is 13.8.

▶ **EXERCISES**

Use a graphing calculator to solve the equation. Round to the nearest tenth.

1. $19.65x + 2.2(x - 6.05) = 255.65$

2. $16.2(3.1 - x) - 31.55x = -19.5$

3. $3.56x + 2.43 = 6.17x - 11.40$

4. $3.5(x - 5.6) + 0.03x = 4.2x - 25.5$

3.7

Formulas and Functions

What you should learn

GOAL 1 Solve a formula for one of its variables.

GOAL 2 Rewrite an equation in function form.

Why you should learn it

▼ To solve **real-life** problems about rate, time, and distance as in *Pathfinder*'s flight to Mars in **Example 4**.

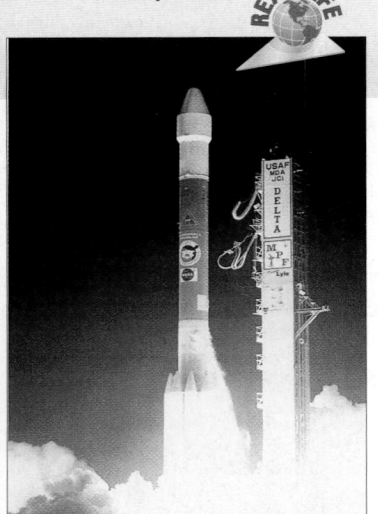

GOAL 1 **SOLVING FORMULAS**

In this lesson you will work with equations that have more than one variable. A **formula** is an algebraic equation that relates two or more real-life quantities.

EXAMPLE 1 *Solving and Using an Area Formula*

Use the formula for the area of a rectangle, $A = lw$.

a. Find a formula for l in terms of A and w.

b. Use the new formula to find the length of a rectangle that has an area of 35 square feet and a width of 7 feet.

SOLUTION

a. Solve for length l.

$$A = lw \qquad \text{Write original formula.}$$

$$\frac{A}{w} = l \qquad \text{To isolate } l\text{, divide each side by } w.$$

b. Substitute the given values into the new formula.

$$l = \frac{A}{w} = \frac{35}{7} = 5$$

▶ The length of the rectangle is 5 feet.

EXAMPLE 2 *Solving a Temperature Conversion Formula*

Solve the temperature formula $C = \frac{5}{9}(F - 32)$ for F.

SOLUTION

$$C = \frac{5}{9}(F - 32) \qquad \text{Write original formula.}$$

$$\frac{9}{5} \cdot C = \frac{9}{5} \cdot \frac{5}{9}(F - 32) \qquad \text{Multiply each side by } \tfrac{9}{5}.$$

$$\frac{9}{5}C = F - 32 \qquad \text{Simplify.}$$

$$\frac{9}{5}C + 32 = F - 32 + 32 \qquad \text{Add 32 to each side.}$$

$$\frac{9}{5}C + 32 = F \qquad \text{Simplify.}$$

EXAMPLE 3 *Solving and Using an Interest Formula*

a. The simple interest I on an investment of P dollars at an interest rate r for t years is given by $I = Prt$. Solve this formula for r.

b. Find the interest rate r for an investment of $1500 that earned $54 in simple interest in one year.

SOLUTION

a. $I = Prt$ Write original formula.

$\dfrac{I}{Pt} = \dfrac{Prt}{Pt}$ Divide each side by *Pt*.

$\dfrac{I}{Pt} = r$ Simplify.

b. $r = \dfrac{I}{Pt} = \dfrac{54}{1500 \cdot 1} = \dfrac{54}{1500} = 0.036$, or 3.6%

EXAMPLE 4 *Solving and Using a Distance Formula*

PATHFINDER The *Pathfinder* was launched on December 4, 1996. During its 212-day flight to Mars, it traveled about 310 million miles. Estimate the time the *Pathfinder* would have taken to reach Mars traveling at the following speeds.

a. 30,000 miles per hour

b. 40,000 miles per hour

c. 60,000 miles per hour

d. 80,000 miles per hour

Which of the four speeds is the best estimate of *Pathfinder's* average speed?

PATHFINDER
Since its landing on July 4, 1997, the Mars Pathfinder has returned 2.6 billion bits of information, including more than 16,550 images. ▶ Source: NASA

SOLUTION

Use the formula $d = rt$ and solve for the time t.

$d = rt$ Write original formula.

$\dfrac{d}{r} = \dfrac{rt}{r}$ Divide each side by *r*.

$\dfrac{d}{r} = t$ Simplify.

a. $t = \dfrac{d}{r} = \dfrac{310,000,000}{30,000} = 10,333$ hours ≈ 431 days

b. $t = \dfrac{d}{r} = \dfrac{310,000,000}{40,000} = 7,750$ hours ≈ 323 days

c. $t = \dfrac{d}{r} = \dfrac{310,000,000}{60,000} \approx 5,167$ hours ≈ 215 days

d. $t = \dfrac{d}{r} = \dfrac{310,000,000}{80,000} = 3,875$ hours ≈ 161 days

▶ The trip took 212 days, so *Pathfinder's* average speed was about 60,000 mi/h.

GOAL 2 REWRITING EQUATIONS IN FUNCTION FORM

A two-variable equation is written in *function form* if one of its variables is isolated on one side of the equation. The isolated variable is the output and is a function of the input. For instance, the equation $P = 4s$ describes the perimeter P of a square as a function of its side length s.

EXAMPLE 5   *Rewriting an Equation in Function Form*

STUDENT HELP

▸ **Look Back** For help with functions, see page 46.

HOMEWORK HELP
Visit our Web site www.mcdougallittell.com for extra examples.

Rewrite the equation $3x + y = 4$ so that y is a function of x.

SOLUTION

$3x + y = 4$	Write original equation.
$3x + y - 3x = 4 - 3x$	Subtract $3x$ from each side.
$y = 4 - 3x$	Simplify.

▸ The equation $y = 4 - 3x$ represents y as a function of x.

EXAMPLE 6   *Rewriting an Equation in Function Form*

a. Rewrite the equation $3x + y = 4$ so that x is a function of y.

b. Use the result to find x when $y = -2, -1, 0,$ and 1.

SOLUTION

a.

$3x + y = 4$	Write original equation.
$3x + y - y = 4 - y$	Subtract y from each side.
$3x = 4 - y$	Simplify.
$\dfrac{3x}{3} = \dfrac{4 - y}{3}$	Divide each side by 3.
$x = \dfrac{4 - y}{3}$	Simplify.

▸ The equation $x = \dfrac{4 - y}{3}$ represents x as a function of y.

b. It is helpful to organize your work in columns.

INPUT	SUBSTITUTE	OUTPUT
$y = -2$	$x = \dfrac{4 - (-2)}{3}$	$x = 2$
$y = -1$	$x = \dfrac{4 - (-1)}{3}$	$x = \dfrac{5}{3}$
$y = 0$	$x = \dfrac{4 - (0)}{3}$	$x = \dfrac{4}{3}$
$y = 1$	$x = \dfrac{4 - (1)}{3}$	$x = 1$

GUIDED PRACTICE

Vocabulary Check ✓

1. Give an example of a formula. State what real-life quantity each variable represents.

Concept Check ✓

Tell whether the formula shows correctly the relationships among perimeter, length, and width of a rectangle.

2. $P = 2l + 2w$

3. $P = l + w \cdot 2$

4. $P = 2(l + w)$

5. $l = \dfrac{P - 2w}{2}$

6. $l = \dfrac{P}{2w} - 2$

7. $w = \dfrac{P}{2} - 2l$

8. Write a formula that describes the side length s of a square as a function of its perimeter P.

Skill Check ✓

9. Rewrite the equation $2x + 2y = 10$ so that y is a function of x.

10. Use the result of Exercise 9 to find y when $x = -2, -1, 0, 1,$ and 2.

PRACTICE AND APPLICATIONS

STUDENT HELP

▶ **Extra Practice**
to help you master
skills is on p. 799.

SOLVING A FORMULA **Solve for the indicated variable.**

11. Area of a Triangle

Solve for b: $A = \frac{1}{2}bh$

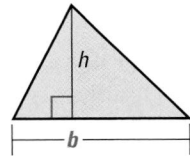

12. Volume of a Rectangular Prism

Solve for h: $V = \ell wh$

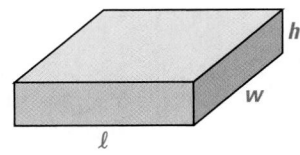

13. Volume of a Circular Cylinder

Solve for h: $V = \pi r^2 h$

14. Area of a Trapezoid

Solve for b_2: $A = \frac{1}{2}h(b_1 + b_2)$

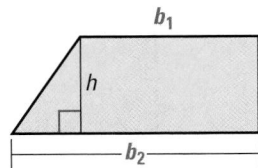

REWRITING EQUATIONS **Rewrite the equation so that y is a function of x.**

15. $2x + y = 5$

16. $3x + 5y = 7$

17. $13 = 12x - 2y$

18. $2x = -3y + 10$

19. $9 - y = 1.5x$

20. $1 + 7y = 5x - 2$

21. $\dfrac{y}{5} - 7 = -2x$

22. $\dfrac{1}{4}y + 3 = -5x$

23. $-3x + 4y - 5 = -14$

24. $7x - 4x + 12 = 36 - 5y$

25. $\dfrac{1}{3}(y + 2) + 3x = 7x$

STUDENT HELP

▶ **HOMEWORK HELP**
Examples 1–4: Exs. 11–14,
34–38
Example 5: Exs. 15–29
Example 6: Exs. 30–33

26. $5(y - 3x) = 8 - 2x$

27. $4x - 3(y - 2) = 15 + y$

28. $3(x - 2y) = -12(x + 2y)$

29. $\dfrac{1}{5}(25 - 5y) = 4x - 9y + 13$

3.7 *Formulas and Functions*   **177**

SUBSTITUTION Rewrite the equation so that *x* is a function of *y*. Then use the result to find *x* when *y* = −2, −1, 0, and 1.

30. $2x + y = 5$

31. $3y - x = 12$

32. $4(5 - y) = 14x + 3$

33. $5y - 2(x - 7) = 20$

🌐 **DISCOUNTS** In Exercises 34 and 35, use the relationship between the sale price *S*, the list price *L*, and the discount rate *r*.

34. Solve for *r* in the formula $S = L - rL$.

Skills Review
For help with writing decimals as percents, see pages 784–785.

35. Use the new formula to find the discount rate as a decimal and as a percent.

  a. Sale price: $80
  List price: $100

  b. Sale price: $72
  List price: $120

  c. Sale price: $12.50
  List price: $25

36. *Writing* You can solve the formula $d = rt$ for any of its variables. This means that you need to learn only one formula to solve a problem asking for distance, rate, or time. Explain.

🌐 **SCUBA DIVING** In Exercises 37–39, use the following information.
If a scuba diver starts at sea level, the pressure on the diver at a depth of *d* feet is given by the formula $P = 64d + 2112$, where *P* represents the total pressure in pounds per square foot. Suppose the current pressure on a diver is 4032 pounds per square foot.

37. Solve the formula for *d*.

38. What is the diver's current depth?

39. In the original equation, is *P* a function of *d* or is *d* a function of *P*? Explain.

KEYSTROKE HELP
Visit our Web site
www.mcdougallittell.com
to see keystrokes for several models of calculators.

🖩 **CIRCLE RELATIONSHIPS** In Exercises 40–44, use the information at the right. Use the *Table* feature on a graphing calculator (or spreadsheet software) as indicated.

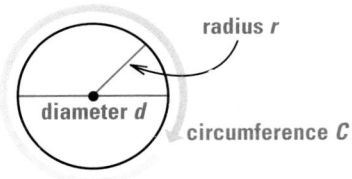

40. In the formula, is the circumference a function of the radius or is the radius a function of the circumference?

41. If *X* is the radius, what expression gives the circumference? On your graphing calculator enter this expression as Y_1.

42. Solve the circumference formula for *r*. If Y_1 is the circumference, what expression involving Y_1 equals the radius? On your graphing calculator enter this expression as Y_2. To enter Y_1 into your expression, use the *Variables* menu.

43. **LOGICAL REASONING** Enter 10 different values for the radius of a circle in the *X*-column. (You may need to choose "Ask" on the Table Setup menu to do this.) View your table and then explain the relationship between the three columns.

44. 🌐 **GIANT SEQUOIA** The *General Sherman* tree, a sequoia tree in Sequoia National Park, has the greatest volume of any tree in the world. The distance around the tree (the circumference) measures 102.6 feet. Show how to find the distance straight through the center of the tree (the diameter) without measuring it directly. Then find this value to the nearest tenth of a foot.

45. MULTIPLE CHOICE Which of the choices shows how to rewrite the equation $2y - 3(y - 2x) = 8(x - 1) + 3$ so that y is a function of x?

(A) $x = \dfrac{5 - y}{2}$

(B) $x = \dfrac{-y + 5}{10}$

(C) $y = -14x + 5$

(D) $y = -2x + 5$

46. MULTIPLE CHOICE The formula $A = \frac{1}{2}h(b_1 + b_2)$ relates the area and the dimensions of a trapezoid. Which way can you rewrite this relationship?

(A) $A = \frac{1}{2}hb_1 + b_2$

(B) $h = \dfrac{2A}{b_1 + b_2}$

(C) $h = \dfrac{A}{b_1 + b_2}$

(D) $b_1 = 2A - b_2$

★ **Challenge**

🌎 **ROPE AROUND THE WORLD** In Exercises 47–49, imagine a rope wrapped around Earth at the equator (Earth's circumference C). Then think of adding d feet to the rope's length so it can now circle Earth at a distance h feet above the equator at all points.

47. Write an equation to model this situation.

48. Solve your equation in Exercise 47 for d.

49. How much rope do you need to insert if you want the rope to circle Earth 500 feet above the equator? Use 3.14 as an approximation for π.

Length of rope = $C + d$

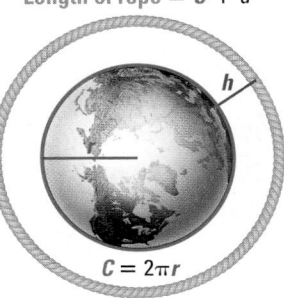

h

$C = 2\pi r$

MIXED REVIEW

CHECKING SOLUTIONS Check whether the given number is a solution of the inequality. **(Review 1.4)**

50. $y - 5 > 4; 9$

51. $4 + 7y > 12; 1$

52. $3x - 3 \geq x + 3; 5$

SIMPLIFYING EXPRESSIONS Simplify the variable expression. **(Review 2.5)**

53. $-(2)^3(b)$

54. $(-2)^3(b)$

55. $3(-x)(-x)(-x)$

56. $(-4)(-c)(-c)(-c)$

57. $(-4)^2(t)(t)$

58. $(-5)^2(-y)(-y)$

🌎 **TEEN ATTENDANCE** Each bar shows the percent of teens that attend the activity in a 12-month period. **(Review 1.6 for 3.8)**

59. Which activity shown is attended by the most teens?

60. What percent attend rock concerts?

61. How many out of 100 attend art museums?

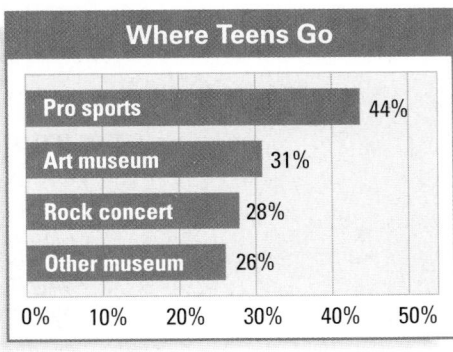

Where Teens Go

Pro sports	44%
Art museum	31%
Rock concert	28%
Other museum	26%

0% 10% 20% 30% 40% 50%

▶ Source: *YOUTHviews*

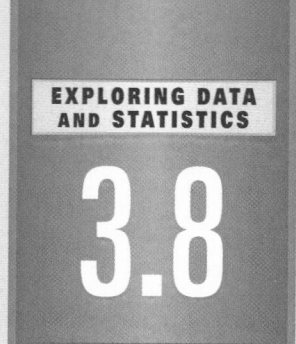

Rates, Ratios, and Percents

GOAL 1 USING RATES AND RATIOS

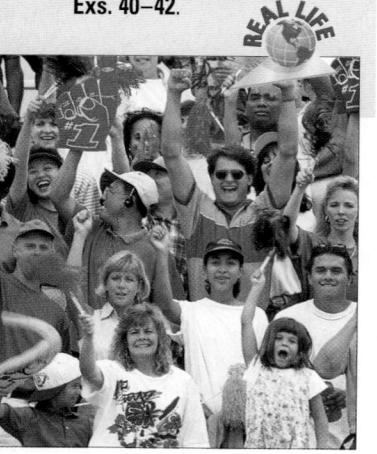

In this lesson you will apply rates, ratios, and percents and use your equation solving skills to solve problems. If a and b are two quantities measured in different units, then the **rate of a per b** is $\frac{a}{b}$. Rates are often expressed as *unit rates*. A **unit rate** is a rate per one given unit, such as 60 miles per 1 gallon.

EXAMPLE 1 Interpreting Large Numbers

SPENDING How can you relate this information to individual spending?

Estimated Spending for Clothes and Food in the United States in 1996		
Clothing & Shoes	Restaurants	Food at home
$183 billion	$190 billion	$300 billion

 DATA UPDATE of U.S. Bureau of Labor Statistics at www.mcdougallittell.com

SOLUTION One solution is to find the average rate of spending *per person* so that people can compare themselves to the average. You can do this by dividing by the total population, which was about 266 million in 1996.

Clothing and shoes: about $688 per person

Restaurants: about $714 per person

Food at home: about $1128 per person

EXAMPLE 2 Using Collected Data

MILEAGE You have recorded your car mileage and gasoline use for 2 months. Estimate the number of miles you can drive on a full 18-gallon tank of gasoline.

Number of miles	290	242	196	237	184
Number of gallons	12.1	9.8	8.2	9.5	7.8

SOLUTION You drove a total of 1149 miles and used 47.4 gallons of gasoline, so your average rate was $1149 \div 47.4$, or about 24.2 miles per gallon. Let x represent the number of miles you can drive on 18 gallons. To estimate x, you can solve the following equation.

$$\text{Number of miles} \longrightarrow \frac{x}{18} = 24.2 \longleftarrow \text{Average rate in miles per gallon}$$
$$\text{Number of gallons} \longrightarrow$$

▶ The solution is $x = 435.6$, so your estimate is 436 miles on an 18-gallon tank.

Exchange Rates

EXAMPLE 3 *Applying Unit Analysis*

a. You are visiting Mexico and you want to exchange $180 for pesos. The rate of currency exchange is 9.990 pesos per United States dollar. You want to find out how many pesos you will receive.

UNIT ANALYSIS You can use unit analysis to write an equation.

$$\text{dollars} \cdot \frac{\text{pesos}}{\text{dollar}} = \text{pesos}$$

$$D \cdot \frac{9.990}{1} = P \qquad \text{Write equation.}$$

$$180 \cdot \frac{9.990}{1} = P \qquad \text{Substitute 180 for } D \text{ dollars.}$$

$$1798.2 = P \qquad \text{Simplify.}$$

▶ You will receive 1798 pesos.

b. When you leave Mexico, you are surprised to find that you have exactly 180 pesos left. You want to find out how many United States dollars you will receive. The rate of currency exchange is now 9.987 pesos per dollar.

UNIT ANALYSIS $\text{pesos} \cdot \dfrac{\text{dollar}}{\text{pesos}} = \text{dollars}$

$$P \cdot \frac{1}{9.987} = D \qquad \text{Write equation.}$$

$$180 \cdot \frac{1}{9.987} = D \qquad \text{Substitute 180 for } P \text{ pesos.}$$

▶ After simplifying, you find that $D \approx 18.02343046$. You will receive $18.

EXAMPLE 4 *Using Ratios to Write an Equation*

FOCUS ON APPLICATIONS

TULIPS You tested a sample of 50 tulip bulbs from a shipment of 4500 bulbs for resistance to a type of mold. You found that 32 of the bulbs had a natural resistance, and 18 did not. Use these results to estimate the number of bulbs in the shipment that will have a natural resistance to the mold.

SOLUTION

One way to answer the question is to write a ratio. Let x represent the number of resistant bulbs in the shipment.

$$\frac{\text{Resistant bulbs in sample}}{\text{Total bulbs in sample}} = \frac{\text{Resistant bulbs in shipment}}{\text{Total bulbs in shipment}}$$

$$\frac{32}{50} = \frac{x}{4500} \qquad \text{Write equation.}$$

$$4500 \cdot \frac{32}{50} = x \qquad \text{Multiply each side by 4500.}$$

$$2880 = x \qquad \text{Simplify.}$$

▶ About 2880 of the 4500 bulbs in the shipment will be resistant to the mold.

TULIPS About 25% of tulip bulbs sold in the United States are grown in the United States. The Skagit Valley area, shown above, is the largest U.S. producer of tulips.

GOAL 2 USING PERCENTS

Survey

EXAMPLE 5 *Finding Percents*

What percent of 15–17-year-olds said that they are dating?

A Survey of Teen Dating		
Age Group	Number Surveyed	Number Who Are Dating
12–14-year-olds	1074	216
15–17-year-olds	992	482
18–19-year-olds	307	205

▶ Source: Simmons Market Research Bureau

SOLUTION To find the percent, divide the number who are dating by the number surveyed and then write the result as a percent.

$\frac{482}{992} \approx 0.485887097$, so about 49% of 15–17-year-olds said that they are dating.

EXAMPLE 6 *Using a Graph*

GLASS RECYCLING The circle graph shows the percent of glass containers recycled in the United States in a recent year. About 3.2 million tons of glass containers were recycled. Estimate the total weight of glass containers used that year.

Glass Containers

Recycled 29%

Not recycled 71%

 DATA UPDATE of U.S. Environmental Protection Agency data at www.mcdougallittell.com

FOCUS ON APPLICATIONS

GLASS RECYCLING When one glass bottle is recycled, the energy saved could light a 100-watt light bulb for four hours.

SOLUTION

VERBAL MODEL	Percent of glass containers recycled (in decimal form)	·	Total weight of glass containers used	=	Weight of glass containers recycled

LABELS

Percent of glass containers recycled = **0.29**   (no units)

Total weight of glass containers used = **x**   (tons)

Weight of glass containers recycled = **3,200,000**   (tons)

ALGEBRAIC MODEL

$0.29 \cdot x = 3{,}200{,}000$ Write algebraic model.

$x = \frac{3{,}200{,}000}{0.29}$ Divide each side by 0.29.

$x \approx 11{,}034{,}482.76$ Simplify.

▶ About 11.0 million tons of glass containers were used that year.

182   **Chapter 3** *Solving Linear Equations*

GUIDED PRACTICE

Vocabulary Check ✓   **1.** Explain the difference between a rate and a ratio.

Concept Check ✓   **2.** Which model would you use to change 14 yards to feet? Explain.

A. 14 yards · $\dfrac{1 \text{ yard}}{3 \text{ feet}}$ **B.** 14 yards · $\dfrac{3 \text{ feet}}{1 \text{ yard}}$

3. **SURVEY** You took a survey of your class and found that 18 out of the 31 students have a pet at home. Explain how you can use your results to make a prediction for the 1746 students in your school.

Skill Check ✓   **4.** Look back at Example 1. Find the per person rate of spending for a month for each of the given categories.

EXCHANGE RATES **Convert the currency using the given exchange rate.**

5. Convert 200 euros to United States dollars. (1 euro is 1.066 dollar.)

6. Convert 340 U.S. dollars to South African rand. (1 rand is 0.607 dollar.)

In Exercises 7–9, write and solve an equation to find the unknown number.

7. 45% of 280 = _?_   **8.** 7.5% of 340 = _?_   **9.** 20% of _?_ = 15

10. 🌐 **TIPPING** What percent was the server's tip if the customer left $1.75 for a $12.50 meal?

PRACTICE AND APPLICATIONS

STUDENT HELP

↳ **Extra Practice**
to help you master
skills is on p. 799.

UNIT RATES **Find the unit rate.**

11. $2 for 5 cans of dog food   **12.** $121.50 for working 18 hours

13. $1.39 for $1\frac{1}{2}$ quarts of juice   **14.** 6 ounces for 2.5 servings

FINDING SPEEDS **In Exercises 15–18, find the average speed.**

15. Fly 1200 miles in 4 hours   **16.** Hike 52 miles in 3 days

17. Swim 2 miles in 40 minutes   **18.** Drive 69 kilometers in $\frac{3}{4}$ hour

19. *Writing* A store sells a box of 5 frozen yogurt bars for $1.20. The store also sells a box containing 7 of the same frozen yogurt bars for $1.59. Which is the better buy? Explain how you decided.

🌐 **IN ONE YEAR** **In Exercises 20 and 21, find the average rate as indicated.**

20. The United States postal service receives 38 million changes of address per year. Find the rate per day. Round to the nearest thousand.

21. 1,100,000,000 miles are driven to move the mail in the United States per year. Find the rate per week. Round to the nearest million miles.

22. 🖩 **EQUATION SOLVING** Give a calculator keystroke sequence that you could use to find the value of x in Example 4.

STUDENT HELP

↳ HOMEWORK HELP
Example 1: Exs. 11–21
Example 2: Exs. 11–21,
    27–29
Example 3: Exs. 23–26,
    30–31
Example 4: Ex. 32
Example 5: Exs. 33–37
Example 6: Exs. 38–42

MEASUREMENT In Exercises 23–26, convert the measure. Round your answer to the nearest tenth.

23. 12 fluid ounces to cups (1 cup = 8 fluid ounces)

24. 21 inches to centimeters (1 inch = 2.54 centimeters)

25. 56 miles to kilometers (1 mile = 1.609 kilometers)

26. length of a football field (100 yards, not including the end zones) to meters (1 yard = 0.9144 meter)

27. 🌐 **CAR MILEAGE** A car uses fuel at a rate of 15 miles per gallon. Estimate how many miles the car can travel on 20 gallons of fuel.

🌐 **BOOKS** **A library has 14,588 books which fill its 313 equal-size shelves.**

28. What is the average number of books per shelf?

29. The library plans to install 50 new shelves of this size. Write and solve an equation to estimate how many more books the library will be able to hold.

🌐 **EXCHANGE RATES** **In Exercises 30 and 31, use 114.520 yen per United States dollar as the rate of currency exchange. You are visiting Japan and have taken $325 to spend on your trip.**

30. If you exchange the entire amount, how many yen will you receive?

31. You have 605 yen left after your trip. How many dollars will you get back?

32. 🌐 **CALLING FROM THE AIR** You are conducting a survey on the use of airplane phones. You survey 320 adults and find that 288 of them never made a phone call from an airplane. If you surveyed 3500 adults, how many of them would you predict *have* made a phone call from an airplane? Explain.

FINDING PERCENTS Find the percent. Round to the nearest whole percent.

33. $2.25 tip on a cab fare of $14   **34.** Tax of $.68 on an item priced at $11.29

35. 292 people in favor out of 450 people surveyed

🌐 **MOON ROCKS** **In Exercises 36–38, round to the nearest tenth. A total of 382 kilograms of lunar samples (rocks, dust, and so on) were collected during the six Apollo moon landings between 1969 and 1972.**

36. The largest rock collected weighs 11.7 kilograms. This single rock is what percent of the total weight of the samples?

37. The 110.5 kilograms of lunar samples collected by the Apollo 17 astronauts represent what percent of the total weight of the samples?

38. About 7.5% of the lunar samples (by weight) have been analyzed and then returned for storage in the Return Sample Vault at NASA's Johnson Space Center. What is the combined weight of the samples in this vault?

39. 🌐 **CONSUMER ACTION** Americans ages 18 years and older were asked, *"Have you ever stopped buying a product specifically because the manufacturer of that product pollutes the environment?"* Of those surveyed, 719 said no. About how many people took part in the survey?

▶ Source: Wirthlin Worldwide

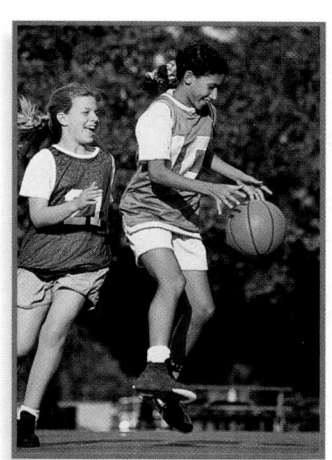

In the survey, Basketball was the most popular team sport.

 INTERPRETING DATA In Exercises 40–42, use the graph. It shows the percent of 16-to-24-year-olds participating in the top seven categories of outdoor recreation.

40. Viewing activities include sightseeing, visiting a nature center, and so on. Estimate how many students participate in viewing activities in a college with 1400 students.

41. Estimate the survey size if a survey of 16-to-24-year-olds found that 270 of them participate in fitness activities.

42. Write your own question based on the survey data. Then find the answer.

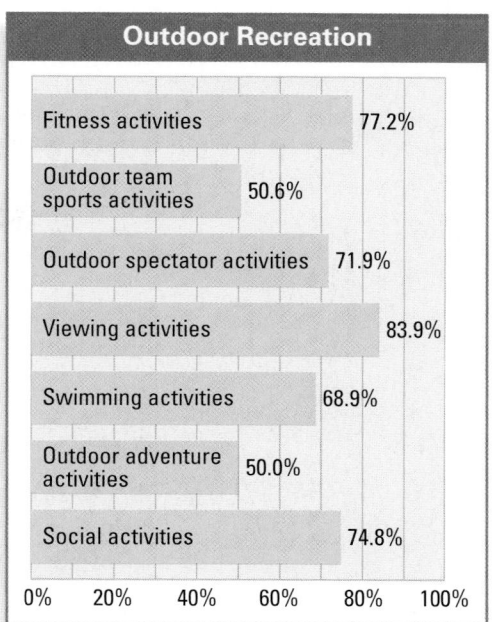

▶Source: National Survey on Recreation and the Environment

43. CRITICAL THINKING Compare Example 2 and Example 4 in Goal 1. How are the methods shown alike? How are they different?

Test Preparation

QUANTITATIVE COMPARISON In Exercises 44–46, choose the statement below that is true about the given values of *x*.

(A) The value of *x* in column A is greater.

(B) The value of *x* in column B is greater.

(C) The two values of *x* are equal.

(D) The relationship cannot be determined from the given information.

	Column A	Column B
44.	The solution of the equation $160\% \text{ of } 400 = x$	The solution of the equation $16\% \text{ of } 4000 = x$
45.	The solution of the equation $\dfrac{x}{3} = \dfrac{7}{8}$	The solution of the equation $\dfrac{x}{8} = \dfrac{7}{3}$
46.	The solution of the equation $15\% \text{ of } x = 30$	The solution of the equation $30\% \text{ of } x = 15$

★ Challenge

LITERATURE CONNECTION **Use this information in Exercises 47 and 48.**
In *Citizen of the Galaxy* by Robert Heinlein, Thorby learns that he owns "an interest in a company . . . through a chain of six companies—18% of 31% of 43% of 19% of 44% of 27%, a share so microscopic that he lost track." Let *x* represent the total worth of the company in which Thorby owns a share.

47. Write and simplify an expression to show Thorby's share of the company.

48. Suppose Thorby's share of the company is worth 1000 credits. Write and solve an equation to find the total worth of the company.

WRITING INEQUALITIES Graph the numbers on a number line. Then write two inequalities that compare the two numbers. (Review 2.1)

49. 4 and -3 **50.** -2.4 and 3.2 **51.** -0.2 and -0.21

52. -1.8 and -2 **53.** $\frac{3}{4}$ and $-\frac{5}{6}$ **54.** $-1\frac{1}{3}$ and -1.75

SOLVING EQUATIONS Solve the equation. Round the result to the nearest hundredth. Check the rounded solution. (Review 3.6)

55. $-11a - 16 = 5$ **56.** $2(4 - 3x) = -x$

57. $2.62x - 4.03 = 7.65 - 5.34x$ **58.** $2.6(4.2y - 6.5) = -7.1y - 2.8$

59. 🌐 **POPULATION PROJECTIONS** The table shows the projected number (in millions) of people 85 years and older in the United States for different years. Make a line graph of the data. (Review 1.6 for 4.1)

Year	2000	2010	2020	2030	2040	2050
Number of people 85 years and older (in millions)	4.1	5.0	5.0	5.8	8.3	9.6

▶Source: *Statistical Abstract of the United States, 1997*

QUIZ 3

Self-Test for Lessons 3.7 and 3.8

Write y as a function of x and evaluate when x is -2, 0, and 2. (Lesson 3.7)

1. $3x + 2y = 12$ **2.** $\frac{y}{3} - 4 = x$ **3.** $\frac{1}{2}(2x + 10y) = 8$

Solve the given formula for the specified variable. (Lesson 3.7)

4. Solve $V = lwh$ for w.   **5.** Solve $A = \frac{1}{2}bh$ for h.   **6.** Solve $P = C + rC$ for r.

Convert the given currency or measure. (Lesson 3.8)

7. 125 Swiss francs to United States dollars (1 Swiss franc is 0.746 dollar.)

8. 50.8 centimeters to inches (1 inch = 2.54 centimeters)

In Exercises 9–11, write and solve an equation to find the answer. (Lesson 3.8)

9. 🌐 **CAR MILEAGE** A car uses fuel at a rate of 33 miles per gallon. Estimate how many miles the car will travel on 12 gallons of fuel.

10. 🌐 **POPULATION** A school's population increased by 42 students. This was a 3% increase. About how many students attended before the increase?

11. 🌐 **SURVEY** Out of 525 people surveyed, 210 answered yes. Estimate how many people would answer yes if 900 people were surveyed.

12. Use the information in Exercise 11. What percent of the 525 people surveyed answered yes? (Lesson 3.8)

Extension

Inductive and Deductive Reasoning

What you should learn

GOAL Identify and use inductive and deductive reasoning.

Why you should learn it

To use logical reasoning in mathematics and in everyday life as in **Examples 3 and 4.**

GOAL **USING INDUCTIVE AND DEDUCTIVE REASONING**

Reasoning is used in mathematics, science, and everyday life. When you reach a conclusion, called a **generalization,** based on several observations, you are using **inductive reasoning.** Such a generalization is not always true. If a counterexample is found, then the generalization is proved to be false.

EXAMPLE 1 *Inductive Reasoning in Everyday Life*

You go to the school library every day for a week to do research for a paper. You notice that the computer you plan to use is not in use at 3:00 each day.

   a. Using inductive reasoning, what would you conclude about the computer?

   b. What counterexample would show that your generalization is false?

SOLUTION

   a. From your observations, you conclude that the computer is available every weekday at 3:00.

   b. A counterexample would be to find the computer in use one day at 3:00.

· · · · · · · · ·

STUDENT HELP

↳ **Look Back**
For help with counterexamples, see p. 66.

You use inductive reasoning when you make generalizations about number patterns. You assume the next number in the sequence will follow the pattern.

EXAMPLE 2 *Inductive Reasoning and Sequences*

Using inductive reasoning, name the next three numbers of the sequence 1, 5, 9, 13, 17, 21, ...

SOLUTION

The first step is to look for a pattern in the list of numbers. In this case, each number in the list is 4 more than the previous number ($1 + 4 = $ **5**, $5 + 4 = $ **9**, $9 + 4 = $ **13**, $13 + 4 = $ **17**). The next three numbers would be $21 + 4 = $ **25**, $25 + 4 = $ **29**, and $29 + 4 = $ **33**.

· · · · · · · · ·

When you use facts, definitions, rules, or properties to reach a conclusion, you are using **deductive reasoning.** A conclusion reached in this way is proved to be true. Deductive reasoning often uses **if-then statements.** The *if* part is called the **hypothesis** and the *then* part is called the **conclusion.** When deductive reasoning has been used to *prove* an if-then statement then the fact that the hypothesis is true implies that the conclusion is true.

EXAMPLE 3 *Use of If-Then Statements*

During the last week of a class, your teacher tells you that if you receive an A on the final exam, you will have earned an A average in the course.

a. Identify the hypothesis and the conclusion of the if-then statement.

b. Supose you receive an A on the final exam. What will your final grade be?

SOLUTION

a. The hypothesis is "you receive an A on the final exam." The conclusion is "you will have earned an A average in the course."

b. You can conclude that you have earned an A in the course.

EXAMPLE 4 *Deductive Reasoning in Mathematics*

STUDENT HELP

Look Back
For help with the properties of addition, see p. 73.

To show that the statement "If a, b, and c are real numbers, then $(a + b) + c = (c + b) + a$" is true by deductive reasoning, you can write each step and justify it using the properties of addition.

$$(a + b) + c = c + (a + b) \quad \text{Commutative property}$$
$$= c + (b + a) \quad \text{Commutative property}$$
$$= (c + b) + a \quad \text{Associative property}$$

EXERCISES

In Exercises 1–4, identify the reasoning as inductive or deductive. Explain.

1. The tenth number in the list 1, 4, 9, 16, 25, . . . is 100.

2. You know that in your neighborhood, if it is Sunday, then no mail is delivered. It is Sunday, so you conclude that the mail will not be delivered.

3. If the last digit of a number is 2, then the number is divisible by 2. You conclude that 98,765,432 is divisible by 2.

4. You notice that for several values of x the value of x^2 is greater than x. You conclude that the square of a number is greater than the number itself.

5. Find a counterexample to show that the conclusion in Exercise 4 is false.

6. Give an example of inductive reasoning and an example of deductive reasoning. Do not use any of the examples already given.

7. Name the next three numbers of the sequence: 0, 3, 6, 9, 12, 15, 18, . . .

In Exercises 8 and 9, identify the hypothesis and the conclusion of the if-then statement.

8. If you add two odd numbers, then the answer will be an even number.

9. If you are in Minnesota in January, then you will be cold.

10. Use deductive reasoning and the properties of addition to show that if z is a real number, then $(z + 2) + (-2) = z$.

Chapter Summary

WHAT did you learn?

Solve a linear equation
- using addition and subtraction. (3.1)
- using multiplication and division. (3.2)
- using two or more transformations. (3.3)
- with variables on both sides. (3.4)
- involving decimals. (3.6)

Write an equation using equal ratios. (3.2)

Solve a formula for one of its variables. (3.7)

Rewrite an equation in function form, and find the output given the input. (3.7)

Use linear equations to model and solve real-life problems
- using a diagram. (3.5)
- using a table or a graph to check. (3.5)

- involving rates, ratios, and percents. (3.8)

WHY did you learn it?

Model and find increases and decreases. (p. 134)
Find your distance from a thunderstorm. (p. 143)
Find the temperature below Earth's surface. (p. 147)
Decide whether a membership is economical. (p. 156)
Find the expansion gap for a bridge. (p. 171)

Find unknown side lengths in similar triangles. (p. 141)

Estimate the speed on Pathfinder's flight to Mars. (p. 175)

Prepare for graphing linear equations in two variables. (p. 176)

Design a high school yearbook. (p. 160)
Understand when a gazelle is a safe distance from a cheetah. (p. 162)
Estimate how far a car can travel on a tank of gasoline. (p. 180)

How does Chapter 3 fit into the BIGGER PICTURE of algebra?

In Chapters 1 and 2 you used mental math to solve simple equations. In this chapter you learned systematic equation-solving techniques that allow you to solve more complicated equations such as $0.5(x - 4) - (x - 8) = 16$. These techniques are based on the rules of algebra and the methods for simplifying you learned in Chapter 2.

You will need to solve linear equations when you solve linear inequalities in Chapter 6 and systems of equations in Chapter 7.

STUDY STRATEGY

How did you use your formula cards?

One of the formula cards you made, using the **Study Strategy** on p. 130, may look like this one.

> **The Distance Formula**
>
> $$D = rt$$
> D = distance (in feet, miles, kilometers, etc.)
> t = time (in minutes, hours, etc.)
> r = rate (in feet per minute, miles per hour, etc.)
>
> For example: If D is in kilometers and t is in hours, then r is in kilometers per hour.

Chapter Review

VOCABULARY

- equivalent equations, p. 132
- inverse operations, p. 132
- solution step, p. 133

- linear equation in one variable, p. 133
- properties of equality, p. 139
- ratio of a to b, p. 140

- similar triangles, p. 140
- identity, p. 155
- round-off error, p. 166

- formula, p. 174
- rate of a per b, p. 180
- unit rate, p. 180

3.1–3.2   SOLVING EQUATIONS USING ONE OPERATION

Examples on
pp. 132–134, 138–141

EXAMPLES Use inverse operations to isolate the variable.

$y - 4 = -6$	Write original equation.	$2 - x = 12$	Write original equation.
$y = -2$	Add 4 to each side.	$-x = 10$	Subtract 2 from each side.
		$x = -10$	x is the opposite of 10.
$\frac{1}{8}m = -5$	Write original equation.	$-7n = 28$	Write original equation.
$m = -40$	Multiply each side by 8.	$n = -4$	Divide each side by -7.

Solve the equation.

1. $y - 15 = -4$ **2.** $-7 + x = -3$ **3.** $25 = -35 - c$ **4.** $-11 = z - (-15)$

5. $36 = \dfrac{h}{-12}$ **6.** $-\dfrac{2}{3}w = -70$ **7.** $6m = -72$ **8.** $\dfrac{y}{4} = \dfrac{15}{6}$

3.3   SOLVING MULTI-STEP EQUATIONS

Examples on
pp. 145–147

EXAMPLE Solving some equations requires two or more transformations.

$-2p - (-5) - 2p = 13$	Write original equation.
$-4p + 5 = 13$	Simplify.
$-4p = 8$	Subtract 5 from each side.
$p = -2$	Divide each side by -4.

Solve the equation.

9. $26 - 9p = -1$ **10.** $\dfrac{4}{5}c - 12 = -32$ **11.** $\dfrac{y}{4} + 2 = 0$ **12.** $-2(4 - x) - 7 = 5$

13. $6r - 2 - 9r = 1$ **14.** $16 = 5(1 - x)$ **15.** $-\dfrac{2}{3}(6 - 2a) = 6$ **16.** $n - 4(1 + 5n) = -2$

SOLVING EQUATIONS WITH VARIABLES ON BOTH SIDES

Examples on pp. 154–156

EXAMPLES To solve, try to collect the variable terms on one side of the equation.

An equation with one solution:

$$-21d + 15 = -5d + 7$$
$$15 = 16d + 7$$
$$8 = 16d$$
$$\frac{1}{2} = d$$

An equation with no solution:

$$-3(2x - 5) = -(15 + 6x)$$
$$-6x + 15 = -15 - 6x$$
$$15 = -15$$

$15 \neq -15$ for any value of x, so the original equation has no solution.

An equation with many solutions:

$$2s - 5s + 11 = 2 - 3s + 9$$
$$-3s + 11 = 11 - 3s$$
$$11 = 11$$

The equation $11 = 11$ is always true, so all values of s are solutions.

Solve the equation if possible.

17. $9z + 24 = -3z$

18. $12 - 4h = -18 + 11h$

19. $24a - 8 - 10a = -2(4 - 7a)$

20. $9(-5 - r) = -10 - 2r$

21. $\frac{2}{3}(3x - 9) = 4(x + 6)$

22. $6m - 3 = 10 - 6(2 - m)$

LINEAR EQUATIONS AND PROBLEM SOLVING

Examples on pp. 160–162

EXAMPLE A diagram can help you to understand a problem. Two runners leave the starting line at the same time. The first runner crosses the finish line in 25 minutes and averages 12 kilometers per hour. The second runner crosses the finish line 5 minutes after the first runner. Find the second runner's speed.

Runner 1 runs 12 km/h.
25 min
25 + 5 = 30 min
Runner 2 runs ? km/h.
Start   Finish

VERBAL MODEL

| Speed of first runner | · | Time of first runner | = | Speed of second runner | · | Time of second runner |

LABELS

Speed of first runner = **12** (kilometers per hour)

Time of first runner = $\frac{5}{12}$ (hour)

Speed of second runner = **x** (kilometers per hour)

Time of second runner = $\frac{1}{2}$ (hour)

23. Write and solve the equation for the example. Then answer the question.

24. 🌐 **TOMATOES** One tomato plant is 12 inches tall and grows $1\frac{1}{2}$ inches per week. Another tomato plant is 6 inches tall and grows 2 inches per week. When will the plants be the same height? Use a table or a graph to check.

SOLVING DECIMAL EQUATIONS

Examples on pp. 166–168

EXAMPLE For some equations, you need to give an approximate solution.

$3.45m = -2.93m - 2.95$	**Write original equation.**
$6.38m = -2.95$	**Add 2.93m to each side.**
$m \approx -0.462382445$	**Using a calculator, divide each side by 6.38.**
$m \approx -0.46$	**Round answer. (Use hundredths, as in original equation.)**

Solve the equation. Round the result to the nearest tenth.

25. $13.7t - 4.7 = 9.9 + 8.1t$ **26.** $4.6(2a + 3) = 3.7a - 0.4$ **27.** $-6(5.61x - 3.21) = 4.75$

FORMULAS AND FUNCTIONS

Examples on pp. 174–176

EXAMPLE You can solve the formula for the volume of a cone for the height h.

$V = \dfrac{1}{3}\pi r^2 h$	**Write original formula.**
$3V = \pi r^2 h$	**Multiply each side by 3.**
$\dfrac{3V}{\pi r^2} = h$	**Divide each side by πr^2.**

In Exercises 28–30, solve for the indicated variable.

28. $S = 2\pi rh$ for h **29.** $S = \pi s(R + r)$ for r **30.** $R = \dfrac{pV}{nT}$ for p

31. Rewrite the equation $3x + 2y - 4 = 2(5 - y)$ so that y is a function of x. Then use the result to find y when $x = -2$, 0, 1, and 5.

RATES, RATIOS, AND PERCENTS

Examples on pp. 180–182

EXAMPLE For a United States flag, the ratio $\dfrac{\text{length}}{\text{width}}$ is $\dfrac{1.9}{1}$. How long is a 5-inch-wide flag?

length of small flag $\longrightarrow \dfrac{x}{5} = \dfrac{1.9}{1}$ $\longleftarrow$ **standard length to width ratio**
width of small flag $\longrightarrow$

The solution of the equation is $x = 9.5$, so the flag is 9.5 inches long.

32. You earn $210 in 40 hours. At this rate, how much do you earn in 55 hours?

33. A cab driver typically receives about 15% of the fare charged as a tip. To earn a total of $30 in tips, about how much would a driver need to collect in fares?

34. Convert 470 Ethiopian birrs to U.S. dollars. (1 dollar is 7.821 birrs.)

CHAPTER 3 Chapter Test

Solve the equation if possible.

1. $2 + x = 8$

2. $19 = a - 4$

3. $-3y = -18$

4. $\frac{x}{4} = 5$

5. $17 = 5 - 3p$

6. $-\frac{3}{4}x - 2 = -8$

7. $\frac{5}{3}(9 - w) = -10$

8. $-3(x - 2) = x$

9. $-5r - 6 + 4r = -r + 2$

10. $-4y - (5y + 6) = -7y + 3$

Solve the equation. Round the result to the nearest hundredth.

11. $13.2x + 4.3 = 2(2.7x - 3.6)$

12. $-4(2.5x + 8.7) = (1.4 - 9.2x)(6)$

In Exercises 13 and 14, solve for the indicated variable.

13. $C = 2\pi r$, r

14. $S = B + \frac{1}{2}Pl$, l

15. Rewrite $3x + 4y = 15 + 6y$ so that y is a function of x.

16. Use the result in Exercise 15 to find y when $x = -1$, 0, and 2.

17. How many feet are in 3.5 kilometers? (Hint: 1 km ≈ 3281 ft)

18. 🌎 **SHOVELING SNOW** You shovel snow. You charge $7 per driveway and earn $42. Let x represent the number of driveways you shoveled. Which of the following equations is an algebraic model for the situation?

A. $42x = 7$ **B.** $\frac{1}{7}x = 42$ **C.** $7x = 42$ **D.** $\frac{1}{42}x = 7$

🌎 **EARNINGS** **In Exercises 19 and 20, your cousin earns about $25 per week baby-sitting and receives one $5 bonus. You earn about $15 per week mowing lawns and $12 per week running errands. After working the same number of weeks, you have $11 more than your cousin.**

19. Write and solve an equation to find how many weeks you worked.

20. Check your solution in Exercise 19 with a table or a graph.

21. 🌎 **SAVINGS INTEREST** You invest $400. After one year, the total of the investment is $414.40. Use the formula $A = P + Prt$ to find the annual simple interest rate for the investment, where A is the total of the investment, P is the principal (amount invested), r is the annual simple interest rate, and t is the time in years.

In Exercises 22 and 23, write and solve an equation to answer the question.

22. 🌎 **VOLUNTEER WORK** You stuffed 108 envelopes in 45 minutes. At this rate, how many envelopes can you stuff in 2 hours?

23. 🌎 **WAGES** After an 8% increase in your wages, you receive $.94 more per hour. About how much did you receive per hour before the increase in your wages?

CHAPTER 3

Chapter Standardized Test

● **TEST TAKING STRATEGY** As soon as the testing time begins, start working. Keep moving and stay focused on the test.

1. **MULTIPLE CHOICE** Solve $4 - x = -5$.

   (A) -1 (B) 1 (C) -9

   (D) 9 (E) $\frac{5}{4}$

2. **MULTIPLE CHOICE** Which of these steps can you use to solve the equation $\frac{3}{5}x = 12$?

   I. Multiply by $\frac{3}{5}$.   **II.** Divide by $\frac{5}{3}$.

   III. Divide by $\frac{3}{5}$.   **IV.** Multiply by $\frac{5}{3}$.

   (A) **I** only   (B) **III** only

   (C) **I** and **II**   (D) **III** and **IV**

   (E) None of the above

3. **MULTIPLE CHOICE** The perimeter of the rectangle is 30. Find the value of x.

   $3x$
   $x - 1$

   (A) 3 (B) $\frac{31}{4}$ (C) 10

   (D) 4 (E) 31

4. **MULTIPLE CHOICE** If $9x - 4(3x - 2) = 4$, then $x = \underline{\ ?\ }$.

   (A) $\frac{4}{3}$ (B) $-\frac{4}{3}$ (C) -4

   (D) 4 (E) 2

5. **MULTIPLE CHOICE** How many solutions does the equation $-2y + 3(4 - y) = 12 - 5y$ have?

   (A) none   (B) one   (C) two

   (D) three   (E) an infinite number

6. **MULTIPLE CHOICE** Solve the equation $\frac{1}{3}(27x + 18) = 12 + 6(x - 4)$.

   (A) -6 (B) -3 (C) -2

   (D) 2 (E) 14

7. **MULTIPLE CHOICE** If $0.75t = 12$, then $t = \underline{\ ?\ }$.

   (A) 2 (B) 8 (C) 9

   (D) 12 (E) 16

8. **MULTIPLE CHOICE** You sell hot dogs for $1.25 each. Which equation can you use to find how many hot dogs you sold if you have $60 from selling hot dogs?

   (A) $\frac{x}{60} = 1.25$ (B) $60x = 1.25$

   (C) $1.25x = 60$ (D) $\frac{x}{1.25} = 60$

   (E) $(1.25)(60) = x$

9. **MULTIPLE CHOICE** Find the value of y if $13.56y - 14.76 = 3(4.12y - 6.72)$.

   (A) -4.5 (B) -2.56 (C) -1.2

   (D) 1.2 (E) 2.70

10. **MULTIPLE CHOICE** Use the equation $2(2 - y) = 3x$. What are the values of y when $x = -4, 0, \frac{2}{3}$, and 3?

    (A) $4, 2, 1, -\frac{5}{2}$ (B) $4, \frac{4}{3}, \frac{8}{9}, -\frac{2}{3}$

    (C) $8, 2, 1, -\frac{5}{2}$ (D) $16, 4, 2, -5$

    (E) $-8, -2, -1, \frac{5}{2}$

11. **MULTIPLE CHOICE** The sales tax is 6%. Which is the total charge for your meal before tax if the sales tax came to $.87?

    (A) 14.30 (B) 5.22 (C) 6.90

    (D) 1.45 (E) 14.50

12. **MULTIPLE CHOICE** If $x = -5$ is a solution of $2x + tx - 5 = 30$, what is the value of t?

    (A) -9 (B) -7 (C) -5

    (D) 3 (E) 9

QUANTITATIVE COMPARISON **In Exercises 13 and 14, choose the statement that is true about the value of the variable.**

(A) The value in column A is greater.

(B) The value in column B is greater.

(C) The two values are equal.

(D) The relationship cannot be determined from the given information.

	Column A	Column B
13.	The value of b in the formula $A = \frac{1}{2}bh$ when $A = 39$ and $h = 6$	The value of b in the formula $A = \frac{1}{2}bh$ when $A = 78$ and $h = 12$
14.	The value of A in the formula $A = \frac{1}{2}bh$ when $h = 32$	The value of A in the formula $A = \frac{1}{2}bh$ when $h = 5$

15. MULTIPLE CHOICE Out of 225 people surveyed, 183 said yes. Which equation can you use to estimate how many people would say yes if 600 people were surveyed?

(A) $\dfrac{225}{183} = \dfrac{x}{600}$ (B) $\dfrac{x}{600} = \dfrac{183}{225}$ (C) $600 = x \cdot \dfrac{183}{225}$ (D) $\dfrac{225}{600} = \dfrac{x}{183}$ (E) none of them

16. MULTI-STEP PROBLEM Karim and his three children enjoy ice skating. The town ice skating rink charges $10.00 for adults and $6.50 for children per visit. The rink also offers a one-year family membership for $650.00. The membership offers a family unlimited ice skating throughout the year.

Karim's schedule is so busy that he has at most two days each month to go ice skating with his children. Karim wants to decide whether it is worthwhile for him to purchase the one-year membership.

a. Let r represent the number of times Karim's family (Karim and his children) visits the ice skating rink during the year. Write a variable expression for each of the following costs: the cost of one child's visits to the rink during the year, the cost of Karim's visits to the rink during the year, the total cost of the family's visits to the rink during the year.

b. Karim decides to compare the total cost of the family's visits during the year to the membership cost. Write an equation that models the situation. Then solve the equation.

c. How much money will Karim lose or save by purchasing the membership if he and his children find the time to visit the skating rink 27 times in the year? if they only visit the skating rink once a month?

d. *Writing* Based on your results in parts (b) and (c), make a recommendation to Karim. Should he buy the one-year membership with unlimited visits or should he pay for each visit? Explain your reasoning.

Cumulative Practice

Evaluate the numerical expression. (1.3, 2.1, 2.7)

1. $5 + 3(18 \div 6)$

2. $3.6 \div (2 + 4) + 1.2$

3. $[2(9 - 5) + 1] \cdot 3^2$

4. $|6 - 14| - 2.5(7)$

5. $2(3.5) - |13.2 - 7.21|$

6. $4(12.7 - 31.2) + 3.6$

7. $(20 - 3 + 7) \div (-8)$

8. $\dfrac{4(9 - 2)}{(7)(8)}$

9. $\dfrac{2^3 - 2(9)}{-5}$

Evaluate the variable expression. (1.3, 2.5, 2.7)

10. $-20 - 4y$ when $y = -3$

11. $r + 6(5 - r)$ when $r = 10$

12. $\dfrac{x - y}{3}$ when $x = 22$ and $y = 7$

13. $\dfrac{15x - 21}{y}$ when $x = 3$ and $y = 6$

14. $\dfrac{10x^2 - 8}{y}$ when $x = -2$ and $y = 11$

15. $\dfrac{x^2 y^2}{4x - 10}$ when $x = 10$ and $y = -\dfrac{1}{2}$

Check whether the number is a solution of the equation or inequality. (1.4)

16. $4 + 2x = 12; 2$

17. $6x - 5 = 13; 3$

18. $3y + 7 = 4y - 2; 8$

19. $x - 4 < 6; 9$

20. $5x + 3 > 8; 1$

21. $9 - x \le x + 3; 3$

Write the verbal phrase or sentence as an expression, an equation, or an inequality. (1.5)

22. A number cubed minus eight

23. The sum of four times a number and seventeen

24. Four less than twice a number is equal to ten.

25. The product of negative three and a number is greater than twelve.

26. The quotient of twenty and a number is less than one.

Perform the indicated matrix operation. (2.4)

27. $\begin{bmatrix} 8 & -2 \\ 1 & -5 \end{bmatrix} + \begin{bmatrix} -3 & 6 \\ -7 & 0 \end{bmatrix}$

28. $\begin{bmatrix} -5 & 5 \\ -2 & -1 \\ 8 & 4 \end{bmatrix} - \begin{bmatrix} -2 & 0 \\ 4 & -5 \\ 1 & -10 \end{bmatrix}$

29. $\begin{bmatrix} 23 & -6 & 1 \\ -47 & 15 & 4 \end{bmatrix} + \begin{bmatrix} 3 & 20 & -7 \\ -7 & -18 & 31 \end{bmatrix}$

30. $[4 \quad -2 \quad -7 \quad 1] - [6 \quad -4 \quad -8 \quad -1]$

Find the probability of choosing the indicated letter from a bag that contains the letters of the word. (2.8)

31. Letter: A

Word: MATHEMATICS

32. Letter: I

Word: DIAMETER

33. Letter: P

Word: PHILADELPHIA

34. Letter: A

Word: ALEXANDRIA

Solve the equation. (3.1–3.4)

35. $x + 11 = 19$ **36.** $-7 - x = -2$ **37.** $9b = 135$

38. $35 = 3c - 19$ **39.** $\dfrac{p}{2} - 9 = -1$ **40.** $4(2x - 9) = 6(10x - 6)$

41. $3(q - 12) = 5q + 2$ **42.** $-\dfrac{3}{4}(2x + 5) = 6$ **43.** $9(2p + 1) - 3p = 4p - 6$

Solve the equation. Round the result to the nearest hundredth. (3.6)

44. $-3.46y = -5.78$ **45.** $4.17n + 3.29 = 2.74n$

46. $4.2(0.3 + x) = 8.7$ **47.** $23.5a + 12.5 = 5.2(9.3a - 4.8)$

In Exercises 48–50, rewrite the equation so that x is a function of y. Then use the result to find x when $y = -2, 0, 1.5,$ and 3. (3.7)

48. $x + \dfrac{1}{2}y = -3$ **49.** $2(3y - 1) = 4x$ **50.** $-3(x + y) + 4 = 7y$

51. 🌐 **TEMPERATURE** Suppose the temperature outside is 82°F. What is the temperature in degrees Celsius? Use the formula $C = \dfrac{5}{9}(F - 32)$. (1.1)

52. 🌐 **SILVER PRODUCTION** The table shows the amount (in metric tons) of silver produced in the United States for different years. Make a line graph of the data. (1.6)

Year	1991	1992	1993	1994	1995	1996
Amount (metric tons)	1860	1800	1640	1480	1560	1570

▶ Source: U.S. Geological Survey

53. 🌐 **FUND RAISER** Your school band is planning to attend a competition. The total cost for the fifty band members to attend is $750. Each band member will pay $3 toward this cost and the rest of the money will be raised by selling wrapping paper. For each roll of wrapping paper sold, the band makes $2. Write and solve an equation to find how many rolls the band members need to sell. (3.3)

54. **GEOMETRY** ▸ **CONNECTION**   The volume of a circular cylinder with a radius of 1.5 inches is about 42.4 cubic inches. Find the cylinder's height. Round to the nearest tenth. (*Hint:* Volume of a circular cylinder $= \pi r^2 h$) (3.7)

🌐 **VACATION IN SWEDEN In Exercises 55–57, use the following information. You are vacationing in Sweden and have taken $620 to spend. The rate of currency exchange in Sweden is 7.827 kronor (plural of krona) per United States dollar.** (3.8)

55. If you exchange $\dfrac{3}{4}$ of the entire amount, how many kronor will you receive?

56. After your vacation, you have 1255 kronor left. If the exchange rate is the same, how many dollars will you get back?

57. If you exchanged the entire amount at the start of your vacation, how many kronor would you have received?

Running a Business

OBJECTIVE Comparing the expenses and income of a business to determine profitability.

Materials: paper, pencil, graphing calculator or computer (optional)

INVESTIGATION

In Exercises 1–8, use the financial plan below.

> My summer window-cleaning business: Financial Plans
>
> 1. Expenses:
>   - Paper towels cost $.90 for a 60-sheet roll.
>   - Spray window cleaner costs $1.98 for a 33-ounce bottle.
>   - A step ladder costs $25.00.
>
> 2. Income (per window):
>
> | Number of windows | 1–14 | 15 or more |
> |---|---|---|
> | Outside only | $.60 | $.50 |
> | Outside and inside | $1.10 | $1.00 |

1. You use two paper towels and 0.5 ounce of window cleaner to clean one side of a window. What is the total cost of materials to clean one side of a window?

2. Write an equation to find the cost C of cleaning one side of x windows.

3. Copy and complete the table. You may want to use a spreadsheet.

Number of windows	5	9	15	25
Cost for one side	?	?	?	?
Cost for both sides	?	?	?	?

4. Write an equation for the income I for cleaning both sides of x windows when $x < 15$.

5. How much profit will you make for cleaning both sides of 15 windows?

6. What is your total profit for cleaning the windows of 6 houses (inside and outside) with 12, 17, 13, 9, 14, and 10 windows respectively?

7. How many windows do you have to clean to pay for your step ladder? Explain your reasoning.

8. What would it mean if you found a negative profit?

PRESENT YOUR RESULTS

Write a report about your window cleaning plans.

- Include a discussion of income and expenses.

- Include your answers to Exercises 1–8.

- Explain how the cost of the ladder is a different kind of expense from the cost of paper towels and the window cleaner.

You may want to find out whether this business would work in your neighborhood.

- Survey some of your neighbors to find the price they would be willing to pay to have their windows cleaned.

- Do some research to find out what local businesses pay workers for similar work.

- Find out what the minimum hourly wage is. How many windows would you have to clean each hour to earn that amount?

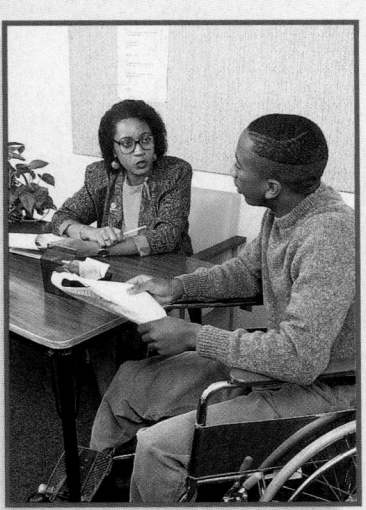

EXTENSION

Think of a business that you would like to start.

1. If you can, interview someone who has experience with the type of business you are interested in. What advice can that person give you?

2. Do some research to find out what kind of supplies or equipment you would need to get started and the cost of these items.

3. Decide what you could charge customers for this service.

4. Survey some of your friends and neighbors to find the price they would be willing to pay for such a product or service.

5. Write a financial plan for your business.

GRAPHING LINEAR EQUATIONS AND FUNCTIONS

▶ *How do you solve the problem of transporting people up steep hills?*

APPLICATION: Transportation

Before 1873, public transportation in San Francisco was
provided by horse-drawn wagons.

To design a transportation system,
people needed a mathematical
way to describe and measure
steepness.

Think & Discuss

1. What are some other real-life situations when
steepness is important? When is steepness
helpful? When is steepness a problem?

2. How would you describe the steepness of the
sections of street shown below?

(cross section of side view)

Learn More About It

Slope is a measure of steepness. You will calculate
the slope of this street in Exercise 55 on p. 231.

APPLICATION LINK Visit www.mcdougallittell.com
for more information about cable cars.

Study Guide

What's the chapter about?

Chapter 4 is about **graphing linear equations**. In Chapter 4, you'll learn

- how to graph linear equations.
- two ways to graph linear equations quickly.
- how to tell whether an equation or a graph represents a function.

KEY VOCABULARY

▶ **Review**
- variable expression, p. 3
- solution of an equation, p. 24
- function, p. 46
- linear equation, p. 133

▶ **New**
- coordinate plane, p. 203
- scatter plot, p. 204
- graph of a linear equation, p. 210
- x-intercept, p. 218

- y-intercept, p. 218
- slope, p. 226
- rate of change, p. 229
- slope-intercept form, p. 241
- function notation, p. 257

Are you ready for the chapter?

SKILL REVIEW Do these exercises to review key skills that you'll apply in this chapter. See the given **reference page** if there is something you don't understand.

Rewrite as a decimal and as a fraction in lowest terms. (Skills Review, p. 784)

1. 50%   **2.** 75%   **3.** 1%   **4.** 20%

Use the function $y = 5x + 70$, where $x \geq 0$. (Review Examples 1 and 2, pp. 46–47)

5. For several inputs x, use the function to calculate an output y.

6. Represent the data with a line graph.

7. Describe the domain and range of the function.

Evaluate the expression for the given values of the variables.
(Review Example 3, p. 109)

8. $\dfrac{x - y}{2}$ when $x = -3$ and $y = -1$ **9.** $\dfrac{x + 2y}{x}$ when $x = 6$ and $y = 3$

▶ **Study Tip**
"Student Help" boxes throughout the chapter give you study tips and tell you where to look for extra help in this book and on the Internet.

Here's a study strategy!

Getting Your Questions Answered

Each day after you finish your math homework, write a list of questions about things you don't understand. Ask your teacher or another student to answer your questions and write the explanations in your notebook.

Coordinates and Scatter Plots

GOAL 1 PLOTTING POINTS IN A COORDINATE PLANE

A **coordinate plane** is formed by two real number lines that intersect at a right angle. Each point in the plane corresponds to an **ordered pair** of real numbers.

The first number in an ordered pair is the **x-coordinate** and the second number is the **y-coordinate**. The ordered pair $(3, -2)$ has an x-coordinate of 3 and a y-coordinate of -2 as shown in the graph at the left below.

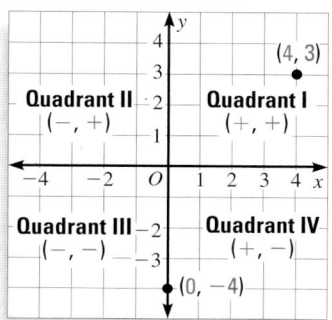

The x-axis and the y-axis (the *axes*) divide the coordinate plane into four quadrants. You can tell which quadrant a point is in by looking at the signs of its coordinates.

In the diagram at the right above, the point $(4, 3)$ is in Quadrant I. The point $(0, -4)$ is on the y-axis and is not inside any of the four quadrants.

The point in the plane that corresponds to an ordered pair (x, y) is called the **graph** of (x, y). To plot a point, you draw the point in the coordinate plane that corresponds to an ordered pair of numbers.

EXAMPLE 1 *Plotting Points in a Coordinate Plane*

a. To plot the point $(3, 4)$, start at the origin. Move 3 units to the right and 4 units up.

b. To plot the point $(-2, -3)$, start at the origin. Move 2 units to the left and 3 units down.

c. To plot the point $(2, 0)$, start at the origin. Move 2 units to the right and 0 units up.

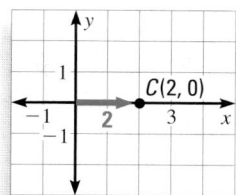

GOAL 2 USING A SCATTER PLOT

Many real-life situations can be described in terms of pairs of numbers. Medical charts record both the height and weight of the patient, while weather reports may include both temperature and windspeed. One way to analyze the relationships between two quantities is to graph the pairs of data on a coordinate axis. Such a graph is called a **scatter plot**.

Sports

EXAMPLE 2   *Making a Scatter Plot*

You are the student manager of your high school soccer team. You are working on the team's program guide and have recorded the height and weight of the eleven starting players in the given table.

Height (in.)	72	70	71	70	69	70	69	73	66	70	76
Weight (lb)	190	170	180	175	160	160	150	180	150	150	200

a. Make a scatter plot of the data. Put height *h* on the horizontal axis and weight *w* on the vertical axis.

b. Use the scatter plot to estimate the weight of a player who is 69 inches tall and of one who is 71 inches tall.

c. In general, how does weight change as height changes?

d. What would you expect a player who is 74 inches tall to weigh?

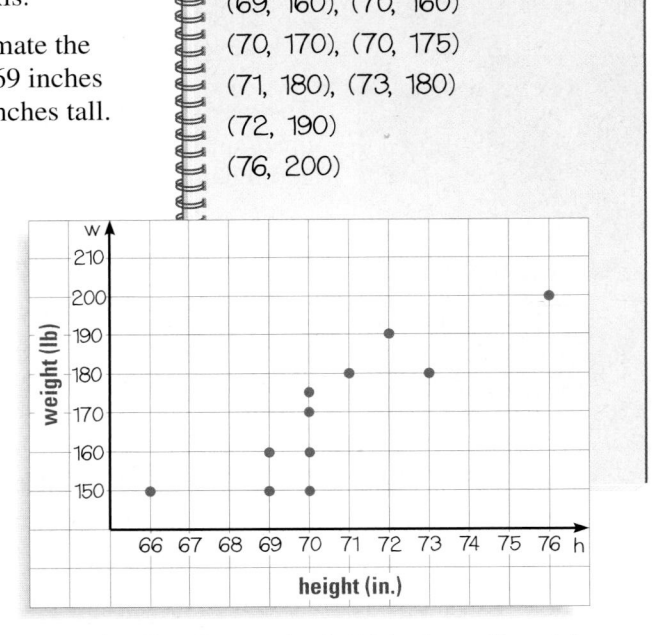

(66, 150), (69, 150), (70, 150)
(69, 160), (70, 160)
(70, 170), (70, 175)
(71, 180), (73, 180)
(72, 190)
(76, 200)

SOLUTION

a. Plot each ordered pair, as shown at the right.

b. The two players who are 69 inches tall weigh 150 pounds and 160 pounds, so a good estimate would be about 155 pounds. The player who is 71 inches tall weighs 180 pounds, so a possible estimate would be about 180 pounds.

c. As height increases, it appears that weight increases.

d. There is no given data value for a player who is 74 inches tall. However, the 72-inch-tall player weighs 190 pounds, the 73-inch-tall player weighs 180 pounds, and the 76-inch-tall player weighs 200 pounds, so a good estimate of the weight of a 74-inch-tall player would be between 190 and 195 pounds.

STUDENT HELP

INTERNET

HOMEWORK HELP
Visit our Web site
www.mcdougallittell.com
for extra examples.

You can use scatter plots to see trends in data and to make predictions about the future.

EXAMPLE 3 *Describing Patterns from a Scatter Plot*

WINTER SPORTS EQUIPMENT The amount (in millions of dollars) spent in the United States on snowmobiles and ski equipment is shown in the table.

  a. Draw a scatter plot of each set of data in the same coordinate plane.

  b. Describe the pattern of the amount spent on snowmobiles.

  c. Describe the pattern of the amount spent on ski equipment.

Year	1990	1991	1992	1993	1994	1995	1996
Snowmobiles	322	362	391	515	715	924	970
Ski equipment	606	577	627	611	652	607	644

DATA UPDATE of National Sporting Goods Association data at www.mcdougallittell.com

SOLUTION

  a. Because you want to see how spending changes over time, put time *t* on the horizontal axis and spending *s* on the vertical axis. Let *t* be the number of years since 1990. The scatter plot is shown below.

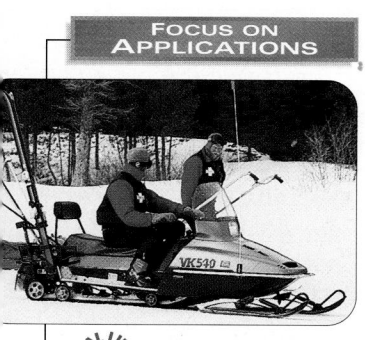

SNOWMOBILES have proven essential in the search and rescue field. They can often reach mountainous areas more quickly than an aircraft.

  b. From the scatter plot, you can see that the amount spent on snowmobiles has been increasing rapidly since 1990.

  c. The amount spent on ski equipment has been fairly constant since 1990. The amount spent has stayed around $600 million.

GUIDED PRACTICE

Vocabulary Check ✓

1. In the ordered pair (4, 9), the *x*-coordinate is __?__ .

Concept Check ✓

2. Decide whether the following statement is *true* or *false*. *Each point in a coordinate plane corresponds to an ordered pair of real numbers.*

Skill Check ✓

3. Write the ordered pairs that correspond to the points labeled *A*, *B*, and *C* in the coordinate plane at the right.

Plot the ordered pairs in a coordinate plane.

4. $A(4, -1)$, $B(5, 0)$

5. $A(-2, -3)$, $B(-3, -2)$

6. The point $(-2, 5)$ lies in Quadrant __?__ .

Ex. 3

SCATTER PLOT In Exercises 7 and 8, draw a scatter plot of the given data.

7.

Time	1:00	3:00	5:00	7:00
Temp.	71°	74°	68°	63°

8.

TV size	19 in.	27 in.	32 in.	36 in.
Price	$179	$349	$499	$659

9. 🌐 **SNOWMOBILE SALES** Use the scatter plot in Example 3. If you were given the amounts spent on snowmobiles from 1990 through 1992 only, would your description of the pattern be different than the one given in the Example?

PRACTICE AND APPLICATIONS

STUDENT HELP

▶ **Extra Practice**
to help you master
skills is on p. 800.

IDENTIFYING ORDERED PAIRS Write the ordered pairs that correspond to the points labeled *A, B, C,* and *D* in the coordinate plane.

10.

11.

12.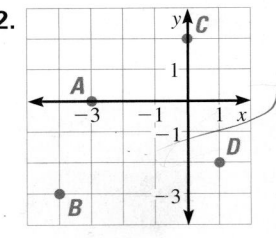

PLOTTING POINTS Plot and label the ordered pairs in a coordinate plane.

13. $A(0, 3)$, $B(-2, -1)$, $C(2, 0)$

14. $A(5, 2)$, $B(4, 3)$, $C(-2, -4)$

15. $A(4, 1)$, $B(0, -3)$, $C(3, 3)$

16. $A(0, 0)$, $B(2, -2)$, $C(-2, 0)$

17. $A(-4, 1)$, $B(-1, 5)$, $C(0, -4)$

18. $A(3, -5)$, $B(1.5, 3)$, $C(-3, -1)$

STUDENT HELP

▶ **HOMEWORK HELP**
Example 1: Exs. 10–26
Example 2: Exs. 33–37
Example 3: Exs. 27–32

IDENTIFYING QUADRANTS Without plotting the point, tell whether it is in Quadrant I, Quadrant II, Quadrant III, or Quadrant IV.

19. $(5, -3)$

20. $(-2, 7)$

21. $(6, 17)$

22. $(14, -5)$

23. $(-4, -2)$

24. $(3, 9)$

25. $(-5, -2)$

26. $(-5, 6)$

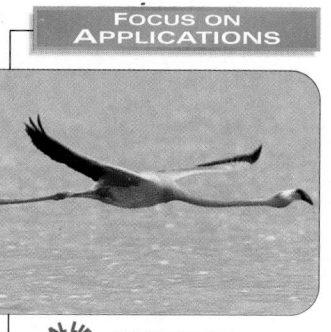

STUDENT HELP

▶ **Look Back**
For help with breaks in the scale of a graph, see p. 41.

🌐 **CAR COMPARISONS** In Exercises 27–32, use the scatter plots.

27. In the Weight vs. Length graph, what are the units on the horizontal axis? What are the units on the vertical axis?

28. In the Weight vs. Length graph, estimate the coordinates of the point for a car that weighs about 4000 pounds.

29. Which of the following is true?

   A. Length tends to decrease as weight increases.

   B. Length is constant as weight increases.

   C. Length tends to increase as weight increases.

   D. Length is not related to weight.

30. In the Weight vs. Gas Mileage graph, what is the value of w in the ordered pair (2010, 29)? What is the value of G?

31. **INTERPRETING DATA** In the Weight vs. Gas Mileage graph, how does gas mileage tend to change as weight increases?

32. **CRITICAL THINKING** How would you expect the length of a car to affect its gas mileage? Explain your reasoning.

33. **GATHERING DATA** Write a list of ten songs in alphabetical order. Put songs you like on the list and some you don't like. Make two copies. On one copy, rank the songs from 1 to 10 (1 for the most liked and 10 for the least liked). Then ask a friend to rank the songs without looking at your rankings.

34. **INTERPRETING A GRAPH** Make a scatter plot with your song ratings from Exercise 33 on the horizontal axis and your friend's ratings on the vertical axis. What conclusions (if any) can you draw from the scatter plot?

BIOLOGY ▷ **CONNECTION** In Exercises 35–37, the table shows the wing length in millimeters and the wing-beat rate in beats per second.

Bird	Flamingo	Shellduck	Velvet Scoter	Fulmar	Great Egret
Wing length	400	375	281	321	437
Wing-beat rate	2.4	3.0	4.3	3.6	2.1

FOCUS ON APPLICATIONS

35. Make a scatter plot that shows the wing lengths and wing-beat rates for the six birds. Use the horizontal axis to represent the wing length.

36. What is the slowest wing-beat rate shown on the scatter plot? What is the fastest? Where are these located on your scatter plot?

37. **INTERPRETING DATA** Describe the relationship between the wing length and the wing-beat rate.

AMERICAN FLAMINGOES have distinctive and unusual features. Their extremely long neck and legs give the impression that the bird could fly backwards. When the flamingo's wings are fully extended, you can see the black in its wings.

38. MULTI-STEP PROBLEM The table below shows the number of rolls of film developed for the United States media at the Winter Olympics.

Number of years since 1980, *t*	4	8	12	14	18
Rolls of film, *f*	48,200	53,750	60,500	67,500	75,000

    a. Construct a scatter plot of the data. Describe the pattern of the number of rolls of film developed for the Winter Olympics from 1984 to 1998.

    b. *Writing* Predict the number of rolls of film that will be developed for the Winter Olympics in the year 2002. Explain how you made your prediction.

★ Challenge

🌐 **MUSIC** **Sara thought that there might be a relationship between the number of songs and the number of minutes of music recorded on a CD. She collected the following data from five CDs she had on her desk.**

Number of songs, *s*	15	12	13	16	18
Number of minutes, *m*	44.9	31.5	40.6	50.5	71.6

39. Make a scatter plot of Sara's data. What relationship do the data suggest?

40. To check her findings, Sara collected data from five more CDs. Make a new scatter plot of these data. What relationship do the data suggest?

Number of songs, *s*	12	13	9	11	10
Number of minutes, *m*	46.8	40.6	67.0	53.0	56.1

41. CRITICAL THINKING Do you think there is a relationship between the number of songs and the number of minutes on a CD? Explain your reasoning. How could you test whether there is a relationship?

EXTRA CHALLENGE

↳ www.mcdougallittell.com

MIXED REVIEW

EVALUATING EXPRESSIONS **Evaluate the expression for the given value of the variable.** (Review 1.3 and 2.5 for 4.2)

42. $3x + 9$ when $x = 2$

43. $13 - (y + 2)$ when $y = 4$

44. $4.2t + 17.9$ when $t = 3$

45. $-3x - 9y$ when $x = -2$ and $y = -1$

USING EXPONENTS **Evaluate the expression.** (Review 1.2)

46. $x^2 - 3$ when $x = 4$

47. $12 + y^3$ when $y = 3$

ABSOLUTE VALUE **In Exercises 48–51, evaluate the expression.** (Review 2.1)

48. $|-2.6|$

49. $|1.07|$

50. $\left|\dfrac{9}{10}\right|$

51. $\left|\dfrac{-2}{3}\right|$

52. 🌐 **TEEN SAVINGS** In a survey of 500 teens, 345 said they have a savings account. What is the experimental probability that a randomly chosen teen in the survey has a savings account? (Review 2.8)

● ACTIVITY 4.1

Using Technology

Graphing a Scatter Plot

▶ **EXAMPLE**

The table below shows the maximum time allowed for boys in the 1-mile run to qualify for the President's Physical Fitness Award. Use a graphing calculator or a computer to make a scatter plot of the data.

Age (years)	10	11	12	13	14	15	16	17
Time (minutes)	7.95	7.53	7.18	6.83	6.43	6.33	6.13	6.10

▶ **SOLUTION**

❶ Write the data as a set of ordered pairs. Use age as the x-coordinate and time as the y-coordinate, for example (10, 7.95). Use the STAT EDIT feature to enter the ordered pairs as List 1 and List 2.

❷ Use WINDOW to describe the size of the graph. The x-values are between 0 and 20. The y-values are between 0 and 10.

The x-scale is the number of units per mark on the x-axis of the graph.

❸ Use STAT PLOT. In this window, select scatter plot, List 1 for the x-values, and List 2 for the y-values.

❹ Use GRAPH to draw the scatter plot.

Tick marks will be 5 units apart on the x-axis.

▶ **EXERCISES**

1. **LOOK FOR A PATTERN** Describe any patterns you see in the scatter plot you made in the example above.

The table below shows the maximum time allowed for girls in the 1-mile run to qualify for the President's Physical Fitness Award.

Age (years)	10	11	12	13	14	15	16	17
Time (minutes)	9.32	9.03	8.38	8.22	7.98	8.13	8.38	8.25

2. Use a graphing calculator to make a scatter plot of the data.

3. **LOOK FOR A PATTERN** Describe any patterns you see in the scatter plot.

4. How does this scatter plot differ from the scatter plot for the boys' times?

Graphing Linear Equations

What you should learn

GOAL 1 Graph a linear equation using a table or a list of values.

GOAL 2 Graph horizontal and vertical lines.

Why you should learn it

▼ To solve **real-life** problems such as finding the amount of calories burned while training for Triathlon in **Exs. 71–73**.

GOAL 1 GRAPHING A LINEAR EQUATION

A **solution of an equation** in two variables x and y is an ordered pair (x, y) that makes the equation true. The **graph of an equation** in x and y is the set of *all* points (x, y) that are solutions of the equation. In this lesson you will see that the graph of a *linear* equation is a line.

EXAMPLE 1 *Verifying Solutions of an Equation*

Use the graph to decide whether the point lies on the graph of $x + 3y = 6$. Justify your answer algebraically.

   a. $(1, 2)$

   b. $(-3, 3)$

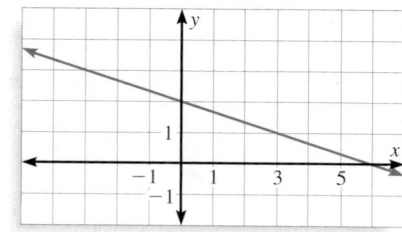

SOLUTION

   a. The point $(1, 2)$ is *not* on the graph of $x + 3y = 6$. This means that $(1, 2)$ is not a solution. You can check this algebraically.

$$x + 3y = 6 \qquad \text{Write original equation.}$$

$$1 + 3(2) \stackrel{?}{=} 6 \qquad \text{Substitute 1 for } x \text{ and 2 for } y.$$

$$7 \neq 6 \qquad \text{Simplify. Not a true statement}$$

   ▶ $(1, 2)$ is not a solution of the equation $x + 3y = 6$, so it is not on the graph.

   b. The point $(-3, 3)$ is on the graph of $x + 3y = 6$. This means that $(-3, 3)$ is a solution. You can check this algebraically.

$$x + 3y = 6 \qquad \text{Write original equation.}$$

$$-3 + 3(3) \stackrel{?}{=} 6 \qquad \text{Substitute } -3 \text{ for } x \text{ and 3 for } y.$$

$$6 = 6 \qquad \text{Simplify. True statement}$$

   ▶ $(-3, 3)$ is a solution of the equation $x + 3y = 6$, so it is on the graph.

· · · · · · · · · ·

In Example 1 the point $(-3, 3)$ is on the graph of $x + 3y = 6$, but how many points does the graph have in all? The answer is that most graphs have too many points to list. Then how can you ever graph an equation? One way is to make a table or a list of a few values, plot enough solutions to recognize a pattern, and then connect the points. Even then, the graph extends without limit to the left of the smallest input and to the right of the largest input.

When you make a table of values to graph an equation, you may want to choose values for x that include negative values, zero, and positive values. This way you will see how the graph behaves to the left and right of the y-axis.

STUDENT HELP

Look Back
For help with rewriting equations in function form, see p. 176.

EXAMPLE 2 *Graphing an Equation*

Use a table of values to graph the equation $y + 2 = 3x$.

SOLUTION

Rewrite the equation in function form by solving for y.

$y + 2 = 3x$	Write original equation.
$y = 3x - 2$	Subtract 2 from each side.

Choose a few values for x and make a table of values.

Choose x.	Substitute to find the corresponding y-value.
-2	$y = 3(-2) - 2 = -8$
-1	$y = 3(-1) - 2 = -5$
0	$y = 3(0) - 2 = -2$
1	$y = 3(1) - 2 = 1$
2	$y = 3(2) - 2 = 4$

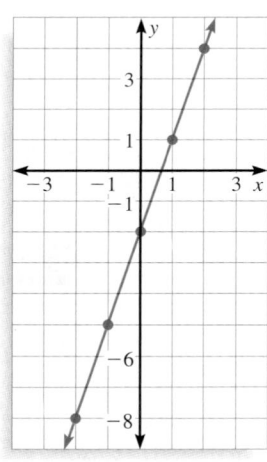

With this table of values you have found the five solutions $(-2, -8)$, $(-1, -5)$, $(0, -2)$, $(1, 1)$, and $(2, 4)$.

Plot the points. Note that they appear to lie on a straight line.

▶ The line through the points is the graph of the equation.

· · · · · · · · ·

STUDENT HELP

HOMEWORK HELP
Visit our Web site
www.mcdougallittell.com
for extra examples.

In Lesson 3.1 you saw examples of linear equations in one variable. The solution of an equation such as $2x - 1 = 3$ is a real number. Its graph is a point on the real number line. The equation $y + 2 = 3x$ in Example 2 is a linear equation in *two variables*. Its graph is a straight line.

GRAPHING A LINEAR EQUATION

STEP ❶ Rewrite the equation in function form, if necessary.

STEP ❷ Choose a few values of x and make a table of values.

STEP ❸ Plot the points from the table of values. A line through these points is the graph of the equation.

EXAMPLE 3 *Graphing a Linear Equation*

Use a table of values to graph the equation $3x + 2y = 1$.

SOLUTION

1 Rewrite the equation in function form by solving for y. This will make it easier to make a table of values.

$$3x + 2y = 1$$ Write original equation.

$$2y = -3x + 1$$ Subtract 3x from each side.

$$y = -\frac{3}{2}x + \frac{1}{2}$$ Divide each side by 2.

STUDENT HELP

▶ **Skills Review**
For help with fraction operations, see pp. 780–782.

2 Choose a few values of x and make a table of values.

Choose x.	-2	0	2
Evaluate y.	$\frac{7}{2}$	$\frac{1}{2}$	$-\frac{5}{2}$

With this table of values you have found three solutions.

$$\left(-2, \frac{7}{2}\right), \left(0, \frac{1}{2}\right), \left(2, -\frac{5}{2}\right)$$

3 Plot the points and draw a line through them.

▶ The graph of $3x + 2y = 1$ is shown at the right.

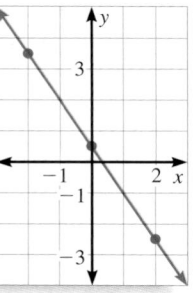

EXAMPLE 4 *Using the Graph of a Linear Model*

Internet Access

An Internet Service Provider estimates that the number of households h (in millions) with Internet access can be modeled by $h = 6.76t + 14.9$, where t represents the number of years since 1996. Graph this model. Describe the graph in the context of the real-life situation.

SOLUTION

Make a table of values. Use $0 \le t \le 6$ for 1996–2002.

t	h
0	14.90
1	21.66
2	28.42
3	35.18
4	41.94
5	48.70
6	55.46

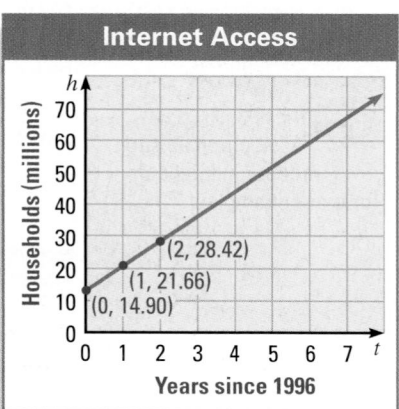

▶ From the table and the graph, you can see that the number of households with Internet access is projected to increase by about 7 million households per year.

GOAL 2 HORIZONTAL AND VERTICAL LINES

All linear equations in x and y can be written in the form $Ax + By = C$. When $A = 0$ the equation reduces to $By = C$ and the graph is a horizontal line. When $B = 0$ the equation reduces to $Ax = C$ and the graph is a vertical line.

EQUATIONS OF HORIZONTAL AND VERTICAL LINES

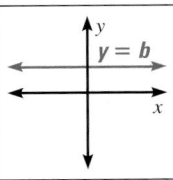

In the coordinate plane, the graph of $y = b$ is a horizontal line.

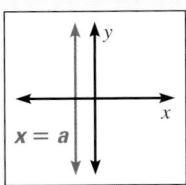

In the coordinate plane, the graph of $x = a$ is a vertical line.

EXAMPLE 5   *Graphing y = b*

Graph the equation $y = 2$.

SOLUTION

The equation does not have x as a variable. The y-value is always 2, regardless of the value of x. For instance, here are some points that are solutions of the equation:

$$(-3, 2), (0, 2), (3, 2).$$

▶ The graph of the equation is a horizontal line 2 units above the x-axis.

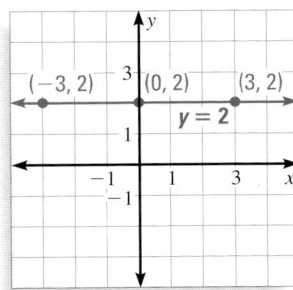

STUDENT HELP

↳ **Study Tip**
The equations $y = 2$ and $0x + 1y = 2$ are equivalent. For any value of x, the ordered pair $(x, 2)$ is a solution of $y = 2$.

EXAMPLE 6   *Graphing x = a*

Graph the equation $x = -3$.

SOLUTION

The x-value is always -3, regardless of the value of y. For instance, here are some points that are solutions of the equation:

$$(-3, -2), (-3, 0), (-3, 3).$$

▶ The graph of the equation is a vertical line 3 units to the left of the y-axis.

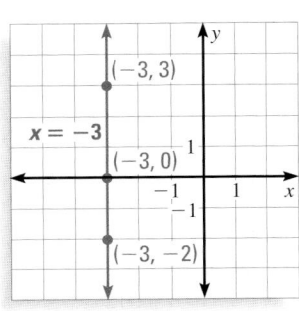

4.2 Graphing Linear Equations   **213**

GUIDED PRACTICE

Vocabulary Check ✓

1. Complete the following sentence: An ordered pair that makes an equation in two variables true is called a(n) ? .

Concept Check ✓

2. In Example 2, if you choose a value of x different from those in the table of values, will you find a solution that lies on the same line? Explain.

3. Decide whether the following statement is *true* or *false*. *The graph of the equation $x = 3$ is a horizontal line.* Explain.

Skill Check ✓

Use a table of values to graph the equation.

4. $6x - 3y = 12$ 5. $x = 1.5$ 6. $y = -2$

Tell whether the point is a solution of the equation $4x - y = 1$.

7. $(-1, 3)$ 8. $(1, 3)$ 9. $(1, 0)$ 10. $(1, 4)$

11. 🌐 **INTERNET ACCESS** Using the graph or the model in Example 4, estimate the number of households that had Internet access in 1999.

PRACTICE AND APPLICATIONS

STUDENT HELP

▶ **Extra Practice**
to help you master
skills is on p. 800.

VERIFYING SOLUTIONS Use the graph to decide whether the point lies on the graph of the line. Justify your answer algebraically.

12. $3x - 4y = 10$

  a. $(2, -1)$

  b. $(-1, 2)$

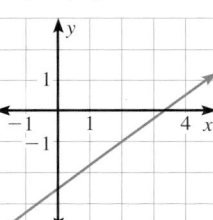

13. $y = 5$

  a. $(5, 0)$

  b. $(0, 5)$

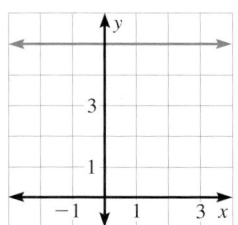

14. $x = 0$

  a. $(0, 14)$

  b. $(14, 0)$

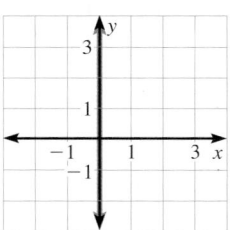

CHECKING SOLUTIONS Decide whether the given ordered pair is a solution of the equation.

15. $2y - 4x = 8, (-2, 8)$ 16. $-5x - 8y = 15, (-3, 0)$

17. $y = -2, (-2, -2)$ 18. $x = -4, (1, -4)$

19. $6y - 3x = -9, (2, -1)$ 20. $-2x - 9y = 7, (-1, -1)$

STUDENT HELP

▶ HOMEWORK HELP
Example 1: Exs. 12–20
Example 2: Exs. 21–55
Example 3: Exs. 21–55
Example 4: Exs. 67–70
Example 5: Exs. 44–55,
    60–65
Example 6: Exs. 44–55,
    60–65

FINDING SOLUTIONS Find three different ordered pairs that are solutions of the equation.

21. $y = 3x - 5$ 22. $y = 7 - 4x$ 23. $y = -2x - 6$

24. $x = 2$ 25. $x = \dfrac{1}{2}$ 26. $y = -6$

27. $y = \dfrac{1}{2}(4 - 2x)$ 28. $y = 3(6x - 1)$ 29. $y = 4\left(\dfrac{1}{2}x - 1\right)$

FUNCTION FORM Rewrite the equation in function form.

30. $-3x + y = 12$ **31.** $2x + 3y = 6$ **32.** $x + 4y = 48$

33. $5x + 5y = 19$ **34.** $\frac{1}{2}x + \frac{5}{2}y = 1$ **35.** $-x - y = 5$

GRAPHING EQUATIONS Use a table of values to graph the equation.

36. $y = -x + 4$ **37.** $y = -2x + 5$ **38.** $y = -(3 - x)$ **39.** $y = -2(x - 6)$

40. $y = 3x + 2$ **41.** $y = 4x - 1$ **42.** $y = \frac{4}{3}x + 2$ **43.** $y = -\frac{3}{4}x + 1$

44. $x = 9$ **45.** $y = -1$ **46.** $y = 0$ **47.** $y = -3x + 1$

48. $x = 0$ **49.** $x - 2y = 6$ **50.** $4x + 4y = 2$ **51.** $x + 2y = -8$

MATCHING EQUATIONS WITH GRAPHS Match the equation with its graph.

A. $x = -2$ **B.** $2x - y = 3$

C. $6x + 3y = 0$ **D.** $-x + 2y = 6$

52.

53.

54.

55.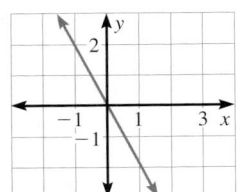

56. CRITICAL THINKING Robin always finds at least three different ordered pairs when making a table to graph an equation. Why do you think she does this?

STUDENT HELP

Look Back
For help with scatter plots, see p. 204.

PLOTTING POINTS In Exercises 57–59, use the ordered pairs below.
$(-3, -9), (-2, -7), (-1.6, -5.5), (0.4, -2.2), (3.1, 3.2), (5.2, 7.4)$

57. Use a graphing calculator or a computer to graph the ordered pairs.

58. The line that fits most of the points is the graph of $y = 2x - 3$. One of the points does not appear to fall on the line with the others. Which point is it?

59. Show algebraically that one point does not lie on this line.

POINTS OF INTERSECTION In Exercises 60–65, graph the two lines in the same coordinate plane. Then find the coordinates of the point at which the lines cross.

60. $x = -5, y = 2$ **61.** $y = 11, x = -8$ **62.** $y = -6, x = 1$

63. $x = 4, y = -4$ **64.** $y = -1, x = 0$ **65.** $x = 3, y = 0$

66. VISUAL THINKING Name a point that would be on the graphs of both $x = -3$ and $y = 2$. Sketch both graphs to verify your answer.

LANDSCAPING BUSINESS In Exercises 67–70, use the following information.

One summer you charge $20 to mow a lawn and $10 to trim bushes. You want to make $300 in one week. An algebraic model for your earnings is $20x + 10y = 300$, where x is the number of lawns you mow and y is the number of bushes you trim.

67. Solve the equation for y.

68. Use the equation in function form from Exercise 67 to make a table of values for $x = 5$, $x = 10$, and $x = 15$.

69. Look at the graph at the right. Does the line shown appear to pass through the points from your table of values?

70. If you do not trim any bushes during the week, how many lawns will you have to mow to earn $300?

Summer Earnings

[Graph: y-axis labeled "Bushes trimmed" with values 0, 5, 10, 15, 20, 25, 30; x-axis labeled "Lawns mowed" with values 0, 5, 10, 15, 20; a line descending from upper left to lower right.]

 TRAINING FOR A TRIATHLON In Exercises 71–73, Mary Gordon is training for a triathlon. Like most triathletes she regularly trains in two of the three events every day. On Saturdays she expects to burn about 800 calories during her workout by running and swimming.

Running:	7.1 calories per minute
Swimming:	10.1 calories per minute
Bicycling:	6.2 calories per minute

71. Copy and complete the model below. Let x represent the number of minutes she spends running, and let y represent the number of minutes she spends swimming.

REAL LIFE **TRIATHLON**
In 1998, over 1500 people competed in Hawaii's Ironman Triathlon World Championship.

APPLICATION LINK
www.mcdougallittell.com

VERBAL MODEL	Calories burned while running	$\cdot$	?	$+$	?	$\cdot$	Swimming Time	$=$	Total calories burned

LABELS   Calories burned while running = ? (calories/minute)

Running time = x (minutes)

? = **10.1** (calories/minute)

? = y (minutes)

Total calories burned = **800** (calories)

ALGEBRAIC MODEL   ? $\cdot x +$? $\cdot y = 800$ Write a linear model.

72. Make a table of values and graph the equation from Exercise 71.

73. If Mary Gordon spends 45 minutes running, about how many minutes will she have to spend swimming to burn 800 calories?

CHOOSING A MODEL In Exercises 74 and 75, decide whether a graph of the data would be points that appear to lie on a *horizontal line*, a *vertical line*, or *neither*. Explain. Let the *x*-axis represent time.

74. The number of books read by Avery each year from 1999 to 2005.

75. The number of senators in the United States Congress each year from 1991 to 2000.

Test
Preparation

76. **MULTIPLE CHOICE** Which point lies on the graph of $2x + 5y = 6$?

   Ⓐ $(-2, 2)$ Ⓑ $(3, 0)$ Ⓒ $(0, 3)$ Ⓓ both A and B

77. **MULTIPLE CHOICE** Which point does *not* lie on the graph of $y = 3$?

   Ⓐ $(0, 3)$ Ⓑ $(-3, 3)$ Ⓒ $(3, -3)$ Ⓓ $\left(\frac{1}{3}, 3\right)$

78. **MULTIPLE CHOICE** The ordered pair $(-3, 5)$ is a solution of ? .

   Ⓐ $y = 5$ Ⓑ $x = 5$ Ⓒ $y = \frac{1}{2}x - 2$ Ⓓ $y = -\frac{1}{2}x - 2$

★ **Challenge**

MISINTERPRETING GRAPHS Even though they provide an accurate representation of data, some graphs are easy to misinterpret. In Exercises 79 and 80, use the following.

Based on actual and projected data from 1995 to 2000, a linear model for a company's profit P is $P = 3,005,000 - 900t$, where t represents the number of years since 1995.

79. Sketch two graphs of the model. In the first graph, divide the vertical axis into $1,000,000 intervals. In the second graph start at $3,000,000 and use $1000 intervals.

EXTRA CHALLENGE
www.mcdougallittell.com

80. **CRITICAL THINKING** What are the advantages and disadvantages of each graph?

MIXED REVIEW

EVALUATING EXPRESSIONS Evaluate the expression. (Review 2.2)

81. $5 + 2 + (-3)$ 82. $-6 + (-14) + 8$ 83. $-18 + (-10) + (-1)$

84. $-\frac{1}{3} + 6 + \frac{1}{3}$ 85. $\frac{4}{7} + \frac{3}{7} - 1$ 86. $-\frac{7}{9} + \frac{1}{3} + 2$

MATRICES Find the sum of the matrices. (Review 2.4)

87. $\begin{bmatrix} 1 & 6 \\ -4 & 2 \end{bmatrix} + \begin{bmatrix} 15 & -3 \\ 0 & 16 \end{bmatrix}$ 88. $\begin{bmatrix} 2 & 5 \\ 3 & 10 \end{bmatrix} + \begin{bmatrix} -14 & -5 \\ 12 & 7 \end{bmatrix}$

89. $\begin{bmatrix} 4 & 10 \\ -1 & 9 \end{bmatrix} + \begin{bmatrix} -20 & 40 \\ -8 & 10 \end{bmatrix}$ 90. $\begin{bmatrix} 5 & -2 \\ 5 & -1 \end{bmatrix} + \begin{bmatrix} -1 & -16 \\ 11 & -3 \end{bmatrix}$

SOLVING EQUATIONS Solve the equation. (Review 3.2 for 4.3)

91. $-2z = -26$ 92. $9x = 3$ 93. $6p = -96$ 94. $24 = 8c$

95. $\frac{2}{3}t = -10$ 96. $-\frac{p}{7} = -9$ 97. $\frac{n}{15} = \frac{3}{5}$ 98. $\frac{c}{6} = \frac{2}{3}$

4.3

Quick Graphs Using Intercepts

GOAL 1 **FINDING THE INTERCEPTS OF A LINE**

What you should learn

GOAL 1 Find the intercepts of the graph of a linear equation.

GOAL 2 Use intercepts to make a quick graph of a linear equation as in **Example 4**.

Why you should learn it

▼ To solve **real-life** problems, such as finding numbers of school play tickets to be sold to reach a fundraising goal in **Ex. 63**.

In Lesson 4.2 you graphed a linear equation by writing a table of values, plotting the points, and drawing a line through the points.

In this lesson, you will learn a quicker way to graph a linear equation. To do this, you need to realize that only two points are needed to determine a line. Two points that are usually convenient to use are points where a graph crosses the axes.

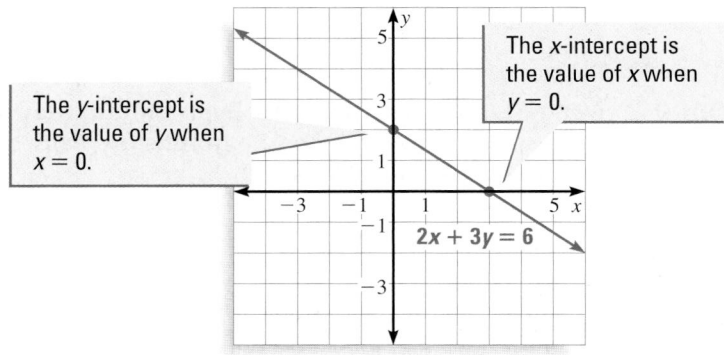

The y-intercept is the value of y when x = 0.

The x-intercept is the value of x when y = 0.

$2x + 3y = 6$

An **x-intercept** is the x-coordinate of a point where a graph crosses the x-axis. A **y-intercept** is the y-coordinate of a point where a graph crosses the y-axis.

EXAMPLE 1 *Finding Intercepts*

Find the x-intercept and the y-intercept of the graph of the equation $2x + 3y = 6$.

SOLUTION

To find the x-intercept of $2x + 3y = 6$, let $y = 0$.

$2x + 3y = 6$	**Write original equation.**
$2x + 3(0) = 6$	**Substitute 0 for y.**
$x = 3$	**Solve for x.**

▶ The x-intercept is 3. The line crosses the x-axis at the point $(3, 0)$.

To find the y-intercept of $2x + 3y = 6$, let $x = 0$.

$2x + 3y = 6$	**Write original equation.**
$2(0) + 3y = 6$	**Substitute 0 for x.**
$y = 2$	**Solve for y.**

▶ The y-intercept is 2. The line crosses the y-axis at the point $(0, 2)$.

EXAMPLE 2 *Making a Quick Graph*

Graph the equation $3.5x + 7y = 14$.

SOLUTION

Find the intercepts.

$3.5x + 7y = 14$	Write original equation.
$3.5x + 7(0) = 14$	Substitute 0 for *y*.
$x = \dfrac{14}{3.5} = 4$	The *x*-intercept is 4.
$3.5x + 7y = 14$	Write original equation.
$3.5(0) + 7y = 14$	Substitute 0 for *x*,
$y = \dfrac{14}{7} = 2$	The *y*-intercept is 2.

Draw a coordinate plane that includes the points
$(4, 0)$ and $(0, 2)$.

Plot the points $(4, 0)$ and $(0, 2)$ and draw a line
through them.

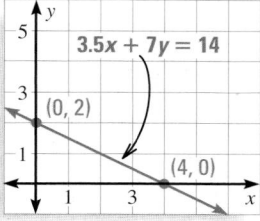

EXAMPLE 3 *Drawing Appropriate Scales*

Graph the equation $y = 4x + 40$.

SOLUTION

Find the intercepts, by substituting 0 for *y* and then 0 for *x*.

$y = 4x + 40$	$y = 4x + 40$
$0 = 4x + 40$	$y = 4(0) + 40$
$-40 = 4x$	$y = 40$
$-10 = x$	The *y*-intercept is 40.

The *x*-intercept is -10.

Draw a coordinate plane that includes the points
$(-10, 0)$ and $(0, 40)$. With these values, it is
reasonable to use tick marks at 10-unit intervals.

You may want to draw axes with at least two tick
marks to the left of -10 and to the right of 0 on the
x-axis and two tick marks below 0 and above 40 on
the *y*-axis.

Plot the points $(-10, 0)$ and $(0, 40)$ and draw a line
through them.

EXAMPLE 4 **Writing and Using a Linear Model**

ZOO FUNDRAISING You are organizing the annual spaghetti dinner to raise funds for a zoo. Your goal is to sell $1500 worth of tickets. Assuming 200 adults and 100 students will attend the dinner, how much should you charge for an adult ticket and for a student ticket?

SOLUTION

PROBLEM SOLVING STRATEGY

VERBAL MODEL

$$\boxed{\begin{array}{c}\text{Number}\\\text{of}\\\text{adults}\end{array}} \cdot \boxed{\begin{array}{c}\text{Adult}\\\text{ticket}\\\text{price}\end{array}} + \boxed{\begin{array}{c}\text{Number}\\\text{of}\\\text{students}\end{array}} \cdot \boxed{\begin{array}{c}\text{Student}\\\text{ticket}\\\text{price}\end{array}} = \boxed{\begin{array}{c}\text{Total}\\\text{sales}\end{array}}$$

LABELS

Number of adults = **200**   (people)

Adult ticket price = x (dollars per person)

Number of students = **100**   (people)

Student ticket price = y (dollars per person)

Total sales = **1500**   (dollars)

ALGEBRAIC MODEL

$200 x + 100 y = 1500$ Write linear model.

$2x + y = 15$ Divide by 100 to simplify model.

This equation has many solutions. To get a better idea of the possible prices, make a quick graph.

Find the intercepts.

$2x + y = 15$	$2x + y = 15$
$2x + 0 = 15$	$2(0) + y = 15$
$x = 7.5$ ◄— *x*-intercept	$y = 15$ ◄— *y*-intercept

Draw a coordinate plane that includes the points (7.5, 0) and (0, 15).

Plot the points (7.5, 0) and (0, 15) and draw a line through them. From the graph, you can determine several possible prices to charge.

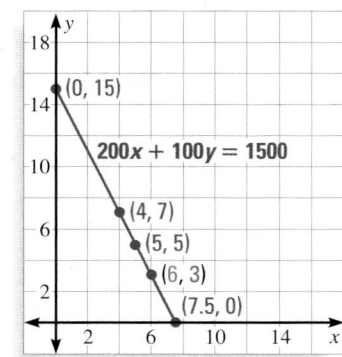

ZOO EXPENSES The American Zoo and Aquarium Institute estimates that it costs a zoo about $22,000 per year to house, feed, and care for a lion and about $18,500 for a polar bear.

APPLICATION LINK
www.mcdougallittell.com

Possible Prices to Raise $1500	
Adult	**Student**
$0.00	$15.00
$4.00	$7.00
$5.00	$5.00
$6.00	$3.00
$7.50	$0.00

▶ One reasonable price to charge is $6 for adults and $3 for students.

GUIDED PRACTICE

Vocabulary Check ✓

1. Decide whether 2 is the *x-intercept* or the *y-intercept* of the line $y = 2x + 2$. Explain your choice.

Concept Check ✓

2. How many points are needed to determine a line?

3. Describe a line that has no *x*-intercept.

Skill Check ✓

Find the *x*-intercept of the graph of the equation.

4. $y = 2x + 20$
5. $y = 0.1x + 0.3$
6. $y = x - \dfrac{1}{4}$

In Exercises 7–12, find the *x*-intercept and the *y*-intercept of the graph of the equation. Graph the equation.

7. $y = x + 2$
8. $y - 2x = 3$
9. $2x - y = 4$

10. $3y = -6x + 3$
11. $5y = 5x + 15$
12. $x - y = 1$

13. 🌐 **FUNDRAISING** If your goal for the fundraising dinner in Example 4 is $2000, find reasonable prices for adult tickets and student tickets.

PRACTICE AND APPLICATIONS

STUDENT HELP

▶ **Extra Practice**
to help you master
skills is on p. 800.

USING GRAPHS TO FIND INTERCEPTS Use the graph to find the *x*-intercept and the *y*-intercept of the line.

14.

15.

16.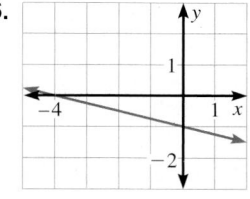

FINDING X-INTERCEPTS Find the *x*-intercept of the graph of the equation.

17. $x + 3y = 5$
18. $x - 2y = 6$
19. $2x + 2y = -10$

20. $3x + 4y = 12$
21. $5x - y = 45$
22. $-x + 3y = 27$

23. $-7x - 3y = 42$
24. $2x + 6y = -24$
25. $-12x - 20y = 60$

FINDING Y-INTERCEPTS Find the *y*-intercept of the graph of the equation.

26. $y = -2x + 5$
27. $y = 3x - 4$
28. $y = 8x + 27$

29. $y = 7x - 15$
30. $4x - 5y = -35$
31. $6x - 9y = 72$

32. $3x + 12y = -84$
33. $-x + 1.7y = 5.1$
34. $2x - 6y = -18$

USING INTERCEPTS Graph the line that has the given intercepts.

35. *x*-intercept: -2
    y-intercept: 5
36. *x*-intercept: 4
    y-intercept: 6
37. *x*-intercept: -7
    y-intercept: -3

38. *x*-intercept: -3
    y-intercept: -7
39. *x*-intercept: -12
    y-intercept: -8
40. *x*-intercept: -7
    y-intercept: 15

STUDENT HELP

▶ HOMEWORK HELP
Example 1: Exs. 17–34
Example 2: Exs. 35–55
Example 3: Exs. 44–55
Example 4: Exs. 60–63

MATCHING GRAPHS AND EQUATIONS Match the equation with its graph.

A. $8x - 2y = 16$ **B.** $8x - 2y = 8$ **C.** $8x - 2y = -8$

41.

42.

43.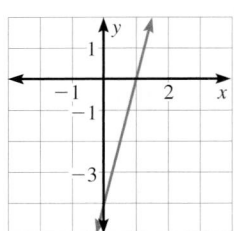

GRAPHING LINES Find the *x*-intercept and the *y*-intercept of the line. Graph the equation. Label the points where the line crosses the axes.

44. $y = x + 2$

45. $y = x - 3$

46. $y = 4x + 8$

47. $y = -6 + 3x$

48. $y = 5x + 15$

49. $2x + 4y = 16$

50. $-4x + 3y = 24$

51. $x - 7y = 21$

52. $6x - y = 36$

53. $2x + 9y = -36$

54. $4x + 5y = 20$

55. $0.5y = -2x + 8$

LOGICAL REASONING In Exercises 56–59, tell whether the statement is *true* or *false*. Justify your answer.

56. The *y*-intercept of the graph of $3x + 5y = 30$ is 10.

57. The *x*-intercept of the graph of $3x + 5y = 30$ is 10.

58. The point (3, 5) is on the graph of $3x + 5y = 30$.

59. The graph of the equation $x = 4$ is a horizontal line.

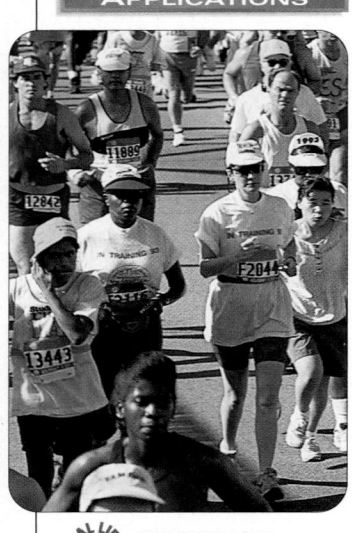

SCHOOL PLAY In Exercises 60–63, use the following information.
Your school drama club is putting on a play next month. By selling tickets for the play, the club hopes to raise $600 for the drama fund for new costumes, scripts, and scenery for future plays. Let *x* represent the number of adult tickets they sell at $8 each, and let *y* represent the number of student tickets they sell at $5 each.

60. Graph the linear function $8x + 5y = 600$.

61. What is the *x*-intercept? What does it represent in this situation?

62. What is the *y*-intercept? What does it represent in this situation?

63. What are three possible numbers of adult and student tickets to sell that will make the drama club reach its goal?

MARATHON In Exercises 64–66, you are running in a marathon. You either run 8 miles per hour or walk 4 miles per hour.

64. Write an equation to show the relationship between time run and time walked during the 26.2-mile course.

65. Graph the equation from Exercise 64. What are some possible running and walking times if you complete the 26.2-mile course?

66. If you walk for a total of 1 hour during the course, how long will you have spent running when you cross the finish line of the marathon?

🌐 **MOVIE PRICES** In Exercises 67 and 68, a theater charges $4 per person before 6:00 P.M. and $7 per person after 6:00 P.M. The total ticket sales for Saturday were $11,228.

67. Make a graph showing the possible number of people who attended the theater before and after 6:00 P.M.

68. Suppose no one attended the theater before 6:00 P.M. How many people attended the theater after 6:00 P.M.? Explain how you know.

Test Preparation

69. MULTI-STEP PROBLEM The number of people who worked for the railroads in the United States each year from 1989 to 1995 can be modeled by the equation $y = -6.61x + 229$, where x represents the number of years since 1989 and y represents the number of railroad employees (in thousands).

🌐 **DATA UPDATE** of U.S. Bureau of the Census data at www.mcdougallittell.com

a. Find the y-intercept of the line. What does it represent?

b. Find the x-intercept of the line. What does it represent?

c. About how many people worked for the railroads in 1995?

d. *Writing* Do you think the line in the graph will continue to be a good model for the next 50 years? Explain.

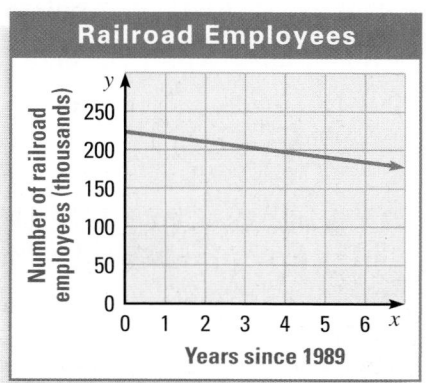

★ **Challenge**

70. CRITICAL THINKING Consider the equation $6x + 8y = k$. What numbers could replace k so that the x-intercept and the y-intercept are both integers? Explain.

MIXED REVIEW

EVALUATING DIFFERENCES **Find the difference.** (Review 2.3 for 4.4)

71. $5 - 9$ **72.** $17 - 6$ **73.** $-8 - 9$ **74.** $|8| - 12.6$

75. $-\frac{2}{3} - \left(-\frac{7}{3}\right)$ **76.** $13.8 - 6.9$ **77.** $7 - |-1|$ **78.** $-4.1 - (-5.1)$

EVALUATING QUOTIENTS **In Exercises 79–86, find the quotient.**
(Review 2.7 for 4.4)

79. $54 \div 9$ **80.** $-72 \div 8$ **81.** $12 \div \left(-\frac{1}{5}\right)$ **82.** $3 \div \frac{1}{4}$

83. $26 \div (-13)$ **84.** $-1 \div 8$ **85.** $-20 \div \left(-2\frac{1}{2}\right)$ **86.** $\frac{1}{8} \div \frac{1}{2}$

87. 🌐 **SCHOOL BAKE SALE** You have one hour to make cookies for your school bake sale. You spend 20 minutes mixing the dough. It then takes 12 minutes to bake each tray of cookies. If you bake one tray at a time, which model can you use to find how many trays you can bake? (Review 3.3 and 3.6)

A. $x(20 + 12) = 60$ **B.** $12x + 20 = 60$

Plot and label the ordered pairs in a coordinate plane. (Lesson 4.1)

1. $A(-4, 1)$, $B(0, 2)$, $C(-3, 0)$ **2.** $A(-1, -5)$, $B(0, -7)$, $C(1, 6)$

3. $A(-4, -6)$, $B(1, -3)$, $C(-1, 1)$ **4.** $A(2, -6)$, $B(5, 0)$, $C(0, -4)$

Find three different ordered pairs that are solutions of the equation. Graph the equation. (Lesson 4.2)

5. $y = 2x - 6$ **6.** $y = 4x - 1$ **7.** $y = 2(-3x + 1)$

8. $x = 3$ **9.** $y = -3(x - 4)$ **10.** $y = -5$

Find the *x*-intercept and the *y*-intercept of the line. Graph the line. Label the points where the line crosses the axes. (Lesson 4.3)

11. $y = 4 - x$ **12.** $y = -5 + 2x$ **13.** $y = 3x + 12$

14. $3x + 3y = 27$ **15.** $-6x + y = -3$ **16.** $y = 10x + 50$

MATH & History

Graphing Mathematical Relationships

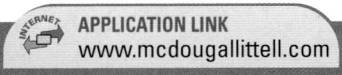

APPLICATION LINK
www.mcdougallittell.com

THEN

400 YEARS AGO, this chapter would not have been in your algebra book. In 1637 René Descartes published a method for drawing algebraic equations on a coordinate grid—introducing a new connection between algebra and geometry that linked the two branches more closely than ever before.

Descartes was interested in studying curves that are more complicated than the lines you have seen in this chapter.

Descartes was interested in equations like $x^3 + y^3 = 3axy$ when $a = 10$, which is graphed at the right. Use algebra to show whether the point is on the graph of the equation.

1. $(15, 15)$ **2.** $(0, 0)$ **3.** $(-1, -1)$ **4.** $(3, 0.3)$

NOW

TODAY, using a coordinate plane to graph an equation is one of the first things you learn in Algebra 1. Computers that can process large amounts of data have enabled mathematicians to study mathematical systems whose outputs are too complicated to graph by hand.

The first graphing calculator produced

1985

Now

1596–1650

1637

René Descartes

Publication of Descartes's text: *La Géométrie*

Computers used to graph mathematical equations

ACTIVITY 4.4

Developing Concepts

Investigating Slope

GROUP ACTIVITY
Work with a partner.

MATERIALS
• several books
• two metric rulers

▶ **QUESTION** How can you use numbers to describe the steepness of a ramp?

The *slope* of a ramp describes its steepness. For the ramp at the right:

$$\text{slope} = \frac{\text{rise}}{\text{run}} = \frac{2 \text{ m}}{5 \text{ m}} = \frac{2}{5}$$

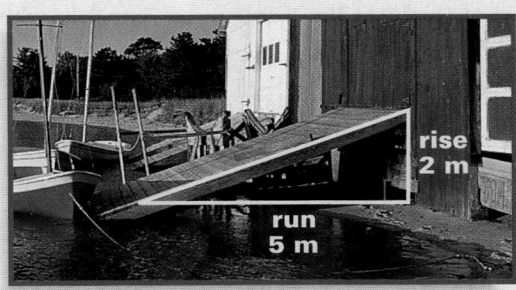

rise
2 m

run
5 m

Height of books	Distance between ruler and books	Rise	Run	Slope
7 cm	12 cm	7	12	$\frac{7}{12}$
11 cm	5.5 cm	?	?	?

▶ **EXPLORING THE CONCEPT**

1 Copy and complete the table at the left.

2 Make a pile of three books. Measure the height of the pile of books. Use one ruler to create a ramp. Measure the distance from the bottom of the ruler to the books. Use this information to add a row to your table.

3 Without changing the rise, create at least four ramps that have different runs. Record information about these ramps in your table.

4 Place a piece of paper under the edge of your pile of books and make a mark on it that is 15 cm away from the books. Place the end of your ramp on the mark. Add this ramp to your table.

5 Change the rise by adding or removing books. Without changing the run, create at least four ramps that have different rises. Add them to your table.

▶ **DRAWING CONCLUSIONS**

In Exercises 1 and 2, give examples to support your answer.

1. If the run of a ramp increases and the rise stays the same, how does the slope of the ramp change?

2. If the rise of a ramp increases and the run stays the same, how does the slope of the ramp change?

In Exercises 3–5, you will summarize what you have learned about slope.

3. If a ramp has a slope of 1, what is the relationship between its rise and run?

4. If a ramp has a slope greater than 1, is it steeper than a ramp with a slope of 1? Describe the relationship between its rise and run.

5. If a ramp has a slope less than 1, is it steeper than a ramp with a slope of 1? Describe the relationship between its rise and run.

4.4

The Slope of a Line

What you should learn

GOAL 1 Find the slope of a line using two of its points.

GOAL 2 Interpret slope as a rate of change in **real-life** situations like the parachute problem in **Example 6**.

Why you should learn it

▼ To solve **real-life** problems about the steepness of a hill or the grade of a road in **Ex. 51**.

GOAL 1 FINDING THE SLOPE OF A LINE

The **slope** m of a nonvertical line is the number of units the line rises or falls for each unit of horizontal change from left to right.

The slanted line at the right rises 3 units for each 2 units of horizontal change from left to right. So, the slope m of the line is $\frac{3}{2}$.

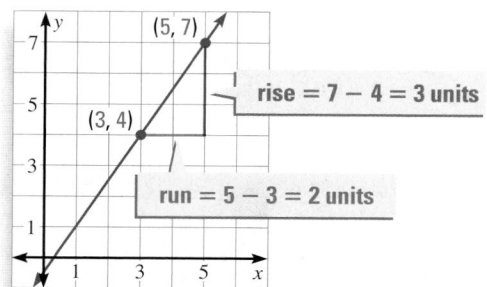

$$\text{slope} = \frac{\text{rise}}{\text{run}} = \frac{7-4}{5-3} = \frac{3}{2}$$

Two points on a line are all that is needed to find its slope.

FINDING THE SLOPE OF A LINE

The slope m of the nonvertical line passing through the points (x_1, y_1) and (x_2, y_2) is

$$m = \frac{\text{rise}}{\text{run}} = \frac{\text{change in } y}{\text{change in } x} = \frac{y_2 - y_1}{x_2 - x_1}.$$

Read x_1 as "x sub one." Think "x-coordinate of the first point."

Read y_2 as "y sub two." Think "y-coordinate of the second point."

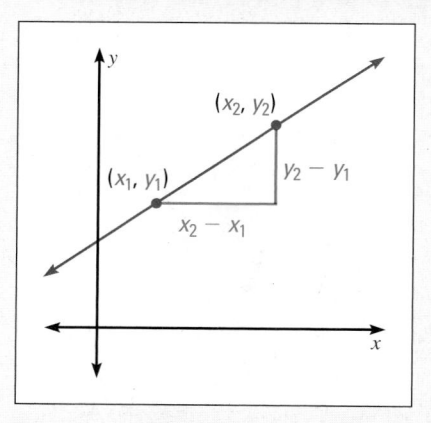

When you use the formula for slope, the order of the subtraction is important. Given two points on a line, you can label either point as (x_1, y_1) and the other point as (x_2, y_2). After doing this, however, you must form the numerator and the denominator using the *same* order of subtraction.

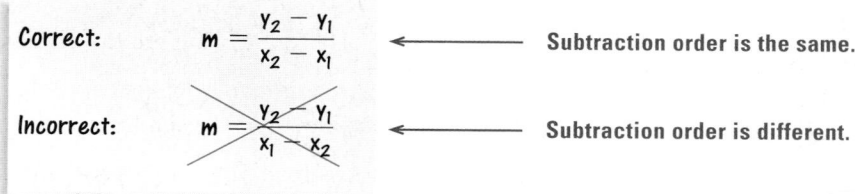

Correct: $m = \dfrac{y_2 - y_1}{x_2 - x_1}$ ⟵   **Subtraction order is the same.**

Incorrect: $m = \dfrac{y_2 - y_1}{x_1 - x_2}$ ⟵   **Subtraction order is different.**

EXAMPLE 1 **A Line with a Positive Slope Rises**

Find the slope of the line passing through $(-2, 2)$ and $(3, 4)$.

SOLUTION

STUDENT HELP

► **Look Back**
For help with evaluating expressions, see p. 79.

Let $(x_1, y_1) = (-2, 2)$ and $(x_2, y_2) = (3, 4)$.

$$m = \frac{y_2 - y_1}{x_2 - x_1}$$ ← Rise: Difference of *y*-values
← Run: Difference of *x*-values

$$= \frac{4 - 2}{3 - (-2)}$$ Substitute values.

$$= \frac{2}{3 + 2}$$ Simplify.

$$= \frac{2}{5}$$ Slope is positive.

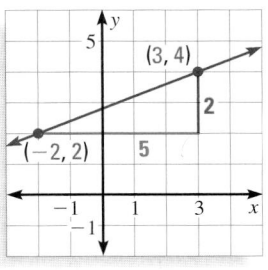

Positive slope: line rises from left to right.

EXAMPLE 2 **A Line with a Zero Slope is Horizontal**

Find the slope of the line passing through $(-1, 2)$ and $(3, 2)$.

SOLUTION

Let $(x_1, y_1) = (-1, 2)$ and $(x_2, y_2) = (3, 2)$.

$$m = \frac{y_2 - y_1}{x_2 - x_1}$$ ← Rise: Difference of *y*-values
← Run: Difference of *x*-values

$$= \frac{2 - 2}{3 - (-1)}$$ Substitute values.

$$= \frac{0}{4}$$ Simplify.

$$= 0$$ Slope is zero.

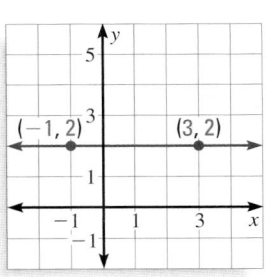

Zero slope: line is horizontal.

EXAMPLE 3 **A Line with a Negative Slope Falls**

Find the slope of the line passing through $(0, 0)$ and $(3, -3)$.

SOLUTION

Let $(x_1, y_1) = (0, 0)$ and $(x_2, y_2) = (3, -3)$

$$m = \frac{y_2 - y_1}{x_2 - x_1}$$ ← Rise: Difference of *y*-values
← Run: Difference of *x*-values

$$= \frac{-3 - 0}{3 - 0}$$ Substitute values.

$$= \frac{-3}{3}$$ Simplify.

$$= -1$$ Slope is negative.

STUDENT HELP

► **Skills Review**
For help with simplifying fractions, see p. 780.

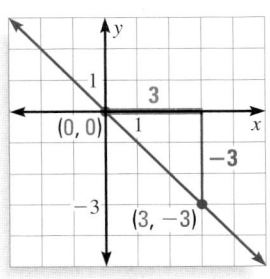

Negative slope: line falls from left to right.

EXAMPLE 4 *Slope of a Vertical Line is Undefined*

Find the slope of the line passing through (2, 4) and (2, 1).

SOLUTION   Let $(x_1, y_1) = (2, 1)$ and $(x_2, y_2) = (2, 4)$.

$$m = \frac{y_2 - y_1}{x_2 - x_1}$$ ← Rise: Difference of *y*-values
← Run: Difference of *x*-values

$$= \frac{4 - 1}{2 - 2}$$ Substitute values.

$$= \frac{3}{0}$$ Division by 0 is undefined.

▶ Because division by 0 is undefined, the expression $\frac{3}{0}$ has no meaning. The slope of a vertical line is undefined.

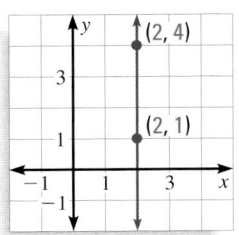

Undefined slope: line is vertical.

CONCEPT SUMMARY   **CLASSIFICATION OF LINES BY SLOPE**

A line with positive slope *rises* from left to right.	A line with negative slope *falls* from left to right.	A line with zero slope is *horizontal*.	A line with undefined slope is *vertical*.
			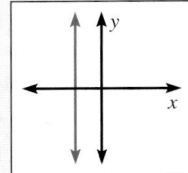
$m > 0$	$m < 0$	$m = 0$	m is undefined.

EXAMPLE 5   *Given the Slope, Find a y-Coordinate*

Find the value of *y* so that the line passing through the points $(-2, 1)$ and $(4, y)$ has a slope of $\frac{2}{3}$.

SOLUTION   Let $(x_1, y_1) = (-2, 1)$ and $(x_2, y_2) = (4, y)$.

$$m = \frac{y_2 - y_1}{x_2 - x_1}$$ Write formula for slope.

$$\frac{2}{3} = \frac{y - 1}{4 - (-2)}$$ Substitute values for *m*, x_1, y_1, x_2, and y_2.

$$\frac{2}{3} = \frac{y - 1}{6}$$ Simplify.

$$6 \cdot \frac{2}{3} = 6 \cdot \frac{y - 1}{6}$$ Multiply each side by 6.

$$4 = y - 1$$ Simplify.

$$5 = y$$ Add 1 to each side.

STUDENT HELP

HOMEWORK HELP
Visit our Web site
www.mcdougallittell.com
for extra examples.

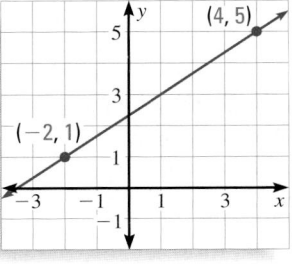

GOAL 2 INTERPRETING SLOPE AS A RATE OF CHANGE

A **rate of change** compares two different quantities that are changing. For example, the rate at which distance is changing with time is called *velocity*. Slope provides an important way of visualizing a rate of change.

Parachuting

EXAMPLE 6 *Slope as a Rate of Change*

You are parachuting. At time $t = 0$ seconds, you open your parachute at height $h = 2500$ feet above the ground. At time $t = 35$ seconds, you are at height $h = 2115$ feet.

a. What is your rate of change in height?

b. About when will you reach the ground?

SOLUTION

a. Use the formula for slope to find the rate of change. The change in time is $35 - 0 = 35$ seconds. Subtract in the same order. The change in height is $2115 - 2500 = -385$ feet.

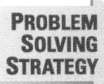
PROBLEM
SOLVING
STRATEGY

VERBAL MODEL

$$\text{Rate of change} = \frac{\boxed{\text{Change in height}}}{\boxed{\text{Change in time}}}$$

LABELS

Rate of change = m (ft/sec)

Change in height = -385 (ft)

Change in time = 35 (sec)

ALGEBRAIC MODEL

$$m = \frac{-385}{35}$$

▶ Your rate of change is -11 ft/sec. The negative value indicates that you are falling.

b. Falling at a rate of 11 ft/sec, find the time it will take you to fall 2500 feet.

$$\text{Time} = \frac{\text{Distance}}{\text{Rate}} = \frac{2500 \text{ ft}}{11 \text{ ft/sec}} \approx 227 \text{ sec}$$

▶ You will reach the ground about 227 seconds after opening your parachute.

UNIT ANALYSIS Check that *seconds* are the units of the solution.

$$\frac{\text{ft}}{\text{ft/sec}} = \text{ft} \cdot \frac{\text{sec}}{\text{ft}} = \text{sec}$$

GUIDED PRACTICE

Vocabulary Check ✔ 1. Draw a ramp and label its rise and run. Explain what is meant by the slope of the ramp.

Concept Check ✔ 2. **ERROR ANALYSIS** Describe the error at the right. Then calculate the correct slope.

The slope of the line through (3, 2) and (1, 4) is

$$m = \frac{4 - 2}{3 - 1}.$$

Ex. 2

3. Explain what happens when the formula for slope is applied to a vertical line.

4. **CRITICAL THINKING** How can you tell that the slope of the line through (2, 2) and (−3, 5) is negative without calculating?

Skill Check ✔ **In Exercises 5–10, plot the points and draw a line through them. Find the slope of the line passing through the points.**

5. (0, 0), (1, 2) 6. (0, 0), (−1, −1) 7. (1, 2), (2, 1)

8. (3, 2), (1, 4) 9. (2, 2), (3, 5) 10. (−3, −2), (1, 6)

11. Find the value of y so that the line passing through the points (0, 3) and (4, y) has a slope of −3.

PRACTICE AND APPLICATIONS

STUDENT HELP

▶ **Extra Practice**
to help you master
skills is on p. 800.

DESCRIBING SLOPE Plot the points and draw a line through them. Without calculating, state whether the slope of the line is *positive, negative, zero,* or *undefined*. Explain your reasoning.

12. (6, 9), (4, 3) 13. (7, 4), (−1, 8) 14. (5, 10), (5, −4) 15. (1, 1), (4, −3)

16. (−2, 5), (3, 5) 17. (0, 0), (−5, 3) 18. (1, 3), (−2, 1) 19. (2, −2), (2, −6)

GRAPH AND CALCULATE Plot the points and find the slope of the line passing through the points.

20. (4, 5), (2, 3) 21. (1, 5), (5, 2) 22. (2, 3), (−3, 0)

23. (0, −6), (8, 0) 24. (0, 6), (8, 0) 25. (2, 4), (4, −4)

26. (−6, −1), (−6, 4) 27. (0, −10), (−4, 0) 28. (1, −2), (−2, 2)

29. (3, 6), (3, 0) 30. (−6, 2), (4, −2) 31. (−1, −1), (−3, −6)

32. $\left(0, \frac{1}{2}\right)$, (0, 0) 33. (2, 2), (−3, 5) 34. (4, 1), (6, 1)

STUDENT HELP

▶ **HOMEWORK HELP**
Example 1: Exs. 12–37
Example 2: Exs. 12–37
Example 3: Exs. 12–37
Example 4: Exs. 12–37
Example 5: Exs. 38–46
Example 6: Exs. 56, 57

GRAPHICAL REASONING Find the slope of each line.

35.

36.

37.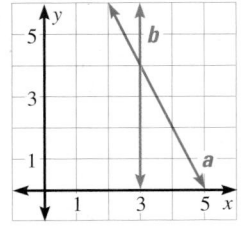

FINDING A COORDINATE Find the value of *y* so that the line passing through the two points has the given slope.

38. $(2, y), (4, 5), m = 2$ 　　**39.** $(0, -2), (2, y), m = 3$ 　　**40.** $(-5, 3), (3, y), m = -\frac{1}{2}$

41. $(0, y), (2, 5), m = 2$ 　　**42.** $(-1, 5), (3, y), m = 5$ 　　**43.** $(-1, 3), (5, y), m = -1$

44. $(5, 7), (8, y), m = \frac{4}{3}$ 　　**45.** $(3, y), (1, 4), m = -\frac{1}{2}$ 　　**46.** $(2, -15), (5, y), m = \frac{4}{5}$

INDUCTIVE REASONING Choose three different pairs of points on the line. Find the slope of the line using each pair. What do you notice?

47.

48.
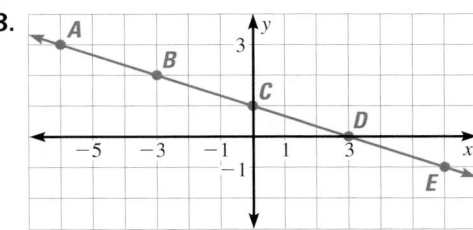

49. GEOMETRY ▶ CONNECTION Use the concept of slope to decide whether the points $(-2, 4), (2, -2),$ and $(6, 0)$ are on the same line. Explain your reasoning and include a diagram.

50. FINDING SLOPE To find the slope of a line, can you choose any two points on the line? Explain your reasoning. What are some guidelines that you could use to choose convenient points for calculating slope?

51. 🌐 **ROAD GRADES** The U.S. Department of Transportation requires surveyors to place signs on steep sections of roads. The grade of a road is measured as a percent. For instance, the grade of the road shown below is 6%. What is the slope of the road? Explain the relationship between road grade and slope.

WHAT ARE THE UNITS? In Exercises 52–54, find the rate of change between the two points. Give the units of measure for the rate.

52. $(2, 2)$ and $(9, 23)$; *x* in minutes, *y* in inches

53. $(3, 5)$ and $(11, 69)$; *x* in years, *y* in dollars.

54. $(53, 44)$ and $(32, 14)$; *x* in seconds, *y* in liters.

55. CABLE CARS In the 1870s a cable car system was built in San Francisco to climb the steep streets. San Francisco was the site of the first cable car used for public transportation in America. Calculate each labeled slope from left to right in the diagram.

(cross section of side view)

56. **SPACE SHUTTLE** A space shuttle achieves orbit at 9:23 A.M. At 9:31 A.M. it has traveled 2,309.6 miles in orbit. Find the rate of change in miles per minute.

57. **PROFIT** In 1990, a company had a profit of $173,000,000. In 1996, the profit was $206,000,000. If the profit increased the same amount each year, find the rate of change of the company's profit in dollars per year.

MOVIE PRICES In Exercises 58–61, the graph shows the price of a movie ticket at the Midtown Theater for the years 1960–1995.

58. Estimate the rate of change from 1960 to 1995 in the price in dollars per year.

59. Estimate the rate of change from 1985 to 1990 in the price in dollars per year.

60. Which five-year period had the smallest price increase?

61. *Writing* Use the graph to estimate the cost of going to a movie at the Midtown Theater this year. Why might your estimate be different from the actual cost?

MOVIE THEATER TICKETS

POPULATION RATES In Exercises 62–65, use the line graph below.

62. During which decade did the population of the South increase the most? Estimate the rate of change for this decade in people per year.

63. During which decade did the population of the Midwest increase the most? Estimate the rate of change for this decade in people per year.

64. **INTERPRETING A GRAPH** The line graph for the Northeast appears to be horizontal between 1970 and 1980. Write a sentence about what this means in terms of the real-life situation.

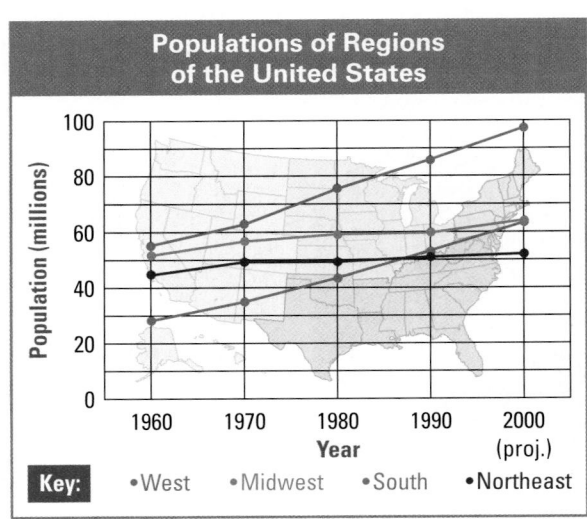

Populations of Regions of the United States

Key: •West •Midwest •South •Northeast

DATA UPDATE of U.S. Bureau of the Census data at www.mcdougallittell.com

65. **RESEARCH** Find the population of your state in 1980 and in 1990. Find the annual rate of change of this population.

66. MATHEMATICAL REASONING When you use the formula $\frac{y_2 - y_1}{x_2 - x_1}$ to find the slope of a line passing through two points, does it matter which point you choose to use as (x_1, y_1)? Give three different examples to support your answer.

Test Preparation

67. MULTIPLE CHOICE The slope of the line passing through the points $(0, 5)$ and $(0, -3)$ is   ? .

  (A) positive   **(B)** negative   **(C)** zero   **(D)** undefined

68. MULTIPLE CHOICE The slope of the line passing through the points $(8, 0)$ and $(0, 8)$ is   ? .

  (A) positive   **(B)** negative   **(C)** zero   **(D)** undefined

69. MULTIPLE CHOICE What is the slope of the line passing through the points $(-3, 4)$ and $(5, -11)$?

  (A) $\frac{-7}{8}$ **(B)** $\frac{-7}{2}$ **(C)** $\frac{15}{-8}$ **(D)** $\frac{15}{8}$

★ **Challenge**

70. FINDING AN X-COORDINATE Write an expression for the slope of a line passing through the points $(0, 3)$ and $(x, -9)$. What value of x will make the fraction equivalent to -2?

EXTRA CHALLENGE
www.mcdougallittell.com

71. Use your answers to Exercise 70 to find the value of x so that the line passing through the points $(0, 3)$ and $(x, -9)$ will have a slope of -3.

MIXED REVIEW

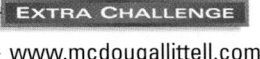

EVALUATING EXPRESSIONS Evaluate the expression for the given value of the variable. (Review 1.3)

72. $12x + 3$ when $x = 5$ **73.** $\frac{3}{4}p$ when $p = 16$ **74.** $8n$ when $n = \frac{3}{16}$

75. $\frac{7}{2}y - 3$ when $y = 4$ **76.** $5x + x$ when $x = 7$ **77.** $\frac{6}{5}z + 2$ when $z = 5$

SIMPLIFYING EXPRESSIONS Simplify the variable expression. (Review 2.5)

78. $(-6)(y)$ **79.** $(-1)(x)(-x)$ **80.** $-(-3)^2(-y)$

81. $\left(\frac{2}{5}\right)(5)(-x)(x)$ **82.** $(y)(-23)(-y^2)$ **83.** $\left(\frac{1}{8}\right)(-4)(-x)(-x)$

WRITING IN FUNCTION FORM Solve for y. (Review 3.7 for 4.5)

84. $9x - 2y = 14$ **85.** $5x + 9y = 18$ **86.** $-2x - 2y = 7$

87. $-x + 4y = 36$ **88.** $6x - 3y = 21$ **89.** $3x + 5y = 17$

FINDING INTERCEPTS Find the x-intercept and the y-intercept of the graph of the equation. (Review 4.3)

90. $y = x + 8$ **91.** $y = 2x + 12$ **92.** $y = 3x + 9$

93. $y = -6 + 2x$ **94.** $y = -2x + 16$ **95.** $3y = 6x + 3$

4.5

Direct Variation

What you should learn

GOAL 1 Write linear equations that represent direct variation.

GOAL 2 Use a ratio to write an equation for direct variation, such as the ratio of tail length to body length in alligators in **Example 4**.

Why you should learn it

▼ To solve **real-life** problems such as lengths of several stringed instruments in **Exs. 36 and 37**.

GOAL 1 **RECOGNIZING AND USING DIRECT VARIATION**

Two variables x and y *vary directly* if there is a nonzero number k such that the following is true.

$$y = kx \quad \longleftarrow \text{ Model for direct variation}$$

The number k is the **constant of variation**. Two quantities that vary directly are said to have **direct variation**.

EXAMPLE 1 *Graphs of Direct Variation Models*

Find the constant of variation and the slope of each direct variation model.

a. $y = 2x$

b. $y = -\frac{1}{2}x$

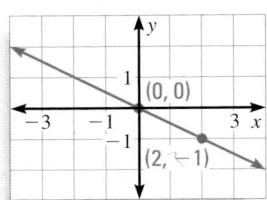

SOLUTION

a. For the equation $y = 2x$, the constant of variation is $k = 2$.

To find the slope of the line, use the slope formula.

$$m = \frac{y_2 - y_1}{x_2 - x_1}$$

$$m = \frac{2 - 0}{1 - 0} = 2$$

b. For the equation $y = -\frac{1}{2}x$, the constant of variation is $k = -\frac{1}{2}$.

To find the slope of the line, use the slope formula.

$$m = \frac{y_2 - y_1}{x_2 - x_1}$$

$$m = \frac{-1 - 0}{2 - 0} = -\frac{1}{2}$$

PROPERTIES OF GRAPHS OF DIRECT VARIATION MODELS

- The graph of $y = kx$ is a line through the origin.

- The slope of the graph of $y = kx$ is k.

$k < 0$

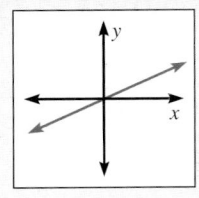

$k > 0$

---

234   **Chapter 4** *Graphing Linear Equations and Functions*

EXAMPLE 2 *Writing a Direct Variation Equation*

The variables x and y vary directly. When $x = 5$, $y = 20$.

  a. Write an equation that relates x and y.

  b. Find the value of y when $x = 10$.

SOLUTION

  a. Because x and y vary directly, the equation is of the form $y = kx$. You can solve for k as follows.

$y = kx$	**Write model for direct variation.**
$20 = k(5)$	**Substitute 5 for *x* and 20 for *y*.**
$4 = k$	**Divide each side by 5.**

    ▶ An equation that relates x and y is $y = 4x$.

  b.

$y = 4(10)$	**Substitute 10 for *x* in *y* = 4*x*.**
$y = 40$	

    ▶ When $x = 10$, $y = 40$.

EXAMPLE 3 *Writing a Direct Variation Model*

ZEPPELIN In 1852 Henri Giffard built the first airship successfully used for transportation. It had a volume of 88,000 cubic feet and could support 5650 pounds. The *Graf Zeppelin II*, built in 1937, had a volume of 7,063,000 cubic feet, making it one of the two largest airships ever built. The weight an airship can support varies directly with its volume. How much weight could the *Graf Zeppelin II* support?

SOLUTION

Use the data about the first airship. Find a model that relates the volume V (in cubic feet) to the weight w (in pounds) that an airship can support.

$w = kV$	**Write model for direct variation.**
$5650 = k(88,000)$	**Substitute 5650 for *w* and 88,000 for *V*.**
$\dfrac{5650}{88,000} = k$	**Divide each side by 88,000.**
$0.064 \approx k$	**Solve for *k*.**

A direct variation model for the weight an airship can support is $w = 0.064V$.

Use the model to find the weight the *Graf Zeppelin II* could support.

$w = 0.064V$	**Write the model for direct variation.**
$w = 0.064(7,063,000)$	**Substitute 7,063,000 for *V*.**
$w = 452,032$	**Simplify.**

▶ The *Graf Zeppelin II* could support about 452,000 pounds.

GOAL 2 USING A RATIO TO MODEL DIRECT VARIATION

The model $y = kx$ for direct variation can be rewritten as follows.

$$k = \frac{y}{x} \longleftarrow \text{ Ratio form of direct variation model}$$

The ratio form tells you that if x and y have *direct variation*, then the ratio of y to x is the same for all values of x and y. Sometimes real-life data can be approximated by a direct variation model, even though the data may not fit the model exactly.

EXAMPLE 4 *Using a Ratio Based on Data to Write a Model*

ANIMAL STUDIES The tail and body lengths (in feet) of 8 alligators are shown below. The ages range from 2 years to over 50 years. ▶ Source: St. Augustine Alligator Farm

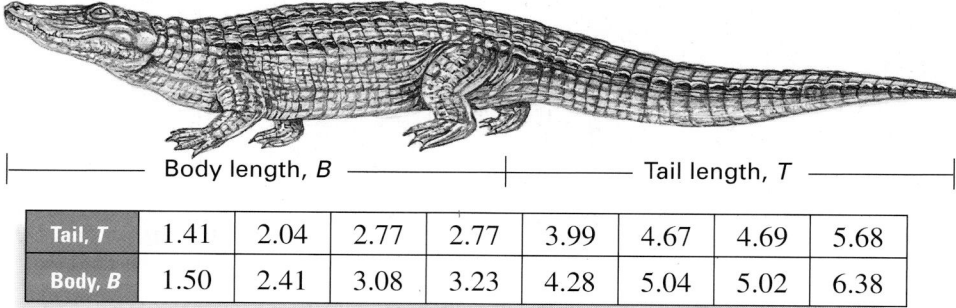

Tail, T	1.41	2.04	2.77	2.77	3.99	4.67	4.69	5.68
Body, B	1.50	2.41	3.08	3.23	4.28	5.04	5.02	6.38

a. Write a model that relates the tail length T to the body length B.

b. Estimate the body length of an alligator whose tail length is 4.5 feet.

SOLUTION

a. Begin by finding the ratio of tail length to body length for each alligator.

Tail, T	1.41	2.04	2.77	2.77	3.99	4.67	4.69	5.68
Body, B	1.50	2.41	3.08	3.23	4.28	5.04	5.02	6.38
Ratio	0.94	0.85	0.90	0.86	0.93	0.93	0.93	0.89

The ratio is about 0.9 for each alligator, so use a direct variation model.

$$k = \frac{T}{B} \qquad \text{Write ratio model for direct variation.}$$

$$0.9 = \frac{T}{B} \qquad \text{Substitute 0.9 for } k.$$

$$0.9B = T \qquad \text{Multiply each side by } B.$$

b. Use the model $0.9B = T$ to estimate the body length of the alligator.

$$0.9B = 4.5 \qquad \text{Substitute 4.5 for } T.$$

$$B = 5 \qquad \text{Divide each side by 0.9.}$$

▶ You estimate that the alligator's body is about 5 feet long.

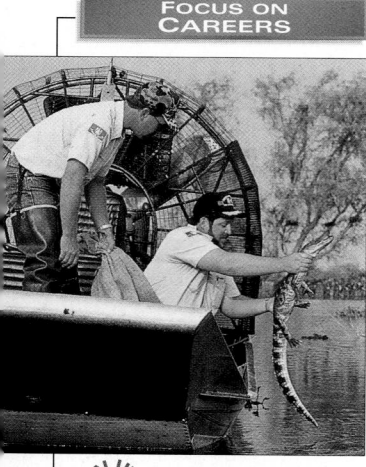

GUIDED PRACTICE

1. Explain what it means for x and y to vary directly.

2. In a direct variation equation, how are the constant of variation and the slope related?

Graph the equation. State whether the two quantities have direct variation. If they have direct variation, find the constant of variation and the slope of the direct variation model.

3. $y = x$

4. $y = 4x$

5. $y = \frac{1}{2}x$

6. $y = 2x$

7. $y = x - 4$

8. $y - 0.1x = 0$

🌎 **SALARY** In Exercises 9–11, you work a different number of hours each day. The table shows your total pay p and the number of hours h you worked.

Total pay, p	$18	$42	$48	$30
Hours worked, h	3	7	8	5
Ratio	?	?	?	?

9. Copy and complete the table by finding the ratio of your total pay each day to the number of hours you worked that day.

10. Write a model that relates the variables p and h.

11. If you work 6 hours on the fifth day, what will your total pay be?

PRACTICE AND APPLICATIONS

STUDENT HELP

▶ **Extra Practice**
to help you master skills is on p. 800.

DIRECT VARIATION MODEL Find the constant of variation and the slope.

12. $y = 3x$

13. $y = -\frac{2}{5}x$

14. $y = 0.75x$

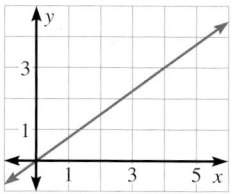

CONSTANT OF VARIATION Graph the equation. Find the constant of variation and the slope of the direct variation model.

15. $y = -3x$

16. $y = -5x$

17. $y = 0.4x$

18. $y = -x$

19. $y = \frac{5}{4}x$

20. $y = -\frac{1}{5}x$

STUDENT HELP

▶ **HOMEWORK HELP**
Example 1: Exs. 12–20
Example 2: Exs. 23–31
Example 3: Exs. 21–22, 32
Example 4: Exs. 36–37

RECOGNIZING DIRECT VARIATION In Exercises 21 and 22, state whether the two quantities have direct variation.

21. 🌎 **BICYCLING** You ride your bike at an average speed of 14 miles per hour. The number of miles m you ride during h hours is modeled by $m = 14h$.

22. **GEOMETRY** ▶ **CONNECTION** The circumference C of a circle and its diameter d are related by the equation $C = \pi d$.

**VALENTINA V.
TERESHKOVA**
In 1963 the Soviet astronaut
Valentina Tereshkova was
the first woman to travel
in space.

FINDING EQUATIONS In Exercises 23–31, the variables *x* and *y* vary directly.
Use the given values to write an equation that relates *x* and *y*.

23. $x = 4, y = 12$

24. $x = 7, y = 35$

25. $x = 18, y = 4$

26. $x = 22, y = 11$

27. $x = 5.5, y = 1.1$

28. $x = 16.5, y = 3.3$

29. $x = -1, y = -1$

30. $x = 7\frac{1}{5}, y = -9$

31. $x = -9, y = 3$

32. SCIENCE ▸ CONNECTION   The volume *V* of blood pumped from your heart each
minute varies directly with your pulse rate *p*. Each time your heart beats, it
pumps approximately 0.06 liter of blood.

   a. Find an equation that relates *V* and *p*.

   b. COLLECTING DATA Take your pulse and find out how much blood your
    heart pumps per minute.

33. 🌐 **ASTRONAUTS** Weight varies directly with gravity. With his equipment
Buzz Aldrin weighed 360 pounds on Earth but only 60 pounds on the moon.
If Valentina V. Tereshkova had landed on the moon with her equipment and
weighed 54 pounds, how much would she have weighed on Earth with
equipment?

🖩 **SWIMMING POOLS** In Exercises 34 and 35, use the following
information about several sizes of pools. The amount of chlorine
needed in a pool varies with the amount of water in the pool.

Amount of water (gallons)	6250	5000	12,500	15,000
Chlorine (pounds)	0.75	0.60	1.50	1.80

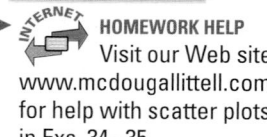
34. Use a graphing calculator or a computer to make a scatter plot of the data.
Sketch the graph.

35. Does the scatter plot you made in Exercise 34 show direct variation?

🌐 **VIOLIN FAMILY** In Exercises 36 and 37, use the following information.
The violin family includes the bass, the cello, the
viola, and the violin. The size of each instrument
determines its tone. The shortest produces the
highest tone, while the longest produces the
deepest (lowest) tone.

Total length, *t*

Body length, *b*

Violin family	Bass	Cello	Viola	Violin
Total length *t* (inches)	72	47	26	23
Body length *b* (inches)	44	30	16	14

36. Write a direct variation model that you can use to relate the body length of a
member of the violin family to its total length.

37. Another instrument in the violin family has a body length of 28 inches. Use
your model from Exercise 36 to estimate the total length of the instrument. Is
its tone higher or lower than a viola's tone?

38. MULTIPLE CHOICE The variables x and y vary directly. When $x = 4$, $y = 24$. Which equation correctly relates x and y?

   Ⓐ $x = 4y$ **Ⓑ** $y = 4x$ **Ⓒ** $x = 6y$ **Ⓓ** $y = 6x$

39. MULTIPLE CHOICE Which equation models the ratio form of direct variation?

   Ⓐ $\dfrac{-4}{3} = \dfrac{y}{x}$ **Ⓑ** $-3y = 4x - 1$ **Ⓒ** $\dfrac{4}{-3} = x + y$ **Ⓓ** $y = -\dfrac{4}{3}x + 6$

40. MULTIPLE CHOICE Find the constant of variation of the direct variation model $3x = y$.

   Ⓐ 3 **Ⓑ** $\dfrac{1}{3}$ **Ⓒ** y **Ⓓ** x

41. MULTIPLE CHOICE You buy some oranges for $.80 per pound. Which direct variation model relates the total cost x to the number of pounds of oranges y?

   Ⓐ $y = 8x$ **Ⓑ** $x = 0.8y$ **Ⓒ** $y = 0.8x$ **Ⓓ** $x = 8y$

★ **Challenge**

42. **GEOMETRY** **CONNECTION** Write an equation for the perimeter of the regular hexagon at the right. Does your equation model direct variation?

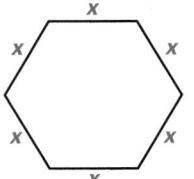

EXTRA CHALLENGE
www.mcdougallittell.com

43. LOGICAL REASONING If a varies directly with b, then does b vary directly with a? Explain your reasoning.

MIXED REVIEW

SOLVING EQUATIONS Solve the equation. (Review 3.4)

44. $7z + 30 = -5$ **45.** $4b = 26 - 9b$ **46.** $2(w - 2) = 2$

47. $9x + 65 = -4x$ **48.** $55 - 5y = 9y + 27$ **49.** $7c - 3 = 4(c - 3)$

FUNCTIONS In Exercises 50 and 51, rewrite the equation so that x is a function of y. (Review 3.7)

50. $15 = 7(x - y) + 3x$ **51.** $3x + 12 = 5(x + y)$

52. 🌐 **HOURLY WAGE** You get paid $152.25 for working 21 hours. Find your hourly rate of pay. (Review 3.8)

53. ORDERED PAIRS Plot and label the points $R(2, 4)$, $S(0, -1)$, $T(3, 6)$, and $U(-1, -2)$ in a coordinate plane. (Review 4.1)

CHECKING SOLUTIONS Decide whether the given point lies on the line. Justify your answer both algebraically and graphically. (Review 4.2)

54. $x - y = 10$; $(5, -5)$ **55.** $3x - 6y = -2$; $(-4, -2)$

56. $5x + 6y = -1$; $(1, -1)$ **57.** $-4x - 3y = -8$; $(-4, 2)$

FINDING INTERCEPTS Find the *x*-intercept and the *y*-intercept of the graph of the equation. (Review 4.3 for 4.6)

58. $2x + y = 6$ **59.** $x - 1.1y = 10$ **60.** $x - 6y = 4$

61. $x + 5y = 10$ **62.** $y = x - 5$ **63.** $y = \dfrac{1}{3}x - \dfrac{7}{3}$

● ACTIVITY 4.6

Developing Concepts

Graphing Families of Linear Equations

GROUP ACTIVITY
Work in a small group.

MATERIALS
• desk
• textbooks
• graph paper
• meter stick or metric ruler

▶ **QUESTION** What are some relationships that exist between members of a family of equations?

▶ **EXPLORING THE CONCEPT**

You can use a linear equation $y = mx + b$ to model the height from the floor to the top of a stack of books that are m centimeters thick sitting on a desk b centimeters high.

❶ Measure the thickness of your algebra textbook. Measure the height of the top of your desk to the floor.

❷ Write a model for the height y from the floor to the top of a stack of x algebra books the same size as yours sitting on your desk.

❸ Graph and label your model from **Step 2**.

❹ Measure the thickness of your English textbook. Write a model for the height y from the floor to the top of a stack of x English books the same size as yours sitting on your desk. Graph this model in the coordinate plane you drew in **Step 3**.

❺ Repeat **Step 4** using another book.

▶ **DRAWING CONCLUSIONS**

1. Equations that have characteristics in common can be thought of as a *family of equations*. List all of the characteristics that the equations have in common. List all of the characteristics that their graphs have in common.

2. Suppose in **Step 2** you used the same book but on a desk or a table of a different height. Write models for the height of a stack of algebra books on a desk 74 cm tall and on a computer table 68 cm tall. Graph these models in the same coordinate plane. What characteristics do the equations share? What characteristics do their graphs share?

3. What characteristics are shared by the family of equations in which $m = 4$?

4. What is true about the family of linear equations with graphs passing through the point (0, 5)?

4.6

Quick Graphs Using Slope-Intercept Form

What you should learn

GOAL 1 Graph a linear equation in slope-intercept form.

GOAL 2 Graph and interpret equations in slope-intercept form that model **real-life** situations, such as the snowstorm in **Exs. 56–59**.

Why you should learn it

▼ To model **real-life** situations, such as a flooding river in **Example 4**.

Mississippi and Ohio Rivers flooding

GOAL 1 GRAPHING USING SLOPE-INTERCEPT FORM

In Lesson 4.4 you learned to find the slope of a line given two points on the line. There is also a method for finding the slope given an equation of a line.

▶ ACTIVITY
Developing Concepts

Investigating Slope-Intercept Form

Copy and complete the table. Then write a generalization about the meaning of m and b in $y = mx + b$.

	Equation	Two solutions	Slope	y-Intercept
1.	$y = 2x + 1$	$(0, ?), (?, 0)$	?	?
2.	$y = -2x - 3$	$(0, ?), (?, 0)$	?	?
3.	$y = x + 4$	$(0, ?), (?, 0)$	?	?
4.	$y = 0.5x - 2.5$	$(0, ?), (?, 0)$	?	?

In this activity, you may have discovered the following idea, which applies only when an equation is in slope-intercept form.

SLOPE-INTERCEPT FORM OF THE EQUATION OF A LINE

The linear equation $y = mx + b$ is written in **slope-intercept form**. The slope of the line is m. The y-intercept is b.

$y = 2x + 3$

Slope is **2**.

y-intercept is **3**.

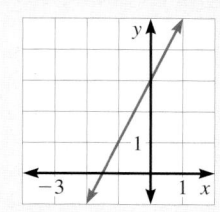

EXAMPLE 1   *Writing Equations in Slope-Intercept Form*

	EQUATION	SLOPE-INTERCEPT FORM	SLOPE	y-INTERCEPT
a.	$y = -x + 2$	$y = (-1)x + 2$	$m = -1$	$b = 2$
b.	$y = \dfrac{x + 3}{2}$	$y = \dfrac{1}{2}x + \dfrac{3}{2}$	$m = \dfrac{1}{2}$	$b = \dfrac{3}{2}$
c.	$y = -4$	$y = 0x - 4$	$m = 0$	$b = -4$
d.	$2x - 4y = 16$	$y = 0.5x - 4$	$m = 0.5$	$b = -4$

EXAMPLE 2 *Graphing Using Slope and y-Intercept*

Graph the equation $3x + y = 2$.

SOLUTION

Write the equation in slope-intercept form.

$$y = -3x + 2$$

Find the slope and the *y*-intercept.

$$m = -3 \qquad b = 2$$

Plot the point $(0, b)$.

Draw a slope triangle to locate a second point on the line.

$$m = \frac{-3}{1} = \frac{\text{rise}}{\text{run}}$$

Draw a line through the two points.

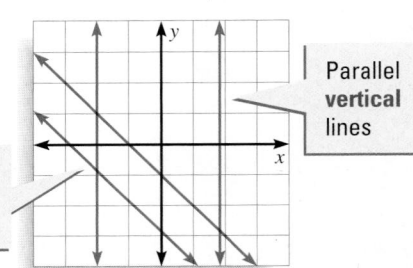

· · · · · · · · · ·

Two different lines in the same plane are **parallel** if they do not intersect.

In a coordinate plane, any two vertical lines are parallel. Any two nonvertical lines are parallel if and only if they have the same slope.

Parallel lines with slope of $m = -1$

Parallel vertical lines

EXAMPLE 3 *Identifying a Family of Parallel Lines*

Which of the following lines are parallel?

    line *a*: $-x + 2y = 6$ **line *b*:** $-x + 2y = -2$ **line *c*:** $x + 2y = 4$

SOLUTION Begin by writing each equation in slope-intercept form.

    line *a*: $y = \frac{1}{2}x + 3$ **line *b*:** $y = \frac{1}{2}x - 1$ **line *c*:** $y = -\frac{1}{2}x + 2$

Lines *a* and *b* are parallel because each has a slope of $\frac{1}{2}$.

Line *c* is not parallel to either of the other two lines because it has a slope of $-\frac{1}{2}$.

✔**CHECK** The graph gives you a visual check. It shows that line *c* intersects each of the two parallel lines.

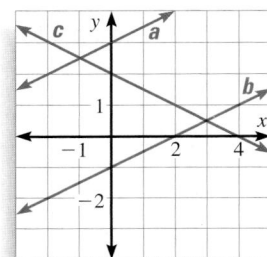

▶ Line *a* and line *b* are parallel.

EXAMPLE 4 *Graphing Using Slope-Intercept Form*

CITY PLANNING You are an intern at a city planner's office and are asked to create a graph for a planning board meeting. The graph will represent different heights of a local river during a flood.

You are given the following equations to model the changing river heights. In each equation, h represents the height of the river (in feet) and t represents the time (in hours) since the flooding began.

Stage 1 (first 60 hours):	$h = \frac{1}{2}t + 24$	$0 \le t \le 60$
Stage 2 (next 12 hours):	$h = 54$	$60 < t \le 72$
Stage 3 (last 48 hours):	$h = -\frac{5}{8}t + 99$	$72 < t \le 120$

SOLUTION

You decide to graph all three equations in the same coordinate plane and label the graph to describe the three stages of flooding. You notice that each equation is in slope-intercept form. The slope in each equation represents the rate at which the river's height is changing during a particular period of time.

Stage 1: During the first 60 hours, the slope is $\frac{1}{2}$. The river height increased $\frac{1}{2}$ foot per hour, from 24 feet to 54 feet.

Stage 2: During the next 12 hours, the river stayed at a constant peak height of 54 feet.

Stage 3: During the last 48 hours, the slope is $-\frac{5}{8}$. The river height decreased $-\frac{5}{8}$ foot per hour, from 54 feet to a normal 24 feet.

To graph each model, you plot each stage within each domain.

GUIDED PRACTICE

Vocabulary Check ✓
1. Why is the equation $y = mx + b$ called the *slope-intercept form*?

Concept Check ✓
2. Explain how to graph $2x - 3y = 6$ using slope-intercept form.

3. Decide whether the graphs of $y = x + 2$ and $y = x - 4$ are parallel lines.

Skill Check ✓
4. Choose the equation whose graph is shown at the right.

A. $y = \frac{1}{2}x - 2$ **B.** $y = 2x - 2$ **C.** $y = 2x$

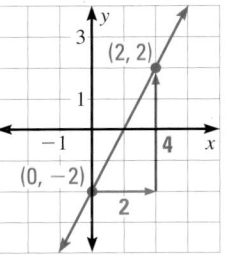

Find the slope and the *y*-intercept of the graph of the equation.

5. $y = 2x + 1$ **6.** $y = 11x$ **7.** $y = x + 3$

8. $y = -1.5x$ **9.** $y = 5x - 3$ **10.** $y = -x - 2$

🌐 **SAVINGS ACCOUNT** In Exercises 11 and 12, you have $50 in your savings account at the beginning of the year. Each month you save $30. Assuming no interest is paid, the equation $s = 30m + 50$ models the amount of money s in your savings account after m months.

11. What is the slope of the graph of the line? What is the *y*-intercept?

12. Graph your total savings.

PRACTICE AND APPLICATIONS

STUDENT HELP

▶ **Extra Practice**
to help you master
skills is on p. 800.

SLOPE AND *y*-INTERCEPT **Find the slope and the *y*-intercept of the graph of the equation.**

13. $y = 6x + 4$ **14.** $y = 3x + 1$ **15.** $y = 2x - 3$

16. $y - 9x = 0$ **17.** $y = -2$ **18.** $3x + 4y = 16$

19. $y = \dfrac{x + 2}{4}$ **20.** $y = \dfrac{6 - x}{3}$ **21.** $12x + 4y - 2 = 0$

GRAPHING LINES **Graph the equation.**

22. $y = x + 3$ **23.** $y = 2x - 1$ **24.** $y = x + 5$

25. $y = -x + 4$ **26.** $y = 6 - x$ **27.** $y = 3x + 7$

28. $y = 4x + 4$ **29.** $y = x + 9$ **30.** $y = 4x + 9$

31. $y = \frac{2}{3}x$ **32.** $y = -\frac{1}{2}x - 3$ **33.** $y = 2$

STUDENT HELP

▶ **HOMEWORK HELP**
Example 1: Exs. 13–21
Example 2: Exs. 22–45,
52–55
Example 3: Exs. 46–51
Example 4: Exs. 56–59

GRAPHING LINES **Write the equation in slope-intercept form. Then graph the equation.**

34. $y = -2$ **35.** $3x - 6y = 9$ **36.** $4x + 5y = 15$

37. $4x - y - 3 = 0$ **38.** $x - y + 4 = 0$ **39.** $x + y = 0$

40. $x - y = 0$ **41.** $x + 3y - 3 = 0$ **42.** $2x - 3y - 6 = 0$

43. $y - 0.5 = 0$ **44.** $5(x + 3 + y) = 10x$ **45.** $2x + 3y - 4 = x + 5$

PARALLEL LINES Decide whether the graphs of the two equations are parallel lines. Explain your answer.

46. $y = -3x + 2$, $y + 3x = -4$ **47.** $2x - 12 = y$, $y = 10 + 2x$

48. $y + 6x - 8 = 0$, $2y = 12x - 4$ **49.** $3y - 4x = 3$, $3y = -4x + 9$

50. $y + 3x = 6x + 1$, $9x - 3y = 7$ **51.** $-x + 3 + y = 2x + 3$, $y + 4 = 3x$

MATCHING EQUATIONS AND GRAPHS Match the equation with its graph.

A. $y = \frac{1}{2}x + 1$ **B.** $y = \frac{1}{2}x - 1$ **C.** $y = x + 2$ **D.** $y = -x - 1$

52.   **53.**   **54.**   **55.**

SNOWSTORM In Exercises 56–59, snow fell for 9 hours at a rate of $\frac{1}{2}$ inch per hour. Before the snowstorm began, there were already 6 inches of snow on the ground. The equation $y = \frac{1}{2}x + 6$ models the depth y of snow on the ground after x hours.

56. What is the slope of $y = \frac{1}{2}x + 6$? What is the y-intercept?

57. CRITICAL THINKING Explain what the slope and the y-intercept mean in the snowstorm model.

58. Graph the amount of snow on the ground during the storm.

59. *Writing* In the Apple County School District, school is canceled if there is a foot or more of snow on the ground. If this 9-hour storm occurred in Apple County, would school be canceled? Explain your reasoning.

SNOWSTORMS
Each year an average of 105 snowstorms affect the continental United States.

PHONE CALL In Exercises 60 and 61, the cost of a long-distance telephone call is $.87 for the first minute and $.15 for each additional minute.

60. PLOTTING POINTS Let c represent the total cost of a call that lasts t minutes. Plot points for the costs of calls that last 1, 2, 3, 4, 5, and 6 minutes.

61. CRITICAL THINKING Draw a line through the points you plotted in Exercise 60. Find the slope. What does the slope represent?

GEOMETRY **CONNECTION** In Exercises 62–63, use the following linear equations.

line *a:* $y = -x + 2$ line *b:* $y = -1$ line *c:* $y = x + 2$

62. Which of the lines are parallel? Explain.

63. Graph each equation in the same coordinate plane. What type of polygon do they form? Find the area of the polygon. Justify your method.

MODELING REAL LIFE In Exercises 64 and 65, graph the situation.

64. You start from home and drive 55 miles per hour for 3 hours, where d is your distance from home.

65. You start 165 miles from home and drive toward home at 55 miles per hour for 3 hours, where d is your distance from home.

🌐 **ROLLER COASTER** **In Exercises 66–68, use the following information.**
You are supervising the construction of a roller coaster for young children. For
the first 20 feet of horizontal distance, the track must rise off the ground at a
constant rate. After your crew has constructed 5 feet of horizontal distance, the
track is 1 foot off the ground.

66. Plot points for the heights of the track at 5-foot intervals. Draw a line through
    the points. Find the slope of the line. What does the slope represent?

67. After 20 feet of horizontal distance is constructed, you are at the highest
    point of your roller coaster. How high off the ground is the track?

68. During construction, the park passes a regulation that the track for any roller
    coaster for young children must not be higher than 5 feet off the ground.
    Will your roller coaster pass inspection when it is completed?

**Test
Preparation**

69. **MULTIPLE CHOICE** What is the slope of a line parallel to the graph of the
    equation $1.6x - 3.2y = 16$?

    Ⓐ -5 Ⓑ 0.5 Ⓒ -0.5 Ⓓ 5

70. **MULTIPLE CHOICE** If $y + 8 = 0$, what is the slope of the graph?

    Ⓐ Undefined   Ⓑ 1 Ⓒ 0 Ⓓ -1

★ **Challenge**

GEOMETRY **CONNECTION** **In Exercises
71–73, graph the two equations in
the same coordinate plane. Use the
following information to decide
whether the lines are perpendicular.**

It can be shown that two different
nonvertical lines in the same plane with
slopes m_1 and m_2 are perpendicular if
and only if m_2 is the negative reciprocal
of m_1.

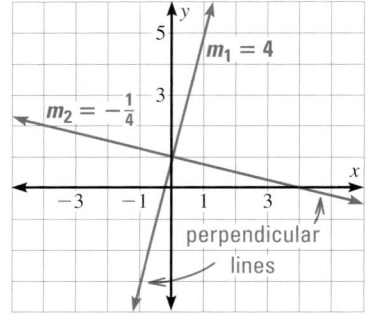

71. $y = 2x + 4$ 72. $y = -\frac{1}{3}x - 4$ 73. $y = 1 + \frac{2}{3}x$

    $y = -\frac{1}{2}x + 2$ $y = 3x + 2$ $y = \frac{3}{2}x - 2$

PERPENDICULAR LINES **In Exercises 74–76, use Exercises 71–73 to help you
write an equation of a line that is perpendicular to the given line.**

74. $y = 3x - 4$ 75. $y = -2x + 1$ 76. $y = \frac{4}{3}x - 3$

77. **PARALLEL LINES** Is it possible to find another line that is parallel to
    $3x + 9y = 1$ and passes through the point $\left(0, \frac{1}{9}\right)$? Explain your reasoning.

MIXED REVIEW

SOLVING EQUATIONS **Solve the equation.** (Review 3.3, 3.4 for 4.7)

78. $x + 6 = 14$ **79.** $9 - y = 4$ **80.** $7b = 21$

81. $\frac{a}{4} = 3$ **82.** $\frac{1}{3}g - 2 = 1$ **83.** $3p - 12 = 6$

84. $2(v + 1) = 4$ **85.** $3(r - 1) = 2(r - 2)$ **86.** $5(w - 5) = 25$

87. **COIN COLLECTION** You have 32 coins in a jar. Each coin is either copper or silver. You have 8 more copper coins than silver coins. Let c be the number of copper coins. Which equation correctly models the situation? (Review 1.5)

     A. $(c - 8) + c = 32$ **B.** $c + (c + 8) = 32$

COST OF RAISING A CHILD **In Exercises 88 and 89, the table shows estimated costs of raising a child born in 1996 to a low income family for the child's first seven years.** (Review 1.6)

Year	1996	1997	1998	1999	2000	2001	2002
Cost (in dollars)	5670	5960	6280	6730	7080	7450	8000

DATA UPDATE of USDA data at www.mcdougallittell.com

88. Make a line graph of the data.

89. During which year did the cost increase the most?

QUIZ 2

Find the slope of the line passing through the points. (Lesson 4.4)

     1. $(0, 0), (5, 2)$ **2.** $(1, -3), (-4, -5)$ **3.** $(3, 3), (-6, -4)$

     4. $(-3, 2), (-5, -2)$ **5.** $(0, -4), (5, -4)$ **6.** $(1, -2), (-7, 6)$

The variables x and y vary directly. Given one pair of values for x and y, find an equation that relates the variables. (Lesson 4.5)

     7. $x = 2, y = 10$ **8.** $x = 8, y = 64$ **9.** $x = 12, y = 72$

     10. $x = 16, y = 12$ **11.** $x = 10, y = 7$ **12.** $x = 18, y = 8$

Write the equation in slope-intercept form. Then graph the equation. (Lesson 4.6)

     13. $y = 2x - 4$ **14.** $6x + 12y + 4 = 0$ **15.** $x - 2y = 12$

     16. $x - y + 2 = 0$ **17.** $x + 2y - 2 = 0$ **18.** $\frac{3}{2}x + \frac{3}{2}y = \frac{3}{4}$

19. **BUSINESS** On January 1, a company had $365,800 in its account. On June 1, the company had $215,400 in its account. If the amount in the company's account changed by an equal amount each month, find the rate of change. Give your answer in dollars per month. (Lesson 4.4)

● ACTIVITY 4.6
Using Technology

Graphing a Linear Equation

In Lesson 4.6 you learned how to graph a linear equation using the slope and the *y*-intercept. With a graphing calculator or a computer, you can graph a linear equation and find solutions.

▶ **EXAMPLE 1**

Use a graphing calculator to graph $2x - 3y = 33$.

▶ **SOLUTION**

❶ Rewrite the equation in terms of *x* and *y* if necessary. Then solve the equation for *y*.

$$2x - 3y = 33$$
$$-3y = -2x + 33$$
$$y = \frac{2}{3}x - 11$$

❷ Press $\boxed{Y=}$ $\boxed{(}$ 2 $\boxed{\div}$ 3 $\boxed{)}$ *x* $\boxed{-}$ 11 $\boxed{ENTER}$.

Without parentheses, the calculator may interpret the fraction as $\frac{2}{3x}$.

❸ Think of the screen as a "window" that lets you look at part of a coordinate plane. Press $\boxed{WINDOW}$ to set the size of the graph.

❹ Press $\boxed{GRAPH}$ to graph the equation. A standard viewing window is shown.

❺ To see the point where the graph crosses the *x*-axis, you can adjust the viewing window. Press $\boxed{WINDOW}$ and enter new values. Then press $\boxed{GRAPH}$ to graph the equation.

▶ **EXAMPLE 2**

Estimate the value of y when $x = -7$ in the equation $y = \frac{2}{3}x - \frac{45}{8}$.

▶ **SOLUTION**

① Graph the equation $y = \frac{2}{3}x - \frac{45}{8}$ using a viewing window that will show the graph when $x \approx -7$.

```
WINDOW
 Xmin=-10
 Xmax=5
 Xscl=1
 Ymin=-15
 Ymax=5
 Yscl=1
```

② Press **TRACE** and a flashing cursor appears. The x-coordinate and y-coordinate of the cursor's location are at the bottom of the screen. Press right and left arrows to move it. Move the trace cursor until the x-coordinate of the point is at about -7.

```
X=-7.02        Y=-10.305
```

STUDENT HELP

▸ **Study Tip**
You can continue to use zoom until the y-coordinate is to the nearest tenth, hundredth, or any other decimal place you need.

③ Use the **ZOOM** feature to get a more accurate estimate. A common way to zoom is to press **ZOOM** and select *Zoom In*. You now have a closer look at the graph at that point. Repeat **Step 2**.

```
X=-7          Y=-10.291
```

▶ When $x = -7$, $y \approx -10.3$.

▶ **EXERCISES**

Use the standard viewing window to graph the equation.

1. $y = -2x - 3$ **2.** $y = 2x + 2$ **3.** $x + 2y = -1$ **4.** $x - 3y = 3$

Use the indicated viewing window to graph the equation.

5. $y = x + 25$
Xmin = –10
Xmax = 10
Xscl = 1
Ymin = –5
Ymax = 35
Yscl = 5

6. $y = 0.1x$
Xmin = –10
Xmax = 10
Xscl = 1
Ymin = –5
Ymax = 1
Yscl = 0.1

7. $y = 100x + 2500$
Xmin = 0
Xmax = 100
Xscl = 10
Ymin = 0
Ymax = 15000
Yscl = 1000

Determine an appropriate viewing window for the graph of the equation.

8. $y = x - 330$ **9.** $y = x - 0.3$ **10.** $y = 120x$ **11.** $y = 40{,}000 - 1500x$

Use a graph of the equation to estimate the value of y for the given value of x.

12. $y = -9x$ when $x = -1.05$ **13.** $y = 5x + 651$ when $x = 2.3$

14. $y + \frac{1}{3}x = \frac{1}{5}$ when $x = 19$ **15.** $y = -2x - 3$ when $x = 954$

4.7 Solving Linear Equations Using Graphs

What you should learn

GOAL 1 Solve a linear equation graphically.

GOAL 2 Use a graph to solve **real-life** problems, such as estimating when there will be 2.5 million registered nurses in **Example 4.**

Why you should learn it

▼ To solve **real-life** problems such as finding production costs of a small business in **Ex. 44.**

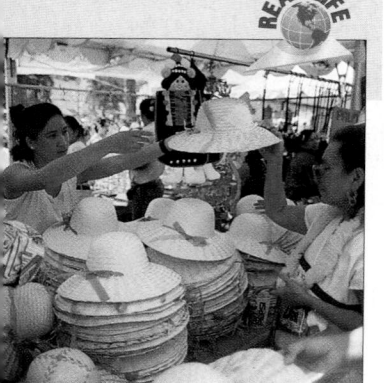

GOAL 1 SOLVING LINEAR EQUATIONS GRAPHICALLY

Up to this point, you have been solving linear equations and checking the solutions *algebraically* (by using algebra). In this lesson you will learn how to solve linear equations and check solutions *graphically* (by using a graph).

STEPS FOR SOLVING LINEAR EQUATIONS GRAPHICALLY

The solution of a linear equation can be found graphically using the following steps:

STEP 1 Write the equation in the form $ax + b = 0$.

STEP 2 Write the related function $y = ax + b$.

STEP 3 Graph the equation $y = ax + b$.

The solution of $ax + b = 0$ is the x-intercept of $y = ax + b$.

EXAMPLE 1 *Using a Graphical Check for a Solution*

Solve $2x - 5 = 1$ algebraically. Check your solution graphically.

SOLUTION

$$2x - 5 = 1 \qquad \text{Write original equation.}$$
$$2x = 6 \qquad \text{Add 5 to each side.}$$
$$x = 3 \qquad \text{Divide each side by 2.}$$

✓ **CHECK** Solve $2x - 5 = 1$ graphically as a check.

1 Write the equation in the form $ax + b = 0$.

$$2x - 5 = 1$$
$$2x - 6 = 0$$

2 Write the related function in two variables.

$$y = 2x - 6$$

3 Graph the related function

$$y = 2x - 6.$$

Notice that the x-intercept is 3, which is the solution of $2x - 6 = 0$. This confirms that 3 is the solution of $2x - 5 = 1$.

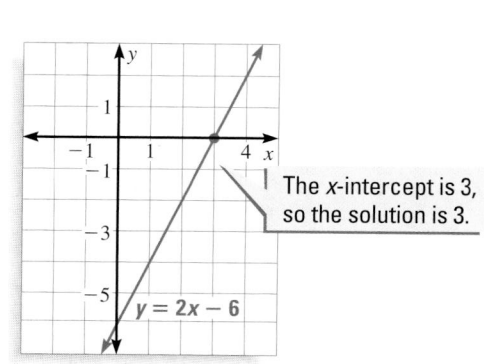

The x-intercept is 3, so the solution is 3.

$y = 2x - 6$

Study Tip
When you know two
ways to solve a problem,
it's a good idea to use
one method to get a
solution and the other
method to check the
solution. This is done in
Examples 1 and 2.

EXAMPLE 2 *Solving an Equation Graphically*

Solve $\frac{4}{3}x + 3 = 2x$ graphically. Check your solution algebraically.

SOLUTION

① Write the equation in the form $ax + b = 0$.

$$\frac{4}{3}x + 3 = 2x \qquad \text{Write original equation.}$$

$$-\frac{2}{3}x + 3 = 0 \qquad \text{Subtract 2x from each side.}$$

② Write the related function $y = -\frac{2}{3}x + 3$.

③ Graph the equation
$y = -\frac{2}{3}x + 3$.
The x-intercept
appears to be $\frac{9}{2}$.

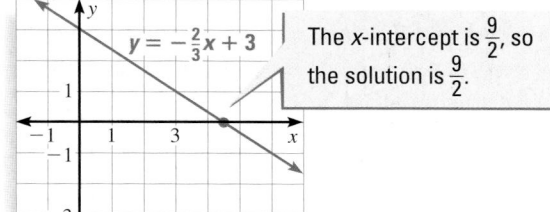

$y = -\frac{2}{3}x + 3$

The x-intercept is $\frac{9}{2}$, so
the solution is $\frac{9}{2}$.

✓ CHECK Use substitution.

$$\frac{4}{3}x + 3 = 2x$$

$$\frac{4}{3}\left(\frac{9}{2}\right) + 3 \stackrel{?}{=} 2\left(\frac{9}{2}\right)$$

$$6 + 3 = 9 \longleftarrow \text{True statement}$$

▶ The solution of $\frac{4}{3}x + 3 = 2x$ is $\frac{9}{2}$.

EXAMPLE 3 *Using a Graphing Calculator*

Use a graphing calculator to approximate the solution of the linear equation
$2.65(4x - 9) = -8.85 + 7.6x$.

SOLUTION

When you graph an equation using a graphing calculator, you do not need to
simplify the equation before entering it.

$$2.65(4x - 9) + 8.85 - 7.6x = 0 \qquad \text{Rewrite equation so one side is 0.}$$

Then use a graphing calculator
(or a computer) to graph the
related function

$$y = 2.65(4x - 9) + 8.85 - 7.6x.$$

X=5   Y=0

▶ The x-intercept appears to be 5. Check
that 5 is a solution of the original equation.

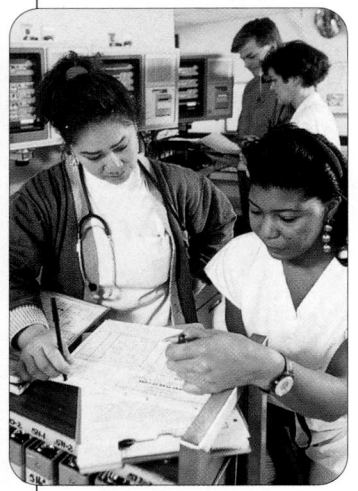
GOAL 2 **APPROXIMATING SOLUTIONS IN REAL LIFE**

Example 4 shows how to apply the graphical approach of Examples 1–3 to a real-life problem. Example 5 shows another graphical approach to this problem.

EXAMPLE 4 *Approximating a Real-Life Solution*

NURSES Based on data from 1980 to 1997, a model for the number n (in millions) of registered nurses in the United States is $n = 0.055t + 1.26$, where t is the number of years since 1980. According to this model, in what year will the United States have 2.5 million registered nurses? ▶ Source: U.S. Public Health Service

SOLUTION

Substitute 2.5 for n in the linear model. You can answer the question by solving the resulting linear equation, $2.5 = 0.055t + 1.26$.

Write the equation in the form $ax + b = 0$.

$$2.5 = 0.055t + 1.26$$

$$0 = 0.055t - 1.24$$

Graph the related function.

$$y = 0.055t - 1.24$$

The t-intercept is about 22.5.

The t-intercept is about 22.5. This is where $0.055t - 1.24 = 0$.

$y = 0.055t - 1.24$

▶ Because t is the number of years since 1980, you can estimate that there will be 2.5 million registered nurses sometime in 2002.

EXAMPLE 5 *Solving by Graphing Both Sides*

Another graphical approach that you can use to solve the equation $2.5 = 0.055t + 1.26$ in Example 4 is to write and graph a function for each side of the equation.

$$2.5 = 0.055t + 1.26 \qquad \text{Original equation.}$$

$$y = 2.5 \qquad \text{Function for left side of equation.}$$

$$y = 0.055t + 1.26 \qquad \text{Function for right side of equation.}$$

Then graph both functions in the same coordinate plane. The graphs cross where the value of y for both functions is about 2.5.

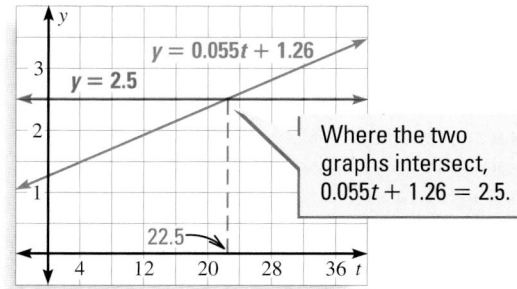

$y = 0.055t + 1.26$

$y = 2.5$

Where the two graphs intersect, $0.055t + 1.26 = 2.5$.

22.5

▶ The t-coordinate where the graphs intersect is about 22.5, the same value found by the method in Example 4.

GUIDED PRACTICE

Vocabulary Check ✓   **1.** Explain how to solve a linear equation in one variable *graphically*.

Concept Check ✓   **2.** In Example 2, explain why the *x*-intercept of the line $y = -\frac{2}{3}x + 3$ is the solution of the equation $0 = -\frac{2}{3}x + 3$.

Solve the equation graphically. Check your answer algebraically.

3. $x - 3 = 7$ **4.** $2 - x = -5$ **5.** $5x + 6 = -9$

Skill Check ✓   **In Exercises 6–10, match the one-variable equation with its related function.**

6. $2x = 10$ **A.** $y = 2x - 16$

7. $2x - 10 = 6$ **B.** $y = -2x - 11$

8. $5x + 4 = 3x + 5$ **C.** $y = 2x - 10$

9. $-4x - 6 = -2x + 5$ **D.** $y = 2x - 1$

10. $19x + 3 = x$ **E.** $y = 18x + 3$

PRACTICE AND APPLICATIONS

STUDENT HELP

▶ **Extra Practice**
to help you master
skills is on p. 800.

MATCHING EQUATIONS AND GRAPHS Match the equation with the line whose *x*-intercept is the solution of the equation.

A. $2x - 4 = 0$ **B.** $x + 6 = 0$ **C.** $x - 6 = 0$

11.   **12.**   **13.**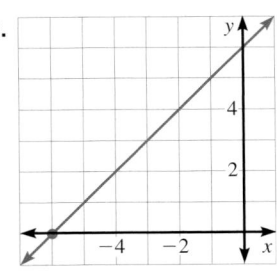

RELATED FUNCTIONS Write the equation in the form *ax* + *b* = 0. Then write the related function *y* = *ax* + *b*.

14. $7x - 3 = 3$ **15.** $6 - 4x = 13$ **16.** $9 + 5x = 19$

17. $12x + 5 = 8x$ **18.** $-4x - 5 = 3x + 8$ **19.** $6 - \frac{4}{7}x = 13 + \frac{3}{7}x$

STUDENT HELP

▶ HOMEWORK HELP
Example 1: Exs. 11–28
Example 2: Exs. 11–37
Example 3: Exs. 38–43
Example 4: Exs. 44, 45
Example 5: Exs. 44, 45

SOLVING EQUATIONS Solve the equation algebraically. Check your solution graphically.

20. $5x + 3 = -2$ **21.** $-3x + 11 = 2$ **22.** $-x = -2$

23. $2x + 7 = 10$ **24.** $\frac{1}{4}x + 1 = -\frac{1}{2}$ **25.** $\frac{1}{2}x + 5 = 3$

26. $-\frac{2}{3}x - 6 = -4$ **27.** $-\frac{3}{4}x + 3 = \frac{9}{4}$ **28.** $\frac{2}{3}x - \frac{2}{3} = 2$

SOLVING GRAPHICALLY Solve the equation graphically. Check your solution algebraically.

29. $2x - 7 = -5$
30. $5x - 2 = 8$
31. $-4x = -12$

32. $6x + 9 = 3$
33. $7 - 9x = -11$
34. $3x + 10 = -2x$

35. $-5x + 4 = 12 - 3x$
36. $\frac{1}{3}x + 1 = 4$
37. $\frac{1}{2}x + 5 = 3$

SOLVING GRAPHICALLY Use a graphing calculator to find the solution of the equation. Check your solution algebraically.

38. $4(x + 2) = 3(x + 5)$
39. $-1.6(1.5x + 7.5) = 0.6(6x + 30)$

40. $\frac{1}{2}(x + 7) = \frac{1}{3}(10x + 2)$
41. $0.7(3x - 20) = 22 - 3.9x$

42. $\frac{3}{4}(4x - 15) = -\frac{3}{2}(4x - 18)$
43. $\frac{1}{3}(10x + 27) = -\frac{1}{5}\left(\frac{55}{3}x + 25\right)$

44. 🌐 **PRODUCTION COSTS** Chai has a small business making decorated hats. She calculates her monthly cost y of producing x hats using the function $y = 1.9x + 350$. In January, her cost was $458.30. How many hats did she make that month? Solve algebraically and graphically.

STUDENT HELP

🔗 **INTERNET**
APPLICATION LINK
Visit our Web site
www.mcdougallittell.com
for more information
about tourism in Ex. 45.

45. 🌐 **TOURISM** Based on data from 1991–1995, a model for the annual number of visitors v from the United States to Europe is

$$v = 559,100t + 6,423,000$$

where t is the number of years since 1991. According to this model, in what year will the number of visitors to Europe reach 11,000,000?

▶ Source: U.S. Bureau of the Census

Venice, Italy

🌐 **VIEWING HABITS** In Exercises 46–49, use the models below. They can be used to estimate the average number of hours h per week that a household in the United States watches television programs. In all three models, t is the number of years since 1985. ▶ Source: Media Dynamics, Inc.

Hours spent watching television:	$h = 0.57t + 54.85$
Hours spent watching talk shows:	$h = 0.35t + 4.06$
Hours spent watching game shows:	$h = -0.2t + 3.4$

46. According to the model, in what year will a household watch television an average of 70 hours per week?

47. According to the model, in what year will a household watch an average of 10 hours of talk shows per week?

48. According to the model, in what year will the average number of hours per week that a household watches game shows be zero?

49. *Writing* Did you solve Exercises 46–48 algebraically or graphically? Give a reason for your choice.

50. MULTI-STEP PROBLEM The U.S. Bureau of Labor Statistics projects job growth by using three models to make low, moderate, and high estimates. The equations below model the projected number of auto mechanics m from 1994 to 2005. In all three models, t is the number of years since 1994.

Model 1: $m = 13{,}272t + 736{,}000$

Model 2: $m = 9455t + 736{,}000$

Model 3: $m = 11{,}455t + 736{,}000$

a. For each model, write an equation that enables you to predict the year in which the number of auto mechanics will reach 800,000.

b. In the same coordinate plane, graph the related function for each equation that you found in part (a). According to each model, in what year will the number of auto mechanics reach 800,000?

c. VISUAL THINKING Which model gives a high estimate of the number of mechanics? a low estimate? How can you tell this from the graphs of the models?

★ Challenge

51. COMPARING METHODS Below, Tanya and Dwight solve $3x - 5 = 2x - 3$ graphically. Does each method give a correct solution? Explain.

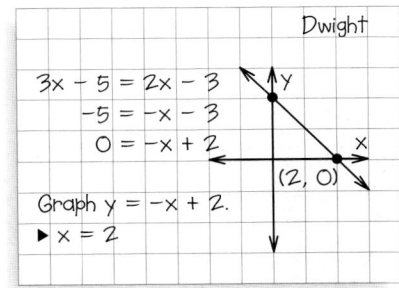

EXTRA CHALLENGE
www.mcdougallittell.com

MIXED REVIEW

CHECKING SOLUTIONS Is the given number a solution of the inequality? (Review 1.4)

52. $x + 3 > 5$; 7

53. $-2 - x \le -9$; -7

54. $3x - 11 \ge 2$; 4

55. $8 + 5x < -2$; -2

56. $4x - 1 > 10$; 3

57. $2x + 4 \le 3x - 3$; 5

DISTRIBUTIVE PROPERTY Apply the distributive property. (Review 2.6)

58. $4(x + 7)$

59. $-8(8 - y)$

60. $(3 - b)9$

61. $(q + 4)(-3q)$

62. $10(6x + 2)$

63. $-2(d - 5)$

64. $(7 - 2a)(4a)$

65. $-5w(-3 + 2w)$

66. 🌐 FLOWER SERVICE You start a daily flower club and charge $10 to join and $.50 per day. Every day each member of the club gets a fresh flower. Let n represent the number of club members and let I represent your income for four weeks. A model for the situation is $I = [10 + 4 \cdot 7(0.5)]n$. Write an input-output table that shows your income for 2, 4, 6, 8, and 10 club members. (Review 1.7)

Functions and Relations

GOAL ① **IDENTIFYING FUNCTIONS**

In defining functions, you learned that for every input there corresponds exactly one output, as in the case of linear functions defined by the rule $y = mx + b$. However, there are rules that associate more than one output with an input, as in $x = y^2$ where the input $x = 4$ corresponds to the outputs $y = 2$ and $y = -2$. A rule of this type, where an input can have more than one output, is a *relation*. A **relation** is defined to be any set of ordered pairs.

EXAMPLE 1 *Identifying Functions*

Decide whether the relation is a function. If so, give the domain and the range.

a. Input Output

b. Input Output

SOLUTION

a. The relation is a function. For each input there is exactly one output. The domain of the function is the set of input values 1, 2, 3, and 4. The range is the set of output values 2, 4, and 5.

b. The relation is not a function because the input 1 has two outputs: 5 and 7.

· · · · · · · · · ·

When you graph a relation, the input is given by the horizontal axis and the output is given by the vertical axis.

VERTICAL LINE TEST FOR FUNCTIONS

A relation is a function of the horizontal-axis variable if and only if no vertical line passes through two or more points on the graph.

function

function

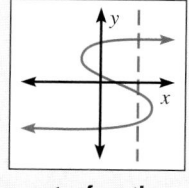

not a function

not a function

STUDENT HELP

▶ **Look Back**
For help with domain and range, see p. 47.

When a function is defined by an equation, it is convenient to give the function a name. In making a table of values for the equation $y = 3x + 2$, you apply the rule *multiply by three and add two* to transform an input x into the output y. By giving the rule *multiply by three and add two* the name f, you have a shorthand notation for applying this rule to different numbers and variables. The fact that this rule transforms the input 1 into the output 5 can now be written $f(1) = 5$.

In general, the symbol $f(x)$ replaces y and is read as "the value of f at x" or simply as "f of x." It does not mean f times x. $f(x)$ is called **function notation**.

EXAMPLE 2 *Evaluating a Function*

STUDENT HELP

▸ **Study Tip**
You don't have to use f to name a function. You can use other letters, such as g and h.

Evaluate the function for the given value of the variable.

    a. $f(x) = 2x - 3$ when $x = -2$ **b.** $g(x) = -5x$ when $x = 0$

SOLUTION

    a. $f(x) = 2x - 3$ **Write original function.**

        $f(-2) = 2(-2) - 3$ **Substitute −2 for x.**

             $= -7$ **Simplify.**

    b. $g(x) = -5x$ **Write original function.**

        $g(0) = -5(0)$ **Substitute 0 for x.**

           $= 0$ **Simplify.**

Since function notation allows you to write $f(x)$ in place of y, the **graph of a function** f is the set of all points $(x, f(x))$, where x is in the domain of the function. To graph a linear function, you may want to rewrite the function using x-y notation.

EXAMPLE 3 *Graphing a Linear Function*

Graph $f(x) = -\frac{1}{2}x + 3$.

SOLUTION

Rewrite the function as $y = -\frac{1}{2}x + 3$.

The y-intercept is 3, so plot $(0, 3)$.

The slope is $-\frac{1}{2}$.

Draw a slope triangle to locate a second point on the line.

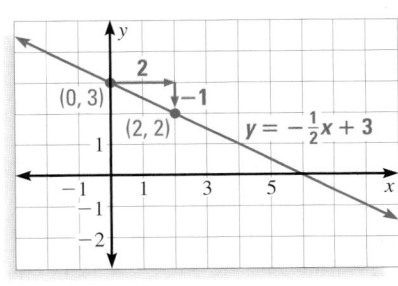

EXAMPLE 4 *Writing and Using a Linear Function*

BUTTERFLIES Use the diagram about monarch butterfly migration.

a. Write a linear function that models the distance traveled by a migrating butterfly.

b. Use the model to estimate the distance traveled after 30 days of migration.

c. Graph your model and label the point that represents the distance traveled after 30 days.

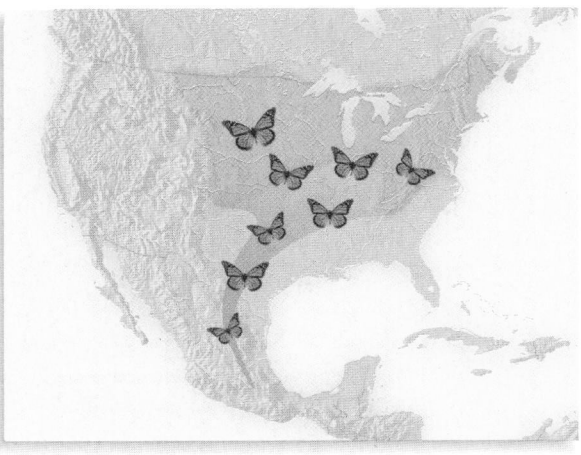

Monarch butterflies migrate from the northern United States to Mexico.

SOLUTION

a. You can see in the photo caption below that the butterflies travel about 2000 miles in 40 days. Their average speed is 50 miles per day. To create a linear model, we approximate the actual speed with this constant.

PROBLEM SOLVING STRATEGY

| **VERBAL MODEL** | **Distance traveled** = | **Average speed** | • **Time** |

LABELS
Time = t (days)

Average speed = **50**   (miles per day)

Distance traveled = $f(t)$ (miles)

ALGEBRAIC MODEL $f(t) = 50\,t$

b. To estimate the distance traveled after 30 days, substitute 30 for t.

$f(t) = 50t$ **Write linear function.**

$f(30) = 50 \cdot 30$ **Substitute 30 for *t*.**

$\qquad = 1500$ **Simplify.**

The distance traveled after 30 days is 1500 miles.

UNIT ANALYSIS You can use unit analysis to check that *miles* are the units of the solution.

$$\frac{\text{miles}}{\text{day}} \cdot \text{days} = \text{miles}$$

c. From the graph, you can see that distance traveled is a function of time.

Butterfly Migration

(30, 1500)

MONARCH BUTTERFLY
Thousands of monarch butterflies migrate in one large flock. The 2000-mile trip takes about 40 days.

GUIDED PRACTICE

Vocabulary Check ✓
Concept Check ✓
Skill Check ✓

1. Is every function a relation? Is every relation a function? Explain.

2. Describe a line that cannot be the graph of a linear function.

Evaluate the function $f(x) = 3x - 10$ for the given value of x.

3. $x = 0$ 　　　　**4.** $x = 20$ 　　　　**5.** $x = -2$ 　　　　**6.** $x = \dfrac{2}{3}$

In Exercises 7–9, decide whether the relation is a function. If it is a function, give the domain and the range.

7. Input　Output

8. Input　Output

9.
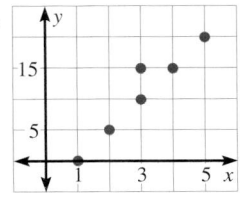

10. 🌎 **CAR TRAVEL** Your average speed during a trip is 40 miles per hour. Write a linear function that models the distance you travel $d(t)$ as a function of t, the time spent traveling.

PRACTICE AND APPLICATIONS

STUDENT HELP

▶ **Extra Practice**
to help you master
skills is on p. 800.

GRAPHICAL REASONING Decide whether the graph represents y as a function of x. Explain your reasoning.

11.

12.

13.
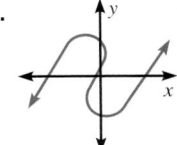

RELATIONS AND FUNCTIONS In Exercises 14–19, decide whether the relation is a function. If it is a function, give the domain and the range.

14. Input　Output

15. Input　Output

16. Input　Output
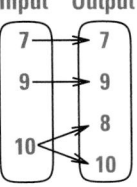

STUDENT HELP

▶ HOMEWORK HELP
Example 1: Exs. 11–19
Example 2: Exs. 20–28
Example 3: Exs. 29–40
Example 4: Exs. 50–52

17.

Input	Output
0	2
1	4
2	6
3	8

18.

Input	Output
0	1
2	2
4	3
2	4

19.

Input	Output
1	1
3	2
5	3
7	1

EVALUATING FUNCTIONS Evaluate the function when $x = 2$, $x = 0$, and $x = -3$.

20. $f(x) = 10x + 1$ **21.** $g(x) = 8x - 2$ **22.** $h(x) = 3x + 6$

23. $g(x) = 1.25x$ **24.** $h(x) = 0.75x + 8$ **25.** $f(x) = 0.33x - 2$

26. $h(x) = \frac{3}{4}x - 4$ **27.** $g(x) = \frac{2}{5}x + 7$ **28.** $f(x) = \frac{2}{7}x + 4$

GRAPHICAL REASONING Match the function with its graph.

  A. $f(x) = 3x - 2$ **B.** $f(x) = 2x + 2$ **C.** $f(x) = \frac{1}{2}x - 2$

29.   **30.**   **31.**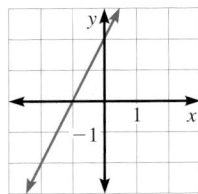

GRAPHING FUNCTIONS In Exercises 32–40, graph the function.

32. $f(x) = -2x + 5$ **33.** $g(x) = -x + 4$ **34.** $h(x) = 5x - 6$

35. $g(x) = 2x - 3$ **36.** $h(x) = -\frac{1}{3}x + 2$ **37.** $f(x) = -\frac{1}{2}x + 1$

38. $f(x) = 4x + 1$ **39.** $h(x) = 5$ **40.** $g(x) = -3x - 2$

41. *Writing* Describe how to find the slope of the graph of linear function f given that $f(1) = 2$ and $f(3) = -1$.

STUDENT HELP

HOMEWORK HELP
Visit our Web site
www.mcdougallittell.com
for help with Exs. 42–49.

FINDING SLOPE Find the slope of the graph of the linear function f.

42. $f(2) = -3, f(-2) = 5$ **43.** $f(0) = 4, f(4) = 0$

44. $f(-3) = -9, f(3) = 9$ **45.** $f(6) = -1, f(3) = 8$

46. $f(9) = -1, f(-1) = 2$ **47.** $f(-2) = -1, f(2) = 6$

48. $f(2) = 2, f(3) = 3$ **49.** $f(-1) = 2, f(3) = 2$

HIGH SCHOOL AND COLLEGE STUDENTS In Exercises 50–52, use the graph below. It shows the projected number of high school and college students in the United States for different years. Let x be the number of years since 1980.

50. Is the projected high school enrollment a function of the year? Is the projected college enrollment a function of the year? Explain.

51. Let $f(x)$ represent the projected number of high school students in year x. Estimate $f(2005)$.

52. Let $g(x)$ represent the projected number of college students in year x. Estimate $g(2005)$.

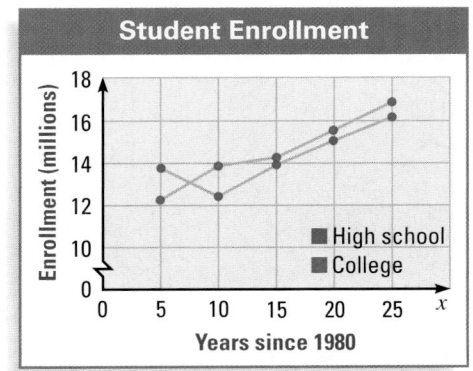

DATA UPDATE of National Center for Education Statistics data at www.mcdougallittell.com

53. 🌐 **ZYDECO MUSIC** The graph shows the number of people who attended the Southwest Louisiana Zydeco Music Festival for different years, where k is the number of years since 1980. Is the number of people who attended the festival a function of the year? Explain.

▶ Source: Louisiana Zydeco Music Festival

Music Festival

(graph: Attendance vs. Years since 1980)

54. 🌐 **MASTERS TOURNAMENT** The table shows information about the top 7 winners of the 1997 Masters Tournament in Augusta, Georgia. Graph the relation. Is the money earned a function of the score? Explain. ▶ Source: Golfweb

Score	270	282	283	284	285	285	286
Prize ($)	486,000	291,600	183,600	129,600	102,600	102,600	78,570

55. **SCIENCE** **CONNECTION** It takes 4.25 years for starlight to travel 25 trillion miles. Let t be the number of years and let $f(t)$ be trillions of miles traveled. Write a linear function $f(t)$ that expresses the distance traveled as a function of time.

Test Preparation

QUANTITATIVE COMPARISON In Exercises 56–58, choose the statement that is true about the given quantities.

Ⓐ The number in column A is greater.

Ⓑ The number in column B is greater.

Ⓒ The two numbers are equal.

Ⓓ The relationship cannot be determined from the given information.

	Column A	Column B
56.	$f(x) = -7x + 4$ when $x = -4$	$f(x) = -7x + 4$ when $x = -5$
57.	$f(x) = \frac{1}{2}x - 3$ when $x = 7$	$f(x) = \frac{1}{2}x - 5$ when $x = 11$
58.	$g(x) = 6x - \frac{1}{7}$ when $x = \frac{2}{7}$	$h(t) = 6t - \frac{1}{7}$ when $t = \frac{2}{7}$

★ **Challenge**

RESTRICTING DOMAINS In Exercises 59–62, use the equations $y = \frac{1}{x}$ and $y = \frac{1}{x + 3}$.

59. Use a graphing calculator or computer to graph both equations.

60. Explain why each equation is not a function for all real values of x.

61. How can you restrict the domain of each equation so that it is a function?

62. Describe what happens to the graph of $y = \frac{1}{x}$ near the value(s) of x for which the graph is not a function.

MIXED REVIEW

MATRICES Find the sum or the difference of the matrices. (Review 2.4)

63. $\begin{bmatrix} 4 & -8 \\ 7 & 0 \end{bmatrix} - \begin{bmatrix} -5 & 3 \\ -5 & -7 \end{bmatrix}$

64. $\begin{bmatrix} -6.5 & -4.2 \\ 0 & 3.7 \end{bmatrix} + \begin{bmatrix} 2.4 & -5.1 \\ 4.3 & -3 \end{bmatrix}$

65. $\begin{bmatrix} 6.2 & -12 \\ -2.5 & -4.4 \\ 3.4 & -5.8 \end{bmatrix} - \begin{bmatrix} -3.6 & 5.9 \\ 9.8 & -4.3 \\ -9 & 7.4 \end{bmatrix}$

66. $\begin{bmatrix} 9 & 1 & 6 \\ -4 & -7 & 1 \\ -5 & 0 & -1 \end{bmatrix} + \begin{bmatrix} -6 & 3 & -5 \\ -2 & 4 & -4 \\ 0 & 5 & 1 \end{bmatrix}$

SOLVING EQUATIONS Solve the equation if possible. (Review 3.4)

67. $4x + 8 = 24$

68. $3n = 5n - 12$

69. $9 - 5z = -8z$

70. $-5y + 6 = 4y + 3$

71. $3b + 8 = 9b - 7$

72. $-7q - 13 = 4 - 7q$

GRAPHING LINES In Exercises 73–78, write the equation in slope-intercept form. Then graph the equation. (Review 4.6 for 5.1)

73. $2x - y + 3 = 0$

74. $x + 2y - 6 = 0$

75. $y - 2x = -7$

76. $5x - y = 4$

77. $x - 2y + 4 = 2$

78. $4y + 12 = 0$

79. 🌐 **CHARITY WALK** You start 5 kilometers from the finish line and walk $1\frac{1}{2}$ kilometers per hour for 2 hours, where d is your distance from the finish line. Graph the situation. (Review 4.6 for 5.1)

QUIZ 3

Self-Test for Lessons 4.7 and 4.8

Solve the equation graphically. Check your solution algebraically. (Lesson 4.7)

1. $4x + 3 = -5$

2. $6x - 12 = -9$

3. $8x - 7 = x$

4. $-5x - 4 = 3x$

5. $\frac{1}{3}x + 5 = -\frac{2}{3}x - 8$

6. $\frac{3}{4}x + 2 = -\frac{3}{4}x - 6$

Evaluate the function when $x = 3$, $x = 0$, and $x = -4$. (Lesson 4.8)

7. $h(x) = 5x - 9$

8. $g(x) = -4x + 3$

9. $f(x) = 1.75x - 2$

10. $h(x) = -1.4x$

11. $f(x) = \frac{1}{4}x + 9$

12. $g(x) = \frac{4}{7}x + \frac{2}{7}$

In Exercises 13–18, graph the function. (Lesson 4.8)

13. $f(x) = -5x$

14. $h(x) = 4x - 7$

15. $f(x) = 3x - 2$

16. $h(x) = \frac{2}{5}x - 1$

17. $f(x) = \frac{1}{4}x + \frac{1}{2}$

18. $g(x) = -6x + 5$

19. 🌐 **LUNCH BOX BUSINESS** You have a small business making and delivering box lunches. You calculate your average weekly cost y of producing x lunches using the function $y = 2.1x + 75$. Last week your cost was $600. How many lunches did you make last week? Solve algebraically and graphically. (Lesson 4.7)

Chapter Summary

WHAT did you learn?

Plot points and draw scatter plots. (4.1)

Graph a linear equation in two variables
  • using a table of values. (4.2)
  • using intercepts. (4.3)

  • using slope-intercept form. (4.6)

Find the slope of a line passing through two points. (4.4)

Interpret slope as a rate of change. (4.4)

Write and graph direct variation equations. (4.5)

Use a graph to check or approximate the solution of a linear equation. (4.7)

Identify, evaluate, and graph functions. (4.8)

WHY did you learn it?

See relationships between two real-life quantities and make predictions. (p. 205)

Model earnings from a business. (p. 216)
Make a quick graph to help plan a fundraiser. (p. 220)
Make a quick graph of a river's heights. (p. 243)
Represent the steepness of a road. (p. 231)

Describe the rate of change of a parachutist's height above the ground. (p. 229)

Model the relationship between lengths of stringed instruments. (p. 238)

Model production costs for a business. (p. 254)

Model projected school enrollments. (p. 260)

How does Chapter 4 fit into the BIGGER PICTURE of algebra?

In this chapter you saw that relationships between variables may be expressed in algebraic form as an equation or in geometric form as a graph. Recognizing and using the connection between equations and graphs is one of the most important skills you can acquire to help you solve real-life problems.

STUDY STRATEGY

How did you use your list of questions?

The list of questions and answers you made, using the **Study Strategy** on page 202, may resemble this one.

Getting Questions Answered

1. In Lesson 4.1, Exercises 19–26, how can I find the quadrant without plotting the points?

Answer: Mary told me that I just need to look at each coordinate to see the direction I move.

For example, with (4, −5), I go right and then down, so the point is in Quadrant IV.

Chapter Review

- coordinate plane, p. 203
- ordered pair, p. 203
- *x*-coordinate, p. 203
- *y*-coordinate, p. 203
- *x*-axis, p. 203
- *y*-axis, p. 203

- origin, p. 203
- quadrants, p. 203
- graph of an ordered pair, p. 203
- scatter plot, p. 204
- solution of an equation, p. 210

- graph of an equation, p. 210
- *x*-intercept, p. 218
- *y*-intercept, 218
- slope, p. 226
- rate of change, p. 229
- constant of variation, p. 234

- direct variation, p. 234
- slope-intercept form, p. 241
- parallel lines, p. 242
- relation, p. 256
- function notation, p. 257
- graph of a function, p. 257

4.1   COORDINATES AND SCATTER PLOTS

Examples on pp. 203–205

EXAMPLES

To plot the point $(4, -2)$, start at the origin. Move 4 units to the right and 2 units down.

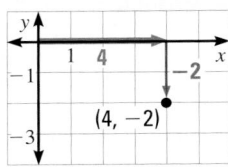

To plot the point $(-3, 1)$, start at the origin. Move 3 units to the left and 1 unit up.

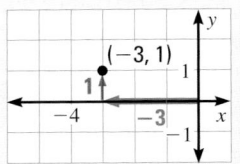

1. Make a scatter plot of the data in the table at the right.

Time (h)	1	1.5	3	4.5
Distance (mi)	20	24	32.5	41

Plot and label the ordered pair in a coordinate plane.

2. $A(4, 6)$ **3.** $B(0, -3)$ **4.** $C(-3.5, 5)$ **5.** $D(4, 0)$

4.2   GRAPHING LINEAR EQUATIONS

Examples on pp. 210–213

EXAMPLE To graph $3y = x - 6$, solve the equation for *y*, make a table of values, and plot the points.

x	-1	0	1
y	$-2\frac{1}{3}$	-2	$-1\frac{2}{3}$

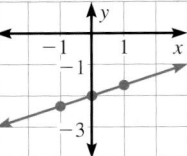

$3y = x - 6$ **Write original equation.**

$y = \dfrac{x - 6}{3}$ **Divide each side by 3.**

Graph the equation.

6. $y = 2x + 2$ **7.** $y = 7 - \frac{1}{2}x$ **8.** $y = -4(x + 1)$ **9.** $x - 10 = 2y$

4.3 QUICK GRAPHS USING INTERCEPTS

> **EXAMPLE** To graph $y + 2x = 10$, first find the intercepts.
>
> $y + 2x = 10$ $\qquad$ $y + 2x = 10$
>
> $0 + 2x = 10$ $\qquad$ $y + 2(0) = 10$
>
> $\qquad x = 5$ $\qquad\qquad$ $y = 10$
>
> Plot $(5, 0)$ and $(0, 10)$. Then draw a line through the points.

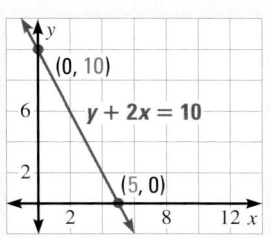

Graph the equation. Label the intercepts.

10. $-x + 4y = 8$ $\qquad$ **11.** $3x + 5y = 15$ $\qquad$ **12.** $4x - 5y = -20$ $\qquad$ **13.** $2x + 3y = 12$

4.4 THE SLOPE OF A LINE

> **EXAMPLE** To find the slope of the line passing through the points $(-2, 5)$ and $(4, -7)$, let $(x_1, y_1) = (-2, 5)$ and $(x_2, y_2) = (4, -7)$.
>
> $m = \dfrac{y_2 - y_1}{x_2 - x_1}$ $\qquad$ Write formula for slope.
>
> $m = \dfrac{-7 - 5}{4 - (-2)}$ $\qquad$ Substitute values.
>
> $m = \dfrac{-12}{6}$ $\qquad$ Simplify.
>
> $m = -2$ $\qquad$ Slope is negative.

Plot the points and find the slope of the line passing through the points.

14. $(2, 1), (3, 4)$ $\qquad$ **15.** $(0, 8), (-1, 2)$ $\qquad$ **16.** $(2, 4), (5, 0)$ $\qquad$ **17.** $(0, 5), (-4, 5)$

4.5 DIRECT VARIATION

> **EXAMPLE** If x and y vary directly, the equation that relates x and y is of the form $y = kx$. If $x = 3$ when $y = 18$, then you can write an equation that relates x and y.
>
> $y = kx$ $\qquad$ Write model for direct variation.
>
> $18 = k(3)$ $\qquad$ Substitute 3 for x and 18 for y.
>
> $6 = k$ $\qquad$ Divide each side by 3.
>
> An equation that relates x and y is $y = 6x$.

The variables x and y vary directly. Use the given values of the variables to write an equation that relates x and y.

18. $x = 7, y = 35$ $\qquad$ **19.** $x = 12, y = -4$ $\qquad$ **20.** $x = 4, y = -16$ $\qquad$ **21.** $x = 3, y = 10.5$

4.6 QUICK GRAPHS USING SLOPE-INTERCEPT FORM

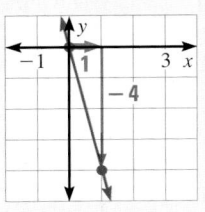

EXAMPLE Use the following steps to graph $4x + y = 0$.

STEP ① Write the equation in $y = mx + b$ form: $y = -4x$.

STEP ② Find the slope and the y-intercept: $m = -4$, $b = 0$.

STEP ③ Plot the point $(0, 0)$. Draw a slope triangle to locate a second point on the line. Draw a line through the two points.

Graph the equation.

22. $y = -x - 2$ **23.** $x - 4y = 12$ **24.** $-x + 6y = -24$

4.7 SOLVING LINEAR EQUATIONS USING GRAPHS

EXAMPLE You can solve the equation $2x - 4 = 2$ graphically.

$2x - 4 = 2$	**Write original equation.**
$2x - 6 = 0$	**Write in form $ax + b = 0$.**
$y = 2x - 6$	**Write related function $y = ax + b$.**

Graph $y = 2x - 6$. The x-intercept is 3, so the solution is $x = 3$.

✓ CHECK

$2x - 4 = 2$	**Write original equation.**
$2(3) - 4 \stackrel{?}{=} 2$	**Substitute 3 for x.**
$2 = 2$	**True statement.**

Solve the equation graphically. Check your solution algebraically.

25. $3x - 6 = 0$ **26.** $-5x - 3 = 0$ **27.** $3x + 8 = 4x$ **28.** $-4x - 1 = 7$

4.8 FUNCTIONS AND RELATIONS

EXAMPLE To evaluate the function $f(x) = -\frac{1}{5}x + 1$ when $x = 15$, substitute the given value for x.

$f(x) = -\frac{1}{5}x + 1$	**Write original function.**
$f(15) = -\frac{1}{5}(15) + 1$	**Substitute 15 for x.**
$f(15) = -2$	**Simplify.**

Evaluate the function for the given value of x. Then graph the function.

29. $f(x) = x - 7$ when $x = -2$ **30.** $f(x) = -x + 4$ when $x = 4$

31. $f(x) = 2x + 6$ when $x = -3$ **32.** $f(x) = 1.5x - 4.2$ when $x = -9$

Chapter Test

Plot and label the points in a coordinate plane.

1. $A(2, 6)$, $B(-4, -1)$, $C(-1, 4)$, $D(3, -5)$

2. $A(-5, 1)$, $B(0, 3)$, $C(-1, -5)$, $D(4, 6)$

3. $A(7, 3)$, $B(-2, -2)$, $C(0, 4)$, $D(6, -2)$

4. $A(0, -1)$, $B(-5, -6)$, $C(7, -2)$, $D(2, 4)$

Graph the line that has the given intercepts.

5. x-intercept: 3
y-intercept: -1

6. x-intercept: -5
y-intercept: 4

7. x-intercept: 6
y-intercept: 6

8. x-intercept: $-\frac{1}{2}$
y-intercept: -3

Use a table of values to graph the equation.

9. $y = -x + 3$

10. $y = 4$

11. $y = -(5 - x)$

12. $x = 6$

Graph the equation. Tell which method you used.

13. $2x + y - 11 = 0$

14. $3x - 2y - 2 = 0$

15. $-7x - y + 49 = 0$

16. $\frac{2}{3}x + y - 32 = 0$

Plot the points and find the slope of the line passing through the points.

17. $(0, 1)$, $(-2, -6)$

18. $(-4, -1)$, $(5, -7)$

19. $(-3, 5)$, $(2, -2)$

20. $(-3, -1)$, $(2, -1)$

The variables x and y vary directly. Use the given values of the variables to write an equation that relates x and y.

21. $x = -2$, $y = -2$

22. $x = 2$, $y = 10$

23. $x = -3$, $y = 7$

24. $x = \frac{1}{2}$, $y = 6$

25. $x = 1.3$, $y = 3.9$

26. $x = 16$, $y = 3.2$

In Exercises 27 and 28, decide whether the graphs of the two equations are parallel lines. Explain your answer.

27. $y = 4x + 3$, $y = -4x - 5$

28. $10y + 20 = 6x$, $5y = 3x + 35$

29. Solve $x - 2 = -3x$ graphically. Check your solution algebraically.

In Exercises 30–32, evaluate the function when $x = 3$, $x = 0$, and $x = -4$.

30. $f(x) = 6x$

31. $f(x) = -(x - 2)$

32. $g(x) = 3.2x + 2.8$

33. 🌎 **FLOOD WATERS** A river has risen 6 feet above flood stage. Beginning at time $t = 0$, the water level drops at a rate of two inches per hour. The number of feet above flood stage y after t hours is given by $y = 6 - \frac{1}{6}t$.
Graph the equation over the 12-hour period from $t = 0$ to $t = 12$.

34. 🌎 **SHOE SIZES** The table below shows how foot length relates to women's shoe sizes. Is shoe size a function of foot length? Why or why not?

Foot length (in inches), x	$9\frac{1}{4}$	$9\frac{1}{2}$	$9\frac{5}{8}$	$9\frac{3}{4}$	$9\frac{15}{16}$	$10\frac{1}{4}$	$10\frac{1}{2}$
Shoe size, y	$6\frac{1}{2}$	7	7	8	8	$9\frac{1}{2}$	$9\frac{1}{2}$

▶ **TEST-TAKING STRATEGY** Read all of the answer choices before deciding which is the correct one.

1. MULTIPLE CHOICE What is the equation of the line shown?

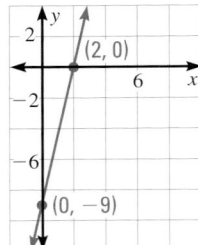

   (A) $9x - 2y = -18$

   (B) $-9x - 2y = 18$

   (C) $9x + 2y = 18$

   (D) $9x + 2y = -18$

   (E) $-9x + 2y = -18$

2. MULTIPLE CHOICE What is the y-intercept of the line $-4x - \frac{1}{2}y = 10$?

   (A) -20 **(B)** -4

   (C) $-\frac{5}{2}$ **(D)** 5

   (E) 20

3. MULTIPLE CHOICE Write the equation $3x - 4y = 20$ in slope-intercept form.

   (A) $y = -\frac{3}{4}x - 5$

   (B) $y = -\frac{3}{4}x + 5$

   (C) $y = \frac{3}{4}x - 5$

   (D) $y = \frac{3}{4}x + 5$

   (E) $y = 20 - 3x$

4. MULTIPLE CHOICE Find the slope of the line passing through the points $(1, 2)$ and $(2, 1)$.

   (A) 1 **(B)** 3

   (C) 2 **(D)** -1

   (E) -2

5. MULTIPLE CHOICE What is the slope of the line shown?

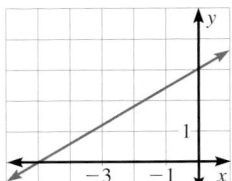

   (A) -5 **(B)** $-\frac{3}{5}$

   (C) $\frac{3}{5}$ **(D)** $\frac{5}{3}$

   (E) 3

6. MULTIPLE CHOICE What is the slope of the graph of the equation $5x - y = -2$?

   (A) -5 **(B)** 5

   (C) 1 **(D)** -2

   (E) 2

7. MULTIPLE CHOICE Which point does *not* lie on the graph of $x = -12$?

   (A) $(-12, 0)$

   (B) $(-12, -12)$

   (C) $(-12, 1)$

   (D) $(-1, -12)$

   (E) $(-12, 12)$

8. MULTIPLE CHOICE What is the x-intercept of $-13x - y = -65$?

   (A) -65 **(B)** -5

   (C) 0 **(D)** 5

   (E) 65

9. MULTIPLE CHOICE Find the value of $f(x) = -x^2 - 6x - 7$ when $x = -2$.

   (A) -23 **(B)** -15

   (C) 1 **(D)** 7

   (E) 9

QUANTITATIVE COMPARISON **In Exercises 10–12, choose the statement below that is true about the given numbers.**

(A) The number in column A is greater.

(B) The number in column B is greater.

(C) The two numbers are equal.

(D) The relationship cannot be determined from the given information.

	Column A	Column B
10.	The slope of the line through $(4, -3)$ and $(-12, -3)$	0
11.	The slope of the line through $(4.5, 6)$ and $(-7, 4)$	The slope of the line through $(-6, 4.5)$ and $(4, -7)$
12.	The slope of the line through $(3.5, y)$ and $(6.8, 4)$	The slope of the line through $(3.5, q)$ and $(6.8, 4)$

13. **MULTI-STEP PROBLEM** An Internet provider offers three different levels of monthly service.

   Standard: $10 for the first 10 hours and $1 for each additional hour.

   Upgrade: $15 for the first 20 hours and $1 for each additional hour.

   Unlimited: $20 per month with no hourly charge.

   a. Tell whether each graph represents Standard, Upgrade, or Unlimited service. Explain your reasoning.

I.

II.

III.

   b. Write an equation for the total cost T per month for Upgrade service as a function of the number of additional hours used b.

   c. If you use the Internet 13 hours per month, which service will cost the least? Explain.

   d. If you use the Internet 24 hours per month, which service will cost the least? Explain.

   e. The equation $C = 10 + a$ gives the total cost C per month for Standard service as a function of the number of additional hours used a. Explain how this model is different from the one you labeled Standard in part (a).

WRITING LINEAR EQUATIONS

▶ *How can you figure out how old an artifact is?*

APPLICATION: Archaeology

Archaeologists use radiocarbon dating to estimate the age of an artifact. To do this, they use an instrument to measure the amount of carbon-14 remaining in a sample.

Think & Discuss

In Exercises 1–3, use the graph below.

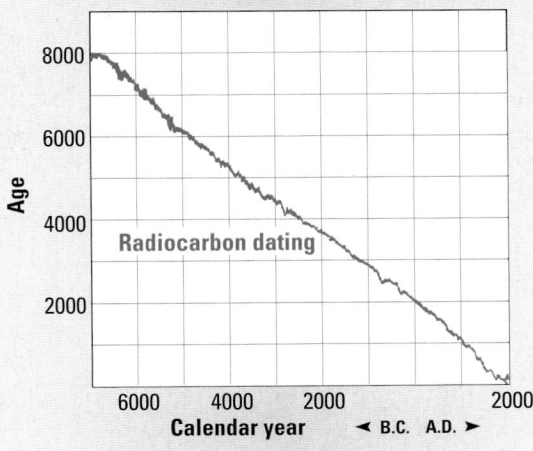

Radiocarbon dating

Age — Calendar year ◄ B.C. A.D. ►

1. What calendar year corresponds to an artifact that has a radiocarbon age of 7000?

2. What is the radiocarbon age of an object from 4000 B.C.?

3. For which calendar years does radiocarbon dating produce the most accurate results?

Learn More About It

You will learn more about archaeological dating in the Math & History on p. 306.

APPLICATION LINK Visit www.mcdougallittell.com for more information about archaeology.

Study Guide

PREVIEW

What's the chapter about?

Chapter 5 is about writing **different forms of linear equations**. You'll learn

- three forms of linear equations.
- to write a linear equation given a slope and a point, or given two points.
- to write an equation of a line perpendicular to another line.
- to fit a line to data and use linear interpolation or linear extrapolation.

KEY VOCABULARY

▶ **Review**
- scatter plot, p. 204
- *x*-intercept, p. 218
- *y*-intercept, p. 218
- slope, p. 226

▶ **New**
- slope-intercept form, p. 273
- best-fitting line, p. 292
- correlation, p. 295
- point-slope form, p. 300
- standard form, p. 308
- linear interpolation, p. 318
- linear extrapolation, p. 318

PREPARE

Are you ready for the chapter?

SKILL REVIEW Do these exercises to review key skills that you'll apply in this chapter. See the given **reference page** if there is something you don't understand.

Solve the equation. (Review Example 3, p. 155)

1. $4(x + 8) = 20x$ **2.** $2x + 2 = 3x - 8$ **3.** $9a = 4a - 24 + a$

Plot the ordered pairs in a coordinate plane. (Review Example 1, p. 203)

4. $A(5, -7), B(-6, -8), C(-9, 0)$ **5.** $A(8, -5), B(7, 3), C(-2, 0)$

Find the *x*-intercept and the *y*-intercept in the equation. Graph the line.
(Review Example 2, p. 219)

6. $4x + 9y = 18$ **7.** $-x - 5y = 15 + 2x$ **8.** $-6x - 2y = 8$

STUDY
STRATEGY

Here's a study strategy!

Practice Test

Writing and taking a practice test are good ways to determine how ready you are for an actual test. Review the chapter. Create a test and exchange it with a classmate. After taking the tests, correct and discuss them. You should study any topics that gave you difficulty.

5.1

Writing Linear Equations in Slope-Intercept Form

What you should learn

GOAL 1 Use the slope-intercept form to write an equation of a line.

GOAL 2 Model a **real-life** situation with a linear function, such as the population of California in **Example 3**.

Why you should learn it

▼ To model **real-life** situations, such as finding the cost of renting a bicycle in **Exs. 9–11**.

GOAL 1 USING SLOPE-INTERCEPT FORM

In this lesson you will learn to write an equation of a line using its slope and y-intercept. To do this, you need to use the **slope-intercept form** of the equation of a line.

$$y = mx + b \longleftarrow \text{Slope-intercept form}$$

In the equation, m is the slope and b is the y-intercept. Recall that the y-intercept is the y-coordinate of the point where the line crosses the y-axis.

EXAMPLE 1 *Writing an Equation of a Line*

Write an equation of the line whose slope m is -2 and whose y-intercept b is 5.

SOLUTION

You are given the slope $m = -2$ and the y-intercept $b = 5$.

$y = mx + b$	Write slope-intercept form.
$y = -2x + 5$	Substitute -2 for m and 5 for b.

EXAMPLE 2 *Writing an Equation of a Line from a Graph*

Write an equation of the line shown in the graph.

SOLUTION

The line intersects the y-axis at $(0, -4)$, so the y-intercept b is -4. The line also passes through the point $(2, 0)$. Find the slope of the line:

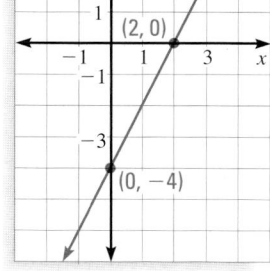

$$m = \frac{\text{rise}}{\text{run}} = \frac{-4 - 0}{0 - 2} = \frac{-4}{-2} = 2$$

Knowing the slope and y-intercept, you can write an equation of the line.

STUDENT HELP

→ **Study Tip**
In Example 2, you can also find the slope of the line by reading the graph.
$$\frac{\text{rise}}{\text{run}} = \frac{4}{2} = 2$$

$y = mx + b$	Write slope-intercept form.
$y = 2x + (-4)$	Substitute 2 for m and -4 for b.
$y = 2x - 4$	Simplify.

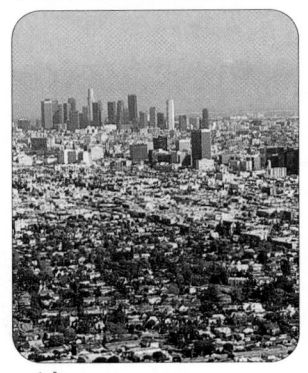

POPULATION DATA In 1990, California had a population of about 29.76 million. During the next 15 years, the state's population was expected to increase by an average of about 0.31 million people per year.

▶ Source: U.S. Bureau of the Census

GOAL 2 MODELING A REAL-LIFE SITUATION

In Lesson 4.8 you saw examples of linear functions.

$f(x) = mx + b$ ◀——— **Linear function**

A *linear model* is a linear function that is used to model a real-life situation. In a linear model, *m* is the rate of change and *b* is the initial amount. In such models, sometimes line graphs can be used to approximate change that occurs in discrete steps.

EXAMPLE 3 *A Linear Model for Population*

POPULATION CHANGE Linear functions can approximate population change.

a. Write a linear equation to approximate the expected population of California in any year between 1990 and 2005. Use the information below the photo.

b. Use the equation to predict the population of California in 2005.

SOLUTION

a. **VERBAL MODEL**

$$\boxed{\text{California Population}} = \boxed{\text{1990 Population}} + \boxed{\text{Increase per year}} \cdot \boxed{\text{Years since 1990}}$$

LABELS California Population = **P**   (million people)

1990 Population = **29.76**   (million people)

Increase per year = **0.31**   (million people per year)

Years since 1990 = **t**   (years)

ALGEBRAIC MODEL $P = 29.76 + 0.31 \cdot t$ **Linear model**

UNIT ANALYSIS Check that *people* are the units in the algebraic model:

$$people = \text{people} + \frac{\text{people}}{\text{year}} \cdot \text{year}$$

b. When $t = 15$, the year will be 2005. Substitute in your equation.

$P = 29.76 + 0.31(15)$

$= 29.76 + 4.65$

$= 34.41$

▶ In 2005 the population will be about 34.4 million people. The graph represents this prediction.

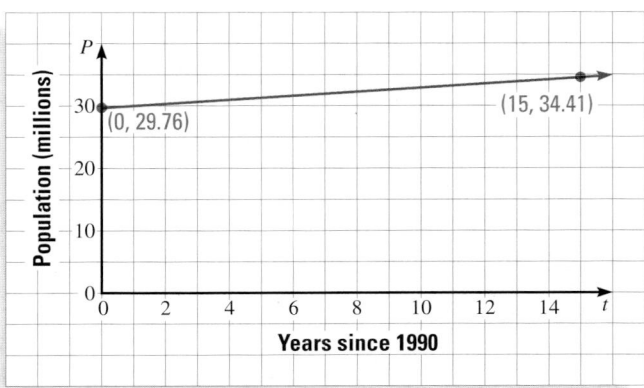

STUDENT HELP

↳ **Look Back**
For help with graphing linear equations, see p. 219.

EXAMPLE 4 **A Linear Model for Telephone Charges**

Telephone Charges

You can approximate collect telephone call charges using a linear function.

a. Write a linear equation to approximate the cost of collect telephone calls. Use the information shown on the telephone bill to create your model.

b. How much would a 9-minute collect telephone call cost?

Date	Time	Area Number	1st Min.	Rate	Add'l Min	Amount
Jan 7	857PM	360 555-1829	$3.44	$0.24	4	$4.40
Jan 16	558PM	360 555-1829	$3.44	$0.24	1	$3.68
Jan 17	837PM	360 555-1829	$3.44	$0.24	17	$7.52
Jan 22	601PM	360 555-1829	$3.44	$0.24	9	$5.60
Feb 3	859PM	360 555-1829	$3.44	$0.24	10	$5.84

SOLUTION

PROBLEM SOLVING STRATEGY

a. **VERBAL MODEL**

$$\boxed{\text{Total cost}} = \boxed{\begin{array}{c}\text{Cost} \\ \text{for first} \\ \text{minute}\end{array}} + \boxed{\begin{array}{c}\text{Rate per} \\ \text{additional} \\ \text{minute}\end{array}} \cdot \boxed{\begin{array}{c}\text{Number of} \\ \text{additional} \\ \text{minutes}\end{array}}$$

LABELS

Total cost = C (dollars)

Cost for first minute = **3.44**   (dollars)

Rate per additional minute = **0.24**   (dollars per minute)

Number of additional minutes = t (minutes)

ALGEBRAIC MODEL

$C = 3.44 + 0.24 \cdot t$ **Linear model**

UNIT ANALYSIS Check that *dollars* are the units in the algebraic model:

$$dollars = \text{dollars} + \frac{\text{dollars}}{\text{min}} \cdot \text{min}$$

b. A 9-minute call would involve 8 additional minutes. Substitute in your equation.

$C = 3.44 + 0.24 \cdot t$

$\quad = 3.44 + 0.24(8)$

$\quad = 5.36$

▶ A 9-minute call would cost $5.36. The graph represents this prediction.

GUIDED PRACTICE

Vocabulary Check ✓ **1.** Is 5 the *x-intercept* or the *y-intercept* of the line $y = 3x + 5$? Explain.

Concept Check ✓ **2.** Describe the rate of change in the context of Example 3 on page 274.

Write an equation of the line in slope-intercept form.

Skill Check ✓ **3.** The slope is 1; the *y*-intercept is 0.   **4.** The slope is -7; the *y*-intercept is $-\frac{2}{3}$.

5. The slope is -1; the *y*-intercept is 3.   **6.** The slope is -2; the *y*-intercept is 0.

7. The slope is -3; the *y*-intercept is $\frac{1}{2}$.   **8.** The slope is 4; the *y*-intercept is -6.

🌐 **RENTING A BIKE** Suppose that bike rentals cost \$4 plus \$1.50 per hour.

9. Write an equation to model the total cost *y* of renting a bike for *x* hours.

10. Graph the equation. Label the *y*-intercept.

11. Use the equation to find the cost of renting a bike for 12 hours.

PRACTICE AND APPLICATIONS

STUDENT HELP

▶ **Extra Practice**
to help you master
skills is on p. 801.

WRITING EQUATIONS Write an equation of the line in slope-intercept form.

12. The slope is 3; the *y*-intercept is -2.   **13.** The slope is 1; the *y*-intercept is 2.

14. The slope is 0; the *y*-intercept is 4.   **15.** The slope is 2; the *y*-intercept is -1.

16. The slope is $\frac{3}{2}$; the *y*-intercept is 3.   **17.** The slope is $-\frac{1}{4}$; the *y*-intercept is 1.

18. The slope is -6; the *y*-intercept is $\frac{3}{4}$.   **19.** The slope is -3; the *y*-intercept is $-\frac{1}{2}$.

GRAPHICAL REASONING Write an equation of the line shown in the graph.

20.   **21.**   **22.**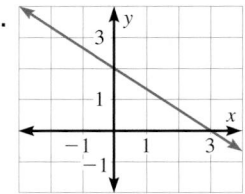

PARALLEL LINES Write an equation of each line in slope-intercept form.

23.   **24.**   **25.**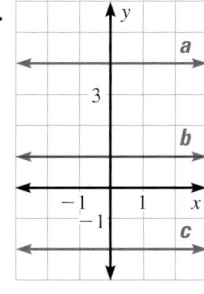

STUDENT HELP

▶ HOMEWORK HELP
Example 1: Exs. 12–19
Example 2: Exs. 20–25
Example 3: Exs. 26, 27
Example 4: Exs. 28, 29

SOUTH CAROLINA POPULATION In Exercises 26 and 27, use the following information. In 1990 the population of South Carolina was approximately 3,486,000. During the next five years, the population increased by approximately 37,400 people per year.

> **DATA UPDATE** of U.S. Bureau of the Census data at www.mcdougallittell.com

26. Write an equation to model the population P of South Carolina in terms of t, the number of years since 1990.

27. Estimate the population of South Carolina in 1996.

RENTING A MOVING VAN In Exercises 28 and 29, a rental company charges a flat fee of $30 and an additional $.25 per mile to rent a moving van.

28. Write an equation to model the total charge y (in dollars) in terms of x, the number of miles driven.

29. Copy and complete the table using the equation you found in Exercise 28.

Miles (x)	25	50	75	100
Cost (y)	?	?	?	?

UNIT ANALYSIS In Exercises 30–32, write a linear equation to model the situation. Use unit analysis to check your model.

30. You borrow $40 from your sister. To repay the loan, you pay her $5 a week.

31. Your uncle weighed 180 pounds. He has lost 2 pounds a month for 8 months.

32. You have walked 5 miles on a hiking trail. You continue to walk at the rate of 2 miles per hour for 6 hours.

33. **TRAVELING HOME** You are traveling home in a bus whose speed is 50 miles per hour. At noon you are 200 miles from home. Write an equation that models your distance y from home in terms of t, the number of hours since noon. Why does the line given by this equation have a negative slope?

STUDENT HELP

HOMEWORK HELP
Visit our Web site
www.mcdougallittell.com
for help with Exs. 34–37.

FUNDRAISING In Exercises 34–37, you are designing a calendar as a fund-raising project for your Biology Club. The cost of printing is $500, plus $2.50 per calendar.

34. Write an equation to model the total cost C of printing x calendars.

35. You sell each calendar for $5.00. Write an equation to model the total income T for selling x calendars.

36. Graph both equations in the same coordinate plane. Estimate the point at which the two lines intersect. Explain the significance of this point of intersection in the context of the real-life problem.

37. **ANALYZING DATA** You estimate the club can sell 200 calendars. Write an analysis of how effective this fundraising project will be for the club.

Calendar Sales

(Money (dollars): 500, 1000, 1500; Number of calendars: 0, 100, 200, 300, 400)

🌐 **FLORIDA POPULATION** **In Exercises 38 and 39, use the following information.**
The U.S. Bureau of the Census predicted that the population of Florida would be about 17.4 million in 2010 and then would increase by about 0.22 million per year until 2025.

38. **MULTIPLE CHOICE** Choose the linear model that predicts the population P of Florida (in millions) in terms of t, the number of years since 2010.

    Ⓐ $P = 17.4t + 0.22$ Ⓑ $P = -0.22t + 17.4$

    Ⓒ $P = 0.22t + 17.4$ Ⓓ $P = -17.4t + 0.22$

39. **MULTIPLE CHOICE** According to the correct model, the population of Florida in 2011 will be about <u>?</u> million.

    Ⓐ 17.18   Ⓑ 3.8   Ⓒ 17.62   Ⓓ 39.4

★ **Challenge**

40. 🌐 **CLASS SIZE** In January, your ceramics class begins with 12 students. In every month after January, three new students join and one student drops out.

    a. Write a linear equation to model the situation.

    b. Graph the model.

    c. Predict the size of your ceramics class in May and June.

EXTRA CHALLENGE
www.mcdougallittell.com

MIXED REVIEW

EVALUATING EXPRESSIONS **Evaluate the expression when $x = -3$ and $y = 6$.** (Review 2.7)

41. $\dfrac{3x}{x + y}$ **42.** $\dfrac{x}{x + 2}$ **43.** $\dfrac{y^2 + x}{x}$

🌐 **SCHOOL NEWSPAPER** **You are designing a newspaper page with three photos. The page is $13\frac{1}{4}$ inches wide with 1 inch margins on both sides. You need to allow $\frac{3}{4}$ inch between photographs. How wide should you make the photos if they are of equal size?** (Review 3.5)

44. Sketch a diagram of the newspaper page.

45. Write an equation to model the problem. Use the diagram to help.

46. Solve the equation and answer the question.

🌐 **WINDSURFING** **Match the description with the linear model $y = 10$ or the linear model $y = 10x$. Graph the model.** (Review 4.2)

47. You rent a sailboard for $10 per hour.

48. You rent a life jacket for a flat fee of $10.

GRAPHING LINEAR EQUATIONS **Find the slope and the y-intercept of the graph of the equation. Then graph the equation.** (Review 4.6 for 5.2)

49. $y + 2x = 2$ **50.** $3x - y = -5$ **51.** $2y - 3x = 6$

52. $4x + 2y = 6$ **53.** $4y + 12x = 16$ **54.** $25x - 5y = 30$

55. $x + 3y = 15$ **56.** $x + 6y = 12$ **57.** $x - y = 10$

5.2

Writing Linear Equations Given the Slope and a Point

What you should learn

GOAL 1 Use slope and any point on a line to write an equation of the line.

GOAL 2 Use a linear model to make predictions about a **real-life** situation, such as the number of vacation trips in **Example 3**.

Why you should learn it

▼ To model a **real-life** situation, such as finding the total cost of a taxi ride in **Ex. 48**.

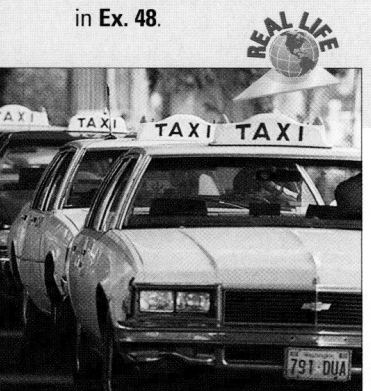

GOAL 1 USING SLOPE AND A POINT ON A LINE

In Lesson 5.1 you learned how to write an equation of a line when given the slope and the y-intercept of the line. You used the slope-intercept form of the equation of a line, $y = mx + b$.

In this lesson you will learn to write an equation of a line when given its slope and *any* point on the line.

EXAMPLE 1 *Writing an Equation of a Line*

Write an equation of the line that passes through the point $(6, -3)$ and has a slope of -2.

SOLUTION

Find the y-intercept. Because the line has a slope of $m = -2$ and passes through the point $(x, y) = (6, -3)$, you can substitute the values $m = -2$, $x = 6$, and $y = -3$ into the slope-intercept form and solve for b.

$y = mx + b$ Write slope-intercept form.

$-3 = (-2)(6) + b$ Substitute -2 for m, 6 for x, and -3 for y.

$-3 = -12 + b$ Simplify.

$9 = b$ Solve for b.

The y-intercept is $b = 9$.

Write an equation of the line. Because you now know both the slope and the y-intercept, you can use the slope-intercept form.

$y = mx + b$ Write slope-intercept form.

$y = -2x + 9$ Substitute -2 for m and 9 for b.

✓**CHECK** You can check your result by graphing $y = -2x + 9$.

Note that the line crosses the y-axis at the point $(0, 9)$ and passes through the given point $(6, -3)$.

You can count the number of units in the rise and the run to check that the slope is -2.

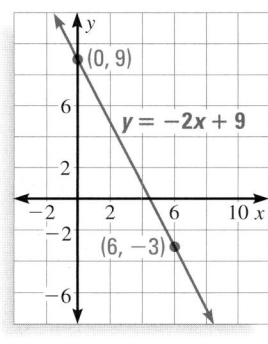

WRITING AN EQUATION OF A LINE GIVEN ITS SLOPE AND A POINT

STEP ❶ **First find the *y*-intercept.** Substitute the slope *m* and the coordinates of the given point (*x*, *y*) into the slope-intercept form, $y = mx + b$. Then solve for the *y*-intercept *b*.

STEP ❷ **Then write an equation of the line.** Substitute the slope *m* and the *y*-intercept *b* into the slope-intercept form, $y = mx + b$.

EXAMPLE 2 *Writing Equations of Parallel Lines*

STUDENT HELP

↳ **Look Back**
For help with parallel lines, see p. 242.

Two nonvertical lines are parallel if and only if they have the same slope. Write an equation of the line that is parallel to the line $y = \frac{2}{3}x - 2$ and passes through the point $(-2, 1)$.

SOLUTION

❶ The given line has a slope of $m = \frac{2}{3}$. Because parallel lines have the same slope, a parallel line through $(-2, 1)$ must also have a slope of $m = \frac{2}{3}$. Use this information to find the *y*-intercept.

$y = mx + b$ **Write slope-intercept form.**

$1 = \frac{2}{3}(-2) + b$ **Substitute $\frac{2}{3}$ for *m*, −2 for *x*, and 1 for *y*.**

$1 = -\frac{4}{3} + b$ **Simplify.**

$\frac{7}{3} = b$ **Solve for *b*.**

The *y*-intercept is $b = \frac{7}{3}$.

❷ Write an equation using the slope-intercept form.

$y = mx + b$ **Write slope-intercept form.**

$y = \frac{2}{3}x + \frac{7}{3}$ **Substitute $\frac{2}{3}$ for *m* and $\frac{7}{3}$ for *b*.**

✓ **CHECK** You can check your result graphically. The original line $y = \frac{2}{3}x - 2$ is parallel to $y = \frac{2}{3}x + \frac{7}{3}$.

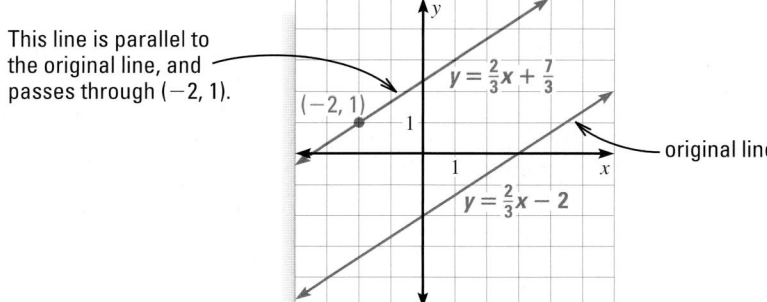

This line is parallel to the original line, and passes through (−2, 1).

$y = \frac{2}{3}x + \frac{7}{3}$

$(-2, 1)$

original line

$y = \frac{2}{3}x - 2$

STUDENT HELP

INTERNET **HOMEWORK HELP**
Visit our Web site
www.mcdougallittell.com
for extra examples.

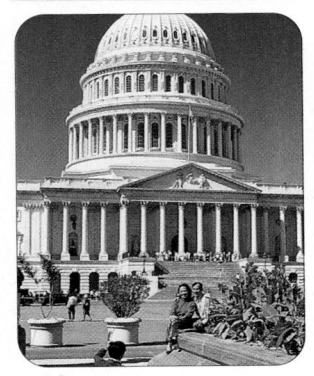
GOAL **2** WRITING AND USING REAL-LIFE MODELS

EXAMPLE 3 *Writing and Using a Linear Model*

VACATION TRIPS Between 1985 and 1995, the number of vacation trips in the United States taken by United States residents increased by about 26 million per year. In 1993, United States residents went on 740 million vacation trips within the United States. ⟿ **DATA UPDATE** of Travel Industry of America at www.mcdougallittell.com

> **a.** Write a linear equation that models the number of vacation trips y (in millions) in terms of the year t. Let t be the number of years since 1985.
>
> **b.** Estimate the number of vacation trips in the year 2005.

SOLUTION

a. The number of trips increased by about 26 million per year, so you know the slope is $m = 26$. You also know that $(t, y) = (8, 740)$ is a point on the line, because 740 million trips were taken in 1993, 8 years after 1985.

$y = mt + b$	Write slope-intercept form.
$740 = (26)(8) + b$	Substitute 26 for m, 8 for t, and 740 for y.
$740 = 208 + b$	Simplify.
$532 = b$	The y-intercept is $b = 532$.

Write an equation of the line using $m = 26$ and $b = 532$.

$y = mt + b$	Write slope-intercept form.
$y = 26t + 532$	Substitute 26 for m and 532 for b.

b. You can estimate the number of vacation trips in the year 2005 by substituting $t = 20$ into the linear model.

$y = 26t + 532$	Write linear model.
$= 26(20) + 532$	Substitute 20 for t.
$= 1052$	Simplify.

▶ You can estimate that United States residents will take about 1052 million vacation trips in the year 2005. A graph can help check this result. The line goes through $(20, 1052)$.

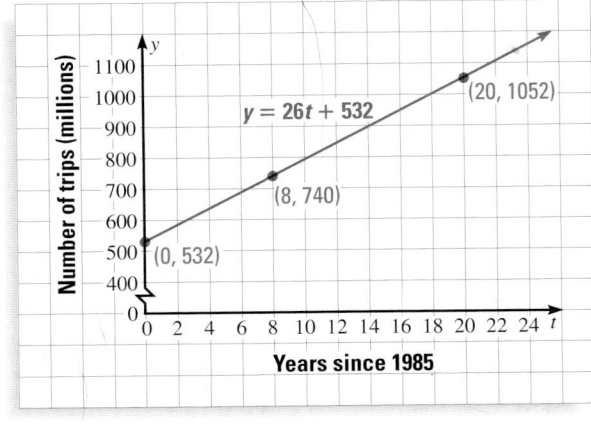

GUIDED PRACTICE

Vocabulary Check ✓

Concept Check ✓

Skill Check ✓

1. Two nonvertical lines that have the same slope must be _?_ .

2. Explain how to find the equation of a line given its slope and a point on the line.

Write an equation of the line that passes through the point and has the given slope. Write the equation in slope-intercept form.

3. $(3, 4)$, $m = \frac{1}{2}$ **4.** $(2, -4)$, $m = -5$ **5.** $(10, -10)$, $m = \frac{2}{3}$

6. $(-12, 2)$, $m = -2$ **7.** $(4, 8)$, $m = 5$ **8.** $(0, -5)$, $m = 0$

Write an equation of the line that is parallel to the given line and passes through the point.

9. $y = \frac{1}{2}x + 8$, $(-6, 4)$ **10.** $y = -3x - 3$, $(-4, -3)$

11. 🌐 **BANKING** Christina has her savings in a bank account. She withdraws $8.25 per week from her account. After 10 weeks, the balance is $534. Write an equation that models the balance y of Christina's account in terms of the number of weeks x. Do not consider any interest earned by the account.

PRACTICE AND APPLICATIONS

STUDENT HELP

▶ **Extra Practice**
to help you master
skills is on p. 801.

WRITING EQUATIONS Write an equation of the line that passes through the point and has the given slope. Write the equation in slope-intercept form.

12. $(1, 4)$, $m = 3$ **13.** $(2, -3)$, $m = 2$ **14.** $(-4, 2)$, $m = -1$

15. $(1, -3)$, $m = -4$ **16.** $(-3, -5)$, $m = -2$ **17.** $(1, 3)$, $m = 4$

18. $(2, 5)$, $m = \frac{1}{2}$ **19.** $(-3, 2)$, $m = \frac{1}{3}$ **20.** $(0, 2)$, $m = 3$

21. $(0, -2)$, $m = 4$ **22.** $(3, 4)$, $m = 0$ **23.** $(-2, 4)$, $m = 0$

GRAPHICAL REASONING Write an equation of the line shown in the graph.

24.

25.

26.

27.

28.

29.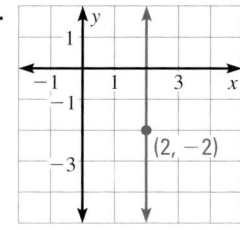

STUDENT HELP

▶ **HOMEWORK HELP**
Example 1: Exs. 12–29
Example 2: Exs. 32–41
Example 3: Exs. 42–45

USING *x*-INTERCEPTS **Write an equation of the line that has the given *x*-intercept and slope.**

30. *x*-intercept = 2, $m = -\dfrac{2}{3}$ **31.** *x*-intercept = 4, $m = 3$

PARALLEL LINES **Write an equation of the line that is parallel to the given line and passes through the given point.**

32. $y = 2x + 2$, $(3, 2)$ **33.** $y = x + 4$, $(-2, 0)$ **34.** $y = -2x + 3$, $(4, 4)$

35. $y = -3x + 1$, $(4, 2)$ **36.** $y = \dfrac{2}{3}x - 2$, $(2, 1)$ **37.** $y = -\dfrac{1}{3}x - 1$, $(4, 1)$

38. $y = -4x - 2$, $(5, 3)$ **39.** $y = 6x + 9$, $(5, -3)$ **40.** $y = -9x - 8$, $(7, -2)$

41. **GEOMETRY** **CONNECTION** $\overline{AB}$ is part of a line with a slope of $\dfrac{1}{2}$. To begin to draw a parallelogram, you want to draw a line parallel to $\overline{AB}$ through point C. Write an equation of the line.

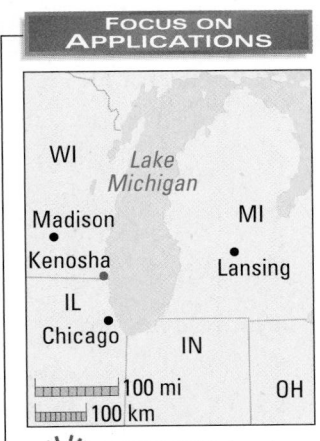

KENOSHA borders Lake Michigan and originally had an economy dominated by the shipping industry.

🌎 **POPULATION** **In Exercises 42 and 43, use the following information.**
In 1991, the population of Kenosha, Wisconsin, was 132,000. Between 1991 and 1996, the population of Kenosha increased by approximately 2000 people per year. ▶ Source: U.S. Bureau of the Census

42. Write an equation that models the population *y* of Kenosha in terms of *x*, where *x* represents the number of years since 1991.

43. Use the model to estimate the population of Kenosha in 2006.

🌎 **SALARY** **In Exercises 44 and 45, use the following information.**
At the start of your second year as a veterinary technician, you receive a raise of $750. You expect to receive the same raise every year. Your total yearly salary after your first raise is $18,000 per year.

44. Write an equation that models your total salary *s* in terms of the number of years *n* since you started as a technician.

45. Calculate your yearly salary after six years as a veterinary technician.

🌎 **CELLULAR RATES** **In Exercises 46 and 47, use the following information.**
You are moving to Houston, Texas, and are switching your cellular phone company. Your new peak air time rate in Houston is $.23 per minute. Your bill also includes a monthly access charge. For 110 minutes of peak air time your bill is $51.30.

46. Write an equation that models the cost *C* of your monthly bill in terms of the number of minutes *m* used. (All of your minutes are during peak air time.)

47. How much is your monthly bill for 60 minutes of peak air time?

🌎 **TAXI RIDE** **In Exercises 48 and 49, the cost of a taxi ride is an initial fee plus $1.50 for each mile. Your fare for 9 miles is $15.50.**

48. Write an equation that models the total cost *y* of a taxi ride in terms of the number of miles *x*.

49. How much is the initial fee?

50. MULTI-STEP PROBLEM After 6 weeks on a fitness program, Greg jogs 35 miles per week. His average mileage gain has been 2 miles per week.

   a. Write an equation that models Greg's weekly mileage m in terms of the number of weeks n that he stays on the program.

   b. When will Greg jog over 45 miles per week?

   c. *Writing* According to the equation, what will be Greg's weekly mileage after 52 weeks? Do you think this is realistic? Explain.

★ **Challenge**

51. **RENTING A CAR** You are comparing the costs of car rental agencies for a one-day car rental. Car Rental Agency A charges $30 a day plus $.08 per mile. Car Rental Agency B charges a flat fee of $40 a day.

   a. Write an equation in slope-intercept form that models the cost of renting a car from each car rental agency.

   b. Use a graphing calculator to graph the two equations on the same coordinate plane.

   c. Under what conditions would the cost of renting a car from either rental agency be the same?

   d. Under what conditions would the cost of renting a car from Car Rental Agency A be the best deal? Under what conditions would it be cheaper for you to rent a car from Car Rental Agency B?

EXTRA CHALLENGE
www.mcdougallittell.com

MIXED REVIEW

EVALUATING EXPONENTIAL EXPRESSIONS Use a calculator to evaluate the power. *(Review 1.2)*

52. 5^7 **53.** 8^5 **54.** 9^6 **55.** 3^{12}

56. 2^8 **57.** 4^3 **58.** 8^4 **59.** 10^4

60. 7^8 **61.** 6^9 **62.** 5^{11} **63.** 9^{13}

RULES OF ADDITION Find the sum. *(Review 2.2)*

64. $-7 + (-1)$ **65.** $4 + \left(-4\frac{1}{2}\right)$ **66.** $-9 + 11$

67. $-10 + (-1)$ **68.** $2 + (-6)$ **69.** $-18 + (-2)$

70. $6 + (-8) - 4$ **71.** $4 - (-7) + 3$ **72.** $5 + (-3) + (-5)$

FINDING SLOPE Find the slope of the line. *(Review 4.4 for 5.3)*

73.

74.

75.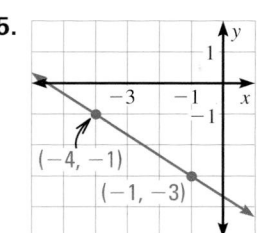

5.3

Writing Linear Equations Given Two Points

What you should learn

GOAL 1 Write an equation of a line given two points on the line.

GOAL 2 Use a linear equation to model a **real-life** problem, such as estimating height in **Example 3**.

Why you should learn it

▼ To model a **real-life** situation, such as the distance an echo travels across a canyon in **Ex. 57**.

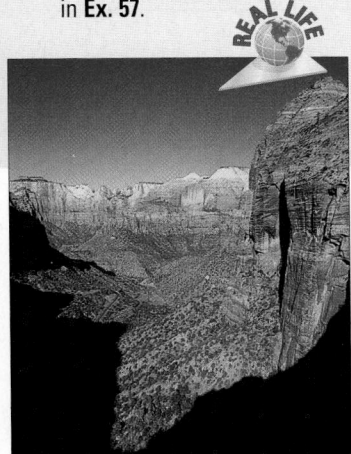

GOAL 1 USING TWO POINTS TO WRITE AN EQUATION

So far in this chapter, you have been writing equations of lines for which you were given the slope. In this lesson you will work with problems in which you must first find the slope. To do this, you can use the formula given in Chapter 4.

$$m = \frac{\text{rise}}{\text{run}} = \frac{y_2 - y_1}{x_2 - x_1} \longleftarrow \text{Slope of a line through } (x_1, y_1) \text{ and } (x_2, y_2)$$

EXAMPLE 1 *Writing an Equation Given Two Points*

Write an equation of the line that passes through the points $(1, 6)$ and $(3, -4)$.

SOLUTION

❶ Find the slope of the line. Let $(x_1, y_1) = (1, 6)$ and $(x_2, y_2) = (3, -4)$.

$$m = \frac{y_2 - y_1}{x_2 - x_1} \qquad \text{Write formula for slope.}$$

$$= \frac{-4 - 6}{3 - 1} \qquad \text{Substitute.}$$

$$= \frac{-10}{2} = -5 \qquad \text{Simplify.}$$

❷ Find the y-intercept. Let $m = -5$, $x = 1$, and $y = 6$ and solve for b.

$y = mx + b$ Write slope-intercept form.

$6 = (-5)(1) + b$ Substitute –5 for *m*, 1 for *x*, and 6 for *y*.

$6 = -5 + b$ Simplify.

$11 = b$ Solve for *b*.

❸ Write an equation of the line.

$y = mx + b$ Write slope-intercept form.

$y = -5x + 11$ Substitute –5 for *m* and 11 for *b*.

✓**CHECK** You can use a graph to check your work. Plot the two given points, $(1, 6)$ and $(3, -4)$, and draw a line through them. Then check that the line has a y-intercept of 11 and a slope of -5.

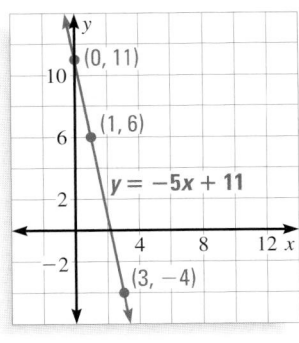

WRITING AN EQUATION OF A LINE GIVEN TWO POINTS

STEP ❶ Find the slope. Substitute the coordinates of the two given

points into the formula for slope, $m = \dfrac{y_2 - y_1}{x_2 - x_1}$.

STEP ❷ Find the y-intercept. Substitute the slope m and the coordinates of one of the points into the slope-intercept form, $y = mx + b$, and solve for the y-intercept b.

STEP ❸ Write an equation of the line. Substitute the slope m and the y-intercept b into the slope-intercept form, $y = mx + b$.

STUDENT HELP

HOMEWORK HELP
Visit our Web site
www.mcdougallittell.com
for extra examples.

EXAMPLE 2 *Writing Equations of Perpendicular Lines*

GEOMETRY CONNECTION Two different nonvertical lines are perpendicular if and only if their slopes are negative reciprocals of each other.

a. Show that $\overline{AB}$ and $\overline{BC}$ are perpendicular sides of figure $ABCD$.

b. Write equations for the lines containing $\overline{AB}$ and $\overline{BC}$.

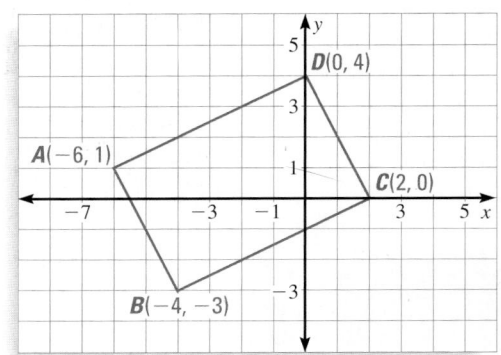

SOLUTION

a. Find the slopes.

Slope of $\overline{AB}$: $\quad m = \dfrac{1 - (-3)}{-6 - (-4)} = -2$

Slope of $\overline{BC}$: $\quad m = \dfrac{0 - (-3)}{2 - (-4)} = \dfrac{1}{2}$

▶ $\overline{AB}$ and $\overline{BC}$ are perpendicular because $\dfrac{1}{2}$ is the negative reciprocal of -2.

b. Find the y-intercepts of the lines containing $\overline{AB}$ and $\overline{BC}$. Substitute the slopes from part (a) and the coordinates of one point into $y = mx + b$.

For $\overline{AB}$	For $\overline{BC}$
$y = mx + b$	$y = mx + b$
$-3 = (-2)(-4) + b$	$-3 = \left(\dfrac{1}{2}\right)(-4) + b$
$-11 = b$	$-1 = b$

Write an equation in slope-intercept form by substituting for m and b.

Equation of line containing $\overline{AB}$	Equation of line containing $\overline{BC}$
$y = mx + b$	$y = mx + b$
$y = -2x - 11$	$y = \dfrac{1}{2}x - 1$

EXAMPLE 3 *Writing and Using a Linear Model*

ARCHAEOLOGY While working at an archaeological dig, you find an upper leg bone (femur) that belonged to an adult human male. The bone is 43 centimeters long. In humans, femur length is linearly related to height. To estimate the height of the person, you measure the femur and height of two complete adult male skeletons found at the same excavation.

Person 1: 40-centimeter femur, 162-centimeter height

Person 2: 45-centimeter femur, 173-centimeter height

Estimate the height of the person whose femur was found.

SOLUTION

Write a linear equation to model the height of a person in terms of the femur length. Let x represent femur length (in centimeters) and let y represent the height of the person (in centimeters).

Find the slope of the line through the points (40, 162) and (45, 173).

$$m = \frac{173 - 162}{45 - 40}$$

$$= \frac{11}{5} = 2.2$$

Find the y-intercept.

$y = mx + b$	Write slope-intercept form.
$173 = 2.2(45) + b$	Substitute for y, m, and x.
$74 = b$	Solve for b.

Write a linear equation.

$y = mx + b$	Write slope-intercept form.
$y = 2.2x + 74$	Substitute 2.2 for m and 74 for b.

Femur Length and Height

Estimate the height of the person whose femur is 43 centimeters by substituting 43 for x in the equation you wrote.

$$y = 2.2x + 74$$

$$y = 2.2(43) + 74$$

$$y = 168.6$$

▶ The person was about 169 centimeters tall.

FOCUS ON CAREERS

ANTHROPOLOGIST
Physical anthropologists examine bones from archaeological digs to investigate the height, weight, and diet of members of a culture.

CAREER LINK
www.mcdougallittell.com

GUIDED PRACTICE

Vocabulary Check ✔   **1.** Compare writing linear equations given the slope and a point with writing linear equations given two points.

Concept Check ✔   **2.** Explain why you should find the slope m first when finding the equation of a line passing through two points.

Skill Check ✔   **Give the slope of a line perpendicular to the given line.**

3. $y = -4x + 2$ **4.** $y = \frac{1}{2}x - 3$ **5.** $y = x - 3$

Write an equation in slope-intercept form of the line shown in the graph.

6.   **7.**   **8.**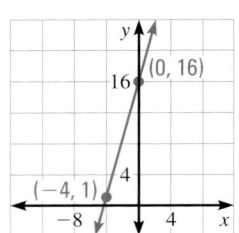

Write an equation in slope-intercept form of the line that passes through the points.

9. $(-1, 1), (4, 5)$ **10.** $(3, -2), (-6, 4)$ **11.** $(-4, 3), (-1, -7)$

12. $(-2, 5), (-6, -8)$ **13.** $(-8, -4), (4, 2)$ **14.** $(-1, -3), (-8, -9)$

15. $(5, 3), (4, -3)$ **16.** $(6, -10), (-3, -8)$ **17.** $(12, 2), (7, 2)$

PRACTICE AND APPLICATIONS

STUDENT HELP

→ **Extra Practice**
to help you master skills is on p. 801.

WRITING EQUATIONS Write an equation in slope-intercept form of the line shown in the graph.

18.   **19.**   **20.**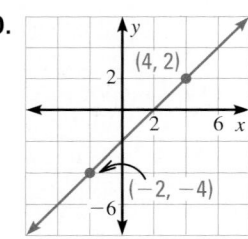

GRAPHING Graph the points and draw a line through them. Write an equation in slope-intercept form of the line that passes through the points.

21. $(-1, -2), (2, 6)$ **22.** $(1, 4), (5, -1)$ **23.** $(-1, -2), (3, -2)$

24. $(2, 0), (-2, 6)$ **25.** $(2, -3), (-3, 7)$ **26.** $(0, -5), (3, 4)$

27. $(6, -4), (-1, 2)$ **28.** $(-2, -1), (8, 8)$ **29.** $(1, 1), (7, 4)$

30. $(2, 4), (1, -2)$ **31.** $(5, -6), (5, -3)$ **32.** $(-3, -5), (1, 9)$

33. $(-5, 2), (6, 1)$ **34.** $(-6, 2), (-4, 11)$ **35.** $(-1, 10), (12, -4)$

STUDENT HELP

→ **HOMEWORK HELP**
Example 1: Exs. 18–44
Example 2: Exs. 45–49
Example 3: Exs. 53–55

SLOPE-INTERCEPT FORM Write an equation in slope-intercept form of the line that passes through the points.

36. $(-6, -5), (1, 4)$ **37.** $(2, 3), (4, 3)$ **38.** $(5, -10), (12, -7)$

39. $(14, -3), (-6, 9)$ **40.** $(-7, 9), (-3, 8)$ **41.** $(-8, 9), (10, -3)$

42. $\left(\frac{1}{4}, 2\right), \left(-5, \frac{2}{3}\right)$ **43.** $\left(\frac{1}{2}, -\frac{1}{2}\right), \left(\frac{1}{9}, \frac{3}{9}\right)$ **44.** $(-8.5, 6.75), (3.33, -9.75)$

45. PERPENDICULAR LINES Which of the lines are perpendicular? Explain.

line p: $y = \frac{1}{5}x + 2$ **line q:** $y = 5x - \frac{1}{2}$ **line r:** $y = -5x + 3$

46. Write an equation of a line through $(0, 2)$ that is perpendicular to $y = -4x + 6$.

47. Write an equation of a line through $(4, 5)$ that is perpendicular to $y = \frac{1}{2}x + 3$.

GEOMETRY ▸ **CONNECTION**   **In Exercises 48–50, use the graph.**

48. Find the perpendicular sides of trapezoid *WXYZ*. How do you know mathematically that these sides are perpendicular?

49. Write equations of the lines containing the perpendicular sides.

50. Write equations of the lines containing the two parallel sides. How do you know these sides are parallel?

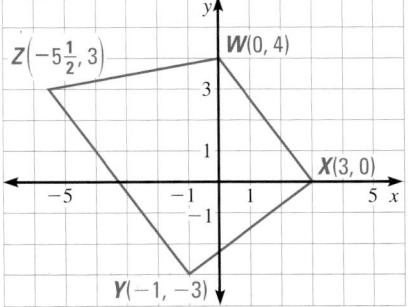

🌐 **CHUNNEL** **In Exercises 51 and 52, use the diagram of the *Chunnel*, a railroad tunnel built under the English channel. It is one of the most ambitious engineering feats of the twentieth century.**

51. Write an equation of the line from point *A* to point *B*. What is the slope of the line?

52. Write an equation of the line from point *C* to point *D*. What is the slope of the line? Is the Chunnel steeper on the French side or on the English side?

In Exercises 53–55, use the following information.
At sea level, the speed of sound in air is linearly related to the air temperature. If it is 35°C, sound will travel at a rate of 352 meters per second. If it is 15°C, sound will travel at a rate of 340 meters per second.

53. Write a linear equation that models speed of sound s in terms of air temperature T.

54. How fast will sound travel at sea level if it is 25°C outside?

55. If sound travels at a rate of 346 meters per second at sea level, what is the temperature?

ECHOES In Exercises 56 and 57, use the following information.
You yell across a canyon. Your sound travels at a rate of 343 meters per second.

56. Use your equation from Exercise 53 to determine the air temperature.

57. After you shout, it takes 4 seconds to hear your echo. How far are you from the canyon wall?

Test Preparation

58. MULTIPLE CHOICE What is the equation of the line that passes through the points $(7, 4)$ and $(-5, -2)$?

Ⓐ $y = \frac{1}{2}x - \frac{1}{2}$ Ⓑ $y = -\frac{1}{2}x + \frac{1}{2}$

Ⓒ $y = -\frac{1}{2}x - \frac{1}{2}$ Ⓓ $y = \frac{1}{2}x + \frac{1}{2}$

59. MULTIPLE CHOICE What is the equation of the line shown in the graph?

Ⓐ $y = 5x + 11$ Ⓑ $y = 5x - 17$

Ⓒ $y = \frac{11}{5}x + \frac{1}{5}$ Ⓓ $y = \frac{1}{5}x + \frac{11}{5}$

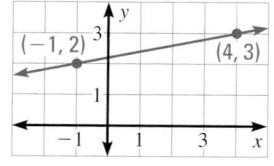

60. MULTIPLE CHOICE Choose which lines are perpendicular.

Line p passes through $(4, 0)$ and $(6, 4)$

Line q passes through $(0, 4)$ and $(6, 4)$

Line r passes through $(0, 4)$ and $(0, 0)$

Ⓐ line p and line q Ⓑ line p and line r

Ⓒ line q and line r Ⓓ none of these

★ Challenge

CRITICAL THINKING In Exercises 61–64, use a graph to determine whether the given three points seem to lie on the same line. If they do, prove algebraically that they lie on the same line and write an equation of the line.

61. $(-3, -1), (0, 1), (12, 9)$ **62.** $(4, -2), (-1, 2), (-8, 9)$

63. $(-2, -1), (3, 2), (7, 5)$ **64.** $(3, -3), (-1, 13), (1, 5)$

65. What is an equation of the line that passes through the points $\left(3\frac{1}{2}, 4\right)$ and $\left(-5, -\frac{9}{2}\right)$?

MIXED REVIEW

SIMPLIFYING EXPRESSIONS Simplify the expression. (Review 2.7)

66. $\dfrac{6x + 12y}{24}$

67. $\dfrac{48a - 56b}{16}$

68. $\dfrac{14x}{-28y - 1}$

SOLVING EQUATIONS Solve the equation. (Review 3.4)

69. $4x - 11 = -31$

70. $5x - 7 + x = 19$

71. $18 = 4 - \dfrac{2x}{5}$

72. $2x - 6 = 20$

73. $\dfrac{1}{2}a + 8\dfrac{1}{2}a = 3$

74. $7y = 9y - 8$

PLOTTING POINTS Plot the points in the table. Determine whether the slope of the line given by the points is *positive* or *negative*. (Review 4.1, 4.4 for 5.4)

75.

x	−1	0	1	2	3	4
y	−7	−4	−1	2	5	8

76.

x	−2	−1	0	1	2	3
y	7	5	3	1	−1	−3

QUIZ 1

Self-Test for Lessons 5.1–5.3

Write an equation of the line. (Lesson 5.1)

1.

2.

3.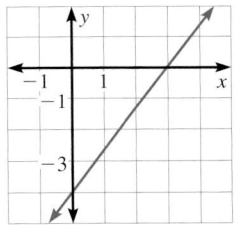

Write an equation of the line that passes through the point and has the given slope. Write the equation in slope-intercept form. (Lesson 5.2)

4. $(-5, 4)$, $m = 2$

5. $(2, 1)$, $m = -3$

6. $(-3, -6)$, $m = 1$

7. Find an equation of the line that is perpendicular to the line $y = -x + 6$ and passes through $(-2, -4)$. (Lesson 5.3)

Write an equation in slope-intercept form of the line that passes through the points. (Lesson 5.3)

8. $(8, -3)$, $(5, -2)$

9. $(-2, 6)$, $(-5, -7)$

10. $(4, 4)$, $(-7, 4)$

CANOE RENTAL In Exercises 11–13, suppose your family rents a canoe for a deposit of \$10 plus \$28 per day. (Lesson 5.1)

11. Write an equation to model the total cost y of renting a canoe for x days.

12. Graph the equation. Label the y-intercept.

13. Use the equation to find the cost of renting a canoe for 3 days.

5.4

Fitting a Line to Data

GOAL 1 FITTING A LINE TO DATA

What you should learn

GOAL 1 Find a linear equation that approximates a set of data points.

GOAL 2 Determine whether there is a positive or negative correlation or no correlation in a set of **real-life** data, like the Olympic data in **Example 3.**

Why you should learn it

To investigate trends in **real-life** data and to make predictions such as future football salaries in **Exs. 23** and **24.**

In this lesson you will learn how to write a linear model to represent a collection of data points.

Usually there is no single line that passes through all of the data points, so you try to find the line that best fits the data, as shown at the right. This is called the **best-fitting line**.

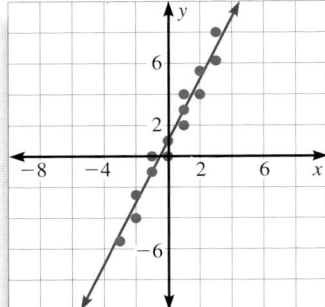

There is a mathematical definition of the best-fitting line that is called *least squares approximation*. Many calculators have a built-in program for finding the equation of the best-fitting line. Since least squares approximation is not part of Algebra 1, you will be asked to use a graphical approach for drawing a line that is probably close to the best-fitting line.

> **▶ ACTIVITY**
> Developing
> Concepts
>
> ## Approximating a Best-Fitting Line

With your group, use the following steps to approximate a best-fitting line.

1 Carefully plot the following points on graph paper.

(0, 3.3), (0, 3.9), (1, 4.2), (1, 4.5), (1, 4.8), (2, 4.7), (2, 5.1), (3, 4.9), (3, 5.6), (4, 6.1), (5, 6.4), (5, 7.1), (6, 6.8), (7, 7.5), (8, 7.8)

2 Use a ruler to sketch the line that you think best approximates the data points. Describe your strategy.

3 Locate two points on the line. Approximate the *x*-coordinate and the *y*-coordinate for each point. (These do not have to be two of the original data points.)

4 Use the method from Lesson 5.3 to find an equation of the line that passes through the two points.

MIXED REVIEW

SIMPLIFYING EXPRESSIONS Simplify the expression. (Review 2.7)

66. $\dfrac{6x + 12y}{24}$

67. $\dfrac{48a - 56b}{16}$

68. $\dfrac{14x}{-28y - 1}$

SOLVING EQUATIONS Solve the equation. (Review 3.4)

69. $4x - 11 = -31$

70. $5x - 7 + x = 19$

71. $18 = 4 - \dfrac{2x}{5}$

72. $2x - 6 = 20$

73. $\dfrac{1}{2}a + 8\dfrac{1}{2}a = 3$

74. $7y = 9y - 8$

PLOTTING POINTS Plot the points in the table. Determine whether the slope of the line given by the points is *positive* or *negative*. (Review 4.1, 4.4 for 5.4)

75.

x	−1	0	1	2	3	4
y	−7	−4	−1	2	5	8

76.

x	−2	−1	0	1	2	3
y	7	5	3	1	−1	−3

QUIZ 1

Write an equation of the line. (Lesson 5.1)

1.

2.

3.
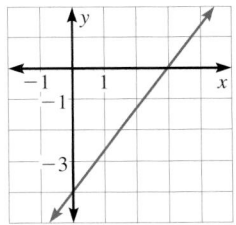

Write an equation of the line that passes through the point and has the given slope. Write the equation in slope-intercept form. (Lesson 5.2)

4. $(-5, 4)$, $m = 2$

5. $(2, 1)$, $m = -3$

6. $(-3, -6)$, $m = 1$

7. Find an equation of the line that is perpendicular to the line $y = -x + 6$ and passes through $(-2, -4)$. (Lesson 5.3)

Write an equation in slope-intercept form of the line that passes through the points. (Lesson 5.3)

8. $(8, -3)$, $(5, -2)$

9. $(-2, 6)$, $(-5, -7)$

10. $(4, 4)$, $(-7, 4)$

🌎 **CANOE RENTAL** In Exercises 11–13, suppose your family rents a canoe for a deposit of $10 plus $28 per day. (Lesson 5.1)

11. Write an equation to model the total cost y of renting a canoe for x days.

12. Graph the equation. Label the y-intercept.

13. Use the equation to find the cost of renting a canoe for 3 days.

Fitting a Line to Data

In this lesson you will learn how to write a linear model to represent a collection of data points.

Usually there is no single line that passes through all of the data points, so you try to find the line that best fits the data, as shown at the right. This is called the **best-fitting line**.

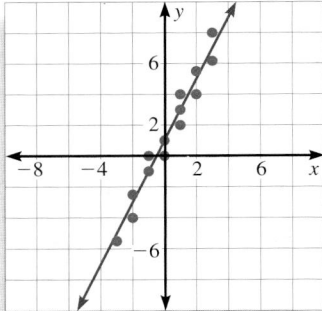

There is a mathematical definition of the best-fitting line that is called *least squares approximation*. Many calculators have a built-in program for finding the equation of the best-fitting line. Since least squares approximation is not part of Algebra 1, you will be asked to use a graphical approach for drawing a line that is probably close to the best-fitting line.

▶ **ACTIVITY**

Developing
Concepts

Approximating a Best-Fitting Line

With your group, use the following steps to approximate a best-fitting line.

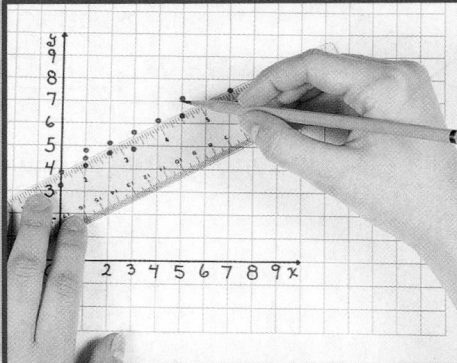

❶ Carefully plot the following points on graph paper.

(0, 3.3), (0, 3.9), (1, 4.2), (1, 4.5), (1, 4.8), (2, 4.7), (2, 5.1), (3, 4.9), (3, 5.6), (4, 6.1), (5, 6.4), (5, 7.1), (6, 6.8), (7, 7.5), (8, 7.8)

❷ Use a ruler to sketch the line that you think best approximates the data points. Describe your strategy.

❸ Locate two points on the line. Approximate the *x*-coordinate and the *y*-coordinate for each point. (These do not have to be two of the original data points.)

❹ Use the method from Lesson 5.3 to find an equation of the line that passes through the two points.

Biology

EXAMPLE 1 *Approximating a Best-Fitting Line*

The data in the table show the forearm lengths and foot lengths (without shoes) of 18 students in an algebra class. After graphing these data points, draw a line that corresponds closely to the data. Write an equation of your line.

Forearm length	Foot length
22 cm	24 cm
20 cm	19 cm
24 cm	24 cm
21 cm	23 cm
25 cm	23 cm
18 cm	18 cm
20 cm	21 cm
23 cm	23 cm
24 cm	25 cm
20 cm	22 cm
19 cm	19 cm
25 cm	25 cm
23 cm	22 cm
22 cm	23 cm
18 cm	19 cm
24 cm	23 cm
21 cm	24 cm
22 cm	22 cm

SOLUTION

Let x represent the forearm length and let y represent the foot length. To begin, plot the points given by the ordered pairs. Then sketch the line that appears to best fit the points.

Next, find two points that lie on the line. You might choose the points $(19, 20)$ and $(26, 26)$. Find the slope of the line through these two points.

$$m = \frac{y_2 - y_1}{x_2 - x_1}$$ **Write slope formula.**

$$m = \frac{26 - 20}{26 - 19}$$ **Substitute.**

$$m = \frac{6}{7}$$ **Simplify.**

$$\approx 0.86$$ **Decimal approximation.**

To find the y-intercept of the line, substitute the values $m = 0.86$, $x = 19$, and $y = 20$ in the slope-intercept form.

$$y = mx + b$$ **Write slope-intercept form.**

$$20 = (0.86)(19) + b$$ **Substitute 0.86 for *m*, 19 for *x*, and 20 for *y*.**

$$20 = 16.34 + b$$ **Simplify.**

$$3.66 = b$$ **Solve for *b*.**

▶ An approximate equation of the best-fitting line is $y = 0.86x + 3.66$. In general, if a student has a long forearm, then that student also has a long foot.

STUDENT HELP

↳ **Study Tip**
If you choose different points, you might get a different linear model. Be sure to choose points that will give you a line that is close to most of the points.

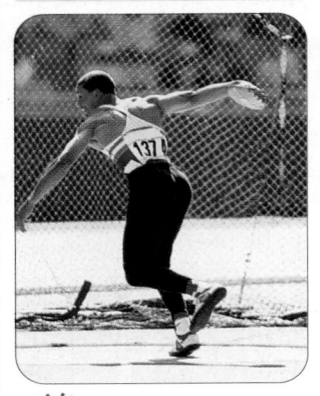

DISCUS EVENT
The discus throw is one of the original Olympic events. New records for the distance an athlete can throw the discus continue to be set.

EXAMPLE 2 *Approximating a Best-Fitting Line*

DISCUS THROWS The winning Olympic discus throws from 1908 to 1996 are shown in the table. After graphing these data points, draw a line that corresponds closely to the data. Write an equation of your line.

SOLUTION

Let x represent the years since 1900. Let y represent the winning throw. To begin, plot the points given by the ordered pairs. Then sketch the line that appears to best fit the points.

Olympic year	Winning throw
1908	134.1 ft
1912	148.3 ft
1920	146.6 ft
1924	151.4 ft
1928	155.3 ft
1932	162.4 ft
1936	165.6 ft
1948	173.2 ft
1952	180.5 ft
1956	184.9 ft
1960	194.2 ft
1964	200.1 ft
1968	212.5 ft
1972	211.3 ft
1976	221.5 ft
1980	218.7 ft
1984	218.5 ft
1988	225.8 ft
1992	213.7 ft
1996	227.7 ft

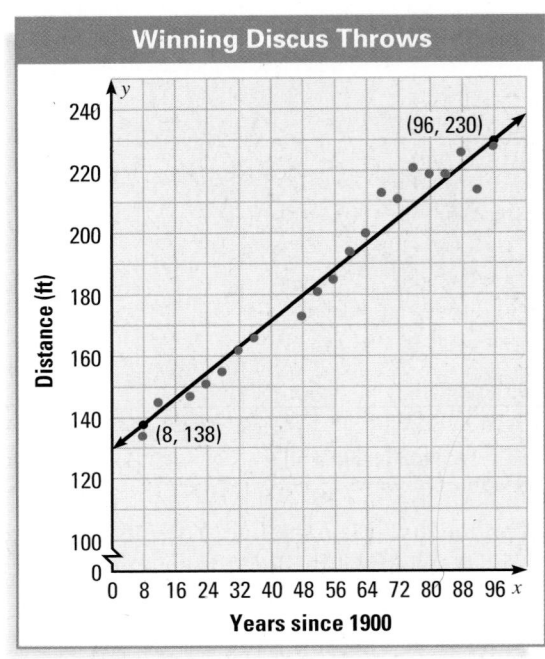

Winning Discus Throws

DATA UPDATE of *Information Please Almanac* at www.mcdougallittell.com

Next, find two points that lie on the line, such as (8, 138) and (96, 230). Find the slope of the line through these points.

$$m = \frac{y_2 - y_1}{x_2 - x_1} = \frac{230 - 138}{96 - 8} = \frac{92}{88} \approx 1.05$$

To find the y-intercept of the line, substitute the values $m = 1.05$, $x = 8$, and $y = 138$ in the slope-intercept form.

$y = mx + b$	Write slope-intercept form.
$138 = (1.05)(8) + b$	Substitute 1.05 for *m*, 8 for *x*, and 138 for *y*.
$138 = 8.4 + b$	Simplify.
$129.6 = b$	Solve for *b*.

▶ An approximate equation of the best-fitting line is $y = 1.05x + 129.6$. In most years, the winner of the discus throw was able to throw the discus farther than the previous winner.

Correlation is a number *r* satisfying $-1 \le r \le 1$ that indicates how well a particular set of data can be approximated by a straight line. The Activity on page 299 shows how to find an *r*-value using a calculator. In this course you will describe a correlation without actually finding *r*-values, as described below.

When the points on a scatter plot can be approximated by a line with positive slope, *x* and *y* have a **positive correlation**. When the points can be approximated by a line with negative slope, *x* and *y* have a **negative correlation**. When the points cannot be well approximated by a straight line, we say that there is **relatively no correlation.**

Positive correlation

Negative correlation

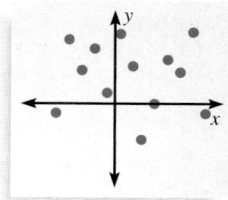

Relatively no correlation

EXAMPLE 3 *Using Correlation*

In swimming events, performance is positively correlated with time.

a. The two graphs show the winning 100-meter women's freestyle swimming times and the winning women's long jump distances for the Olympics from 1948 through 1996. Which is which? Explain your reasoning.

b. Describe the correlation of each set of data.

Year

▶ Source: *Information Please Almanac*

Year

▶ Source: *Information Please Almanac*

SOLUTION

a. The first graph must represent the long jump distances because the winners have tended to jump farther with each Olympic year. The second graph must represent the swimming times because the winners have tended to swim faster with each Olympic year, so their times have been decreasing.

b. The first graph shows a positive correlation between the year and the winning distance. The second graph shows a negative correlation between the year and the winning time.

GUIDED PRACTICE

Vocabulary Check ✔ **1.** The line that most closely fits a set of data is called the <u> ? </u>.

Concept Check ✔ **Draw a scatter plot of data that have the given correlation.**

2. Positive   **3.** Negative   **4.** Relatively no

5. 🌐 **DISCUS THROWS** Predict the distance of the winning throw in the year 2005 from the data in Example 2. Explain your reasoning.

Skill Check ✔ **Draw a scatter plot of the data. State whether *x* and *y* have a *positive correlation*, a *negative correlation*, or *relatively no correlation*. If possible, draw a line that closely fits the data and write an equation of the line.**

6.
x	y
1	2
2	9
3	8
4	1
5	4
6	8

7.
x	y
−3	8
−2	6
−1	5
0	3
1	2
2	0

8.
x	y
1.1	5.1
1.7	5.5
2.2	5.9
2.6	6.3
3.3	7.5
3.5	7.6

9.
x	y
5.5	0.4
6.2	1.0
7.7	2.5
8.1	2.9
9.2	4.3
9.7	5.5

PRACTICE AND APPLICATIONS

STUDENT HELP

▶ **Extra Practice**
to help you master skills is on p. 801.

FITTING LINES Copy the graph and draw a line that corresponds closely to the data. Write an equation of your line.

10.

11.

12.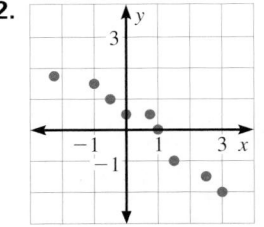

FITTING LINES Draw a scatter plot of the data. Draw a line that corresponds closely to the data and write an equation of the line.

STUDENT HELP

▶ **HOMEWORK HELP**
Example 1: Exs. 10–16, 23
Example 2: Exs. 10–16, 23
Example 3: Exs. 17–22

13.
x	y
1.0	3.8
1.5	4.2
1.7	5.3
2.0	5.8
2.0	5.5
1.5	6.7

14.
x	y
3.0	7.1
3.4	8.1
4.0	8.5
4.1	8.9
4.8	9.6
5.2	9.8

15.
x	y
3.0	9.9
3.5	9.7
3.7	8.6
4.0	8.1
4.0	8.4
4.5	7.4

16.
x	y
5.0	6.8
5.4	5.8
6.0	5.6
6.1	5.2
6.8	4.3
7.2	3.5

GRAPHICAL REASONING State whether *x* and *y* have a *positive correlation*, a *negative correlation*, or *relatively no correlation*.

17.

18.

19.

20.

21.

22.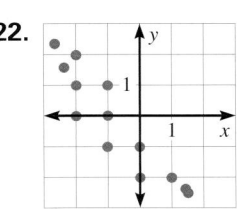

STUDENT HELP

INTERNET

HOMEWORK HELP
Visit our Web site
www.mcdougallittell.com
for help with Exs. 23 and
24.

FOOTBALL SALARIES
In Exercises 23 and 24, use the following information.
The median base salary for players in the National Football League from 1983 to 1997 is shown in the scatter plot at the right. In the scatter plot, *y* represents the salary and *x* represents the number of years since 1980.

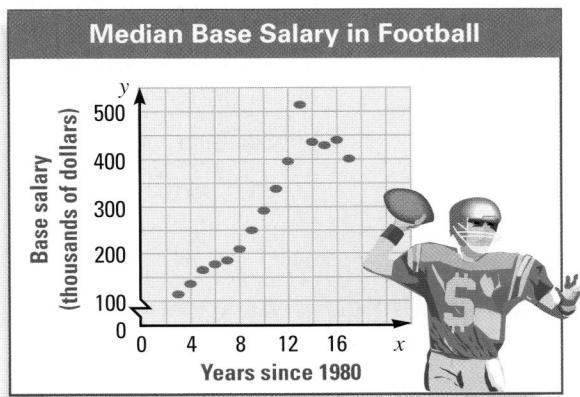

► Source: National Football League Players Association

23. Find an equation of the line that you think closely fits the data.

24. Use the equation from Exercise 23 to approximate the median base salary in the year 2010.

BIOLOGY ▸ **CONNECTION** In Exercises 25–27, use the following information.
As people grow older, the size of their pupils tends to get smaller. The average diameter (in millimeters) of one person's pupils is given in the table.

25. Draw a scatter plot of the day diameters and another of the night diameters. Let *x* represent the person's age and let *y* represent pupil diameters.

26. Find an equation of the line that closely fits the day and the night sets of data for pupil diameters.

Sample Pupil Diameters		
Age (years)	Day	Night
20	4.7	8.0
30	4.3	7.0
40	3.9	6.0
50	3.5	5.0
60	3.1	4.1
70	2.7	3.2
80	2.3	2.5

27. **CRITICAL THINKING** Do the two lines have the same slope? Explain your answer in the context of the real-life data.

MULTI-STEP PROBLEM In Exercises 28–31, use the scatter plots. They show a library's annual book budget *B* and the average price *P* of a book.

Library Book Budget

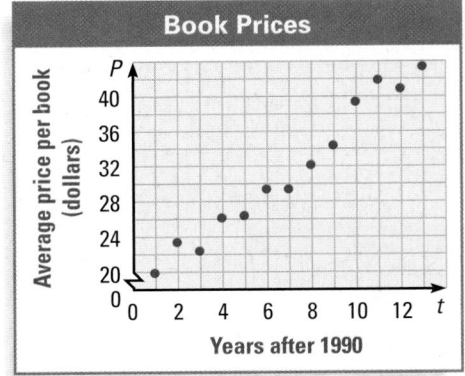

Book Prices

28. Find an equation of the line that you think best represents the library's budget for purchasing books.

29. Find an equation of the line that you think best represents the average price of a new book purchased by the library.

30. Interpret the slopes of the two lines in the context of the problem.

31. **CRITICAL THINKING** Suppose that you want to ask town officials to increase the library's annual book budget. Use your results and the information above to write a letter that explains why the library budget should be increased.

★ **Challenge**

ANALYZING DATA In Exercises 32–34, use the Book Prices scatter plot above.

32. Explain why you would not want to choose the points for the years 1992 and 1997 to write an equation that represents the data.

33. Will choosing the two points that are the farthest apart always give you the closest line? Explain why or why not. If not, sketch a counterexample.

EXTRA CHALLENGE
www.mcdougallittell.com

34. Explain how to choose a good pair of points to find a line that is probably close to the best-fitting line.

MIXED REVIEW

HORIZONTAL AND VERTICAL LINES Decide whether the line is *horizontal* or *vertical*. Then graph the line. (Review 4.2)

35. $y = -2$ **36.** $y = 3$ **37.** $x = 4$ **38.** $x = -5$

VISUAL REASONING Without calculating, state whether the slope of the line through the points is *positive, negative, zero,* or *undefined.* (Review 4.4)

39. $(1, 4), (3, 5)$ **40.** $(2, 5), (4, 1)$ **41.** $(6, 1), (3, 1)$ **42.** $(5, 2), (4, 3)$

WRITING EQUATIONS OF LINES Write an equation of the line that passes through the points. (Review 5.3 for 5.5)

43. $(2, 5), (6, 4)$ **44.** $(1, 4), (3, 7)$ **45.** $(3, 7), (7, 3)$ **46.** $(5, 2), (4, 3)$

47. $(-3, 1), (4, -2)$ **48.** $(-2, -3), (0, 4)$ **49.** $(5, 1), (3, -6)$ **50.** $(0, -6), (-1, 7)$

▶ ACTIVITY 5.4

Using Technology

Best-Fitting Lines

A graphing calculator can be used to find a best-fitting line. One way to tell how well a line fits a set of data is to look at the *r*-value. The closer the absolute value of *r* is to 1, the better the line fits the data.

STUDENT HELP

Look Back
For help with scatter plots, see p. 209.

KEYSTROKE HELP
See keystrokes for several models of calculators at www.mcdougallittell.com

▶ EXAMPLE

Use a graphing calculator to find the best-fitting line for the data.
$(38, 62), (28, 46), (56, 102), (56, 88), (24, 36), (77, 113), (40, 69), (46, 60)$

▶ SOLUTION

1 Enter the ordered pairs into the graphing calculator. Make a scatter plot of the data.

2 Use linear regression to find the best-fitting line. Select L_1 as the x list and L_2 as the y list.

3 The equation $y = 1.49x + 3.85$ is the line of best fit with an r-value of approximately 0.95.

4 Graph the equation $y = 1.49x + 3.85$ with the data points.

▶ The r-value of 0.95 is close to 1. The equation $y = 1.49x + 3.85$ fits the data points well.

▶ EXERCISES

Find the best-fitting line for the points.

1. $(0.1, 2.1), (1.0, 2.5), (2.2, 2.9), (2.9, 3.4), (4.0, 4.0), (4.9, 4.3)$

2. $(31, 114), (40, 136), (49, 165), (62, 177), (70, 185), (78, 209)$

3. $(0, 1), (1, 2), (1, 3), (2, 3), (2, 3.5), (3, 4), (3, 4.5), (4, 5.5), (4, 6),$
$(5, 5), (5, 6), (5, 6.5), (6, 7), (6, 8), (7, 7.5)$

4. $(0, 8), (1, 7.5), (1, 6), (2, 6.5), (2, 6), (3, 5.5), (3, 5), (4, 4), (4, 3.5),$
$(5, 3), (5, 2.5), (6, 2), (6, 1.5), (7, 1), (7, 0)$

5.5 Point-Slope Form of a Linear Equation

What you should learn

GOAL 1 Use the point-slope form to write an equation of a line.

GOAL 2 Use the point-slope form to model a **real-life** situation, such as running pace in **Example 3**.

Why you should learn it

▼ To estimate the **real-life** time it will take a mountain climber to reach the top of a cliff in **Ex. 63**.

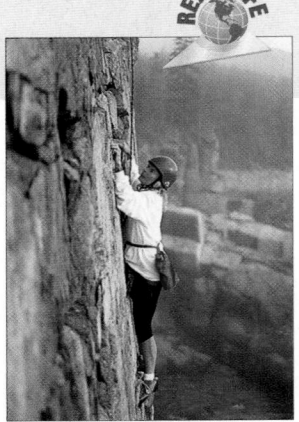

GOAL 1 USING THE POINT-SLOPE FORM

In Lesson 5.2 you learned one strategy for writing a linear equation when given the slope and a point on the line. In this lesson you will learn a different strategy—one that uses the **point-slope form** of an equation of a line.

EXAMPLE 1 *Developing the Point-Slope Form*

Write an equation of the line. Use the points $(2, 5)$ and (x, y).

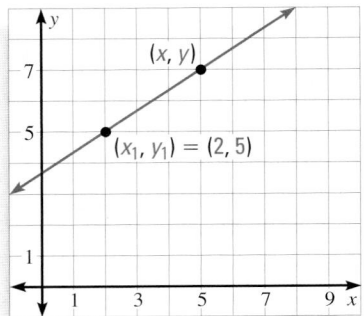

SOLUTION

You are given one point on the line. Let (x, y) be any point on the line. Because $(2, 5)$ and (x, y) are two points on the line, you can write the following expression for the slope of the line.

$$m = \frac{y - 5}{x - 2} \qquad \text{Use formula for slope.}$$

The graph shows that the slope is $\frac{2}{3}$. Substitute $\frac{2}{3}$ for m in the formula for slope.

$$\frac{y - 5}{x - 2} = \frac{2}{3} \qquad \text{Substitute } \tfrac{2}{3} \text{ for } m.$$

$$y - 5 = \frac{2}{3}(x - 2) \qquad \text{Multiply each side by } (x - 2).$$

The equation $y - 5 = \frac{2}{3}(x - 2)$ is written in point-slope form.

POINT-SLOPE FORM OF THE EQUATION OF A LINE

The **point-slope form** of the equation of the nonvertical line that passes through a given point (x_1, y_1) with a slope of m is

$$y - y_1 = m(x - x_1).$$

You can use the point-slope form when you are given the slope and a point on the line. In the point-slope form, (x_1, y_1) is the given point and (x, y) is any other point on the line. You can also use the point-slope form when you are given two points on the line. First find the slope. Then use either given point as (x_1, y_1).

EXAMPLE 2 *Using the Point-Slope Form*

STUDENT HELP

INTERNET

HOMEWORK HELP
Visit our Web site
www.mcdougallittell.com
for extra examples.

Write an equation of the line shown at the right.

SOLUTION

First find the slope. Use the points
$(x_1, y_1) = (-3, 6)$ and $(x_2, y_2) = (1, -2)$.

$$m = \frac{y_2 - y_1}{x_2 - x_1}$$

$$= \frac{-2 - 6}{1 - (-3)}$$

$$= \frac{-8}{4}$$

$$= -2$$

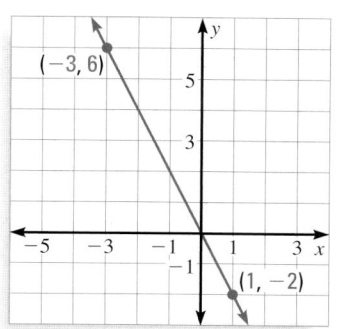

STUDENT HELP

▶ **Study Tip**
The point-slope form
$y - y_1 = m(x - x_1)$ has
two minus signs. Be sure
to account for these
signs when the point
(x_1, y_1) has negative
coordinates.

Then use the slope to write the point-slope form. Choose either point as (x_1, y_1).

$y - y_1 = m(x - x_1)$	Write point-slope form.
$y - 6 = -2[x - (-3)]$	Substitute for m, x_1, and y_1.
$y - 6 = -2(x + 3)$	Simplify.
$y - 6 = -2x - 6$	Use distributive property.
$y = -2x$	Add 6 to each side.

● ACTIVITY

Developing
Concepts

Investigating the Point-Slope Form

The line shown at the right is labeled
with four points.

❶ Each person in your group should
use a different pair of points to
write an equation of the line in
point-slope form.

❷ Compare the equations of the
people in your group. Discuss
whether the following statement
seems to be always, sometimes, or
never true. *Any two points on a line
can be used to find an equation of the line.*

> **LAMECK AGUTA**
> of Kenya won the
> Boston Marathon in 1997.
> The high temperature on that
> day was 52° and the low
> temperature was 42°.

EXAMPLE 3 *Writing and Using a Linear Model*

MARATHON The information below was taken from an article that appeared in a newspaper.

> Section C   9   °F
>
> **Temperature Affects Running Speed**
>
> The best temperature for running is below 60°F. If a person ran optimally at 17.6 feet per second, he or she would slow by about 0.3 foot per second for every 5° increase in temperature above 60°F.

a. Use the information to write a linear model for optimal running pace.

b. Use the model to find the optimal running pace for a temperature of 80°F.

SOLUTION

a. Let T represent the temperature in degrees Fahrenheit. Let P represent the optimal pace in feet per second.

From the article, you know that the optimal running pace at 60° F is 17.6 feet per second so one point on the line is $(T_1, P_1) = (60, 17.6)$. Find the slope of the line.

$$m = \frac{\text{change in } P}{\text{change in } T} = \frac{-0.3}{5} = -0.06.$$

Use the point-slope form to write the model.

$P - P_1 = m(T - T_1)$	**Write point-slope form.**
$P - 17.6 = (-0.06)(T - 60)$	**Substitute for m, T_1, and P_1.**
$P - 17.6 = -0.06T + 3.6$	**Use distributive property.**
$P = -0.06T + 21.2$	**Add 17.6 to each side.**

b. Use the model to find the optimal pace at 80°F.

$$P = -0.06(80) + 21.2$$
$$= 16.4$$

▶ At 80°F the optimal running pace is 16.4 feet per second.

✓**CHECK** A graph can help you check this result. You can see that as the temperature increases the optimal running pace decreases.

Optimal Pace

GUIDED PRACTICE

Vocabulary Check ✔

Concept Check ✔

Skill Check ✔

1. Name the following form of the equation of a line: $y - y_1 = m(x - x_1)$.

2. What are the values of m, x_1, and y_1 in the equation $y - (-1) = 3(x - 2)$?

Write an equation of the line in point-slope form.

3.

4.

5.
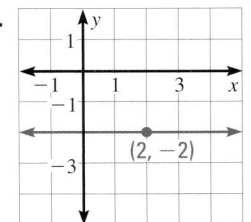

Write an equation of the line in point-slope form that passes through the given point and has the given slope.

6. $(2, -1)$, $m = 3$

7. $(3, 4)$, $m = \dfrac{1}{2}$

8. $(-5, -7)$, $m = -2$

9. $(-3, 10)$, $m = 4$

10. $(-2, -9)$, $m = 4$

11. $(7, -7)$, $m = -8$

Write an equation of the line that passes through the given points.

12. $(5, 12)$, $(6, -2)$

13. $(-4, -1)$, $(-9, 2)$

14. $(-17, -8)$, $(-7, -4)$

15. $(2, 12)$, $(7, 2)$

16. $(3, -12)$, $(8, 4)$

17. $(-4, -7)$, $(2, 2)$

PRACTICE AND APPLICATIONS

STUDENT HELP

▸ **Extra Practice**
to help you master
skills is on p. 801.

USING A GRAPH Write an equation of the line in point-slope form.

18.

19.

20.
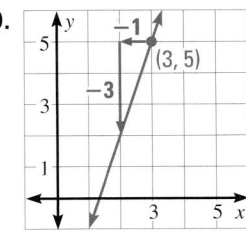

POINT-SLOPE FORM Write an equation in point-slope form of the line that passes through the given points.

21. $(1, 5)$, $(-1, -5)$

22. $(-2, -5)$, $(7, -6)$

23. $(-9, 10)$, $(-4, -3)$

24. $(4, -5)$, $(-2, -7)$

25. $(-5, 10)$, $(-4, -2)$

26. $(-3, -2)$, $(-3, -8)$

27. $(-3, -9)$, $(-6, -8)$

28. $(-3, -7)$, $(-4, -8)$

29. $(1, -7)$, $(-1, -5)$

WRITING EQUATIONS Write an equation in point-slope form of the line that passes through the given point and has the given slope.

STUDENT HELP

▸ **HOMEWORK HELP**
Example 1: Exs. 18–20
Example 2: Exs. 21–29
Example 3: Exs. 57–61

30. $(-1, -3)$, $m = 4$

31. $(-6, 2)$, $m = -5$

32. $(-10, 0)$, $m = 2$

33. $(-8, -2)$, $m = 2$

34. $(-4, 3)$, $m = -6$

35. $(-3, 4)$, $m = 6$

36. $(12, 2)$, $m = -7$

37. $(8, -1)$, $m = 0$

38. $(5, -12)$, $m = -11$

COMPARING FORMS Write the point-slope form of the equation of the line that passes through the point and has the given slope. Then rewrite the equation in slope-intercept form.

39. $(1, 4)$, $m = 2$ **40.** $(-2, 4)$, $m = 3$ **41.** $(6, 2)$, $m = \dfrac{1}{2}$

42. $(-3, -1)$, $m = 4$ **43.** $(5, -1)$, $m = -1$ **44.** $(-5, -5)$, $m = -2$

45. $(-1, 1)$, $m = -\dfrac{1}{8}$ **46.** $(4, -2)$, $m = \dfrac{1}{4}$ **47.** $(-9, -6)$, $m = -\dfrac{2}{3}$

WRITING EQUATIONS Write an equation of the line.

48.   **49.**   **50.**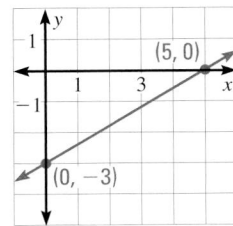

WRITING EQUATIONS GIVEN TWO POINTS Write the point-slope form of the equation of the line that passes through the two points.

51. $(1, 3)$, $(2, 5)$ **52.** $(-2, 3)$, $(2, -5)$ **53.** $(7, -10)$, $(15, -22)$

54. $(2, 6)$, $(5, 1)$ **55.** $(-3, -4)$, $(1, -1)$ **56.** $(4, -2)$, $(-9, 5)$

🌎 **FIELD TRIP** In Exercises 57–59, you are going on a trip to the Natural History Museum. At 9:00 A.M., you leave for the museum, which is 120 miles away. At 10:15 A.M., you are 63 miles away from the museum.

57. Write a linear equation that gives the distance d (in miles) from the museum in terms of the time t. Let t represent the number of minutes since 9:00 A.M.

58. Find the distance you are from the museum after you have traveled 2 hours.

59. According to your equation, when will you reach the museum?

🌎 **TRAVEL** In Exercises 60 and 61, you are flying from Montreal to Miami in a plane. The plane leaves Montreal at 8:00 A.M. and at 9:15 A.M. is flying over Washington, DC.

60. Use the map to write a linear equation that gives the distance y (in kilometers) remaining in the flight in terms of the number of minutes x since 8:00 A.M.

61. When will you reach Miami? (Assume that the plane is flying at a constant speed.)

🌎 **MOUNTAIN CLIMBING** In Exercises 62 and 63, a mountain climber is scaling a 300-foot cliff at a constant rate. The climber starts at the bottom at 12:00 P.M. By 12:30 P.M., the climber has moved 62 feet up the cliff.

62. Write an equation that gives the distance d (in feet) remaining in the climb in terms of the time t (in hours). What is the slope of the line?

63. At what time will the mountain climber reach the top of the cliff?

64. MULTIPLE CHOICE The time t (in hours) needed to produce x units of a product is modeled by $t = px + s$. If it takes 265 hours to produce 200 units and 390 hours to produce 300 units, what is the value of s?

 A 1.25   **B** 15   **C** 100   **D** 125

65. MULTIPLE CHOICE What is the equation in point-slope form of the line in the graph?

 A $y - 3 = 3(x - 0)$

 B $y = 3x + 3$

 C $y - (-1) = 3(x - 3)$

 D $y - 3 = 3[x - (-1)]$

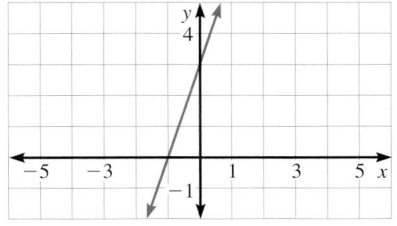

66. MULTIPLE CHOICE What is the equation in point-slope form of the line perpendicular to the line in the graph and through $(2, -1)$?

 A $y = -x + 1$

 B $y - (-1) = -1(x - 2)$

 C $y - 4 = -1(x + 3)$

 D $y - (-1) = 1(x - 2)$

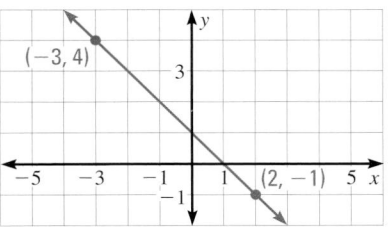

★ **Challenge**   **Find the value of k so that the line through the given points has slope m.**

67. $(2k, 3), (1, k); m = 2$ **68.** $(k + 1, k - 1), (k, -k); m = k + 1$

69. $(k, k + 1), (3, 2); m = 3$ **70.** $(k + 1, 3 + 2k), (k - 1, 1 - k); m = k$

MIXED REVIEW

CHECKING SOLUTIONS OF INEQUALITIES **Check whether the given number is a solution of the inequality.** (Review 1.4)

71. $2x < 24; 8$ **72.** $7y + 6 \geq 10; 3$ **73.** $16p - 9 \leq 71; 5$

74. $12a \leq a - 9; -2$ **75.** $4x \leq 28; 7$ **76.** $6c - 4 > 14; 3$

GRAPHING FUNCTIONS **Graph the function.** (Review 4.8 for 5.6)

77. $f(x) = -3x + 4$ **78.** $g(x) = -x - 7$ **79.** $h(x) = 2x - 8$

80. $f(x) = -5x - 7$ **81.** $f(x) = 6x + 7$ **82.** $f(x) = 3 - 7x$

83. $g(x) = -\frac{1}{2}x - 3$ **84.** $f(x) = 8x + \frac{2}{3}$ **85.** $h(x) = \frac{6}{5}x + 5$

86. 🌐 **TEEN SURVEY** In a school of 500 teens, 40 have taken drum lessons. What are the odds that a randomly chosen teen has not taken drum lessons? (Review 2.8)

87. **PROBABILITY** ▸ **CONNECTION**   A jar contains 10 blue marbles, 7 red marbles, and 4 yellow marbles. Without looking, you reach into the jar and choose one marble. What is the probability that the marble is red? (Review 2.8)

Copy the graph and draw a best-fitting line for the scatter plot. Find an equation of the line. State whether *x* and *y* have a *positive correlation* or a *negative correlation*. (Lesson 5.4)

1.

2.

3.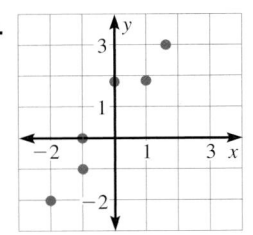

Write an equation in point-slope form of the line that passes through the given point and has the given slope. (Lesson 5.5)

4. $(1, -4), m = -1$

5. $(2, 5), m = 2$

6. $(-3, -2), m = -2$

7. $(-3, -3), m = 0$

8. $(-6, 6), m = \frac{1}{2}$

9. $(3, 8), m = 7$

Write an equation in point-slope form of the line that passes through the given points. (Lesson 5.5)

10. $(0, 0), (-3, -1)$

11. $(-5, -2), (-6, -2)$

12. $(-5, -3), (1, 6)$

MATH & History

Archaeological Dating

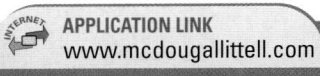
APPLICATION LINK
www.mcdougallittell.com

THEN

BY THE MIDDLE OF THE TWENTIETH CENTURY, radiocarbon dating was being used to find the ages of objects. During the 1950s, increasing differences emerged between the radiocarbon dates and the historical dates of civilizations.

NOW

TODAY, archaeologists calibrate tree ring dates with radiocarbon dates to accurately determine the age of an object.

1. Radiocarbon dates calibrate well with tree ring dates after approximately what year?

2. Does radiocarbon dating produce calendar years that are earlier or later than those based on tree ring dating?

1929

An excavation unearths pottery at Mesa Verde.

1930

A. E. Douglass uses tree rings to date Mesa Verde sites.

Modern archaeologists use a variety of dating methods.

1990

● ACTIVITY 5.6

Developing Concepts

Investigating the
Standard Form of a Linear Equation

GROUP ACTIVITY
Work in a small group.

MATERIALS
graph paper

▶ **QUESTION** How can you model possible combinations of two stocks you can buy with a limited amount of money?

▶ **EXPLORING THE CONCEPT**

Your social studies class is learning about the stock market. Each person in class "invests" up to $80 in either GFE stock, which costs $8 per share, or JIH stock, which costs $20 per share.

1 Copy and complete the table.

Number of GFE shares	0	1	2	3	4	5
Number of JIH shares	1	1	1	1	1	1
Total cost (dollars)	?	?	?	?	?	?

2 Total costs that represent different combinations of the two stocks are written at points on the graph. Locate the values from your table on the graph.

3 Find the cost of 5 shares of GFE stock and 2 shares of JIH stock. What does the red line on the graph represent?

4 Write an equation of the line in slope-intercept form.

▶ **DRAWING CONCLUSIONS**

1. Each member of the group should copy the graph and choose a different amount to invest from the following list: $48, $64, $96, and $108.

2. Draw a line that represents the combinations of stocks you can invest in using all of your money. Write an equation of the line in slope-intercept form.

3. Use the verbal model below to write an equation that models the combinations of stocks you can buy using your investment amount as the total cost.

4. *Writing* You have modeled your investments using a graph and two forms of equations. Compare the results of each person in the group. What do you notice about the lines? about the equations from Exercises 2 and 3?

5.6 The Standard Form of a Linear Equation

What you should learn

GOAL 1 Write a linear equation in standard form.

GOAL 2 Use the standard form of an equation to model **real-life** situations, such as the amount of food to purchase for a barbecue in **Example 4**.

Why you should learn it

▼ To model **real-life** situations, such as buying combinations of bird seeds in **Exs. 64–66**.

GOAL 1 WRITING AN EQUATION IN STANDARD FORM

Most of the linear equations in this chapter are written in slope-intercept form.

> **Slope-intercept form:** $y = mx + b$

Another commonly used form is the **standard form** of the equation of a line.

> **Standard (or general) form:** $Ax + By = C$

In this form, notice that the variable terms are on the left side of the equation and the constant term is on the right. A, B, and C represent real numbers and A and B are not both zero.

▶ ACTIVITY
Developing Concepts
Investigating Forms of Equations

1 Graph each of these equations.

    a. $y = \frac{4}{3}x - 2$ **b.** $-4x + 3y = -6$ **c.** $4x - 3y = 6$

2 Which, if any, of the equations are equivalent? How do you know?

EXAMPLE 1 *Writing an Equation in Standard Form*

Write $y = \frac{2}{5}x - 3$ in standard form with integer coefficients.

SOLUTION

To write the equation in standard form, isolate the variable terms on the left and the constant term on the right.

$$y = \frac{2}{5}x - 3 \qquad \text{Write original equation.}$$

$$5y = 5\left(\frac{2}{5}x - 3\right) \qquad \text{Multiply each side by 5.}$$

$$5y = 2x - 15 \qquad \text{Use distributive property.}$$

$$-2x + 5y = -15 \qquad \text{Subtract 2\textit{x} from each side.}$$

. . . .

A linear equation can have more than one standard form. For instance, if you multiply each side of the standard form above by -1, you get $2x - 5y = 15$, which is also in standard form.

STUDENT HELP

↪ **Look Back**
For help with solving linear equations, see p. 155.

EXAMPLE 2 *Writing a Linear Equation*

Write the standard form of an equation of the line passing through $(-4, 3)$ with a slope of -2.

SOLUTION

You are given a point on the line and its slope, so you can write the point-slope form of the equation of the line.

$y - y_1 = m(x - x_1)$	Write point-slope form.
$y - 3 = -2[x - (-4)]$	Substitute for y_1, m, and x_1.
$y - 3 = -2(x + 4)$	Simplify.
$y - 3 = -2x - 8$	Use distributive property.
$2x + y = -5$	Add $2x$ and 3 to each side.

▶ The equation $2x + y = -5$ is in standard form.

EXAMPLE 3 *Horizontal and Vertical Lines*

Write the standard form of an equation

  a. of the horizontal line.

  b. of the vertical line.

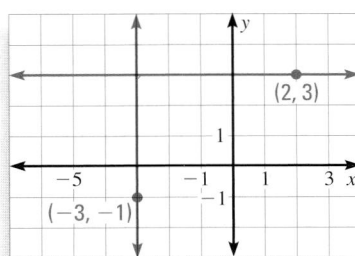

SOLUTION

  a. The horizontal line has a point with a y-coordinate of 3. The standard form of the equation is $y = 3$.

  b. The vertical line has a point with an x-coordinate of -3. The standard form of the equation is $x = -3$.

· · · · · · · · · ·

You have now studied all of the commonly used forms of linear equations. They are summarized in the following list.

CONCEPT SUMMARY	EQUATIONS OF LINES
SLOPE-INTERCEPT FORM:	$y = mx + b$
POINT-SLOPE FORM:	$y - y_1 = m(x - x_1)$
VERTICAL LINE (UNDEFINED SLOPE):	$x = a$
HORIZONTAL LINE (ZERO SLOPE):	$y = b$
STANDARD FORM:	$Ax + By = C$, where A, B, and C are real numbers; A and B are not both zero.

GOAL 2 MODELING A REAL-LIFE SITUATION

EXAMPLE 4 *Writing and Using a Linear Model*

BARBECUE You are in charge of buying the hamburger and boned chicken for a barbecue. The hamburger costs $2 per pound and the boned chicken costs $3 per pound. You have $30 to spend.

a. Write an equation that models the different amounts of hamburger and chicken that you can buy.

b. Make a table and a graph that illustrate several different amounts of hamburger and chicken that you can buy.

SOLUTION

a. Model the possible combinations of hamburger and chicken.

PROBLEM SOLVING STRATEGY

| **VERBAL MODEL** | Price of hamburger | • | Weight of hamburger | + | Price of chicken | • | Weight of chicken | = | Total cost |

LABELS Price of hamburger = **2**   (dollars per pound)

Weight of hamburger = **x**   (pounds)

Price of chicken = **3**   (dollars per pound)

Weight of chicken = **y**   (pounds)

Total cost = **30**   (dollars)

ALGEBRAIC MODEL $2x + 3y = 30$ **Linear model**

b. Use the algebraic model to make a table.

Hamburger (lb), x	0	3	6	9	12	15
Chicken (lb), y	10	8	6	4	2	0

The points corresponding to these different amounts are shown in the graph. Note that as the number of pounds of hamburger you purchase increases, the number of pounds of chicken you purchase decreases, and vice versa.

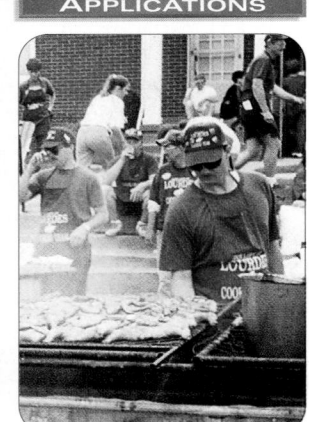

FOCUS ON APPLICATIONS

▶ **BARBECUE** The International Bar-B-Que Festival in Owensboro, Kentucky, uses over 5000 chickens in its annual cookout.

GUIDED PRACTICE

Vocabulary Check ✔

1. Name the following form of the equation of a line: $y = mx + b$.

2. Name the following form of the equation of a line: $Ax + By = C$.

Concept Check ✔

3. The equations $y = -\frac{2}{3}x + 3$ and $2x + 3y = 9$ are equivalent. Describe how you would use each equation to graph the equation.

Skill Check ✔

Write the equation in standard form with integer coefficients.

4. $y = 2x - 9$

5. $y = 6 - 5x$

6. $y = 9 + 1x$

7. $y = \frac{1}{2}x + 8$

8. $y = 7x + 3$

9. $y = -2 + \frac{3}{2}x$

Write an equation in standard form of the line that passes through the given point and has the given slope.

10. $(-3, 4)$, $m = -4$

11. $(1, -2)$, $m = 5$

12. $(2, 5)$, $m = 3$

13. $(5, -8)$, $m = -1$

14. $(-5, -6)$, $m = 3$

15. $(4, -3)$, $m = -2$

16. 🌎 **VEGETABLES** You have $10 to buy tomatoes and carrots for a salad. Tomatoes cost $2 per pound and carrots cost $1.25 per pound. Write a linear equation that models the different amounts of tomatoes x and carrots y that you can buy.

17. Copy and complete the table using the linear model in Exercise 16.

Tomatoes (lb), x	0	1.25	2.5	3.75	5
Carrots (lb), y	?	?	?	?	?

PRACTICE AND APPLICATIONS

STUDENT HELP

▶ **Extra Practice**
to help you master
skills is on p. 801.

EQUATIONS Write the equation in standard form with integer coefficients.

18. $4x - y - 7 = 0$

19. $x + 3y - 4 = 0$

20. $-4x + 5y + 16 = 0$

21. $2x - 3y - 14 = 0$

22. $x - 5 = 0$

23. $y + 3 = 0$

24. $y = -5x + 2$

25. $y = 3x - 8$

26. $y = -0.4x + 1.2$

27. $3x + 9 = \frac{7}{2}y$

28. $y = 9x + \frac{1}{2}$

29. $y = \frac{5}{2}x + 9$

30. $y = -\frac{3}{4}x + \frac{5}{4}$

31. $y = -\frac{1}{7}x + \frac{6}{7}$

32. $y = -\frac{1}{3}x - 4$

WRITING EQUATIONS Write an equation in standard form of the line that passes through the given point and has the given slope.

STUDENT HELP

▶ **HOMEWORK HELP**
Example 1: Exs. 18–32
Example 2: Exs. 33–50
Example 3: Exs. 51–61
Example 4: Exs. 64–69

33. $(-8, 3)$, $m = 2$

34. $(-2, 7)$, $m = -4$

35. $(-1, 4)$, $m = -3$

36. $(-6, -7)$, $m = -1$

37. $(3, -2)$, $m = 5$

38. $(10, 6)$, $m = 7$

39. $(2, 9)$, $m = -7$

40. $(5, -8)$, $m = 10$

41. $(7, 3)$, $m = -2$

42. $(-4, 2)$, $m = -2$

43. $(0, 3)$, $m = 1$

44. $(-3, 3)$, $m = 4$

WRITING EQUATIONS Write an equation in standard form of the line that passes through the two points.

45. $(1, 4), (5, 7)$ **46.** $(-3, -3), (7, 2)$ **47.** $(-4, 1), (2, -5)$

48. $(9, -2), (-3, 2)$ **49.** $(0, 0), (2, 0)$ **50.** $(4, -7), (5, -1)$

HORIZONTAL AND VERTICAL LINES Write an equation in standard form of the horizontal line and the vertical line.

51.   **52.**   **53.**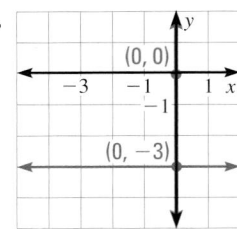

HORIZONTAL AND VERTICAL LINES Write an equation in standard form of the horizontal line and the vertical line that pass through the point.

54. $(1, 3)$ **55.** $(-4, 4)$ **56.** $(-2, -5)$ **57.** $(6, -1)$

58. $(0, 7)$ **59.** $(-9, 0)$ **60.** $(-3, 7)$ **61.** $(10, -3)$

ERROR ANALYSIS In Exercises 62 and 63, describe the error.

62.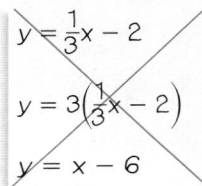

63.
$$y - 4 = -3[x - (-6)]$$
$$y - 4 = -3(x - 6)$$
$$y - 4 = -3x + 18$$
$$y = -3x + 22$$

 FEEDING HABITS The American Goldfinch uses its feet to extract seeds. Before a storm, American Goldfinches increase the amount they eat tremendously and gain weight. ▶ Source: Canadian Wildlife Service

BIRD SEED MIXTURE In Exercises 64–66, use the following information. You are buying $20 worth of bird seed that consists of two types of seed. Thistle seed attracts finches and costs $2 per pound. Dark oil sunflower seed attracts many kinds of song birds and costs $1.50 per pound.

64. Write an equation that represents the different amounts of $2 thistle seed x and $1.50 dark oil sunflower seed y that you could buy.

65. Graph the line representing the possible seed mixtures in Exercise 64.

66. Copy and complete the table. Label the points from the table on the graph created in Exercise 65.

Thistle seed (lb), x	0	2	4	6	8
Dark oil sunflower seed (lb), y	?	?	?	?	?

PRIZES In Exercises 67–69, you are in charge of buying prizes for a school contest. A one-strand rosette ribbon costs $2.00 and a three-strand rosette ribbon costs $3.00. You have $10 to spend.

67. Write an equation that represents the different numbers of one-strand and three-strand rosette ribbons that you can purchase.

68. What is the greatest number of students that can receive a ribbon?

69. What is the least number of students that can receive a ribbon?

COLOR PRINTING **In Exercises 70–74, use the following information.**
In printing, different shades of color are often formed by *overprinting* different percents of two or more primary colors such as magenta (red) and cyan (blue). For instance, combining a 40% magenta screen with a 20% cyan screen produces a more reddish purple than combining a 20% magenta screen with a 40% cyan screen. This process reduces the number of colors of ink needed.

CMYK DOT PATTERN

TWO COLOR PROCESS CHART

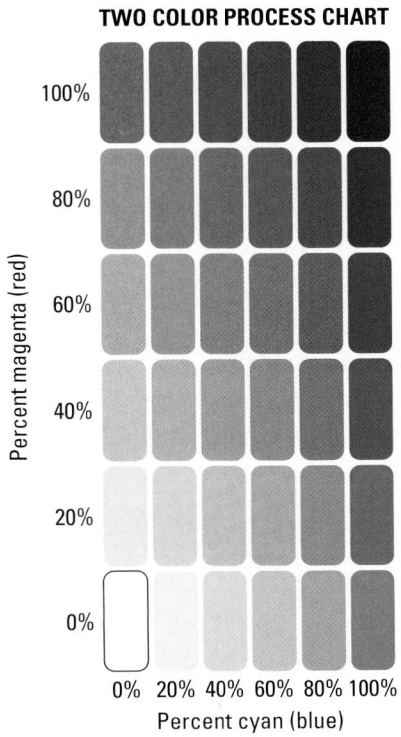

70. You are designing an advertising piece. You want the *combined* percent of magenta and cyan screens for a background color to be 60%. Write a linear equation that models the different percents of magenta and cyan you can use. Let *x* represent the percent of magenta, and let *y* represent the percent of cyan.

71. Trace the magenta-cyan color palette matrix at the right and identify the possible shades you can use for a combined percent of 60%.

72. Write a linear equation that models the different percents of magenta and cyan you can use for a background color of 80%.

73. Trace the magenta-cyan color palette matrix and identify the possible shades you can use for a combined percent of 80%.

74. How do the patterns formed by the possible shades relate to the lines whose equations you found in Exercises 70 and 72?

Test Preparation

75. **MULTIPLE CHOICE** Choose the equation in standard form of the line that passes through the point $(-1, -4)$ and has a slope of 2.

Ⓐ $2x + y = -2$ Ⓑ $-2x + y = -2$

Ⓒ $2x + y = 2$ Ⓓ $2x - y = -2$

76. **MULTIPLE CHOICE** Choose the standard form of the equation shown in the graph.

Ⓐ $3x + y = 3$

Ⓑ $-3y = x + (-9)$

Ⓒ $-x - y = 9$

Ⓓ $-x - 3y = -9$

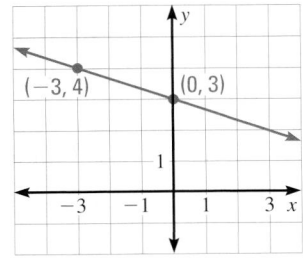

In Exercises 77–80, use the equation $2x + 7y = 14$.

77. What is the x-intercept?

78. What is the y-intercept?

79. Multiply each term in the equation by $\frac{1}{14}$.

80. Find a relationship between the denominators on the left side of the equation and the x-intercept and the y-intercept.

★ **Challenge**

FINDING EQUATIONS In Exercises 81–83, use the following information. The equation represents the intercept form of the equation of a line. In the equation, the x-intercept is a and the y-intercept is b.

$$\frac{x}{a} + \frac{y}{b} = 1$$

81. Write the intercept form of the equation of the line whose x-intercept is 2 and y-intercept is 3.

82. Write the equation in Exercise 81 in standard form.

EXTRA CHALLENGE
www.mcdougallittell.com

83. Write the equation in Exercise 82 in slope-intercept form.

MIXED REVIEW

SOLVING EQUATIONS Solve the equation. Check the result. (Review 3.4)

84. $8 + y = 3$
85. $y - 9 = 2$
86. $-6(q + 22) = 5q$

87. $2(x + 5) = 18$
88. $7 - 2a = -14$
89. $-2 + 4c = 19$

GRAPHING EQUATIONS Use a table of values to graph the equation. Label the x-intercept and the y-intercept. (Review 4.2, 4.3)

90. $y = -x + 8$
91. $y = 4x - 4$
92. $y = x + 5$

93. $y = -9 + 3x$
94. $y = -x - 1$
95. $y = 10 - x$

SLOPE-INTERCEPT FORM Graph the line that passes through the points. Write its equation in slope-intercept form. (Review 5.3 for 5.7)

96. $(2, 3), (-4, 1)$
97. $(7, 6), (5, -9)$
98. $(-5, -2), (-1, 12)$

99. $(6, -2), (-5, -8)$
100. $(2, 9), (4, 7)$
101. $(19, -2), (4, -1)$

102. $(5, -8), (7, -3)$
103. $(14, -9), (-5, -3)$
104. $(-5, 9), (5, 4)$

105. 🌎 **BUYING A CD PLAYER** You have $125.79 to spend for a CD player. The sales tax is 6%. What is your price limit for the CD player? (Review 3.6)

106. 🌎 **BUYING A CALENDAR** You have $15 to spend for a calendar. The sales tax is 8.5%. What is your price limit for the calendar? (Review 3.6)

107. 🌎 **LEAVING A TIP** You leave a $1.50 tip for a lunch of $6.00. What percent tip did you leave? (Review 3.8)

108. 🌎 **SHOPPING** A coat regularly sells for $84. You buy the coat on sale and save $10. What percent is the discount? (Review 3.8)

▶ ACTIVITY 5.7

Developing Concepts

GROUP ACTIVITY
Work in a small group.

MATERIALS
• toothpicks
• graph paper

Investigating Linear Modeling

▶ **QUESTION** How can you decide whether data can be represented by a linear model?

▶ **EXPLORING THE CONCEPT**

The following figures represent the first five stages in a sequence.

1 Copy and complete the table showing the number of toothpicks used to make each figure.

Number of squares in figure	1	2	3	4	5
Number of toothpicks	4	?	?	?	?

2 Make a scatter plot of the data. Put the number of squares on the horizontal axis. What do you observe about the data points?

3 Choose two points on the line and calculate the slope.

4 Write the equation of the line in slope-intercept form.

5 Use the equation to predict the number of toothpicks necessary to construct a figure with 10 squares. Check your result.

▶ **DRAWING CONCLUSIONS**

The figures show the first three stages in a sequence. Each group member should choose one sequence and answer Exercises 1–4 individually.

A.

B.

C.

1. Use toothpicks to make the next three figures in the sequence.

2. Make a table of the results. For each stage, give the number of small squares or small triangles in the figure and the number of toothpicks used.

3. Make a scatter plot of the number of small squares or small triangles as a function of the stage number.

4. Make a scatter plot of the number of toothpicks as a function of the number of small squares or small triangles.

5. Compare your scatter plots with those of others in your group. Which of the sequences can be modeled with a linear model? Which cannot? Explain.

6. If the data appear to fit a linear model, find an equation of the line.

Predicting with Linear Models

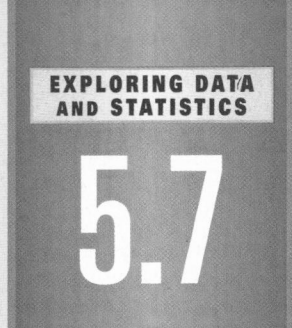

GOAL 1 DECIDING WHEN TO USE A LINEAR MODEL

Two of your major goals in this course are to learn about different types of models and to learn which type of model to use in a specific real-life situation.

In this lesson you will learn how to decide when a linear model can be used to represent real-life data.

EXAMPLE 1 *Which Data Set is More Linear?*

The amount (in millions of dollars) spent on advertising in broadcast television and on the Internet from 1995 through 2001 is given in the table. Which data are better modeled with a linear model?

Year	1995	1997	1999	2001
Broadcast television advertising expenditures (in millions)	32,720	36,893	41,230*	46,140*
Internet advertising expenditures (in millions)	24	1300	15,000*	46,000*

▶ Sources: Veronis, Suhler & Associates Communications Industry Forecast and *Activ* Media

*Projected data

SOLUTION

A good way to decide whether data can be represented by a linear model is to draw a scatter plot of the data.

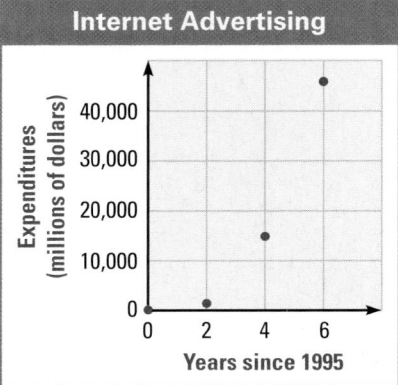

From the two scatter plots, you can see that the broadcast television data fall almost exactly on a line. The Internet data are much less linear. That is, the data points don't lie as close to a straight line.

What you should learn

GOAL 1 Determine whether a linear model is appropriate.

GOAL 2 Use a linear model to make a **real-life** prediction, such as spending on advertising in **Example 3**.

Why you should learn it

▼ To predict the cost of college tuition in the future in **Exs. 29 and 30**.

Advertising

EXAMPLE 2 *Writing a Linear Model*

Write a linear model for the amounts spent on television advertising given in the table in Example 1.

SOLUTION

METHOD 1 Make a scatter plot of the data and draw the line that best fits the points. The line does not need to pass through any of the data points.

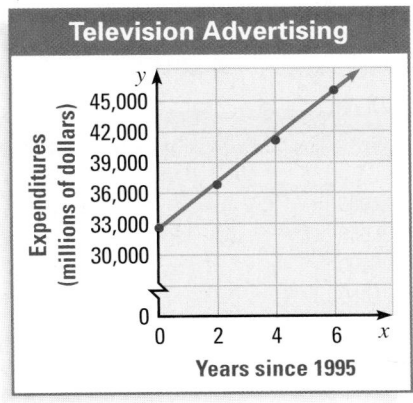

STUDENT HELP

▸ **Look Back**
For help with best-fitting lines, see p. 293.

Find two points on the best-fitting line such as (0, 32,720) and (6, 46,140). Use these points to find the slope of the best-fitting line.

$$m = \frac{y_2 - y_1}{x_2 - x_1} = \frac{46,140 - 32,720}{6 - 0} \approx 2236.67 \approx 2237$$

Using a *y*-intercept of $b = 32,720$ and a slope of $m = 2237$ you can write an equation of the line.

$y = mx + b$ **Write slope-intercept form.**

$y = 2237x + 32,720$ **Substitute 2237 for *m* and 32,720 for *b*.**

▸ A linear model for the amounts spent on television advertising is $y = 2237x + 32,720$.

METHOD 2 You can use a graphing calculator and follow the procedure given on page 299.

STUDENT HELP

▸ **Study Tip**
In Example 2, notice that the two methods give slightly different results. The equation found using the graphing calculator is the more accurate model.

The linear regression program gives you the results shown at the right. A linear model for spending on television advertising is $y = 2229.85x + 32,556.2$. The *r*-value of about 0.999 indicates that the linear model is a very good fit.

STUDENT HELP

HOMEWORK HELP
Visit our Web site
www.mcdougallittell.com
for extra examples.

INTERPOLATION AND EXTRAPOLATION When you use a linear model to estimate data points that are not given, you are using *linear interpolation* or *linear extrapolation*. **Linear interpolation** is a method of estimating the coordinates of a point that lies between two given data points. **Linear extrapolation** is a method of estimating the coordinates of a point that lies to the right or left of all of the given data points.

EXAMPLE 3 *Linear Interpolation and Linear Extrapolation*

ADVERTISING Use the linear model you found in Example 2 to estimate the amount spent on advertising in broadcast television in the given year. Tell whether you use *linear interpolation* or *linear extrapolation*.

a. 1996   **b.** 2015

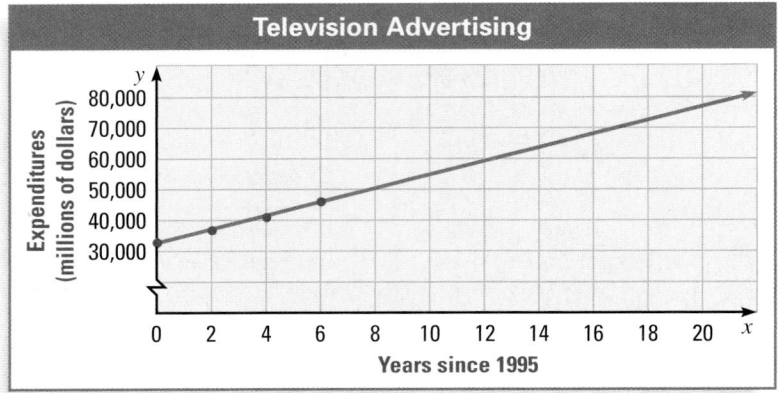

Television Advertising

a. You used data for 1995 and 2001 to write the model. Because 1996 is between these two dates, you will use *linear interpolation*. Because x represents the number of years since 1995, you can estimate the amount spent in 1996 by substituting $x = 1$ into the linear model from Example 2.

$y = 2237x + 32{,}720$ **Write linear model.**

$= 2237(1) + 32{,}720$ **Substitute 1 for x.**

$= 34{,}957$ **Simplify.**

▶ The model predicts that almost $35,000 million, or $35 billion, was spent in 1996.

b. Because 2015 is to the right of all of the given data, you will use *linear extrapolation*. You can estimate the amount spent in 2015 by substituting $x = 20$ into the linear model from Example 2.

$y = 2237x + 32{,}720$ **Write linear model.**

$= 2237(20) + 32{,}720$ **Substitute 20 for x.**

$= 77{,}460$ **Simplify.**

▶ The model predicts that about $77,000 million, or about $77 billion, will be spent in 2015.

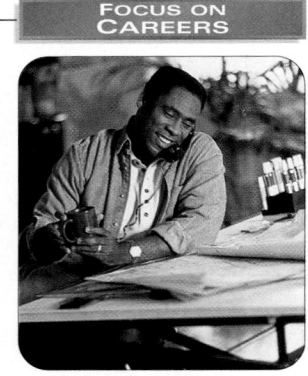

GUIDED PRACTICE

Vocabulary Check ✓

1. Explain the difference between linear interpolation and linear extrapolation.

Concept Check ✓

2. Explain how to decide whether a data set can be represented by a linear model.

Tell whether it is reasonable for the graph to be represented by a linear model.

3.

4.

5.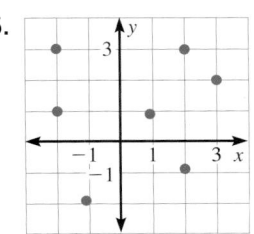

Skill Check ✓

🌐 **BOTTLED WATER** In Exercises 6–10, use the data on bottled water consumption per person.

6. Make a scatter plot of the data.

7. Write a linear model for the data.

Use your model to estimate the consumption of bottled water in the given year. Tell whether you use *linear interpolation* or *linear extrapolation*.

8. 1994   **9.** 2010   **10.** 1979

Year	Water (in gallons)
1980	2.4
1985	4.5
1990	8.0
1995	11.6

▶ Source: *Statistical Abstract of the United States*

PRACTICE AND APPLICATIONS

STUDENT HELP

▶ **Extra Practice**
to help you master skills is on p. 801.

REPRESENTING DATA Tell whether it is reasonable for the graph to be represented by a linear model.

11.

12.

13.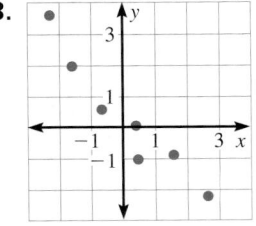

STUDENT HELP

▶ **HOMEWORK HELP**
Example 1: Exs. 11–16, 17–19
Example 2: Exs. 20, 23, 25
Example 3: Exs. 21, 22, 24, 26, 27

14.

15.

16.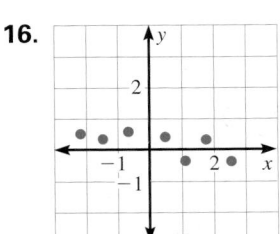

Year	1975	1980	1985	1990	1995
Indoor screens (in thousands)	11	14	18	23	27
Drive-in screens (in thousands)	4	4	3	1	1

🔄 **DATA UPDATE** of Motion Picture Association of America, Inc. data at www.mcdougallittell.com

17. Make a scatter plot of the number of indoor movie screens in terms of the year t. Let t represent the number of years since 1975.

18. Make a scatter plot of the number of drive-in movie screens in terms of the year t. Let t represent the number of years since 1975.

19. Which data are better modeled with a linear model?

20. Write a linear model for the number of indoor movie screens.

21. Use the linear model to estimate the number of indoor movie screens in 2005.

22. Use the linear model to estimate the number of indoor movie screens in 1989. Did you use *linear interpolation* or *linear extrapolation*?

🌐 **BOOKS AND MAPS** In Exercises 23 and 24, use the table which shows the number of dollars (in billions) spent on books and maps in the United States from 1990 through 1995.

Years since 1990	0	1	2	3	4	5
Billions of dollars	16.5	16.9	17.7	19.0	20.1	20.9

▶ Source: U.S. Bureau of Economic Analysis

23. Write a linear model for the amount spent on books and maps.

24. Use the linear model to estimate the amount spent in 2005. Did you use *linear interpolation* or *linear extrapolation*?

🌐 **TOYS AND SPORT SUPPLIES** In Exercises 25–27, use the table which shows the number of dollars (in billions) spent on toys and sport supplies in the United States from 1990 through 1995.

25. Write a linear model for the amount spent on toys and sport supplies.

26. Use the linear model to estimate the amount spent in 1992. Did you use *linear interpolation* or *linear extrapolation*?

27. Use the linear model to estimate the amount spent in 2005. Did you use *linear interpolation* or *linear extrapolation*?

Years since 1990	Billions of dollars
0	31.6
1	32.8
2	?
3	36.5
4	40.1
5	42.7

▶ Source: U.S. Bureau of Economic Analysis

FOCUS ON APPLICATIONS

🌐 **SPORTS EQUIPMENT** Life jackets should be chosen by the type of water activities, as well as the expected water conditions. Type I can be used in rough, offshore water while Type III are appropriate for calm, inland waters.

COLLEGE TUITION In Exercises 28–30, use the table which shows the average tuition for attending a private and a public four-year college.

Year	Public college	Private college
1990	$2,035	$10,348
1991	$2,159	$11,379
1992	$2,410	$12,192
1993	$2,604	$13,055
1994	$2,820	$13,874
1995	$2,977	$14,537
1996	$3,151	$15,581

▶ Source: U.S. National Center for Education Statistics

28. Write a linear model of the tuition for attending a public and of the tuition for attending a private college.

29. Use linear extrapolation to estimate the tuition for attending a public college when you graduate from high school.

30. Use linear extrapolation to estimate the tuition for attending a private college when you graduate from high school.

Test Preparation

MULTI-STEP PROBLEM In Exercises 31–34, use the following information. You are the produce manager at a new grocery store. It is your job to decide how much fruit to order for the week of the grand opening. You find a table that shows yearly per person consumption of pounds of bananas.

31. What was the average *weekly* consumption per person of bananas in 1995? What was the average *monthly* consumption?

32. Write a linear model for the average weekly consumption per person of bananas in pounds.

33. Use the linear model to estimate the average weekly consumption per person of bananas in pounds for this year.

Year	Pounds of bananas
1990	24.4
1991	25.1
1992	27.3
1993	26.8
1994	28.1
1995	27.4

▶ Source: U.S. Department of Agriculture

34. If you expect 1750 customers for the week of the grand opening, how many pounds of bananas should you order?

★ Challenge

In Exercises 35–37, use the data from Exercises 28–30 and a graphing calculator. Let *x* represent years since 1990 and let *y* represent the average tuition at a public college.

35. Enter the data for the tuition for public colleges and graph the equation.

36. Locate the *x*-intercept of the graph. What does this point represent?

37. *Writing* What are the reasonable limits of linear extrapolation in terms of college tuition?

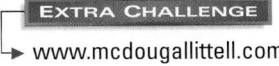

WRITING INEQUALITIES Graph the numbers on a number line. Then write two inequalities that compare the two numbers. (Review 2.1 for 6.1)

38. -7 and 3

39. -2 and -1

40. 12 and -12

41. $-\frac{1}{2}$ and $\frac{3}{2}$

42. -7 and 2

43. -3 and $-\frac{7}{2}$

SLOPE-INTERCEPT FORM Write an equation of the line in slope-intercept form. (Review 5.1)

44. The slope is 2; the y-intercept is -5. **45.** The slope is $\frac{1}{2}$; the y-intercept is -8.

46. The slope is -4; the y-intercept is 7. **47.** The slope is -2; the y-intercept is -6.

WRITING EQUATIONS Write an equation in slope-intercept form of the line that passes through the point and has the given slope. (Review 5.2)

48. $(6, 5)$, $m = 2$

49. $(-3, 7)$, $m = 7$

50. $(8, 2)$, $m = 7$

51. $(8, 4)$, $m = -5$

52. $(3, 1)$, $m = 7$

53. $(-8, 7)$, $m = 2$

54. FEATHER GROWTH At nine days old, a flight feather of a night heron is 17 millimeters. At 30 days, the flight feather is 150 millimeters. Write a linear model that gives feather length f in terms of age a. (Review 5.5)

QUIZ 3

Self-Test for Lessons 5.6 and 5.7

Write the equation in standard form with integer coefficients. (Lesson 5.6)

1. $y = \frac{1}{2}x + 3$

2. $3y + 9x - 18 = 0$

3. $6y - 2x = 8$

4. $y = 9x + 12$

5. $y = \frac{2}{3}x + 6$

6. $-8y = \frac{1}{2} - 7x$

Write an equation in standard form of the line that passes through the point and has the given slope. (Lesson 5.6)

7. $(6, -8)$, $m = -2$

8. $(4, 1)$, $m = -\frac{1}{2}$

9. $(1, 5)$, $m = -3$

10. $(-3, -1)$, $m = 2$

11. $(-12, 4)$, $m = 3$

12. $(-16, -2)$, $m = 6$

🌐 **LIFE EXPECTANCY** In Exercises 13–15, use the table on projected life expectancy at birth. (Lesson 5.7)

13. Write a linear equation of the data.

14. Interpolate the life expectancy for a baby born in 1989.

15. Extrapolate the life expectancy for a baby born in 2015.

Birth year	Life expectancy
1985	74.7
1990	75.4
1995	76.3
2000*	76.7
2005*	77.3
2010*	77.9

▶ Source: U.S. National Center for Health Statistics *Projected

Chapter Summary

WHAT did you learn?

Write an equation of a line in slope-intercept form.

- given its slope and its *y*-intercept **(5.1)**
- given its slope and one of its points **(5.2)**
- given two of its points **(5.3)**

Write equations of perpendicular lines. **(5.3)**

Fit a line to data. **(5.4)**

Write an equation of a line in point-slope form. **(5.5)**

Write an equation of a line in standard form. **(5.6)**

Create a linear model for a real-life situation. **(5.1–5.6)**

Predict using a linear model. **(5.7)**

WHY did you learn it?

Calculate the cost of a phone call. **(p. 275)**

Predict the number of vacations trips in 2005. **(p. 281)**

Estimate height at an archaeological dig. **(p. 287)**

Write equations for sides of geometric figures. **(p. 286)**

Represent winning Olympic discus throws. **(p. 294)**

Find the optimal running pace for a given temperature. **(p. 302)**

Plan possible purchases. **(p. 310)**

Make predictions and estimates. **(pp. 274 and 281)**

Estimate the amount spent in 2015 on advertising. **(p. 318)**

How does Chapter 5 fit into the BIGGER PICTURE of algebra?

In this chapter you studied techniques for writing equations of lines. Using the slope-intercept form that you saw in Chapter 4, you learned the point-slope form and standard form of an equation. You used many techniques you learned in earlier chapters: the problem-solving strategies in Chapter 1; the rules of simplification in Chapter 2; the equation solving in Chapter 3; and the graphing methods in Chapter 4.

Knowing which form of a linear equation is best to use is a basic problem solving strategy you will continue to apply in the following chapters.

STUDY STRATEGY

How did you use your practice test?

A practice test you may have written using the **Study Strategy** on page 272 may have begun like this one.

Practice Test

Lesson 5.1 Write an equation of the line in slope-intercept form.

1. $m = 3; b = -2$

2. $m = -\frac{1}{2}; b = 5$

Lesson 5.2 Write an equation of the line that passes through the point and has the given slope.

4. $(2, 6), m = \frac{2}{3}$

5. $(-3, -3), m = -1$

Chapter Review

- slope-intercept form, p. 273
- best-fitting line, p. 292
- positive correlation, p. 295
- negative correlation, p. 295
- point-slope form, p. 300
- standard form, p. 308
- linear interpolation, p. 318
- linear extrapolation, p. 318

5.1   WRITING LINEAR EQUATIONS: SLOPE-INTERCEPT FORM

Examples on pp. 273–275

EXAMPLES   Write an equation of the line with a slope of $\frac{1}{2}$ and a y-intercept of -2.

$y = mx + b$ Write slope-intercept form.

$y = \frac{1}{2}x - 2$ Substitute $\frac{1}{2}$ for m and -2 for b.

Write an equation of the line with the given slope and *y*-intercept.

1. $m = 2; b = -2$ **2.** $m = -\frac{1}{2}; b = 5$ **3.** $m = -8; b = -3$

5.2   WRITING LINEAR EQUATIONS GIVEN THE SLOPE AND A POINT

Examples on pp. 279–281

EXAMPLES   Write an equation of the line through $(2, -1)$ with a slope of 3.

$y = mx + b$ Write slope-intercept form.

$-1 = 3(2) + b$ Substitute -1 for y, 2 for x, and 3 for m.

$-7 = b$ Simplify and solve for b.

$y = 3x - 7$ Substitute 3 for m and -7 for b in slope-intercept form.

Write an equation of the line that passes through the point and has the given slope.

4. $(4, -3), m = 6$ **5.** $(-9, 4), m = 2$ **6.** $(-3, 2), m = -1$

5.3   WRITING LINEAR EQUATIONS GIVEN TWO POINTS

Examples on pp. 285–287

EXAMPLES   Write an equation of the line that passes through $(-2, -6)$ and $(3, 4)$.

$m = \dfrac{y_2 - y_1}{x_2 - x_1} = \dfrac{4 - (-6)}{3 - (-2)} = \dfrac{10}{5} = 2$ Find the slope of the line.

Now use the slope $m = 2$ and one of the given points to write an equation of the line as in the Example for Lesson 5.2 above. An equation is $y = 2x - 2$.

Write the slope-intercept form of an equation of the line that passes through the points.

7. $(4, -9), (-3, 2)$ **8.** $(1, 8), (-2, -1)$ **9.** $(2, 5), (-8, 2)$

10. Write the slope-intercept form of an equation of the line perpendicular to the line in Exercise 7 with a y-intercept of -3.

5.4   FITTING A LINE TO DATA

Examples on pp. 292–295

EXAMPLES On the scatter plot, sketch a line to approximate the data. Choose two points on your line, say $(11, 5)$ and $(6, -5)$. Find the slope.

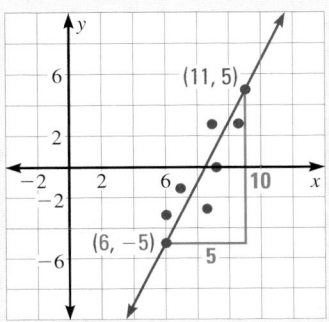

$$m = \frac{y_2 - y_1}{x_2 - x_1} = \frac{5 - (-5)}{11 - 6} = \frac{10}{5} = 2$$

$y = mx + b$ Write slope-intercept form.

$-5 = 2(6) + b$ Substitute for *y*, *x*, and *m*.

$-17 = b$ Solve for *b*.

An equation that approximates the best-fitting line is $y = 2x - 17$.

Draw a scatter plot of the data. Find an equation of the line that corresponds closely to the data and that best fits the data.

11.

x	−1	−3	5	9	12
y	−1	−4	9	20	25

12.

x	2	1	−2	−4	−6
y	10	5	0	−5	−10

5.5   POINT-SLOPE FORM OF A LINEAR EQUATION

Examples on pp. 300–302

EXAMPLES Write an equation of the line through $(5, -4)$ and $(-3, 4)$.

$$m = \frac{y_2 - y_1}{x_2 - x_1} = \frac{4 - (-4)}{-3 - 5} = \frac{8}{-8} = -1$$

$y - y_1 = m(x - x_1)$ Write point-slope form.

$y - (-4) = (-1)(x - 5)$ Substitute for *m*, x_1, and y_1.

$y = -x + 1$ Simplify.

Write an equation in point-slope form of the line that passes through the two points. Then rewrite the equation in slope-intercept form.

13. $(-4, 4), (2, 5)$ **14.** $(-2, 3), (5, 0)$ **15.** $(1, -2), (-1, 8)$

THE STANDARD FORM OF A LINEAR EQUATION

Examples on pp. 308–310

EXAMPLES The standard form of a linear equation is $Ax + By = C$.

Write the equation $y = -\frac{2}{3}x + 6$ in standard form with integer coefficients.

$$y = -\frac{2}{3}x + 6 \qquad \text{Write given form.}$$

$$3y = -2x + 18 \qquad \text{Multiply each side by 3.}$$

$$2x + 3y = 18 \qquad \text{Add 2x to each side.}$$

Rewrite the equation in standard form with integer coefficients.

16. $y = 2x + 9$ 　　　　**17.** $3y = -8x + 2$ 　　　　**18.** $2y = -2x + 6$

19. $y = -\frac{1}{3}x + \frac{2}{3}$ 　　　**20.** $y = \frac{3}{4}x + \frac{1}{2}$ 　　　**21.** $\frac{1}{2}y = \frac{2}{3}x - 2$

PREDICTING WITH LINEAR MODELS

Examples on pp. 316–318

EXAMPLES You can use linear models to make predictions. Use the graph showing the number of World Wide Web users (in millions) for different years, with x representing the number of years since 1996. Predict the number of World Wide Web users in the year 2005.

$$m = \frac{66 - 34}{3 - 1} = 16 \qquad \text{Find slope using} \\ \text{(1, 34) and (3, 66).}$$

$$34 = (16)1 + b \qquad \text{Substitute 34 for } y, \text{ 1 for } x, \\ \text{and 16 for } m \text{ in } y = mx + b.$$

$$b = 18 \qquad \text{Simplify and solve for } b.$$

$$y = 16x + 18 \qquad \text{Write equation with } m \text{ and } b.$$

$$y = 16(9) + 18 \qquad \text{Substitute 9 to represent 2005.}$$

$$y = 162 \qquad \text{Simplify and solve.}$$

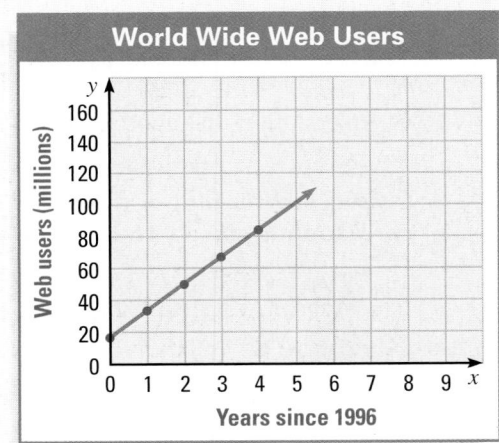

World Wide Web Users

Web users (millions) vs. Years since 1996

▶ Source: IDC Link

Using the linear model $y = 16x + 18$, you can estimate the number of World Wide Web users in 2005 to be 162 million.

Use the linear model in the Example above to estimate the number of World Wide Web users in the given year. Tell whether you use a *linear interpolation* or *linear extrapolation*.

22. 1995 　　　　**23.** 2010 　　　　**24.** 2002 　　　　**25.** 2006

Chapter Test

Write an equation of the line with the given slope and *y*-intercept. Write the equation in slope-intercept form.

1. $m = 2, b = -1$

2. $m = -4, b = 3$

3. $m = 6, b = 9$

4. $m = \frac{1}{4}, b = -3$

5. $m = -3, b = 3$

6. $m = 0, b = 4$

Write an equation of the line that passes through the given point and has the given slope. Write the equation in slope-intercept form.

7. $(2, 6), m = 2$

8. $(3, -9), m = -5$

9. $(-5, -6), m = -3$

10. $(1, 8), m = -4$

11. $(4, -2), m = \frac{1}{2}$

12. $\left(\frac{1}{3}, -5\right), m = 8$

Graph the line that passes through the points. Then write an equation of the line in slope-intercept form.

13. $(-3, 2), (4, -1)$

14. $(6, 2), (8, -4)$

15. $(-2, 5), (2, 4)$

16. $(-2, -8), (-1, 0)$

17. $(-5, 2), (2, 4)$

18. $(9, -1), (1, -9)$

19. Write an equation of a line that is perpendicular to $y = -2x + 6$ and passes through $(-4, 7)$.

In Exercises 20–25, rewrite the equation in standard form with integer coefficients.

20. $4y = 24 + 2x$

21. $y = 7x + 8$

22. $6y = -18x + 3$

23. $\frac{1}{2} - x = 9y$

24. $5y = 25x$

25. $-2y + \frac{1}{2}x = 4$

26. Rewrite the equation $y = \frac{5}{13}x + 4$ in standard form with integer coefficients.

27. **NICKELS AND DIMES** Maria needs \$2.20 to buy a magazine. The only money she has is a jar of nickels and dimes. Write an equation in standard form for the different amounts of nickels x and dimes y she could use.

28. **MONTHLY PAY** A salesperson for an appliance store earns a monthly pay of \$1250 plus a 4% commission on the sales. Write an equation in slope-intercept form that gives the total monthly pay y in terms of sales x.

CELLULAR PHONE INDUSTRY **In Exercises 29–33, use the following information. The table shows the number of employees in the cellular telephone industry in the United States from 1990 through 1995.**

▶ Source: Cellular Telecommunications Industry Association

29. Make a scatter plot and fit a line to the data.

30. Write an equation of the line in slope-intercept form.

31. Use the linear model to estimate the number of employees in 1994. Did you use *linear interpolation* or *linear extrapolation*?

32. Use the linear model to estimate the number of employees in 2004. Did you use *linear interpolation* or *linear extrapolation*?

33. Use the linear model to estimate the year in which the number of employees was 0. Did you use *linear interpolation* or *linear extrapolation*? Is this a realistic prediction? Why or why not?

Cellular Telephone Industry	
Years since 1990	Employees
0	21,400
1	26,300
2	34,300
3	39,800
4	?
5	68,200

Chapter Standardized Test

▶ **TEST-TAKING STRATEGY** Avoid spending too much time on one question. Skip questions that are too difficult for you, and spend no more than a few minutes on each question.

1. **MULTIPLE CHOICE** What is an equation of the line that passes through the points $(-4, 2)$ and $(6, 6)$?

   (A) $y = \frac{2}{5}x + \frac{18}{5}$ **(B)** $y = \frac{2}{5}x - \frac{12}{5}$

   (C) $y = 2x - 6$ **(D)** $y = \frac{2}{5}x - \frac{18}{5}$

   (E) $y = 2x + 18$

2. **MULTIPLE CHOICE** An equation of the line perpendicular to the line $y = -2x - 3$ with a y-intercept of $-\frac{3}{4}$ is _?_.

   (A) $y = -2x + \frac{3}{4}$ **(B)** $y = -2x - \frac{3}{4}$

   (C) $y = 2x - \frac{3}{4}$ **(D)** $y = \frac{1}{2}x - \frac{3}{4}$

   (E) $y = -\frac{1}{2}x + \frac{3}{4}$

3. **MULTIPLE CHOICE** A line with a slope of -1 passes through the point $(2, -1)$. If $(-4, p)$ is another point on the line, what is the value of p?

   (A) -5 **(B)** -1 **(C)** 1

   (D) 2 **(E)** 5

4. **MULTIPLE CHOICE** What is an equation of a line that best fits the scatter plot?

   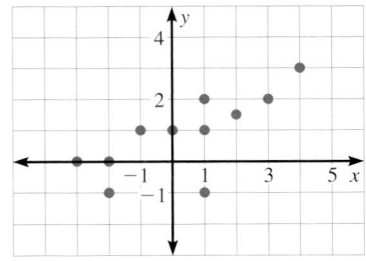

   (A) $y = \frac{1}{2}x + 1$ **(B)** $y = 1$

   (C) $y = -\frac{1}{2}x + 1$ **(D)** $y = x + 1$

   (E) $y = x - 1$

5. **MULTIPLE CHOICE** A bike rental shop charges \$8 to rent a bike, plus \$1.50 for every half hour you ride. If the shop charges you and your friend a total of \$25, how many hours did you each ride? (Assume that you each rode a separate bike for an equal amount of time.)

   (A) 1   **(B)** 1.5

   (C) 2   **(D)** 2.5

   (E) 3

6. **MULTIPLE CHOICE** What is an equation of the line that passes through the point $(4, -5)$ and has a slope of $\frac{1}{2}$?

   (A) $y = x - 5$ **(B)** $y = -\frac{1}{2}x + 7$

   (C) $y = \frac{1}{2}x + 7$ **(D)** $y = -\frac{1}{2}x - 7$

   (E) $y = \frac{1}{2}x - 7$

7. **MULTIPLE CHOICE** An equation of the line whose x-intercept is 3 and whose y-intercept is 5 is _?_.

   (A) $y = \frac{5}{3}x + 5$ **(B)** $y = -\frac{3}{5}x + 5$

   (C) $y = -\frac{5}{3}x + 5$ **(D)** $y = \frac{3}{5}x + 5$

   (E) $y = -\frac{5}{3}x - 5$

8. **MULTIPLE CHOICE** Which two points lie on the line $y = -2x + 7$?

   (A) $(0, 7), (1, -5)$ **(B)** $(4, 0), (-2, -8)$

   (C) $(-3, -4), (2, 6)$ **(D)** $(-1, 9), (3, 1)$

   (E) $(2, -1), (-3, -11)$

9. **MULTIPLE CHOICE** Which equation is in standard form with integer coefficients?

   (A) $x - \frac{1}{2}y = \frac{5}{2}$ **(B)** $y = 2x + -5$

   (C) $y = -5 + 2x$ **(D)** $x = \frac{1}{2}y + \frac{5}{2}$

   (E) $-2x + y = -5$

10. MULTIPLE CHOICE An equation in standard form of the line that passes through the point $(-6, 1)$ and has a slope of -2 is ? .

   (A) $2x + y = 13$ (B) $2x - y = 11$

   (C) $2x + y = -11$ (D) $2x + y = -13$

   (E) $2x - y = -13$

11. MULTIPLE CHOICE An equation in standard form of a line that is perpendicular to the line that passes through the points $(3, -4)$ and $(6, 1)$ is ? .

   (A) $5x + 3y - 6 = 0$ (B) $x + 3y - 6 = 0$

   (C) $y = \dfrac{-3}{5}x + 6$ (D) $3x + 5y = 6$

   (E) $5y = -3x + 6$

QUANTITATIVE COMPARISON In Exercises 12–14, choose the statement that is true.

   (A) The number in Column A is greater.

   (B) The number in Column B is greater.

   (C) The two numbers are equal.

   (D) The relationship cannot be determined from the information given.

	Column A	Column B
12.	slope of $2x + 3y = 12$	slope of $-5y = 6 + 10x$
13.	y-intercept of $2x + 3y = 12$	y-intercept of $-5y = 6 + 10x$
14.	x-intercept of $\dfrac{2}{3}x + 6y = 8$	x-intercept of $3y = -7 + 2x$

MULTI-STEP PROBLEM In Exercises 15–20, all students in a class were surveyed after they took a chapter test. The teacher wanted to know if studying at home produced good test grades. After the survey was taken, the following data were recorded in a table.

Hours spent studying the chapter	0	.25	.5	.75	1	1.5	2	3	5	7
Average grade on the chapter test	29	32	35	38	40	47	54	66	79	89

15. Make a scatter plot of the data.

16. Make a linear model of the average grade on the chapter test based on the number of hours spent studying the chapter at home.

17. If you study for four hours, approximately what grade can you expect to earn on the chapter test according to the model?

18. Use linear extrapolation to estimate the number of hours needed to earn a grade of 93 on the chapter test.

19. Use linear interpolation to find the average grade on the chapter test by students who study for 4.5 hours.

20. *Writing* If you were the parent of a child studying this chapter, what advice would you give your child about studying at home for the chapter test? Explain your reasoning.

SOLVING AND GRAPHING LINEAR INEQUALITIES

▶ *How are sounds produced?*

APPLICATION: Music

Musical instruments produce vibrations in the air that we hear as music. Not all instruments produce these vibrations in the same way, and different instruments produce sounds in different frequencies.

A flute player blows across an opening in the flute, which causes the air inside to vibrate. A clarinet or saxophone player blows on a wooden reed whose vibrations cause the air inside to vibrate.

Frequency Ranges of Instruments

Think & Discuss

1. Estimate the frequency range of each instrument.

2. Which of these instruments has the greatest frequency range?

3. Estimate the frequency range that a flute can play that a soprano clarinet cannot.

Learn More About It

You will write inequalities to describe frequency ranges in Exercises 66 and 67 on p. 338.

APPLICATION LINK Visit www.mcdougallittell.com for more information about music.

Study Guide

PREVIEW

What's the chapter about?

Chapter 6 is about **solving and graphing linear inequalities**, many of which model real-life applications. In Chapter 6 you'll learn

- how to solve and graph inequalities.
- how to solve and graph absolute-value equations and inequalities.
- how to use measures of central tendency and statistical plots.

> ### KEY VOCABULARY
>
> ▶ **Review**
> - equation, p. 24
> - inequality, p. 26
> - absolute value, p. 65
> - graph of an equation, p. 210
>
> ▶ **New**
> - graph of a linear inequality, p. 334
> - compound inequality, p. 346
> - solution of a linear inequality, p. 360
>
> - stem-and-leaf plot, p. 368
> - mean, median, mode, p. 369
> - box-and-whisker plot, p. 375

PREPARE

Are you ready for the chapter?

SKILL REVIEW Do these exercises to review skills that you'll apply in this chapter. See the given **reference page** if there is something you don't understand.

> **STUDENT HELP**
>
> ▶ **Study Tip**
> "Student Help" boxes throughout the chapter give you study tips and tell you where to look for extra help in this book and on the Internet.

Decide whether 5 is a solution of the inequality. (Review Example 4, p. 26)

1. $3x + 2 < 18$ **2.** $x - 3 > 2$ **3.** $4 + 4x \geq 24$

4. $1 + 2x \leq 5$ **5.** $8 + x < 12$ **6.** $2x^2 > 45$

Solve the equation. (Review Examples 1–3, pp. 145–146)

7. $\frac{1}{2}x + 10 = 15$ **8.** $\frac{2}{3}x - 4 = 12$ **9.** $20 = 2(x + 1)$

10. $4x + 5x - 1 = 53$ **11.** $6x - 2x + 8 = 36$ **12.** $4(5 - x) = 12$

Graph the equation. (Review Examples, pp. 211, 219, and 242)

13. $y = -4x$ **14.** $y = -2x + 5$ **15.** $2y - x = 4$ **16.** $-2x + y = 3$

STUDY STRATEGY

Here's a study strategy!

Showing Your Work

Show all the steps when you do your homework. Showing your work makes it easier to find the place where you made a mistake. Write corrections next to the errors.

● ACTIVITY 6.1

Developing Concepts

Investigating Inequalities

GROUP ACTIVITY
Work in a small group.

MATERIALS
• paper
• pencil

▶ **QUESTION** How do operations change an inequality?

▶ **EXPLORING THE CONCEPT**

❶ Each member of your group should write a different inequality by choosing two numbers and placing $>$ or $<$ between them to show which is greater.

❷ Apply each rule below to both sides of your inequality. Write the correct inequality symbol between the two resulting numbers.

  a. Add 4.   **b.** Subtract 4.

  c. Multiply by 4.   **d.** Divide by 4.

  e. Multiply by -4.   **f.** Divide by -4.

❸ In **Step 2**, when did you have to change the direction of the inequality symbol?

❹ Use your inequality from **Step 1**. Repeat **Step 2**, but change 4 and -4 to some other positive and negative numbers. When did you have to change the direction of the inequality symbol?

▶ **DRAWING CONCLUSIONS**

In Exercises 1–6, predict whether the direction of the inequality symbol will change when you apply the given rule. Check your prediction.

  1. $4 < 9$; add 7   **2.** $15 > 12$; subtract -4 **3.** $4 > -3$; multiply by 5

  4. $2 > -11$; add -7 **5.** $-6 < 2$; divide by -3 **6.** $1 < 8$; multiply by -10

7. Copy and complete the table.

Does the inequality symbol change directions?		
	a positive number	a negative number
Add	?	?
Subtract	?	?
Multiply by	?	?
Divide by	?	?

Apply the given rule to solve the inequality.

  8. $x + 3 > 9$; subtract 3   **9.** $x + 7 \leq 12$; add -7

  10. $4x \geq 15$; divide by 4   **11.** $-3x > 11$; divide by -3

  12. $2x < 11$; multiply by $\frac{1}{2}$ **13.** $-\frac{1}{3}x \leq 12$; multiply by -3

  14. $x + 6 < 15$; subtract 6   **15.** $x - 2 \geq 90$; add 2

  16. $5x \leq 25$; divide by 5   **17.** $-6x > 30$; multiply by $-\frac{1}{6}$

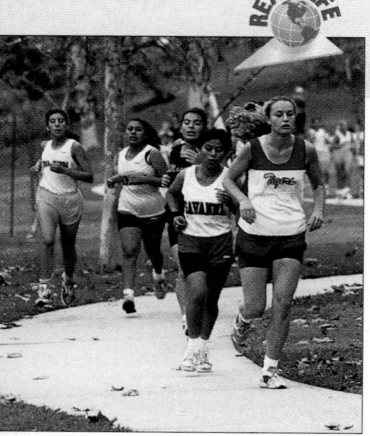

GOAL 1 GRAPHING LINEAR INEQUALITIES

The **graph** of a linear inequality in one variable is the set of points on a number line that represent all solutions of the inequality.

VERBAL PHRASE	INEQUALITY	GRAPH
All real numbers less than 2	$x < 2$	−3 −2 −1 0 1 2 3
All real numbers greater than −2	$x > -2$	−3 −2 −1 0 1 2 3
All real numbers less than or equal to 1	$x \le 1$	−3 −2 −1 0 1 2 3
All real numbers greater than or equal to 0	$x \ge 0$	−3 −2 −1 0 1 2 3

An open dot is used for $<$ or $>$ and a solid dot for $\le$ or $\ge$.

EXAMPLE 1 Write and Graph a Linear Inequality

Sue ran a 2-kilometer race in 8 minutes. Write an inequality to describe the average speeds of runners who were faster than Sue. Graph the inequality.

SOLUTION Average speed is $\dfrac{\text{distance}}{\text{time}}$. A faster runner's average speed must be greater than Sue's average speed.

VERBAL MODEL	Faster average speed $>$ $\dfrac{\text{Distance}}{\text{Sue's time}}$	
LABELS	Faster average speed $= s$	(kilometers per minute)
	Distance $= 2$	(kilometers)
	Sue's time $= 8$	(minutes)
ALGEBRAIC MODEL	$s > \dfrac{2}{8}$	Write linear inequality.
	$s > \dfrac{1}{4}$	Simplify.

$-\frac{1}{4}$ 0 $\frac{1}{4}$ $\frac{1}{2}$ $\frac{3}{4}$ 1 $1\frac{1}{4}$ $1\frac{1}{2}$ $1\frac{3}{4}$ 2

STUDENT HELP

▶ **Look Back**
For help with inequalities, see p. 26.

STUDENT HELP

↳ **Look Back**
For help with solving equations with addition and subtraction, see pp. 132–134.

GOAL 2 **SOLVING ONE-STEP LINEAR INEQUALITIES**

Solving a linear inequality in one variable is much like solving a linear equation in one variable. To solve the inequality, you isolate the variable on one side using transformations that produce **equivalent inequalities,** which have the same solution(s).

TRANSFORMATIONS THAT PRODUCE EQUIVALENT INEQUALITIES

	Original Inequality		Equivalent Inequality
• Add the same number to *each* side.	$x - 3 < 5$	Add 3.	$x < 8$
• Subtract the same number from *each* side.	$x + 6 \geq 10$	Subtract 6.	$x \geq 4$

EXAMPLE 2 *Using Subtraction to Solve an Inequality*

Solve $x + 5 \geq 3$. Graph the solution.

SOLUTION

$x + 5 \geq 3$ Write original inequality.

$x + 5 - 5 \geq 3 - 5$ Subtract 5 from each side.

$x \geq -2$ Simplify.

▶ The solution is all real numbers greater than or equal to -2. Check several numbers that are greater than or equal to -2 in the original inequality.

EXAMPLE 3 *Using Addition to Solve an Inequality*

Solve $-2 > n - 4$. Graph the solution.

STUDENT HELP

↳ **Study Tip**
Check several possible solutions by substituting them in the original inequality. Also try some numbers that are *not* solutions to make sure that they do *not* satisfy the original inequality.

SOLUTION

$-2 > n - 4$ Write original inequality.

$-2 + 4 > n - 4 + 4$ Add 4 to each side.

$2 > n$ Simplify.

▶ The solution is all real numbers less than 2. Check several numbers that are less than 2 in the original inequality.

STUDENT HELP

Look Back
For help with solving equations with multiplication and division, see p. 138.

USING MULTIPLICATION AND DIVISION The operations used to solve linear inequalities are similar to those used to solve linear equations, but there are important differences. When you multiply or divide each side of an inequality by a *negative* number, you must *reverse* the inequality symbol to maintain a true statement. For instance, to reverse $>$, replace it with $<$.

TRANSFORMATIONS THAT PRODUCE EQUIVALENT INEQUALITIES

	Original inequality		Equivalent inequality
• Multiply each side by the same *positive* number.	$\frac{1}{2}x > 3$	Multiply by 2.	$x > 6$
• Divide each side by the same *positive* number.	$3x \leq 9$	Divide by 3.	$x \leq 3$
• Multiply each side by the same *negative* number and *reverse* the inequality symbol.	$-x < 4$	Multiply by (-1).	$x > -4$
• Divide each side by the same *negative* number and *reverse* the inequality symbol.	$-2x \leq 6$	Divide by (-2).	$x \geq -3$

EXAMPLE 4 *Using Multiplication or Division to Solve an Inequality*

a.

$\dfrac{a}{3} \leq 12$	Original inequality
$3 \cdot \dfrac{a}{3} \leq 3 \cdot 12$	Multiply each side by positive 3.
$a \leq 36$	Simplify.

▶ The solution is all real numbers less than or equal to 36. Check several numbers that are less than or equal to 36 in the original inequality.

b.

$-4.2m > 6.3$	Original inequality
$\dfrac{-4.2m}{-4.2} < \dfrac{6.3}{-4.2}$	Divide each side by -4.2 and reverse inequality symbol.
$m < -1.5$	Simplify.

▶ The solution is all real numbers less than -1.5. Check several numbers that are less than -1.5 in the original inequality.

STUDENT HELP

HOMEWORK HELP
Visit our Web site
www.mcdougallittell.com
for extra examples.

GUIDED PRACTICE

Vocabulary Check ✓   **1.** Since $x - 3 < 5$ and $x < 8$ have the same solution, they are _?_ inequalities.

Concept Check ✓   **Write a verbal phrase that describes the inequality.**

    2. $x > -7$ **3.** $x < 1$ **4.** $9 \le x$ **5.** $10 \ge x$

ERROR ANALYSIS   **Describe and correct the error.**

6.

7.

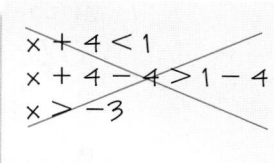

Tell whether you should use an *open dot* or a *closed dot* on the graph of the inequality.

    8. $x < 3$ **9.** $x > 10$ **10.** $x \ge 5$

    11. $3x + 5 < 4$ **12.** $5x - 3 \ge 12$ **13.** $-2x - 1 \le 3$

Skill Check ✓   **Solve the inequality and graph its solution.**

    14. $-2 + x < 5$ **15.** $-3 \le y + 2$ **16.** $-2b \le -8$

    17. $x - 4 > 10$ **18.** $5x > -45$ **19.** $-6y \le 36$

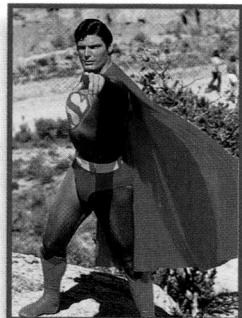

🌐 **COLLECTIBLES**   **In 1997 a software executive bid $19,550 for Superman's cape from the 1978 movie *Superman*. This was the highest bid.**

    20. Let b represent the amount of a bid for the cape. Write an inequality for b.

    21. Graph the inequality.

PRACTICE AND APPLICATIONS

STUDENT HELP

→ **Extra Practice**
to help you master
skills is on p. 802.

GRAPHING   **Graph the inequality.**

    22. $x > -2$ **23.** $x < 16$ **24.** $x \le 7$

    25. $x \ge -6$ **26.** $2 \ge x$ **27.** $2.5 \le x$

    28. $1 \ge -x$ **29.** $-10 \le -x$ **30.** $x < -0.5$

STUDENT HELP

→ **HOMEWORK HELP**
Example 1: Exs. 22–30,
  61–63
Examples 2, 3:
  Exs. 31–45, 55–60
Example 4: Exs. 46–60

SOLVING AND GRAPHING   **Solve the inequality and graph its solution.**

    31. $x + 6 < 8$ **32.** $-5 < 4 + x$ **33.** $-4 + x < 20$

    34. $8 + x \le -9$ **35.** $p - 12 \ge -1$ **36.** $-2 > b - 5$

    37. $x - 3 > 2$ **38.** $x - 5 \ge 1$ **39.** $6 \le c + 2$

    40. $-8 \le x - 14$ **41.** $m + 7 \ge -10$ **42.** $-6 > x - 4$

    43. $-2 + x < 0$ **44.** $-10 > a - 6$ **45.** $5 + x \ge -5$

SOLVING INEQUALITIES Solve the inequality.

46. $15p < 60$

47. $-10a > 100$

48. $-\frac{n}{5} < 17$

49. $11 \geq -2.2m$

50. $-18.2x \geq -91$

51. $2.1x \leq -10.5$

52. $13 \leq -\frac{x}{3}$

53. $-\frac{a}{10} \leq -2$

54. $\frac{x}{4} \leq -9$

SOLVING AND MATCHING In Exercises 55–60, solve the inequality. Then match its solution with its graph.

A. number line with points at $-1, 0, 1, 2, 3$; filled dot at 0, arrow right

B. number line with points at $-10, -9, -8, -7, -6$; filled dot at -8, arrow left

C. number line with points at $3, 4, 5, 6, 7$; open dot at 5, arrow right

D. number line with points at $-1, 0, 1, 2, 3$; filled dot at 2, arrow left

E. number line with points at $3, 4, 5, 6, 7$; open dot at 5, arrow left

F. number line with points at $-10, -9, -8, -7, -6$; filled dot at -8, arrow right

55. $x - 3.2 < 1.8$

56. $x + 4 \leq 6$

57. $10x > 50$

58. $x - 2 \geq -10$

59. $-\frac{x}{2} \leq 0$

60. $-3.5x \geq 28$

61. 🌐 **WALKING RACE** You finish a three-mile walking race in 27.5 minutes. Write an inequality that describes the average speed of a walker who finished after you did.

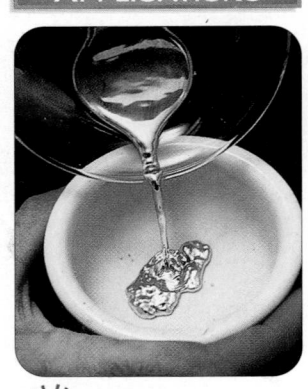
62. **SCIENCE** **CONNECTION** Mercury is the metallic element with the lowest melting point, $-38.87°C$. Write an inequality that describes the melting point p (in degrees Celsius) of any other metallic element.

63. 🌐 **LARGEST MARLIN** The world record for the largest Pacific blue marlin is 1376 pounds. It was caught in Kaaiwi Point, Kona, Hawaii. Let M represent the weight of a Pacific blue marlin that has been caught. Write an inequality for M. Graph the inequality. ▶ Source: International Game Fish Association

64. 🌐 **BOWLING TOURNAMENT** After two games of bowling, Brenda has a total score of 475. To win the tournament, she needs a total score of 684 or higher. Let x represent the score she needs for her third game to win the tournament. Write an inequality for x. What is the lowest score she can get for her third game and win the tournament?

65. 🌐 **STEEL ARCH BRIDGE** The longest steel arch bridge in the world is the New River Gorge Bridge near Fayetteville, West Virginia, at 1700 feet. Write an inequality that describes the length l (in feet) of any other steel arch bridge. Graph the inequality.

🌐 **MUSICAL INSTRUMENTS** Write an inequality to describe the frequency range f of the instrument.

66. The frequency range of a guitar is from 73 hertz to 698 hertz.

67. The frequency range of cymbals is from 131 hertz to 587 hertz.

68. MULTI-STEP PROBLEM You start your own business making wind chimes. Your equipment costs $48. It costs $3.50 to make each wind chime. You sell each wind chime for $7.50. The graph shows your total costs.

Wind Chime Sales

a. Copy the graph. On the same graph draw the line that represents the total revenue for different numbers of wind chimes sold.

b. How many wind chimes must you sell before you start making a profit?

c. Write an inequality that describes the number of wind chimes you must sell before you start making a profit.

★ **Challenge**

69. REVERSING INEQUALITIES Explain why you must reverse the direction of the inequality symbol when multiplying by a negative number. Give two examples to support your reasoning.

70. LOGICAL REASONING Explain why multiplying by x to solve the inequality $\frac{4}{x} > 2$ might lead to an error.

MIXED REVIEW

SOLVING EQUATIONS **Solve the equation.** (Review 3.3 for 6.2)

71. $45b - 3 = 2$ **72.** $-5x + 50 = 300$ **73.** $-3s - 2 = -44$

74. $\frac{1}{3}x + 5 = -4$ **75.** $\frac{x}{4} + 4 = 18$ **76.** $-8 = \frac{3}{5}a - 5$

77. $x + 2x + 5 = 14$ **78.** $3(x - 6) = 12$ **79.** $9 = -\frac{3}{2}(x - 2)$

WRITING EQUATIONS **Write the slope-intercept form of the equation of the line that passes through the two points. Graph the line. Label the points where the line crosses the axes.** (Review 4.3, 5.3)

80. $(1, 2), (4, -1)$ **81.** $(2, 0), (-4, -3)$ **82.** $(1, 1), (-3, 5)$

83. $(-1, 4), (2, 4)$ **84.** $(-1, -3), (2, 3)$ **85.** $(5, 0), (5, -2)$

86. EXAM GRADES There are 20 questions on an exam, each worth 5 points. Your percent grade p varies directly with the number n of correct answers. Find an equation that relates p and n. What is your percent grade if you get 17 correct answers? (Review 4.5)

87. BIKE RIDING The table shows the time t (in minutes) and the distance d (in miles) that Maria rode her bike each week. Write a model that relates the variables d and t. (Review 4.5)

Time (minutes), t	3	5	10	12
Distance (miles), d	0.36	0.60	1.20	1.44

6.2

Solving Multi-Step Linear Inequalities

What you should learn

GOAL 1 Solve multi-step linear inequalities.

GOAL 2 Use linear inequalities to model and solve **real-life** problems, as in the business problem in **Example 4**.

Why you should learn it

▼ To describe **real-life** problems, such as city population growth in Nashville, Tennessee, in **Example 3**.

GOAL 1 SOLVING MULTI-STEP INEQUALITIES

In Lesson 6.1 you solved inequalities using one step. In this lesson you will learn how to solve linear inequalities using two or more steps.

EXAMPLE 1 *Using More than One Step*

Solve $2y - 5 < 7$.

SOLUTION

$2y - 5 < 7$	Write original inequality.
$2y < 12$	Add 5 to each side.
$y < 6$	Divide each side by 2.

▶ The solution is all real numbers less than 6.

EXAMPLE 2 *Multiplying or Dividing by a Negative Number*

Solve the inequality.

a. $5 - x > 4$ **b.** $2x - 4 \geq 4x - 1$

SOLUTION

a.

$5 - x > 4$	Write original inequality.
$-x > -1$	Subtract 5 from each side.
$(-x)(-1) < (-1)(-1)$	Multiply each side by −1. *Reverse* inequality symbol.
$x < 1$	Simplify.

▶ The solution is all real numbers less than 1.

b.

$2x - 4 \geq 4x - 1$	Write original inequality.
$2x \geq 4x + 3$	Add 4 to each side.
$-2x \geq 3$	Subtract 4x from each side.
$x \leq -\dfrac{3}{2}$	Divide each side by −2. *Reverse* inequality symbol.

▶ The solution is all real numbers less than or equal to $-\dfrac{3}{2}$.

In part (b) of Example 2, you could begin by subtracting $2x$ from each side. Your solution would still be all real numbers less than or equal to $-\dfrac{3}{2}$.

STUDENT HELP

HOMEWORK HELP
Visit our Web site
www.mcdougallittell.com
for extra examples.

EXAMPLE 3 *Writing a Linear Model*

Population

In 1990 Nashville, Tennessee, had a population of 985,000. From 1990 through 1996, the population increased at an average rate of about 22,000 per year. Write a linear model for the population of Nashville.

SOLUTION

To write a linear model of the population of Nashville, express the population as the 1990 population plus 22,000 per year.

Let N represent the population of Nashville.

Let t represent the number of years since 1990.

Population = 1990 population + 22,000 · Years since 1990

$$N = 985{,}000 + 22{,}000t$$

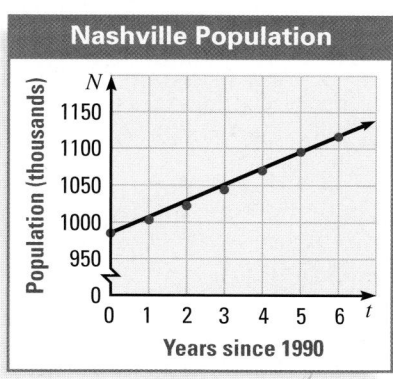

Nashville Population

DATA UPDATE of U.S. Bureau of the Census data at www.mcdougallittell.com

· · · · · · · · · ·

In the Activity below, you will compare populations of Nashville and Las Vegas.

● ACTIVITY

Developing
Concepts

Investigating Problem Solving

❶ In 1990 Las Vegas, Nevada, had a population of 853,000. From 1990 through 1996, the population increased at an average rate of about 58,000 per year. Write a linear model for the population of Las Vegas. Let L represent the population of Las Vegas.

❷ Graph your linear model from **Step 1**. Graph the linear model from Example 3 in the same coordinate plane. According to the models, in what year will the populations be the same?

❸ Write and solve a linear inequality to find the year that the population of Las Vegas exceeded the population of Nashville.

❹ In which years was the population of Las Vegas less than the population of Nashville?

❺ Write an inequality to represent the numbers of years y (since 1990) in which the population of Las Vegas was less than the population of Nashville.

EXAMPLE 4 *Writing and Using a Linear Model*

Fly Fishing

You see an advertisement for instructions on how to tie flies for fishing. The cost of materials for each fly is $.15. You plan to sell each fly for $.58, and you want to make a profit of at least $200. How many flies will you need to tie and sell?

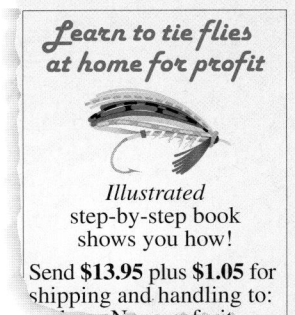

Learn to tie flies at home for profit

Illustrated step-by-step book shows you how!

Send **$13.95** plus **$1.05** for shipping and handling to:

SOLUTION

Your total expenses will be $.15 per fly, plus $15 for the instruction book.

PROBLEM SOLVING STRATEGY

VERBAL MODEL

$$\boxed{\text{Price per fly}} \cdot \boxed{\text{Number of flies sold}} - \boxed{\text{Total expenses}} \geq \boxed{\text{Desired profit}}$$

LABELS

Price per fly = **0.58**   (dollars per fly)

Number of flies sold = **x**   (flies)

Total expenses = **0.15x + 15**   (dollars)

Desired profit = **200**   (dollars)

ALGEBRAIC MODEL

$0.58\,x - (0.15x + 15) \geq 200$ **Write algebraic model.**

$0.58x - 0.15x - 15 \geq 200$ **Use distributive property.**

$0.43x - 15 \geq 200$ **Combine like terms.**

$0.43x \geq 215$ **Add 15 to each side.**

$x \geq 500$ **Divide each side by 0.43.**

▶ You need to tie and sell at least 500 flies.

✓**CHECK** You can check your result graphically by graphing equations for sales and for expenses separately.

FOCUS ON APPLICATIONS

FLY FISHING In fly fishing, flies are made of feathers, hair, or other materials. They are intended to look like insects.

GUIDED PRACTICE

Vocabulary Check ✔

1. Explain why an inequality such as $3a + 6 \geq 0$ is called a *multi-step* inequality. Give another example of a multi-step inequality.

Concept Check ✔

2. Describe the steps you could use to solve the inequality $-3y + 2 > 11$.

ERROR ANALYSIS Describe and correct the error.

3.

$$-4y + 10 < 15$$
$$-4y < 5$$
$$\frac{-4y}{-4} < \frac{5}{-4}$$
$$y < -\frac{5}{4}$$

4.

$$6x - 4 \geq 2x + 1$$
$$6x \geq 2x - 3$$
$$4x \geq -3$$
$$x \geq -\frac{3}{4}$$

Skill Check ✔

Solve the inequality.

5. $y + 2 > -1$
6. $-2x < -14$
7. $-4x \geq -12$

8. $4y - 3 < 13$
9. $5x + 12 \leq 62$
10. $10 - c \geq 6$

11. $2 - x > 6$
12. $3x + 2 \leq 7x$
13. $2x - 1 > 6x + 2$

14. 🌐 **BUSINESS** In Example 4, how many flies will you need to tie and sell to make a profit of at least $150?

PRACTICE AND APPLICATIONS

STUDENT HELP

▶ **Extra Practice**
to help you master
skills is on p. 802.

SOLVING INEQUALITIES Solve the inequality.

15. $x + 5 > -13$
16. $15 - x < 7$
17. $-5 \leq 6x - 12$

18. $-6 + 5x < 19$
19. $7 - 3x \leq 16$
20. $-3x - 0.4 > 0.8$

21. $6x + 5 < 23$
22. $-17 > 5x - 2$
23. $-x + 9 \geq 14$

24. $4x - 1 \leq -17$
25. $12 > -2x - 6$
26. $-x - 4 > 3x - 2$

27. $\frac{2}{3}x + 3 \geq 11$
28. $6 \geq \frac{7}{3}x - 1$
29. $-\frac{1}{2}x + 3 < 7$

30. $3x + 1.2 < -7x - 1.3$
31. $x + 3 \leq 2(x - 4)$

32. $2x + 10 \geq 7(x + 1)$
33. $-x + 4 < 2(x - 8)$

34. $-x + 6 > -(2x + 4)$
35. $-2(x + 3) < 4x - 7$

STUDENT HELP

▶ **HOMEWORK HELP**
Example 1: Exs. 15–35
Example 2: Exs. 15–35
Example 3: Ex. 36
Example 4: Exs. 37, 39

36. 🌐 **POPULATION** In 1990 Tampa, Florida, had a population of 280,015. From 1990 through 1996, the population increased at an average rate of about 850 per year. Write a linear model for the population of Tampa.
▶ Source: U.S. Bureau of the Census

37. 🌐 **AMUSEMENT PARK** An amusement park charges $5 for admission and $1.25 for each ride. You go to the park with $25. Write an inequality that represents the possible number of rides you can go on. What is the maximum number of rides you can go on?

38. 🌐 **SWEETENERS** From 1980 to 1995, the per capita consumption of sugar sweeteners dropped from 83.6 pounds to 65.5 pounds. The per capita consumption of corn syrup rose from 38.2 pounds to 83.2 pounds. For which years did the per capita consumption of corn syrup exceed sugar sweeteners?

39. 🌐 **PIZZA** You have $18.50 to spend on pizza. It costs $14 plus $.75 for each additional topping, tax included. Solve an inequality to find the maximum number of toppings the pizza can have.

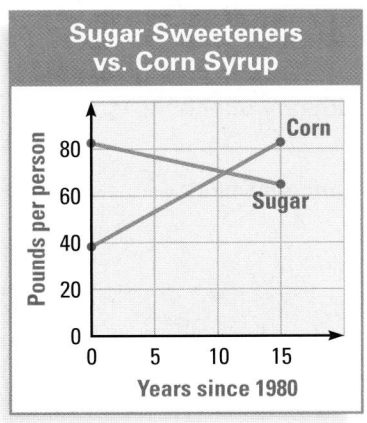

Sugar Sweeteners vs. Corn Syrup

▶ Source: U.S. Department of Agriculture

🌐 **ANIMATED FILMS** In Exercises 40–42, you are working as an animator. Each frame in an animated feature film takes at least one hour to draw.

When projected, 35-millimeter film runs at 24 frames per second. A $2\frac{1}{2}$-hour movie has about 216,000 frames.

40. Write an inequality that describes the number of hours it would take to draw the frames needed for a $1\frac{1}{2}$-hour animated feature film.

41. You are part of a team of 36 artists, each working 40 hours per week for 45 weeks per year. How many years would it take your team to draw the $1\frac{1}{2}$-hour animated feature film?

42. LOGICAL REASONING If you doubled the size of your team, how would that affect the time it would take to draw the film?

GEOMETRY **CONNECTION** **Write an inequality for the values of x.**

43. Area > 36 square meters

9 m

44. Area ≥ 25 square meters

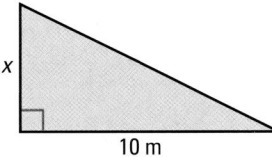

10 m

45. Area < 30 square feet

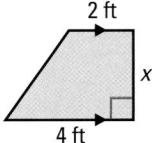

2 ft

4 ft

46. Area < 144 square inches

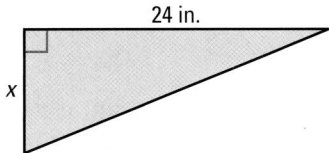

24 in.

47. Area ≤ 25 square inches

5 in.

48. Area > 60 square centimeters

12 cm

49. MULTIPLE CHOICE At a grocery store, four oranges cost $2.39 and kiwi fruit costs $.69 each. If you have $5 to spend and you buy four oranges, which inequality represents the number of kiwi fruit you can buy?

    (A) $x \le 3$ **(B)** $x \ge 3$ **(C)** $x > 3$ **(D)** $x < 7$

50. MULTIPLE CHOICE The Glee Club budgeted $250 for food for the annual Spaghetti Supper. Each meal costs $1.75 to prepare. Which inequality represents the number of meals that can be prepared without going over the budget?

    (A) $x \le 143$ **(B)** $x \ge 143$ **(C)** $x \le 142$ **(D)** $x \ge 142$

51. MULTIPLE CHOICE For Park College's basketball games, it costs $15 to attend. A season's pass costs $170. At most, how many games could you attend at the $15 price before spending more than the cost of a season's pass?

    (A) 10   **(B)** 11   **(C)** 15   **(D)** 17

★ **Challenge**

52. GRAPHICAL REASONING Use the graph of $y = \frac{2}{3}x - 2$ to solve the inequality $\frac{2}{3}x - 2 < 0$. Explain your reasoning.

EXTRA CHALLENGE
www.mcdougallittell.com

53. GRAPHICAL REASONING Use the graph of $y = -2x + 4$ to solve the inequality $-2x + 4 > 0$. Explain your reasoning.

MIXED REVIEW

EVALUATING EXPRESSIONS **Evaluate the expression.** (Review 1.3, 2.7)

54. $(a + 4) - 8$ when $a = 7$ **55.** $3x + 2$ when $x = -4$

56. $b^3 - 5$ when $b = 2$ **57.** $2(r + s)$ when $r = 2$ and $s = 4$

58. $x^2 - 3x$ when $x = 5$ **59.** $\dfrac{a^2}{8 - b}$ when $a = 4$ and $b = -9$

TRANSLATING VERBAL SENTENCES **Translate the verbal sentence into an equation or an inequality.** (Review 1.5 for 6.3)

60. Sarah's height S is 4 inches more than Joanne's height J.

61. The number of tickets t sold this week is more than twice the number of tickets l sold last week.

WRITING INTEGERS **In Exercises 62 and 63, write an integer to represent the situation.** (Review 2.1)

62. a loss of $12   **63.** three feet above ground

64. 🌐 **SHOPPING TRIP** You buy a pair of shoes for $42.99, a shirt for $14.50, and a pair of jeans for $29.99. You have a coupon for $10 off your purchase. How much did you spend? (Review 1.3)

65. 🌐 **PROBABILITY** You put 20 slips of paper in a hat. Eight slips are yellow, five slips are blue, and the rest are red. Without looking, you reach into the hat and choose a slip of paper. What is the probability that the slip of paper is not blue? (Review 2.8)

Solving Compound Inequalities

GOAL 1 SOLVING COMPOUND INEQUALITIES

In Lesson 6.1 you studied four types of simple inequalities. In this lesson you will study *compound inequalities*. A **compound inequality** consists of two inequalities connected by *and* or *or*.

EXAMPLE 1 *Writing Compound Inequalities*

Write an inequality that represents the set of numbers and graph the inequality.

a. All real numbers that are greater than zero *and* less than or equal to 4.

b. All real numbers that are less than -1 *or* greater than 2.

SOLUTION

a. $0 < x \leq 4$

This inequality is also written as $0 < x$ *and* $x \leq 4$.

b. $x < -1$ *or* $x > 2$

EXAMPLE 2 *Compound Inequalities in Real Life*

Write an inequality that describes the elevations of the regions of Mount Rainier.

a. Timber region below 6000 ft

b. Alpine meadow region below 7500 ft

c. Glacier and permanent snow field region

SOLUTION Let y represent the approximate elevation (in feet).

a. Timber region:
$2000 \leq y < 6000$

b. Alpine meadow region:
$6000 \leq y < 7500$

c. Glacier and permanent snow field region:
$7500 \leq y \leq 14{,}410$

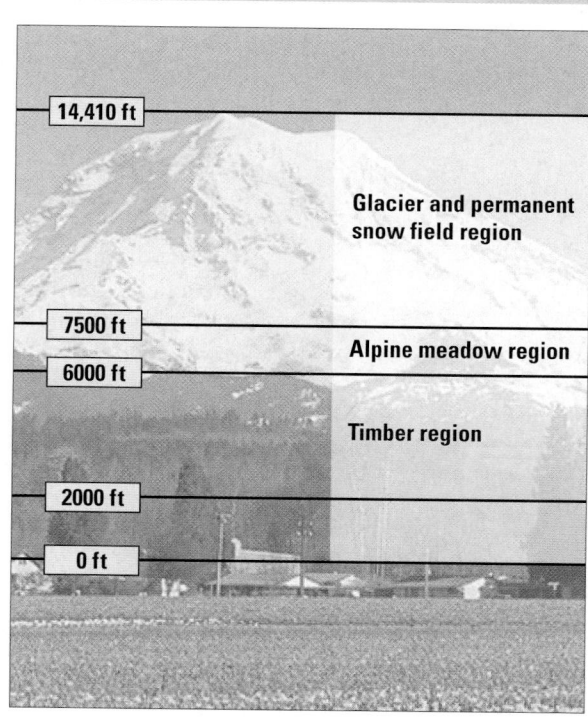

14,410 ft

Glacier and permanent snow field region

7500 ft

Alpine meadow region

6000 ft

Timber region

2000 ft

0 ft

STUDENT HELP

HOMEWORK HELP
Visit our Web site
www.mcdougallittell.com
for extra examples.

EXAMPLE 3 *Solving a Compound Inequality with And*

Solve $-2 \le 3x - 8 \le 10$. Graph the solution.

SOLUTION

Isolate the variable x between the two inequality symbols.

$-2 \le 3x - 8 \le 10$	**Write original inequality.**
$6 \le 3x \le 18$	**Add 8 to each expression.**
$2 \le x \le 6$	**Divide each expression by 3.**

▶ The solution is all real numbers that are greater than or equal to 2 *and* less than or equal to 6.

EXAMPLE 4 *Solving a Compound Inequality with Or*

Solve $3x + 1 < 4$ *or* $2x - 5 > 7$. Graph the solution.

SOLUTION A solution of this inequality is a solution of either of its simple parts. You can solve each part separately.

$$3x + 1 < 4 \quad or \quad 2x - 5 > 7$$
$$3x < 3 \quad or \quad 2x > 12$$
$$x < 1 \quad or \quad x > 6$$

▶ The solution is all real numbers that are less than 1 *or* greater than 6.

STUDENT HELP

➔ **Study Tip**
When you multiply or divide by a negative number to solve a compound inequality, remember that you have to reverse *both* inequality symbols.

EXAMPLE 5 *Reversing Both Inequality Symbols*

Solve $-2 < -2 - x < 1$. Graph the solution.

SOLUTION

Isolate the variable x between the two inequality signs.

$-2 < -2 - x < 1$	**Write original inequality.**
$0 < -x < 3$	**Add 2 to each expression.**
$0 > x > -3$	**Multiply each expression by −1 and *reverse* both inequality symbols.**

▶ To match the order of numbers on a number line, this compound inequality is usually written as $-3 < x < 0$. The solution is all real numbers that are greater than -3 *and* less than 0.

EXAMPLE 6 *Modeling with a Compound Inequality*

Distances

You have a friend Bill who lives three miles from school and another friend Mary who lives two miles from the same school. You wish to estimate the distance d that separates their homes.

   a. What is the smallest value d might have?

   b. What is the largest value d might have?

   c. Write an inequality that describes all the possible values that d might have.

SOLUTION

PROBLEM SOLVING STRATEGY

DRAW A DIAGRAM A good way to begin this problem is to draw a diagram with the school at the center of a circle.

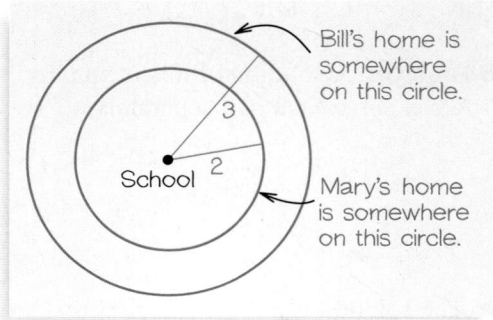

Bill's home is somewhere on the circle with radius 3 miles and center at the school.

Mary's home is somewhere on the circle with radius 2 miles and center at the school.

   a. If both homes are on the same line going toward school, the distance is 1 mile.

   b. If both homes are on the same line but in opposite directions from school, the distance is 5 miles.

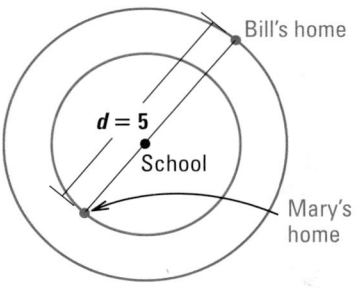

   c. The values of d can be described by the inequality $1 \le d \le 5$.

GUIDED PRACTICE

Vocabulary Check ✓

Concept Check ✓

Skill Check ✓

1. Write a compound inequality and explain why it is a compound inequality.

2. Write a compound inequality that describes the graph at the right.

$$-5 \quad -4 \quad -3 \quad -2 \quad -1 \quad 0 \quad 1$$

WRITING INEQUALITIES Write an inequality that represents the statement and graph the inequality.

3. x is less than 5 and greater than 2.

4. x is greater than 3 or less than -1.

Solve the inequality.

5. $7 < 4 + x < 8$

6. $-1 < 2x + 3 \leq 13$

7. $6 < 4x - 2 \leq 14$

8. $4x - 1 > 7$ or $5x - 1 < -6$

9. $2x + 3 < -1$ or $3x - 5 > -2$

10. $4 \leq -8 - x < 7$

11. In Example 6, write an inequality that describes the situation if you live two miles from school and your friend lives one mile from the same school.

PRACTICE AND APPLICATIONS

STUDENT HELP

▶ **Extra Practice**
to help you master
skills is on p. 802.

WRITING INEQUALITIES Write an inequality that represents the statement and graph the inequality.

12. x is less than 8 and greater than 3.

13. x is greater than 7 or less than 5.

14. x is less than 5 and is at least 0.

15. x is less than 4 and is at least -9.

16. x is less than -2 and is at least -4.

17. x is greater than -6 and less than -1.

SOLVING INEQUALITIES Solve the inequality. Write a sentence that describes the solution.

18. $6 < x - 6 \leq 8$

19. $-5 < x - 3 < 6$

20. $-4 < 2 + x < 1$

21. $8 \leq 2x + 6 \leq 18$

22. $6 + 2x > 20$ or $8 + x \leq 0$

23. $-3x - 7 \geq 8$ or $-2x - 11 \leq -31$

24. $-4 \leq -3x - 13 \leq 26$

25. $-13 \leq 5 - 2x < 9$

GRAPHING INEQUALITIES Solve the inequality and graph the solution.

26. $3 \leq 2x < 7$

27. $-25 < 5x < -20$

28. $-5 < 3x + 4 < 19$

29. $-4 \leq 9x - 1 < 5$

30. $2x + 7 < 3$ or $5x + 5 \geq 10$

31. $3x + 8 > 17$ or $2x + 5 \leq 7$

STUDENT HELP

▶ **HOMEWORK HELP**
Example 1: Exs. 12–17
Example 2: Exs. 36–38
Example 3: Exs. 18–35
Example 4: Exs. 18–35
Example 5: Exs. 18–35
Example 6: Exs. 41–44

CHECKING SOLUTIONS Solve the inequality and graph the solution. Then check graphically whether the given x-value is a solution by graphing the x-value on the same number line.

32. $-4 < 4x - 8 < 12$; $x = 1$

33. $-1 < 7x - 15 \leq 20$; $x = 5$

34. $-2x \geq 6$ or $2x + 1 > 5$; $x = 0$

35. $7 \leq -2x + 21 < 31$; $x = 0$

FINE ART
The painting above is *Still Life with Apples* by Paul Cézanne. Another of Cézanne's paintings, *Still Life with Curtain, Pitcher and Bowl of Fruit,* sold at auction for $60.5 million in 1999.

36. 🌐 **PRICES OF FINE ART** In 1958, the painting *Still Life with Apples* by Paul Cézanne sold at auction for $252,000. The painting was auctioned again in 1993 and sold for $28.6 million. Write a compound inequality that represents the different values that the painting probably was worth between 1958 and 1993.

37. 🌐 **TELEVISION ADVERTISING** In 1967 a 60-second TV commercial during the first Super Bowl cost $85,000. In 1998 advertisers paid $2.6 million for 60 seconds of commercial time (two 30-second spots). Write a compound inequality that represents the different prices that 60 seconds of commercial time during the Super Bowl probably cost between 1967 and 1998.

38. 🌐 **ANTELOPES** The table gives the weights of some adult antelopes. The eland is the largest antelope in Africa. The royal antelope is the smallest of all. Write a compound inequality that represents the different weights of these adult antelopes.

Antelope	Weight (lb)
Eland	2000
Kudu	700
Nyala	280
Springbok	95
Royal	7

39. LOGICAL REASONING Explain why the inequality $3 < x < 1$ has no solution.

40. LOGICAL REASONING Explain why the inequality $x < 2 \ or \ x > 1$ has every real number as a solution.

SCIENCE CONNECTION Use the diagram of distances in our solar system.

41. Which compound inequality best describes the distance d (in miles) between the Sun and any of the nine planets?

A. $10^7 < d < 10^{10}$

B. $10^6 < d < 10^{11}$

C. $10^8 < d < 10^{11}$

42. Write an inequality to describe an estimate of the distance d (in miles) between the Sun and Mercury.

43. Write an inequality to describe an estimate of the distance d (in miles) between the Sun and Saturn.

44. The Moon's distance d (in miles) from Earth varies from about 220,000 miles to about 250,000 miles. Write an inequality to represent this fact.

Not drawn to scale

45. MULTI-STEP PROBLEM You have a friend Kiko who lives one mile from a pool. Another friend D'evon lives 0.5 mile from Kiko. Kiko walks from her home to the pool, where she meets D'evon. They both walk from the pool to D'evon's home and then to Kiko's home.

a. Write an inequality that describes the values, *d*, of the possible distances that D'evon could live from the pool.

b. Write an inequality that describes the values, *D*, of the possible distances that Kiko could have walked. (Assume that each part of the walk followed a straight path.)

The pool is on this circle.

Kiko's home

D'evon lives somewhere on this circle.

GEOMETRY CONNECTION Write a compound inequality that must be satisfied by the length of the side labeled *x*. Use the fact that the sum of the lengths of any two sides of a triangle is greater than the length of the third side.

46.

47.

48.

MIXED REVIEW

EVALUATING EXPRESSIONS Evaluate the expression. (Review 1.1)

49. $x + 5$ when $x = 2$
50. $6.5a$ when $a = 4$
51. $m - 20$ when $m = 30$

52. $\dfrac{x}{15}$ when $x = 30$
53. $5x$ when $x = 3.3$
54. $4.2p$ when $p = 4.1$

SOLVING EQUATIONS Solve the equation. (Review 3.1, 3.2 for 6.4)

55. $x + 17 = 9$
56. $8 = x + 2\frac{1}{2}$
57. $x - 4 = 12$
58. $x - (-9) = 15$

59. $\frac{1}{2}x = -6$
60. $-3x = -27$
61. $4x = -28$
62. $-\frac{3}{4}x = 21$

63. $x + 3.2 = 11$
64. $x - 4 = 16.7$
65. $\dfrac{x}{-6} = -\dfrac{1}{2}$
66. $\frac{5}{6}x = -25$

67. 🌐 **ICE SKATING** An ice skating rink charges $4.75 for admission and skate rental. If you bring your own skates, the admission is $3.25. You can buy a pair of ice skates for $45. How many times must you go ice skating to justify buying your own skates? (Review 3.4)

🌐 **HIKING** **You are hiking a six-mile trail at a constant rate in Topanga Canyon. You begin at 10 A.M. At noon you are two miles from the end of the trail.** (Review 5.5)

68. Write a linear equation that gives the distance *d* (in miles) from the end of the trail in terms of time *t*. Let *t* represent the number of hours since 10 A.M.

69. Find the distance you are from the end of the trail at 11 A.M.

In Exercises 1–13, solve the inequality and graph the solution.
(Lessons 6.2 and 6.3)

1. $x + 2 < 7$ **2.** $-3 + x \le -11$ **3.** $3.4x \le 13.6$

4. $5 \le -\dfrac{x}{2}$ **5.** $-4x - 2 \ge 14$ **6.** $-5 < x - 8 < 4$

7. $-x - 4 > 3x - 12$ **8.** $x + 3 \le 2(x - 7)$ **9.** $-10 \le -4x - 18 \le 30$

10. $-3 < x + 6$ or $-\dfrac{x}{3} > 4$ **11.** $2 - x < -3$ or $2x + 14 < 12$

12. $2x - 6 < -8$ or $10 - 5x < -19$ **13.** $6x - 2 > -7$ or $-3x - 1 > 11$

14. 🌐 **AMUSEMENT PARK** A person must be at least 52 inches tall to ride the *Power Tower* ride at Cedar Point in Ohio. Write an inequality that describes the required heights. **(Lesson 6.1)**

15. 🌐 **TEMPERATURES** The lowest temperature ever recorded was $-128.6°F$ at the Soviet station Vostok in Antarctica. The highest temperature ever recorded was $136°F$ at Azizia, Libya. Write a compound inequality whose solution includes all of the other temperatures T ever recorded. **(Lesson 6.3)**

▶ Source: National Climatic Data Center

MATH & History   **History of Communication**   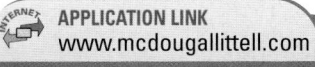 **APPLICATION LINK** www.mcdougallittell.com

THEN   **IN 1860** you could send a message from St. Joseph, Missouri, to Sacramento, California, in 10 to 11 days via Pony Express. By 1884 you could send a message in at least $4\frac{1}{2}$ days by transcontinental railroad.

NOW   **BY 1972** it took less than a second to send a message across the country via e-mail.

Write an inequality to represent the time it took to send the message.

1. Via Pony Express. Let t represent the time (in days).

2. Via transcontinental railroad. Let t represent the time (in hours).

3. Via e-mail. Let t represent the time (in seconds).

Pony Express   1860

Transcontinental Railroad   1884

U.S. MAIL   1920   Air mail

e-mail   1972

6.4 Solving Absolute-Value Equations and Inequalities

What you should learn

GOAL 1 Solve absolute-value equations.

GOAL 2 Solve absolute-value inequalities.

Why you should learn it

▼ To solve **real-life** problems such as finding the wavelengths of different colors of fireworks in **Exs. 65–68**.

GOAL 1 SOLVING ABSOLUTE-VALUE EQUATIONS

You can solve some absolute-value equations using mental math. For instance, you learned in Lesson 2.1 that the equation $|x| = 8$ has *two* solutions: 8 and -8.

To solve absolute-value equations, you can use the fact that the expression inside the absolute value symbols can be either positive or negative.

EXAMPLE 1 *Solving an Absolute-Value Equation*

Solve $|x - 2| = 5$.

SOLUTION

Because $|x - 2| = 5$, the expression $x - 2$ can be equal to 5 or to -5.

$x - 2$ IS POSITIVE	**$x - 2$ IS NEGATIVE**
$|x - 2| = 5$	$|x - 2| = 5$
$x - 2 = +5$	$x - 2 = -5$
$x = 7$	$x = -3$

▶ The equation has two solutions: 7 and -3.

✓**CHECK** Substitute both values into the original equation.

$$|7 - 2| = |5| = 5 \qquad\qquad |-3 - 2| = |-5| = 5$$

EXAMPLE 2 *Solving an Absolute-Value Equation*

Solve $|2x - 7| - 5 = 4$.

SOLUTION

Isolate the absolute-value expression on one side of the equation.

$2x - 7$ IS POSITIVE	**$2x - 7$ IS NEGATIVE**
$|2x - 7| - 5 = 4$	$|2x - 7| - 5 = 4$
$|2x - 7| = 9$	$|2x - 7| = 9$
$2x - 7 = +9$	$2x - 7 = -9$
$2x = 16$	$2x = -2$
$x = 8$	$x = -1$

▶ The equation has two solutions: 8 and -1. Check these solutions in the original equation.

GOAL 2 SOLVING ABSOLUTE-VALUE INEQUALITIES

Recall that $|x|$ is the distance between x and 0. If $|x| < 8$, then any number between -8 and 8 is a solution of the inequality.

▶ ACTIVITY
Developing Concepts
Investigating Absolute-Value Inequalities

Use Guess, Check, and Revise to find values of x that satisfy each absolute-value inequality. Graph the solution set on a number line. Then use a compound inequality to describe the solution set.

1. $|x| < 2$ **2.** $|x + 2| \geq 1$ **3.** $|x - 3| \leq 2$

You can use these properties to solve absolute-value inequalities and equations.

SOLVING ABSOLUTE-VALUE EQUATIONS AND INEQUALITIES

Each absolute-value equation or inequality is rewritten as two equations or two inequalities joined by *and* or *or*.

- $|ax + b| < c$ **means**   ⟶ $ax + b < c$ *and* $ax + b > -c.$
- $|ax + b| \leq c$ **means**   ⟶ $ax + b \leq c$ *and* $ax + b \geq -c.$
- $|ax + b| = c$ **means**   ⟶ $ax + b = c$ *or* $ax + b = -c.$
- $|ax + b| > c$ **means**   ⟶ $ax + b > c$ *or* $ax + b < -c.$
- $|ax + b| \geq c$ **means**   ⟶ $ax + b \geq c$ *or* $ax + b \leq -c.$

Notice that when an absolute value is *less than* a number, the inequalities are connected by *and*. When an absolute value is *greater than* a number, the inequalities are connected by *or*.

EXAMPLE 3   *Solving an Absolute-Value Inequality*

Solve $|x - 4| < 3$.

SOLUTION

x − 4 IS POSITIVE	**x − 4 IS NEGATIVE**
$|x - 4| < 3$	$|x - 4| < 3$
$x - 4 < +3$	$x - 4 > -3$ ⟵ **Reverse inequality symbol.**
$x < 7$	$x > 1$

▶ The solution is all real numbers greater than 1 *and* less than 7, which can be written as $1 < x < 7$.

EXAMPLE 4 *Solving an Absolute-Value Inequality*

Solve $|2x + 1| - 3 \geq 6$. Then graph the solution.

SOLUTION

2x + 1 IS POSITIVE	**2x + 1 IS NEGATIVE**
$|2x + 1| - 3 \geq 6$	$|2x + 1| - 3 \geq 6$
$|2x + 1| \geq 9$	$|2x + 1| \geq 9$
$2x + 1 \geq +9$	$2x + 1 \leq -9$ ◄—— **Reverse inequality symbol.**
$2x \geq 8$	$2x \leq -10$
$x \geq 4$	$x \leq -5$

▶ The solution of $|2x + 1| - 3 \geq 6$ is all real numbers greater than or equal to
4 *or* less than or equal to -5, which can be written as the compound inequality
$x \leq -5$ *or* $x \geq 4$.

EXAMPLE 5 *Writing an Absolute-Value Inequality*

You work in the quality control department of a manufacturing company.
The diameter of a drill bit must be between 0.62 inch and 0.63 inch.

a. Write an absolute-value inequality to represent this requirement.

b. A bit has a diameter of 0.623 inch. Does it meet the requirement?

SOLUTION

a. Let d represent the diameter (in inches) of the drill bit.

   Write a compound inequality.

     $0.62 \leq d \leq 0.63$

   Find the halfway point: 0.625.

   Subtract 0.625 from each part of the
compound inequality.

     $0.62 - 0.625 \leq d - 0.625 \leq 0.63 - 0.625$

       $-0.005 \leq d - 0.625 \leq 0.005$

   Rewrite as an absolute-value inequality:

     $|d - 0.625| \leq 0.005$

   This inequality can be read as "the actual
diameter must differ from 0.625 inch by no
more than 0.005 inch."

b. Because $|0.623 - 0.625| \leq 0.005$,
the bit does meet the requirement.

0.623 in.

GUIDED PRACTICE

Vocabulary Check ✓

1. $|x + 3| = 8$ is an example of a(n) _?_ and $|x + 3| \leq 8$ is an example of a(n) _?_ .

Concept Check ✓

2. Explain each step you should use to solve $|x + 3| = 8$.

3. Explain why $|x - 5| < 2$ means that $x - 5$ is between -2 and 2.

Complete the sentence using the word *and* or the word *or*.

4. $|x - 5| < 2$ means $x - 5 < 2$ _?_ $x - 5 > -2$.

5. $|x - 5| > 2$ means $x - 5 > 2$ _?_ $x - 5 < -2$.

Skill Check ✓

Solve the equation.

6. $|n| = 5$

7. $|a| = 0$

8. $|x + 3| = 6$

9. $|x - 4| = 10$

10. $|2n - 3| + 4 = 8$

11. $|3x + 2| + 2 = 5$

Match the inequality with the graph of its solution.

12. $|x + 2| \geq 1$

A.

13. $|x + 2| \leq 1$

B.

14. $|x + 2| > 1$

C.

Solve the inequality.

15. $|x + 6| < 4$

16. $|x - 2| > 9$

17. $|3x + 1| \leq 5$

18. **⚙ MANUFACTURING** In Example 5, suppose the diameter of the drill bit could be 0.5 inch, plus or minus as much as 0.005 inch. Write an absolute value inequality to represent this requirement.

PRACTICE AND APPLICATIONS

STUDENT HELP

▶ **Extra Practice**
to help you master
skills is on p. 802.

STUDENT HELP

▶ **HOMEWORK HELP**
Example 1: Exs. 19–39
Example 2: Exs. 19–39

continued on p. 357

SOLVING EQUATIONS Solve the equation.

19. $|x| = 7$

20. $|x| = 10$

21. $|x| = 25$

22. $|x - 4| = 6$

23. $|x + 5| = 11$

24. $|x + 8| = 9$

25. $|x - 5| = 2$

26. $|x - 1| = 4$

27. $|x + 3| = 9$

28. $|x + 1| = 6$

29. $|x - 3.2| = 7$

30. $|x + 5| = 6.5$

31. $|4x - 2| = 22$

32. $|6x - 4| = 2$

33. $|3x + 5| = 23$

34. $|5 - 4x| - 3 = 4$

35. $|2x - 4| - 8 = 10$

36. $|7x + 3| + 2 = 33$

37. $|x + 3.6| = 4.6$

38. $|x - 1.2| - 2 = 5$

39. $\left|x - \dfrac{1}{2}\right| = \dfrac{5}{2}$

STUDENT HELP

→ HOMEWORK HELP
continued from p. 356

Example 3: Exs. 40–60
Example 4: Exs. 40–60
Example 5: Exs. 61, 62

SOLVING INEQUALITIES Solve the inequality.

40. $|x + 3| < 8$ **41.** $|2x - 9| \le 11$ **42.** $|x + 10| \ge 20$

43. $|x - 2.2| > 3$ **44.** $|4x + 2| - 1 < 5$ **45.** $|5x - 15| - 4 \ge 21$

SOLVING AND GRAPHING Solve the inequality. Then graph the solution.

46. $|9 + x| \le 7$ **47.** $|4 - x| < 5$ **48.** $|x + 12| > 36$

49. $|x - 3| \le 17$ **50.** $|x + 5| \ge 1$ **51.** $|x + 3| \ge 8$

52. $|10 - 4x| \le 2$ **53.** $|2x + 3| > 4$ **54.** $|x + 2| - 5 \ge 8$

55. $|3 + x| + 7 < 10$ **56.** $|3x + 2| - 1 \ge 10$ **57.** $|5x + 1| - 8 \le 16$

58. $|5x + 3| - 4 \ge 9$ **59.** $|2x + 5| - 1 < 6$ **60.** $|3x - 9| + 2 > 7$

61. 🌐 **BASKETBALL** On your basketball team, the starting players' scoring averages are between 8 and 22 points per game. Write an absolute-value inequality describing the scoring averages for the players.

62. 🌐 **TEST SCORES** The test scores in your class range from 60 to 100. Write an absolute-value inequality describing the range of the test scores.

63. 🌐 **CAR MILEAGE** Your car averages 28 miles per gallon in the city. The actual mileage varies from the average by at most 4 miles per gallon. Write an absolute-value inequality that shows the range for the mileage your car gets.

64. 🌐 **BOXING** The cruiser weight division in boxing is centered at 183 pounds. A boxer's weight can be as much as 7 pounds more than or less than 183 pounds. Write an absolute-value inequality for this weight requirement.

🌐 **FIREWORKS** When a firework star bursts, the color of the "stars" is determined by the chemical compounds in the firework. The wavelengths for different colors in the spectrum are shown below.

65. A firework star contains strontium. When it is burned, strontium emits light at wavelengths given by $|w - 643| < 38$. What colors could the star be?

66. A firework star contains a copper compound. When it is burned, the compound emits light at wavelengths given by $|w - 455| < 23$. Determine the color of the star.

67. A firework star contains barium chlorate. When it is burned, barium chlorate emits light at wavelengths given by $|w - 519.5| < 12.5$. What color is the star?

Color	Wavelength, w
Ultraviolet	$w < 400$
Violet	$400 \le w < 424$
Blue	$424 \le w < 491$
Green	$491 \le w < 575$
Yellow	$575 \le w < 585$
Orange	$585 \le w < 647$
Red	$647 \le w < 700$
Infrared	$700 \le w$

68. A firework star contains a sodium compound. When it is burned, the compound emits light at wavelengths given by $|w - 600| < 5$. Determine the color of the star.

FOCUS ON APPLICATIONS

Stars
Launch tube

FIREWORKS
The diagram above shows what happens when a firework is launched.

🌐 APPLICATION LINK
www.mcdougallittell.com

69. MULTIPLE CHOICE Solve $|x - 7| < 6$.

   (A) $-6 < x < 6$ **(B)** $-7 < x < 7$ **(C)** $1 < x < 13$ **(D)** $-1 < x < 13$

70. MULTIPLE CHOICE Solve $|3x + 3| > 12$.

   (A) $-5 < x < 3$ **(B)** $3 < x < -5$ **(C)** $x > 3$ or $x < -5$ **(D)** $x > 3$

71. MULTIPLE CHOICE Solve $|2x - 4| \leq 3$.

   (A) $2 \leq x \leq 7$ **(B)** $\frac{1}{2} \leq x \leq \frac{7}{2}$ **(C)** $-\frac{7}{2} \leq x \leq \frac{1}{2}$ **(D)** $-\frac{7}{2} \leq x \leq \frac{7}{2}$

★ **Challenge**

   SCIENCE CONNECTION **In Exercises 72 and 73, use the diagram below. It shows how light is absorbed in seawater.**

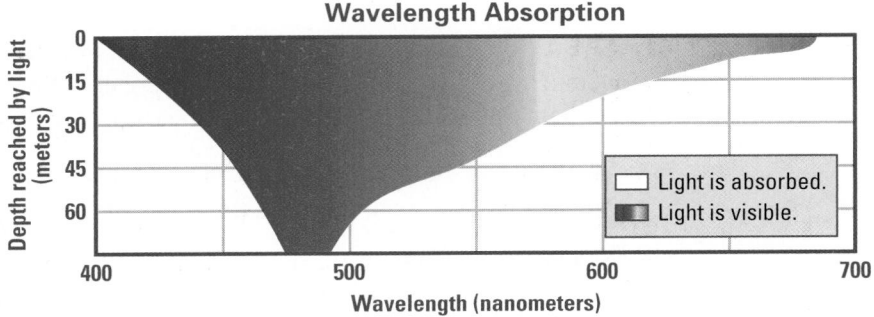

72. Write an absolute-value inequality approximating the wavelengths (w) of light that reach a depth of 30 meters in seawater.

73. Write an absolute-value inequality approximating the wavelengths (w) of light that reach a depth of 60 meters in seawater.

MIXED REVIEW

MATRICES Find the sum or difference of the matrices. (Review 2.4)

74. $\begin{bmatrix} -2 & 7 \\ 0 & 4 \end{bmatrix} + \begin{bmatrix} 3 & -6 \\ -1 & -5 \end{bmatrix}$ **75.** $\begin{bmatrix} -4 & -9 \\ -1 & 0 \end{bmatrix} - \begin{bmatrix} -12 & 8 \\ -10 & -5 \end{bmatrix}$

SLOPE-INTERCEPT FORM Rewrite the equation in slope-intercept form. (Review 3.7, 4.6 for 6.5)

76. $x + 5y = 20$ **77.** $6x + 9y = 36$ **78.** $3x - 7y = 42$

EQUATIONS Graph the equation. (Review 4.6)

79. $x = -1$ **80.** $3y = 15$ **81.** $x + y = 7$

WRITING EQUATIONS Write the point-slope form of the equation of the line that passes through the point and has the given slope. Then rewrite the equation in slope-intercept form. (Review 5.5)

82. $(0, 4)$, $m = 3$ **83.** $(2, -5)$, $m = -2$ **84.** $(-3, 1)$, $m = \frac{2}{3}$

85. 🌎 **TRAVELING** It is 368 miles from New York City to Pittsburgh. You make the trip in $6\frac{1}{2}$ hours. What was your average speed? Round your answer to the nearest mile per hour. (Review 1.1)

ACTIVITY 6.4

Using Technology

Graphing Absolute-Value Equations

▶ **EXAMPLE**

Solve the equation $|2x + 1| - 2 = 5$ using a graphing calculator.

▶ **SOLUTION**

To solve the equation, graph both sides of the equation and find the intersections.

1 Enter the equations $y = |2x + 1| - 2$ and $y = 5$.

2 Using a standard viewing window, graph both equations.

3 Use the *Intersect* feature to estimate a point where the graphs intersect. If you need to select a graph, use the direction keys to move the cursor to one of the graphs.

4 Move the cursor to the approximate intersection point. Follow your calculator's procedure to display the coordinate values. Repeat the steps to find the other intersection point.

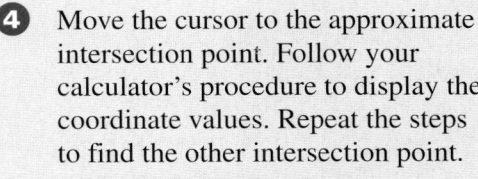

▶ The solutions are 3 and −4.

▶ **EXERCISES**

Use a graphing calculator or computer to solve the absolute-value equation. Check your solutions algebraically. Use a standard viewing window.

1. $|x + 3| - 1 = 3$

2. $|4x - 4| + 1 = 6$

3. $\left|\frac{1}{2}x - 2\right| + 1 = 8$

4. $|x - 1.67| - 3.24 = -1.1$

5. $|2x - 60| - 55 = 13$

6. $\left|\frac{1}{3}x + 1\right| + 2 = 4$

7. $|x - 4.3| + 2.8 = 5.3$

8. $|x - 7.2| - 7.6 = 10.9$

9. $|x + 36| + 35 = 49$

6.5 Graphing Linear Inequalities in Two Variables

What you should learn

GOAL 1 Graph a linear inequality in two variables.

GOAL 2 Model a **real-life** situation using a linear inequality in two variables, such as purchasing produce in **Ex. 64**.

Why you should learn it

▼ To model **real-life** situations, such as salvaging coins from a shipwreck in **Example 5**.

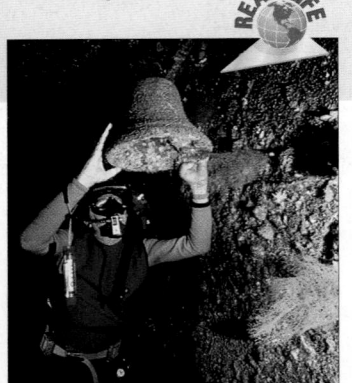

GOAL 1 GRAPHING LINEAR INEQUALITIES

A **linear inequality** in x and y is an inequality that can be written as follows.

$$ax + by < c \qquad ax + by \le c \qquad ax + by > c \qquad ax + by \ge c$$

An ordered pair (x, y) is a **solution** of a linear inequality if the inequality is true when the values of x and y are substituted into the inequality.

EXAMPLE 1 *Checking Solutions of a Linear Inequality*

Check whether the ordered pair is a solution of $2x - 3y \ge -2$.

a. $(0, 0)$ **b.** $(0, 1)$ **c.** $(2, -1)$

SOLUTION

(x, y)	$2x - 3y \ge -2$	Conclusion
a. $(0, 0)$	$2(0) - 3(0) = 0 \ge -2$	$(0, 0)$ is a solution.
b. $(0, 1)$	$2(0) - 3(1) = -3 \not\ge -2$	$(0, 1)$ is not a solution.
c. $(2, -1)$	$2(2) - 3(-1) = 7 \ge -2$	$(2, -1)$ is a solution.

· · · · · · · · ·

The **graph** of a linear inequality in two variables is the graph of the solutions of the inequality. For instance, the graph of $2x - 3y \ge -2$ is shown. Every point in the shaded region and on the line is a solution of the inequality. Every other point in the plane is not a solution.

The line is the graph of $2x - 3y = -2$.

GRAPHING A LINEAR INEQUALITY

STEP 1 Graph the corresponding equation. Use a *dashed* line for inequalities with $>$ or $<$ to show that the points on the line are not solutions. Use a *solid* line for inequalities with $\ge$ or $\le$ to show that the points on the line are solutions.

STEP 2 The line you drew separates the coordinate plane into two **half-planes**. Test a point in one of the half-planes to find whether it is a solution of the inequality.

STEP 3 If the test point is a solution, shade the half-plane it is in. If not, shade the other half-plane.

EXAMPLE 2 **Graphing a Linear Inequality**

Sketch the graph of $x < -2$.

SOLUTION

❶ Graph the corresponding equation $x = -2$, a vertical line. Use a dashed line.

❷ Test a point. The origin $(0, 0)$ is *not* a solution and it lies to the right of the line. So, the graph of $x < -2$ is all points to the left of the line $x = -2$.

❸ Shade the region to the left of the line.

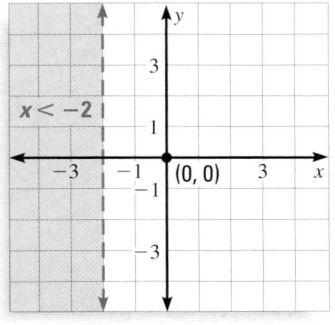

EXAMPLE 3 **Graphing a Linear Inequality**

Sketch the graph of $y \leq 1$.

SOLUTION

❶ Graph the corresponding equation $y = 1$, a horizontal line. Use a solid line.

❷ Test a point. The origin $(0, 0)$ *is* a solution and it lies below the line. So, the graph of $y \leq 1$ is all points on or below the line $y = 1$.

❸ Shade the region below the line.

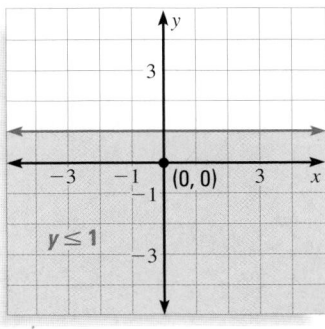

EXAMPLE 4 **Writing in Slope-Intercept Form**

Sketch the graph of $x + y > 3$.

SOLUTION

The corresponding equation is $x + y = 3$. To graph this line, you can first write the equation in slope-intercept form.

$$y = -x + 3$$

Then graph the line that has a slope of -1 and a y-intercept of 3. Use a dashed line.

The origin $(0, 0)$ is *not* a solution and it lies below the line. So, the graph of $x + y > 3$ is all points above the line $y = -x + 3$.

✓**CHECK** Test any point above the line. Any point you choose will satisfy the inequality.

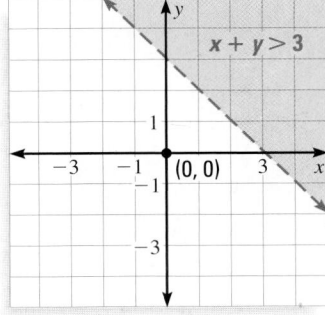

STUDENT HELP

↪ **Study Tip**
You can use any point that is not on the line as a test point. The origin is often used because it is convenient to evaluate expressions in which 0 is substituted for each variable.

GOAL 2 MODELING A REAL-LIFE SITUATION

Treasure Diving

EXAMPLE 5 *Modeling with a Linear Inequality*

You are on a treasure-diving ship that is hunting for gold and silver coins. Objects collected by the divers are placed in a wire basket. One of the divers signals you to reel in the basket. It feels as if it contains no more than 50 pounds of material.

If each gold coin weighs about 0.5 ounce and each silver coin weighs about 0.25 ounce, what are the different amounts of coins that could be in the basket?

SOLUTION

Find the number of ounces in the basket. There are 16 ounces in a pound.

$$16 \cdot 50 = 800$$

Write an algebraic model.

PROBLEM SOLVING STRATEGY

| VERBAL MODEL | Weight per gold coin | · | Number of gold coins | + | Weight per silver coin | · | Number of silver coins | ≤ | Weight in basket |

LABELS	Weight per gold coin = **0.5**	(ounces per coin)
	Number of gold coins = **x**	(coins)
	Weight per silver coin = **0.25**	(ounces per coin)
	Number of silver coins = **y**	(coins)
	Maximum weight in basket = **800**	(ounces)

ALGEBRAIC MODEL $0.5\,x + 0.25\,y \leq 800$ **Write algebraic model.**

Graph the inequality to see the possible solutions. To make a quick graph of the corresponding equation, find the *x*-intercept and the *y*-intercept. The *x*-intercept is (1600, 0). The *y*-intercept is (0, 3200). Then graph the line, test the origin, and shade the graph of the inequality.

FOCUS ON APPLICATIONS

GOLD found in the ocean can look brand new. Most other metals deteriorate quickly in salt water.

APPLICATION LINK
www.mcdougallittell.com

The graph shows all the solutions of the inequality. The possible numbers of gold and silver coins, however, are only the ordered pairs of integers in the graph.

One solution is all gold coins.

(1600, 0)

Another solution is all silver coins.

(0, 3200)

There are many other solutions, including no gold or silver coins.

(0, 0)

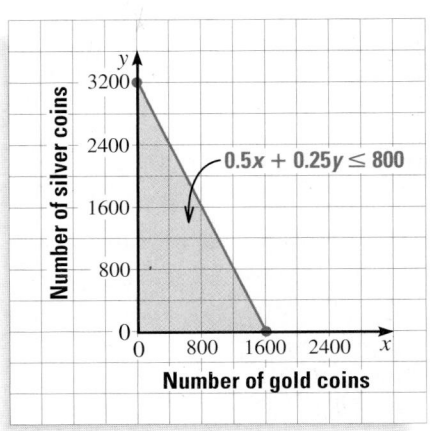

GUIDED PRACTICE

Vocabulary Check ✓
Concept Check ✓

1. Explain what a *solution* of a linear inequality in x and y is.

2. In the graph in Example 5, why is shading shown only in Quadrant 1? Use the real-life context to explain your reasoning.

3. Choose the inequality whose solution is shown by the graph. Explain your reasoning.

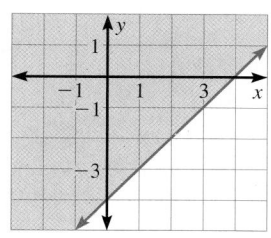

A. $x - y > 4$

B. $x - y < 4$

C. $x - y \geq 4$

D. $x - y \leq 4$

Skill Check ✓

Check whether (0, 0) is a solution. Then sketch the graph of the inequality.

4. $y < -2$ **5.** $x > -2$ **6.** $x + y \geq -1$

7. $x - y \leq -2$ **8.** $x + y < 4$ **9.** $x - y \leq 5$

10. $x + y > 3$ **11.** $3x - y < 3$ **12.** $x - 3y \geq 12$

🌐 **BASKETBALL SCORES** With two minutes left in a basketball game, your team is 12 points behind. What are two different numbers of 2-point and 3-point shots your team could score to earn at least 12 points?

13. Write a verbal model for the situation. Assign labels to each part of the verbal model and write an inequality.

14. Sketch the graph of the inequality. Then name two ways your team could score at least 12 points.

PRACTICE AND APPLICATIONS

STUDENT HELP

▶ **Extra Practice**
to help you master
skills is on p. 802.

CHECKING SOLUTIONS Is each ordered pair a solution of the inequality?

15. $x + y > -3$; $(0, 0)$, $(-6, 3)$ **16.** $2x + 2y \leq 0$; $(-1, -1)$, $(1, 1)$

17. $2x + 5y \geq 10$; $(1, 2)$, $(6, 1)$ **18.** $4x + 7y \leq 26$; $(3, 2)$, $(2, 3)$

19. $0.6x + 0.6y > 2.4$; $(2, 2)$, $(3, -3)$ **20.** $1.8x - 3.8y \geq 5$; $(0, 0)$, $(1, -1)$

21. $\frac{3}{4}x - \frac{3}{4}y < 2$; $(8, 8)$, $(8, -8)$ **22.** $\frac{5}{6}x + \frac{5}{3}y > 4$; $(6, -12)$, $(8, -8)$

SKETCHING GRAPHS Sketch the graph of the inequality.

STUDENT HELP

▶ HOMEWORK HELP
Example 1: Exs. 15–22
Example 2: Exs. 23–42
Example 3: Exs. 23–42
Example 4: Exs. 43–60
Example 5: Exs. 64–66

23. $x \geq 4$ **24.** $x \leq 5$ **25.** $y > -3$ **26.** $y < 9$

27. $x + 3 > -2$ **28.** $7 - x \leq 16$ **29.** $y + 6 > 5$ **30.** $8 - y \leq 0$

31. $4x < -12$ **32.** $-2x \geq 10$ **33.** $5y \leq -25$ **34.** $8y > 24$

35. $-3x \geq 15$ **36.** $6y \leq 24$ **37.** $-4y < 8$ **38.** $-5x > -10$

39. $x < \frac{1}{2}$ **40.** $y \geq 1.5$ **41.** $2y > 1$ **42.** $x \leq 3.5$

MATCHING GRAPHS Match the inequality with its graph.

A. $2x - y \leq 1$　　　　**B.** $-2x - y < 1$　　　　**C.** $2x - y \geq 1$

D. $2x - y > 1$　　　　　**E.** $2x - y < 1$　　　　　**F.** $-2x - y > 1$

43. 　　　**44.** 　　　**45.**

46. 　　　**47.** 　　　**48.**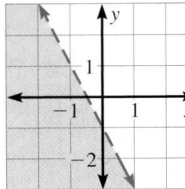

SKETCHING GRAPHS Sketch the graph of the inequality.

49. $x + y > -8$　　**50.** $x - y \geq 4$　　**51.** $y - x \leq 11$　　**52.** $-x - y < 3$

53. $x + 6y \leq 12$　　**54.** $3x - y \geq 5$　　**55.** $2x + y > 6$　　**56.** $y - 5x < 0$

57. $4x + 3y \leq 24$　　**58.** $9x - 3y \geq 18$　　**59.** $\frac{1}{4}x + \frac{1}{2}y < 1$　　**60.** $\frac{1}{3}x - \frac{2}{3}y \geq 2$

WRITING INEQUALITIES FROM GRAPHS Write an inequality whose solution
is shown in the graph.

61. 　　　**62.** 　　　**63.**

64. 🌐 **PURCHASING PRODUCE** You have $12 to spend on fruit for a meeting.
Grapes cost $1 per pound and peaches cost $1.50 per pound. Let x represent
the number of pounds of grapes you can buy. Let y represent the number of
pounds of peaches you can buy. Write and graph an inequality to model the
amounts of grapes and peaches you can buy.

65. 🌐 **FOOTBALL** In the last quarter of a high school football game, your team
is behind by 21 points. A field goal is 3 points and a touchdown (with the
point-after-touchdown) is 7 points. Let x represent the number of field goals
scored. Let y represent the number of touchdowns scored.

　a. Write and graph an inequality that models the different numbers of field
　goals and touchdowns your team could score and still not win or tie.
　(Assume the other team scores no more points.)

　b. Does every point on the graph represent a solution of the real-life
　problem? Give examples to support your answer.

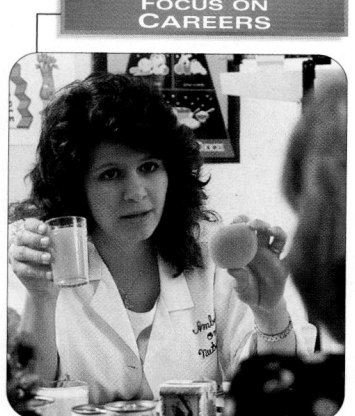
66. 🌐 **CAR SALES** You are a car dealer. You have $1,408,000 available to purchase compact cars and sport utility vehicles for your lot. The compact car costs $11,000 and the sport utility vehicle costs $22,000. Let *x* represent the number of compact cars and let *y* represent the number of sport utility vehicles you purchase. Write an inequality that models the different numbers of compact cars and sport utility vehicles that you could purchase.

NUTRITION In Exercises 67–69, use the following information. You are planning a breakfast that supplies at most 500 calories. The table shows the numbers of calories in certain foods.

67. a. You select tomato juice, some cereal, and milk. What different amounts of cups of cereal and milk could you choose along with one glass of tomato juice to supply at most 500 calories?

   b. Describe a reasonable meal of tomato juice, cereal, and milk that supplies at most 500 calories.

   c. Find reasonable amounts of cups of cereal and milk, with a glass of tomato juice, to supply at most 600 calories.

Breakfast food	Calories
Bagel, 1 plain	200
Cereal, 1 cup	88
Juice, Apple, 1 glass	120
Juice, Tomato, 1 glass	43
Egg	75
Milk, skim, 1 cup	85
Margarine, 1 tsp	33

68. a. Another morning you choose a bagel with some margarine, and apple juice. Find different numbers of teaspoons of margarine and glasses of apple juice, with a bagel, to supply at most 500 calories.

   b. Describe a reasonable meal of a bagel with margarine, and apple juice, that supplies at most 500 calories.

69. *Writing* Describe two methods you could use to solve part (a) of Exercise 68.

Test Preparation

70. MULTIPLE CHOICE Choose the inequality whose graph is shown.

   Ⓐ $2y - 6x < -4$

   Ⓑ $2y - 6x \leq -4$

   Ⓒ $2y - 6x > -4$

   Ⓓ $6x + 2y > 4$

71. MULTIPLE CHOICE Choose the inequality whose graph is shown.

   Ⓐ $2y - 6x < -4$

   Ⓑ $2y - 6x \leq -4$

   Ⓒ $2y - 6x \geq -4$

   Ⓓ $6x + 2y > 4$

   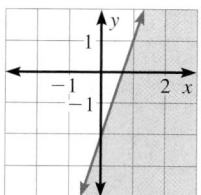

★ Challenge

72. Sketch the graph of $|y| < 2$ in a coordinate plane. Find the domain and the range.

73. Sketch the graph of $|x + 3| \leq y$ in a coordinate plane.

MIXED REVIEW

EVALUATING EXPRESSIONS Evaluate the expression. (Review 1.3 for 6.6)

74. $\dfrac{16 + 11 + 18}{3}$

75. $\dfrac{20 + 15 + 22 + 19}{4}$

76. $\dfrac{37 + 65 + 89 + 72 + 82}{5}$

SOLVING A FORMULA Solve for the indicated variable. (Review 3.7)

77. Distance traveled
Solve for r: $d = rt$

78. Volume of a pyramid
Solve for h: $V = \dfrac{1}{3}Bh$

GRAPHING EQUATIONS Use a table of values to graph the equation. (Review 4.2)

79. $y = -6x + 7$

80. $y = 3x - 7$

81. $-2x + 2y = 5$

82. $3x + 4y = 20$

FINDING SLOPES AND Y-INTERCEPTS Find the slope and the *y*-intercept of the line. (Review 4.6)

83. $y = -5x + 2$

84. $y = \dfrac{x}{2} - 2$

85. $5x - 5y = 1$

86. $6x + 2y = 14$

87. $y = -2$

88. $y = 5$

89. $y = 3x - 6.5$

90. $y = -4x + \dfrac{1}{2}$

91. $3x + 2y = 10$

QUIZ 2

Self-Test for Lessons 6.4 and 6.5

Solve the equation. (Lesson 6.4)

1. $|x| = 15$

2. $|x| = 22$

3. $|x + 3| = 6$

4. $|x - 2| = 10$

5. $|2x + 7| = 7$

6. $|3x - 2| - 2 = 5$

Solve the inequality. Then graph its solution on a number line. (Lesson 6.4)

7. $|x - 4| > 1$

8. $|x + 7| < 2$

9. $|x - 12| \le 9$

10. $\left|x - \dfrac{1}{4}\right| > \dfrac{9}{4}$

11. $|2x + 7| \le 25$

12. $|4x + 2| - 5 > 17$

Is each ordered pair a solution of the inequality? (Lesson 6.5)

13. $x + y \le 4$; $(0, -1)$, $(2, 2)$

14. $y - 3x > 0$; $(0, 0)$, $(-4, 1)$

15. $-2x + 5y \ge 5$; $(2, 1)$, $(-1, 2)$

16. $-x - 2y < 4$; $(1, -1)$, $(2, -3)$

Sketch the graph of the inequality in a coordinate plane. (Lesson 6.5)

17. $y - 5x > 0$

18. $y \ge 3$

19. $x \le -4$

20. $y < -2x$

21. $2x - y \ge 10$

22. $3x + y > 15$

23. **STOCK MARKET** You purchase shares of a technology company's stock and hold onto them for one year. During that time period, the price per share ranged from \$65 to \$143. Write an absolute-value inequality that shows the range of stock prices for the year. (Lesson 6.4)

Using Technology

Graphing Inequalities

▶ **EXAMPLE**

Graph the solution of the inequality $x - 2y \leq -6$.

▶ **SOLUTION**

① Rewrite the inequality so that y is isolated on the left.

$x - 2y \leq -6$	**Write original inequality.**
$-2y \leq -x - 6$	**Subtract *x* from each side.**
$y \geq \dfrac{x}{2} + 3$	**Divide each side by −2 and reverse inequality symbol.**

② Use your calculator's procedure for graphing and shading an inequality. You may need to decide whether the graph of the corresponding equation is part of the solution, because that may not be clear on the screen.

The graph of $y = \dfrac{x}{2} + 3$ is part of the solution.

③ The corresponding equation should be shown with a solid line, because in this case the inequality is "less than or equal to."

▶ **EXERCISES**

In Exercises 1–12, use a graphing calculator or a computer to graph the inequality. (For Exercises 1–8, use a standard viewing rectangle. For Exercises 9–12, use the indicated viewing rectangle.)

1. $y < -2x - 3$ **2.** $y > 2x + 2$ **3.** $x + 2y \leq -1$ **4.** $x - 3y \geq 3$

5. $y > 0.5x + 2$ **6.** $y < 3.2x - 3$ **7.** $\dfrac{3}{4}x + y \geq 1$ **8.** $\dfrac{x}{2} - 2y \leq 2$

9. $y < x + 25$
Xmin = −10
Xmax = 10
Xscl = 1
Ymin = −5
Ymax = 35
Yscl = 5

10. $y > -x + 25$
Xmin = −10
Xmax = 10
Xscl = 1
Ymin = −5
Ymax = 35
Yscl = 5

11. $y \leq 0.1x$
Xmin = −10
Xmax = 10
Xscl = 1
Ymin = −1
Ymax = 1
Yscl = 0.1

12. $y \geq 100x + 2500$
Xmin = 0
Xmax = 100
Xscl = 10
Ymin = 0
Ymax = 15000
Yscl = 1000

13. Write an inequality that represents all points that lie above the line $y = x$. Use a graphing calculator or a computer to check your answer.

14. Write an inequality that represents all points that lie below the line $y = x + 2$. Use a graphing calculator or a computer to check your answer.

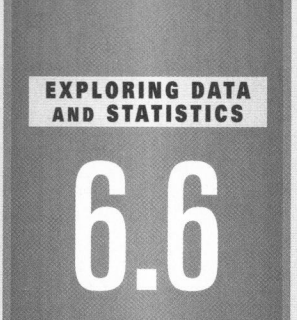

Stem-and-Leaf Plots and Mean, Median, and Mode

GOAL 1 **MAKING STEM-AND-LEAF PLOTS**

What you should learn

GOAL 1 Make and use a stem-and-leaf plot to put data in order.

GOAL 2 Find the mean, median, and mode of data, such as tire usage in **Example 3**.

Why you should learn it

▼ To describe **real-life** data, such as the ages of the residents of Alcan, Alaska, in **Example 1**.

A **stem-and-leaf plot** is an arrangement of digits that is used to display and order numerical data.

EXAMPLE 1 *Making a Stem-and-Leaf Plot*

The following data show the ages of the 27 residents of Alcan, Alaska. Make a stem-and-leaf plot to display the data. ▶ Source: U.S. Bureau of the Census

45	1	52	42	10	40	50	40	7
46	19	35	3	11	31	6	41	12
43	37	8	41	48	42	55	30	58

SOLUTION

Use the digits in the tens' place for the *stems* and the digits in the ones' place for the *leaves*. The key shows you how to interpret the digits.

Unordered stem-and-leaf plot

```
        0 | 1 7 3 6 8
        1 | 0 9 1 2
        2 |
Stems   3 | 5 1 7 0            Leaves
        4 | 5 2 0 0 6 1 3 1 8 2
        5 | 2 0 5 8            Key: 4|5 = 45
```

You can order the leaves to make an *ordered* stem-and-leaf plot.

Ordered stem-and-leaf plot

```
        0 | 1 3 6 7 8
        1 | 0 1 2 9
        2 |
Stems   3 | 0 1 5 7            Leaves
        4 | 0 0 1 1 2 2 3 5 6 8
        5 | 0 2 5 8            Key: 4|5 = 45
```

Your choice of place values for the stem and the leaves will depend on the data. For data between 0 and 100, the leaves are the digits in the ones' place. Be sure to include a key that explains how to interpret the digits.

A **measure of central tendency** is a number that is used to represent a typical number in a data set. What value is "most typical" may depend on the type of data, and it may be a matter of opinion. There are three commonly used measures of central tendency of a collection of numbers: the *mean*, the *median*, and the *mode*.

CONCEPT SUMMARY	MEASURES OF CENTRAL TENDENCY

- The **mean,** or **average,** of *n* numbers is the sum of the numbers divided by *n*.

- The **median** of *n* numbers is the middle number when the numbers are written in order. If *n* is even, the median is taken to be the average of the two middle numbers.

- The **mode** of *n* numbers is the number that occurs most frequently. A set of data can have more than one mode or no mode.

Population

EXAMPLE 2 *Finding the Mean, Median, and Mode*

Find the measure of central tendency of the ages of the residents of Alcan, Alaska, given in Example 1.

   a. mean   **b.** median   **c.** mode

SOLUTION

  a. To find the mean, add the 27 ages and divide by 27.

$$\text{mean} = \frac{1 + 3 + \cdots + 55 + 58}{27} \qquad \text{\textbf{Definition of mean}}$$

$$= \frac{853}{27} \qquad\qquad\qquad \text{\textbf{Add ages.}}$$

    The mean is $\frac{853}{27}$, or about 32.

  b. To find the median, write the ages in order and find the middle number. To order the ages, use the ordered stem-and-leaf plot in Example 1.

1	3	6	7	8	10	11	12	19
30	31	35	37	**40**	40	41	41	42
42	43	45	46	48	50	52	55	58

    From this list, you can see that the median age is 40. Half of the ages fall below 40 and half of the ages are 40 or older.

  c. To find the mode, use the ordered list in part (b).

    There are three modes, 40, 41, and 42.

Many collections of numbers in real life have graphs that are *bell shaped.* For such collections, the mean, the median, and the mode are about equal.

Manufacturing

STUDENT HELP

Look Back
For help with graphs, see p. 41.

EXAMPLE 3 *A Bell-Shaped Distribution*

A tire manufacturer conducted a survey of 118 people who had purchased a particular type of tire. Each person was asked to report the number of miles driven before replacing the tires. Responses are shown in the histogram. Find the median and the mode of the data.

SOLUTION The tallest bar is at 20,000 miles, so that is the mode. The number of responses to the left of that bar is the same as the number of responses to the right, so 20,000 miles is also the median. The mean is also 20,000 miles.

EXAMPLE 4 *Interpreting Measures of Central Tendency*

80-Year-Old Graduates at Elliot School

Elliot School had 28 graduates this year. The town turned out to witness the graduation of John Wilson, age 80. Of the other graduates, seven were 17 years old, nineteen were 18 years old, and one was 19 years old. One person remarked, "The average age of the graduates must be about 35 years."

Was the person's estimate of the average age correct? Would the mean be the most representative measure of central tendency?

SOLUTION

$$\text{Mean} = \frac{7(17) + 19(18) + 1(19) + 1(80)}{28} = \frac{560}{28} = 20$$

The person's estimate was wrong, because the mean is 20.

Because both the median and the mode of the ages are 18 years, the mean is not the most representative measure of central tendency.

· · · · · · · · · ·

People usually use the mean to represent a typical number in a data set. If some data are very different, the median may be more representative of the data.

GUIDED PRACTICE

Vocabulary Check ✓
Concept Check ✓
Skill Check ✓

1. Define the *mean*, the *median*, and the *mode* of a collection of numbers.

2. Explain why you might make a stem-and-leaf plot for a data collection.

3. Give an example in which the mean of a collection of numbers is *not* representative of a typical number in the collection.

4. Make a stem-and-leaf plot for the data at the right.

   22, 34, 11, 55, 13, 22,
   30, 21, 39, 48, 38, 46

Find the mean, the median, and the mode of the collection of numbers.

5. 2, 2, 2, 2, 4, 4, 5

6. 5, 10, 15, 1, 2, 3, 7, 8

7. −4, 8, 9, −6, −2, 1

8. 6.5, 3.2, 1.7, 10.1, 3.2

9. Use the stem-and-leaf plot below to order the data set.

```
1 | 6 3 8 1 7 5 3
2 | 8 2 5 0 7 7 0
3 | 8 3 1 4 7        Key: 3 | 8 = 38
```

10. 🌐 **AGES** If someone said that the mean age of everyone in your algebra class is about $16\frac{1}{2}$ years, do you think the age of the teacher was included in the calculation? Explain.

PRACTICE AND APPLICATIONS

STUDENT HELP

▶ **Extra Practice**
to help you master skills is on p. 802.

MAKING STEM-AND-LEAF PLOTS **Make a stem-and-leaf plot for the data. Use the result to list the data in increasing order.**

11. 60, 74, 75, 63, 78, 70, 50, 74, 52, 74, 65, 78, 54

12. 24, 29, 17, 50, 39, 51, 19, 22, 40, 45, 20, 18, 23, 30

13. 4, 31, 22, 37, 39, 24, 2, 28, 1, 26, 28, 30, 28, 3, 20, 20, 5

14. 15, 39, 13, 31, 46, 9, 38, 17, 32, 10, 12, 45, 30, 1, 32, 23, 32, 41

15. 87, 61, 54, 77, 79, 86, 30, 76, 52, 44, 48, 76, 87, 68, 82, 61, 84, 33, 39, 68, 37, 80, 62, 81, 76

16. 48, 10, 48, 25, 40, 42, 44, 23, 21, 13, 50, 17, 18, 19, 21, 57, 35, 33, 25, 50, 13, 12, 46

FINDING MEAN, MEDIAN, AND MODE **Find the mean, the median, and the mode of the collection of numbers.**

STUDENT HELP

▶ HOMEWORK HELP
Example 1: Exs. 11–16, 32–34
Example 2: Exs. 17–27
Example 3: Exs. 36, 37
Example 4: Exs. 29, 30

17. 4, 2, 10, 6, 10, 7, 10

18. 1, 2, 1, 2, 1, 3, 3, 4, 3

19. 8, 5, 6, 5, 6, 6

20. 4, 4, 4, 4, 4, 4

21. 5, 3, 10, 13, 8, 18, 5, 17, 2, 7, 9, 10, 4, 1

22. 12, 5, 6, 15, 12, 9, 13, 1, 4, 6, 8, 14, 12

23. 3.56, 4.40, 6.25, 1.20, 8.52, 1.20

24. 161, 146, 158, 150, 156, 150

BASEBALL **In Exercises 25–28, use the following information.**

The table shows the number of shutouts that ten baseball pitchers had in their careers. A shutout is a complete game pitched without allowing a run.

25. Find the mean and the median for the set of data.

26. Write the numbers in decreasing order.

27. Does the set of data have a mode? If so, what is it?

28. **CRITICAL THINKING** What number could you add to the set of data to make it have more than one mode? Explain why you chose the number.

Pitcher	Shutouts
Warren Spahn	63
Christy Mathewson	80
Eddie Plank	69
Nolan Ryan	61
Bert Blyleven	60
Don Sutton	58
Grover Alexander	90
Walter Johnson	110
Cy Young	76
Tom Seaver	61

▶ Source: *The Baseball Encyclopedia*

STUDENT HELP

HOMEWORK HELP
Visit our Web site www.mcdougallittell.com for help with problem solving in Ex. 29.

29. **AVERAGE SALARY** A small town has an adult population of 100. One person is a multimillionaire who makes $5,000,000 per year. The mean annual salary in the town is $74,750. Is the mean a fair measure of a typical salary in the town? What is the mean annual salary of the other 99 adults?

30. **NUMBER OF HOUSEHOLDS** The U.S. Bureau of the Census reports on the number of households (in thousands) in each state. Some of the data are shown in the table. Is one measure of central tendency the most representative of the typical number of households in these states? Explain your reasoning.

31. Use the data in Exercise 30. If you exclude California from the data, is one measure of central tendency the most representative of the data? Explain your reasoning.

State	Households
Arizona	1,687
California	11,101
Colorado	1,502
Idaho	430
Montana	341
Nevada	619
New Mexico	619
Utah	639
Wyoming	184

DATA UPDATE Visit our Web site www.mcdougallittell.com

32. **CRITICAL THINKING** Create two different sets of data, each having 10 ages. Create one set so that the mean age is 16 and the median age is 18. Create the other set so that the median age is 16 and the mean age is 18.

33. **BIRTHDAYS** Use a stem-and-leaf plot (months as stems, days as leaves) to write the birthdays in order from earliest in the year to latest (1 = January, 2 = February, and so on). Include a key with your stem-and-leaf plot.

10-11	4-14	7-31	12-28	4-17
2-22	8-21	1-24	9-12	1-3
4-30	10-17	6-5	1-25	5-10
12-9	4-1	8-26	12-15	3-17
4-30	2-3	11-11	6-13	11-4
6-24	6-3	4-8	2-20	11-28

34. **WEIGHTS** The numbers shown below represent the weights (in pounds) of twelve high school students. Use a stem-and-leaf plot to order the weights of the students from least to greatest. (*Hint:* Use 17 | 7 = 177 for your key.)

177, 164, 108, 158, 195, 206, 106, 126, 143, 118, 148, 146

35. **ASTEROIDS** The numbers below are the mean distances from the sun (in millions of miles) of the first ten asteroids. Use a stem-and-leaf plot to order the distances from least to greatest. (*Hint:* Use 25 | 70 = 257.0 for your key.)

257.0, 257.4, 247.8, 219.3, 239.3, 225.2, 221.4, 204.4, 221.7, 222.6

VACATIONS In Exercises 36–38, use the following information.

A business conducted a survey of its employees who go on vacation every year. Each person was asked to report the number of miles traveled (to the nearest hundred) on the last vacation. The responses are shown in the histogram.

36. Find the median of the data.

37. Find the mode of the data.

38. *Writing* Suppose a new employee traveled 400 miles on the last vacation. Decide whether this would affect the median or the mode. Explain your thinking.

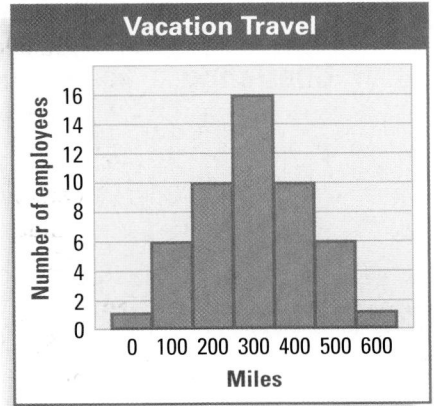

EXTENSION: DOUBLE STEM-AND-LEAF PLOT In Exercises 39 and 40, use the following information.

Another type of visual model that you can use is a *double stem-and-leaf plot*. This type of visual model is used to compare two sets of data. The Stem column is in the middle of the plot, so that the "stem" can apply to both sets of data.

The double stem-and-leaf plot below shows the number of all-time tournament wins by the top 17 male and female professional golfers.

▶ Source: Professional Golfers Association

Male	Stem	Female
	1 | 8	8 2
	0 | 7	
3	0 | 6	
2	1 | 5	7 5 0
0	0 | 4	4 2 2
0 1 8 6 3 2	1 | 3	8 5 2 1 1 1
9 9	2 | 2	9 9 6

Key: 1 | 3 | 8 = 31, 38

39. What conclusions can be drawn from the double stem-and-leaf plot?

40. Use the data in the double stem-and-leaf plot to make two conventional stem-and-leaf plots. Explain what changes you need to make.

QUANTITATIVE COMPARISON In Exercises 41 and 42, choose the statement below that is true about the given numbers.

Ⓐ The number in column A is greater.

Ⓑ The number in column B is greater.

Ⓒ The two numbers are equal.

Ⓓ The relationship cannot be determined from the given information.

	Column A	Column B
41.	The mean of 1, 2, 3, 4, 5, 5, 10	The mean of 2, 3, 4, 5, 5, 10, 11
42.	The mode of $-2, -2, -2, 4$	The mode of $-2, -2, -3, -3, -3$

★ **Challenge**

43. 🌐 **TEST SCORES** You have test scores of 84, 92, and 76. There will be one more test in the marking period. You want your mean test score for the marking period to be 85 or higher.

   a. Let x represent your last test score. Write an expression for the mean of your test scores for the marking period.

   b. Write and solve an inequality to find what you must score on the last test.

   c. Solve the problem without using algebra. Describe your method. Do your answers agree?

EXTRA CHALLENGE
➡ www.mcdougallittell.com

MIXED REVIEW

EVALUATING EXPRESSIONS Evaluate the expression. (Review 1.3 for 6.7)

44. $35 + 40 \div 2$ **45.** $120 \times 3 - 2$ **46.** $237 - 188 \div 4$

CHECKING SOLUTIONS Check whether the given number is a solution of the inequality. (Review 1.4)

47. $x + 5 > 11$; 6   **48.** $2z - 3 < 4$; 4

49. 🌐 **ROAD TRIP** You and two friends each agree to drive $\frac{1}{3}$ of a 75-mile trip. Which equation would you use to find the number of miles each of you must drive? (Review 1.5)

   A. $3x = 75$ **B.** $\frac{1}{3}x = 75$

FINDING SLOPE Find the slope of the graph of the linear function f. (Review 4.8)

50. $f(2) = -1, f(5) = 5$ **51.** $f(0) = 5, f(5) = 0$

52. $f(-3) = -12, f(3) = 12$ **53.** $f(0) = 1, f(4) = -1$

SOLVING INEQUALITIES Solve the inequality and graph the solution. (Review 6.2–6.4)

54. $-x + 7 > 13$ **55.** $16 - x \leq 7$ **56.** $-4 < x + 3 < 7$

57. $7 < 3 - 2x \leq 19$ **58.** $|x - 3| < 12$ **59.** $|x + 16| \geq 9$

6.7

Box-and-Whisker Plots

What you should learn

GOAL ① Draw a box-and-whisker plot to organize **real-life** data.

GOAL ② Read and interpret a box-and-whisker plot of **real-life** data.

Why you should learn it

▼ To interpret **real-life** data, such as data about the lengths of commuters' trips to work, as in **Exs. 31–33**.

A **box-and-whisker plot** is a data display that divides a set of data into four parts. The median or **second quartile** separates the set into two halves: the numbers that are below the median and the numbers that are above the median. The **first quartile** is the median of the lower half. The **third quartile** is the median of the upper half.

EXAMPLE 1 *Finding Quartiles*

Use this set of data: 11, 19, 5, 34, 9, 25, 28, 16, 17, 11, 12, 7.

a. Find the first, second, and third quartiles of the data.

b. Draw a box-and-whisker plot of the data.

SOLUTION

a. Begin by writing the numbers in increasing order. You must find the second quartile before you find the first and third quartiles.

Second quartile: $\frac{12 + 16}{2} = 14$

5, 7, 9, | 11, 11, 12, | 16, 17, 19, | 25, 28, 34

First quartile: $\frac{9 + 11}{2} = 10$ Third quartile: $\frac{19 + 25}{2} = 22$

b. *Draw* a number line that includes the least number and the greatest number in the data set.

Plot the least number, the first quartile, the second quartile, the third quartile, and the greatest number. Draw a line from the least number to the greatest number below your number line. Plot the same points on that line.

The "box" extends from the first to the third quartile. Draw a vertical line in the box at the second quartile. The "whiskers" connect the box to the least and greatest numbers.

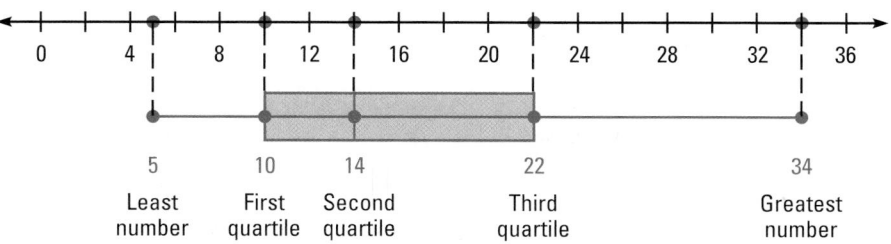

EXAMPLE 2 *Organizing Data*

Retail Prices

You found the following prices of 24 different brands of backpacks.

a. Draw a stem-and-leaf plot to order the data.

b. Draw a box-and-whisker plot of the data.

c. Describe the results.

$15	$25	$50	$42	$29
$50	$33	$27	$35	$32
$40	$35	$28	$40	$40
$35	$35	$75	$40	$40
$25	$50	$35	$50	

...ack

...of backpacks

Navy

School Days
Style 44302 $35.00
Size: 18" x 13" x 9"
Colors: Black, Navy

Tan

Ultimate Pack
Style 44336 $50.00
Size: 15" x 24" x 13"
Colors: Black, Navy, Tan

SOLUTION

a. Draw an ordered stem-and-leaf plot.

```
1 | 5
2 | 5  5  7  8  9
3 | 2  3  5  5  5  5  5
4 | 0  0  0  0  0  2
5 | 0  0  0  0
6 |
7 | 5
```

Key: 5|0 = 50

STUDENT HELP

Study Tip
A stem with no leaves shows that there are no data in the set that begin with that stem number.

From this plot, you can order the data.

$15	$25	$25	$27	$28	$29	$32	$33
$35	$35	$35	$35	$35	$40	$40	$40
$40	$40	$42	$50	$50	$50	$50	$75

b. Use the ordered data to find the quartiles.

Second quartile: $\dfrac{35 + 35}{2} = 35$

First quartile: $\dfrac{29 + 32}{2} = 30.5$

Third quartile: $\dfrac{40 + 42}{2} = 41$

c. One half of the prices are between $30.50 and $41. The median price is $35. Three fourths of the backpacks cost $41 or less. The least price is $15 and the greatest price is $75.

GOAL 2 **READING BOX-AND-WHISKER PLOTS**

You can use a box-and-whisker plot to see how data are grouped within a set of data. You can also use a box-and-whisker plot to compare two different sets of data.

Meteorology

EXAMPLE 3 *Interpreting a Box-and-Whisker Plot*

The box-and-whisker plots below show the annual precipitation (in inches) in Chicago, Illinois, and in San Diego, California, recorded over the last 30 years.

Precipitation in Chicago, Illinois

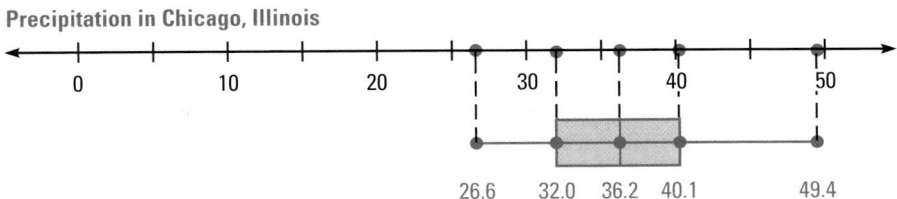

Precipitation in San Diego, California

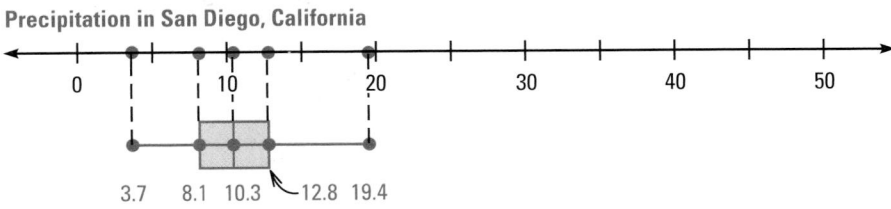

a. What is the median amount of precipitation in Chicago? in San Diego?

b. Which city has had more precipitation in the last 30 years?

c. *Writing* How else do the data sets differ?

SOLUTION

a. The median amount of precipitation in Chicago is about 36.2 inches. The median amount of precipitation in San Diego is about 10.3 inches.

b. Chicago has had more precipitation than San Diego. The lowest "whisker" in the Chicago plot represents a greater amount than the highest "whisker" in the San Diego plot.

c.

Chicago has had between 26.6 inches and 49.4 inches of precipitation. San Diego has had between 3.7 inches and 19.4 inches of precipitation. The difference between the extremes of precipitation in Chicago is about 22.8 inches. The difference between the extremes of precipitation in San Diego is about 15.7 inches.

In about half of the years, Chicago had a precipitation between 32 inches and 40 inches. In about half of the years, San Diego had a precipitation between 8 inches and 13 inches.

GUIDED PRACTICE

Vocabulary Check ✔

1. Another expression for the median of an ordered set of numbers is ? .

Concept Check ✔

2. Describe the "box" of a box-and-whisker plot. What does it represent?

3. Describe the "whiskers" of a box-and-whisker plot. What do they represent?

Skill Check ✔

In Exercises 4–7, find the first, second, and third quartiles of the data.

4. 1, 2, 3, 1, 2, 1, 2, 1, 2

5. 5, 6, 7, 2, 1, 3, 4

6. 12, 30, 19, 15, 18, 22

7. 4, 20, 14, 6, 8, 18, 2, 10, 12, 16

8. Draw a box-and-whisker plot of the following ages of horses in a stable.

2, 5, 12, 3, 18, 23, 7, 8, 11, 24, 4, 10, 3, 5, 12

9. Tell which set of data is shown by the box-and-whisker plot.

    A. 0, 10, 15, 18, 25   **B.** 5, 10, 15, 18, 30   **C.** 5, 10, 15, 18, 25

10. Use the box-and-whisker plots in Example 3. Is it true that 50% of the yearly precipitation in San Diego is less than 8.1 inches? Explain.

PRACTICE AND APPLICATIONS

STUDENT HELP

▶ **Extra Practice**
to help you master
skills is on p. 802.

FINDING QUARTILES Find the first, second, and third quartiles of the data.

11. 12, 5, 3, 8, 10, 7, 6, 5

12. 20, 73, 31, 53, 22, 64, 47

13. 1, 12, 6, 5, 4, 7, 5, 10, 3, 4

14. 2.3, 5.6, 3.4, 4.5, 3.8, 1.2, 9.7

DRAWING BOX-AND-WHISKER PLOTS In Exercises 15–22, draw a box-and-whisker plot of the data.

15. 6, 7, 10, 6, 2, 8, 7, 7, 8

16. 10, 5, 9, 50, 10, 3, 4, 15, 20, 6

17. 12, 13, 7, 6, 25, 25, 5, 10, 15, 10, 16, 14, 29

18. 8, 8, 10, 10, 1, 12, 8, 6, 5, 1, 9, 10

19. Number of days of rainfall in a year: 39, 46, 26, 12, 34, 57, 38, 37, 69, 15, 44, 47, 38, 58, 75, 29, 40, 35, 22, 69, 22, 37, 51, 55, 46, 27, 19, 36, 72, 49

20. Dogs' weights (in pounds): 88, 23, 75, 46, 77, 22, 83, 75, 97, 89, 46, 79, 69, 72, 91, 20, 75, 78, 83, 35, 39, 98, 59, 77, 84, 69, 82, 79, 57, 91

STUDENT HELP

▶ **HOMEWORK HELP**
Example 1: Exs. 11–22
Example 2: Exs. 25–29
Example 3: Exs. 31–33

21. Attendance at early showing of a movie: 48, 60, 40, 68, 51, 47, 57, 41, 65, 61, 20, 65, 49, 34, 63, 53, 52, 35, 45, 35, 65, 65, 48, 36, 24, 53, 64, 48, 40

22. Weekly tips earned (in dollars): 167, 191, 190, 154, 188, 174, 192, 166, 180, 155, 157, 161, 163, 172, 169, 167, 182, 184, 158, 160, 176

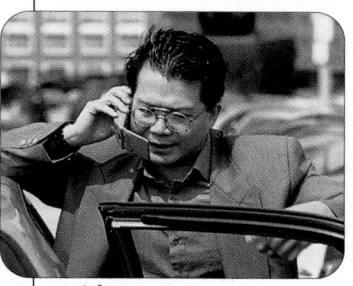
CREATING DATA SETS Create a collection of 16 numbers that could be represented by the box-and-whisker plot.

23.

10 13   19   27   38

24.
106   124   150 162   193

CELLULAR TELEPHONES In Exercises 25–29, use the table that lists the weights (in ounces) and operating times (in minutes) for 10 cellular telephones.

25. Make a stem-and-leaf plot to order the weights of the phones.

26. Draw a box-and-whisker plot of the weights of the phones.

27. Make a stem-and-leaf plot to order the operating times of the phones.

28. Draw a box-and-whisker plot of the operating times of the phones.

29. *Writing* Using the plot in Exercise 28, describe the distribution of the operating time data. What does this mean in terms of operating time?

Weight	Operating Time
8.8	140
7.7	80
4.8	90
7.0	90
7.1	90
8.4	70
3.8	60
3.6	260
6.7	75
6.2	135

DATA UPDATE Visit our Web site
www.mcdougallittell.com

30. **MILK PRODUCTION** To increase the amount of milk produced by the herd, a dairy farmer changes the cows' feed. The data show the average daily milk yield (in pints) for 10 cows before the feed change and one month after the feed change. Did the feed change increase the average daily milk yield of a cow? Use box-and-whisker plots to support your answer.

Before	39	42	43	44	39	40	42	51	40	47
After	52	53	50	46	39	49	50	49	51	44

COMMUTING In Exercises 31–33, use the box-and-whisker plot that shows the lengths (in hours) of commuters' trips to work.

0   0.5   1.0   1.5   2.0   2.5   3.0

31. How long is the median trip to work?

32. Compare the number of people whose trip is 0–0.5 hour long to the number of people whose trip is 1–3 hours long. Explain your reasoning.

33. Do more people travel 1–3 hours than travel 0.5–1 hour? Explain.

DRAWING BOX-AND-WHISKER PLOTS Draw a box-and-whisker plot of the data.

34.

35.

36. MULTI-STEP PROBLEM The heights (in meters) of some of the world's tallest skyscrapers are given in the table below.

Skyscraper, location	Height (m)
One Liberty Place, Philadelphia	288
Columbia Seafirst Center, Seattle	287
First Interstate World Center, Los Angeles	310
Society Tower, Cleveland	289
One Peachtree Center, Atlanta	275
Texas Commerce Tower, Houston	305
Two Prudential Center, Chicago	274
First Interstate Plaza, Houston	300
Bank of China, Hong Kong	305
Citicorp Center, New York City	279
Empire State, New York City	381
John Hancock Center, Chicago	343
Overseas Union Bank, Singapore	280
Aon Center, Chicago	346

a. Make a stem-and-leaf plot of the heights. List the heights from largest to smallest.

b. Draw a box-and-whisker plot of the heights.

c. CRITICAL THINKING Explain which type of plot you would prefer to use to answer this question: What is the median height of the skyscrapers that are listed in the table?

★ Challenge

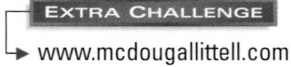
37. ANALYZING DATA In Exercises 36(a) and 36(b) you made a stem-and-leaf plot and a box-and-whisker plot. Compare the types of plots. Include a discussion of how to find the measures of central tendency with each plot. Also include an explanation of the types of conclusions you can draw from the plots.

FUNCTIONS Rewrite the equation so that *x* is a function of *y*. Then use the result to find *x* when $y = -2, -1, 0,$ and **1**. (Review 3.7)

38. $3x + y = 7$

39. $4x - y = 4$

40. $3(2 - y) = -9x + 8$

41. $6y - 4(x + 3) = -2$

UNIT RATES Find the unit rate. (Review 3.8)

42. 12 ounces for 4 servings

43. $420 for 40 hours

FINDING POINTS Decide whether the given ordered pair is a solution of the equation. (Review 4.2 for 7.1)

44. $3x - 2y = 2;$ $(1, 3)$

45. $5x + 4y = 6;$ $(-2, 4)$

46. $-2x - 2y = -6;$ $(4, -1)$

47. $x = 3;$ $(-3, 3)$

🌎 **UNITED STATES HOUSEHOLDS** Use the table that shows the number of households in the United States from 1970 to 1995. (Review 5.5)

48. Find the year in the table in which the number of households first exceeded 80,000,000.

49. Write a linear model for the number of households in the United States.

50. Use the linear model to estimate the number of households in 2005.

Years since 1970	Households (in thousands)
0	63,401
5	71,120
10	80,776
15	86,789
20	93,347
25	98,990

▶ Source: *Statistical Abstract of the United States*

QUIZ 3

Self-Test for Lessons 6.6 and 6.7

Make a stem-and-leaf plot for the data. Use the result to list the data in increasing order. (Lesson 6.6)

1. 23, 16, 24, 31, 38, 10, 32, 29, 5, 25, 37, 7, 20

2. 33, 59, 27, 44, 47, 12, 61, 46, 18, 33, 42, 26

Find the mean, the median, and the mode of the data. (Lesson 6.6)

3. 9, 9, 5, 10, 7, 10, 6

4. 42, 43, 50, 20, 30, 40

Find the first, second, and third quartiles of the data. Then draw a box-and-whisker plot of the data. (Lesson 6.7)

5. 13, 10, 16, 25, 5, 12, 20, 7, 15

6. 50, 70, 75, 60, 30, 10, 40, 80, 15, 20

7. 57, 48, 9, 27, 8, 80, 56, 55, 6, 33

8. 2, 6, 11, 16, 10, 7, 3, 12, 20, 5, 1, 14

9. 🌎 **BASKETBALL WINS** The data represent the number of wins by some NBA basketball teams for the 1996–1997 season. Find the mean, the median, and the mode of the data to the nearest whole number. (Lesson 6.6)

64, 57, 24, 20, 14, 40, 21, 15, 61, 57, 22, 26, 45, 44, 57, 30, 34, 56, 49

ACTIVITY 6.7

Using Technology

Box-and-Whisker Plots

You can draw a box-and-whisker plot using a graphing calculator or computer. Technology is especially useful for large groups of data or multiple sets of data.

▶ EXAMPLE

Draw a box-and-whisker plot of the following data.

32, 24, 39, 55, 67, 35, 23, 61, 11, 44, 43, 30, 29

▶ SOLUTION

STUDENT HELP

INTERNET KEYSTROKE HELP

See keystrokes for several models of calculators at www.mcdougallittell.com

Calculators vary but follow the same general instructions for graphing box-and-whisker plots. Be sure to set reasonable WINDOW settings.

1 Clear all lists and enter the given data.

2 Choose to sketch a box-and-whisker plot.

3 Use **ZOOM** to set a statistics viewing window. Press **GRAPH** to sketch the box-and-whisker plot.

4 Use **TRACE** and the direction arrows to find quartile values.

▶ EXERCISES

Use a graphing calculator or computer to draw a box-and-whisker plot of the data. List the first, second, and third quartiles.

1. Ages of students' brothers: 19, 12, 14, 9, 14, 4, 17, 13, 19, 11, 6, 19

2. Cost of CDs (in dollars): 11, 10, 12, 14, 17, 16, 14, 6, 8, 14, 20

3. Temperatures in February (in degrees Fahrenheit): 20.1, 43.4, 34.9, 23.9, 33.5, 24.1, 22.5, 42.4, 25.7

4. Miles traveled on weekends: 78.4, 76.3, 107.5, 78.5, 93.2, 90.3, 77.8, 37.1, 97.1, 75.5, 58.8, 65.6, 3.2

Chapter Summary

WHAT did you learn?

Write, solve, and graph an inequality in one variable.
- Simple linear inequalities (6.1)

- Multi-step linear inequalities (6.2)
- Compound inequalities (6.3)
- Absolute-value inequalities (6.4)

Write, solve, and graph a linear inequality in two variables. (6.5)

Use an inequality to model a real-life situation. (6.1–6.5)

Make a stem-and-leaf plot for data. (6.6)

Use measures of central tendency to represent data. (6.6)

Draw a box-and-whisker plot of data. (6.7)

WHY did you learn it?

Summarize the melting points of metallic elements. (p. 338)

Model and predict city population growth. (p. 341)

Describe distances between planets. (p. 350)

Determine wavelengths of colors of fireworks. (p. 357)

Find different amounts of coins collected on a treasure-diving ship. (p. 362)

Analyze real-life situations. (p. 342)

Display and order population data. (p. 368)

Describe the average age of a high school graduate. (p. 370)

Organize and compare backpack prices. (p. 376)

How does Chapter 6 fit into the BIGGER PICTURE of algebra?

You studied solving and graphing linear inequalities in one and two variables and absolute-value inequalities. Many real-life situations can be described with phrases like "at most" or "less than," which can be modeled using inequalities.

You also organized data using stem-and-leaf plots, measures of central tendency, and box-and-whisker plots. When reviewing this chapter, look for connections between solving and graphing equations and solving and graphing inequalities.

STUDY STRATEGY

How did showing all your work help you make corrections?

When you show all your work, using the **Study Strategy** on p. 332, the solution steps may be like these.

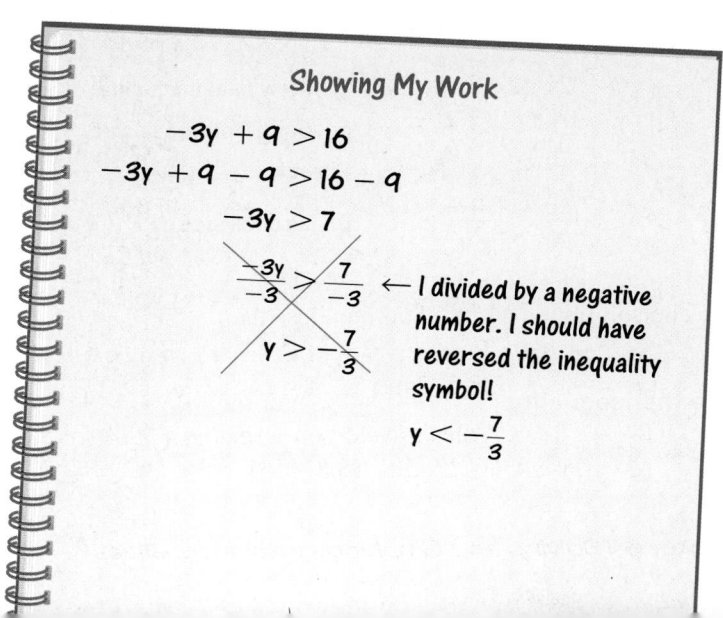

Showing My Work

$$-3y + 9 > 16$$
$$-3y + 9 - 9 > 16 - 9$$
$$-3y > 7$$
$$\frac{-3y}{-3} > \frac{7}{-3}$$ ← I divided by a negative number. I should have reversed the inequality symbol!
$$y > -\frac{7}{3}$$
$$y < -\frac{7}{3}$$

• graph of a linear inequality in one variable, p. 334

• equivalent inequalities, p. 335

• compound inequality, p. 346

• linear inequality in *x* and *y*, p. 360

• solution of a linear inequality, p. 360

• graph of a linear inequality in two variables, p. 360

• half-plane, p. 360

• stem-and-leaf plot, p. 368

• measure of central tendency, p. 369

• mean, or average, p. 369

• median, p. 369

• mode, p. 369

• box-and-whisker plot, p. 375

• quartiles, p. 375

6.1   SOLVING ONE-STEP LINEAR INEQUALITIES

Examples on pp. 334–336

EXAMPLE   Solve $-0.9x \geq 3.6$. Graph the solution.

$-0.9x \geq 3.6$ Write original inequality.

$\dfrac{-0.9x}{-0.9} \leq \dfrac{3.6}{-0.9}$ Divide each side by -0.9 and *reverse* the inequality symbol.

$x \leq -4$ Simplify.

▶ The solution is all real numbers less than or equal to -4.

Solve the inequality and graph its solution.

1. $x - 5 \leq -3$

2. $\dfrac{3}{4} + x > 1$

3. $\dfrac{x}{3} < -5$

4. $-6x \geq -30$

6.2   SOLVING MULTI-STEP LINEAR INEQUALITIES

Examples on pp. 340–342

EXAMPLE   Solve $7 + 2x < -3$.

$7 + 2x < -3$ Write original inequality.

$7 - 7 + 2x < -3 - 7$ Subtract 7 from each side.

$2x < -10$ Simplify.

$\dfrac{2x}{2} < \dfrac{-10}{2}$ Divide each side by 2.

$x < -5$ Simplify.

▶ The solution is all real numbers less than -5.

Solve the inequality.

5. $6x + 8 > 4$

6. $10 - 3x < 5$

7. $9 - 4x \geq -11$

8. $5 - \dfrac{1}{2}x \leq -3$

SOLVING COMPOUND INEQUALITIES

Examples on
pp. 346–348

EXAMPLE Solve $1 < -2x + 3 < 9$.

$1 < -2x + 3 < 9$ **Write original inequality.**

$-2 < -2x < 6$ **Subtract 3 from each expression.**

$1 > x > -3$ **Divide each expression by −2. Reverse both inequality symbols.**

▶ The solution is all real numbers greater than −3 and less than 1.

Solve the inequality. Write a sentence that describes the solution.

9. $3 < x + 1 < 6$

10. $6 \le 2x + 3 \le 10$

11. $x + \frac{1}{2} \le -\frac{3}{4}$ or $\frac{1}{4}x - 1 > \frac{3}{4}$

SOLVING ABSOLUTE-VALUE EQUATIONS AND INEQUALITIES

Examples on
pp. 353–355

EXAMPLE To solve both absolute-value equations and inequalities, remember that expressions inside absolute-value symbols can be either positive or negative.

Solve $|x - 4| > 3$.

x − 4 is positive.	**x − 4 is negative.**
$x - 4 > 3$	$x - 4 < -3$
$x > 7$	$x < 1$

▶ The solution is all real numbers greater than 7 or less than 1, or $x < 1$ or $x > 7$.

Solve the equation or the inequality.

12. $|x| = 12$

13. $|x - 5| = 11$

14. $|x + 0.5| = 0.25$

15. $|5 + x| \le 6$

16. $|7 - x| > 2$

17. $|3x + 2| - 4 \le 8$

GRAPHING LINEAR INEQUALITIES IN TWO VARIABLES

Examples on
pp. 360–362

EXAMPLE To graph $2x + y < 1$, first sketch the graph of the corresponding equation $2x + y = 1$. Use a dashed line because the inequality symbol is $<$. Next, test a point. The origin $(0, 0)$ *is* a solution, so the graph of $2x + y < 1$ includes $(0, 0)$ and all points below the line.

Graph the inequality.

18. $x < 2$

19. $-2x + y > 4$

20. $\frac{1}{3}x - 3y \le 3$

21. $2y - 6x \ge -2$

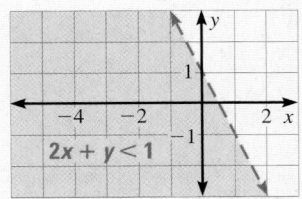

STEM-AND-LEAF PLOTS AND MEAN, MEDIAN, AND MODE

Examples on
pp. 368–370

EXAMPLE To make a stem-and-leaf plot for the following data, use the digits in the tens' place for the stem and the digits in the ones' place for the leaves.

40, 60, 34
43, 68, 45
61, 64, 54
51, 64, 52

Stems

3	4
4	0 3 5
5	1 2 4
6	0 1 4 4 8

Leaves

Key: 6 | 0 = 60

The mean of the data is the sum of the numbers divided by 12, which is 53.

The median of the data is the average of the two middle numbers, which is 53.

The mode of the data is the number that occurs most often, which is 64.

22. The data below show the monthly water temperature (in degrees Fahrenheit) of the Gulf of Mexico near Pensacola, Florida. Make a stem-and-leaf plot of the data: 56, 58, 63, 71, 78, 84, 85, 86, 82, 78, 65, 58.

23. Find the mean, the median, and the mode of the data in Exercise 22.

BOX-AND-WHISKER PLOTS

Examples on
pp. 375–377

EXAMPLE The data show the average temperature (in degrees Celsius) for each month in Tokyo: 5.2, 5.6, 8.5, 14.1, 18.6, 21.7, 25.2, 27.1, 23.2, 17.6, 12.6, 7.9.

Write the numbers in order and find the quartiles of the data.

5.2 5.6 7.9 8.5 12.6 14.1 17.6 18.6 21.7 23.2 25.2 27.1

$$\text{Second quartile} = \frac{14.1 + 17.6}{2} = 15.85$$

$$\text{First quartile} = \frac{7.9 + 8.5}{2} = 8.2 \qquad \text{Third quartile} = \frac{21.7 + 23.2}{2} = 22.45$$

To make a box-and-whisker plot, draw a box that extends from the first to the third quartiles. Connect the least and greatest numbers to the box as the "whiskers."

24. The data below show the average temperature (in degrees Celsius) for each month in Paris. Make a box-and-whisker plot of the data.

3.5, 4.2, 6.6, 9.5, 13.2, 16.3, 15.9, 16.0, 14.7, 12.2, 8.9, 7.3

25. Compare the box-and-whisker plot in Exercise 24 to the one in the Example. How do the data sets differ?

Chapter Test

Solve the inequality. Graph the solution on a number line.

1. $x - 3 < 10$

2. $-6 > x + 5$

3. $-32x > 64$

4. $\dfrac{x}{4} \leq 8$

5. $\dfrac{2}{3}x + 2 \leq 4$

6. $6 - x > 15$

7. $3x + 5 \leq 2x - 1$

8. $(x + 6) \geq 2(1 - x)$

9. $-2x + 8 > 3x + 10$

Solve the inequality. Write a sentence that describes the solution.

10. $-15 \leq 5x < 20$

11. $-3 \leq 4x + 5 \leq 7$

12. $8x - 11 < 5$ or $4x - 7 > 13$

13. $-2x > 8$ or $3x + 1 \geq 7$

14. $12 > 4 - x > -5$

15. $6x + 9 \geq 21$ or $9x - 5 \leq 4$

Write a compound inequality that describes the graph.

16.

17.

Solve the equation or the inequality.

18. $|x + 7| = 11$

19. $|x - 8| - 3 \leq 10$

20. $|x + 4.2| + 3.6 = 16.2$

21. $|2x - 6| > 14$

22. $|4x + 5| - 6 \leq 1$

23. $|3x - 9| + 6 = 18$

Sketch the graph of the inequality.

24. $x > -1$

25. $x - 1 \leq -3$

26. $-4x \leq 8$

27. $x + 2y > 6$

28. $3x + 4y \geq 12$

29. $7y - 2x + 3 < 17$

EXERCISE BICYCLE PRICES In Exercises 30–33, use these prices:

$1130, $695, $900, $220, $350, $500, $630, $180, $170, $145, $185, $140.

30. Make a stem-and-leaf plot for the data. List the data in increasing order.

31. Find the mean, the median, and the mode of the data.

32. Find the first, second, and third quartiles. Which quartile is the median?

33. Draw a box-and-whisker plot of the data.

34. **PAPER MAKING** One kind of machine makes paper in a roll that can be as wide as 33 feet or as narrow as 12 feet. Write a compound inequality for the possible widths of a roll of paper that this machine can produce.

35. **WALKING DISTANCE** Walking at a rate of 210 feet per minute, you take 12 minutes to walk from your home to school. Your uncle's home is closer to school than your home is. Write an inequality for the distance d (in feet) that your uncle lives from your school.

36. **RAFTING** Members of an outdoor club rent several rafts and launch all of the rafts at the same time. The first raft finishes in 36 minutes. The last raft finishes in 48 minutes. Write an absolute-value inequality that describes the finishing times.

Chapter Standardized Test

TEST-TAKING STRATEGY Work as fast as you can through the easier problems, but not so fast that you are careless.

1. MULTIPLE CHOICE Which graph represents the solution of $x + 10 < 17$?

Ⓐ

Ⓑ

Ⓒ

Ⓓ

Ⓔ

2. MULTIPLE CHOICE Describe the solution of the inequality $x + 3 \le 7$.

Ⓐ All real numbers less than 4

Ⓑ All real numbers less than or equal to 10

Ⓒ All real numbers less than or equal to 4

Ⓓ All real numbers less than or equal to -4

Ⓔ None of these

3. MULTIPLE CHOICE Which inequality is equivalent to $2 - 3x \ge -4$?

Ⓐ $x \ge 2$ Ⓑ $x \le 2$

Ⓒ $x \le -\dfrac{2}{3}$ Ⓓ $x \ge -2$

Ⓔ None of these

4. MULTIPLE CHOICE Describe the solution of the compound inequality $-3x + 2 > 11$ or $5x + 1 > 6$.

Ⓐ All real numbers less than -3 or greater than 1

Ⓑ All real numbers greater than 3 or less than 1

Ⓒ All real numbers less than 3 or greater than -1

Ⓓ All real numbers less than -3 and greater than 1

Ⓔ None of these

5. MULTIPLE CHOICE For which values of x is the inequality $5(3x + 4) \le 5x - 10$ true?

Ⓐ $x \ge -3$ Ⓑ $x \le -3$

Ⓒ $x \le -1$ Ⓓ $x \le 1$

Ⓔ $x \le 3$

6. MULTIPLE CHOICE Which graph represents the solution of $|2x - 10| \ge 6$?

Ⓐ

Ⓑ

Ⓒ

Ⓓ

Ⓔ

7. MULTIPLE CHOICE Which numbers are solutions to the absolute-value equation $|x - 7| + 5 = 17$?

Ⓐ 5 and -19 Ⓑ 5 and -5

Ⓒ 12 and -5 Ⓓ 19 and -19

Ⓔ 19 and -5

8. MULTIPLE CHOICE Which point *is not* a solution of $y < x + 5$?

Ⓐ $(4, -4)$ Ⓑ $(1, 4)$

Ⓒ $(-1, 4)$ Ⓓ $(-3, 1)$

Ⓔ $(4, 6)$

9. MULTIPLE CHOICE Choose the inequality whose solution is shown in the graph.

Ⓐ $2x + y < 4$

Ⓑ $2x + y \ge 4$

Ⓒ $2x + y > 4$

Ⓓ $y - 2x > 4$

Ⓔ $y - 2x \le 4$

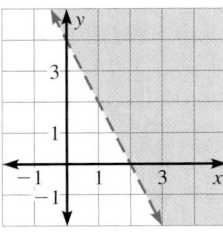

10. **MULTIPLE CHOICE** The stem-and-leaf plot shows the ages of 20 people. What percent of people are under 20 years old?

    (A) 7%   (B) 8%   (C) 10%   (D) 20%   (E) 40%

0	5 7 1 2
1	1 3 3 8
2	2 4 5 9 4 2
3	0 3 3 5 3 8

    Key: 3 | 0 = 30

11. **MULTIPLE CHOICE** What is the mean of the collection of numbers: 25, 29, 33, 38, 40, 45, 51, 53, 66, 73?

    (A) 40   (B) 42.5   (C) 45   (D) 45.3   (E) 73

12. **MULTIPLE CHOICE** Which set of numbers is represented by the box-and-whisker plot?

    15   19   24   28   30

    (A) 20, 24, 15, 20, 25, 18, 19   (B) 19, 18, 15, 23, 25, 28, 30

    (C) 24, 22, 18, 16, 29, 28, 18, 20, 21, 20, 19   (D) 25, 23, 17, 15, 19, 21, 28, 28, 30, 26

    (E) 20, 18, 14, 13, 22, 26, 22, 25, 29

QUANTITATIVE COMPARISON In Exercises 13 and 14, choose the statement below that is true about the given numbers.

    (A) The number in column A is greater.

    (B) The number in column B is greater.

    (C) The two numbers are equal.

    (D) The relationship cannot be determined from the given information.

	Column A	Column B
13.	The mean of 2, 3, 4, 5, 6	The median of 2, 3, 4, 5, 6
14.	$\lvert a + 2 \rvert$	$\lvert a - 2 \rvert$

15. **MULTI-STEP PROBLEM** You own a printing shop and order paper each week to meet your customers' printing needs. Company A charges $4.50 for a ream of 500 sheets of paper plus a $25 delivery fee for each order. Company B charges only $4.00 for a ream but charges a $75 delivery fee for each order.

    a. Let x represent the number of reams of paper you purchase. Write an expression that represents the total cost of purchasing paper from Company A. Write an expression that represents the total cost of purchasing paper from Company B.

    b. Choose two different amounts of paper between 50 reams and 150 reams that you could purchase. Calculate the charges from each supplier.

    c. *Writing* Draw a graph to show the costs of ordering up to 200 reams of paper from each supplier. Explain how to use the graph to determine which company charges the lower price for the same order.

    d. Write an inequality that represents orders for which Company A offers the lower price. Write an inequality that represents orders for which Company B offers the lower price.

Evaluate the expression. (1.1–1.3)

1. $x + 8$ when $x = -1$

2. $3x - 2$ when $x = 7$

3. $x(4 + x)$ when $x = 5$

4. $(x - 5)^2$ when $x = 1$

5. $2\left(\dfrac{x + 8}{x}\right)$ when $x = 4$

6. $x^3 - 3x + 1$ when $x = 2$

Evaluate the expression. (2.2 and 2.3)

7. $2 - (-6) + (-14)$

8. $3.1 + (-3.3) - 1.8$

9. $20 - |-5.5|$

Find the sum or the difference of the matrices. (2.4)

10. $\begin{bmatrix} 3 & 2 \\ 8 & -2 \end{bmatrix} + \begin{bmatrix} -4 & -2 \\ -1 & 0 \end{bmatrix}$

11. $\begin{bmatrix} -2 & 7 & -3 \\ 5 & 4 & 1 \end{bmatrix} - \begin{bmatrix} -8 & 0 & 3 \\ 10 & 5 & -4 \end{bmatrix}$

Simplify the expression. (2.5 and 2.6)

12. $4(y - 4)$

13. $3(6 + x)$

14. $2y(5 + y)$

15. $-5t(3 - t)$

16. $20x - 17x$

17. $4b + 7 + 7b$

18. $5x^2 - 3x^2$

19. $4.2y + 1.1y$

Solve the equation. (3.1–3.4, 3.6)

20. $x + 4 = -1$

21. $-3 = n - 15$

22. $5b = -25$

23. $\dfrac{x}{4} = 6$

24. $3x + 4 = 13$

25. $6 + \dfrac{2}{3}x = 14$

26. $5(x - 2) = 15$

27. $14x + 50 = 75$

28. $x + 8 = 3(x - 4)$

29. $-(x - 7) = \dfrac{1}{2}x + 1$

30. $3x - 15.6 = 75.3$

31. $5.5x + 2.1 = 7.6$

Rewrite the equation so that *y* is a function of *x*. (3.7)

32. $x = y + 3$

33. $4x - 5y = 13$

34. $3(y - x) = 10 - 4x$

Find the unit rate. (3.8)

35. $1 for two cans of dog food

36. $440 for working 40 hours

Plot and label the ordered pairs in a coordinate plane. (4.1)

37. $A(2, 3)$, $B(2, -3)$, $C(-1, 1)$

38. $A(0, -2)$, $B(-3, -3)$, $C(2, 0)$

39. $A(2, 4)$, $B(3, 0)$, $C(-1, -4)$

40. $A(1, -4)$, $B(-2, 4)$, $C(0, -1)$

Plot the points and find the slope of the line passing through the points. (4.4)

41. $(3, 1)$, $(-3, -1)$

42. $(2, 2)$, $(-5, 2)$

43. $(-4, 1)$, $(-4, -2)$

44. $(-2, 0)$, $(0, -4)$

Graph the equation. (4.2, 4.3, and 4.6)

45. $x - y = 4$

46. $2x - y + 1 = 0$

47. $x + 2y - 4 = 0$

48. $x + 3y = 7x$

49. $x + 4y - 1 = 0$

50. $y - 2.5 = 0$

Write an equation of the line in slope-intercept form. (5.1)

51. The slope is 1; the *y*-intercept is -3.

52. The slope is -2; the *y*-intercept is 5.

Write an equation of the line that passes through the point and has the given slope. Write the equation in slope-intercept form. (5.2)

53. $(-1, 1)$, $m = 2$

54. $(3, -1)$, $m = \frac{1}{4}$

55. $(-3, 6)$, $m = -5$

Write an equation in slope-intercept form of the line that passes through the points. (5.3)

56. $(-1, -7)$, $(-2, 1)$

57. $(0, 3)$, $(2, 4)$

58. $(4.2, -3.6)$, $(7.0, 3.4)$

Solve the inequality. (6.1–6.4)

59. $6 > 3x$

60. $-6 \leq x + 12$

61. $-\frac{x}{6} \geq 8$

62. $-4 - 5x \leq 31$

63. $-4x + 3 > -21$

64. $-x + 2 < 2(x - 5)$

65. $-3.2 + x \geq 6.9$

66. $-4 \leq -2x \leq 10$

67. $5 < 4x - 11 < 13$

68. $-2 < x - 7 \leq 15$

69. $|x - 8| > 10$

70. $|2x + 5| \leq 7$

Find the mean, the median, and the mode of the collection of numbers. (6.6)

71. 10, 5, 25, 5, 10, 15, 20, 50, 5, 15

72. 8, 7, 5, 2, 3, 5, 2, 3, 2, 7, 1, 2

73. **PURCHASES** You have $25. You buy two CDs that cost $9.99 each, tax included. Do you have enough money left over to buy a cassette that costs $5.95? Explain. (1.4)

74. **PHOTO COSTS** A photography studio charges $65 for a basic graduation package of photos, plus $3 for each additional wallet photo. Use the equation $65 + 3n = C$, where n represents the number of additional wallet photos and C represents the total cost, to make an input-output table of the costs for ordering 0 through 6 additional wallet photos. (1.7)

75. **VELOCITY** Recall that the speed of an object is the absolute value of its velocity. A hot-air balloon drops at a rate of 100 feet per minute. What are its velocity and speed? (2.1)

76. **TEMPERATURES** On February 21, 1918, the temperature in Granville, North Dakota, rose from $-33°F$ to $50°F$. By how many degrees did the temperature rise? (3.1)

77. **SALES TAX** You are shopping for a pen. The sales tax is 6%. You have a total of $10.50 to spend. What is your price limit for the pen? (3.6)

AMUSEMENT PARKS **In Exercises 78–80, use the table that shows the number of dollars (in millions) spent at amusement parks in the United States from 1991 through 1995.** (4.1 and 5.4)

Years since 1991	0	1	2	3	4
Dollars (in millions)	4820	5366	5663	5905	6376

▶ Source: U.S. Bureau of the Census

78. Draw a scatter plot of the data.

79. Write a linear model for the amount spent at amusement parks.

80. Use the linear model to estimate the amount spent in 2005.

Investigating Elasticity

OBJECTIVE **Explore the relationship between the length of a rubber band and the weight suspended from it.**

Materials: paper cup, paper clip, masking tape, metric ruler, string, rubber band, hole punch, scissors, 100 pennies, graph paper or graphing calculator (optional)

COLLECTING THE DATA

❶ Punch two holes in the paper cup about $\frac{1}{2}$ inch from the top of the rim directly across from each other. Thread the string through the two holes. Tie off the string on both sides of the cup. Cut off any extra string on either end. Then attach the rubber band to the string.

❷ Tape the paper clip to the edge of a table or desk so that one end hangs over the edge. Attach the rubber band to the end of the paper clip so the cup is hanging on the rubber band over the side of the table.

❸ Tape the ruler to the edge of the table next to the rubber band with 0 on the ruler next to the top of the rubber band. Record the distance from the top of the rubber band to the bottom of the cup. This is the initial distance.

❹ Add 10 pennies to the cup. Record the number of pennies you added to the cup and the distance from the top of the rubber band to the bottom of the cup.

❺ Repeat **Step 4** several more times, each time increasing the number of pennies placed in the cup until you have 50 pennies in the cup.

INVESTIGATING THE DATA

1. Make a scatter plot of the data you have collected. Describe any patterns you see.

2. Find an equation for a best-fitting line. You may want to use a graphing calculator or a computer.

3. Explain what the *y*-intercept and the slope mean in terms of your data.

4. Describe a reasonable domain and the range of your equation. Write inequalities to represent both.

MAKING CONJECTURES

5. Make a conjecture about what the distance from the top of the rubber band to the bottom of the cup would be if you placed 100 pennies in the cup.

6. Test your conjecture. What relationship do you see between the number of pennies used and the length of the stretch?

In Exercises 7 and 8, discuss your results with others in your class.

7. Make a conjecture about how the length of the rubber band might affect the total distances. Would the equations be the same or different? Give examples to support your answer.

8. How would your graph be different if you measured from the floor up to the bottom of the rubber band? Explain your answer.

PRESENTING YOUR RESULTS

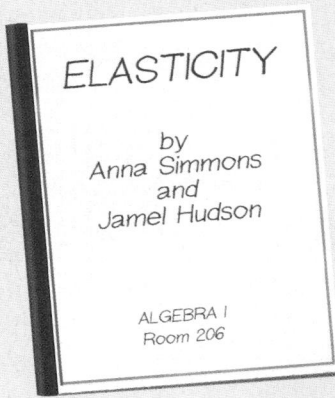

ELASTICITY

by
Anna Simmons
and
Jamel Hudson

ALGEBRA I
Room 206

Write a report or make a poster to report your results.

- Include a table with your data.

- Include your answers to Exercises 1–4.

- Describe the conjectures that you made in Exercises 5–8 and your reasons for believing them to be true.

- Describe any patterns you found when you discussed results with others in your class.

- What advice would you give to someone else who is going to do this project?

EXTENDING THE PROJECT

- How does the thickness of the rubber band affect the distance it stretches? Do a second experiment with a thicker rubber band to find out.

- A grocery store scale operates in a similar way. When you put fruits or vegetables on a scale, the spring inside the scale stretches. The heavier the item, the larger the stretch. Can you think of other items that work in a similar way?

Unweighted spring   Spring with weight attached

Amount of
stretch

weight

SYSTEMS OF LINEAR EQUATIONS AND INEQUALITIES

▶ *How can you analyze the need for low-income housing?*

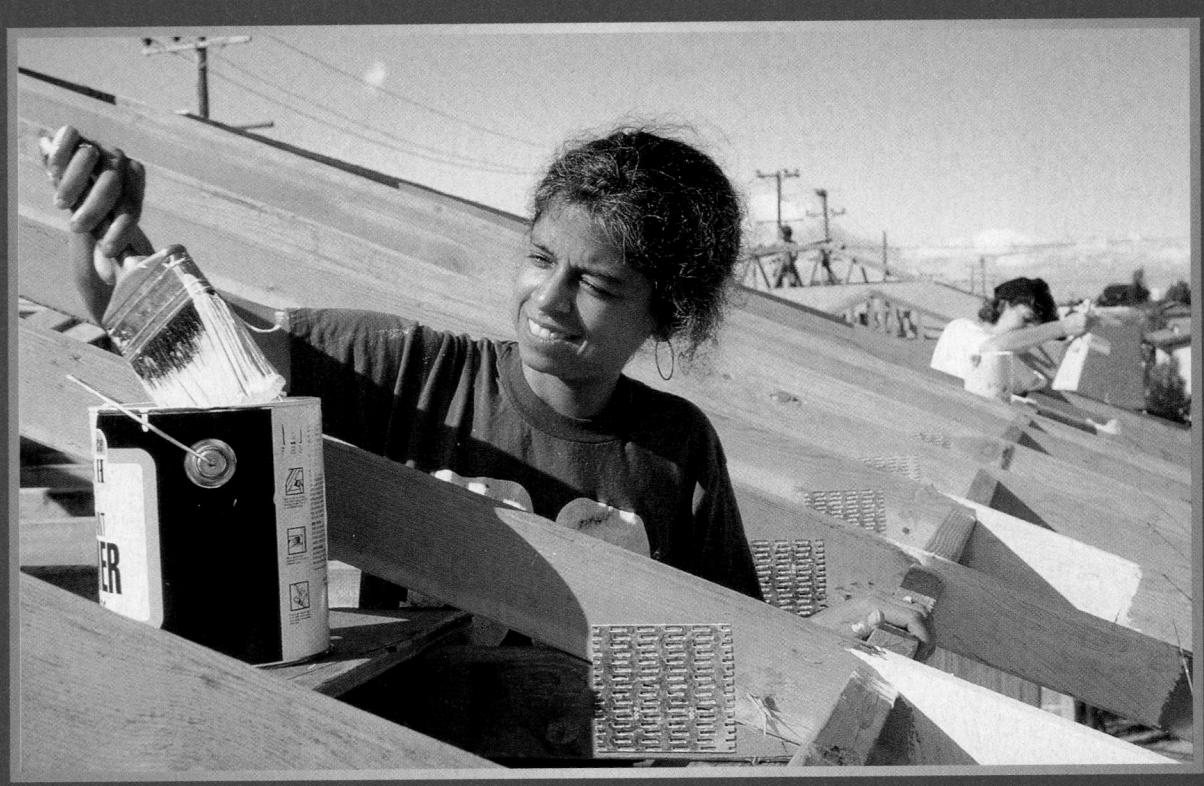

CHAPTER

7

APPLICATION: Housing

To see how the need for low-income rental housing has changed over time, you can look at a model. The graph below shows the number of households with annual earnings of $12,000 or less that need to rent housing and the number of rental units available that they can afford.

In this chapter, you will learn how to use pairs of linear models to analyze problems.

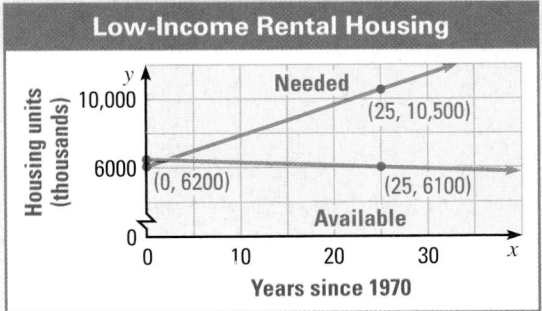

Low-Income Rental Housing

Think & Discuss

Use the graph to answer the following questions.

1. How many low-cost housing units were available in 1995?

2. In 1995, how many more low-income renters were there than low-cost units?

Learn More About It

You will use a linear system to analyze the need for low-income housing in Ex. 51 on p. 422.

 APPLICATION LINK www.mcdougallittell.com

Study Guide

PREVIEW

What's the chapter about?

Chapter 7 is about **systems of equations**. In Chapter 7, you'll learn
- three methods for solving a system of linear equations.
- to determine the number of solutions of a linear system.
- to graph and solve a system of linear inequalities.

KEY VOCABULARY		
▶ **Review**	▶ **New**	• system of linear inequalities, p. 432
• coefficient, p. 102	• linear system, p. 398	• solution of a system of inequalities, p. 432
• linear equation, p. 210	• solution of a linear system, p. 398	• graph of a system of inequalities, p. 432
• ordered pair, p. 203	• linear combination, p. 411	
• parallel lines, p. 242		

PREPARE

Are you ready for the chapter?

SKILL REVIEW Do these exercises to review key skills that you'll apply in this chapter. See the given **reference page** if there is something you don't understand.

STUDENT HELP

▶ **Study Tip**
"Student Help" boxes throughout the chapter give you study tips and tell you where to look for extra help in this book and on the Internet.

Simplify the expression. (Review Example 5, p. 102)

1. $13x + 8x$ **2.** $9r + (-45r)$ **3.** $0.1d - 1.1d$

4. $\frac{1}{2}w + \frac{3}{4}w$ **5.** $-\frac{3}{7}g + \left(-\frac{1}{3}\right)g$ **6.** $-\frac{3}{10}y + \frac{7}{8}y$

Solve the equation if possible. (Review Example 3 and Example 4, p. 155)

7. $2x + 6(x + 1) = -2$ **8.** $5y + 8 = 5y$

9. $1 + 4x = 4x + 1$ **10.** $2(4y - 1) + 2y = 3$

Decide whether the given ordered pair is a solution of the equation or inequality. (Review Example 1, p. 210 and Example 1, p. 360)

11. $2x + y = 1, (1, -1)$ **12.** $5x + 5y = 10, (2, 1)$

13. $3y - x \geq 9, (3, -2)$ **14.** $7y - 8x > 56, (112, 7)$

STUDY STRATEGY

Here's a study strategy!

Solving Problems

It's important to sort out the useful information in a problem. Then you can organize the information and plan how to answer the question.

In your notebook, keep a list of different types of problems you find and how to solve them. Once you have a plan for finding a solution, you can calculate the answer.

▶ ACTIVITY 7.1

Developing Concepts

Investigating Graphs of Linear Systems

GROUP ACTIVITY
Work as a class.

MATERIALS
graph paper

▶ **QUESTION** **Can two different linear equations have a solution in common?**

In this activity, use the following linear equations.

$x - y = -2$ **Equation 1**
$x + y = 4$ **Equation 2**

▶ **EXPLORING THE CONCEPT**

1 Turn your classroom into a coordinate grid by arranging your desks into rows. Every position in your grid should be occupied.

2 Choose one student's position to represent the origin. Write down the ordered pair you represent. A sample classroom grid is shown.

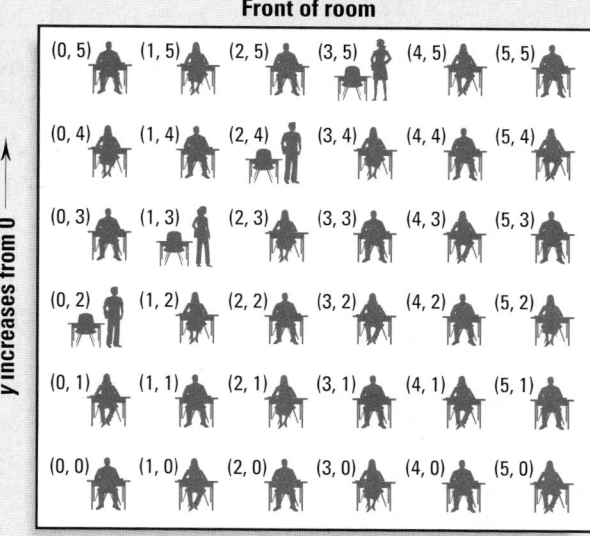

Front of room

y increases from 0 ——▶

x increases from 0 ——▶

STUDENT HELP

↱ **Look Back**
For help with checking solutions, see p. 210.

3 Substitute the *x*-value and *y*-value that you represent into Equation 1. If you get a true statement, stand up.

4 What do you notice about the positions of the students standing up? On graph paper, draw axes and plot a point for each student who is standing.

5 Have everyone sit down. Then repeat **Step 3** and **Step 4** using Equation 2.

▶ **DRAWING CONCLUSIONS**

1. Look at your graph and describe what you observe. Which student's ordered pair do you think will make both equations true? Is this the only ordered pair that is a solution of both equations? Explain.

In Exercises 2–5, use the class as a coordinate grid to find an ordered pair that is a solution of both equations.

2. $x - y = -1$
$x + y = 3$

3. $x + y = 4$
$-x + y = -2$

4. $-x + y = 0$
$x + y = 6$

5. $x = 3$
$y = 2$

6. *Writing* In this activity your class has been modeling the solutions of pairs of linear equations. What have you learned about the solutions of two linear equations whose graphs intersect at one point?

Solving Linear Systems by Graphing

What you should learn

GOAL ① Solve a system of linear equations by graphing.

GOAL ② Model a **real-life** problem using a linear system, such as predicting the number of visits at Internet sites in **Example 3**.

Why you should learn it

▼ To solve **real-life** problems, such as comparing the number of people who live inland to the number of people living on the coastline in **Exs. 37–39**.

GOAL ① GRAPHING A LINEAR SYSTEM

In this chapter you will study *systems of linear equations* in two variables. Here are two equations that form a **system of linear equations** or simply a **linear system**.

$$x + 2y = 5 \qquad \text{Equation 1}$$
$$2x - 3y = 3 \qquad \text{Equation 2}$$

A **solution of a system of linear equations** in two variables is an ordered pair (x, y) that satisfies each equation in the system.

Because the solution of a linear system satisfies each equation in the system, the solution must lie on the graph of both equations. When the solution has integer values, it is possible to find the solution by graphical methods.

EXAMPLE 1 *Checking the Intersection Point*

Use the graph at the right to solve the system of linear equations. Then check your solution algebraically.

$$3x + 2y = 4 \qquad \text{Equation 1}$$
$$-x + 3y = -5 \qquad \text{Equation 2}$$

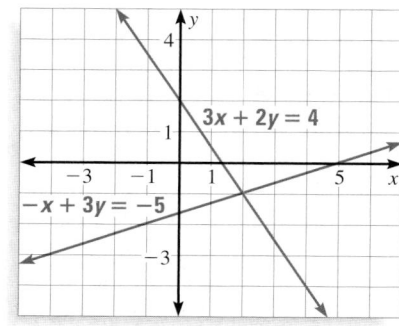

SOLUTION

The graph gives you a visual model of the solution.

The lines appear to intersect once at $(2, -1)$.

✓ **CHECK** To check $(2, -1)$ as a solution algebraically, substitute 2 for x and -1 for y in each equation.

EQUATION 1	EQUATION 2
$3x + 2y = 4$	$-x + 3y = -5$
$3(2) + 2(-1) \stackrel{?}{=} 4$	$-(2) + 3(-1) \stackrel{?}{=} -5$
$6 - 2 \stackrel{?}{=} 4$	$-2 - 3 \stackrel{?}{=} -5$
$4 = 4$	$-5 = -5$

STUDENT HELP

↳ **Look Back**
For help with checking solutions, see p. 210.

▶ Because $(2, -1)$ is a solution of each equation, $(2, -1)$ is the solution of the system of linear equations. Because the lines in the graph of this system intersect at only one point, $(2, -1)$ is the only solution of the linear system.

SOLVING A LINEAR SYSTEM USING GRAPH-AND-CHECK

To use the graph-and-check method to solve a system of linear equations in two variables, use the following steps.

STEP ① Write each equation in a form that is easy to graph.

STEP ② Graph both equations in the same coordinate plane.

STEP ③ Estimate the coordinates of the point of intersection.

STEP ④ Check the coordinates algebraically by substituting into each equation of the original linear system.

STUDENT HELP

HOMEWORK HELP
Visit our Web site
www.mcdougallittell.com
for extra examples.

EXAMPLE 2 *Using the Graph-and-Check Method*

Solve the linear system graphically. Check the solution algebraically.

$x + y = -2$ **Equation 1**
$2x - 3y = -9$ **Equation 2**

SOLUTION

① Write each equation in a form that is easy to graph, such as slope-intercept form.

$y = -x - 2$ Slope: -1, y-intercept: -2

$y = \frac{2}{3}x + 3$ Slope: $\frac{2}{3}$, y-intercept: 3

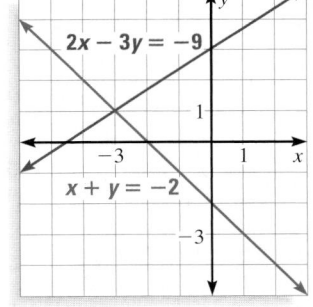

② Graph these equations.

③ The two lines appear to intersect at $(-3, 1)$.

④ To check $(-3, 1)$ as a solution algebraically, substitute -3 for x and 1 for y in each original equation.

EQUATION 1	**EQUATION 2**
$x + y = -2$	$2x - 3y = -9$
$-3 + 1 \stackrel{?}{=} -2$	$2(-3) - 3(1) \stackrel{?}{=} -9$
$-2 = -2$	$-6 - 3 \stackrel{?}{=} -9$
	$-9 = -9$

▶ Because $(-3, 1)$ is a solution of each equation in the linear system, it is a solution of the linear system.

· · · · · · · · · ·

In Example 2 you used the slope-intercept form of each equation in the system to graph the lines. However, there are other methods. For instance, in Lesson 4.3 you learned how to make a quick graph of a linear equation using intercepts.

In the Graphing Calculator Activity at the end of this lesson, you will learn how to graph a system of linear equations using a graphing calculator.

GOAL 2 **MODELING A REAL-LIFE PROBLEM**
··

EXAMPLE 3 | *Writing and Using a Linear System*
──

INTERNET In the fall, the math club and the science club each created an Internet site. You are the webmaster for both sites. It is now January and you are comparing the number of times each site is visited each day.

> **Science Club:** There are currently 400 daily visits and the visits are increasing at a rate of 25 daily visits per month.

> **Math Club:** There are currently 200 daily visits and the visits are increasing at a rate of 50 daily visits per month.

Predict when the number of visits at the two sites will be the same.

SOLUTION

PROBLEM SOLVING STRATEGY

VERBAL MODEL

$$\boxed{\text{Daily visits}} = \boxed{\text{Current visits to science site}} + \boxed{\text{Monthly increase (sci)}} \cdot \boxed{\text{Number of months}}$$

$$\boxed{\text{Daily visits}} = \boxed{\text{Current visits to math site}} + \boxed{\text{Monthly increase (math)}} \cdot \boxed{\text{Number of months}}$$

LABELS

Daily visits = **V**   (daily visits)

Current visits (science) = **400**   (daily visits)

Increase (science) = **25**   (daily visits per month)

Number of months = **t**   (months)

Current visits (math) = **200**   (daily visits)

Increase (math) = **50**   (daily visits per month)

ALGEBRAIC MODEL

$V = 400 + 25\,t$ **Equation 1 (science)**

$V = 200 + 50\,t$ **Equation 2 (math)**

WEBMASTER
Webmasters build Web sites for clients. They often update their technical skills to meet the demands for first-class Web sites. Some also help design Web pages and are responsible for updating the content.

CAREER LINK
www.mcdougallittell.com

Use the graph-and-check method to solve the system. The point of intersection of the two lines appears to be (8, 600). Check this solution in Equation 1 and in Equation 2.

$600 = 400 + 25(8)$

$600 = 200 + 50(8)$

▶ If the monthly increases continue at the same rates, the sites will have the same number of visits by the eighth month after January, which is September.

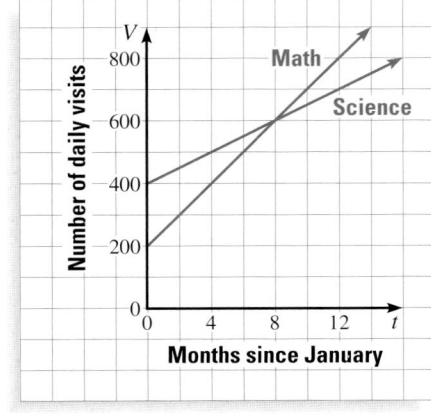

GUIDED PRACTICE

Vocabulary Check ✓

1. Explain what it means to solve a system of linear equations.

Concept Check ✓

2. Explain how to use the graph at the right to solve the system of linear equations.

$$y = -x + 2$$
$$y = x + 2$$

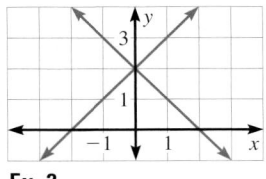

Ex. 2

Skill Check ✓

Graph the linear system below. Then decide if the ordered pair is a solution of the system.

$$-x + y = -2$$
$$2x + y = 10$$

3. $(-4, -2)$ **4.** $(4, -2)$ **5.** $(-4, 2)$ **6.** $(4, 2)$

7. Confirm your answer for Exercise 3 algebraically.

Use the graph-and-check method to solve the system of linear equations.

8. $y = 2x - 1$
$y = x + 1$

9. $y = -2x + 3$
$y = x - 3$

10. $y = \frac{1}{2}x + 2$
$y = -x + 5$

PRACTICE AND APPLICATIONS

STUDENT HELP

▶ **Extra Practice**
to help you master
skills is on p. 803.

CHECKING FOR SOLUTIONS Decide whether the ordered pair is a solution of the system of linear equations.

11. $3x - 2y = 11$
$-x + 6y = 7$ $(5, 2)$

12. $6x - 3y = -15$
$2x + y = -3$ $(-2, 1)$

13. $x + 3y = 15$
$4x + y = 6$ $(3, -6)$

14. $-5x + y = 19$
$x - 7y = 3$ $(-4, -1)$

15. $-15x + 7y = 1$
$3x - y = 1$ $(3, 5)$

16. $-2x + y = -11$
$-x - 9y = -15$ $(6, 1)$

SOLVING SYSTEMS GRAPHICALLY Use the graph to solve the linear system. Check your solution algebraically.

17. $-x + 2y = 6$
$x + 4y = 24$

18. $2x - y = -2$
$4x - y = -6$

19. $x + y = 3$
$-2x + y = -6$

STUDENT HELP

▶ **HOMEWORK HELP**
Example 1: Exs. 11–19
Example 2: Exs. 20–34
Example 3: Exs. 35, 36

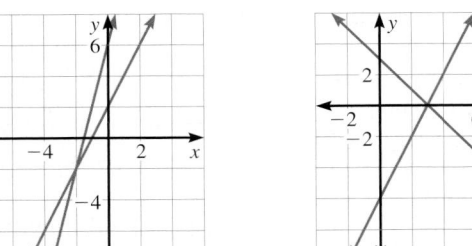

Graph and check to solve the linear system.

20. $y = -x + 3$
$y = x + 1$

21. $y = -6$
$x = 6$

22. $y = 2x - 4$
$y = -\frac{1}{2}x + 1$

23. $2x - 3y = 9$
$x = -3$

24. $5x + 4y = 16$
$y = -16$

25. $x - y = 1$
$5x - 4y = 0$

26. $3x + 6y = 15$
$-2x + 3y = -3$

27. $7y = -14x + 42$
$7y = 14x + 14$

28. $0.5x + 0.6y = 5.4$
$-x + y = 9$

29. $15x - 10y = -80$
$6x + 8y = -80$

30. $-3x + y = 10$
$7x + y = 20$

31. $x - 8y = -40$
$-5x + 8y = 8$

32. $\frac{1}{5}x + \frac{3}{5}y = \frac{12}{5}$
$-\frac{1}{5}x + \frac{3}{5}y = \frac{6}{5}$

33. $\frac{3}{4}x - \frac{1}{4}y = -\frac{1}{2}$
$\frac{1}{4}x - \frac{3}{4}y = \frac{3}{2}$

34. $2.8x + 1.4y = 1.4$
$0.7x - 0.7y = 1.4$

35. 🌎 **COMPARING CARS** Car model X costs $22,000 to purchase and an average of $.12 per mile to maintain. Car model Y costs $24,500 to purchase and an average of $.10 per mile to maintain. Use the graph to determine how many miles must be driven for the total cost of the two models to be the same.

Ex. 35

36. 🌎 **AEROBICS CLASSES** A fitness club offers two water aerobics classes. There are currently 40 people regularly going to the morning class, and attendance is increasing at a rate of 2 people per month. There are currently 22 people regularly going to the evening class, and attendance is increasing at a rate of 8 people per month. Predict when the number of people in each class will be the same.

🌎 **COASTAL POPULATION** **In Exercises 37–39, use the table below, which gives the percents of people in the contiguous United States living within 50 miles of a coastal shoreline and those living further inland.**

Population in United States	1940	1997
Living within 50 miles of a coastal shoreline	46%	53%
Living farther inland	54%	47%

 DATA UPDATE U.S. Bureau of the Census at www.mcdougallittell.com

37. For each location, write a linear model to represent the percent at time t, where t represents the number of years since 1940.

38. Graph the linear equations you wrote.

39. From your graphs, estimate when the percent of people living near the coast equaled the percent living inland.

40. 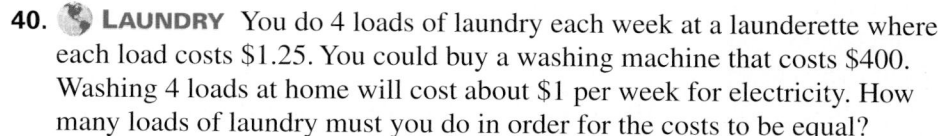 **LAUNDRY** You do 4 loads of laundry each week at a launderette where each load costs $1.25. You could buy a washing machine that costs $400. Washing 4 loads at home will cost about $1 per week for electricity. How many loads of laundry must you do in order for the costs to be equal?

Test Preparation

41. MULTIPLE CHOICE Which ordered pair is a solution of the linear system?

$$x + y = 0.5$$
$$x + 2y = 1$$

(A) $(0, -2)$ **(B)** $(-0.5, 0)$ **(C)** $(0, 0.5)$ **(D)** $(0, -0.5)$

42. MULTIPLE CHOICE If $y - x = -3$ and $4x + y = 2$, then $x = \underline{\ ?\ }$.

(A) 1 **(B)** -1 **(C)** 5 **(D)** -5

★ **Challenge**

43. SOLVE USING A SYSTEM You know how to solve the equation $\frac{1}{2}x + 2 = \frac{3}{2}x - 12$ algebraically. This equation can also be solved graphically by solving the linear system.

$$y = \frac{1}{2}x + 2$$

$$y = \frac{3}{2}x - 12$$

  a. Explain how the linear system is related to the original equation.

  b. Solve the system graphically.

  c. Check that the *x*-coordinate from part (b) satisfies the original equation $\frac{1}{2}x + 2 = \frac{3}{2}x - 12$ by substituting the *x*-coordinate for *x*.

EXTRA CHALLENGE
www.mcdougallittell.com

Use the method shown in Exercise 43 to solve the equation graphically.

44. $\frac{4}{5}x = 3x - 11$ **45.** $x + 1 = \frac{3}{2}x + 2$ **46.** $1.2x - 2 = 3.4x - 13$

MIXED REVIEW

SOLVING EQUATIONS **Solve the equation.** (Review 3.3 for 7.2)

47. $3x + 7 = -2$ **48.** $15 - 2a = 7$ **49.** $21 = 7(w - 2)$

50. $2y + 5 = 3y$ **51.** $2(z - 3) = 12$ **52.** $-(3 - x) = -7$

WRITING EQUATIONS **Write an equation of the line that passes through the point and has the given slope. Use slope-intercept form.** (Review 5.2)

53. $(3, 0)$, $m = -4$ **54.** $(-4, 3)$, $m = 1$ **55.** $(1, -5)$, $m = 4$

56. $(-4, -1)$, $m = -2$ **57.** $(2, 3)$, $m = 2$ **58.** $(-1, 5)$, $m = \frac{2}{3}$

59. **SUSPENSION BRIDGES** The Verrazano-Narrows Bridge in New York City is the longest suspension bridge in North America, with a main span of 4260 feet. Write an inequality that describes the length in feet *x* of every other suspension bridge in North America. Graph the inequality on a number line. (Review 6.1)

Verrazano-Narrows Bridge

ACTIVITY 7.1
Using Technology

Solving Linear Systems by Graphing

▶ **EXAMPLE**

Solve the linear system by graphing.

$$y = -0.3x + 1.8 \qquad \textbf{Equation 1}$$
$$y = 0.6x - 1.5 \qquad \textbf{Equation 2}$$

STUDENT HELP

INTERNET **KEYSTROKE HELP**

See keystrokes for several models of calculators at www.mcdougallittell.com

▶ **SOLUTION**

1 Enter the equations.

2 Set an appropriate viewing window to graph both equations.

3 Graph both equations. You can use the direction keys to move the cursor to the approximate intersection point.

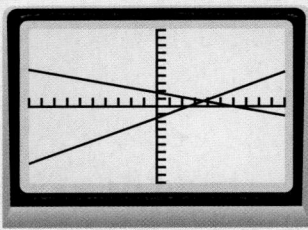

4 Use the *Intersection* feature to estimate a point where the graphs intersect. Follow your calculator's procedure to display the coordinate values.

▶ The solution of the system of linear equations is approximately (3.7, 0.7).

▶ **EXERCISES**

In Exercises 1–4, solve the linear system. Check the result in each of the original equations.

1. $y = x + 6$
$y = -x - 1$

2. $3x + y = -2$
$x - y = -8$

3. $-0.25x - y = 2.25$
$-1.25x + 1.25y = -1.25$

4. $-0.8x + 0.6y = -12.0$
$1.25x - 1.50y = 12.75$

5. Graph the linear system at the right. $\quad 3x + 9y = 8$
$\qquad\qquad\qquad\qquad\qquad\qquad\qquad\quad 2x + 6y = 7$

Describe the lines, and explain why the linear system has no solution.

7.2 Solving Linear Systems by Substitution

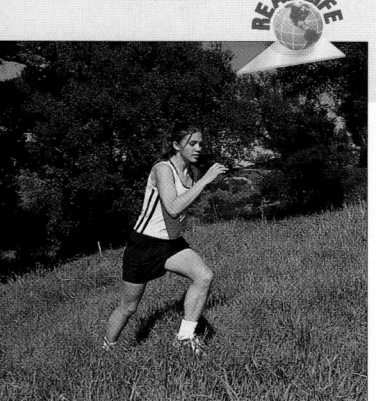

What you should learn

GOAL ① Use substitution to solve a linear system.

GOAL ② Model a **real-life** situation using a linear system, such as the average number of visitors to a Museum in **Example 3**.

Why you should learn it

▼ To solve **real-life** problems such as finding a distance run in **Exs. 46** and **47**.

GOAL ① USING SUBSTITUTION

In this lesson you will study an algebraic method for solving a linear system.

SOLVING A LINEAR SYSTEM BY SUBSTITUTION

STEP ① Solve one of the equations for one of its variables.

STEP ② Substitute the expression from Step 1 into the other equation and solve for the other variable.

STEP ③ Substitute the value from Step 2 into the revised equation from Step 1 and solve.

STEP ④ Check the solution in each of the original equations.

EXAMPLE 1 *The Substitution Method*

Solve the linear system.

$$-x + y = 1 \qquad \text{Equation 1}$$
$$2x + y = -2 \qquad \text{Equation 2}$$

SOLUTION

① Solve for y in Equation 1.

$$y = x + 1 \qquad \text{Revised Equation 1}$$

② Substitute $x + 1$ for y in Equation 2 and solve for x.

$2x + y = -2$	Write Equation 2.
$2x + (x + 1) = -2$	Substitute $x + 1$ for y.
$3x + 1 = -2$	Simplify.
$3x = -3$	Subtract 1 from each side.
$x = -1$	Solve for x.

③ To find the value of y, substitute -1 for x in the revised Equation 1.

$y = x + 1$	Write revised Equation 1.
$y = -1 + 1$	Substitute -1 for x.
$y = 0$	Solve for y.

④ Check that $(-1, 0)$ is a solution by substituting -1 for x and 0 for y in each of the original equations.

▶ The solution is $(-1, 0)$.

EXAMPLE 2 **The Substitution Method**

Solve the linear system.

$$2x + 2y = 3 \qquad \textbf{Equation 1}$$
$$x - 4y = -1 \qquad \textbf{Equation 2}$$

SOLUTION

Solve for *x* in Equation 2 because it is easy to isolate *x*.

$$x = 4y - 1 \qquad \textbf{Revised Equation 2}$$

Substitute $4y - 1$ for *x* in Equation 1 and solve for *y*.

$$2x + 2y = 3 \qquad \text{Write Equation 1.}$$
$$2(4y - 1) + 2y = 3 \qquad \text{Substitute } 4y - 1 \text{ for } x.$$
$$8y - 2 + 2y = 3 \qquad \text{Distribute the 2.}$$
$$10y - 2 = 3 \qquad \text{Simplify.}$$
$$10y = 5 \qquad \text{Add 2 to each side.}$$
$$y = \frac{1}{2} \qquad \text{Solve for } y.$$

Substitute $\frac{1}{2}$ for *y* in the revised Equation 2 to find the value of *x*.

$$x = 4y - 1 \qquad \text{Write revised Equation 2.}$$
$$x = 4\left(\frac{1}{2}\right) - 1 \qquad \text{Substitute } \frac{1}{2} \text{ for } y.$$
$$x = 1 \qquad \text{Solve for } x.$$

Check by substituting 1 for *x* and $\frac{1}{2}$ for *y* in each of the original equations.

EQUATION 1	**EQUATION 2**
$2x + 2y = 3$	$x - 4y = -1$
$2(1) + 2\left(\frac{1}{2}\right) \stackrel{?}{=} 3$	$1 - 4\left(\frac{1}{2}\right) \stackrel{?}{=} -1$
$2 + 1 \stackrel{?}{=} 3$	$1 - 2 \stackrel{?}{=} -1$
$3 = 3$	$-1 = -1$

▶ The solution is $\left(1, \frac{1}{2}\right)$.

. . . .

When you use the substitution method, you can still use a graph to check the reasonableness of your solution. For instance, the graph at the right shows a graphic check for Example 2.

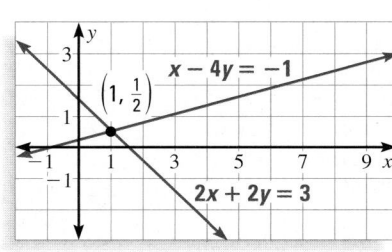

EXAMPLE 3 *Writing and Using a Linear System*

MUSEUM ADMISSIONS In one day the National Civil Rights Museum in Memphis, Tennessee, collected $1590 from 321 people admitted to the museum. The price of each adult admission is $6. People with the ages of 4–17 pay the child admission, $4. Estimate how many adults and how many children were admitted that day.

SOLUTION

Use a verbal model to find the number of adults and children admitted to the museum that day.

 PROBLEM SOLVING STRATEGY

VERBAL MODEL

| Number of adults | + | Number of children | = | Total number admitted |

| Number of adults | · | Price of adult admission | + | Number of children | · | Price of child admission | = | Total amount collected |

LABELS

Number of adults = x (people)

Number of children = y (people)

Total number admitted = **321**   (people)

Price of adult admission = **6**   (dollars per person)

Price of child admission = **4**   (dollars per person)

Total amount collected = **1590**   (dollars)

ALGEBRAIC MODEL

$x + y = 321$ Equation 1 (Number admitted)

$6x + 4y = 1590$ Equation 2 (Amount collected)

NATIONAL CIVIL RIGHTS MUSEUM
The National Civil Rights Museum educates people about the history of the civil rights movement through its unique collections and powerful exhibits.

APPLICATION LINK
www.mcdougallittell.com

Using the substitution method, you can determine that $x = 153$ when $y = 168$. The solution is the ordered pair (153, 168).

The graphs of the two equations appear to intersect at (153, 168). The solution checks graphically.

▶ You can conclude that 153 adults were admitted and 168 children were admitted to the National Civil Rights Museum that day.

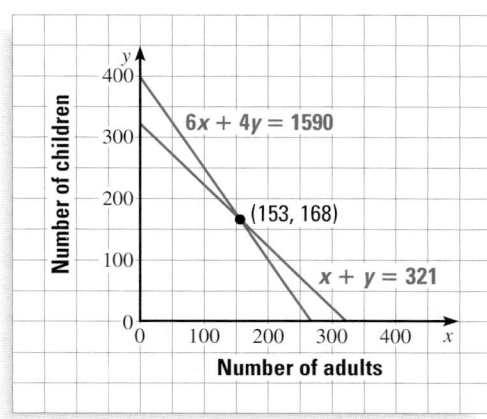

GUIDED PRACTICE

Concept Check ✓

In Exercises 1–5, use the linear system below.

$$-x + y = 5 \qquad \textbf{Equation 1}$$
$$\tfrac{1}{2}x + y = 8 \qquad \textbf{Equation 2}$$

1. Which equation would you choose to solve for y? Why?

2. Solve for y in the equation that you chose.

3. Substitute the expression into the other equation and solve for x.

4. Substitute the value of x into your equation from Exercise 2. What is the solution of the linear system?

5. Explain how you can check the solution algebraically and graphically.

Skill Check ✓

Use substitution to solve the linear system.

6. $3x + y = 3$
   $7x + 2y = 1$

7. $2x - y = -1$
   $2x + y = -7$

8. $3x - y = 0$
   $5y = 15$

9. $2x + y = 4$
   $-x + y = 1$

10. $x - y = 0$
   $x + y = 2$

11. $x + y = 1$
   $2x - y = 2$

12. $-x + 4y = 10$
   $x - 3y = 11$

13. $x + y = 1$
   $x - y = 2$

PRACTICE AND APPLICATIONS

STUDENT HELP

→ **Extra Practice**
to help you master
skills is on p. 803.

REASONING **Tell which equation you would use to isolate a variable. Explain your reasoning.**

14. $2x + y = -10$
   $3x - y = 0$

15. $m + 4n = 30$
   $m - 2n = 0$

16. $5c + 3d = 11$
   $5c - d = 5$

SOLVING LINEAR SYSTEMS **Use the substitution method to solve the linear system.**

17. $y = x - 4$
   $4x + y = 26$

18. $s = t + 4$
   $2t + s = 19$

19. $2c - d = -2$
   $4c + d = 20$

20. $2a = 8$
   $a + b = 2$

21. $2x + 3y = 31$
   $y = x + 7$

22. $p + q = 4$
   $4p + q = 1$

23. $x - 2y = -25$
   $3x - y = 0$

24. $u - v = 0$
   $7u + v = 0$

25. $x - y = 0$
   $12x - 5y = -21$

26. $m + 2n = 1$
   $5m + 3n = -23$

27. $x - y = -5$
   $x + 4 = 16$

28. $-3a + b = 4$
   $-9a + 5b = -1$

29. $3w - 2u = 12$
   $w - u = 60$

30. $y = 3x$
   $x = 3y$

31. $x + y = 5$
   $0.5x + 6.0y = 8.0$

STUDENT HELP

→ **HOMEWORK HELP**
Example 1: Exs. 14–34
Example 2: Exs. 14–34
Example 3: Exs. 42–44

32. $x + y = 12$
   $x + \tfrac{3}{2}y = \tfrac{3}{2}$

33. $7g + h = -2$
   $g - 2h = 9$

34. $\tfrac{1}{8}p + \tfrac{3}{4}q = 7$
   $\tfrac{3}{2}p - q = 4$

35. ERROR ANALYSIS You are helping a friend with tonight's math homework. Answer your friend's questions.

$$3x + y = 9 \quad \leftarrow \text{Equation 1}$$
$$-2x + y = 4 \quad \leftarrow \text{Equation 2}$$
$$3x + y = 9$$
$$y = -3x + 9$$

$$3x + (-3x + 9) = 9$$
$$3x - 3x + 9 \overset{\underset{\cdot}{}}{=} 9$$
$$9 = 9$$

What does this mean?

How do I find the answer?

 SOLVING LINEAR SYSTEMS In Exercises 36–41, use substitution to solve the linear system. Then use a graphing calculator or a computer to check your solution.

36. $x - y = 2$
$2x + y = 1$

37. $2y = x$
$4y = 300 - x$

38. $x - 2y = 9$
$1.5x + 0.5y = 6.5$

39. $0.50x + 0.25y = 2.00$
$x + y = 1$

40. $x + y = 20$
$\frac{1}{5}x + \frac{1}{2}y = 8$

41. $1.5x - y = 40.0$
$0.5x + 0.5y = 10.0$

42. 🌎 **TICKET SALES** You are selling tickets for a high school play. Student tickets cost $4 and general admission tickets cost $6. You sell 525 tickets and collect $2876. How many of each type of ticket did you sell?

43. 🌎 **ORDERING SOFTBALLS** You are ordering softballs for two softball leagues. The Pony League uses an 11-inch softball priced at $2.75. The Junior League uses a 12-inch softball priced at $3.25. The bill smeared in the rain, but you know the total was 80 softballs for $245. How many of each size did you order?

44. 🌎 **MATH TEST** Your math teacher tells you that next week's test is worth 100 points and contains 38 problems. Each problem is worth either 5 points or 2 points. Because you are studying systems of linear equations, your teacher says that for extra credit you can figure out how many problems of each value are on the test. How many of each value are there?

45. 🌎 **INVESTING IN STOCKS** The value of your EFG stock is three times the value of your PQR stock. If the total value of the stocks is $4500, how much is invested in each company?

🌎 **RUNNING** In Exercises 46 and 47, you can run 250 meters per minute downhill and 180 meters per minute uphill. One day you run a total of 1557 meters in 7.6 minutes on a route that goes both uphill and downhill.

46. Assign labels to the verbal model below. Then write an algebraic model.

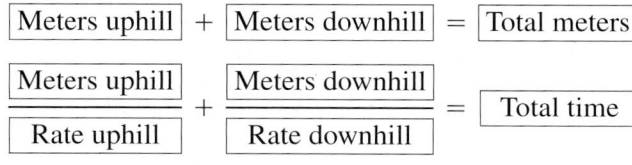

$$\boxed{\text{Meters uphill}} + \boxed{\text{Meters downhill}} = \boxed{\text{Total meters}}$$

$$\frac{\boxed{\text{Meters uphill}}}{\boxed{\text{Rate uphill}}} + \frac{\boxed{\text{Meters downhill}}}{\boxed{\text{Rate downhill}}} = \boxed{\text{Total time}}$$

47. Find the number of meters you ran uphill and the number of meters you ran downhill.

MULTI-STEP PROBLEM In Exercises 48–51, use the linear system below.

$$y = x + 3$$
$$y = 2x + 3$$

48. Graph the system. Explain what the graph shows.

49. Solve the linear system using substitution. What does the solution mean?

50. Which method do you think is easier for solving this linear system?

51. *Writing* Describe the advantages and disadvantages of each method.

★ Challenge

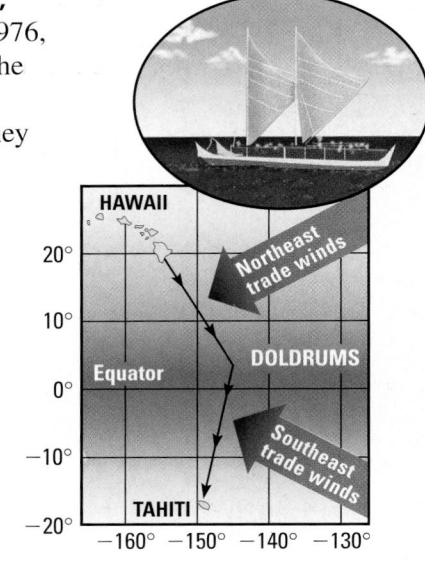

HISTORY CONNECTION In Exercises 52 and 53, use the following information. On May 1, 1976, a team of adventurers set sail to discover how the ancient Polynesians regularly navigated the 3000-nautical-mile route shown at the right. They sailed from Hawaii to Tahiti on a traditional twin-hulled canoe called the *Hokule'a*.

Sailing into northeast trade winds, the crew maintained a course represented by

$$y = -\frac{3}{2}x - 215.$$

Sailing into southeast trade winds, the crew maintained a course represented by

$$y = 7x + 1026.$$

At the point of intersection, the team became caught in the "doldrums" and made little headway for 5 to 6 days.

52. Find the coordinates of the point where the team was caught in the doldrums.

EXTRA CHALLENGE
www.mcdougallittell.com

53. The equation of the straight line passing through Hawaii and Tahiti is $36x + 7y = -5483$. Find the coordinates of Hawaii and Tahiti.

MIXED REVIEW

SIMPLIFYING EXPRESSIONS Simplify the variable expression.
(Review 2.6 for 7.3)

54. $4g + 3h + 2g - 3h$

55. $3x + 2y - (5x + 2y)$

56. $6(2p - m) - 3m - 12p$

57. $4(3x + 5y) + 3(-4x + 2y)$

GRAPHING LINES Write the equation in slope-intercept form. Then graph the equation. (Review 4.6)

58. $6x + y = 0$

59. $8x - 4y + 16 = 0$

60. $3x + y + 5 = 0$

61. $5x + 3y = 3$

62. $x + y = 0$

63. $y = -2$

SOLVING AND GRAPHING Solve the inequality. Then graph its solution.
(Review 6.3, 6.4)

64. $-5 < -x \le -1$

65. $|x + 5| \le 14$

66. $3 > -x > -1$

67. $2x - 6 < -7$ or $2x - 6 > 5$

68. $3x - 2 > 4$ or $3x - 2 < -5$

7.3

Solving Linear Systems by Linear Combinations

What you should learn

GOAL 1 Use linear combinations to solve a system of linear equations.

GOAL 2 Model a **real-life** problem using a system of linear equations, such as the mixture problem in **Example 4**.

Why you should learn it

▼ To solve **real-life** problems such as finding the speed of the current in a river in **Ex. 48**.

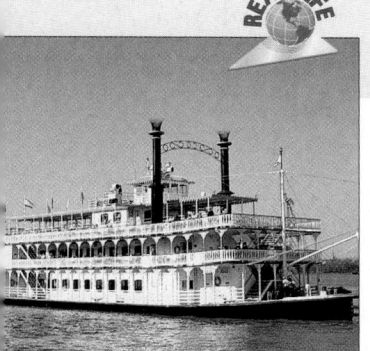

GOAL 1 USING LINEAR COMBINATIONS

Sometimes when you want to solve a linear system, it is not easy to isolate one of the variables. In that case, you can solve the system by *linear combinations*. A **linear combination** of two equations is an equation obtained by adding one of the equations (or a multiple of one of the equations) to the other equation.

SOLVING A LINEAR SYSTEM BY LINEAR COMBINATIONS

STEP 1 Arrange the equations with like terms in columns.

STEP 2 Multiply one or both of the equations by a number to obtain coefficients that are opposites for one of the variables.

STEP 3 Add the equations from Step 2. Combining like terms will eliminate one variable. Solve for the remaining variable.

STEP 4 Substitute the value obtained in Step 3 into either of the original equations and solve for the other variable.

STEP 5 Check the solution in each of the original equations.

EXAMPLE 1 *Using Addition*

Solve the linear system. $4x + 3y = 16$ **Equation 1**
$2x - 3y = 8$ **Equation 2**

SOLUTION

1 The equations are already arranged.

2 The coefficients for y are already opposites.

3 Add the equations to get an equation in one variable.

$$4x + 3y = 16$$ Write Equation 1.
$$\underline{2x - 3y = 8}$$ Write Equation 2.
$$6x = 24$$ Add equations.
$$x = 4$$ Solve for x.

4 Substitute 4 for x in the first equation and solve for y.

$$4(4) + 3y = 16$$ Substitute 4 for x.
$$y = 0$$ Solve for y.

5 Check by substituting 4 for x and 0 for y in each of the original equations.

▶ The solution is $(4, 0)$.

EXAMPLE 2 *Using Multiplication First*

Solve the linear system. $3x + 5y = 6$ **Equation 1**
                          $-4x + 2y = 5$ **Equation 2**

SOLUTION

The equations are already arranged. You can get the coefficients of x to be opposites by multiplying the first equation by 4 and the second equation by 3.

$$\begin{array}{ll} 3x + 5y = 6 & \textbf{Multiply by 4.} \\ -4x + 2y = 5 & \textbf{Multiply by 3.} \end{array} \qquad \begin{array}{l} 12x + 20y = 24 \\ -12x + 6y = 15 \end{array}$$

$$26y = 39 \qquad \textbf{Add equations.}$$

$$y = 1.5 \qquad \textbf{Solve for } y.$$

Substitute 1.5 for y in the second equation and solve for x.

$$-4x + 2y = 5 \qquad \textbf{Write Equation 2.}$$

$$-4x + 2(\mathbf{1.5}) = 5 \qquad \textbf{Substitute 1.5 for } y.$$

$$-4x + 3 = 5 \qquad \textbf{Simplify.}$$

$$x = -0.5 \qquad \textbf{Solve for } x.$$

▶ The solution is $(-0.5, 1.5)$. Check this in the original equations.

EXAMPLE 3 *Arranging Like Terms in Columns*

Solve the linear system. $3x + 2y = 8$ **Equation 1**
                          $2y = 12 - 5x$ **Equation 2**

SOLUTION

First arrange the equations.

$$\begin{array}{ll} 3x + 2y = 8 & \textbf{Write Equation 1.} \\ 5x + 2y = 12 & \textbf{Rearrange Equation 2.} \end{array}$$

You can get the coefficients of y to be opposites by multiplying the second equation by -1.

$$\begin{array}{ll} 3x + 2y = 8 \\ 5x + 2y = 12 & \textbf{Multiply by } -1. \end{array} \qquad \begin{array}{l} 3x + 2y = 8 \\ -5x - 2y = -12 \end{array}$$

$$-2x = -4 \qquad \textbf{Add equations.}$$

$$x = 2 \qquad \textbf{Solve for } x.$$

Substitute 2 for x into the first equation and solve for y.

$$3x + 2y = 8 \qquad \textbf{Write Equation 1.}$$

$$3(\mathbf{2}) + 2y = 8 \qquad \textbf{Substitute 2 for } x.$$

$$6 + 2y = 8 \qquad \textbf{Simplify.}$$

$$y = 1 \qquad \textbf{Solve for } y.$$

▶ The solution is $(2, 1)$. Check this in the original equations.

Legend has it that Archimedes used the relationship between the weight of an object and its volume to prove that his king's gold crown was not pure gold. If the crown was all gold, it would have had the same volume as an equal amount of gold.

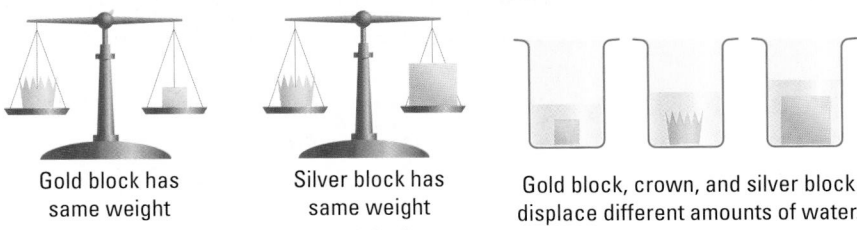

Gold block has same weight as crown.

Silver block has same weight as crown.

Gold block, crown, and silver block displace different amounts of water.

EXAMPLE 4 *Writing and Using a Linear System*

GOLD AND SILVER A gold crown, suspected of containing some silver, was found to have a weight of 714 grams and a volume of 46 cubic centimeters. The density of gold is about 19 grams per cubic centimeter. The density of silver is about 10.5 grams per cubic centimeter. What percent of the crown is silver?

SOLUTION

VERBAL MODEL

$$\boxed{\text{Gold volume}} + \boxed{\text{Silver volume}} = \boxed{\text{Total volume}}$$

$$\boxed{\text{Gold density}} \cdot \boxed{\text{Gold volume}} + \boxed{\text{Silver density}} \cdot \boxed{\text{Silver volume}} = \boxed{\text{Total weight}}$$

LABELS

Volume of gold = G (cubic centimeters)

Volume of silver = S (cubic centimeters)

Total volume = 46   (cubic centimeters)

Density of gold = 19   (grams per cubic centimeter)

Density of silver = 10.5   (grams per cubic centimeter)

Total weight = 714   (grams)

ALGEBRAIC MODEL

$G + S = 46$ **Equation 1**

$19G + 10.5S = 714$ **Equation 2**

ARCHIMEDES In the third century B.C., Archimedes supposedly used the relationship between the weight of an object and its volume to uncover a fraud in the manufacture of a gold crown.

APPLICATION LINK
www.mcdougallittell.com

Use linear combinations to solve for S.

$$
\begin{array}{ll}
-19G - 19S = -874 & \text{\textbf{Multiply Equation 1 by }}-19. \\
\underline{19G + 10.5S = 714} & \text{\textbf{Write Equation 2.}} \\
\qquad\quad -8.5S = -160 & \text{\textbf{Add equations.}}
\end{array}
$$

▶ The volume of silver is about 19 cm³. The crown has a volume of 46 cm³, so the crown is $\frac{19}{46} \approx 41\%$ silver by volume.

GUIDED PRACTICE

Vocabulary Check ✓

1. When you use the linear combinations method to solve a linear system, what is the purpose of using multiplication as the first step?

Concept Check ✓

ERROR ANALYSIS Find and describe the error. Then correctly solve the linear system by using linear combinations.

2.

3.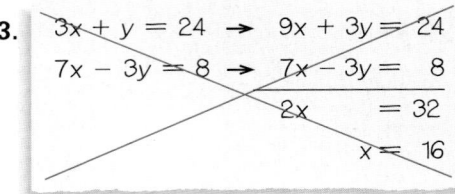

Skill Check ✓

Explain the steps you would use to solve the system of equations using linear combinations. Then solve the system.

4. $x + 3y = 6$
   $x - 3y = 12$

5. $x - 3y = 0$
   $x + 10y = 13$

6. $3x - 4y = 7$
   $2x - y = 3$

7. $2y = -2 + 2x$
   $2x + 3y = 12$

PRACTICE AND APPLICATIONS

STUDENT HELP

→ **Extra Practice**
to help you master
skills is on p. 803.

USING ADDITION Use linear combinations to solve the system of linear equations.

8. $2x + y = 4$
   $x - y = 2$

9. $a - b = 8$
   $a + b = 20$

10. $y - 2x = 0$
   $6y + 2x = 0$

11. $m + 3n = 2$
   $-m + 2n = 3$

12. $p + 4q = 23$
   $-p + q = 2$

13. $3v - 2w = 1$
   $2v + 2w = 4$

14. $\frac{1}{2}g + h = 2$
   $-g - h = 2$

15. $6.5x - 2.5y = 4.0$
   $1.5x + 2.5y = 4.0$

USING MULTIPLICATION FIRST Use linear combinations to solve the system of linear equations.

16. $x - y = 0$
   $-3x - y = 2$

17. $v - w = -5$
   $v + 2w = 4$

18. $x + 3y = 3$
   $x + 6y = 3$

19. $2g - 3h = 0$
   $3g - 2h = 5$

20. $2p - q = 2$
   $2p + 3q = 22$

21. $2a + 6z = 4$
   $3a - 7z = 6$

22. $5e + 4f = 9$
   $4e + 5f = 9$

23. $10m + 16n = 140$
   $5m - 8n = 60$

24. $9x - 3z = 20$
   $3x + 6z = 2$

STUDENT HELP

→ **HOMEWORK HELP**
Example 1: Exs. 8–15
Example 2: Exs. 16–24,
          31–42
Example 3: Exs. 25–42
Example 4: Ex. 43

ARRANGING LIKE TERMS Use linear combinations to solve the system of linear equations.

25. $x + 3y = 12$
   $-3y + x = 30$

26. $3b + 2c = 46$
   $5c + b = 11$

27. $y = x - 9$
   $x + 8y = 0$

28. $2q = 7 - 5p$
   $4p - 16 = q$

29. $2v = 150 - u$
   $2u = 150 - v$

30. $0.1g - h + 4.3 = 0$
   $3.6 = -0.2g + h$

Look Back
For help with simplifying expressions, see p. 102.

SOLVING LINEAR SYSTEMS In Exercises 31–42, use linear combinations to solve the system of linear equations.

31. $x + 2y = 5$
$5x - y = 3$

32. $3p - 2 = -q$
$-q + 2p = 3$

33. $3g - 24 = -4h$
$-2 + 2h = g$

34. $t + r = 1$
$2r - t = 2$

35. $x + 1 - 3y = 0$
$2x = 7 - 3y$

36. $3a + 9b = 8b - a$
$5a - 10b = 4a - 9b + 5$

37. $2m - 4 = 4n$
$m - 2 = n$

38. $3y = -5x + 15$
$-y = -3x + 9$

39. $3j + 5k = 19$
$4j - 8k = -4$

40. $1.5v - 6.5w = 3.5$
$0.5v + 2w = -3$

41. $5y - 20 = -4x$
$y = -\frac{5}{4}x + 4$

42. $9g - 7h = \frac{2}{3}$
$3g + h = \frac{1}{3}$

43. 🌐 **WEIGHT OF GOLD** A gold and copper bracelet weighs 238 grams. The volume of the bracelet is 15 cubic centimeters. Gold weighs 19.3 grams per cubic centimeter, and copper weighs 9 grams per cubic centimeter. How many grams of copper are mixed with the gold?

44. 🌐 **HONEY BEE PATHS** A farmer is tracking two wild honey bees in his field. He maps the first bee's path back to the hive on the line $y = \frac{9}{7}x$. The second bee's path follows the line $y = -3x + 12$. Their paths cross at the hive. At what coordinates will the farmer find the hive?

FOCUS ON APPLICATIONS

HONEY BEES In 1990, unusually cold weather and predators destroyed 90% of the wild honey bee colonies in the United States. If a colony is destroyed, farmers may need to rent bee hives to pollinate their crops.

🔗 **APPLICATION LINK**
www.mcdougallittell.com

🌐 **AIRPLANE SPEED** In Exercises 45–47, use the following information.
It took 3 hours for a plane, flying against the wind, to travel 900 miles from Alabama to Minnesota. The "ground speed" of the plane is 300 miles per hour. On the return trip, the flight took only 2 hours with a ground speed of 450 miles per hour. During both flights the speed and the direction of the wind were the same. The plane's speed decreases or increases because of the wind as the verbal model below shows.

| Speed in still air | − | Wind speed | = | Ground speed against wind |

| Speed in still air | + | Wind speed | = | Ground speed with wind |

45. Assign labels to the verbal model shown above. Use the labels to translate the verbal model into a system of linear equations.

46. Solve the linear system.

47. What was the speed of the plane in still air? What was the speed of the wind?

48. 🌐 **STEAMBOAT SPEED** A steamboat went 8 miles upstream in 1 hour. The return trip took only 30 minutes. Assume that the speed of the current and the direction were constant during both parts of the trip. Find the speed of the boat in still water and the speed of the current.

SOLVING EFFICIENTLY In Exercises 49–51, decide which variable to eliminate when using linear combinations to solve the system. Explain your thinking.

49. $2x + 3y = 1$
$4x - 2y = 10$

50. $5y - 3x = 7$
$x + 3y = 7$

51. $\frac{1}{3}x + 6y = 6$
$-x + 3y = 3$

52. *Writing* Describe a general method for deciding which variable to eliminate when using linear combinations.

Test Preparation

QUANTITATIVE COMPARISON In Exercises 53–55, solve the system. Then choose the statement below that is true about the solution of the system.

Ⓐ The value of x is greater than the value of y.

Ⓑ The value of y is greater than the value of x.

Ⓒ The values of x and y are equal.

Ⓓ The relationship cannot be determined from the given information.

53. $x + y = 4$
$x - 2y = 1$

54. $x - 5y + 1 = 6$
$x = 12y$

55. $3x + 5y = -8$
$x - 2y = 1$

★ Challenge

56. SYSTEM OF THREE EQUATIONS Solve for x, y, and z in the system of equations. Explain each of your solution steps.

$3x + 2y + z = 42$
$2y + z + 12 = 3x$
$x - 3y = 0$

EXTRA CHALLENGE
www.mcdougallittell.com

MIXED REVIEW

WRITING EQUATIONS Write an equation of the line in slope-intercept form that passes through the two points, or passes through the point and has the given slope. (Review 5.2, 5.3)

57. $(-2, -1), (4, 2)$

58. $(-2, 4), m = 3$

59. $(6, 5), (2, 1)$

60. $(5, 1), m = 5$

61. $(9, 3), m = -\frac{1}{3}$

62. $(4, -5), (-1, -3)$

CHECKING SOLUTIONS Check whether each ordered pair is a solution of the inequality. (Review 6.5)

63. $3x - 2y < 2; (1, 3), (2, 0)$

64. $5x + 4y \geq 6; (-2, 4), (5, 5)$

65. $5x + y > 5; (5, 5), (-5, -5)$

66. $12y - 3x \leq 3; (-2, 4), (1, -1)$

SOLVING SYSTEMS Use substitution to solve the linear system. (Review 7.2 for 7.4)

67. $-6x - 5y = 28$
$x - 2y = 1$

68. $m + 2n = 1$
$5m - 4n = -23$

69. $g - 5h = 20$
$4g + 3h = 34$

70. $p + 4q = -9$
$2p - 3q = 4$

71. $\frac{3}{5}b - a = 0$
$1 + b = 2a$

72. $d - e = 8$
$\frac{1}{5}d = e + 4$

Graph and check to solve the linear system. (Lesson 7.1)

1. $3x + y = 5$
$-x + y = -7$

2. $\frac{1}{2}x + \frac{3}{4}y = 9$
$-2x + y = -4$

3. $x - 2y = 0$
$3x - y = 0$

Use substitution to solve the linear system. (Lesson 7.2)

4. $4x + 3y = 31$
$y = 2x + 7$

5. $-12x + y = 15$
$3x + 2y = 3$

6. $x + \frac{1}{2}y = 7$
$3x + 2y = 18$

Use linear combinations to solve the linear system. (Lesson 7.3)

7. $x + 7y = 12$
$3x - 5y = 10$

8. $3x - 5y = -4$
$-9x + 7y = 8$

9. $\frac{2}{3}x + \frac{1}{6}y = \frac{2}{3}$
$-y = 12 - 2x$

10. 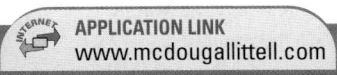 **COMPACT DISC SALE** A store is selling compact discs for \$10.50 and \$8.50. You buy 10 discs and spend a total of \$93. How many compact discs did you buy that cost \$10.50? that cost \$8.50? (Lessons 7.1–7.3)

MATH & History

Systems of Linear Equations

APPLICATION LINK
www.mcdougallittell.com

THEN THE FIRST KNOWN SYSTEM of linear equations appeared in a Chinese book about 2000 years ago. The problem below appeared in the book *Shu-shu chiu-chang* in 1247.

A storehouse has three kinds of stuff: cotton, floss silk, and raw silk. They take inventory of the materials and wish to cut out and make garments for the army. As for the cotton, if we use 8 rolls for 6 men, we have a shortage of 160 rolls; if we use 9 rolls for 7 men, there is a surplus of 560 rolls. . . . We wish to know the number of men [we can clothe] and the amounts of cotton [we will use]. . .

$$-x = -\frac{8y}{6} + 160$$

$$x = \frac{9y}{7} + 560$$

$$0 = \frac{9y}{7} - \frac{8y}{6} + 720$$

1. In the equations above, what does x represent? What does y represent?

2. Solve the linear system and interpret the solution.

NOW CASH REGISTERS can keep track of inventory and notify a store's manager when inventory needs to be ordered.

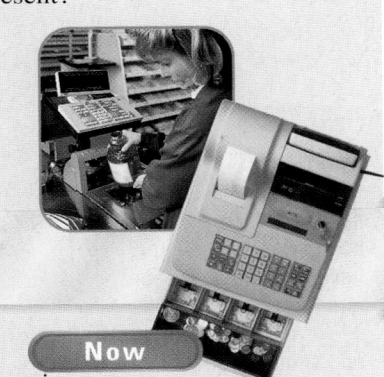

c. 3000 B.C.

The first abacus

1879

Cash register is invented.

Now

Modern cash registers have scanners.

Applications of Linear Systems

GOAL 1 CHOOSING A SOLUTION METHOD

CONCEPT SUMMARY	WAYS TO SOLVE A SYSTEM OF LINEAR EQUATIONS

GRAPHING: A useful method for approximating a solution, checking the reasonableness of a solution, and providing a visual model. (**Examples 1–3, pp. 398–400**)

SUBSTITUTION: A useful method when one of the variables has a coefficient of 1 or −1. (**Examples 1–3, pp. 405–407**)

LINEAR COMBINATIONS: A useful method when none of the variables has a coefficient of 1 or −1. (**Examples 1–4, pp. 411–413**)

EXAMPLE 1 *Choosing a Solution Method*

SELLING SHOES A store sold 28 pairs of cross-trainer shoes for a total of $2220. Style A sold for $70 per pair and Style B sold for $90 per pair. How many of each style were sold?

SOLUTION

PROBLEM SOLVING STRATEGY

VERBAL MODEL

$$\boxed{\text{Number of Style A}} + \boxed{\text{Number of Style B}} = \boxed{\text{Total number sold}}$$

$$\boxed{\text{Price of Style A}} \cdot \boxed{\text{Number of Style A}} + \boxed{\text{Price of Style B}} \cdot \boxed{\text{Number of Style B}} = \boxed{\text{Total receipts}}$$

LABELS

Number of Style A = x (pairs of shoes)

Number of Style B = y (pairs of shoes)

Total number sold = **28**   (pairs of shoes)

Price of Style A = **70**   (dollars per pair)

Price of Style B = **90**   (dollars per pair)

Total receipts = **2220**   (dollars)

ALGEBRAIC MODEL

$$x + y = 28 \qquad \text{Equation 1}$$

$$70x + 90y = 2220 \qquad \text{Equation 2}$$

Because the coefficients of x and y are 1 in Equation 1, substitution is most convenient. Solve Equation 1 for x and substitute the result into Equation 2. Simplify to obtain $y = 13$. Substitute 13 for y in Equation 1 and solve for x.

▶ The solution is 15 pairs of Style A and 13 pairs of Style B.

EXAMPLE 2 *Solving a Mixture Problem*

CAR MAINTENANCE Your car's manual recommends that you use at least 89-octane gasoline. Your car's 16-gallon gas tank is almost empty. How much regular gasoline (87-octane) do you need to mix with premium gasoline (92-octane) to produce 16 gallons of 89-octane gasoline?

SOLUTION

An octane rating is the percent of isooctane in the gasoline, so 16 gallons of 89-octane gasoline contains 89% of 16, or 14.24, gallons of isooctane.

PROBLEM SOLVING STRATEGY

VERBAL MODEL

$$\boxed{\text{Volume of regular}} + \boxed{\text{Volume of premium}} = \boxed{\text{Volume of 89-octane}}$$

$$\boxed{\text{Isooctane in regular}} + \boxed{\text{Isooctane in premium}} = \boxed{\text{Isooctane in 89-octane}}$$

LABELS

Volume of regular = x (gallons)

Volume of premium = y (gallons)

Volume of 89-octane = **16**   (gallons)

Isooctane in regular = **0.87x**   (gallons)

Isooctane in premium = **0.92y**   (gallons)

Isooctane in 89-octane = **14.24**   (gallons)

ALGEBRAIC MODEL

$$x + y = 16 \qquad \text{Equation 1}$$

$$0.87x + 0.92y = 14.24 \qquad \text{Equation 2}$$

Use substitution. Solve Equation 1 for y and substitute into Equation 2.

$y = 16 - x$	Solve Equation 1 for *y*.
$0.87x + 0.92(16 - x) = 14.24$	Substitute 16 − *x* for *y* in Equation 2.
$-0.05x = -0.48$	Simplify.
$x = 9.6$	Solve for *x*.
$9.6 + y = 16$	Substitute 9.6 for *x* in Equation 1.
$y = 6.4$	Solve for *y*.

✓**CHECK** Substitute in each equation to check your result.

EQUATION 1	**EQUATION 2**
$9.6 + 6.4 \stackrel{?}{=} 16$	$0.87(9.6) + 0.92(6.4) \stackrel{?}{=} 14.24$
$16.0 = 16$	$8.352 + 5.888 = 14.24$

▶ You need to mix 9.6 gallons of regular gasoline with 6.4 gallons of premium gasoline to get 16 gallons of 89-octane gasoline.

FOCUS ON APPLICATIONS

Fuel and air

Exhaust

Spark plug

Piston

Cylinder

Crank shaft

CAR ENGINE In a car engine, fuel and air in the cylinder are ignited by a spark to provide power to drive the engine. Using a fuel with the correct octane rating makes the engine run more smoothly.

APPLICATION LINK
www.mcdougallittell.com

EXAMPLE 3 *Making a Decision*

Career Decisions

You are offered two different sales jobs. Job A offers an annual salary of $30,000 plus a year-end bonus of 1% of your total sales. Job B offers an annual salary of $24,000 plus a year-end bonus of 2% of your total sales.

a. How much would you have to sell to earn the same amount in each job?

b. You believe you can sell between $500,000 and $800,000 of merchandise per year. Which job should you choose?

SOLUTION

a. First find a linear system that models the situation.

> **PROBLEM SOLVING STRATEGY**

VERBAL MODEL

Total earnings = **Job A salary** + **1%** · **Total sales**

Total earnings = **Job B salary** + **2%** · **Total sales**

LABELS

Total earnings = **y**   (dollars)

Total sales = **x**   (dollars)

Salary for Job A = **30,000**   (dollars)

Salary for Job B = **24,000**   (dollars)

ALGEBRAIC MODEL

y = **30,000 + 0.01 x**   **Equation 1 (Job A)**

y = **24,000 + 0.02 x**   **Equation 2 (Job B)**

Use linear combinations to solve this system of linear equations because you can easily get the coefficients of y to be opposites.

$$y = 30,000 + 0.01x \qquad \text{Write Equation 1.}$$
$$\underline{-y = -24,000 - 0.02x} \qquad \text{Multiply Equation 2 by } -1.$$
$$0 = 6000 - 0.01x \qquad \text{Add equations.}$$

$$0.01x = 6000 \qquad \text{Add } 0.01x \text{ to each side.}$$

$$x = 600,000 \qquad \text{Solve for } x.$$

The solution of the linear system is $x = 600,000$ and $y = 36,000$.

▶ You would have to sell $600,000 worth of merchandise to earn the same amount of money in each job.

b. One way to decide which job to choose is to draw a graph of the linear system.

▶ From the graph you can see that if your sales are greater than $600,000, Job B would pay better than Job A.

GUIDED PRACTICE

Concept Check ✓   1. Solve the linear system in Example 3 using the substitution method.

2. You have seen three ways to solve the linear system in Example 3. Which method or methods do you prefer for solving the linear system in Example 3? Why?

Skill Check ✓   **Choose a method to solve the linear system. Explain your choice.**

3. $x + y = 300$
$x + 3y = 18$

4. $3x + 5y = 25$
$2x - 6y = 12$

5. $2x + y = 0$
$x + y = 5$

🌐 **PRICE PER GALLON** **In Exercises 6–9, use the following problem.**
The total cost of 10 gallons of regular gasoline and 15 gallons of premium gasoline is \$32.75. Premium costs \$.20 more per gallon than regular. What is the cost per gallon of each type of gasoline?

6. Write a verbal model for the problem.

7. Assign labels to the verbal model.

8. Write a linear system as an algebraic model.

9. Solve the system and answer the question.

PRACTICE AND APPLICATIONS

STUDENT HELP

▶ **Extra Practice**
to help you master
skills is on p. 803.

COMPARING METHODS **Solve the linear system using all three methods on page 418.**

10. $x + y = 2$
$6x + y = 2$

11. $x - y = 1$
$x + y = 5$

12. $3x - y = 3$
$-x + y = 3$

CHOOSING A SOLUTION METHOD **Choose a method to solve the linear system. Explain your choice.**

13. $6x + y = 2$
$9x - y = 5$

14. $2x + 3y = 3$
$5x + 5y = 10$

15. $-3x = 36$
$-6x + y = 1$

16. $2x - 5y = 0$
$x - y = 3$

17. $3x + 2y = 10$
$2x + 5y = 3$

18. $6.2x - 0.5y = -27.8$
$0.3x + 0.4y = 68.7$

SOLVING LINEAR SYSTEMS **Choose a method to solve the linear system. Explain your choice, and then solve the system.**

19. $2x + y = 5$
$x - y = 1$

20. $2x - y = 3$
$4x + 3y = 21$

21. $x - 2y = 4$
$6x + 2y = 10$

22. $3x + 6y = 8$
$-6x + 3y = 2$

23. $x + y = 0$
$3x + 2y = 1$

24. $2x - 3y = -7$
$3x + y = -5$

STUDENT HELP

▶ HOMEWORK HELP
Example 1: Exs. 10–48
Example 2: Exs. 10–48
Example 3: Exs. 10–48

25. $3y + 4x = 5$
$x + y = 1$

26. $8x + y = 15$
$9 = 2y + 2x$

27. $100 - 9x = 5y$
$0 = 5y - 9x$

28. $x + 2y = 2$
$x + 4y = -2$

29. $-y = -4$
$x + 2y = 4$

30. $0.2x - 0.5y = -3.8$
$0.3x + 0.4y = 10.4$

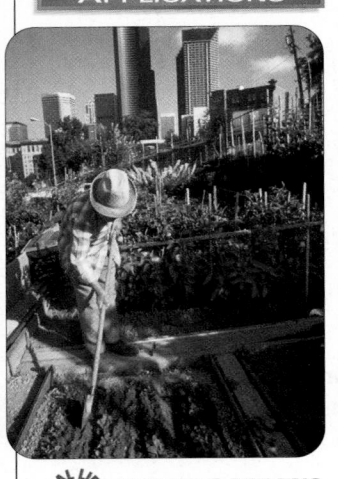

URBAN GARDENS
Cities are blossoming with thousands of gardens. They provide green areas of plant life amid acres of steel and concrete.

APPLICATION LINK
www.mcdougallittell.com

CHOOSING A METHOD In Exercises 31–45, solve the linear system.

31. $6x - y = 18$
$8x + y = 24$

32. $x - y = -4$
$2y + x = 5$

33. $x + 2y = 8$
$3x - 2y = 8$

34. $x + 2y = 1$
$5x - 4y = -23$

35. $8x + 4y = 8$
$-2x + 3y = 12$

36. $3x - 5y = 8$
$-2x + 3y = 3$

37. $2x - y = 6$
$y - x = 0$

38. $8x + 9y = 42$
$6x - y = 16$

39. $7x + 4y = 22$
$-5x - 9y = 15$

40. $3x - 5y = 3$
$9x - 20y = 6$

41. $0.5x + 2.2y = 9$
$6x + 0.4y = -22$

42. $1.5x - 2.5y = 8.5$
$6x + 30y = 24$

43. $3x + 9y = 1$
$2x + 3y = \frac{2}{3}$

44. $3x - 2y = 8$
$x + \frac{3}{2}y = 20$

45. $\frac{1}{2}x - y = -5$
$x - \frac{1}{3}y = 0$

46. 🌱 **GARDEN PLANTS** In early spring, you buy 6 potted tomato plants for your container garden. The plants contained in 8-inch pots sell for $5 and the plants contained in 10-inch pots sell for $8. If you spend $36, how many of each size are you buying?

| Number of 8-inch pots | + | Number of 10-inch pots | = | Total number buying |

| Cost of all 8-inch pots | + | Cost of all 10-inch pots | = | Total cost |

47. **SCIENCE CONNECTION** In your chemistry class you have a bottle of 5% boric acid solution and a bottle of 2% boric acid solution. You need 60 milliliters of a 3% boric acid solution for an experiment. How much of each solution do you need to mix together?

48. 🌲 **TREE GROWTH** You plant a 14-inch hemlock tree in your backyard that grows at a rate of 4 inches per year and an 8-inch blue spruce tree that grows at a rate of 6 inches per year. In how many years after you plant the trees will the two trees be the same height? How tall will each tree be?

🌍 **PARTY PLANNING** In Exercises 49 and 50, you are planning a birthday party for your 8-year-old cousin. You can have the party at a pizza place for $8 per person plus $30 for favors and a small cake or at a taco place for $12 per person plus $14 for a large cake.

49. How many children would you have to invite to the party for the cost to be the same for both places?

50. How many children would you have to invite to the party for the cost to be less at the pizza place?

51. 🌍 **LOW-INCOME HOUSING** The graph at the right represents the demands for low-income rental housing in the United States and the number of affordable rental units. Use the coordinates given to write a linear system. Solve the system. What does the point of intersection represent in the context of the situation?

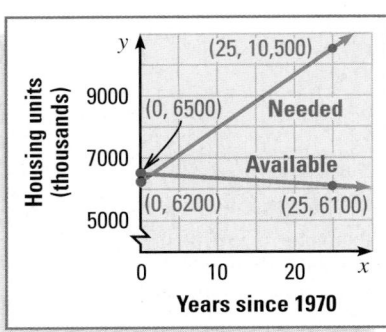

🌐 **DRAWING PORTRAITS** In Exercises 52–54, you are earning extra money drawing sketches for your friends and family. You receive $12 per sketch. Your expenses for art supplies are $50.

52. Write an equation that models only your income.

53. Suppose you plan to spend an additional $7 per sketch for a frame. Write an equation that models only your expenses.

54. How many framed sketches do you have to sell in order for your income to equal your expenses?

55. 🌐 **TREADMILLS** You exercised on a treadmill for 1.5 hours. You ran at 4 miles per hour, then you sprinted at 6 miles per hour. If the treadmill monitor says that you ran and sprinted 7 miles, how long did you run at each speed?

56. 🌐 **TRAVEL TIME** You are driving to a concert. To arrive on time, you plan to travel at an average speed of 45 miles per hour. For the first two hours of the trip you travel at 40 miles per hour. Find the expression for the total time you traveled. Then use the following verbal models to find how many hours you traveled at 55 miles per hour to arrive on time.

$$\boxed{\text{Distance at 40 mi/h}} + \boxed{\text{Distance at 55 mi/h}} = \boxed{\text{Total distance}}$$

$$\boxed{\text{Average speed}} \cdot \boxed{\text{Total time}} = \boxed{\text{Total distance}}$$

SCIENCE CONNECTION In Exercises 57–60, a chemist is calculating absolute zero using the procedure below. Absolute zero is the lowest possible temperature for all substances. It is believed to be the temperature at which the volume of an ideal gas (at constant pressure) contracts to zero.

- On page 1811, I found several readings for the volume and the temperature of three gases.

- I made a scatter plot of the data.

- I found a linear equation that relates the volume (in liters) and the temperature (in degrees Celsius) of each gas by fitting a line to the data.

  Methane: $-2T + 302V = 546.4$
  Water: $-T + 228V = 273.2$
  Nitrous oxide: $-3T + 1872V = 819.6$

- I solved the linear system.

57. What methods could the chemist use to solve the linear system?

58. Use the chemist's graph to predict what absolute zero is on the Celsius scale.

59. Does the chemist need to solve all three equations to find T? Explain.

60. Solve the system algebraically.

STUDENT HELP

🌐 **HOMEWORK HELP**
Visit our Web site
www.mcdougallittell.com
for help with Ex. 55.

STUDENT HELP

🌐 **APPLICATION LINK**
Visit our Web site
www.mcdougallittell.com
for more information
about absolute zero.

🌎 **MARBLES** In Exercises 61–63, consider a bag containing 12 marbles that are either red or blue. A marble is drawn at random. There are three times as many red marbles as there are blue marbles in the bag.

61. Write a linear system to describe this situation.

62. How many red marbles are in the bag?

63. PROBABILITY ▸ CONNECTION   What is the probability of drawing a red marble?

64. **MULTIPLE CHOICE** At what point do the lines $3x - 2y = 0$ and $5x + 2y = 0$ intersect?

Ⓐ $(1, 2)$ Ⓑ $(5, 2)$ Ⓒ $(3, 2)$ Ⓓ $(0, 0)$

65. **MULTIPLE CHOICE** Find the x-value of the solution for the linear system below.
$$y = 2x - 2$$
$$y = 3x + 1$$

Ⓐ -8 Ⓑ -3 Ⓒ 3 Ⓓ 8

★ **Challenge**

66. 🌎 **RELAY RACE** The total time for a two-member team to complete a 5765-meter relay race was 19 minutes. The first runner averaged 285 meters per minute and the second runner averaged 335 meters per minute. Use the verbal model to find how many minutes the first runner ran.

| Time for 1st runner | + | Time for 2nd runner | = | Total time |

| Distance for 1st runner | + | Distance for 2nd runner | = | Total distance |

EXTRA CHALLENGE
www.mcdougallittell.com

MIXED REVIEW

PARALLEL LINES Decide whether the graphs of the two equations are parallel lines. (Review 4.6 for 7.5)

67. $y = 4x + 3$; $2y - 8x = -3$ **68.** $4y + 5x = 1$; $10x + 2y = 2$

69. $3x + 9y + 2 = 0$; $2y = -6x + 3$ **70.** $4y - 1 = 5$; $6y + 2 = 8$

GRAPHING FUNCTIONS Graph the function. (Review 4.8)

71. $f(x) = 2x + 3$ **72.** $h(x) = x + 5$ **73.** $g(x) = -3x - 1$

🌎 **CD-ROM DRIVES** In Exercises 74 and 75, the number of United States households with CD-ROM drives in their computers is shown in the scatter plot at the right. (Review 5.4 and 5.7)

74. Find an equation of the line that you think best fits the data. Notice that x represents the number of years since 1993 and y represents the number of households out of 100.

75. Use a linear model to estimate the number of households that will have computer-installed CD-ROM drives in 2003.

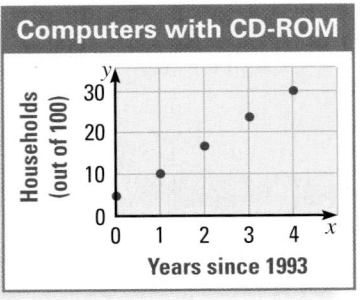

Computers with CD-ROM

Households (out of 100)

Years since 1993

🌐 DATA UPDATE
www.mcdougallittell.com

▶ **ACTIVITY 7.5**

Developing Concepts

Investigating
Special Types of Linear Systems

GROUP ACTIVITY
Work in a small group.

MATERIALS
• graph paper

▶ **QUESTION** How can you identify the number of solutions of a linear system by graphing?

▶ **EXPLORING THE CONCEPT**

1 Each member of your group should choose a different one of the linear systems below and graph it.

a. $x + y = 0$
$3x - 2y = 10$

b. $2x - 4y = 6$
$x - 2y = 3$

c. $x - y = 1$
$-3x + 3y = 3$

2 Share your graphs. How are the three graphs different?

3 For the system you graphed, write both equations in the form $y = mx + b$.

4 Share your results from **Step 3** with the others in your group. How are the equations within each system alike or different?

▶ **DRAWING CONCLUSIONS**

1. Repeat **Steps 1** through **4** above using the following systems.

a. $x - 3y = 9$
$-2x + 6y = -18$

b. $x - \frac{1}{4}y = 5$
$5x + \frac{1}{4}y = 7$

c. $x + 2y = 3$
$x + 2y = 6$

STUDENT HELP

↳ **Look Back**
For help with graphing linear systems, see p. 399.

Write a linear system for the graphical model. If only one line is shown, write two different equations for the line.

2.

3.

4.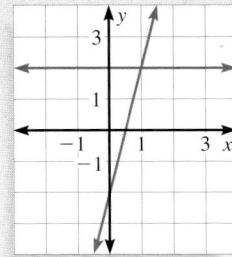

CRITICAL THINKING In Exercises 5–7, the graph of a linear system is described. Decide whether the system has *no solution*, *exactly one solution*, or *many solutions*. Explain your reasoning.

5. The slope and the *y*-intercept of the lines are the same.

6. The lines have different slopes and *y*-intercepts.

7. The lines have the same slope but different *y*-intercepts.

Have each member of your group give an example of a linear system that has the given number of solutions. Compare your results.

8. No solution

9. Exactly one solution

10. Many solutions

Special Types of Linear Systems

What you should learn

GOAL 1 Identify linear systems as having one solution, no solution, or infinitely many solutions.

GOAL 2 Model **real-life** problems using a linear system, as in **Ex. 30**.

Why you should learn it

▼ To solve **real-life** problems such as finding the heights of statues on Easter Island in **Example 4**.

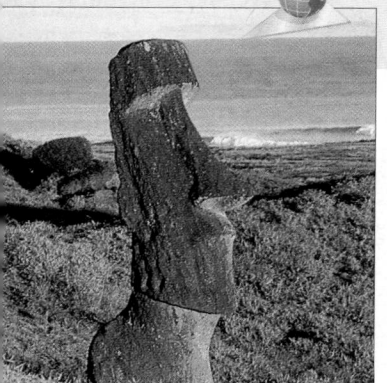

GOAL 1 IDENTIFYING THE NUMBER OF SOLUTIONS

In Lessons 7.1 through 7.4, each linear system in two variables has exactly one solution. The summary below shows that there are two other possibilities.

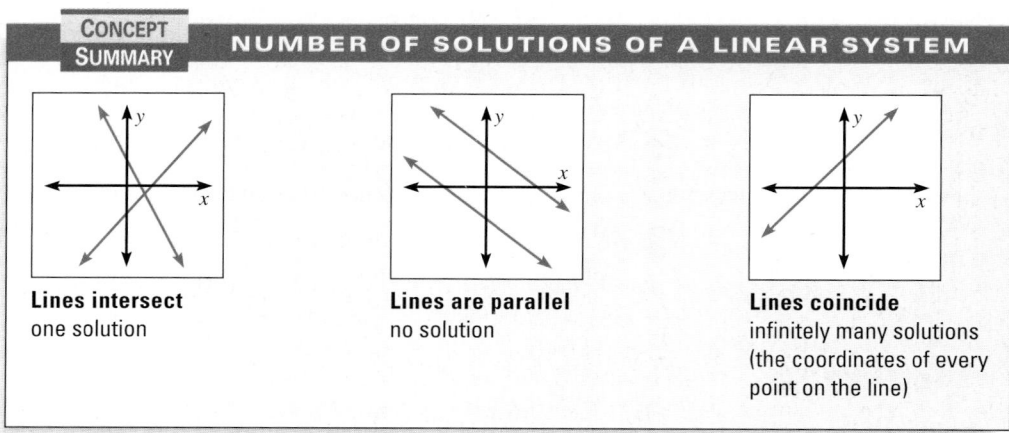

CONCEPT SUMMARY NUMBER OF SOLUTIONS OF A LINEAR SYSTEM

Lines intersect
one solution

Lines are parallel
no solution

Lines coincide
infinitely many solutions
(the coordinates of every point on the line)

EXAMPLE 1 *A Linear System with No Solution*

Show that the linear system has no solution.

$$2x + y = 5 \quad \textbf{Equation 1}$$
$$2x + y = 1 \quad \textbf{Equation 2}$$

SOLUTION

Method 1: GRAPHING Rewrite each equation in slope-intercept form. Then graph the linear system.

$$y = -2x + 5 \quad \textbf{Revised Equation 1}$$
$$y = -2x + 1 \quad \textbf{Revised Equation 2}$$

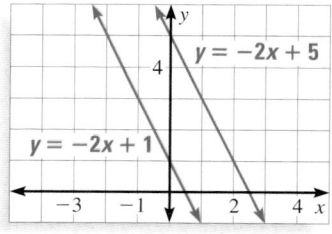

▶ Because the lines have the same slope but different *y*-intercepts, they are parallel. Parallel lines do not intersect, so the system has no solution.

Method 2: SUBSTITUTION Because Equation 2 can be revised to $y = -2x + 1$, you can substitute $-2x + 1$ for *y* in Equation 1.

$$2x + y = 5 \quad \textbf{Write Equation 1.}$$
$$2x + (-2x + 1) = 5 \quad \textbf{Substitute } -2x + 1 \textbf{ for } y.$$
$$1 = 5 \quad \textbf{Simplify. False statement}$$

STUDENT HELP

Look Back
For help with equations in one variable with no solution, see p. 155.

▶ The variables are eliminated and you are left with a statement that is not true regardless of the values of *x* and *y*. This tells you the system has no solution.

EXAMPLE 2 *A Linear System with Many Solutions*

Show that the linear system has infinitely many solutions.

$$-2x + y = 3 \qquad \textbf{Equation 1}$$
$$-4x + 2y = 6 \qquad \textbf{Equation 2}$$

STUDENT HELP

↳ **Study Tip**
When both equations of a system are in the form $y = mx + b$, you can determine the number of solutions.
- different slopes: one solution
- same slopes, different y-intercepts: no solution
- same slopes, same y-intercepts: infinitely many solutions

SOLUTION

Method 1: GRAPHING Rewrite each equation in slope-intercept form.

$$y = 2x + 3 \qquad \textbf{Revised Equation 1}$$
$$y = 2x + 3 \qquad \textbf{Revised Equation 2}$$

▶ From these equations you can see that the equations represent the same line. Any point on the line is a solution.

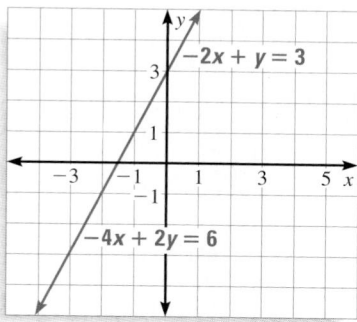

Method 2: LINEAR COMBINATIONS You can multiply Equation 1 by -2.

$$4x - 2y = -6 \qquad \textbf{Multiply Equation 1 by } -2.$$
$$\underline{-4x + 2y = 6} \qquad \textbf{Write Equation 2.}$$
$$0 = 0 \qquad \textbf{Add equations. True statement}$$

▶ The variables are eliminated and you are left with a statement that is true regardless of the values of x and y. This result tells you that the linear system has infinitely many solutions.

· · · · · · · · · ·

Notice in Example 2 that $-2x + y = 3$ can be transformed to look exactly like $-4x + 2y = 6$ by multiplying by 2. The two equations are *equivalent*. That is why your result is $0 = 0$.

EXAMPLE 3 *Identifying the Number of Solutions*

Solve the system and interpret the results.

a. $3x + y = -1$
$-9x - 3y = 3$

b. $x - 2y = 5$
$-2x + 4y = 2$

c. $2x + y = 4$
$4x - 2y = 0$

SOLUTION

a. Using the substitution method, you get $3 = 3$. This is true regardless of the values of x and y. This linear system has infinitely many solutions.

b. Using linear combinations, you get $0 = 12$. This is not true for any values of x and y. This linear system has no solution.

c. Using the substitution method to eliminate y, you get the equation $x = 1$. This linear system has exactly one solution—the ordered pair $(1, 2)$.

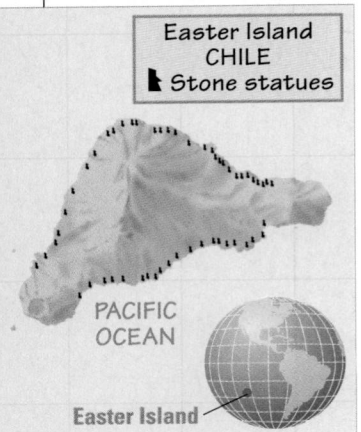

Easter Island
CHILE
Stone statues

PACIFIC
OCEAN

Easter Island

EASTER ISLAND is located in the South Pacific. On the island there are more than 600 massive stone statues called *moai*. The statues were carved hundreds of years ago, and some are over 40 feet high.

GOAL 2 MODELING A REAL-LIFE PROBLEM

EXAMPLE 4 *Error Analysis*

GEOMETRY CONNECTION Two students are visiting the mysterious statues on Easter Island in the South Pacific. To find the heights of two statues that are too tall to measure, they tried a technique involving proportions. They measured the shadow lengths of the statues at 2:00 P.M. and again at 3:00 P.M. Why were they unable to use their measurements to determine the heights of the statues?

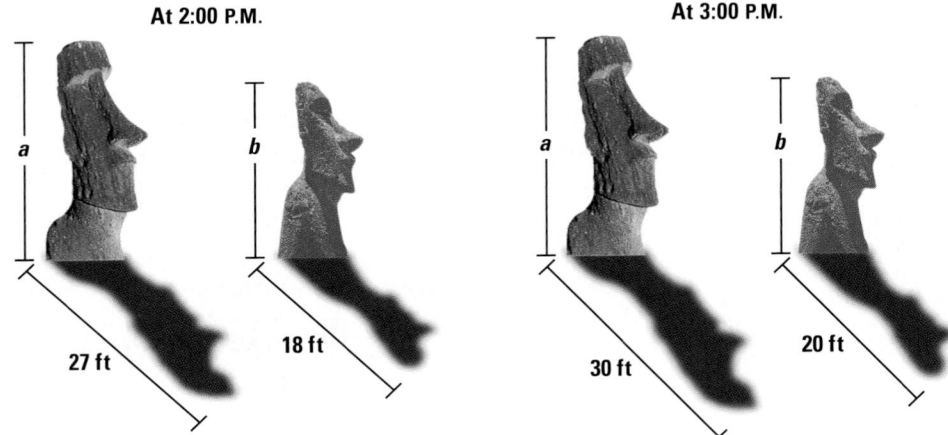

At 2:00 P.M.   At 3:00 P.M.

a   *b*   *a*   *b*

27 ft   18 ft   30 ft   20 ft

SOLUTION They let a and b represent the heights of the two statues. Because the ratios of corresponding sides of similar triangles are equal, the students wrote the following two equations.

a b a b

27   18   30   20

2:00 P.M. $\dfrac{a}{27} = \dfrac{b}{18}$ 3:00 P.M. $\dfrac{a}{30} = \dfrac{b}{20}$

$a = \dfrac{27}{18}b$ $a = \dfrac{30}{20}b$

$a = \dfrac{3}{2}b$ $a = \dfrac{3}{2}b$

▶ They got stuck because the equations that they wrote are equivalent. All that the students found from these measurements was that $a = \dfrac{3}{2}b$. In other words, the height of the first statue is one and one half times the height of the second.

· · · · · · · · · ·

To find the heights of the two statues, the students need to measure the shadow length of something else whose height they know or can measure. For instance, if at 2:00 P.M. a student 5 feet tall casts a shadow 3 feet long, the proportion $3:5 = 27:a$ can be used to find the height of the taller statue.

GUIDED PRACTICE

Vocabulary Check ✓ **In Exercises 1–3, describe the graph of a linear system that has the given number of solutions. Sketch an example.**

1. no solution   **2.** infinitely many solutions   **3.** exactly one solution

Concept Check ✓ **4. ERROR ANALYSIS** Patrick says that the graph of the linear system shown at the right has no solution. Why is he wrong?

5. Explain how you can tell if the system of linear equations has a solution. Then solve the system.

$$x - y = 2$$
$$4x - 4y = 8$$

Ex. 4

Skill Check ✓ **Graph the system of linear equations. Does the system have *exactly one solution, no solution,* or *infinitely many solutions*?**

6. $2x + y = 5$
    $-6x - 3y = -15$

7. $-6x + 2y = 4$
    $-9x + 3y = 12$

8. $2x + y = 7$
    $3x - y = -2$

Use the substitution method or linear combinations to solve the linear system and tell how many solutions the system has.

9. $-x + y = 7$
    $2x - 2y = -18$

10. $-4x + y = -8$
    $-12x + 3y = -24$

11. $-4x + y = -8$
    $2x - 2y = -14$

PRACTICE AND APPLICATIONS

STUDENT HELP

▸ **Extra Practice**
to help you master
skills is on p. 803.

MATCHING GRAPHS Match the graph with its linear system. Does the system have *exactly one solution, no solution,* or *infinitely many solutions*?

A. $-2x + 4y = 1$
    $3x - 6y = 9$

B. $2x - 2y = 4$
    $-x + y = -2$

C. $2x + y = 4$
    $-4x - 2y = -8$

D. $-x + y = 1$
    $x - y = 1$

E. $5x + 3y = 17$
    $x - 3y = -2$

F. $x - y = 0$
    $5x - 2y = 6$

12.

13.

14.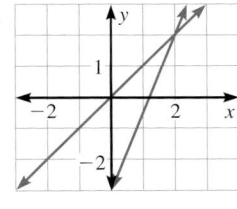

STUDENT HELP

▸ **HOMEWORK HELP**
Example 1: Exs. 12–29
Example 2: Exs. 12–29
Example 3: Exs. 18–29
Example 4: Ex. 30

15.

16.

17.

INTERPRETING ALGEBRAIC RESULTS Use the substitution method or linear combinations to solve the linear system and tell how many solutions the system has.

18. $-7x + 7y = 7$
$2x - 2y = -18$

19. $4x + 4y = -8$
$2x + 2y = -4$

20. $2x + y = -4$
$4x - 2y = 8$

21. $15x - 5y = -20$
$-3x + y = 4$

22. $-6x + 2y = -2$
$-4x - y = 8$

23. $2x + y = -1$
$-6x - 3y = -15$

INTERPRETING GRAPHING RESULTS Use the graphing method to solve the linear system and tell how many solutions the system has.

24. $x + y = 8$
$x + y = -1$

25. $3x - 2y = 3$
$-6x + 4y = -6$

26. $x - y = 2$
$-2x + 2y = 2$

27. $-x + 4y = -20$
$3x - 12y = 48$

28. $6x - 2y = 4$
$-4x + 2y = -\frac{8}{3}$

29. $\frac{3}{4}x + \frac{1}{2}y = 10$
$-\frac{3}{2}x - y = 4$

30. 🌐 **JEWELRY** You have a necklace and matching bracelet with 2 types of beads. There are 30 small beads and 6 large beads on the necklace. The bracelet has 10 small beads and 2 large beads. The necklace weighs 3.6 grams and the bracelet weighs 1.2 grams. If the chain has no significant weight, can you find the weight of one large bead? Explain.

🌐 **CARPENTRY SUPPLIES** In Exercises 31 and 32, use the following information.
A carpenter is buying supplies for a job. The carpenter needs 4 sheets of oak paneling and 2 sheets of shower tileboard. The carpenter pays $99.62 for these supplies. For the next job the carpenter buys 12 sheets of oak paneling and 6 sheets of shower tileboard and pays $298.86.

31. Could you find how much the carpenter is spending on 1 sheet of oak paneling? Explain.

32. If the carpenter later spends a total of $139.69 for 1 sheet of shower tileboard and 8 sheets of oak paneling, could you find how much 1 sheet of oak paneling costs? Explain.

33. **CRITICAL THINKING** Use linear systems to determine where the x-coordinate is equal to the y-coordinate on the graph of $2x + 3y = 25$.

📊 **USING A SPREADSHEET** In Exercises 34 and 35, use the spreadsheet at the right to investigate the linear system.

$y = 2x + 3$
$y = 2x - 9$

34. What do the results mean? Explain how you know.

35. Use a spreadsheet or a table of values to verify your answers to Exercises 6–8.

	A	B	C	D
		linear system		
1	x	y = 2x + 3	y = 2x – 9	col. B – col. C
2	–3	–3	–15	12
3	–2	–1	–13	12
4	–1	1	–11	12
5	0	3	–9	12
6	1	5	–7	12
7	2	7	–5	12
8	3	9	–3	12
9	4	11	–1	12

Exs. 34 and 35

MULTI-STEP PROBLEM In Exercises 36–38, use the description shown below.

36. Write a linear equation for the description. Let x represent the number that is chosen and let y represent the final result.

37. To find the number a person would have chosen to obtain a final result of 1, solve the linear system consisting of the equation you wrote in Exercise 36 and the equation $y = 1$. Explain your result.

> Choose any number.
> Add 10 to the number.
> Multiply the result by 2.
> Subtract 18 from the result.
> Multiply the result by one half.
> Subtract the original number.

38. LOGICAL REASONING Write a number trick of your own that will give similar results. Explain why your trick works.

★ **Challenge**

ALTERING LINEAR SYSTEMS In Exercises 39–42, perform parts (a)–(c).

  a. Find a value of n so that the linear system has infinitely many solutions.

  b. Find a value of n so that the linear system has no solution.

  c. Graph both results.

EXTRA CHALLENGE
www.mcdougallittell.com

39. $x - y = 3$
$4x - 4y = n$

40. $x - y = 4$
$-2x + 2y = n$

41. $6x - 9y = n$
$-2x + 3y = 3$

42. $9x + 6y = n$
$1.8x + 1.2y = 3$

MIXED REVIEW

MATCHING GRAPHS Match the inequality with its graph. (Review 6.5 for 7.6)

  A. $2x + y \leq 3$ **B.** $2x + y < 3$ **C.** $2x + y \geq 3$ **D.** $2x + y > 3$

43.

44.

45.

46.
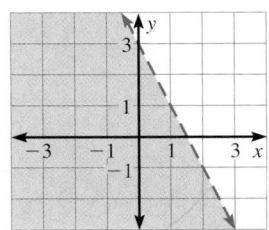

🌐 **ROCK CLIMBING** In Exercises 47 and 48, you are climbing a 500-foot cliff. By 1:00 P.M. you have climbed 125 feet up the cliff. By 4:00 P.M. you have reached a height of 290 feet. (Review 4.4)

47. What is your rate of change in height?

48. If you continue climbing the cliff at the same rate, at what time will you reach the top?

Solving Systems of Linear Inequalities

What you should learn

GOAL 1 Solve a system of linear inequalities by graphing.

GOAL 2 Use a system of linear inequalities to model a **real-life** situation such as earnings from two jobs in **Exs. 38 and 39.**

Why you should learn it

▼ To model **real-life** situations, such as buying spotlights for a concert hall in **Example 4.**

GOAL 1 SOLVING INEQUALITIES BY GRAPHING

From Lesson 6.5, remember that the graph of a linear inequality in two variables is a half-plane. The boundary line of the half-plane is dashed if the inequality is $<$ or $>$ and solid if the inequality is $\le$ or $\ge$.

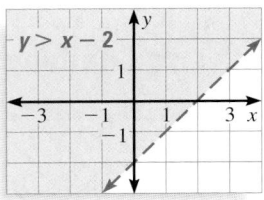

Two or more linear inequalities form a **system of linear inequalities** or simply a *system of inequalities*. A **solution** of a system of linear inequalities is an ordered pair that is a solution of each inequality in the system. The **graph** of a system of linear inequalities is the graph of *all solutions* of the system.

EXAMPLE 1 *A Triangular Solution Region*

Graph the system of linear inequalities.

$y < 2$	**Inequality 1**
$x \ge -1$	**Inequality 2**
$y > x - 2$	**Inequality 3**

SOLUTION

Graph all three inequalities in the same coordinate plane. The graph of the system is the overlap, or *intersection*, of the three half-planes shown.

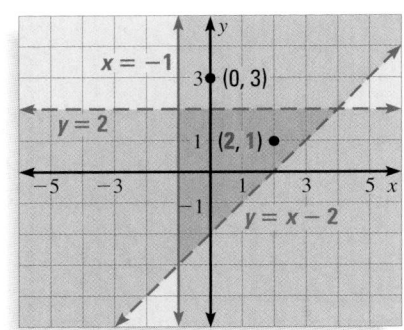

✓ **CHECK** You can see from the graph that the point $(2, 1)$ is a solution of the system. To check this, substitute the point into each inequality.

$1 < 2$	**True**
$2 \ge -1$	**True**
$1 > 2 - 2$	**True**

The point $(0, 3)$ is not in the graph of the system. Notice $(0, 3)$ is not a solution of Inequality 1. This point is not a solution of the system.

· · · · · · · · · ·

When graphing a system of inequalities, it is helpful to find each corner point (or *vertex*). For instance, the graph in Example 1 has three corner points: $(-1, 2)$, $(-1, -3)$, and $(4, 2)$.

EXAMPLE 2 *Solution Region Between Parallel Lines*

Write a system of inequalities that defines the shaded region at the right.

SOLUTION

The graph of one inequality is the half-plane *below* the line $y = 3$.

The graph of the other inequality is the half-plane *above* the line $y = 1$.

The shaded region of the graph is the horizontal band that lies *between* the two horizontal lines, $y = 3$ and $y = 1$, but not *on* the lines.

▶ The system of linear inequalities at the right defines the shaded region.

$y < 3$ **Inequality 1**
$y > 1$ **Inequality 2**

EXAMPLE 3 *A Quadrilateral Solution Region*

STUDENT HELP

Study Tip
When you are graphing a system of inequalities, try shading with several colored pencils. The graph of the system is the region that has been shaded by every color.

Graph the system of linear inequalities. Label each vertex of the solution region. Describe the shape of the region.

$x \geq 0$ **Inequality 1**
$y \geq 0$ **Inequality 2**
$y \leq 2$ **Inequality 3**
$y \leq -\dfrac{1}{2}x + 3$ **Inequality 4**

SOLUTION

The graph of the first inequality is the half-plane *on and to the right* of the *y*-axis.

The graph of the second inequality is the half-plane *on and above* the *x*-axis.

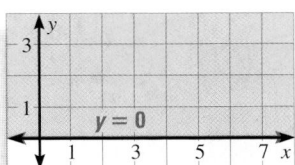

The graph of the third inequality is the half-plane *on and below* the horizontal line $y = 2$.

The graph of the fourth inequality is the half-plane *on and below* the line $y = -\dfrac{1}{2}x + 3$.

▶ The region that lies in all four half-planes is a *quadrilateral* with vertices at $(0, 2)$, $(0, 0)$, $(6, 0)$, and $(2, 2)$. Note that the point $(0, 3)$ is not a vertex of the solution region even though two boundary lines meet at that point.

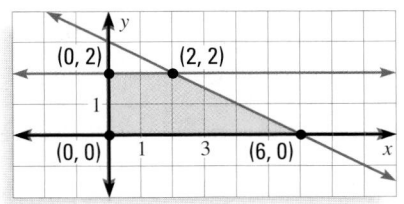

EXAMPLE 4 *Writing a System of Linear Inequalities*

LIGHTING You are ordering lighting for a theater so the spotlights can follow the performers. The lighting technician needs at least 3 medium-throw spotlights and at least 1 long-throw spotlight. A medium-throw spotlight costs $1000 and a long-throw spotlight costs $3500. The minimum order for free delivery is $10,000.

a. Write and graph a system of linear inequalities that shows how many medium-throw spotlights and long-throw spotlights should be ordered to get the free delivery.

b. Will an order of 4 medium-throw spotlights and 1 long-throw spotlight be delivered free?

SOLUTION

PROBLEM SOLVING STRATEGY

a. **VERBAL MODEL**

$$\boxed{\begin{array}{c}\text{Number of} \\ \text{medium-} \\ \text{throws}\end{array}} \geq 3$$

$$\boxed{\begin{array}{c}\text{Number of} \\ \text{long-} \\ \text{throws}\end{array}} \geq 1$$

$$\boxed{\begin{array}{c}\text{Number of} \\ \text{medium-} \\ \text{throws}\end{array}} \cdot \boxed{\begin{array}{c}\text{Price of a} \\ \text{medium-} \\ \text{throw}\end{array}} + \boxed{\begin{array}{c}\text{Number of} \\ \text{long-} \\ \text{throws}\end{array}} \cdot \boxed{\begin{array}{c}\text{Price of a} \\ \text{long-} \\ \text{throw}\end{array}} \geq 10{,}000$$

LABELS

Number of medium-throws = x (no units)

Number of long-throws = y (no units)

Price of a medium-throw = **1000**   (dollars)

Price of a long-throw = **3500**   (dollars)

ALGEBRAIC MODEL

$x \geq 3$ Inequality 1

$y \geq 1$ Inequality 2

$1000\ x + 3500\ y \geq 10{,}000$ Inequality 3

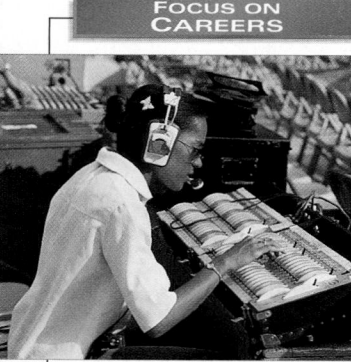
The graph of the system of inequalities is shown. Any point in the shaded region of the graph is a solution of the system. A fraction of a spotlight cannot be ordered, so only ordered pairs of integers in the shaded region will correctly answer the problem.

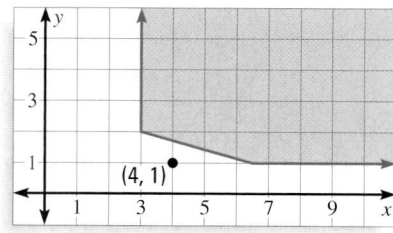

b. The point (4, 1) is outside the solution region, so an order of 4 medium-throw spotlights and 1 long-throw spotlight would not be delivered free.

GUIDED PRACTICE

Vocabulary Check ✓

1. Determine whether the following statement is *true* or *false*. *A solution of a system of linear inequalities is an ordered pair that is a solution of any one of the inequalities in the system.* Explain.

Concept Check ✓

2. How is graphing a system of linear inequalities the same as graphing a system of linear equations? How is it different?

3. After you graph a system of linear inequalities, how can you use algebra to check whether the correct region is shaded?

Skill Check ✓

In Exercises 4 and 5, use both the student graph at the right and the system of linear inequalities shown below.

$y > -1$
$x \geq 2$
$y > x - 4$

4. Describe the errors the student made while graphing the system.

5. Graph the system correctly.

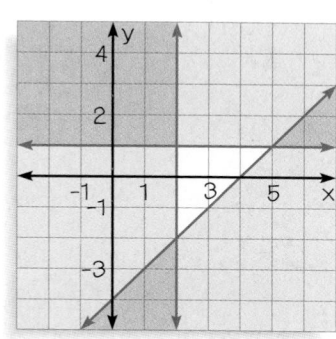

Ex. 4

Graph the system of linear inequalities.

6. $y > -2x + 2$
$y \leq -1$

7. $y > x$
$x \leq 1$

8. $x + 1 > y$
$y \geq 0$

PRACTICE AND APPLICATIONS

STUDENT HELP

▶ **Extra Practice**
to help you master skills is on p. 803.

MATCHING GRAPHS **Match the system of linear inequalities with its graph.**

A. $2x + y < 4$
$-2x + y \leq 4$

B. $2x + y \geq -4$
$x - 2y < 4$

C. $2x + y \leq 4$
$2x + y \geq -4$

9.

10.

11.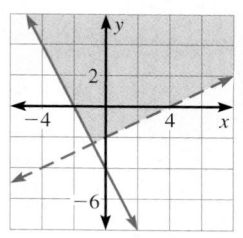

STUDENT HELP

▶ **HOMEWORK HELP**
Example 1: Exs. 9–11, 15–26
Example 2: Exs. 12–14
Example 3: Exs. 15–26
Example 4: Exs. 34–38

WRITING A SYSTEM **Write a system of linear inequalities that defines the shaded region.**

12.

13.

14.

15. $2x + y > 2$
$6x + 3y < 12$

16. $2x - 2y < 6$
$x - y < 9$

17. $x - 3y \geq 12$
$x - 6y \leq 12$

18. $x + y < 4$
$x + y > -2$

19. $x + y \leq 6$
$x \geq 1$
$y \geq 0$

20. $\frac{3}{2}x + y < 3$
$x > 0$
$y > 0$

21. $x \geq 0$
$y \geq 0$
$x \leq 3$
$y \leq 5$

22. $x > -2$
$y \geq -2$
$x \leq 1$
$y \leq 4$

23. $-\frac{3}{2}x + y \leq 3$
$\frac{1}{4}x + y > -\frac{1}{2}$
$4x + y < 2$

24. $2x + y \geq 2$
$x \leq 3$
$y \leq \frac{1}{2}$

25. $x \geq 2$
$x - 2y \geq 3$
$3x + y \geq 9$
$x + y \leq 7$

26. $x \geq 1$
$x - 2y \leq 3$
$3x + 2y \geq 9$
$x + y \leq 6$

GRAPHING A SYSTEM **Use a graphing calculator or a computer to graph the system of inequalities. Give the coordinates of each vertex of the solution region.**

27. $x + y \leq 11$
$5x - 3y \leq 15$
$x \geq 0$

28. $5x - 3y \geq -7$
$3x + y \leq 7$
$x + 5y \geq -7$

29. $x + 2y \geq 0$
$5x - 2y \leq 0$
$-x + y \leq 3$

GEOMETRY CONNECTION **In Exercises 30–33, plot the points and draw line segments connecting the points to create the polygon. Then write a system of linear inequalities that defines the polygonal region.**

30. Triangle: $(-2, 0)$, $(2, 0)$, $(0, 2)$

31. Rectangle: $(1, 1)$, $(7, 1)$, $(7, 6)$, $(1, 6)$

32. Triangle: $(0, 0)$, $(-7, 0)$, $(-3, 5)$

33. Trapezoid: $(-1, 1)$, $(1, 3)$, $(4, 3)$, $(6, 1)$

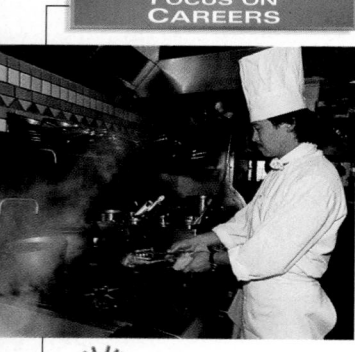

FOOD BUDGET **In Exercises 34 and 35, use the following information.**
You are planning the menu for your restaurant. Each evening you offer two different meals and have at least 240 customers. For Saturday night you plan to offer roast beef and teriyaki chicken. You expect that fewer customers will order the beef than will order the chicken. The beef costs you $5 per serving and the chicken costs you $3 per serving. You have a budget of at most $1200 for meat for Saturday night.

34. Write a system of linear inequalities that shows the various numbers of roast beef and teriyaki chicken meals you could make for Saturday night.

35 Graph the system of linear inequalities.

36. LOCAL MAGAZINE A monthly magazine is hiring reporters to cover school events and local events. In each magazine, the managing editor wants at least 4 reporters covering local news and at least 1 reporter covering school news. The budget allows for not more than 9 different reporters' articles to be in one magazine. Graph the region that shows the possible combinations of local and school events covered in a magazine.

37. GEOMETRY CONNECTION What is the area of the region described by the system of linear inequalities $x \leq 3$, $y \leq 1$, and $x + y \geq 0$?

EARNING MONEY **In Exercises 38–39, use the following information.**
Suppose you can work a total of no more than 20 hours per week at your two jobs. Baby-sitting pays $5 per hour, and your cashier job pays $6 per hour. You need to earn at least $90 per week to cover your expenses.

38. Write a system of inequalities that shows the various numbers of hours you can work at each job. Graph the result.

39. Give two possible ways you could divide your hours between the two jobs.

EXTENSION: LINEAR PROGRAMMING **In Exercises 40 and 41, use the following information.**
You own a bottle recycling center that receives bottles that are either sorted by color or unsorted. To sort and recycle all of the bottles, you can use up to 4200 hours of human labor and up to 2400 hours of machine time. The system below represents the number of hours your center spends sorting and recycling bottles where x is the number of tons of unsorted bottles and y is the number of tons of sorted bottles.

$4x + y \leq 4200$ **Human labor: up to 4200 hours**
$2x + y \leq 2400$ **Machine time: up to 2400 hours**
$x \geq 0, y \geq 0$ **Cannot have negative number of tons**

40. Graph the system of linear inequalities.

41. a. Find the vertices of your graph.

     b. You will earn $30 per ton for bottles that are sorted by color and earn $10 per ton for unsorted bottles. Let P be the maximum profit. Substitute the ordered pairs from part (a) into the following equation and solve.

$$P = 10x + 30y$$

     c. Assuming that the maximum profit occurs at one of the four vertices, what is the maximum profit?

Test Preparation

42. MULTI-STEP PROBLEM Use the tree farm shown at the right.

     a. Write a system of inequalities that defines the region containing maple trees.

     b. Write a system of inequalities that defines the region containing sycamore trees.

     c. Write a system of inequalities that defines the region containing oak trees.

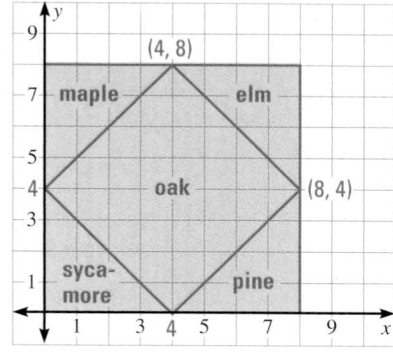

     d. Calculate the area of the oak tree region. Explain your method.

★ Challenge

43. CRITICAL THINKING Explain why the system of inequalities has no solution.
$$2x - y > 4$$
$$y > 2x - 2$$

44. VISUAL THINKING Describe the graph of the system of inequalities.
$$2x + 3y > -6$$
$$2x + 3y \geq 6$$

MIXED REVIEW

EVALUATING NUMERICAL EXPRESSIONS Evaluate the expression.
(Review 1.2, 1.3 for 8.1)

45. $3 \cdot 3 \cdot 3 \cdot 3 \cdot 3$

46. $8^2 - 17$

47. $5^3 + 12$

48. $(3^3 - 20)^2$

49. $2^6 - 31$

50. $5 \cdot 5 + 3 \cdot 3 \cdot 3$

EVALUATING ALGEBRAIC EXPRESSIONS In Exercises 51–56, evaluate the
exponential expression. (Review 1.2)

51. $(x + y)^2$ when $x = 5$ and $y = 2$

52. $(b - c)^2$ when $b = 2$ and $c = 1$

53. $g - h^2$ when $g = 4$ and $h = 8$

54. $x^2 + z$ when $x = 8$ and $z = 12$

55. $m^3 + 1$ when $m = 2$

56. $v^3 + w$ when $v = 3$ and $w = 5$

57. **MEAN, MEDIAN, AND MODE** Find the mean, the median, and the mode of
the collection of numbers shown below. (Review 6.6)

57, 40, 57, 57, 30, 56, 40, 30, 56

58. 🌐 **TEST QUESTIONS** Your teacher is giving a test worth 250 points. There
are 68 questions. Some questions are worth 5 points and the rest are worth 2
points. How many of each question are on the test? (Review 7.3)

QUIZ 2

1. **GEOMETRY** ▸ **CONNECTION**   The perimeter of the rectangle
is 22 feet. The perimeter of the triangle is 12 feet.
Find the dimensions of the rectangle. (Lesson 7.4)

**Use the graphing method to solve the linear system
and tell how many solutions the system has.** (Lesson 7.5)

2. $5x - 2y = 0$
$5x - 2y = -4$

3. $3x + 2y = 12$
$9x + 6y = 18$

4. $-4x + 11y = 44$
$4x - 11y = -44$

5. $3x + y = 9$
$2x + y = 4$

6. $4x + 8y = 8$
$x + y = 1$

7. $3x + 6y = 30$
$4x + 8y = 40$

Graph the system of linear inequalities. (Lesson 7.6)

8. $x - 2y < -6$
$5x - 3y < -9$

9. $-3x + 2y < 6$
$x - 4y > -2$
$2x + y < 3$

10. $x + y < 3$
$x \geq 0$
$y \geq 1$

11. $x \geq 0$
$y \geq 1$
$x \leq 3$
$y \leq 5$

12. $x + y \leq \frac{1}{2}$
$-x + y \leq \frac{1}{2}$
$y \geq 0$

13. $x + y < 26$
$-x + 4y \geq 40$
$2x > 4$

14. 🌐 **INVESTMENTS** A total of $16,000 is invested in two individual
retirement accounts paying 5% and 6% annual interest. The combined
annual interest is $860. How much of the $16,000 is invested in each
account? (Lesson 7.4)

Chapter Summary

WHAT did you learn?

Solve a system of linear equations
- by graphing. **(7.1)**
- by substitution. **(7.2)**
- by linear combinations. **(7.3)**

Choose the best method to solve a linear system. **(7.4)**

Identify the number of solutions of a linear system. **(7.5)**

Use a system of linear equations to model a real-life situation. **(7.1–7.5)**

Solve a system of linear inequalities. **(7.6)**

Use a system of linear inequalities to model a real-life situation. **(7.6)**

WHY did you learn it?

Predict traffic at two Internet sites. **(p. 400)**
Analyze a museum's ticket sales. **(p. 407)**
Model compositions of chemical mixtures. **(p. 413)**

Make a decision about two job offers. **(p. 420)**

Interpret results when modeling with linear systems. **(p. 428)**

Find the speed of an airplane flying against the wind. **(p. 415)**

Plan a minimum order for free delivery. **(p. 434)**

Find ways to work within a budget. **(p. 436)**

How does Chapter 7 fit into the BIGGER PICTURE of algebra?

You saw in this chapter how to choose and apply an appropriate method to solve systems of linear equations and systems of linear inequalities. Knowing the advantages and disadvantages of each method is part of becoming an efficient problem solver.

Linear systems often occur as models of real-life situations. The information you gain from studying systems that model real-life problems will help you analyze situations and make decisions.

STUDY STRATEGY

How did you use your list of problem types?

One type of problem that you listed in your notebook, using the **Study Strategy** on page 396, may be this one.

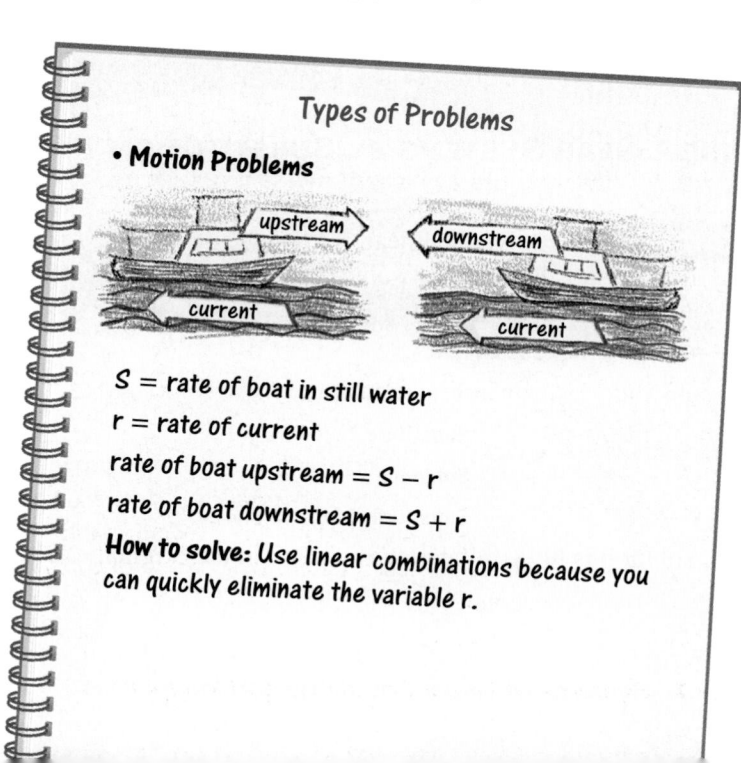

Types of Problems

• **Motion Problems**

upstream

downstream

current

current

S = rate of boat in still water
r = rate of current
rate of boat upstream = $S - r$
rate of boat downstream = $S + r$
How to solve: Use linear combinations because you can quickly eliminate the variable r.

Chapter Review

• system of linear equations, or linear system (p. 398)

• solution of a system of linear equations (p. 398)

• linear combination (p. 411)

• system of linear inequalities (p. 432)

• solution of a system of linear inequalities (p. 432)

• graph of a system of linear inequalities (p. 432)

7.1   **SOLVING LINEAR SYSTEMS BY GRAPHING**

Examples on pp. 398–400

EXAMPLE   To solve a linear system by graphing, you can graph each equation using a table of values, the intercepts, or slope-intercept form.

Graph and solve the system. $y = x + 3$ **Equation 1**

$y = -x + 7$ **Equation 2**

The two lines seem to intersect at the point $(2, 5)$.
Check this solution algebraically in both equations.

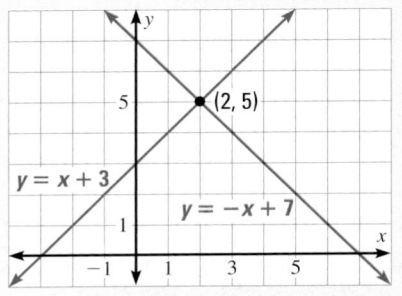

EQUATION 1:

$y = x + 3$

$5 \overset{?}{=} 2 + 3$

$5 = 5$

EQUATION 2:

$y = -x + 7$

$5 \overset{?}{=} -(2) + 7$

$5 = 5$

▶ The solution is $(2, 5)$.

Graph and check to solve the linear system.

1. $x + y = 6$
   $x - y = 12$

2. $4x - y = 3$
   $3x + y = 4$

3. $x + 9y = 9$
   $3x + 6y = 6$

4. $5x - y = -5$
   $3x + 6y = -3$

5. $7x + 8y = 24$
   $x - 8y = 8$

6. $2x - 3y = -3$
   $x + 6y = -9$

7.2   **SOLVING LINEAR SYSTEMS BY SUBSTITUTION**

Examples on pp. 405–407

EXAMPLE   To solve the linear system
at the right by substitution, first solve one
equation for one of its variables.

$4x - 2y = 0$ **Equation 1**

$8x - 2y = 16$ **Equation 2**

$y = 2x$ **Revised Equation 1**

Then substitute $2x$ for y in Equation 2 and solve for x.

$8x - 2(2x) = 16$ Substitute $2x$ for y.

$x = 4$ Solve for x.

$y = 2(4) = 8$ Substitute 4 for x in $y = 2x$.

▶ The solution is $(4, 8)$. Check the solution in the original equations.

Use the substitution method to solve the linear system.

7. $x + 3y = 9$
$4x - 2y = -6$

8. $-2x - 5y = 7$
$7x + y = -8$

9. $4x - 3y = -2$
$4x + y = 4$

10. $-x + 3y = 24$
$5x + 8y = -5$

11. $4x + 9y = 2$
$2x + 6y = 1$

12. $9x + 6y = 3$
$3x - 7y = -26$

7.3 SOLVING LINEAR SYSTEMS BY LINEAR COMBINATIONS

Examples on pp. 411–413

EXAMPLE To solve the linear system, get coefficients for x or y that are opposites.

$2x - 15y = -10$ **Equation 1**
$-4x + 5y = -30$ **Equation 2**

$\begin{aligned} 4x - 30y &= -20 \\ -4x + 5y &= -30 \\ \hline -25y &= -50 \\ y &= 2 \end{aligned}$

Multiply Equation 1 by 2.
Write Equation 2.
Add the equations.
Solve for y.

Then substitute 2 for y in Equation 2 and solve for x.

$-4x + 5y = -30$ Write Equation 2.

$-4x + 5(2) = -30$ Substitute 2 for y.

$x = 10$ Solve for x.

▶ The solution is $(10, 2)$. Check the solution in the original equations.

Use linear combinations to solve the linear system.

13. $-4x - 5y = 7$
$x + 5y = 8$

14. $2x + y = 0$
$5x - 4y = 26$

15. $3x + 5y = -16$
$-2x + 6y = -36$

16. $9x + 6y = 3$
$3y + 6x = 18$

17. $2 - 7x = 9y$
$2y - 4x = 6$

18. $4x - 9y = 1$
$-5x + 6y = 4$

7.4 APPLICATIONS OF LINEAR SYSTEMS

Examples on pp. 418–420

EXAMPLES After you model a real-life problem with a linear system, you have a choice of three methods for solving the system.

GRAPHING: Use to approximate a solution.

SUBSTITUTION: Use when one variable has a coefficient of 1 or -1.

LINEAR COMBINATIONS: Use when no variable has a coefficient of 1 or -1.

19. **CARNIVAL** You have 50 tickets to ride the Ferris wheel and the roller coaster. If you ride 12 times, using 3 tickets for each Ferris wheel ride and 5 tickets for each roller coaster ride, how many times did you go on each ride?

20. **RENTING MOVIES** You spend $13 to rent five movies for the weekend. Since new releases rent for $3 and regular movies rent for $2, how many regular movies did you rent? How many new releases did you rent?

Chapter 7 *Chapter Review* **441**

SPECIAL TYPES OF LINEAR SYSTEMS

Examples on pp. 426–428

EXAMPLES A system of linear equations in two variables can have exactly one solution, no solution, or infinitely many solutions.

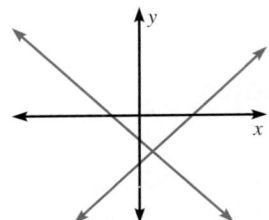

Since the lines intersect, there is one solution.

Since the lines are parallel, there is no solution.

Since the lines coincide, there are infinitely many solutions.

Solve the linear system and tell how many solutions the linear system has.

21. $\frac{1}{3}x + y = 2$
$2x + 6y = 12$

22. $2x - 3y = 1$
$-2x + 3y = 1$

23. $-6x + 5y = 18$
$7x + 2y = 26$

24. $10x + 4y = 25$
$5x + 8y = 11$

25. $14x + 7y = 0$
$-2x + y = 13$

26. $21x + 28y = 14$
$9x + 12y = 6$

SOLVING SYSTEMS OF LINEAR INEQUALITIES

Examples on pp. 432–434

EXAMPLE The boundary line of the graph of a linear inequality in two variables is dashed if the inequality is $<$ or $>$ and solid if the inequality is $\leq$ or $\geq$.

The graph of the system of linear inequalities below is the intersection of the three half-planes shown at the right.

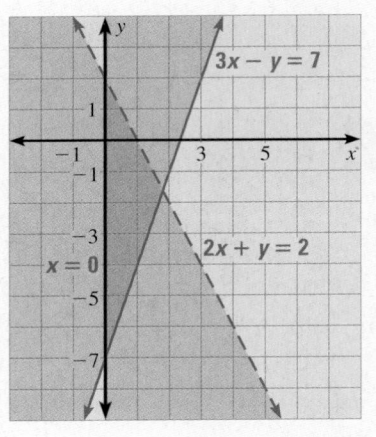

$x \geq 0$	**Inequality 1**
$3x - y \leq 7$	**Inequality 2**
$2x + y < 2$	**Inequality 3**

The graph of the first inequality is the half-plane *on and to the right* of the line $x = 0$.

The graph of the second inequality is the half-plane *on and above* the line $y = 3x - 7$.

The graph of the third inequality is the half-plane *below* the line $y = -2x + 2$.

Graph the system of linear inequalities.

27. $x > -5$
$y < -2$

28. $2x - 10y > 8$
$x - 5y < 12$

29. $-x + 3y \leq 15$
$9x \geq 27$

30. $x < 5$
$y > -2$
$x + 2y > -4$

31. $x + y < 8$
$x - y < 0$
$y \geq -4$

32. $7y > -49$
$-7x + y \geq -14$
$x + y \leq 10$

Chapter Test

Graph and check to solve the linear system.

1. $y = 2x - 3$
$-y = 2x - 1$

2. $6x + 2y = 16$
$-2x + y = -2$

3. $4x - y = 10$
$-2x + 4y = 16$

4. $-4x + y = -10$
$6x + 2y = 22$

5. $3x + 5y = -10$
$-x + 2y = 18$

6. $2x - 3y = 12$
$-x - 3y = -6$

Use the substitution method to solve the linear system.

7. $-4x + 7y = -2$
$-x - y = 5$

8. $7x + 4y = 5$
$x - 6y = -19$

9. $-3x + 6y = 24$
$-2x - y = 1$

10. $5x - y = 7$
$4x + 8y = -12$

11. $x + 6y = 9$
$-x + 4y = 11$

12. $8x + 3y = 0$
$-x - 9y = 92$

Use linear combinations to solve the linear system.

13. $6x + 7y = 5$
$4x - 2y = -10$

14. $-7x + 2y = -5$
$10x - 2y = 6$

15. $-3x + 3y = 12$
$4x + 2y = 20$

16. $3x + 4y = 9$
$4y - 3x = -1$

17. $8x - 2 + y = 0$
$9x - y = 219$

18. $5y - 3x = 1$
$4y + 2x = 80$

Solve the system using the method of your choice and tell how many solutions the system has.

19. $8x + 4y = -4$
$2x - y = -3$

20. $-6x + 3y = -6$
$2x + 6y = 30$

21. $-x + \frac{1}{3}y = -6$
$3x - y = -16$

22. $3x + y = 8$
$4x + 6y = 6$

23. $3x - 4y = 8$
$\frac{9}{2}x - 6y = 12$

24. $6x + y = 12$
$-4x - 2y = 0$

Graph the system of linear inequalities.

25. $x \le 4$
$y \ge 1$
$y \le x + 2$

26. $x < 5$
$y \le 6$
$y > -2x + 3$

27. $y > \frac{3}{2}x + \frac{3}{2}$
$y < -\frac{1}{4}x - \frac{1}{2}$

Write a system of linear inequalities that defines the shaded region.

28.

29.

30.

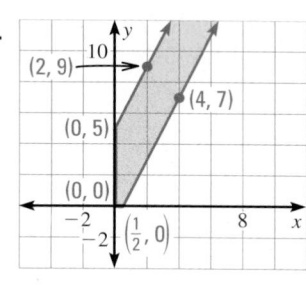

31. 🐦 **WILD BIRD FOOD** You buy six bags of wild bird food to fill the feeders in your yard. Oyster shell grit, a natural calcium source, sells for $4.00 a bag, and sunflower seeds sell for $4.45 a bag. If you spend $25.80, how many bags of each type of feed are you buying?

Chapter Standardized Test

▶ **TEST-TAKING STRATEGY** Go back and check as much of your work as you can.

1. MULTIPLE CHOICE Which point represents the solution of the system of linear equations?

$$y = x - 2$$
$$y = -x - 4$$

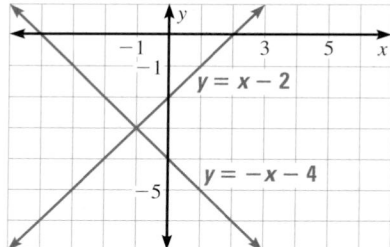

A $(2, 0)$ **B** $(-3, -1)$ **C** $(1, -1)$

D $(-1, -3)$ **E** $(0, -4)$

2. MULTIPLE CHOICE What is the solution of the system of linear equations?

$$\frac{4}{5}x + \frac{1}{2}y = 16$$
$$x + y = 24$$

A $(8, 16)$ **B** $(10, 14)$

C $\left(\frac{40}{3}, \frac{32}{3}\right)$ **D** $\left(\frac{41}{4}, \frac{55}{4}\right)$

E $(2, 22)$

3. MULTIPLE CHOICE If $x + y = 15$ and $x - y = -19$, then $xy = \underline{\ ?\ }$.

A -76 **B** -68 **C** -34

D 15 **E** 34

4. MULTIPLE CHOICE If $-2x + 7y = -8$ and $x - 6y = 10$, then $x - y = \underline{\ ?\ }$.

A -2 **B** 0 **C** $\frac{3}{2}$

D $\frac{5}{2}$ **E** 4

5. MULTIPLE CHOICE If $-\frac{3}{4}x + \frac{7}{10}y = 5$ and $\frac{1}{4}x - \frac{3}{10}y = -5$, then $x + y = \underline{\ ?\ }$.

A -90 **B** -10 **C** $-\frac{25}{8}$

D 10 **E** 90

6. MULTIPLE CHOICE If $y = 5x - 2$, then $-3y = \underline{\ ?\ }$.

A $5x - 6$ **B** $15x - 6$ **C** $15x + 6$

D $-15x - 6$ **E** $-15x + 6$

7. MULTIPLE CHOICE Your teacher is giving a test worth 150 points. There is a total of 42 five-point and two-point questions. How many two-point questions are on the test?

A 18 **B** 20 **C** 22

D 24 **E** 26

8. MULTIPLE CHOICE How many solutions does the linear system have?

$$4x - 2y = 6$$
$$7x + y = 15$$

A None   **B** Exactly one   **C** Two

D Infinitely many   **E** Cannot be determined

9. MULTIPLE CHOICE How many solutions does the linear system have?

$$y = 2x + 4$$
$$y = 2$$

A None   **B** Exactly one   **C** Two

D Infinitely many   **E** Cannot be determined

10. MULTIPLE CHOICE The ordered pair $(3, 4)$ is a solution of $\underline{\ ?\ }$.

A $x + y = 7$ **B** $x - y = 1$
       $x + 2y = 11$ $2x - y = 9$

C $x - y = 1$ **D** $x + y = 7$
       $2x + y = 10$ $2x - 2y = 14$

E Cannot be determined

11. MULTIPLE CHOICE Which point is a solution of the system of linear inequalities?

$$y < -x$$
$$y < x$$

A $(2, 6)$ **B** $(6, -2)$ **C** $(-2, 6)$

D $(-1, -6)$ **E** $(-6, -1)$

12. MULTIPLE CHOICE Which system of inequalities is represented by the graph at the right?

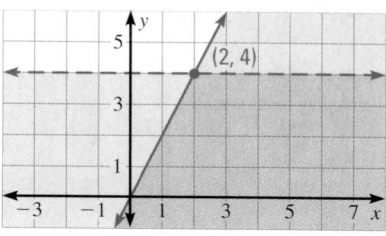

Ex. 12

A $y \le 4$
$y < 2x + 1$

B $y < 4$
$y \ge 2x$

C $y < 4$
$y \le 2x$

D $y < 4$
$y < 2x$

E $y < 4$
$y \le 2x + 1$

13. MULTIPLE CHOICE A ship is traveling toward a lighthouse following the line $4x - y = 10$. Another ship is traveling toward the lighthouse following the line $x + y = 5$. What are the coordinates of the lighthouse?

A $(3, -2)$ **B** $(2, 3)$ **C** $(-2, -3)$ **D** $(-2, 3)$ **E** $(3, 2)$

14. MULTIPLE CHOICE Which point lies on the graph of the system?

$3y = 3$
$x + 2y = 4$

A $(3, 1)$ **B** $(2, 1)$ **C** $(4, 1)$

D $\left(\frac{3}{2}, 1\right)$ **E** Cannot be determined

15. QUANTITATIVE COMPARISON Solve the linear system. Then choose the statement below that is true about the solution of the system.

$2x + 6y = 13$
$x - 4y = 3$

A The value of x is greater.   **B** The value of y is greater.

C The values of x and y are equal.

D The relationship cannot be determined from the given information.

16. MULTI-STEP PROBLEM The members of the city cultural center have decided to put on a play once a night for a week. Their auditorium holds 500 people. By selling tickets, the members would like to raise $3150 every night to cover all expenses. Let x represent the number of adult tickets sold at $7.50 each. Let y represent the number of student tickets sold at $4.50 each.

a. Write a linear equation that models the $3150 income the members hope to raise from the sale of adult and student tickets for one night.

b. Write a second linear equation that models the number of tickets they sell if all 500 seats are filled for a single night's performance.

c. If all 500 seats are filled for a performance, how many of each type of ticket must have been sold for the members to raise exactly $3150?

d. At one performance there were three times as many adult tickets sold as student tickets. If there were 400 tickets sold, how much below the goal of $3150 did the ticket sales fall?

e. *Writing* At another performance, only adults attended. The members know they raised at least $3150 that night. Find the possible numbers of tickets that could have been sold. Explain your method.

EXPONENTS AND EXPONENTIAL FUNCTIONS

▶ *How does switching gears cause a chain reaction?*

CHAPTER
8

APPLICATION: Bicycle Racing

Shifting into high gear helps a racer increase speed on level or downhill surfaces, but pedaling becomes more difficult. When the racer exerts energy the brain sends a message to increase the rate and depth of breathing.

The relationship between breathing rate and bicycle speed can be represented with a type of mathematical model that you'll study in Chapter 8.

Think & Discuss

1. Construct a scatter plot of the data below. Draw a smooth curve through the points.

Bicycle speed, *x* (miles per hour)	Breathing rate, *y* (liters per minute)
0	6.4
5	10.7
10	18.1
15	30.5
20	51.4

2. Describe the change in breathing rate after each increase of 5 mi/h in bike speed. Does it increase by the same amount? the same percent?

Learn More About It

You will use an exponential model that relates the breathing rate to bike speed in Ex. 17 on p. 480.

 APPLICATION LINK Visit www.mcdougallittell.com for more information about bicycle racing.

447

Study Guide

PREVIEW

What's the chapter about?

Chapter 8 is about **exponents**. In Chapter 8 you'll learn

- how to multiply and divide expressions with exponents
- how to use scientific notation in problem solving
- how to use exponential growth and decay models to solve real-life problems

---

KEY VOCABULARY

▶ Review	▶ New	
• power, p. 9	• exponential function, p. 458	• growth factor, p. 477
• base, p. 9	• scientific notation, p. 470	• initial amount, p. 477, 484
• function, p. 46	• exponential growth, p. 477	• exponential decay, p. 484
		• decay factor, p. 484

PREPARE

Are you ready for the chapter?

SKILL REVIEW Do these exercises to review key skills that you'll apply in this chapter. See the given **reference page** if there is something you don't understand.

STUDENT HELP

▸ **Study Tip**
"Student Help" boxes throughout the chapter give you study tips and tell you where to look for extra help in this book and on the Internet.

Write the expression in exponential form. (Review Example 1, p. 9)

1. six squared   **2.** four cubed   **3.** $2y \cdot 2y \cdot 2y \cdot 2y \cdot 2y$

Find the probability of choosing a blue marble from the given bag of red and blue marbles. (Review Example 1, p. 114)

4. Number of blue marbles: 20
Total number of marbles: 80

5. Number of blue marbles: 6
Total number of marbles: 54

6. Number of red marbles: 12
Total number of marbles: 48

7. Number of red marbles: 25
Total number of marbles: 50

Find the unit rate. (Review pp. 180–182)

8. $123.75 for working 15 hours   **9.** $3.16 for 4 cantaloupes

10. $6 for 12 cans of cat food   **11.** 270 miles for 6 gallons of gasoline

STUDY
STRATEGY

Here's a study strategy!

Planning Your Time:

A schedule or weekly planner can be a useful tool that allows you to coordinate your study time with time for other activities and responsibilities.

- Make a plan for each day of the week.
- Study every day, not just the day before a test.

● ACTIVITY 8.1

Developing Concepts

SETUP
Work in a small group.

MATERIALS
• paper
• pencil

Investigating Powers

▶ **QUESTION** How can you use addition to multiply exponential expressions? How can you use multiplication to raise an exponential expression to a power?

▶ **EXPLORING THE CONCEPT: PRODUCT OF POWERS**

① Copy and complete the table. To simplify an expression, expand the product. Then count the factors.

Product of powers	Expanded product	Number of factors	Product as a power
$7^3 \cdot 7^2$	$(7 \cdot 7 \cdot 7) \cdot (7 \cdot 7)$	5	7^5
$2^4 \cdot 2^4$	$(2 \cdot 2 \cdot 2 \cdot 2) \cdot (2 \cdot 2 \cdot 2 \cdot 2)$	8	?
$x^4 \cdot x^5$	$(x \cdot x \cdot x \cdot x) \cdot (x \cdot x \cdot x \cdot x \cdot x)$	?	?

② Add a column to your table that shows the sum of the exponents that are in the first column. What pattern do you notice?

▶ **EXPLORING THE CONCEPT: POWER OF A POWER**

③ Copy and complete the table. To simplify an expression, expand the product. Then count the factors.

Power of a power	Expanded product	Expanded product	Number of factors	Product as a power
$(5^2)^3$	$(5^2) \cdot (5^2) \cdot (5^2)$	$(5 \cdot 5) \cdot (5 \cdot 5) \cdot (5 \cdot 5)$	6	5^6
$[(-3)^2]^2$	$[(-3)^2] \cdot [(-3)^2]$	?	?	?
$(b^2)^4$	?	?	?	?

④ Add a column to your table that shows the product of the exponents that are in the first column. What pattern do you notice?

▶ **DRAWING CONCLUSIONS**

Expand the product. Then write your answer as a power.

1. $6^3 \cdot 6^2$ **2.** $(-2) \cdot (-2)^4$ **3.** $p^4 \cdot p^6$ **4.** $x^{12} \cdot x^7$

5. $(4^2)^6$ **6.** $[(-5)^2]^4$ **7.** $(d^5)^5$ **8.** $[(-n)^3]^8$

9. What operation do you use to simplify a product of powers? Give examples.

10. What operation do you use to simplify a power of a power? Give examples.

11. **CRITICAL THINKING** Does $x^3 \cdot y^5 = xy^8$? Explain your answer.

8.1

Multiplication Properties of Exponents

What you should learn

GOAL 1 Use properties of exponents to multiply exponential expressions.

GOAL 2 Use powers to model **real-life** problems, such as finding the area of crop irrigation circles in **Example 5**.

Why you should learn it

▼ To solve **real-life** problems such as calculating the power generated by a windmill in **Ex. 77**.

GOAL 1 MULTIPLYING EXPONENTIAL EXPRESSIONS

To multiply two powers that have the same base, you add exponents. Here is an example.

$$
a^2 \cdot a^3 = \underbrace{a \cdot a}_{\text{2 factors}} \cdot \underbrace{a \cdot a \cdot a}_{\text{3 factors}} = a^5 = a^{2+3}
$$

5 factors

To find a power of a power, you multiply exponents. Here is an example.

$$
(a^2)^3 = \overbrace{a^2 \cdot a^2 \cdot a^2}^{\text{3 factors}} = \overbrace{a \cdot a \cdot a \cdot a \cdot a \cdot a}^{\text{6 factors}} = a^6 = a^{2 \cdot 3}
$$

These two rules for exponents and the rule for raising a product to a power are summarized below.

CONCEPT SUMMARY   **MULTIPLICATION PROPERTIES OF EXPONENTS**

Let a and b be numbers and let m and n be positive integers.

PRODUCT OF POWERS PROPERTY
To multiply powers having the same base, add the exponents.
$a^m \cdot a^n = a^{m+n}$ **Example:** $3^2 \cdot 3^7 = 3^{2+7} = 3^9$

POWER OF A POWER PROPERTY
To find a power of a power, multiply the exponents.
$(a^m)^n = a^{m \cdot n}$ **Example:** $(5^2)^4 = 5^{2 \cdot 4} = 5^8$

POWER OF A PRODUCT PROPERTY
To find a power of a product, find the power of each factor and multiply.
$(a \cdot b)^m = a^m \cdot b^m$ **Example:** $(2 \cdot 3)^6 = 2^6 \cdot 3^6$

EXAMPLE 1   *Using the Product of Powers Property*

a. $5^3 \cdot 5^6 = 5^{3+6}$
      $= 5^9$

b. $x^2 \cdot x^3 \cdot x^4 = x^{2+3+4}$
      $= x^9$

STUDENT HELP

► **Look Back**
For help with exponential expressions, see page 9.

c. $3 \cdot 3^5 = 3^1 \cdot 3^5$
      $= 3^{1+5}$
      $= 3^6$

d. $(-2)(-2)^4 = (-2)^1 \cdot (-2)^4$
      $= (-2)^{1+4}$
      $= (-2)^5$

EXAMPLE 2 *Using the Power of a Power Property*

a. $(3^5)^2 = 3^{5 \cdot 2}$

$\qquad = 3^{10}$

b. $(y^2)^4 = y^{2 \cdot 4}$

$\qquad = y^8$

c. $[(-3)^3]^2 = (-3)^{3 \cdot 2}$

$\qquad = (-3)^6$

d. $[(a+1)^2]^5 = (a+1)^{2 \cdot 5}$

$\qquad = (a+1)^{10}$

· · · · · · · · · ·

When you use the power of a power property, it is the quantity within the parentheses that is raised to the power *not* the individual terms.

Correct: $\qquad (a+1)^3 = (a+1)(a+1)(a+1) \qquad \longleftarrow$ **3 factors**

Incorrect: $\qquad \cancel{(a+1)^3 = a^3 + 1^3} \qquad \longleftarrow$ **2 terms**

EXAMPLE 3 *Using the Power of a Product Property*

a. $(6 \cdot 5)^2 = 6^2 \cdot 5^2$ $\qquad$ **Raise each factor to a power.**

$\qquad = 36 \cdot 25$ $\qquad$ **Evaluate each power.**

$\qquad = 900$ $\qquad$ **Multiply.**

b. $(4yz)^3 = (4 \cdot y \cdot z)^3$ $\qquad$ **Identify factors.**

$\qquad = 4^3 \cdot y^3 \cdot z^3$ $\qquad$ **Raise each factor to a power.**

$\qquad = 64y^3z^3$ $\qquad$ **Simplify.**

c. $(-2w)^2 = (-2 \cdot w)^2$ $\qquad$ **Identify factors.**

$\qquad = (-2)^2 \cdot w^2$ $\qquad$ **Raise each factor to a power.**

$\qquad = 4w^2$ $\qquad$ **Simplify.**

d. $-(2w)^2 = -(2 \cdot w)^2$ $\qquad$ **Identify factors.**

$\qquad = -(2^2 \cdot w^2)$ $\qquad$ **Raise each factor to a power.**

$\qquad = -4w^2$ $\qquad$ **Simplify.**

EXAMPLE 4 *Using All Three Properties*

Simplify $(4x^2y)^3 \cdot x^5$.

SOLUTION

$(4x^2y)^3 \cdot x^5 = 4^3 \cdot (x^2)^3 \cdot y^3 \cdot x^5$ $\qquad$ **Power of a product**

$\qquad = 64 \cdot x^6 \cdot y^3 \cdot x^5$ $\qquad$ **Power of a power**

$\qquad = 64x^{11}y^3$ $\qquad$ **Product of powers**

GOAL 2 USING POWERS IN REAL LIFE

Irrigation

EXAMPLE 5 *Using the Power of a Product Property*

Some farmers use *center-pivot irrigation,* which is a sprinkler system that revolves around a center pivot. The large irrigation circles help farmers to conserve water, maximize crop yield, and reduce the cost of pesticides.

a. Find the ratio of the area of the larger irrigation circle to the area of the smaller irrigation circle.

b. Write a general statement about *doubling* the radius of an irrigation circle.

SOLUTION

a. Ratio $= \dfrac{\pi(2r)^2}{\pi r^2} = \dfrac{\pi \cdot 2^2 \cdot r^2}{\pi \cdot r^2} = \dfrac{\pi \cdot 4 \cdot r^2}{\pi \cdot r^2} = \dfrac{4}{1}$

b. Doubling the radius of an irrigation circle makes the area *four* times as large.

EXAMPLE 6 *Using the Product of Powers Property*

PROBABILITY CONNECTION A true-false test has two parts. There are 2^{10} ways to answer the 10 questions in Part A. There are 2^{15} ways to answer the 15 questions in Part B.

a. How many ways are there to answer all 25 questions?

b. If you guess each answer, what is the probability you will get them all right?

SOLUTION

STUDENT HELP

Skills Review
For help with the counting principle, see page 788.

a. For each of the 2^{10} ways to answer the questions in Part A, there are 2^{15} ways to answer the questions in Part B. Use the counting principle to find the total number of ways to answer for both parts. The number of ways to answer the 25 questions is the product of 2^{10} and 2^{15}.

$$2^{10} \cdot 2^{15} = 2^{10 + 15} \qquad \text{Use product of powers property.}$$

$$= 2^{25} \qquad \text{Add exponents.}$$

$$= 33{,}554{,}432 \qquad \text{Use a calculator.}$$

▶ The number of ways to answer the 25 questions is 33,554,432.

b. Probability $= \dfrac{\text{Ways to get all right}}{\text{Ways to answer}} = \dfrac{1}{33{,}554{,}432}$

▶ The probability of guessing and getting all answers correct is about 0.00000003.

GUIDED PRACTICE

Vocabulary Check ✔

1. In the expression a^5, a is called the __?__ of the expression.

Concept Check ✔

2. How are the expressions $x^7 \cdot x^3$ and $(x^7)^3$ different? Explain your answer.

3. Can $a^3 \cdot b^4$ be simplified? Explain your answer.

Skill Check ✔

Use the product of powers property to simplify the expression.

4. $c \cdot c \cdot c$ **5.** $m \cdot m^2$ **6.** $2^2 \cdot 2^3$

7. $3^2 \cdot 3^5$ **8.** $a^4 \cdot a^6$ **9.** $x^4 \cdot x^5$

Use the power of a power property to simplify the expression.

10. $(3)^2$ **11.** $(-2)^2$ **12.** $(2^4)^3$

13. $(4^3)^3$ **14.** $(y^4)^5$ **15.** $(m^4)^8$

Use the power of a product property to simplify the expression.

16. $(2m^2)^3$ **17.** $(ab^2)^2$ **18.** $(5x)^2$

19. $(x^3y^5)^4$ **20.** $(x^3y^8)^5$ **21.** $(-2x^3)^3$

PRACTICE AND APPLICATIONS

STUDENT HELP

▶ **Extra Practice**
to help you master
skills is on p. 804.

SIMPLIFYING EXPRESSIONS Simplify, if possible. Write your answer as a power or as a product of powers.

22. $3^4 \cdot 3^6$ **23.** $5^8 \cdot 5^3$ **24.** $(2^3)^2$ **25.** $(7^4)^2$

26. $x \cdot x^6$ **27.** $(3 \cdot 7)^2$ **28.** $(2x)^2$ **29.** $(-5a)^3$

30. $(-2m^4n^6)^2$ **31.** $[(-4)^2]^3$ **32.** $[(-5xy)^2]^5$ **33.** $[(5+x)^3]^6$

34. $[(2x+3)^3]^2$ **35.** $(3b)^3 \cdot b$ **36.** $5^3 \cdot (5a^4)^2$

37. $4x \cdot (x \cdot x^3)^2$ **38.** $(-3a)^5 \cdot (4a)^2$ **39.** $-(3x)^2 \cdot (7x^4)^2$

40. $2x^3 \cdot (3x)^2$ **41.** $3y^2 \cdot (2y)^3$ **42.** $(-ab)(a^2b)^2$

43. $(-rs)(rs^3)^2$ **44.** $(-2xy)^3(-x^2)$ **45.** $(-3cd)^3(-d^2)$

46. $(5b^2)^3\left(\frac{1}{2}b^3\right)^2$ **47.** $(6a^4)^2\left(\frac{1}{4}a^3\right)^2$ **48.** $(2t)^3(-t^2)$

49. $(-w^3)(3w^2)^2$ **50.** $(-y)^3(-y)^4(-y)^5$ **51.** $(-x)^4(-x)^3(-x)^2$

52. $(abc^2)^3(a^2b)^2$ **53.** $-(r^2st^3)^2(s^4t)^3$ **54.** $(-3xy^2)^3(-2x^2y)^2$

STUDENT HELP

▶ HOMEWORK HELP
Example 1: Exs. 22–62
Example 2: Exs. 22–62
Example 3: Exs. 22–62
Example 4: Exs. 36–62
Example 5: Exs. 77, 78
Example 6: Ex. 79

EVALUATING EXPRESSIONS Simplify. Then evaluate the expression when $a = 1$ and $b = 2$.

55. $a^2 \cdot a^3$ **56.** $b \cdot b^4$ **57.** $(a^3)^2$ **58.** $(-b)^3 \cdot b^2$

59. $(a \cdot b^2)^2$ **60.** $(a^2b)^4$ **61.** $-(ab^3)^2$ **62.** $(b^2 \cdot b^3) \cdot (b^2)^4$

WRITING INEQUALITIES Complete the statement using > or <.

63. $(5 \cdot 6)^4$ _?_ $5 \cdot 6^4$

64. $5^2 \cdot 3^6$ _?_ $(5 \cdot 3)^6$

65. $(3^6 \cdot 3^{12})$ _?_ 3^{72}

66. $4^2 \cdot 4^8$ _?_ 4^{16}

67. $(7^2)^3$ _?_ 7^5

68. $(6^2 \cdot 3)^3$ _?_ $6^5 \cdot 3^3$

EVALUATING POWERS In Exercises 69–74, simplify the expression. Then use a calculator to evaluate the expression. Round the result to the nearest tenth when appropriate.

69. $(2.1 \cdot 4.4)^3$

70. $6.5^3 \cdot 6.5^4$

71. $2.6^4 \cdot 2.6^2$

72. $(5.0 \cdot 4.9)^2$

73. $(3.7^3)^5$

74. $(8.4^2)^4$

75. **GEOMETRY** **CONNECTION** The volume of a sphere is given by $V = \frac{4}{3}\pi r^3$, where r is the radius and π is approximately 3.14. What is the volume of the sphere in terms of a?

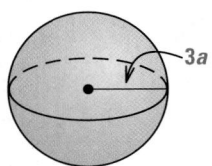

76. **GEOMETRY** **CONNECTION** The volume of a cone is given by $V = \frac{1}{3}\pi r^2 h$, where r is the radius of the base, h is the height, and $\pi \approx 3.14$. What is the volume of the cone in terms of b?

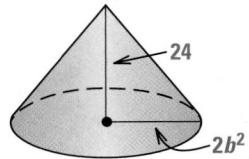

WINDMILLS In Exercises 77 and 78, use the following information. The power generated by a windmill can be modeled by the equation $w = 0.015s^3$, where w is the power measured in watts and s is the wind speed in miles per hour.

77. Find the ratio of the power generated by a windmill when the wind speed is 20 miles per hour to the power generated when the wind speed is 10 miles per hour.

78. *Writing* Write a general statement about how doubling the wind speed affects the amount of power generated by a windmill.

79. **PROBABILITY** **CONNECTION** Part A of a test has 10 true-false questions. Part B has 10 multiple-choice questions. Each of the multiple-choice questions has 4 possible answers. There are 2^{10} ways to answer the 10 questions in Part A. There are 4^{10} ways to answer the 10 questions in Part B.

a. How many ways are there to answer all 20 questions?

b. If you guess the answer to each question, what is the probability that you will get them all right?

PROBABILITY **CONNECTION** In Exercises 80 and 81, suppose you put one red marble, one green marble, and one blue marble in each of six bags. There are 3^6 possible orderings of the colors of the marbles you can get when you choose one marble from each bag.

80. If you use 8 bags, there are 3^8 possible orderings of colors. What is the probability that the marbles you choose will all be red?

81. If you use 14 bags, how many different orderings of colors are there? What is the probability that the marbles you choose will all be red?

FOCUS ON CAREERS

ENGINEERING TECHNICIANS
use science, engineering, and math to solve technical problems in the development, construction, inspection, and maintenance of industrial machinery.

CAREER LINK
www.mcdougallittell.com

MULTI-STEP PROBLEM Use the results of Exercise 82 for Exercise 83.

82. a. Copy and complete the table of values.

x	0	1	2	3	4
2x	?	?	?	?	?
2^x	?	?	?	?	?

b. Sketch the graphs of $y = 2x$ and $y = 2^x$ in the same coordinate plane.

c. Compare the graphs. How are they the same? How are they different?

83. CRITICAL THINKING You are offered a job that pays $2x$ dollars or 2^x dollars for x hours of work. Assuming you must work at least 2 hours, which method of payment would you choose? Explain your reasoning.

★ **Challenge**

84. LOGICAL REASONING Fill in the blanks and give a reason for each step to complete a convincing argument that the power of a power property is true.

$$(a^2)^3 = a^2 \cdot \underline{?} \cdot \underline{?}$$
$$= \underline{?} \cdot \underline{?} \cdot \underline{?} \cdot \underline{?} \cdot \underline{?} \cdot \underline{?}$$
$$= \underline{?}$$

EXTRA CHALLENGE
www.mcdougallittell.com

85. LOGICAL REASONING Write a convincing argument to show that the power of a product property is true.

MIXED REVIEW

EXPONENTIAL EXPRESSIONS Evaluate the expression. (Review 1.3 for 8.2)

86. b^2 when $b = 8$

87. $(5y)^4$ when $y = 2$

88. $\frac{1}{2}n^3$ when $n = -2$

89. $\frac{1}{y^2}$ when $y = 5$

90. $\frac{24}{x^3}$ when $x = 2$

91. $\frac{45}{a^2}$ when $a = 2$

GRAPHING EQUATIONS Use a table of values to graph the equation. (Review 4.2)

92. $y = x + 2$

93. $y = -(x - 4)$

94. $y = \frac{1}{2}x - 5$

95. $y = \frac{3}{4}x + 2$

96. $y = 2$

97. $x = -3$

GRAPHING INEQUALITIES Sketch the graph of the inequality. (Review 6.1)

98. $x < 4$

99. $x > 15$

100. $x \geq -9$

101. $x \leq 3$

SOLVING INEQUALITIES Solve the inequality. (Review 6.2)

102. $-x - 2 < -5$

103. $8 + 3x \geq -2$

104. $2 < 2x + 7$

105. **PRICE OF MILK** In 1910, a quart of milk cost $.07. In 1994, a quart of milk cost $.71. After 1910, the price of milk increased steadily, never falling below $.07 per quart again. During the period 1910–1994, the maximum price of a quart was $.71. Write a compound inequality that represents the possible costs of a quart of milk between 1910 and 1994. (Review 6.3)

8.2 Zero and Negative Exponents

What you should learn

GOAL 1 Evaluate powers that have zero and negative exponents.

GOAL 2 Graph exponential functions.

Why you should learn it

▼ To solve **real-life** problems such as predicting a player's average score per game in **Example 6**.

GOAL 1 USING ZERO AND NEGATIVE EXPONENTS

In this lesson you will study how to use the multiplication properties of exponents when working with negative exponents.

ACTIVITY
Developing Concepts

Investigating Zero and Negative Exponents

1 Copy the table and discuss any patterns you see. Use the patterns to complete the table. Write non-integers as fractions in simplest form.

Exponent, n	3	2	1	0	-1	-2	-3
Power, 2^n	8	4	2	?	?	?	?
Power, 3^n	27	9	3	?	?	?	?
Power, 4^n	64	16	4	?	?	?	?

2 What appears to be the value of a^0 for any number a?

3 How can you evaluate an expression of the form a^{-n}?

DEFINITION OF ZERO AND NEGATIVE EXPONENTS

Let a be a nonzero number and let n be a positive integer.

• A nonzero number to the zero power is 1: $a^0 = 1$, $a \neq 0$.

• a^{-n} is the reciprocal of a^n: $a^{-n} = \dfrac{1}{a^n}$, $a \neq 0$.

EXAMPLE 1 *Powers with Zero and Negative Exponents*

a. $2^{-2} = \dfrac{1}{2^2} = \dfrac{1}{4}$ 2^{-2} is the reciprocal of 2^2.

b. $(-2)^0 = 1$ a^0 is 1.

c. $5^{-x} = \dfrac{1}{5^x}$ 5^{-x} is the reciprocal of 5^x.

d. $\left(\dfrac{1}{3}\right)^{-1} = 3$ The reciprocal of $\dfrac{1}{3}$ is 3.

e. $0^{-3} = \dfrac{1}{0^3}$ (Undefined)   Zero has no reciprocal.

STUDENT HELP

INTERNET **HOMEWORK HELP**
Visit our Web site
www.mcdougallittell.com
for extra examples.

EXAMPLE 2 *Simplifying Exponential Expressions*

STUDENT HELP

Study Tip
Informally, you can think of rewriting expressions with positive exponents as "moving factors" from the denominator to the numerator or vice versa.

$$\frac{1}{3x^{-4}} = \frac{x^4}{3}$$

Rewrite with positive exponents.

a. $5(2^{-x})$ **b.** $2x^{-2}y^{-3}$

SOLUTION

a. $5\left(2^{-x}\right) = 5\left(\dfrac{1}{2^x}\right) = \dfrac{5}{2^x}$ **b.** $2x^{-2}y^{-3} = 2 \cdot \dfrac{1}{x^2} \cdot \dfrac{1}{y^3} = \dfrac{2}{x^2 y^3}$

EXAMPLE 3 *Evaluating Exponential Expressions*

Evaluate the expression.

a. $3^{-2} \cdot 3^2$ **b.** $\left(2^{-3}\right)^{-2}$ **c.** 3^{-4}

SOLUTION

a. $3^{-2} \cdot 3^2 = 3^{-2+2}$ Use product of powers property.

          $= 3^0$ Add exponents.

          $= 1$ a^0 is 1.

b. $\left(2^{-3}\right)^{-2} = 2^{-3 \cdot (-2)}$ Use power of a power property.

          $= 2^6$ Multiply exponents.

          $= 64$ Evaluate.

STUDENT HELP

KEYSTROKE HELP
Use or to input the exponent -4.

c. You might want to evaluate 3^{-4} with a calculator.

KEYSTROKES   **DISPLAY**

3 ⌷y^x⌷ 4 ⌷+/−⌷ ⌷=⌷   ⌷.01234568⌷

EXAMPLE 4 *Simplifying Exponential Expressions*

Rewrite with positive exponents.

a. $(5a)^{-2}$ **b.** $\dfrac{1}{d^{-3n}}$

SOLUTION

a. $(5a)^{-2} = 5^{-2} \cdot a^{-2}$ Use power of a product property.

          $= \dfrac{1}{5^2} \cdot \dfrac{1}{a^2}$ Write reciprocals of 5^2 and a^2.

          $= \dfrac{1}{25a^2}$ Multiply fractions.

b. $\dfrac{1}{d^{-3n}} = \left(d^{-3n}\right)^{-1}$ Use definition of negative exponents.

          $= d^{(-3n) \cdot (-1)}$ Use power of a power property.

          $= d^{3n}$ Multiply exponents.

So far we have used expressions of the form b^n where $b \neq 0$ and n is an integer. To model some situations, we need an **exponential function** of the form $y = a \cdot b^x$ where x is a real number, $b > 0$, and $b \neq 1$. To graph the exponential function $y = a \cdot b^x$, make a table using integer values for x and plot the corresponding points. To complete the graph for all real values of x, connect the points with a smooth curve.

EXAMPLE 5 *Graphing an Exponential Function*

To sketch the graph of $y = 2^x$, make a table that includes negative x-values.

x	-2	-1	0	1	2	3
2^x	$2^{-2} = \frac{1}{4}$	$2^{-1} = \frac{1}{2}$	$2^0 = 1$	2	4	8

Draw a coordinate plane and plot the six points given by the table. Then draw a smooth curve through the points.

Notice that the graph has a y-intercept of 1, and that it gets closer to the negative side of the x-axis as the x-values get smaller.

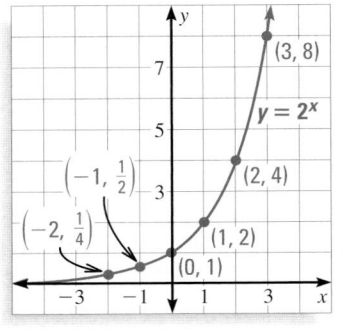

. . . .

In real-life applications of $y = ab^x$, x is often the time period.

Basketball

EXAMPLE 6 *Evaluating an Exponential Function*

A professional basketball player's first year in the NBA was 1998. Suppose it were estimated that from 1998 to 2010 his average points per game could be modeled by $P = 18.5(1.038)^t$, where $t = 0$ represents the year 2000.

  a. Estimate the player's average points per game in 1998.

  b. Estimate his average points per game in the year 2000.

SOLUTION

  a. $P = 18.5 \cdot 1.038^{-2}$ Substitute -2 for t.

    ≈ 17.17 Use a calculator.

  ▶ In the year 1998 his average points per game was about 17.2 points.

  b. $P = 18.5 \cdot 1.038^0$ Substitute 0 for t.

    $= 18.5$ a^0 is 1.

  ▶ In the year 2000 his average points per game was about 18.5 points.

GUIDED PRACTICE

Vocabulary Check ✔

Concept Check ✔

Skill Check ✔

1. The function $y = ab^x$ is a(n) __?__ function.

2. ERROR ANALYSIS Describe the error at the right.

$$5x^{-3} = \frac{1}{5x^3}$$

Evaluate the expression.

3. 3^{-1}　　　　**4.** 0^{-4}　　　　**5.** 0^0　　　　**6.** $6 \cdot 3^0$

Rewrite as an expression with positive exponents.

7. m^{-2}　　**8.** $3c^{-5}$　　**9.** $a^5 b^{-8}$　　**10.** $\dfrac{1}{(2x)^{-3}}$

11. Does the graph at the right appear to be the graph of the exponential function $y = 3^x$?

12. Tell whether the following statement is true.

If a is positive, then a^{-n} is positive.

Explain your reasoning.

Ex. 11

13. 🌐 **BASKETBALL** Use the information in Example 6. If the player's final year in the NBA is 2010, estimate his average points per game in his final year.

PRACTICE AND APPLICATIONS

STUDENT HELP

▶ **Extra Practice**
to help you master
skills is on p. 804.

EVALUATING EXPRESSIONS Evaluate the exponential expression. Write fractions in simplest form.

14. 4^{-2}　　**15.** 3^{-4}　　**16.** $\left(\dfrac{1}{5}\right)^{-1}$　　**17.** $8\left(\dfrac{1}{4}\right)^{-1}$

18. $4(4^{-2})$　　**19.** $\left(\dfrac{1}{10}\right)^{-2}$　　**20.** $-6^0 \cdot \dfrac{1}{3^{-2}}$　　**21.** $2^{-3} \cdot 2^2$

22. $8^3 \cdot 0^{-1}$　　**23.** $7^4 \cdot 7^{-4}$　　**24.** $8^{-7} \cdot 8^7$　　**25.** $-4 \cdot (-4)^{-1}$

26. $(5^{-3})^2$　　**27.** $(-3^{-2})^{-1}$　　**28.** $11 \cdot 11^{-1}$　　**29.** $4^0 \cdot 5^{-3}$

SIMPLIFYING EXPRESSIONS Rewrite the expression with positive exponents.

STUDENT HELP

▶ **HOMEWORK HELP**
Example 1: Exs. 14–29
Example 2: Exs. 30–45
Example 3: Exs. 14–29,
　　　　　49–52
Example 4: Exs. 30–45
Example 5: Exs. 53–63
Example 6: Exs. 64, 65

30. x^{-5}　　**31.** $3x^{-4}$　　**32.** $\dfrac{1}{2x^{-5}}$　　**33.** $x^{-2}y^4$

34. $x^4 y^{-7}$　　**35.** $8x^{-2}y^{-6}$　　**36.** $\dfrac{1}{9x^{-3}y^{-1}}$　　**37.** $\dfrac{1}{4x^{-10}y^{14}}$

38. $(-9)^0 x$　　**39.** $(-4x)^{-3}$　　**40.** $(-10a)^0$　　**41.** $(3xy)^{-2}$

42. $(6a^{-3})^3$　　**43.** $\dfrac{8}{m^{-2}}$　　**44.** $\dfrac{1}{(4x)^{-5}}$　　**45.** $\left(\dfrac{-4x^2}{2x^{-1}}\right)^{-1}$

MATCHING THE GRAPH Match the equation with its graph.

A.

B.

C.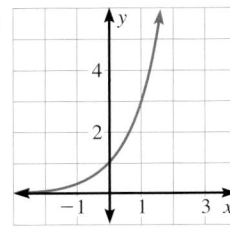

46. $y = 2x$

47. $y = 3^x$

48. $y = 5^x$

EVALUATING EXPONENTIAL EXPRESSIONS Use a calculator to evaluate the expression. Round your answer to the nearest hundred thousandth.

49. 2^{-5}

50. $(1.1)^{-2}$

51. $55 \cdot 5^{-6}$

52. $3^{-5} \div 0.9$

CHECKING POINTS Does the graph of the function contain the point (0, 1)?

53. $y = -3^x$

54. $y = 4^x$

55. $y = 4 \cdot 1^x$

56. $y = 60^x$

GRAPHING FUNCTIONS In Exercises 57–60, graph the exponential function.

57. $y = \left(\dfrac{1}{3}\right)^x$

58. $y = \left(\dfrac{1}{5}\right)^x$

59. $y = 4^{-x}$

60. $y = 5^x$

61. VISUAL THINKING Sketch the graphs of $y = 2^x$ and $y = \left(\dfrac{1}{2}\right)^x$. How are the graphs related?

62. CRITICAL THINKING Sketch the graphs of $y = 3^x$ and $y = \left(\dfrac{1}{3}\right)^x$. Use these graphs and the ones you sketched in Exercise 61 to predict how the graphs of $y = b^x$ and $y = \left(\dfrac{1}{b}\right)^x$ are related.

63. COMMON POINTS What point do all graphs of the form $y = a^x$ have in common? Is there a point that all graphs of the form $y = 2(a)^x$ have in common? If so, name the point.

64. ⊕ SAVINGS ACCOUNT You started a savings account in 1990. The balance A is modeled by $A = 450(1.06)^t$, where $t = 0$ represents the year 2000. What is the balance in the account in 1990? in 2000? in 2010?

65. ⊕ SHIPWRECKS Suppose that from 1860 to 1980 the number of shipwrecks in the Gulf of Mexico increased by about the same percent each year and that the number of shipwrecks S for each decade t can be modeled by $S = 292(1.2)^t$, where $t = 0$ represents the decade 1920 to 1929.

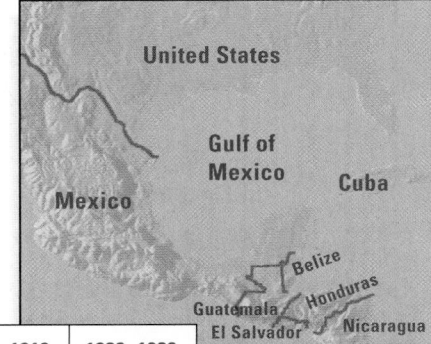

a. Copy and complete the table below.

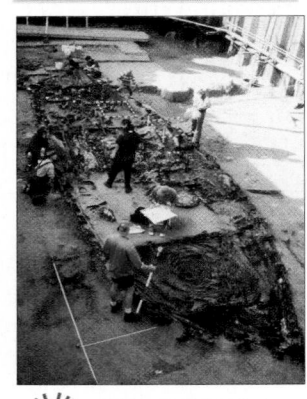
	1870–1879	1880–1889	1900–1909	1910–1919	1920–1929
t	-5	-4	-2	-1	0
S	?	?	?	?	?

b. Graph the function and check your results.

Test Preparation

QUANTITATIVE COMPARISON In Exercises 66–68, evaluate each function. Then choose the statement below that is true about the given values of *y*.

Ⓐ The value of *y* in column A is greater.

Ⓑ The value of *y* in column B is greater.

Ⓒ The two values of *y* are equal.

Ⓓ The relationship cannot be determined from the given information.

		Column A	Column B
66.	When $x = 3$,	$y = 2x$	$y = 2^x$
67.	When $x = 1$,	$y = 2^x$	$y = 2^{-x}$
68.	When $x = 0$,	$y = \left(\dfrac{1}{2}\right)^x$	$y = \left(\dfrac{1}{2}\right)^{-x}$

69. MULTIPLE CHOICE What is a possible equation of the graph?

Ⓐ $y = 2^x$ Ⓑ $y = 3^x$

Ⓒ $y = \left(\dfrac{1}{2}\right)^x$ Ⓓ $y = \left(\dfrac{1}{3}\right)^x$

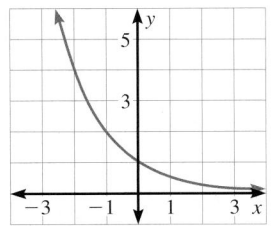

★ **Challenge**

70. *Writing* Suppose you did not know that for $b \neq 0$, $b^0 = 1$. Based on the equation $b^2 \cdot b^0 = b^{2+0} = b^2$, explain why you might want to make this definition.

MIXED REVIEW

EVALUATING EXPRESSIONS Evaluate the expression. (Review 1.3 for 8.3)

71. $\left(\dfrac{2}{5}\right)^2$ **72.** $\left(\dfrac{1}{2}\right)^3$ **73.** $\left(-\dfrac{9}{10}\right)^3$ **74.** $\left(\dfrac{1}{5}\right)^4$

SOLVE AND GRAPH Solve the inequality. Then sketch a graph of the solution on a number line. (Review 6.4)

75. $|5 + x| + 4 \leq 11$ **76.** $|3x + 7| - 4 > 9$ **77.** $|x + 2| - 1 \leq 8$

78. $|3 - x| - 6 > -4$ **79.** $|9 - 2x| + 3 < 4$ **80.** $|3x + 2| + 9 \geq -1$

STATISTICS Draw a box-and-whisker plot of the data. (Review 6.7)

81. 48, 10, 48, 25, 40, 42, 44, 23, 21, 13, 50, 17

82. 85, 61, 55, 78, 79, 86, 30, 76, 76, 87, 68, 82

SOLVING SYSTEMS Use substitution to solve the system. (Review 7.2)

83. $2x - y = -2$
$4x + y = 5$

84. $-3x + y = 4$
$-9x + 5y = 10$

85. $x + 4y = 300$
$x - 2y = 0$

86. $2x - 3y = 10$
$3x + 3y = 15$

87. $x + 15y = 6$
$-x - 5y = 84$

88. $4x - y = 5$
$2x + 4y = 15$

8.2 *Zero and Negative Exponents*   **461**

◗ ACTIVITY 8.2

Using Technology

Graphing Exponential Functions

You can use a graphing calculator to graph an exponential function.

▶ EXAMPLE

Graph $y = \left(\frac{1}{2}\right)^x$.

▶ SOLUTION

❶ To enter the function in your graphing calculator, press ⬚Y=⬚. Enter the function as

 .

```
Y1 ▤ 0.5^X
Y2=
Y3=
Y4=
Y5=
Y6=
Y7=
```

❷ Adjust the *viewing window* to get the best scale for your graph.

```
WINDOW
 Xmin=-10
 Xmax=10
 Xscl=2
 Ymin=-10
 Ymax=10
 Yscl=2
```

❸ Now you are ready to graph the function. Press ⬚GRAPH⬚ to see the graph.

▶ EXERCISES

Use a graphing calculator to graph the exponential function.

1. $y = 2^x$ **2.** $y = 10^x$ **3.** $y = -3^x$

4. $y = 5^{-x}$ **5.** $y = (0.27)^x$ **6.** $y = -\left(\frac{2}{3}\right)^x$

CRITICAL THINKING Use your results from Exercises 1–6 to answer the following questions.

7. If $a > 1$, what does the graph of $y = a^x$ look like?

8. If $0 < a < 1$, what does the graph of $y = a^x$ look like?

9. If $a > 1$, what does the graph of $y = -\left(a^x\right)$ look like?

10. If $0 < a < 1$, what does the graph of $y = -\left(a^x\right)$ look like?

8.3 Division Properties of Exponents

What you should learn

GOAL 1 Use the division properties of exponents to evaluate powers and simplify expressions.

GOAL 2 Use the division properties of exponents to find a probability as in **Example 5**.

Why you should learn it

▼ To solve **real-life** problems such as comparing the top speeds of boats in an Olympic rowing competition in **Ex. 58**.

GOAL 1 DIVIDING WITH EXPONENTS

In Lesson 8.1 you learned that you multiply powers with the same base by adding exponents. To divide powers with the same base, you subtract exponents. Here is an example.

$$\frac{4^5}{4^3} = \frac{\overbrace{4 \cdot 4 \cdot 4 \cdot 4 \cdot 4}^{5\ \text{factors}}}{\underbrace{4 \cdot 4 \cdot 4}_{3\ \text{factors}}} = \underbrace{4 \cdot 4}_{2\ \text{factors}} = 4^{5-3} = 4^2$$

CONCEPT SUMMARY   DIVISION PROPERTIES OF EXPONENTS

Let a and b be numbers and let m and n be integers.

QUOTIENT OF POWERS PROPERTY
To divide powers having the same base, subtract exponents.

$$\frac{a^m}{a^n} = a^{m-n}, \ a \neq 0$$

Example: $\dfrac{3^7}{3^5} = 3^{7-5} = 3^2$

POWER OF A QUOTIENT PROPERTY
To find a power of a quotient, find the power of the numerator and the power of the denominator and divide.

$$\left(\frac{a}{b}\right)^m = \frac{a^m}{b^m}, \ b \neq 0$$

Example: $\left(\dfrac{4}{5}\right)^3 = \dfrac{4^3}{5^3}$

EXAMPLE 1 *Using the Quotient of Powers Property*

a. $\dfrac{6^5}{6^4} = 6^{5-4}$

$\quad\quad = 6^1$

$\quad\quad = 6$

b. $\dfrac{(-5)^2}{(-5)^2} = (-5)^{2-2}$

$\quad\quad\quad = (-5)^0$

$\quad\quad\quad = 1$

c. $\dfrac{9^4 \cdot 9^2}{9^7} = \dfrac{9^6}{9^7}$

$\quad\quad\quad = 9^{6-7}$

$\quad\quad\quad = 9^{-1}$

$\quad\quad\quad = \dfrac{1}{9}$

d. $\dfrac{1}{y^5} \cdot y^3 = \dfrac{y^3}{y^5}$

$\quad\quad\quad = y^{3-5}$

$\quad\quad\quad = y^{-2}$

$\quad\quad\quad = \dfrac{1}{y^2}$

EXAMPLE 2 *Using the Power of a Quotient Property*

STUDENT HELP

HOMEWORK HELP
Visit our Web site
www.mcdougallittell.com
for extra examples.

Simplify the expression.

a. $\left(\dfrac{2}{3}\right)^2$ **b.** $\left(-\dfrac{3}{y}\right)^3$ **c.** $\left(\dfrac{7}{4}\right)^{-3}$

SOLUTION

a. $\left(\dfrac{2}{3}\right)^2 = \dfrac{2^2}{3^2} = \dfrac{4}{9}$ **Square numerator and denominator and simplify.**

b. $\left(-\dfrac{3}{y}\right)^3 = \left(\dfrac{-3}{y}\right)^3$ **Rewrite fraction.**

$= \dfrac{(-3)^3}{y^3}$ **Power of a quotient**

$= \dfrac{-27}{y^3}$ **Simplify.**

c. $\left(\dfrac{7}{4}\right)^{-3} = \dfrac{7^{-3}}{4^{-3}}$ **Power of a quotient**

$= \dfrac{4^3}{7^3}$ **Definition of negative exponents**

$= \dfrac{64}{343}$ **Simplify.**

EXAMPLE 3 *Simplifying Expressions*

Simplify the expression.

a. $\dfrac{2x^2 y}{3x} \cdot \dfrac{9xy^2}{y^4}$ **b.** $\left(\dfrac{2x}{y^2}\right)^4$

SOLUTION

a. $\dfrac{2x^2 y}{3x} \cdot \dfrac{9xy^2}{y^4} = \dfrac{(2x^2 y)(9xy^2)}{(3x)(y^4)}$ **Multiply fractions.**

$= \dfrac{18x^3 y^3}{3xy^4}$ **Product of powers**

$= 6x^2 y^{-1}$ **Quotient of powers**

$= \dfrac{6x^2}{y}$ **Definition of negative exponents**

b. $\left(\dfrac{2x}{y^2}\right)^4 = \dfrac{(2x)^4}{(y^2)^4}$ **Power of a quotient**

$= \dfrac{2^4 \cdot x^4}{y^{2 \cdot 4}}$ **Product of a product and power of a power**

$= \dfrac{16x^4}{y^8}$ **Simplify.**

EXAMPLE 4 *Using the Quotient of Powers Property*

STOCK EXCHANGE The number of shares N (in billions) listed on the New York Stock Exchange from 1977 through 1997 can be modeled by

$$N = 92.56 \cdot (1.112)^t$$

where $t = 0$ represents 1990. Find the ratio of shares listed in 1997 to the shares listed in 1977. ▶ Source: Federal Reserve Bank of New York

SOLUTION

Use $t = -13$ for 1977 and $t = 7$ for 1997.

$$\frac{\text{Number listed in 1997}}{\text{Number listed in 1977}} = \frac{92.56 \cdot (1.112)^7}{92.56 \cdot (1.112)^{-13}}$$

$$= 1.112^{7 - (-13)}$$

$$= 1.112^{20}$$

$$\approx 8.4$$

▶ The ratio of shares listed in 1997 to the shares listed in 1977 is 8.4 to 1. There were about 8.4 times as many listed in 1997 as in 1977.

EXAMPLE 5 *Using the Power of a Quotient Property*

PROBABILITY CONNECTION You toss a fair coin ten times. Show that the probability that the coin lands heads up each time is about 0.001.

SOLUTION

Probability that the first toss is heads: $\dfrac{1}{2}$

Probability that the first two tosses are heads: $\left(\dfrac{1}{2}\right)^2$

Probability that the first three tosses are heads: $\left(\dfrac{1}{2}\right)^3$

$\vdots$ $\vdots$

Probability that the first nine tosses are heads: $\left(\dfrac{1}{2}\right)^9$

Probability that the first ten tosses are heads: $\left(\dfrac{1}{2}\right)^{10}$

Use the power of a quotient property to evaluate.

$$\left(\frac{1}{2}\right)^{10} = \frac{1}{2^{10}} = \frac{1}{1024} \approx 0.001$$

▶ The probability is $\left(\dfrac{1}{2}\right)^{10}$ or about 0.001.

STUDENT HELP

Look Back
For help with probability, see page 114.

GUIDED PRACTICE

Vocabulary Check ✔ **1.** The expression $\dfrac{a^4}{a^6}$ can be simplified by using the ? property.

Concept Check ✔ **2.** Can $\dfrac{x^8}{y^3}$ be simplified? Explain your answer.

Skill Check ✔ **Use the quotient of powers property to simplify the expression.**

3. $\dfrac{5^4}{5^1}$ **4.** $\dfrac{7^6}{7^9}$ **5.** $\dfrac{a^{12}}{a^9}$ **6.** $\dfrac{m^5}{m^{11}}$

7. $\dfrac{a^5}{a^2}$ **8.** $\dfrac{(-2)^8}{(-2)^3}$ **9.** $\dfrac{5^3 \cdot 5^5}{5^9}$ **10.** $\dfrac{x^7 \cdot x}{x^{-2}}$

Use the power of a quotient property to simplify the expression.

11. $\left(\dfrac{1}{2}\right)^5$ **12.** $\left(\dfrac{3}{5}\right)^3$ **13.** $\left(\dfrac{5}{m}\right)^2$ **14.** $\left(\dfrac{2}{b}\right)^4$

15. $\left(\dfrac{5}{4}\right)^{-3}$ **16.** $\left(\dfrac{x^4}{2^3}\right)^2$ **17.** $\left(\dfrac{x^3}{y^5}\right)^6$ **18.** $\left(\dfrac{a^6}{b^9}\right)^5$

PRACTICE AND APPLICATIONS

STUDENT HELP

▶ **Extra Practice**
to help you master
skills is on p. 804.

EVALUATING EXPRESSIONS Evaluate the expression. Write fractions in simplest form.

19. $\dfrac{5^6}{5^3}$ **20.** $\dfrac{8^3}{8^1}$ **21.** $\dfrac{(-3)^6}{-3^6}$ **22.** $\dfrac{(-3)^9}{(-3)^9}$

23. $\dfrac{3^3}{3^{-4}}$ **24.** $\dfrac{8^3 \cdot 8^2}{8^5}$ **25.** $\dfrac{5 \cdot 5^4}{5^8}$ **26.** $\left(\dfrac{3}{4}\right)^2$

27. $\left(\dfrac{6}{2}\right)^3$ **28.** $\left(-\dfrac{2}{3}\right)^3$ **29.** $\left(-\dfrac{3}{5}\right)^2$ **30.** $\left(\dfrac{9}{6}\right)^{-1}$

SIMPLIFYING EXPRESSIONS Simplify the expression. The simplified expression should have no negative exponents.

31. $\left(\dfrac{3}{x}\right)^4$ **32.** $\dfrac{x^4}{x^5}$ **33.** $\left(\dfrac{1}{x}\right)^5$ **34.** $x^3 \cdot \dfrac{1}{x^2}$

35. $x^5 \cdot \dfrac{1}{x^8}$ **36.** $\left(\dfrac{a^9}{a^5}\right)^{-1}$ **37.** $\left(\dfrac{y^2}{y^3}\right)^{-2}$ **38.** $\dfrac{m^3 \cdot m^5}{m^2}$

39. $\dfrac{(r^3)^4}{(r^3)^8}$ **40.** $\left(\dfrac{-6x^2y}{2xy^3}\right)^3$ **41.** $\left(\dfrac{2x^3y^4}{3xy}\right)^3$ **42.** $\dfrac{16x^3y}{-4xy^3} \cdot -\dfrac{2xy}{-x^{-1}}$

43. $\dfrac{4x^3y^3}{2xy} \cdot \dfrac{5xy^2}{2y}$ **44.** $\dfrac{36a^8b^2}{ab} \cdot \left(\dfrac{6}{ab^2}\right)^{-1}$

STUDENT HELP

▶ **HOMEWORK HELP**
Example 1: Exs. 19–50
Example 2: Exs. 19–48
Example 3: Exs. 31–50
Example 4: Exs. 51–59
Example 5: Exs. 60, 61

45. $\dfrac{16x^5y^{-8}}{x^7y^4} \cdot \left(\dfrac{x^3y^2}{8xy}\right)^4$ **46.** $\dfrac{6x^{-2}y^2}{xy^{-3}} \cdot \dfrac{(4x^2y)^{-2}}{xy^2}$

47. $\dfrac{5x^{-3}y^2}{x^5y^{-1}} \cdot \dfrac{(2xy^3)^{-2}}{xy}$ **48.** $\left(\dfrac{2xy^{-2}y^4}{3x^{-1}y}\right)^{-2} \cdot \left(\dfrac{4xy}{2x^{-1}y^{-3}}\right)^2$

ERROR ANALYSIS In Exercises 49 and 50, find and correct the errors.

49.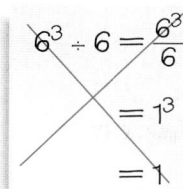
$$6^3 \div 6 = \frac{6^3}{6}$$
$$= 1^3$$
$$= 1$$

50.
$$\frac{x^{-9}}{x^{-3}} = x^{-9-3}$$
$$= x^{-12}$$
$$= \frac{1}{x^{-12}}$$

51. 🌎 **EARTH AND MOON** The volume of a sphere is given by $V = \frac{4}{3}\pi r^3$, where r is the radius of the sphere. Assuming that the radius of the Moon is $\frac{1}{4}$ the radius of Earth, find the ratio of the volume of Earth to the volume of the Moon. Let r represent the radius of Earth.

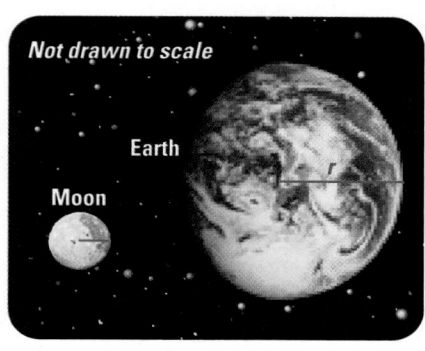

Not drawn to scale

Earth

Moon

52. 🌎 **RETAIL SALES** From 1994 to 1998, the sales for a national clothing store increased by about the same percent each year. The sales S (in millions of dollars) for year t can be modeled by
$$S = 3723\left(\frac{6}{5}\right)^t$$
where $t = 0$ corresponds to 1994. Find the ratio of 1998 sales to 1995 sales.

Sales (millions of dollars)

Years since 1994

53. 🌎 **BASEBALL SALARIES** The average salary for a professional baseball player in the United States can be approximated by $y = 283(1.2)^t$, where $t = 0$ represents the year 1984. Using this approximation, find the ratio of an average salary in 1988 to an average salary in 1994.

🌎 **ATLANTIC COD** In Exercises 54–56, use the following information. The average weight w (in pounds) of an Atlantic cod t years old can be modeled by the equation $w = 1.16(1.44)^t$. ▶ Source: National Marine Fisheries Service, Northeast Science Center

54. Find the ratio of the weight of a 5-year-old cod to the weight of a 2-year-old cod. Express this ratio as a power of 1.44.

55. A 5-year-old cod weighs how many times as much as a 2-year-old cod?

56. According to the model, what is the average weight of an Atlantic cod when it is hatched? How did you get your answer?

ATLANTIC COD
Adult Atlantic cod average about 3 feet in length and weigh from 10 to 25 pounds, though some may grow much larger.

57. 🌎 **SALES** From 1995 through 1999, the sales for a national furniture store increased by about the same percent each year. The sales s (in millions of dollars) for year t can be modeled by $s = 476(1.13)^t$, where $t = 0$ represents 1995. Find the ratio of 1997 sales to 1999 sales.

58. **OLYMPIC ROWING** The racing shells (boats) used in rowing competition usually have 1, 2, 4, or 8 rowers. Top speeds for racing shells in the Olympic 2000-meter races can be modeled by $s = 16.3(1.0285)^n$, where s is the speed in kilometers per hour and n is the number of rowers. Use the model to estimate the ratio of the speed of an 8-rower shell to the speed of a 2-rower shell.

59. 🌐 **LEARNING SPANISH** You memorized a list of 200 Spanish vocabulary words. Unfortunately, each week you forget one fifth of the words you knew the previous week. The number of words S you remember after n weeks can be approximated by the following equation.

Vocabulary words remembered: $S = 200\left(\dfrac{4}{5}\right)^n$

a. Copy and complete the table showing the number of words you remember after n weeks.

Weeks, n	0	1	2	3	4	5	6
Words, S	?	?	?	?	?	?	?

b. CRITICAL THINKING How many weeks does it take to forget all but three words? Explain your answer.

60. **PROBABILITY** **CONNECTION** You roll a die eight times. What is the probability that you will roll eight sixes in a row?

61. **PROBABILITY** **CONNECTION** You roll a die six times. What is the probability that you will roll six even numbers in a row?

Test Preparation

MULTI–STEP PROBLEM In Exercises 62–65, use the following information. You work for a real estate company that wants to build a new apartment complex. A team is formed to decide in which state to build the complex. One team member wants to build in Arizona. Another team member wants to build in Michigan. Your boss asks you to decide where to build the complex.

62. You find that the population P of Arizona (in thousands) in 1995 projected through 2025 can be modeled by $P = 4264(1.0208)^t$, where $t = 0$ represents 1995. Find the ratio of the population in 2025 to the population in 2000.

    DATA UPDATE of U.S. Bureau of the Census data at www.mcdougallittell.com

63. You find that the population P of Michigan (in thousands) in 1995 projected through 2025 can be modeled by $P = 9540(1.0026)^t$, where $t = 0$ represents 1995. Find the ratio of the population in 2025 to the population in 2000.

    ▶ Source: U.S. Bureau of the Census

64. Which population is projected to grow more rapidly?

65. *Writing* Use the results from Exercises 62–64 to decide where to build the complex. Write a memo to your boss explaining your decision.

★ Challenge

66. 🌐 **STACKING PAPER** A piece of notebook paper is about 0.0032 inch thick. If you begin with a stack consisting of a single sheet and double the stack 25 times, how tall will the stack be in inches? How tall will it be in feet? (*Hint:* Write and solve an exponential equation to find the height of the stack in inches. Then use unit analysis to find the height in feet.)

MIXED REVIEW

POWERS OF TEN Evaluate the expression. (Review 1.2, 8.2 for 8.4)

67. 10^5 **68.** 10^3 **69.** 10^{-4} **70.** 10^{-8}

SKETCHING GRAPHS Sketch the graph of the inequality in a coordinate plane. (Review 6.5)

71. $x \geq 5$ **72.** $x + 3 < 4$ **73.** $y > -2$ **74.** $y \leq -1.5$

75. $x \geq 2.5$ **76.** $3x - y < 0$ **77.** $y \leq \frac{x}{2}$ **78.** $\frac{3}{4}x + \frac{1}{4}y \geq 1$

CHECKING FOR SOLUTIONS Decide whether the ordered pair is a solution of the system. (Review 7.1)

79. $2x + 4y = 2$
$-x + 5y = 13$ $(-3, 2)$

80. $x - 5y = 9$
$3x + y = 11$ $(1, -4)$

81. $8a + 4b = 6$
$4a + b = 3$ $\left(\frac{3}{4}, 0\right)$

82. $3c - 8d = 11$
$c + 6d = 8$ $\left(5, -\frac{1}{2}\right)$

SOLVING LINEAR SYSTEMS Use linear combinations to solve the system. (Review 7.3)

83. $x - y = 4$
$x + y = 12$

84. $-x + 2y = 12$
$x + 6y = 20$

85. $2a + 3b = 17$
$3a + 4b = 24$

QUIZ 1

Self-Test for Lessons 8.1–8.3

Evaluate the expression. (Lessons 8.1, 8.2, and 8.3)

1. $3^3 \cdot 3^4$ **2.** $\left(2^2\right)^4$ **3.** $\left[(8 + 2)^2\right]^2$ **4.** 7^{-4}

5. $4^{-3} \cdot 4^{-4}$ **6.** $\left(\frac{6}{7}\right)^{-1}$ **7.** $\frac{5^{-3}}{5^2}$ **8.** $\frac{3^4 \cdot 3^6}{3^3}$

9. $\left(\frac{5}{4}\right)^{-3}$ **10.** $\frac{(-2)^9}{(-2)^2}$ **11.** $6^0 \cdot \frac{1}{4^{-3}}$ **12.** $\frac{2^3 \cdot 2^{-4}}{2^{-3}}$

Simplify the expression. Write your answer with no negative exponents. (Lessons 8.1, 8.2, and 8.3)

13. $x^4 \cdot x^5$ **14.** $(-2x)^5$ **15.** $-\frac{3}{a^{-5}}$ **16.** $200^0 c^5$

17. $\frac{x^6}{x^4}$ **18.** $\frac{x^{-5}}{x^{-6}}$ **19.** $\left(\frac{-2m^2 n}{3mn^2}\right)^4$ **20.** $x^4 \cdot \frac{1}{x^3}$

21. $(3a)^3 \cdot (-4a)^3$ **22.** $\left(8m^3\right)^2 \left(\frac{1}{2}m^2\right)^2$ **23.** $\frac{20x^3 y}{4xy^2} \cdot \frac{-6xy}{-x}$

24. 🌎 **SAVINGS ACCOUNT** You started a savings account in 1994. The balance A is given by $A = 250(1.08)^t$, where $t = 0$ represents the year 2001. What is the balance in the account in 1994? in 1999? in 2001? (Lesson 8.2)

Scientific Notation

GOAL 1 USING SCIENTIFIC NOTATION

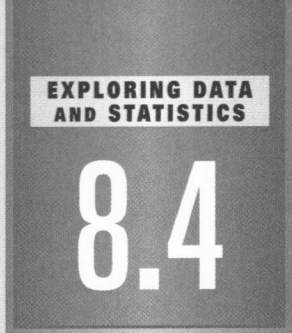

What you should learn

GOAL 1 Use scientific notation to represent numbers.

GOAL 2 Use scientific notation to describe **real-life** situations, such as the price per acre of the Alaska purchase in **Example 6**.

Why you should learn it

▼ To solve **real-life** problems, such as finding the amount of water discharged by the Amazon River each year in **Example 5**.

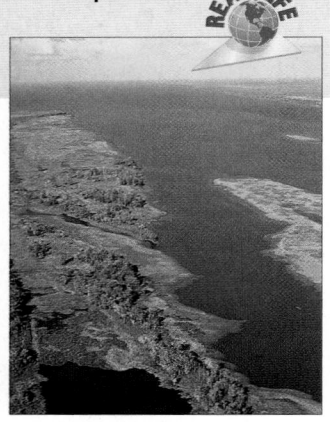

A number is written in **scientific notation** if it is of the form $c \times 10^n$, where $1 \le c < 10$ and n is an integer.

> **ACTIVITY**
>
> **Developing Concepts**
>
> ### Investigating Scientific Notation
>
> **1** Rewrite each number in decimal form.
>
>   **a.** 6.43×10^4 **b.** 3.072×10^6 **c.** 4.2×10^{-2} **d.** 1.52×10^{-3}
>
> **2** Describe a general rule for writing the decimal form of a number given in scientific notation. How many places do you move the decimal point? Do you move the decimal point left or right?

EXAMPLE 1   *Rewriting in Decimal Form*

Rewrite in decimal form.

  a. 2.834×10^2 **b.** 4.9×10^5 **c.** 7.8×10^{-1} **d.** 1.23×10^{-6}

SOLUTION

  a. $2.834 \times 10^2 = 283.4$ Move decimal point right 2 places.

  b. $4.9 \times 10^5 = 490{,}000$ Move decimal point right 5 places.

  c. $7.8 \times 10^{-1} = 0.78$ Move decimal point left 1 place.

  d. $1.23 \times 10^{-6} = 0.00000123$ Move decimal point left 6 places.

EXAMPLE 2   *Rewriting in Scientific Notation*

  a. $34{,}690 = 3.469 \times 10^4$ Move decimal point left 4 places.

  b. $1.78 = 1.78 \times 10^0$ Move decimal point 0 places.

  c. $0.039 = 3.9 \times 10^{-2}$ Move decimal point right 2 places.

  d. $0.000722 = 7.22 \times 10^{-4}$ Move decimal point right 4 places.

  e. $5{,}600{,}000{,}000 = 5.6 \times 10^9$ Move decimal point left 9 places.

STUDENT HELP

INTERNET
HOMEWORK HELP
Visit our Web site
www.mcdougallittell.com
for extra examples.

To multiply, divide, or find powers of numbers in scientific notation, use the properties of exponents.

EXAMPLE 3 *Computing with Scientific Notation*

Evaluate the expression. Write the result in scientific notation.

a. $(1.4 \times 10^4)(7.6 \times 10^3)$

b. $(1.2 \times 10^{-1}) \div (4.8 \times 10^{-4})$

c. $(4.0 \times 10^{-2})^3$

SOLUTION

a. $(1.4 \times 10^4)(7.6 \times 10^3)$

$\quad = (1.4 \cdot 7.6) \times (10^4 \cdot 10^3)$ — Associative property of multiplication

$\quad = 10.64 \times 10^7$ — Simplify.

$\quad = 1.064 \times 10^8$ — Write in scientific notation.

b. $\dfrac{1.2 \times 10^{-1}}{4.8 \times 10^{-4}} = \dfrac{1.2}{4.8} \times \dfrac{10^{-1}}{10^{-4}}$ — Rewrite as a product.

$\quad = 0.25 \times 10^3$ — Simplify.

$\quad = 2.5 \times 10^2$ — Write in scientific notation.

c. $(4.0 \times 10^{-2})^3 = 4^3 \times (10^{-2})^3$ — Power of a product

$\quad = 64 \times 10^{-6}$ — Power of a power

$\quad = 6.4 \times 10^{-5}$ — Write in scientific notation.

· · · · · · · · · ·

Many calculators automatically switch to scientific notation to display large or small numbers. Try multiplying 98,900,000 by 500. If your calculator follows standard conventions, it will display the product using scientific notation.

$\boxed{\text{4.945 E10}}$ ◀—— Calculator display for 4.945×10^{10}

EXAMPLE 4 *Using a Calculator*

 Use a calculator to multiply 0.000000748 by 2,400,000,000.

SOLUTION

Enter 0.000000748 as 7.48×10^{-7} and 2,400,000,000 as 2.4×10^9.

STUDENT HELP

INTERNET
KEYSTROKE HELP
If your
calculator does not have
an ⌊EE⌋ function, you can
enter the number in scientific
notation as a product.
7.48 ⌊×⌋ 10 ⌊yˣ⌋ 7 ⌊+/-⌋

KEYSTROKES	DISPLAY
7.48 ⌊EE⌋ 7 ⌊+/-⌋ ⌊×⌋ 2.4 ⌊EE⌋ 9 ⌊ENTER⌋	$\boxed{\text{1.7952 E3}}$

▶ The product is 1.7952×10^3, or 1795.2.

AMAZON RIVER
The Amazon River
in Brazil contributes more
water to Earth's oceans than
any other river. Each second,
it discharges 4.2×10^6 cubic
feet of water into the Atlantic
Ocean.

GOAL 2 SOLVING REAL-LIFE PROBLEMS

EXAMPLE 5 *Multiplying with Scientific Notation*

AMAZON RIVER How much water does the Amazon River discharge into the
Atlantic Ocean each year?

SOLUTION

First find the number of seconds in a year. Then multiply the amount of water
discharged per second by the number of seconds per year to find the total amount
of water discharged into the Atlantic Ocean.

Use unit analysis to find the number of seconds in a year.

$$\frac{\text{days}}{\text{year}} \cdot \frac{\text{hours}}{\text{day}} \cdot \frac{\text{minutes}}{\text{hour}} \cdot \frac{\text{seconds}}{\text{minute}} = \frac{\text{seconds}}{\text{year}}$$

$$\frac{365}{1} \cdot \frac{24}{1} \cdot \frac{60}{1} \cdot \frac{60}{1} = 31{,}536{,}000 \approx 3.2 \times 10^7$$

There are about 3.2×10^7 seconds in a year.

Multiply to find the total amount of water discharged by the Amazon River into
the Atlantic Ocean in one year.

$$\text{Total amount of water} = \frac{4.2 \times 10^6 \text{ cubic feet}}{1 \text{ second}} \cdot \frac{3.2 \times 10^7 \text{ seconds}}{1 \text{ year}}$$

$$= \left(4.2 \times 10^6\right) \cdot \left(3.2 \times 10^7\right)$$

$$= 13.44 \times 10^{13}$$

$$= 1.344 \times 10^{14}$$

▶ One trillion is 1×10^{12}, so the total amount of water discharged into the
Atlantic Ocean by the Amazon River is about 134 trillion cubic feet per year.

History

EXAMPLE 6 *Dividing with Scientific Notation*

In 1867, the United States purchased Alaska from Russia for $7.2 million. The
total area of Alaska is about 3.78×10^8 acres. What was the price per acre?

STUDENT HELP

▸ **Look Back**
For help with unit rates,
see p. 180.

SOLUTION The price per acre is a unit rate.

$$\text{Price per acre} = \frac{\text{Total price}}{\text{Number of acres}}$$

$$= \frac{7.2 \times 10^6}{3.78 \times 10^8} \quad \longleftarrow \quad \text{7.2 million} = \text{7.2} \times \text{10}^6$$

$$= \frac{7.2}{3.78} \times 10^{-2}$$

$$\approx 0.019$$

▶ The price was about 2¢ per acre.

GUIDED PRACTICE

Vocabulary Check ✓
Concept Check ✓

Skill Check ✓

1. Is the number 12.38×10^2 in scientific notation? Explain.

2. Given the number 6.39×10^7, would you move the decimal point to the *left* or to the *right* to rewrite the number in decimal form?

Rewrite in decimal form.

3. 4.3×10^2 **4.** 8.11×10^3 **5.** 2.45×10^{-1} **6.** 9.38×10^5

Rewrite in scientific notation.

7. 39.6   **8.** 0.72   **9.** 1200   **10.** 0.0003

11. 6,900,000   **12.** 0.0000205   **13.** 72,000,000   **14.** 0.000000006

15. 🌐 **ASTRONOMY** The distance between the ninth planet Pluto and the Sun is 5.9×10^9 kilometers. Light travels at a speed of about 3.0×10^5 kilometers per second. How long does it take light to travel from the Sun to Pluto?

PRACTICE AND APPLICATIONS

STUDENT HELP

▶ **Extra Practice**
to help you master
skills is on p. 804.

DECIMAL FORM **Rewrite in decimal form.**

16. 2.14×10^4 **17.** 98×10^{-2} **18.** 7.75×10^0

19. 8.6521×10^3 **20.** 4.65×10^{-4} **21.** 6.002×10^{-6}

22. 4.332×10^8 **23.** 1.00012×10^8 **24.** 1.1098×10^{10}

SCIENTIFIC NOTATION **Rewrite in scientific notation.**

25. 0.05   **26.** 95.2   **27.** 0.0422   **28.** 370.207

29. 700,000,000   **30.** 19.314   **31.** 0.008551   **32.** 2,730,000,000

33. 0.000459   **34.** 0.00032954   **35.** 88,000,000   **36.** 0.0000288

EVALUATING EXPRESSIONS **Evaluate the expression without using a calculator. Write the result in scientific notation and in decimal form.**

37. $(4 \times 10^{-2}) \cdot (3 \times 10^6)$ **38.** $(7 \times 10^{-3}) \cdot (8 \times 10^{-4})$

39. $(6 \times 10^5) \cdot (2.5 \times 10^{-1})$ **40.** $(1.2 \times 10^{-6}) \cdot (2.3 \times 10^4)$

41. $\dfrac{8 \times 10^{-3}}{5 \times 10^{-5}}$ **42.** $\dfrac{1.4 \times 10^{-1}}{3.5 \times 10^{-4}}$ **43.** $\dfrac{6.6 \times 10^{-1}}{1.1 \times 10^{-1}}$

44. $(3.0 \times 10^{-3})^2$ **45.** $(9 \times 10^3)^2$ **46.** $(3 \times 10^{-2})^4$

STUDENT HELP

▶ HOMEWORK HELP
Example 1: Exs. 16–24
Example 2: Exs. 25–36
Example 3: Exs. 37–46
Example 4: Exs. 47–52
Example 5: Exs. 61, 62
Example 6: Exs. 58–60

🖩 **CALCULATOR** **Use a calculator to evaluate the expression. Write the result in scientific notation and in decimal form.**

47. $2,000,000 \cdot 12,000$ **48.** $6,000,000 \cdot 324,000$

49. $0.000279 \cdot 3,940,000,000$ **50.** $654,000 \cdot 0.000042$

51. $(2.4 \times 10^{-4})^2$ **52.** 0.000094^3

53. LIGHTNING The speed of a lightning bolt is 120,000,000 feet per second.

54. WORLD POPULATION In 1997, the population of the world was estimated at 5,852,000,000. DATA UPDATE of U.S. Bureau of the Census data at www.mcdougallittell.com

55. ASTRONOMY The star Sirius in the constellation Canis Major is about 50,819,000,000,000 miles from Earth.

56. CHEMISTRY The mass of a carbon atom is 0.00000000000000000000002 gram.

57. SIZE OF JUPITER Jupiter, the largest planet in our solar system, has a radius of about 4.4×10^4 miles. Use the equation $V = \frac{4}{3}\pi r^3$ to find Jupiter's volume.

STUDENT HELP

APPLICATION LINK
Visit our Web site
www.mcdougallittell.com
for more information
about the purchase of
Alaska, the Louisiana
Purchase, and the
Gadsden Purchase in
Example 6 and Exs. 58–60.

HISTORY CONNECTION **In Exercises 58–60, use the following information.**
In 1803, the Louisiana Purchase added 8.28×10^5 square miles to the United States. The cost of this land was $15 million. In 1853, the Gadsden Purchase added 2.94×10^4 square miles, and the cost was $10 million.

58. Find the average cost of a square mile for each of the purchases.

59. Find the average cost of an acre for each of the purchases. (*Hint:* There are 640 acres in a square mile.)

60. *Writing* Describe a factor that you think might explain the difference in the price per acre for these two purchases.

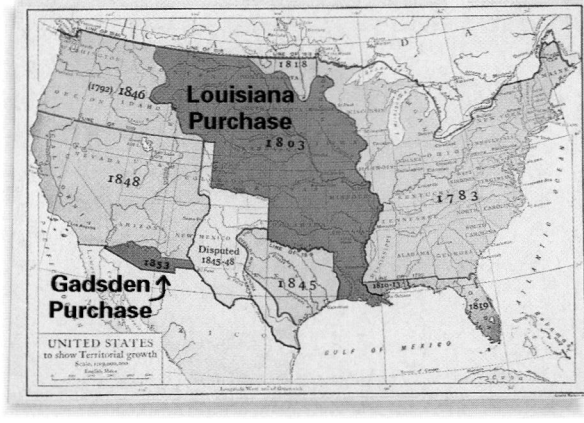

61. WATERFALL Stanley Falls in Congo, Africa, has an average flow of about 1.7×10^4 cubic meters per second. How much water goes over Stanley Falls in a typical 30-day month?

62. HEARTBEATS Consider a person whose heart beats 70 times per minute and who lives to be 85 years old. Estimate the number of times the person's heart beats during his or her life. Do not acknowledge leap years. Write your answer in decimal form and in scientific notation.

STUDENT HELP

HOMEWORK HELP
Visit our Web site
www.mcdougallittell.com
for help with Ex. 62.

63. TELEPHONE SURVEY Use the table which shows the population and the number of local telephone calls made in five states in 1994 to find the number of local calls made per person in each state.

State	Local Calls	Population
Texas	3.9×10^{10}	1.8×10^7
Minnesota	7.0×10^9	4.6×10^6
Pennsylvania	1.9×10^{10}	1.2×10^7
Vermont	4.7×10^8	5.8×10^5
California	5.6×10^{10}	3.1×10^7

▶ Source: U.S. Bureau of the Census

64. MULTIPLE CHOICE Which number is not in scientific notation?

Ⓐ 1×10^4 Ⓑ 3.4×10^{-3} Ⓒ 9.02×10^2 Ⓓ 12.25×10^{-5}

65. MULTIPLE CHOICE Evaluate $\dfrac{1.1 \times 10^{-1}}{5.5 \times 10^{-5}}$ using scientific notation.

Ⓐ 0.2×10^{-4} Ⓑ 2.0×10^4 Ⓒ 2.0×10^3 Ⓓ 0.2×10^4

★ **Challenge**

66. 🌐 **BASEBALL** A baseball pitcher can throw a ball to home plate in about 0.5 second. The distance between the pitcher's mound and home plate is 60.5 feet.

Pitcher's mound

60.5 ft

Home plate

a. Fill in the missing numbers and simplify the following expression to find the rate, in scientific notation, at which the ball is traveling in millimeters per second.

$$\frac{? \text{ feet}}{? \text{ second}} \cdot \frac{1 \text{ meter}}{3.3 \text{ feet}} \cdot \frac{? \text{ millimeters}}{1 \text{ meter}} \approx \underline{\ ?\ } \times 10^? \text{ millimeters per second}$$

b. To hit a home run, a batter has a leeway of about 200 millimeters in the point of contact between the bat and the ball. What is the most the batter's timing could be off and still hit a home run? Explain your calculations. (*Hint:* Find the time it takes the ball to travel 200 millimeters.)

c. CRITICAL THINKING You are at bat. The pitcher throws you a pitch. Your timing is off by 0.006 second. Could you hit a home run on this pitch? Explain your answer.

EXTRA CHALLENGE
www.mcdougallittell.com

MIXED REVIEW

PERCENTS AS DECIMALS Write the percent as a decimal. (Skills Review page 784 for 8.5)

67. 22% **68.** 87.5% **69.** 0.07% **70.** 8.42%

71. $\frac{1}{2}\%$ **72.** $\frac{3}{4}\%$ **73.** 255% **74.** $1\frac{1}{4}\%$

GRAPHING LINEAR SYSTEMS Use the graphing method to solve the linear system and describe its solution(s). (Review 7.5)

75. $4x + 2y = 12$
$-6x + 3y = 6$

76. $3x - 2y = 0$
$3x - 2y = -4$

GRAPHING Graph the system of linear inequalities. (Review 7.6)

77. $2x + y \le 1$
$-2x + y \le 1$

78. $x + 2y < 3$
$x - 3y > 1$

79. $2x + y \ge 2$
$x \le 2$

SIMPLIFYING EXPRESSIONS Simplify the expression. (Review 8.2 and 8.3)

80. 2^{-4} **81.** $\left(\dfrac{1}{10}\right)^{-3}$ **82.** $\dfrac{1}{(2x)^{-2}}$ **83.** $\dfrac{7^4 \cdot 7}{7^7}$

◉ ACTIVITY 8.5

Developing Concepts

Linear and Exponential Growth Models

SET UP
Work in a small group.

MATERIALS
graph paper

▶ **QUESTION** How are linear growth models and exponential growth models different?

▶ **EXPLORING THE CONCEPT**

1 The equation $y = 5x + 20$ is a *linear growth model*. Copy and complete the table.

x	0	1	2	3	4	5
y	20	25	?	?	?	?

2 Graph $y = 5x + 20$.

3 The equation $y = 5^x$ is an *exponential growth model*. Copy and complete the table.

x	0	1	2	3	4	5
y	1	5	?	?	?	?

4 Graph $y = 5^x$.

5 Which of the graphs below shows a *linear growth model*? Which shows an *exponential growth model*? Explain how you know.

a.

b.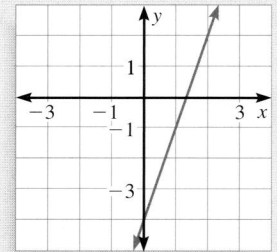

▶ **DRAWING CONCLUSIONS**

In Exercises 1–6, identify the equation as a *linear* growth model or an *exponential* growth model.

1. $y = x + 5$

2. $y = 3^x$

3. $y = 10 + 2x$

4. $y = 15 + 2^x$

5. $y = 5(4x - 7)$

6. $y = 10(1.2)^x$

7. Look at your data and graph in Steps 1 and 2 to complete the statement.

A linear growth model increases the __?__ amount for each unit on the x-axis.

8. Describe the rate of increase in an exponential growth model.

9. **CRITICAL THINKING** You accept a job that pays $20,000 your first year. Would you rather receive a raise of $500 each year or a raise of 3% of your current salary each year? Does your answer depend on how long you plan to stay at the job? Explain your reasoning.

8.5

Exponential Growth Functions

What you should learn

GOAL 1 Write and use models for exponential growth.

GOAL 2 Graph models for exponential growth.

Why you should learn it

▼ To solve **real-life** problems such as finding the weight of a channel catfish in **Example 2**.

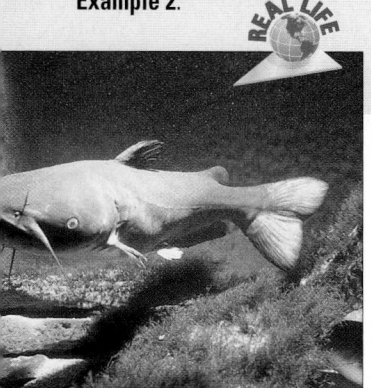

GOAL 1 WRITING EXPONENTIAL GROWTH MODELS

A quantity is *growing exponentially* if it increases by the same percent in each unit of time. This is called **exponential growth**.

EXPONENTIAL GROWTH MODEL

C is the **initial amount**. ────────────┐   ┌──── t is the **time period.**

$$y = C(1 + r)^t$$

The **percent of increase** is 100r. $(1 + r)$ is the **growth factor,**
          r is the **growth rate.**

EXAMPLE 1   *Finding the Balance in an Account*

COMPOUND INTEREST You deposit $500 in an account that pays 8% annual interest compounded yearly. What is the account balance after 6 years?

SOLUTION

Method 1 SOLVE A SIMPLER PROBLEM

Find the account balance A_1 after 1 year and multiply by the growth factor to find the balance for each of the following years. The growth rate is 0.08, so the growth factor is $1 + 0.08 = 1.08$.

$A_1 = 500(1.08) = 540$	**Balance after 1 year**
$A_2 = 500(1.08)(1.08) = 583.20$	**Balance after 2 years**
$A_3 = 500(1.08)(1.08)(1.08) = 629.856$	**Balance after 3 years**
$\vdots$	$\vdots$
$A_6 = 500(1.08)^6 \approx 793.437$	**Balance after 6 years**

▶ The account balance after 6 years will be about $793.44.

Method 2 USE A FORMULA

Use the exponential growth model to find the account balance A. The growth rate is 0.08. The initial value is 500.

$A = C(1 + r)^t$	**Exponential growth model**
$\quad = 500(1 + 0.08)^6$	**Substitute 500 for *C*, 0.08 for *r*, and 6 for *t*.**
$\quad = 500(1.08)^6$	**Simplify.**
$\quad \approx 793.437$	**Evaluate.**

▶ The balance after 6 years will be about $793.44.

Catfish Growth

EXAMPLE 2 *Writing an Exponential Growth Model*

A newly hatched channel catfish typically weighs about 0.3 gram. During the first six weeks of life, its growth is approximately exponential, increasing by about 10% each day.

a. Write a model for the weight during the first six weeks.

b. Find the weight at the end of six weeks.

SOLUTION

a. Let W represent the weight in grams, and let t represent the time in days. The initial weight is $C = 0.3$ and the growth rate is 0.10.

$$W = C(1 + r)^t \qquad \text{Exponential growth model}$$

$$= 0.3(1 + 0.10)^t \qquad \text{Substitute 0.3 for } C \text{ and 0.10 for } r.$$

$$= 0.3(1.1)^t \qquad \text{Simplify.}$$

b. To find the weight at the end of 6 weeks (or 42 days), substitute 42 for t.

$$W = 0.3(1.1)^{42} \qquad \text{Substitute.}$$

$$\approx 16.42910977 \qquad \text{Use a calculator.}$$

$$\approx 16.4 \qquad \text{Round to the nearest tenth.}$$

▶ The weight is about 16.4 grams.

Population Growth

EXAMPLE 3 *Writing an Exponential Growth Model*

A population of 20 rabbits is released into a wild-life region. The population triples each year for 5 years.

a. What is the percent of increase each year?

b. What is the population after 5 years?

SOLUTION

a. The population triples each year, so the growth factor is 3.

$$1 + r = 3$$

▶ So, the growth rate r is 2 and the percent of increase each year is 200%.

b. After 5 years, the population is

$$P = C(1 + r)^t \qquad \text{Exponential growth model}$$

$$= 20(1 + 2)^5 \qquad \text{Substitute for } C, r, \text{ and } t.$$

$$= 20 \cdot 3^5 \qquad \text{Simplify.}$$

$$= 4860 \qquad \text{Evaluate.}$$

▶ There will be about 4860 rabbits after 5 years.

┌─STUDENT HELP
│
│ ▸ **Study Tip**
Notice that the growth factor and the percent of increase are not the same. In Example 3, the growth factor is 3 but the percent of increase is 200%.

GOAL 2 GRAPHING EXPONENTIAL GROWTH MODELS

You can graph exponential growth models in the same way you graphed exponential functions in Lesson 8.2.

EXAMPLE 4 *A Model with a Small Growth Factor*

Compound Interest

Graph the exponential growth model in Example 1.

SOLUTION

Use the values found in Method 1 of Example 1 to plot points in a coordinate plane. Then, draw a smooth curve through the points.

EXAMPLE 5 *A Model with a Large Growth Factor*

Population Growth

Graph the exponential growth model in Example 3.

SOLUTION

Make a table of values, plot the points in a coordinate plane, and draw a smooth curve through the points.

t	0	1	2	3	4	5
P	20	60	180	540	1620	4860

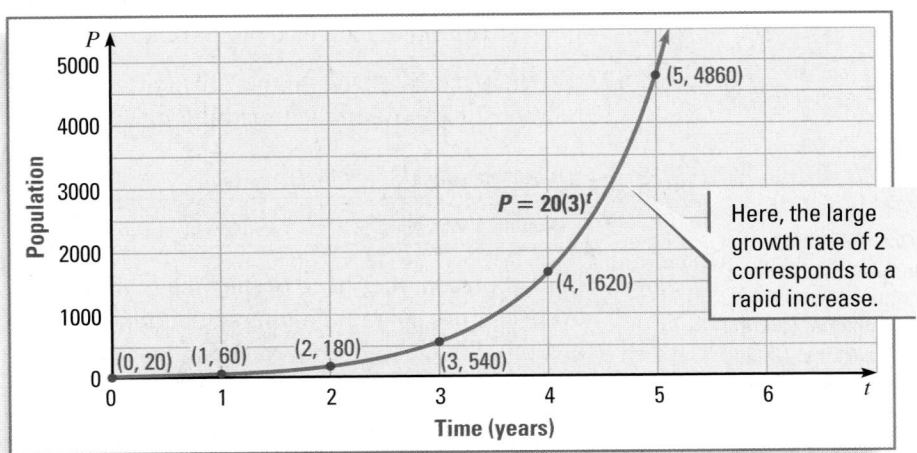

GUIDED PRACTICE

Vocabulary Check ✓

1. In the exponential growth model, $y = C(1 + r)^t$, C is the __?__ and $(1 + r)$ is the __?__ .

Concept Check ✓

2. Look back at Example 1. Suppose that you got a 12% annual interest rate. Write a new exponential growth model for the balance in the account.

3. Look back at Example 3. Suppose that the rabbit population doubled every year for 5 years. What was the percent of increase? the growth factor?

Skill Check ✓

4. **ACCOUNT BALANCE** You deposit $500 in an account that pays 4% interest compounded yearly. What is the balance after 5 years? after 10 years?

5. **CHOOSE A MODEL** Which model best represents the growth curve shown in the graph at the right?

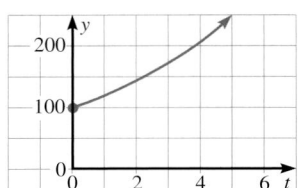

   A. $y = 100(1.08)^t$

   B. $y = 100(1.2)^t$

   C. $y = 200(1.08)^t$

PRACTICE AND APPLICATIONS

STUDENT HELP

▸ **Extra Practice**
to help you master
skills is on p. 804.

FIND THE BALANCE **You deposit $1400 in an account that pays 6% interest compounded yearly. Find the balance for the given time period.**

6. 5 years   7. 8 years   8. 12 years   9. 20 years

FIND THE BALANCE **Find the balance after 5 years of an account that pays 4.8% interest compounded yearly given the following investment amounts.**

10. $250   11. $300   12. $350   13. $400

14. 🌐 **ACCOUNT BALANCE** A principal of $200 is deposited in an account that pays 4.2% interest compounded yearly. Find the balance after 5 years.

15. 🌐 **INVESTING** How much must you deposit in an account that pays 3.5% interest compounded yearly to have a balance of $400 after 6 years?

16. 🌐 **INVESTING** How much must you deposit in an account that pays 6% interest compounded yearly to have a balance of $1000 after 8 years?

17. 🌐 **BICYCLE RACING** In the Chapter Opener you learned that there is a relationship between the breathing rate of a cyclist and the bicycle speed.

Bicycle speed, x	0	5	10	15	20
Breathing rate, y	6.4	10.7	18.1	30.5	51.4

STUDENT HELP

▸ HOMEWORK HELP
Example 1: Exs. 6–17
Example 2: Exs. 21, 22
Example 3: Ex. 24
Example 4: Exs. 18–20
Example 5: Exs. 25–28

Let x represent the speed of the bike in miles per hour, and let y represent the cyclist's breathing rate in liters of air taken into the lungs per minute. The breathing rate of a cyclist can be modeled by $y = 6.37(1.11)^x$. What is the cyclist's breathing rate if the bike is traveling 19 miles per hour? 25 miles per hour?

MATCHING THE GRAPH Match the description with its graph.

A.

B.

C.
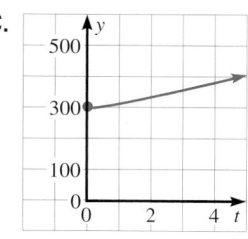

18. Deposit: $300
Annual rate: 6%

19. Deposit: $300
Annual rate: 12%

20. Deposit: $300
Annual rate: 20%

🌐 **BUSINESS** In Exercises 21 and 22, write an exponential growth model.

21. A business had a $10,000 profit in 1990. Then the profit increased by 25% per year for the next 10 years.

22. A business had a $20,000 profit in 1990. Then the profit increased by 20% per year for the next 10 years.

23. VISUAL THINKING Graph the exponential growth models in Exercises 21 and 22 in the same coordinate plane. Which business would you rather own? Explain.

24. 🌐 **POPULATION GROWTH** A population of 30 mice is released in a wildlife region. The population doubles each year for 4 years. What is the population after 4 years?

BIOLOGY ▶ CONNECTION   In Exercises 25–28, use the following information.

The average of the diameters of the two cross-sections shown can be related to the length of the adult bird. This average for a robin's egg is 25 millimeters (mm); for a bluebird, 19 mm; and for a chickadee, 13 mm. The graph shows the relationship between the average A of the two diameters and the length L (in centimeters) of an adult bird.

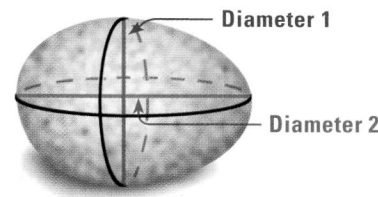

25. CHOOSING A MODEL Which model best represents the growth curve shown in the graph?

A. $L = (0.09)(1.23)^A$

B. $L = 12 + (0.09)(1.23)^A$

C. $L = 12 + [(0.09)(1.23)]^A$

26. Estimate the length of an adult bluebird from the graph.

27. Estimate the length of an adult bluebird using the exponential growth model. How does it compare to the length you found in Exercise 26?

28. Use the exponential growth model to find the ratio of the length of a chickadee to the length of a robin.

29. MULTIPLE CHOICE The hourly rate of your new job is $5.00 per hour. You expect a raise of 9% each year. At the end of your first year, you receive your first raise. What will your hourly rate be at the end of your fifth year?

(A) $5.45　　(B) $7.25　　(C) $7.69　　(D) $7.76

30. MULTIPLE CHOICE What is the equation of the graph?

(A) $y = 2(0.88)^x$　(B) $y = 4(0.88)^x$

(C) $y = 2(1.3)^x$　(D) $y = 4(1.3)^x$

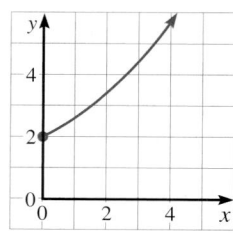

★ Challenge

31. EXTENSION: COMPOUND INTEREST What is the value of an $8000 investment after 5 years if it earns 8% annual interest compounded quarterly? To solve, use the compound interest formula, $A = P(1 + i)^n$, where P is the original value of the investment, i is the interest rate per compounding period, n is the total number of compounding periods, and A is the value of the investment after n periods.

  a. What is the interest rate per quarter?

  b. How many compounding periods (quarters) are there in 5 years?

  c. Use the formula $A = P(1 + i)^n$ to find the value of the investment after 5 years.

EXTRA CHALLENGE
➤ www.mcdougallittell.com

MIXED REVIEW

PERCENT OF A NUMBER Find the percent of a number. (Skills Review page 786)

32. 12% of 56　　　　**33.** 75% of 235　　　　**34.** 1.25% of 90

35. 200% of 130　　　**36.** 2% of 105　　　　**37.** 0.8% of 120

EVALUATING VARIABLE EXPRESSIONS Evaluate the expression. (Review 1.3)

38. $24 + m^3$ when $m = 5$

39. $\dfrac{a^2 - b^2}{ab}$ when $a = 3$ and $b = 5$

40. $x^6 - 1$ when $x = 1.2$

41. $3y^4 + 15y$ when $y = -0.02$

42. $(1 - x)^t$ when $x = 0.5$ and $t = 3$

43. $\dfrac{(1 - x)^t}{2}$ when $x = 0.09$ and $t = 2$

44. BREAKFAST You are in charge of bringing breakfast for your scout troop. You buy 6 bagels and 8 donuts for a total of $4.10. Then you decide to buy 3 extra of each for a total of $1.80. How much did each bagel and donut cost? (Review 7.4)

SOLVING EQUATIONS Solve the equation. (Review 3.3, 3.4, 3.6)

45. $-2(7 - 5x) = 10$

46. $25 - (6x + 5) = 4(3x - 5) + 4$

47. $\dfrac{3}{2}(8m - 30) = -3m$

48. $1.4(6.4y - 3.5) = -9.54y + 22.85$

● ACTIVITY 8.6

Developing Concepts

Investigating Exponential Decay

SET UP
Work in a small group.

MATERIALS
• 100 pennies
• cup

▶ **QUESTION** Can an exponential decay model show a decreasing amount?

▶ **EXPLORING THE CONCEPT**

① Make a table to record your results.

Number of toss	0	1	2	3	4	5	6	7
Number of pennies remaining	?	?	?	?	?	?	?	?

② Place the pennies in the cup. Shake the pennies in the cup then spill them onto a flat surface. Remove all of the pennies that land face up. Count and record the number of pennies remaining.

③ Repeat **Step 2** until there are no pennies left in the cup.

④ Make a scatter plot of the data you have collected.

▶ **DRAWING CONCLUSIONS**

1. Describe any patterns suggested by the scatter plot.

2. Look at your data and scatter plot to complete the following statement.

> Each time the cup is emptied, the number of pennies you remove is about ? of the number in the cup.

3. Write an exponential equation to model this situation.

4. Compare your equations and graphs with those of other groups. Describe any patterns you see.

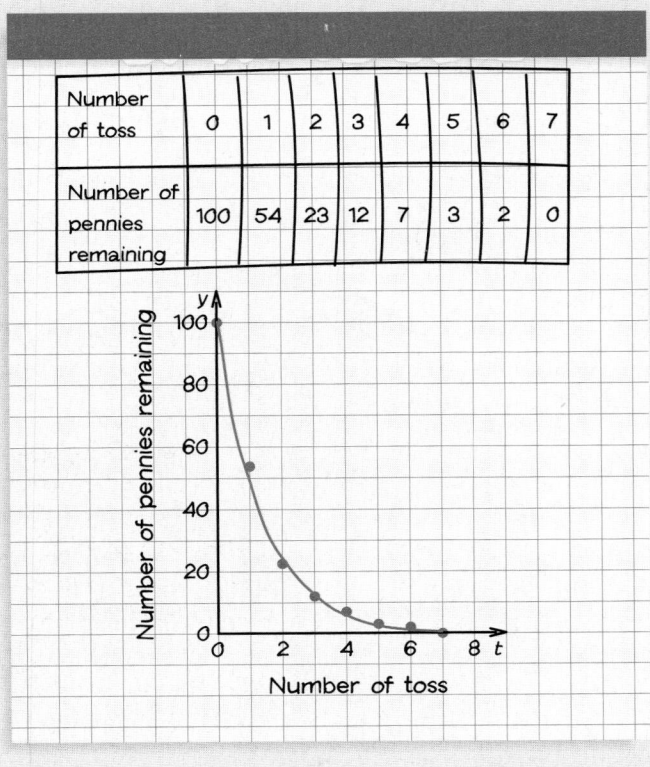

Number of toss	0	1	2	3	4	5	6	7
Number of pennies remaining	100	54	23	12	7	3	2	0

8.6

Exponential Decay Functions

What you should learn

GOAL 1 Write and use models for exponential decay.

GOAL 2 Graph models for exponential decay.

Why you should learn it

▼ To solve **real-life** problems, such as comparing the buying power of a dollar in different years as in **Example 1**.

GOAL 1 **WRITING EXPONENTIAL DECAY MODELS**

In Lesson 8.5, you learned that a quantity is *growing exponentially* if it *increases* by the same percent in each unit of time. A quantity is *decreasing exponentially* if it *decreases* by the same percent in each unit of time. This is called **exponential decay**.

EXPONENTIAL DECAY MODEL

C is the **initial amount**.   *t* is the **time period**.

$$y = C(1 - r)^t$$

$(1 - r)$ is the **decay factor**, *r* is the **decay rate**. To assure $1 > (1 - r) > 0$, it is necessary that $0 < r < 1$.

The **percent of decrease** is 100*r*.

EXAMPLE 1 *Writing an Exponential Decay Model*

PURCHASING POWER From 1982 through 1997, the purchasing power of a dollar decreased by about 3.5% per year. Using 1982 as the base for comparison, what was the purchasing power of a dollar in 1997?

▶ Source: *Statistical Abstract of the United States: 1998.*

SOLUTION Let *y* represent the purchasing power and let $t = 0$ represent the year 1982. The initial amount is $1. Use an exponential decay model.

$y = C(1 - r)^t$ **Exponential decay model**

$= (1)(1 - 0.035)^t$ **Substitute 1 for *C* and 0.035 for *r*.**

$= 0.965^t$ **Simplify.**

Because 1997 is 15 years after 1982, substitute 15 for *t*.

$y = 0.965^{15}$ **Substitute 15 for *t*.**

≈ 0.59 **Use a calculator.**

▶ The purchasing power of a dollar in 1997 compared to 1982 was $.59.

✔**CHECK** You can check your result by using a graphing calculator to make a table of values. Enter the exponential decay model and use the *Table* feature. Notice that as the prices *inflate*, the purchasing power of a dollar *deflates*.

x	Y2
11	.67577
12	.65212
13	.6293
14	.60727
15	.58602

Y1=.586016305535

Depreciation

EXAMPLE 2 *Writing an Exponential Decay Model*

You bought a used car for $18,000. The value of the car will be less each year because of depreciation. The car depreciates (loses value) at the rate of 12% per year.

    a. Write an exponential decay model to represent this situation.

    b. Estimate the value of your car in 8 years.

SOLUTION

STUDENT HELP

▶ **Skills Review**
For help with writing a percent as a decimal, see page 784.

  a. The initial value C is $18,000. The decay rate r is 0.12. Let y be the value and let t be the age of the car in years.

$$y = C(1 - r)^t \qquad \text{Exponential decay model}$$
$$= 18{,}000(1 - 0.12)^t \qquad \text{Substitute 18,000 for } C \text{ and 0.12 for } r.$$
$$= 18{,}000(0.88)^t \qquad \text{Simplify.}$$

    ▶ The exponential decay model is $y = 18{,}000(0.88)^t$.

  b. To find the value in 8 years, substitute 8 for t.

$$y = 18{,}000(0.88)^t \qquad \text{Exponential decay model}$$
$$= 18{,}000(0.88)^8 \qquad \text{Substitute 8 for } t.$$
$$\approx 6473 \qquad \text{Use a calculator.}$$

    ▶ According to this model, the value of your car in 8 years will be about $6473.

Depreciation

EXAMPLE 3 *Making a List to Verify a Model*

Verify the model you found in Example 2. Find the value of the car for each year by multiplying the value in the previous year by the decay factor.

SOLUTION The decay rate is 0.12. Decay factor = $1 - 0.12 = 0.88$.

Year	Value
0	18,000
1	0.88(**18,000**) = **15,840**
2	0.88(**15,840**) ≈ 13,939
3	0.88(13,939) ≈ 12,266
4	0.88(12,266) ≈ 10,794
5	0.88(10,794) ≈ 9499
6	0.88(9499) ≈ 8359
7	0.88(8359) ≈ 7356
8	0.88(7356) ≈ 6473

◀——— Initial value of the car

From the list you can see that the value of the car in 8 years will be about $6473, which is consistent with your model.

Purchasing Power

EXAMPLE 4 *Graphing an Exponential Decay Model*

Graph the exponential decay model in Example 1.

SOLUTION

Use your graphing calculator to graph the model. Set the viewing rectangle so that $0 \leq x \leq 20$ and $0 \leq y \leq 1$.

Depreciation

EXAMPLE 5 *Graphing an Exponential Decay Model*

a. Graph the exponential decay model in Example 2.

b. Use the graph to estimate the value of your car in 10 years.

SOLUTION

a. Use the table of values in Example 3. Plot the points in a coordinate plane, and draw a smooth curve through the points.

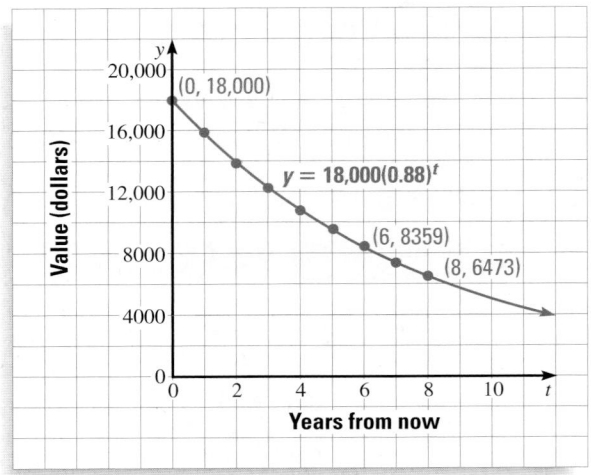

b. From the graph, the value of your car in 10 years will be about $5000.

· · · · · · · · · ·

An exponential model $y = a \cdot b^t$ represents exponential growth if $b > 1$ and exponential decay if $0 < b < 1$.

EXAMPLE 6 *Comparing Growth and Decay Models*

Classify each model as *exponential growth* or *exponential decay*. In each case identify the growth or decay factor and the percent of increase or percent of decrease per time period. Then graph each model.

a. $y = 30(1.2)^t$

b. $y = 30\left(\dfrac{3}{5}\right)^t$

SOLUTION

a. Because $1.2 > 1$, the model $y = 30(1.2)^t$ is an exponential growth model.

The growth factor $(1 + r)$ is 1.20.

The growth rate is 0.2, so the percent of increase is 20%.

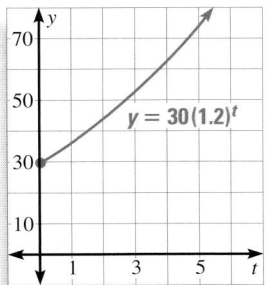

b. Because $0 < \dfrac{3}{5} < 1$, the model $y = 30\left(\dfrac{3}{5}\right)^t$ is an exponential decay model.

The decay factor $(1 - r) = \dfrac{3}{5}$.

The decay rate is $\dfrac{2}{5}$ or 0.4, so the percent of decrease is 40%.

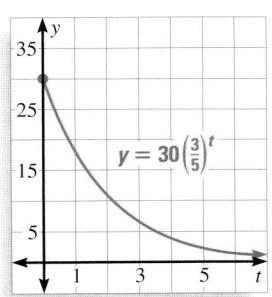

CONCEPT SUMMARY **EXPONENTIAL GROWTH AND DECAY MODELS**

EXPONENTIAL GROWTH MODEL

$y = C(1 + r)^t$ ← time period

initial amount   growth factor

$1 + r > 1$

EXPONENTIAL DECAY MODEL

$y = C(1 - r)^t$ ← time period

initial amount   decay factor

$0 < 1 - r < 1$

(0, C)

(0, C)

GUIDED PRACTICE

Vocabulary Check ✓

1. In the exponential decay model, $y = C(1 - r)^t$, what is the decay factor?

Concept Check ✓

2. Is $y = 1.02^t$ an exponential decay model? Explain.

3. Look back at Example 2. Suppose that the car was depreciating at the rate of 20% per year. Write a new exponential decay model.

Skill Check ✓

🌎 **CAR VALUE You buy a used car for $7000. The car depreciates at the rate of 6% per year. Find the value of the car in the given years.**

4. 2 years   **5.** 5 years   **6.** 8 years   **7.** 10 years

8. 🌎 **BUSINESS DECLINE** A business earned $85,000 in 1990. Then its earnings decreased by 2% each year for 10 years. Write an exponential decay model for the earnings E in year t. Let $t = 0$ represent 1990.

9. CHOOSE A MODEL Which model best represents the decay curve shown in the graph at the right?

A. $y = 60(0.80)^t$

B. $y = 60(1.20)^t$

C. $y = 60(0.40)^t$

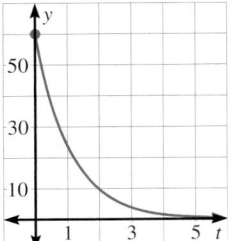

PRACTICE AND APPLICATIONS

STUDENT HELP

→ **Extra Practice**
to help you master skills is on p. 804.

🌎 **TRUCK VALUE You buy a used truck for $20,000. It depreciates at the rate of 15% per year. Find the value of the truck in the given years.**

10. 3 years   **11.** 8 years   **12.** 10 years   **13.** 12 years

MATCHING THE GRAPH Match the equation with its graph.

A.   **B.**   **C.**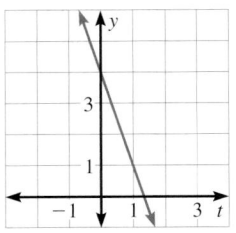

STUDENT HELP

→ **HOMEWORK HELP**
Examples 1, 2: Exs. 10–13, 23–29
Example 3: Exs. 30–33
Examples 4, 5: Exs. 14–16, 30, 33
Example 6: Exs. 14–22

14. $y = 4 - 3t$ **15.** $y = 4(1.6)^t$ **16.** $y = 4(0.6)^t$

RECOGNIZING MODELS Classify the model as *exponential growth* or *exponential decay*. Identify the growth or decay factor and the percent of increase or decrease per time period.

17. $y = 24(1.18)^t$ **18.** $y = 14(0.98)^t$ **19.** $y = 35\left(\dfrac{5}{4}\right)^t$

20. $y = 112(0.4)^t$ **21.** $y = 9\left(\dfrac{2}{5}\right)^t$ **22.** $y = 97(1.01)^t$

PHARMACISTS
Pharmacists must understand the use, composition, and effects of drugs.

CAREER LINK
www.mcdougallittell.com

SCIENCE CONNECTION **In Exercises 23–25, use the following information.**
The concentration of aspirin in a person's bloodstream can be modeled by the equation $y = A(0.8)^t$, where y represents the concentration of aspirin in a person's bloodstream in milligrams (mg), A represents the amount of aspirin taken, and t represents the number of hours since the medication was taken. Find the amount of aspirin remaining in a person's bloodstream at the given dosage.

23. Dosage: 250 mg
Time: after 2 hours

24. Dosage: 500 mg
Time: after 3.5 hours

25. Dosage: 750 mg
Time: after 5 hours

26. **BUYING A TRUCK** You buy a used truck in 1996 for $10,500. Each year the truck depreciates by 10%. Write an exponential decay model to represent this situation. Then estimate the value of the truck in 10 years.

BASKETBALL **In Exercises 27–29, use the following information.**
Each year in the month of March, the NCAA basketball tournament is held to determine the national champion. At the start of the tournament there are 64 teams, and after each round, one half of the remaining teams are eliminated.

27. Write an exponential decay model showing the number of teams N left in the tournament after round t.

28. How many teams remain after 3 rounds? after 4 rounds?

29. **CRITICAL THINKING** If a team won 6 games in a row in the tournament, does it mean that it won the national championship? Explain your reasoning.

30. **SUMMER CAMP** A summer youth camp had a declining enrollment from 1995 to 2000. The enrollment in 1995 was 320 people. Each year for the next five years, the enrollment decreased by 2%. Copy and complete the table showing the enrollment for each year. Sketch a graph of the results.

Year	1995	1996	1997	1998	1999	2000
Enrollment	?	?	?	?	?	?

CABLE CARS **In Exercises 31–33, use the following information. From 1894 to 1903 the number of miles of cable car track decreased by about 10% per year. There were 302 miles of track in 1894.**

31. Write an exponential decay model showing the number of miles M of cable car track left in year t.

32. Copy and complete the table. You may want to use a calculator.

Year	1894	1896	1898	1899	1900	1901	1903
Miles of track	?	?	?	?	?	?	?

33. Sketch a graph of the results.

34. **CRITICAL THINKING** A store is having a sale on sweaters. On the first day the price of a sweater is reduced by 20%. The price will be reduced another 20% each day until the sweater is sold. Denise thinks that on the fifth day of the sale the sweater will be free. Is she right? Explain.

Test Preparation

35. MULTIPLE CHOICE In 1995, you purchase a parcel of land for $8000. The value of the land depreciates by 4% every year. What will the approximate value of the land be in 2002?

Ⓐ $5760   Ⓑ $5771   Ⓒ $6012   Ⓓ $6262

36. MULTIPLE CHOICE Which model best represents the decay curve shown in the graph at the right?

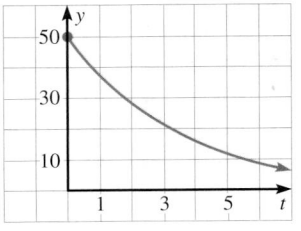

Ⓐ $y = 20(1.16)^t$

Ⓑ $y = 50(0.75)^t$

Ⓒ $y = 20(0.75)^t$

Ⓓ $y = 50 + 20(1.16)^t$

★ **Challenge**

UNDERSTANDING GRAPHS In Exercises 37–39, use a graphing calculator.

37. Make an input-output table for the equations $y = 4^t$ and $y = \left(\frac{1}{4}\right)^t$. Use -3, -2, -1, 0, 1, 2, and 3 as the input. Then sketch the graph of each equation.

38. VISUAL THINKING Interpret the graphs. How are they related?

39. VISUAL THINKING The graph at the right is $y = 2.26^t$. Based on the relationships between the graphs in Exercise 37, predict the graph of $y = \left(\frac{1}{2.26}\right)^t$.

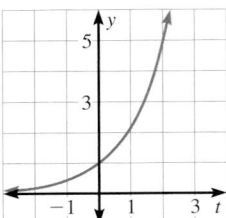

EXTRA CHALLENGE
www.mcdougallittell.com

MIXED REVIEW

VARIABLE EXPRESSIONS Evaluate the expression. (Review 1.3 for 9.1)

40. $4a^2 + 11$ when $a = 5$

41. $c^3 + 6cd$ when $c = 2$ and $d = 1$

42. $b^2 - 4ac$ when $a = 1$, $b = 3$, and $c = 5$

43. $\frac{a^2 - b^2}{2c^2} + 9$ when $a = -3$, $b = 5$, and $c = -2$

SOLVING EQUATIONS Solve the equation. Round the result to the nearest tenth if necessary. (Review 3.6)

44. $12m - 9 = 5m - 2$

45. $5(2x + 2.3) - 11.2 = 6x - 5$

46. $-1.3y + 3.7 = 4.2 - 5.4y$

47. $2.5(3.5p + 6.4) = 18.2p - 6.5$

48. 🌐 **TELEVISION** A TV station's local news program has 50,000 viewers. The managers of the station plan to increase the number of viewers by 2% per month. Write an exponential growth model to represent the number of viewers in t months. (Review 8.5)

SCIENTIFIC NOTATION **Rewrite in scientific notation.** (Lesson 8.4)

1. 0.011205   **2.** 140,000,000   **3.** 0.000000067   **4.** 30,720,000,000

DECIMAL FORM **Rewrite in decimal form.** (Lesson 8.4)

5. 4.82×10^3 **6.** 5×10^9 **7.** 7.04×10^{-6} **8.** 1.112×10^{-2}

9. 🌐 **INVESTMENT** In 1995, you bought a baseball card for $50 that you expect to increase in value 5% each year for the next 10 years. Write an exponential growth model and estimate the value of the baseball card in 2002. (Lesson 8.5)

10. 🌐 **BUYING A CAMPER** You buy a used camper in 1995 for $20,000. Each year the camper depreciates by 15%. Write an exponential decay model to represent this situation. Then estimate the value of the camper in 5 years. (Lesson 8.6)

MATH & History

> **History of Microscopes**

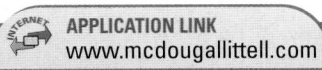

APPLICATION LINK
www.mcdougallittell.com

THEN

THE EARLIEST MICROSCOPES consisted of a single, strongly curved lens mounted on a metal plate. These simple microscopes used visible light to illuminate the object being viewed and could magnify objects as much as 400 times.

NOW

TODAY, scientists use microscopes that use electrons instead of light. The *transmission electron microscope* (or TEM) can resolve two objects as close together as 0.0000005 millimeter (mm) with magnifications up to 1,000,000 times. At this magnification, a sneaker would be long enough to reach from Boston to New York City.

1. Write 0.0000005 mm in scientific notation.

2. The distance from Boston to New York City is 1,003,200 feet. Write this number in scientific notation.

3. How many times stronger is the magnification of the TEM compared to the earliest microscopes? Write your answer in scientific notation.

Anton van Leeuwenhoek was the first to see red blood cells.

1670

Max Knoll and Ernst Ruska of Germany developed the first TEM.

1931

Today

This TEM image shows a white blood cell at a magnification of 9600 times. The image has been colored to show the different parts of the cell.

ACTIVITY 8.6

Using Technology

Fitting Exponential Models

In Chapter 5, you learned that you can use a graphing calculator to find a best-fitting line. A graphing calculator can also be used to find a best-fitting exponential growth or decay model.

▶ **EXAMPLE**

A rubber ball is dropped from a height of 0.82 meter. Using a CBL unit, the height of the ball on each successive bounce was recorded. The *x*-values represent the bounce and the *y*-values represent the height. Use a graphing calculator to find an exponential model for these data.

x	0	1	2	3	4	5	6	7	8	9
y	0.82	0.64	0.50	0.39	0.30	0.24	0.18	0.14	0.11	0.08

▶ **SOLUTION**

1 Enter the ordered pairs into the graphing calculator. Select L_1 as the *x* list and L_2 as the *y* list.

2 Use exponential regression to find an exponential model. The equation $y = 0.8335(0.7744)^x$ is the best-fitting exponential model.

3 Set the viewing rectangle so that $0 \le x \le 20$ and $0 \le y \le 1$.

4 Graph the equation $y = 0.8335(0.7744)^x$.

▶ **EXERCISES**

Use a graphing calculator to find the best-fitting exponential growth model for the points.

1. (0, 1), (1, 1.4), (2, 3), (3, 5), (4, 8), (5, 12), (6, 20), (7, 30), (8, 50), (9, 80)

2. (0, 0.5), (2, 0.8), (3, 1), (4, 1.4), (5, 1.8), (6, 2.7), (7, 3.6), (8, 4.9), (9, 7)

Chapter Summary

WHAT did you learn?

Evaluate exponential expressions

- using multiplication properties of exponents. (8.1)

- that have negative and zero exponents. (8.2)

- using division properties of exponents. (8.3)

Convert numbers from scientific notation to decimal form. (8.4)

Convert numbers from decimal form to scientific notation. (8.4)

Perform operations with numbers in scientific notation. (8.4)

Use scientific notation in problem solving. (8.4)

Use exponential growth models. (8.5)

Use exponential decay models. (8.6)

Sketch the graphs of exponential growth and decay models. (8.5 and 8.6)

WHY did you learn it?

Find the power generated by a windmill. (p. 454)

Predict a basketball player's average score per game. (p. 458)

Estimate the speed of an Olympic rowing team. (p. 468)

Find the amount of water discharged by the Amazon River each year. (p. 472)

Find the price per acre of the Alaska purchase. (p. 472)

Find how long it takes light to travel from the Sun to Pluto. (p. 473)

Estimate the number of heartbeats in a person's life. (p. 474)

Find the weight of a channel catfish. (p. 478)

Find the buying power of a dollar. (p. 484)

Find the balance on a savings account. (p. 480)

How does Chapter 8 fit into the BIGGER PICTURE of algebra?

In Chapters 3–7, you learned how to solve linear equations such as $4(x - 3y) = 24$. In this chapter you learned how to use the properties of exponents and scientific notation to solve exponential functions such as $y = 42(1.2)^x$. You will need to know how to use the properties of exponents when you solve quadratic equations in Chapter 9 and polynomial equations in Chapter 10.

STUDY STRATEGY

How did you use your schedule?

A schedule that you made using the **Study Strategy** on p. 448 may resemble this one.

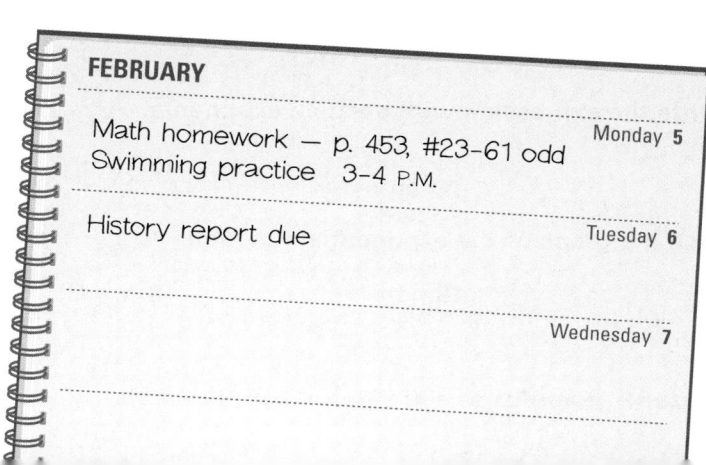

FEBRUARY

Math homework — p. 453, #23–61 odd   Monday 5
Swimming practice   3–4 P.M.

History report due   Tuesday 6

Wednesday 7

VOCABULARY

- exponential function, p. 458
- scientific notation, p. 470
- exponential growth, p. 477
- growth factor, p. 477
- initial amount, pp. 477, 484
- time period, pp. 474, 484
- percent of increase, p. 477
- growth rate, p. 477
- exponential decay, p. 484
- decay factor, p. 484
- decay rate, p. 484
- percent of decrease, p. 484

8.1 MULTIPLICATION PROPERTIES OF EXPONENTS

Examples on pp. 450–452

EXAMPLES Use the multiplication properties of exponents.

a. $4^2 \cdot 4^7 = 4^{2+7} = 4^9$ **Product of powers property**

b. $(5^2)^3 = 5^{2 \cdot 3} = 5^6$ **Power of a power property**

c. $(6 \cdot x)^3 = 6^3 \cdot x^3$ **Power of a product property**

Simplify the expression.

1. $2^2 \cdot 2^7$ **2.** $(4^3)^2$ **3.** $(3a)^3 \cdot (2a)^2$ **4.** $(w^3x^4y)^2 \cdot (wx^2y^3)^4$

Simplify. Then evaluate the expression when $s = 2$ and $t = 3$.

5. $s^3 \cdot s^4$ **6.** $s^4 \cdot (-t)^3$ **7.** $(s^3 \cdot t)^2$ **8.** $-(st^2)^2$

8.2 ZERO AND NEGATIVE EXPONENTS

Examples on pp. 456–458

EXAMPLES Use zero and negative exponents.

a. $6^0 = 1$ **A nonzero number to the zero power is 1.**

b. $7(x^{-3}) = 7\left(\dfrac{1}{x^3}\right) = \dfrac{7}{x^3}$ a^{-n} **is the reciprocal of** a^n.

Evaluate the expression. Write fractions in simplest form.

9. 5^{-3} **10.** $7^{-4} \cdot 7^6$ **11.** $16\left(\dfrac{1}{2}\right)^{-1}$ **12.** $2^0 \cdot \left(\dfrac{1}{4^{-2}}\right)$

Rewrite the expression with positive exponents.

13. x^6y^{-6} **14.** $\dfrac{1}{5p^8q^{-3}}$ **15.** $(a^2b)^0$ **16.** $(-2y)^{-4}$

Sketch the graph of the exponential function.

17. $y = 4^x$ **18.** $y = \left(\dfrac{1}{2}\right)^x$ **19.** $y = 3^{-x}$ **20.** $y = \left(\dfrac{2}{3}\right)^{-x}$

DIVISION PROPERTIES OF EXPONENTS

Examples on pp. 463–465

EXAMPLES Using the division properties of exponents.

a. $\dfrac{6^4}{6^2} = 6^{4-2} = 6^2 = 36$ **Quotient of powers property**

b. $\left(\dfrac{2}{3}\right)^3 = \dfrac{2^3}{3^3} = \dfrac{8}{27}$ **Power of a quotient property**

Evaluate the expression. Write fractions in simplest form.

21. $\dfrac{3^2}{3^5}$ **22.** $\dfrac{5^2}{5^{-2}}$ **23.** $\left(-\dfrac{4}{9}\right)^2$ **24.** $\left(\dfrac{10}{7}\right)^{-1}$

Simplify the expression. The simplified expression should have no negative exponents.

25. $\left(\dfrac{9}{b}\right)^6$ **26.** $\dfrac{x^{12}}{x^6}$ **27.** $\left(\dfrac{m^7}{m^4}\right)^2$ **28.** $\dfrac{(p^2)^3}{(p^2)^5}$

29. $\left(\dfrac{-9a^2b^2}{3ab}\right)^3$ **30.** $\left(\dfrac{25a^4b^5}{-5a^2b}\right)^3$ **31.** $\dfrac{32a^4b^{-2}}{2a^3b^3} \cdot \dfrac{3a^2b^7}{-2a}$ **32.** $\dfrac{9x^{-3}y^6}{x^4y^{-5}} \cdot \dfrac{(3x^2y)^{-2}}{xy^3}$

33. 🌏 **SALES** From 1994 through 1999, the sales for a national book store increased by about the same percent each year. The sales s (in millions of dollars) for year t can be modeled by $s = 1686(1.17)^t$ where $t = 0$ represents 1994. Find the ratio of 1994 sales to 1999 sales.

SCIENTIFIC NOTATION

Examples on pp. 470–472

EXAMPLES Rewriting numbers in decimal form and scientific notation.

a. $1.247 \times 10^2 = 124.7$ **Move decimal point right 2 places.**

b. $1.045 \times 10^{-3} = 0.001045$ **Move decimal point left 3 places.**

c. $79,500 = 7.95 \times 10^4$ **Move decimal point left 4 places.**

d. $0.0588 = 5.88 \times 10^{-2}$ **Move decimal point right 2 places.**

Rewrite the number in decimal form.

34. 6.667×10^{-3} **35.** 7.68×10^5 **36.** 3.75×10^{-1} **37.** 2×10^{-4}

Rewrite the number in scientific notation.

38. 523,000,000 **39.** 0.000679 **40.** 0.0000000233

41. 🌏 **SPACE TRAVEL** Astronaut Shannon W. Lucid holds the United States single-mission, space-flight endurance record. Upon completion of her 1996 mission aboard the Russian Space Station *Mir*, Dr. Lucid had traveled 75,200,000 miles. Write 75,200,000 miles in scientific notation.

42. 🌏 **ASTRONOMY** The distance from Earth to the star Alpha Centauri is about 4.07×10^{13} kilometers (km). Light travels at a speed of about 3.0×10^5 km per second. How long does it take light to travel from this star to Earth?

EXPONENTIAL GROWTH FUNCTIONS

Examples on pp. 477–479

EXAMPLE

You deposited $1200 in a savings account that pays 9% annual interest compounded yearly. What is the balance after 8 years?

$$y = C(1 + r)^t$$ **Exponential growth model**

$$= 1200(1 + 0.09)^t$$ **Substitute 1200 for C and 0.09 for r.**

$$= 1200(1.09)^t$$ **Simplify.**

After 8 years, the balance would be

$$y = 1200(1.09)^8$$ **Substitute 8 for t.**

$$\approx 2391.08$$ **Use a calculator.**

After 8 years, the balance would be $2391.08.

FITNESS PROGRAM In Exercises 43 and 44, use the following information. You start a walking program. The first week you walk 2 miles. Over the next 9 weeks, you increase your distance 5% per week.

43. Write an exponential growth model to represent the number of miles w you are walking after x weeks.

44. How far are you walking in the tenth week?

EXPONENTIAL DECAY FUNCTIONS

Examples on pp. 484–487

EXAMPLE

In 1995 you bought a 32-inch television for $600. The television is depreciating at the rate of 8% per year. Write an exponential decay model and estimate the value of the television in 6 years.

$$y = C(1 - r)^t$$ **Exponential decay model**

$$= 600(1 - 0.08)^t$$ **Substitute 600 for C and 0.08 for r.**

$$= 600(0.92)^t$$ **Simplify.**

After 6 years, the balance would be

$$y = 600(0.92)^6$$ **Substitute 6 for t.**

$$\approx 363.81$$ **Use a calculator.**

After 6 years, the television would be worth $363.81.

TENNIS CLUB In Exercises 45 and 46, use the following information. A tennis club had a declining enrollment from 1993 to 2000. The enrollment in 1993 was 125 people. Each year for 7 years, the enrollment decreased by 3%.

45. Write an exponential decay model to represent enrollment e after x weeks.

46. Estimate the enrollment in 2000.

Chapter Test

In Exercises 1–12, simplify the expression. The simplified expression should have no negative exponents.

1. $x^3 \cdot x^4$

2. $a^0 \cdot a^4$

3. $b^2 \cdot b^{-5}$

4. $5y^{-4}$

5. $\left(x^3\right)^7$

6. $\left(a^{-2}\right)^3$

7. $\dfrac{n^3}{n^5}$

8. $(2b)^3\left(b^{-4}\right)$

9. $(mn)^2 \cdot n^4$

10. $3a^5 \cdot 5a^{-2} \cdot a^3$

11. $\left(\dfrac{x^3}{xy^4}\right)\left(\dfrac{y}{x}\right)^5$

12. $\dfrac{a^{-1}b^2}{ab} \cdot \dfrac{a^2b^3}{b^{-2}}$

In Exercises 13–20, evaluate the expression.

13. $5^4 \cdot 5^{-1}$

14. 4^{-3}

15. $\left(425^2\right)^0$

16. $\left(\dfrac{5}{2}\right)^{-2}$

17. $\dfrac{3 \cdot 3^5}{3^4}$

18. $\left(\dfrac{3}{4}\right)^3 \cdot 4^2 \cdot 3^0$

19. $(5 \cdot 4)^3 \cdot 5^{-2}$

20. $\left[(-2)^5\right]^2$

In Exercises 21–24, write the number in decimal form.

21. $4.27 \cdot 10^5$

22. $6.283 \cdot 10^{-9}$

23. 4.56×10^{10}

24. 5×10^{-12}

In Exercises 25–28, write the number in scientific notation.

25. 9,875,000

26. 0.00125

27. 6,557,000,000

28. 0.0000000317

In Exercises 29–31, sketch a graph of the equation.

29. $y = 2^x$

30. $y = \left(\dfrac{1}{3}\right)^x$

31. $y = 10(1.4)^x$

32. GEOMETRY ▶ CONNECTION The volume of a cube is given by $V = s^3$, where s is the length of a side. The cube has a side of length $3a$. What is the volume of the cube if $a = 2$?

33. SAVINGS ACCOUNT You started a savings account in 1996. The balance A is given by $A = 400(1.1)^t$, where $t = 0$ represents the year 1996. What is the balance in 2000? in 2003?

34. SALES In 1996, you started your own business. In the first year, your sales totaled $88,500. Then each year for the next 4 years, your sales increased by 20%. Write an exponential growth model to represent this situation. Then estimate your sales in 2001.

35. RADIOISOTOPES The amount of time it takes for a radioactive substance to reduce to half of its original amount is called its half-life. The half-life of carbon 11 (^{11}C) is 20 minutes. If you start with 16 grams of ^{11}C, the number of grams remaining after h half-life periods would be $W = 16(0.5)^h$. Copy and complete the table and use the results to sketch the graph.

Half-life periods, h	0	1	2	3	4
Grams remaining, W	?	?	?	?	?

Chapter Standardized Test

🔘 **TEST-TAKING STRATEGY** Be aware of how much time you have left, but keep focused on your work.

1. **MULTIPLE CHOICE** Simplify $7^4 \cdot 7^7$. Write the answer as a power.

    Ⓐ 7^3 Ⓑ 7^{11} Ⓒ 7^{28}

    Ⓓ 49^{11} Ⓔ 49^{28}

2. **MULTIPLE CHOICE** Evaluate $\left[(a + 1)^2\right]^2 \cdot a^3$ when $a = 2$.

    Ⓐ 72   Ⓑ 128   Ⓒ 136

    Ⓓ 200   Ⓔ 648

3. **MULTIPLE CHOICE** Evaluate $(5^{-3})^2$.

    Ⓐ -3125 Ⓑ $-\dfrac{1}{15,625}$

    Ⓒ $\dfrac{1}{3125}$ Ⓓ $\dfrac{1}{15,625}$

    Ⓔ $15,625$

4. **MULTIPLE CHOICE** Evaluate $-8^0 \cdot 2^x \cdot 10^y$ when $x = -2$ and $y = -3$.

    Ⓐ $-\dfrac{1}{4000}$ Ⓑ $-\dfrac{1}{500}$

    Ⓒ $\dfrac{1}{500}$ Ⓓ $\dfrac{1}{4000}$

    Ⓔ 4000

5. **MULTIPLE CHOICE** Simplify $\dfrac{4x^2y^2}{4xy} \cdot \dfrac{8xy^3}{4y}$.

    Ⓐ $2x^2y^3$ Ⓑ $4x^2y$

    Ⓒ $2xy^2$ Ⓓ $2x^2y^4$

    Ⓔ $2xy^3$

6. **MULTIPLE CHOICE** Which expression simplifies to x^3?

    Ⓐ $\dfrac{x^2}{x^5}$ Ⓑ $\dfrac{x^5}{x^{-2}}$

    Ⓒ $\dfrac{x^5}{x^2}$ Ⓓ $x^5 \cdot x^2$

    Ⓔ $x^5 - x^2$

7. **MULTIPLE CHOICE** Which of the following numbers *is not* written in scientific notation?

    Ⓐ 8.62×10^4 Ⓑ 2.12×10^{-12}

    Ⓒ 21.2×10^{-5} Ⓓ 9.9132×10^{-1}

    Ⓔ 2.0001×10^{-3}

8. **MULTIPLE CHOICE** Rewrite 3.6×10^{-6} in decimal form.

    Ⓐ 0.000036   Ⓑ 3,600,000

    Ⓒ 0.00000036   Ⓓ 36,000,000

    Ⓔ 0.0000036

9. **MULTIPLE CHOICE** Evaluate the product $(6.2 \times 10^4) \cdot (2.4 \times 10^5)$. Write the result in scientific notation.

    Ⓐ 1.488×10^8 Ⓑ 1.488×10^{10}

    Ⓒ 14.88×10^1 Ⓓ 14.88×10^{10}

    Ⓔ 14.88×10^{20}

10. **MULTIPLE CHOICE** Evaluate $\dfrac{(2.3622 \times 10^4)}{(3.81 \times 10^{-3})}$.

    Write the result in scientific notation.

    Ⓐ 6.2×10^6 Ⓑ 6.2×10^8

    Ⓒ 0.62×10^6 Ⓓ 6.2×10^1

    Ⓔ 6.2×10^{-12}

11. **MULTIPLE CHOICE** Which model best represents the growth curve shown below?

    Ⓐ $y = 50(1.4)^t$

    Ⓑ $y = 100(1.4)^t$

    Ⓒ $y = 50(1.12)^t$

    Ⓓ $y = 50(1.4)^{-t}$

    Ⓔ $y = 200(1.08)^t$

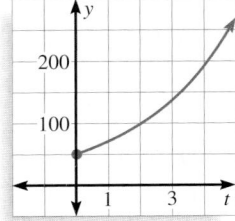

12. **MULTIPLE CHOICE** You deposit $450 into a savings account that pays 6% interest compounded yearly. How much money is in the account after 6 years? Assume you make no more deposits or withdrawals.

    Ⓐ $477.00   Ⓑ $602.20

    Ⓒ $638.33   Ⓓ $676.63

    Ⓔ $693.33

13. MULTIPLE CHOICE In 1994 you bought a rare stamp for $500 that you expect to increase in value 12% each year for the next 15 years. Write an exponential growth model and estimate the value of the stamp in 2002.

   (**A**) $881.17   (**B**) $986.91   (**C**) $1557.92   (**D**) $1237.98   (**E**) $2000

QUANTITATIVE COMPARISON **In Exercises 14–16, evaluate each function. Then choose the statement below that is true about the given values of *y*.**

   A. The value of y in column A is greater.

   B. The value of y in column B is greater.

   C. The two values of y are equal.

   D. The relationship cannot be determined from the given information.

		Column A	Column B
14.	When $x = 3$,	$y = 3x$	$y = 3^x$
15.	When $x = -2$,	$y = 3^x$	$y = \left(\frac{1}{3}\right)^x$
16.	When $x = 1$,	$y = 3^{-x}$	$y = \left(\frac{1}{3}\right)^x$

17. MULTIPLE CHOICE The concentration of an allergy medication in a person's bloodstream in nanograms per milliliter (ng/mL) can be modeled by the equation $y = 263(0.92)^t$, where t represents the number of hours since the medication was taken. What is the concentration of the medication remaining in the person's bloodstream after 4 hours?

   (**A**) 263 ng/mL   (**B**) 222 ng/mL   (**C**) 205 ng/mL   (**D**) 188 ng/mL   (**E**) 170 ng/mL

18. MULTIPLE CHOICE A business had a profit of $142,000 in 1994. Then its profit decreased by 8% each year for the next 6 years. Which exponential decay model would you use to find how much the business earned in the year 2000? Let E represent the earnings and let t represent the year.

   (**A**) $E = 142{,}000(0.08)^t$ (**B**) $E = 142{,}000(0.96)^t$ (**C**) $E = 142{,}000(0.92)^t$

   (**D**) $t = 142{,}000(0.08)^E$ (**E**) $E = 0.92(142{,}000)^t$

19. MULTIPLE CHOICE Which models below are exponential decay models?

   I $y = 1.25^t$ **II** $y = 0.97^t$ **III** $y = \left(\frac{4}{3}\right)^t$ **IV** $y = \left(\frac{2}{3}\right)^t$

   (**A**) I and II   (**B**) III and IV   (**C**) II and III   (**D**) I and III   (**E**) II and IV

20. MULTI-STEP PROBLEM The population in one midwestern town was tracked over several years. Based on the data for the town, population experts determined that the population, in thousands of people, could be represented by the expression $2(1.175)^t$, where t is the number of years from now.

   a. What is the population this year?

   b. What is the estimated population 5 years from now?

   c. What was the population 2 years ago?

   d. *Writing* What advice would you give to the city planners who are trying to decide whether or not to build freeways? Include in your advice a population prediction for 10 years and 20 years from now.

QUADRATIC EQUATIONS AND FUNCTIONS

▶ *What is the path of a home run ball?*

CHAPTER

9

APPLICATION: Baseball

A batter usually scores a home run by hitting a ball over the outfield fence. Mathematical models can be used to find how long it takes for a baseball to reach the ground.

You'll use quadratic equations to solve different types of vertical motion problems in Chapter 9.

Think & Discuss

1. Use the graph to approximate the maximum height the ball reaches.

2. Use the graph to approximate the maximum horizontal distance it travels.

Learn More About It

You will use a quadratic model to learn more about the path of a ball in Exercise 84 on p. 538.

 APPLICATION LINK Visit www.mcdougallittell.com for more information about baseball.

PREVIEW

What's the chapter about?

Chapter 9 is about **solving quadratic equations and graphing quadratic functions**, many of which model real-life applications. In Chapter 9 you'll learn

- how to evaluate and approximate square roots.
- how to simplify radicals.
- how to solve a quadratic equation.
- how to sketch the graph of a quadratic function and a quadratic inequality.

KEY VOCABULARY

▶ **Review**
- linear equation, p. 133
- x-intercept, p. 218
- exponential growth, p. 477
- exponential decay, p. 484

▶ **New**
- square root, p. 503
- irrational number, p. 504
- radical expression, p. 504
- quadratic equation, p. 505

- quadratic function, p. 518
- parabola, p. 518
- roots, p. 526
- discriminant, p. 541
- quadratic inequalities, p. 548

PREPARE

Are you ready for the chapter?

SKILL REVIEW Do these exercises to review key skills that you'll apply in this chapter. See the given **reference page** if there is something you don't understand.

STUDENT HELP

▶ **Study Tip**
"Student Help" boxes throughout the chapter give you study tips and tell you where to look for extra help in this book and on the Internet.

Evaluate the expression. (Review pp. 94 and 109)

1. $3x^2 - 108$ when $x = -4$

2. $8x^2 \div \frac{2}{3}$ when $x = -1$

3. $x^2 - 4xy$ when $x = -2$ and $y = 5$

4. $-\frac{x}{2y}$ when $x = 12$ and $y = -3$

Use a table of values to graph the equation. (Review Examples 2 and 3, pp. 211–212)

5. $y = \frac{1}{2}x + 3$

6. $y + 3 = -2x + 2$

7. $x + 7y = 14$

Check whether the ordered pair is a solution. (Review Example 1, p. 360)

8. $3x + 4y < 5, (-1, 2)$

9. $\frac{1}{2}x - \frac{2}{3}y \geq -6, (0, 0)$

10. $6x - 2y > -8, (2, -3)$

STUDY STRATEGY

Here's a study strategy!

Explaining Ideas

Sometimes explaining things to another person can help you understand a topic better. Or, someone else's questions may point out something that you don't fully understand. Talking about math is a good way to check how well you know the material and to work through questions.

9.1 Solving Quadratic Equations by Finding Square Roots

What you should learn

GOAL 1 Evaluate and approximate square roots.

GOAL 2 Solve a quadratic equation by finding square roots.

Why you should learn it

▼ To solve **real-life** problems such as finding the time it takes an egg to hit the ground in an engineering contest in **Example 7**.

GOAL 1 EVALUATING SQUARE ROOTS

You know how to find the square of a number. For instance, the square of 3 is $3^2 = 9$. The square of -3 is also 9.

In this lesson you will study the reverse problem: finding a *square root* of a number.

SQUARE ROOT OF A NUMBER

If $b^2 = a$, then b is a **square root** of a.

Example: If $3^2 = 9$, then 3 is a square root of 9.

All positive real numbers have two square roots: a **positive square root** (or principal square root) and a **negative square root**. Square roots are written with a radical symbol $\sqrt{}$. The number or expression inside a radical symbol is the **radicand**. In the following examples, 9 is the radicand.

Meaning	Positive square root	Negative square root	The positive and negative square roots
Symbol	$\sqrt{}$	$-\sqrt{}$	$\pm\sqrt{}$
Example	$\sqrt{9} = 3$	$-\sqrt{9} = -3$	$\pm\sqrt{9} = \pm3 = +3$ or -3

The symbol $\pm$ is read as "plus or minus" and refers to both the positive square root and the negative square root. Zero has only one square root: zero. Negative numbers have no real square roots, because the square of every real number is either positive or zero.

EXAMPLE 1 *Finding Square Roots of Numbers*

Evaluate the expression.

   a. $\sqrt{64}$ **b.** $-\sqrt{64}$ **c.** $\sqrt{0}$ **d.** $\pm\sqrt{0.25}$ **e.** $\sqrt{-4}$

SOLUTION

   a. $\sqrt{64} = 8$ **Positive square root**

   b. $-\sqrt{64} = -8$ **Negative square root**

   c. $\sqrt{0} = 0$ **Square root of zero**

   d. $\pm\sqrt{0.25} = \pm0.5$ **Two square roots**

   e. $\sqrt{-4}$ (undefined)   **No real square root**

Numbers whose square roots are integers or quotients of integers are called **perfect squares.** The square roots of numbers that are not perfect squares must be written using the radical symbol or approximated. These numbers are part of the set of *irrational numbers.* An **irrational number** is a number that cannot be written as the quotient of two integers.

EXAMPLE 2 *Evaluating Square Roots*

STUDENT HELP

▸ **Square Root Table**
For a table of square roots, see p. 811.

Evaluate the expression. Use a calculator if necessary.

a. $-\sqrt{121}$ b. $-\sqrt{1.44}$ c. $\sqrt{0.09}$ d. $\sqrt{7}$

SOLUTION

a. $-\sqrt{121} = -11$ 121 is a perfect square: $11^2 = 121$.

b. $-\sqrt{1.44} = -1.2$ 1.44 is a perfect square: $1.2^2 = 1.44$.

c. $\sqrt{0.09} = 0.3$ 0.09 is a perfect square: $0.3^2 = 0.09$.

d. $\sqrt{7} \approx 2.65$ Round to the nearest hundredth.

· · · · · · · · · ·

A **radical expression** involves square roots (or *radicals*). If the symbol $\pm$ precedes the radical, the expression represents two different numbers, as in Example 4. The square root symbol is a grouping symbol. Operations inside a radical symbol must be performed before the square root is evaluated.

EXAMPLE 3 *Evaluating a Radical Expression*

Evaluate $\sqrt{b^2 - 4ac}$ when $a = 1$, $b = -2$, and $c = -3$.

SOLUTION

$$\sqrt{b^2 - 4ac} = \sqrt{(-2)^2 - 4(1)(-3)}$$ Substitute values.

$$= \sqrt{4 + 12}$$ Simplify.

$$= \sqrt{16}$$ Simplify.

$$= 4$$ Positive square root

EXAMPLE 4 *Evaluating an Expression with a Calculator*

Evaluate $\dfrac{1 \pm 2\sqrt{3}}{4}$ to the nearest hundredth.

STUDENT HELP

▸ **KEYSTROKE HELP**
To find the square root of 3 on your calculator you may need to press
[√] [3] or
[3] [√]. Test your calculator to find out which order is correct.

SOLUTION This expression represents two numbers.

[(] 1 [+] 2 [×] 3 [√] [)] [÷] 4 [ENTER] (1.116025404)

[(] 1 [−] 2 [×] 3 [√] [)] [÷] 4 [ENTER] (−0.61602540)

▸ Rounded to the nearest hundredth, the expression represents 1.12 and −0.62.

GOAL 2 SOLVING A QUADRATIC EQUATION

A **quadratic equation** is an equation that can be written in the following **standard form**.

$$ax^2 + bx + c = 0, \text{ where } a \neq 0$$

In standard form, a is the **leading coefficient**.

When $b = 0$, this equation becomes $ax^2 + c = 0$. To solve quadratic equations of this form, isolate x^2 on one side. Then find the square root(s) of each side.

CONCEPT SUMMARY — **SOLVING $x^2 = d$ BY FINDING SQUARE ROOTS**

- If $d > 0$, then $x^2 = d$ has two solutions: $x = \pm\sqrt{d}$.

- If $d = 0$, then $x^2 = d$ has one solution: $x = 0$.

- If $d < 0$, then $x^2 = d$ has no real solution.

EXAMPLE 5 Solving Quadratic Equations

Solve each equation.

  a. $x^2 = 4$ **b.** $x^2 = 5$ **c.** $x^2 = 0$ **d.** $x^2 = -1$

SOLUTION

  a. $x^2 = 4$ has two solutions: $x = +2$ and $x = -2$.

  b. $x^2 = 5$ has two solutions: $x = \sqrt{5}$ and $x = -\sqrt{5}$.

  c. $x^2 = 0$ has one solution: $x = 0$.

  d. $x^2 = -1$ has no real solution.

EXAMPLE 6 Rewriting Before Finding Square Roots

Solve $3x^2 - 48 = 0$.

STUDENT HELP

↳ **Study Tip**
When checking solutions of quadratic equations, remember to check *all* solutions in the original equation. In Example 6, check both 4 and −4.

$3(4)^2 - 48 \stackrel{?}{=} 0$

$3(-4)^2 - 48 \stackrel{?}{=} 0$

SOLUTION

$3x^2 - 48 = 0$	**Write original equation.**
$3x^2 = 48$	**Add 48 to each side.**
$x^2 = 16$	**Divide each side by 3.**
$x = \pm\sqrt{16}$	**Find square roots.**
$x = \pm 4$	**16 is a perfect square: $4^2 = 16$, $(-4)^2 = 16$.**

▶ The solutions are 4 and −4. Check both solutions in the original equation. Both 4 and −4 make the equation true, so $3x^2 - 48 = 0$ has two solutions.

FALLING OBJECT MODEL When an object is dropped, the speed with which it falls continues to increase. Ignoring air resistance, its height h can be approximated by the falling object model.

$$h = -16t^2 + s \quad \longleftarrow \text{ Falling object model}$$

Here h is measured in feet, t is the number of seconds the object has fallen, and s is the initial height from which the object was dropped.

The object's increase in speed is due to Earth's gravitational pull. On a planet whose gravitational pull is different from that of Earth, the factor -16 would be replaced by another constant.

Engineering

EXAMPLE 7 *Using a Falling Object Model*

An engineering student is in an "egg dropping contest." The goal is to create a container for an egg so it can be dropped from a height of 32 feet without breaking the egg. To the nearest tenth of a second, about how long will it take for the egg's container to hit the ground? Assume there is no air resistance.

SOLUTION Write an equation to model the egg container's height h as function of time t, where the initial height $s = 32$.

$h = -16t^2 + s$	Write falling object model.
$h = -16t^2 + 32$	Substitute 32 for s.

The falling object model for the egg container is $h = -16t^2 + 32$.

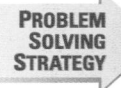

PROBLEM SOLVING STRATEGY

Method 1 **MAKE A TABLE** One way to solve the problem is to find the height h for different values of time t in the function $h = -16t^2 + 32$. Organize the data in a table. The egg container will hit the ground when $h = 0$.

Time (sec)	0.0	0.5	1.0	1.1	1.2	1.3	1.4	1.5
Height (ft)	32	28	16	12.64	8.96	4.96	0.64	−4

▶ From the table, you can see that $h = 0$ between 1.4 and 1.5 seconds. The egg container will take between 1.4 and 1.5 seconds to hit the ground.

Method 2 **USE AN EQUATION** Another way to approach the problem is to solve the quadratic equation for the time t that gives a height of $h = 0$ feet.

$h = -16t^2 + 32$	Write falling egg model.
$0 = -16t^2 + 32$	Substitute 0 for h.
$-32 = -16t^2$	Subtract 32 from each side.
$2 = t^2$	Divide each side by -16.
$\sqrt{2} = t$	Find positive square root.
$1.4 \approx t$	Use a calculator.

STUDENT HELP

▸ **Look Back**
For help with using a table of values to graph an equation, see pp. 211–212.

▶ The egg container will hit the ground in about 1.4 seconds. You can ignore the negative square root, because -1.4 seconds is not a reasonable solution.

GUIDED PRACTICE

Vocabulary Check ✔ **1.** State the meanings of the symbols $\sqrt{\ }$, $-\sqrt{\ }$, and $\pm\sqrt{\ }$.

2. Give an example of a perfect square and an example of an irrational number.

Concept Check ✔ **3.** Explain how to find solutions of an equation of the form $ax^2 + c = 0$.

If the statement is *true*, give an example. If false, give a counterexample.

4. Some numbers have no real square root.

5. No number has only one square root.

6. All positive numbers have two different square roots.

7. The square root of the sum of two numbers is equal to the sum of the square roots of the numbers.

Skill Check ✔ **Evaluate the expression.**

8. $\sqrt{36}$ **9.** $\sqrt{0.81}$ **10.** $-\sqrt{0.04}$ **11.** $\pm\sqrt{9}$

Evaluate the radical expression when *a* = 2 and *b* = 4.

12. $\sqrt{b^2 + 10a}$ **13.** $\dfrac{10 \pm 2\sqrt{b}}{a}$ **14.** $\sqrt{b^2 - 8a}$

Solve the equation. If there is no solution, state the reason.

15. $2x^2 - 8 = 0$ **16.** $x^2 + 25 = 0$ **17.** $x^2 - 1.44 = 0$ **18.** $5x^2 = -15$

🌀 **FALLING OBJECTS If an object is dropped from an initial height *s*, how long will it take to reach the ground? Assume there is no air resistance.**

19. $s = 48$ **20.** $s = 96$ **21.** $s = 192$

22. If you double the height from which the object falls, do you double the falling time? If not, why?

PRACTICE AND APPLICATIONS

STUDENT HELP

➤ **Extra Practice**
to help you master
skills is on p. 805.

FINDING SQUARE ROOTS Find all square roots of the number or write *no square roots*. Check the results by squaring each root.

23. 49   **24.** 144   **25.** -4 **26.** -25

27. 0   **28.** 100   **29.** 0.09   **30.** 0.16

EVALUATING SQUARE ROOTS Evaluate the expression. Give the exact value if possible. Otherwise, approximate to the nearest hundredth.

31. $-\sqrt{169}$ **32.** $\sqrt{64}$ **33.** $\sqrt{13}$ **34.** $-\sqrt{125}$

35. $\sqrt{0.04}$ **36.** $\pm\sqrt{0.75}$ **37.** $-\sqrt{0.1}$ **38.** $\pm\sqrt{6.25}$

STUDENT HELP

➤ **HOMEWORK HELP**
Example 1: Exs. 23–30
Example 2: Exs. 31–38
Example 3: Exs. 39–44

continued on p. 508

EVALUATING EXPRESSIONS Evaluate $\sqrt{b^2 - 4ac}$ for the given values.

39. $a = 4, b = 5, c = 1$ **40.** $a = -2, b = 8, c = -8$ **41.** $a = 3, b = -7, c = 6$

42. $a = 2, b = 4, c = 0.5$ **43.** $a = -3, b = 7, c = 5$ **44.** $a = 6, b = -8, c = 4$

EVALUATING EXPRESSIONS Use a calculator to evaluate the expression. Round the results to the nearest hundredth.

45. $\dfrac{3 \pm 4\sqrt{6}}{3}$ **46.** $\dfrac{6 \pm 4\sqrt{2}}{-1}$ **47.** $\dfrac{2 \pm 5\sqrt{3}}{5}$

48. $\dfrac{1 \pm 6\sqrt{8}}{6}$ **49.** $\dfrac{7 \pm 3\sqrt{2}}{-1}$ **50.** $\dfrac{2 \pm 5\sqrt{6}}{2}$

51. $\dfrac{5 \pm 6\sqrt{3}}{3}$ **52.** $\dfrac{3 \pm 4\sqrt{5}}{4}$ **53.** $\dfrac{7 \pm 0.3\sqrt{12}}{-6}$

QUADRATIC EQUATIONS Solve the equation or write *no solution*. Write the solutions as integers if possible. Otherwise write them as radical expressions.

54. $x^2 = 36$ **55.** $b^2 = 64$ **56.** $5x^2 = 500$

57. $x^2 = 16$ **58.** $x^2 = 0$ **59.** $x^2 = -9$

60. $3x^2 = 6$ **61.** $a^2 + 3 = 12$ **62.** $x^2 - 7 = 57$

63. $2s^2 - 5 = 27$ **64.** $5x^2 + 5 = 20$ **65.** $7x^2 + 30 = 9$

66. $x^2 + 4.0 = 0$ **67.** $6x^2 - 54 = 0$ **68.** $7x^2 - 63 = 0$

SOLVING EQUATIONS Use a calculator to solve the equation or write *no solution*. Round the results to the nearest hundredth.

69. $4x^2 - 3 = 57$ **70.** $6y^2 + 22 = 34$ **71.** $2x^2 - 4 = 10$

72. $\frac{2}{3}n^2 - 6 = 2$ **73.** $\frac{4}{5}x^2 + 12 = 5$ **74.** $\frac{1}{2}x^2 + 3 = 8$

75. $3x^2 + 7 = 31$ **76.** $6s^2 - 12 = 0$ **77.** $5a^2 + 10 = 20$

78. CRITICAL THINKING Write your own example of a quadratic equation in the form $x^2 = d$ for each of the following.

   a. An equation that has no real solution.

   b. An equation that has one solution.

   c. An equation that has two solutions.

ROAD SAFETY In Exercises 79–82, a boulder falls off the top of a cliff during a storm. The cliff is 60 feet high. Find how long it will take for the boulder to hit the road below.

79. Write the falling object model for $s = 60$.

80. Try to determine the time when $h = 0$ from an input-output table for this model.

81. Solve the falling object model for $h = 0$.

82. *Writing* Which problem solving method do you prefer? Why?

FALLING OBJECT MODEL In Exercises 83–86, an object is dropped from a height *s*. How long does it take to reach the ground? Assume there is no air resistance.

83. $s = 144$ feet   **84.** $s = 256$ feet   **85.** $s = 400$ feet   **86.** $s = 600$ feet

87. 🌐 **HOME COMPUTER SALES** The sales S (in millions of dollars) of home computers in the United States from 1988 to 1995 can be modeled by $S = 145.63t^2 + 3327.56$, where t is the number of years since 1988. Use this model to estimate the year in which sales of home computers will be $36,000 million. ▶ Source: Electronic Industries Association

88. 🌐 **COMPUTER SOFTWARE SALES** The sales S (in millions of dollars) of computer software in the United States from 1990 to 1995 can be modeled by $S = 61.98t^2 + 1001.15$, where t is the number of years since 1990. Use this model to estimate the year in which sales of computer software will be $7200 million. ▶ Source: Electronic Industries Association

🌐 **MINERALS In Exercises 89–94, use the following information.**
Mineralogists use the Vickers scale to measure the hardness of minerals. The hardness H of a mineral can be determined by hitting the mineral with a pyramid-shaped diamond and measuring the depth d of the indentation. The harder the mineral, the smaller the depth of the indentation. A model that relates mineral hardness with the indentation depth (in millimeters) is $Hd^2 = 1.89$.

Use a calculator to find the depth of the indentation for the mineral with the given value of H. Round to the nearest hundredth of a millimeter.

89. Graphite: $H = 12$ **90.** Gold: $H = 50$ **91.** Galena: $H = 80$

92. Platinum: $H = 125$ **93.** Copper: $H = 140$ **94.** Hematite: $H = 755$

Test Preparation

QUANTITATIVE COMPARISON In Exercises 95–96, choose the statement below that is true about the given numbers.

(A) The number in column A is greater.

(B) The number in column B is greater.

(C) The two numbers are equal.

(D) The relationship cannot be determined from the given information.

	Column A	Column B
95.	$-\sqrt{121}$	$-2\sqrt{121}$
96.	The positive value of x in $2x^2 - 14 = 18$	The positive value of x in $2x^2 + 14 = 46$

SCIENCE CONNECTION **In Exercises 97–100, use the following information.**
Scientists simulate a gravity-free environment called *microgravity* in free-fall situations. A similar microgravity environment can be felt on free-fall rides at amusement parks or when stepping off a high diving platform. The distance d (in meters) that an object that is dropped falls in t seconds can be modeled by the equation $d = \frac{1}{2}g(t^2)$, where g is the acceleration due to gravity (9.8 meters per second per second).

97. The NASA Lewis Research Center has two microgravity facilities. One provides a 132-meter drop into a hole and the other provides a 24-meter drop inside a tower. How long will each free-fall period be?

98. In Japan a 490-meter-deep mine shaft has been converted into a microgravity facility. This creates the longest period of free fall currently available on Earth. How long will a period of free-fall be?

99. If you want to double the free-fall time, how much do you have to increase the height from which the object was dropped?

100. CRITICAL THINKING How are these formulas similar?

$$d = \frac{1}{2}g(t^2) \text{ when } d \text{ is distance, } g \text{ is gravity, and } t \text{ is time}$$

$$h = -16t^2 + s \text{ when } h \text{ is height, } s \text{ is initial height, and } t \text{ is time}$$

MIXED REVIEW

FACTORING INTEGERS **Write the prime factorization.** (Skills Review, p. 777)

101. 11   **102.** 24   **103.** 72   **104.** 108

GRAPH AND CHECK **Use a graph to solve the linear system. Check your solution algebraically.** (Review 7.1)

105. $-3x + 4y = -5$
$\quad\ \ 4x + 2y = -8$

106. $4x + 5y = 20$
$\quad\ \ \frac{5}{4}x + y = 4$

107. $\frac{1}{2}x + 3y = 18$
$\quad\ \ 2x + 6y = -12$

SOLVING SYSTEMS **In Exercises 109–111, use linear combinations to solve the system.** (Review 7.3)

108. $12x - 4y = -32$
$\quad\ \ x + 3y = 4$

109. $10x - 3y = 17$
$\quad\ \ -7x + y = 9$

110. $8x - 5y = 100$
$\quad\ \ 2x + \frac{1}{2}y = 4$

111. 🌐 **BASKETBALL TICKETS** You are selling tickets at a high school basketball game. Student tickets cost $2 and general admission tickets cost $3. You sell 2342 tickets and collect $5801. How many of each type of ticket did you sell? (Review 7.2)

112. 🌐 **FLOWERS** You are buying a combination of irises and white tulips for a flower arrangement. The irises are $1 each and the white tulips are $.50. You spend $20 total to purchase an arrangement of 25 flowers. How many of each kind did you purchase? (Review 7.2)

9.2

Simplifying Radicals

GOAL 1 **SIMPLIFYING RADICALS**

What you should learn

GOAL ① Use properties of radicals to simplify radicals.

GOAL ② Use quadratic equations to model **real-life** problems, such as the speed of a tsunami in **Ex. 55**.

Why you should learn it

▼ To compare the speeds of two different-sized sailboats in a **real-life** boat race in **Example 3**.

In this lesson you will learn how to simplify radical expressions and how to recognize when a radical is written in simplest form.

▶ **ACTIVITY**

Developing Concepts

Investigating Properties of Radicals

① Evaluate the radical expressions $\sqrt{ab}$ and $\sqrt{a} \cdot \sqrt{b}$ for the given values of a and b.

a. $a = 4, b = 9$ **b.** $a = 64, b = 100$ **c.** $a = 25, b = 4$

d. $a = 36, b = 16$ **e.** $a = 100, b = 625$ **f.** $a = 121, b = 49$

② What can you conclude?

③ Evaluate the radical expressions $\sqrt{\dfrac{a}{b}}$ and $\dfrac{\sqrt{a}}{\sqrt{b}}$ for the given values of a and b.

a. $a = 4, b = 49$ **b.** $a = 16, b = 64$ **c.** $a = 25, b = 36$

d. $a = 225, b = 4$ **e.** $a = 144, b = 100$ **f.** $a = 9, b = 81$

④ What can you conclude?

In the activity you may have discovered the following two properties that can be used to simplify expressions that contain radicals.

PROPERTIES OF RADICALS

PRODUCT PROPERTY The square root of a product equals the product of the square roots of the factors.

$$\sqrt{ab} = \sqrt{a} \cdot \sqrt{b} \text{ where } a \geq 0 \text{ and } b \geq 0$$

Example: $\sqrt{4 \cdot 100} = \sqrt{4} \cdot \sqrt{100}$

QUOTIENT PROPERTY The square root of a quotient equals the quotient of the square roots of the numerator and denominator.

$$\sqrt{\dfrac{a}{b}} = \dfrac{\sqrt{a}}{\sqrt{b}} \text{ where } a \geq 0 \text{ and } b > 0$$

Example: $\sqrt{\dfrac{9}{25}} = \dfrac{\sqrt{9}}{\sqrt{25}}$

An expression with radicals is in **simplest form** if the following are true:

- No perfect square factors other than 1 are in the radicand.

  $\sqrt{8}$ ⟹ $\sqrt{4 \cdot 2}$ ⟹ $2\sqrt{2}$

- No fractions are in the radicand.

  $\sqrt{\dfrac{5}{16}}$ ⟹ $\dfrac{\sqrt{5}}{\sqrt{16}}$ ⟹ $\dfrac{\sqrt{5}}{4}$

- No radicals appear in the denominator of a fraction.

  $\dfrac{1}{\sqrt{4}}$ ⟹ $\dfrac{1}{2}$

EXAMPLE 1 *Simplifying with the Product Property*

Simplify the expression $\sqrt{50}$.

SOLUTION

You can use the product property to simplify a radical by removing perfect square factors from the radicand.

STUDENT HELP

↳ **Skills Review**
For help with factoring, see pp. 777–778.

$$\sqrt{50} = \sqrt{25 \cdot 2} \qquad \text{Factor using perfect square factor.}$$
$$= \sqrt{25} \cdot \sqrt{2} \qquad \text{Use product property.}$$
$$= 5\sqrt{2} \qquad \text{Simplify.}$$

EXAMPLE 2 *Simplifying with the Quotient Property*

Simplify the expression.

a. $\sqrt{\dfrac{3}{4}}$ 　　　　 b. $\dfrac{\sqrt{20}}{4}$ 　　　　 c. $\sqrt{\dfrac{32}{50}}$

SOLUTION

a. $\sqrt{\dfrac{3}{4}} = \dfrac{\sqrt{3}}{\sqrt{4}}$ 　　 Use quotient property.

$\qquad = \dfrac{\sqrt{3}}{2}$ 　　 Simplify.

b. $\dfrac{\sqrt{20}}{4} = \dfrac{\sqrt{4 \cdot 5}}{4}$ 　　 Factor using perfect square factor.

$\qquad = \dfrac{2\sqrt{5}}{4}$ 　　 Remove perfect square factors.

$\qquad = \dfrac{\sqrt{5}}{2}$ 　　 Divide out common factors.

c. $\sqrt{\dfrac{32}{50}} = \sqrt{\dfrac{2 \cdot 16}{2 \cdot 25}}$ 　　 Factor using perfect square factor.

$\qquad = \sqrt{\dfrac{16}{25}}$ 　　 Divide out common factors.

$\qquad = \dfrac{\sqrt{16}}{\sqrt{25}}$ 　　 Use quotient property.

$\qquad = \dfrac{4}{5}$ 　　 Simplify.

STUDENT HELP

 HOMEWORK HELP
Visit our Web site
www.mcdougallittell.com
for extra examples.

GOAL 2 USING QUADRATIC MODELS IN REAL LIFE

Quadratic equations can be used to model real-life situations, such as comparing the maximum speeds of two sailboats with different water line lengths.

EXAMPLE 3 *Simplifying Radical Expressions*

BOAT RACING The maximum speed s (in knots or nautical miles per hour) that some kinds of boats can travel can be modeled by

$$s^2 = \frac{16}{9}x,$$ where x is the length of the water line in feet.

A sailboat with a 16-foot water line is racing against a sailboat with a 32-foot water line. The smaller sailboat is traveling at a maximum speed of 5.3 knots.

a. Find the maximum speed of the sailboat with the 32-foot water line. Find the speed to the nearest tenth.

b. Is the maximum speed of the sailboat with the 32-foot water line twice that of the sailboat with the 16-foot water line? Explain.

32 ft waterline   16 ft waterline

SOLUTION

a. Write the model for maximum speed of a sailboat and let $x = 32$ feet.

$s^2 = \frac{16}{9}x$	Write quadratic model.
$s^2 = \frac{16}{9} \cdot 32$	Substitute 32 for *x*.
$\sqrt{s^2} = \sqrt{\frac{16}{9} \cdot 32}$	Find square root of both sides.
$s = \frac{\sqrt{16}}{\sqrt{9}} \cdot \sqrt{32}$	Use quotient and product properties.
$= \frac{\sqrt{16}}{\sqrt{9}} \cdot \sqrt{16} \cdot \sqrt{2}$	Identify perfect square factors.
$= \frac{4}{3} \cdot 4\sqrt{2}$	Remove perfect square factors.
$= \frac{16\sqrt{2}}{3}$	Simplify.
≈ 7.5	Use a calculator or square root table.

b. No, because 7.5 knots is not twice 5.3 knots. The maximum speed of the smaller sailboat is $s = \sqrt{\frac{16^2}{9}}$, or $\frac{16}{3}$, so the longer sailboat's maximum speed is only $\sqrt{2}$ times the smaller sailboat's maximum speed.

GUIDED PRACTICE

Vocabulary Check ✔

1. Is the radical expression in simplest form? Explain.

   a. $\frac{3}{5}\sqrt{2}$ **b.** $\sqrt{\frac{3}{16}}$ **c.** $5\sqrt{40}$

Concept Check ✔

2. Explain how to use the product property of radicals to simplify $\sqrt{3} \cdot \sqrt{15}$.

3. Explain how to use the quotient property of radicals to simplify $\sqrt{\frac{4}{25}}$.

Skill Check ✔

Match the radical expression with its simplified form.

A. $3\sqrt{6}$ **B.** $9\sqrt{6}$ **C.** $2\sqrt{2}$ **D.** $4\sqrt{2}$

4. $\sqrt{32}$ **5.** $\sqrt{54}$ **6.** $\sqrt{486}$ **7.** $\sqrt{8}$

8. 🌐 **SAILING** Find the maximum speed of a sailboat with a 25-foot water line using the formula in Example 3.

9. **ERROR ANALYSIS** Describe the error. Simplify correctly.

$$\sqrt{50} = \sqrt{5 \cdot 10}$$
$$= 5\sqrt{10}$$

PRACTICE AND APPLICATIONS

STUDENT HELP

➤ **Extra Practice**
to help you master
skills is on p. 805.

PRODUCT PROPERTY Simplify the expression.

10. $\sqrt{44}$ **11.** $\sqrt{27}$ **12.** $\sqrt{48}$ **13.** $\sqrt{75}$

14. $\sqrt{90}$ **15.** $\sqrt{125}$ **16.** $\sqrt{200}$ **17.** $\sqrt{80}$

18. $\frac{1}{2}\sqrt{112}$ **19.** $\frac{1}{3}\sqrt{54}$ **20.** $\sqrt{2} \cdot \sqrt{8}$ **21.** $\sqrt{6} \cdot \sqrt{8}$

QUOTIENT PROPERTY Simplify the expression.

22. $\sqrt{\frac{7}{9}}$ **23.** $\sqrt{\frac{11}{16}}$ **24.** $2\sqrt{\frac{5}{4}}$ **25.** $18\sqrt{\frac{5}{81}}$

26. $2\sqrt{\frac{10}{2}}$ **27.** $3\sqrt{\frac{9}{3}}$ **28.** $8\sqrt{\frac{13}{9}}$ **29.** $3\sqrt{\frac{8}{64}}$

30. $4\sqrt{\frac{16}{4}}$ **31.** $3\sqrt{\frac{3}{16}}$ **32.** $5\sqrt{\frac{6}{2}}$ **33.** $8\sqrt{\frac{20}{4}}$

SIMPLIFYING Simplify the expression.

34. $\frac{\sqrt{32}}{\sqrt{25}}$ **35.** $\sqrt{\frac{27}{36}}$ **36.** $\frac{\sqrt{49}}{\sqrt{4}}$ **37.** $\frac{\sqrt{36}}{\sqrt{9}}$

38. $\frac{\sqrt{9}}{\sqrt{49}}$ **39.** $\frac{\sqrt{48}}{\sqrt{81}}$ **40.** $\frac{\sqrt{64}}{\sqrt{16}}$ **41.** $\frac{\sqrt{120}}{\sqrt{4}}$

STUDENT HELP

➤ **HOMEWORK HELP**
Example 1: Exs. 10–21
Example 2: Exs. 22–41
Example 3: Exs. 42–57

42. $\frac{1}{2}\sqrt{32} \cdot \sqrt{2}$ **43.** $3\sqrt{63} \cdot \sqrt{4}$ **44.** $\sqrt{9} \cdot 4\sqrt{25}$ **45.** $-2\sqrt{27} \cdot \sqrt{3}$

46. $\sqrt{7} \cdot \frac{\sqrt{18}}{\sqrt{2}}$ **47.** $-\sqrt{4} \cdot \frac{\sqrt{81}}{\sqrt{36}}$ **48.** $\frac{\sqrt{10} \cdot \sqrt{16}}{\sqrt{5}}$ **49.** $\frac{-2\sqrt{20}}{\sqrt{100}}$

STUDENT HELP

► **Skills Review**
For help with area of
geometric figures,
see pp. 790–791.

GEOMETRY **CONNECTION** **Find the area of the figure. Give both the exact answer in simplified form and the decimal approximation rounded to the nearest hundredth.**

50.

51.

52.

🌐 **BODY SURFACE AREA In Exercises 53 and 54, use the following information.**

Physicians can approximate the Body Surface Area of an adult (in square meters) using an index called *BSA* where *H* is height in centimeters and *W* is weight in kilograms.

Body Surface Area: $\sqrt{\dfrac{HW}{3600}}$

53. Find the *BSA* of a person who is 180 centimeters tall and weighs 75 kilograms.

54. Find the *BSA* of a person who is 160 centimeters tall and weighs 50 kilograms.

🌐 **TSUNAMI In Exercises 55–57, use the following information.**

A *tsunami* is a destructive, fast-moving ocean wave that is caused by an undersea earthquake, landslide, or volcano. The Pacific Tsunami Warning Center is responsible for monitoring earthquakes that could potentially cause tsunamis in the Pacific Ocean. Through measuring the water level and calculating the speed of a tsunami, scientists can predict arrival times of tsunamis.

The speed *s* (in meters per second) at which a tsunami moves is determined by the depth *d* (in meters) of the ocean.

$s = \sqrt{gd}$, where *g* is 9.8 meters per second per second

55. Find the speed of a tsunami in a region of the ocean that is 1000 meters deep. Write the result in simplified form.

56. Find the speed of a tsunami in a region of the ocean that is 4000 meters deep. Write the result in simplified form.

57. **CRITICAL THINKING** Is the speed of a tsunami at a depth of 4000 meters four times the speed of a tsunami at 1000 meters? Explain why or why not.

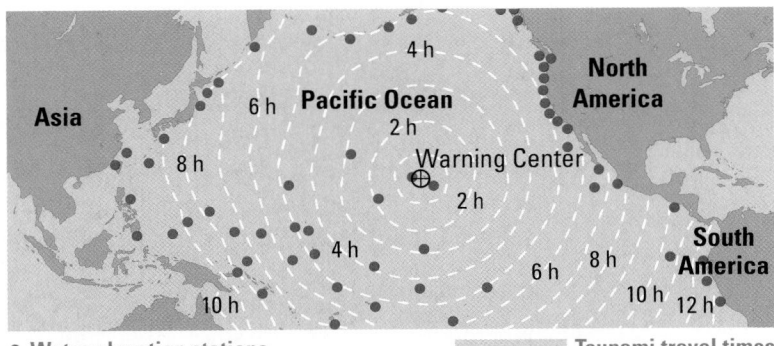

● Water elevation stations   ┄┄┄┄┄ Tsunami travel times
(in hours) to Honolulu, Hawaii

58. MULTIPLE CHOICE Which is the simplified form of $4\dfrac{\sqrt{125}}{\sqrt{25}}$?

(A) $2\sqrt{5}$　　　(B) $4\sqrt{5}$　　　(C) $20\sqrt{5}$　　　(D) $\dfrac{4\sqrt{5}}{5}$

59. MULTIPLE CHOICE Which is the simplified form of $33\sqrt{\dfrac{2}{121}}$?

(A) $\dfrac{2\sqrt{33}}{\sqrt{11}}$　　　(B) $33\sqrt{2}$　　　(C) $3\sqrt{2}$　　　(D) $\dfrac{3\sqrt{2}}{\sqrt{11}}$

60. MULTIPLE CHOICE Which is the simplified form of $\dfrac{6\sqrt{52}}{\sqrt{2}\cdot\sqrt{8}}$?

(A) $\dfrac{3\sqrt{13}}{\sqrt{2}}$　　　(B) $3\sqrt{13}$　　　(C) $3\sqrt{26}$　　　(D) $\dfrac{6\sqrt{13}}{\sqrt{2}}$

★ **Challenge**

EXTENSION: FRACTIONAL EXPONENTS Sometimes $\sqrt{3}$ is written as $3^{1/2}$.

61. You can obtain a graphical representation of the relationship $2^{1/2} = \sqrt{2}$ by investigating the graph of $f(x) = 2^x$.

　　a. Graph $f(x) = 2^x$.

　　b. Use the *Trace* feature to find values of f when $x = \dfrac{1}{2}$.

　　c. Compare the value from part (b) with the value of $\sqrt{2}$.

EXTRA CHALLENGE
www.mcdougallittell.com

Using the fact that $x^{1/2} = \sqrt{x}$, rewrite in simplest radical form.

62. $6x^{1/2}$　　　　**63.** $x^{1/2} \cdot 4\sqrt{2}$　　　　**64.** $18^{1/2}x \cdot 9x^{1/2}x$

MIXED REVIEW

GRAPHING EQUATIONS Use a table of values to graph the equation.
(Review 4.2 for 9.3)

65. $y = -x + 5$　　　**66.** $y = x - 7$　　　**67.** $y = 3x - 1$

EVALUATING EXPRESSIONS Simplify the expression. Then evaluate the expression when $a = 1$ and $b = 2$. (Review 8.1)

68. $\left(a^3\right)^2$　　　**69.** $b^6 \cdot b^2$　　　**70.** $\left(a^3b\right)^4$

REWRITING EXPRESSIONS Rewrite the expression using positive exponents. (Review 8.2)

71. $\dfrac{1}{2x^{-5}}$　　　**72.** $\dfrac{1}{4x^{-7}}$　　　**73.** $x^{-4}y^3$　　　**74.** $6x^{-2}y^{-6}$

75. **BUSINESS** From 1994 to 1999, the sales for a chain of home furnishing stores increased by about the same annual rate. The sales S (in millions of dollars) in year t can be modeled by $S = 455\left(\dfrac{13}{10}\right)^t$ where t represents years since 1994. Find the ratio of 1999 sales to 1995 sales. (Review 8.3)

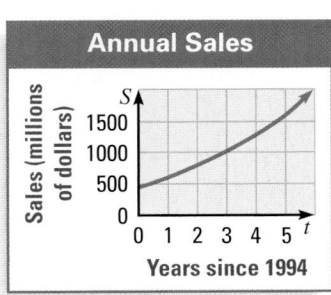

Annual Sales

Sales (millions of dollars)

Years since 1994

○ ACTIVITY 9.3

Developing Concepts

GROUP ACTIVITY
Work in a small group.

MATERIALS
graphing calculator

STUDENT HELP

▸ **KEYSTROKE**
HELP

See keystrokes for
several models of
calculators at
www.mcdougallittell.com

Investigating Graphs of Quadratic Functions

▸ **QUESTION** How do the coefficients *a, b,* and *c* affect the shape of the graph of the quadratic function $y = ax^2 + bx + c$?

▸ **EXPLORING THE CONCEPT**

① Use a graphing calculator to graph $y = ax^2$ using $-2, -1, -0.5, 0.5, 1,$ and 2 as values of *a*. Adjust the viewing window if necessary. Discuss your results with others in your group.

Write a sentence that describes how the value of *a* affects the graph of $y = ax^2$.

② Use a graphing calculator to graph $y = x^2 + bx$ using $-4, -2, -1, 0, 1, 2,$ and 4 as values of *b*. Adjust the viewing window if necessary. Discuss your results with others in your group.

Write a sentence that describes how the value of *b* affects the graph of $y = x^2 + bx$.

③ Use a graphing calculator to graph $y = x^2 + c$ using $-5, -3, -1, 1, 3,$ and 5 as values of *c*. Adjust the viewing window if necessary. Discuss your results with others in your group.

Write a sentence that describes how the value of *c* affects the graph of $y = x^2 + c$.

▸ **DRAWING CONCLUSIONS**

ANALYZING GRAPHS From the graph, what can you tell about the *a, b,* and *c* values of the function?

1.

2.

3.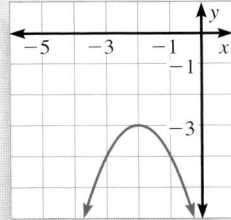

SKETCHING GRAPHS Sketch the graph of the function. Use the *a, b,* and *c* values.

4. $y = 5x^2$ **5.** $y = 5x^2 + 10x$ **6.** $y = 5x^2 + 10x - 5$

7. $y = -2x^2$ **8.** $y = -2x^2 - 7x$ **9.** $y = -2x^2 - 7x + 6$

10. GRAPHING FUNCTIONS Which of the quadratic functions could be shown by the graph at the right? Explain your reasoning.

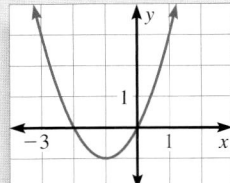

A. $y = x^2 - 2$ **B.** $y = x^2 + 2$

C. $y = 2x^2$ **D.** $y = x^2 + 2x$

Graphing Quadratic Functions

What _you should learn_

GOAL 1 Sketch the graph of a quadratic function.

GOAL 2 Use quadratic models in **real-life** settings, such as finding the winning distance of a shot put in **Example 3**.

Why _you should learn it_

▼ To model **real-life** parabolic situations, such as the height above the water of a jumping dolphin in **Exs. 65 and 66**.

GOAL 1 SKETCHING A QUADRATIC FUNCTION

A **quadratic function** is a function that can be written in the **standard form**

$$y = ax^2 + bx + c, \text{ where } a \neq 0.$$

Every quadratic function has a U-shaped graph called a **parabola**. If the leading coefficient a is positive, the parabola *opens up*. If the leading coefficient is negative, the parabola *opens down* in the shape of an upside down U.

The graph on the left has a positive leading coefficient so it opens up. The graph on the right has a negative leading coefficient so it opens down.

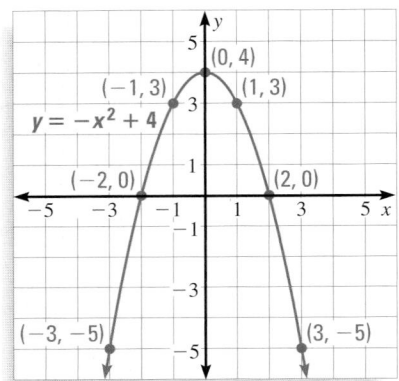

The **vertex** is the lowest point of a parabola that opens up and the highest point of a parabola that opens down. The parabola on the left has a vertex of $(0, 0)$ and the parabola on the right has a vertex of $(0, 4)$.

The line passing through the vertex that divides the parabola into two symmetric parts is called the **axis of symmetry**. The two symmetric parts are mirror images of each other.

GRAPH OF A QUADRATIC FUNCTION

The graph of $y = ax^2 + bx + c$ is a parabola.

- If a is positive, the parabola opens up.

- If a is negative, the parabola opens down.

- The vertex has an x-coordinate of $-\dfrac{b}{2a}$.

- The axis of symmetry is the vertical line $x = -\dfrac{b}{2a}$.

GRAPHING A QUADRATIC FUNCTION

STEP ❶ Find the *x*-coordinate of the vertex.

STEP ❷ Make a table of values, using *x*-values to the left and right of the vertex.

STEP ❸ Plot the points and connect them with a smooth curve to form a parabola.

EXAMPLE 1 *Graphing a Quadratic Function with a Positive a-value*

Sketch the graph of $y = x^2 - 2x - 3$.

SOLUTION

❶ Find the *x*-coordinate of the vertex when $a = 1$ and $b = -2$.

$$-\frac{b}{2a} = -\frac{-2}{2(1)} = 1$$

❷ Make a table of values, using *x*-values to the left and right of $x = 1$.

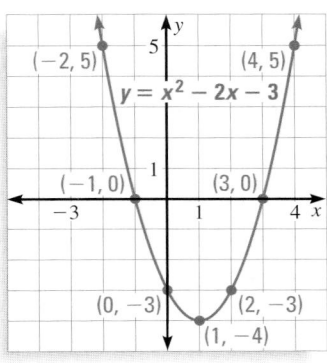

x	−2	−1	0	1	2	3	4
y	5	0	−3	−4	−3	0	5

❸ Plot the points. The vertex is $(1, -4)$ and the axis of symmetry is $x = 1$. Connect the points to form a parabola that opens up since *a* is positive.

EXAMPLE 2 *Graphing a Quadratic Function with a Negative a-value*

Sketch the graph of $y = -2x^2 - x + 2$.

SOLUTION

❶ Find the *x*-coordinate of the vertex when $a = -2$ and $b = -1$.

$$-\frac{b}{2a} = -\frac{-1}{2(-2)} = -\frac{1}{4}$$

STUDENT HELP

▶ Study Tip
If the *x*-coordinate of the vertex is a fraction, you can still choose whole numbers when you make a table.

❷ Make a table of values, using *x*-values to the left and right of $x = -\frac{1}{4}$.

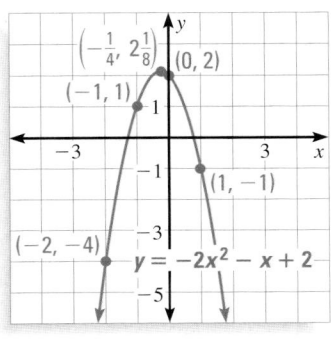

x	−2	−1	−$\frac{1}{4}$	0	1	2
y	−4	1	$2\frac{1}{8}$	2	−1	−8

❸ Plot the points. The vertex is $\left(-\frac{1}{4}, 2\frac{1}{8}\right)$ and the axis of symmetry is $x = -\frac{1}{4}$. Connect the points to form a parabola that opens down since *a* is negative.

GOAL 2 **USING QUADRATIC MODELS IN REAL LIFE**

When an object has little air resistance, its path through the air can be approximated by a parabola.

EXAMPLE 3 *Using a Quadratic Model*

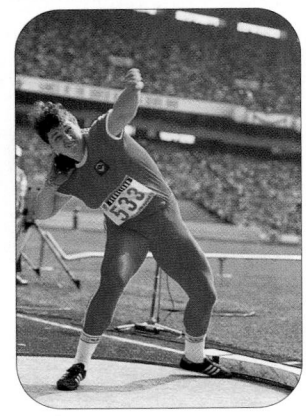

NATALYA LISOVSKAYA
In 1987, the women's world record in shot put was set by Lisovskaya. She also won an Olympic gold medal in 1988.

TRACK AND FIELD Natalya Lisovskaya holds the world record for the women's shot put. The path of her record-breaking throw can be modeled by $y = -0.01347x^2 + 0.9325x + 5.5$, where x is the horizontal distance in feet and y is the height (in feet). The initial height is represented by 5.5, the height at which the shot (a 4-kilogram metal ball) was released.

a. What was the maximum height (in feet) of the shot thrown by Lisovskaya?

b. What was the distance of the throw to the nearest hundredth of a foot?

SOLUTION

a. The maximum height of the throw occurred at the vertex of the parabolic path. Find the x-coordinate of the vertex. Use $a = -0.01347$ and $b = 0.9325$.

$$-\frac{b}{2a} = -\frac{0.9325}{2(-0.01347)} \approx 34.61$$

Substitute 34.61 for x in the model to find the maximum height.

$$y = -0.01347(34.61)^2 + 0.9325(34.61) + 5.5 \approx 21.6$$

▶ The maximum height of the shot was about 21.6 feet.

b. To find the distance of the throw, sketch the parabolic path of the shot. Because a is negative, the graph opens down. Use (35, 22) as the vertex. The y-intercept is 5.5. Sketch a symmetric curve.

The distance of the throw is the x-value that yields a y-value of 0. The graph shows that the distance was between 74 and 75 feet. You can use a table to refine this estimate.

Distance, x	74.5 ft	74.6 ft	74.7 ft	74.8 ft
Height, y	0.209 ft	0.102 ft	−0.006 ft	−0.114 ft

▶ The shot hit the ground at a distance between 74.6 and 74.7 feet.

GUIDED PRACTICE

Vocabulary Check ✔

1. Identify the values of a, b, and c for the quadratic function in standard form $y = -5x^2 + 7x - 4$.

2. Why is the vertical line that passes through the vertex of a parabola called the axis of symmetry?

Concept Check ✔

3. Explain how you can decide whether the graph of $y = 3x^2 + 2x - 4$ opens up or down.

4. Find the coordinates of the vertex of the graph of $y = 2x^2 + 4x - 2$.

Skill Check ✔

Tell whether the graph opens up or down. Write an equation of the axis of symmetry.

5. $y = x^2 + 4x - 1$ **6.** $y = 3x^2 + 8x - 6$ **7.** $y = x^2 + 7x - 1$

8. $y = -x^2 - 4x + 2$ **9.** $y = 5x^2 - 2x + 4$ **10.** $y = -x^2 + 4$

Sketch the graph of the function. Label the vertex.

11. $y = -3x^2$ **12.** $y = -3x^2 + 6x + 2$ **13.** $y = -5x^2 + 10$

14. $y = x^2 + 4x + 7$ **15.** $y = x^2 - 6x + 8$ **16.** $y = 5x^2 + 5x - 2$

17. $y = -4x^2 - 4x + 12$ **18.** $y = 3x^2 - 6x + 1$ **19.** $y = 2x^2 - 8x + 3$

20. 🏀 **BASKETBALL** You throw a basketball whose path can be modeled by $y = -16x^2 + 15x + 6$, where x represents time (in seconds) and y represents height of the basketball (in feet).

  a. What is the maximum height that the basketball reaches?

  b. In how many seconds will the basketball hit the ground if no one catches it?

PRACTICE AND APPLICATIONS

STUDENT HELP

▶ **Extra Practice**
to help you master
skills is on p. 805.

PREPARING TO GRAPH Complete these steps for the function.

  a. Tell whether the graph of the function opens up or down.

  b. Find the coordinates of the vertex.

  c. Write an equation of the axis of symmetry.

21. $y = 2x^2$ **22.** $y = -7x^2$ **23.** $y = 6x^2$ **24.** $y = \frac{1}{2}x^2$

25. $y = -5x^2$ **26.** $y = -4x^2$ **27.** $y = -16x^2$ **28.** $y = 5x^2 - x$

29. $y = 2x^2 - 10x$ **30.** $y = -7x^2 + 2x$ **31.** $y = -10x^2 + 12x$

32. $y = 6x^2 + 2x + 4$ **33.** $y = 5x^2 + 10x + 7$ **34.** $y = -4x^2 - 4x + 8$

35. $y = 2x^2 - 7x - 8$ **36.** $y = 2x^2 + 7x - 21$ **37.** $y = -x^2 + 8x + 32$

38. $y = \frac{1}{2}x^2 + 3x - 7$ **39.** $y = 4x^2 + \frac{1}{4}x - 8$ **40.** $y = -10x^2 + 5x - 3$

41. $y = 0.78x^2 - 4x - 8$ **42.** $y = 3.5x^2 + 2x - 8$ **43.** $y = -10x^2 - 7x + 2.66$

STUDENT HELP

▶ HOMEWORK HELP
Example 1: Exs. 21–64
Example 2: Exs. 21–64
Example 3: Exs. 65–75

SKETCHING GRAPHS Sketch the graph of the function. Label the vertex.

44. $y = x^2$

45. $y = -2x^2$

46. $y = 4x^2$

47. $y = x^2 + 4x - 1$

48. $y = -3x^2 + 6x - 9$

49. $y = 4x^2 + 8x - 3$

50. $y = 2x^2 - x$

51. $y = 6x^2 - 4x$

52. $y = 3x^2 - 2x$

53. $y = x^2 + x + 4$

54. $y = x^2 + x + \frac{1}{4}$

55. $y = 3x^2 - 2x - 1$

56. $y = 2x^2 + 6x - 5$

57. $y = -3x^2 - 2x - 1$

58. $y = -4x^2 + 32x - 20$

59. $y = -4x^2 + 4x + 7$

60. $y = -3x^2 - 3x + 4$

61. $y = -2x^2 + 6x - 5$

62. $y = -\frac{1}{3}x^2 + 2x - 3$

63. $y = -\frac{1}{2}x^2 - 4x + 6$

64. $y = -\frac{1}{4}x^2 - x - 1$

DOLPHIN In Exercises 65 and 66, use the following information.
A bottlenose dolphin jumps out of the water. The path the dolphin travels can be modeled by $h = -0.2d^2 + 2d$, where h represents the height of the dolphin and d represents horizontal distance.

65. What is the maximum height the dolphin reaches?

66. How far did the dolphin jump?

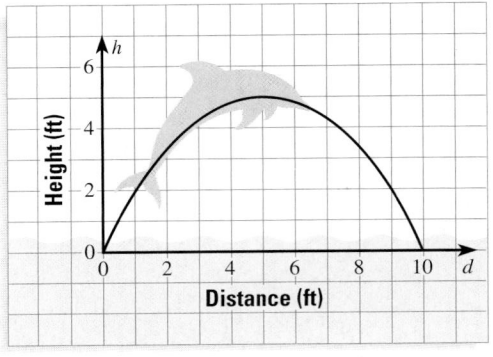

WATER ARC In Exercises 67 and 68, use the following information.
On one of the banks of the Chicago River, there is a water cannon, called the Water Arc, that sprays recirculated water across the river. The path of the Water Arc is given by the model

$$y = -0.006x^2 + 1.2x + 10$$

where x is the distance (in feet) across the river, y is the height of the arc (in feet), and 10 is the number of feet the cannon is above the river.

67. What is the maximum height of the water sprayed from the Water Arc?

68. How far across the river does the water land?

GOLD PRODUCTION In Exercises 69–71, use the following information.
In Ghana from 1980 to 1995, the annual production of gold G in thousands of ounces can be modeled by $G = 12t^2 - 103t + 434$, where t is the number of years since 1980.

69. From 1980 to 1995, during which years was the production of gold in Ghana decreasing?

70. From 1980 to 1995, during which years was the production of gold increasing?

71. How are the questions asked in Exercises 69 and 70 related to the vertex of the graph?

STUDENT HELP

INTERNET
HOMEWORK HELP
Visit our Web site
www.mcdougallittell.com
for help with Exs. 72–75.

TABLE TENNIS **In Exercises 72–75, use the following information.**
Suppose a table-tennis ball is hit in such a way that its path can be modeled by $h = -4.9t^2 + 2.07t$, where h is the height in meters above the table and t is the time in seconds.

72. Estimate the maximum height reached by the table-tennis ball. Round to the nearest tenth.

73. About how many seconds did it take for the table-tennis ball to reach its maximum height after its initial bounce? Round to the nearest tenth.

74. About how many seconds did it take for the table-tennis ball to travel from the initial bounce to land on the other side of the net? Round to the nearest tenth.

75. CRITICAL THINKING What factors would change the path of the table-tennis ball? What combination of factors would result in the table-tennis ball bouncing the highest? What combination of factors would result in the table-tennis ball bouncing the lowest?

Test Preparation

76. 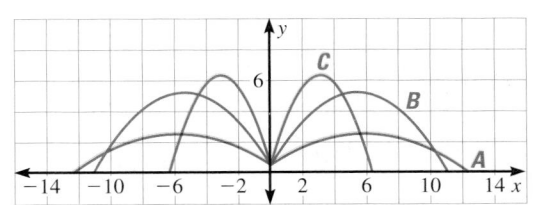 **MULTI-STEP PROBLEM** A sprinkler can eject water at an angle of 35°, 60°, or 75° with the ground. For these settings, the paths of the water can be modeled by the equations below where x and y are measured in feet.

35°: $y = -0.06x^2 + 0.70x + 0.5$

60°: $y = -0.16x^2 + 1.73x + 0.5$

75°: $y = -0.60x^2 + 3.73x + 0.5$

a. Find the maximum height of the water for each setting.

b. Find how far from the sprinkler the water reaches for each setting.

c. CRITICAL THINKING Do you think there is an angle setting for the sprinkler that will reach farther than any of the settings above? How do the angle and reach represented by the graph of $y = -0.08x^2 + x + 0.5$ compare with the others? What angle setting would reach the least distance?

★ **Challenge**

77. UNDERSTANDING GRAPHS Sketch the graphs of the three functions in the same coordinate plane. Describe how the three graphs are related.

a. $y = x^2 + x + 1$
$y = \frac{1}{2}x^2 + x + 1$
$y = 2x^2 + x + 1$

b. $y = x^2 - 1x + 1$
$y = x^2 - 5x + 1$
$y = x^2 - 10x + 1$

c. $y = x^2 - x + 1$
$y = x^2 - x + 3$
$y = x^2 - x - 2$

78. How does a change in the value of a change the graph of $y = ax^2 + bx + c$?

79. How does a change in the value of b change the graph of $y = ax^2 + bx + c$?

EXTRA CHALLENGE

www.mcdougallittell.com

80. How does a change in the value of c change the graph of $y = ax^2 + bx + c$?

MIXED REVIEW

GRAPHING Write the equation in slope-intercept form, and then graph the equation. Label the *x*- and *y*-intercepts on the graph. (Review 4.6 for 9.4)

81. $-3x + y + 6 = 0$

82. $-x + y - 7 = 0$

83. $4x + 2y - 12 = 0$

84. $x + 2y - 7 = 5x + 1$

GRAPHING LINEAR INEQUALITIES Graph the system of linear inequalities. (Review 7.6)

85. $x - 3y \geq 3$
$x - 3y \leq 12$

86. $x + y \leq 5$
$x \geq 2$
$y \geq 0$

87. $x + y < 10$
$2x + y > 10$
$x - y < 2$

SIMPLIFYING EXPRESSIONS Simplify. Write your answer as a power or as an expression containing powers. (Review 8.1)

88. $4^5 \cdot 4^8$

89. $(3^3)^2$

90. $(3^6)^3$

91. $a \cdot a^5$

92. $(3b^4)^2$

93. $6x \cdot (6x)^2$

94. $(3t)^3(-t^4)$

95. $(-3a^2b^2)^3$

SCIENTIFIC NOTATION Rewrite the number in scientific notation. (Review 8.4)

96. 0.0012

97. $987,000$

98. $3,984,328$

99. $1,229,000,000$

100. 0.000432

101. 0.00999

QUIZ 1

Evaluate the expression. Give the exact value if possible. Otherwise, approximate to the nearest hundredth. (Review 9.1)

1. $\sqrt{144}$

2. $-\sqrt{196}$

3. $-\sqrt{676}$

4. $-\sqrt{27}$

5. $\sqrt{6}$

6. $\sqrt{1.5}$

7. $\sqrt{0.16}$

8. $\sqrt{2.25}$

Solve the equation. (Review 9.1)

9. $x^2 = 169$

10. $4x^2 = 64$

11. $12x^2 = 120$

12. $-6x^2 = -48$

Simplify the expression. (Review 9.2)

13. $\sqrt{18}$

14. $\sqrt{5} \cdot \sqrt{20}$

15. $\dfrac{2\sqrt{121}}{\sqrt{4}}$

16. $\sqrt{\dfrac{45}{36}}$

Tell whether the graph of the function opens up or down. Find the coordinates of the vertex. Write the equation of the axis of symmetry of the function. (Review 9.3)

17. $y = x^2 + 2x - 11$

18. $y = 2x^2 - 8x - 6$

19. $y = 3x^2 + 6x - 10$

20. $y = \frac{1}{2}x^2 + 5x - 3$

21. $y = 7x^2 - 7x + 7$

22. $y = x^2 + 9x$

Sketch a graph of the function. (Review 9.3)

23. $y = -x^2 + 5x - 5$

24. $y = 3x^2 + 3x + 1$

25. $y = -2x^2 + x - 3$

● ACTIVITY 9.3

Using Technology

MATERIALS
CBL (optional)

Graphing Quadratic Curves of Best Fit

▶ **EXAMPLE**

A falling object is dropped from a height of 5.23 feet. Using a CBL unit, the height of the object was recorded. Use a graphing calculator to find a quadratic model for the data.

Time	0.0	0.04	0.12	0.16	0.22	0.26	0.32	0.36	0.41
Height	5.23	5.16	4.85	4.63	4.20	3.85	3.23	2.77	1.98

▶ **SOLUTION**

1 Let L_1 represent time (x) and L_2 represent height (y). Enter the ordered pairs.

2 Set the viewing window so the range of x is from 0 to 1 and the range of y is from 0 to 6. Make a scatter plot.

3 Use quadratic regression to find a quadratic model. Approximate to the nearest hundredths place.

4 Graph the equation $y = -16.80x^2 - 0.90x + 5.22$ with the initial points.

QuadReg
$y = ax^2 + bx + c$
a = -16.80264011
b = -.8974844214
c = 5.218564216

▶ From the scatter plot and the curve, you can see that the data appear to be part of a parabola that opens downward.

▶ **EXERCISES**

In Exercises 1 and 2, find the best-fitting quadratic model for the points.

1. (1, 16), (3, 138), (5, 366), (7, 652), (9, 970), (11, 1310), (13, 1660)

2. (3.9, −2.8), (5.1, −8.2), (6.3, −16.3), (−3.1, −16.1), (−2.8, −8.9), (−1.3, −2.5), (0, 2), (1.8, 4.1), (2.7, 2.8)

3. If you have access to a CBL unit, collect data for three different falling objects such as a basketball, a baseball, and a table-tennis ball. Find a quadratic model for the height of each object. Are the values of a very different for different objects?

Solving Quadratic Equations by Graphing

What you should learn

GOAL 1 Solve a quadratic equation graphically.

GOAL 2 Use quadratic models in **real-life** settings, such as the consumption of Swiss cheese in the United States in **Ex. 52**.

Why you should learn it

▼ To make predictions with **real-life** situations, such as the length of a shot put in **Example 4**.

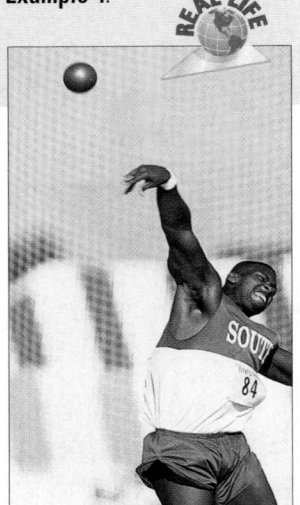

GOAL 1 SOLVING QUADRATIC EQUATIONS GRAPHICALLY

In Lesson 4.7 you learned to use the x-intercept of a linear graph to estimate the solution of a linear equation. A similar procedure applies to quadratic equations.

SOLVING QUADRATIC EQUATIONS USING GRAPHS

The solution of a quadratic equation in one variable x can be solved or checked graphically with the following steps.

STEP 1 Write the equation in the form $ax^2 + bx + c = 0$.

STEP 2 Write the related function $y = ax^2 + bx + c$.

STEP 3 Sketch the graph of the function $y = ax^2 + bx + c$. The solutions, or **roots**, of $ax^2 + bx + c = 0$ are the x-intercepts.

EXAMPLE 1 *Representing a Solution Using a Graph*

Solve $\frac{1}{2}x^2 = 8$ algebraically. Represent your solutions as the x-intercepts of a graph.

SOLUTION

$\frac{1}{2}x^2 = 8$	Write original equation.
$x^2 = 16$	Multiply each side by 2.
$x = \pm 4$	Find the square root of each side.

Represent these solutions using a graph.

1 Write the equation in the form $ax^2 + bx + c = 0$.

$\frac{1}{2}x^2 = 8$	Rewrite original equation.
$\frac{1}{2}x^2 - 8 = 0$	Subtract 8 from each side.

2 Write the related function $y = ax^2 + bx + c$.

$$y = \frac{1}{2}x^2 - 8$$

3 Sketch the graph of $y = \frac{1}{2}x^2 - 8$. The x-intercepts are ± 4, which are the algebraic solutions.

STUDENT HELP

INTERNET **HOMEWORK HELP**
Visit our Web site
www.mcdougallittell.com
for extra examples.

EXAMPLE 2 *Solving an Equation Graphically*

Solve $x^2 - x = 2$ graphically. Check your solution algebraically.

SOLUTION

❶ Write the equation in the form $ax^2 + bx + c = 0$.

$$x^2 - x = 2 \qquad \text{Write original equation.}$$

$$x^2 - x - 2 = 0 \qquad \text{Subtract 2 from each side.}$$

❷ Write the related function $y = ax^2 + bx + c$.

$$y = x^2 - x - 2$$

❸ Sketch the graph of the function $y = x^2 - x - 2$.

From the graph, the x-intercepts appear to be $x = -1$ and $x = 2$.

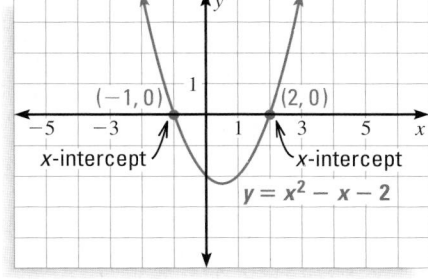

✓**CHECK** You can check this by substitution.

Check $x = -1$:	Check $x = 2$:
$x^2 - x = 2$	$x^2 - x = 2$
$(-1)^2 - (-1) \overset{?}{=} 2$	$2^2 - 2 \overset{?}{=} 2$
$1 + 1 = 2$	$4 - 2 = 2$

EXAMPLE 3 *Using a Graphing Calculator*

STUDENT HELP

► **Look Back**
For help with using a graphing calculator to graph equations, see p. 248.

 Use a graphing calculator to approximate the solution of $x^2 + 4x - 12 = 0$. Check your solution algebraically.

SOLUTION

$$x^2 + 4x - 12 = 0 \qquad \text{Write original equation.}$$

$$y = x^2 + 4x - 12 \qquad \text{Write related function.}$$

Use a graphing calculator to graph the function.

From the graph, you can see that the x-intercepts appear to be $x = 2$ and $x = -6$.

✓**CHECK** You can check this by substitution.

Check $x = 2$:	Check $x = -6$:
$x^2 + 4x - 12 = 0$	$x^2 + 4x - 12 = 0$
$2^2 + 4(2) - 12 \overset{?}{=} 0$	$(-6)^2 + 4(-6) - 12 \overset{?}{=} 0$
$4 + 8 - 12 = 0$	$36 + (-24) - 12 = 0$

Shot Put

EXAMPLE 4 *Comparing Two Quadratic Models*

A shot put champion performs an experiment for your math class. Assume that both times he releases the shot with the same initial speed but at different angles. The path of each put can be modeled by one of the equations below, where x represents the horizontal distance (in feet) and y represents the height (in feet).

Initial angle of 35°: $\qquad y = -0.010735x^2 + 0.700208x + 6$

Initial angle of 65°: $\qquad y = -0.040330x^2 + 2.144507x + 6$

Which angle results in a farther throw?

SOLUTION

Begin by graphing both models in the same coordinate plane. Use only positive x-values because x represents the distance of the throw.

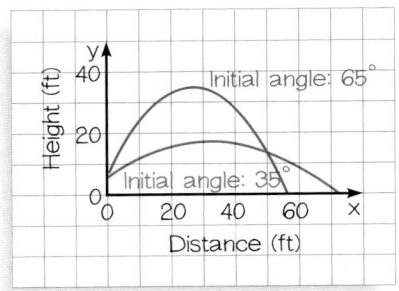

You can see that the 35° angle produced a greater distance.

· · · · · · · · ·

PARABOLIC MOTION It can be shown that an angle of 45° produces the maximum distance if an object is propelled from ground level. An angle smaller than 45° is better when a shot is released above the ground. If a shot is released from 6 feet above the ground, a 43° angle produces a maximum distance of 74.25 feet.

GUIDED PRACTICE

Vocabulary Check ✓

Concept Check ✓

1. Define the roots of a quadratic equation.

2. Write the steps for solving a quadratic equation using a graph.

Match the quadratic equation with the graph of its related function.

A. $x^2 = 3$

B. $x^2 + x = 4$

C. $-x^2 = -2x - 1$

3. **4.** **5.**

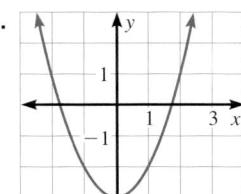

Skill Check ✓

Solve the equation algebraically. Check the solution graphically.

6. $3x^2 = 12$

7. $4x^2 = 16$

8. $5x^2 = 125$

9. $3x^2 = 27$

10. $8x^2 = 32$

11. $-2x^2 = -18$

Solve the equation graphically. Check the solutions algebraically.

12. $3x^2 = 48$

13. $x^2 - 4 = 5$

14. $-x^2 + 7x - 10 = 0$

15. $2x^2 + 6x = -4$

16. $\frac{1}{3}x^2 + x - 6 = 0$

17. $x - x^2 = -20$

PRACTICE AND APPLICATIONS

STUDENT HELP

▶ **Extra Practice**
to help you master
skills is on p. 805.

ESTIMATING ROOTS **For each quadratic equation, use the graph to estimate the roots of the equation.**

18. $-x^2 + 3x - 2 = 0$

19. $x^2 + 4x - 1 = 0$

20. $-3x^2 - 2x + 1 = 0$

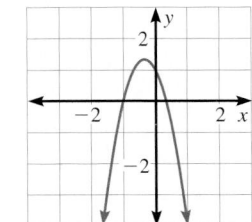

STUDENT HELP

▶ HOMEWORK HELP
Example 1: Exs. 21–32
Example 2: Exs. 18–20,
           33–44
Example 3: Exs. 45–50
Example 4: Exs. 51–56

CHECKING GRAPHICALLY **Solve the equation algebraically. Check the solutions graphically.**

21. $2x^2 = 32$

22. $4x^2 = 16$

23. $4x^2 = 100$

24. $\frac{1}{3}x^2 = 3$

25. $\frac{1}{4}x^2 = 36$

26. $\frac{1}{2}x^2 = 18$

27. $x^2 - 11 = 14$

28. $x^2 - 13 = 36$

29. $x^2 - 4 = 12$

30. $x^2 - 53 = 11$

31. $x^2 + 37 = 118$

32. $2x^2 - 89 = 9$

GRAPHICAL REPRESENTATION Represent the solution graphically. Check the solution algebraically.

33. $x^2 - x = 6$ **34.** $x^2 + 2x = 3$ **35.** $-x^2 + x = -2$

36. $-x^2 + 3x = -4$ **37.** $2x^2 + 4x = 6$ **38.** $3x^2 + 3x = 6$

39. $x^2 - 4x - 5 = 0$ **40.** $x^2 - x = 12$ **41.** $x^2 + 4x = 21$

42. $8x^2 - 4 = 4x$ **43.** $-7x^2 - 21x = 14$ **44.** $-2x^2 - 4x = -30$

APPROXIMATING SOLUTIONS Use a graphing calculator to approximate the solution of the equation.

45. $x^2 - 3x - 4 = 0$ **46.** $x^2 + 6x - 7 = 0$

47. $5x^2 + 5x - 1 = 0$ **48.** $-8x^2 - 24x + 32 = 0$

49. $\frac{1}{2}x^2 + 2x - 16 = 0$ **50.** $\frac{5}{4}x^2 + 15x + 40 = 0$

51. **SHOT PUT** A shot put champion releases the shot at a 55° angle. The path of the shot is modeled by the equation below where x represents the horizontal distance (in feet) and y represents the height (in feet).

$$y = -0.021895x^2 + 1.428148x + 6$$

How far does the shot travel? Assume the initial speed is the same as in Example 4. Compare the results with the results in Example 4.

52. **SWISS CHEESE** The consumption of Swiss cheese in the United States from 1970 to 1996 can be modeled by $P = -0.002t^2 + 0.056t + 0.889$, where P is the number of pounds per person and t is the number of years since 1970. According to the graph of the model, in what year would the consumption of Swiss cheese drop to 0? Is this a realistic prediction?

▶ Source: U.S. Department of Agriculture

RV SALES In Exercises 53–56, use the following information.
The number of recreational vehicles (RVs) sold in the United States from 1985 to 1991 can be modeled by $N = -9.5t^2 + 48.9t + 343.5$, where N represents the number of vehicles sold (in thousands) and t represents the number of years since 1985.

 DATA UPDATE of Recreation Vehicle Industry Association data at www.mcdougallittell.com

53. Sketch a graph of the model for positive values of x and y.

54. Use the graph to estimate a positive root of the equation

$$0 = -9.5t^2 + 48.9t + 343.5.$$

55. According to the model, in what year will the number of RVs sold in the United States drop to 0?

56. Do you think this prediction is realistic? What factors might explain a decrease or an increase in the number of sales of recreational vehicles?

RECREATIONAL VEHICLES
Motorized homes, travel and camping trailers, and truck campers are all considered recreational vehicles.

57. MULTIPLE CHOICE What are the x-intercepts of $y = x^2 - 2x - 3$?

(A) 1 and -3 **(B)** -2 and -3 **(C)** 6 and -1 **(D)** 3 and -1

58. MULTIPLE CHOICE Choose the equation whose roots are shown in the graph below.

(A) $5x^2 - 1 = 0$

(B) $\frac{1}{5}x^2 - 5 = 0$

(C) $x^2 - 5 = 0$

(D) $\frac{1}{5}x^2 - 1 = 0$

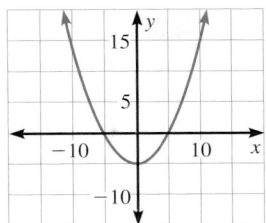

★ **Challenge**

SOLVING EQUATIONS WITH A GRAPHING CALCULATOR The solution of a quadratic equation can be found by graphing each side separately and locating the points of intersection. You may wish to consult page 532 for help in approximating solutions.

59. $3x^2 + 2x + 5 = 6x^2$

60. $-5x^2 + 4x = 2x^2 - 8$

61. $-2x^2 + 5x = 8x^2 - 2$

62. $-x^2 - 2 = 4x^2 + 6x - 3$

63. $0.75x^2 + 2.67x = 6.22x^2 - 4.1$

64. $-4.87x^2 + 1.44x = 5.22x^2 + 6x$

MIXED REVIEW

SOLVING LINEAR SYSTEMS Solve the system of linear equations if possible. Does the system have exactly *one solution, no solution,* or *infinitely many solutions*? (Review 7.5)

65. $-2x + 8y = 11$
$x + 6y = 2$

66. $4x + 5y = 37$
$-5x + 3y = 0$

67. $-2x + 2y = 4$
$x - y = -2$

68. $8x + 4y = -4$
$4x - y = -20$

69. $10x - 6y = -5$
$3y = 5x + 2$

70. $4y = -5x - 3$
$15x + 12y = 9$

EVALUATING EXPRESSIONS Evaluate the expression to the nearest hundredth. (Review 9.1 for 9.5)

71. $\dfrac{5 \pm 3\sqrt{6}}{2}$

72. $\dfrac{2 \pm 6\sqrt{3}}{3}$

73. $\dfrac{-3 \pm 2\sqrt{5}}{-1}$

74. $\dfrac{-2 \pm 4\sqrt{2}}{-2}$

SIMPLIFYING RADICAL EXPRESSIONS Simplify the radical expression. (Review 9.2)

75. $\sqrt{40}$

76. $\sqrt{24}$

77. $\sqrt{60}$

78. $\sqrt{200}$

79. $\frac{1}{2}\sqrt{80}$

80. $\frac{1}{3}\sqrt{27}$

81. $\frac{1}{8}\sqrt{32}$

82. $\frac{2}{3}\sqrt{300}$

83. 🌐 **LUNCH TIME** At lunch, you order 2 pasta dishes and 1 type of salad. Your friend orders 1 pasta dish and 2 types of salads. The restaurant charges the same price for each pasta dish and the same price for each salad. Your bill is $13.85 and your friend's bill is $9.85. How much did each pasta dish and each salad cost? (Review 7.4)

ACTIVITY 9.4

Using Technology

Approximating Solutions by Graphing

You can use the root or zero feature of a graphing calculator to approximate the solutions, or roots, of a quadratic equation.

▶ **EXAMPLE**

Approximate the roots of $2x^2 + 3x - 4 = 0$.

▶ **SOLUTION**

The four screens below show the steps in approximating the roots of an equation.

❶ Enter the related function $y = 2x^2 + 3x - 4$ into the graphing calculator.

❷ Adjust the viewing window so you can see the graph cross the x-axis twice. Graph the function.

❸ Choose the *Root* or *Zero* feature.

❹ Follow your graphing calculator's procedure to find one root.

▶ The approximate positive root is 0.85. Follow similar steps to find the negative root, −2.35.

▶ **EXERCISES**

APPROXIMATING ROOTS Use a graphing calculator to approximate both roots of the quadratic equation to the nearest hundredth.

1. $3x^2 - 20x + 5 = 0$

2. $-4x^2 + 6x + 7 = 0$

3. $-x^2 + 5x - 1 = 0$

4. $6x^2 + 4x - 5.1 = 0$

5. $-1.4x^2 + 5.2x - 4.8 = 0$

6. $2.87x^2 - 9.43x - 4.53 = 0$

7. $-0.53x^2 + 5x - 10.3 = 0$

8. $4.72x^2 + 8x - 7.65 = 0$

9.5 Solving Quadratic Equations by the Quadratic Formula

What you should learn

GOAL 1 Use the quadratic formula to solve a quadratic equation.

GOAL 2 Use quadratic models for **real-life** situations, such as the hot-air balloon competition in **Example 4**.

Why you should learn it

▼ To model **real-life** situations, such as the maximum height of a baseball in **Ex. 84**.

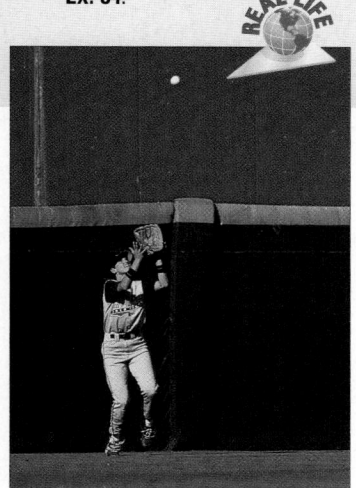

GOAL 1 USING THE QUADRATIC FORMULA

In Lesson 9.1 you learned how to solve quadratic equations of the form $ax^2 + c = 0$ by finding square roots. In this lesson you will learn how to use the **quadratic formula** to solve *any* quadratic equation.

THE QUADRATIC FORMULA

The solutions of the quadratic equation $ax^2 + bx + c = 0$ are

$$x = \frac{-b \pm \sqrt{b^2 - 4ac}}{2a}$$ when $a \neq 0$ and $b^2 - 4ac \geq 0$.

You can read this formula as "x equals the opposite of b, plus or minus the square root of b squared minus $4ac$, all divided by $2a$."

EXAMPLE 1 Using the Quadratic Formula

Solve $x^2 + 9x + 14 = 0$.

SOLUTION

Use the quadratic formula.

$1x^2 + 9x + 14 = 0$ **Identify $a = 1$, $b = 9$, and $c = 14$.**

$x = \dfrac{-9 \pm \sqrt{9^2 - 4(1)(14)}}{2(1)}$ **Substitute values in the quadratic formula.**

$x = \dfrac{-9 \pm \sqrt{81 - 56}}{2}$ **Simplify.**

$x = \dfrac{-9 \pm \sqrt{25}}{2}$ **Simplify.**

$x = \dfrac{-9 \pm 5}{2}$ **Solutions**

▶ The equation has two solutions:

$$x = \frac{-9 + 5}{2} = -2 \text{ and } x = \frac{-9 - 5}{2} = -7.$$

✓Check these solutions in the original equation.

Check $x = -2$:	Check $x = -7$:
$x^2 + 9x + 14 = 0$	$x^2 + 9x + 14 = 0$
$(-2)^2 + 9(-2) + 14 \overset{?}{=} 0$	$(-7)^2 + 9(-7) + 14 \overset{?}{=} 0$
$0 = 0$	$0 = 0$

STUDENT HELP

HOMEWORK
HELP

Visit our Web site
www.mcdougallittell.com
for extra examples.

EXAMPLE 2 *Writing in Standard Form*

Solve $2x^2 - 3x = 8$.

SOLUTION

$2x^2 - 3x = 8$	Write original equation.
$2x^2 - 3x - 8 = 0$	Rewrite equation in standard form.
$x = \dfrac{-(-3) \pm \sqrt{(-3)^2 - 4(2)(-8)}}{2(2)}$	Substitute values into the quadratic formula: $a = 2$, $b = -3$, $c = -8$.
$x = \dfrac{3 \pm \sqrt{9 + 64}}{4}$	Simplify.
$x = \dfrac{3 \pm \sqrt{73}}{4}$	Solutions

▶ The equation has two solutions:

$$x = \frac{3 + \sqrt{73}}{4} \approx 2.89 \text{ and } x = \frac{3 - \sqrt{73}}{4} \approx -1.39.$$

EXAMPLE 3 *Finding the x-Intercepts of a Graph*

Find the x-intercepts of the graph of $y = -x^2 - 2x + 5$.

SOLUTION

The x-intercepts occur when $y = 0$.

$y = -x^2 - 2x + 5$	Write original equation.
$0 = -x^2 - 2x + 5$	Substitute 0 for y.
$x = \dfrac{-(-2) \pm \sqrt{(-2)^2 - 4(-1)(5)}}{2(-1)}$	Substitute values into the quadratic formula: $a = -1$, $b = -2$, and $c = 5$.
$x = \dfrac{2 \pm \sqrt{4 + 20}}{-2}$	Simplify.
$x = \dfrac{2 \pm \sqrt{24}}{-2}$	Solutions

▶ The two solutions,

$$x = \frac{2 + \sqrt{24}}{-2} \approx -3.45 \text{ and}$$

$$x = \frac{2 - \sqrt{24}}{-2} \approx 1.45,$$

are the x-intercepts of the graph of
$y = -x^2 - 2x + 5$.

✓ Check your solution graphically.
You can see that the graph shows
the x-intercepts between -3 and -4
and between 1 and 2.

STUDENT HELP

→ **Study Tip**
Note that the x-intercepts
are x-coordinates of
points that are the same
distance from the axis of
symmetry.

$y = -x^2 - 2x + 5$

$x \approx -3.45$ $x \approx 1.45$

GOAL 2 USING QUADRATIC MODELS IN REAL LIFE

In Lesson 9.1 you studied the model for the height of a falling object that is *dropped*. For an object that is *thrown* down or up, the model has an extra term to take into account, the initial velocity. Problems involving these two models are called *vertical motion* problems.

VERTICAL MOTION MODELS

OBJECT IS DROPPED: $h = -16t^2 + s$

OBJECT IS THROWN: $h = -16t^2 + vt + s$

h = height (feet) t = time in motion (seconds)

s = initial height (feet) v = initial velocity (feet per second)

In these models the coefficient of t^2 is one half the acceleration due to gravity. On the surface of Earth, this acceleration is approximately 32 feet per second per second.

Remember that velocity v can be positive (for an object moving up), negative (for an object moving down), or zero (for an object that is not moving). Speed is the absolute value of velocity.

EXAMPLE 4   *Modeling Vertical Motion*

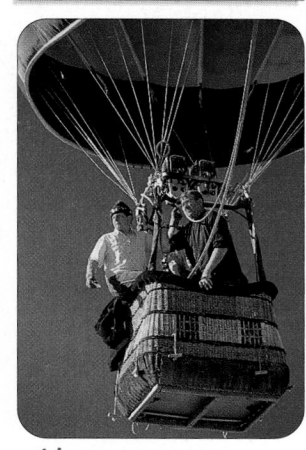

**HOT-AIR
BALLOONS**
The annual Albuquerque International Balloon Fiesta has several competitive events including the Field Target Event and Prize Grab. There is also a Special Shapes Rodeo and a night time Balloon Glow event.

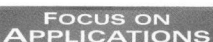 **APPLICATION LINK**
www.mcdougallittell.com

BALLOON COMPETITION You are competing in the Field Target Event at a hot-air balloon festival. You throw a marker down from an altitude of 200 feet toward a target. When the marker leaves your hand, its speed is 30 feet per second. How long will it take the marker to hit the target?

SOLUTION

Because the marker is thrown down, the initial velocity is $v = -30$ feet per second. The initial height is $s = 200$ feet. The marker will hit the target when the height is 0.

$h = -16t^2 + vt + s$ Choose the vertical motion model for a thrown object.

$h = -16t^2 + (-30)t + 200$ Substitute values for v and s into the vertical motion model.

$0 = -16t^2 - 30t + 200$ Substitute 0 for h. Write in standard form.

$t = \dfrac{-(-30) \pm \sqrt{(-30)^2 - 4(-16)(200)}}{2(-16)}$ Substitute values for a, b, and c into the quadratic formula.

$t = \dfrac{30 \pm \sqrt{13,700}}{-32}$ Simplify.

$t \approx 2.72$ or -4.60 Solutions

▸ The weighted marker will hit the target about 2.72 seconds after it was thrown. As a solution, -4.60 doesn't make sense in the problem.

GUIDED PRACTICE

Vocabulary Check ✓

1. What formula can you use to solve any quadratic equation?

Concept Check ✓

2. Explain how to use the quadratic formula to solve $-2x^2 + 5x = -7$.

3. What is the difference between the two models for vertical motion?

Skill Check ✓

Use the quadratic formula to solve the equation.

4. $x^2 + 6x - 7 = 0$　　**5.** $x^2 - 2x - 15 = 0$　　**6.** $x^2 + 12x + 36 = 0$

7. $4x^2 - 8x + 3 = 0$　　**8.** $3x^2 + x - 1 = 0$　　**9.** $x^2 + 6x - 3 = 0$

Write in standard form. Use the quadratic formula to solve the equation.

10. $2x^2 = -x + 6$　　**11.** $6x = -8x^2 + 2$　　**12.** $3 = 3x^2 + 8x$

13. $-14x = -2x^2 + 36$　　**14.** $-x^2 + 4x = 3$　　**15.** $4x^2 + 4x = -1$

Find the *x*-intercepts of the graph of the equation.

16. $y = x^2 - 11x + 24$　　**17.** $y = x^2 + 10x + 16$　　**18.** $y = 2x^2 + 4x - 30$

19. $y = 2x^2 + 6x - 9$　　**20.** $y = 5x^2 + 8x - 8$　　**21.** $y = 4x^2 + 8x - 1$

22. 🌐 **FIELD TARGET EVENT** From a hot-air balloon directly over a target, you throw a marker with an initial downward velocity of -40 feet per second from a height of 180 feet. How long does it take the marker to reach the target?

PRACTICE AND APPLICATIONS

STUDENT HELP

▶ **Extra Practice**
to help you master
skills is on p. 805.

FINDING VALUES Find the value of $b^2 - 4ac$ for the equation.

23. $x^2 - 3x - 4 = 0$　　**24.** $4x^2 + 5x + 1 = 0$　　**25.** $x^2 - 11x + 30 = 0$

26. $5w^2 - 3w - 2 = 0$　　**27.** $s^2 - 13s + 42 = 0$　　**28.** $3x^2 - 5x - 12 = 0$

29. $5x^2 + 5x + \frac{1}{5} = 0$　　**30.** $\frac{1}{2}a^2 + 5a - 8 = 0$　　**31.** $\frac{1}{4}v^2 - 6v - 3 = 0$

SOLVING EQUATIONS Use the quadratic formula to solve the equation.

32. $4x^2 - 13x + 3 = 0$　　**33.** $y^2 + 11y + 10 = 0$　　**34.** $7x^2 + 8x + 1 = 0$

35. $-3y^2 + 2y + 8 = 0$　　**36.** $6n^2 - 10n + 3 = 0$　　**37.** $9x^2 + 14x + 3 = 0$

38. $8m^2 + 6m - 1 = 0$　　**39.** $7x^2 + 2x - 1 = 0$　　**40.** $-6x^2 - 3x + 2 = 0$

41. $-\frac{1}{2}x^2 + 6x + 13 = 0$　　**42.** $-10a^2 + 3a + 2 = 0$　　**43.** $-2d^2 - 5d + 19 = 0$

STUDENT HELP

▶ HOMEWORK HELP
Example 1: Exs. 23–43
Example 2: Exs. 44–52
Example 3: Exs. 53–61
Example 4: Exs. 71–80

STANDARD FORM Write the quadratic equation in standard form. Solve using the quadratic formula.

44. $2x^2 = 4x + 30$　　**45.** $2 - 3x + x^2 = 0$　　**46.** $16 = -x^2 + 11x$

47. $5x - 1 = -6x^2$　　**48.** $2q^2 - 6 = -4q$　　**49.** $5z - 2z^2 + 15 = 8$

50. $-1 + 3x^2 = 2x$　　**51.** $-5c^2 + 9c = 4$　　**52.** $-16b = -8b^2 - 8$

FINDING INTERCEPTS Find the *x*-intercepts of the graph of the equation.

53. $y = 3x^2 - 6x - 24$ **54.** $y = 2x^2 - 6x - 8$ **55.** $y = 2x^2 - 2x - 12$

56. $y = -2x^2 + 6x + 9$ **57.** $y = x^2 + x - 4$ **58.** $y = x^2 + 7x - 2$

59. $y = -3x^2 - 2x + 1$ **60.** $y = -4x^2 + 8x - 2$ **61.** $y = -5x^2 + 5x + 5$

CHOOSING A METHOD Solve the quadratic equation by finding square roots or by using the quadratic formula. Explain why you chose the method.

62. $6x^2 + 20x + 5 = 0$ **63.** $m^2 = 32$ **64.** $x^2 - 625 = 0$

65. $4y^2 - 49 = 0$ **66.** $-2x^2 + 6x + 1 = 0$ **67.** $h^2 + 18h + 81 = 0$

68. $5x^2 = 25$ **69.** $9y^2 - 3y = 1$ **70.** $v^2 = 8v + 2$

 FIELD TARGET EVENT In Exercises 71–76, six balloonists compete in the Field Target Event at a hot-air balloon festival. Calculate the amount of time it takes for the marker to hit the target when thrown down from the given initial height (in feet) with the given initial velocity (in feet per second).

71. $s = 200; v = -50$ **72.** $s = 150; v = -25$ **73.** $s = 100; v = -10$

74. $s = 150; v = -33$ **75.** $s = 80; v = -40$ **76.** $s = 50; v = 0$

VERTICAL MOTION In Exercises 77–80, use a vertical motion model to find how long it will take for the object to reach the ground.

77. You drop keys from a window 30 feet above ground to your friend below. Your friend does not catch them.

78. An acorn falls 45 feet from the top of a tree.

79. A lacrosse player throws a ball upward from her playing stick with an initial height of 7 feet, at an initial speed of 90 feet per second.

80. You throw a ball downward with an initial speed of 10 feet per second out of a window to a friend 20 feet below. Your friend does not catch the ball.

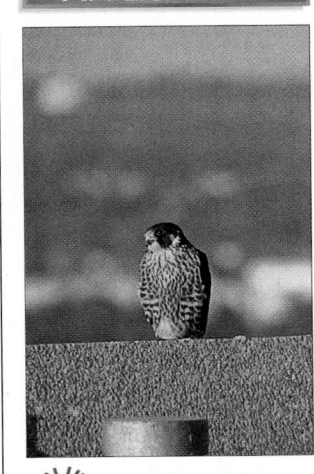
81. **PEREGRINE FALCON** A falcon dives toward a pigeon on the ground. When the falcon is at a height of 100 feet the pigeon sees the falcon, which is diving at 220 feet per second. Estimate the time the pigeon has to escape.

82. **RED-TAILED HAWK** A hawk dives toward a snake. When the hawk is at a height of 200 feet the snake sees the hawk, which is diving at 105 feet per second. Estimate the time the snake has to escape.

Falcon

100 ft

Pigeon

83. **BALD EAGLE** An eagle dives toward a mouse. When the eagle is at a height of 125 feet the mouse sees the eagle, which is diving at 145 feet per second. Estimate the time the mouse has to escape.

84. MULTI-STEP PROBLEM In parts (a)–(d), a batter hits a pitched baseball when it is 3 feet off the ground. After it is hit, the height h (in feet) of the ball at time t (in seconds) is modeled by

$$h = -16t^2 + 80t + 3$$

where t is the time (in seconds).

a. Find the time when the ball hits the ground in the outfield.

b. Write a quadratic equation that you can use to find the time when the baseball is at its maximum height of 103 feet. Solve the quadratic equation.

c. [calculator] Use a graphing calculator to graph the function. Use the zoom feature to approximate the time when the baseball is at its maximum height. Compare your results with those you obtained in part (b).

d. **CRITICAL THINKING** What factors change the path of a baseball? What factors would contribute to hitting a home run?

★ **Challenge**

85. VISUAL THINKING Write an equation of the axis of symmetry of the graph and show that it lies halfway between the two x-intercepts.

86. *Writing* Explain how you can use this two-part form of the quadratic formula

$$x = \frac{-b}{2a} \pm \frac{\sqrt{b^2 - 4ac}}{2a}$$

EXTRA CHALLENGE
www.mcdougallittell.com

to find the distance between the axis of symmetry of a parabola and either of its x-intercepts.

Ex. 85

MIXED REVIEW

EVALUATING EXPRESSIONS **Evaluate the expression.** (Review 1.3 for 9.6)

87. x^2 when $x = -5$ **88.** $-y^2$ when $y = -1$

89. $-4xy$ when $x = -2$ and $y = -6$ **90.** $y^2 - y$ when $y = -2$

INEQUALITIES **Solve the inequality and graph the solution.** (Review 6.3, 6.4)

91. $2 \leq x < 5$ **92.** $8 > 2x > -4$ **93.** $-12 < 2x - 6 < 4$

94. $-3 < -x < 1$ **95.** $|x + 5| \geq 10$ **96.** $|2x + 9| \leq 15$

SKETCHING GRAPHS **Sketch the graph of the function. Label the vertex.**
(Review 9.3)

97. $y = 6x^2 - 4x - 1$ **98.** $y = -3x^2 - 5x + 3$ **99.** $y = -2x^2 - 3x + 2$

100. $y = \frac{1}{2}x^2 + 2x - 1$ **101.** $y = 4x^2 - \frac{1}{4}x + 4$ **102.** $y = -5x^2 - 0.5x + 0.5$

103. 🌐 **RECREATION** There were 1.4×10^7 people who visited Golden Gate Recreation Area in California in 1996. On average, how many people visited per day? per month? ▶ Source: National Park Service (Review 8.4)

● ACTIVITY 9.5
Using Technology

Writing a Program for the Quadratic Formula

A graphing calculator or a computer can be programmed to use the quadratic formula to solve a quadratic equation. Both graphing calculators and computers use step-by-step instructions to perform operations.

▶ EXAMPLE

Write a graphing calculator program to solve the equation $5x^2 - 5.5x + 1.5 = 0$.

▶ SOLUTION

An algorithm is a step-by-step model. The algorithm below shows the steps needed when writing a program that uses the quadratic formula to solve a quadratic equation.

1 Enter values for a, b, and c.

2 Calculate the value of $b^2 - 4ac$.

3 If $b^2 - 4ac < 0$, display "No solution."

4 If $b^2 - 4ac \geq 0$, proceed to the next step.

5 Find the first solution: $\dfrac{-b + \sqrt{b^2 - 4ac}}{2a}$.

6 Display the first solution.

7 Find the second solution: $\dfrac{-b - \sqrt{b^2 - 4ac}}{2a}$.

8 Display the second solution.

```
PROGRAM:QUADFORM
:Prompt A,B,C
:B²-4AC→D
:If D<0
:Then
:Disp "NO
SOLUTION"
:Pause
```

Follow your graphing calculator's procedure to enter a program. Run the program. The program produces the solutions 0.6 and 0.5.

✓ Check these solutions in the original equation.

```
prgmQUADFORM
A=?5
B=?-5.5
C=?1.5
THE FIRST
SOLUTION IS...
              .6
```

▶ EXERCISES

QUADRATIC FORMULA Use your graphing calculator or a computer program to find the solutions of the quadratic equation.

1. $x^2 + x - 30 = 0$

2. $2x^2 + x - 21 = 0$

3. $x^2 + 4x + 4 = 0$

4. $x^2 - 6x + 10 = 0$

5. $-3x^2 - 6x - 4 = 0$

6. $x^2 - 3x + 3 = 0$

7. $0.25x^2 + 0.35x - 0.60 = 0$

8. $x^2 - 1.38x - 4.32 = 0$

9. $x^2 + 8.51x + 13.716 = 0$

10. $0.032x^2 + 0.712x - 9 = 0$

◉ ACTIVITY 9.6

Developing Concepts

Investigating Applications of the Discriminant

GROUP ACTIVITY
Work in a small group.

MATERIALS
• graph paper
• graphing calculator
  (optional)

▶ **QUESTION** How can you determine the number of solutions of a quadratic equation?

▶ **EXPLORING THE CONCEPT**

In Lesson 9.4 you learned that the solutions of a quadratic equation $ax^2 + bx + c = 0$ are the x-intercepts of the graph of the related function $y = ax^2 + bx + c$.

❶ Begin with the equation $x^2 + 3x - 2 = 0$. Graph the related function $y = x^2 + 3x - 2$.

❷ How many x-intercepts does your graph have?

❸ How many solutions does the equation $x^2 + 3x - 2 = 0$ have?

❹ Repeat **Steps 1–3** for each of the following equations.

$$x^2 - 6x + 9 = 0$$

$$x^2 + 3 = 0$$

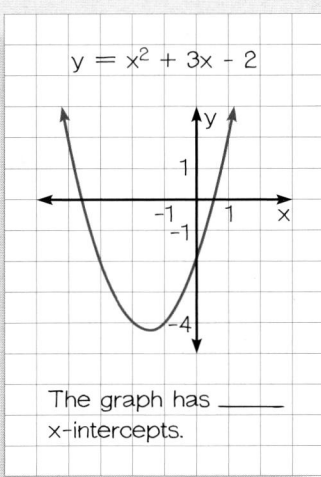

$y = x^2 + 3x - 2$

The graph has _____ x-intercepts.

❺ Compare the graphs you have drawn. How many intercepts did you find?

▶ **DRAWING CONCLUSIONS**

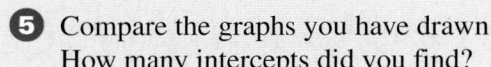

In Exercises 1–9, begin with the given quadratic equation. Follow Steps 1–3 for each equation.

1. $9x^2 - 24x + 16 = 0$ **2.** $2x^2 - 5x - 4 = 0$ **3.** $3x^2 - x + 2 = 0$

4. $-x^2 - 4x + 3 = 0$ **5.** $-5x^2 - 5x - 12 = 0$ **6.** $-2x^2 - 4x - 2 = 0$

7. $4x^2 + 8x - 2 = 0$ **8.** $-6x^2 + 2x - \frac{1}{2} = 0$ **9.** $x^2 + 2x - 1 = 0$

10. Compare your results in Exercises 1–9 with those of others in your group. How are the graphs alike? How are they different? How many intercepts did you find? How are the parabolas positioned with respect to the x-axis?

11. Each of the equations in Exercises 1–9 is in the form $ax^2 + bx + c = 0$. For each equation, calculate the value of $b^2 - 4ac$. Write the value next to the sketch of the related graph.

12. CRITICAL THINKING Use your results of Exercises 1–11 to write a rule that relates the number of solutions of a quadratic equation to the value of $b^2 - 4ac$.

STUDENT HELP

▶ **Look Back**
For help with using a graphing calculator to graph equations, see p. 248.

Applications of the Discriminant

What you should learn

GOAL 1 Use the discriminant to find the number of solutions of a quadratic equation.

GOAL 2 Apply the discriminant to solve **real-life** problems, such as financial analysis in **Exs. 29 and 30**.

Why you should learn it

▼ To model a **real-life** situation, such as storing your food while camping in **Example 4**.

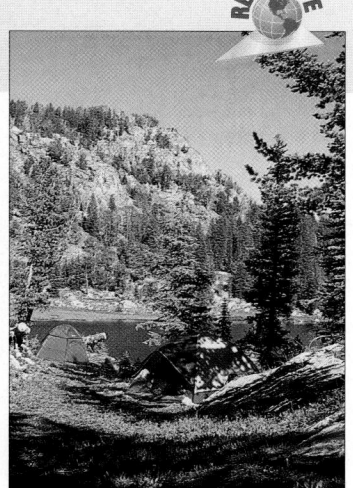

GOAL 1 **NUMBER OF SOLUTIONS OF A QUADRATIC**

In the quadratic formula, the expression inside the radical is the **discriminant**.

$$x = \frac{-b \pm \sqrt{b^2 - 4ac}}{2a}$$ ⟵ Discriminant

The discriminant $b^2 - 4ac$ of a quadratic equation can be used to find the number of solutions of the quadratic equation.

THE NUMBER OF SOLUTIONS OF A QUADRATIC EQUATION

Consider the quadratic equation $ax^2 + bx + c = 0$.

- If $b^2 - 4ac$ is positive, then the equation has two solutions.
- If $b^2 - 4ac$ is zero, then the equation has one solution.
- If $b^2 - 4ac$ is negative, then the equation has no real solution.

EXAMPLE 1 *Finding the Number of Solutions*

Find the value of the discriminant and use the value to tell if the equation has *two solutions*, *one solution*, or *no solution*.

a. $x^2 - 3x - 4 = 0$ **b.** $-x^2 + 2x - 1 = 0$ **c.** $2x^2 - 2x + 3 = 0$

SOLUTION

a. $b^2 - 4ac = (-3)^2 - 4(1)(-4)$ Substitute 1 for *a*, −3 for *b*, −4 for *c*.

$= 9 + 16$ Simplify.

$= 25$ Discriminant is positive.

▶ The discriminant is positive, so the equation has two solutions.

b. $b^2 - 4ac = (2)^2 - 4(-1)(-1)$ Substitute −1 for *a*, 2 for *b*, −1 for *c*.

$= 4 - 4$ Simplify.

$= 0$ Discriminant is zero.

▶ The discriminant is zero, so the equation has one solution.

c. $b^2 - 4ac = (-2)^2 - 4(2)(3)$ Substitute 2 for *a*, −2 for *b*, 3 for *c*.

$= 4 - 24$ Simplify.

$= -20$ Discriminant is negative.

▶ The discriminant is negative, so the equation has no real solution.

The number of x-intercepts of the graph of $y = ax^2 + bx + c$ is the same as the number of real solutions of the equation $ax^2 + bx + c = 0$.

EXAMPLE 2   *Finding the Number of x-Intercepts*

Use the related equation to find the number of x-intercepts of the graph of the function.

a. $y = x^2 + 2x - 2$ **b.** $y = x^2 + 2x + 1$ **c.** $y = x^2 + 2x + 3$

STUDENT HELP

INTERNET

HOMEWORK HELP
Visit our Web site
www.mcdougallittell.com
for extra examples.

SOLUTION

For each function, let $y = 0$. Then find the value of the discriminant.

a. $b^2 - 4ac = 2^2 - 4(1)(-2)$ $a = 1, b = 2, c = -2$

$\quad\quad\quad\quad = 4 + 8$ Simplify.

$\quad\quad\quad\quad = 12$ Discriminant is positive.

▶ The discriminant is positive, so the equation has two solutions *and* the graph has two x-intercepts.

b. $b^2 - 4ac = 2^2 - 4(1)(1)$ $a = 1, b = 2, c = 1$

$\quad\quad\quad\quad = 4 - 4$ Simplify.

$\quad\quad\quad\quad = 0$ Discriminant is zero.

▶ The discriminant is zero, so the equation has one solution *and* the graph has one x-intercept.

c. $b^2 - 4ac = 2^2 - 4(1)(3)$ $a = 1, b = 2, c = 3$

$\quad\quad\quad\quad = 4 - 12$ Simplify.

$\quad\quad\quad\quad = -8$ Discriminant is negative.

▶ The discriminant is negative, so the equation has no real solutions *and* the graph has no x-intercepts.

EXAMPLE 3   *Changing the Value of c*

STUDENT HELP

▶ **Look Back**
For help with sketching
a quadratic function,
see p. 518.

Sketch the graphs of the equations in Example 2 to check the number of x-intercepts. What effect does changing the value of c have on the graph?

SOLUTION

By changing the value of c, you can move the graph of $y = x^2 + 2x + c$ up or down in the coordinate plane.

If the graph is moved high enough, it will not have an x-intercept and the equation $x^2 + 2x + c = 0$ will have no real solution.

GOAL 2 USING THE DISCRIMINANT IN REAL LIFE

Camping

EXAMPLE 4 *Using the Discriminant*

You and a friend are camping in Glacier National Park in Montana. You want to hang a food pack from a high tree branch in order to protect your food from bears. You attach a stick to a rope and your friend is preparing to throw it over a tree branch that is 20 feet from the ground.

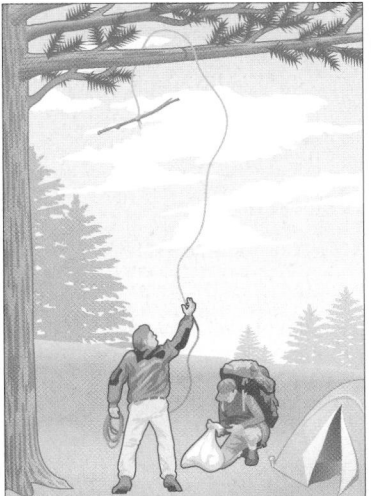

Not drawn to scale

a. Your friend can throw the stick upward with an initial velocity of 29 feet per second from an initial height of 6 feet. Will the stick reach the branch when it is thrown?

b. You can throw a stick upward with an initial velocity of 32 feet per second from the same initial height as your friend. Will the stick reach the branch when it is thrown?

SOLUTION

In both situations, you can use a vertical motion model $h = -16t^2 + vt + s$ where h is the height you are trying to reach, t is the time in motion, v is the initial velocity, and s is the initial height.

Because the initial height for you and your friend is 6 feet, the vertical motion model is $h = -16t^2 + vt + 6$. After you substitute for the initial velocity, evaluating the discriminant will tell you whether the stick reaches the tree branch.

a. Solve for an initial velocity v of 29. Use the discriminant to decide if the equation has a solution when $h = 20$.

$h = -16t^2 + vt + 6$	**Write vertical motion model.**
$20 = -16t^2 + 29t + 6$	**Substitute 20 for *h* and 29 for *v*.**
$0 = -16t^2 + 29t - 14$	**Rewrite in standard form.**

Evaluate $b^2 - 4ac = 29^2 - 4(-16)(-14)$. The discriminant is -55.

▶ Because the discriminant is negative, the equation has no solution. The stick thrown by your friend *will not* reach the branch.

b. Solve for an initial velocity v of 32. Use the discriminant to decide if the equation has a solution when $h = 20$.

$h = -16t^2 + vt + 6$	**Write vertical motion model.**
$20 = -16t^2 + 32t + 6$	**Substitute 20 for *h* and 32 for *v*.**
$0 = -16t^2 + 32t - 14$	**Rewrite in standard form.**

Evaluate $b^2 - 4ac = 32^2 - 4(-16)(-14)$. The discriminant is 128.

▶ Because the discriminant is positive, the equation has two solutions. The stick that you throw *will* reach the branch.

STUDENT HELP

 APPLICATION LINK
www.mcdougallittell.com

GUIDED PRACTICE

Vocabulary Check ✔

1. Write the quadratic formula and circle the part that is the discriminant.

Concept Check ✔

2. How can you use the discriminant to tell the number of solutions of $ax^2 + bx + c = 0$ and the number of x-intercepts of the graph of the equation?

Skill Check ✔

Find the discriminant for the equation. Then tell if the equation has *two solutions*, *one solution*, or *no real solution*.

3. $3x^2 - 2x + 5 = 0$　　　**4.** $-3x^2 + 6x - 3 = 0$　　　**5.** $x^2 - 5x - 10 = 0$

Match the discriminant with the graph.

A. $b^2 - 4ac = 2$　　　　**B.** $b^2 - 4ac = 0$　　　　**C.** $b^2 - 4ac = -3$

6. 　　**7.** 　　**8.**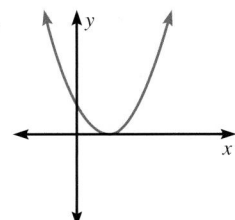

PRACTICE AND APPLICATIONS

STUDENT HELP

▶ **Extra Practice**
to help you master
skills is on p. 805.

USING THE DISCRIMINANT **Tell if the equation has *two solutions*, *one solution*, or *no real solution*.**

9. $x^2 - 3x + 2 = 0$　　　**10.** $2x^2 - 4x + 3 = 0$　　　**11.** $-3x^2 + 5x - 1 = 0$

12. $-\frac{1}{3}x^2 + x + 4 = 0$　　　**13.** $6x^2 - 2x + 4 = 0$　　　**14.** $3x^2 - 6x + 3 = 0$

NUMBER OF *X*-INTERCEPTS **Use the related equation to find the number of *x*-intercepts the graph of the function has. Then match the function with its graph.**

A. 　　**B.** 　　**C.**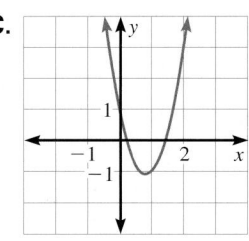

15. $y = 2x^2 + 4x + 2$　　　**16.** $y = 3x^2 - 5x + 1$　　　**17.** $y = x^2 + 2x + 5$

STUDENT HELP

▶ **HOMEWORK HELP**
Example 1: Exs. 9–14
Example 2: Exs. 15–20
Example 3: Exs. 21–23
Example 4: Exs. 24–26

INTERPRETING THE DISCRIMINANT **Consider the equation $\frac{1}{2}x^2 + \frac{2}{3}x - 3 = 0$.**

18. Evaluate the discriminant.

19. How many solutions does the equation have?

20. What does the discriminant tell you about the graph of $y = \frac{1}{2}x^2 + \frac{2}{3}x - 3$? Does the graph cross the x-axis?

CHANGING C-VALUES In Exercises 21–23, find values of c so that the equation will have two solutions, one solution, and no real solution. Then sketch the graph of the equation for each value of c that you chose.

21. $x^2 + 4x + c = 0$ **22.** $x^2 - 2x + c = 0$ **23.** $2x^2 + 3x + c = 0$

24. 🌐 **FIREFIGHTING** You see a firefighter aim a fire hose from 4 feet above the ground at a window that is 26 feet above the ground. The equation $h = -0.01d^2 + 1.06d + 4$ models the path of the water when h equals height in feet. Estimate, to the nearest whole number, the possible horizontal distances d (in feet) between the firefighter and the building.

🌐 **BASKETBALL** In Exercises 25 and 26, use the vertical motion model $h = -16t^2 + vt + s$ (p. 535) and the following information.

You and a friend are playing basketball. You can jump with an initial velocity of 12 feet per second. You need to jump 2.2 feet to dunk a basketball. Your friend can jump with an initial velocity of 14 feet per second. Your friend needs to jump 3.4 feet to dunk a basketball.

25. Can you dunk the ball? Can your friend? Justify your answers.

26. Suppose you can jump with an initial velocity of 11.5 feet per second and your friend can jump with an initial velocity of 15.5 feet per second. How, if at all, would this change your answers to Exercise 25?

🖩 **GOVERNMENT PAYROLL** In Exercises 27 and 28, use a graphing calculator and the following information.

For a recent 12-year period, the total government payroll (local, state, and federal) in the United States can be modeled by $P = 26t^2 + 1629t + 19{,}958$, where P is the payroll in millions of dollars and t is the number of years since the beginning of the 12-year period. ▶ Source: U.S. Bureau of the Census

27. Use the discriminant to show that the payroll will reach 80 billion dollars in the future according to the model.

28. Use a graphing calculator to find out how many years it will take for the total payroll to reach 80 billion dollars according to the model.

🖩 **FINANCIAL ANALYSIS** In Exercises 29 and 30, use a graphing calculator and the following information.

You are a financial analyst for a software company. You have been asked to project the net profit of your company. The net profit of the company from 1993 to 1998 can be modeled by $P = 6.84t^2 - 3.76t + 9.29$ where P is the profit in millions of dollars and t represents the number of years since 1993.

29. Use the model to predict whether the net profit will reach 650 million dollars.

30. Use a graphing calculator to estimate how many years it will take for the company's net profit to reach 475 million dollars according to the model.

31. MULTI-STEP PROBLEM You are on a team that is building a roller coaster. The vertical height of the first hill of the roller coaster is supposed to be 220 feet. According to the design, the path of the first hill can be modeled by $y = 0.039x^2 - 0.331x + 1.850$, where y is the vertical height in feet and x is the horizontal distance in feet. The first hill can use only 75 feet of horizontal distance.

a. Use the model to determine whether the first hill will reach a height of 220 feet.

b. What minimum horizontal distance is needed for the first hill to reach a vertical height of 220 feet?

c. *Writing* Can you build the first hill high enough? Explain your findings.

d. CRITICAL THINKING Is the shape of the graph the same as the shape of the hill? Why or why not?

★ **Challenge**

LOGICAL REASONING Consider the equation $ax^2 + bx + c = 0$ and use the quadratic formula to justify the statement.

32. If $b^2 - 4ac$ is positive, then the equation has two solutions.

33. If $b^2 - 4ac$ is zero, then the equation has one solution.

EXTRA CHALLENGE
www.mcdougallittell.com

34. If $b^2 - 4ac$ is negative, then the equation has no real solution.

MIXED REVIEW

GRAPHING FUNCTIONS Graph the function. (Review 4.8)

35. $f(x) = -x + 1$ **36.** $f(x) = -6x + 1$ **37.** $f(x) = 3x - 9$

SOLVING INEQUALITIES Solve the inequality. (Review 6.1)

38. $\frac{x}{6} \le -2$ **39.** $-\frac{x}{3} \ge 15$ **40.** $-12.3x > 86.1$ **41.** $11.2x \le 134.4$

SKETCHING GRAPHS Sketch the graph of the inequality. (Review 6.5 for 9.7)

42. $3x + y > 9$ **43.** $y - 4x < 0$ **44.** $-2x - y \ge 4$ **45.** $-y - 3x \le 6$

🌐 **COMPUTER MODEMS** In Exercises 46–48, use the following data which list the prices of several computer modems. (Review 6.6, 6.7)

$230, $220, $170, $215, $190, $200, $200, $150, $170

46. Use a stem-and-leaf plot to order the data from least to greatest.

47. Make a box-and-whisker plot of the data.

48. Use your results to describe the prices.

SOLVING GRAPHICALLY Solve the equation graphically. Check the results algebraically. (Lesson 9.4)

1. $x^2 - 3x = 10$ **2.** $x^2 - 12x = -36$ **3.** $3x^2 + 12x = -9$

USING THE FORMULA Use the quadratic formula to solve the equation. (Lesson 9.5)

4. $x^2 + 6x + 9 = 0$ **5.** $2x^2 + 13x + 6 = 0$ **6.** $-x^2 + 6x + 16 = 0$

7. $-2x^2 + 7x - 6 = 0$ **8** $-3x^2 - 5x + 12 = 0$ **9** $5x^2 + 8x + 3 = 0$

USING THE DISCRIMINANT Tell if the equation has *two solutions, one solution*, or *no real solution*. (Lesson 9.6)

10. $x^2 - 15x + 56 = 0$ **11.** $x^2 + 8x + 16 = 0$ **12.** $x^2 - 3x + 4 = 0$

13. 🌐 **THROWING A BASEBALL** Your friend is standing on a 45-foot balcony. He asks you to throw a baseball up to him. You throw the baseball with an initial upward velocity of 50 feet per second. Assuming that you released the baseball 6 feet above the ground, did it reach your friend? Explain. (Lesson 9.6)

MATH & History

History of the Quadratic Formula

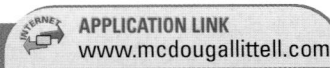

APPLICATION LINK
www.mcdougallittell.com

THEN

OVER 3700 YEARS AGO, in Mesopotamia, math exercises using quadratic equations were written on cuneiform tablets. A cuneiform tablet contains the math exercise:

A region consists of two nonoverlapping squares of total area 1000. The side of one square is two-thirds of the side of the other square, diminished by ten. What are the sides of the two squares?

1. Use the equations $x^2 + y^2 = 1000$ and $y = \frac{2}{3}x - 10$ to write a quadratic equation to find the length of a side x of the figure.

2. Use the discriminant to find the number of solutions. How many reasonable solutions are there?

3. Solve the quadratic equation. What are the lengths of both sides of the figure?

TODAY, there are many modern applications of quadratic equations. NASA relies on aircraft that fly in a parabolic arc in which to train astronauts.

NOW

Cuneiform tablets record knowledge of quadratic equations.

c. 1775 B.C.

1535 A.D.

Mathematician Niccolo Tartaglia solves cubic equations.

Astronaut Mary Cleave trains in a low gravity environment.

1985

low gravity

Altitude

Horizontal distance

9.6 *Applications of the Discriminant*   **547**

9.7 Graphing Quadratic Inequalities

What you should learn

GOAL 1 Sketch the graph of a quadratic inequality.

GOAL 2 Use quadratic inequalities as **real-life** models, as in bridge building in **Example 4**.

Why you should learn it

▼ To model a **real-life** situation such as the height of the two towers on the Golden Gate Bridge in **Ex. 32**.

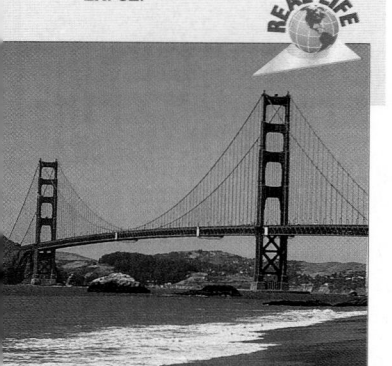

GOAL 1 GRAPHING A QUADRATIC INEQUALITY

In this lesson you will study the following types of **quadratic inequalities**.

$$y < ax^2 + bx + c \qquad\qquad y \le ax^2 + bx + c$$
$$y > ax^2 + bx + c \qquad\qquad y \ge ax^2 + bx + c$$

The **graph** of a quadratic inequality consists of the graph of all ordered pairs (x, y) that are solutions of the inequality.

EXAMPLE 1 *Checking Points*

Sketch the graph of $y = x^2 - 3x - 3$. Plot and label the points $A\ (3, 2)$, $B\ (1, 4)$, and $C\ (4, -3)$. Tell whether each point lies inside or outside the parabola.

SOLUTION

① Sketch the graph of $y = x^2 - 3x - 3$.

② Plot and label the points $A(3, 2)$, $B(1, 4)$, and $C(4, -3)$.

   A and B lie inside the parabola while C lies outside.

· · · · · · · · ·

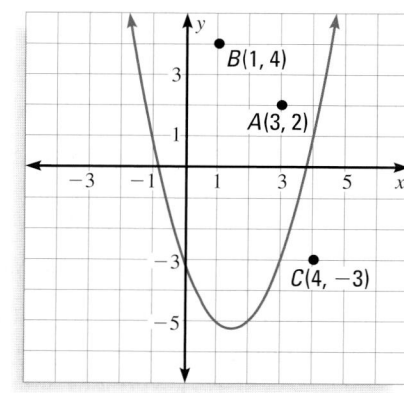

Checking points helps you graph quadratic inequalities by telling you which region to shade. You can use the following guidelines to graph any quadratic inequality.

SKETCHING THE GRAPH OF A QUADRATIC INEQUALITY

STEP ① Sketch the graph of the equation $y = ax^2 + bx + c$ that corresponds to the inequality. Sketch a dashed parabola for inequalities with $<$ or $>$ to show that the points on the parabola are *not* solutions. Sketch a solid parabola for inequalities with $\le$ or $\ge$ to show that the points on the parabola are solutions.

STEP ② The parabola you drew separates the coordinate plane into two regions. Test a point that is not on the parabola to find whether it is a solution of the inequality.

STEP ③ If the test point is a solution, shade its region. If not, shade the other region.

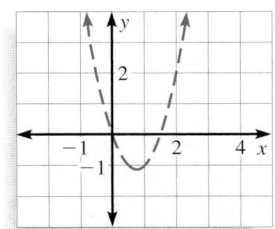

EXAMPLE 2 *Graphing a Quadratic Inequality*

Sketch the graph of $y < 2x^2 - 3x$.

SOLUTION

STEP ❶ Sketch the equation $y = 2x^2 - 3x$ that corresponds to the inequality $y < 2x^2 - 3x$. Use a dashed line since the inequality is $<$. The parabola opens up.

STUDENT HELP

▶ **Look Back**
For help with checking ordered pairs as solutions, see p. 360.

STEP ❷ Test a point that is not on the parabola, say $(0, 2)$.

$$y < 2x^2 - 3x \qquad \text{Write original inequality.}$$

$$2 \overset{?}{<} 2(0)^2 - 3(0) \qquad \text{Substitute 0 for } x \text{ and 2 for } y.$$

$$2 \not< 0 \qquad \text{2 is not less than 0.}$$

Because 2 is not less than 0, the ordered pair $(0, 2)$ is not a solution.

STEP ❸ The point $(0, 2)$ is not a solution and it is inside the parabola, so the graph of $y < 2x^2 - 3x$ is all the points outside, but not on, the parabola.

EXAMPLE 3 *Graphing a Quadratic Inequality*

Sketch the graph of $y \le -x^2 - 5x + 4$.

SOLUTION

STEP ❶ Sketch the equation $y = -x^2 - 5x + 4$ that corresponds to the inequality $y \le -x^2 - 5x + 4$. Use a solid line since the inequality is $\le$. The parabola opens down.

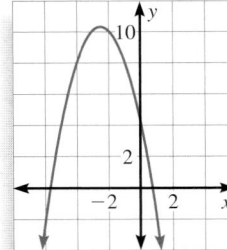

STEP ❷ Test a point that is not on the parabola, say $(0, 0)$.

$$y \le -x^2 - 5x + 4 \qquad \text{Write original inequality.}$$

$$0 \overset{?}{\le} -(0)^2 - 5(0) + 4 \qquad \text{Substitute 0 for } x \text{ and } y.$$

$$0 \le 4 \qquad \text{True.}$$

Because 0 *is* less than or equal to 4, the ordered pair $(0, 0)$ is a solution.

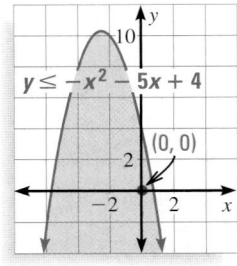

STEP ❸ The point $(0, 0)$ is a solution and it is inside the parabola, so the graph of $y \le -x^2 - 5x + 4$ is all the points inside or on the parabola $y = -x^2 - 5x + 4$.

EXAMPLE 4 *Using a Quadratic Inequality Model*

BRIDGE BUILDING The Akashi Kaikyo Bridge in Japan is the longest suspension bridge in the world. The shape of the main cable between the two main towers can be modeled by

$$y = 0.000188x^2 + 15$$

where x is the distance (in meters) from the center of the bridge and y is the height (in meters) above the road.

BRIDGE BUILDING
The Akashi Kaikyo
Bridge is part of a network of
bridges built to connect all of
Japan's four main islands. It
connects the cities of Kobe
and Awaji.

APPLICATION LINK
www.mcdougallittell.com

a. How high are the towers above the road?

b. Write a system of inequalities that describes the region under the main cable, above the roadbed, and between the main towers. Assume that the roadbed is modeled by $y = 0$. Graph the system.

SOLUTION

a. The diagram shows that the distance between the two towers is 1990 meters. Because the vertex of the parabola is at the center of the bridge, the x-coordinates of the tops of the towers are ±995. Substitute either value.

$y = 0.000188x^2 + 15$	**Write quadratic equation.**
$= 0.000188(\mathbf{995})^2 + 15$	**Substitute 995 for x.**
≈ 201.12	**Approximate with a calculator.**

▶ The towers are about 201 meters above the road.

b. The parabola $y = 0.000188x^2 + 15$ opens up. To include the region below the parabola and the main cable, use the inequality ≤.

Region below the cable: $y \leq 0.00188x^2 + 15$

Region between the towers: $-995 \leq x \leq 995$

Region above the roadbed: $y \geq 0$

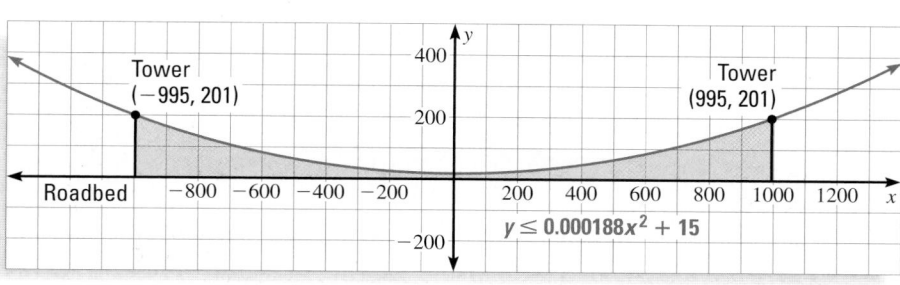

GUIDED PRACTICE

Vocabulary Check ✔

1. Give an example of each of the types of quadratic inequalities.

Concept Check ✔

2. Describe the steps used to sketch the graph of a quadratic inequality.

3. Is $(0, 3)$ inside or outside the graph of $y = x^2 + 3x + 2$?

Skill Check ✔ **Decide whether each labeled ordered pair is a solution of the inequality.**

4. $y < -x^2$

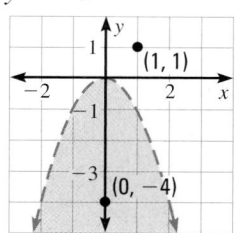

5. $y \geq x^2 - 2$

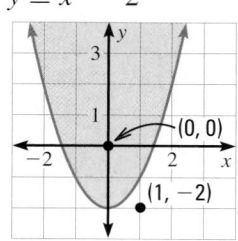

6. $y \leq 2x^2 + 5x$

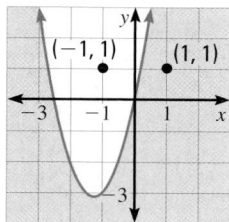

Sketch the graph of the inequality.

7. $y \leq x^2$

8. $y > -x^2 + 3$

9. $y < x^2 + 2x$

10. $y \geq x^2 - 2x$

11. $y > -2x^2 + 5x$

12. $y < 4x^2 - 2x + 1$

PRACTICE AND APPLICATIONS

SOLUTIONS **Decide whether the ordered pair is a solution of the inequality.**

13. $y \geq 2x^2 - x$, $(2, 6)$

14. $y < x^2 + 9x$, $(-3, 10)$

15. $y > 4x^2 - 7x$, $(2, -10)$

16. $y \geq x^2 - 13x$, $(-1, 14)$

MATCHING INEQUALITIES **In Exercises 17–22, match the graph with its inequality.**

A. $y \geq -2x^2 - 2x + 1$

B. $y > -2x^2 + 4x + 3$

C. $y \leq 2x^2 + x + 1$

D. $y \geq 4x^2 - 6x + 5$

E. $y < 2x^2 - x - 3$

F. $y > -4x^2 + 6x - 5$

17.

18.

19.

20.

21.

22.

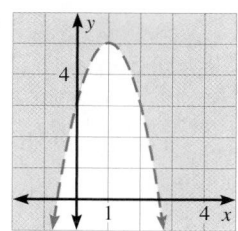

9.7 *Graphing Quadratic Inequalities* **551**

SKETCHING GRAPHS Sketch the graph of the inequality.

23. $y < -x^2 + x$ **24.** $y \geq x^2 - 3$ **25.** $y \geq x^2 - 5x$

26. $y < -x^2 - 3x - 1$ **27.** $y < x^2 + x + 8$ **28.** $y \leq -x^2 + 3x + 2$

29. $y > -4x^2 - 8x - 4$ **30.** $y \geq -4x^2 - 3x + 8$ **31.** $y \geq 2x^2 + 5x + 3$

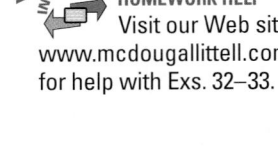

HOMEWORK HELP
Visit our Web site
www.mcdougallittell.com
for help with Exs. 32–33.

🌐 **GOLDEN GATE BRIDGE** **Use the following information for Exercises 32 and 33.**

The Golden Gate Bridge connects northern California to San Francisco. The vertical cables that are suspended from the main cable lie in the region given by $0 \leq y \leq 0.000112x^2 + 5$ where x is horizontal distance from the middle of the bridge (in feet) and y is vertical distance (in feet) above the road.

4200 ft

32. How high are the towers above the road?

33. Sketch a graph of the region between the towers and under the main cable.

🌐 **DIAMONDS** **In Exercises 34–38, use the equations below which represent the sample price y (in hundreds of dollars) of diamonds of x carats with different grades of flawlessness.**

Flawlessness	Equation
IF	$y = 82.12x^2 + 119.13x - 48.15$
VS2	$y = 38.88x^2 + 26.62x - 5.07$
I3	$y = 1.87x^2 + 14.83x - 2.3$

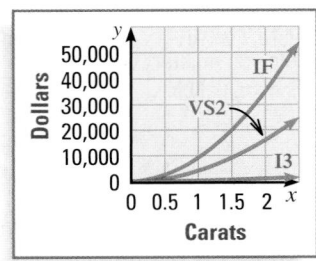

34. Which of the three grades of diamond is the least flawed? How do you know?

35. Which of the three grades of diamond is the most flawed? How do you know?

36. A two-carat diamond is selling for the wholesale price of $55,000. The diamond is described as having the highest quality. Describe the region in the graph that contains the point (2, 55,000). Is this the highest quality for a two-carat diamond? Explain.

37. The wholesale price of a one-carat diamond is $12,000. Assume that the price fairly represents the flawlessness of the diamond. Which region contains the point (1, 12,000)? What grade of flawlessness is the diamond?

A. $y > 1.87x^2 + 14.83x - 2.3$ **B.** $y < 1.87x^2 + 14.83x - 2.3$

38. You see a $\frac{1}{2}$-carat diamond on display for a wholesale price of $4000. Next to it is a two-carat diamond for a wholesale price of $12,000. Is the more expensive one necessarily less flawed?

39. MULTIPLE CHOICE Which ordered pair is *not* a solution of the inequality $y \geq 2x^2 - 7x - 10$?

Ⓐ $(0, -4)$　　Ⓑ $(-1, -1)$　　Ⓒ $(4, -13)$　　Ⓓ $(5, 15)$

40. MULTIPLE CHOICE Identify the graph of $y \leq 3x^2 + 2x - 5$.

Ⓐ　　Ⓑ　　Ⓒ　　Ⓓ

★ **Challenge**

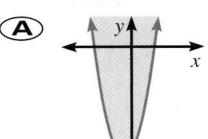 **MILK CONSUMPTION** **In Exercises 41–43, use the following information.**
The per capita consumption (pounds per person) of whole milk W and reduced fat milk R from 1980 to 1995 can be modeled by the equations below where t represents years since 1980. ▶ Source: U.S. Department of Agriculture

Whole milk: $W = 0.09t^2 - 5.29t + 114.69$

Reduced fat: $R = -0.23t^2 + 2.40t + 71.39$

41. Sketch a graph of each equation on the same coordinate plane.

42. Shade the region where the per capita consumption of reduced fat milk was greater than that of whole milk. What inequalities represent this region?

43. Find the points where the parabolas intersect. What does each of these points represent?

MIXED REVIEW

GRAPHING EQUATIONS **Graph the equation.** (Review 4.3, 9.3 for 9.8)

44. $y = x + 4$　　**45.** $3x + 6y = -18$　　**46.** $2x - 4y = 24$

47. $y = x^2 + x + 2$　　**48.** $y = -x^2 + 4x + 1$　　**49.** $y = 3x^2 - 2x + 6$

DIRECT VARIATION **The variables *x* and *y* vary directly. Use the given values to write an equation that relates *x* and *y*.** (Review 4.5)

50. $x = 6, y = 42$　　**51.** $x = 54, y = -9$　　**52.** $x = 7, y = 5$

53. $x = -13, y = -52$　　**54.** $x = \frac{3}{4}, y = 3$　　**55.** $x = 4.6, y = 1.2$

GRAPHING EXPONENTIAL EQUATIONS **Sketch the graph of the exponential equation.** (Review 8.5, 8.6)

56. $y = 2^x$　　**57.** $y = 0.5^x$　　**58.** $y = \frac{1}{2}(2)^x$

59. $y = 0.9^x$　　**60.** $y = 4(1.5)^x$　　**61.** $y = 5(0.5)^x$

SOLVING QUADRATIC EQUATIONS **Use the quadratic formula to solve the equation.** (Review 9.5)

62. $x^2 - 2x - 3 = 0$　　**63.** $2x^2 - 6x + 4 = 0$　　**64.** $2x^2 - 2x - 12 = 0$

65. $-\frac{2}{3}x^2 - 3x + 1 = 0$　　**66.** $-7x^2 - 2.5x + 3 = 0$　　**67.** $2x^2 + 4x - 3 = 0$

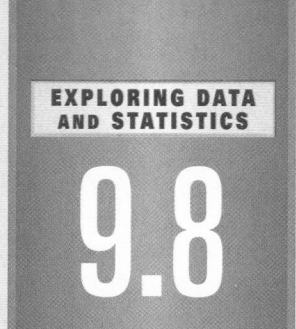
Comparing Linear, Exponential, and Quadratic Models

Chambered Nautilus

GOAL 1 CHOOSING A MODEL

This lesson will help you choose the type of model that best fits a collection of data.

CONCEPT SUMMARY — **THREE BASIC MODELS**

LINEAR MODEL
$$y = mx + b$$

EXPONENTIAL MODEL
$$y = C(1 \pm r)^t$$

QUADRATIC MODEL
$$y = ax^2 + bx + c$$

EXAMPLE 1 Choosing a Model

Name the type of model that best fits each data collection.

a. $(-3, 4)$, $\left(-2, \frac{7}{2}\right)$, $(-1, 3)$, $\left(0, \frac{5}{2}\right)$, $(1, 2)$, $\left(2, \frac{3}{2}\right)$, $(3, 1)$

b. $(-3, 4)$, $(-2, 2)$, $(-1, 1)$, $\left(0, \frac{1}{2}\right)$, $\left(1, \frac{1}{4}\right)$, $\left(2, \frac{1}{8}\right)$, $\left(3, \frac{1}{16}\right)$

c. $(-3, 4)$, $\left(-2, \frac{7}{3}\right)$, $\left(-1, \frac{4}{3}\right)$, $(0, 1)$, $\left(1, \frac{4}{3}\right)$, $\left(2, \frac{7}{3}\right)$, $(3, 4)$

SOLUTION

Make scatter plots of the data. Then decide whether the points appear to lie on a line (linear model), an exponential curve (exponential model), or a parabola (quadratic model).

a. Linear Model   **b.** Exponential Model   **c.** Quadratic Model

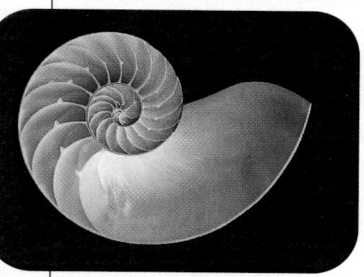

REAL LIFE **CHAMBERED NAUTILUS**
is a marine animal whose soft body is covered with a shell. The nautilus lives in the outermost chamber. Shown here is a cross section of the shell.

EXAMPLE 2 *Writing a Model*

NAUTILUS As a chambered nautilus grows, its chambers get larger and larger. The relationship between the volume and consecutive chambers usually follows the same pattern.

The volumes *v* (in cubic centimeters) of nine consecutive chambers of a chambered nautilus are given in the table. The chambers are numbered from 0 to 8, with 0 being the first and smallest chamber.

Decide which type of model best fits the data. Write a model.

Chamber, *n*	Volume (cm³), *v*
0	0.787
1	0.837
2	0.889
3	0.945
4	1.005
5	1.068
6	1.135
7	1.207
8	1.283

SOLUTION

Draw a scatter plot of the data. You can see that the graph has a slight curve.

Test whether an exponential model fits the data by finding the ratios of consecutive volumes of the chambers.

$$\frac{\text{Volume of Chamber 1}}{\text{Volume of Chamber 0}} = \frac{0.837}{0.787} \approx 1.064$$

$$\frac{\text{Volume of Chamber 2}}{\text{Volume of Chamber 1}} = \frac{0.889}{0.837} \approx 1.062$$

$$\frac{\text{Volume of Chamber 3}}{\text{Volume of Chamber 2}} = \frac{0.945}{0.889} \approx 1.063$$

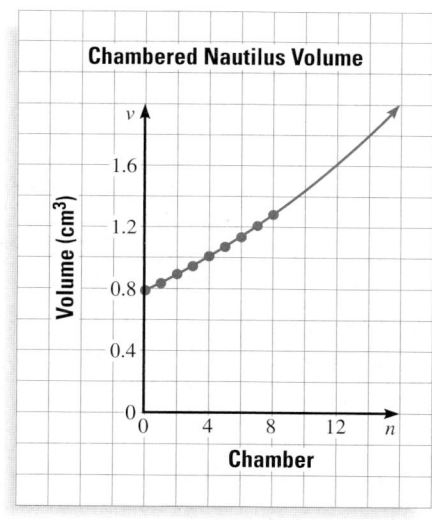

Chambered Nautilus Volume

STUDENT HELP

Look Back
For help writing an exponential growth model, see p. 477.

The ratios show that each chamber's volume is about 0.063, or 6.3%, larger than the volume of the chamber just before it. Assuming this pattern applies to all data points, it is appropriate to use an exponential growth model $v = C(1 + r)^n$.

The rate of growth *r* is 0.063 and the initial volume in chamber 0 is 0.787.

✓**CHECK** Check values of *n* in the exponential model $v = 0.787(1.063)^n$.

$$v = 0.787(1.063)^n \qquad\qquad v = 0.787(1.063)^n$$
$$v = 0.787(1.063)^3 \qquad\qquad v = 0.787(1.063)^8$$
$$v = 0.945 \qquad\qquad\qquad v = 1.283$$

The exponential model $v = 0.787(1.063)^n$ fits the data.

EXAMPLE 3 *Writing a Model*

PENDULUMS A simple pendulum can be constructed with a string hung from a fixed point and a weight attached at the other end. The time it takes for the pendulum to swing from one side to the other and all the way back again is called its *period*. The period t (in seconds) of the pendulum is related to its length d (in inches). The table gives values of t and d for several different pendulums. Decide which type of model best fits the data. Write a model.

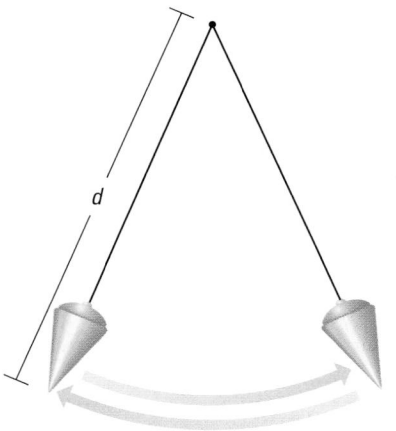

Period (sec), t	Length (in.), d
0.25	0.61
0.50	2.45
0.75	5.50
1.00	9.78
1.25	15.28
1.50	22.00
1.75	29.95
2.00	39.12

SOLUTION

Draw a scatter plot for the data. From the scatter plot, you can see that the pattern is not linear.

You can test whether an exponential model fits by finding the ratios of consecutive pendulum lengths. Since the lengths do not increase by the same percent, an exponential model does not fit the data.

Test whether a quadratic model fits. Write the simple quadratic model $d = at^2$. To find a, substitute any known values of d and t.

Length and Period of a Pendulum

$$d = at^2 \qquad \text{Write quadratic model.}$$

$$9.78 = a(1^2) \qquad \text{Substitute 9.78 for } d \text{ and } 1 \text{ for } t.$$

$$9.78 = a \qquad \text{Solve for } a.$$

$$d = 9.78t^2 \qquad \text{Substitute } a \text{ in the equation.}$$

✓**CHECK** Check values of t in the quadratic model $d = 9.78t^2$

$$d = 9.78t^2 \qquad\qquad\qquad d = 9.78t^2$$

$$d = 9.78(0.25)^2 \qquad\qquad d = 9.78(2.0)^2$$

$$d = 0.61 \qquad\qquad\qquad\quad d = 39.12$$

▶ The quadratic model $d = 9.78t^2$ fits the data.

FOCUS ON APPLICATIONS

PENDULUM CLOCKS One of the first clocks to use a pendulum was invented by the Dutch physicist, astronomer, and mathematician, Christiaan Huygens in the 1650s.

GUIDED PRACTICE

Vocabulary Check ✓

1. Name, sketch, and write an equation for each of the three types of algebraic models you have studied.

Concept Check ✓

2. Describe the steps you would follow to decide which of the three basic models best fits a collection of data.

Skill Check ✓

Name the type of model suggested by the graph.

3.

4.

5.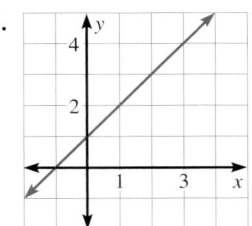

Use the data: (0, 1), (1, 1.25), (2, 2), (3, 3.25), (4, 5), (5, 7.25).

6. Draw a scatter plot of the data.

7. Decide which type of model best fits the data. Explain your reasoning.

8. Write a model that fits the data.

PRACTICE AND APPLICATIONS

STUDENT HELP

▸ **Extra Practice**
to help you master
skills is on p. 805.

CHOOSING MODELS **Make a scatter plot of the data. Then name the type of model that best fits the data.**

9. $(-1, -6), (-3, 4), (2, 9), (-2, -3), (0, -5), (1, 0)$

10. $(0, 3), (8, 3), (-4, -1), (4, 4), (-6, -3), (10, 1)$

11. $(1, 3), (2.5, 16.5), (0.5, 1.5), (-2, 0.1), (0, 1), (1.5, 5)$

12. $(-2, -1), (-1, -2.5), (0, -3), (1, -2.5), (2, -1), (3, 1.5)$

13. $(-3, 2), \left(-2, \frac{5}{2}\right), \left(-1, \frac{7}{2}\right), (0, 5), (1, 7), \left(2, \frac{19}{2}\right)$

14. $(-2, 2), \left(-1, \frac{5}{2}\right), (0, 3), \left(1, \frac{7}{2}\right), (2, 4), \left(3, \frac{9}{2}\right)$

STUDENT HELP

▸ **HOMEWORK HELP**
Example 1: Exs. 9–17
Example 2: Exs. 18–20
Example 3: Exs. 18–20

15.

x	y
5	4
0	-6
7	-6
-1	-14
6	0
3	6

16.

x	y
-1	8
1	2
-2	16
3	0.5
0	4
2	1

17.

x	y
0	5
2	-3
-2	13
1	1
4	-11
3	-7

18. **GEOMETRY** **CONNECTION** The surface area S of a sphere with radius r is shown in the table. Write a model that best fits the data.

Radius, r	1	2	3	4	5
Surface area, S	4π	16π	36π	64π	100π

19. 🌐 **BODY MASS INDEX** Body mass index is a measure of weight in relation to height. The table shows the body mass index B of a person who is 152 centimeters tall and weighs w kilograms. Which type of model best fits the data? Write a model.

Weight, w	45.40	49.94	54.48	59.02	63.56	68.10	72.64
Body mass index, B	19.55	21.50	23.46	25.41	27.37	29.32	31.28

▶ Source: Reuters Health Information

20. **SCIENCE** **CONNECTION** Different masses M (in kilograms) are hung from a spring. The distances d (in centimeters) that the spring stretches are shown in the table. Test different models to see which type of model best fits the data. Write a model that accurately represents the data.

Mass, M	1	2	3	4	5	6	7
Distance, d	2.6	5.2	7.8	10.4	13	15.6	18.2

STUDENT HELP

> **HOMEWORK HELP**
> Visit our Web site
> www.mcdougallittell.com
> for help with Exs. 21
> and 22.

🖩 **NHL ATTENDANCE In Exercises 21 and 22, use the following information.**
The regular season attendance A (in thousands) of National Hockey League games during a recent five-year period can be modeled by

$$A = 341.93t^2 - 583.61t + 12{,}580.66$$

where t is the number of years since the beginning of the five-year period.

🔗 **DATA UPDATE** of National Hockey League data at www.mcdougallittell.com

21. Copy and complete the table.

Year t	Attendance A	Change in A from previous year
0	12,580,660	——
1	?	?
2	?	?
3	?	?
4	?	?

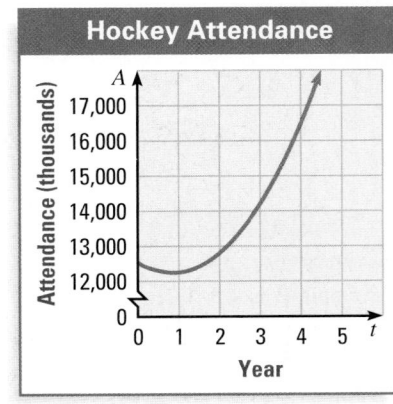

22. Describe the pattern in the change of attendance.

EXTENSION: ABSOLUTE-VALUE EQUATIONS

In Exercises 23–26, use the V-shaped graph. It is the graph of an absolute-value equation of the form $y = a|x - b| + c$.

23. Write an equation of the line passing through the points *A* and *B*. What is its slope?

24. Write an equation of the line passing through the points *D* and *E*. What is its slope?

25. The intersection of the two lines in Exercises 23 and 24 is the vertex of the graph. Find the intersection of the two lines.

26. Find values of *a*, *b*, and *c* such that the equation of the graph is of the form $y = a|x - b| + c$, where *a* is the slope of the line to the right of the vertex and (*b*, *c*) is the vertex.

Test Preparation

27. MULTIPLE CHOICE The graph shows the number of NCAA men's college basketball teams during a recent ten-year period, where *t* is the number of years since the beginning of the period. Which type of model best fits the data?

▶ Source: National College Athletic Association

  Ⓐ Exponential   Ⓑ Quadratic

  Ⓒ Linear   Ⓓ None

28. MULTIPLE CHOICE In 1970 the population *A* of Arizona was 1,775,000. Since then, the average annual percent of increase has been about 3.41%. Which model best fits the situation where *t* is the number of years since 1970?

▶ Source: U.S. Bureau of the Census

  Ⓐ $A = 3.41t + 1{,}775{,}000$ Ⓑ $A = 60{,}527.5t + 1{,}775{,}000$

  Ⓒ $A = 1{,}835{,}527.5t^2$ Ⓓ $A = 1{,}775{,}000(1.0341)^t$

29. MULTIPLE CHOICE The area of an ellipse whose semi-minor and semi-major axes are *r* and *r* + 1 respectively is given below. Which model best fits the data?

Radius, *r*	1	2	3	4	5	6
Area *A*	2π	6π	12π	20π	30π	42π

  Ⓐ $A = \pi r + 2$ Ⓑ $A = \pi r(r + 1)$ Ⓒ $A = \pi(1 + r)^t$ Ⓓ $A = r^2 + \pi r + 2$

★ Challenge

CHOOSING A MODEL Use a graphing calculator to graph the points. Which type of model best fits the data?

30. $(-3, 4), \left(-2, \frac{7}{2}\right), (-1, 3), \left(0, \frac{5}{2}\right), (1, 2), \left(2, \frac{3}{2}\right), (3, 1)$

31. $(-3, 4), (-2, 2), (-1, 1), \left(0, \frac{1}{2}\right), \left(1, \frac{1}{4}\right), \left(2, \frac{1}{8}\right), \left(3, \frac{1}{16}\right)$

32. $(-3, 4), \left(-2, \frac{7}{3}\right), \left(-1, \frac{4}{3}\right), (0, 1), \left(1, \frac{4}{3}\right), \left(2, \frac{7}{3}\right), (3, 4)$

MIXED REVIEW

FINDING TERMS List the terms of the expression. (Review 2.3)

33. $-3 + x$ **34.** $a - 5$ **35.** $-5 - 8x$ **36.** $-4r + s - 1$

SIMPLIFYING EXPRESSIONS Simplify the variable expression.
(Review 2.5 for 10.1)

37. $-(-5)(y)(-y)$ **38.** $(-3)^3(x)(x)$ **39.** $(-2)(-r)(-r)(-r)$

40. $(-n)(-n)(-4)$ **41.** $-(y)^3$ **42.** $(-1)(-x)^4$

SOLVING EQUATIONS Solve the equation. Round the result to two decimal places. (Review 3.6)

43. $15.67x + 23.61 = 1.56 + 45.8x$ **44.** $17.87 - 2.87x = 1.87 - 4.92x$

45. $6.35x - 9.94 = 3.88 + 40.34x$ **46.** $5.6(1.2 + 1.9x) = 20.4x + 6.8$

WRITING EQUATIONS Write an equation of the line that passes through the two points. (Review 5.3)

47. $(3, -2), (5, 4)$ **48.** $(-3, -9), (5, 7)$ **49.** $(2, 3), (-4, 6)$

QUIZ 3

Self-Test for Lessons 9.7 and 9.8

Decide whether the ordered pair is a solution of the inequality. (Lesson 9.7)

1. $y \geq 2x^2 - x + 9, (2, 10)$ **2.** $y > 4x^2 - 64x + 115, (12, -60)$

3. $y < x^2 + 6x + 12, (-1, 6)$ **4.** $y \leq x^2 - 7x + 9, (-1, 16)$

Match the inequality with its graph. (Lesson 9.7)

A.   **B.**   **C.**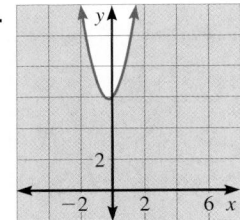

5. $y > -x^2 + 12x - 1$ **6.** $y \leq 2x^2 + x + 6$ **7.** $y \geq 3x^2 + 9x - 1$

Graph the equation. Name the model it represents. (Lesson 9.8)

8. $y = 3x - 6$ **9.** $y = 0.5(1.4)^x$ **10.** $y = 2x^2 + 8x - 4$

Make a scatter plot of the data. Then name the type of model that best fits the data and write a model. (Lesson 9.8)

11. $(-8.5, 20), (-8, 19), (-2, 7), (0, 3), (1, 1), (6, -9), (7.5, -12), (10, -17)$

12. $(-3, 1.5), (-1.5, 2.7), (-0.5, 4), (0, 5), (1, 7.5), (3, 17)$

13. $(3.3, 15.0), (2.1, 11.7), (1.0, 6.8), (0, 2.9), (-1.1, -0.9)$

Chapter Summary

WHAT did you learn?

Evaluate and approximate square roots. **(9.1)**

Solve a quadratic equation.
- by finding square roots **(9.1)**
- by sketching its graph **(9.4)**
- by using the quadratic formula. **(9.5)**

Simplify radicals. **(9.2)**

Sketch the graph of a quadratic function. **(9.3)**

Find the number of solutions of a quadratic equation by using the discriminant. **(9.6)**

Sketch the graph of a quadratic inequality. **(9.7)**

Choose an algebraic model that best fits a collection of data. **(9.8)**

Why did you learn it?

Find solutions using a quadratic model for mineral hardness. **(p. 509)**

Estimate the time for an object to fall. **(p. 506)**
Compare shot-put throws. **(p. 528)**
Model vertical motion problems. **(p. 535)**

Compare the speeds of two sailboats. **(p. 513)**

Estimate the maximum height of a water spray. **(p. 522)**

Decide whether an outcome is possible in a camping situation. **(p. 543)**

Sketch the region between the towers and under the main cable of a suspension bridge. **(p. 550)**

Recognize the characteristics of different models in real-life settings. **(pp. 555 and 556)**

How does Chapter 9 fit into the BIGGER PICTURE of algebra?

A quadratic equation contains the square of a variable. Try to remember the "algebra-geometry" connection between equations in one and two variables. For instance, the equation $x^2 - 9 = 0$ has two solutions, or roots, which correspond to the two x-intercepts of the graph of the function $y = x^2 - 9$. A quadratic function has a U-shaped graph called a *parabola*.

This chapter focuses on quadratic models, which have many applications, such as vertical motion and parabolic path problems. The last lesson helps you decide whether to apply a linear, an exponential, or a quadratic model to fit a collection of real-life data.

STUDY STRATEGY

How did explaining ideas help you to understand a topic?

Talking with a classmate about Lesson 9.4 may have led you to think about ideas that you would understand fully in Lesson 9.6.

Talking about x-intercepts following Lesson 9.4

"Let's see what the graph of $y = x^2$ looks like. It has only one x-intercept. When I solve $x^2 = 0$, I get $x = \sqrt{0} = 0$. It has only one solution, too!"

"If a quadratic function has a graph with no x-intercepts, then I don't think the equation will have any solutions either."

Chapter Review

VOCABULARY

- square root, p. 503
- positive square root, p. 503
- negative square root, p. 503
- radicand, p. 503
- perfect square, p. 504
- irrational number, p. 504

- radical expression, p. 504
- quadratic equation in standard form, p. 505
- leading coefficient, p. 505
- simplest form of a radical expression, p. 512

- quadratic function in standard form, p. 518
- parabola, p. 518
- vertex, p. 518
- axis of symmetry, p. 518
- roots, p. 526

- quadratic formula, p. 533
- discriminant, p. 541
- quadratic inequalities, p. 548
- graph of a quadratic inequality, p. 548

9.1 SOLVING QUADRATIC EQUATIONS BY FINDING SQUARE ROOTS

Examples on pp. 503–506

> **EXAMPLE** To find the real solutions of a quadratic equation of the form $ax^2 + c = 0$, isolate x^2 and then find the square root of each side.
>
> | | |
> |---|---|
> | $2x^2 - 98 = 0$ | Write original equation. |
> | $2x^2 = 98$ | Add 98 to each side. |
> | $x^2 = 49$ | Divide each side by 2. |
> | $x = \pm\sqrt{49}$ | Find square roots. |
> | $x = \pm 7$ | 49 is a perfect square. |

Solve the equation.

1. $x^2 - 144 = 0$

2. $8y^2 = 968$

3. $4t^2 + 19 = 19$

4. $16y^2 - 80 = 0$

5. $\frac{1}{5}a^2 = 5$

6. $\frac{1}{3}x^2 - 7 = -4$

9.2 SIMPLIFYING RADICALS

Examples on pp. 511–513

> **EXAMPLES** Use the product property and the quotient property.
>
> **a.** $\sqrt{28} = \sqrt{4 \cdot 7}$ Factor using perfect square factor.
>
> $\quad = \sqrt{4} \cdot \sqrt{7} = 2\sqrt{7}$ Use product property and simplify.
>
> **b.** $\sqrt{\dfrac{169}{625}} = \dfrac{\sqrt{169}}{\sqrt{625}} = \dfrac{13}{25}$ Use quotient property and simplify.

Simplify the expression.

7. $\sqrt{45}$

8. $\sqrt{441}$

9. $\sqrt{\dfrac{36}{64}}$

10. $\sqrt{\dfrac{99}{25}}$

GRAPHING QUADRATIC FUNCTIONS

Examples on pp. 518–520

EXAMPLE To sketch the graph of $y = x^2 - 4x - 3$, first find the x-coordinate of the vertex: $-\dfrac{b}{2a} = -\dfrac{-4}{2(1)} = 2$. Make a table of values using x-values to the left and right of $x = 2$. Plot the points and connect them to form a parabola.

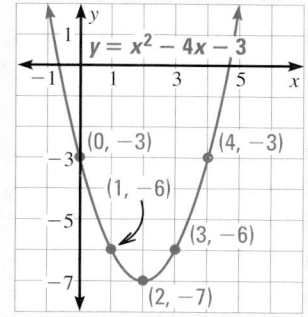

x	−1	0	1	2	3	4	5
y	2	−3	−6	−7	−6	−3	2

Sketch the graph of the function. Label the vertex.

11. $y = x^2 - x - 5$ **12.** $y = -x^2 - 3x + 2$ **13.** $y = -4x^2 + 6x + 3$

SOLVING QUADRATIC EQUATIONS BY GRAPHING

Examples on pp. 526–528

EXAMPLE To solve the quadratic equation $-x^2 + 3x = 2$ by graphing, first rewrite the equation in the form $ax^2 + bx + c = 0$.

$$-x^2 + 3x - 2 = 0.$$

Sketch the graph of the related function $y = -x^2 + 3x - 2$.

▶ From the graph, the x-intercepts appear to be $x = 1$ and $x = 2$. Check these in the original equation.

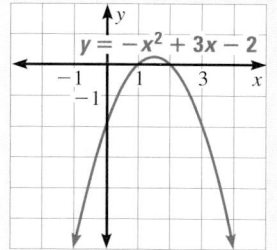

Solve the equation by graphing. Check the solution algebraically.

14. $x^2 + 2 = 3x$ **15.** $x^2 - 2x = 15$ **16.** $\dfrac{1}{2}x^2 + 5x = -8$ **17.** $-x^2 - 2x = -24$

SOLVING QUADRATIC EQUATIONS BY THE QUADRATIC FORMULA

Examples on pp. 533–535

EXAMPLE Solve equations of the form $ax^2 + bx + c = 0$ by substituting the values of a, b, and c into the quadratic formula. Solve $x^2 + 6x - 16 = 0$.

$$x = \frac{-6 \pm \sqrt{6^2 - 4(1)(-16)}}{2(1)} = \frac{-6 \pm \sqrt{36 + 64}}{2} = \frac{-6 \pm \sqrt{100}}{2} = \frac{-6 \pm 10}{2}$$

▶ The equation has two solutions: $x = \dfrac{-6 + 10}{2} = 2$ and $x = \dfrac{-6 - 10}{2} = -8$.

Use the quadratic formula to solve the equation.

18. $3x^2 - 4x + 1 = 0$ **19.** $-2x^2 + x + 6 = 0$ **20.** $10x^2 - 11x + 3 = 0$

9.6 APPLICATIONS OF THE DISCRIMINANT

Examples on
pp. 541–543

EXAMPLES Use the discriminant, $b^2 - 4ac$, to find the number of solutions of a quadratic equation $ax^2 + bx + c = 0$.

EQUATION	DISCRIMINANT	NUMBER OF SOLUTIONS
$3x^2 + 6x + 2 = 0$	$6^2 - 4(3)(2) = 12$	2
$2x^2 + 8x + 8 = 0$	$8^2 - 4(2)(8) = 0$	1
$x^2 + 7x + 15 = 0$	$7^2 - 4(1)(15) = -11$	0

Tell if the equation has *two solutions*, *one solution*, or *no real solution*.

21. $3x^2 - 12x + 12 = 0$ **22.** $2x^2 + 10x + 6 = 0$ **23.** $-x^2 + 3x - 5 = 0$

9.7 GRAPHING QUADRATIC INEQUALITIES

Examples on
pp. 548–550

EXAMPLE To sketch the graph of the quadratic inequality $y < x^2 - 9$, first sketch the graph of the parabola $y = x^2 - 9$. Use a dashed parabola for inequalities with > or <, and a solid parabola for inequalities with ≥ or ≤.

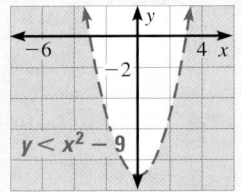

Then test a point that is not on the parabola, say $(0, 0)$. If the test point is a solution, shade its region. If not, shade the other region.

Sketch the graph of the inequality.

24. $x^2 - 3 \geq y$ **25.** $-x^2 - 2x + 3 \leq y$ **26.** $\frac{1}{2}x^2 + 3x - 4 < y$

9.8 COMPARING LINEAR, EXPONENTIAL, AND QUADRATIC MODELS

Examples on
pp. 554–556

EXAMPLE To choose the type of model that best fits a set of data, first make a scatter plot of the data. Then decide whether the points lie on a line, an exponential curve, or a parabola.

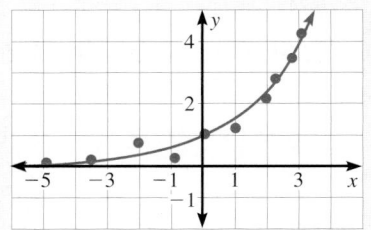

The points in the graph appear to lie on an exponential curve. An exponential model could be used to model the set of data.

Make a scatter plot and name the type of model that best fits the data.

27. $(-3, 4), (-2, 1), (-1, 0), (0, 1), (1, 4), (2, 9), (3, 16)$

28. $(-3, -7), (-2, -4), (-1, -1), (0, 2), (1, 5), (2, 8), (3, 11)$

29. $\left(-3, \frac{1}{8}\right), \left(-2, \frac{1}{4}\right), \left(-1, \frac{1}{2}\right), (0, 1), (1, 2), (2, 4), (3, 8)$

Chapter Test

Simplify the expression.

1. $-\sqrt{9}$

2. $\sqrt{0.0064}$

3. $\pm\sqrt{121}$

4. $\sqrt{8^2 - 4(2)(8)}$

5. $\sqrt{192}$

6. $\sqrt{5} \cdot \sqrt{30}$

7. $\sqrt{\dfrac{27}{147}}$

8. $\dfrac{10\sqrt{8}}{\sqrt{16}}$

Solve the equation by finding square roots or using the quadratic formula.

9. $8x^2 = 800$

10. $4x^2 + 11 = 12$

11. $2x^2 + 5x - 7 = 0$

12. $-2x^2 + 4x + 6 = 0$

13. $64x^2 - 5 = 11$

14. $10x^2 + 17x - 11 = 0$

Match the equation or inequality with its graph.

A.

B.

C.

D.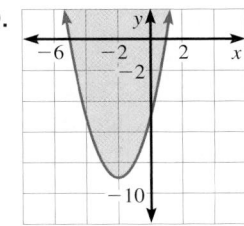

15. $y = x^2 - 2x + 3$

16. $y = -x^2 + 3x - 4$

17. $y \geq x^2 + 4x - 5$

18. $y \leq -x^2 - 2x - 1$

Decide how many solutions the equation has. Check the results by graphing.

19. $5x^2 - 20x - 60 = 0$

20. $-3x^2 + 4x - 2 = 0$

21. $x^2 - 4x + 4 = 0$

Sketch the graph of the equation or the inequality.

22. $y = \dfrac{1}{3}x^2 + 2x - 3$

23. $y = -x^2 + 5x - 6$

24. $y < x^2 + 7x + 6$

25. $y \leq -\dfrac{1}{2}x^2 + 2x + \dfrac{5}{2}$

Name the type of model suggested by the graph.

26.

27.

28.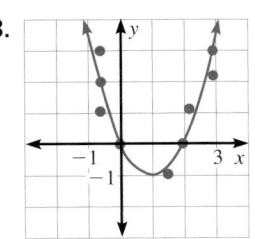

VERTICAL MOTION In Exercises 29–31, you are standing on a bridge over a creek, holding a stone 20 feet above the water.

29. You release the stone. How long will it take the stone to hit the water?

30. You take another stone and toss it straight up with an initial velocity of 30 feet per second. How long will it take the stone to hit the water?

31. If you throw a stone straight up into the air with an initial velocity of 50 feet per second, could the stone reach a height of 60 feet above the water?

Chapter Standardized Test

▶ **TEST-TAKING STRATEGY** Before you give up on a question, try to eliminate some of your choices so you can make an educated guess.

1. MULTIPLE CHOICE Which one of the following is *not* a quadratic equation?

(A) $x^2 - 4 = 0$ (B) $x^2 + 10x + 21 = 0$

(C) $-9 + x^2 = 0$ (D) $-7x + 12 = 0$

(E) $-2 + 9x + x^2 = 0$

2. MULTIPLE CHOICE Which one of the following is a solution of the equation $\frac{2}{3}t^2 - 7 = 17$?

(A) -6 (B) -4 (C) 4

(D) $\sqrt{15}$ (E) $\sqrt{24}$

3. MULTIPLE CHOICE You drop a rock from a bridge 320 feet above a river. How long will it take the rock to hit the river?

(A) 2.5 sec   (B) 3.5 sec   (C) 3.8 sec

(D) 4.5 sec   (E) 5.5 sec

4. MULTIPLE CHOICE The surface area S of a cube is 150 square feet. What is the length (in feet) of each edge of the cube? $\left(S = 6s^2\right)$

(A) ± 5

(B) $5\sqrt{6}$

(C) 5

(D) 25

(E) None of these

5. MULTIPLE CHOICE Find the area of the rectangle.

(A) $20\sqrt{3}$

(B) 240

(C) 60

(D) $12\sqrt{5}$

(E) $4\sqrt{15}$

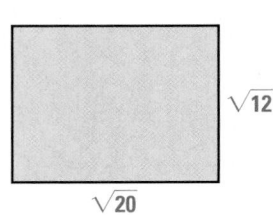

$\sqrt{12}$

$\sqrt{20}$

6. MULTIPLE CHOICE What is the value of x when $3x^2 - 78 = 114$?

(A) $\pm 2\sqrt{3}$ (B) $\pm 4\sqrt{3}$ (C) ± 6

(D) ± 8 (E) $\pm 2\sqrt{29}$

QUANTITATIVE COMPARISON **In Questions 7 and 8, perform the indicated operation and simplify the result. Then choose the statement below that is true about the given numbers.**

(A) The number in column A is greater.

(B) The number in column B is greater.

(C) The two numbers are equal.

(D) The relationship cannot be determined from the given information.

	Column A	Column B
7.	$\sqrt{24} \cdot \sqrt{6}$	$\sqrt{25} \cdot \sqrt{5}$
8.	$\dfrac{\sqrt{27}\sqrt{3}}{\sqrt{9}}$	$\dfrac{\sqrt{30}\sqrt{6}}{\sqrt{12}}$

9. MULTIPLE CHOICE What is the x-coordinate of the vertex for the graph of the equation $y = -\frac{1}{2}x^2 - x + 8$?

(A) -2 (B) -1 (C) $-\frac{1}{2}$

(D) $\frac{1}{2}$ (E) 1

10. MULTIPLE CHOICE What are the x-intercepts of the graph of $y = -x^2 - 6x + 40$?

(A) 4 and 10   (B) -7 and 1

(C) -10 and 4   (D) -8 and 2

(E) -11 and 5

11. MULTIPLE CHOICE Which one of the following is a solution of $-3x^2 + 22x + 93 = 0$?

(A) -7 (B) 3 (C) $-\frac{6}{31}$

(D) -3 (E) $\frac{31}{6}$

12. MULTIPLE CHOICE Which one of the following is a solution of $4x^2 - 17x + 13 = 0$?

(A) $-\frac{17}{13}$ (B) -1 (C) $\frac{4}{13}$

(D) 13 (E) 1

13. MULTIPLE CHOICE What is the discriminant of the equation $-7x^2 - 2x + 5 = 0$?

   (A) 12   (B) 144   (C) -12 (D) 136   (E) 1

14. MULTIPLE CHOICE Which of the following inequalities is represented by the graph?

   (A) $y > -4x^2 + 8x - 5$

   (B) $y < 4x^2 + 8x - 5$

   (C) $y > 4x^2 + 8x - 5$

   (D) $y \leq -4x^2 + 8x - 5$

   (E) $y < -4x^2 + 8x - 5$

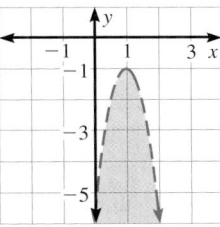

15. MULTIPLE CHOICE Name the type of model suggested by the graph.

   (A) Quadratic

   (B) Exponential decay

   (C) Exponential growth

   (D) Linear

   (E) None of these

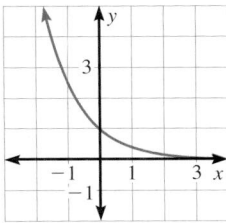

16. MULTI-STEP PROBLEM Use the data in the table below.

x	−5	−4	−2	0	1	2
y	0.3	0.5	1.5	5	9	16.2

   a. Make a scatter plot of the data.

   b. Name the type of model that best fits the data.

   c. Write a model that best fits the data.

17. MULTI-STEP PROBLEM A bird flying above the edge of a cliff sees a fish several meters below the surface of the water in a lake bounded by the cliff. The bird makes a dive to catch the fish. The path of the dive follows a parabolic curve given by the function $y = x^2 - 12x + 32$. At the right is a graph of this function. Imagine that the x-axis runs along the surface of the lake and that the y-axis runs along the edge of the cliff.

   a. How far from the side of the cliff is the fish if it is at the vertex of the curve?

   b. How far below the surface of the water does the bird have to dive to catch the fish?

   c. How far from the side of the cliff will the bird enter and exit the water (x-intercepts)?

   d. Approximate the height of the cliff (y-intercept).

   e. *Writing* If the bird enters the water 4 meters from the side of the cliff and exits it 8 meters from the cliff, write an inequality to represent the region in which the fish can swim safely.

Not drawn to scale

Cumulative Practice

Does the table represent a function? Explain. (1.7)

1.

Input	1	2	3	4
Output	5	8	11	14

2.

Input	5	3	5	2
Output	8	7	4	3

3.

Input	3	6	9	12
Output	5	8	5	8

Find the probability of choosing a green marble from a bag of green and yellow marbles. Then find the odds of choosing a green marble. (2.8)

4. Number of green marbles: 30
Total number of marbles: 84

5. Number of green marbles: 16
Total number of marbles: 72

In Exercises 6 and 7, the two triangles are similar. Write an equation and solve it to find the length of the side marked *x*. (3.2)

6.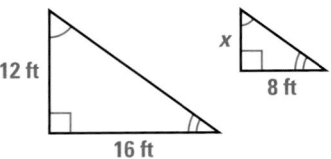
12 ft
16 ft
x
8 ft

7.
35 in.
15 in.
x
6 in.

Find the value of *y* so that the line passing through the two points has the given slope. (4.4)

8. $(2, y), (11, 8), m = \frac{1}{3}$

9. $(7, 3), (6, y), m = -1$

10. $(5, -10), (8, y), m = 4$

11. $(5, y), (-5, 7), m = -\frac{1}{2}$

12. $(0, -12), (3, y), m = 5$

13. $(-4, y), (3, -8), m = -2$

Write the equation in standard form with integer coefficients. (5.6)

14. $3x - 5y + 6 = 0$

15. $6y = 2x + 4$

16. $-2x + 7y - 15 = 0$

Find the first, second, and third quartiles of the data. (6.7)

17. 8, 5, 7, 5, 6, 9, 8, 5, 7

18. 10, 12, 7, 30, 25, 8, 6, 10, 5, 8

19. 4, 4, 8, 2, 10, 8, 4, 6, 2, 10, 4

Solve the linear system. (7.1–7.4)

20. $x + y = 8$
$2x + y = 10$

21. $\frac{1}{4}x - y = 7$
$x + 4y = 0$

22. $-2x + 20y = 10$
$x - 5y = -5$

23. $3.2x + 1.1y = -19.3$
$-32x + 4y = 148$

24. $\frac{1}{10}x - \frac{3}{2}y = -1$
$-10x + 3y = 2$

25. $1.4x + 2.1y = 1.75$
$2.8x - 4.2y = 34.58$

Sketch the graph of the system of linear inequalities. (7.6)

26. $x \geq 0$
$y \geq 0$
$x < 5$
$y < \frac{5}{2}$

27. $x > 2$
$x - y \leq 2$
$\frac{1}{2}x + y \leq 3$

28. $3x + 5y \geq 15$
$x - 2y < 10$
$x > 1$

29. $-\frac{1}{4}x + y \leq 2$
$-4x + y \geq -4$
$2x + y \geq -4$

Simplify the expression. (8.1–8.3)

30. $\left(\dfrac{1}{x^2}\right)^7$

31. $\dfrac{x^8}{x^{10}}$

32. $\dfrac{4}{(2x)^{-3}}$

33. $\left(\dfrac{-8x^3}{4xy^5}\right)^2$

34. $5x \cdot \left(x \cdot x^{-4}\right)^2$

35. $\left(6a^3\right)^2\left(\dfrac{1}{2}a^3\right)^2$

36. $\left(r^2st^5\right)^0\left(s^4t^2\right)^3$

37. $\dfrac{6x^4y^4}{3xy} \cdot \dfrac{5x^2y^3}{2y^2}$

Evaluate the expression. Write the result in scientific notation and in decimal form. (8.4)

38. $\left(5 \times 10^{-2}\right) \cdot \left(3 \times 10^4\right)$

39. $\left(6 \times 10^{-4}\right) \cdot \left(7 \times 10^{-5}\right)$

40. $\left(20 \times 10^{-4}\right) \div \left(2.5 \times 10^{-8}\right)$

41. $\left(7 \times 10^3\right)^{-3}$

42. $\left(8.8 \times 10^{-1}\right) \div \left(11 \times 10^{-1}\right)$

43. $\left(2.8 \times 10^{-2}\right)^3$

Match the graph with its description. (8.5)

A. Deposit: $300,
   Annual rate: 2.5%

B. Deposit: $300,
   Annual rate: 4%

C. Deposit: $250,
   Annual rate: 2%

D. Deposit: $250,
   Annual rate: 4.5%

44.

45.

46.

47.

Simplify the expression. (9.2)

48. $\sqrt{48}$

49. $\sqrt{\dfrac{28}{36}}$

50. $\dfrac{1}{4}\sqrt{84}$

51. $\dfrac{\sqrt{112}}{\sqrt{49}}$

52. $\sqrt{12} \cdot \sqrt{63}$

53. $\sqrt{9} \cdot \dfrac{\sqrt{18}}{\sqrt{54}}$

54. $\dfrac{-2\sqrt{98}}{\sqrt{7}}$

55. $\dfrac{\sqrt{33} \cdot \sqrt{75}}{\sqrt{11}}$

Sketch the graph of the function or the inequality. (9.3 and 9.7)

56. $y = -3x^2 + 12x - 7$

57. $y \geq 5x^2 + 20x + 13$

58. $y \leq \dfrac{1}{2}x^2 + 4x + 1$

Use the quadratic formula to solve the equation. (9.5)

59. $x^2 + 10x + 9 = 0$

60. $-x^2 + 5x - 6 = 0$

61. $3x^2 + 8x - 5 = 0$

62. $-2x^2 + 5x + 12 = 0$

63. $-\dfrac{1}{2}x^2 + 3x - \dfrac{5}{2} = 0$

64. $7x^2 + 12x - 2 = 0$

65. ⊛ **COMPOUND INTEREST** Your savings account earns 4.8% interest, compounded annually. Another bank in town is offering 5.1% interest, compounded annually. The balance in your account is $567. How much additional interest could you earn in 5 years by moving your account to the bank with the 5.1% interest? in 10 years? (8.5)

⊛ **SENDING UP FLARES** In Exercises 69 and 70, a flare is fired straight up from ground level with an initial velocity of 100 feet per second. (9.5)

66. How long will it take the flare to reach an altitude of 150 feet?

67. Will the flare reach an altitude of 180 feet? Explain.

68. GEOMETRY ▶ CONNECTION Is it possible for a rectangle with a perimeter of 52 centimeters to have an area of 148.75 square centimeters? Explain. (9.5–9.6)

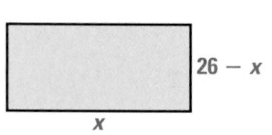

$26 - x$

x

Fitting a Model to Data

OBJECTIVE Fitting a model to data and then using the model to predict future outcomes.

Materials: graph paper, graphing calculator or computer (optional)

COLLECTING YOUR DATA

You opened a pizza business eight years ago, and you want to write an equation to represent the growth of the business since you opened.

1. Copy and complete the table.

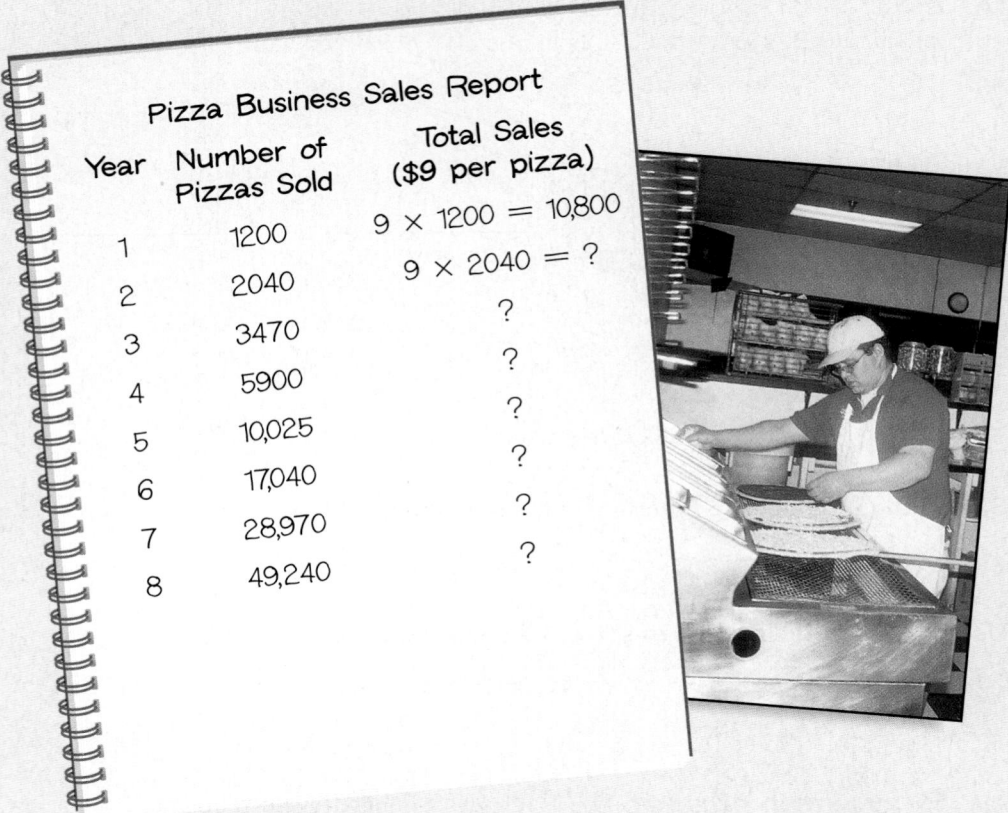

Pizza Business Sales Report

Year	Number of Pizzas Sold	Total Sales ($9 per pizza)
1	1200	9 × 1200 = 10,800
2	2040	9 × 2040 = ?
3	3470	?
4	5900	?
5	10,025	?
6	17,040	?
7	28,970	?
8	49,240	?

INVESTIGATING YOUR DATA

2. Make a scatter plot of the data. Describe any patterns you see.

3. To write an equation that represents your data, test a linear model, a quadratic model, and an exponential model to determine which fits the data best. You may want to use a graphing calculator or computer. (See the Graphing Calculator Activity in Chapter 8, page 492, on how to fit a model to a given set of data.) Explain why you think that each model either fits or doesn't fit the data.

4. Make a prediction on what the total sales would be in the tenth year.

INVESTIGATING ANOTHER BUSINESS

5. Find the annual sales for at least four years for a business or an industry that interests you. Make a table of the data.

6. Make a scatter plot of the data. Try to fit a linear model, a quadratic model, and an exponential model to the data. Which model fits best?

7. Can you use the best-fitting model from Exercise 6 to predict future sales for this business or industry? If you can, use your model to predict sales five years from now. If you cannot, explain why not.

PRESENT YOUR RESULTS

Write a report or make a poster to report your results.

- Include your answers to Exercises 1–4.

- Include all the curves you tried and your explanations of whether they fit or not.

- Describe the business or industry you looked at in Exercises 5–7. Tell where you found your data. Explain whether you were able to fit a model to your data. Include your answers to Exercises 5–7.

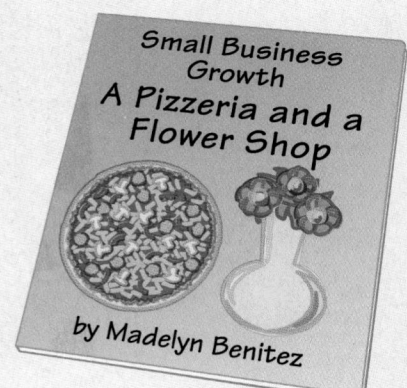

- If you used a graphing calculator or a computer to create your models, give the *r*-value for each model and explain what the values mean.

- Describe what you learned about fitting a model to data. For example, what information or values helped you to determine the best model to use?

EXTENSION

- Find sales data for a business or industry related to the one you used for Exercises 5–7. Compare the two sets of data. Compare the growth in sales in the two businesses or industries.

- Do some research to find a stock market index that you can use to compare the performance of the business or industry you used in the project with the performance of stocks during the same period of time.

POLYNOMIALS AND FACTORING

▶ *Where can scientists dish up astronomical research projects?*

APPLICATION: Arecibo Observatory

The Arecibo radio telescope is the largest single-dish radio telescope in the world. Its enormous reflector dish, built in a natural limestone sinkhole in Puerto Rico, is sensitive enough to collect radio waves originating 7000 trillion miles from Earth.

The cross section of many radio telescopes, such as the one shown below, where *x* and *y* are in feet, can be modeled by a polynomial equation whose graph is a parabola. You will solve polynomial equations in Chapter 10.

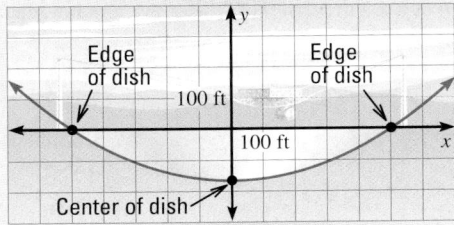

Think & Discuss

Use the graph modeling a cross section of the telescope's reflector dish for Exercises 1 and 2.

1. Find the *x*-intercepts. How can you use this information to find the diameter of the dish?

2. Estimate the depth of the dish.

Learn More About It

You will use an algebraic model of a radio telescope in Exercises 53 and 54 on page 601.

 APPLICATION LINK Visit www.mcdougallittell.com for more information about the Arecibo Observatory.

Study Guide

What's the chapter about?

Chapter 10 is about **polynomials and factoring**. In Chapter 10 you'll learn

- how to add, subtract, and multiply polynomials.
- how to factor polynomials.
- how to solve polynomial equations by factoring.

KEY VOCABULARY

▶ **Review**

- distributive property, p. 100
- like terms, p. 102
- x-intercept, p. 218
- parabola, p. 518

- quadratic formula, p. 533
- vertical motion model, p. 535
- discriminant, p. 541

▶ **New**

- polynomial, p. 576
- FOIL pattern, p. 585
- factored form, p. 597
- zero-product property, p. 597

- factor a quadratic expression, p. 604
- factor completely, p. 625

Are you ready for the chapter?

SKILL REVIEW Do these exercises to review key skills that you'll apply in this chapter. See the given **reference page** if there is something you don't understand.

STUDENT HELP

▶ **Study Tip**
"Student Help" boxes throughout the chapter give you study tips and tell you where to look for extra help in this book and on the Internet.

Apply the distributive property. Combine like terms. (Review Examples 2 and 3, p. 101 and Example 5, p. 102)

1. $3x(x + 6)$ **2.** $(2 - 4x)7$ **3.** $-4(x + 5)$ **4.** $(8 - 2x)(-8)$

5. $2(x - 3) + x$ **6.** $5x + 3(1 - x)$ **7.** $-(x + 4) - x$ **8.** $2x^2 - x(1 + x)$

Simplify the expression. (Review pp. 450 and 451)

9. $x^5 \cdot x^4 \cdot x$ **10.** $(x^6)^2$ **11.** $(-2ab)^3$ **12.** $(3xy^4)^2 \cdot x^2$

Find the discriminant. Tell if the equation has *two solutions, one solution,* **or** *no real solution.* (Review Example 1, p. 541)

13. $3x^2 - 4x + 6 = 0$ **14.** $5x^2 + 6x - 8 = 0$ **15.** $2x^2 - 12x + 18 = 0$

Here's a study strategy!

Working on Trouble Spots

Look through the chapter and identify your trouble spots: questions that you had difficulty answering or homework exercises that you solved incorrectly. Review the material covering these topics and then try to answer the questions again.

▶ ACTIVITY 10.1

Developing Concepts

SET UP
Work with a partner.

MATERIALS
algebra tiles

Modeling Addition of Polynomials

▶ **QUESTION** How can you model the addition of polynomials with algebra tiles?

▶ **EXPLORING THE CONCEPT**

Algebra tiles can be used to model polynomials.

1   −1

These 1-by-1 square
tiles have an area of
1 square unit.

x $-x$

These 1-by-x rectangular
tiles have an area of
x square units.

x^2 $-x^2$

These x-by-x square tiles
have an area of
x^2 square units.

1 You can use algebra tiles to add the polynomials $x^2 + 4x + 2$ and $2x^2 - 3x - 1$.

x^2 + $4x$ + 2 $2x^2$ − $3x$ − 1

2 To add the polynomials, combine like terms. Group the x^2-tiles, the x-tiles, and the 1-tiles.

3 Rearrange the tiles to form zero pairs. Remove the zero pairs. The sum is $3x^2 + x + 1$.

▶ **DRAWING CONCLUSIONS**

In Exercises 1–6, use algebra tiles to find the sum. Sketch your solution.

1. $(-x^2 + x - 1) + (4x^2 + 2x - 3)$ **2.** $(3x^2 + 5x - 6) + (-2x^2 - 3x - 6)$

3. $(5x^2 - 3x + 4) + (-x^2 + 3x - 2)$ **4.** $(2x^2 - x - 1) + (-2x^2 + x + 1)$

5. $(-x^2 + 3x + 7) + (x^2 - 7)$ **6.** $(4x^2 + 5) + (4x^2 + 5x)$

7. Describe how to use algebra tiles to model *subtraction* of polynomials.

Use algebra tiles to find the difference.

8. $(x^2 + 3x + 4) - (x^2 + 3)$ **9.** $(x^2 - 2x + 5) - (3 - 2x)$

10. $(2x^2 + 5) - (-x^2 + 3)$ **11.** $(x^2 + 4) - (2x^2 + x)$

10.1

Adding and Subtracting Polynomials

What you should learn

GOAL 1 Add and subtract polynomials.

GOAL 2 Use polynomials to model **real-life** situations, such as energy use in **Exs. 67–69**.

Why you should learn it

▼ To represent **real-life** situations, like mounting a photo on a mat in **Example 5**.

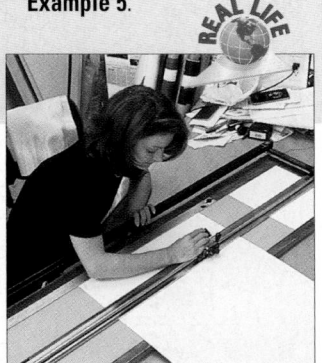

GOAL 1 ADDING AND SUBTRACTING POLYNOMIALS

An expression which is the sum of terms of the form ax^k where k is a nonnegative integer is a **polynomial**. Polynomials are usually written in **standard form**, which means that the terms are placed in descending order, from largest degree to smallest degree.

Leading coefficient ⟶ —Degree —Constant term

Polynomial in standard form: $2x^3 + 5x^2 - 4x + 7$

The **degree** of each term of a polynomial is the exponent of the variable. The **degree of a polynomial** is the largest degree of its terms. When a polynomial is written in standard form, the coefficient of the first term is the **leading coefficient**.

EXAMPLE 1 *Identifying Polynomial Coefficients*

Identify the coefficients of $-4x^2 + x^3 + 3$.

SOLUTION First write the polynomial in standard form. Account for each degree, even if you must use a zero coefficient.

$$-4x^2 + x^3 + 3 = (1)x^3 + (-4)x^2 + (0)x + 3$$

▶ The coefficients are 1, −4, 0, and 3.

· · · · · · · · · ·

A polynomial with only one term is called a **monomial**. A polynomial with two terms is called a **binomial**. A polynomial with three terms is called a **trinomial**.

EXAMPLE 2 *Classifying Polynomials*

POLYNOMIAL	DEGREE	CLASSIFIED BY DEGREE	CLASSIFIED BY NUMBER OF TERMS
a. 6	0	constant	monomial
b. $-2x$	1	linear	monomial
c. $3x + 1$	1	linear	binomial
d. $-x^2 + 2x - 5$	2	quadratic	trinomial
e. $4x^3 - 8x$	3	cubic	binomial
f. $2x^4 - 7x^3 - 5x + 1$	4	quartic	polynomial

To add or subtract two polynomials, add or subtract the like terms. You can use a vertical format or a horizontal format.

EXAMPLE 3 *Adding Polynomials*

Find the sum. Write the answer in standard form.

a. $(5x^3 - x + 2x^2 + 7) + (3x^2 + 7 - 4x) + (4x^2 - 8 - x^3)$

b. $(2x^2 + x - 5) + (x + x^2 + 6)$

SOLUTION

a. **Vertical format:** Write each expression in standard form. Align like terms.

$$5x^3 + 2x^2 - \ x + 7$$
$$3x^2 - 4x + 7$$
$$\underline{-x^3 + 4x^2 \qquad - 8}$$
$$4x^3 + 9x^2 - 5x + 6$$

b. **Horizontal format:** Add like terms.

$$(2x^2 + x - 5) + (x + x^2 + 6) = (2x^2 + x^2) + (x + x) + (-5 + 6)$$
$$= 3x^2 + 2x + 1$$

EXAMPLE 4 *Subtracting Polynomials*

Find the difference.

a. $(-2x^3 + 5x^2 - x + 8) - (-2x^3 + 3x - 4)$

b. $(x^2 - 8) - (7x + 4x^2)$

c. $(3x^2 - 5x + 3) - (2x^2 - x - 4)$

SOLUTION

a. Use a vertical format. To subtract, you *add the opposite*. This means that you can multiply each term in the subtracted polynomial by -1 and add.

$$\begin{array}{r} (-2x^3 + 5x^2 - x + 8) \\ -\ \underline{(-2x^3 + 3x - 4)} \end{array} \quad \textbf{Add the opposite.} \quad \begin{array}{r} -2x^3 + 5x^2 - \ x + 8 \\ +\ \underline{2x^3 \qquad - 3x + 4} \\ 5x^2 - 4x + 12 \end{array}$$

b.
$$\begin{array}{r} (x^2 - 8) \\ -\ \underline{(7x + 4x^2)} \end{array} \quad \textbf{Add the opposite.} \quad \begin{array}{r} x^2 \qquad - 8 \\ +\ \underline{-4x^2 - 7x} \\ -3x^2 - 7x - 8 \end{array}$$

c. Use a horizontal format.

$$(3x^2 - 5x + 3) - (2x^2 - x - 4) = 3x^2 - 5x + 3 - 2x^2 + x + 4$$
$$= (3x^2 - 2x^2) + (-5x + x) + (3 + 4)$$
$$= x^2 - 4x + 7$$

GOAL 2 **USING POLYNOMIALS IN REAL LIFE**

Geometry

EXAMPLE 5 *Subtracting Polynomials*

You are enlarging a 5-inch by 7-inch photo by a scale factor of *x* and mounting it on a mat. You want the mat to be twice as wide as the enlarged photo and 2 inches less than twice as high as the enlarged photo.

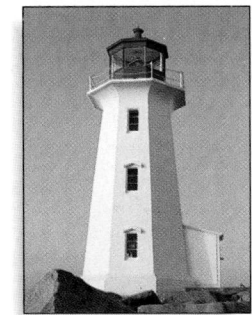

a. Draw a diagram to represent the described situation. Label the dimensions.

b. Write a model for the area of the mat around the photograph as a function of the scale factor.

SOLUTION

a. Use rectangles to represent the mat and the photo. Use the description of the problem to label the dimensions as shown in the sample diagram below.

The dimensions of the photo are enlarged by a scale factor of *x*.

7x   14x − 2

The mat is 2 inches less than twice as high as the enlarged photo.

5x

10x

The mat is twice as wide as the enlarged photo.

b. Use a verbal model. Use the diagram to find expressions for the labels.

PROBLEM
SOLVING
STRATEGY

VERBAL MODEL
$$\boxed{\text{Area of mat}} = \boxed{\text{Total area}} - \boxed{\text{Area of photo}}$$

LABELS
Area of mat = A (square inches)

Total area = $(10x)(14x - 2)$ (square inches)

Area of photo = $(5x)(7x)$ (square inches)

ALGEBRAIC MODEL
$A = (10x)(14x - 2) - (5x)(7x)$
$= 140x^2 - 20x - 35x^2$
$= 105x^2 - 20x$

▶ A model for the area of the mat around the photograph as a function of the scale factor *x* is $A = 105x^2 - 20x$.

Internet

EXAMPLE 6 *Adding Polynomials*

From 1991 through 1998, the number of commercial C and education E Internet Web sites can be modeled by the following equations, where t is the number of years since 1991. ▶ Source: Network Wizards

Commercial sites (in millions): $C = 0.321t^2 - 1.036t + 0.698$

Education sites (in millions): $E = 0.099t^2 - 0.120t + 0.295$

Find a model for the total number S of commercial and education sites.

SOLUTION

You can find a model for S by adding the models for C and E.

$$0.321t^2 - 1.036t + 0.698$$
$$+ \quad 0.099t^2 - 0.120t + 0.295$$
$$\overline{\quad 0.42t^2 - 1.156t + 0.993}$$

▶ The model for the sum is $S = 0.42t^2 - 1.156t + 0.993$.

GUIDED PRACTICE

Vocabulary Check ✔

1. Is $9x^2 + 8x - 4x^3 + 3$ a polynomial with a degree of 2? Explain.

Concept Check ✔

In Exercises 2–4, consider the polynomial expression $5x + 6 - 3x^3 - 4x^2$.

2. Write the expression in standard form and name its terms.

3. Name the coefficients of the terms. Which is the leading coefficient?

4. What is the degree of the polynomial?

ERROR ANALYSIS Describe the error shown.

5.
$$7x^3 - 3x^2 + 5$$
$$+ \quad 2x^3 - 5x - 7$$
$$\overline{\quad 9x^3 - 8x^2 - 2}$$

6.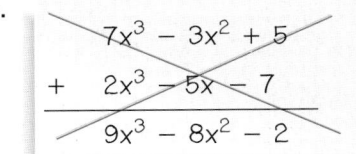
$$(4x^2 - 9x) - (-8x^2 + 3x - 7)$$
$$= (4x^2 + 8x^2) + (-9x + 3x) - 7$$
$$= 12x^2 - 6x - 7$$

Skill Check ✔

Classify the polynomial by degree and by the number of terms.

7. $-9y + 5$

8. $12x^2 + 7x$

9. $4w^3 - 8w + 9$

10. $\frac{1}{2}x - \frac{3}{4}x^2$

11. -4.3

12. $7y + 2y^3 - y^2 + 3y^4$

Find the sum or the difference.

13. $(x^2 - 4x + 3) + (3x^2 - 3x - 5)$

14. $(-x^2 + 3x - 4) - (2x^2 + x - 1)$

15. $(-3x^2 + x + 8) - (x^2 - 8x + 4)$

16. $(5x^2 - 2x - 1) + (-3x^2 - 6x - 2)$

17. $(4x^2 - 2x - 9) + (x - 7 - 5x^2)$

18. $(2x - 3 + 7x^2) - (3 - 9x^2 - 2x)$

PRACTICE AND APPLICATIONS

STUDENT HELP

→ **Extra Practice**
to help you master
skills is on p. 806.

CLASSIFYING POLYNOMIALS Identify the leading coefficient, and classify
the polynomial by degree and by number of terms.

19. $-3w + 7$

20. $-4x^2 + 2x - 1$

21. $8 + 5t^2 - 3t + t^3$

22. $8 + 5y^2 - 3y$

23. -6

24. $14w^4 + 9w^2$

25. $-\dfrac{2}{3}x + 5x^4 - \dfrac{5}{6}$

26. $-4.1b^2 + 7.4b^3$

27. $-9t^2 + 3t^3 - 4t^4 - 15$

28. $9y^3 - 5y^2 + 4y - 1$

29. $-16x^3$

30. $-8z^2 + 74 + 39z - 95z^4$

VERTICAL FORMAT Use a vertical format to add or subtract.

31. $(12x^3 + 10) - (18x^3 - 3x^2 + 6)$

32. $(a + 3a^2 + 2a^3) - (a^4 - a^3)$

33. $(2m - 8m^2 - 3) + (m^2 + 5m)$

34. $(8y^2 + 2) + (5 - 3y^2)$

35. $(3x^2 + 7x - 6) - (3x^2 + 7x)$

36. $(4x^2 - 7x + 2) + (-x^2 + x - 2)$

37. $(8y^3 + 4y^2 + 3y - 7) + (2y^2 - 6y + 4)$

38. $(7x^4 - x^2 + 3x) - (x^3 + 6x^2 - 2x + 9)$

HORIZONTAL FORMAT Use a horizontal format to add or subtract.

39. $(x^2 - 7) + (2x^2 + 2)$

40. $(-3a^2 + 5) + (-a^2 + 4a - 6)$

41. $(x^3 + x^2 + 1) - x^2$

42. $12 - (y^3 + 4)$

43. $(3n^3 + 2n - 7) - (n^3 - n - 2)$

44. $(3a^3 - 4a^2 + 3) - (a^3 + 3a^2 - a - 4)$

45. $(6b^4 - 3b^3 - 7b^2 + 9b + 3) + (4b^4 - 6b^2 + 11b - 7)$

46. $(x^3 - 6x) - (2x^3 + 9) - (4x^2 + x^3)$

POLYNOMIAL ADDITION AND SUBTRACTION Use a vertical format or a
horizontal format to add or subtract.

47. $(9x^3 + 12) + (16x^3 - 4x + 2)$

48. $(-2t^4 + 6t^2 + 5) - (-2t^4 + 5t^2 + 1)$

49. $(3x + 2x^2 - 4) - (x^2 + x - 6)$

50. $(u^3 - u) - (u^2 + 5)$

51. $(-7x^2 + 12) - (6 - 4x^2)$

52. $(10x^3 + 2x^2 - 11) + (9x^2 + 2x - 1)$

53. $(-9z^3 - 3z) + (13z - 8z^2)$

54. $(21t^4 - 3t^2 + 43) - (19t^3 + 33t - 58)$

55. $(6t^2 - 19t) - (3 - 2t^2) - (8t^2 - 5)$

56. $(7y^2 + 15y) + (5 - 15y + y^2) + (24 - 17y^2)$

57. $\left(x^4 - \dfrac{1}{2}x^2\right) + \left(x^3 + \dfrac{1}{3}x^2\right) + \left(\dfrac{1}{4}x^2 - 9\right)$

STUDENT HELP

→ **HOMEWORK HELP**
Example 1: Exs. 19–30
Example 2: Exs. 19–30
Example 3: Exs. 31–62
Example 4: Exs. 31–62
Example 5: Exs. 63, 64
Example 6: Exs. 65–69

58. $(10w^3 + 20w^2 - 55w + 60) + (-25w^2 + 15w - 10) + (-5w^2 + 10w - 20)$

59. $(9x^4 - x^2 + 7x) + (x^3 - 6x^2 + 2x - 9) - (4x^3 + 3x + 8)$

60. $(6.2b^4 - 3.1b + 8.5) + (-4.7 + 5.8b^2 - 2.4b^4)$

61. $(-3.8y^3 + 6.9y^2 - y + 6.3) - (-3.1y^3 + 2.9y - 4.1)$

62. $\left(\dfrac{2}{5}a^4 - 2a + 7\right) - \left(-\dfrac{3}{10}a^4 + 6a^3\right) - (2a^2 - 7)$

🌐 **BUILDING A HOUSE** In Exercises 63 and 64, you plan to build a house that is $1\frac{1}{2}$ times as long as it is wide. You want the land around the house to be 20 feet wider than the width of the house, and twice as long as the length of the house, as shown at the right.

63. Write an expression for the area of the land surrounding the house.

64. If $x = 30$ feet, what is the area of the house? What is the area of the entire property?

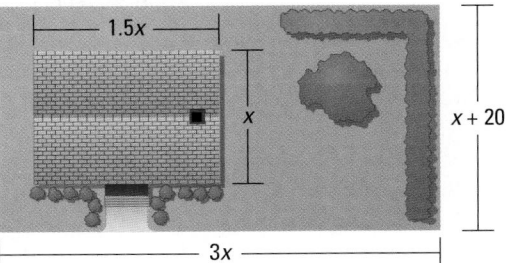

🌐 **POPULATION** In Exercises 65 and 66, use the following information. Projected from 1950 through 2010, the total population P and the male population M of the United States (in thousands) can be modeled by the following equations, where t is the number of years since 1950.

DATA UPDATE of U.S. Bureau of the Census data at www.mcdougallittell.com

Total population model: $P = 2387.74t + 155{,}211.46$

Male population model: $M = 1164.16t + 75{,}622.43$

65. Find a model that represents the female population F of the United States from 1950 through 2010.

66. For the year 2010, the value of P is 298,475.86 and the value of M is 145,472.03. Use these figures to predict the female population in 2010.

🌐 **ENERGY USE** In Exercises 67–69, use the following information. From 1989 through 1993, the amounts (in billions of dollars) spent on natural gas N and electricity E by United States residents can be modeled by the following equations, where t is the number of years since 1989.

▶ Source: U.S. Energy Information Administration

Gas spending model: $N = 1.488t^2 - 3.403t + 65.590$

Electricity spending model: $E = -0.107t^2 + 6.897t + 169.735$

67. Find a model for the total amount A (in billions of dollars) spent on natural gas *and* electricity by United States residents from 1989 through 1993.

68. According to the models, will more money be spent on natural gas or on electricity in 2020?

69. The graph at the right shows U.S. energy spending starting in 1989. Models N, E, and A are shown. Copy the graph and label the models N, E, and A.

FOCUS ON CAREERS

🌐 **ELECTRICAL ENGINEERS**
design, test, and monitor the performance of electrical equipment. This includes equipment used by power utilities to generate and transmit electricity.

🌐 **CAREER LINK**
www.mcdougallittell.com

70. MULTI-STEP PROBLEM The table below shows the amounts that Megan and Sara plan to deposit in their savings accounts to buy a used car. Their savings accounts have the same annual growth rate g.

Date	1/1/00	1/1/01	1/1/02	1/1/03
Megan	$250	$400	$170	$625
Sara	$475	$50	$300	$540

a. On January 1, 2003, the value of Megan's account M can be modeled by $M = 250g^3 + 400g^2 + 170g + 625$, where g is the annual growth rate. Find a model for the value of Sara's account S on January 1, 2003.

b. Find a model for the total value of Megan's and Sara's accounts together on January 1, 2003.

c. The annual growth rate g is equal to $1 + r$, where r is the annual interest rate. The annual interest rate on both accounts is 2.5% for the three-year period. Find the combined value of the two accounts on January 1, 2003.

d. If the used car that Megan and Sara want to buy costs $2500, will they have enough money?

★ **Challenge**

71. The sum of any two consecutive integers can be written as $(x) + (x + 1)$. Show that the sum of any two consecutive integers is always odd.

EXTRA CHALLENGE
www.mcdougallittell.com

72. Use algebra to show that the sum of any four consecutive integers is always even.

MIXED REVIEW

DISTRIBUTIVE PROPERTY Simplify the expression. (Review 2.6 for 10.2)

73. $-3(x + 1) - 2$

74. $(2x - 1)(2) + x$

75. $11x + 3(8 - x)$

76. $(5x - 1)(-3) + 6$

77. $-4(1 - x) + 7$

78. $-12x - 5(11 - x)$

79. BEST-FITTING LINES Draw a scatter plot. Then draw a line that approximates the data and write an equation of the line. (Review 5.4)

$$(-7, 19), (-6, 16), (-5, 12), (-2, 12), (-2, 9), (0, 7),$$

$$(2, 4), (6, -3), (6, 2), (9, -4), (9, -7), (12, -10)$$

EXPONENTIAL EXPRESSIONS In Exercises 80–85, simplify. Then use a calculator to evaluate the expression. Round the result to two decimal places when appropriate. (Review 8.1)

80. $\left(4 \cdot 3^2 \cdot 2^3\right)^4$

81. $\left(2^4 \cdot 2^4\right)^2$

82. $\left(-6 \cdot 3^4\right)^3$

83. $(1.1 \cdot 3.3)^3$

84. $5.5^3 \cdot 5.5^4$

85. $\left(2.9^3\right)^5$

86. 🌎 **ALABAMA** The population P of Alabama (in thousands) for 1995 projected through 2025 can be modeled by $P = 4227(1.0104)^t$, where t is the number of years since 1995. Find the ratio of the population in 2025 to the population in 2000. Compare this ratio with the ratio of the population in 2000 to the population in 1995. ▶ Source: U.S. Bureau of the Census (Review 8.3)

Graphing Polynomial Functions

You can use a graphing calculator or a computer to check an answer when finding the sum or difference of polynomials.

► **EXAMPLE**

One of the expressions below is the difference of $2x^2 + 3x - 1$ and $-x^2 - 2x + 3$. Use a graphing calculator to check which is correct.

A. $x^2 + 5x - 4$ **B.** $3x^2 + 5x - 4$

► **SOLUTION**

1 Enter $(2x^2 + 3x - 1) - (-x^2 - 2x + 3)$ as equation Y1.

Enter $x^2 + 5x - 4$ as equation Y2.

Enter $3x^2 + 5x - 4$ as equation Y3.

2 Graph equations Y1 and Y2 on the same screen.

The graphs do not coincide, so

$$(2x^2 + 3x - 1) - (-x^2 - 2x + 3)$$

is not equal to $x^2 + 5x - 4$.

3 Graph equations Y1 and Y3 on the same screen.

The graphs coincide, so

$$(2x^2 + 3x - 1) - (-x^2 - 2x + 3)$$

equals $3x^2 + 5x - 4$.

► **EXERCISES**

Tell whether the given answer is a correct sum or difference. If it is incorrect, find the correct answer.

1. $(2x^2 - 3x + 5) + (-x^2 + 2x - 6) \stackrel{?}{=} x^2 - x - 1$

2. $(-x^2 - 3x - 1) - (-2x^2 + 4x + 5) \stackrel{?}{=} -3x^2 + x + 4$

Find the sum or difference. Then use a graphing calculator or a computer to check your answer.

3. $(2x^2 - 6x - 3) + (x^2 - 3x + 3)$ **4.** $(x^2 - 14x + 5) + (-2x^2 - 3x + 2)$

5. $(x^2 + 12x + 6) - (3x^2 - 2x + 2)$ **6.** $(-3x^2 + 5x - 8) - (x^2 - 5x - 8)$

7. $(2x^2 + 10x + 3) + (4x^2 + 2x - 4)$ **8.** $(x^2 - 4x + 5) - (-2x^2 - 3x + 7)$

10.2

Multiplying Polynomials

What you should learn

GOAL ① Multiply two polynomials.

GOAL ② Use polynomial multiplication in **real-life** situations, such as calculating the area of a window in **Example 5**.

Why you should learn it

▼ To solve **real-life** problems such as finding a model for movie ticket revenue in **Exs. 58** and **59**.

GOAL ① MULTIPLYING POLYNOMIALS

In Lesson 2.6 you learned how to multiply a polynomial by a monomial by using the distributive property.

$$(3x)(2x^2 - 5x + 3) = (3x)(2x^2) + (3x)(-5x) + (3x)(3) = 6x^3 - 15x^2 + 9x$$

In the following activity, you will see how an area model illustrates the multiplication of two binomials.

> **● ACTIVITY**
> **Developing Concepts**
> ## Investigating Binomial Multiplication
>
> The rectangle shown at the right has a width of $(x + 2)$ and a height of $(2x + 1)$.
>
> **①** Copy the model. What is the area of each part of the rectangle?
>
> **②** Find the product of $(x + 2)$ and $(2x + 1)$ by adding the areas of the parts to get an expression for total area.
>
> **③** Copy and complete the equation: $(x + 2)(2x + 1) = $? .
>
> **④** Use an area model to multiply $(x + 3)$ and $(2x + 4)$.

Another way to multiply two binomials is to use the distributive property *twice*.

First use $(a + b)(c + d) = a(c + d) + b(c + d)$.

Then use $a(c + d) = ac + ad$ and $b(c + d) = bc + bd$.

This shows that $(a + b)(c + d) = ac + ad + bc + bd$.

This property can also be applied to binomials of the form $a - b$ or $c - d$.

EXAMPLE 1 *Using the Distributive Property*

Find the product $(x + 2)(x - 3)$.

STUDENT HELP

▶ **Look Back**
For help with the distributive property, see p. 100.

SOLUTION

$$(x + 2)(x - 3) = x(x - 3) + 2(x - 3) \qquad (b + c)a = ba + ca$$

$$= x^2 - 3x + 2x - 6 \qquad a(b - c) = ab - ac$$

$$= x^2 - x - 6 \qquad \text{Combine like terms.}$$

When you multiply two binomials, you can remember the results given by the distributive property by means of the **FOIL** pattern. Multiply the **F**irst, **O**uter, **I**nner, and **L**ast terms.

| Product of First terms | Product of Outer terms | Product of Inner terms | Product of Last terms |

$$(3x + 4)(x + 5) = 3x^2 + 15x + 4x + 20$$
$$= 3x^2 + 19x + 20$$

STUDENT HELP

HOMEWORK HELP
Visit our Web site
www.mcdougallittell.com
for extra examples.

EXAMPLE 2 *Multiplying Binomials Using the FOIL Pattern*

$$\begin{array}{cccc} \textbf{F} & \textbf{O} & \textbf{I} & \textbf{L} \\ \downarrow & \downarrow & \downarrow & \downarrow \end{array}$$
$$(3x - 4)(2x + 1) = 6x^2 + 3x - 8x - 4 \qquad \text{Mental math}$$
$$= 6x^2 - 5x - 4 \qquad \text{Simplify.}$$

. . . .

To multiply two polynomials that have three or more terms, remember that *each term of one polynomial must be multiplied by each term of the other polynomial.* Use a vertical or a horizontal format. Write each polynomial in standard form.

EXAMPLE 3 *Multiplying Polynomials Vertically*

Find the product $(x - 2)(5 + 3x - x^2)$.

SOLUTION Align like terms in columns.

$$\begin{array}{rl} -x^2 + 3x + 5 & \text{Standard form} \\ \underline{\times \qquad\qquad x - 2} & \text{Standard form} \\ 2x^2 - 6x - 10 & \longleftarrow -2(-x^2 + 3x + 5) \\ \underline{-x^3 + 3x^2 + 5x \qquad\quad} & \longleftarrow x(-x^2 + 3x + 5) \\ -x^3 + 5x^2 - x - 10 & \text{Combine like terms.} \end{array}$$

EXAMPLE 4 *Multiplying Polynomials Horizontally*

Find the product $(4x^2 - 3x - 1)(2x - 5)$.

STUDENT HELP

Look Back
For help with multiplying
exponential expressions,
see p. 451.

SOLUTION Multiply $2x - 5$ by each term of $4x^2 - 3x - 1$.

$$(4x^2 - 3x - 1)(2x - 5) = 4x^2(2x - 5) - 3x(2x - 5) - 1(2x - 5)$$
$$= 8x^3 - 20x^2 - 6x^2 + 15x - 2x + 5$$
$$= 8x^3 - 26x^2 + 13x + 5$$

EXAMPLE 5 *Multiplying Binomials to Find an Area*

Carpentry

The diagram at the right shows
the basic dimensions for a window.
The glass portion of the window
has a height-to-width ratio of 3 : 2.
The framework adds 6 inches to the
width and 10 inches to the height.

a. Write a polynomial expression
that represents the total area of
the window, including the
framework.

b. Find the area when $x = 10, 11,$
$12, 13,$ and $14.$

SOLUTION

a. Use a verbal model.

PROBLEM
SOLVING
STRATEGY

**VERBAL
MODEL**

| Total area | $=$ | Height of window | $\cdot$ | Width of window |

LABELS

Total area $= A$ (square inches)

Height of window $= \mathbf{3x + 10}$ (inches)

Width of window $= \mathbf{2x + 6}$ (inches)

**ALGEBRAIC
MODEL**

$$A = \left(\mathbf{3x + 10} \right) \cdot \left(\mathbf{2x + 6} \right) \quad \text{Area model}$$
$$= 6x^2 + 18x + 20x + 60 \quad \text{FOIL pattern}$$
$$= 6x^2 + 38x + 60 \quad \text{Combine like terms.}$$

b. You can evaluate the polynomial expression $6x^2 + 38x + 60$ by substituting
x-values. For instance, to find the total area of the window when $x = 10$,
substitute 10 for x.

$$A = 6x^2 + 38x + 60$$
$$= 6(\mathbf{10})^2 + 38(\mathbf{10}) + 60$$
$$= 600 + 380 + 60$$
$$= 1040$$

▶ The areas for all five x-values are listed in the table.

x (in.)	10	11	12	13	14
A (in.²)	1040	1204	1380	1568	1768

GUIDED PRACTICE

Vocabulary Check ✓

1. How do the letters in "FOIL" help you remember how to multiply two binomials?

Concept Check ✓

2. Write an equation that represents the product of two binomials as shown in the area model at the right.

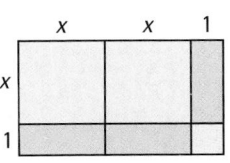

Explain how to use the distributive property to find the product.

3. $(2x - 3)(x + 4)$ **4.** $(x + 1)(x^2 - x + 1)$

Skill Check ✓

Use the given method to find the product $(2x + 3)(4x + 1)$.

5. Use an area model.

6. Use the distributive property.

7. Use the FOIL pattern.

8. Which of the methods you used in Exercises 5–7 do you prefer? Explain.

Find the product.

9. $(4x + 7)(-2x)$ **10.** $-4x^2(3x^2 + 2x - 6)$ **11.** $(-y - 2)(y + 8)$

12. $(w - 3)(2w + 5)$ **13.** $(x + 6)(x + 9)$ **14.** $(-2x - 4)(8x + 3)$

15. $(b + 8)(6 - 2b)$ **16.** $(-4y + 5)(-7 - 3y)$ **17.** $(3w^2 - 9)(5w - 1)$

PRACTICE AND APPLICATIONS

STUDENT HELP

▶ **Extra Practice**
to help you master
skills is on p. 806.

MULTIPLYING EXPRESSIONS **Find the product.**

18. $(2x - 5)(-4x)$ **19.** $3t^2(7t - t^3 - 3)$ **20.** $2x(x^2 - 8x + 1)$

21. $(-y)(6y^2 + 5y)$ **22.** $4w^2(3w^3 - 2w^2 - w)$ **23.** $-b^2(6b^3 - 16b + 11)$

DISTRIBUTIVE PROPERTY **Use the distributive property to find the product.**

24. $(t + 8)(t + 5)$ **25.** $(2d + 3)(3d + 1)$ **26.** $(4y^2 + y - 7)(2y - 1)$

27. $(3s^2 - s - 1)(s + 2)$ **28.** $(a^2 + 8)(a^2 - a - 3)$ **29.** $(x + 6)(x^2 - 6x - 2)$

USING THE FOIL PATTERN **Use the FOIL pattern to find the product.**

30. $(4q - 1)(3q + 8)$ **31.** $(2z + 7)(3z + 2)$ **32.** $(x + 6)(x - 6)$

33. $(2w - 5)(w + 5)$ **34.** $(x - 9)(2x + 15)$ **35.** $(5t - 3)(2t + 3)$

MULTIPLYING EXPRESSIONS **Find the product.**

36. $(d - 5)(d + 3)$ **37.** $(4x + 1)(x - 8)$ **38.** $(3b - 1)(b - 9)$

39. $(9w + 8)(11w - 10)$ **40.** $(11t - 30)(5t - 21)$ **41.** $(9.4y - 5.1)(7.3y - 12.2)$

42. $(3x + 4)\left(\dfrac{2}{3}x + 1\right)$ **43.** $\left(n + \dfrac{6}{5}\right)(4n - 10)$ **44.** $\left(x + \dfrac{1}{8}\right)\left(x - \dfrac{9}{8}\right)$

45. $(2.5z - 6.1)(z + 4.3)$ **46.** $(t^2 + 6t - 8)(t - 6)$ **47.** $(-4s^2 + s - 1)(s + 4)$

STUDENT HELP

▶ **HOMEWORK HELP**
Example 1: Exs. 18–29
Example 2: Exs. 30–35
Example 3: Exs. 36–47
Example 4: Exs. 36–47
Example 5: Exs. 52–55

USING A GRAPH TO CHECK **Find the product. Check your result by comparing a graph of the given expression with a graph of the product.**

48. $(x + 5)(x + 4)$ **49.** $(2x + 1)(x - 6)$

50. $(3x^2 - 8x - 1)(9x + 4)$ **51.** $(x + 7)(-x^2 - 6x + 2)$

GEOMETRY CONNECTION **Find an expression for the area of the figure.** (*Hint:* the *Table of Formulas* is on p. 813.) **Give your answer as a quadratic polynomial.**

52.

53.

FOOTBALL **In Exercises 54 and 55, a football field's dimensions can be represented by a width of $\left(\frac{1}{2}x + 10\right)$ feet and a length of $\left(\frac{5}{4}x - 15\right)$ feet.**

54. Find an expression for the area A of a football field. Give your answer as a quadratic trinomial.

55. An actual football field is 160 feet wide and 360 feet long. For what value of x does the expression you wrote in Exercise 54 give these dimensions?

$\left(\frac{1}{2}x + 10\right)$ ft

$\left(\frac{5}{4}x - 15\right)$ ft

VIDEOCASSETTES **In Exercises 56 and 57, use the following information about videocassette sales from 1987 to 1996, where t is the number of years since 1987.**

The annual number of blank videocassettes B sold in the United States can be modeled by $B = 15t + 281$, where B is measured in millions. The wholesale price P for a videocassette can be modeled by $P = -0.21t + 3.52$, where P is measured in dollars. ▶ Source: EIA Market Research Department

56. Find a model for the revenue from annual sales of blank videocassettes. Give the model as a quadratic trinomial.

57. Describe what happens to revenue during the period from 1987 to 1996.

BOX OFFICE **In Exercises 58 and 59, use the following information about movie theater admissions from 1980 to 1996, where t is the number of years since 1980.**

The annual number of admissions D into movie theaters can be modeled by $D = 13.75t + 1057.36$, where D is measured in millions. The admission price P can be modeled by $P = 0.11t + 2.90$, where P is the price per person. ▶ Source: Motion Picture Association of America

58. Find a model for the annual box office revenue. Give the model as a quadratic trinomial.

59. What conclusions can you make from your model?

60. MULTI-STEP PROBLEM Use the table, which gives annual data on cows and milk production (in pounds) in the United States from 1985 to 1996, where *t* is the number of years since 1985.

Year (*t*)	0	5	6	7	8	9	10	11
Milk production (1000s of lb/cow)	13	14.8	15	15.6	15.7	16.2	16.4	16.5
Millions of cows	11	10	9.8	9.7	9.6	9.5	9.5	9.4

 DATA UPDATE of U.S. Department of Agriculture data at www.mcdougallittell.com

a. Make a scatter plot of the milk production data.

b. Make a scatter plot of the annual data on the number of cows.

c. Write a linear model for each set of data. (Use the line-fitting technique in Lesson 5.4.)

d. Find a model for the total amount of milk produced. Check to see whether the model matches the information in the table below.

Year (*t*)	0	5	6	7	8	9	10	11
U.S. milk production (billion lb)	143	148	148	151	151	154	155	154

▶ Source: U.S. Department of Agriculture

e. What conclusions can you make based on the information?

 Challenge

61. a. PATTERNS Find each product: $(x - 1)(x + 1)$, $(x - 1)(x^2 + x + 1)$, and $(x - 1)(x^3 + x^2 + x + 1)$. Find a pattern in the results.

b. Use the pattern to predict the product $(x - 1)(x^4 + x^3 + x^2 + x + 1)$. Verify your guess by multiplying or graphing.

MIXED REVIEW

SIMPLIFYING EXPRESSIONS Simplify. (Review 8.1 for 10.3)

62. $(7x)^2$ **63.** $\left(\frac{1}{3}m\right)^2$ **64.** $\left(\frac{2}{5}y\right)^2$ **65.** $(0.5w)^2$

66. $9^3 \cdot 9^5$ **67.** $(4^2)^4$ **68.** $b^2 \cdot b^5$ **69.** $(4c^2)^4$

70. $(2t)^4 \cdot 3^3$ **71.** $(-w^4)^3$ **72.** $(-3xy)^3(2y)^2$ **73.** $(8x^2y^8)^3$

FINDING SOLUTIONS Tell how many solutions the equation has. (Review 9.6)

74. $2x^2 - 3x - 1 = 0$ **75.** $4x^2 + 4x + 1 = 0$ **76.** $3x^2 - 7x + 5 = 0$

77. $7x^2 - 8x - 6 = 0$ **78.** $10x^2 - 13x - 9 = 0$ **79.** $6x^2 - 12x - 6 = 0$

SKETCHING GRAPHS Sketch the graph of the inequality. (Review 9.7)

80. $y \geq 4x^2 - 7x$ **81.** $y < x^2 - 3x - 10$ **82.** $y > -2x^2 + 4x + 16$

83. $y < 6x^2 - 1$ **84.** $y \geq x^2 - 3x + 1$ **85.** $y \leq 8x^2 - 3$

Special Products of Polynomials

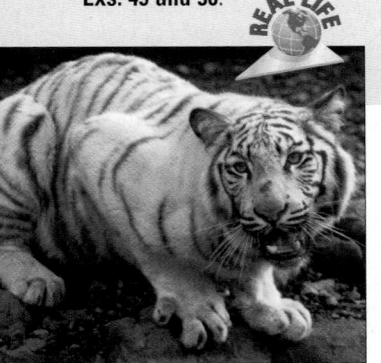

GOAL 1 **USING SPECIAL PRODUCT PATTERNS**

As you learned in Lesson 10.2, you can always use the FOIL pattern to multiply two binomials. Some pairs of binomials have *special products*. If you learn to recognize these pairs, finding the product of two binomials will sometimes be quicker and easier.

● ACTIVITY

Developing Concepts

Investigating Special Product Patterns

① Use the FOIL pattern to find the products in each group.

1. $(x - 2)(x + 2)$ **2.** $(x + 3)^2$ **3.** $(z - 2)^2$

  $(2n + 3)(2n - 3)$ $(3m + 1)^2$ $(6x - 4)^2$

  $(4t - 1)(4t + 1)$ $(5s + 2)^2$ $(5p - 7)^2$

  $(x + y)(x - y)$ $(x + y)^2$ $(x - y)^2$

② Describe any patterns that you see in each group.

In this activity, you may have noticed that the product of the sum and difference of two terms has no "middle term." Also, you may have noticed that in the square of a binomial the middle term is twice the product of the terms in the binomial.

SPECIAL PRODUCT PATTERNS

SUM AND DIFFERENCE PATTERN

$$(a + b)(a - b) = a^2 - b^2$$ Example: $(3x - 4)(3x + 4) = 9x^2 - 16$

SQUARE OF A BINOMIAL PATTERN

$$(a + b)^2 = a^2 + 2ab + b^2$$ Example: $(x + 4)^2 = x^2 + 8x + 16$

$$(a - b)^2 = a^2 - 2ab + b^2$$ Example: $(2x - 6)^2 = 4x^2 - 24x + 36$

The area model shown at the right gives a geometric representation of the *square of a binomial* pattern $(a + b)^2 = a^2 + 2ab + b^2$.

The area of the large square is $(a + b)^2$, which is equal to the sum of the areas of the two small squares and two rectangles. Note that the two rectangles with area ab produce the middle term $2ab$.

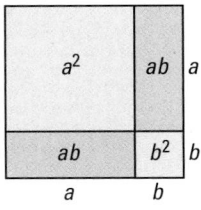

EXAMPLE 1 *Using the Sum and Difference Pattern*

Find the product $(5t - 2)(5t + 2)$.

SOLUTION

$(a - b)(a + b) = a^2 - b^2$	Write pattern.
$(5t - 2)(5t + 2) = (5t)^2 - 2^2$	Apply pattern.
$= 25t^2 - 4$	Simplify.

✓**CHECK** You can use the FOIL pattern to check your answer.

$(5t - 2)(5t + 2) = (5t)(5t) + (5t)(2) + (-2)(5t) + (-2)(2)$	Use FOIL.
$= 25t^2 - 4$	Simplify.

EXAMPLE 2 *Squaring a Binomial*

Find the product.

a. $(3n + 4)^2$ **b.** $(2x - 7y)^2$

SOLUTION

a.
$(a + b)^2 = a^2 + 2ab + b^2$	Write pattern.
$(3n + 4)^2 = (3n)^2 + 2(3n)(4) + 4^2$	Apply pattern.
$= 9n^2 + 24n + 16$	Simplify.

b.
$(a - b)^2 = a^2 - 2ab + b^2$	Write pattern.
$(2x - 7y)^2 = (2x)^2 - 2(2x)(7y) + (7y)^2$	Apply pattern.
$= 4x^2 - 28xy + 49y^2$	Simplify.

· · · · · · · · · ·

The special product patterns can help you use mental math to find products.

EXAMPLE 3 *Special Products and Mental Math*

Use mental math to find the product.

a. $17 \cdot 23$ **b.** 29^2

SOLUTION

a.
$17 \cdot 23 = (20 - 3)(20 + 3)$	Write as product of difference and sum.
$= 400 - 9$	Apply pattern.
$= 391$	Simplify.

b.
$29^2 = (30 - 1)^2$	Write as square of binomial.
$= 900 - 60 + 1$	Apply pattern.
$= 841$	Simplify.

EXAMPLE 4 *Finding an Area*

GEOMETRY CONNECTION Find an expression for the area of the blue region.

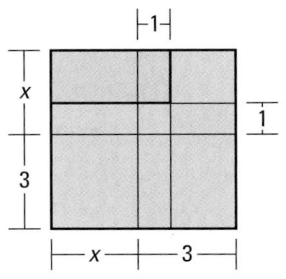

SOLUTION

PROBLEM SOLVING STRATEGY

VERBAL MODEL

| Area of blue region | = | Area of entire square | − | Area of red region |

LABELS

Area of blue region = A (square units)

Area of entire square = $(x + 3)^2$ (square units)

Area of red region = $(x + 1)(x - 1)$ (square units)

ALGEBRAIC MODEL

$A = (x + 3)^2 - (x + 1)(x - 1)$ Write algebraic model.

$ = (x^2 + 6x + 9) - (x^2 - 1)$ Apply pattern.

$ = x^2 + 6x + 9 - x^2 + 1$ Use distributive property.

$ = 6x + 10$ Simplify.

EXAMPLE 5 *Modeling a Punnett Square*

SCIENCE CONNECTION The Punnett square at the right is an area model that shows the possible results of crossing two pink snapdragons, each with one red gene R and one white gene W. Each parent snapdragon passes along only one gene for color to its offspring. Show how the square of a binomial can be used to model the Punnett square.

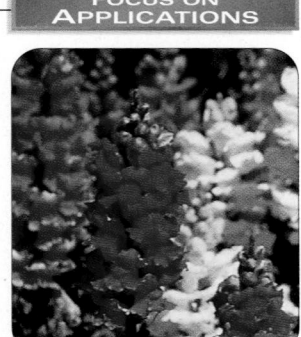

REAL LIFE PUNNETT SQUARES
are used in genetics to model the mixing of parents' genes in the resulting offspring.

SOLUTION

Each parent snapdragon has half red genes and half white genes. You can model the genetic makeup of each parent as $0.5R + 0.5W$. The genetic makeup of the offspring can be modeled by the product $(0.5R + 0.5W)^2$.

$$(0.5R + 0.5W)^2 = (0.5R)^2 + 2(0.5R)(0.5W) + (0.5W)^2$$

$$= 0.25R^2 + 0.5RW + 0.25W^2$$

 Red Pink White

▶ 25% of the offspring will be red, 50% will be pink, and 25% will be white.

GUIDED PRACTICE

Vocabulary Check ✔

Concept Check ✔

1. What is the sum and difference pattern?

2. Write two expressions for the product shown by the area model at the right.

3. Tell whether the following statement is *true* or *false*. The product of $(a + b)$ and $(a + b)$ is $a^2 + b^2$. Explain.

4. Find the missing term: $(a - b)^2 = a^2 - \boxed{?} + b^2$.

Skill Check ✔

5. Show the product $(x + 2)^2$ using an area model or algebra tiles. Draw a sketch of the model and use it to help you write $(x + 2)^2$ as a trinomial.

Use a special product pattern to find the product.

6. $(x - 6)^2$

7. $(w + 11)(w - 11)$

8. $(6 + p)^2$

9. $(2y - 3)^2$

10. $(3z + 2)^2$

11. $(t - 6)(t + 6)$

12. $(x - 3)(x - 3)$

13. $(2y + 5)(2y - 5)$

14. $(4n + 3)^2$

PRACTICE AND APPLICATIONS

STUDENT HELP

↳ **Extra Practice**
to help you master
skills is on p. 806.

SUM AND DIFFERENCE PATTERN Write the product of the sum and difference.

15. $(x + 3)(x - 3)$

16. $(y - 1)(y + 1)$

17. $(2m + 2)(2m - 2)$

18. $(3b - 1)(3b + 1)$

19. $(3 + 2x)(3 - 2x)$

20. $(6 - 5n)(6 + 5n)$

SQUARE OF A BINOMIAL Write the square of the binomial as a trinomial.

21. $(x + 5)^2$

22. $(a + 8)^2$

23. $(3t + 1)^2$

24. $(2s - 4)^2$

25. $(4b - 3)^2$

26. $(x - 7)^2$

SPECIAL PRODUCT PATTERNS Find the product.

27. $(x + 4)(x - 4)$

28. $(x - 3)(x + 3)$

29. $(3x + 1)(3x - 1)$

30. $(6x + 5)(6x - 5)$

31. $(a + 2b)(a - 2b)$

32. $(4n - 8m)(4n + 8m)$

33. $(3y + 8)^2$

34. $(9 - 4t)(9 + 4t)$

35. $\left(2x + \dfrac{1}{2}\right)\left(2x - \dfrac{1}{2}\right)$

36. $(-5 - 4x)^2$

37. $(3s + 4t)(3s - 4t)$

38. $(-a - 2b)^2$

STUDENT HELP

↳ **HOMEWORK HELP**
Example 1: Exs. 15–20,
    27–42
Example 2: Exs. 21–42
Example 3: Exs. 43–46
Example 4: Exs. 47, 48
Example 5: Exs. 49–52

CHECKING SOLUTIONS Tell whether the statement is *true* or *false*. If the statement is false, rewrite the right-hand side to make the statement true.

39. $(9x + 8)(9x - 8) \stackrel{?}{=} 81x^2 - 64$

40. $(6y - 7w)^2 \stackrel{?}{=} 36y^2 - 49w^2$

41. $\left(\dfrac{1}{3}a + 3b\right)^2 \stackrel{?}{=} \dfrac{1}{9}a^2 + 2ab + 9b^2$

42. $\left(\dfrac{2}{7}n - 3m\right)\left(\dfrac{2}{7}n - 3m\right) \stackrel{?}{=} \dfrac{4}{49}n^2 - 9m^2$

MENTAL MATH Use mental math to find the product.

43. $26 \cdot 34$

44. $45 \cdot 55$

45. 16^2

46. 41^2

AREA MODELS Write two expressions for the area of the figure. Describe the special product pattern that is represented.

47.

48.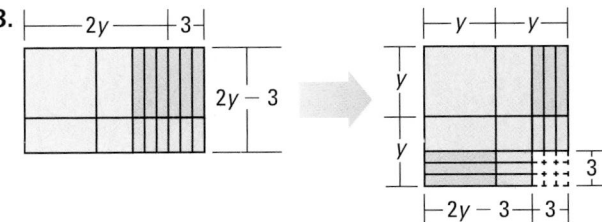

SCIENCE **CONNECTION** In tigers, the normal color gene *C* is *dominant* and the white color gene *c* is *recessive*. This means that a tiger whose color genes are *CC* or *Cc* will have normal coloring. A tiger whose color genes are *cc* will be white.

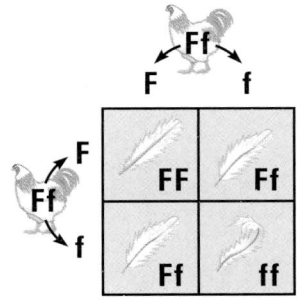

49. The Punnett square at the right shows the possible results of crossing two tigers that have recessive white genes. Find a model that can be used to represent the Punnett square and write the model as a polynomial.

50. What percent of the offspring will have normal coloring? What percent will be white?

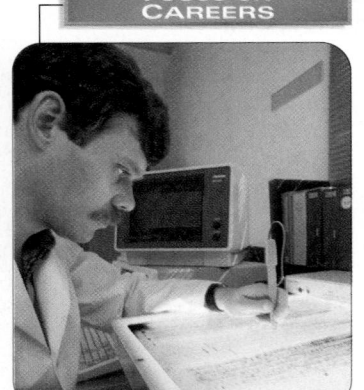
SCIENCE **CONNECTION** In Exercises 51 and 52, use the following information. In chickens, neither the normal-feathered gene *F* nor the frizzle-feathered gene *f* is dominant. So chickens whose feather genes are *FF* will have normal feathers. Chickens with *Ff* will have mildly frizzled feathers. Chickens with *ff* will have extremely frizzled feathers.

51. The Punnett square at the right shows the possible results of crossing two chickens with mildly frizzled feathers. Find a model that can be used to represent the Punnett square and write the model as a polynomial.

52. What percent of the offspring will have normal feathers? What percent will have mildly frizzled feathers? What percent will have extremely frizzled feathers?

INVESTMENT VALUE In Exercises 53–55, an investment of *P* dollars that gains *r* percent of its value in one year is worth $P(1 + r)$ at the end of that year. An investment that loses *r* percent of its value in one year is worth $P(1 - r)$ at the end of that year.

53. Write a model for the value of an investment *P* that loses *r* percent one year, then gains *r* percent the following year.

54. According to the model, did the investment increase or decrease in value? By how much?

55. If the investment gains *r* percent the first year and loses *r* percent the second year, what is the increase or decrease in the value of the investment?

QUANTITATIVE COMPARISON In Exercises 56 and 57, choose the statement that is true about the given numbers.

Ⓐ The number in column A is greater.

Ⓑ The number in column B is greater.

Ⓒ The two numbers are equal.

Ⓓ The relationship cannot be determined from the given information.

	Column A	Column B
56.	$(3x - 7)(3x + 7)$ when $x = 4$	$(3x - 7)^2$ when $x = 4$
57.	$a^2 + b^2$ when $a = 1$ and $b = -2$	$(a + b)^2$ when $a = 1$ and $b = -2$

58. MULTIPLE CHOICE Which of the following is equal to $(3x + 2)^2 - (x + 5)(x - 5)$?

Ⓐ $8x^2 + 29$ Ⓑ $8x^2 + 12x - 21$

Ⓒ $10x^2 + 6x + 29$ Ⓓ $8x^2 + 12x + 29$

★ **Challenge**

WRITING FACTORS Write a pair of factors that have the given product.

59. $x^2 + 12x + 36$ **60.** $x^2 - 4$

61. $25x^2 - 30x + 9$ **62.** $49x^2 - 169$

MIXED REVIEW

SIMPLIFYING EXPRESSIONS Simplify the expression. The simplified expression should have no negative exponents. (Review 8.3)

63. $\left(\dfrac{x}{4}\right)^3$ **64.** $\dfrac{x^3}{x^2}$ **65.** $\left(\dfrac{4x}{y^3}\right)^3$

66. $x^7 \cdot \dfrac{1}{x^4}$ **67.** $\dfrac{3x^2y}{2x} \cdot \dfrac{6xy^2}{y^3}$ **68.** $\dfrac{5x^4y}{3xy^2} \cdot \dfrac{9xy}{x^2y}$

FINDING PARTS OF A GRAPH Find the coordinates of the vertex and write the equation of the axis of symmetry. (Review 9.3 for 10.4)

69. $y = 2x^2 + 3x + 6$ **70.** $y = 3x^2 - 9x - 12$ **71.** $y = -x^2 + 4x + 16$

72. $y = -4x^2 - 2x + 5$ **73.** $y = -\dfrac{1}{2}x^2 + 6x - 4$ **74.** $y = \dfrac{1}{6}x^2 - \dfrac{1}{3}x + 2$

CHECKING GRAPHICALLY Solve the equation algebraically. Check the solutions graphically. (Review 9.4)

75. $x^2 - 10 = 6$ **76.** $x^2 + 12 = 48$ **77.** $\dfrac{1}{5}x^2 = 5$

78. $3x^2 = 192$ **79.** $\dfrac{2}{3}x^2 = 6$ **80.** $2x^2 - 66 = 96$

81. GEOMETRY CONNECTION Is it possible for a rectangle with a perimeter of 52 centimeters to have an area of 148.75 square centimeters? Explain. (Review 9.6)

Use a vertical format or a horizontal format to add or subtract. (Lesson 10.1)

1. $(2x^2 + 7x + 1) + (x^2 - 2x + 8)$ **2.** $(-4x^3 - 5x^2 + 2x) - (2x^3 + 9x^2 + 2)$

3. $(7t^2 - 3t + 5) - (4t^2 + 10t - 9)$ **4.** $(5x^3 - x^2 + 3x + 3) + (x^3 - 4x^2 + x)$

Find the product. (Lesson 10.2)

5. $(x + 8)(x - 1)$ **6.** $(4n + 7)(4n - 7)$ **7.** $(-2x^2 + x - 4)(x - 2)$

8. $(9m - 4)(3m + 1)$ **9.** $\left(\frac{1}{2}x - 3\right)\left(\frac{1}{2}x + 5\right)$ **10.** $-x^2(12x^3 - 11x^2 + 3)$

Use special products to find the product. (Lesson 10.3)

11. $(x - 6)(x + 6)$ **12.** $(4x + 3)(4x - 3)$ **13.** $(5 + 3b)(5 - 3b)$

14. $(2x - 7y)(2x + 7y)$ **15.** $(3x + 6)^2$ **16.** $(-6 - 8x)^2$

17. 🌐 **NEW PATIO** You are making a square concrete patio. You want a brick border that is 8 inches wide around the outer edge of the patio, and the total length of a side is $2x$ inches. Draw a diagram and write a polynomial for the area of the floor of the patio not including the brick border. (Lesson 10.3)

MATH & **History**   ▶ **Plant Genetics**

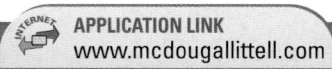

APPLICATION LINK
www.mcdougallittell.com

THEN ▶ **IN 1866,** Gregor Mendel identified the pattern in which pea plants passed their characteristics on to the next generation of plants. In Lesson 10.3, you used special products to model genetic patterns, as shown in Punnett squares.

Mendel identified the pattern for pea plants by breeding many plants under identical circumstances. This enabled him to calculate the experimental probability that a given generation of pea plants would have a given characteristic.

Use the table. Find the experimental probability. (see p. 115)

1. In trial 1, what is the probability that a pea plant is tall?

2. In trial 2, what is the probability that a pea plant is short?

	Short plants	Tall plants
Trial 1	39	121
Trial 2	81	235

NOW ▶ **TODAY,** knowledge of genetics helps researchers grow disease-resistant crops, more nutritious vegetables, taller trees, and more varieties of flowers.

Machinery dramatically increases farm production.

1860–1890

1896

Barbara McClintock receives Nobel Prize for her work on the genetics of corn.

1983

George Washington Carver heads Agriculture Dept. at Tuskegee Institute.

10.4 Solving Polynomial Equations in Factored Form

What you should learn

GOAL 1 Solve a polynomial equation in factored form.

GOAL 2 Relate factors and *x*-intercepts.

Why you should learn it

▼ To solve **real-life** problems like estimating the dimensions of the Gateway Arch in **Exs. 55 and 56**.

GOAL 1 SOLVING FACTORED EQUATIONS

In Chapter 9 you learned how to solve quadratic equations in standard form.

> **Standard form:** $2x^2 + 7x - 15 = 0$

In this lesson you will learn how to solve quadratic and other polynomial equations in *factored form*. A polynomial is in **factored form** if it is written as the product of two or more linear factors.

> **Factored form:** $(2x - 3)(x + 5) = 0$

> **Factored form:** $(2x - 3)(x + 5)(x - 7) = 0$

▶ ACTIVITY

Developing Concepts

Investigating Factored Equations

1 Copy and complete the table by substituting the *x*-values into the given expression.

Expression	x-value						
	−3	−2	−1	0	1	2	3
$(x - 3)(x + 2)$	$(-6)(-1) = 6$	?	?	?	?	?	?
$(x + 1)(x + 3)$	?	?	?	?	?	?	?
$(x - 2)(x - 2)$	?	?	?	?	?	?	?
$(x - 1)(x + 2)$	?	?	?	?	?	?	?

2 Use the table to solve each of the following equations.

a. $(x - 3)(x + 2) = 0$ **b.** $(x + 1)(x + 3) = 0$

c. $(x - 2)(x - 2) = 0$ **d.** $(x - 1)(x + 2) = 0$

3 Write a general rule for solving an equation that is in factored form.

In this activity, you may have noticed that the product of two factors is zero *only* when at least one of the factors is zero. This is because the real numbers satisfy the **zero-product property**.

ZERO-PRODUCT PROPERTY

Let *a* and *b* be real numbers. If *ab* = 0, then *a* = 0 or *b* = 0.

Examples 1, 2, and 3 show how to use this property to solve factored equations.

EXAMPLE 1 *Using the Zero-Product Property*

Solve the equation $(x - 2)(x + 3) = 0$.

SOLUTION Use the zero-product property: either $x - 2 = 0$ or $x + 3 = 0$.

$(x - 2)(x + 3) = 0$ Write original equation.

$x - 2 = 0$ Set first factor equal to 0.

$x = 2$ Solve for *x*.

$x + 3 = 0$ Set second factor equal to 0.

$x = -3$ Solve for *x*.

▶ The solutions are 2 and -3. Check these in the original equation.

EXAMPLE 2 *Solving a Repeated-Factor Equation*

Solve $(x + 5)^2 = 0$.

SOLUTION

This equation has a *repeated* factor. To solve the equation you need to set only $x + 5$ equal to zero.

$(x + 5)^2 = 0$ Write original equation.

$x + 5 = 0$ Set repeated factor equal to 0.

$x = -5$ Solve for *x*.

▶ The solution is -5. Check this in the original equation.

EXAMPLE 3 *Solving a Factored Cubic Equation*

Solve $(2x + 1)(3x - 2)(x - 1) = 0$.

SOLUTION

$(2x + 1)(3x - 2)(x - 1) = 0$ Write original equation.

$2x + 1 = 0$ Set first factor equal to 0.

$x = -\dfrac{1}{2}$ Solve for *x*.

$3x - 2 = 0$ Set second factor equal to 0.

$x = \dfrac{2}{3}$ Solve for *x*.

$x - 1 = 0$ Set third factor equal to 0.

$x = 1$ Solve for *x*.

▶ The solutions are $-\dfrac{1}{2}$, $\dfrac{2}{3}$, and 1. Check these in the original equation.

STUDENT HELP

↳ **Study Tip**
A polynomial equation in one variable can have as many solutions as it has linear factors that include the variable. As you saw in Example 2, an equation may have fewer solutions than factors if a factor is repeated.

CONCEPT SUMMARY **FACTORS, SOLUTIONS, AND *X*-INTERCEPTS**

For any quadratic polynomial $ax^2 + bx + c$, if one of the following statements is true, then all three statements are true.

- $(x - p)$ is a factor of the quadratic expression $ax^2 + bx + c$.
    Example: $(x - 4)$ and $(x + 3)$ are factors of $x^2 - x - 12$.

- $x = p$ is a solution of the quadratic equation $ax^2 + bx + c = 0$.
    Example: $x = 4$ and $x = -3$ are solutions of $x^2 - x - 12 = 0$.

- p is an *x*-intercept of the graph of the function $y = ax^2 + bx + c$.
    Example: 4 and -3 are *x*-intercepts of $y = x^2 - x - 12$.

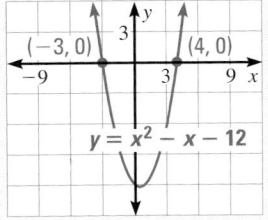

EXAMPLE 4 *Relating x-Intercepts and Factors*

STUDENT HELP

→ **Study Tip**
The statements above about factors, solutions, and *x*-intercepts are *logically equivalent* because each statement implies the truth of the other statements.

To sketch the graph of $y = (x - 3)(x + 2)$:

First solve $(x - 3)(x + 2) = 0$ to find the *x*-intercepts: 3 and -2.

Then find the coordinates of the vertex.

- The *x*-coordinate of the vertex is the average of the *x*-intercepts.

$$x = \frac{3 + (-2)}{2} = \frac{1}{2}$$

- Substitute to find the *y*-coordinate.

$$y = \left(\frac{1}{2} - 3\right)\left(\frac{1}{2} + 2\right) = -\frac{25}{4}$$

- The coordinates of the vertex are $\left(\frac{1}{2}, -\frac{25}{4}\right)$.

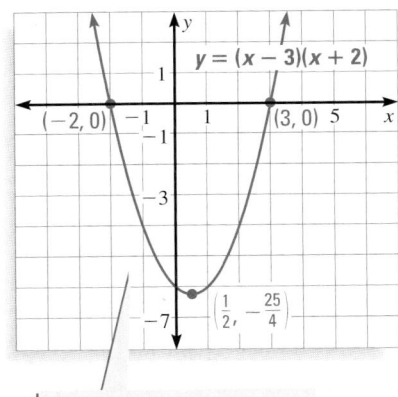

Sketch the graph by using the *x*-intercepts and vertex coordinates.

Archways

EXAMPLE 5 *Using a Quadratic Model*

An arch is modeled by the equation $y = -0.15(x - 8)(x + 8)$, with *x* and *y* measured in feet. How wide is the arch at the base? How high is the arch?

SOLUTION Sketch a graph of the model.

- The *x*-intercepts are $x = 8$ and $x = -8$.

- The vertex is at $(0, 9.6)$.

▶ The arch is $8 - (-8)$, or 16 feet wide at the base and 9.6 feet high.

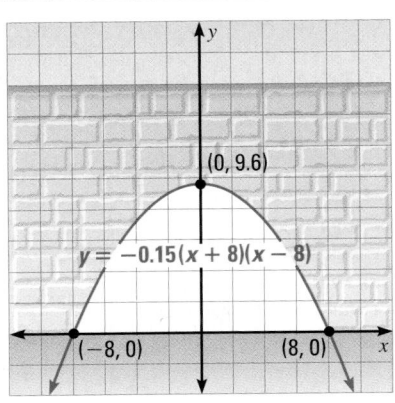

GUIDED PRACTICE

Vocabulary Check ✔

1. What is the zero-product property?

Concept Check ✔

2. Are 1 and -4 the solutions of $(x + 1)(x - 4) = 0$? Explain.

3. Are -5, 2, and 3 the solutions of $3(x - 2)(x + 5) = 0$? Explain.

Tell whether the statement about $x^2 + 12x + 32$ is *true* or *false*.

4. $x^2 + 12x + 32 = (x + 4)(x + 8)$

5. $x = -4$ and $x = -8$ are solutions of $x^2 + 12x + 32 = 0$.

6. $(x + 4)$ and $(x + 8)$ are factors of $x^2 + 12x + 32$.

7. The x-intercepts of the graph of $y = x^2 + 12x + 32$ are -4 and -8.

Skill Check ✔

Does the graph of the function have x-intercepts of 4 and -5?

8. $y = 2(x + 4)(x - 5)$ **9.** $y = 4(x - 4)(x - 5)$

10. $y = -(x - 4)(x + 5)$ **11.** $y = 3(x + 5)(x - 4)$

In Exercises 12–17, use the zero-product property to solve the equation.

12. $(b + 1)(b + 3) = 0$ **13.** $(t - 3)(t - 5) = 0$

14. $(x - 7)^2 = 0$ **15.** $(y + 9)(y - 2) = 0$

16. $(3d + 6)(2d + 5) = 0$ **17.** $\left(2w + \dfrac{1}{2}\right)^2 = 0$

18. Sketch the graph of $y = (x - 2)(x + 5)$. Label the vertex and the x-intercepts.

PRACTICE AND APPLICATIONS

STUDENT HELP

▶ **Extra Practice**
to help you master
skills is on p. 806.

ZERO-PRODUCT PROPERTY Use the zero-product property to solve the equation.

19. $(x + 4)(x + 1) = 0$ **20.** $(y + 3)^2 = 0$ **21.** $(t + 8)(t - 6) = 0$

22. $(w - 17)^2 = 0$ **23.** $(b - 9)(b + 8) = 0$ **24.** $(d + 7)^2 = 0$

25. $(y - 2)(y + 1) = 0$ **26.** $(z + 2)(z + 3) = 0$ **27.** $(v - 7)(v - 5) = 0$

28. $\left(t + \dfrac{1}{2}\right)(t - 4) = 0$ **29.** $4(c + 9)^2 = 0$ **30.** $(u - 3)\left(u - \dfrac{2}{3}\right) = 0$

31. $(y - 5.6)^2 = 0$ **32.** $(a - 40)(a + 12) = 0$ **33.** $7(b - 5)^3 = 0$

SOLVING FACTORED EQUATIONS Solve the equation.

34. $(4x - 8)(7x + 21) = 0$ **35.** $(2d + 8)(3d + 12) = 0$

36. $5(3m + 9)(5m - 15) = 0$ **37.** $8(9n + 27)(6n - 9) = 0$

STUDENT HELP

▶ HOMEWORK HELP
Example 1: Exs. 19–43
Example 2: Exs. 19–43
Example 3: Exs. 38–43
Example 4: Exs. 44–52
Example 5: Exs. 53–58

38. $(6b - 18)(2b + 2)(2b + 2) = 0$ **39.** $(4y - 5)(2y - 6)(3y - 4) = 0$

40. $(x + 44)(3x - 2)^2 = 0$ **41.** $(5x - 9.5)^2(3x + 6.3) = 0$

42. $\left(\dfrac{1}{2}x + 2\right)\left(\dfrac{2}{3}x + 6\right)\left(\dfrac{1}{6}x - 1\right) = 0$ **43.** $\left(2n - \dfrac{1}{4}\right)\left(5n + \dfrac{3}{10}\right)\left(3n - \dfrac{2}{3}\right) = 0$

MATCHING FUNCTIONS AND GRAPHS Match the function with its graph.

A. $y = (x + 2)(x - 4)$ **B.** $y = (x - 2)(x + 4)$ **C.** $y = (x + 4)(x + 2)$

44.

45.

46.
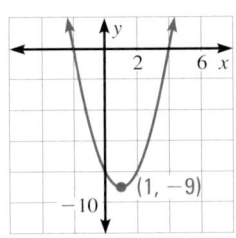

SKETCHING GRAPHS Find the *x*-intercepts and the vertex of the graph of the function. Then sketch the graph of the function.

47. $y = (x - 4)(x + 2)$ **48.** $y = (x + 5)(x + 3)$ **49.** $y = (-x - 2)(x + 2)$

50. $y = (-x - 1)(x + 7)$ **51.** $y = (x - 2)(x - 6)$ **52.** $y = (-x + 4)(x + 3)$

STUDENT HELP

HOMEWORK HELP
Visit our Web site
www.mcdougallittell.com
for help with Exs. 53–58.

🌐 **RADIO TELESCOPE** In Exercises 53 and 54, use the cross section of the radio telescope dish shown below.

The cross section of the telescope's dish can be modeled by the polynomial function

$$y = \frac{167}{500^2}(x + 500)(x - 500)$$

where *x* and *y* are measured in feet, and the center of the dish is where $x = 0$.

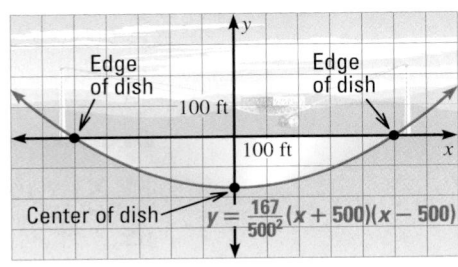

53. Explain how to use the algebraic model to find the width of the dish.

54. Use the model to find the coordinates of the center of the dish.

🌐 **GATEWAY ARCH** In Exercises 55 and 56, use the following information.
The Gateway Arch in St. Louis, Missouri, has the shape of a *catenary* (a U-shaped curve similar to a parabola). It can be approximated by the following model, where *x* and *y* are measured in feet. ▶ Source: National Park Service

    Gateway Arch model: $y = -\dfrac{7}{1000}(x + 300)(x - 300)$

55. According to the model, how far apart are the legs of the arch?

56. How high is the arch?

🌐 **BARRINGER METEOR CRATER** In Exercises 57 and 58, use the following equation, where *x* and *y* are measured in meters, to model a cross section of the Barringer Meteor Crater, near Winslow, Arizona.
▶ Source: Jet Propulsion Laboratory

    Barringer Meteor Crater model: $y = \dfrac{1}{1800}(x - 600)(x + 600)$

57. Assuming the lip of the crater is at $y = 0$, how wide is the crater?

58. What is the depth of the crater?

FOCUS ON APPLICATIONS

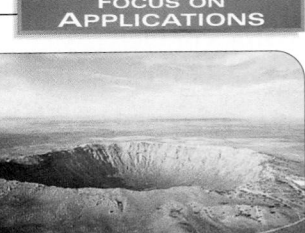

THE BARRINGER METEOR CRATER
was formed about 49,000 years ago when a nickel and iron meteorite struck the desert at about 25,000 miles per hour.

59. MULTI-STEP PROBLEM You sell hot dogs for $1.00 each at your concession stand at a baseball park and have about 200 customers. You want to increase the price of a hot dog. You estimate that you will lose three sales for every $.10 increase. The following equation models your hot dog sales revenue R, where n is the number of $.10 increases.

Concession stand revenue model: $R = (1 + 0.1n)(200 - 3n)$

a. To find your revenue from hot dog sales, you multiply the price of each hot dog sold by the number of hot dogs sold. In the formula above, what does $1 + 0.1n$ represent? What does $200 - 3n$ represent?

b. How many times would you have to raise the price by $.10 to reduce your revenue to zero? Make a graph to help find your answer.

c. Decide how high you should raise the price to make the most money. Explain how you got your answer.

★ **Challenge**

60. *Writing* Write your own multi-step problem about selling a product like the one in Exercise 59. Include a model that shows the relationship between price and number of items sold. Explain what each factor in the model represents.

MIXED REVIEW

DECIMAL FORM Rewrite in decimal form. **(Review 8.4)**

61. 2.1×10^5 **62.** 4.443×10^{-2} **63.** 8.57×10^8 **64.** 1.25×10^6

65. 3.71×10^{-3} **66.** 9.96×10^6 **67.** 7.22×10^{-4} **68.** 8.17×10^7

MULTIPLYING EXPRESSIONS Find the product. **(Review 10.2 for 10.5)**

69. $(x - 2)(x - 7)$ **70.** $(x + 8)(x - 8)$ **71.** $(x - 4)(x + 5)$

72. $(x + 6)(x - 7)$ **73.** $\left(x + \frac{2}{3}\right)\left(x - \frac{1}{3}\right)$ **74.** $(x - 3)\left(x - \frac{1}{6}\right)$

75. $(2x + 7)(3x - 1)$ **76.** $(5x - 1)(5x + 2)$ **77.** $(3x + 1)(8x - 3)$

78. $(2x - 4)\left(\frac{1}{4}x - 2\right)$ **79.** $(x + 10)(x + 10)$ **80.** $(3x + 5)\left(\frac{2}{3}x - 3\right)$

EXPONENTIAL MODELS Tell whether the situation can be represented by a model of *exponential growth* or *exponential decay*. Then write a model that represents the situation. **(Review 8.5, 8.6)**

81. 🌎 **COMPUTER PRICES** From 1996 to 2000, the average price of a computer company's least expensive home computer system decreased by 16% per year.

82. 🌎 **MUSIC SALES** From 1995 to 1999, the number of CDs a band sold increased by 23% per year.

83. 🌎 **COOKING CLUB** From 1996 to 2000, the number of members in the cooking club decreased by 3% per year.

84. 🌎 **INTERNET SERVICE** From 1993 to 1998, the total revenues for a company that provides Internet service increased by about 137% per year.

● ACTIVITY 10.5

Developing Concepts

GROUP ACTIVITY
Work with a partner.

MATERIALS
algebra tiles

Modeling the Factorization of $x^2 + bx + c$

▶ **QUESTION** How can you model the factorization of a trinomial of the form $x^2 + bx + c$ using algebra tiles?

▶ **EXPLORING THE CONCEPT**

You can use algebra tiles to create a model that can be used to factor a trinomial that has a leading coefficient of 1. Factor the trinomial $x^2 + 5x + 6$ as follows.

❶ Use algebra tiles to model $x^2 + 5x + 6$.

x^2 + $5x$ + 6

❷ With the x^2-tile at the upper left, arrange the x-tiles and the 1-tiles around the x^2-tile to form a rectangle.

❸ The width of the rectangle is _?_, and the length of the rectangle is _?_.

Complete the statement: $x^2 + 5x + 6 = $ _?_ • _?_ .

▶ **EXERCISES**

Use the model to write the factors of the trinomial.

1.

2.

In Exercises 3–8, use algebra tiles to factor the trinomial. Sketch your model.

3. $x^2 + 7x + 6$ **4.** $x^2 + 6x + 8$ **5.** $x^2 + 8x + 15$

6. $x^2 + 6x + 9$ **7.** $x^2 + 4x + 4$ **8.** $x^2 + 7x + 10$

9. Use algebra tiles to show why the trinomial $x^2 + 3x + 4$ cannot be factored.

10.5 Factoring $x^2 + bx + c$

GOAL 1 FACTORING A QUADRATIC TRINOMIAL

What you should learn

GOAL 1 Factor a quadratic expression of the form $x^2 + bx + c$.

GOAL 2 Solve quadratic equations by factoring.

Why you should learn it

▼ To help solve **real-life** problems, such as finding the width of a stone border in **Example 7**.

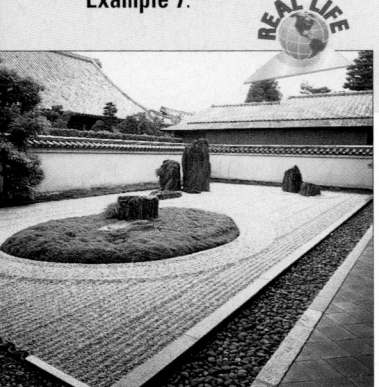

To **factor** a quadratic expression means to write it as the product of two linear expressions. In this lesson, you will learn how to factor quadratic trinomials that have a leading coefficient of 1.

FACTORING $x^2 + bx + c$

You know from the FOIL method that $(x + p)(x + q) = x^2 + (p + q)x + pq$. So to factor $x^2 + bx + c$, you need to find numbers p and q such that

$$p + q = b \quad \text{and} \quad pq = c$$

because $x^2 + (p + q)x + pq = x^2 + bx + c$ if and only if $p + q = b$ and $pq = c$.

Example: $x^2 + 6x + 8 = (x + 4)(x + 2)$ $4 + 2 = 6$ and $4 \cdot 2 = 8$

EXAMPLE 1   *Factoring when b and c are Positive*

Factor $x^2 + 3x + 2$.

SOLUTION

For this trinomial, $b = 3$ and $c = 2$. You need to find two numbers whose sum is 3 and whose product is 2.

$$x^2 + 3x + 2 = (x + p)(x + q) \qquad \text{Find } p \text{ and } q \text{ when } p + q = 3 \text{ and } pq = 2.$$
$$= (x + 1)(x + 2) \qquad p = 1 \text{ and } q = 2$$

✓**CHECK:** You can check the result by multiplying.

$$(x + 1)(x + 2) = x^2 + 2x + x + 2 \qquad \text{Use FOIL to check.}$$
$$= x^2 + 3x + 2 \qquad \text{Simplify.}$$

EXAMPLE 2   *Factoring when b is Negative and c is Positive*

Factor $x^2 - 5x + 6$.

SOLUTION

Because b is negative and c is positive, both p and q must be negative numbers. Find two numbers whose sum is -5 and whose product is 6.

$$x^2 - 5x + 6 = (x + p)(x + q) \qquad \text{Find } p \text{ and } q \text{ when } p + q = -5 \text{ and } pq = 6.$$
$$= (x - 2)(x - 3) \qquad p = -2 \text{ and } q = -3$$

STUDENT HELP

┌─────────────┐
│ INTERNET   │
│ ┌───┐   │ HOMEWORK HELP
│ │   │   │ Visit our Web site
└─────────────┘ www.mcdougallittell.com
                 for extra examples.

EXAMPLE 3 *Factoring when b and c are Negative*

Factor $x^2 - 2x - 8$.

SOLUTION For this trinomial, $b = -2$ and $c = -8$. Because c is negative, you know that p and q cannot both have negative values.

$$x^2 - 2x - 8 = (x + p)(x + q) \qquad \text{Find } p \text{ and } q \text{ when } p + q = -2 \text{ and } pq = -8.$$
$$= (x + 2)(x - 4) \qquad p = 2 \text{ and } q = -4$$

✓**CHECK:** Use a graphing calculator.
Graph $y = x^2 - 2x - 8$ and
$y = (x + 2)(x - 4)$ on the same screen.

The graphs coincide, so your answer
is correct.

EXAMPLE 4 *Factoring when b is Positive and c is Negative*

Factor $x^2 + 7x - 18$.

SOLUTION For this trinomial, $b = 7$ and $c = -18$. Because c is negative, you know that p and q cannot both have negative values.

$$x^2 + 7x - 18 = (x + p)(x + q) \qquad \text{Find } p \text{ and } q \text{ when } p + q = 7 \text{ and } pq = -18.$$
$$= (x + 9)(x - 2) \qquad p = 9 \text{ and } q = -2$$

. . . .

STUDENT HELP

► **Look Back**
 For help with finding the
 discriminant, see p. 541.

It is important to realize that *many* quadratic trinomials with integer coefficients cannot be factored into linear factors with integer coefficients. A quadratic trinomial $x^2 + bx + c$ can be factored (using integer coefficients) only if the *discriminant* is a perfect square.

EXAMPLE 5 *Using the Discriminant*

Tell whether the trinomial can be factored.

a. $x^2 + 3x - 4$ **b.** $x^2 + 3x - 6$

SOLUTION Find the discriminant.

a. $b^2 - 4ac = 3^2 - 4(1)(-4) \qquad a = 1, b = 3, \text{ and } c = -4$
$$= 25 \qquad \text{Simplify.}$$

▶ The discriminant is a perfect square, so the trinomial can be factored.

b. $b^2 - 4ac = 3^2 - 4(1)(-6) \qquad a = 1, b = 3, \text{ and } c = -6$
$$= 33 \qquad \text{Simplify.}$$

▶ The discriminant is not a perfect square, so the trinomial cannot be factored.

GOAL 2 SOLVING QUADRATIC EQUATIONS BY FACTORING

EXAMPLE 6   Solving a Quadratic Equation

$x^2 - 3x = 10$	Write equation.
$x^2 - 3x - 10 = 0$	Write in standard form.
$(x - 5)(x + 2) = 0$	Factor left side.
$(x - 5) = 0$ or $(x + 2) = 0$	Use zero-product property.
$x - 5 = 0$	Set first factor equal to 0.
$x = 5$	Solve for x.
$x + 2 = 0$	Set second factor equal to 0.
$x = -2$	Solve for x.

▶ The solutions are 5 and −2. Check these in the original equation.

EXAMPLE 7   Writing a Quadratic Model

LANDSCAPE DESIGN You are putting a stone border along two sides of a rectangular Japanese garden that measures 6 yards by 15 yards. Your budget limits you to only enough stone to cover 46 square yards. How wide should the border be?

SOLUTION

Begin by drawing and labeling a diagram.

Area of border	=	Total area	−	Garden area

$46 = (x + 15)(x + 6) - (15)(6)$	Write quadratic model.
$46 = x^2 + 21x + 90 - 90$	Multiply.
$0 = x^2 + 21x - 46$	Write in standard form.
$0 = (x + 23)(x - 2)$	Factor.
$(x + 23) = 0$ or $(x - 2) = 0$	Use zero-product property.
$x + 23 = 0$	Set first factor equal to 0.
$x = -23$	Solve for x.
$x - 2 = 0$	Set second factor equal to 0.
$x = 2$	Solve for x.

▶ The solutions are −23 and 2. Only $x = 2$ is a reasonable solution, because negative values for dimension do not make sense. Make the border 2 yards wide.

GUIDED PRACTICE

Vocabulary Check ✔

1. What does it mean to factor a quadratic expression?

Concept Check ✔

2. Factor $x^2 - 4x + 3$. When testing possible factorizations, why is it unnecessary to test $(x - 1)(x + 3)$ and $(x + 1)(x - 3)$?

3. Factor $x^2 + 2x - 3$. When testing possible factorizations, why is it unnecessary to test $(x - 1)(x - 3)$ and $(x + 1)(x + 3)$?

4. Can a trinomial $x^2 + bx + c$, where b and c are integers, be factored with integer coefficients if its discriminant is 35? Explain.

Skill Check ✔

Match the trinomial with a correct factorization.

5. $x^2 - x - 20$

6. $x^2 + x - 20$

7. $x^2 + 9x + 20$

8. $x^2 - 9x + 20$

A. $(x + 5)(x - 4)$

B. $(x + 4)(x + 5)$

C. $(x - 4)(x - 5)$

D. $(x + 4)(x - 5)$

Use the discriminant to decide whether the equation can be solved by factoring. Explain your reasoning.

9. $x^2 - 4x + 4 = 0$

10. $x^2 - 4x - 5 = 0$

11. $x^2 - 4x - 6 = 0$

PRACTICE AND APPLICATIONS

STUDENT HELP

▶ **Extra Practice**
to help you master
skills is on p. 806.

FACTORED FORM Choose the correct factorization. If neither is correct, find the correct factorization.

12. $x^2 + 7x + 12$

    A. $(x + 6)(x + 2)$

    B. $(x + 4)(x + 3)$

13. $x^2 - 10x + 16$

    A. $(x - 4)(x - 4)$

    B. $(x - 8)(x - 2)$

14. $x^2 + 11x - 26$

    A. $(x - 13)(x + 2)$

    B. $(x - 13)(x - 2)$

FACTORING TRINOMIALS Factor the trinomial.

15. $x^2 + 8x - 9$

16. $t^2 - 10t + 21$

17. $b^2 + 5b - 24$

18. $w^2 + 13w + 36$

19. $y^2 - 3y - 18$

20. $c^2 + 14c + 40$

21. $m^2 - 7m - 30$

22. $32 + 12n + n^2$

23. $44 - 15s + s^2$

24. $z^2 + 65z + 1000$

25. $x^2 - 45x + 450$

26. $d^2 - 33d - 280$

STUDENT HELP

▶ HOMEWORK HELP
Examples 1–4:
  Exs. 12–26, 48–51
Example 5: Exs. 42–47
Example 6: Exs. 27–41
Example 7: Exs. 56–60

SOLVING QUADRATIC EQUATIONS Solve the equation by factoring.

27. $x^2 + 7x + 10 = 0$

28. $x^2 + 5x - 14 = 0$

29. $x^2 - 9x = -14$

30. $x^2 + 32x = -220$

31. $x^2 + 16x = -15$

32. $x^2 + 3x = 54$

33. $x^2 + 8x = 65$

34. $-x + x^2 = 56$

35. $x^2 - 20x = -51$

36. $x^2 - 5x = 84$

37. $x^2 + 3x - 31 = -3$

38. $x^2 - 2x - 19 = -4$

39. $x^2 - x - 8 = 82$

40. $x^2 + 42 = 13x$

41. $x^2 - 9x + 18 = 2x$

USING THE DISCRIMINANT Tell whether the quadratic expression can be factored with integer coefficients. If it can, find the factors.

42. $t^2 + 7t - 144$ **43.** $y^2 + 19y + 60$ **44.** $x^2 - 11x + 24$

45. $w^2 - 6w + 16$ **46.** $z^2 - 26z - 87$ **47.** $b^2 + 14b + 35$

CHECKING GRAPHICALLY Solve the equation by factoring. Then use a graphing calculator to check your answer.

48. $x^2 - 17x + 30 = 0$ **49.** $x^2 + 8x = 105$

50. $x^2 - 20x + 21 = 2$ **51.** $x^2 + 52x + 680 = 40$

WRITING EQUATIONS Write a quadratic equation with the given solutions.

52. 12 and -21 **53.** -5 and -6 **54.** -41 and 5   **55.** 427 and 0

STUDENT HELP

TABLE OF FORMULAS
For help with area, see the Table of Formulas, p. 813.

GEOMETRY CONNECTION In Exercises 56–58, consider a rectangle having one side of length $x - 6$ and having an area given by $A = x^2 - 17x + 66$.

56. Use factoring to find an expression for the other side of the rectangle.

57. If the area of the rectangle is 84 square feet, what are possible values of x?

58. For the value of x found in Exercise 57, what are the dimensions of the rectangle?

GEOMETRY CONNECTION Consider a circle whose radius is greater than 9 and whose area is given by $A = \pi(x^2 - 18x + 81)$. (Use $\pi \approx 3.14$.)

59. Use factoring to find an expression for the radius of the circle.

60. If the area of the circle is 12.56 square meters, what is the value of x?

MAKING A SIGN In Exercises 61 and 62, a triangular sign has a base that is 2 feet less than twice its height. A local zoning ordinance restricts the surface area of street signs to no more than 20 square feet.

61. Write an inequality involving the height of the triangle that represents the largest triangular sign allowed.

62. Find the base and height of the largest triangular sign that meets the zoning ordinance.

FOCUS ON APPLICATIONS

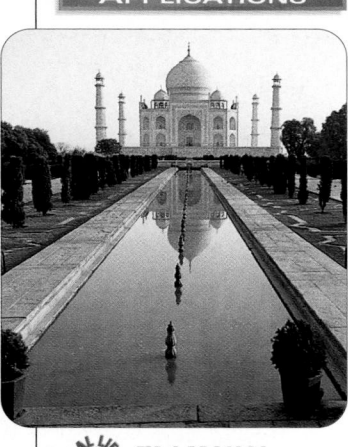

TAJ MAHAL
It took more than 20,000 daily workers 22 years to complete the Taj Mahal around 1643 in India. Constructed primarily of white marble and red sandstone, the Taj Mahal is renowned for its beauty.

APPLICATION LINK
www.mcdougallittell.com

THE TAJ MAHAL In Exercises 63 and 64, refer to the illustration at the right of the Taj Mahal.

63. The platform is about 38 meters wider than the main building. The total area of the platform is about 9025 square meters. Find the dimensions of the platform and the base of the building. (Assume each is a square.)

64. The entire complex of the Taj Mahal is about 245 meters longer than it is wide. The area of the entire complex is about 167,750 square meters. What are the dimensions of the entire complex? Explain your steps in finding the solution.

Building

Platform

65. **MULTIPLE CHOICE** The length of a rectangular plot of land with an area of 880 square meters is 24 meters more than its width. A paved area measuring 8 meters by 12 meters is placed on the plot. If w represents the width of the plot of land in meters, which of the following equations can be factored to find possible values of the width of the land?

   Ⓐ $w^2 + 24w = 880$ Ⓑ $w^2 - 24w = 880$

   Ⓒ $w^2 + 24w = -880$ Ⓓ $w^2 - 24w = -880$

66. **MULTIPLE CHOICE** A triangle's base is 16 feet less than 2 times its height. If h represents the height in feet, and the total area of the triangle is 48 square feet, which of the following equations can be used to determine the height?

   Ⓐ $2h + 2(h + 4) = 48$ Ⓑ $h^2 - 8h = 48$

   Ⓒ $h^2 + 8h = 48$ Ⓓ $2h^2 - 16h = 48$

67. **MULTIPLE CHOICE** Which of the following equations does *not* have solutions that are integers?

   Ⓐ $x^2 + 21x + 100 = -10$ Ⓑ $x^2 - 169 = 0$

   Ⓒ $x^2 - 8x - 105 = 0$ Ⓓ $x^2 - 15x - 75 = 0$

★ Challenge

FACTORING CHALLENGE In Exercises 68–71, *n* is a positive integer. Factor the expression. (*Hint*: $(a^n)^2 = a^{2n}$)

68. $a^{2n} - b^{2n}$ **69.** $a^{2n} + 2a^n b^n + b^{2n}$

EXTRA CHALLENGE
www.mcdougallittell.com

70. $a^{2n} + 18a^n b^n + 81b^{2n}$ **71.** $5a^{2n} - 9a^n b^n - 2b^{2n}$

MIXED REVIEW

FINDING THE GCF Find the greatest common factor. (Skills Review, p. 777)

72. 30, 45   **73.** 49, 64   **74.** 412, 18

75. 77, 91   **76.** 20, 32, 40   **77.** 36, 54, 162

MULTIPLYING EXPRESSIONS Find the product. (Review 10.2, 10.3)

78. $3q(q^3 - 5q^2 + 6)$ **79.** $(y + 9)(y - 4)$ **80.** $(7x - 11)^2$

81. $(5 - w)(12 + 3w)$ **82.** $(3a - 2)(4a + 6)$ **83.** $(2b - 4)(b^3 + 4b^2 + 5b)$

84. $(9x + 8)(9x - 8)$ **85.** $\left(6z + \dfrac{1}{3}\right)^2$ **86.** $(5t - 3)(4t - 10)$

SOLVING FACTORED EQUATIONS Solve the equation. (Review 10.4)

87. $(x + 12)(x + 7) = 0$ **88.** $(z + 2)(z + 3) = 0$ **89.** $(t - 19)^2 = 0$

90. $\left(b - \dfrac{2}{5}\right)\left(b - \dfrac{5}{6}\right) = 0$ **91.** $(x - 9)(x - 6) = 0$ **92.** $(y + 47)(y - 27) = 0$

93. $(z - 1)(4z + 2) = 0$ **94.** $(3a - 8)(a + 5) = 0$ **95.** $(4n - 6)^3 = 0$

96. 🌎 **DISASTER RELIEF** You drop a box of supplies from a helicopter at an altitude of 40 feet above a drop area. Use a vertical motion model to find the time it takes the box to reach the ground. (Review 9.5 for 10.6)

● ACTIVITY 10.6

Developing Concepts

SET UP
Work in a small group.

MATERIALS
algebra tiles

Modeling the Factorization of $ax^2 + bx + c$

▶ **QUESTION** How can you model the factorization of a trinomial of the form $ax^2 + bx + c$ using algebra tiles?

▶ **EXPLORING THE CONCEPT**

You can use algebra tiles to create a model that can be used to factor a trinomial that has a leading coefficient other than 1. Factor the trinomial $2x^2 + 5x + 3$ as follows.

❶ Use algebra tiles to model $2x^2 + 5x + 3$.

$2x^2$ $+$ $5x$ $+$ 3

❷ With the x^2-tiles at the upper left, arrange the x-tiles and the 1-tiles around the x^2-tiles to form a rectangle.

❸ The width of the rectangle is _?_, and the length of the rectangle is _?_.

Complete the statement: $2x^2 + 5x + 3 = $ _?_ • _?_

▶ **EXERCISES**

Use algebra tiles to factor the trinomial. Sketch your model.

1. $2x^2 + 9x + 9$ **2.** $2x^2 + 7x + 3$ **3.** $3x^2 + 4x + 1$

4. $3x^2 + 10x + 3$ **5.** $3x^2 + 10x + 8$ **6.** $4x^2 + 5x + 1$

ERROR ANALYSIS The algebra tile model is incorrect. Sketch the correct model, and use the model to factor the trinomial.

7. $2x^2 + 3x + 1$ **8.** $2x^2 + 4x + 2$ **9.** $4x^2 + 4x + 1$

  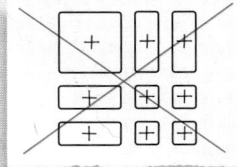

10.6 Factoring $ax^2 + bx + c$

What you should learn

GOAL 1 Factor a quadratic expression of the form $ax^2 + bx + c$.

GOAL 2 Solve quadratic equations by factoring.

Why you should learn it

▼ To help solve **real-life** problems, such as finding the time it takes a cliff diver to reach the water in **Example 6**.

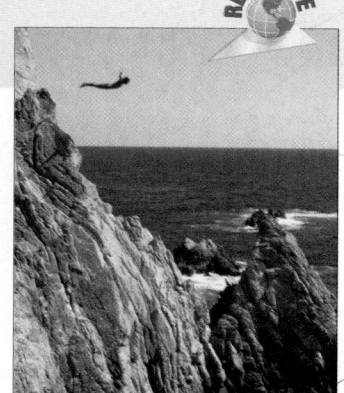

In this lesson, you will learn to factor quadratic polynomials whose leading coefficient is not 1. Find the factors of a (m and n) and the factors of c (p and q) so that the sum of the outer and inner products (mq and pn) is b.

$$c = pq$$
$$ax^2 + bx + c = (mx + p)(nx + q) \qquad b = mq + pn$$
$$a = mn$$

Example:
$$20 = 5 \cdot 4$$
$$6x^2 + 22x + 20 = (3x + 5)(2x + 4) \qquad 22 = (3 \cdot 4) + (5 \cdot 2)$$
$$6 = 3 \cdot 2$$

EXAMPLE 1 One Pair of Factors for a and c

Factor $2x^2 + 11x + 5$.

SOLUTION Test the possible factors of a (1 and 2) and c (1 and 5).
Try $a = 1 \cdot 2$ and $c = 1 \cdot 5$.

$$(1x + 1)(2x + 5) = 2x^2 + 7x + 5 \qquad \text{Not correct}$$

Now try $a = 1 \cdot 2$ and $c = 5 \cdot 1$.

$$(1x + 5)(2x + 1) = 2x^2 + 11x + 5 \qquad \text{Correct}$$

▶ The correct factorization of $2x^2 + 11x + 5$ is $(x + 5)(2x + 1)$.

EXAMPLE 2 One Pair of Factors for a and c

Factor $3x^2 - 4x - 7$.

SOLUTION

FACTORS OF a AND c	PRODUCT	CORRECT?
$a = 1 \cdot 3$ and $c = (-1)(7)$	$(x - 1)(3x + 7) = 3x^2 + 4x - 7$	No
$a = 1 \cdot 3$ and $c = (7)(-1)$	$(x + 7)(3x - 1) = 3x^2 + 20x - 7$	No
$a = 1 \cdot 3$ and $c = (1)(-7)$	$(x + 1)(3x - 7) = 3x^2 - 4x - 7$	Yes
$a = 1 \cdot 3$ and $c = (-7)(1)$	$(x - 7)(3x + 1) = 3x^2 - 20x - 7$	No

▶ The correct factorization of $3x^2 - 4x - 7$ is $(x + 1)(3x - 7)$.

EXAMPLE 3 *Several Pairs of Factors for a and c*

Factor $6x^2 - 19x + 15$.

SOLUTION

Both factors of c must be negative, because b is negative and c is positive. Test the possible factors of a and c.

FACTORS OF *a* AND *c*	PRODUCT	CORRECT?
$a = 1 \cdot 6$ and $c = (-1)(-15)$	$(x - 1)(6x - 15) = 6x^2 - 21x + 15$	No
$a = 1 \cdot 6$ and $c = (-15)(-1)$	$(x - 15)(6x - 1) = 6x^2 - 91x + 15$	No
$a = 1 \cdot 6$ and $c = (-3)(-5)$	$(x - 3)(6x - 5) = 6x^2 - 23x + 15$	No
$a = 1 \cdot 6$ and $c = (-5)(-3)$	$(x - 5)(6x - 3) = 6x^2 - 33x + 15$	No
$a = 2 \cdot 3$ and $c = (-1)(-15)$	$(2x - 1)(3x - 15) = 6x^2 - 33x + 15$	No
$a = 2 \cdot 3$ and $c = (-15)(-1)$	$(2x - 15)(3x - 1) = 6x^2 - 47x + 15$	No
$a = 2 \cdot 3$ and $c = (-3)(-5)$	$(2x - 3)(3x - 5) = 6x^2 - 19x + 15$	Yes
$a = 2 \cdot 3$ and $c = (-5)(-3)$	$(2x - 5)(3x - 3) = 6x^2 - 21x + 15$	No

▶ The correct factorization of $6x^2 - 19x + 15$ is $(2x - 3)(3x - 5)$.

EXAMPLE 4 *A Common Factor for a, b, and c*

Factor $6x^2 - 2x - 8$.

SOLUTION

Begin by factoring out the common factor 2.

$$6x^2 - 2x - 8 = 2(3x^2 - x - 4)$$

Now factor $3x^2 - x - 4$ by testing the possible factors of a and c.

FACTORS OF *a* AND *c*	PRODUCT	CORRECT?
$a = 1 \cdot 3$ and $c = (-1)(4)$	$(x - 1)(3x + 4) = 3x^2 + x - 4$	No
$a = 1 \cdot 3$ and $c = (4)(-1)$	$(x + 4)(3x - 1) = 3x^2 + 11x - 4$	No
$a = 1 \cdot 3$ and $c = (1)(-4)$	$(x + 1)(3x - 4) = 3x^2 - x - 4$	Yes
$a = 1 \cdot 3$ and $c = (-4)(1)$	$(x - 4)(3x + 1) = 3x^2 - 11x - 4$	No
$a = 1 \cdot 3$ and $c = (-2)(2)$	$(x - 2)(3x + 2) = 3x^2 - 4x - 4$	No
$a = 1 \cdot 3$ and $c = (2)(-2)$	$(x + 2)(3x - 2) = 3x^2 + 4x - 4$	No

▶ The correct factorization is $6x^2 - 2x - 8 = 2(x + 1)(3x - 4)$.

· · · · · · · · · ·

> **STUDENT HELP**
>
> ► **Study Tip**
> You may find it easier to factor quadratic trinomials that have positive leading coefficients. If the leading coefficient is negative, factor out −1 first. For instance, $-2x^2 + 3x - 1 = (-1)(2x^2 - 3x + 1)$.

In Examples 1 through 4, each test is shown for the sake of completeness. But when you factor, you can stop testing once you find the correct factorization.

EXAMPLE 5 *Solving a Quadratic Equation*

$$21n^2 + 14n + 7 = 6n + 11 \qquad \text{Write equation.}$$

$$21n^2 + 8n - 4 = 0 \qquad \text{Write in standard form.}$$

$$(3n + 2)(7n - 2) = 0 \qquad \text{Factor left side.}$$

$$(3n + 2) = 0 \quad \text{or} \quad (7n - 2) = 0 \qquad \text{Use zero-product property.}$$

$$3n + 2 = 0 \qquad\qquad 7n - 2 = 0$$

$$n = -\frac{2}{3} \qquad\qquad n = \frac{2}{7}$$

▶ The solutions are $-\frac{2}{3}$ and $\frac{2}{7}$.

✓ **CHECK** Substitute $-\frac{2}{3}$ and $\frac{2}{7}$ for n in $21n^2 + 14n + 7 = 6n + 11$.

$$21\left(-\frac{2}{3}\right)^2 + 14\left(-\frac{2}{3}\right) + 7 = 6\left(-\frac{2}{3}\right) + 11$$

$$7 = 7$$

$$21\left(\frac{2}{7}\right)^2 + 14\left(\frac{2}{7}\right) + 7 = 6\left(\frac{2}{7}\right) + 11$$

$$\frac{89}{7} = \frac{89}{7}$$

Cliff Diving

EXAMPLE 6 *Writing a Quadratic Model*

When a diver jumps from a ledge, the vertical component of his motion can be modeled by the vertical motion model. Suppose the ledge is 48 feet above the ocean and the initial upward velocity is 8 feet per second. How long will it take until the diver enters the water?

STUDENT HELP

▶ **Look Back**
For help with using a vertical motion model, see p. 535.

SOLUTION Use a vertical motion model.
Let $v = 8$ and $s = 48$.

$$h = -16t^2 + vt + s \qquad \text{Vertical motion model}$$

$$= -16t^2 + 8t + 48 \qquad \text{Substitute values.}$$

To find the time when the diver enters the water, let $h = 0$ and solve the resulting equation for t.

$$0 = -16t^2 + 8t + 48 \qquad \text{Write quadratic model.}$$

$$0 = (-8)(2t^2 - t - 6) \qquad \text{Factor out } -8.$$

$$0 = (-8)(t - 2)(2t + 3) \qquad \text{Factor.}$$

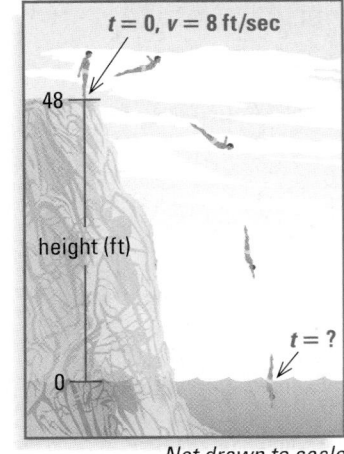

t = 0, v = 8 ft/sec

48

height (ft)

t = ?

0

Not drawn to scale

▶ The solutions are 2 and $-\frac{3}{2}$. Negative values for time do not make sense, so the only reasonable solution is $t = 2$. It will take the diver 2 seconds.

GUIDED PRACTICE

Concept Check ✔

1. Tell whether the following statement is *true* or *false*. If $(5x - 1)(x + 3) = 1$, then $5x - 1 = 1$ or $x + 3 = 1$. Explain.

2. **ERROR ANALYSIS** Describe the error at the right. Then solve the equation by factoring correctly.

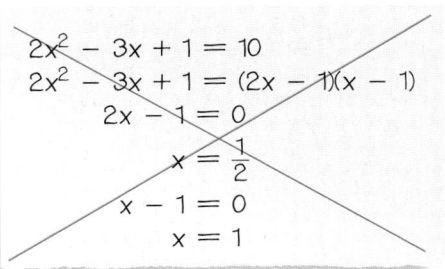

$$2x^2 - 3x + 1 = 10$$
$$2x^2 - 3x + 1 = (2x - 1)(x - 1)$$
$$2x - 1 = 0$$
$$x = \frac{1}{2}$$
$$x - 1 = 0$$
$$x = 1$$

3. Can a quadratic expression be factored if its discriminant is 1? Explain.

4. The sum of a number and its square is zero. Write and solve an equation to find numbers that fit this description.

Skill Check ✔ **Match the trinomial with the correct factorization.**

5. $3x^2 - 17x - 6$ **A.** $(3x + 2)(x + 3)$

6. $3x^2 + 7x - 6$ **B.** $(3x + 1)(x - 6)$

7. $3x^2 + 11x + 6$ **C.** $(3x - 1)(x + 6)$

8. $3x^2 + 17x - 6$ **D.** $(3x - 2)(x + 3)$

Use the discriminant to decide whether the expression can be factored. If it can be factored, factor the expression.

9. $2x^2 - 3x - 2$ 10. $-3y^2 - 4y + 7$ 11. $6t^2 - 4t - 5$

Solve the equation.

12. $3b^2 + 26b + 35 = 0$ 13. $2z^2 + 15z = 8$ 14. $-7n^2 - 40n = -12$

PRACTICE AND APPLICATIONS

┌─ **STUDENT HELP**

↳ **Extra Practice**
to help you master
skills is on p. 806.

FACTORIZATIONS **Choose the correct factorization. If neither is correct, find the correct factorization.**

15. $3x^2 + 2x - 8$ 16. $6y^2 - 29y - 5$ 17. $4w^2 - 14w - 30$

   A. $(3x - 4)(x + 2)$ **A.** $(2y + 1)(3y - 5)$ **A.** $(2w + 3)(2w - 10)$

   B. $(3x - 4)(x - 2)$ **B.** $(6y - 1)(y + 5)$ **B.** $(4w + 15)(w - 2)$

┌─ **STUDENT HELP**

↳ **HOMEWORK HELP**
Example 1: Exs. 15–32
Example 2: Exs. 15–32
Example 3: Exs. 15–32
Example 4: Exs. 15–32
Example 5: Exs. 33–47
Example 6: Exs. 64–66

FACTORING TRINOMIALS **Factor the trinomial if possible. If it cannot be factored, write *not factorable*.**

18. $3t^2 + 16t + 5$ 19. $6b^2 - 11b - 2$ 20. $4n^2 - 26n - 42$

21. $5w^2 - 9w - 2$ 22. $4x^2 + 27x + 35$ 23. $6y^2 - 11y - 10$

24. $6x^2 - 21x - 9$ 25. $3c^2 - 37c + 44$ 26. $10x^2 + 17x + 6$

27. $14y^2 - 15y + 4$ 28. $4z^2 + 32z + 63$ 29. $6t^2 + t - 70$

30. $8b^2 + 2b - 3$ 31. $2z^2 + 19z - 10$ 32. $12m^2 + 48m + 96$

SOLVING EQUATIONS Solve the equation by factoring.

33. $2x^2 - 9x - 35 = 0$ 34. $7x^2 - 10x + 3 = 0$ 35. $3x^2 + 34x + 11 = 0$

36. $4x^2 - 21x + 5 = 0$ 37. $2x^2 - 17x - 19 = 0$ 38. $5x^2 - 3x - 26 = 0$

39. $2x^2 + 19x = -24$ 40. $4x^2 - 8x = -3$ 41. $6x^2 - 23x = 18$

42. $8x^2 - 34x + 24 = -11$ 43. $10x^2 + x - 10 = -2x + 8$

44. $28x^2 - 9x - 1 = -4x + 2$ 45. $24x^2 + 39x + 15 = 0$

46. $30x^2 - 80x + 50 = 7x - 4$ 47. $18x^2 - 30x - 100 = 67x + 30$

STUDENT HELP

▶ **Look Back**
For help with using square roots to solve quadratic equations, see p. 505.

▶ For help with the quadratic formula, see p. 533.

CHOOSING A METHOD Solve the equation by factoring, by finding square roots, or by using the quadratic formula.

48. $\frac{1}{16}s^2 = 4$ 49. $x^2 - 10x = -25$ 50. $y^2 - 7y + 6 = -6$

51. $4n^2 + 2n = 0$ 52. $12t^2 = 0$ 53. $35b^2 - 61b + 24 = 0$

54. $9x^2 - 19 = -3$ 55. $20d^2 - 10d = 100$ 56. $8c^2 - 27c - 24 = -6$

57. $56w^2 - 61w = 22$ 58. $3n^2 + 12n + 9 = -1$ 59. $24z^2 + 46z - 55 = 10$

MULTIPLY AND SOLVE Multiply each side of the equation by an appropriate power of ten to obtain integer coefficients. Then solve by factoring.

60. $0.8x^2 + 3.2x + 2.40 = 0$ 61. $0.23t^2 - 0.54t + 0.16 = 0$

62. $0.3n^2 - 2.2n + 8.4 = 0$ 63. $0.119y^2 - 0.162y + 0.055 = 0$

VERTICAL COMPONENT OF MOTION In Exercises 64–66, use the vertical motion model $h = -16t^2 + vt + s$, where h is the height (in feet), t is the time in motion (in seconds), v is the initial velocity (in feet per second), and s is the initial height (in feet). Solve by factoring.

STUDENT HELP

HOMEWORK HELP
Visit our Web site www.mcdougallittell.com for help with Exs. 64–66.

64. **GYMNASTICS** A gymnast dismounts the uneven parallel bars at a height of 8 feet with an initial upward velocity of 8 feet per second. Find the time t (in seconds) it takes for the gymnast to reach the ground. Is your answer reasonable?

65. **CIRCUS ACROBATS** An acrobat is shot out of a cannon and lands in a safety net that is 10 feet above the ground. Before being shot out of the cannon, she was 4 feet above the ground. She left the cannon with an initial upward velocity of 50 feet per second. Find the time t (in seconds) it takes for her to reach the net. Explain why only one of the two solutions is reasonable.

66. **T-SHIRT CANNON** At a basketball game, T-shirts are rolled-up into a ball and shot from a "T-shirt cannon" into the crowd. The T-shirts are released from a height of 6 feet with an initial upward velocity of 44 feet per second. If you catch a T-shirt at your seat 30 feet above the court, how long was it in the air before you caught it? Is your answer reasonable?

🌐 **WARP AND WEFT** **In Exercises 67 and 68, use the following information.**
In every square inch of sailcloth, the warp (lengthwise threads) intersects the weft (crosswise threads) about 9000 times. The density (number of threads per inch) of the weft threads to the warp threads is about 5 to 2.

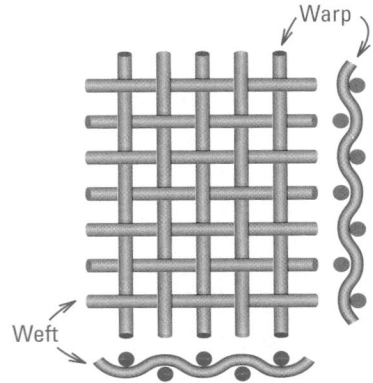

Warp

Weft

67. Write an equation that you can solve to find the number of threads per square inch. Let x represent the number of warp threads.

68. How many threads are there in each square inch of sailcloth?

EXTENSION: WRITING EQUATIONS **In Exercises 69–72, you are tutoring a friend and want to create some quadratic equations that can be solved by factoring. Find a quadratic equation that has the given solutions and explain the procedure you used to obtain the equation.**

69. 4 and -3 **70.** 8 and -8 **71.** $-\dfrac{1}{2}$ and $\dfrac{1}{3}$ **72.** $-\dfrac{5}{4}$ and $-\dfrac{8}{3}$

Test Preparation

73. MULTIPLE CHOICE Which one of the following equations *cannot* be solved by factoring with integer coefficients?

Ⓐ $12x^2 - 15x - 63 = 0$ Ⓑ $12x^2 + 46x - 8 = 0$

Ⓒ $6x^2 - 38x - 28 = 0$ Ⓓ $8x^2 - 49x - 68 = 0$

74. MULTIPLE CHOICE Which one of the following is a correct factorization of the expression $-16x^2 + 36x + 52$?

Ⓐ $(-16x + 26)(x - 2)$ Ⓑ $(-4x - 13)(4x + 4)$

Ⓒ $-1(4x - 13)(4x + 4)$ Ⓓ $-1(4x - 4)(4x + 13)$

75. MULTIPLE CHOICE Which one of the following is a solution of the equation $7x^2 - 11x - 6 = 0$?

Ⓐ -2 Ⓑ $-\dfrac{3}{7}$ Ⓒ $-\dfrac{2}{7}$ Ⓓ $\dfrac{3}{7}$

76. MULTIPLE CHOICE A pebble is thrown upward from the edge of a building 132 feet above the ground with an initial upward velocity of 4 feet per second. How long does it take to reach the ground?

Ⓐ $2\dfrac{1}{2}$ seconds   Ⓑ $2\dfrac{3}{4}$ seconds   Ⓒ 3 seconds   Ⓓ 6 seconds

★ **Challenge**

🌐 **SAVING FOR A TRIP** **You are saving money for a trip to Europe that costs $3600. You make an investment of $1000 two years before the trip and an investment of $1800 one year before the trip.**

77. Use $(1 + r)$ as a growth factor to write an equation that can be solved to find the growth rate r that you need in order to have $3600 at the time of the trip to Europe.

78. Can the equation be solved by factoring? Solve the equation. What growth rate do you need in order to have $3600 at the time of the trip to Europe?

MIXED REVIEW

SOLVING SYSTEMS Use linear combinations to solve the system. (Review 7.3)

79. $4x + 5y = 7$
$6x - 2y = -18$

80. $6x - 5y = 3$
$-12x + 8y = 5$

81. $2x + y = 120$
$x + 2y = 120$

SOLVING INEQUALITIES Decide whether the ordered pair is a solution of the inequality. (Review 9.7)

82. $y > 2x^2 - x + 7$; $(2, 15)$

83. $y \geq 4x^2 - 64x + 92$; $(1, 30)$

SPECIAL PRODUCT PATTERNS Find the product. (Review 10.3 for 10.7)

84. $(4t - 1)^2$

85. $(b + 9)(b - 9)$

86. $(3x + 5)(3x + 5)$

87. $(2a - 7)(2a + 7)$

88. $(11 - 6x)^2$

89. $(100 + 27x)^2$

90. BASKETBALL The graph shows the number of women's college basketball teams from 1985 projected through 2000. Which type of model best fits the data?

▶ Source: National Collegiate Athletic Association

(Review 9.8)

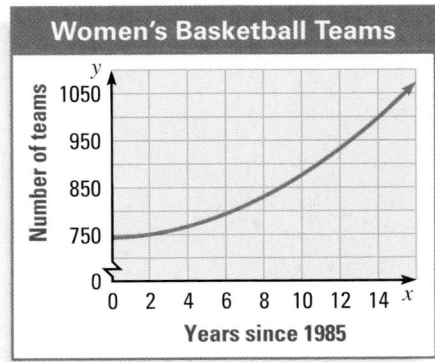

Women's Basketball Teams

QUIZ 2

Self-Test for Lessons 10.4–10.6

Solve the equation. (Lesson 10.4)

1. $(x + 5)(2x + 10) = 0$

2. $(4x - 6)(5x - 20) = 0$

3. $(2x + 7)(3x - 12) = 0$

4. $\left(4x + \dfrac{1}{3}\right)^2 = 0$

5. $(2x + 8)^2 = 0$

6. $(x - 4)(x + 7)(x + 1) = 0$

Name the *x*-intercepts and the vertex of the graph of the function. Then sketch the graph of the function. (Lesson 10.4)

7. $y = \left(x - \dfrac{1}{2}\right)(x + 2)$

8. $y = (x + 4)(x - 4)$

9. $y = (3x - 1)(x + 2)$

Factor the trinomial. (Lessons 10.5 and 10.6)

10. $y^2 + 3y - 4$

11. $w^2 + 13w + 22$

12. $n^2 + 16n - 57$

13. $x^2 + 17x + 66$

14. $t^2 - 41t - 86$

15. $-45 + 14z - z^2$

16. $12b^2 - 17b - 99$

17. $2t^2 + 63t + 145$

18. $18d^2 - 54d + 28$

Solve the equation by factoring. (Lessons 10.5 and 10.6)

19. $y^2 + 5y - 6 = 0$

20. $n^2 + 26n + 25 = 0$

21. $t^2 - 11t = -18$

22. $w^2 - 29w = 170$

23. $x^2 + 35x + 3 = 77$

24. $2a^2 + 33a + 136 = 0$

25. $15n^2 + 41n = -14$

26. $18b^2 - 89b = -36$

27. $6x^2 + x - 96 = 80$

10.6 *Factoring ax² + bx + c* **617**

● ACTIVITY 10.7

Developing Concepts

Modeling the Factorization of $(ax)^2 + 2abx + b^2$

SET UP
Work in a small group.

MATERIALS
• algebra tiles

▶ **QUESTION**

How can you model the factorization of a trinomial of the form $(ax)^2 + 2abx + b^2$ using algebra tiles?

▶ **EXPLORING THE CONCEPT**

You can use algebra tiles to create a model that can be used to factor a trinomial in which the first and last terms are perfect squares and the middle term is twice the product of the square roots of the first and last terms. Factor the trinomial $x^2 + 6x + 9$ as follows.

❶ Use algebra tiles to model $x^2 + 6x + 9$.

x^2 + $6x$ + 9

❷ Arrange the tiles to form a square.

❸ The length of each side of the square is _?_. Complete this statement:
$x^2 + 6x + 9 = (\underline{?})(\underline{?}) = (\underline{?})^2$

▶ **DRAWING CONCLUSIONS**

Use algebra tiles to factor the trinomial.

1. $x^2 + 4x + 4$ **2.** $x^2 + 8x + 16$

3. $4x^2 + 4x + 1$ **4.** $4x^2 + 12x + 9$

5. Look for a pattern in the factorizations in Exercises 1–4. Complete this statement: $a^2 + 2ab + b^2 = (\underline{?})(\underline{?}) = \underline{?}$

Use the pattern from Exercise 5 to factor the trinomial.

6. $9x^2 + 6x + 1$ **7.** $16x^2 + 56x + 49$ **8.** $49x^2 + 28x + 4$

9. Make a conjecture about how to complete this statement:
$a^2 - 2ab + b^2 = (\underline{?})(\underline{?}) = \underline{?}$

Factoring Special Products

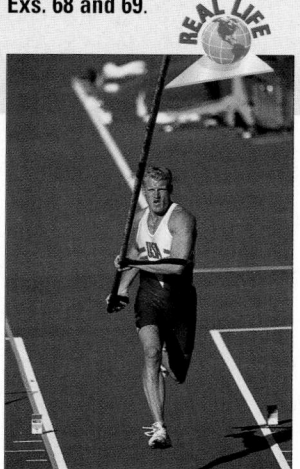

What you should learn

GOAL 1 Use special product patterns to factor quadratic polynomials.

GOAL 2 Solve quadratic equations by factoring.

Why you should learn it

▼ To solve **real-life** problems, such as finding the velocity of a pole-vaulter in **Exs. 68 and 69**.

GOAL 1 **FACTORING QUADRATIC POLYNOMIALS**

Each of the special product patterns you studied in Lesson 10.3 can be used to factor polynomials. Note that there are two forms of perfect square trinomials.

FACTORING SPECIAL PRODUCTS

DIFFERENCE OF TWO SQUARES PATTERN

$a^2 - b^2 = (a + b)(a - b)$

Example

$9x^2 - 16 = (3x + 4)(3x - 4)$

PERFECT SQUARE TRINOMIAL PATTERN

$a^2 + 2ab + b^2 = (a + b)^2$

$a^2 - 2ab + b^2 = (a - b)^2$

Example

$x^2 + 8x + 16 = (x + 4)^2$

$x^2 - 12x + 36 = (x - 6)^2$

EXAMPLE 1 *Factoring the Difference of Two Squares*

a. $m^2 - 4 = m^2 - 2^2$ Write as $a^2 - b^2$.

$= (m + 2)(m - 2)$ Factor using pattern.

b. $4p^2 - 25 = (2p)^2 - 5^2$ Write as $a^2 - b^2$.

$= (2p + 5)(2p - 5)$ Factor using pattern.

c. $50 - 98x^2 = 2(25 - 49x^2)$ Factor out common factor.

$= 2[5^2 - (7x)^2]$ Write as $a^2 - b^2$.

$= 2(5 + 7x)(5 - 7x)$ Factor using pattern.

EXAMPLE 2 *Factoring Perfect Square Trinomials*

a. $x^2 - 4x + 4 = x^2 - 2(x)(2) + 2^2$ Write as $a^2 - 2ab + b^2$.

$= (x - 2)^2$ Factor using pattern.

b. $16y^2 + 24y + 9 = (4y)^2 + 2(4y)(3) + 3^2$ Write as $a^2 + 2ab + b^2$.

$= (4y + 3)^2$ Factor using pattern.

c. $3x^2 - 30x + 75 = 3(x^2 - 10x + 25)$ Factor out common factor.

$= 3[x^2 - 2(x)(5) + 5^2]$ Write as $a^2 - 2ab + b^2$.

$= 3(x - 5)^2$ Factor using pattern.

EXAMPLE 3   *Graphical and Analytical Reasoning*

Solve the equation $-2x^2 + 12x - 18 = 0$.

SOLUTION

$-2x^2 + 12x - 18 = 0$	**Write original equation.**
$-2(x^2 - 6x + 9) = 0$	**Factor out common factor.**
$-2\left[x^2 - 2(3x) + 3^2\right] = 0$	**Write as $a^2 - 2ab + b^2$.**
$-2(x - 3)^2 = 0$	**Factor using pattern.**
$x - 3 = 0$	**Set repeated factor equal to 0.**
$x = 3$	**Solve for x.**

▶ The solution is 3.

✓ **CHECK:** You can check your answer by
substitution or by graphing.

Graph $y = -2x^2 + 12x - 18$.

Graph the x-axis, $y = 0$.

Use your graphing calculator's *Intersect*
feature to find the x-intercept, where
$-2x^2 + 12x - 18 = 0$.

When $x = 3$, $-2x^2 + 12x - 18 = 0$,
which appears to confirm your solution.

EXAMPLE 4   *Solving a Quadratic Equation*

Solve $x^2 + x + \frac{1}{4} = 0$.

SOLUTION

$x^2 + x + \frac{1}{4} = 0$	**Write original equation.**
$x^2 + 2\left(\frac{1}{2}x\right) + \left(\frac{1}{2}\right)^2 = 0$	**Write as $a^2 + 2ab + b^2$.**
$\left(x + \frac{1}{2}\right)^2 = 0$	**Factor using pattern.**
$x + \frac{1}{2} = 0$	**Set repeated factor equal to 0.**
$x = -\frac{1}{2}$	**Solve for x.**

▶ The solution is $-\frac{1}{2}$. Check this in the original equation.

A block and tackle makes it easier to lift a heavy object. For instance, using a block and tackle with 4 pulleys, you can lift 1000 pounds with only 250 pounds of applied force.

EXAMPLE 5 *Writing and Using a Quadratic Model*

BLOCK AND TACKLE An object lifted with a rope or wire should not weigh more than the *safe working load* for the rope or wire. The safe working load S (in pounds) for a natural fiber rope is a function of C, the circumference of the rope in inches.

Safe working load model: $150 \cdot C^2 = S$

You are setting up a block and tackle to lift a 1350-pound safe. What size natural fiber rope do you need to have a safe working load?

SOLUTION Use the model to find a safe rope size. Substitute 1350 for S.

$150C^2 = S$	Write model.
$150C^2 = 1350$	Substitute.
$150C^2 - 1350 = 0$	Subtract 1350 from each side.
$150(C^2 - 9) = 0$	Factor out common factor.
$150(C - 3)(C + 3) = 0$	Factor.
$(C - 3) = 0$ or $(C + 3) = 0$	Use zero-product property.
$C - 3 = 0$	Set first factor equal to 0.
$C = 3$	Solve for C.
$C + 3 = 0$	Set second factor equal to 0.
$C = -3$	Solve for C.

▶ The negative solution makes no sense. You need a rope with a circumference of at least 3 inches.

EXAMPLE 6 *Writing and Using a Quadratic Model*

If you project a ball straight up from the ground with an initial velocity of 64 feet per second, will the ball reach a height of 64 feet? If it does, how long will it take to reach that height?

SOLUTION Use a vertical motion model where $v = 64$, $s = 0$, and $h = 64$.

$-16t^2 + vt + s = h$	Vertical motion model
$-16t^2 + 64t + 0 = 64$	Substitute for v, s, and h.
$-16t^2 + 64t - 64 = 0$	Write in standard form.
$-16(t^2 - 4t + 4) = 0$	Factor out common factor.
$-16(t - 2)^2 = 0$	Factor.
$t - 2 = 0$	Set repeated factor equal to 0.
$t = 2$	Solve for t.

▶ Because there is a solution, you know that the ball will reach a height of 64 feet. The solution is $t = 2$, so it will take 2 seconds to reach that height.

GUIDED PRACTICE

Vocabulary Check ✓

Concept Check ✓

1. What is the difference of two squares pattern?

2. **ERROR ANALYSIS** Describe the error at the right. Then solve the equation correctly.

3. Look back to Lesson 10.3. Describe the relationship between the special products shown in Lesson 10.3 and the polynomials you factored in this lesson.

4. Write the three special product factoring patterns. Give an example of each pattern.

5. Factor out the common factor in $3x^2 - 6x + 9$.

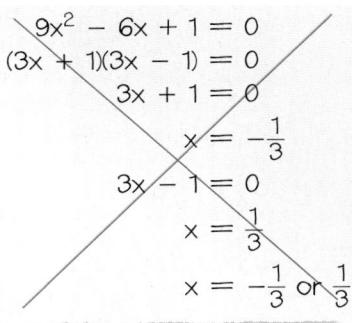

$$9x^2 - 6x + 1 = 0$$
$$(3x + 1)(3x - 1) = 0$$
$$3x + 1 = 0$$
$$x = -\frac{1}{3}$$
$$3x - 1 = 0$$
$$x = \frac{1}{3}$$
$$x = -\frac{1}{3} \text{ or } \frac{1}{3}$$

Skill Check ✓

Factor the expression.

6. $x^2 - 9$

7. $t^2 + 10t + 25$

8. $w^2 - 16w + 64$

9. $16 - t^2$

10. $6y^2 - 24$

11. $18 - 2z^2$

Use factoring to solve the equation.

12. $x^2 + 6x + 9 = 0$

13. $144 - y^2 = 0$

14. $s^2 - 14s + 49 = 0$

15. $-25 + x^2 = 0$

16. $7x^2 + 28x + 28 = 0$

17. $-4y^2 + 24y - 36 = 0$

PRACTICE AND APPLICATIONS

STUDENT HELP

▶ **Extra Practice**
to help you master
skills is on p. 806.

DIFFERENCE OF TWO SQUARES Factor the expression.

18. $n^2 - 16$

19. $100x^2 - 121$

20. $6m^2 - 150$

21. $60y^2 - 540$

22. $16 - 81r^2$

23. $98 - 2t^2$

24. $w^2 - y^2$

25. $9t^2 - 4q^2$

26. $-28y^2 + 7t^2$

PERFECT SQUARES Factor the expression.

27. $x^2 + 8x + 16$

28. $x^2 - 20x + 100$

29. $y^2 + 30y + 225$

30. $b^2 - 14b + 49$

31. $9x^2 + 6x + 1$

32. $4r^2 + 12r + 9$

33. $25n^2 - 20n + 4$

34. $36m^2 - 84m + 49$

35. $18x^2 + 12x + 2$

36. $48y^2 - 72xy + 27x^2$

37. $-16w^2 - 80w - 100$

38. $-3k^2 + 42k - 147$

STUDENT HELP

▶ HOMEWORK HELP
Example 1: Exs. 18–26,
        39–50
Example 2: Exs. 27–50
Example 3: Exs. 51–62
Example 4: Exs. 51–62
Example 5: Exs. 63–66
Example 6: Ex. 67

FACTORING EXPRESSIONS Factor the expression. Tell which special product factoring pattern you used.

39. $z^2 - 25$

40. $y^2 + 12y + 36$

41. $4n^2 - 36$

42. $32 - 18x^2$

43. $4b^2 - 40b + 100$

44. $-27t^2 - 18t - 3$

45. $-2x^2 + 52x - 338$

46. $169 - x^2$

47. $x^2 - 10,000w^2$

48. $-108 + 147x^2$

49. $x^2 + \frac{2}{3}x + \frac{1}{9}$

50. $\frac{3}{4} - 12x^2$

SOLVING EQUATIONS Use factoring to solve the equation. Use a graphing calculator to check your solution if you wish.

51. $2x^2 - 72 = 0$ **52.** $3x^2 - 24x + 48 = 0$ **53.** $25x^2 - 4 = 0$

54. $\frac{1}{5}x^2 - 2x + 5 = 0$ **55.** $27 - 12x^2 = 0$ **56.** $50x^2 + 60x + 18 = 0$

57. $\frac{1}{3}x^2 - 6x + 27 = 0$ **58.** $90x^2 - 120x + 40 = 0$

59. $x^2 - \frac{5}{3}x + \frac{25}{36} = 0$ **60.** $112x^2 - 252 = 0$

61. $-16x^2 + 56x - 49 = 0$ **62.** $-\frac{4}{5}x^2 - \frac{4}{5}x - \frac{1}{5} = 0$

🌐 **SAFE WORKING LOAD** In Exercises 63 and 64, the safe working load S (in tons) for a *wire* rope is a function of D, the diameter of the rope in inches.

   Safe working load model for wire rope: $4 \cdot D^2 = S$

63. What diameter of wire rope do you need to lift a 9-ton load and have a safe working load?

64. When determining the safe working load S of a rope that is old or worn, decrease S by 50%. Write a model for S when using an old wire rope. What diameter of old wire rope do you need to safely lift a 9-ton load?

🌐 **HANG TIME** In Exercises 65 and 66, use the following information about *hang time*, the length of time a basketball player is in the air after jumping.

The maximum height h jumped (in feet) is a function of t, where t is the hang time (in seconds).

   Hang time model: $h = 4t^2$

65. If you jump 1 foot into the air, what is your hang time?

66. If a professional player jumps 4 feet into the air, what is the hang time?

$h = 4t^2$

67. VERTICAL MOTION An object is propelled from the ground with an initial upward velocity of 224 feet per second. Will the object reach a height of 784 feet? If it does, how long will it take the object to reach that height? Solve by factoring.

🌐 **POLE-VAULTING** In Exercises 68 and 69, use the following information.
In the sport of pole-vaulting, the height h (in feet) reached by a pole-vaulter is a function of v, the velocity of the pole-vaulter, as shown in the model below. The constant g is approximately 32 feet per second per second.

   Pole-vaulter height model: $h = \dfrac{v^2}{2g}$

68. To reach a height of 9 feet, what is the pole-vaulter's velocity?

69. To reach a height of 16 feet, what is the pole-vaulter's velocity?

Test Preparation

70. MULTIPLE CHOICE Which of the following is a correct factorization of $-12x^2 + 147$?

    Ⓐ $-3(2x + 7)^2$ Ⓑ $3(2x - 7)(2x + 7)$

    Ⓒ $-2(2x - 7)(2x + 7)$ Ⓓ $-3(2x - 7)(2x + 7)$

71. MULTIPLE CHOICE Which of the following is a correct factorization of $72x^2 - 24x + 2$?

    Ⓐ $-9(3x - 1)^2$ Ⓑ $8\left(9x - \dfrac{1}{2}\right)^2$

    Ⓒ $8\left(3x - \dfrac{1}{2}\right)\left(3x - \dfrac{1}{2}\right)$ Ⓓ $-8\left(3x - \dfrac{1}{2}\right)^2$

72. MULTIPLE CHOICE Which of the following is the solution of the equation $-4x^2 + 24x - 36 = 0$?

    Ⓐ -6 Ⓑ -3 Ⓒ 2 Ⓓ 3

★ Challenge

73. 🌐 **SAFE WORKING LOAD** Example 5 on page 621 models the safe working load of a natural fiber rope as a function of its *circumference*. Exercises 63 and 64 use a model for the safe working load of a wire rope as a function of its *diameter*. Find a way to use these models to compare the strength of a wire rope to the strength of a natural fiber rope.

┌─ **EXTRA CHALLENGE**

↳ www.mcdougallittell.com

MIXED REVIEW

FINDING THE GCF Find the greatest common factor of the numbers. (Skills Review, p. 777)

74. 9 and 12   **75.** 15 and 45   **76.** 55 and 132   **77.** 14 and 18

CHECKING FOR SOLUTIONS Decide whether or not the ordered pair is a solution of the system of linear equations. (Review 7.1)

78. $x + 9y = -11$
    $-4x + y = -30$ $(7, -2)$

79. $2x + 6y = 22$
    $-x - 4y = -13$ $(-5, -2)$

80. $-2x + 7y = -41$
    $3x + 5y = 15$ $(-10, 3)$

81. $-5x - 8y = 28$
    $9x - 2y = 48$ $(4, -6)$

SOLVING LINEAR SYSTEMS Use the substitution method to solve the linear system. (Review 7.2)

82. $x - y = 2$
    $2x + y = 1$

83. $x - 2y = 10$
    $3x - y = 0$

84. $-x + y = 0$
    $2x + y = 0$

85. $2x + 3y = -5$
    $x - 2y = -6$

SIMPLIFYING RADICAL EXPRESSIONS Simplify the expression. (Review 9.2)

86. $\sqrt{216}$ **87.** $\sqrt{5} \cdot \sqrt{15}$ **88.** $\sqrt{10} \cdot \sqrt{20}$ **89.** $\sqrt{4} \cdot 3\sqrt{9}$

90. $\sqrt{\dfrac{28}{49}}$ **91.** $\dfrac{10\sqrt{8}}{\sqrt{25}}$ **92.** $\dfrac{12\sqrt{4}}{\sqrt{9}}$ **93.** $\dfrac{-6\sqrt{12}}{\sqrt{4}}$

SOLVING EQUATIONS Use the quadratic formula to solve the equation. (Review 9.5 for 10.8)

94. $9x^2 - 14x - 7 = 0$ **95.** $9d^2 - 58d + 24 = 0$ **96.** $7y^2 - 9y - 17 = 0$

10.8 Factoring Using the Distributive Property

What you should learn

GOAL 1 Use the distributive property to factor a polynomial.

GOAL 2 Solve polynomial equations by factoring.

Why you should learn it

▼ To solve some types of **real-life** problems, such as modeling the effect of gravity in **Exs. 51–54**.

Shannon Lucid on Space Station *Mir*

GOAL 1 FACTORING AND THE DISTRIBUTIVE PROPERTY

In dealing with polynomials, you have already been using the distributive property to factor out integers common to the various terms of the expression.

$$9x^2 - 15 = 3(3x^2 - 5) \qquad \text{Factor out common factor.}$$

In many situations, it is important to factor out common *variable* factors. To save steps, you should factor out the *greatest common factor* (GCF).

EXAMPLE 1 *Finding the Greatest Common Factor*

Factor the greatest common factor out of $14x^4 - 21x^2$.

SOLUTION First find the greatest common factor. It is the product of all the common factors.

$$14x^4 = 2 \cdot 7 \cdot x \cdot x \cdot x \cdot x$$

$$21x^2 = 3 \cdot 7 \cdot x \cdot x$$

$$\text{GCF} = 7 \cdot x \cdot x = 7x^2$$

Then use the distributive property to factor the greatest common factor out of the polynomial.

$$14x^4 - 21x^2 = 7x^2(2x^2 - 3)$$

· · · · · · · · ·

In this lesson we restrict the polynomials we consider to polynomials having integer coefficients. A polynomial is **prime** if it is not the product of polynomials having integer coefficients. To **factor a polynomial completely**, write it as the product of these types of factors:

- monomial factors
- prime factors with at least two terms

EXAMPLE 2 *Recognizing Complete Factorization*

Tell whether the polynomial is factored completely.

a. $2x^2 + 8 = 2(x^2 + 4)$ **b.** $2x^2 - 8 = 2(x^2 - 4)$

SOLUTION

a. This polynomial is factored completely because $x^2 + 4$ cannot be factored using integer coefficients.

b. This polynomial is not factored completely because $x^2 - 4$ can be factored as $(x - 2)(x + 2)$.

┌─ STUDENT HELP

↳ **Skills Review**
For help with finding a greatest common factor, see p. 777.

EXAMPLE 3 *Factoring Completely*

Factor $4x^3 + 20x^2 + 24x$ completely.

SOLUTION

$$4x^3 + 20x^2 + 24x = 4x(x^2 + 5x + 6)$$
$$= 4x\underbrace{(x + 2)(x + 3)}$$

Monomial factor ⎤   ⎡ Prime factors

EXAMPLE 4 *Factoring Completely*

Factor $45x^4 - 20x^2$ completely.

SOLUTION

$$45x^4 - 20x^2 = 5x^2(9x^2 - 4) \qquad \text{Factor out GCF.}$$
$$= 5x^2(3x - 2)(3x + 2) \qquad \text{Factor difference of squares.}$$

. . . .

GROUPING Another use of the distributive property is in factoring polynomials that have four terms. Sometimes you can factor the polynomial by grouping into two groups of terms and factoring the greatest common factor out of each term.

EXAMPLE 5 *Factoring by Grouping*

Factor $x^3 + 2x^2 + 3x + 6$ completely.

SOLUTION

$$x^3 + 2x^2 + 3x + 6 = \left(x^3 + 2x^2\right) + (3x + 6) \qquad \text{Group terms.}$$
$$= x^2(x + 2) + 3(x + 2) \qquad \text{Factor each group.}$$
$$= (x + 2)(x^2 + 3) \qquad \text{Use distributive property.}$$

EXAMPLE 6 *Factoring by Grouping*

Factor $x^3 - 2x^2 - 9x + 18$ completely.

SOLUTION

$$x^3 - 2x^2 - 9x + 18 = \left(x^3 - 2x^2\right) - (9x - 18) \qquad \text{Group terms.}$$
$$= x^2(x - 2) - 9(x - 2) \qquad \text{Factor each group.}$$
$$= (x^2 - 9)(x - 2) \qquad \text{Use distributive property.}$$
$$= (x - 3)(x + 3)(x - 2) \qquad \text{Factor difference of squares.}$$

626 **Chapter 10** *Polynomials and Factoring*

EXAMPLE 7 *Solving a Polynomial Equation*

Solve $8x^3 - 18x = 0$.

SOLUTION

$8x^3 - 18x = 0$	Write original equation.
$2x(4x^2 - 9) = 0$	Factor out GCF.
$2x(2x - 3)(2x + 3) = 0$	Factor difference of squares.

▶ By setting each variable factor equal to zero, you can find that the solutions are 0, $\frac{3}{2}$, and $-\frac{3}{2}$.

EXAMPLE 8 *Writing and Using a Polynomial Model*

The width of a box is 1 inch less than the length. The height is 4 inches greater than the length. The box has a volume of 12 cubic inches. What are the dimensions of the box?

Height

Length   Width

SOLUTION

VERBAL MODEL

Length · **Width** · **Height** = ⎡Volume⎤

LABELS

Length = **x**   (inches)

Width = **$x - 1$**   (inches)

Height = **$x + 4$**   (inches)

Volume = ⎡12⎤   (cubic inches)

ALGEBRAIC MODEL

$x\ (x - 1)\ (x + 4) = 12$	Write model.
$x^3 + 3x^2 - 4x = 12$	Multiply.
$(x^3 + 3x^2) - (4x + 12) = 0$	Write in standard form and group terms.
$x^2(x + 3) - 4(x + 3) = 0$	Factor each group of terms.
$(x^2 - 4)(x + 3) = 0$	Use distributive property.
$(x - 2)(x + 2)(x + 3) = 0$	Factor difference of squares.

▶ By setting each factor equal to zero, you can see that the solutions are 2, -2, and -3. The only positive solution is $x = 2$. The dimensions of the box are 2 inches by 1 inch by 6 inches.

WAYS TO SOLVE POLYNOMIAL EQUATIONS

GRAPHING: Can be used to solve any equation, but gives only approximate solutions. Examples 2 and 3, p. 527

THE QUADRATIC FORMULA: Can be used to solve any *quadratic* equation. Examples 1–3, pp. 533–534

FACTORING: Can be used with the zero-product property to solve an equation that is factorable.

- **Factoring $x^2 + bx + c$:** Examples 1–6, pp. 604–606

    $x^2 + 9x + 18 = (x + 3)(x + 6)$

- **Factoring $ax^2 + bx + c$:** Examples 1–5, pp. 611–613

    $3x^2 + 10x + 7 = (3x + 7)(x + 1)$

- **Special Products:** Examples 1–4, pp. 619–620

    $a^2 - b^2 = (a + b)(a - b)$　　　**Example:** $4x^2 - 36 = (2x + 6)(2x - 6)$

    $a^2 + 2ab + b^2 = (a + b)^2$　　　**Example:** $x^2 + 18x + 81 = (x + 9)^2$

    $a^2 - 2ab + b^2 = (a - b)^2$　　　**Example:** $x^2 - 16x + 64 = (x - 8)^2$

- **Factoring Completely:** Examples 1–7, pp. 625–627

STUDENT HELP

HOMEWORK HELP
Visit our Web site
www.mcdougallittell.com
for extra examples.

EXAMPLE 9　*Solving Quadratic and Other Polynomial Equations*

Solve the equation.

a. $-30x^4 + 58x^3 - 24x^2 = 0$　　　　**b.** $18x^3 - 30x^2 = 60x$

SOLUTION

a.　$-30x^4 + 58x^3 - 24x^2 = 0$　　　**Write original equation.**

　　$-2x^2(15x^2 - 29x + 12) = 0$　　　**Factor out $-2x^2$.**

　　$-2x^2(5x - 3)(3x - 4) = 0$　　　**Find correct factorization for trinomial.**

▸ Set each variable factor equal to zero. The solutions are 0, $\frac{3}{5}$, and $\frac{4}{3}$.

✓ **CHECK** Graph $y = -30x^4 + 58x^3 - 24x^2$. Use your calculator's TRACE feature to estimate the x-intercepts.

The graph appears to confirm the solutions.

b. $18x^3 - 30x^2 - 60x = 0$　　　**Rewrite equation in standard form.**

　　$6x(3x^2 - 5x - 10) = 0$　　　**Factor out GCF.**

▸ $6x$ factors out, so one solution is 0. Because $3x^2 - 5x - 10$ is not factorable, use the quadratic formula to find the other solutions, $x \approx 2.84$ and $x \approx -1.17$.

GUIDED PRACTICE

Vocabulary Check ✓

1. In writing a polynomial as the product of polynomials of lesser degrees, what does it mean to say that a factor is *prime*?

Concept Check ✓

2. To factor a polynomial completely, you must write it as the product of what two types of factors?

3. Name three ways to find the solution(s) of a quadratic equation. Which way do you prefer? Explain.

ERROR ANALYSIS Describe and correct the factoring error.

4.

$4x^3 + 36x$
$= 4x(x^2 + 9)$
$= 4x(x + 3)(x - 3)$

5.

$-2b^3 + 12b^2 - 14b$
$= -2b(b^2 + 6b - 7)$
$= -2b(b + 7)(b - 1)$

Skill Check ✓

Find the greatest common factor and factor it out of the expression.

6. $5n^3 - 20n$

7. $6x^2 + 3x^4$

8. $6y^4 + 14y^3 - 10y^2$

Tell whether the expression is factored completely. If the expression is not factored completely, write the complete factorization.

9. $7x^3 - 11x$

10. $9t(t^2 + 49)$

11. $3w(9w^2 - 16)$

Solve the equation. Tell which method you used.

12. $y^2 - 4y - 5 = 0$

13. $z^2 + 11z + 30 = 0$

14. $5a^2 + 11a + 2 = 0$

PRACTICE AND APPLICATIONS

STUDENT HELP

► **Extra Practice**
to help you master
skills is on p. 806.

FACTORING OUT THE GCF Find the greatest common factor and factor it out of the expression.

15. $6v^3 - 18v$

16. $4q^4 + 12q$

17. $3x - 9x^2$

18. $24t^5 + 6t^3$

19. $4a^5 + 8a^3 - 2a^2$

20. $18d^6 - 6d^2 + 3d$

FACTORING COMPLETELY Factor the expression completely.

21. $24x^3 + 18x^2$

22. $-3w^4 + 21w^3$

23. $2y^3 - 10y^2 - 12y$

24. $5s^3 + 30s^2 + 40s$

25. $-7m^3 + 28m^2 - 21m$

26. $2d^4 + 2d^3 - 60d^2$

27. $4t^3 - 144t$

28. $-12z^4 + 3z^2$

29. $c^4 + c^3 - 12c - 12$

30. $x^3 - 3x^2 + x - 3$

31. $6b^4 + 5b^3 - 24b - 20$

32. $3y^3 - y^2 - 21y + 7$

33. $a^3 + 6a^2 - 4a - 24$

34. $t^3 - t^2 - 16t + 16$

35. $3m^3 - 15m^2 - 6m + 30$

36. $7n^5 + 7n^4 - 3n^2 - 6n - 3$

STUDENT HELP

► **HOMEWORK HELP**
Example 1: Exs. 15–20
Examples 2–6: Exs. 21–36
Example 7: Exs. 37–50
Example 8: Exs. 55–57
Example 9: Exs. 37–50

SOLVING EQUATIONS Solve the equation. Tell which solution method you used.

37. $y^2 + 7y + 12 = 0$

38. $x^2 - 3x - 4 = 0$

39. $b^2 + 4b - 117 = 0$

40. $t^2 - 16t + 65 = 0$

41. $27 + 6w - w^2 = 0$

42. $x^2 - 21x + 84 = 0$

43. $5x^4 - 80x^2 = 0$

44. $-16x^3 + 4x = 0$

45. $10x^3 - 290x^2 + 620x = 0$

46. $34x^4 - 85x^3 + 51x^2 = 0$

47. $8x^2 + 9x - 7 = 0$

48. $18x^2 - 21x + 28 = 0$

49. $24x^3 + 18x^2 - 168x = 0$

50. $-14x^4 + 118x^3 + 72x^2 = 0$

VERTICAL MOTION In Exercises 51–54, use the vertical motion models, where *h* is the initial height (in feet), *v* is the initial velocity (in feet per second) and *t* is the time (in seconds) the object spends in the air. (Note that the acceleration due to gravity on the Moon is $\frac{1}{6}$ that of Earth.)

Model for vertical motion on Earth: $h = 16t^2 - vt$

Model for vertical motion on the Moon: $h = \frac{16}{6}t^2 - vt$

51. 🌎 **EARTH** On Earth, you toss a tennis ball from a height of 96 feet with an initial upward velocity of 16 feet per second. How long will it take the tennis ball to reach the ground?

52. 🌎 **MOON** On the Moon, you toss a tennis ball from a height of 96 feet with an initial upward velocity of 16 feet per second. How long will it take the tennis ball to reach the surface of the moon?

53. *Writing* Do objects fall faster on Earth or on the Moon? Use your results from Exercises 51 and 52 and the vertical motion models shown above to support your answer.

54. **CRITICAL THINKING** The coefficient of the t^2-term in the vertical motion models is one-half the acceleration of a falling object due to gravity. On the surface of Jupiter, the acceleration due to gravity is about 2.4 times that on the surface of Earth. Write a vertical motion model for Jupiter.

🌎 **PACKAGING** In Exercises 55–57, use the following information. Refer to the diagram at the right.

The length ℓ of a box is 3 inches less than the height h. The width w is 9 inches less than the height. The box has a volume of 324 cubic inches.

55. Copy and complete the diagram by labeling the dimensions.

56. Write a model that you can solve to find the length, height, and width of the box.

57. What are the dimensions of the box?

EXTENSION: BRITISH METHOD Another method for finding the binomial factors of factorable trinomials of the form $ax^2 + bx + c$ is sometimes called the *British method*. To factor $6x^2 - x - 2$ by the British method, use the following steps.

① Find the "magic" number ac.
$$6 \cdot (-2) = -12$$

② Write the magic number as the product of two factors whose sum is b.
$$-12 = 3 \cdot (-4)$$

③ Rewrite the trinomial using the factors.
$$6x^2 - x - 2 = 6x^2 + 3x - 4x - 2$$

④ Factor using the distributive property.
$$6x^2 + 3x - 4x - 2 = 3x(2x + 1) - 2(2x + 1)$$
$$= (3x - 2)(2x + 1)$$

Use the British method to factor the trinomials.

58. $8x^2 - 2x - 3$ **59.** $3x^2 + 13x + 14$ **60.** $5x^2 + 27x - 18$

Test Preparation

61. MULTIPLE CHOICE Which of the following is the complete factorization of $x^3 - 5x^2 + 4x - 20$?

Ⓐ $(x + 2)(x + 2)(x - 5)$ Ⓑ $(x + 2)(x - 2)(x - 5)$

Ⓒ $(x^2 + 4)(x - 5)$ Ⓓ $(x - 4)(x - 1)(x - 20)$

62. MULTIPLE CHOICE Which of the following equations have real solutions?

I. $6x^2 + x - 12 = 0$ **II.** $6x^2 + 7x - 12 = 0$ **III.** $6x^2 + 7x - 13 = 0$

Ⓐ I only   Ⓑ II only   Ⓒ III only   Ⓓ All

63. MULTIPLE CHOICE The length l of a box is 3 centimeters more than half the height h. The width w is 2 centimeters more than one fifth of the height. The box has a volume of 3780 cubic centimeters. Which of the following equations can be used to find the height of the box?

Ⓐ $h\left(\frac{1}{5}h + 2\right)\left(\frac{1}{2}h + 3\right) = 3780$ Ⓑ $h\left(\frac{1}{2}h + 2\right)\left(\frac{1}{5}h + 3\right) = 3780$

Ⓒ $\frac{1}{10}h(h + 2)(h + 3) = 3780$ Ⓓ $h\left(\frac{1}{2}w + 2\right)\left(\frac{1}{5}l + 3\right) = 3780$

★ Challenge

CUBIC EQUATIONS Sums and differences of *cubes* can be factored using the following patterns.

Sum of cubes pattern: $a^3 + b^3 = (a + b)(a^2 - ab + b^2)$

Difference of cubes pattern: $a^3 - b^3 = (a - b)(a^2 + ab + b^2)$

In Exercises 64–67, use the patterns above to factor the cubic expression completely. Use the distributive property to verify your results.

64. $y^3 - 125$ **65.** $b^3 + 27$ **66.** $\frac{1}{8} + 8x^3$ **67.** $216 - 343t^3$

EXTRA CHALLENGE
www.mcdougallittell.com

68. Set each expression in Exercises 64–67 equal to zero and solve the equation.

MIXED REVIEW

SOLVING AND GRAPHING INEQUALITIES Solve the inequality and graph its solution. (Review 6.1, 6.2)

69. $7 + x \leq -9$ **70.** $-3 > 2x - 5$ **71.** $-x + 6 \leq 13$

SOLVING EQUATIONS Solve the equation. (Review 6.4)

72. $|x| = 3$ **73.** $|x - 5| = 7$ **74.** $|x + 6| = 13$

75. $|x + 8| - 2 = -12$ **76.** $|2x - 5| + 7 = 16$ **77.** $\left|x + \frac{3}{4}\right| = \frac{9}{4}$

SKETCHING GRAPHS Sketch the graph of the inequality. (Review 6.5)

78. $x + y < 9$ **79.** $y - 3x \geq 2$ **80.** $y - 4x \leq 10$

81. 🌎 **HEIGHT** One of the tallest people in the world is Ri Myong-hun of North Korea, who is about 93 inches tall. The average height of a United States male is about 69 inches. Compare Ri Myong-hun's height to the average U.S. male height using a ratio and a percent. (Review 3.8 for 11.1)

82. 🌎 **COMPARING ROOMS** One bedroom in a house is 10 feet by 12 feet. The living room is 24 feet by 15 feet. Compare the areas of the two rooms using a ratio. (Review 3.8 for 11.1)

QUIZ 3

Self-Test for Lessons 10.7 and 10.8

Factor the expression. Tell which special product factoring pattern you used. (Lesson 10.7)

1. $49x^2 - 64$ **2.** $121 - 9x^2$ **3.** $4t^2 + 20t + 25$

4. $72 - 50y^2$ **5.** $9y^2 + 42y + 49$ **6.** $3n^2 - 36n + 108$

Use factoring to solve the equation. (Lesson 10.7)

7. $3x^2 - 192 = 0$ **8.** $4x^2 + 32x + 64 = 0$ **9.** $9x^2 + 96x + 256 = 0$

10. $\frac{1}{2}x^2 - 4x + 8 = 0$ **11.** $216x^2 - 96 = 0$ **12.** $-3x^2 - 2x - \frac{1}{3} = 0$

Find the greatest common factor and factor it out of the expression. (Lesson 10.8)

13. $3x^3 + 12x^2$ **14.** $6x^2 + 3x$ **15.** $18x^4 - 9x^3$ **16.** $8x^5 + 4x^2 - 2x$

Factor the expression completely. (Lesson 10.8)

17. $2x^3 - 6x^2 + 4x$ **18.** $48x^3 - 75x$ **19.** $x^3 + 3x^2 + 4x + 12$

Solve the equation. Tell which solution method you used. (Lesson 10.8)

20. $12x^4 - 27x^2 = 0$ **21.** $-3x^2 - 4x + 15 = 0$ **22.** $3x^3 - 6x^2 + 5x - 10 = 0$

23. $56x^3 + 98x = 170x^2$ **24.** $17x^6 = 17x^5 + 204x^4$ **25.** $6x^3 + 45x^2 + 15x = 0$

Chapter Summary

WHAT did you learn?

Classify a polynomial by degree and by number of terms. **(10.1)**

Add and subtract polynomials. **(10.1)**

Multiply polynomials
- using the FOIL pattern. **(10.2)**

- using special product patterns. **(10.3)**

Solve polynomial equations in factored form. **(10.4)**

Factor quadratic trinomials. **(10.5–10.6)**

Factor a polynomial
- using special product patterns. **(10.7)**
- using the distributive property. **(10.8)**

Solve polynomial equations by factoring. **(10.5–10.8)**

WHY did you learn it?

Understand how to use polynomials to model real-life situations. **(p. 578)**

Represent the growth in the number of Internet sites. **(p. 579)**

Evaluate a polynomial expression to find the area of a window. **(p. 586)**

Find products of some polynomials more easily. **(p. 591)**

Find the dimensions of an archway. **(p. 599)**

Find the time it takes a diver to reach the water. **(p. 613)**

Find the size of rope needed to lift a safe. **(p. 621)**
Find the dimensions of a box. **(p. 627)**

Apply factoring skills to write models for real-life situations. **(pp. 604–632)**

How does Chapter 10 fit into the BIGGER PICTURE of algebra?

Polynomials can model a great variety of real-life situations. You were already familiar with three types of polynomial models: $y = a$ (constant model), $y = ax + b$ (linear model), and $y = ax^2 + bx + c$ (quadratic model).

In this chapter you learned how to add, subtract and multiply polynomials. You also learned how to "undo" multiplication by a process called factoring. This chapter has many connections with the mathematics you studied in Chapter 9. For instance, in this chapter you learned how to use factoring to solve quadratic equations.

STUDY STRATEGY

How did identifying trouble spots help you review?

One of your notes about trouble spots, using the **Study Strategy** on p. 574, may look like this.

Trouble Spots:

Lesson 10.1

Remember to change all of the signs when subtracting.
$(x^2 + 4x) - (x^2 - 3x + 1)$
$= x^2 + 4x - x^2 + 3x - 1$
$= 7x - 1$

10.1 ADDING AND SUBTRACTING POLYNOMIALS

Examples on pp. 576–579

EXAMPLES To add or subtract polynomials, add or subtract like terms.

Horizontal Format	Vertical Format

$$(4x^3 + 6x - 8) - (-x^2 + 7x - 2)$$

$$= 4x^3 + 6x - 8 + x^2 - 7x + 2$$

$$= 4x^3 + x^2 - x - 6$$

$$-2x^3 - 4x^2 - x + 5$$
$$3x^3 + 2x^2 - 4x + 9$$
$$+ \quad -x^3 + 5x^2 - x - 1$$
$$\overline{\qquad 3x^2 - 6x + 13}$$

Find the sum or the difference.

1. $(-x^2 + x + 2) + (3x^2 + 4x + 5)$

2. $(x^2 + 3x - 1) - (4x^2 - 5x + 6)$

3. $(x^3 + 5x^2 - 4x) - (3x^2 - 6x + 2)$

4. $(4x^3 + x^2 - 1) + (2 - x - x^2)$

10.2 MULTIPLYING POLYNOMIALS

Examples on pp. 584–586

EXAMPLES To multiply polynomials, use the distributive property or the FOIL pattern.

a. $(3x + 2)(5x^2 - 4x + 1) = 5x^2(3x + 2) - 4x(3x + 2) + 1(3x + 2)$

$$= 15x^3 + 10x^2 - 12x^2 - 8x + 3x + 2$$

$$= 15x^3 - 2x^2 - 5x + 2$$

$$\begin{array}{cccc} \text{F} & \text{O} & \text{I} & \text{L} \\ \downarrow & \downarrow & \downarrow & \downarrow \end{array}$$

b. $(4x + 5)(-3x - 6) = -12x^2 - 24x - 15x - 30$

$$= -12x^2 - 39x - 30$$

Find the product.

5. $(-x)(8x^3 - 12x^2)$

6. $4x^3(-x^2 + 2x - 7)$

7. $(x + 3)(x + 11)$

8. $(7x - 1)(5x + 2)$

9. $(x + 5)(2x^2 + x - 10)$

10. $(4x^2 + 9x)(-x^2 - 3)$

SPECIAL PRODUCTS OF POLYNOMIALS

Examples on pp. 590–592

EXAMPLES Use special product patterns to multiply some polynomials.

$$(a + b)(a - b) = a^2 - b^2 \qquad\qquad (a + b)^2 = a^2 + 2ab + b^2$$

$$(3x + 7)(3x - 7) = (3x)^2 - 7^2 \qquad (5t + 4)^2 = (5t)^2 + 2(5t)(4) + 4^2$$

$$= 9x^2 - 49 \qquad\qquad\qquad = 25t^2 + 40t + 16$$

Find the product.

11. $(x + 15)(x - 15)$ **12.** $(5x - 2)(5x + 2)$ **13.** $(x + 2)^2$ **14.** $(7m - 6)^2$

SOLVING POLYNOMIAL EQUATIONS IN FACTORED FORM

Examples on pp. 597–599

EXAMPLE Solve the equation $(x + 1)(x - 5) = 0$.

$(x + 1) = 0 \quad$ or $\quad (x - 5) = 0 \qquad$ **Use zero-product property.**

$x + 1 = 0 \qquad\qquad x - 5 = 0$

$x = -1 \qquad\qquad x = 5$

▶ The solutions are -1 and 5. Check these in the original equation.

Solve the equation.

15. $(x + 1)(x + 10) = 0$ **16.** $(x - 3)(x - 2) = 0$

17. $(x + 9)^2 = 0$ **18.** $(3x + 6)(4x - 1)(x - 4) = 0$

FACTORING $x^2 + bx + c$

Examples on pp. 604–606

EXAMPLE Solve the equation $x^2 - 9x = -14$ by factoring.

$x^2 - 9x = -14 \qquad\qquad$ **Write original equation.**

$x^2 - 9x + 14 = 0 \qquad\qquad$ **Write in standard form.**

$(x - 2)(x - 7) = 0 \qquad\qquad$ **Factor.**

$(x - 2) = 0$ or $(x - 7) = 0 \qquad$ **Use zero-product property.**

$x - 2 = 0 \qquad x - 7 = 0$

$x = 2 \qquad\qquad x = 7$

▶ The solutions are 2 and 7. Check these in the original equation.

Solve the equation by factoring.

19. $x^2 - 21x + 108 = 0$ **20.** $x^2 + 10x - 200 = 0$ **21.** $x^2 + 26x = -169$

FACTORING $ax^2 + bx + c$

Examples on
pp. 611–613

EXAMPLE To factor $3x^2 - x - 2$, test the possible factors of a (1 and 3) and of c (-2 and 1 or 2 and -1).

$(x - 2)(3x + 1) = 3x^2 - 5x - 2$	**Not correct**
$(x + 1)(3x - 2) = 3x^2 + x - 2$	**Not correct**
$(x + 2)(3x - 1) = 3x^2 + 5x - 2$	**Not correct**
$(x - 1)(3x + 2) = 3x^2 - x - 2$	**Correct**

Factor the trinomial.

22. $12x^2 + 7x + 1$ **23.** $2x^2 + 5x - 12$ **24.** $6x^2 + 4x - 10$ **25.** $4x^2 - 12x + 9$

FACTORING SPECIAL PRODUCTS

Examples on
pp. 619–621

EXAMPLES Factor using special product patterns to solve the equations.

$a^2 - b^2 = (a + b)(a - b)$ $a^2 - 2ab + b^2 = (a - b)^2$

$4x^2 - 64 = 0$ $x^2 - 4x + 4 = 0$

$(2x + 8)(2x - 8) = 0$ $x^2 - 2(x)(2) + 2^2 = 0$

$2x + 8 = 0$ or $2x - 8 = 0$ $(x - 2)^2 = 0$

▶ The solutions are -4 and 4. $x - 2 = 0$

                                         ▶ The solution is 2.

Use factoring to solve the equation.

26. $100x^2 - 121 = 0$ **27.** $16x^2 + 24x + 9 = 0$ **28.** $9x^2 - 18x + 9 = 0$

FACTORING USING THE DISTRIBUTIVE PROPERTY

Examples on
pp. 625–628

EXAMPLES Use the distributive property to factor out common variable factors.

$3x^3 - 27x = 3x(x^2 - 9)$ $x^4 - 4x^3 + x^2 - 4x = (x^4 + x^2) + (-4x^3 - 4x)$

$= 3x(x + 3)(x - 3)$ $= x^2(x^2 + 1) - 4x(x^2 + 1)$

                                      $= (x^2 - 4x)(x^2 + 1)$

                                      $= x(x - 4)(x^2 + 1)$

Factor the expression completely.

29. $-2x^5 - 2x^4 + 4x^3$ **30.** $2x^4 - 32x^2$

31. $3x^3 + x^2 + 15x + 5$ **32.** $x^3 + 3x^2 - 4x - 12$

Chapter Test

Use a vertical format or a horizontal format to add or subtract.

1. $(x^2 + 4x - 1) + (5x^2 + 2)$

2. $(5t^2 - 9t + 1) - (8t + 13)$

3. $(7n^3 + 2n^2 - n - 4) - (4n^3 - 3n^2 + 8)$

4. $(x^4 + 6x^2 + 7) + (2x^4 - 3x^2 + 1)$

Find the product.

5. $(x + 3)(2x + 3)$

6. $(9x - 1)(7x + 4)$

7. $(w - 6)(4w^2 + w - 7)$

8. $(5t^3 + 2)(4t^2 + 8t - 7)$

9. $(3z^3 - 5z^2 + 8)(z + 2)$

10. $(4x + 1)\left(\frac{1}{2}x - \frac{3}{8}\right)$

11. $(x - 12)^2$

12. $(7x + 2)^2$

13. $(8x + 3)(8x - 3)$

Use the zero-product property to solve the equation.

14. $(6x - 5)(x + 2) = 0$

15. $(x + 8)^2 = 0$

16. $(4x + 3)(x - 1)(3x + 9) = 0$

Find the x-intercepts and the vertex of the graph. Then sketch the graph.

17. $y = (x + 1)(x - 5)$

18. $y = (x + 2)(x + 6)$

19. $y = (-x - 4)(x + 7)$

Solve the equation by factoring.

20. $x^2 + 13x + 30 = 0$

21. $x^2 - 19x + 84 = 0$

22. $x^2 - 34x - 240 = 0$

23. $2x^2 + 15x - 108 = 0$

24. $9x^2 - 9x = 28$

25. $18x^2 - 57x = -35$

Factor the expression.

26. $x^2 - 196$

27. $16x^2 - 36$

28. $128 - 50x^2$

29. $x^2 - 6x + 9$

30. $4x^2 + 44x + 121$

31. $2x^2 + 28x + 98$

32. $9t^2 - 54$

33. $4x^2 + 38x + 34$

34. $x^3 + 2x^2 - 16x - 32$

Solve the equation by a method of your choice.

35. $x^2 - 60 = -11$

36. $2x^2 + 15x - 8 = 0$

37. $x^2 - 13x = -40$

38. $x(x - 16) = 0$

39. $12x^2 + 3x = 0$

40. $8x^2 + 6x = 5$

41. $12x^2 + 17x = 7$

42. $81x^2 - 6 = 30$

43. $16x^2 - 34x - 15 = 0$

44. 🌐 **TIC-TAC-TOE** You are making a tic-tac-toe board. Each square will have sides of x inches. The board will have a border with a width of 1 inch. Draw a diagram and label the dimensions. Write a polynomial expression for the area of the board.

45. 🌐 **ROOM DIMENSIONS** A room's length is 3 feet less than twice its width. The area of the room is 135 square feet. What are the room's dimensions?

46. 🌐 **KICKING A FOOTBALL** You kick a football into the air. The vertical component of this motion can be modeled by the vertical motion model. Suppose the football has an initial upward velocity of 31 feet per second. The ball makes contact with your foot about 2 feet above the ground. Find the time t (in seconds) for the football to reach the ground. Use the vertical motion model on page 621.

CHAPTER
10

Chapter Standardized Test

▶ **TEST-TAKING STRATEGY** Some questions involve more than one step. Reading too quickly might lead to mistaking the answer to a preliminary step for your final answer.

1. **MULTIPLE CHOICE** Classify $3x^2 - 7 + 4x^3 - 5x$ by degree and by the number of terms.

   Ⓐ quadratic trinomial

   Ⓑ cubic polynomial

   Ⓒ quartic polynomial

   Ⓓ quadratic polynomial

   Ⓔ cubic trinomial

2. **MULTIPLE CHOICE** Which of the following is equal to $(-x^2 - 5x + 7) + (-7x^2 + 5x - 2)$?

   Ⓐ $8x^2 - 5$ Ⓑ $-8x^2 + 10x + 5$

   Ⓒ $6x^2 + 5$ Ⓓ $-8x^2 - 10x + 5$

   Ⓔ $-8x^2 + 5$

3. **MULTIPLE CHOICE** Which of the following is equal to $(5x^3 + 3x^2 - x + 1) - (2x^3 + x - 5)$?

   Ⓐ $3x^3 + 3x^2 - 4$

   Ⓑ $3x^3 + 3x^2 - 2x - 4$

   Ⓒ $3x^3 + 3x^2 - 2x - 6$

   Ⓓ $3x^3 + 3x^2 - 2x + 6$

   Ⓔ $7x^3 + 3x^2 - 2x + 6$

4. **MULTIPLE CHOICE** The base of a triangular sail is x feet and its height is $\frac{1}{2}x + 7$ feet. Which expression represents the sail's area? $\left(\text{The area of a triangle is } A = \frac{1}{2}bh.\right)$

   Ⓐ $\frac{1}{2}x^2 + 7x$ Ⓑ $\frac{1}{4}x^2 + \frac{7}{2}x$

   Ⓒ $\frac{1}{2}x^2 + \frac{7}{2}x$ Ⓓ $\frac{7}{2}x^2 + \frac{1}{2}x$

   Ⓔ $\frac{1}{4}x^2 + 7x$

5. **MULTIPLE CHOICE** Which of the following is equal to $(4x - 9)(7x - 2)$?

   Ⓐ $28x^2 - 71x + 18$ Ⓑ $28x^2 - 55x + 18$

   Ⓒ $28x^2 - 71x - 18$ Ⓓ $28x^2 + 55x + 18$

   Ⓔ $28x^2 - 69x + 18$

6. **MULTIPLE CHOICE** Which trinomial represents the area of the trapezoid? (The area of a trapezoid is $A = \frac{1}{2}h(b_1 + b_2)$.)

   Ⓐ $\frac{5}{2}x^2 + 19x + 12$ Ⓑ $5x^2 + 19x + 6$

   Ⓒ $\frac{5}{2}x^2 + \frac{19}{2}x + 6$ Ⓓ $5x^2 + 19x - 6$

   Ⓔ $\frac{5}{2}x^2 + \frac{17}{2}x + 6$

7. **MULTIPLE CHOICE** Which of the following is equal to $(2x - 9)^2$?

   Ⓐ $x^2 + 81$ Ⓑ $x^2 - 18x - 81$

   Ⓒ $4x^2 + 36x + 81$ Ⓓ $4x^2 - 18x + 81$

   Ⓔ $4x^2 - 36x + 81$

8. **MULTIPLE CHOICE** What are the coordinates of the vertex of the graph of $y = (x - 6)(x + 5)$?

   Ⓐ $\left(-\frac{1}{2}, -24\frac{1}{2}\right)$ Ⓑ $\left(\frac{1}{2}, -25\frac{1}{2}\right)$

   Ⓒ $(2, -28)$ Ⓓ $\left(\frac{1}{2}, -30\frac{1}{4}\right)$

   Ⓔ $\left(-\frac{1}{2}, -24\frac{1}{4}\right)$

9. **MULTIPLE CHOICE** Which of the following is one of the solutions of the equation $x^2 - 2x = 120$?

   Ⓐ -12 Ⓑ -10 Ⓒ 10

   Ⓓ 20 Ⓔ 60

10. **MULTIPLE CHOICE** The area of a circle is given by $A = \pi(9x^2 + 30x + 25)$. Which expression represents the radius of the circle?

    Ⓐ $|3x + 5|$ Ⓑ $9x^2 - 25$ Ⓒ $(3x - 5)^2$

    Ⓓ $9x^2 + 25$ Ⓔ $(3x + 5)^2$

11. **MULTIPLE CHOICE** If $x = -2$ is a solution of $x^2 - bx - 16 = 0$, what is the value of b?

    (A) -8 (B) -6 (C) 6 (D) 8 (E) 10

12. **MULTIPLE CHOICE** A ball is tossed into the air from a height of 10 feet with an initial upward velocity of 12 feet per second. Find the time in seconds for the ball to reach the ground.

    (A) $\frac{1}{2}$ (B) $\frac{4}{5}$ (C) $1\frac{1}{4}$ (D) $1\frac{1}{2}$ (E) 2

13. **MULTIPLE CHOICE** Which of the following is a correct factorization of $-45x^2 + 150x - 125$?

    (A) $5(-3x + 5)$ (B) $-5(3x + 5)^2$ (C) $-5(3x + 5)(3x - 5)$

    (D) $-5(3x - 5)^2$ (E) $-5(-3x + 5)(-3x - 5)$

QUANTITATIVE COMPARISON In Exercises 14 and 15, evaluate the expression for the given values and choose the statement that is true about the results.

    (A) The number in Column A is greater.   (B) The number in Column B is greater.

    (C) The two numbers are equal.   (D) The relationship cannot be determined from the information given.

	Column A	Column B
14.	$(a + b)^2$ when $a = 17$ and $b = -8$	$(a - b)^2$ when $a = 17$ and $b = -8$
15.	$(a^2 - b^2)$ when $a = 3$ and $b = -4$	$(a - b)^2$ when $a = 3$ and $b = -4$

16. **MULTIPLE CHOICE** Which of the following is equal to the expression $x^3 - 2x^2 - 11x + 22$?

    (A) $(x - 2)(x - 11)$ (B) $(x - 2)(x^2 + 11)$ (C) $(x - 2)(x^2 - 11)$

    (D) $(x - 2)(x + 11)$ (E) none of these

17. **MULTI-STEP PROBLEM** You have made clay animals to sell for charity. Each animal is about 6 inches long by 8 inches wide by 8 inches tall. You want to package each animal in a box with the top of its head showing. You will not use a lid for the box. You have received a donation of cardboard sheets that are 24 inches by 20 inches to make the boxes. You must cut out corner regions of x^2 so that the flaps can be folded up to form each box.

24 in.

20 in.

    a. Write a polynomial expression for the area of the box bottom. Find the area of the box bottom in terms of x.

    b. Write a polynomial expression for the volume of the box. Find the volume of the box in terms of x.

    c. Is it possible to use squares that are 12 inches for the corners? Explain your reasoning.

    d. Is it possible to use the donated cardboard sheets to make boxes that will be large enough to hold the clay animals? Explain.

RATIONAL EQUATIONS AND FUNCTIONS

▶ *How do scale models fit into the design process?*

CHAPTER
11

APPLICATION: Scale Models

An architectural scale model is a smaller, three-dimensional representation of a structure. Models can be built for a single building or an entire city. Architects, builders, and city planners use them.

The dimensions of a scale model can be determined by solving a proportion. In Chapter 11 you'll learn ways to solve proportions and other rational equations.

Think & Discuss

Use the drawing of a scale model for Exercises 1–2.

Scale of 1 in. to 48 in.

7 in.

1. Solve the equation $\frac{7}{1} = \frac{x}{48}$ to find the height x of the actual house. Write your answer in feet.

2. A shutter on the house is 1 foot wide. How wide is it on the model? Write your answer in inches.

Learn More About It

You will write and use a proportion for a problem about a scale model in Exercise 43 on page 647.

APPLICATION LINK Visit www.mcdougallittell.com for more information about scale models.

What's the chapter about?

Chapter 11 is about **rational expressions**. In Chapter 11 you'll learn

- how to solve rational equations.
- how to add, subtract, multiply, and divide rational expressions.
- how to graph rational functions, including inverse variation functions.

KEY VOCABULARY

▶ **Review**
- equivalent equations, p. 132
- transformations, p. 132
- direct variation, p. 234
- polynomial, p. 576
- zero-product property, p. 597

▶ **New**
- proportion, p. 643
- extraneous solution, p. 644
- inverse variation, p. 656
- rational number, p. 664
- rational expression, p. 664

- geometric probability, p. 666
- rational equation, p. 690
- rational function, p. 692
- hyperbola, p. 692

Are you ready for the chapter?

SKILL REVIEW These exercises will help you review skills that you'll apply in this chapter. See the given **reference page** if there is something you don't understand.

Find the value of the expression. Write the answer as a fraction or mixed number in lowest terms. (Skills Review, p. 781–783)

1. $\dfrac{11}{14} - \dfrac{4}{14}$ **2.** $\dfrac{9}{15} + \dfrac{7}{10}$ **3.** $\dfrac{6}{11} - \dfrac{3}{5}$ **4.** $\dfrac{8}{12} + \dfrac{11}{18}$

Simplify the expression. (Review Examples 1 and 2, pp. 108–109)

5. $\dfrac{36x}{15} \div \dfrac{9}{5}$ **6.** $49x^2 \div \dfrac{-7x}{3}$ **7.** $\dfrac{15x + 25}{5}$ **8.** $\dfrac{16 - 4x}{8}$

Solve the equation by finding square roots or by factoring.
(Review pp. 505 and 613)

9. $3x^2 - 65 = 178$ **10.** $4x^2 - 10x + 6 = 0$ **11.** $10x^2 - 30x - 40 = 0$

Here's a study strategy!

Previewing and Reviewing

Preview the chapter. Write down what you already know about each topic. After studying the chapter, go back to each topic and write down what you then know about it. Compare the two sets of notes. See what you have learned.

11.1

Ratio and Proportion

What you should learn

GOAL ① Solve proportions.

GOAL ② Use proportions to solve **real-life** problems, such as making estimates about an archaeological dig in **Example 4**.

Why you should learn it

▼ To solve **real-life** problems such as creating a mural in **Exs. 41 and 42**.

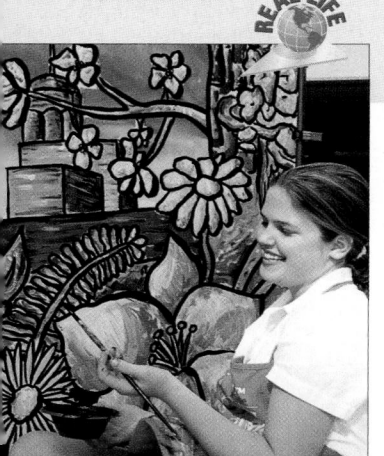

GOAL ① **SOLVING PROPORTIONS**

In Chapter 3 you solved problems involving ratios. An equation that states that two ratios are equal is a **proportion**.

$$\frac{a}{b} = \frac{c}{d} \qquad b \text{ and } d \text{ are nonzero.}$$

This proportion is read as "a is to b as c is to d." When the ratios are written in this order, the numbers a and d are the **extremes** of the proportion and the numbers b and c are the **means** of the proportion.

PROPERTIES OF PROPORTIONS

RECIPROCAL PROPERTY
If two ratios are equal, their reciprocals, if they exist, are also equal.

If $\frac{a}{b} = \frac{c}{d}$, then $\frac{b}{a} = \frac{d}{c}$. **Example:** $\frac{2}{3} = \frac{4}{6}$ ⟹ $\frac{3}{2} = \frac{6}{4}$

CROSS PRODUCT PROPERTY
The product of the extremes equals the product of the means.

If $\frac{a}{b} = \frac{c}{d}$, then $ad = bc$. **Example:** $\frac{2}{3} = \frac{4}{6}$ ⟹ $2 \cdot 6 = 3 \cdot 4$

When a proportion involves a single variable, finding the value of that variable is called **solving the proportion**.

EXAMPLE 1 *Using the Reciprocal Property*

Solve the proportion $\frac{3}{y} = \frac{5}{8}$.

SOLUTION

$\frac{3}{y} = \frac{5}{8}$ **Write original proportion.**

$\frac{y}{3} = \frac{8}{5}$ **Use reciprocal property.**

$y = 3 \cdot \frac{8}{5}$ **Multiply each side by 3.**

$y = \frac{24}{5}$ **Simplify.**

✓**CHECK** When you substitute to check, $\dfrac{3}{\frac{24}{5}}$ becomes $3 \cdot \frac{5}{24}$ which simplifies to $\frac{5}{8}$.

EXAMPLE 2 *Using the Cross Product Property*

Solve the proportion $\frac{x}{3} = \frac{12}{x}$.

SOLUTION

$$\frac{x}{3} = \frac{12}{x} \qquad \text{Write original proportion.}$$

$$x \cdot x = 3 \cdot 12 \qquad \text{Use cross product property.} \qquad \frac{x}{3} \diagup\hspace{-0.9em}\diagdown \frac{12}{x}$$

$$x^2 = 36 \qquad \text{Simplify.}$$

$$x = \pm 6 \qquad \text{Take square root of each side.}$$

▶ The solutions are $x = 6$ and $x = -6$. Check these in the original proportion.

· · · · · · · · · ·

Up to now, you have been checking solutions to make sure that you didn't make errors in the solution process. Even with no mistakes, it can happen that a trial solution does not satisfy the original equation. This type of solution is called **extraneous.** An extraneous solution should not be listed as an actual solution.

EXAMPLE 3 *Checking Solutions*

Solve the proportion $\dfrac{y^2 - 9}{y + 3} = \dfrac{y - 3}{2}$.

SOLUTION

$$\frac{y^2 - 9}{y + 3} = \frac{y - 3}{2} \qquad \text{Write original proportion.}$$

$$2(y^2 - 9) = (y + 3)(y - 3) \qquad \text{Use cross product property.}$$

$$2y^2 - 18 = y^2 - 9 \qquad \text{Use distributive property.}$$

$$y^2 = 9 \qquad \text{Isolate variable term.}$$

$$y = \pm 3 \qquad \text{Take square root of each side.}$$

At this point, the solutions appear to be $y = 3$ and $y = -3$.

✔**CHECK** Check each solution by substituting it into the original proportion.

y = 3:

$$\frac{y^2 - 9}{y + 3} = \frac{y - 3}{2}$$

$$\frac{3^2 - 9}{3 + 3} \overset{?}{=} \frac{3 - 3}{2}$$

$$\frac{0}{6} \overset{?}{=} \frac{0}{2}$$

$$0 = 0$$

y = -3:

$$\frac{y^2 - 9}{y + 3} = \frac{y - 3}{2}$$

$$\frac{(-3)^2 - 9}{(-3) + 3} \overset{?}{=} \frac{(-3) - 3}{2}$$

$$\frac{0}{0} \neq \frac{-6}{2}$$

▶ You can conclude that $y = -3$ is extraneous because the check results in a false statement. The only solution is $y = 3$.

STUDENT HELP

→ **Study Tip**
Remember to check your solution in the original proportion. Notice that Example 2 has two solutions so you need to check both of them.

STUDENT HELP

→ **Look Back**
For help with solving an equation by finding square roots or by factoring, see pp. 505 and 613.

644 **Chapter 11** *Rational Equations and Functions*

GOAL 2 USING PROPORTIONS IN REAL LIFE

When writing a proportion to model a situation, you can set up your proportion in more than one way.

EXAMPLE 4 *Writing and Using a Proportion*

ARCHAEOLOGY Archaeologists excavated three pits containing the clay army. To estimate the number of warriors in Pit 1 shown below, an archaeologist might excavate three sites. The sites at the ends together contain 450 warriors. The site in the central region contains 282 warriors. This 10-meter-wide site is thought to be representative of the 200-meter central region. Estimate the number of warriors in the central region. Then estimate the total number of warriors in Pit 1.

Not drawn to scale

ARCHAEOLOGY
In 1974, archaeologists discovered the tomb of Emperor Qin Shi Huang (259–210 B.C.) in China. Buried close to the tomb was an entire army of life-sized clay warriors.

APPLICATION LINK
www.mcdougallittell.com

SOLUTION Let *n* represent the number of warriors in the 200-meter central region. You can find the value of *n* by solving a proportion.

$$\frac{\text{Number of warriors found}}{\text{Total number of warriors}} = \frac{\text{Number of meters excavated}}{\text{Total number of meters}}$$

$$\frac{282}{n} = \frac{10}{200}$$

▶ The solution is $n = 5640$, indicating that there are about 5640 warriors in the central region. With the 450 warriors at the ends, that makes a total of about 6090 warriors in Pit 1.

Model Making

EXAMPLE 5 *Writing and Using a Proportion*

You want to make a scale model of one of the clay horses found in the tomb. The clay horse is 1.5 meters tall and 2 meters long. Your scale model will be 18 inches long. How tall should it be?

SOLUTION Let *h* represent the height of the model.

$$\frac{\text{Height of actual statue}}{\text{Length of actual statue}} = \frac{\text{Height of model}}{\text{Length of model}}$$

$$\frac{1.5}{2} = \frac{h}{18}$$

▶ The solution is $h = 13\frac{1}{2}$. Your scale model should be $13\frac{1}{2}$ inches tall.

GUIDED PRACTICE

Vocabulary Check ✓

1. Write the extremes and the means of the proportion $\frac{3}{4} = \frac{9}{12}$.

Concept Check ✓ Write *yes* or *no* to tell whether the equation is a consequence of $\frac{a}{b} = \frac{c}{d}$.

2. $ac = bd$ **3.** $ba = dc$ **4.** $ad = bc$

5. $\frac{a}{b} = \frac{d}{c}$ **6.** $\frac{b}{a} = \frac{d}{c}$ **7.** $\frac{a}{d} = \frac{b}{c}$

8. Solve the proportion $\frac{4}{x+1} = \frac{7}{2}$ two ways—using the reciprocal property and using the cross product method. Which method do you prefer? Why?

Skill Check ✓ Solve the proportion. Check for extraneous solutions.

9. $\frac{x}{3} = \frac{2}{7}$ **10.** $\frac{6}{x} = \frac{5}{3}$ **11.** $\frac{2}{2x+1} = \frac{1}{5}$

12. $\frac{3}{x} = \frac{x+1}{4}$ **13.** $\frac{t-2}{t} = \frac{2}{t+3}$ **14.** $\frac{2u-3}{4u} = \frac{u-1}{u}$

🌐 **MODEL MAKING** In Exercises 15 and 16, use Example 5. The proportion used in Example 5 compares height to length, but the situation could be described using other comparisons instead.

15. Set up a different proportion to represent the situation in Example 5.

16. Solve the proportion you wrote in Exercise 15. Do you get the same solution as in Example 5?

PRACTICE AND APPLICATIONS

STUDENT HELP

▶ **Extra Practice**
to help you master
skills is on p. 807.

SOLVING PROPORTIONS Solve the proportion. Check for extraneous solutions.

17. $\frac{16}{4} = \frac{12}{x}$ **18.** $\frac{4}{2x} = \frac{7}{3}$ **19.** $\frac{5}{8} = \frac{c}{9}$

20. $\frac{x}{3} = \frac{2}{5}$ **21.** $\frac{5}{3c} = \frac{2}{3}$ **22.** $\frac{24}{5} = \frac{9}{y+2}$

23. $\frac{6}{3} = \frac{x+8}{-1}$ **24.** $\frac{r+4}{3} = \frac{r}{5}$ **25.** $\frac{w+4}{2w} = \frac{-5}{6}$

26. $\frac{5}{2y} = \frac{7}{y-3}$ **27.** $\frac{x+6}{3} = \frac{x-5}{2}$ **28.** $\frac{x-2}{4} = \frac{x+10}{10}$

29. $\frac{8}{x+2} = \frac{3}{x-1}$ **30.** $\frac{x-3}{18} = \frac{3}{x}$ **31.** $\frac{-2}{a-7} = \frac{a}{5}$

STUDENT HELP

▶ **HOMEWORK HELP**
Example 1: Exs. 17–40
Example 2: Exs. 17–40
Example 3: Exs. 17–40
Example 4: Exs. 41–43
Example 5: Exs. 41–43

32. $\frac{u}{3} = \frac{1}{2u-1}$ **33.** $\frac{d}{d+4} = \frac{d-2}{d}$ **34.** $\frac{3x}{4x-1} = \frac{1}{x}$

35. $\frac{x-3}{x} = \frac{x}{x+6}$ **36.** $\frac{5}{m+1} = \frac{4m}{m}$ **37.** $\frac{2}{3t} = \frac{t-1}{t}$

38. $\frac{2}{6x+1} = \frac{2x}{1}$ **39.** $\frac{-2}{q} = \frac{q+1}{q^2}$ **40.** $\frac{6}{19n} = \frac{-2}{n^2+2}$

🌐 **MURAL PROJECT** In Exercises 41–42, use the following information.

The *Art is the Heart of the City* fence mural project in Charlotte, North Carolina, involved artists Cordelia Williams and Paul Rousso along with 22 students in grades 11 and 12. Students created drawings on paper. Slides of the drawings were made and projected to fit onto 4-foot-wide by 8-foot-long sheets of plywood used for the fence panels. Students traced and later painted the enlarged images.

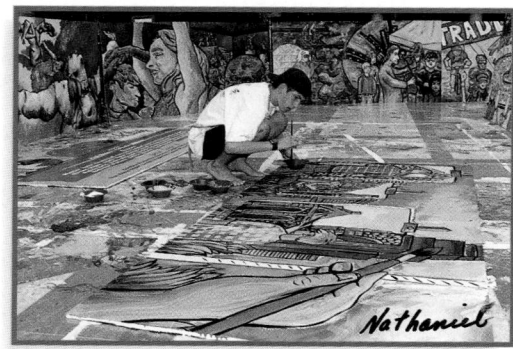

41. If the paper used for the original drawings was 11 inches wide, how long did it need to be?

42. Suppose the length of the paintbrush on the panel shown is $2\frac{1}{2}$ feet. Use Exercise 41 to find the length of the paintbrush in the student's drawing.

43. 🌐 **SCALE MODELS** A scale model uses a scale of $\frac{1}{16}$ inch to represent 1 foot. Explain how you can use a proportion and cross products to show that a scale of $\frac{1}{16}$ in. to 1 ft is the same as a scale of 1 in. to 192 in.

🌐 **WHAT STUDENTS BUY** In Exercises 44–46, use the table. It shows the results of a survey in which 100 students were asked how they spent money last week.

44. Estimate the number of students out of 500 that bought clothes or accessories in the last week.

45. Choose 3 items that were bought by different numbers of students. Based on the survey, how many students out of 20 would you predict to have bought each item?

46. **COLLECTING DATA** Choose one item from Exercise 45. Ask 20 students whether they bought that item. Compare the results with your prediction. Are the results what you expected? Explain.

How 100 students spent money	
Item	Number of students
Food	78
Clothes, accessories	20
Books, magazines, comics	15
Toys, stickers, games	14
Movie tickets	14
Arcade games	14
Gifts	13
Movie rentals	13
Music	12
Footwear	11
Grooming products	11

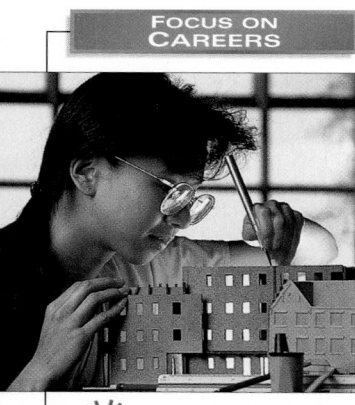
47. 🌐 **SAMPLING FISH POPULATIONS** Researchers studying fish populations at Dryden Lake in New York caught, marked, and then released 232 Chain pickerel. Later a sample of 329 Chain pickerel were caught and examined. Of these, 16 were found to be marked. Use the proportion below to estimate the total Chain pickerel population in the lake.

$$\frac{\text{Marked pickerel in sample}}{\text{Total pickerel in sample}} = \frac{\text{Marked pickerel in lake}}{\text{Total pickerel in lake}}$$

48. MULTI-STEP PROBLEM Base your answers on the 1997 population data shown in the table for people 25 years and older in the United States.

Total population (in thousands)	Number of people out of 100 with education level			
	Not a high school graduate	High school graduate	Some college, but less than 4 yr	At least 4 yr of college
170,581	17.9	33.8	24.5	23.8

 DATA UPDATE of U.S. Bureau of the Census data at www.mcdougallittell.com

a. Out of 200 people aged 25 years or older, about how many would you expect to have just a high school education? to have at least 4 years of college?

b. Write and solve a proportion to estimate the number of people in the United States aged 25 years or older with at least 4 years of college.

c. Suppose a town has 20,000 residents aged 25 years or older. Write and solve a proportion to estimate the number of town residents 25 years or older who have completed at least 4 years of college.

d. *Writing* Suppose another town has 15,860 people aged 25 years or older and that 7581 of these people have completed at least 4 years of college. Explain how you can find out whether the number of college graduates in that town is typical for a town of that size.

★ Challenge

 EXTRA CHALLENGE
www.mcdougallittell.com

49. LOGICAL REASONING One way to prove that two proportions are equivalent is to apply the properties of equality to transform one of the proportions into the other proportion. Give a sequence of steps that transforms the proportion $\frac{a}{b} = \frac{c}{d}$ into $\frac{a}{c} = \frac{b}{d}$.

MIXED REVIEW

50. DECIMAL AND PERCENT FORM Copy and complete the table. If necessary, round to the nearest tenth of a percent. **(Skills Review, pages 784–785)**

Decimal	?	0.2	?	0.073	0.666…	?	?	2
Percent	78%	?	3%	?	?	176%	110%	?

FINDING SQUARE ROOTS Find all square roots of the number or write *no square roots*. Check the results by squaring each root. **(Review 9.1)**

51. 64   **52.** −9   **53.** 12   **54.** 169

55. −20   **56.** 50   **57.** $\frac{9}{25}$ **58.** 0.04

SIMPLIFYING RADICAL EXPRESSIONS Simplify the radical expression. **(Review 9.2)**

59. $\sqrt{18}$ **60.** $\sqrt{20}$ **61.** $\sqrt{80}$ **62.** $\sqrt{162}$

63. $9\sqrt{36}$ **64.** $\sqrt{\frac{11}{9}}$ **65.** $\frac{1}{2}\sqrt{28}$ **66.** $4\sqrt{\frac{5}{4}}$

Percents

What you should learn

GOAL 1 Use equations to solve percent problems.

GOAL 2 Use percents in **real-life** problems, such as finding the number of known insect species in **Example 4**.

Why you should learn it

▼ To model and solve **real-life** problems, such as comparing two discounted prices in **Ex. 45**.

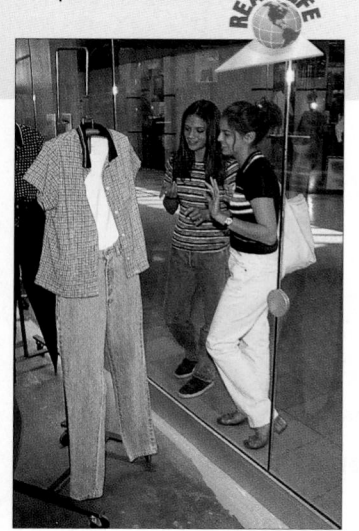

GOAL 1 SOLVING PERCENT PROBLEMS

In the percent equation "8 is 40% of 20," you compare 8 to the *base number* 20 by writing $\frac{8}{20} = \frac{40}{100}$. The percent for $\frac{8}{20}$ can be written as 40%, as the fraction $\frac{40}{100}$, or as the decimal 0.4. When you work with percents in equations, you usually write the percent as a fraction or as a decimal. In any percent equation the **base number** is the number you are comparing to. You can write a verbal model to help you solve the equation.

VERBAL MODEL	**Number being compared to base** is a **percent** of **base number**
LABELS	Number compared to base $= a$ (same units as b)
	Percent $= p$ (no units)
	Base number $= b$ (assigned units)
ALGEBRAIC MODEL	$a = p \cdot b$

In Examples 1–3 you will see how the basic verbal model above can be applied to the three different cases of percent problems—finding a, finding p, or finding b. As shown in these examples, percents are usually converted to decimal form before performing arithmetic operations.

EXAMPLE 1 *Number Compared to Base is Unknown*

What is 30% of 70 feet?

SOLUTION

VERBAL MODEL	a is $\boxed{p \text{ percent}}$ of $\boxed{b}$
LABELS	Number compared to base $= a$ (feet)
	Percent $= 30\% = \mathbf{0.3}$ (no units)
	Base number $= \mathbf{70}$ (feet)
ALGEBRAIC MODEL	$a = (\mathbf{0.3})(\mathbf{70})$
	$a = 21$

▶ 21 feet is 30% of 70 feet.

EXAMPLE 2 Base Number is Unknown

Fourteen dollars is 25% of what amount of money?

SOLUTION

VERBAL MODEL

$\boxed{a}$ is $\boxed{p \text{ percent}}$ of b

LABELS

Number compared to base = **14**   (dollars)

Percent = 25% = **0.25**   (no units)

Base number = b (dollars)

ALGEBRAIC MODEL

$$14 = (0.25)\,b$$

$$\frac{14}{0.25} = b$$

$$56 = b$$

▶ $14 is 25% of $56.

STUDENT HELP

Study Tip

You can check your work by using a different method. In Example 2, you are comparing $14 to an unknown number of dollars b. You can use the proportion $\frac{14}{b} = \frac{25}{100}$.

EXAMPLE 3 Percent is Unknown

One hundred thirty-five is what percent of 27?

SOLUTION

VERBAL MODEL

$\boxed{a}$ is $\boxed{p \text{ percent}}$ of $\boxed{b}$

LABELS

Number compared to base = **135**   (no units)

Percent = p (no units)

Base number = **27**   (no units)

ALGEBRAIC MODEL

$$135 = p\,(27)$$

$$\frac{135}{27} = p$$

$$5 = p \qquad \text{Decimal form}$$

$$500\% = p \qquad \text{Percent form} \left(5 = \frac{500}{100} \right)$$

CONCEPT SUMMARY

THREE FORMS OF PERCENT PROBLEMS $a = pb$

QUESTION	GIVEN	NEED TO FIND	EXAMPLE
What is p percent of b?	b and p	a	Example 1
a is p percent of **what**?	a and p	b	Example 2
a is **what percent** of b?	a and b	p	Example 3

STUDENT HELP

INTERNET HOMEWORK HELP
Visit our Web site
www.mcdougallittell.com
for extra examples.

GOAL 2 **USING PERCENTS IN REAL LIFE**

EXAMPLE 4 *Modeling and Using Percents*

SCIENCE CONNECTION
There are about 170,000 species of butterflies and moths world-wide. Butterflies and moths make up about 17% of all classified insect species. Estimate how many insect species have been classified.

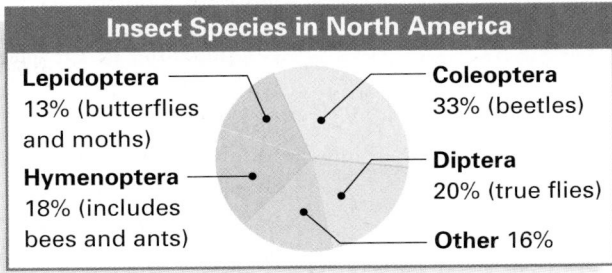

Insect Species in North America

Lepidoptera 13% (butterflies and moths)
Coleoptera 33% (beetles)
Hymenoptera 18% (includes bees and ants)
Diptera 20% (true flies)
Other 16%

Note: the percents for the world-wide species are slightly different.

SOLUTION

Method 1 Use the percent equation $a = pb$.

PROBLEM SOLVING STRATEGY

VERBAL MODEL

| Number of butterfly and moth species | is | *p* percent | of | Total number of insect species |

LABELS

Number of butterfly and moth species = **170,000**   (species)

Percent = 17% = **0.17**   (no units)

Total number of insect species = *b*   (species)

ALGEBRAIC MODEL

$$170,000 = 0.17\,b$$

$$\frac{170,000}{0.17} = b$$

$$1,000,000 = b$$

▶ About 1,000,000 species of insects have been classified.

Method 2 Use a proportion.

Write ratios that compare the part to the whole. Let *b* represent the total number of insect species that have been classified.

$$\frac{\text{Number of butterfly and moth species}}{\text{Total number of insect species}} = \frac{17}{100}$$ Write proportion.

$$\frac{170,000}{b} = \frac{17}{100}$$ Substitute.

$$17b = 170,000 \cdot 100$$ Use cross products.

$$b = \frac{17,000,000}{17}$$ Divide each side by 17.

$$b = 1,000,000$$ Simplify.

▶ About 1,000,000 species of insects have been classified.

CLASSIFYING INSECTS
Butterflies and moths together make up the insect order *Lepidoptera*. About 17,000 species of butterflies and about 153,000 species of moths have been classified.

APPLICATION LINK
www.mcdougallittell.com

Cars

EXAMPLE 5 *Using Percents to Compare*

The circle graph shows the average costs (in percents) of owning an automobile in 1996.

Suppose that in 1996 a car owner spent $650 on gasoline for a car whose total costs were $3750. Was the percent spent on gasoline about the same as the national average?

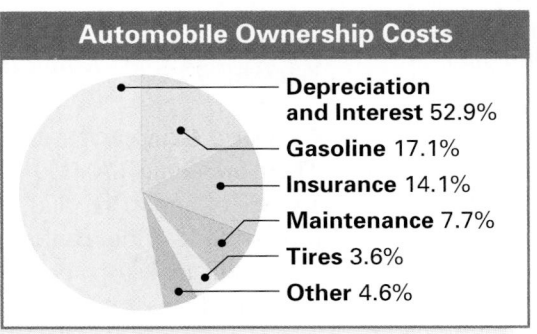

Automobile Ownership Costs

Depreciation and Interest 52.9%
Gasoline 17.1%
Insurance 14.1%
Maintenance 7.7%
Tires 3.6%
Other 4.6%

▶ Source: Runzheimer International

SOLUTION Use the percent equation $a = pb$.

PROBLEM SOLVING STRATEGY

VERBAL MODEL

| Amount spent on gasoline | is | p percent | of | Total costs of owning a car |

LABELS

Amount spent on gasoline = **650** (dollars)

Percent = **p** (no units)

Total costs of owning a car = **3750** (dollars)

ALGEBRAIC MODEL

$650 = p\,(3750)$

▶ $p \approx 0.173$ or 17.3%, which is about the national average of 17.1%.

GUIDED PRACTICE

Vocabulary Check ✓

1. Write an equation that represents the statement "10% of 160 is 16." What is the base number?

Concept Check ✓

🌐 **DISCOUNTS** In Exercises 2–4, the sale price of a shirt is $17.25 after a 25% discount is taken.

2. The sale price is what percent of the regular price?

3. You can model the situation with an equation of the form a is p percent of b. Is the base b the sale price or the regular price?

4. Write and solve an equation to find the regular price of the shirt.

Skill Check ✓

In Exercises 5–8, solve the percent problem.

5. 35 is what percent of 20?

6. 12% of 5 is what number?

7. 18 is 37.5% of what number?

8. 13.2 is 120% of what number?

9. 🌐 **SALES TAX** The price of a book without tax is $5.99 and the sales tax rate is 6%. Find the amount of the tax by using an equation of the form $a = pb$ and by using a proportion. How are the two methods similar?

PRACTICE AND APPLICATIONS

STUDENT HELP

▶ **Extra Practice**
to help you master
skills is on p. 807.

UNDERSTANDING PERCENT EQUATIONS Match the percent problem with
the equation that represents it.

A. $a = (0.39)(50)$ **B.** $39 = p(50)$ **C.** $39 = 0.50b$

10. 39 is 50% of what number?

11. 39% of 50 is what number?

12. $39 is what percent of $50?

SOLVING PERCENT PROBLEMS Solve the percent problem.

13. What number is 25% of 80?   **14.** 85% of 300 is what number?

15. 18 is what percent of 60?   **16.** 52 is 12.5% of what number?

17. 14% of 220 feet is what distance?   **18.** How much money is 35% of $750?

19. 42 feet is 50% of what length?   **20.** What distance is 24% of 710 miles?

21. 16% of what number is 8?   **22.** $4 is 2.5% of what amount?

23. 33 grams is 22% of what weight?   **24.** 55 years is what percent of 20 years?

25. How much is 8.2% of 800 tons?   **26.** 9 people is what percent of 60 people?

27. 62 hours is what percent of 3 days?   **28.** 30 inches is what percent of 40 feet?

29. $240 is what percent of $50?   **30.** 2 percent of what amount is $200?

GEOMETRY CONNECTION In Exercises 31 and 32, what percent of the region is
shaded blue? What percent is shaded yellow? All figures are rectangles.

31.

32.
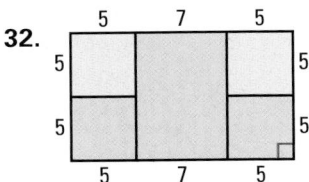

🌎 **OIL CHANGES** The histogram shows how 861 people answered a survey question about when they usually change the oil in their cars.

33. How many of the people change their oil between 3001 and 4000 miles?

34. How many of the people change their oil between 4001 and 6000 miles?

STUDENT HELP

▶ **HOMEWORK HELP**
Example 1: Exs. 10–30
Example 2: Exs. 10–30
Example 3: Exs. 10–30
Example 4: Exs. 33–39
Example 5: Exs. 42, 43

35. If you surveyed 2500 people, about how many people do you expect to answer "2001 to 3000 miles?"

▶ Source: Maritz Marketing Research Inc.

🌎 **CHOOSING A COLLEGE** In Exercises 36–39, use the graph. It shows the responses of 3500 seniors from high schools around the United States.

36. What percent of the seniors said location was the reason for their choice?

37. What percent of the seniors said academic reputation was the reason for their choice?

Reason for Choosing a College

Other 280 — Cost 945
Size 175 — Availability of Major 735
Academic Reputation 630 — Location 735

▶ Source: Careers and Colleges

38. What percent of the seniors said size or cost most influences their choice?

39. Use the survey results to predict the number of seniors in a class of 2000 students who would say that availability of major most influences their choice.

40. ERROR ANALYSIS Find and correct the mistake in the restaurant bill. The tax rate is 8%.

Food	$24.93
Beverages	$5.25
Subtotal	$30.18
Tax	$4.22
Total	$34.40

41. 🌎 **TIPPING** Use the corrected bill from Exercise 40. In the United States, the standard tip for a waiter or waitress is 15%–20%. You leave a $4.75 tip. Is your tip within the standard range if the tip is figured before tax is added? if the tip is figured on the total including tax?

🌎 **OZONE LAYER SURVEY** In Exercises 42–44, use the graph.

42. In the survey 572 people said they think the ozone layer is getting worse. What was the total number of people surveyed?

43. Use the result from Exercise 42. About how many of the people surveyed think the ozone layer is staying the same?

Do You Believe the Ozone Layer Is...

Getting worse 55%
Staying the same 38%
Improving 4%
Don't know 3%

▶ Source: Worthlin Worldwide

44. CRITICAL THINKING In this survey the researchers tried to use a representative sample of people 18 years old and over in the United States. Would this sample be reasonable to use in predicting the responses of scientists? Explain.

45. 🌎 **THE BETTER BUY** You are shopping and find a coat that is on sale for 30% off. It is regularly priced at $80. Your friend tells you that she saw the same coat for $80 in another store, but it was 20% off plus an additional 10% off. Will you save money by going to the other store? Explain why or why not.

ALTERNATIVE MODELS In Exercises 46 and 47, the charge for a cab ride is $11.50, and you give a 20% tip. Using the model, find the total cost of the cab ride. Describe what the variable a represents.

46. Model 1: a is 20% of $11.50.

47. Model 2: a is 120% of $11.50.

Test Preparation

QUANTITATIVE COMPARISON In Exercises 48–50, choose the statement below that is true about the given numbers.

   Ⓐ The number in column A is greater.

   Ⓑ The number in column B is greater.

   Ⓒ The two numbers are equal.

   Ⓓ The relationship cannot be determined from the given information.

	Column A	Column B
48.	104% of 150	100% of 150 + 4% of 150
49.	The solution of the equation 24% of $x = 450$	The solution of the equation 12% of $x = 225$
50.	The solution of the equation 16% of $x = 28$	The solution of the equation $\dfrac{16}{100} = \dfrac{x}{28}$

★ Challenge

51. CRITICAL THINKING You earn 10% more money at your summer job than your sister earns at her summer job. Does this mean that your sister earns 10% less money than you? Explain your answer.

52. CRITICAL THINKING A student claims that if a price is now 220% more than it was before, then it is 320% of what it was before, and what it was before is 31.25% of what it is now. Do you agree? Explain your answer.

EXTRA CHALLENGE

www.mcdougallittell.com

MIXED REVIEW

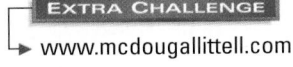

FINDING EQUATIONS The variables x and y vary directly. Use the given values of the variables to write an equation that relates x and y. **(Review 4.5 for 11.3)**

53. $x = 4, y = 8$ **54.** $x = 33, y = 9$ **55.** $x = -2, y = -1$

56. $x = 6.3, y = 1.5$ **57.** $x = 5\frac{1}{3}, y = 8$ **58.** $x = 9.8, y = 3.6$

CHECKING SOLUTIONS Decide whether the ordered pair is a solution of the inequality. **(Review 9.7)**

59. $y < x^2 + 6x + 12; (-1, 4)$ **60.** $y \le x^2 - 7x + 9; (-1, 2)$

61. $y > 2x^2 - 7x - 15; (2, 5)$ **62.** $y \ge x^2 + 6x + 12; (1, -4)$

FACTORING EXPRESSIONS Completely factor the expression. **(Review 10.8)**

63. $x^2 + 5x - 14$ **64.** $7x^2 + 8x + 1$ **65.** $5x^2 - 51x + 54$

66. $4x^2 - 28x + 49$ **67.** $6x^2 + 16x$ **68.** $36x^5 - 90x^3$

69. $3x^3 + 21x^2 + 30x$ **70.** $36x^3 - 9x$ **71.** $15x^4 - 50x^3 - 40x^2$

72. 🌏 **TEXAS POPULATION** The population P of Texas (in thousands) for 1995 projected through 2025 can be modeled by $P = 18{,}870(1.0124)^t$, where $t = 0$ represents 1995. Find the ratio of the population in 2025 to the population in 2000. **(Review 8.3)** ▶ Source: U.S. Bureau of the Census

11.3

Direct and Inverse Variation

GOAL 1
USING DIRECT AND INVERSE VARIATION

What you should learn

GOAL 1 Use direct and inverse variation.

GOAL 2 Use direct and inverse variation to model **real-life** situations, such as the snowshoe problem in **Exs. 43 and 44**.

Why you should learn it

▼To solve **real-life** situations such as relating the banking angle of a bicycle to its turning radius in **Example 3**.

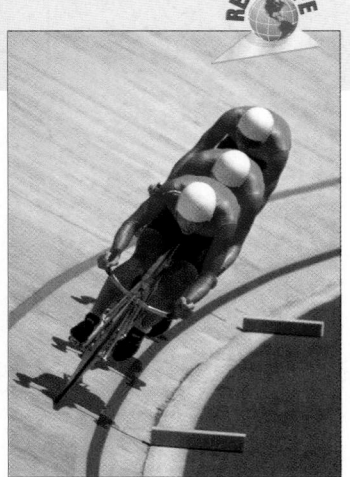

In Lesson 4.5 you studied *direct variation*. Now you will review variation problems and learn about a different type of variation, called **inverse variation**.

MODELS FOR DIRECT AND INVERSE VARIATION

DIRECT VARIATION   The variables x and y *vary directly* if for a constant k

$$\frac{y}{x} = k, \text{ or } y = kx, k \neq 0.$$

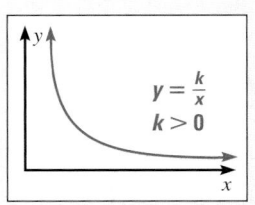

$y = kx$
$k > 0$

INVERSE VARIATION   The variables x and y *vary inversely* if for a constant k

$$xy = k, \text{ or } y = \frac{k}{x}, k \neq 0.$$

$y = \frac{k}{x}$
$k > 0$

The number k is the **constant of variation**.

EXAMPLE 1   *Using Direct and Inverse Variation*

When x is 2, y is 4. Find an equation that relates x and y in each case.

a. x and y vary directly   **b.** x and y vary inversely

SOLUTION

a. $\dfrac{y}{x} = k$ **Write direct variation model.**

$\dfrac{4}{2} = k$ **Substitute 2 for x and 4 for y.**

$2 = k$ **Simplify.**

▶ The direct variation that relates x and y is $\dfrac{y}{x} = 2$, or $y = 2x$.

b. $xy = k$ **Write inverse variation model.**

$(2)(4) = k$ **Substitute 2 for x and 4 for y.**

$8 = k$ **Simplify.**

▶ The inverse variation that relates x and y is $xy = 8$, or $y = \dfrac{8}{x}$.

EXAMPLE 2 *Comparing Direct and Inverse Variation*

Compare the direct variation model and the inverse variation model you found in Example 1 using $x = 1, 2, 3,$ and 4.

a. numerically   **b.** graphically

SOLUTION

a. Use the models $y = 2x$ and $y = \dfrac{8}{x}$ to make a table.

Direct Variation: Because k is positive, y increases as x increases. As x increases by 1, y increases by 2.

Inverse Variation: Because k is positive, y decreases as x increases. As x doubles (from 1 to 2), y is halved (from 8 to 4).

x-value	1	2	3	4
Direct, $y = 2x$	2	4	6	8
Inverse, $y = \dfrac{8}{x}$	8	4	$\dfrac{8}{3}$	2

b. Use the table of values. Plot the points and then connect the points with a smooth curve.

Direct Variation: The graph for this model is a line passing through the origin.

Inverse Variation: The graph for this model is a curve that approaches the x-axis as x increases and approaches the y-axis as x gets close to 0.

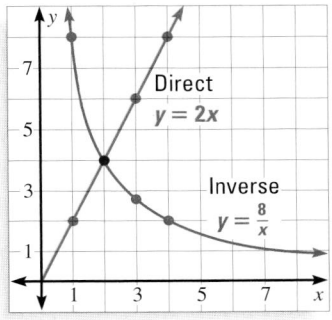

· · · · · · · · · ·

Direct and inverse variation models represent functions because for each value of x there is exactly one value of y. For inverse variation, the domain excludes 0.

▶ **ACTIVITY**

Developing Concepts

Investigating Direct and Inverse Variation

Make a table and draw a graph for each situation. Then decide whether the quantities vary *directly*, *inversely*, or *neither*.

❶ You are walking at a rate of 5 miles per hour. How are your distance d and time t related?

❷ You take a 5-mile walk. How are your rate r and time t related?

❸ A ball is dropped from a height of 32 feet. How are the height h and time t related?

❹ A rectangle has an area of 12 square inches. How are the length l and width w related?

EXAMPLE 3 *Writing and Using a Model*

BICYCLING The graph below shows a model for the relationship between the banking angle and the turning radius for a bicycle traveling at a particular speed. For the values shown, the banking angle B and the turning radius r can be approximated by an inverse variation.

bicycle's path

turning radius

a. Find an inverse variation model that approximately relates B and r.

b. Use the model to approximate the angle for a radius of 5 feet.

c. Use the graph to describe how the banking angle changes as the turning radius gets smaller.

SOLUTION

a. From the graph, you can see that $B = 32°$ when $r = 3.5$ feet.

$$B = \frac{k}{r}$$ **Write inverse variation model.**

$$32 = \frac{k}{3.5}$$ **Substitute 32 for *B* and 3.5 for *r*.**

$$112 = k$$ **Solve for *k*.**

▶ The model is $B = \dfrac{112}{r}$, where B is in degrees and r is in feet.

b. Substitute 5 for r in the model found in part (a).

$$B = \frac{112}{5} = 22.4$$

▶ When the turning radius is 5 feet, the banking angle is about 22°.

c. As the turning radius gets smaller, the banking angle becomes greater. The bicyclist leans at greater angles. Notice that the increase in the banking angle becomes more rapid when the turning radius is small. For instance, the increase in the banking angle is about 10° for a 1-foot decrease from 4 feet to 3 feet. The increase in the banking angle is only about 4° for a 1-foot decrease from 6 feet to 5 feet.

BICYCLE BANKING A bicyclist tips the bicycle when making a turn. The angle B of the bicycle from the vertical direction is called the *banking angle*.

GUIDED PRACTICE

Vocabulary Check ✔

1. What does it mean for two quantities to vary directly? to vary inversely?

Concept Check ✔

Does the graph show *direct variation*, *inverse variation*, or *neither*? Explain.

2.

3.

4.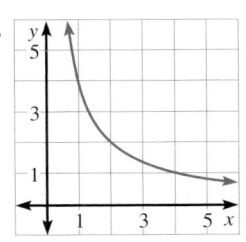

5. One student says that the equation $y = -2x$ is an example of direct variation. Another student says it is inverse variation. Which is correct? Explain.

Skill Check ✔

Does the equation model *direct variation*, *inverse variation*, or *neither*?

6. $x = \dfrac{4}{y}$ 7. $y = 7x - 2$ 8. $a = 12b$ 9. $ab = 9$

When $x = 4$, $y = 6$. For the given type of variation, find an equation that relates x and y. Then find the value of y when $x = 8$.

10. x and y vary directly   11. x and y vary inversely

PRACTICE AND APPLICATIONS

STUDENT HELP

▶ **Extra Practice**
to help you master
skills is on p. 807.

DIRECT VARIATION EQUATIONS The variables x and y vary directly. Use the given values to write an equation that relates x and y.

12. $x = 3, y = 9$ 13. $x = 2, y = 8$ 14. $x = 18, y = 6$

15. $x = 8, y = 24$ 16. $x = 36, y = 12$ 17. $x = 27, y = 3$

18. $x = 24, y = 16$ 19. $x = 45, y = 81$ 20. $x = 54, y = 27$

INVERSE VARIATION EQUATIONS The variables x and y vary inversely. Use the given values to write an equation that relates x and y.

21. $x = 2, y = 5$ 22. $x = 3, y = 7$ 23. $x = 16, y = 1$

24. $x = 11, y = 2$ 25. $x = \dfrac{1}{2}, y = 8$ 26. $x = \dfrac{13}{5}, y = 5$

27. $x = 12, y = \dfrac{3}{4}$ 28. $x = 5, y = \dfrac{1}{3}$ 29. $x = 30, y = 7.5$

30. $x = 1.5, y = 50$ 31. $x = 45, y = \dfrac{3}{5}$ 32. $x = 10.5, y = 7$

STUDENT HELP

▶ **HOMEWORK HELP**
Example 1: Exs. 12–32
Example 2: Exs. 33–38
Example 3: Exs. 43–46

DIRECT OR INVERSE VARIATION Make a table of values for $x = 1, 2, 3$, and 4. Use the table to sketch a graph. Decide whether x and y vary *directly* or *inversely*.

33. $y = \dfrac{4}{x}$ 34. $y = \dfrac{3}{2x}$ 35. $y = 3x$ 36. $y = \dfrac{6}{x}$

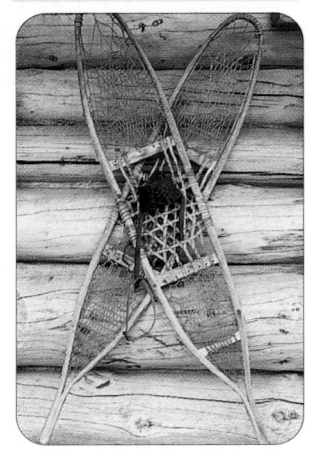
VARIATION MODELS FROM DATA Decide if the data in the table show *direct* or *inverse* variation. Write an equation that relates the variables.

37.

x	1	3	5	10	0.5
y	5	15	25	50	2.5

38.

x	1	3	4	10	0.5
y	30	10	7.5	3	60

🌐 **VARIATION MODELS IN CONTEXT** State whether the variables have *direct variation*, *inverse variation*, or *neither*.

39. BASE AND HEIGHT The area B of the base and the height h of a prism with a volume of 10 cubic units are related by the equation $Bh = 10$.

40. MASS AND VOLUME The mass m and the volume V of a substance are related by the equation $2V = m$, where 2 is the density of the substance.

41. DINNER AND BREAKFAST Alicia cut a pizza into 8 pieces. The number of pieces d that Alicia ate for dinner and the number of pieces b that she can eat for breakfast are related by the equation $b = 8 - d$.

42. HOURS AND PAY RATE The number of hours h that you must work to earn $480 and your hourly rate of pay p are related by the equation $ph = 480$.

🌐 **SNOWSHOES** In Exercises 43 and 44, use the following information.
When a person walks, the pressure P on each boot sole varies inversely with the area A of the sole. Denise is walking through deep snow, wearing boots that have a sole area of 29 square inches each. The boot-sole pressure is 4 pounds per square inch when she stands on one foot.

43. The constant of variation is Denise's weight in pounds. What is her weight?

44. If Denise wears snowshoes, each with an area 11 times that of her boot soles, what is the snowshoe pressure when she stands on one foot?

🌐 **OCEAN TEMPERATURES** The graph for Exercises 45 and 46 shows water temperatures for part of the Pacific Ocean. Assume temperature varies inversely with depth at depths greater than 900 meters.

45. Find a model that relates the temperature T and the depth d. Round k to the nearest hundred.

46. Find the temperature at a depth of 5000 meters. Round to the nearest tenth of a degree.

Pacific Ocean Temperatures

(3700, 1.2)

Temperature (°C)

Depth (meters)

🌐 **FUEL MILEAGE** In Exercises 47–49, you are taking a trip on the highway in a car that gets a gas mileage of about 26 miles per gallon for highway driving. You start with a full tank of 12 gallons of gasoline.

47. Find your rate of gas consumption (the gallons of gas used to drive 1 mile).

48. Use Exercise 47 to write an equation relating the number of gallons of gas in your tank g and the number of miles m that you have driven on your trip.

49. Do the variables g and m vary *directly*, *inversely*, or *neither*? Explain.

50. MULTI-STEP PROBLEM Use x to represent one dimension of a rectangle, and use y to represent the other dimension.

    a. Make a table of possible values of x and y if the area of the rectangle is 12 square inches. Then use your table to sketch a graph.

    b. Do x and y vary *directly*, *inversely*, or *neither*? Explain your reasoning.

    c. Make a table of possible values of x and y if the area of the rectangle is 24 square inches. Then use your table to sketch a graph in the same coordinate plane you used for your graph in part (a).

    d. CRITICAL THINKING How is the area of the first rectangle related to the area of the second rectangle? For a given value of x, how is the value of y for the first rectangle related to the value of y for the second rectangle? For a given value of y, how are the values of x related?

★ **Challenge**

CONSTANT RATIOS In Exercises 51 and 52, use the following information.

In a direct variation, the ratio $\frac{y}{x}$ is constant. If (x_1, y_1) and (x_2, y_2) are solutions of the equation $\frac{y}{x} = k$, then $\frac{y_1}{x_1} = k$ and $\frac{y_2}{x_2} = k$. Use the proportion $\frac{y_1}{x_1} = \frac{y_2}{x_2}$ to find the missing value.

51. Find x_2 when $x_1 = 2$, $y_1 = 3$, and $y_2 = 6$.

52. Find y_2 when $x_1 = -4$, $y_1 = 8$, and $x_2 = -1$.

CONSTANT PRODUCTS In an inverse variation, the product xy is constant. If (x_1, y_1) and (x_2, y_2) are solutions of $xy = k$, then $x_1 y_1 = x_2 y_2$. Use this equation to find the missing value.

EXTRA CHALLENGE
www.mcdougallittell.com

53. Find y_2 when $x_1 = 4$, $y_1 = 5$, and $x_2 = 8$.

54. Find x_2 when $x_1 = 9$, $y_1 = -3$, and $y_2 = 12$.

MIXED REVIEW

SIMPLIFYING FRACTIONS Simplify the fraction. (Skills Review, p. 781–783)

55. $\frac{36}{48}$ **56.** $\frac{27}{108}$ **57.** $\frac{96}{180}$ **58.** $\frac{-15}{125}$

PROBABILITY Find the probability. (Review 2.8 for 11.4)

59. You roll a die. What is the probability that you will roll a four?

60. You roll a die. What is the probability that you will roll an odd number?

SIMPLIFYING FRACTIONS Simplify the fraction. (Review 8.3 for 11.4)

61. $\frac{y^4 \cdot y^7}{y^5}$ **62.** $\frac{5xy}{5x^2}$ **63.** $\frac{-3xy^3}{3x^3y}$ **64.** $\frac{56x^2y^5}{64x^2y}$

CLASSIFYING POLYNOMIALS Identify the leading coefficient, and classify the polynomial by degree and by number of terms. (Review 10.1)

65. $-5x - 4$ **66.** $8x^4 + 625$ **67.** $x - x^3$ **68.** $16 - 4x + 3x^2$

Solve the proportion. (Lesson 11.1)

1. $\dfrac{x}{10} = \dfrac{4}{5}$ **2.** $\dfrac{3}{x} = \dfrac{7}{9}$ **3.** $\dfrac{x}{4x-8} = \dfrac{2}{x}$ **4.** $\dfrac{6x+4}{5} = \dfrac{2}{x}$

The variables x and y vary inversely. Use the given values to write an equation that relates x and y. (Lesson 11.3)

5. $x = 3,\ y = 4$ **6.** $x = 12,\ y = 1$ **7.** $x = 24,\ y = \dfrac{3}{4}$

 CAR WASH In Exercises 8 and 9, use the survey results. (Lesson 11.2)

8. In the survey, 413 people said they hand-wash their cars at home. How many people were surveyed? Round to the nearest whole number.

9. Use the result of Exercise 8 to find the number of people in the survey who wash their cars at an automatic car wash.

Method	Percent of people
Hand-wash at home	45.7
Automatic car wash	22.6
Manually wash it myself at a car wash	16.3
Others manually wash it at a car wash	14.8
Other	0.7

▶ Source: Maritz Marketing Research

MATH & History

History of Polling

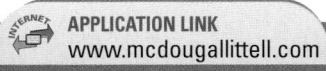 **APPLICATION LINK**
www.mcdougallittell.com

THEN **IN THE 1930S,** opinion polls were conducted by interviewers knocking on people's doors. Later telephone polling became popular and a sampling method using random digit-dialing was developed.

NOW **DURING THE 1990S,** television stations used computers to evaluate exit poll data and present real-time election results.

After the polls closed in one of the 1998 governor's races, exit poll data reported that the top three candidates had 37%, 34%, and 28% of the vote.

1. A total of 2,075,280 votes had been counted so far. If the exit polls accurately described the vote count, about how many votes did each candidate have?

2. Use your results from Exercise 1. The final vote count included 16,486 more votes. If these votes were all for one candidate instead of being distributed as exit polls predicted, would the outcome of the election have been changed?

1948
Opinion polls incorrectly predict Dewey's win.

1970s on
Telephone polling becomes common

Now
Internet sites enable voters to learn early results

▶ ACTIVITY 11.3

Using Technology

Modeling Inverse Variation

You can use a graphing calculator or a computer to decide whether quantities vary directly, inversely, or neither.

▶ EXAMPLE

x	y
20	1.06771
19	1.11276
18	1.17583
17	1.24341
16	1.32450
15	1.40559
14	1.51371
13	1.62183
12	1.74347
11	1.90566

During a chemistry experiment, the volume of a fixed mass of air was decreased and the pressure at different volumes was recorded. The data are at the left, where x is the volume (in cubic centimeters) and y is the pressure (in atmospheres). Use a graphing calculator to determine if the data vary directly, inversely, or neither. Then make a scatter plot to check your model.

▶ SOLUTION

1 Let L_1 represent the volume x and L_2 represent the pressure y. Enter the ordered pairs into the graphing calculator. Then create lists L_3 and L_4 as shown to find whether the data vary directly or inversely.

2 Notice that the values in L_3 are all different while the values in L_4 are all about 21.1. This means that x and y vary inversely.

3 To find the constant of variation k, find the mean of the values in L_4. Use this value to write an inverse variation model in the form $y = \dfrac{k}{x}$.

4 Set the viewing rectangle so that $11 \le x \le 20$ and $1 \le y \le 2$. Make a scatter plot of L_1 and L_2. Then graph $y = \dfrac{21.12}{x}$ on the same screen.

```
mean(L4)
           21.123503
```

▶ EXERCISES

Use a graphing calculator to decide if the data vary directly or inversely and to find the constant of variation. Then write a model for the data.

1. (10, 8.25), (9, 7.425), (8, 6.6), (7, 5.775), (6, 4.95), (5, 4.125), (4, 3.3)
2. (18, 1.389), (17, 1.471), (16, 1.563), (15, 1.667), (14, 1.786), (13, 1.923)

11.4
Simplifying Rational Expressions

What you should learn

GOAL 1 Simplify a rational expression.

GOAL 2 Use rational expressions to find geometric probability.

Why you should learn it

▼ To model **real-life** situations, such as finding the probability of a meteor strike in **Exs. 36–38**.

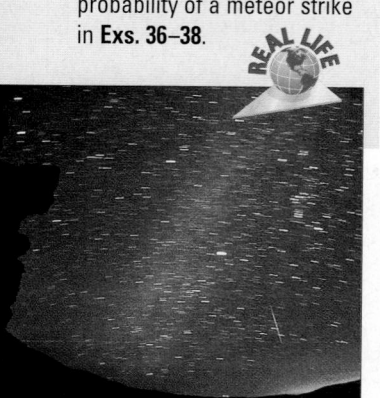

GOAL 1 SIMPLIFYING A RATIONAL EXPRESSION

A **rational number** is a number that can be written as the quotient of two integers, such as $\frac{1}{2}$, $\frac{4}{3}$, and $\frac{7}{1}$. A fraction whose numerator, denominator, or both numerator and denominator are nonzero polynomials is a **rational expression**. Here are some examples.

$$\frac{3}{x+4} \qquad\qquad \frac{2x}{x^2-9} \qquad\qquad \frac{3x+1}{x^2+1}$$

A rational expression is *undefined* when the denominator is equal to zero. For instance, in the first expression x can be any real number except -4.

To simplify a fraction, you factor the numerator and the denominator and then divide out any common factors. A rational expression is **simplified** if its numerator and denominator have no factors in common (other than ± 1).

SIMPLIFYING FRACTIONS

Let *a, b,* and *c* be nonzero numbers.

$$\frac{ac}{bc} = \frac{a \cdot \cancel{c}}{b \cdot \cancel{c}} = \frac{a}{b}$$

Example: $\dfrac{28}{35} = \dfrac{4 \cdot \cancel{7}}{5 \cdot \cancel{7}} = \dfrac{4}{5}$

EXAMPLE 1 *When and When Not to Divide Out*

Simplify the expression.

a. $\dfrac{2x}{2(x+5)}$ 　　 **b.** $\dfrac{x(x^2+6)}{x^2}$ 　　 **c.** $\dfrac{x+4}{x}$

SOLUTION

a. $\dfrac{2x}{2(x+5)} = \dfrac{\cancel{2} \cdot x}{\cancel{2}(x+5)}$ 　　 You can divide out the common factor 2.

$= \dfrac{x}{x+5}$ 　　 Simplified form

b. $\dfrac{x(x^2+6)}{x^2} = \dfrac{\cancel{x}(x^2+6)}{\cancel{x} \cdot x}$ 　　 You can divide out the common factor x.

$= \dfrac{x^2+6}{x}$ 　　 Simplified form

c. $\dfrac{x+4}{x}$ 　　 You cannot divide out the common term x.

STUDENT HELP

▶ **Study Tip**
When you simplify rational expressions, you can divide out only factors, not terms.

STUDENT HELP

INTERNET

HOMEWORK HELP
Visit our Web site
www.mcdougallittell.com
for extra examples.

EXAMPLE 2 *Factoring Numerator and Denominator*

Simplify $\dfrac{2x^2 - 6x}{6x^2}$.

SOLUTION

$$\dfrac{2x^2 - 6x}{6x^2} = \dfrac{2x(x - 3)}{2 \cdot 3 \cdot x \cdot x}$$ Factor numerator and denominator.

$$= \dfrac{2x(x - 3)}{2x(3x)}$$ Divide out common factor 2x.

$$= \dfrac{x - 3}{3x}$$ Simplified form

EXAMPLE 3 *Recognizing Opposite Factors*

Simplify $\dfrac{4 - x^2}{x^2 - x - 2}$.

SOLUTION

$$\dfrac{4 - x^2}{x^2 - x - 2} = \dfrac{(2 - x)(2 + x)}{(x - 2)(x + 1)}$$ Factor numerator and denominator.

$$= \dfrac{-(x - 2)(2 + x)}{(x - 2)(x + 1)}$$ Factor −1 from (2 − x).

$$= \dfrac{-(x - 2)(x + 2)}{(x - 2)(x + 1)}$$ Divide out common factor x − 2.

$$= -\dfrac{x + 2}{x + 1}$$ Simplified form

EXAMPLE 4 *Recognizing when an Expression is Undefined*

In Examples 2 and 3, are the original expression and the simplified expression defined for the same values of the variable?

STUDENT HELP

Look Back
For help with using the zero-product property, see p. 597.

SOLUTION A rational expression is undefined when the denominator is 0. Think of setting the denominator equal to 0 and then solving that equation.

Example 2: Yes, $6x^2 = 0$ and $3x = 0$ have the same solution: $x = 0$. Both expressions are undefined when $x = 0$.

Example 3: No, $x^2 - x - 2 = 0$ and $x + 1 = 0$ do not have the same solutions. To see this set the denominator of the original expression equal to zero.

$$x^2 - x - 2 = 0$$ Set denominator equal to 0.

$$(x - 2)(x + 1) = 0$$ Factor denominator.

$$x - 2 = 0 \quad \text{or} \quad x + 1 = 0$$ Use zero-product property.

$$x = 2 \qquad\qquad x = -1$$ Solve for x.

▶ The original expression is undefined when $x = 2$ and $x = -1$. The simplified expression is undefined only when $x = -1$.

GOAL 2 APPLYING RATIONAL EXPRESSIONS

Rational expressions can be useful in modeling situations such as finding averages, ratios, and probabilities. In Chapter 2 you learned to find theoretical probability by comparing the number of favorable outcomes to the total number of outcomes. In some cases, you can give theoretical probabilities a geometric interpretation in terms of areas.

GEOMETRIC PROBABILITY

Region *B* is contained in Region *A*. An object is tossed onto Region *A* and is equally likely to land on any point in the region.

The **geometric probability** that it lands in Region *B* is

$$P = \frac{\text{Area of Region } B}{\text{Area of Region } A}.$$

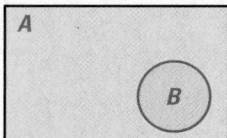

EXAMPLE 5 *Writing and Using a Rational Model*

A coin is tossed onto the large rectangular region shown at the right. It is equally likely to land on any point in the region.

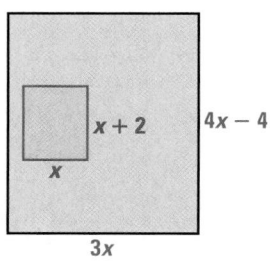

a. Write a model that gives the probability that the coin will land in the small rectangle.

b. Evaluate the model when $x = 10$.

SOLUTION

a. $P = \dfrac{\text{Area of small rectangle}}{\text{Area of large rectangle}}$ **Formula for geometric probability**

$ = \dfrac{x(x + 2)}{3x(4x - 4)}$ **Find areas.**

$ = \dfrac{x \cdot (x + 2)}{3x \cdot 4(x - 1)}$ **Divide out common factors.**

$ = \dfrac{x + 2}{12(x - 1)}$ **Simplified form**

b. To find the probability when $x = 10$, substitute 10 for x in the model.

$$P = \frac{x + 2}{12(x - 1)} = \frac{10 + 2}{12(10 - 1)} = \frac{12}{108} = \frac{1}{9}$$

▶ The probability of landing in the small rectangle is $\dfrac{1}{9}$.

GUIDED PRACTICE

Vocabulary Check ✓   **1.** Define a rational expression. Then give an example of a rational expression.

Concept Check ✓   **ERROR ANALYSIS** Describe the error.

2.
$$\frac{3+x}{5+2x} = \frac{3+\cancel{x}}{5+2x}$$
$$= \frac{4}{7}$$

3.
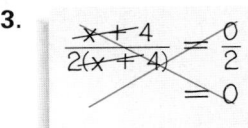

Skill Check ✓   **For what values of the variable is the rational expression undefined?**

4. $\dfrac{6}{8x}$

5. $\dfrac{x-1}{x-5}$

6. $\dfrac{2}{x^2 - x - 2}$

7. Which of the following is the simplified form of $\dfrac{6+2x}{x^2+5x+6}$?

   A. $\dfrac{2x}{x^2+5x}$ **B.** $\dfrac{2}{x+5}$ **C.** $\dfrac{2}{x+2}$

8. Which ratio represents the ratio of the area of the smaller rectangle to the area of the larger rectangle?

   A. $\dfrac{1}{2x}$ **B.** $\dfrac{1}{4x}$

PRACTICE AND APPLICATIONS

STUDENT HELP

▶ **Extra Practice**
to help you master
skills is on p. 807.

SIMPLIFYING EXPRESSIONS Simplify the expression if possible.

9. $\dfrac{4x}{20}$

10. $\dfrac{15x}{45}$

11. $\dfrac{-18x^2}{12x}$

12. $\dfrac{14x^2}{50x^4}$

13. $\dfrac{3x^2 - 18x}{-9x^2}$

14. $\dfrac{42x - 6x^3}{36x}$

15. $\dfrac{7x}{12x + x^2}$

16. $\dfrac{x + 2x^2}{x + 2}$

17. $\dfrac{12 - 5x}{10x^2 - 24x}$

18. $\dfrac{x^2 + 25}{2x + 10}$

19. $\dfrac{5 - x}{x^2 - 8x + 15}$

20. $\dfrac{2x^2 + 11x - 6}{x + 6}$

21. $\dfrac{x^2 + x - 20}{x^2 + 2x - 15}$

22. $\dfrac{x^3 + 9x^2 + 14x}{x^2 - 4}$

23. $\dfrac{x^3 - x}{x^3 + 5x^2 - 6x}$

UNDEFINED VALUES For what values of the variable is the rational expression undefined?

STUDENT HELP

▶ **HOMEWORK HELP**
Example 1: Exs. 9–23
Example 2: Exs. 9–23
Example 3: Exs. 9–23
Example 4: Exs. 24–29
Example 5: Exs. 30–33

24. $\dfrac{7}{x - 3}$

25. $\dfrac{11}{x - 8}$

26. $\dfrac{4}{x^2 - 1}$

27. $\dfrac{x + 3}{x^2 - 9}$

28. $\dfrac{x + 9}{x^2 + x - 12}$

29. $\dfrac{x - 3}{x^2 + 5x - 6}$

GEOMETRIC PROBABILITY A coin is tossed onto the large rectangular region shown. It is equally likely to land on any point in the region. Write a model that gives the probability that the coin will land in the red region. Then evaluate the model when $x = 3$.

30.

31.

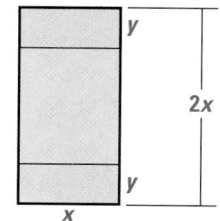

CARNIVAL GAMES In Exercises 32–34, use the following information. You are designing a game for a school carnival. Players will drop a coin into a basin of water, trying to hit a target on the bottom. The water is kept moving randomly, so the coin is equally likely to land anywhere. You use a rectangular basin twice as long as it is wide. You place the blue rectangular target an equal distance from each end.

32. Express the two dimensions of the target in terms of the variables x and y.

33. Write a model that gives the probability that the coin will land on the target.

34. **CRITICAL THINKING** You want players to win about half the time. Give a set of values you could use for x and y if the basin's area is between 72 and 120 square inches.

35. *Writing* Create three problems of the form $\dfrac{ax^2 + bx + c}{dx^2 + ex + f}$ in which the numerator and the denominator have a common factor. Describe the process you used to create your problems.

METEOR STRIKES In Exercises 36–38, use this information. A meteorite is equally likely to hit anywhere on Earth. The probability that a meteorite lands in the

Torrid Zone is $\dfrac{\text{Area of Torrid Zone}}{\text{Total surface area of Earth}}$.

Let R represent Earth's radius.

36. Write an expression to estimate the area of the Torrid Zone. You can think of the distance between the tropics (about 3250 miles) as the height of a cylindrical belt around Earth at the equator. The length of the belt is Earth's circumference $2\pi R$.

37. The surface area of a sphere with radius R is $4\pi R^2$. Write and simplify an expression for the probability that a meteorite lands in the Torrid Zone.

38. Find the probability in Exercise 37. Use 3963 miles for Earth's radius.

39. MULTI-STEP PROBLEM In this exercise you will look for a pattern.

a. Copy and complete the table by evaluating the expression for each x-value.

x-values	−2	−1	0	1	2	3	4
$\dfrac{x^2 - x - 6}{x - 3}$	?	?	?	?	?	?	?
$x + 2$	?	?	?	?	?	?	?

b. Describe the relationship between $\dfrac{x^2 - x - 6}{x - 3}$ and $x + 2$. What does the table tell you about this relationship?

c. CRITICAL THINKING Write another pair of expressions that have this relationship. Describe the procedure you used to find your example.

★ **Challenge**

40. RATIOS Write the ratio in simplest form comparing the area of the smaller rectangle to the area of the larger rectangle.

41. PROPORTIONS Solve the proportion.

$$\frac{x^2 + 5x + 6}{x^2 - 2x - 8} = \frac{x^2 - 4x - 5}{x^2 - 8x + 15}$$

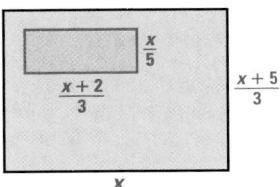

Ex. 40

MIXED REVIEW

PRODUCTS AND QUOTIENTS **Simplify.** (Review 2.5 and 2.7 for 11.5)

42. $\left(-\dfrac{1}{2}\right)\left(\dfrac{2}{3}\right)$ **43.** $(-15)\left(-\dfrac{5}{6}\right)$ **44.** $\dfrac{2}{7} \div \dfrac{14}{24}$ **45.** $\dfrac{4}{9} \div (-36)$

46. $\left(-\dfrac{3}{4}\right)\left(\dfrac{3y}{-5}\right)$ **47.** $\dfrac{2m}{3} \cdot 6m^2$ **48.** $\dfrac{36}{45a} \div \dfrac{-9a}{5}$ **49.** $-18c^3 \div \dfrac{-27c}{-4}$

50. GEOMETRY The area of the triangle is 192 square meters. What is the value of x? What is the perimeter? (Review 9.1)

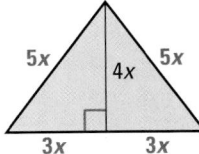

SKETCHING GRAPHS **Sketch the graph of the function.** (Review 9.3)

51. $y = x^2$ **52.** $y = 4 - x^2$ **53.** $y = \dfrac{1}{2}x^2$

54. $y = 5x^2 + 4x - 5$ **55.** $y = 4x^2 - x + 6$ **56.** $y = -3x^2 - x + 7$

57. 🌐 **POPULATION DENSITY** Population density is the number of people per square mile. Suppose the population density of a city decreases by 8% for every mile you travel from the center of the city. In the center of the city, the population density is 2500 people per square mile. Find an exponential decay model for the population density. Copy and complete the table. (Review 8.6)

Distance from center of city (miles)	2	3	4	5	6
Population density (people per square mile)	?	?	?	?	?

11.5 Multiplying and Dividing Rational Expressions

What you should learn

GOAL 1 Multiply and divide rational expressions.

GOAL 2 Use rational expressions as **real-life** models, as when comparing parts of the service industry to the total in **Exs. 38–41**.

Why you should learn it

▼ To model **real-life** situations, such as describing the average car sales per dealership in **Example 6**.

GOAL 1 FINDING PRODUCTS AND QUOTIENTS

Because the variables in a rational expression represent real numbers, the rules for multiplying and dividing rational expressions are the same as the rules for multiplying and dividing numerical fractions.

MULTIPLYING AND DIVIDING RATIONAL EXPRESSIONS

Let *a, b, c,* and *d* be nonzero polynomials.

TO MULTIPLY, multiply numerators and denominators. $\dfrac{a}{b} \cdot \dfrac{c}{d} = \dfrac{ac}{bd}$

TO DIVIDE, multiply by the reciprocal of the divisor. $\dfrac{a}{b} \div \dfrac{c}{d} = \dfrac{a}{b} \cdot \dfrac{d}{c}$

EXAMPLE 1 Multiplying Rational Expressions Involving Monomials

Simplify $\dfrac{3x^3}{4x} \cdot \dfrac{8x^2}{15x^4}$.

SOLUTION

$$\frac{3x^3}{4x} \cdot \frac{8x^2}{15x^4} = \frac{24x^5}{60x^5}$$ Multiply numerators and denominators.

$$= \frac{2 \cdot \cancel{12} \cdot \cancel{x^5}}{5 \cdot \cancel{12} \cdot \cancel{x^5}}$$ Factor, and divide out common factors.

$$= \frac{2}{5}$$ Simplified form

┌─ STUDENT HELP

▶ **Study Tip**
When multiplying, you usually factor as far as possible to identify all common factors. Note, however, that you do not need to write the prime factorizations of 24 and 60 in Example 1, if you recognize 12 as their greatest common factor.

EXAMPLE 2 Multiplying Rational Expressions Involving Polynomials

Simplify $\dfrac{x}{3x^2 - 9x} \cdot \dfrac{x - 3}{2x^2 + x - 3}$.

SOLUTION

$$\frac{x}{3x^2 - 9x} \cdot \frac{x - 3}{2x^2 + x - 3} = \frac{x(x - 3)}{(3x^2 - 9x)(2x^2 + x - 3)}$$ Multiply numerators and denominators.

$$= \frac{\cancel{x}\cancel{(x - 3)}}{3\cancel{x}\cancel{(x - 3)}(x - 1)(2x + 3)}$$ Factor, and divide out common factors.

$$= \frac{1}{3(x - 1)(2x + 3)}$$ Simplified form

EXAMPLE 3 *Multiplying by a Polynomial*

Simplify $\dfrac{7x}{x^2 + 5x + 4} \cdot (x + 4)$.

SOLUTION

$$\dfrac{7x}{x^2 + 5x + 4} \cdot (x + 4) = \dfrac{7x}{x^2 + 5x + 4} \cdot \dfrac{x + 4}{1}$$ Write $x + 4$ as $\dfrac{x + 4}{1}$.

$$= \dfrac{7x(x + 4)}{x^2 + 5x + 4}$$ Multiply numerators and denominators.

$$= \dfrac{7x(x + 4)}{(x + 1)(x + 4)}$$ Factor, and divide out common factors.

$$= \dfrac{7x}{x + 1}$$ Simplified form

EXAMPLE 4 *Dividing Rational Expressions*

Simplify $\dfrac{4n}{n + 5} \div \dfrac{n - 9}{n + 5}$.

SOLUTION

$$\dfrac{4n}{n + 5} \div \dfrac{n - 9}{n + 5} = \dfrac{4n}{n + 5} \cdot \dfrac{n + 5}{n - 9}$$ Multiply by reciprocal.

$$= \dfrac{4n(n + 5)}{(n + 5)(n - 9)}$$ Multiply numerators and denominators.

$$= \dfrac{4n(n + 5)}{(n + 5)(n - 9)}$$ Divide out common factors.

$$= \dfrac{4n}{n - 9}$$ Simplified form

EXAMPLE 5 *Dividing by a Polynomial*

Simplify $\dfrac{x^2 - 9}{4x^2} \div (x - 3)$.

SOLUTION

$$\dfrac{x^2 - 9}{4x^2} \div (x - 3) = \dfrac{x^2 - 9}{4x^2} \cdot \dfrac{1}{x - 3}$$ Multiply by reciprocal.

$$= \dfrac{x^2 - 9}{4x^2(x - 3)}$$ Multiply numerators and denominators.

$$= \dfrac{(x + 3)(x - 3)}{4x^2(x - 3)}$$ Factor, and divide out common factors.

$$= \dfrac{x + 3}{4x^2}$$ Simplified form

GOAL 2 **USING RATIONAL MODELS IN REAL LIFE**
....

Car Sales

EXAMPLE 6 *Writing and Using a Rational Model*
_____

The models below can be created using data collected by the National Automobile Dealers Association in the United States. Five-year intervals from 1975–1995 were used. Let *t* represent the number of years since 1975.

Number of new-car dealerships: $D = \dfrac{30{,}000 + 300t}{1 + 0.03t}$

Total sales (in billions of dollars) of new-car dealerships: $S = \dfrac{80 + 10t}{1 - 0.02t}$

a. Find a model for the average sales per new-car dealership.

b. Use the model to predict the average sales in 2005.

SOLUTION

PROBLEM SOLVING STRATEGY

a.   **VERBAL MODEL**

Average sales per dealership	=	Total sales of dealerships	÷	Number of dealerships

LABELS   Average sales per dealership $= \boxed{A}$

Total sales of dealerships $= \dfrac{\mathbf{80 + 10t}}{\mathbf{1 - 0.02t}}$

Number of dealerships $= \dfrac{\mathbf{30{,}000 + 300t}}{\mathbf{1 + 0.03t}}$

ALGEBRAIC MODEL

$\boxed{A} = \dfrac{\mathbf{80 + 10t}}{\mathbf{1 - 0.02t}} \div \dfrac{\mathbf{30{,}000 + 300t}}{\mathbf{1 + 0.03t}}$ **Write algebraic model.**

$= \dfrac{80 + 10t}{1 - 0.02t} \cdot \dfrac{1 + 0.03t}{30{,}000 + 300t}$ **Multiply by reciprocal.**

$= \dfrac{(80 + 10t)(1 + 0.03t)}{(1 - 0.02t)(30{,}000 + 300t)}$ **Multiply numerators and denominators.**

$= \dfrac{(\cancel{10})(8 + t)(1 + 0.03t)}{(1 - 0.02t)(\cancel{10})(3000 + 30t)}$ **Divide out common factor 10.**

▶ The equation $A = \dfrac{(8 + t)(1 + 0.03t)}{(1 - 0.02t)(3000 + 30t)}$ is a model for the average sales (in billions of dollars) per new-car dealership.

b. In the year 2005, $t = 30$, so substitute 30 for *t* in the model for *A*.

$$\dfrac{(8 + 30)(1 + 0.03 \cdot 30)}{(1 - 0.02 \cdot 30)(3000 + 30 \cdot 30)} = \dfrac{38 \cdot 1.9}{0.4 \cdot 3900} = \dfrac{72.2}{1560} \approx 0.04628$$

▶ The model predicts that the average sales in 2005 will be about $0.0463 billion. Because 1 billion is 1000 million, you can express $0.0463 billion as 0.0463 · 1000 million, or $46.3 million.

GUIDED PRACTICE

Concept Check ✓

1. Describe the steps used to multiply two rational expressions.

2. Describe the steps used to divide two rational expressions.

3. **ERROR ANALYSIS** Describe the error in the problem at the right. Then do the division correctly.

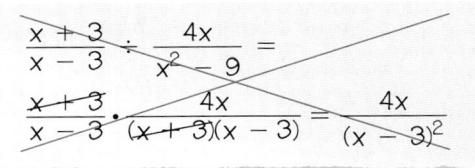

Ex. 3

Skill Check ✓   **Simplify the expression.**

4. $\dfrac{3x}{8x^2} \cdot \dfrac{4x^3}{3x^4}$

5. $\dfrac{x^2 - 1}{x} \cdot \dfrac{2x}{3x - 3}$

6. $\dfrac{x}{x^2 - 25} \cdot \dfrac{x - 5}{x + 5}$

7. $\dfrac{3x}{x^2 - 2x - 15} \cdot (x + 3)$

8. $\dfrac{x}{8 - 2x} \div \dfrac{2x}{4 - x}$

9. $\dfrac{4x^2 - 25}{4x} \div (2x - 5)$

10. $\dfrac{x^2 - 4x + 3}{2x} \div \dfrac{x - 1}{2}$

11. $\dfrac{9x^2 + 6x + 1}{x + 5} \div \dfrac{3x + 1}{x^2 + 5x}$

PRACTICE AND APPLICATIONS

STUDENT HELP

▶ **Extra Practice**
to help you master skills is on p. 807.

SIMPLIFYING EXPRESSIONS **Simplify the expression.**

12. $\dfrac{4x}{3} \cdot \dfrac{1}{x}$

13. $\dfrac{9x^2}{4} \cdot \dfrac{8}{18x}$

14. $\dfrac{7x^2}{6x} \cdot \dfrac{12x^2}{2x}$

15. $\dfrac{16x^2}{8x} \div \dfrac{4x^2}{16x}$

16. $\dfrac{25x^2}{10x} \div \dfrac{5x}{10x}$

17. $\dfrac{13x^4}{7x} \div \dfrac{x^3}{7x}$

18. $\dfrac{5 - 2x}{-2} \cdot \dfrac{24}{10 - 4x}$

19. $\dfrac{4x}{x^2 - 9} \cdot \dfrac{x - 3}{8x^2 + 12x}$

20. $\dfrac{-3}{x - 4} \cdot \dfrac{x - 4}{12(x - 7)}$

21. $\dfrac{3x^2}{10} \div \dfrac{9x^3}{25}$

22. $\dfrac{x}{x + 2} \div \dfrac{x + 5}{x + 2}$

23. $\dfrac{5x + 15}{3x} \div \dfrac{x + 3}{9x}$

24. $\dfrac{2(x + 2)}{5(x - 3)} \div \dfrac{4(x - 2)}{5x - 15}$

25. $\dfrac{x^2 - 36}{-5x^2} \div (x - 6)$

26. $\dfrac{8}{2 + 3x} \cdot (8 + 12x)$

27. $\dfrac{3x}{x^2 - 2x - 24} \cdot \dfrac{x - 6}{6x^2 + 9x}$

28. $\dfrac{x}{3x^2 + 2x - 8} \cdot (3x - 4)$

29. $\dfrac{x + 1}{x^3(3 - x)} \div \dfrac{5}{x(x - 3)}$

30. $(4x^2 + x - 3) \cdot \dfrac{1}{(4x + 3)(x - 1)}$

STUDENT HELP

▶ **HOMEWORK HELP**
Examples 1–5:
          Exs. 12–34
Example 6: Exs. 35–40

31. $\dfrac{x^2 - 8x + 15}{x^2 - 3x} \div (3x - 15)$

32. $\dfrac{6x^2 + 7x - 33}{x + 4} \div (6x - 11)$

33. $\left(\dfrac{x^2}{5} \cdot \dfrac{x + 2}{2} \right) \div \dfrac{x}{30}$

34. $\left(\dfrac{2x^2}{3} \cdot \dfrac{5}{x} \right) \div \dfrac{6x^2}{25}$

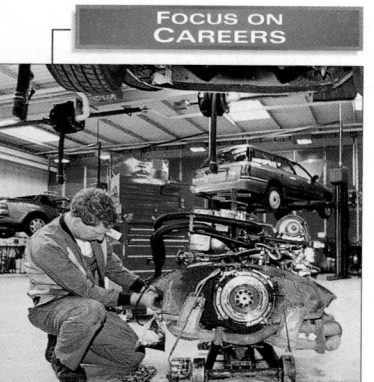
🚂 **RAILROAD TRAVEL** In Exercises 35–37, the models are based on data about train travel from 1990 to 1996 in the United States. Let *t* represent the number of years since 1990. ▶ Source: *Statistical Abstract of the United States*

Miles (in millions) traveled by passengers: $M = \dfrac{6300 - 800t}{1 - 0.12t}$

Passengers (in millions) who traveled by train: $P = \dfrac{222 - 24t}{10 - t}$

35. Find a model for the average number of miles traveled per passenger.

36. Use the model found in Exercise 35 to estimate the average number of miles traveled per passenger in 1995.

37. Use the model to predict the average number of miles traveled per passenger in 2005.

🌐 **SERVICE INDUSTRY** In Exercises 38–41, the models below are based on data collected by the Bureau of Economic Analysis from 1990 to 1997 in the United States. Let *t* represent the number of years since 1990.

Total sales (in billions of dollars) of services: $S = \dfrac{1055 + 23t}{1 - 0.04t}$

Total sales (in billions of dollars) of hotel services: $H = \dfrac{46 + 0.7t}{1 - 0.04t}$

Total sales (in billions of dollars) of auto repair services: $A = \dfrac{48 - t}{1 - 0.06t}$

38. Find the total sales given by each model in 1990.

39. Find a model for the ratio of hotel service sales to total service industry sales. Was this ratio increasing or decreasing from 1990 to 1997? Explain.

40. Find a model for the ratio of auto service sales to total service industry sales. Was this ratio increasing or decreasing from 1990 to 1997? Explain.

41. *Writing* What do your answers in Exercises 38 and 39 tell you about how the sales of the service industry were changing in the period from 1990 to 1997?

PROOF In Exercises 42 and 43, use the *proof* shown below.

Statement	Explanation
1. $\dfrac{ac}{bc} = \dfrac{a}{b} \cdot \dfrac{?}{?}$	**1.** Apply the rule for multiplying rational expressions.
2. $\underline{\ ?\ } = \dfrac{a}{b} \cdot \underline{\ ?\ }$	**2.** Any nonzero number divided by itself is 1.
3. $\underline{\ ?\ } = \dfrac{a}{b}$	**3.** Any nonzero number multiplied by 1 is itself.

42. **LOGICAL REASONING** Copy and complete the *proof* to show why you can divide out common factors.

43. Use the method from Exercise 42 to show that $\dfrac{2x - 4}{x^2 - 4} = \dfrac{2}{x + 2}$.

44. MULTIPLE CHOICE Which of the following represents the expression $\dfrac{x^2 - 3x}{x^2 - 5x + 6} \cdot \dfrac{(x - 2)^2}{2x}$ in simplified form?

Ⓐ $\dfrac{x(x - 3)}{2}$ Ⓑ $\dfrac{x}{2}$ Ⓒ $\dfrac{x - 2}{2}$

Ⓓ $\dfrac{x(x - 3)}{x - 2}$ Ⓔ $\dfrac{x^2 - 4x + 4}{x - 2}$

45. MULTIPLE CHOICE Which product equals the quotient $(2x + 2) \div \dfrac{x^2 + x}{4}$?

Ⓐ $\dfrac{1}{2x + 2} \cdot \dfrac{x^2 + x}{4}$ Ⓑ $\dfrac{2x + 2}{1} \cdot \dfrac{x^2 + x}{4}$ Ⓒ $\dfrac{1}{2x + 2} \cdot \dfrac{4}{x^2 + x}$

Ⓓ $\dfrac{2x + 2}{1} \cdot \dfrac{4}{x^2 + x}$ Ⓔ $\dfrac{2x + 2}{2x + 2} \cdot \dfrac{4}{x^2 + x}$

★ **Challenge**

INDEPENDENT EVENTS In Exercises 46–47, use the following information.
Two events are *independent* if the probability that one
event will occur is not affected by whether or not the other
event occurs. For independent events A and B, the
probability that A *and* B will occur equals the probability
of A times the probability of B.

For example, if you draw a marble from the jar at the
right, put it back, and then draw another one, the
probability that both marbles are red is $\dfrac{3}{5} \cdot \dfrac{3}{5} = \dfrac{9}{25}$.

46. A bag contains n marbles. There are r blue marbles and the rest of the
marbles are yellow. Find the probability of drawing a yellow marble followed
by a blue marble if the first one is put back before drawing again.

EXTRA CHALLENGE
www.mcdougallittell.com

47. Look back at the carnival game in Exercises 32–34 on page 668. Find the
probability of hitting the target two times in a row.

MIXED REVIEW

FINDING THE LCD Find the least common denominator. (Skills Review, pp. 781–783)

48. $\dfrac{3}{4}, \dfrac{2}{5}$ **49.** $\dfrac{2}{9}, \dfrac{3}{18}$ **50.** $\dfrac{1}{16}, \dfrac{9}{20}$ **51.** $\dfrac{14}{54}, \dfrac{31}{81}$

QUADRATIC FORMULA Solve the equation. (Review 9.5)

52. $2x^2 + 12x - 6 = 0$ **53.** $x^2 - 6x + 7 = 0$ **54.** $3x^2 + 11x + 10 = 0$

POLYNOMIALS Add or subtract. (Review 10.1 for 11.6)

55. $(4t^2 + 5t + 2) - (t^2 - 3t - 8)$ **56.** $(16p^3 - p^2 + 24) + (12p^2 - 8p - 16)$

57. $(a^4 - 12a) + (4a^3 + 11a - 1)$ **58.** $(-5x^2 + 2x - 12) - (6 - 9x - 7x^2)$

59. 🌎 **COMPOUND INTEREST** After two years, an investment of $1000
compounded annually at an interest rate r will grow to the amount
$1000(1 + r)^2$ in dollars. Write this product as a trinomial. **(Review 10.3)**

11.6 Adding and Subtracting Rational Expressions

What you should learn

GOAL 1 Add and subtract rational expressions that have like denominators.

GOAL 2 Add and subtract rational expressions that have unlike denominators.

Why you should learn it

▼ To model **real-life** problems, such as planning your route for a car trip in **Example 5**.

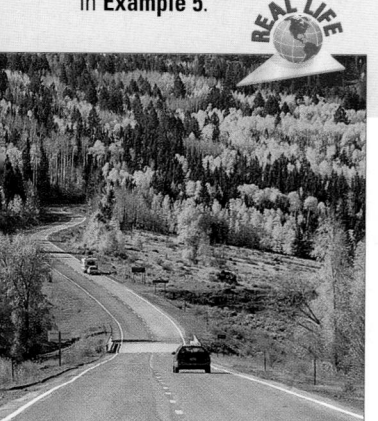

GOAL 1 FRACTIONS WITH LIKE DENOMINATORS

To add or subtract rational expressions with *like* denominators, combine their numerators, and write the result over the common denominator.

ADDING OR SUBTRACTING WITH LIKE DENOMINATORS

Let *a*, *b,* and *c* be polynomials, with $c \neq 0$.

TO ADD, add the numerators.
$$\frac{a}{c} + \frac{b}{c} = \frac{a+b}{c}$$

TO SUBTRACT, subtract the numerators.
$$\frac{a}{c} - \frac{b}{c} = \frac{a-b}{c}$$

EXAMPLE 1 *Adding and Subtracting Expressions*

a. $\dfrac{5}{x} + \dfrac{x-5}{x} = \dfrac{5+x-5}{x}$ Add numerators.

$\qquad\qquad\quad = \dfrac{x}{x}$ Simplify.

$\qquad\qquad\quad = 1$

b. $\dfrac{7}{2m-3} - \dfrac{3m}{2m-3} = \dfrac{7-3m}{2m-3}$ Subtract numerators.

EXAMPLE 2 *Simplifying After Subtracting*

Simplify $\dfrac{4x}{3x^2 - x - 2} - \dfrac{x-2}{3x^2 - x - 2}$.

SOLUTION

$\dfrac{4x}{3x^2 - x - 2} - \dfrac{x-2}{3x^2 - x - 2} = \dfrac{4x - (x-2)}{3x^2 - x - 2}$ Subtract.

$\qquad\qquad\qquad\qquad\qquad = \dfrac{3x+2}{3x^2 - x - 2}$ Simplify.

$\qquad\qquad\qquad\qquad\qquad = \dfrac{3x+2}{(3x+2)(x-1)}$ Factor.

$\qquad\qquad\qquad\qquad\qquad = \dfrac{\cancel{3x+2}}{\cancel{(3x+2)}(x-1)}$ Divide out common factor.

$\qquad\qquad\qquad\qquad\qquad = \dfrac{1}{x-1}$ Simplified form

STUDENT HELP

► **Skills Review**
For help with adding fractions with unlike denominators, see pp. 781–783.

To add or subtract rational expressions with *unlike* denominators, you must first rewrite the expressions so that they have *like* denominators. The like denominator that you usually use is the least common multiple of the original denominators. It is called the **least common denominator** or LCD.

EXAMPLE 3 *Adding with Unlike Denominators*

Simplify $\dfrac{7}{6x} + \dfrac{5}{8x^2}$.

SOLUTION

STUDENT HELP

► **Study Tip**
You can always find a common denominator by multiplying the two denominators, but it is often easier to use the LCD. For instance, using $24x^2$ rather than $48x^3$ in Example 3 makes the expressions in the numerators simpler.

To find the least common denominator, first completely factor the denominators. You get $6x = 2 \cdot 3 \cdot x$ and $8x^2 = 2^3 \cdot x^2$. The LCD contains the highest power of each factor that appears in either denominator, so the LCD is $2^3 \cdot 3 \cdot x^2$, or $24x^2$.

$$\frac{7}{6x} + \frac{5}{8x^2} = \frac{7 \cdot 4x}{6x \cdot 4x} + \frac{5 \cdot 3}{8x^2 \cdot 3} \qquad \text{Rewrite fractions using LCD.}$$

$$= \frac{28x}{24x^2} + \frac{15}{24x^2} \qquad \text{Simplify numerators and denominators.}$$

$$= \frac{28x + 15}{24x^2} \qquad \text{Add fractions.}$$

EXAMPLE 4 *Subtracting with Unlike Denominators*

Simplify $\dfrac{x + 2}{x - 1} - \dfrac{12}{x + 6}$.

SOLUTION

Neither denominator can be factored. The least common denominator is the product $(x - 1)(x + 6)$ because it must contain both of these factors.

$$\frac{x + 2}{x - 1} - \frac{12}{x + 6} = \frac{(x + 2)(x + 6)}{(x - 1)(x + 6)} - \frac{12(x - 1)}{(x - 1)(x + 6)} \qquad \text{Rewrite fractions using LCD.}$$

$$= \frac{x^2 + 8x + 12}{(x - 1)(x + 6)} - \frac{12x - 12}{(x - 1)(x + 6)} \qquad \begin{array}{l}\text{Simplify numerators. Leave}\\ \text{denominators in factored form.}\end{array}$$

$$= \frac{x^2 + 8x + 12 - (12x - 12)}{(x - 1)(x + 6)} \qquad \text{Subtract fractions.}$$

$$= \frac{x^2 + 8x + 12 - 12x + 12}{(x - 1)(x + 6)} \qquad \text{Use distributive property.}$$

$$= \frac{x^2 - 4x + 24}{(x - 1)(x + 6)} \qquad \text{Combine like terms.}$$

Travel Planning

EXAMPLE 5 *Writing and Using a Model*

You are planning a 300-mile car trip. You can make the trip using a combination of two roads: a toll road on which you can average 60 miles per hour and a scenic country road on which you can average 40 miles per hour. To avoid tolls and to enjoy the scenery, you want to spend as much time as possible on the country road. However, you do not want your total trip time to be too long.

Let x represent the number of miles you travel on the country road.

a. Write an expression for the total time.

b. Evaluate the expression at 60-mile intervals.

SOLUTION

PROBLEM SOLVING STRATEGY

a. VERBAL MODEL

$$\boxed{\text{Total time}} = \frac{\text{Distance on country road}}{\text{Speed on country road}} + \frac{\text{Distance on toll road}}{\text{Speed on toll road}}$$

LABELS

Total time $= T$ (hours)

Distance on country road $= x$ (miles)

Speed on country road $= 40$ (miles per hour)

Distance on toll road $= 300 - x$ (miles)

Speed on toll road $= 60$ (miles per hour)

ALGEBRAIC MODEL

$$T = \frac{x}{40} + \frac{300 - x}{60} \qquad \text{Write algebraic model.}$$

$$= \frac{3x}{120} + \frac{2(300 - x)}{120} \qquad \text{Rewrite fractions using LCD.}$$

$$= \frac{3x + 600 - 2x}{120} \qquad \text{Add fractions.}$$

$$= \frac{x + 600}{120} \qquad \text{Combine like terms.}$$

b. Substitute x-values of 0, 60, 120, 180, 240, and 300 into the expression.

Distance (country) x	0	60	120	180	240	300
Total time T	5.0	5.5	6.0	6.5	7.0	7.5

The table can help you decide how many miles to drive on the country road.

GUIDED PRACTICE

Vocabulary Check ✓

1. Explain what is meant by the *least common denominator* of two rational expressions.

Concept Check ✓

2. **ERROR ANALYSIS** Explain the error in the following problem.

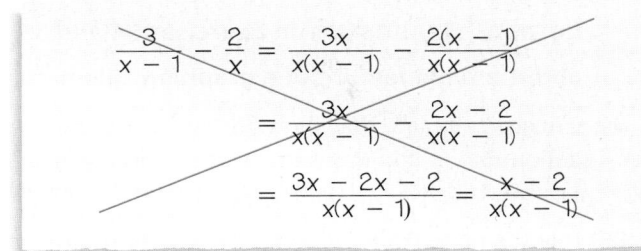

3. You can use $x - 3$ as the LCD when finding the sum $\dfrac{5}{x - 3} + \dfrac{2}{3 - x}$.

What number can you multiply the numerator and the denominator of the second fraction by to get an equivalent fraction with $x - 3$ as the new denominator?

Skill Check ✓

Simplify the expression.

4. $\dfrac{1}{3x} + \dfrac{5}{3x}$

5. $\dfrac{5x}{x + 4} + \dfrac{20}{4 + x}$

6. $\dfrac{x}{x^2 - 9} - \dfrac{3x + 1}{x^2 - 9}$

7. $\dfrac{3}{10x} - \dfrac{1}{4x^2}$

8. $\dfrac{x + 6}{x + 1} - \dfrac{4}{2x + 3}$

9. $\dfrac{x - 2}{2x - 10} + \dfrac{x + 3}{x - 5}$

PRACTICE AND APPLICATIONS

STUDENT HELP

▶ **Extra Practice**
to help you master
skills is on p. 807.

ADDING AND SUBTRACTING **Simplify the expression.**

10. $\dfrac{7}{2x} + \dfrac{x + 2}{2x}$

11. $\dfrac{4}{x + 1} + \dfrac{2x - 2}{x + 1}$

12. $\dfrac{7x}{x^3} - \dfrac{6x}{x^3}$

13. $\dfrac{2}{3x - 1} - \dfrac{5x}{3x - 1}$

14. $\dfrac{3x}{4x + 1} + \dfrac{5x}{4x + 1}$

15. $\dfrac{-8}{3x^2} + \dfrac{11}{3x^2}$

16. $\dfrac{9}{4x} + \dfrac{7}{-5x}$

17. $\dfrac{11}{6x} + \dfrac{2}{13x}$

18. $\dfrac{9}{5x} - \dfrac{2}{x^2}$

19. $\dfrac{4}{x + 4} - \dfrac{7}{x - 2}$

20. $\dfrac{3}{x + 3} + \dfrac{4x}{2x + 6}$

21. $\dfrac{9}{x^2 - 3x} + \dfrac{3}{x - 3}$

22. $\dfrac{2x}{x - 1} - \dfrac{7x}{x + 4}$

23. $\dfrac{x}{x - 10} + \dfrac{x + 4}{x + 6}$

24. $\dfrac{4x}{5x - 2} - \dfrac{2x}{5x + 1}$

25. $\dfrac{x + 8}{3x - 1} + \dfrac{x + 3}{x + 1}$

26. $\dfrac{3x + 10}{7x - 4} - \dfrac{x}{4x + 3}$

27. $\dfrac{2x + 1}{3x - 1} - \dfrac{x + 4}{x - 2}$

28. $\dfrac{x}{x^2 + 5x - 24} + \dfrac{8}{x^2 + 5x - 24}$

29. $\dfrac{x^2 + 1}{x^2 - 4} + \dfrac{5x}{x^2 - 4} - \dfrac{2x + 11}{x^2 - 4}$

30. $\dfrac{x^2 - 9}{x + 3} + \dfrac{x^2 + 9}{x - 3}$

31. $\dfrac{2}{x + 1} + \dfrac{3}{x - 2} + \dfrac{3}{x + 4}$

STUDENT HELP

▶ HOMEWORK HELP
Example 1: Exs. 10–31
Example 2: Exs. 10–31
Example 3: Exs. 16–31
Example 4: Exs. 18–31
Example 5: Exs. 36–38

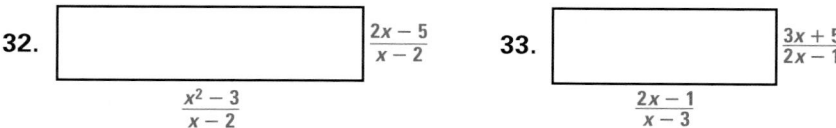

GEOMETRY CONNECTION In Exercises 32 and 33, find an expression for the perimeter of the rectangle.

32.

$\dfrac{2x-5}{x-2}$

$\dfrac{x^2-3}{x-2}$

33.

$\dfrac{3x+5}{2x-1}$

$\dfrac{2x-1}{x-3}$

LOGICAL REASONING In Exercises 34 and 35, use the expression $\dfrac{2x-5}{x-2}$ and the table feature of a graphing calculator or spreadsheet software.

34. Construct a table that shows the value of the numerator, the value of the denominator, and the value of the entire rational expression when the value of x is 10, 100, 1000, 10,000, 100,000, and 1,000,000.

35. Use the table from Exercise 34. As x gets large, what happens to the values of the numerator? of the denominator? of the entire rational expression? Why do you think these results occur?

TRAVEL BY BOAT In Exercises 36–38, use the following information.
A boat moves through still water at x kilometers (km) per hour. It travels 24 km upstream against a current of 2 km per hour and then returns with the current. The rate upstream is $x - 2$ because the boat moves against the current, and the rate downstream is $x + 2$ because the boat moves with the current.

36. Write an expression for the total time for the round trip.

37. Write your answer to Exercise 36 as a single rational expression.

38. Use your answer to Exercise 37 to find how long the round trip will take if the boat travels 10 kilometers per hour through still water.

MOWING LAWNS In Exercises 39–41, use the following information.
You are choosing a business partner for a student lawn-care business you are starting. It takes you an average of 35 minutes to mow a lawn, so your rate is 1 lawn in 35 minutes or $\dfrac{1}{35}$ of a lawn per minute. Let x represent the average time (in minutes) it takes a possible partner to mow a lawn.

39. Write an expression for the partner's rate (that is, the part of a lawn the partner can mow in 1 minute). Then write an expression for the combined rate of you and your partner (the part of a lawn that you both can mow in 1 minute if you work together).

40. Write your answer to Exercise 39 as a single rational expression.

41. The table shows the mowing times of possible partners.

Possible mowing partner	A	B	C
Mowing time (in minutes)	40	45	55

a. Use your expression from Exercise 40 to find the combined rate of you with each possible partner.

b. Which partner(s) can you choose if you want a combined rate of $\dfrac{1}{20}$ of a lawn per minute or faster?

COMBINING OPERATIONS Simplify the expression.

42. $\dfrac{2x}{x+5} - \dfrac{3x+2}{x+5} - \dfrac{4}{x+5}$

43. $\left(\dfrac{3x^2}{56}\right)\left(\dfrac{3}{x} + \dfrac{5}{x}\right)$

44. $\left(\dfrac{3x-5}{x} + \dfrac{1}{x}\right) \div \left(\dfrac{x}{6x-8}\right)$

45. $\dfrac{x-2}{x+6} \div \dfrac{x+8}{4x-24} \cdot \dfrac{x-8}{x-2}$

EXTENSION: TRINOMIAL DENOMINATORS When you add rational expressions, you may need to factor a trinomial to find the LCD. Study the sample below. Then simplify the expressions in Exercises 46–49.

Sample: $\dfrac{2x}{x^2-1} + \dfrac{3}{x^2+x-2} = \dfrac{2x}{(x+1)(x-1)} + \dfrac{3}{(x-1)(x+2)}$

The LCD is $(x+1)(x-1)(x+2)$.

Note: If you just used $(x^2-1)(x^2+x-2)$ as the common denominator, the factor $(x-1)$ would be included twice.

46. $\dfrac{2}{x-3} + \dfrac{x}{x^2+3x-18}$

47. $\dfrac{2}{x^2-4} + \dfrac{3}{x^2+x-6}$

48. $\dfrac{7x+2}{16-x^2} + \dfrac{7}{x-4}$

49. $\dfrac{5x-1}{2x^2-7x-15} - \dfrac{-3x+4}{2x^2+5x+3}$

Test Preparation

50. MULTIPLE CHOICE Find the LCD of $\dfrac{-2}{x+9}$ and $\dfrac{5x}{x^2+9x}$.

(A) x^2+9 **(B)** $x(x+9)$ **(C)** $x(x-9)$ **(D)** $(x+9)(x^2+9x)$

51. MULTIPLE CHOICE Simplify the expression $\dfrac{x}{x-1} - \dfrac{1}{2x+1}$.

(A) $\dfrac{x-1}{(x-1)(2x+1)}$ **(B)** $-\dfrac{x}{x-1}$

(C) $\dfrac{2x^2+1}{(x-1)(2x+1)}$ **(D)** $\dfrac{2x^2-1}{(x-1)(2x+1)}$

52. MULTIPLE CHOICE You are making a 350-mile car trip. You decide to drive a little faster to save time. Choose an expression for the time saved if the car's average speed s is increased by 5 miles per hour.

(A) $\dfrac{350}{s+5}$ **(B)** $\dfrac{s+5}{350} - \dfrac{s}{350}$ **(C)** $\dfrac{350}{s} - \dfrac{350}{s+5}$ **(D)** $350(s+5) - 350s$

★ **Challenge**

AVERAGE SPEED In Exercises 53–55, you will write and simplify a general expression for the average speed traveled when making a round trip. Let d represent the one-way distance. Let x represent the speed while traveling there and let y represent the speed while traveling back.

53. Write an expression for the total time for the round trip. Use addition to write your answer as a single rational expression.

54. To find the average speed on the trip, you need to divide the total distance by the total time. Use your answer from Exercise 53 to write an expression for the average speed. Then simplify that expression as far as possible.

55. What do you notice about the variables in the final answer? If your distance is doubled what happens to the average speed?

SIMPLIFYING EXPRESSIONS Simplify the expression. (Review 8.3 for 11.7)

56. $\dfrac{5}{10x}$ **57.** $\dfrac{4m^2}{6m}$ **58.** $\dfrac{16x^4}{32x^8}$ **59.** $\dfrac{42x^4y^3}{6x^3y^9}$

STANDARD FORM Write the equation in standard form. (Lesson 9.5 for 11.7)

60. $6x^2 = 5x - 7$ **61.** $9 - 6x = 2x^2$ **62.** $-4 + 3y^2 = y$

CHOOSING MODELS FROM DATA Make a scatter plot of the data. Then tell whether a *linear, exponential,* or *quadratic* model fits the data. (Review 9.8)

63. $(-1, 16), (0, 4), (1, -2), (2, -2), (3, 4), (5, 34)$

64. $(-5, 6), (-4, 3), (-2, -3), (-1, -6), (0, -9), (1, -12)$

65. 🌐 **GAME SHOW** A contestant on a television game show must guess the price of a trip within $1000 of the actual price in order to win. The actual price of the trip is $8500. Write an absolute-value inequality that shows the range of possible guesses that will win the trip. (Review 6.4)

QUIZ 2

Self-Test for Lessons 11.4–11.6

Simplify the expression if possible. (Lesson 11.4)

1. $\dfrac{15x^2}{10x}$ **2.** $\dfrac{5x}{11x + x^2}$ **3.** $\dfrac{3 - x}{x^2 - 5x + 6}$ **4.** $\dfrac{x^2 - 7x + 12}{x^2 + 3x + 18}$

Simplify the expression. (Lessons 11.5 and 11.6)

5. $\dfrac{5x^2}{2x} \cdot \dfrac{14x^2}{10x}$ **6.** $\dfrac{5}{10 + 4x} \cdot (20 + 8x)$

7. $\dfrac{3x + 12}{4x} \div \dfrac{x + 4}{2x}$ **8.** $\dfrac{5x^2 - 30x + 45}{x + 2} \div (5x - 15)$

9. $\dfrac{x}{x^2 - 2x - 35} + \dfrac{5}{x^2 - 2x - 35}$ **10.** $\dfrac{4x - 1}{3x^2 + 8x + 5} - \dfrac{x - 6}{3x^2 + 8x + 5}$

🌐 **CANOEING** In Exercises 11–13, use the following information.
You are on a canoe trip. You can paddle your canoe at a rate of x miles per hour in still water. The stream is flowing at a rate of 2 miles per hour, so your rate of travel downstream (with the current) is $x + 2$ miles per hour. You travel 15 miles downstream and 15 miles back upstream. (Lesson 11.6)

11. Write an expression for the travel time downstream and an expression for the travel time upstream.

12. Write and simplify an expression for the total travel time.

13. Find the total travel time if your rate of paddling in still water is about 4 miles per hour.

GOAL 2 USING LONG DIVISION

You can use **polynomial long division** to divide polynomials that do not have common factors. First review the process for long division in arithmetic.

EXAMPLE 2 *The Long Division Algorithm*

Use long division to divide 658 by 28.

SOLUTION

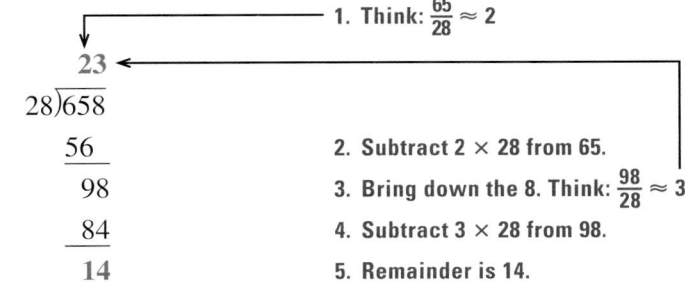

1. Think: $\frac{65}{28} \approx 2$
2. Subtract 2×28 from 65.
3. Bring down the 8. Think: $\frac{98}{28} \approx 3$
4. Subtract 3×28 from 98.
5. Remainder is 14.

$$\text{Dividend} \quad \text{Quotient} \quad \text{Remainder}$$

$$\text{Divisor} \longrightarrow \frac{658}{28} = 23 + \frac{14}{28} = 23 + \frac{1}{2} = 23\frac{1}{2}$$

EXAMPLE 3 *Polynomial Long Division*

Divide $x^2 + 2x + 4$ by $x - 1$.

SOLUTION

1. Think: $\frac{x^2}{x} = x$

2. Subtract $x(x - 1)$.
3. Bring down $+ 4$. Think: $\frac{3x}{x} = 3$
4. Subtract $3(x - 1)$.
5. Remainder is 7.

To subtract $(-x)$ from $2x$, you add x.

$$\text{Dividend} \longrightarrow \text{Divisor} \longrightarrow \frac{x^2 + 2x + 4}{x - 1} = x + 3 + \frac{7}{x - 1} \longleftarrow \text{Remainder}$$

with **Quotient** labeled above $x + 3$.

▶ The answer is $x + 3 + \dfrac{7}{x - 1}$.

When dividing polynomials, remember that the polynomials need to be written in standard form. That is, the terms should be written in descending order according to their degrees.

If a term is missing in the standard form of the dividend, insert a term with a coefficient of 0 to hold the place.

EXAMPLE 4 *Adding a Place-holding Zero*

Divide $6x^2 - 11$ by $x + 2$.

SOLUTION

First insert a place-holding term $0x$ in the dividend: $6x^2 - 11 = 6x^2 + 0x - 11$.

1. Think: $\frac{6x^2}{x} = 6x$

$$
\begin{array}{r}
6x - 12 \\
x + 2 \overline{)6x^2 + 0x - 11} \\
\underline{6x^2 + 12x} \\
-12x - 11 \\
\underline{-12x - 24} \\
13
\end{array}
$$

2. Subtract $(6x)(x + 2)$.

3. Bring down -11. Think: $\frac{-12x}{x} = -12$

4. Subtract $-12(x + 2)$.

5. Remainder is 13.

▶ The answer is $6x - 12 + \dfrac{13}{x + 2}$.

EXAMPLE 5 *Rewriting in Standard Form*

Divide $m^2 - 16m - 21$ by $4 + 2m$.

SOLUTION

First write the divisor $4 + 2m$ in standard form as $2m + 4$.

1. Think: $\frac{m^2}{2m} = \frac{1}{2}m$

$$
\begin{array}{r}
\frac{1}{2}m - 9 \\
2m + 4 \overline{)m^2 - 16m - 21} \\
\underline{m^2 + 2m} \\
-18m - 21 \\
\underline{-18m - 36} \\
15
\end{array}
$$

2. Subtract $\frac{1}{2}m(2m + 4)$.

3. Bring down -21. Think: $\frac{-18m}{2m} = -9$

4. Subtract $-9(2m + 4)$.

5. Remainder is 15.

STUDENT HELP

HOMEWORK HELP
Visit our Web site
www.mcdougallittell.com
for extra examples.

▶ The answer is $\frac{1}{2}m - 9 + \dfrac{15}{2m + 4}$.

GUIDED PRACTICE

Vocabulary Check ✓

1. How is polynomial long division like long division with whole numbers? How is it different?

Concept Check ✓

2. For which of the divisions in Exercises 9–14 do you not need to use long division? Explain why not.

3. For the student's long division work shown at the right, complete the answer.

$$\frac{x^2 - 5}{x - 1} = \text{Quotient} + \frac{\text{Remainder}}{\text{Divisor}}$$

$$= \boxed{?} + \frac{\boxed{?}}{\boxed{?}}$$

$$
\begin{array}{r}
x + 1 \\
x - 1 \overline{)\, x^2 + 0x - 5} \\
\underline{x^2 - x} \\
x - 5 \\
\underline{x - 1} \\
-4
\end{array}
$$

4. Explain how to check the answer to the division in Exercise 3.

Skill Check ✓ **Set up the long division problem, but do not perform the division.**

5. Divide $y^2 + 8$ by $y + 2$.

6. Divide $-x^2 - 4x + 21$ by $-x + 3$.

7. Divide $8y^2 - 2y$ by $3y + 5$.

8. Divide $72 - 18x + x^2$ by $x - 6$.

Divide.

9. Divide 856 by 29.

10. Divide $18x^2 + 45x - 36$ by $9x$.

11. Divide $x^2 - 8x + 15$ by $x - 3$.

12. Divide $y^2 + 6y + 2$ by $y + 3$.

13. Divide $10b^3 - 8b^2 - 5b$ by $-2b$.

14. Divide $2x^2 - x + 4$ by $3x - 6$.

PRACTICE AND APPLICATIONS

STUDENT HELP

▶ **Extra Practice**
to help you master skills is on p. 807.

DIVIDING BY A MONOMIAL Divide.

15. Divide $8x + 13$ by 2.

16. Divide $16y - 9$ by 4.

17. Divide $9c^2 + 3c$ by c.

18. Divide $9m^3 + 4m^2 - 8m$ by m.

19. Divide $-2x^2 - 12x$ by $-2x$.

20. Divide $7p^3 + 18p^2$ by p^2.

21. Divide $9a^2 - 54a - 36$ by $3a$.

22. Divide $16y^3 - 36y^2 - 64$ by $-4y^2$.

CHECKING QUOTIENTS AND REMAINDERS Match the polynomial division problem with the correct answer.

STUDENT HELP

▶ HOMEWORK HELP
Example 1: Exs. 15–22
Example 2: Exs. 23–26
Example 3: Exs. 23–46
Example 4: Exs. 27–46
Example 5: Exs. 27–46

23. $(5x^2 + 2x + 3) \div (x + 2)$

A. $6 + \dfrac{13}{2x - 3}$

24. $(12x - 5) \div (2x - 3)$

B. $5x + 4$

25. $(10x^2 - 7x - 12) \div (2x - 3)$

C. $2x + 1$

26. $(2x^2 + 5x + 2) \div (x + 2)$

D. $5x - 8 + \dfrac{19}{x + 2}$

DIVIDING POLYNOMIALS **Divide.**

27. Divide $a^2 - 3a + 2$ by $a - 1$. **28.** Divide $y^2 + 5y + 7$ by $y + 2$.

29. Divide $2b^2 - 3b - 4$ by $b - 2$. **30.** Divide $3p^2 + 10p + 3$ by $p + 3$.

31. Divide $5g^2 + 14g - 2$ by $g + 3$. **32.** Divide $c^2 - 25$ by $c - 5$.

33. Divide $x^2 - 3x - 59$ by $x - 9$. **34.** Divide $d^2 + 15d + 45$ by $d + 5$.

35. Divide $-x^2 - 6x - 16$ by $x + 2$. **36.** Divide $-x^2 + 9x - 12$ by $-x - 2$.

37. Divide $b^2 - 7b + 4$ by $b + 3$. **38.** Divide $5 - 7m + 3m^2$ by $m - 3$.

39. Divide $x^2 + 9$ by $-x - 4$. **40.** Divide $4x^2 + 12x - 10$ by $x - 2$.

41. Divide $-5m^2 + 2$ by $m - 1$. **42.** Divide $4 + 11q + 6q^2$ by $2q + 1$.

43. Divide $4 - s^2$ by $s + 5$. **44.** Divide $16a^2 - 25$ by $3 + 4a$.

45. Divide $c^2 - 7c + 21$ by $2c - 6$. **46.** Divide $b^2 - 7b - 12$ by $4b + 4$.

GEOMETRY **CONNECTION** **The area and one dimension of the rectangle are shown. Find the missing dimension.**

47.
Area is
$5x^2 - 17x - 12$.
?
$x - 4$

48.
Area is
$7x^2 + 17x + 6$.
?
$x + 2$

49.
Area is
$12x^2 + 5x - 2$.
?
$4x - 1$

 EXERCISE AND OTHER SPORTS EQUIPMENT In Exercises 50–54, use the models below that approximate spending in the United States from 1988 to 1997. Let *t* represent the number of years since 1988.

Dollars spent on exercise equipment (in millions): $E = 200t + 1400$

Total dollars spent on sports equipment (in millions): $S = 900t + 9900$

50. Write a rational model for the ratio of the money spent on exercise equipment to the total money spent on sports equipment. Simplify the model by dividing out the greatest common factor.

51. Use long division to write the model from Exercise 50 in another form.

52. Copy and complete the table. Use the rewritten model from Exercise 51. Round to the nearest thousandth.

Year *t*	0	1	2	3	4	5	6	7	8	9
Ratio of *E* to *S*	?	?	?	?	?	?	?	?	?	?

53. Use the table. Was the ratio increasing or decreasing from 1988 to 1997?

54. **CRITICAL THINKING** Look back at the model you found in Exercise 51. How can you tell from the model if the ratio is increasing or if it is decreasing?

55. MULTI-STEP PROBLEM Suppose you are 14 years old and your brother is 4 years old.

   a. In t years, your age will be $14 + t$. What will your brother's age be?

   b. Write the ratio of your age in t years to your brother's age in t years. Then use long division to rewrite this ratio.

   c. Use the rewritten ratio to find the ratio of your ages now, in 5 years, in 10 years, in 25 years, in 50 years, and in 80 years.

   d. Use your answers to part (c). Is the ratio of your ages getting smaller or larger as time goes by? What value do the ratios approach?

   e. *Writing* Look at the original form of the ratio and the rewritten form of the ratio. Which form of the ratio makes it easier for you to recognize the trend that you described in part (d)? Explain your choice.

★ Challenge

AREA MODELS In Exercises 56–60, use the diagrams.

56. Diagram 1 models $5^2 \div 4$. Write the quotient and the remainder.

57. What division problem does Diagram 2 model? Write the quotient and the remainder.

58. Draw diagrams to model $4^2 \div 3$ and $7^2 \div 6$.

59. LOGICAL REASONING Describe any pattern you observe in Exercises 56–58. Use the pattern to predict the quotient and remainder when x^2 is divided by $x - 1$.

60. Use long division to find $x^2 \div (x - 1)$. Did you get the result you predicted in Exercise 59?

Diagram 1

Diagram 2

MIXED REVIEW

SOLVING EQUATIONS Solve the equation. (Review 3.2 for 11.8)

61. $\dfrac{x}{5} = 3$ **62.** $\dfrac{a}{-3} = 7$ **63.** $\dfrac{c}{4} = \dfrac{6}{8}$ **64.** $\dfrac{y}{-2} = \dfrac{5}{4}$

SOLVING PROPORTIONS In Exercises 65–70, solve the proportion. Check for extraneous solutions. (Review 11.1 for 11.8)

65. $\dfrac{7}{5} = \dfrac{2}{x}$ **66.** $\dfrac{2}{x} = \dfrac{x - 1}{6}$ **67.** $\dfrac{6x - 7}{4} = \dfrac{5}{x}$

68. $\dfrac{8b^2 + 4b}{4b} = \dfrac{2b - 5}{3}$ **69.** $\dfrac{5p^2 - 9}{5} = \dfrac{2p^2 + 3p}{2}$ **70.** $\dfrac{a^2 - 4}{a - 2} = \dfrac{a + 2}{10}$

71. GRAPHING INVERSE VARIATION Use the model $y = \dfrac{12}{x}$. Make a table of values for $x = 1, 2, 3, 4,$ and 5. Sketch the graph. (Review 11.3 for 11.8)

72. BIOLOGY CONNECTION The largest mammal, a blue whale, has a weight of 1.3×10^5 kilograms. The smallest mammal, a pygmy shrew, has a weight of 2.0×10^{-3} kilogram. What is the ratio of the weight of a blue whale to the weight of a pygmy shrew? (Review 8.4)

11.8 Rational Equations and Functions

What you should learn

GOAL 1 Solve rational equations.

GOAL 2 Graph rational functions.

Why you should learn it

▼ To model **real-life** problems as in the fundraising problem in **Exs. 53–54**.

GOAL 1 SOLVING RATIONAL EQUATIONS

A **rational equation** is an equation that contains rational expressions. Examples 1 and 2 show the two basic strategies for solving a rational equation.

EXAMPLE 1 Cross Multiplying

Solve $\dfrac{5}{y+2} = \dfrac{y}{3}$.

SOLUTION

$\dfrac{5}{y+2} = \dfrac{y}{3}$	Write original equation.
$5(3) = y(y+2)$	Cross multiply.
$15 = y^2 + 2y$	Simplify.
$0 = y^2 + 2y - 15$	Write in standard form.
$0 = (y+5)(y-3)$	Factor right side.

▶ If you set each factor equal to 0, you see that the solutions are -5 and 3. Check both solutions in the original equation.

· · · · · · · · · ·

Cross multiplying can be used only for equations in which each side is a single fraction. The second method, multiplying by the LCD, works for any rational equation. Multiplying by the LCD always leads to an equation with no fractions.

EXAMPLE 2 Multiplying by the LCD

Solve $\dfrac{2}{x} + \dfrac{1}{3} = \dfrac{4}{x}$.

SOLUTION

$\dfrac{2}{x} + \dfrac{1}{3} = \dfrac{4}{x}$	The LCD is $3x$.
$3x \cdot \dfrac{2}{x} + 3x \cdot \dfrac{1}{3} = 3x \cdot \dfrac{4}{x}$	Multiply each side by $3x$.
$6 + x = 12$	Simplify.
$x = 6$	Subtract 6 from each side.
✓ **CHECK** $\dfrac{2}{6} + \dfrac{1}{3} \overset{?}{=} \dfrac{4}{6}$	Substitute 6 for x.
$\dfrac{4}{6} = \dfrac{4}{6}$	Simplify.

EXAMPLE 3 *Factoring to Find the LCD*

STUDENT HELP

Study Tip
When you solve rational equations, be sure to check for extraneous solutions. Remember, values of the variable that make any denominator equal to 0 are excluded.

Solve $\dfrac{-4}{y-3} + 1 = \dfrac{-10}{y^2+y-12}$.

SOLUTION The denominator $y^2 + y - 12$ factors as $(y+4)(y-3)$, so the LCD is $(y+4)(y-3)$. Multiply each side of the equation by $(y+4)(y-3)$.

$$\dfrac{-4}{y-3} \cdot (y+4)(y-3) + 1 \cdot (y+4)(y-3) = \dfrac{-10}{y^2+y-12} \cdot (y+4)(y-3)$$

$$\dfrac{-4(y+4)(y-3)}{y-3} + (y+4)(y-3) = \dfrac{-10(y+4)(y-3)}{(y+4)(y-3)}$$

$$-4(y+4) + (y^2+y-12) = -10$$

$$-4y - 16 + y^2 + y - 12 = -10$$

$$y^2 - 3y - 28 = -10$$

$$y^2 - 3y - 18 = 0$$

$$(y-6)(y+3) = 0$$

▶ The solutions are 6 and -3. Check both solutions in the original equation.

EXAMPLE 4 *Writing and Using a Rational Equation*

BATTING AVERAGE You have 35 hits in 140 times at bat. Your batting average is $\dfrac{35}{140} = 0.250$. How many consecutive hits must you get to increase your batting average to 0.300?

SOLUTION If your hits are consecutive, then you must get a hit each time you are at bat, so "future hits" is equal to "future times at bat."

FOCUS ON CAREERS

SPORTS REPORTER
Sports reporters gather statistics and prepare stories that cover all aspects of sports from local sporting events to international sporting events.

CAREER LINK
www.mcdougallittell.com

VERBAL MODEL	Batting average $= \dfrac{\text{Past hits} + \textbf{Future hits}}{\text{Past times at bat} + \textbf{Future times at bat}}$

LABELS	Batting average $= 0.300$	(no units)
	Past hits $= 35$	(no units)
	Future hits $= x$	(no units)
	Past times at bat $= 140$	(no units)
	Future times at bat $= x$	(no units)

ALGEBRAIC MODEL

$$0.300 = \dfrac{35 + x}{140 + x}$$ **Write algebraic model.**

$$0.300(140 + x) = 35 + x$$ **Multiply by LCD.**

$$42 + 0.3x = 35 + x$$ **Use distributive property.**

$$7 = 0.7x$$ **Subtract 0.3x and 35 from each side.**

$$10 = x$$ **Divide each side by 0.7.**

▶ You need to get a hit in each of your next 10 times at bat.

GOAL 2 GRAPHING RATIONAL FUNCTIONS

The inverse variation models you graphed in Lesson 11.3 are a type of *rational function*. A **rational function** is a function of the form

$$f(x) = \frac{\text{polynomial}}{\text{polynomial}}.$$

In this lesson you will learn to graph rational functions whose numerators and denominators are first-degree polynomials. Using long division, such a function can be written in the form

$$y = \frac{a}{x - h} + k.$$

RATIONAL FUNCTIONS WHOSE GRAPHS ARE HYPERBOLAS

The graph of the rational function $y = \frac{a}{x - h} + k$

is a **hyperbola** whose **center** is (h, k).

The vertical and horizontal lines through the center are the *asymptotes* of the hyperbola. An **asymptote** is a line that the graph approaches. While the distance between the graph and the line approaches zero, the asymptote is not part of the graph.

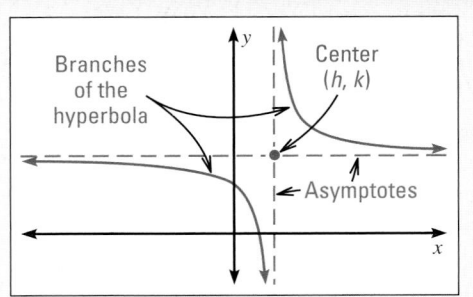

EXAMPLE 5 *Graphing a Rational Function*

Sketch the graph of $y = \frac{1}{x} + 2$.

SOLUTION Think of the function as $y = \frac{1}{x - 0} + 2$. You can see that the center is $(0, 2)$. The asymptotes can be drawn as dashed lines through the center. Make a table of values. Then plot the points and connect them with two smooth branches.

x	y
−4	1.75
−2	1.5
−1	1
−0.5	0
0	undefined
0.5	4
1	3
2	2.5
4	2.25

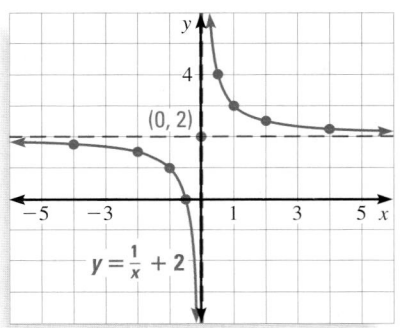

If you have drawn your graph correctly, it should be symmetric about the center (h, k). For example, the points $(0.5, 4)$ and $(−0.5, 0)$ are the same distance from the center $(0, 2)$, but in opposite directions.

Graphing a Rational Function When h is Negative

Sketch the graph of $y = \dfrac{-1}{x+2} + 1$. Describe the domain.

SOLUTION

For this equation, $x - h = x + 2$, so $h = -2$. The graph is a hyperbola with center at $(-2, 1)$. Plot this point and draw a horizontal and a vertical asymptote through it. Then make a table of values, plot the points, and connect them with two smooth branches.

x	y
-6	1.25
-4	1.5
-3	2
-2.5	3
-2	undefined
-1.5	-1
-1	0
0	0.5
2	0.75

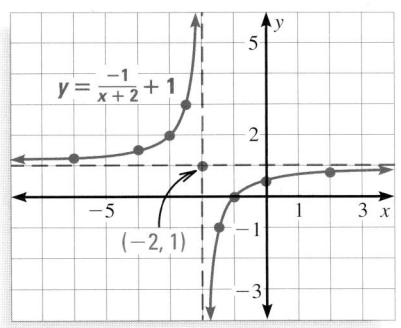

The domain is all real numbers except $x = -2$.

Rewriting before Graphing

Sketch the graph of $y = \dfrac{2x+1}{x+2}$.

SOLUTION   Begin by using long division to rewrite the rational function.

$$x + 2 \overline{)\begin{array}{r} 2 \\ 2x + 1 \\ \underline{2x + 4} \\ -3 \end{array}}$$

$$y = 2 + \frac{-3}{x+2}, \text{ or } y = \frac{-3}{x+2} + 2$$

The graph is a hyperbola with center at $(-2, 2)$. Plot this point and draw a horizontal and a vertical asymptote through it. Make a table of values, plot the points, and connect them with two smooth branches.

When making a table of values, include values of x that are less than h and values of x that are greater than h.

GUIDED PRACTICE

Vocabulary Check ✓   **1.** Describe the shape of a hyperbola. What is an asymptote of a hyperbola?

Concept Check ✓   **In Exercises 2–4, find the least common denominator.**

2. $\dfrac{1}{x}, \dfrac{x}{3}, \dfrac{2}{3x}$

3. $\dfrac{3}{4x}, \dfrac{1}{6x^2}, \dfrac{1}{8x^2}$

4. $\dfrac{1}{x^2 + 6x + 9}, \dfrac{1}{x + 3}$

5. Which of the equations in Exercises 6–11 can you solve using cross multiplying? Explain your answer.

Skill Check ✓   **Solve the equation. Remember to check for extraneous solutions.**

6. $\dfrac{3}{x} = \dfrac{x}{12}$

7. $\dfrac{-4x}{x + 1} = \dfrac{2}{x - 2}$

8. $\dfrac{x}{6} + \dfrac{15}{x} = \dfrac{5}{6}$

9. $\dfrac{4}{x^2 - 2x} = \dfrac{4}{3x - 6}$

10. $\dfrac{4}{x(x + 1)} = \dfrac{3}{x}$

11. $\dfrac{3}{x + 4} + \dfrac{4}{x} = \dfrac{-5}{x^2 + 4x}$

Find the center of the hyperbola. Draw the asymptotes and sketch the graph.

12. $y = \dfrac{4}{x + 5} - 3$

13. $y = \dfrac{2}{x - 2} + 3$

PRACTICE AND APPLICATIONS

STUDENT HELP

↳ **Extra Practice**
to help you master
skills is on p. 807.

CROSS MULTIPLYING Solve the equation by cross multiplying.

14. $\dfrac{x}{5} = \dfrac{7}{3}$

15. $\dfrac{x}{10} = \dfrac{14}{5}$

16. $\dfrac{4}{x} = \dfrac{12}{5(x + 2)}$

17. $\dfrac{5}{x + 4} = \dfrac{5}{3(x + 1)}$

18. $\dfrac{6}{x + 2} = \dfrac{x}{4}$

19. $\dfrac{7}{x + 1} = \dfrac{5}{x - 3}$

MULTIPLYING BY THE LCD Solve the equation by multiplying each side by the least common denominator.

20. $\dfrac{56}{x} = \dfrac{9 - x}{2}$

21. $\dfrac{x}{x + 9} = \dfrac{9}{x + 9} + 2$

22. $\dfrac{7}{3x - 12} - \dfrac{1}{x - 4} = \dfrac{2}{3}$

23. $\dfrac{1}{x - 4} + \dfrac{1}{x + 4} = \dfrac{22}{x^2 - 16}$

24. $\dfrac{1}{x - 4} + 1 = -\dfrac{7}{x^2 + x - 20}$

25. $2 + \dfrac{8}{x - 5} = \dfrac{x + 5}{x^2 - 25}$

CHOOSING A METHOD Solve the equation.

26. $\dfrac{1}{4} + \dfrac{4}{x} = \dfrac{1}{x}$

27. $\dfrac{-3x}{x + 1} = \dfrac{-2}{x - 1}$

28. $\dfrac{1}{5} - \dfrac{2}{5x} = \dfrac{1}{x}$

STUDENT HELP

↳ **HOMEWORK HELP**
Example 1: Exs. 14–19,
         26–38
Example 2: Exs. 20–38
Example 3: Exs. 20–38
Example 4: Exs. 51, 52
Example 5: Exs. 39–50
Example 6: Exs. 39–50
Example 7: Exs. 39–50

29. $\dfrac{x}{9} - \dfrac{8}{x} = \dfrac{1}{9}$

30. $\dfrac{x + 42}{x} = x$

31. $\dfrac{2}{x} - \dfrac{x}{8} = \dfrac{3}{4}$

32. $\dfrac{-3}{x + 7} = \dfrac{2}{x + 2}$

33. $\dfrac{2}{x + 3} + \dfrac{1}{x} = \dfrac{4}{3x}$

34. $\dfrac{10}{x + 3} - \dfrac{3}{5} = \dfrac{10x + 1}{3x + 9}$

35. $\dfrac{x + 3}{x - 5} = \dfrac{56 - 3x}{x^2 - 13x + 40}$

36. $\dfrac{8}{x + 4} + 1 = \dfrac{5x}{x^2 - 2x - 24}$

37. $\dfrac{x}{x - 11} - 1 = \dfrac{22}{x^2 - 5x - 66}$

38. $\dfrac{2x}{x + 3} - \dfrac{x}{x + 7} = \dfrac{x^2 - 1}{x^2 + 10x + 21}$

MATCHING GRAPHS Match the function with its graph.

A.   **B.**   **C.**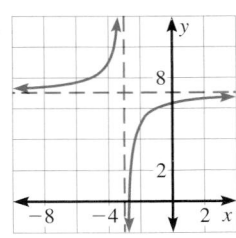

39. $y = -\dfrac{1}{x+7} - 1$ **40.** $y = \dfrac{-2}{x+3} + 7$ **41.** $y = \dfrac{4}{x}$

GRAPHING In Exercises 42–50, graph the function. Describe the domain.

42. $y = \dfrac{1}{x} + 4$ **43.** $y = \dfrac{1}{x-3} - 8$ **44.** $y = \dfrac{2}{x-4} + 6$

45. $y = -\dfrac{3}{x+1} + 8$ **46.** $y = \dfrac{6}{x+9} - 7$ **47.** $y = \dfrac{3x+11}{x+3}$

48. $y = \dfrac{-2x+11}{x-5}$ **49.** $y = \dfrac{9x-6}{x-1}$ **50.** $y = \dfrac{-5x+19}{x-3}$

51. 🌐 **BATTING AVERAGE** After 50 times at bat, a major league baseball player has a batting average of 0.160. How many consecutive hits must the player get to raise his batting average to 0.250?

52. 🌐 **TEST AVERAGES** You have taken 3 tests and have an average of 72 points. If you score 100 points on each of the rest of your tests, how many more tests do you need to take to raise your average to 88 points?

🌐 **FUNDRAISING** In Exercises 53 and 54, a library has received a single large contribution of $5000. A walkathon is also being held in which each sponsor will contribute $10. Let x represent the number of sponsors.

53. Write a function that represents the average contribution per person, including the single large contributor. Sketch the graph of the function.

54. Explain how such averages could be used to misrepresent actual contributions.

🌐 **ORIGAMI CRANES** In Exercises 55–58, you investigate how long it would take you and a friend to fold 1000 origami cranes. You take 2 minutes to fold 1 crane. Let x represent the number of minutes it might take a friend to fold 1 crane.

55. Working alone, you would take 2000 minutes to fold 1000 cranes, so your work rate is $\dfrac{1}{2000}$ of the job per minute. Find your work rate per hour.

56. The expression $\dfrac{60}{1000x}$ is your friend's work rate per hour. Explain why.

57. Write an expression for the combined work rate per hour of you and your friend (the part of the job completed in 1 hour if you both work together).

58. Suppose that together you could complete 1000 cranes in 20 hours. Your combined work rate per hour would be $\dfrac{1}{20}$. To find the time your friend takes to fold 1 crane, set the expression in Exercise 57 equal to $\dfrac{1}{20}$ and solve for x.

INVERSE VARIATION AND RATIONAL FUNCTIONS In Exercises 59 and 60, you will compare the types of graphs in 11.3 with those in this lesson.

59. Graph $f(x) = \dfrac{6}{x}$ and $f(x) = \dfrac{6}{x-2} + 1$ in the same coordinate plane.

60. *Writing* How are the two graphs in Exercise 59 related? Do you think this relationship will hold for any set of functions $f(x) = \dfrac{a}{x-h} + k$ and $f(x) = \dfrac{a}{x}$? Explain.

61. 🖩 **CHANGING CONSTANTS** Use a graphing calculator to graph $f(x) = \dfrac{a}{x}$ for at least ten values of a. Include positive, negative, and non-integer values. How does changing the value of a seem to affect the appearance of the graph?

Test Preparation

62. **MULTIPLE CHOICE** What is the solution of the equation $\dfrac{9}{x+5} = \dfrac{7}{x-5}$?

    Ⓐ 5   Ⓑ 8   Ⓒ 20   Ⓓ 40   Ⓔ 80

63. **MULTIPLE CHOICE** Choose the graph of the function $y = \dfrac{4}{x-2} + 1$.

Ⓐ   Ⓑ   Ⓒ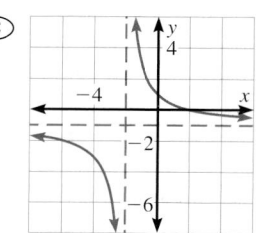

    Ⓓ None of the above

★ **Challenge**

RATIONAL FUNCTIONS In Exercises 64–67, you will look for a pattern.

64. Copy and complete the table. Round your answers to the nearest hundredth.

x	0	20	40	60	80	100
$\dfrac{x^2+6}{x+2}$	?	?	?	?	?	?
$x-2$	?	?	?	?	?	?
$\dfrac{10}{x+2}$	?	?	?	?	?	?

65. What happens to the values of $\dfrac{x^2+6}{x+2}$, $(x-2)$, and $\dfrac{10}{x+2}$ as x increases?

66. Which is the graph of $y = x - 2$? of $y = \dfrac{x^2+6}{x+2}$?

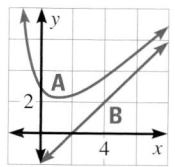

67. **CRITICAL THINKING** Explain the relationship between the two graphs in Exercise 66. Use the table in Exercise 64 to help you.

Exs. 66 and 67

EXTRA CHALLENGE
➤ www.mcdougallittell.com

MIXED REVIEW

FUNCTION VALUES Evaluate the function for $x = 0, 1, 2, 3$, and 4.
(Review 4.8 for 12.1)

68. $f(x) = 4x$ **69.** $f(x) = -x + 9$ **70.** $f(x) = 3x + 1$

71. $f(x) = -x^2$ **72.** $f(x) = x^2 - 1$ **73.** $f(x) = \dfrac{x^2}{2}$

EVALUATING EXPRESSIONS Evaluate the expression. (Review 8.1, 8.2)

74. $2^4 \cdot 2^3$ **75.** $6^3 \cdot 6^{-1}$ **76.** $\left(3^3\right)^2$ **77.** $\left(-4^{-2}\right)^{-1}$

RADICAL EXPRESSIONS Simplify the radical expression. (Review 9.2 for 12.1)

78. $\sqrt{50}$ **79.** $\sqrt{72}$ **80.** $\dfrac{1}{4}\sqrt{112}$ **81.** $\dfrac{1}{2}\sqrt{52}$

82. $\dfrac{1}{4}\sqrt{64}$ **83.** $\sqrt{256}$ **84.** $\dfrac{1}{5}\sqrt{625}$ **85.** $\sqrt{396}$

86. 🌐 **ACCOUNT BALANCE** A principal of $500 is deposited in an account that pays 4% interest compounded yearly. Find the balance after 6 years. (Review 8.5)

QUIZ 3

Self-Test for Lessons 11.7 and 11.8

Divide. (Lesson 11.7)

1. $(x^2 - 8) \div (6x)$ **2.** $\left(6a^3 + 5a^2\right) \div \left(10a^2\right)$

3. $(x^2 + 16) \div (x + 4)$ **4.** $(2y^2 + 8y - 5) \div (2y - 5)$

5. $\left(8 + 4z + z^2\right) \div (3z - 6)$ **6.** $(12x^2 + 17x - 5) \div (3x + 2)$

Solve the equation. (Lesson 11.8)

7. $\dfrac{1}{2} + \dfrac{2}{t} = \dfrac{1}{t}$ **8.** $\dfrac{3}{x} = \dfrac{9}{2(x + 2)}$

9. $\dfrac{1}{x - 5} + \dfrac{1}{x + 5} = \dfrac{x + 3}{x^2 - 25}$ **10.** $\dfrac{7}{8} - \dfrac{16}{s - 2} = \dfrac{3}{4}$

In Exercises 11–13, sketch a graph of the function. (Lesson 11.8)

11. $f(x) = \dfrac{3}{x}$ **12.** $f(x) = \dfrac{6}{x - 4}$ **13.** $f(x) = \dfrac{3}{x + 1} - 2$

14. 🌐 **TELEVISION STATIONS** The models are based on data collected by the Television Bureau of Advertising from 1988 to 1998 in the United States. Let t represent the number of years since 1988.

> **Number of UHF television stations:** $U = 14t + 505$
>
> **Total number of commercial television stations:** $T = 16t + 1048$

Use long division to find a model for the ratio of the number of UHF television stations to the total number of commercial television stations. (Lesson 11.7)

▶ ACTIVITY 11.8

Using Technology

Graphing Rational Functions

▶ **QUESTION** How can you use a graphing calculator or computer to recognize input values that are not in the domain of a rational function?

▶ **EXPLORING THE CONCEPT**

1 Simplify the right-hand side of the equation by factoring the numerator and denominator, and dividing out common factors.

$$y = \frac{4x^2 + 9x + 2}{x^2 - 4}$$

2 Graph the simplified form of the function. Your calculator may show a vertical line at $x = 2$. This is *not* part of the graph. Some calculators draw this line in an attempt to connect the two branches of the graph.

3 Graph the original function in the same viewing rectangle as the simplified form. If you have simplified correctly, the graphs will look identical.

4 To check for undefined values, press [ZOOM] and choose *Decimal*. Then use the trace feature to find *x*-values for which no *y*-values appear in the viewing rectangle. These are the undefined values of the expression.

5 Do the original function and the simplified function have the same domain? Explain.

▶ **DRAWING CONCLUSIONS**

In Exercises 1–6, simplify the right-hand side of the rational function. Then use a graphing calculator or computer to check your answer. Give the domain of the original function and of the simplified function.

1. $y = \dfrac{3x^2 - 13x - 10}{x^2 - 25}$ **2.** $y = \dfrac{x^2 - 6x + 8}{x^2 - 2x - 8}$ **3.** $y = \dfrac{2x^2 + 9x + 4}{x^2 + x - 12}$

4. $y = \dfrac{x^2 - x - 20}{x^2 - 16}$ **5.** $y = \dfrac{2x^2 - 3x - 9}{x^2 - 2x - 3}$ **6.** $y = \dfrac{2x^2 - 5x - 3}{x^2 - 8x + 15}$

7. CRITICAL THINKING Are the functions $y = \dfrac{x - 1}{(x + 3)(x - 1)}$ and $y = \dfrac{1}{x + 3}$ equivalent? Explain your reasoning.

Chapter Summary

WHAT did you learn?

Solve proportions. (11.1)

Use equations to solve percent problems. (11.2)

Use direct and inverse variation. (11.3)

Simplify rational expressions. (11.4)

Find geometric probability. (11.4)

Multiply and divide rational expressions. (11.5)

Add and subtract rational expressions. (11.6)

Divide polynomials. (11.7)

Solve rational equations. (11.8)

Graph rational functions. (11.8)

WHY did you learn it?

Estimate the number of clay figures in an archaeological dig. (p. 645)

Compare responses to a survey. (p. 654)

Relate the banking angle of a bicycle to its turning radius. (p. 658)

Use rational expressions to model real-life situations. (p. 668)

Determine the probability of a meteor strike. (p. 668)

Analyze service industry sales. (p. 674)

Calculate the time it takes to make a trip. (p. 678)

Provide alternate forms of rational expression models. (p. 688)

Study changes in batting averages. (p. 691)

Provide a visual representation of a fundraising problem. (p. 695)

How does Chapter 11 fit into the BIGGER PICTURE of algebra?

In this chapter you studied rational expressions—fractions whose numerators and denominators are polynomials. Rational expressions occur frequently in real life as proportions, percents, probabilities, and direct and inverse variations. Understanding these will enable you to model and solve a variety of real-life problems.

Techniques used in these problems include simplifying, multiplying, dividing, adding, and subtracting rational expressions. Real-life problems can also be modeled with rational equations and represented by graphing rational functions.

STUDY STRATEGY

How did you use your notes to see what you learned?

The notes you made, using the **Study Strategy** on page 642, may include the ideas shown.

Chapter 11 Notes

Preview—Ratio and Proportion:
- ratio of a to b is $\frac{a}{b}$
- Quantities are measured in the same units.

Review—Ratio and Proportion:
- an equation that states that two ratios are equal
- If $\frac{a}{b} = \frac{c}{d}$, then $\frac{b}{a} = \frac{d}{c}$.
- If $\frac{a}{b} = \frac{c}{d}$, then $ad = bc$.

Chapter Review

- proportion, p. 643
- extremes of a proportion, p. 643
- means of a proportion, p. 643
- solving a proportion, p. 643
- extraneous solution, p. 644
- base number of a percent equation, p. 649
- inverse variation, p. 656

- constant of variation, p. 656
- rational number, p. 664
- rational expression, p. 664
- simplified rational expression, p. 664
- geometric probability, p. 666
- least common denominator, p. 677
- polynomial long division, p. 685

- rational equation, p. 690
- rational function, p. 692
- hyperbola, p. 692
- center of a hyperbola, p. 692
- asymptote, p. 692

Examples on pp. 643–645

11.1 RATIO AND PROPORTION

EXAMPLE Solve the proportion $\frac{12}{7} = \frac{5}{x}$.

$\frac{12}{7} = \frac{5}{x}$ Write original proportion.

$12 \cdot x = 7 \cdot 5$ Use cross product property.

$x = \frac{35}{12}$ Divide each side by 12.

Solve the proportion. Check for extraneous solutions.

1. $\frac{x}{2} = \frac{4}{7}$

2. $\frac{7}{10} = \frac{9+x}{x}$

3. $\frac{x^2 - 16}{x + 4} = \frac{x - 4}{3}$

4. $\frac{5}{x + 6} = \frac{x - 6}{x}$

Examples on pp. 649–652

11.2 PERCENTS

EXAMPLES

$20 is 40% of what amount of money?

a is p percent of b

$20 = 0.4 b$

$\frac{20}{0.4} = b$

$50 = b$

▶ $20 is 40% of $50.

$75 is what percent of $60?

a is p percent of b

$75 = p (60)$

$\frac{75}{60} = p$

$1.25 = p$, or $p = 125\%$

▶ $75 is 125% of $60.

Solve the percent problem.

5. How much is 80% of $95?

6. 24 inches is 250% of what length?

7. $90 is 75% of what amount of money?

8. 35 feet is what percent of 175 feet?

DIRECT AND INVERSE VARIATION

Examples on
pp. 656–658

EXAMPLES When x is 5, y is 25. Write an equation that relates x and y in each case.

x and y vary directly:

$$\frac{y}{x} = k$$

$$\frac{25}{5} = k$$

$$5 = k$$

An equation that relates x and y is
$\frac{y}{x} = 5$, or $y = 5x$.

x and y vary inversely:

$$xy = k$$

$$(5)(25) = k$$

$$125 = k$$

An equation that relates x and y is
$xy = 125$, or $y = \frac{125}{x}$.

When x is 17, y is 51. Find an equation that relates x and y in each case.

9. x and y vary directly

10. x and y vary inversely

SIMPLIFYING RATIONAL EXPRESSIONS

Examples on
pp. 664–666

EXAMPLE To simplify a rational expression, look for common factors.

$$\frac{2x^2 + 3x - 2}{2x^2 + 5x + 2} = \frac{(2x - 1)(x + 2)}{(2x + 1)(x + 2)}$$

Factor numerator and denominator.
Divide out common factor ($x + 2$).

$$= \frac{2x - 1}{2x + 1}$$

Simplified form

Simplify the expression.

11. $\dfrac{3x}{9x^2 + 3}$

12. $\dfrac{6x^2}{12x^4 + 18x^2}$

13. $\dfrac{7x^3 - 21x}{-14x^2}$

14. $\dfrac{5x^2 + 21x + 4}{25x + 100}$

MULTIPLYING AND DIVIDING RATIONAL EXPRESSIONS

Examples on
pp. 670–672

EXAMPLE To divide rational expressions, multiply by the reciprocal.

$$\frac{6x^2 + x - 1}{2x + 1} \div (9x - 3) = \frac{6x^2 + x - 1}{2x + 1} \cdot \frac{1}{9x - 3}$$

Multiply by reciprocal.

$$= \frac{(2x + 1)(3x - 1)}{(2x + 1) \cdot 3(3x - 1)}$$

Multiply numerators and denominators.
Factor and divide out common factors.

$$= \frac{1}{3}$$

Simplified form

Simplify the expression.

15. $\dfrac{12x^2}{5x^3} \cdot \dfrac{25x^4}{3x}$

16. $\dfrac{9x^3}{x^3 - x^2} \div \dfrac{x - 8}{x^2 - 9x + 8}$

17. $\dfrac{x^2 + 3x + 2}{x^2 + 7x + 12} \div \dfrac{x^2 + 5x + 4}{x^2 + 5x + 6}$

ADDING AND SUBTRACTING RATIONAL EXPRESSIONS

Examples on pp. 676–678

EXAMPLE Simplify $\dfrac{x}{x-5} - \dfrac{2}{x+2}$. The LCD is $(x-5)(x+2)$.

$$\dfrac{x(x+2)}{(x-5)(x+2)} - \dfrac{2(x-5)}{(x-5)(x+2)} \qquad \text{Rewrite fractions using LCD.}$$

$$= \dfrac{x^2+2x}{(x-5)(x+2)} - \dfrac{2x-10}{(x-5)(x+2)} \qquad \text{Simplify numerators.}$$

$$= \dfrac{(x^2+2x)-(2x-10)}{(x-5)(x+2)} = \dfrac{x^2+10}{(x-5)(x+2)} \qquad \text{Subtract fractions and simplify.}$$

Simplify the expression.

18. $\dfrac{6x}{x+4} - \dfrac{5x-4}{x+4}$ **19.** $\dfrac{2x+1}{8x} - \dfrac{x}{12x}$ **20.** $\dfrac{x+3}{3x-1} + \dfrac{4}{x-3}$ **21.** $\dfrac{-5x-10}{x^2-4} + \dfrac{4x}{x-2}$

DIVIDING POLYNOMIALS

Examples on pp. 684–686

EXAMPLES There are two cases to look for when you divide polynomials.

CASE 1: Monomial divisor

To divide a polynomial by a monomial, divide each term by the monomial.

CASE 2: Binomial divisor

To divide a polynomial by a binomial, factor out common factors if possible. If not, use long division.

Divide.

22. Divide $3x^2 - x - 1$ by $x - 2$.

23. Divide $6x^2 - 36x + 5$ by $6x$.

24. Divide $4x^2 + 6x - 5$ by $2x - 1$.

25. Divide $5x^2 + 13x - 6$ by $5x - 2$.

RATIONAL EQUATIONS AND FUNCTIONS

Examples on pp. 690–693

EXAMPLE Solve the equation $\dfrac{2x}{9} - \dfrac{1}{x} = \dfrac{1}{3}$. The LCD is $9x$.

$$9x \cdot \dfrac{2x}{9} - 9x \cdot \dfrac{1}{x} = 9x \cdot \dfrac{1}{3} \qquad \text{Multiply each side by } 9x.$$

$$2x^2 - 9 = 3x \qquad \text{Simplify.}$$

$$2x^2 - 3x - 9 = 0 \qquad \text{Write in standard form.}$$

$$(2x+3)(x-3) = 0 \qquad \text{Factor left side.}$$

When you set each factor equal to 0, you find that the solutions are $-\dfrac{3}{2}$ and 3.

Solve the equation.

26. $\dfrac{1}{4} - \dfrac{6}{x} = \dfrac{3}{x}$ **27.** $\dfrac{x+2}{2} = \dfrac{4}{x}$ **28.** $\dfrac{6}{x+4} + \dfrac{3}{4} = \dfrac{2x+1}{3x+12}$

Chapter Test

Solve the proportion. Check for extraneous solutions.

1. $\dfrac{6}{x} = \dfrac{17}{5}$

2. $\dfrac{x}{4} = \dfrac{x+8}{x}$

3. $\dfrac{x}{-3} = \dfrac{7}{x-10}$

4. $\dfrac{x^2-64}{x+8} = \dfrac{x-8}{2}$

Solve the percent problem.

5. What is 34% of 100 liters?

6. What is 86% of \$350?

7. 24 yards is 12% of what distance?

8. 36 T-shirts is what percent of 900 T-shirts?

**Make a table of values for $x = 1, 2, 3,$ and 4. Use the table to sketch a graph.
Decide whether x and y vary *directly* or *inversely*.**

9. $y = 4x$

10. $y = \dfrac{50}{x}$

11. $y = \dfrac{9}{2}x$

12. $y = \dfrac{15}{2x}$

Simplify the expression.

13. $\dfrac{56x^6}{4x^4}$

14. $\dfrac{5x^2 - 15x}{15x^4}$

15. $\dfrac{x^2 - x - 6}{x^2 - 4}$

16. $\dfrac{6x^2}{8x} \cdot \dfrac{-4x^3}{2x^2}$

17. $\dfrac{x+3}{x^3 - x^2 - 6x} \div \dfrac{x^2 - 9}{x^2 + x - 12}$

18. $\dfrac{x^3 + x^2}{x^2 - 16} \cdot \dfrac{x+4}{3x^4 + x^3 - 2x^2}$

19. $\dfrac{3x^2 + 6x}{4x} \div \dfrac{15}{8x^2}$

20. $\dfrac{12x - 4}{x - 1} + \dfrac{4x}{x - 1}$

21. $\dfrac{5}{2x^2} + \dfrac{4}{3x}$

22. $\dfrac{8}{5x} - \dfrac{4}{x^2}$

23. $\dfrac{4}{x+3} + \dfrac{3x}{x-2}$

24. $\dfrac{5x+1}{x-3} - \dfrac{2x}{x-1}$

Divide.

25. Divide $4x^3 - 15x^2 - 6x$ by $3x$.

26. Divide $81x^2 - 25$ by $9x - 5$.

27. Divide $2x^2 + 11x + 12$ by $x + 4$.

28. Divide $5x^2 + 4x - 7$ by $x + 2$.

Solve the equation.

29. $\dfrac{3}{4x - 9} = \dfrac{x}{3}$

30. $\dfrac{5}{9} + \dfrac{2}{9x} = \dfrac{3}{x}$

31. $\dfrac{5}{x+3} - \dfrac{3}{x-2} = \dfrac{5}{3x-6}$

Sketch a graph of the function.

32. $y = \dfrac{1}{x-4} + 3$

33. $y = 5 - \dfrac{2}{x}$

34. $y = \dfrac{x-5}{x+2}$

35. 🌐 **BAGEL SHOP** You invest \$30,000 to start a bagel shop. You can
produce bagels for \$1.20 per dozen. How many dozen must you
produce before your average cost per dozen (including your initial
investment of \$30,000) drops to \$1.80?

36. 🌐 **CARNIVAL GAME** At a carnival game, a dart is thrown at the board
shown at the right. Assume it is equally likely to land anywhere on the
board. Write a model that gives the probability that the dart will land in
the small rectangle. Evaluate the model when $x = 5$.

Chapter Standardized Test

▶ **TEST-TAKING STRATEGY** Think positively during a test. This will help keep up your confidence and enable you to focus on each question.

1. **MULTIPLE CHOICE** Which of the following is the solution of the proportion $\dfrac{4}{y+9} = \dfrac{6}{y-7}$?

   A -82 **B** -41 **C** -13

   D 7 **E** 41

2. **QUANTITATIVE COMPARISON** Solve each proportion and choose the statement below that is true about the solutions.

COLUMN A	COLUMN B
$\dfrac{3}{x-2} = \dfrac{2x+2}{x^2-4}$	$\dfrac{5}{y+12} = \dfrac{2}{y+6}$

   A The solution in column A is greater.

   B The solution in column B is greater.

   C The two solutions are equal.

   D The relationship cannot be determined from the given information.

3. **MULTIPLE CHOICE** What is 380% of 52?

   A 0.07 **B** 13.68 **C** 19.76

   D 136.84 **E** 197.6

4. **MULTIPLE CHOICE** 18.6 miles is 15% of what distance?

   A 1.24 miles   **B** 2.79 miles   **C** 105.4 miles

   D 124 miles   **E** 279 miles

5. **MULTIPLE CHOICE** There are 840 students in your school. At a pep rally for a football game, 614 students attend. What percent of the students in your school attended the pep rally?

   A about 136.8%   **B** about 78.8%

   C about 73.1%   **D** about 36.8%

   E about 26.9%

6. **MULTIPLE CHOICE** Which of the following equations models inverse variation?

   A $y = \dfrac{x}{3}$ **B** $y = 3x$ **C** $y = x + 3$

   D $xy = 3$ **E** $y = 3 - x$

7. **MULTIPLE CHOICE** The variables x and y vary inversely. When x is 9, y is 36. If x is 3, what is y?

   A 3 **B** 12 **C** 30

   D 36 **E** 108

8. **MULTIPLE CHOICE** What is the simplified form of the expression $\dfrac{x^3 - 10x^2 + 9x}{x^2 + 5x - 6}$?

   A $\dfrac{x-9}{x+6}$ **B** $\dfrac{x}{x+6}$ **C** $\dfrac{1}{x+6}$

   D $\dfrac{x(x-9)}{x+6}$ **E** $\dfrac{x}{(x-1)(x+6)}$

9. **MULTIPLE CHOICE** A coin is tossed onto the large rectangular region shown below. Assume it is equally likely to land on any point in the region. What is the probability the coin will land in the small rectangle when $x = 3$?

   A $\dfrac{1}{15}$

   B $\dfrac{3}{25}$

   C $\dfrac{1}{5}$

   D $\dfrac{2}{5}$

   E $\dfrac{25}{3}$

   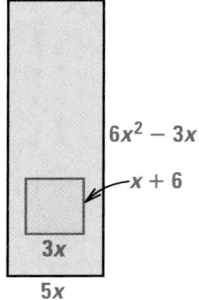

   $6x^2 - 3x$

   $x + 6$

   $3x$

   $5x$

10. **MULTIPLE CHOICE** What is the simplified form of the expression $\dfrac{9x^2}{4x} \cdot \dfrac{16x^3}{x^5}$?

    A $36x$ **B** $\dfrac{9}{x}$ **C** $\dfrac{36}{x}$

    D $36x^3$ **E** $\dfrac{64}{9x^3}$

11. **MULTIPLE CHOICE** What is the simplified form of the expression $\dfrac{x^2 - 64}{3x^2} \div (x - 8)$?

    A $\dfrac{x+8}{3x^2}$ **B** $\dfrac{x-8}{3x^2}$ **C** $\dfrac{1}{3x^2}$

    D $\dfrac{x^3 - 512}{3x}$ **E** $\dfrac{x+8}{3x^2(x-8)}$

12. MULTIPLE CHOICE Find the LCD of $\dfrac{7x}{x^2 - 9}$ and $\dfrac{3}{x^2 + x - 6}$.

(A) $(x + 3)(x - 3)$ (B) $(x^2 - 9)(x^2 + x + 6)$ (C) $(x + 3)(x - 2)$

(D) $(x + 3)(x - 3)(x - 2)$ (E) $(x - 3)(x - 2)$

13. MULTIPLE CHOICE What is the simplified form of the following expression?

$$\frac{2x + 9}{x + 5} - \frac{x - 4}{x - 2}$$

(A) $\dfrac{x^2 + 6x + 2}{(x + 5)(x - 2)}$ (B) $\dfrac{x^2 + 6x - 38}{(x + 5)(x - 2)}$ (C) $\dfrac{x^2 + 6x + 38}{x^2 - 10}$

(D) $\dfrac{x^2 + 4x + 2}{(x + 5)(x - 2)}$ (E) $\dfrac{x^2 + 4x - 38}{(x + 5)(x - 2)}$

14. MULTIPLE CHOICE What is $x^2 + 24x - 3$ divided by $x - 4$?

(A) $x + 28 + \dfrac{109}{x - 4}$ (B) $\dfrac{x + 28}{x - 4} + 109$ (C) $\dfrac{x + 28}{x - 4}$

(D) $\dfrac{x - 4}{x + 28}$ (E) $\dfrac{x - 4}{x + 28} + 109$

15. MULTIPLE CHOICE Which function represents the graph?

(A) $y = \dfrac{1}{x - 1} - 7$

(B) $y = \dfrac{1}{x + 1} - 7$

(C) $y = \dfrac{1}{x - 7} + 1$

(D) $y = \dfrac{1}{x - 1} + 7$

(E) $y = \dfrac{1}{x + 1} + 7$

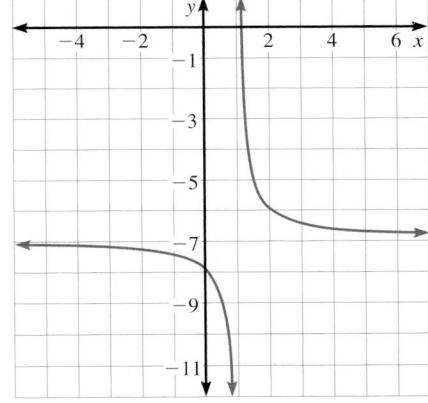

16. MULTI-STEP PROBLEM You are considering buying a new car and want to compare the yearly fuel costs for your car and for the new car. To find the yearly fuel cost you multiply the distance you travel in a year by the price per gallon and then divide by the number of miles per gallon your car averages.

You determine that you drive approximately 20,000 miles in one year and that you pay an average of $1.20 per gallon of gasoline.

Let x equal the number of miles per gallon your car averages.

a. Write an expression to represent the yearly fuel cost for your car.

b. The new car you want to buy gets five more miles to the gallon than your car. Write an expression to represent the yearly fuel cost for the new car.

c. Suppose your yearly fuel cost is $400 less if you buy the new car. Write and solve an equation to find the number of miles per gallon your old car and the new car will get.

d. What is the estimated yearly fuel cost for your old car? for your new car?

RADICALS AND CONNECTIONS TO GEOMETRY

▶ *How are passengers kept in place on an amusement park ride that spins?*

APPLICATION: Spinning Rides

*S*ome amusement park rides spin so fast that the riders "stick" to the walls of the ride. The force exerted by the wall on the rider is called *centripetal force*.

To design an amusement park ride, engineers must figure out the dimensions of the ride and how many times per minute it will spin. You'll learn to calculate the force generated by such a ride in Chapter 12.

Think & Discuss

1. Based on the numbers in the table, is "revolutions per minute" a function of "height"?

Ride name	Height (feet)	Revolutions per minute
Football Ride	34.4	15
Chaos™	36	12
Centrox	44.3	17.5
Galactica	44.3	17

2. You are designing a spinning ride that is 40 feet high. Use the information in the table to decide on a reasonable range for how many revolutions per minute the ride would make.

Learn More About It

You will calculate the centripetal force exerted on a rider in Exercises 66 and 67 on p. 726.

 APPLICATION LINK Visit www.mcdougallittell.com for more information about amusement park rides.

Study Guide

What's the chapter about?

Chapter 12 connects **radicals and geometry**. In Chapter 12 you'll learn

- how to solve radical equations and graph radical functions.
- how to apply the Pythagorean theorem.
- how to use trigonometric ratios.
- how to prove theorems by using algebraic properties.

KEY VOCABULARY

▶ **Review**
- counterexample, p. 66
- similar triangles, p. 140
- perfect square trinomial, p. 619
- extraneous solutions, p. 644

▶ **New**
- square-root function, p. 709
- completing the square, p. 730
- Pythagorean theorem, p. 738
- hypothesis, p. 739
- conclusion, p. 739

- converse, p. 739
- trigonometric ratios, p. 752
- postulate, p. 758
- theorem, p. 759
- indirect proof, p. 760

Are you ready for the chapter?

SKILL REVIEW Do these exercises to review skills that you'll apply in this chapter. See the given **reference page** if there is something you don't understand.

In Exercises 1 and 2, the two triangles are similar. Find the length of the side marked x. (Review Example 5, p. 141)

1.

2.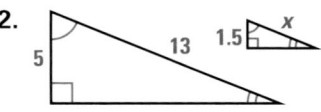

Simplify the expression. (Review Examples 1 and 2, p. 512)

3. $\sqrt{98}$ **4.** $\sqrt{140}$ **5.** $\sqrt{\dfrac{7}{4}}$ **6.** $\dfrac{\sqrt{144}}{\sqrt{16}}$

Factor the trinomial. (Review Examples 1–4, pp. 604 and 605)

7. $x^2 - 3x - 18$ **8.** $x^2 + 2x - 8$ **9.** $4x^2 + 20x + 25$

STUDENT HELP

▶ **Study Tip**
"Student Help" boxes throughout the chapter give you study tips and tell you where to look for extra help in this book and on the Internet.

Here's a study strategy!

Drawing Diagrams

Sometimes it is helpful to include a diagram or another visual when you take notes. Diagrams and tables can also be used to organize related ideas and terms.

12.1

Functions Involving Square Roots

What you should learn

GOAL ① Evaluate and graph a function involving square roots.

GOAL ② Use functions involving square roots to model **real-life** problems, such as an investigation of skid marks in **Ex. 60**.

Why you should learn it

▼ To solve **real-life** problems such as estimating a dinosaur's walking speed in **Example 4**.

GOAL ① **GRAPHING FUNCTIONS INVOLVING SQUARE ROOTS**

● ACTIVITY

Developing Concepts

Investigating the Square Root Function

① Copy the table of values for the function $y = \sqrt{x}$. Use a calculator or the Table of Square Roots on page 811 to complete your table. Round to the nearest tenth. Plot the points. Graph the function.

x	0	1	2	3	4	5
y	?	?	?	?	?	?

② What are the domain and the range of the function?

③ Why are negative values of x not included in the domain?

The **square root function** is defined by the equation $y = \sqrt{x}$. The domain is all nonnegative numbers and the range is all nonnegative numbers. Understanding this function will help you work with other functions involving square roots.

EXAMPLE 1 *Graphing $y = a\sqrt{x}$*

Sketch the graph of $y = 2\sqrt{x}$. Give the domain and the range.

SOLUTION

The radicand of a square root is always nonnegative, so the domain is the set of all nonnegative numbers. Make a table of values. Then plot the points and connect them with a smooth curve.

x	y
0	$y = 2\sqrt{0} = 0$
1	$y = 2\sqrt{1} = 2$
2	$y = 2\sqrt{2} \approx 2.8$
3	$y = 2\sqrt{3} \approx 3.5$
4	$y = 2\sqrt{4} = 4$
5	$y = 2\sqrt{5} \approx 4.5$

Both the domain and the range are all the nonnegative numbers.

STUDENT HELP

HOMEWORK HELP
Visit our Web site
www.mcdougallittell.com
for extra examples.

It is a good idea to find the domain of a function *before* you make a table of values. This will help you choose values of x for the table.

EXAMPLE 2 *Graphing $y = \sqrt{x} + k$*

Find the domain and the range of $y = \sqrt{x} + 1$. Then sketch its graph.

SOLUTION

The domain is the set of all nonnegative numbers. The range is the set of all numbers that are greater than or equal to 1. Make a table of values, plot the points, and connect them with a smooth curve.

x	y
0	$y = \sqrt{0} + 1 = 1$
1	$y = \sqrt{1} + 1 = 2$
2	$y = \sqrt{2} + 1 \approx 2.4$
3	$y = \sqrt{3} + 1 \approx 2.7$
4	$y = \sqrt{4} + 1 = 3$
5	$y = \sqrt{5} + 1 \approx 3.2$

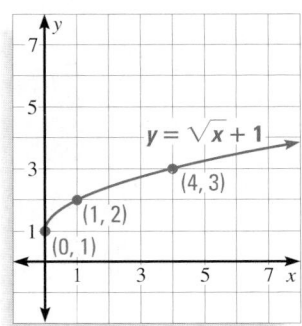

EXAMPLE 3 *Graphing $y = \sqrt{x - h}$*

Find the domain and the range of $y = \sqrt{x - 3}$. Then sketch its graph.

SOLUTION

To find the domain, find the values of x for which the radicand is nonnegative.

$x - 3 \geq 0$ **Write an inequality for the domain.**

$x \geq 3$ **Add 3 to each side.**

The domain is the set of all numbers that are greater than or equal to 3. The range is the set of all nonnegative numbers. Make a table of values, plot the points, and connect them with a smooth curve.

STUDENT HELP

→ **Study Tip**
When you make a table
of values to sketch the
graph of a function
involving square roots,
choose several values to
see the pattern of the
curve.

x	y
3	$y = \sqrt{3 - 3} = 0$
4	$y = \sqrt{4 - 3} = 1$
5	$y = \sqrt{5 - 3} \approx 1.4$
6	$y = \sqrt{6 - 3} \approx 1.7$
7	$y = \sqrt{7 - 3} = 2$
8	$y = \sqrt{8 - 3} \approx 2.2$

EXAMPLE 4 *Using a Model Involving a Square Root*

DINOSAURS In a natural history museum you see leg bones for two species of dinosaurs and want to know how fast they walked. The maximum walking speed S (in feet per second) of an animal can be modeled by the equation below where $g = 32$ ft/sec^2 and L is the length (in feet) of the animal's leg. ▶ Source: *Discover*

Walking speed model: $S = \sqrt{gL}$

PALEONTOLOGIST
A paleontologist studies fossils of animals and plants to better understand the history of life on Earth.

CAREER LINK
www.mcdougallittell.com

a. Use unit analysis to check the units of the model.

b. Sketch the graph of the model.

c. For one dinosaur the length of the leg is 1 foot. For the other dinosaur the length of the leg is 4 feet. Could the taller dinosaur walk four times as fast as the shorter dinosaur?

SOLUTION

a. UNIT ANALYSIS Substitute the units in the model.

$$\sqrt{\frac{ft}{sec^2} \cdot ft} = \sqrt{\frac{ft^2}{sec^2}} = \frac{ft}{sec}$$

b. To sketch the graph of $S = \sqrt{32L}$, make a table of values, plot the points, and draw a smooth curve through the points.

L	S
0	$S = \sqrt{32 \cdot 0} = 0$
1	$S = \sqrt{32 \cdot 1} \approx 5.66$
2	$S = \sqrt{32 \cdot 2} = 8$
3	$S = \sqrt{32 \cdot 3} \approx 9.80$
4	$S = \sqrt{32 \cdot 4} \approx 11.31$
5	$S = \sqrt{32 \cdot 5} \approx 12.65$
6	$S = \sqrt{32 \cdot 6} \approx 13.86$
7	$S = \sqrt{32 \cdot 7} \approx 14.97$
8	$S = \sqrt{32 \cdot 8} = 16$

c. Substitute 1 foot and 4 feet into the model.

When L = 1 foot: $S = \sqrt{32 \cdot 1} \approx 5.66$ feet/second

When L = 4 feet: $S = \sqrt{32 \cdot 4} \approx 11.31$ feet/second

▶ The taller dinosaur could walk about twice as fast as the shorter dinosaur, not four times as fast.

GUIDED PRACTICE

Vocabulary Check ✓ 1. Describe the square root function.

Concept Check ✓ 2. Does the domain of $y = \sqrt{x} + 3$ include negative values of x? Explain.

Skill Check ✓ **Evaluate the function for $x = 0, 1, 2, 3,$ and 4. Round your answer to the nearest tenth.**

3. $y = 4\sqrt{x}$ 4. $y = \frac{1}{2}\sqrt{x}$ 5. $y = 3\sqrt{x} + 4$

6. $y = 6\sqrt{x} - 3$ 7. $y = \sqrt{x+2}$ 8. $y = \sqrt{4x-1}$

Find the domain and the range of the function.

9. $y = 3\sqrt{x}$ 10. $y = \sqrt{x}$ 11. $y = \sqrt{x} - 10$

12. $y = \sqrt{x} + 6$ 13. $y = \sqrt{x+5}$ 14. $y = \sqrt{x-10}$

Sketch the graph of the function.

15. $y = 3\sqrt{x}$ 16. $y = \sqrt{x} + 5$ 17. $y = 3\sqrt{x+1}$

🔥 **FIRE HOSES** For a fire hose with a nozzle that has a diameter of 2 inches, the flow rate f (in gallons per minute) can be modeled by $f = 120\sqrt{p}$ where p is the nozzle pressure in pounds per square inch.

18. Sketch a graph of the model.

19. If the flow rate is 1200 gallons per minute, what is the nozzle pressure?

PRACTICE AND APPLICATIONS

STUDENT HELP

▶ **Extra Practice**
to help you master
skills is on p. 808.

EVALUATING FUNCTIONS Evaluate the function for the given value of x. Round your answer to the nearest tenth.

20. $y = 3\sqrt{x}$; 9 21. $y = \frac{1}{2}\sqrt{x} - 1$; 16

22. $y = \sqrt{x-7}$; 15 23. $y = \sqrt{3x-5}$; 7

24. $y = 6\sqrt{15-x}$; -1 25. $y = \sqrt{21-2x}$; -2

26. $y = \sqrt{\frac{x}{2} - 2}$; 22 27. $y = \sqrt{8x^2 + \frac{3}{2}}$; $\frac{1}{4}$

28. $y = \sqrt{\frac{2x}{3} + 5}$; 6 29. $y = \sqrt{36x - 2}$; $\frac{1}{2}$

FINDING THE DOMAIN Find the domain of the function.

STUDENT HELP

▶ **HOMEWORK HELP**
Example 1: Exs. 20–56
Example 2: Exs. 20–56
Example 3: Exs. 20–56
Example 4: Exs. 57, 58,
61, 62

30. $y = 6\sqrt{x}$ 31. $y = \sqrt{x - 17}$ 32. $y = \sqrt{3x - 10}$

33. $y = \sqrt{x + 5}$ 34. $y = 4 + \sqrt{x}$ 35. $y = \sqrt{x} - 3$

36. $y = 5 - \sqrt{x}$ 37. $y = 4\sqrt{x}$ 38. $y = 2\sqrt{4x}$

39. $y = 0.2\sqrt{x}$ 40. $y = x\sqrt{x}$ 41. $y = \sqrt{x + 9}$

42. $y = 8\sqrt{\frac{5}{2}x}$ 43. $y = \frac{\sqrt{x}}{5}$ 44. $y = \frac{\sqrt{4 - x}}{x}$

GRAPHING FUNCTIONS Find the domain and the range of the function. Then sketch the graph of the function.

45. $y = 7\sqrt{x}$ **46.** $y = 4\sqrt{x}$ **47.** $y = 5\sqrt{x}$

48. $y = \sqrt{x} - 2$ **49.** $y = \sqrt{x} + 4$ **50.** $y = \sqrt{x} - 3$

51. $y = \sqrt{x - 4}$ **52.** $y = \sqrt{x + 1}$ **53.** $y = \sqrt{x - 6}$

54. $y = 2\sqrt{4x + 10}$ **55.** $y = \sqrt{2x + 5}$ **56.** $y = x\sqrt{8x}$

57. 🌐 **MEDICINE** A doctor may use a person's body surface area (*BSA*) as an index to prescribe the correct amount of medicine. You can use the model below to approximate a person's *BSA* (in square meters) where *h* represents height (in inches) and *w* represents weight (in pounds.)

$$BSA = \sqrt{\frac{h \cdot w}{3131}}$$

Find the *BSA* of a person who is 5 feet 2 inches tall and weighs 100 pounds. Round your answer to the nearest hundredth.

58. 🌐 **PENDULUMS** The period *T* (in seconds) of a pendulum is the time it takes for the pendulum to swing back and forth. The period is related to the length *L* (in inches) of the pendulum by the model $T = 2\pi\sqrt{\dfrac{L}{384}}$. Find the length of a pendulum with a period of eight seconds. Give your answer to the nearest tenth.

59. **GEOMETRY** ▸ **CONNECTION** The lateral surface area *S* of a cone with a radius of 14 centimeters can be found using the formula

$$S = \pi \cdot 14\sqrt{14^2 + h^2}$$

where *h* is the height (in centimeters) of the cone.

a. Use unit analysis to check the units of the formula.

b. Sketch the graph of the formula.

c. Find the lateral surface area of a cone with a height of 30 centimeters.

h

— 14 cm

60. 🌐 **INVESTIGATING ACCIDENTS** An accident reconstructionist is responsible for finding how fast cars were going before an accident. To do this, a reconstructionist uses the model below where *S* is the speed of the car in miles per hour, *d* is the length of the tires' skid marks in feet, and *f* is the coefficient of friction for the road.

Car speed model: $S = \sqrt{30df}$

a. In an accident, a car makes skid marks 74 feet long. The coefficient of friction is 0.5. A witness says that the driver was traveling faster than the speed limit of 45 miles per hour. Can the witness's statement be correct? Explain your reasoning.

b. How long would the skid marks have to be in order to know that the car was traveling faster than 45 miles per hour?

COLLECTING DATA In Exercises 61 and 62, use the information from Example 4 on page 711.

61. Measure the length of your leg and calculate your maximum walking speed.

62. Mark a distance of 80 feet. Time yourself to see how long it takes you to walk the distance. Compare your speed from Exercise 61 with your actual speed. What did you find?

Test Preparation

63. **MULTI-STEP PROBLEM** The relationship between a roller coaster's velocity v (in feet per second) at the bottom of a drop and the height of the drop h (in feet) can be modeled by the formula $v = \sqrt{2gh}$ where g represents acceleration due to gravity.

   a. Use the fact that $g = 32$ ft/sec^2 to show that $v = \sqrt{2gh}$ can be simplified to $v = 8\sqrt{h}$.

   b. Sketch the graph of $v = 8\sqrt{h}$.

   c. *Writing* Use the formula or the graph to explain why doubling the height of a drop does not double the velocity of a roller coaster.

★ **Challenge**

64. **CRITICAL THINKING** Find the domain of $y = \dfrac{3}{\sqrt{x} - 2}$.

MIXED REVIEW

SIMPLIFYING RADICAL EXPRESSIONS Simplify the radical expression. (Review 9.2 for 12.2)

65. $\sqrt{24}$ 66. $\sqrt{60}$ 67. $\sqrt{175}$ 68. $\sqrt{9900}$

69. $\sqrt{\dfrac{20}{25}}$ 70. $\dfrac{1}{2}\sqrt{80}$ 71. $\dfrac{3\sqrt{7}}{\sqrt{9}}$ 72. $4\sqrt{\dfrac{11}{16}}$

SOLVING QUADRATIC EQUATIONS Solve the equation. (Review 9.5)

73. $x^2 + 4x - 8 = 0$ 74. $x^2 - 2x - 4 = 0$ 75. $x^2 - 6x + 1 = 0$

76. $x^2 + 3x - 10 = 0$ 77. $2x^2 + x = 3$ 78. $4x^2 - 6x + 1 = 0$

MULTIPLYING EXPRESSIONS Find the product. (Review 10.2 for 12.2)

79. $(x - 2)(x + 11)$ 80. $(x + 4)(3x - 7)$ 81. $(2x - 3)(5x - 9)$

82. $(x - 5)(x - 4)$ 83. $(6x + 2)(x^2 - x - 1)$ 84. $(2x - 1)(x^2 + x + 1)$

SIMPLIFYING EXPRESSIONS Simplify the expression. (Review 11.5)

85. $\dfrac{8x}{3} \cdot \dfrac{1}{x}$ 86. $\dfrac{8x^2}{3} \cdot \dfrac{9}{16x}$ 87. $\dfrac{x}{x + 6} \div \dfrac{x + 1}{x + 6}$

88. 🌐 **MOUNT RUSHMORE** Four American Presidents' faces are carved on Mount Rushmore: Washington, Jefferson, Roosevelt, and Lincoln. Before the faces were carved on the cliff, scale models were made. The ratio of the faces on the cliff to the models was 12 to 1. If the scale model of President Washington's face was 5 feet tall, how tall is his face on Mount Rushmore? (Review 11.1)

●ACTIVITY 12.1

Using Technology

Functions Involving Square Roots

A graphing calculator or a computer can be used to graph functions involving square roots. To graph such a function use the [√] key.

▶ **EXPLORING THE CONCEPT**

❶ Use a graphing calculator to graph $y = a\sqrt{x}$ for $a = 1$.

❷ Repeat **Step 1** for $a = 2, 3,$ and 4. Show all four graphs on the same screen.

❸ Describe the effect that a has on the graph of $y = a\sqrt{x}$.

▶ **EXPLORING THE CONCEPT**

❹ Use a graphing calculator to graph $y = a\sqrt{x}$ for $a = -1$ and $a = 1$.

❺ Graph $y = a\sqrt{x}$ for $a = -4$ and $a = 4$.

❻ Graph $y = a\sqrt{x}$ for $a = -9$ and $a = 9$.

❼ Describe the effect that a has on the graph of $y = a\sqrt{x}$ when a is negative.

STUDENT HELP

INTERNET **KEYSTROKE HELP**

See keystrokes for several models of calculators at www.mcdougallittell.com

▶ **DRAWING CONCLUSIONS**

1. Use a graphing calculator to graph the function $y = \sqrt{x} + k$ for $k = -3, -1, 2,$ and 5. Show all four graphs on the same screen. Then describe the effect that k has on the graph of $y = \sqrt{x} + k$.

2. Use a graphing calculator to graph the function $y = \sqrt{x + k}$ for $k = -3, -1, 2,$ and 5. You may need to use parentheses around the radicand. Show all four graphs on the same screen. Then describe the effect that k has on the graph of $y = \sqrt{x + k}$.

EXTENDING THE CONCEPT **Find the value of *a* or *k* so that the graph of the function matches the given graph.**

3. $y = a\sqrt{x}$

4. $y = \sqrt{x + k}$

5. $y = \sqrt{x} + k$

12.2

Operations with Radical Expressions

What you should learn

GOAL 1 Add, subtract, multiply, and divide radical expressions.

GOAL 2 Use radical expressions in **real-life** situations, as in finding the speed of a pole-vaulter in **Ex. 58**.

Why you should learn it

▼ To solve **real-life** problems such as finding distances to the horizon from a schooner in **Example 5**.

GOAL 1 USING RADICAL OPERATIONS

You can use the distributive property to simplify sums and differences of radical expressions when the expressions have the same radicand.

Sum: $\sqrt{2} + 3\sqrt{2} = (1 + 3)\sqrt{2} = 4\sqrt{2}$

Difference: $\sqrt{2} - 3\sqrt{2} = (1 - 3)\sqrt{2} = -2\sqrt{2}$

In part (b) of Example 1, the first step is to remove a perfect square factor from under the radical sign, as you learned on page 512.

EXAMPLE 1 *Adding and Subtracting Radicals*

a. $2\sqrt{2} + \sqrt{5} - 6\sqrt{2} = -4\sqrt{2} + \sqrt{5}$ Subtract like radicals.

b. $4\sqrt{3} - \sqrt{27} = 4\sqrt{3} - \sqrt{9 \cdot 3}$ Perfect square factor

$\qquad\qquad = 4\sqrt{3} - \sqrt{9} \cdot \sqrt{3}$ Use product property.

$\qquad\qquad = 4\sqrt{3} - 3\sqrt{3}$ Simplify.

$\qquad\qquad = \sqrt{3}$ Subtract like radicals.

EXAMPLE 2 *Multiplying Radicals*

a. $\sqrt{2} \cdot \sqrt{8} = \sqrt{16}$ Use product property.

$\qquad\quad = 4$ Simplify.

b. $\sqrt{2}\left(5 - \sqrt{3}\right) = 5\sqrt{2} - \sqrt{2} \cdot \sqrt{3}$ Use distributive property.

$\qquad\qquad\quad = 5\sqrt{2} - \sqrt{6}$ Use product property.

c. $\left(1 + \sqrt{5}\right)^2 = 1^2 + 2\sqrt{5} + \left(\sqrt{5}\right)^2$ Use square of a binomial pattern.

$\qquad\qquad\quad = 1 + 2\sqrt{5} + 5$ Evaluate powers.

$\qquad\qquad\quad = 6 + 2\sqrt{5}$ Simplify.

d. $\left(a - \sqrt{b}\right)\left(a + \sqrt{b}\right) = a^2 - \left(\sqrt{b}\right)^2$ Use sum and difference pattern.

$\qquad\qquad\qquad\quad = a^2 - b$ Simplify.

The expressions $(a + \sqrt{b})$ and $(a - \sqrt{b})$ are **conjugates**. As you can see in part (d) of Example 2, when a and b are integers, the product $(a + \sqrt{b})(a - \sqrt{b})$ does not involve radicals. Here are some other examples of conjugates.

EXPRESSION	CONJUGATE	PRODUCT
$4 + \sqrt{7}$	$4 - \sqrt{7}$	$4^2 - (\sqrt{7})^2 = 16 - 7 = 9$
$\sqrt{3} - c$	$\sqrt{3} + c$	$(\sqrt{3})^2 - c^2 = 3 - c^2$
$p + \sqrt{q}$	$p - \sqrt{q}$	$p^2 - (\sqrt{q})^2 = p^2 - q$

A simplified fraction does not have a radical in the denominator. To simplify some radical expressions with radicals in the denominator, you can use conjugates. For others, you may be able to write an equivalent expression with a perfect square under the radical sign in the denominator.

STUDENT HELP

INTERNET
HOMEWORK HELP
Visit our Web site
www.mcdougallittell.com
for extra examples.

EXAMPLE 3 *Simplifying Radicals*

a. $\dfrac{3}{\sqrt{5}} = \dfrac{3}{\sqrt{5}} \cdot \dfrac{\sqrt{5}}{\sqrt{5}}$ **Multiply numerator and denominator by $\sqrt{5}$.**

$\qquad = \dfrac{3\sqrt{5}}{\sqrt{5} \cdot \sqrt{5}}$ **Multiply fractions.**

$\qquad = \dfrac{3\sqrt{5}}{5}$ **Simplify.**

b. $\dfrac{1}{c - \sqrt{d}} = \dfrac{1}{c - \sqrt{d}} \cdot \dfrac{c + \sqrt{d}}{c + \sqrt{d}}$ **Multiply numerator and denominator by the conjugate.**

$\qquad = \dfrac{c + \sqrt{d}}{(c - \sqrt{d})(c + \sqrt{d})}$ **Multiply fractions.**

$\qquad = \dfrac{c + \sqrt{d}}{c^2 - d}$ **Simplify.**

EXAMPLE 4 *Checking Quadratic Formula Solutions*

Check that $2 + \sqrt{3}$ is a solution of $x^2 - 4x + 1 = 0$.

SOLUTION

You can check the solution by substituting into the equation.

$x^2 - 4x + 1 = 0$ **Write original equation.**

$(2 + \sqrt{3})^2 - 4(2 + \sqrt{3}) + 1 \stackrel{?}{=} 0$ **Substitute $2 + \sqrt{3}$ for x.**

$4 + 4\sqrt{3} + 3 - 8 - 4\sqrt{3} + 1 \stackrel{?}{=} 0$ **Multiply.**

$0 = 0$ **Solution is correct.**

Sailing

EXAMPLE 5 *Using a Radical Model*

You and a friend are spending the summer working on a schooner. The distance d (in miles) you can see to the horizon can be modeled by the following equation where h is your eye-level height (in feet) above the water.

Distance to horizon: $d = \sqrt{\dfrac{3h}{2}}$

a. Your eye-level height is 32 feet and your friend's eye-level height is 18 feet. Write an expression that shows how much farther you can see than your friend. Simplify the expression.

b. To the nearest tenth of a mile, how much farther can you see?

32 ft
18 ft

SOLUTION

a. Subtract the distance your friend can see from the distance you can see.

PROBLEM SOLVING STRATEGY

| **VERBAL MODEL** | $\boxed{\begin{array}{c}\textbf{Difference}\\\textbf{in distances}\end{array}} = \boxed{\begin{array}{c}\textbf{Your}\\\textbf{distance}\end{array}} - \boxed{\begin{array}{c}\textbf{Your friend's}\\\textbf{distance}\end{array}}$ |

LABELS

Difference in distances $= \boxed{D}$ (miles)

Your distance $= \sqrt{\dfrac{3(32)}{2}}$ (miles)

Your friend's distance $= \sqrt{\dfrac{3(18)}{2}}$ (miles)

ALGEBRAIC MODEL

$\boxed{D} = \sqrt{\dfrac{3(32)}{2}} - \sqrt{\dfrac{3(18)}{2}}$

$= \sqrt{48} - \sqrt{27}$

$= \sqrt{16 \cdot 3} - \sqrt{9 \cdot 3}$

$= 4\sqrt{3} - 3\sqrt{3}$

$= \sqrt{3}$

▶ You can see $\sqrt{3}$ miles farther than your friend.

b. Use a calculator or the Square Root Table on p. 811 to find that $\sqrt{3} \approx 1.7$.

▶ You can see about 1.7 miles farther than your friend.

GUIDED PRACTICE

Vocabulary Check ✓

1. Complete the following sentence: Two radical expressions are _?_ if they have the same radicand.

2. Write a radical expression and its conjugate.

Concept Check ✓

3. Explain how to simplify $\dfrac{\sqrt{3}}{\sqrt{3}-1}$.

Skill Check ✓

Simplify the expression.

4. $4\sqrt{5} + 5\sqrt{5}$

5. $3\sqrt{7} - 2\sqrt{7}$

6. $3\sqrt{6} + \sqrt{24}$

7. $\sqrt{3} \cdot \sqrt{8}$

8. $(2 + \sqrt{3})^2$

9. $\sqrt{3}(5\sqrt{3} - 2\sqrt{6})$

10. $\dfrac{4}{\sqrt{13}}$

11. $\dfrac{3}{8 - \sqrt{10}}$

12. $\dfrac{6}{\sqrt{10}}$

Show whether the expression is a solution of the equation.

13. $6g^2 - 156 = 0;\ \sqrt{26}$

14. $x^2 - 48 = 0;\ -4\sqrt{3}$

15. $x^2 - 12x + 5 = 0;\ 6 + \sqrt{31}$

16. $x^2 - 8x + 8 = 0;\ 4 + 2\sqrt{2}$

17. 🌐 **SAILING** In Example 5, suppose your eye-level height is 24 feet and your friend's is 12 feet. Write an expression that shows how much farther you can see than your friend. Simplify the expression.

PRACTICE AND APPLICATIONS

STUDENT HELP

▶ **Extra Practice**
to help you master
skills is on p. 808.

ADDING AND SUBTRACTING RADICALS Simplify the expression.

18. $5\sqrt{7} + 2\sqrt{7}$

19. $\sqrt{3} + 5\sqrt{3}$

20. $11\sqrt{3} - 12\sqrt{3}$

21. $2\sqrt{6} - \sqrt{6}$

22. $\sqrt{32} + \sqrt{2}$

23. $\sqrt{75} + \sqrt{3}$

24. $\sqrt{80} - \sqrt{45}$

25. $\sqrt{72} - \sqrt{18}$

26. $\sqrt{147} - 7\sqrt{3}$

27. $4\sqrt{5} + \sqrt{125} + \sqrt{45}$

28. $3\sqrt{11} + \sqrt{176} + \sqrt{11}$

29. $\sqrt{24} - \sqrt{96} + \sqrt{6}$

30. $\sqrt{243} - \sqrt{75} + \sqrt{300}$

MULTIPLYING AND DIVIDING RADICALS Simplify the expression.

31. $\sqrt{3} \cdot \sqrt{12}$

32. $\sqrt{5} \cdot \sqrt{8}$

33. $(1 + \sqrt{13})(1 - \sqrt{13})$

34. $\sqrt{3}(5\sqrt{2} + \sqrt{3})$

35. $\sqrt{6}(7\sqrt{3} + 6)$

36. $(\sqrt{6} + 5)^2$

37. $(\sqrt{a} - b)^2$

38. $(\sqrt{c} + d)(3 + \sqrt{5})$

39. $(2\sqrt{3} - 5)^2$

STUDENT HELP

▶ **HOMEWORK HELP**
Example 1: Exs. 18–30
Example 2: Exs. 31–39
Example 3: Exs. 40–48
Example 4: Exs. 52–57
Example 5: Exs. 58, 59

40. $\dfrac{5}{\sqrt{7}}$

41. $\dfrac{2}{\sqrt{2}}$

42. $\dfrac{9}{5 - \sqrt{7}}$

43. $\dfrac{3}{\sqrt{48}}$

44. $\dfrac{6}{10 + \sqrt{2}}$

45. $\dfrac{\sqrt{3}}{\sqrt{3} - 1}$

46. $\dfrac{14}{60 - \sqrt{578}}$

47. $\dfrac{12}{7 - \sqrt{3}}$

48. $\dfrac{4 + \sqrt{3}}{a - \sqrt{b}}$

Find the area. (See Table of Formulas on page 813.)

49.

$\sqrt{68}$

$\sqrt{17} + 9$

50.

$\sqrt{44} + 12$

$\sqrt{99} + 2$

51.

$\sqrt{75} + 10$

$\sqrt{25} + 4$

CHECKING SOLUTIONS In Exercises 52–57, solve the quadratic equation. Check the solutions.

52. $x^2 + 10x + 13 = 0$

53. $x^2 - 4x - 6 = 0$

54. $x^2 - 4x - 15 = 0$

55. $4x^2 - 2x - 1 = 0$

56. $x^2 - 6x - 1 = 0$

57. $a^2 - 6a - 13 = 0$

58. 🌐 **POLE-VAULTING** A pole-vaulter's approach velocity v (in feet per second) and height reached h (in feet) are related by the following equation.

Pole-vaulter model: $v = 8\sqrt{h}$

If you are a pole-vaulter and reach a height of 20 feet and your opponent reaches a height of 16 feet, approximately how much faster were you running than your opponent? Round your answer to the nearest hundredth.

59. 🌐 **BIOLOGY** Many birds drop clams or other shellfish in order to break the shell and get the food inside. The time t (in seconds) it takes for an object such as a clam to fall a certain distance d (in feet) is given by the equation

$$t = \frac{\sqrt{d}}{4}.$$

A gull drops a clam from a height of 50 feet. A second gull drops a clam from a height of 32 feet. Find the difference in the times that it takes for the clams to reach the ground. Round your answer to the nearest hundredth.

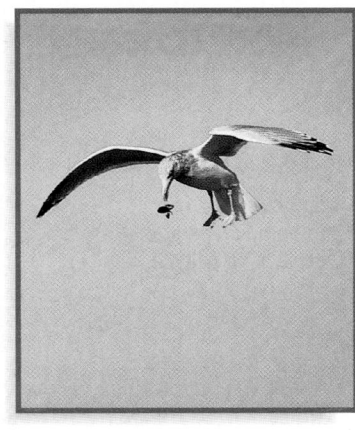

🌐 **FALLING OBJECTS** In Exercises 60–62, use the following information. The average speed of an object S (in feet per second) that is dropped a certain distance d (in feet) is given by the following equation.

Falling object model: $S = \dfrac{d}{\frac{\sqrt{d}}{4}}$

60. Rewrite the equation with the right-hand side in simplest form.

61. Use either equation to find the average speed of an object that is dropped from a height of 400 feet.

62. 📱 **CHECKING GRAPHICALLY** Graph both the falling object model and your equation from Exercise 60 on the same screen to check that you simplified correctly.

63. MULTIPLE CHOICE Simplify $\sqrt{5}\left(6 + \sqrt{5}\right)^2$.

Ⓐ $41 + 2\sqrt{5}$ Ⓑ $53\sqrt{5}$ Ⓒ $41\sqrt{5} + 60$ Ⓓ $101\sqrt{5}$

64. MULTIPLE CHOICE Which of the following is the difference $\sqrt{3} - 5\sqrt{9}$?

Ⓐ $\sqrt{3} - 3$ Ⓑ $\sqrt{3} - 15$ Ⓒ $-4\sqrt{3}$ Ⓓ $\sqrt{3} - 45$

65. MULTIPLE CHOICE Simplify $\dfrac{3}{5 - \sqrt{5}}$.

Ⓐ $\dfrac{15 + 3\sqrt{5}}{20}$ Ⓑ $\dfrac{15 + \sqrt{5}}{20}$ Ⓒ $\dfrac{15 + \sqrt{15}}{20}$ Ⓓ $\dfrac{15 - 3\sqrt{5}}{20}$

★ Challenge

SCIENCE CONNECTION **In Exercises 66–68, use the following information.**
Find a partner to help you with the following experiment. Take a ruler and drop it from a fixed height. Once the ruler is released, your partner should catch it as quickly as possible. Measure how far the ruler falls before your partner catches it. The reaction time can be calculated by the equation

$$t = \sqrt{\frac{d}{192}}$$

where t is the reaction time (in seconds) and d is the distance (in inches) the ruler falls.

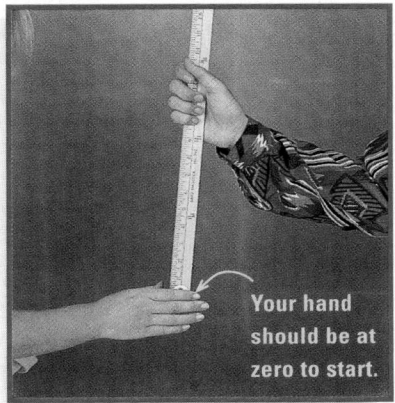

Your hand should be at zero to start.

66. Show how to arrive at this equation from the equation $t = \dfrac{\sqrt{d}}{4}$ in Exercise 59, where d is in feet.

67. Suppose for three trials, the ruler falls 4 inches, 1 inch, and 3 inches. Calculate the average reaction time for the three trials.

68. Perform the experiment several times, recording the distance the ruler falls each time. Organize the results in a table. Calculate the average reaction time for your first five trials. Compare results with your classmates.

EXTRA CHALLENGE
www.mcdougallittell.com

MIXED REVIEW

PERCENT PROBLEMS Solve the percent problem. (Review 11.2)

69. What is 30% of 160?   **70.** 105 is what percent of 240?

SKETCHING GRAPHS Sketch the graph of the function. (Review 11.8)

71. $y = \dfrac{1}{x - 6} - 1$ **72.** $y = \dfrac{1}{x - 5} + 2$ **73.** $y = \dfrac{2}{x - 6} + 9$

FINDING DOMAINS AND RANGES Find the domain and the range of the function. (Review 12.1 for 12.3)

74. $f(x) = \sqrt{x} - 3$ **75.** $f(x) = \sqrt{x - 8}$ **76.** $f(x) = \sqrt{\frac{1}{2}x^2}$

77. $f(x) = \sqrt{x} + 4$ **78.** $f(x) = 6x$ **79.** $f(x) = \sqrt{x + 3}$

12.3

Solving Radical Equations

What you should learn

GOAL 1 Solve a radical equation.

GOAL 2 Use radical equations to solve **real-life** problems, such as finding the centripetal force a person experiences on a ride in **Exs. 66 and 67**.

Why you should learn it

▼ To solve **real-life** problems such as finding the nozzle pressure of antifreeze used to de-ice a plane in **Example 5**.

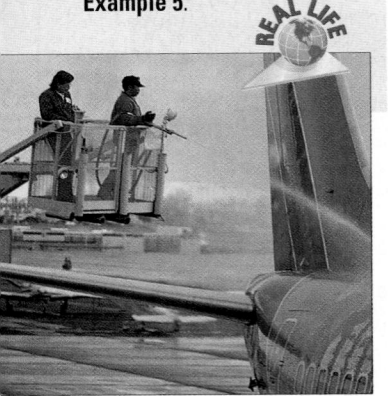

GOAL 1 SOLVING A RADICAL EQUATION

In solving an equation involving radicals, the following property can be extremely useful.

SQUARING BOTH SIDES OF AN EQUATION

Suppose a and b are algebraic expressions.

If $a = b$, then $a^2 = b^2$. **Example:** $\sqrt{4} = 2$, so $(\sqrt{4})^2 = 2^2$.

EXAMPLE 1 *Solving a Radical Equation*

Solve $\sqrt{x} - 7 = 0$.

SOLUTION Isolate the radical expression on one side of the equation.

$$\sqrt{x} - 7 = 0 \qquad \text{Write original equation.}$$
$$\sqrt{x} = 7 \qquad \text{Add 7 to each side.}$$
$$(\sqrt{x})^2 = 7^2 \qquad \text{Square each side.}$$
$$x = 49 \qquad \text{Simplify.}$$

▶ The solution is 49. Check the solution in the original equation.

EXAMPLE 2 *Solving a Radical Equation*

To solve the equation $\sqrt{2x - 3} + 3 = 4$, you need to isolate the radical expression first.

$$\sqrt{2x - 3} + 3 = 4 \qquad \text{Write original equation.}$$
$$\sqrt{2x - 3} = 1 \qquad \text{Subtract 3 from each side.}$$
$$(\sqrt{2x - 3})^2 = 1^2 \qquad \text{Square each side.}$$
$$2x - 3 = 1 \qquad \text{Simplify.}$$
$$2x = 4 \qquad \text{Add 3 to each side.}$$
$$x = 2 \qquad \text{Divide each side by 2.}$$

▶ The solution is 2. Check the solution in the original equation.

EXTRANEOUS SOLUTIONS Squaring both sides of an equation often introduces an extraneous solution of $a^2 = b^2$ that is *not* a solution of $a = b$. When you square both sides of an equation, check each solution in the *original* equation.

EXAMPLE 3   *Checking for Extraneous Solutions*

Solve the equation.

a. $\sqrt{x + 2} = x$ **b.** $\sqrt{x} + 13 = 0$

SOLUTION

a. $\sqrt{x + 2} = x$ **Write original equation.**

$(\sqrt{x + 2})^2 = x^2$ **Square each side.**

$x + 2 = x^2$ **Simplify.**

$0 = x^2 - x - 2$ **Write in standard form.**

$0 = (x - 2)(x + 1)$ **Factor.**

$x = 2 \text{ or } x = -1$ **Zero-product property**

✓**CHECK**   Substitute 2 and -1 in the original equation.

$\sqrt{2 + 2} \stackrel{?}{=} 2$ $\sqrt{-1 + 2} \stackrel{?}{=} -1$

$2 = 2 ✓$ $1 \neq -1$

▶ The only solution is 2, because $x = -1$ is not a solution.

b. $\sqrt{x} + 13 = 0$ **Write original equation.**

$\sqrt{x} = -13$ **Subtract 13 from each side.**

$(\sqrt{x})^2 = (-13)^2$ **Square each side.**

$x = 169$ **Simplify.**

▶ $\sqrt{169} + 13 \neq 0$, so the equation has no solution.

EXAMPLE 4   *Using a Geometric Mean*

The *geometric mean* of a and b is $\sqrt{ab}$. If the geometric mean of a and 6 is 12, what is the value of a?

SOLUTION   Geometric mean $= \sqrt{ab}$

$12 = \sqrt{6a}$ **Substitute.**

$12^2 = (\sqrt{6a})^2$ **Square each side.**

$144 = 6a$ **Simplify.**

$24 = a$ **Solve for a.**

GOAL 2 SOLVING RADICAL EQUATIONS IN REAL LIFE

Plane De-icing

EXAMPLE 5 *Using a Radical Model*

You work for a commercial airline and remove ice from planes. The relationship among the flow rate r (in gallons per minute) of the antifreeze for de-icing, the nozzle diameter d (in inches), and the nozzle pressure P (in pounds per square inch) is shown in the diagram. You want a flow rate of 250 gallons per minute.

a. Find the nozzle pressure for a nozzle whose diameter is 1.25 inches.

b. Find the nozzle pressure for a nozzle whose diameter is 1.75 inches.

c. When you increase the diameter of the nozzle by 40%, do you also change the nozzle pressure by 40%? Explain.

Nozzle diameter d

Flow rate r

Nozzle pressure P

$r = 30d^2\sqrt{P}$

SOLUTION

a.

$r = 30d^2\sqrt{P}$	Write model for water flow.
$250 = 30(1.25)^2\sqrt{P}$	Substitute 1.25 for d and 250 for r.
$250 = 46.875\sqrt{P}$	Simplify.
$\dfrac{250}{46.875} = \sqrt{P}$	Divide each side by 46.875.
$\left(\dfrac{250}{46.875}\right)^2 = P$	Square each side.
$28.4 \approx P$	Use a calculator.

▶ The nozzle pressure will be about 28.4 pounds per square inch.

b.

$r = 30d^2\sqrt{P}$	Write model for water flow.
$250 = 30(1.75)^2\sqrt{P}$	Substitute 1.75 for d and 250 for r.
$\dfrac{250}{91.875} = \sqrt{P}$	Simplify and divide each side by 91.875.
$\left(\dfrac{250}{91.875}\right)^2 = P$	Square each side.
$7.4 \approx P$	Use a calculator.

▶ The nozzle pressure will be about 7.4 pounds per square inch.

c. No, when you increase the nozzle diameter by 40%, the pressure decreases by about 74%.

GUIDED PRACTICE

Vocabulary Check ✔

1. Explain what an *extraneous solution* is.

Concept Check ✔

2. One reason for checking a solution in the original equation is to look for an error in one of the steps of the solution. Give another reason.

3. Is 36 a solution of $\sqrt{x} = -6$? Why or why not?

Skill Check ✔

Solve the equation. Check for extraneous solutions.

4. $\sqrt{x} - 20 = 0$

5. $\sqrt{5x + 1} + 8 = 12$

6. $\sqrt{4x} - 1 = 3$

7. $\sqrt{x} + 6 = 0$

8. $\sqrt{4x + 5} = x$

9. $\sqrt{x + 6} - x = 0$

10. $x = \sqrt{x + 12}$

11. $-5 + \sqrt{x} = 0$

12. $x = \sqrt{5x + 24}$

13. Find a if the geometric mean of 12 and a is 6.

14. 🌐 **PLANE DE-ICING** Use Example 5 to answer the question. What will the nozzle pressure be if the nozzle diameter is 2 inches?

PRACTICE AND APPLICATIONS

STUDENT HELP

→ **Extra Practice**
to help you master
skills is on p. 808.

SOLVING RADICAL EQUATIONS **Solve the equation. Check for extraneous solutions.**

15. $\sqrt{x} - 9 = 0$

16. $\sqrt{x} - 1 = 0$

17. $\sqrt{x} + 5 = 0$

18. $\sqrt{x} - 10 = 0$

19. $\sqrt{x} - 15 = 0$

20. $\sqrt{x} - 0 = 0$

21. $\sqrt{6x} - 13 = 23$

22. $\sqrt{4x + 1} + 5 = 10$

23. $\sqrt{9 - x} - 10 = 14$

24. $\sqrt{5x + 1} + 2 = 6$

25. $\sqrt{6x - 2} - 3 = 7$

26. $4 = 7 - \sqrt{33x - 2}$

27. $10 = 4 + \sqrt{5x + 11}$

28. $-5 - \sqrt{10x - 2} = 5$

29. $\sqrt{-x} - \frac{3}{2} = \frac{3}{2}$

30. $\sqrt{x} + \frac{1}{3} = \frac{13}{3}$

31. $\sqrt{\frac{1}{5}x - 2} - \frac{1}{10} = \frac{7}{10}$

32. $x = \sqrt{\frac{3}{2}x + \frac{5}{2}}$

33. $\sqrt{\frac{1}{4}x - 4} - 3 = 5$

34. $6 - \sqrt{7x - 9} = 3$

35. $\sqrt{\frac{1}{9}x + 1} - \frac{2}{3} = \frac{5}{3}$

36. $x = \sqrt{35 + 2x}$

37. $x = \sqrt{-4x - 4}$

38. $x = \sqrt{6x - 9}$

39. $x = \sqrt{30 - x}$

40. $x = \sqrt{11x - 28}$

41. $\sqrt{-10x - 4} = 2x$

42. $x = \sqrt{200 - 35x}$

43. $\sqrt{110 - x} = x$

44. $2x = \sqrt{-13x - 10}$

45. $x = \sqrt{4x + 45}$

46. $\frac{1}{5}x = \sqrt{x - 6}$

47. $\frac{2}{3}x = \sqrt{24x - 128}$

STUDENT HELP

→ **HOMEWORK HELP**
Example 1: Exs. 15–21
Example 2: Exs. 22–47
Example 3: Exs. 15–47
Example 4: Exs. 48–53
Example 5: Exs. 69, 70

GEOMETRIC MEAN **Two numbers and their geometric mean are given. Find the value of a.**

48. 12 and a; 27

49. 4 and a; 16

50. 6 and a; 27

51. 4 and a; 14

52. 6 and a; 72

53. 8 and a; 104

ERROR ANALYSIS Find and correct the error.

54.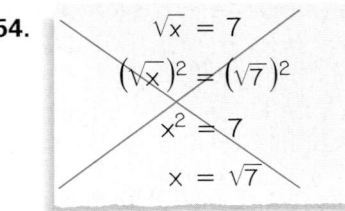
$$\sqrt{x} = 7$$
$$(\sqrt{x})^2 = (\sqrt{7})^2$$
$$x^2 = 7$$
$$x = \sqrt{7}$$

55.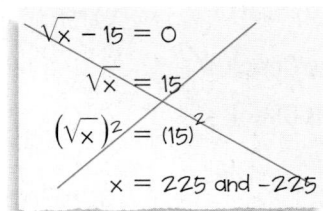
$$\sqrt{x} - 15 = 0$$
$$\sqrt{x} = 15$$
$$(\sqrt{x})^2 = (15)^2$$
$$x = 225 \text{ and } -225$$

STUDENT HELP

▶ **Look Back**
For help with solving an equation using a graphing calculator, see p. 359.

SOLVING GRAPHICALLY In Exercises 56–64, use a graphing calculator to graphically solve the radical equation. Check the solution algebraically.

56. $\sqrt{x + 4} = 3$

57. $\sqrt{x - 5.6} = 2.5$

58. $\sqrt{9.2 - x} = 1.8$

59. $\sqrt{6x - 2} - 3 = 7$

60. $4 + \sqrt{x} = 9$

61. $\sqrt{7x - 12} = x$

62. $\sqrt{2x + 7} = x + 2$

63. $\sqrt{3x - 2} = 4 - x$

64. $\sqrt{15 - 4x} = 2x$

65. **VISUAL THINKING** Use a graphing calculator or a computer to show that the radical equation $\sqrt{11x - 30} = -x$ has no solution. Explain.

GEOMETRY **CONNECTION** Find the value of *x*.

66. Perimeter = 30

6
$\sqrt{x + 6}$

67. Area = $82\frac{1}{2}$

11
$\sqrt{2x - 1}$

68. **LOGICAL REASONING** Write a radical equation that has a solution of 18.

AMUSEMENT PARK RIDE In Exercises 69 and 70, use the following information.

A ride at an amusement park spins in a circle of radius *r* (in meters). The centripetal force *F* experienced by a passenger on the ride is modeled by the equation below, where *t* is the number of seconds the ride takes to complete one revolution and *m* is the mass (in kilograms) of the passenger.

$$t = \sqrt{\frac{4\pi^2 mr}{F}}$$

STUDENT HELP

APPLICATION LINK
Visit our Web site
www.mcdougallittell.com
for more information
about centripetal force.

69. A person whose mass is 67.5 kilograms is on a ride that is spinning in a circle at a rate of 10 seconds per revolution. The radius of the circle is 6 meters. How much centripetal force does the person experience?

70. **CRITICAL THINKING** A person whose mass is 54 kilograms is on the ride. A mass of 54 kilograms is 80% of 67.5 kilograms. Is the centripetal force experienced by the person 80% of the force in Exercise 69? Explain.

BLOTTING PAPER In Exercises 71 and 72, use the following information.
Blotting paper is a thick, soft paper used for absorbing fluids such as water or ink. The distance d (in centimeters) that tap water is absorbed up a strip of blotting paper at a temperature of 28.4°C is given by the equation

$d = 0.444\sqrt{t}$ where t is the time (in seconds).

71. Approximately how many minutes would it take for the water to travel a distance of 28 centimeters up the strip of blotting paper?

72. How far up the blotting paper would the water be after $33\frac{1}{3}$ seconds?

GEOMETRIC MEAN In Exercises 73–76, use the proportion $\frac{a}{b} = \frac{b}{d}$, where a, b, and d are positive numbers.

73. In the proportion $\frac{a}{b} = \frac{b}{d}$, b is called the geometric mean of a and d. Use the cross product property to show that $b = \sqrt{ad}$.

74. Two numbers have a geometric mean of 4. One number is 6 more than the other.

    a. Use the proportion in Exercise 73. Rewrite the proportion substituting the given value for the geometric mean.

    b. Let x represent one of the numbers. How can you represent "one number is 6 more than the other" in the proportion? Rewrite the proportion using x.

    c. Solve the proportion in part (b) to find the numbers.

75. Two numbers have a geometric mean of 10. One number is 21 less than the other. Find the numbers.

76. Two numbers have a geometric mean of 12. One number is 32 more than the other. Find the numbers.

Test Preparation

QUANTITATIVE COMPARISON In Exercises 77–80, choose the statement below that is true about the given quantities.

    (A) The quantity in column A is greater.

    (B) The quantity in column B is greater.

    (C) The two quantities are equal.

    (D) The relationship cannot be determined from the given information.

	Column A	Column B
77.	The geometric mean of 3 and 12	The geometric mean of 1 and 36
78.	The solution of $\sqrt{x} + 4 = 5$	The solution of $\sqrt{x} - 4 = 5$
79.	The solution of $\sqrt{x} - 3 = 5$	The solution of $\sqrt{x - 3} = 5$
80.	The geometric mean of -1 and -64	The geometric mean of -2 and -32

★ **Challenge**

81. LOGICAL REASONING Using $4\sqrt{x} = 2x + k$, find three different expressions that can be substituted for k so that the equation has two solutions, one solution, and no solution. Describe how you found the equations.

MIXED REVIEW

SOLVING EQUATIONS Solve the equation. (Review 9.1, 9.2 for 12.4)

82. $x^2 = 36$

83. $x^2 = 11$

84. $7x^2 = 700$

85. $25x^2 - 9 = -5$

86. $\frac{1}{7}x^2 - 7 = -7$

87. $-16t^2 + 48 = 0$

FINDING PRODUCTS Multiply. (Review 10.3 for 12.4)

88. $(x + 5)^2$

89. $(2x - 3)^2$

90. $(3x + 5y)(3x - 5y)$

91. $(6y - 4)(6y + 4)$

92. $(x + 7y)^2$

93. $(2a - 9b)^2$

FACTORING TRINOMIALS Factor the trinomial. (Review 10.7 for 12.4)

94. $x^2 + 18x + 81$

95. $x^2 - 12x + 36$

96. $4x^2 + 28x + 49$

UNDEFINED VALUES For what values of the variable is the rational expression undefined? (Review 11.4)

97. $\dfrac{5}{x - 4}$

98. $\dfrac{x + 2}{x^2 - 4}$

99. $\dfrac{x + 4}{x^2 + x - 6}$

100. 🌎 **COMPARING COSTS** A discount grocery store offers two types of memberships with annual membership fees of $25 and $100. If you pay the $25 membership fee, you get regular discounted prices. If you pay the $100 membership fee, you get an additional 10% discount. How much money would you have to spend on groceries for the two memberships to cost the same? (Review 7.2)

QUIZ 1

Self-Test for Lessons 12.1–12.3

Identify the domain and the range of the function. Then sketch the graph of the function. (Lesson 12.1)

1. $y = 10\sqrt{x}$

2. $y = \sqrt{x - 9}$

3. $y = \sqrt{2x - 1}$

4. $y = \dfrac{\sqrt{x} - 2}{3}$

Simplify the expression. (Lesson 12.2)

5. $7\sqrt{10} + 11\sqrt{10}$

6. $2\sqrt{7} - 5\sqrt{28}$

7. $4\sqrt{5} + \sqrt{125} - \sqrt{80}$

8. $\sqrt{3}\left(3\sqrt{2} + \sqrt{3}\right)$

9. $\left(\sqrt{7} + 5\right)^2$

10. $\dfrac{15}{8 + \sqrt{7}}$

Solve the equation. (Lesson 12.3)

11. $\sqrt{x} - 12 = 0$

12. $\sqrt{x} - 8 = 0$

13. $\sqrt{3x + 2} + 2 = 3$

14. $\sqrt{3x - 2} + 3 = 7$

15. $\sqrt{77 - 4x} = x$

16. $x = \sqrt{2x + 3}$

17. 🌎 **NOZZLE PRESSURE** The nozzle pressure P (in pounds per square inch) of a hose with diameter d (in inches) and water-flow rate r (in gallons per minute) is given by the equation $r = 30d^2\sqrt{P}$. Find the nozzle pressure in a hose that has a water-flow rate of 250 gallons per minute and a diameter of 2.5 inches. (Lesson 12.3)

⊙ ACTIVITY 12.4

Developing Concepts

GROUP ACTIVITY
Work with a partner.

MATERIALS
algebra tiles

STUDENT HELP

↳ **Look Back**
For help with algebra tiles, see p. 575.

Modeling Completing the Square

▶ **QUESTION** How can you use algebra tiles to represent perfect square trinomials?

▶ **EXPLORING THE CONCEPT**

1 Use algebra tiles to model the expression $x^2 + 6x$.

2 Arrange the x^2-tile and the x-tiles to form part of a square.

3 To complete the square, you need to add nine 1-tiles.

You have completed the square: $x^2 + 6x + 9 = (x + 3)^2$.

▶ **DRAWING CONCLUSIONS**

1. Use algebra tiles to complete the square for each expression in the table. Then copy and complete the table to show your results.

Expression	Number of tiles to complete the square	Number of tiles as a perfect square
$x^2 + 6x$	9	3^2
$x^2 + 8x$	?	?
$x^2 + 4x$	?	?
$x^2 + 2x$	?	?

2. How is the number in the third column related to the coefficient of x in the first column?

3. Use the pattern you found in Exercise 2 to predict how many tiles you would need to add to complete the square for the expression $x^2 + 14x$.

Completing the Square

What you should learn

GOAL 1 Solve a quadratic equation by completing the square.

GOAL 2 Choose a method for solving a quadratic equation.

Why you should learn it

▼ To solve **real-life** problems such as finding the path of the diver in **Ex. 71**.

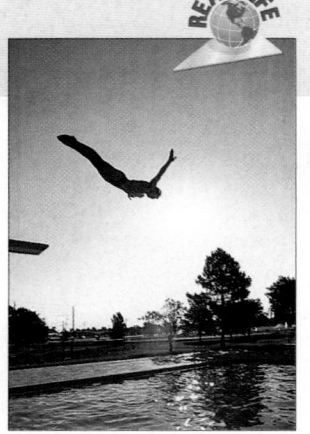

GOAL 1 SOLVING BY COMPLETING THE SQUARE

In the activity on page 729, you completed the square for expressions of the form $x^2 + bx$ where $b = 2, 4, 6$, and 8. In each case, $x^2 + bx + \left(\frac{b}{2} \cdot \frac{b}{2}\right)$ was modeled by a square with sides of length $x + \frac{b}{2}$. By using FOIL to expand $\left(x + \frac{b}{2}\right)\left(x + \frac{b}{2}\right)$, you can show that this pattern holds for any real number b.

COMPLETING THE SQUARE

To complete the square of the expression $x^2 + bx$, add the square of half the coefficient of x.

$$x^2 + bx + \left(\frac{b}{2}\right)^2 = \left(x + \frac{b}{2}\right)^2$$

EXAMPLE 1 *Completing the Square*

What term should you add to $x^2 - 8x$ so that the result is a perfect square?

SOLUTION

The coefficient of x is -8, so you should add $\left(\frac{-8}{2}\right)^2$, or 16, to the expression.

$$x^2 - 8x + \left(\frac{-8}{2}\right)^2 = x^2 - 8x + 16 = (x - 4)^2$$

EXAMPLE 2 *Solving a Quadratic Equation*

Solve $x^2 + 10x = 24$ by completing the square.

SOLUTION

$x^2 + 10x = 24$	Write original equation.
$x^2 + 10x + 5^2 = 24 + 5^2$	Add $\left(\frac{10}{2}\right)^2$, or 5^2, to each side.
$(x + 5)^2 = 49$	Write left side as perfect square.
$x + 5 = \pm 7$	Find square root of each side.
$x = -5 \pm 7$	Subtract 5 from each side.
$x = 2$ or $x = -12$	Simplify.

STUDENT HELP

▶ **Study Tip**
When completing the square to solve an equation, remember that you must always add the term $\left(\frac{b}{2}\right)^2$ to *both* sides of the equation.

▶ The solutions are 2 and -12. Check these in the original equation to see that both are solutions.

EXAMPLE 3 *Solving a Quadratic Equation*

Solve $x^2 - x - 3 = 0$ by completing the square.

SOLUTION

$x^2 - x - 3 = 0$	Write original equation.
$x^2 - x = 3$	Add 3 to each side.
$x^2 - x + \left(-\dfrac{1}{2}\right)^2 = 3 + \dfrac{1}{4}$	Add $\left(-\dfrac{1}{2}\right)^2$, or $\dfrac{1}{4}$, to each side.
$\left(x - \dfrac{1}{2}\right)^2 = \dfrac{13}{4}$	Write left side as perfect square.
$x - \dfrac{1}{2} = \pm\dfrac{\sqrt{13}}{2}$	Find square root of each side.
$x = \dfrac{1}{2} \pm \dfrac{\sqrt{13}}{2}$	Add $\dfrac{1}{2}$ to each side.

▶ The solutions are $\dfrac{1}{2} + \dfrac{\sqrt{13}}{2}$ and $\dfrac{1}{2} - \dfrac{\sqrt{13}}{2}$. Check these in the original equation.

· · · · · · · · · ·

If the leading coefficient of the quadratic is not 1, you should divide each side of the equation by this coefficient *before* completing the square.

EXAMPLE 4 *The Leading Coefficient is Not 1*

Solve $2x^2 - x - 2 = 0$ by completing the square.

SOLUTION

$2x^2 - x - 2 = 0$	Write original equation.
$2x^2 - x = 2$	Add 2 to each side.
$x^2 - \dfrac{1}{2}x = 1$	Divide each side by 2.
$x^2 - \dfrac{1}{2}x + \left(-\dfrac{1}{4}\right)^2 = 1 + \dfrac{1}{16}$	Add $\left(-\dfrac{1}{4}\right)^2$, or $\dfrac{1}{16}$, to each side.
$\left(x - \dfrac{1}{4}\right)^2 = \dfrac{17}{16}$	Write left side as perfect square.
$x - \dfrac{1}{4} = \pm\dfrac{\sqrt{17}}{4}$	Find square root of each side.
$x = \dfrac{1}{4} \pm \dfrac{\sqrt{17}}{4}$	Add $\dfrac{1}{4}$ to each side.

▶ The solutions are $\dfrac{1}{4} + \dfrac{\sqrt{17}}{4} \approx 1.28$ and

$\dfrac{1}{4} - \dfrac{\sqrt{17}}{4} \approx -0.78$.

✓ **CHECK** The graph generated by a graphing calculator appears to confirm the solutions.

X=1.2765957 Y=0

STUDENT HELP

→ **Study Tip**
To solve an equation by completing the square, you first need to isolate the x^2-term and the x-term on one side of the equation.

STUDENT HELP

INTERNET **HOMEWORK HELP**
Visit our Web site
www.mcdougallittell.com
for extra examples.

There are many connections among the five methods for solving a quadratic equation. For instance, in Example 4 you used completing the square to solve the equation, and you used a graphing approach to confirm that the solutions are reasonable.

In the following activity, you will use completing the square to develop the quadratic formula.

> **ACTIVITY**
> Developing
> Concepts   **Investigating the Quadratic Formula**

Consider a general quadratic equation

$$ax^2 + bx + c = 0 \quad \text{where } a \neq 0.$$

Perform the following steps. Then describe how your result is related to the quadratic formula.

1 Subtract c from each side of the equation $ax^2 + bx + c = 0$.

2 Divide each side by a.

3 Add the square of half the coefficient of x to each side.

4 Write the left side as a perfect square.

5 Use a common denominator to express the right side as a single faction.

6 Find the square root of each side. Include $\pm$ on the right side.

7 Solve for x by subtracting the same term from each side.

8 Use a common denominator to express the right side as a single fraction.

You have learned the following five methods for solving quadratic equations. The table will help you choose which method to use to solve an equation.

CONCEPT SUMMARY	METHODS FOR SOLVING $ax^2 + bx + c = 0$	
Method	**Lesson**	**Comments**
FINDING SQUARE ROOTS	9.1	Efficient way to solve $ax^2 + c = 0$.
GRAPHING	9.4	Can be used for *any* quadratic equation. May give only approximate solutions.
USING THE QUADRATIC FORMULA	9.5	Can be used for *any* quadratic equation. Always gives exact solutions to the equation.
FACTORING	10.5–10.8	Efficient way to solve a quadratic equation if the quadratic expression can be factored easily.
COMPLETING THE SQUARE	12.4	Can be used for *any* quadratic equation but is simplest to apply when $a = 1$ and b is an even number.

EXAMPLE 5 *Choosing a Solution Method*

Choose a method to solve the quadratic equation. Explain your choice.

a. $3x^2 - 15 = 0$ **b.** $2x^2 + 3x - 4 = 0$

SOLUTION

a. Because this quadratic equation has the form $ax^2 + c = 0$, it is most efficiently solved by finding square roots.

$3x^2 - 15 = 0$	**Write original equation.**
$3x^2 = 15$	**Add 15 to each side.**
$x^2 = 5$	**Divide each side by 3.**
$x = \pm\sqrt{5}$	**Find square roots.**

▶ The solutions are $\sqrt{5}$ and $-\sqrt{5}$.

b. ▶ Because this quadratic equation is not easily factored, you can use a graphing calculator to approximate the solutions. $\boxed{\text{TRACE}}$ to estimate the *x*-intercepts. The approximate solutions are -2.3 and 0.9.

X=-2.340426 Y=0

✓ **CHECK** Using the quadratic formula, the exact solutions are

$$\frac{-3 + \sqrt{41}}{4} \text{ and } \frac{-3 - \sqrt{41}}{4}.$$

EXAMPLE 6 *Choosing the Quadratic Formula*

VETTISFOSS FALLS The Vettisfoss waterfall falls over a vertical cliff. The path of the water can be modeled by $h = -6.03x^2 + 901$ where h is the height (in feet) above the lower river and x is the horizontal distance (in feet) from the base of the cliff. How far from the base of the cliff does the water hit the lower river?

SOLUTION

When the falling water hits the lower river, $h = 0$. The quadratic equation $0 = -6.03x^2 + 901$ cannot be factored easily and cannot be solved easily by completing the square. The quadratic formula is a good choice.

$x = \dfrac{-b \pm \sqrt{b^2 - 4ac}}{2a}$	**Write quadratic formula.**
$x = \dfrac{0 \pm \sqrt{0 - 4(6.03)901}}{2(-6.03)}$	**Substitute values for *a*, *b*, and *c*.**
$\approx 12.3 \text{ or } -12.3$	**Use a calculator.**

▶ Distance must be positive, so the negative solution is extraneous. The water hits the lower river about 12.3 feet from the base of the cliff. Check this solution in the original equation.

GUIDED PRACTICE

Vocabulary Check ✓
Concept Check ✓
Skill Check ✓

1. The leading coefficient of the polynomial $3x^2 - 8x + 4$ is __?__.

2. Explain why completing the square of the expression $x^2 + bx$ is easier to do when b is an even number.

Find the term that should be added to the expression to create a perfect square trinomial.

3. $x^2 + 20x$ 　　　　**4.** $x^2 + 50x$ 　　　　**5.** $x^2 - 10x$

6. $x^2 - 14x$ 　　　　**7.** $x^2 - 22x$ 　　　　**8.** $x^2 + 100x$

9. Solve $x^2 - 3x = 8$ by completing the square. Solve the equation by using the quadratic formula. Which method did you find easier?

Solve by completing the square.

10. $x^2 - 2x - 18 = 0$ 　　　　**11.** $x^2 + 14x + 13 = 0$

12. $3x^2 + 4x - 1 = 0$ 　　　　**13.** $3x^2 - 7x + 6 = 0$

Choose a method to solve the quadratic equation. What method did you use? Explain your choice.

14. $x^2 - x - 2 = 0$ 　　**15.** $3x^2 + 17x + 10 = 0$ 　　**16.** $x^2 - 9 = 0$

17. $-3x^2 + 5x + 5 = 0$ 　　**18.** $x^2 + 2x - 14 = 0$ 　　**19.** $3x^2 - 2 = 0$

PRACTICE AND APPLICATIONS

STUDENT HELP

▶ **Extra Practice**
to help you master
skills is on p. 808.

PERFECT SQUARE TRINOMIALS Find the term that should be added to the expression to create a perfect square trinomial.

20. $x^2 - 12x$ 　　　　**21.** $x^2 + 8x$ 　　　　**22.** $x^2 + 21x$

23. $x^2 - 22x$ 　　　　**24.** $x^2 + 11x$ 　　　　**25.** $x^2 - 40x$

26. $x^2 + 0.4x$ 　　　　**27.** $x^2 + \frac{3}{4}x$ 　　　　**28.** $x^2 + \frac{4}{5}x$

29. $x^2 - 5.2x$ 　　　　**30.** $x^2 - 0.3x$ 　　　　**31.** $x^2 + \frac{2}{3}x$

COMPLETING THE SQUARE Solve the equation by completing the square.

32. $x^2 + 10x = 39$ 　　**33.** $x^2 + 16x = 17$ 　　**34.** $x^2 - 24x = -44$

STUDENT HELP

▶ **HOMEWORK HELP**
Example 1: Exs. 20–31
Example 2: Exs. 32–40
Example 3: Exs. 35–40
Example 4: Exs. 41–49
Example 5: Exs. 50–67
Example 6: Ex. 71

35. $x^2 - 8x + 12 = 0$ 　　**36.** $x^2 + 5x - \frac{11}{4} = 0$ 　　**37.** $x^2 + 11x + \frac{21}{4} = 0$

38. $x^2 - \frac{2}{3}x - 3 = 0$ 　　**39.** $x^2 + \frac{3}{5}x - 1 = 0$ 　　**40.** $x^2 + x - 1 = 0$

41. $4x^2 + 4x - 11 = 0$ 　　**42.** $3x^2 - 24x - 1 = 0$ 　　**43.** $4x^2 - 40x - 7 = 0$

44. $2x^2 - 8x - 13 = 7$ 　　**45.** $5x^2 - 20x - 20 = 5$ 　　**46.** $3x^2 + 4x + 4 = 3$

47. $4x^2 + 6x - 6 = 2$ 　　**48.** $6x^2 + 24x - 41 = 0$ 　　**49.** $20x^2 - 120x - 109 = 0$

CHOOSING A METHOD Choose a method to solve the quadratic equation. Explain your choice.

50. $x^2 - 5x - 1 = 0$ **51.** $4x^2 - 12 = 0$ **52.** $n^2 + 5n - 24 = 0$

53. $9a^2 - 25 = 0$ **54.** $x^2 - x - 20 = 0$ **55.** $x^2 + 6x - 55 = 0$

SOLVING EQUATIONS Solve the quadratic equation.

56. $x^2 - 10x = 0$ **57.** $c^2 + 2c - 26 = 0$ **58.** $8x^2 + 14x = -5$

59. $x^2 - 16 = 0$ **60.** $x^2 + 12x + 20 = 0$ **61.** $x^2 - 4x = \dfrac{5}{6}$

62. $4x^2 + 4x + 1 = 0$ **63.** $13x^2 - 26x = 0$ **64.** $4p^2 - 12p + 5 = 0$

65. $7z^2 - 46z = 21$ **66.** $11x^2 - 22 = 0$ **67.** $x^2 + 20x + 10 = 0$

GEOMETRY CONNECTION In Exercises 68–70, make a sketch and write a quadratic equation to model the situation. Then solve the equation.

68. In art class you are designing the floor plan of a house. The kitchen is supposed to have 150 square feet of space. What should the dimensions of the kitchen be if you want it to be square?

69. A rectangle is $2x$ feet long and $x + 5$ feet wide. The area is 600 square feet. What are the dimensions of the rectangle?

70. The height of a triangle is 4 more than twice its base. The area of the triangle is 60 square centimeters. What are the dimensions of the triangle?

71. 🌐 **DIVING** The path of a diver diving from a 10-foot high diving board is

$$h = -0.44x^2 + 2.61x + 10$$

where h is the height of the diver above water (in feet) and x is the horizontal distance (in feet) from the end of the board. How far from the end of the board will the diver enter the water?

10 ft

x

🌐 **PENGUINS** In Exercises 72 and 73, use the following information.
You are on a research boat in the ocean. You see a penguin jump out of the water. The path followed by the penguin is given by

$$h = -0.05x^2 + 1.178x$$

where h is the height (in feet) the penguin jumps out of the water and x is the horizontal distance (in feet) traveled by the penguin over the water.

72. Sketch a graph of the equation.

73. How many horizontal feet did the penguin travel over the water before reaching its maximum height?

74. MULTIPLE CHOICE Which of the following is a solution of the equation $2x^2 + 8x - 25 = 5$?

 Ⓐ $\sqrt{17} + 1$ Ⓑ $-\sqrt{19} - 2$ Ⓒ $\sqrt{17} - 2$ Ⓓ $\sqrt{21} - 2$

75. MULTIPLE CHOICE What term should you add to $x^2 - \frac{1}{2}x$ so that the result is a perfect square trinomial?

 Ⓐ $\frac{1}{2}$ Ⓑ $\frac{1}{4}$ Ⓒ $\frac{1}{16}$ Ⓓ $\frac{1}{32}$

76. MULTIPLE CHOICE Solve $x^2 + 8x - 2 = 0$.

 Ⓐ $-4 \pm 3\sqrt{2}$ Ⓑ $4 \pm 3\sqrt{2}$ Ⓒ $-4 \pm 2\sqrt{2}$ Ⓓ $4 \pm \sqrt{16}$

★ **Challenge**

VERTEX FORM The *vertex form* of a quadratic function is $y = a(x - h)^2 + k$. Its graph is a parabola with vertex at (h, k). In Exercises 77–79, use completing the square to write the quadratic function in vertex form. Then give the coordinates of the vertex of the graph of the function.

 77. $y = x^2 + 10x + 25$ **78.** $y = 2x^2 + 12x + 13$ **79.** $y = -x^2 - 5x + 6$

EXTRA CHALLENGE
www.mcdougallittell.com

80. QUADRATIC FORMULA Explain why the quadratic formula gives solutions only if $a \neq 0$ and $b^2 - 4ac \geq 0$.

MIXED REVIEW

MEASURES OF CENTRAL TENDENCY Find the mean, the median, and the mode of the collection of numbers. (Review 6.6)

 81. 1, 5, 2, 4, 3, 6, 1   **82.** 9, 6, 10, 14, 10, 3

 83. -6, 20, -8, -18, 10   **84.** 17, 9, 11, 15, 4, 15, 8, 3, 11

SOLVING LINEAR SYSTEMS Solve the linear system. (Review 7.2, 7.3)

 85. $y = 4x$ **86.** $3x + y = 12$ **87.** $2x - y = 8$
   $x + y = 10$ $9x - y = 36$ $2x + 2y = 2$

SOLVING EQUATIONS Solve the equation. (Review 9.1, 9.2 for 12.5)

 88. $16 + x^2 = 64$ **89.** $x^2 + 81 = 144$ **90.** $x^2 + 25 = 81$

 91. $4x^2 - 144 = 0$ **92.** $x^2 - 30 = -3$ **93.** $x^2 = \frac{9}{25}$

SKETCHING GRAPHS Sketch the graph of the function. (Review 9.3)

 94. $y = x^2 + x + 2$ **95.** $y = -3x^2 - x - 4$ **96.** $y = 2x^2 - 3x + 4$

SOLVING EQUATIONS Solve the equation. (Review 10.4)

 97. $(x + 4)(x - 8) = 0$ **98.** $(x - 3)(x - 2) = 0$ **99.** $(x + 5)(x + 6) = 0$
 100. $(x + 4)^2 = 0$ **101.** $(x - 3)^2 = 0$ **102.** $6(x - 14)^2 = 0$

FACTORING TRINOMIALS Factor the trinomial if possible. (Review 10.5, 10.6)

 103. $x^2 + x - 20$ **104.** $x^2 - 10x + 24$ **105.** $x^2 + 2x + 4$
 106. $3x^2 - 15x + 18$ **107.** $2x^2 - x - 3$ **108.** $14x^2 - 19x - 3$

● ACTIVITY 12.5

Developing Concepts

Investigating the Pythagorean Theorem

▶ **QUESTION** Is the Pythagorean theorem true only for right triangles?

GROUP ACTIVITY
Work in a small group.

MATERIALS
• ruler
• scissors
• glue or tape

▶ **EXPLORING THE CONCEPT**

For the right triangle shown, a, b, and c are the lengths of the sides of the triangle. The Pythagorean theorem states that $a^2 + b^2 = c^2$.

1 Copy the triangle on a piece of paper. Draw a square on each of the triangle's three sides. Label the areas a^2, b^2, and c^2. Then cut out the squares.

2 Cut and rearrange the areas that represent the squares of a and b to see if they fit exactly into the area that represents the square of c.

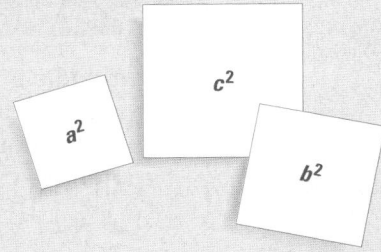

▶ **DRAWING CONCLUSIONS**

1. Each group member should copy a different one of the triangles below. Then draw the areas that represent the squares of the sides. Cut and rearrange them to see how the larger area relates to the sum of the two smaller areas.

Obtuse triangle

Acute triangle

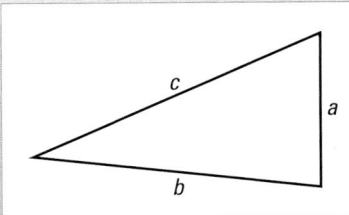

2. Draw any triangle and follow the directions of Exercise 1.

In Exercises 3–5, a, b, and c are the lengths of the sides of a triangle, and c is the greatest length. Use the results of your investigations with triangles to complete the statement with >, <, or =.

3. In an obtuse triangle, $a^2 + b^2 \underline{\ ?\ } c^2$.

4. In a right triangle, $a^2 + b^2 \underline{\ ?\ } c^2$.

5. In an acute triangle, $a^2 + b^2 \underline{\ ?\ } c^2$.

12.5 The Pythagorean Theorem and Its Converse

What you should learn

GOAL 1 Use the Pythagorean theorem and its converse.

GOAL 2 Use the Pythagorean theorem and its converse in **real-life** problems such as finding distance on a baseball field in **Example 4.**

Why you should learn it

▼ To solve **real-life** problems such as installing guy wires in **Ex. 44.**

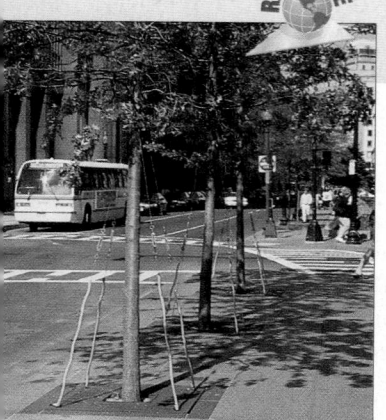

GOAL 1 USING THE THEOREM AND ITS CONVERSE

A *theorem* is a statement that can be proven to be true. The activity on page 737 uses area to explore the *Pythagorean theorem*, but does not prove the theorem.

The **Pythagorean theorem** states a relationship among the sides of a right triangle. The **hypotenuse** is the side opposite the right angle. The other two sides are the **legs.** The theorem is named after the Greek mathematician Pythagoras. However, there are records that suggest earlier use of the basic principle in northern Africa, in Babylonia, and in India.

THE PYTHAGOREAN THEOREM

If a triangle is a right triangle, then the sum of the squares of the lengths of the legs a and b equals the square of the length of the hypotenuse c.

$$a^2 + b^2 = c^2$$

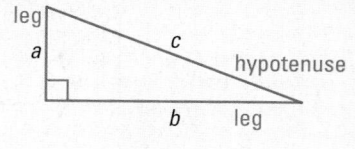

EXAMPLE 1 *Using the Pythagorean Theorem*

a. Given $a = 6$ and $b = 8$, find c.

$$a^2 + b^2 = c^2$$
$$6^2 + 8^2 = c^2$$
$$100 = c^2$$
$$\sqrt{100} = c$$
$$10 = c$$

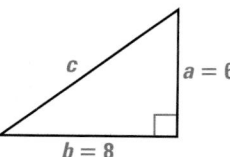

b. Given $a = 5$ and $c = 6$, find b.

$$a^2 + b^2 = c^2$$
$$5^2 + b^2 = 6^2$$
$$b^2 = 6^2 - 5^2$$
$$b^2 = 11$$
$$b = \sqrt{11}, \text{ or about } 3.32$$

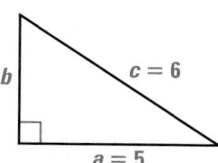

EXAMPLE 2 *Using the Pythagorean Theorem*

A right triangle has one leg that is 3 inches longer than the other leg. The hypotenuse is 15 inches. Find the missing lengths.

SOLUTION

PROBLEM SOLVING STRATEGY

DRAW A DIAGRAM Sketch a right triangle and label the sides. Let x be the length of the shorter leg. Use the Pythagorean theorem to solve for x.

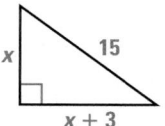

$a^2 + b^2 = c^2$	Write Pythagorean theorem.
$x^2 + (x + 3)^2 = 15^2$	Substitute for a, b, and c.
$x^2 + x^2 + 6x + 9 = 225$	Simplify.
$2x^2 + 6x - 216 = 0$	Write in standard form.
$2(x - 9)(x + 12) = 0$	Factor.
$x = 9$ or $x = -12$	Zero-product property

▶ Length is positive. The sides have lengths 9 inches and $9 + 3 = 12$ inches.

· · · · · · · · · ·

STUDENT HELP

▸ **Look Back**
For help with if-then statements, see p. 189.

LOGICAL REASONING In mathematics an if-then statement is a statement of the form "If p, then q," where p is the **hypothesis** and q is the **conclusion**.

The **converse** of the statement "If p, then q" is the related statement "If q, then p," in which the hypothesis and conclusion are interchanged. The converse of a true statement may be false. However, the converse of the Pythagorean theorem is true.

CONVERSE OF THE PYTHAGOREAN THEOREM

If a triangle has side lengths a, b, and c such that $a^2 + b^2 = c^2$, then the triangle is a right triangle.

EXAMPLE 3 *Determining Right Triangles*

Determine whether the given lengths are sides of a right triangle.

   a. 11.9, 12.0, 16.9   **b.** 5, 11, 12

SOLUTION Use the converse of the Pythagorean theorem.

STUDENT HELP

▸ **Study Tip**
In a right triangle the hypotenuse is always the longest side.

   a. The lengths are sides of a right triangle because

$$11.9^2 + 12.0^2 = 141.61 + 144 = 285.61 = 16.9^2.$$

   b. The lengths are not sides of a right triangle because

$$5^2 + 11^2 = 25 + 121 = 146 \neq 12^2.$$

Baseball

EXAMPLE 4 *Using the Pythagorean Theorem*

The length of each side of a baseball diamond is 90 feet. What is the distance from home plate to second base?

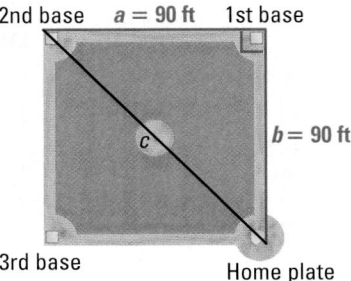

2nd base $a = 90$ ft   1st base

$b = 90$ ft

c

3rd base   Home plate

SOLUTION

The diagonal from home plate to second base is the hypotenuse c of a right triangle. The length of each leg is 90 feet.

$c^2 = a^2 + b^2$	Write Pythagorean theorem.
$c^2 = 90^2 + 90^2$	Substitute 90 for a and for b.
$c^2 = 8100 + 8100$	Multiply.
$c^2 = 16{,}200$	Add.
$c = \sqrt{16{,}200}$	Find positive square root of each side.
$c = 90\sqrt{2}$	Simplify.
$c \approx 127.3$	Use a calculator.

▶ The distance from home plate to second base is about 127.3 feet.

EXAMPLE 5 *Using the Pythagorean Converse*

You can take a rope and tie 12 equally spaced knots in it. You can then use the rope to check that a corner is a right angle. Why does this method work?

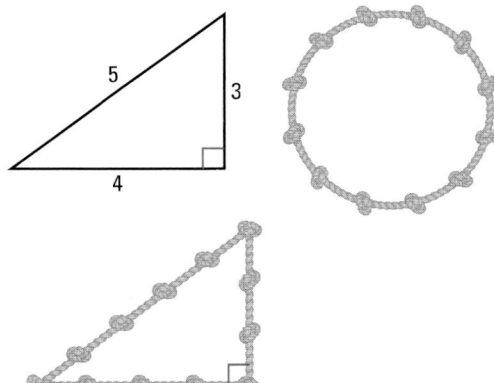

5

3

4

SOLUTION

You can use the rope to form a triangle with a hypotenuse length of 5 and leg lengths of 3 and 4. Use the converse of the Pythagorean theorem to check.

$$5^2 \stackrel{?}{=} 3^2 + 4^2$$

$$25 \stackrel{?}{=} 9 + 16$$

$$25 = 25 \checkmark$$

▶ Because you can use the knots to form the sides of a right triangle, one angle of the triangle must measure 90°. So you can check with the rope that a corner is a right angle.

GUIDED PRACTICE

Vocabulary Check ✓   **1.** The two sides of a right triangle that are not the hypotenuse are the __?__.

2. State the hypothesis and the conclusion of the statement "If x is an even number, then x^2 is an even number."

Concept Check ✓   **3.** Explain how you can use the converse of the Pythagorean theorem to tell whether three given lengths can be sides of a right triangle.

Skill Check ✓   **Find the missing length of the right triangle if a and b are the lengths of the legs and c is the length of the hypotenuse.**

4. $a = 7, b = 24$ **5.** $a = 5, c = 13$ **6.** $b = 15, c = 17$

7. $a = 9, c = 41$ **8.** $b = 11, c = 61$ **9.** $a = 12, b = 35$

Find each missing length.

10.

11.

12.
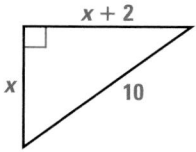

PRACTICE AND APPLICATIONS

STUDENT HELP

► **Extra Practice**
to help you master
skills is on p. 808.

USING THE PYTHAGOREAN THEOREM Find the missing length of the right triangle if a and b are the lengths of the legs and c is the length of the hypotenuse.

13. $a = 3, b = 4$ **14.** $a = 5, c = 10$ **15.** $b = 3, c = 7$

16. $a = 10, b = 24$ **17.** $b = 9, c = 16$ **18.** $a = 14, c = 21$

MISSING LENGTH Find each missing length.

19.

20.

21.

22.

23.

24.
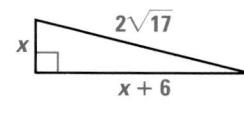

STUDENT HELP

► **HOMEWORK HELP**
Example 1: Exs. 13–18
Example 2: Exs. 19–24
Example 3: Exs. 25–33
Example 4: Exs. 39,
        41–44
Example 5: Ex. 40

DETERMINING RIGHT TRIANGLES Determine whether the given lengths are sides of a right triangle. Explain your reasoning.

25.

26.

27.
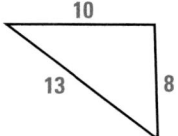

DETERMINING RIGHT TRIANGLES Determine whether the given lengths are sides of a right triangle. Explain your reasoning.

28. 2, 10, 11   **29.** 15, 20, 25   **30.** 5, 12, 13

31. 11, 60, 61   **32.** 7, 24, 26   **33.** 9.9, 2, 10.1

IF-THEN STATEMENTS In Exercises 34–38, state the hypothesis and the conclusion of the statement.

34. If today is Tuesday, then yesterday was Monday.

35. If a polygon is a square, then it is a parallelogram.

36. If $\frac{x}{3} = -15$, then $x = -45$.

37. If the area of a square is 25 square feet, then the length of a side is 5 feet.

38. If a triangle has sides that are 8 inches and 9 inches long, then the length of the third side is greater than 1 inch and less than 17 inches.

39. 🌐 **DIAGONAL OF A FIELD** A field hockey field is a rectangle 60 yards by 100 yards. What is the length of the diagonal from one corner of the field to the opposite corner?

40. *Writing* You have a rope with 30 equally spaced knots in it. How can you use the rope to check that a corner is a right angle?

41. 🌐 **SURVEYING LAND** You are surveying a triangular-shaped piece of land. You have measured and recorded two lengths on a plot plan. What is the length of the property along the street? Round your answer to the nearest hundredth.

🌐 DESIGNING A STAIRCASE In Exercises 42 and 43, you are building the staircase shown at the right.

42. Find the distance d between the edges of each step.

43. The staircase will also have a handrail that is as long as the distance between the edge of the first step and the edge of the top step. How long is the handrail?

44. 🌐 **PLANTING A NEW TREE** You have just planted a new tree. To support the tree in bad weather, you attach guy wires from the trunk of the tree to stakes in the ground. You cut 30 feet of wire into four equal lengths to make the guy wires. You attach four guy wires, evenly spaced around the tree. You put the stakes in the ground five feet from the base of the trunk. Approximately how far up the trunk should you attach the guy wires?

45. MULTI-STEP PROBLEM Amalia and Cindy leave from the same point at the same time. Cindy bicycles east at a rate that is 2 miles per hour faster than Amalia, who bicycles south. After one hour they are 10 miles apart.

    a. Let *r* represent Amalia's rate in miles per hour. Write an expression for the distance each girl has traveled in one hour.

    b. Draw and label a diagram of the situation.

    c. Use the Pythagorean theorem to find how fast each person is traveling.

    d. *Writing* Which method did you use to solve the quadratic equation? Give a reason for your choice.

★ Challenge

In Exercises 46–48, use the fact that a Pythagorean triple is a group of three integers, such as 3, 4, and 5, that could be the lengths of the sides of a right triangle.

46. Find two other Pythagorean triples that are not multiples of 3, 4, 5 or of each other.

47. Notice that $3 \cdot 4 \cdot 5 = 60$. Is the product of the three numbers in each Pythagorean triple evenly divisible by 3? by 4? by 5?

EXTRA CHALLENGE
→ www.mcdougallittell.com

48. Do your observations in Exercise 47 suggest a statement about Pythagorean triples that might be true? Explain.

MIXED REVIEW

PLOTTING ORDERED PAIRS **Plot the ordered pairs in a coordinate plane.** (Review 4.1 for 12.6)

49. $(2, 5), (0, -1), (3, 1)$

50. $(2, -5), (2, 4), (-3, 0)$

51. $(-1, -2), (-4, 5), (0, 2)$

52. $(1, 4), (-2, -1), (3, -1)$

53. $(2, 3), (-2, -3), (4, -2)$

54. $(1, 3), (-3, 1), (3, -4)$

FINDING INTERCEPTS **Find the *x*-intercepts of the graph of the equation.** (Review 9.5)

55. $y = x^2 + 2x + 15$

56. $y = x^2 + 8x + 12$

57. $y = x^2 + x - 10$

58. $y = x^2 + 8x + 16$

59. $y = x^2 + 3x + 1$

60. $y = x^2 - 8x - 11$

61. $y = x^2 + 8x - 10$

62. $y = 3x^2 + 20x + 1$

63. $y = -x^2 + 4x + 1$

FACTORING SPECIAL PRODUCTS **Factor the expression.** (Review 10.7)

64. $x^2 - 64$

65. $16x^2 - 25$

66. $x^2 + 18x + 81$

67. $7x^2 - 28x + 28$

68. $45x^2 - 60x + 20$

69. $-48x^2 + 216x - 243$

70. GEOMETRIC MEAN The geometric mean of 16 and *a* is 32. What is the value of *a*? (Review 12.3)

71. POSTAGE STAMPS In 1960, a first-class United States postage stamp cost $.04. In 1999, a first-class United States postage stamp cost $.33. Write a compound inequality that represents the different prices that a postage stamp could have cost between 1960 and 1999. (Review 6.3)

Solve the equation by completing the square. (Lesson 12.4)

1. $2x^2 - 6x - 15 = 5$ **2.** $4x^2 + 4x - 9 = 0$ **3.** $x^2 + 2x = 2$

Tell whether the given lengths are sides of a right triangle. (Lesson 12.5)

4. 6, 7, 8 **5.** 9, 40, 41 **6.** 12, 35, 37

Find the missing length of the right triangle if a and b are the lengths of the legs and c is the length of the hypotenuse. (Lesson 12.5)

7. $a = 5, b = 12$ **8.** $a = 11, c = 61$ **9.** $b = 63, c = 65$

10. 🌐 **DEPTH OF A SUBMARINE**
The sonar of a Navy cruiser detects a submarine that is 2500 feet away. The point on the water directly above the submarine is 1500 feet away from the front of the cruiser. What is the depth of the submarine? (Lesson 12.5)

1500 ft

2500 ft

Not drawn to scale

MATH & History

History of Pythagorean Theorem

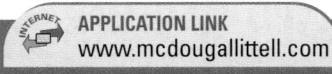

APPLICATION LINK
www.mcdougallittell.com

THEN

THE ANCIENT BABYLONIAN TABLET below suggests that the Babylonians were aware of the theorem now known as the Pythagorean theorem as early as 1650 B.C.

1. The table gives two of three numbers found on the tablet that could be sides of a right triangle. Find the length of the other leg.

NOW

TODAY architects often use right triangles, whose sides show the relationships stated in the Pythagorean theorem.

Leg	Leg	Hypotenuse
119	?	169
56	?	106
161	?	289
65	?	97
2700	?	4500
1771	?	3229

c.1650 B.C.

Babylonian tablet lists Pythagorean triples.

Pythagoras discovers his theorem.

c. 540 B.C.

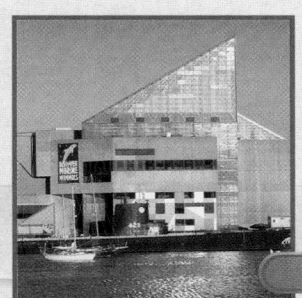

Now

The National Aquarium in Baltimore, Maryland, was designed using right triangles.

12.6

The Distance and Midpoint Formulas

What you should learn

GOAL 1 Find the distance between two points in a coordinate plane.

GOAL 2 Find the midpoint between two points in a coordinate plane.

Why you should learn it

▼ To find distances in **real-life** situations, such as the length of a soccer kick in **Example 3**.

GOAL 1 FINDING THE DISTANCE BETWEEN TWO POINTS

▶ ACTIVITY

Developing Concepts

Investigating Distance

1. Plot $A(2, 1)$ and $B(6, 4)$ on graph paper. Then draw a right triangle that has $\overline{AB}$ as its hypotenuse.

2. Label the coordinates of the vertex C.

3. Find the lengths of the legs of $\triangle ABC$.

4. Use the Pythagorean theorem to find AB.

5. Check the distance by actual measurement.

The steps used in the investigation can be used to develop a general formula for the distance between two points $A(x_1, y_1)$ and $B(x_2, y_2)$. Using the Pythagorean theorem, you can write the equation

$$d^2 = (x_2 - x_1)^2 + (y_2 - y_1)^2.$$

Solving this equation for d produces the **distance formula**.

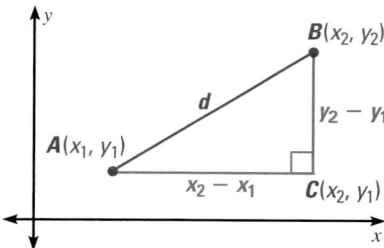

THE DISTANCE FORMULA

The distance d between the points (x_1, y_1) and (x_2, y_2) is
$$d = \sqrt{(x_2 - x_1)^2 + (y_2 - y_1)^2}.$$

EXAMPLE 1 *Finding the Distance Between Two Points*

Find the distance between $(1, 4)$ and $(-2, 3)$.

SOLUTION To find the distance, use the distance formula.

$$d = \sqrt{(x_2 - x_1)^2 + (y_2 - y_1)^2} \qquad \text{Write distance formula.}$$

$$= \sqrt{(-2 - 1)^2 + (3 - 4)^2} \qquad \text{Substitute.}$$

$$= \sqrt{10} \qquad \text{Simplify.}$$

$$\approx 3.16 \qquad \text{Use a calculator.}$$

EXAMPLE 2   *Checking a Right Triangle*

Decide whether the points (3, 2), (2, 0), and (−1, 4) are vertices of a right triangle.

SOLUTION

Use the distance formula to find the lengths of the three sides.

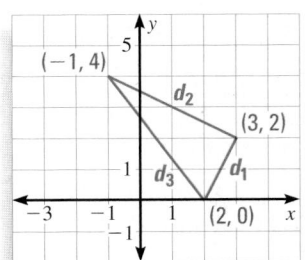

$$d_1 = \sqrt{(3-2)^2 + (2-0)^2} = \sqrt{1+4} = \sqrt{5}$$

$$d_2 = \sqrt{[3-(-1)]^2 + (2-4)^2} = \sqrt{16+4} = \sqrt{20}$$

$$d_3 = \sqrt{[2-(-1)]^2 + (0-4)^2} = \sqrt{9+16} = \sqrt{25}$$

Next find the sum of the squares of the lengths of the two shorter sides.

$$d_1{}^2 + d_2{}^2 = \left(\sqrt{5}\right)^2 + \left(\sqrt{20}\right)^2 \qquad \textbf{Substitute for } d_1 \textbf{ and } d_2.$$

$$= 5 + 20 \qquad\qquad\qquad \textbf{Simplify.}$$

$$= 25 \qquad\qquad\qquad\quad \textbf{Add.}$$

The sum of the squares of the lengths of the shorter sides is 25, which is equal to the square of the length of the longest side, $\left(\sqrt{25}\right)^2$.

▶ The given points are vertices of a right triangle.

· · · · · · · · · ·

When you want to use the distance formula to find a distance in a real-life problem, the first step is to draw a diagram and assign coordinates to the points. This process is called *superimposing* a coordinate system on the diagram.

Soccer

EXAMPLE 3   *Applying the Distance Formula*

A player kicks a soccer ball from a position that is 10 yards from a sideline and 5 yards from a goal line. The ball lands at a position that is 45 yards from the same goal line and 40 yards from the same sideline. How far was the ball kicked?

SOLUTION

You can begin by superimposing a coordinate system on the soccer field. The ball is kicked from the point (10, 5). It lands at the point (40, 45). Use the distance formula.

$$d = \sqrt{(40-10)^2 + (45-5)^2}$$

$$= \sqrt{900 + 1600}$$

$$= \sqrt{2500}$$

$$= 50$$

▶ The ball was kicked 50 yards.

GOAL 2 FINDING THE MIDPOINT BETWEEN TWO POINTS

The **midpoint** of a line segment is the point on the segment that is equidistant from its end-points. The *midpoint between two points* is the midpoint of the line segment connecting them.

THE MIDPOINT FORMULA

The midpoint between (x_1, y_1) and (x_2, y_2) is $\left(\dfrac{x_1 + x_2}{2}, \dfrac{y_1 + y_2}{2}\right)$.

EXAMPLE 4 *Finding the Midpoint Between Two Points*

Find the midpoint between $(-2, 3)$ and $(4, 2)$. Use a graph to check the result.

SOLUTION

$$\left(\frac{-2 + 4}{2}, \frac{3 + 2}{2}\right) = \left(\frac{2}{2}, \frac{5}{2}\right) = \left(1, \frac{5}{2}\right)$$

▶ The midpoint is $\left(1, \dfrac{5}{2}\right)$.

✔**CHECK** From the graph, you can see that the point $\left(1, \dfrac{5}{2}\right)$ appears halfway between $(-2, 3)$ and $(4, 2)$. You can also use the distance formula to check that the distances from the midpoint to each given point are equal.

Computers

EXAMPLE 5 *Applying the Midpoint Formula*

You are using computer software to design a video game. You want to place a buried treasure chest halfway between the center of the base of a palm tree and the corner of a large boulder. Find where you should place the treasure chest.

SOLUTION

Begin by assigning coordinates to the locations of the two landmarks. The center of the base of the palm tree is at $(200, 75)$. The corner of the boulder is at $(25, 175)$. Then use the midpoint formula to find the point that is halfway between the two landmarks.

$$\left(\frac{25 + 200}{2}, \frac{175 + 75}{2}\right) = \left(\frac{225}{2}, \frac{250}{2}\right)$$

$$= (112.5, 125)$$

▶ You should place the treasure chest at $(112.5, 125)$.

GUIDED PRACTICE

Vocabulary Check ✓

1. What is meant by the *midpoint* between two points?

Concept Check ✓

2. Explain how you can use the Pythagorean theorem to find the distance between any two points in a coordinate plane.

Skill Check ✓

Use the coordinate plane to estimate the distance between the two points. Then use the distance formula to find the distance between the points. Round the result to the nearest hundredth.

3. $(1, 5), (-3, 1)$

4. $(-3, -2), (4, 1)$

5. $(5, -2), (-1, 1)$

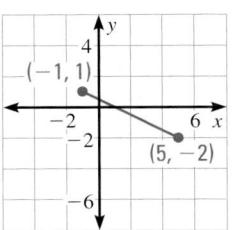

Decide whether the points are vertices of a right triangle.

6. $(0, 0), (20, 0), (20, 21)$

7. $(4, 0), (4, -4), (10, -4)$

8. $(-2, 0), (-1, 0), (1, 7)$

9. $(2, 0), (-2, 2), (-3, -5)$

Find the midpoint between the two points.

10. $(4, 4), (-1, 2)$

11. $(6, 2), (2, -3)$

12. $(-5, 3), (-3, -3)$

13. 🌐 **SOCCER** Suppose the soccer ball in Example 3 lands in a position that is 25 yards from the same goal line and 25 yards from the same sideline. How far was the ball kicked?

PRACTICE AND APPLICATIONS

STUDENT HELP

▶ **Extra Practice**
to help you master
skills is on p. 808

FINDING DISTANCE **Find the distance between the two points. Round the result to the nearest hundredth if necessary.**

14. $(2, 0), (8, -3)$

15. $(2, -8), (-3, 3)$

16. $(3, -1), (0, 3)$

17. $(5, 8), (-2, 3)$

18. $(-3, 1), (2, 6)$

19. $(-6, -2), (-3, -5)$

20. $(4, 5), (-1, 3)$

21. $(-6, 1), (3, 1)$

22. $(-2, -1), (3, -3)$

23. $(3.5, 6), (-3.5, -2)$

24. $\left(\frac{1}{2}, \frac{1}{4}\right), (2, 1)$

25. $\left(\frac{1}{3}, \frac{1}{6}\right), \left(-\frac{2}{3}, \frac{8}{3}\right)$

STUDENT HELP

▶ **HOMEWORK HELP**
Example 1: Exs. 14–25
Example 2: Exs. 26–33
Example 3: Exs. 46–53
Example 4: Exs. 34–45
Example 5: Exs. 54, 55

RIGHT TRIANGLES **Graph the points. Decide whether they are vertices of a right triangle.**

26. $(4, 0), (2, 1), (-1, -5)$

27. $(5, 4), (2, 1), (-3, 2)$

28. $(1, -5), (2, 3), (-3, 4)$

29. $(-1, 1), (-3, 3), (-7, -1)$

30. $(-3, 2), (-3, 5), (0, 2)$

31. $(3, -1), (2, 4), (-3, 0)$

32. $(-2, 2), (3, 4), (4, 2)$

33. $(0, -4), (4, -1), (4, -4)$

FINDING THE MIDPOINT Find the midpoint between the two points.

34. $(3, 0), (-5, 4)$

35. $(0, 0), (0, 8)$

36. $(1, 2), (5, 4)$

37. $(-1, 2), (7, 4)$

38. $(-3, 3), (2, -2)$

39. $(2, 7), (4, 3)$

40. $(-1, 1), (-4, -4)$

41. $(-4, 0), (-1, -5)$

42. $(5, 1), (1, -5)$

43. $(0, -3), (-4, 2)$

44. $(5, -5), (-5, 1)$

45. $(-4, -3), (-1, -5)$

DISTANCES ON MAPS In Exercises 46–48, use the map. Each side of a square in the coordinate plane that is superimposed on the map represents 95 miles. The points represent city locations.

46. Use the distance formula to estimate the distance between Pierre, South Dakota, and Santa Fe, New Mexico.

47. Use the distance formula to estimate the distance between Wichita, Kansas, and Cheyenne, Wyoming.

48. Use the distance formula to estimate the distance between Oklahoma City, Oklahoma, and Des Moines, Iowa.

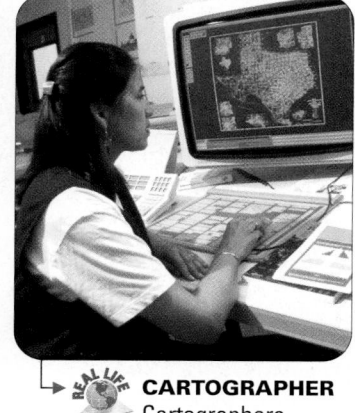
GEOMETRY CONNECTION In Exercises 49–53, use the diagram below.

49. Copy the diagram of triangle ABC on graph paper.

50. Find the length of each side of the triangle.

51. Find the midpoint of each side of the triangle.

52. Join the midpoints to form a new triangle. Find the length of each of its sides.

53. Compare the perimeters of the two triangles.

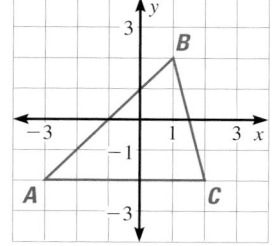

HIKING TRIP In Exercises 54 and 55, use the following information. You and a friend go hiking. You hike 3 miles north and 2 miles west. Starting from the same point, your friend hikes 4 miles east and 1 mile south.

54. How far apart are you and your friend? (*Hint*: Draw a diagram on a grid.)

55. If you and your friend want to meet for lunch, where could you meet so that both of you hike the same distance? How far do you have to hike?

GEOMETRY CONNECTION In Exercises 56–58, use the following information. A trapezoid is *isosceles* if its two opposite nonparallel sides have the same length.

56. Draw the polygon whose vertices are $A(1, 1)$, $B(5, 9)$, $C(2, 8)$, and $D(0, 4)$.

57. Show that the polygon is a trapezoid by showing that only two of the sides are parallel.

58. Use the distance formula to show that the trapezoid is isosceles.

59. MULTIPLE CHOICE What is the distance between $(-6, -2)$ and $(2, 4)$?

  Ⓐ $2\sqrt{5}$ Ⓑ $2\sqrt{7}$ Ⓒ 10 Ⓓ 28

60. MULTIPLE CHOICE What is the midpoint between $(-2, -3)$ and $\left(1, \frac{1}{2}\right)$?

  Ⓐ $\left(-1, -2\frac{1}{2}\right)$ Ⓑ $\left(-\frac{1}{2}, -2\frac{1}{2}\right)$ Ⓒ $\left(-1, -1\frac{1}{4}\right)$ Ⓓ $\left(-\frac{1}{2}, -1\frac{1}{4}\right)$

61. MULTIPLE CHOICE The vertices of a right triangle are $(0, 0)$, $(0, 6)$, and $(6, 0)$. What is the length of the hypotenuse?

  Ⓐ 6 Ⓑ $6\sqrt{2}$ Ⓒ 36 Ⓓ 72

★ **Challenge**

🌐 **TRIP PLANNING** In Exercises 62–64, use the following information. You are planning a family vacation. Each side of a square in the coordinate plane that is superimposed on the map represents 50 miles.

62. How far is it from your home to the amusement park?

63. You leave your home and go to the amusement park. After visiting the amusement park, you go to the beach. You return home. How far did you travel?

64. During your vacation, you want to visit all of the sites on the map. There are two orders in which to visit the sites so that you travel the shortest distance. What are the two orders?

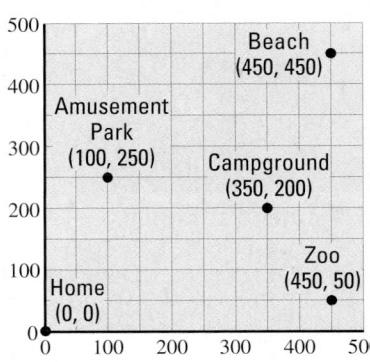

┌ **EXTRA CHALLENGE**
→ www.mcdougallittell.com

MIXED REVIEW

FACTORING Factor the expression completely. (Review 10.8)

65. $3x^3 + 12x^2 - 15x$

66. $x^4 - 3x^2 - 25x^2 + 75$

CLASSIFYING EQUATIONS Does the equation model *direct variation*, *inverse variation*, or *neither*? (Review 11.3)

67. $x = \dfrac{7}{y}$

68. $y = 8x$

69. $y = 9x + 1$

DIVIDING POLYNOMIALS Divide. (Review 11.7)

70. $(6z + 10) \div 2$

71. $\left(7x^3 - 2x^2\right) \div 14x$

GEOMETRY ▶ **CONNECTION** In Exercises 72 and 73, the two triangles are similar. Write an equation and solve it to find the length of the side marked x. (Review 3.2 for 12.7)

72.

73.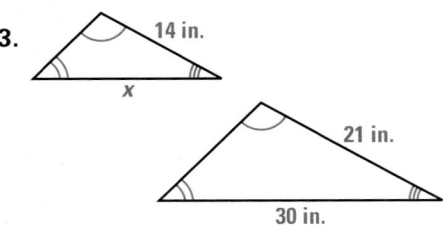

ACTIVITY 12.7

Developing Concepts

Investigating Similar Triangles

GROUP ACTIVITY
Work in a small group.

MATERIALS
• graph paper
• ruler
• protractor

▶ **QUESTION** What relationships are there between the sides of similar right triangles?

▶ **EXPLORING THE CONCEPT**

1 Copy the three triangles onto a sheet of paper. They are similar because their corresponding angles are the same.

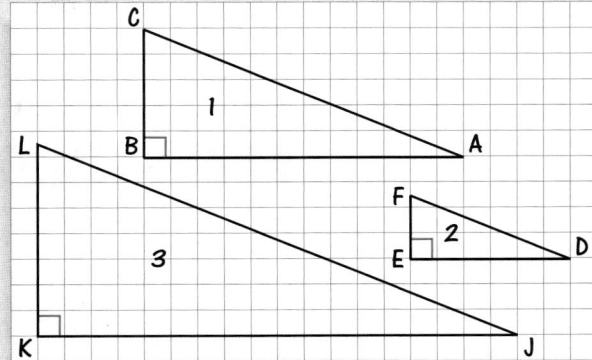

2 Label the lengths of the sides of each triangle to the nearest half unit. Use a strip of graph paper to measure the length of the hypotenuse.

3 Copy and complete the table. Find the ratios to the nearest hundredth.

	Shorter leg	Longer leg	Hypotenuse	$\dfrac{\text{Shorter leg}}{\text{Hypotenuse}}$	$\dfrac{\text{Longer leg}}{\text{Hypotenuse}}$	$\dfrac{\text{Shorter leg}}{\text{Longer leg}}$
△1	?	?	?	?	?	?
△2	?	?	?	?	?	?
△3	?	?	?	?	?	?

▶ **DRAWING CONCLUSIONS**

1. What do you notice about the ratios you found for all three similar triangles?

2. Each person in the group should draw a different triangle that is similar to the triangles at the top of the page. Exchange triangles and use a protractor to check that the triangles are similar.

3. For your triangle, predict what the following ratios will be. Then measure the sides and find each ratio to test your prediction.

    a. $\dfrac{\text{shorter leg}}{\text{hypotenuse}}$ b. $\dfrac{\text{longer leg}}{\text{hypotenuse}}$ c. $\dfrac{\text{shorter leg}}{\text{longer leg}}$

Trigonometric Ratios

What you should learn

GOAL 1 Use the sine, cosine, and tangent of an angle.

GOAL 2 Use trigonometric ratios in **real-life** problems, such as finding cloud height in **Ex. 20**.

Why you should learn it

▼ To solve **real-life** problems, such as finding the height of a parasailer in **Example 3**.

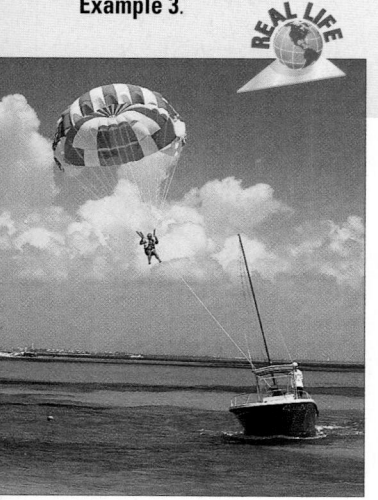

GOAL 1 USING TRIGONOMETRIC RATIOS

In the ancient Greek language, the word *trigonometry* means *measurement of triangles*. A **trigonometric ratio** is a ratio of the lengths of two sides of a right triangle. The three basic trigonometric ratios are **sine**, **cosine**, and **tangent**. You can abbreviate them as *sin*, *cos*, and *tan*.

TRIGONOMETRIC RATIOS

$$\sin A = \frac{\text{side opposite } \angle A}{\text{hypotenuse}} = \frac{a}{c}$$

$$\cos A = \frac{\text{side adjacent to } \angle A}{\text{hypotenuse}} = \frac{b}{c}$$

$$\tan A = \frac{\text{side opposite } \angle A}{\text{side adjacent to } \angle A} = \frac{a}{b}$$

Because all right triangles with a given measure for $\angle A$ are similar, the value of a trigonometric ratio depends only on the measure of $\angle A$. It does not depend on the triangle's size.

EXAMPLE 1 *Finding Trigonometric Ratios*

For $\triangle DEF$, find the sine, the cosine, and the tangent of the angle.

a. $\angle D$

b. $\angle E$

SOLUTION

a. For $\angle D$, the opposite side is 5, and the adjacent side is 12. The hypotenuse is 13.

$$\sin D = \frac{\text{opposite}}{\text{hypotenuse}} = \frac{5}{13}$$

$$\cos D = \frac{\text{adjacent}}{\text{hypotenuse}} = \frac{12}{13}$$

$$\tan D = \frac{\text{opposite}}{\text{adjacent}} = \frac{5}{12}$$

b. For $\angle E$, the opposite side is 12, and the adjacent side is 5. The hypotenuse is 13.

$$\sin E = \frac{\text{opposite}}{\text{hypotenuse}} = \frac{12}{13}$$

$$\cos E = \frac{\text{adjacent}}{\text{hypotenuse}} = \frac{5}{13}$$

$$\tan E = \frac{\text{opposite}}{\text{adjacent}} = \frac{12}{5}$$

STUDENT HELP

→ **Trig Table**
For a table of
trigonometric ratios,
see p. 812.

SOLVING RIGHT TRIANGLES If you know the measure of one angle and the length of one side of a right triangle, then you can use trigonometric ratios and a calculator or a table to find the lengths of the other two sides. This is called *solving a right triangle.*

EXAMPLE 2   *Solving a Right Triangle*

For $\triangle PQR$, $p = 5$ and the measure of $\angle P$ is 30°.

a. Find the length q.

b. Find the length r.

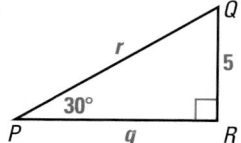

SOLUTION

a. You are given the side opposite $\angle P$, and you need to find the length of the adjacent side.

$$\tan P = \frac{\text{opposite}}{\text{adjacent}}$$ **Definition of tangent**

$$\tan 30° = \frac{5}{q}$$ **Substitute 5 for p and 30° for $\angle P$.**

$$q = \frac{5}{\tan 30°}$$ **Solve for q.**

$$q \approx \frac{5}{0.5774}$$ **Use a calculator or a table.**

$$q \approx 8.66$$ **Simplify.**

▶ The length q is about 8.66 units.

b. You are given the side opposite $\angle P$ and you need to find the length of the hypotenuse.

$$\sin P = \frac{\text{opposite}}{\text{hypotenuse}}$$ **Definition of sine**

$$\sin 30° = \frac{5}{r}$$ **Substitute 5 for p and 30° for $\angle P$.**

$$r = \frac{5}{\sin 30°}$$ **Solve for r.**

$$r = \frac{5}{0.5}$$ **Use a calculator or a table.**

$$r = 10$$ **Simplify.**

▶ The length r is 10 units.

STUDENT HELP

→ **Study Tip**
When you use a calcula-
tor to find trigonometric
ratios, be sure that the
calculator is set in
degree mode.

✓ **CHECK** You can use the Pythagorean theorem to check that the results are reasonable. Because the value of q was rounded, the check will not be exact.

$$p^2 + q^2 = r^2$$ **Pythagorean theorem**

$$5^2 + 8.66^2 \overset{?}{=} 10^2$$ **Substitute for p, q, and r.**

$$99.996 \approx 100$$ **Side lengths are approximately correct.**

GOAL 2 USING TRIGONOMETRIC RATIOS IN REAL LIFE

EXAMPLE 3 *Solving a Right Triangle*

Parasailing

A boat is pulling a parasailer. The line to the parasailer is 800 feet long. The angle between the line and the water is about 25°.

   a. How high is the parasailer?

   b. How far back is the parasailer from the boat?

Not drawn to scale

800 ft

25°

A

B

C

SOLUTION

a. Find the length of the side opposite ∠*A*.

$$\sin A = \frac{\text{opposite}}{\text{hypotenuse}}$$ **Definition of sine**

$$\sin 25° = \frac{a}{800}$$ **Substitute 800 for *c* and 25° for ∠*A*.**

$$800 \cdot \sin 25° \approx a$$ **Multiply each side by 800.**

$$0.4226(800) \approx a$$ **Use a calculator or a table.**

$$338.08 \approx a$$ **Simplify.**

▶ The parasailer is about 338 feet above the water.

b. Find the length of the side adjacent to ∠*A*.

$$\cos A = \frac{\text{adjacent}}{\text{hypotenuse}}$$ **Definition of cosine**

$$\cos 25° = \frac{b}{800}$$ **Substitute 800 for *c* and 25° for ∠*A*.**

$$800 \cdot \cos 25° = b$$ **Multiply each side by 800.**

$$0.9063(800) \approx b$$ **Use a calculator or a table.**

$$725.04 \approx b$$ **Simplify.**

▶ The parasailer is about 725 feet back from the boat.

GUIDED PRACTICE

Vocabulary Check ✓

1. Define *trigonometric ratio*.

Concept Check ✓

2. Is it *true* or *false* that for any right triangle with a 30° angle, sin 30° = 0.5? Explain.

Skill Check ✓

In Exercises 3–5, use △ABC at the right.

3. Find the sine of ∠A.

4. Find the cosine of ∠A.

5. Find the tangent of ∠A.

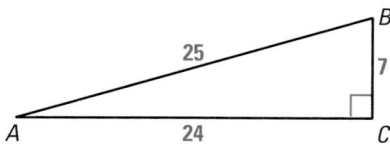

Find the missing lengths of the sides of the triangle. Round to the nearest hundredth. Use the Pythagorean theorem to check the result.

6.

7.

8.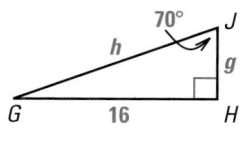

9. 🌐 **PARASAILING** In Example 3, suppose the angle is 35°. How high is the parasailer? How far back is the parasailer?

PRACTICE AND APPLICATIONS

STUDENT HELP

➡ **Extra Practice**
to help you master
skills is on p. 808.

FINDING TRIGONOMETRIC RATIOS Find the sine, the cosine, and the tangent of ∠R and of ∠S.

10.

11.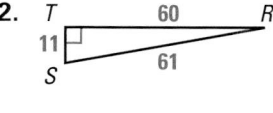

12. T — 60 — R, 11, S, 61

SOLVING RIGHT TRIANGLES Find the missing lengths of the sides of the triangle. Round your answers to the nearest hundredth. Use the Pythagorean theorem to check.

13.

14.

15.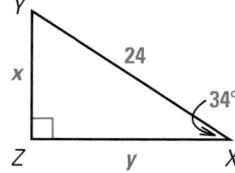

STUDENT HELP

➡ **HOMEWORK HELP**
Example 1: Exs. 10–12
Example 2: Exs. 13–18
Example 3: Exs. 19, 20

16.

17.

18.

19. **CRANE OPERATOR** You are a crane operator using a crane with a 210-foot boom. You lift a load so that the load is directly in front of you. You estimate that the angle between the boom and the line between you and the load is 35°. About how far are you from the load?

Not drawn to scale

210 ft

35°

20. **CLOUD HEIGHT** You are doing an experiment for your science class. You shine a spotlight from the ground straight up onto a cloud to measure the height of the cloud. Your friend stands 500 feet from the spotlight. She estimates that the angle formed between the ground and the line from her feet to the cloud is 25°. Draw a sketch to model the situation. Then find the height of the cloud.

21. **COLLINSVILLE CATSUP BOTTLE** You are standing 197 feet from the base of the world's largest catsup bottle located in Collinsville, Illinois. You estimate that the angle between your eye level and the line from your eyes to the top of the bottle is 40°. If you are 5 feet tall, about how high is the top of the bottle?

Not drawn to scale

40°

197 ft

22. **DINOSAUR TRACKS** You are a paleontologist. You are estimating the length of a dinosaur's hind legs based on its track marks. You measure the pace length as three feet. The pace length represents the base of an isosceles triangle, where the equal sides are the dinosaur's hind legs that enclose the walking angle. Assuming the walking angle is 40°, what is the length of the dinosaur's hind legs?

20°

3 ft

23. **VIEWING ANGLE** A car is traveling on a level road toward a mountain two kilometers high. The angle of elevation from the car to the top of the mountain changes from 6° to 15°. How far has the car traveled?

Test Preparation

24. MULTI-STEP PROBLEM Use the triangle below.

a. Find the length q.

b. Describe two methods for finding the length r.

c. Find the length r.

d. *Writing* Which method did you use in part (c)? Tell why you chose that method.

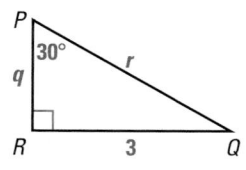

★ **Challenge**

EXTENSION: SLOPE AND ANGLE In Exercises 25 and 26, find the slope of the line that passes through the points. Explain how the slope of the line is related to ∠A.

25.

26.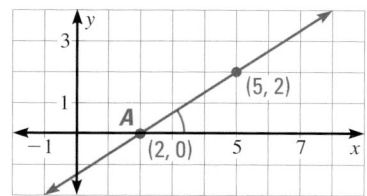

EXTRA CHALLENGE
www.mcdougallittell.com

27. LOGICAL REASONING A line with a positive slope passes through the origin, making a 60° angle with the positive x-axis. Write an equation of the line.

MIXED REVIEW

COUNTEREXAMPLES Decide whether the statement is *true* or *false*. If it is false, give a counterexample. (Review 2.1 for 12.8)

28. The absolute value of a number is always positive.

29. The opposite of a number is always positive.

USING THE DISTRIBUTIVE PROPERTY Use the distributive property to simplify the expression. (Review 2.6 for 12.8)

30. $6(w - 3)$

31. $-p(p + 1)$

32. $-(x - 8)$

33. $(x + 3)x$

34. $(x - 2)5x$

35. $(4 + x)(-6x)$

SUBTRACTING VERTICALLY Use a vertical format to subtract the second polynomial from the first polynomial. (Review 10.1)

36. $6x^2 - 3x + 2, 2x^2 + x + 7$

37. $4x^3 + 3x^2 + 8x + 6, 2x^3 - 3x^2 - 7x$

38. $10x^3 + 15, 17x^3 - 4x + 5$

39. $-2x^3 + 5x^2 - x + 8, -2x^3 + 3x - 4$

SIMPLIFYING RATIONAL EXPRESSIONS Simplify the expression. (Review 11.6)

40. $\dfrac{3}{x} + \dfrac{x + 9}{x}$

41. $\dfrac{8}{4a + 1} - \dfrac{5}{4a + 1}$

42. $\dfrac{2}{2x} + \dfrac{12}{x}$

43. $\dfrac{5}{4x} - \dfrac{7}{3x}$

44. $\dfrac{2x}{x + 1} + \dfrac{5}{x + 3}$

45. $\dfrac{6x}{x + 1} - \dfrac{2x + 4}{x + 1}$

12.8

Logical Reasoning: Proof

What you should learn

GOAL 1 Use logical reasoning and proof to prove a statement is true.

GOAL 2 Prove that a statement is false.

Why you should learn it

▼ To help solve **real-life** problems, such as defending a client in court in **Example 4**.

GOAL 1 PROVING A STATEMENT IS TRUE

LOGICAL REASONING Mathematics is believed to have begun with practical "rules of thumb" that were developed to deal with real-life problems, such as tax records, the surveying of fields, inventories of storehouses, business transactions between merchants, and astronomical calculations. Then, about 2500 years ago, Greek geometers developed a different approach toward mathematics. Starting with a handful of properties that they believed to be true, these geometers insisted on logical reasoning as the basis for developing more elaborate mathematical tools. These more elaborate tools, which can be proved to be true, are called *theorems*.

The basic properties of mathematics that mathematicians accept without proof are called **postulates** or **axioms**. Many of the rules that were discussed in Chapter 2, such as the properties of addition, the properties of multiplication, and the distributive property, fall into this category. The following chart provides a summary of the rules that underlie algebra.

CONCEPT SUMMARY — **THE BASIC AXIOMS OF ALGEBRA**

Let a, b, and c be real numbers.

Axioms of Addition and Multiplication

CLOSURE:	$a + b$ is a real number.	ab is a real number.
COMMUTATIVE:	$a + b = b + a$	$ab = ba$
ASSOCIATIVE:	$(a + b) + c = a + (b + c)$	$(ab)c = a(bc)$
IDENTITY:	$a + 0 = a, 0 + a = a$	$a(1) = a, 1(a) = a$
INVERSE:	$a + (-a) = 0$	$a\left(\dfrac{1}{a}\right) = 1, a \neq 0$

Axiom Relating Addition and Multiplication

DISTRIBUTIVE:	$a(b + c) = ab + ac$	$(a + b)c = ac + bc$

Axioms of Equality

ADDITION:	If $a = b$, then $a + c = b + c$.
MULTIPLICATION:	If $a = b$, then $ac = bc$.
SUBSTITUTION:	If $a = b$, then a can be substituted for b.

Once a list of axioms has been accepted, you can add more rules, formulas, and properties to the list. Some of the new concepts are definitions. You don't have to prove a definition, but it must be consistent with previous definitions and axioms. For instance, the definition of *reciprocal* does not have to be proved.

Other new statements, called **theorems**, do have to be proved. For instance, basic axioms have been used to prove the theorem that for all real numbers b and c, $c(-b) = -cb$. Once a theorem is proved, it can be used as a reason in proofs of other theorems.

EXAMPLE 1 *Proving a Theorem*

┌─ **STUDENT HELP**

▸ **Study Tip**
When you are proving a new theorem, every step must be justified by an axiom, a definition, given information, or a previously proved theorem.

Use the definition of subtraction, $a - b = a + (-b)$, to prove the following theorem: $c(a - b) = ca - cb$.

SOLUTION

$$
\begin{aligned}
c(a - b) &= c[a + (-b)] && \text{Definition of subtraction} \\
&= ca + c(-b) && \text{Distributive property} \\
&= ca + (-cb) && \text{Theorem stated above} \\
&= ca - cb && \text{Definition of subtraction}
\end{aligned}
$$

· · · · · · · · · ·

A **conjecture** is a statement that is thought to be true but is not yet proved. Often it is a statement based on observation.

EXAMPLE 2 *Goldbach's Conjecture*

Christian Goldbach (1690–1764) thought the following statement might be true. It is now referred to as *Goldbach's Conjecture*.

Every even integer, except 2, is equal to the sum of two prime numbers.

The following list shows that every even number between 4 and 30 is equal to the sum of two prime numbers. Does this list prove that *every* even number greater than 2 is equal to the sum of two prime numbers?

$4 = 2 + 2$	$6 = 3 + 3$	$8 = 3 + 5$	$10 = 3 + 7$
$12 = 5 + 7$	$14 = 3 + 11$	$16 = 3 + 13$	$18 = 5 + 13$
$20 = 3 + 17$	$22 = 3 + 19$	$24 = 5 + 19$	$26 = 3 + 23$
$28 = 5 + 23$	$30 = 7 + 23$		

SOLUTION

This list of examples *does not* prove the conjecture. No number of examples can prove that the rule is true for *every* even integer greater than 2. (At the time this book is being written, no one has been able to prove or disprove Goldbach's Conjecture.)

GOAL 2 PROVING A STATEMENT IS FALSE

Sometimes people propose new rules but later find that they *are not* consistent with the axioms, definitions, and theorems in the accepted list. To show that a conjecture is false, you need only one counterexample.

EXAMPLE 3 *Finding a Counterexample*

STUDENT HELP

> **Look Back**
> For help with counter-
> examples, see p. 66.

Assign values to a and b to show that the following conjecture is false.

$$a + (-b) = (-a) + b.$$

SOLUTION

You can choose any values of a and b. For instance, let $a = 1$ and let $b = 2$.

Evaluate the left side of the equation.

$$a + (-b) = 1 + (-2) \qquad \text{Substitute 1 for } a \text{ and 2 for } b.$$
$$= -1 \qquad \text{Simplify.}$$

Evaluate the right side of the equation.

$$(-a) + b = (-1) + 2 \qquad \text{Substitute 1 for } a \text{ and 2 for } b.$$
$$= 1 \qquad \text{Simplify.}$$

Because $-1 \neq 1$, you have shown one case in which $a + (-b) = (-a) + b$ is false. The counterexample of $a = 1$ and $b = 2$ is sufficient to prove that $a + (-b) = (-a) + b$ is false. If the conjecture were true, it would have to work for *any* choices of a and b.

· · · · · · · · · ·

INDIRECT PROOF In this lesson you have used direct proofs to prove that statements are true, and you have used counterexamples to prove that statements are false.

Another type of proof is **indirect proof**. To prove a statement indirectly, assume that the statement is false. If this assumption leads to an impossibility, then you have proved that the original statement is true. An indirect proof is also called a *proof by contradiction*.

EXAMPLE 4 *Use of Contradiction in Real Life*

FOCUS ON CAREERS

LAWYERS
Lawyers represent people in criminal and civil trials by presenting evidence supporting their client's case. They also give advice on legal matters.

CAREER LINK
www.mcdougallittell.com

LAWYERS You are a lawyer. You have been assigned to defend someone accused of violating a law uptown at 10:00 A.M. on March 22. You argue that if guilty, your client must have been there at that time. You have a video of your client being interviewed by a TV reporter at a political rally on the other side of town at the same time.

You argue that it would be impossible for your client to be uptown at 10:00 A.M. and on the other side of town at 10:00 A.M. Therefore your client cannot be guilty.

EXAMPLE 5   *Using an Indirect Proof*

Use an indirect proof to prove that $\sqrt{2}$ is an irrational number.

SOLUTION

Assume that $\sqrt{2}$ is *not* irrational. Then $\sqrt{2}$ is rational and can be written as the quotient of two integers a and b that have no common factors other than 1.

$$\sqrt{2} = \frac{a}{b} \qquad \textbf{Assume } \sqrt{2} \textbf{ is a rational number.}$$

$$2 = \frac{a^2}{b^2} \qquad \textbf{Square each side.}$$

$$2b^2 = a^2 \qquad \textbf{Multiply each side by } b^2.$$

This implies that 2 is a factor of a^2. Therefore 2 is also a factor of a. (You will prove this in Exercise 25 on page 763.) So a can be written as $2c$.

$$2b^2 = (2c)^2 \qquad \textbf{Substitute 2c for } a.$$

$$2b^2 = 4c^2 \qquad \textbf{Simplify.}$$

$$b^2 = 2c^2 \qquad \textbf{Divide each side by 2.}$$

This implies that 2 is a factor of b^2 and also a factor of b. So 2 is a factor of both a and b. But this is impossible because a and b have no common factors. Therefore it must be impossible that $\sqrt{2}$ is a rational number. So you can conclude that $\sqrt{2}$ must be an irrational number.

GUIDED PRACTICE

Vocabulary Check ✓   **1.** Explain the difference between an axiom and a theorem.

2. What is the first step of an indirect proof?

Concept Check ✓   **In Exercises 3–11, state the basic axiom of algebra that is represented.**

3. $y(1) = y$ **4.** $2x + 3 = 3 + 2x$ **5.** $5(x + y) = 5x + 5y$

6. $(4x)y = 4(xy)$ **7.** $y + 0 = y$ **8.** $x + (-x) = 0$

9. $x\left(\dfrac{1}{x}\right) = 1$ **10.** $cd = dc$ **11.** $(x + y) + z = x + (y + z)$

12. Is subtraction closed for the positive real numbers? That is, if a and b are positive real numbers, must $(a - b)$ be a positive real number? Explain your thinking.

Skill Check ✓   **13.** Copy and complete the proof of the statement: If $a = b$ and $c = d$, then $ac = bd$. Each variable represents any real number.

$a = b$	**Given**
$ac = bc$	**Multiplication axiom of equality**
$c = d$	**Given**
$bc = bd$	**?**
$ac = bd$	**?**

PRACTICE AND APPLICATIONS

STUDENT HELP

→ **Extra Practice**
to help you master
skills is on p. 808.

14. SUPPLYING REASONS Copy and complete the proof of the statement: For all real numbers a and b, $(a + b) - b = a$.

$(a + b) - b = (a + b) + (-b)$	**Definition of subtraction**
$(a + b) - b = a + [b + (-b)]$	**Associative property of addition**
$(a + b) - b = a + 0$	**____?____**
$(a + b) - b = a$	**____?____**

PROVING THEOREMS In Exercises 15–17, prove the theorem. (Use the basic axioms of algebra and the definition of subtraction given in Example 1.)

15. If a and b are real numbers, then $a - b = -b + a$.

16. If a, b, and c are real numbers, then $(a - b) - c = a - (b + c)$.

17. If a is any real number, then $-1(a) = -a$.

18. PROVING A CONJECTURE A student proposes the following conjecture. *The sum of the first n odd integers is n^2.* She gives four examples: $1 = 1^2$, $1 + 3 = 4 = 2^2$, $1 + 3 + 5 = 9 = 3^2$, and $1 + 3 + 5 + 7 = 16 = 4^2$. Do the examples prove her conjecture? Explain. Do you think the conjecture is true?

FINDING A COUNTEREXAMPLE In Exercises 19–21, find a counterexample to show that the statement is *not* true.

19. If a and b are real numbers, then $(a + b)^2 = a^2 + b^2$.

20. If a, b, and c are nonzero real numbers, then $(a \div b) \div c = a \div (b \div c)$.

21. If a and b are integers, then $a \div b$ is an integer.

22. **GEOMETRY** ▷ **CONNECTION** Explain how the diagrams below can be used to give a geometrical argument to support the conjecture in Exercise 18.

   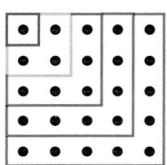

23. THE FOUR-COLOR PROBLEM A famous theorem states that any map can be colored with four different colors so that no two countries that share a border have the same color. No matter how the map shown at the right is colored with three different colors, at least two countries having a common border will have the same color. Does this map serve as a counterexample to the following proposal? Explain.

> *Any map can be colored with three different colors so that no two countries that share a border have the same color.*

STUDENT HELP

→ **HOMEWORK HELP**
Example 1: Exs. 14–17
Example 2: Ex. 18
Example 3: Exs. 19–21
Example 4: Ex. 24
Example 5: Exs. 25–27

INDIRECT PROOF In Exercises 24–27, use an indirect proof to prove that the conclusion is true.

24. Your bus leaves a track meet at 4:30 P.M. and does not travel faster than 60 miles per hour. The meet is 45 miles from home. Your bus will not get you home in time for dinner at 5 P.M.

25. If p is an integer and p^2 is divisible by 2, then p is divisible by 2. (*Hint:* An odd number can be written as $2n + 1$, where n is an integer. An even number can be written as $2n$.)

26. If $a < b$, then $a + c < b + c$.   **27.** If $ac > bc$ and $c > 0$, then $a > b$.

28. PROOF USING THE MIDPOINT Let D represent the midpoint between B and C, as shown at the right. Prove that for any right triangle, the midpoint of its hypotenuse is equidistant from the three vertices of the triangle. In order to prove this, you must first find the distance, BC, between B and C. Using the distance formula, you get $BC = \sqrt{x^2 + y^2}$, so BD and CD must be $\frac{1}{2}\sqrt{x^2 + y^2}$.

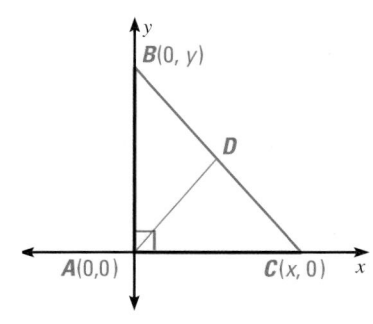

To help you with your proof, use the distance formula to find AD.

29. MULTI-STEP PROBLEM In graph theory, a *complete graph* is one in which every pair of vertices is connected by part of the graph called an *edge*. The following graphs are complete.

| Two vertices | Three vertices | Four vertices | Five vertices |

a. Copy and complete the table.

Vertices	2	3	4	5	6
Edges	1	3	?	?	?

b. Make a conjecture about the relationship between the number of vertices and the number of edges in a complete graph.

c. Use your conjecture to predict how many edges a complete graph with 10 vertices would have.

★ Challenge

30. PYTHAGOREAN THEOREM Explain how the following diagrams could be used to give a geometrical proof of the Pythagorean theorem.

  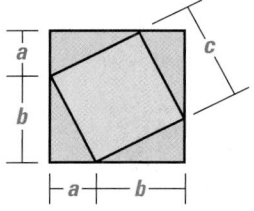

FINDING SOLUTIONS **Decide how many solutions the equation has.** (Review 9.6)

31. $x^2 - 2x + 4 = 0$ **32.** $-2x^2 + 4x - 2 = 0$ **33.** $8x^2 - 8x + 2 = 0$

34. $x^2 - 14x + 49 = 0$ **35.** $-3x^2 - 5x + 1 = 0$ **36.** $6x^2 - x + 5 = 0$

37. $x^2 - 2x - 15 = 0$ **38.** $x^2 + 16x + 64 = 0$ **39.** $x^2 + 11x + 30 = 0$

FINDING SOLUTIONS **Decide whether the ordered pair is a solution of the inequality.** (Review 9.7)

40. $y < x^2 - 2x - 5$; $(1, 1)$ **41.** $y \geq 2x^2 - 8x + 8$; $(3, -2)$

42. $y \leq 2x^2 - 3x + 10$; $(-2, 20)$ **43.** $y > 4x^2 - 48x + 61$; $(1, 17)$

44. $y \geq x^2 + 4x$; $(-2, -4)$ **45.** $y < 3x^2 - 2x$; $(5, 10)$

46. $y > 3x^2 + 50x + 500$; $(-6, 100)$ **47.** $y \geq -x^2 + 3x - \dfrac{15}{4}$; $(2, -3)$

PERCENTS **Solve the percent problem.** (Review 11.2)

48. How much is 15% of $15?   **49.** 41 inches is what percent of 50 inches?

50. 100 is 1% of what number?   **51.** 6 inches is what percent of 3 inches?

52. 1240 is 80% of what number?   **53.** $5 is 33% of what amount of money?

QUIZ 3

Self-Test for Lessons 12.6–12.8

Find the distance between the two points. Round the result to the nearest hundredth if necessary. Then find the midpoint between the two points. (Lesson 12.6)

1. $(1, 3)$, $(7, -9)$ **2.** $(-2, -5)$, $(6, -11)$ **3.** $(0, 0)$, $(8, -14)$

4. $(-8, -8)$, $(-8, 8)$ **5.** $(3, 4)$, $(-3, 4)$ **6.** $(1, 7)$, $(-4, -2)$

7. $(2, 0)$, $(-2, -3)$ **8.** $(-3, 3)$, $(4, 1)$ **9.** $(3, 4)$, $(2, -4)$

Find the sine, the cosine, and the tangent of angles A and B. (Lesson 12.7)

10.

11.

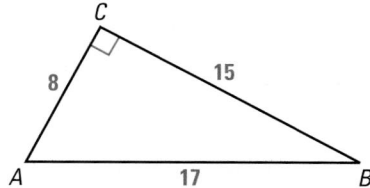

12. Prove the theorem $(a - b)c = ac - bc$. Use only the basic axioms of algebra, the definition of subtraction, and the theorem $(-b)c = -bc$. (Lesson 12.8)

Find a counterexample to show that the statement is *not* true. (Lesson 12.8)

13. If a, b, and c are real numbers and $a < b$, then $ac < bc$.

14. If a and b are real numbers, then $-(a + b) = (-a) - (-b)$.

Chapter Summary

WHAT did you learn?

Evaluate and graph a square-root function. **(12.1)**

Add, subtract, multiply, and divide radical expressions. **(12.2)**

Solve a radical equation. **(12.3)**

Solve a quadratic equation by completing the square. **(12.4)**

Choose a method for solving a quadratic equation. **(12.4)**

Use the Pythagorean theorem and its converse. **(12.5)**

Find the distance and midpoint between two points in a coordinate plane. **(12.6)**

Find the trigonometric ratios *sine*, *cosine*, and *tangent*. **(12.7)**

Use logical reasoning and proof. **(12.8)**

WHY did you learn it?

Investigate walking speeds of dinosaurs. **(p. 711)**

Compare speeds of pole-vaulters. **(p. 720)**

Find how much centripetal force a person experiences on an amusement park ride. **(p. 726)**

Investigate a proof of the quadratic formula. **(p. 732)**

Develop efficient problem solving skills. **(p. 732)**

Calculate the distance from home plate to second base. **(p. 740)**

Apply the distance and midpoint formulas to model real-life situations. **(pp. 746, 747)**

Determine cloud height above the ground. **(p. 756)**

Prove that statements are true or false. **(pp. 759, 760)**

How does Chapter 12 fit into the BIGGER PICTURE of algebra?

Radicals have many applications in geometry and in other fields. In this chapter you learned to add, subtract, multiply, and divide radical expressions and to solve radical equations.

The chapter also contains material that helps prepare you for other courses in mathematics. There are many applications involving geometry; an introduction to the trigonometric ratios sine, cosine, and tangent; and an introduction to some of the formal properties of algebra explored in Algebra 2.

STUDY STRATEGY

How did you use the notes in your notebook?

A map of ideas you made, using the **Study Strategy** on page 708, may look like this one.

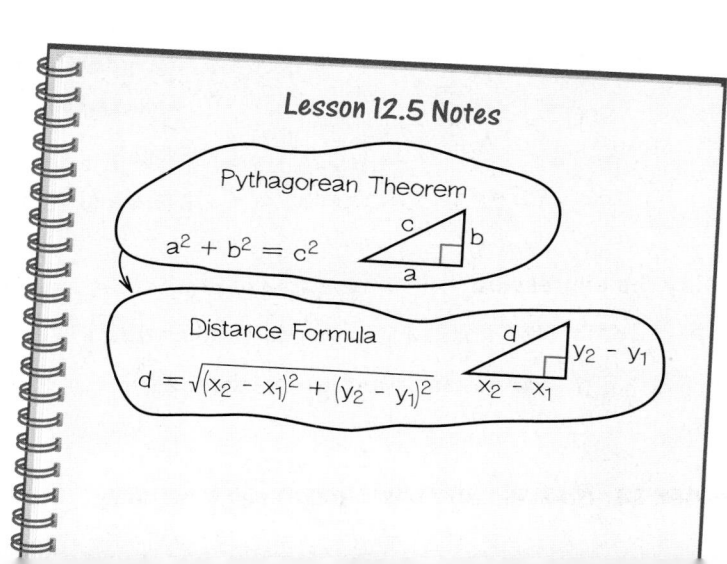

Lesson 12.5 Notes

Pythagorean Theorem

$a^2 + b^2 = c^2$

Distance Formula

$d = \sqrt{(x_2 - x_1)^2 + (y_2 - y_1)^2}$

Chapter Review

- square-root function, p. 709
- conjugates, p. 717
- complete the square, p. 730
- Pythagorean theorem, p. 738
- hypotenuse, p. 738

- legs of a right triangle, p. 738
- hypothesis, p. 739
- conclusion, p. 739
- converse, p. 739
- distance formula, p. 745

- midpoint between two points, p. 747
- midpoint formula, p. 747
- trigonometric ratio, p. 752
- sine, cosine, tangent, p. 752

- postulates, or axioms, p. 758
- theorems, p. 759
- conjecture, p. 759
- indirect proof, p. 760

12.1   **FUNCTIONS INVOLVING SQUARE ROOTS**

Examples on
pp. 709–711

EXAMPLE   To sketch the graph of $y = \sqrt{x} - 2$, note that the domain is the set of all nonnegative numbers. Then make a table of values, plot the points, and connect them with a smooth curve. The range is all numbers greater than or equal to -2.

x	y
0	$y = \sqrt{0} - 2 = -2$
1	$y = \sqrt{1} - 2 = -1$
2	$y = \sqrt{2} - 2 \approx -0.6$
.	.
.	.
.	.

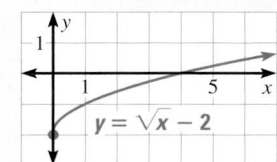

$y = \sqrt{x} - 2$

Identify the domain and the range of the function. Then graph the function.

1. $y = 11\sqrt{x}$

2. $y = 2\sqrt{x - 5}$

3. $y = \sqrt{x} + 3$

12.2   **OPERATIONS WITH RADICAL EXPRESSIONS**

Examples on
pp. 716–718

EXAMPLE   You can use radical operations to simplify radical expressions.

$$4\sqrt{20} - 3\sqrt{5} = 4\sqrt{4 \cdot 5} - 3\sqrt{5} \qquad \text{Perfect square factor}$$

$$= 4\sqrt{2 \cdot 2} \cdot \sqrt{5} - 3\sqrt{5} \qquad \text{Product property}$$

$$= 8\sqrt{5} - 3\sqrt{5} \qquad \text{Simplify.}$$

$$= 5\sqrt{5} \qquad \text{Subtract like radicals.}$$

Simplify the expression.

4. $\sqrt{5} + 2\sqrt{5} - \sqrt{3}$

5. $\sqrt{6}\left(2\sqrt{3} - 4\sqrt{2}\right)$

6. $\left(3 - \sqrt{10}\right)^2$

7. $\left(\sqrt{8} + \sqrt{3}\right)^2$

8. $\dfrac{21}{\sqrt{3}}$

9. $\dfrac{8}{6 - \sqrt{4}}$

SOLVING RADICAL EQUATIONS

Examples on pp. 722–724

EXAMPLE Solve $\sqrt{3x - 2} = x$.

$(\sqrt{3x - 2})^2 = x^2$	Square both sides.
$3x - 2 = x^2$	Simplify.
$0 = x^2 - 3x + 2$	Write in standard form.
$0 = (x - 2)(x - 1)$	Factor.
$x = 2$ or $x = 1$	Zero-product property

Solve the equation.

10. $2\sqrt{x} - 4 = 0$

11. $x = \sqrt{-4x - 4}$

12. $\sqrt{x - 3} + 2 = 8$

COMPLETING THE SQUARE

Examples on pp. 730–733

EXAMPLE Solve $x^2 - 6x - 1 = 6$ by completing the square.

$x^2 - 6x = 7$	Isolate the x^2-term and the x-term.
$x^2 - 6x + 9 = 7 + 9$	Add $\left(-\frac{6}{2}\right)^2$ to each side.
$(x - 3)^2 = 16$	Write left side as perfect square.
$x - 3 = \pm 4$	Find square root of each side.
$x = 7$ or $x = -1$	Solve for x.

Solve the equation by completing the square.

13. $x^2 - 4x - 1 = 7$

14. $x^2 + 20x + 19 = 0$

15. $2x^2 - x - 4 = 10$

THE PYTHAGOREAN THEOREM AND ITS CONVERSE

Examples on pp. 738–740

EXAMPLE Given $a = 6$ and $c = 12$, find b.

$a^2 + b^2 = c^2$	Write Pythagorean theorem.
$6^2 + b^2 = 12^2$	Substitute for a and c.
$b = 6\sqrt{3}$	Solve for b.

Find each missing length.

16.

17.

18.

THE DISTANCE AND MIDPOINT FORMULAS

Examples on pp. 745–747

EXAMPLE Find the distance d and the midpoint m between $(-6, -2)$ and $(4, 3)$.

$$d = \sqrt{(x_2 - x_1)^2 + (y_2 - y_1)^2}$$
$$= \sqrt{[4 - (-6)]^2 + [3 - (-2)]^2}$$
$$= \sqrt{125}$$
$$= 5\sqrt{5}$$
$$m = \left(\frac{x_1 + x_2}{2}, \frac{y_1 + y_2}{2}\right)$$
$$= \left(\frac{-6 + 4}{2}, \frac{-2 + 3}{2}\right)$$
$$= \left(-1, \frac{1}{2}\right)$$

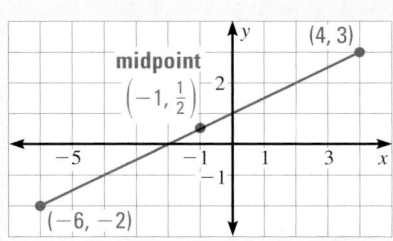

Find the distance and the midpoint between the two points.

19. $(8, 5)$ and $(11, -4)$ **20.** $(-3, 6)$ and $(1, 7)$ **21.** $(-2, -2)$ and $(2, 8)$

TRIGONOMETRIC RATIOS

Examples on pp. 752–754

EXAMPLES

$$\sin A = \frac{\text{side opposite } \angle A}{\text{hypotenuse}} = \frac{a}{c} = \frac{6}{10} = 0.6$$

$$\cos A = \frac{\text{side adjacent to } \angle A}{\text{hypotenuse}} = \frac{b}{c} = \frac{8}{10} = 0.8$$

$$\tan A = \frac{\text{side opposite } \angle A}{\text{side adjacent to } \angle A} = \frac{a}{b} = \frac{6}{8} = 0.75$$

22. Find the sine, the cosine, and the tangent of $\angle B$.

LOGICAL REASONING: PROOF

Examples on pp. 758–761

EXAMPLE Prove that for all numbers a and b, $(a + b) - b = a$.

$(a + b) - b = (a + b) + (-b)$	**Definition of subtraction**
$= a + [b + (-b)]$	**Associative property of addition**
$= a + 0$	**Inverse property of addition**
$= a$	**Identity property of addition**

23. Which basic axiom of algebra is represented by $\left(\frac{2}{3}\right)\left(\frac{4}{5}\right) = \left(\frac{4}{5}\right)\left(\frac{2}{3}\right)$?

24. Prove that $(c)(-b) = -cb$ for all real numbers c and b.

Chapter Test

Identify the domain and the range of the function. Then sketch its graph.

1. $y = 12\sqrt{x}$

2. $y = \sqrt{2x + 7}$

3. $y = \sqrt{3x} - 3$

4. $y = \sqrt{x - 5}$

Simplify the expression.

5. $3\sqrt{2} - \sqrt{2}$

6. $\left(4 + \sqrt{7}\right)\left(4 - \sqrt{7}\right)$

7. $\left(4\sqrt{5} + 1\right)^2$

8. $\dfrac{8}{3 - \sqrt{5}}$

Solve the equation.

9. $\sqrt{y} + 6 = 10$

10. $\sqrt{2m + 3} - 6 = 4$

11. $n = \sqrt{9n - 18}$

12. $p = \sqrt{-3p + 18}$

Solve the equation by completing the square.

13. $x^2 - 6x = -5$

14. $x^2 - 2x = 2$

15. $x^2 + \dfrac{4}{5}x - 1 = 0$

Determine whether the given lengths can be the sides of a right triangle.

16. 6, 18, 36

17. 9, 40, 41

18. 1.5, 3.6, 3.9

In Exercises 19 and 20, use the diagram.

19. Find the perimeter of the parallelogram.

20. Find the coordinates of the midpoint of each side of the parallelogram.

21. Find the perimeter of the parallelogram whose vertices are the midpoints you found in Exercise 20.

22. Compare the perimeters you found in Exercises 19 and 21.

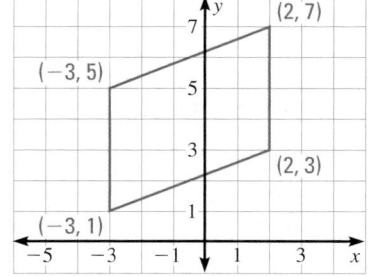

Find the missing lengths of the sides of the triangles. Round your answer to the nearest hundredth.

23.

24.

25.

26. Prove that if a, b, and c are real numbers, and $a + c = b + c$, then $a = b$.

27. 🌎 **PONY EXPRESS** Pony express stations were about 10 miles apart. The latitude-longitude coordinates of two former stations in western Nevada are (39.2 N, 119.0 W) and (39.2 N, 118.5 W). Find the coordinates of the station that was halfway between them.

28. 🌎 **GATEWAY ARCH** You are standing 134 feet from the Gateway Arch in St. Louis, Missouri. You estimate that the angle between the ground and the line from where you stand to the top of the arch is 78°. Estimate the height of the Gateway Arch.

Chapter Standardized Test

▶ **TEST-TAKING STRATEGY** Learn as much as you can about a test ahead of time, such as the types of questions and the topics that the test will cover.

1. **MULTIPLE CHOICE** What is the value of

$$f(x) = \frac{x\sqrt{x^2 - 1}}{x^2 + 8} \text{ when } x = 8?$$

Ⓐ $\frac{3\sqrt{7}}{16}$ Ⓑ $\frac{7}{8}$ Ⓒ $\frac{\sqrt{7}}{3}$

Ⓓ $\frac{8}{9}$ Ⓔ $3\sqrt{7}$

2. **MULTIPLE CHOICE** Which quadrants of the coordinate plane will contain the graph of $y = \sqrt{3x - 1} - 2$?

Ⓐ Quadrant I

Ⓑ Quadrants I and IV

Ⓒ Quadrant IV

Ⓓ Quadrants II and III

Ⓔ Quadrants I and II

3. **MULTIPLE CHOICE** Evaluate the expression $5\sqrt{7} + \sqrt{448} + \sqrt{175} - \sqrt{63}$.

Ⓐ $15\sqrt{7}$ Ⓑ $16\sqrt{7}$ Ⓒ $18\sqrt{7}$

Ⓓ $20\sqrt{7}$ Ⓔ $21\sqrt{7}$

4. **MULTIPLE CHOICE** Which one of the following is the simplified expression of $(3 - \sqrt{6})^2$?

Ⓐ $9 - 5\sqrt{6}$ Ⓑ $3 - 6\sqrt{6}$

Ⓒ 15 Ⓓ $15 - 6\sqrt{6}$

Ⓔ None of these

5. **MULTIPLE CHOICE** The geometric mean of 144 and a is 6. What is a?

Ⓐ $\frac{1}{24}$ Ⓑ $\frac{1}{4}$ Ⓒ $\frac{1}{2}$

Ⓓ 12 Ⓔ 36

6. **MULTIPLE CHOICE** Which one of the following is a solution of the equation $x = \sqrt{880 - 18x}$?

Ⓐ -22 Ⓑ 0 Ⓒ 22

Ⓓ 40 Ⓔ 49

7. **MULTIPLE CHOICE** What term should be added to $x^2 - \frac{4}{3}x$ so that the result is a perfect square trinomial?

Ⓐ $\frac{-2}{3}$ Ⓑ $\frac{64}{9}$ Ⓒ $\frac{4}{9}$

Ⓓ $\frac{-8}{3}$ Ⓔ $\frac{2}{3}$

8. **MULTIPLE CHOICE** What is the length of the missing side of the triangle?

Ⓐ 10 Ⓑ 11

Ⓒ 12 Ⓓ 13

Ⓔ 15

9. **MULTIPLE CHOICE** What is the distance between points P and Q?

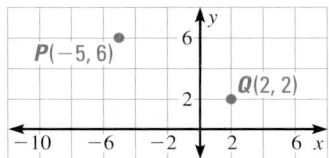

Ⓐ 5 Ⓑ $\sqrt{33}$ Ⓒ $\sqrt{113}$

Ⓓ $\sqrt{73}$ Ⓔ $\sqrt{65}$

10. **MULTIPLE CHOICE** Use the graph in Exercise 9. Find the midpoint between points P and Q.

Ⓐ $\left(-\frac{3}{2}, 4\right)$ Ⓑ $\left(-\frac{7}{2}, 2\right)$ Ⓒ $\left(-\frac{3}{2}, 2\right)$

Ⓓ $\left(-\frac{7}{2}, 4\right)$ Ⓔ $\left(\frac{7}{2}, 2\right)$

11. **MULTIPLE CHOICE** The length of side a is 18. The tangent of angle A is $\frac{9}{5}$. What is the length of the hypotenuse?

Ⓐ 10

Ⓑ 20

Ⓒ $2\sqrt{106}$

Ⓓ $4\sqrt{106}$

Ⓔ $8\sqrt{53}$

QUANTITATIVE COMPARISON In Exercises 12–15, choose the statement below that is true about the numbers.

    Ⓐ The number in column A is greater.

    Ⓑ The number in column B is greater.

    Ⓒ The two numbers are equal.

    Ⓓ The relationship cannot be determined from the given information.

F $e = 6$ D

$d = 3$ $f = 3\sqrt{5}$

E

	Column A	Column B
12.	$\sin D$	$\sin E$
13.	$\cos D$	$\sin D$
14.	$\cos D$	$\cos E$
15.	$\sin E$	$\cos E$

16. MULTIPLE CHOICE Choose the missing reason in the following proof that for all real numbers a and b, $-(a + b) = (-a) + (-b)$.

STATEMENTS	REASONS
1. a and b are real numbers	**1.** Given
2. $-(a + b) = (-1)(a + b)$	**2.** Multiplicative property of -1
3. $-(a + b) = (-1)a + (-1)b$	**3.** _____
4. $-(a + b) = (-a) + (-b)$	**4.** Multiplicative property of -1

    Ⓐ Definition of subtraction

    Ⓑ Associative property of addition

    Ⓒ Inverse property of addition

    Ⓓ Distributive property

    Ⓔ Multiplication axiom of equality

17. MULTI-STEP PROBLEM You have a very small television set in your home now. The length of your little TV screen is 8 inches, but the TV is called a 10-inch TV because the length of the screen's diagonal is 10 inches. After shopping for a larger television, you find two televisions that interest you. One is a 25-inch TV with a screen length of 20 inches. The other TV is advertised as a big screen because it is "double the dimensions of the 25-inch TV."

    a. Write an equation and solve it to find the width of the 25-inch screen.

    b. Find the length and width of the big screen television.

    c. What is the area of the 25-inch screen? of the big screen?

    d. How many times larger is the area of the big screen than the area of the 25-inch screen?

    e. Suppose that the television manufacturer produced a 75-inch screen TV. How many times larger is the area of the 75-inch screen than the area of the 25-inch screen?

Translate the verbal sentence into an equation or an inequality. Then use the information to solve for the variable(s). (1.4–1.5)

1. The quotient of m and 7 is greater than or equal to 16.

2. The sum of 4 and the second power of b is equal to 104.

3. The distance t you travel by train is $3\frac{2}{3}$ times the distance d you live from the train station. You drive 3 miles to get from your house to the train station.

Evaluate the expression for the given value of x. (2.1–2.3, 2.5–2.7)

4. $3 + x + (-4)$, $x = 5$

5. $-x + 12 - 5$, $x = 9$

6. $3.5 - (-x)$, $x = 1.5$

7. $-(-3)^2(x)$, $x = 7$

8. $6x(x + 2)$, $x = 2$

9. $(8x + 1)(-3)$, $x = \frac{1}{2}$

10. $\frac{1}{4}|(-x)(-x)(-x)|$, $x = 4$

11. $\frac{x^2 + 4}{6}$, $x = 8$

12. $\left(-5\right)\left(-\frac{3}{4}x\right)$, $x = 6$

Solve the equation. Round the result to the nearest hundredth. (3.1–3.4, 3.6)

13. $-\frac{2}{9}(x - 5) = 12$

14. $7x - (3x - 2) = 38$

15. $\frac{1}{3}x + 7 = -7x - 5$

16. $8(x + 3) - 2x = 4(x - 8)$

17. $11.47 + 6.23x = 7.62 + 5.51x$

18. $-3(2.98 - 4.1x) = 9.2x + 6.25$

In Exercises 19 and 20, use the graph. (4.3–4.4, 4.6, 5.3)

19. Write an equation of a line that is parallel to the line shown.

20. Write an equation of a line that is perpendicular to the line shown. Graph the equation in the same coordinate plane to check your answer.

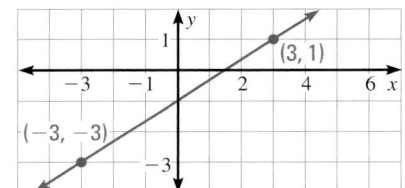

Decide whether the relation is a function. If it is a function, give the domain and the range. (4.8)

21.

Input	Output
−1	−1
1	−1
3	1
5	3
7	5

22.

23.

24.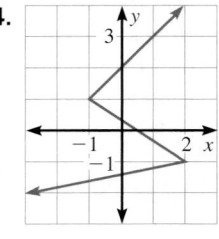

Use the information provided to write an equation of the line in standard form. (5.1–5.2, 5.5–5.6)

25. The slope is $\frac{4}{5}$; the y-intercept is -3.

26. The line passes through $(-1, 2)$; the slope is $\frac{1}{3}$.

Solve the inequality and graph the solution. (6.3–6.4)

27. $-3 < -4x + 9 \le 14$

28. $|3x + 16| + 2 < 10$

29. $3x - 4 > 5$ or $5x + 1 < 11$

Solve the system of linear equations. (7.2–7.3)

30. $4y = -8x + 16$
$2y = 11x - 7$

31. $-2x + 3y = 15$
$10x - 11y = 9$

32. $y = 5x - 2$
$3x + 7y = 5$

Simplify. Then evaluate the expression when $a = 1$ and $b = 2$. (8.1–8.3)

33. $\dfrac{b^8}{b^2}$

34. $3a^4 \cdot a^{-3}$

35. $(-a^3)(2b^2)^3$

36. $4b^3 \cdot (2 + b)^2$

37. $\dfrac{4a^{-3}b^3}{ab^{-2}}$

38. $\dfrac{(5ab^2)^{-2}}{a^{-3}b}$

Decide how many solutions the equation has. Then solve the equation.
(9.1, 9.5–9.6, 10.5)

39. $6x^2 + 8 = 34$

40. $4x^2 - 9x + 5 = 0$

41. $3x^2 + 6x + 3 = 0$

Completely factor the expression. (10.5–10.7)

42. $x^2 + 6x + 8$

43. $x^2 - 24x - 112$

44. $3x^2 + 17x - 6$

45. $4x^2 + 12x + 9$

46. $x^2 + 10x + 25$

47. $x^2 - 14x + 49$

Solve the equation. (10.4–10.8)

48. $(3x + 1)(2x + 7) = 0$

49. $6x^2 - x - 7 = 8$

50. $4x^2 + 16x + 16 = 0$

51. $x^3 + 5x^2 - 4x - 20 = 0$

52. $x^4 + 9x^3 + 18x^2 = 0$

53. $x^2 - \dfrac{4}{3}x + \dfrac{4}{9} = 0$

Simplify the expression. (11.4–11.6)

54. $\dfrac{4x}{12x^2}$

55. $\dfrac{2x + 6}{x^2 - 9}$

56. $\dfrac{3x}{x^2 - 2x - 24} \cdot \dfrac{x - 6}{6x^2 + 9x}$

57. $\dfrac{x^2 - 6x + 8}{x^2 - 2x} \div (3x - 12)$

58. $\dfrac{4}{x + 2} + \dfrac{15x}{3x + 6}$

59. $\dfrac{3x}{x + 4} - \dfrac{x}{x - 1}$

Simplify the expression. (12.2)

60. $4\sqrt{7} + 3\sqrt{7}$

61. $9\sqrt{2} - 12\sqrt{8}$

62. $\sqrt{6}(5\sqrt{3} + 6)$

63. $\dfrac{11}{7 - \sqrt{3}}$

In Exercises 64 and 65, use the triangles at the right. (12.7)

64. Find the sine, the cosine, and the tangent of
$\angle Q$ and $\angle R$. Round your answer to the
nearest hundredth.

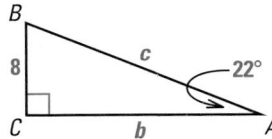

65. Find the lengths of the sides of $\triangle ABC$.
Tan $22° = 0.4040$. Round your answer
to the nearest hundredth.

🌐 **PVR SUBSCRIPTIONS In Exercises 66 and 67, Company A sells a
Personal Video Recorder (PVR) for \$700 and charges a \$5 monthly
subscription fee. Company B sells a PVR for \$500 and charges a \$20
monthly fee.** (6.2, 7.3–7.4)

66. What is the total cost of each PVR after one year? after three years?

67. How many months must the PVRs be used in order for the total costs of the
two models to be the same?

Investigating the Golden Ratio

OBJECTIVE **Explore what the golden ratio is and how it is used.**

Materials: graph paper, metric ruler, graphing calculator (optional)

Over the centuries, the golden rectangle has fascinated artists, architects, and mathematicians. A golden rectangle has the special shape such that when a square is cut from one end, the ratio of length to width of the remaining rectangle is equal to the ratio of length to width of the original rectangle. This ratio, the *golden ratio*, is $\frac{1 + \sqrt{5}}{2}$, or about 1.618034.

It is *not* possible to constuct a golden rectangle with integer sidelengths. However, it *is* possible to construct rectangles with integer sidelengths whose ratios of length to width approximate the golden ratio.

APPROXIMATING A GOLDEN RECTANGLE

1 On graph paper, draw a 1-by-1 square.

2 On one side of the square, add another 1-by-1 square.

3 Build a 2-by-2 square on the longest side of your 1-by-2 rectangle.

4 Build a 3-by-3 square on the longest side of your 2-by-3 rectangle.

INVESTIGATING THE GOLDEN RATIO

One property of golden rectangles is that their lengths and widths are proportional. For example, in the above diagram, $\frac{a + b}{b} = \frac{b}{a}$.

1. Copy and complete the table by using this property to predict the lengths and widths of the next four rectangles you can build on the drawing from **Step 4**.

length, b	3	5	?	?	?	?
width, a	2	3	?	?	?	?

2. Draw the next four rectangles to check your predictions.

3. Add a row to your table and record the ratio of the length to the width of the rectangles. Explain how the ratios are related to the golden ratio.

4. Let $r = \frac{b}{a}$ represent the golden ratio. Use $\frac{a + b}{b} = \frac{b}{a}$ to show that $r = \frac{1 + \sqrt{5}}{2}$ if $a = 1$.

PRESENTING YOUR RESULTS

Write a report or make a poster to present your results.

• Include a sketch of a golden rectangle.

• Include the table you made in Exercise 1.

• Include your answers to Exercises 2–4.

• Describe what you learned about the golden ratio.

EXTENSIONS

• Before the pediment on top of the Parthenon in Athens was destroyed, the front of the building fit almost exactly into a golden rectangle. Do some research on the Parthenon to find out if the golden ratio was used in other aspects of its design.

• The golden rectangle can be found in the works of many artists and in art objects around the world, such as the proportions of a jar from the Ch'ing dynasty of China, shown at the right. Find pictures of works of art and see if you can find any golden rectangles in them.

• The golden ratio can also be found in nature. For example, the average chicken egg fits nicely inside a golden rectangle. Measure at least six chicken eggs and find the average of their ratios.

• Do some research and find other examples of the golden ratio in art, nature, and architecture.

• Find some rectangular objects around you that you think look nice. Measure them to see if they are golden rectangles. You might try a picture frame, a $1 bill, a business card, a 3-by-5 index card, or a TV screen.

Contents
of Student Resources

Skills Review Handbook

FACTORS AND MULTIPLES

The **natural numbers** are all the numbers in the sequence 1, 2, 3, 4, 5, ...
Natural numbers that are multiplied are **factors**. For example, **3** and **7** are
factors of 21, because $3 \cdot 7 = 21$. A **prime number** is a natural number that has
exactly two factors, itself and 1.

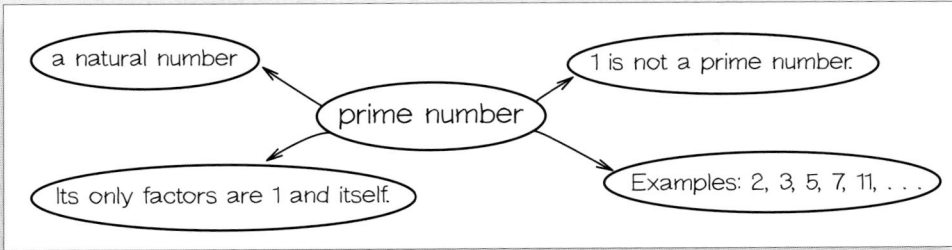

To write the **prime factorization** of a number, write the number as a product of
prime numbers.

EXAMPLE Write the prime factorization of 315.

SOLUTION Use a tree diagram to factor
the number until all factors are prime
numbers. To determine the factors, test
the prime numbers in order.

▶ The prime factorization of 315 is $3 \cdot 3 \cdot 5 \cdot 7$.
 This may also be written as $3^2 \cdot 5 \cdot 7$.

A **common factor** of two natural numbers is a number that is a factor of both
numbers. For example, **7** is a common factor of 35 and 56, because $35 = 5 \cdot 7$
and $56 = 8 \cdot 7$. The **greatest common factor** (GCF) of two natural numbers is
the largest number that is a factor of both.

EXAMPLE Find the greatest common factor of 180 and 84.

SOLUTION First write the prime factorization of each number. Multiply the
common prime factors to find the greatest common factor.

$$180 = 2 \cdot 2 \cdot 3 \cdot 3 \cdot 5$$

$$84 = 2 \cdot 2 \cdot 3 \cdot 7$$

▶ The greatest common factor is $2 \cdot 2 \cdot 3 = 12$.

A **common multiple** of two natural numbers is a number that is a multiple of both numbers. For example, **42** is a common multiple of **6** and **14**, because $42 = 6 \cdot 7$ and $42 = 14 \cdot 3$. The **least common multiple** (LCM) of two natural numbers is the smallest number that is a multiple of both.

EXAMPLE   Find the least common multiple of 24 and 30.

SOLUTION   First write the prime factorization of each number.

$24 = 2 \cdot 2 \cdot 2 \cdot 3$

$30 = 2 \cdot 3 \cdot 5$

▶ The least common multiple is the product of the common prime factors and all the prime factors that are not common. The least common multiple of 24 and 30 is $2 \cdot 3 \cdot 2 \cdot 2 \cdot 5 = 120$.

PRACTICE

List all the factors of the number.

1. 18	**2.** 10	**3.** 77	**4.** 35
5. 27	**6.** 100	**7.** 42	**8.** 49
9. 52	**10.** 81	**11.** 121	**12.** 150

Write the prime factorization of the number if it is not a prime number. If a number is prime, write *prime*.

13. 27	**14.** 24	**15.** 32	**16.** 61
17. 55	**18.** 68	**19.** 48	**20.** 225
21. 90	**22.** 75	**23.** 39	**24.** 1000
25. 728	**26.** 101	**27.** 512	**28.** 210

List all the common factors of the pair of numbers.

29. 15, 30	**30.** 36, 54	**31.** 5, 20	**32.** 14, 21
33. 9, 36	**34.** 24, 28	**35.** 20, 55	**36.** 12, 30

Find the greatest common factor of the pair of numbers.

37. 25, 30	**38.** 32, 40	**39.** 17, 24	**40.** 35, 150
41. 14, 28	**42.** 65, 39	**43.** 102, 51	**44.** 128, 104
45. 36, 50	**46.** 45, 135	**47.** 29, 87	**48.** 35, 48
49. 56, 70	**50.** 88, 231	**51.** 47, 48	**52.** 93, 124

Find the least common multiple of the pair of numbers.

53. 5, 7	**54.** 3, 4	**55.** 3, 16	**56.** 7, 12	**57.** 4, 12
58. 9, 15	**59.** 12, 35	**60.** 6, 14	**61.** 20, 25	**62.** 10, 24
63. 3, 17	**64.** 15, 40	**65.** 70, 14	**66.** 36, 50	**67.** 22, 30

COMPARING AND ORDERING NUMBERS

When you compare two numbers *a* and *b*, there are exactly three possibilities. The possibilities are described at the right in words and in symbols. To compare two whole numbers or decimals, compare the digits of the two numbers from left to right. Find the first place in which the digits are different.

a is *less than* b.	$a < b$
a is *equal to* b.	$a = b$
a is *greater than* b.	$a > b$

EXAMPLE Compare the two numbers. Write the answer using $<$, $=$, or $>$.

a. 4723 and 4732   **b.** 27.52 and 27.39

SOLUTION

a. 4 7 2 3

   4 7 3 2

▶ $2 < 3$, so $4723 < 4732$.

You can picture this on a number line. The numbers on a number line increase from left to right.

4723 is *less* than 4732.

4723 is to the *left* of 4732.

b. 2 7 . 5 2

   2 7 . 3 9

▶ $5 > 3$, so $27.52 > 27.39$.

27.52 is *greater* than 27.39.

27.52 is to the *right* of 27.39.

To compare two fractions that have the same denominator, compare the numerators. If the fractions have different denominators, first rewrite one or both fractions to produce equivalent fractions with a common denominator. The **least common denominator** (LCD) is the least common multiple of the denominators.

EXAMPLE Write the numbers $\frac{3}{4}$, $\frac{7}{8}$, and $\frac{5}{12}$ in order from least to greatest.

SOLUTION The LCD of the fractions is 24.

$$\frac{3}{4} = \frac{3 \cdot 6}{4 \cdot 6} = \frac{18}{24} \qquad\qquad \frac{7}{8} = \frac{7 \cdot 3}{8 \cdot 3} = \frac{21}{24} \qquad\qquad \frac{5}{12} = \frac{5 \cdot 2}{12 \cdot 2} = \frac{10}{24}$$

Compare the numerators: $10 < 18 < 21$, so $\frac{5}{12} < \frac{3}{4} < \frac{7}{8}$.

▶ In order from least to greatest, the fractions are $\frac{5}{12}$, $\frac{3}{4}$, and $\frac{7}{8}$.

EXAMPLE Compare $4\frac{3}{4}$ and $4\frac{2}{3}$. Write the answer using $<$, $=$, or $>$.

SOLUTION The whole number parts of the mixed numbers are the same, so compare the fraction parts.

The LCD of $\frac{3}{4}$ and $\frac{2}{3}$ is 12.

$$\frac{3}{4} = \frac{3 \cdot 3}{4 \cdot 3} = \frac{9}{12} \qquad \frac{2}{3} = \frac{2 \cdot 4}{3 \cdot 4} = \frac{8}{12}$$

Compare the numerators: $9 > 8$, so $\frac{9}{12} > \frac{8}{12}$.

▶ Since $\frac{3}{4} > \frac{2}{3}$, it follows that $4\frac{3}{4} > 4\frac{2}{3}$.

$4\frac{3}{4}$ is to the right of $4\frac{2}{3}$.

PRACTICE

Compare the two numbers. Write the answer using $<$, $=$, or $>$.

1. 12,428 and 15,116   **2.** 905 and 961   **3.** 142,109 and 140,999

4. 16.82 and 14.09   **5.** 0.00456 and 0.40506   **6.** 23.03 and 23.3

7. 1005.2 and 1050.7   **8.** 932,778 and 934,112   **9.** 0.058 and 0.102

10. $\frac{7}{13}$ and $\frac{3}{13}$ **11.** $17\frac{1}{4}$ and $15\frac{11}{12}$ **12.** $\frac{7}{10}$ and $\frac{3}{4}$

13. $\frac{5}{9}$ and $\frac{15}{27}$ **14.** $\frac{1}{2}$ and $\frac{3}{8}$ **15.** $\frac{1}{8}$ and $\frac{1}{9}$

16. $\frac{4}{5}$ and $\frac{2}{3}$ **17.** $42\frac{1}{5}$ and $41\frac{7}{8}$ **18.** 508.881 and 508.793

19. 32,227 and 32,226.5   **20.** $\frac{5}{8}$ and $\frac{2}{3}$ **21.** $17\frac{5}{6}$ and $17\frac{5}{7}$

Write the numbers in order from least to greatest.

22. 1207, 1702, 1220, 1772   **23.** 45,617, 45,242, 40,099, 40,071

24. 23.12, 23.5, 24.0, 23.08, 24.01   **25.** 9.027, 9.10, 9.003, 9.3, 9.27

26. 4.07, 4.5, 4.01, 4.22   **27.** $\frac{1}{3}, \frac{5}{6}, \frac{3}{8}, \frac{5}{4}$ **28.** $\frac{3}{5}, \frac{3}{2}, \frac{3}{4}, \frac{3}{10}, \frac{3}{7}$

29. $1\frac{2}{5}, \frac{7}{4}, \frac{5}{3}, 1\frac{1}{8}, \frac{15}{16}$ **30.** $14\frac{7}{9}, 15\frac{1}{3}, 14\frac{5}{6}, 15\frac{1}{4}$ **31.** $\frac{7}{8}, \frac{5}{4}, 1\frac{1}{3}, \frac{5}{12}$

32. You need a piece of trim $6\frac{5}{8}$ yards long to complete a craft project. You have a piece $6\frac{3}{4}$ yards long left over from another project. Is the trim long enough?

33. Goran finished a ski race in 53.56 seconds. Markus finished in 53.78 seconds. Which skier finished first?

FRACTION OPERATIONS

To add or subtract two fractions with the same denominator, add or subtract the numerators.

EXAMPLE

$$\frac{3}{5} + \frac{4}{5} = \frac{3 + 4}{5}$$ Add numerators.

$$= \frac{7}{5}, \text{ or } 1\frac{2}{5}$$ Simplify.

EXAMPLE

$$\frac{7}{10} - \frac{2}{10} = \frac{7 - 2}{10}$$ Subtract numerators.

$$= \frac{5}{10}$$ Simplify.

$$= \frac{\cancel{5}}{2 \cdot \cancel{5}}$$ Factor numerator and denominator.

$$= \frac{1}{2}$$ Simplify fraction to lowest terms.

To add or subtract two fractions with different denominators, write equivalent fractions with a common denominator.

EXAMPLE

$$\frac{3}{5} + \frac{5}{6} = \frac{18}{30} + \frac{25}{30}$$ Use the LCD, 30.

$$= \frac{18 + 25}{30}$$ Add numerators.

$$= \frac{43}{30}, \text{ or } 1\frac{13}{30}$$ Simplify.

To add or subtract mixed numbers, you can first rewrite them as fractions.

EXAMPLE

$$3\frac{2}{3} - 2\frac{1}{4} = \frac{11}{3} - \frac{9}{4}$$ Rewrite mixed numbers as fractions.

$$= \frac{44}{12} - \frac{27}{12}$$ The LCD is 12.

$$= \frac{44 - 27}{12}$$ Subtract numerators.

$$= \frac{17}{12}, \text{ or } 1\frac{5}{12}$$ Simplify.

To multiply two fractions, multiply the numerators and multiply the denominators.

EXAMPLE

$$\frac{3}{4} \times \frac{5}{6} = \frac{3 \times 5}{4 \times 6}$$ Multiply numerators and multiply denominators.

$$= \frac{15}{24}$$ Simplify.

$$= \frac{\cancel{3} \cdot 5}{\cancel{3} \cdot 8}$$ Factor numerator and denominator.

$$= \frac{5}{8}$$ Simplify fraction to lowest terms.

Two numbers are **reciprocals** of each other if their product is 1. Every number except 0 has a reciprocal.

$5 \times \dfrac{1}{5} = 1$, so 5 and $\dfrac{1}{5}$ are reciprocals.

$\dfrac{2}{3} \times \dfrac{3}{2} = 1$, so $\dfrac{2}{3}$ and $\dfrac{3}{2}$ are reciprocals.

$1\dfrac{1}{4} \times \dfrac{4}{5} = \dfrac{5}{4} \cdot \dfrac{4}{5} = 1$, so $1\dfrac{1}{4}$ and $\dfrac{4}{5}$ are reciprocals.

To find the reciprocal of a number, write the number as a fraction. Then interchange the numerator and the denominator.

EXAMPLE Find the reciprocal of $3\dfrac{1}{4}$.

SOLUTION $3\dfrac{1}{4} = \dfrac{13}{4}$ Write $3\dfrac{1}{4}$ as a fraction.

$\dfrac{13}{4} \longrightarrow \dfrac{4}{13}$ Interchange numerator and denominator.

▶ The reciprocal of $3\dfrac{1}{4}$ is $\dfrac{4}{13}$.

✓ **CHECK** $3\dfrac{1}{4} \times \dfrac{4}{13} = \dfrac{13}{4} \times \dfrac{4}{13} = \dfrac{13 \times 4}{4 \times 13} = 1$

To divide by a fraction, multiply by its reciprocal.

EXAMPLE $\dfrac{3}{4} \div \dfrac{5}{6} = \dfrac{3}{4} \times \dfrac{6}{5}$ The reciprocal of $\dfrac{5}{6}$ is $\dfrac{6}{5}$.

$= \dfrac{3 \times 6}{4 \times 5}$ Multiply numerators and denominators.

$= \dfrac{18}{20}$ Simplify.

$= \dfrac{2 \cdot 9}{2 \cdot 10}$ Factor numerator and denominator.

$= \dfrac{9}{10}$ Simplify fraction to lowest terms.

EXAMPLE $2\dfrac{1}{2} \div 4\dfrac{1}{6} = \dfrac{5}{2} \div \dfrac{25}{6}$ Write mixed numbers as fractions.

$= \dfrac{5}{2} \times \dfrac{6}{25}$ The reciprocal of $\dfrac{25}{6}$ is $\dfrac{6}{25}$.

$= \dfrac{5 \times 6}{2 \times 25}$ Multiply numerators and denominators.

$= \dfrac{30}{50}$ Simplify.

$= \dfrac{3 \times 10}{5 \times 10}$ Factor numerators and denominators.

$= \dfrac{3}{5}$ Simplify fraction to lowest terms.

Add or subtract. Write the answer as a fraction or a mixed number in lowest terms.

1. $\frac{1}{6} + \frac{4}{6}$

2. $\frac{5}{8} - \frac{3}{8}$

3. $\frac{4}{9} - \frac{1}{9}$

4. $\frac{5}{12} + \frac{3}{12}$

5. $\frac{1}{2} + \frac{1}{8}$

6. $\frac{3}{5} - \frac{1}{10}$

7. $\frac{7}{10} + \frac{1}{3}$

8. $\frac{15}{24} - \frac{7}{12}$

9. $5\frac{1}{8} - 2\frac{3}{4}$

10. $1\frac{3}{7} + \frac{1}{2}$

11. $4\frac{3}{8} - 2\frac{5}{6}$

12. $\frac{3}{7} + \frac{3}{4}$

13. $7\frac{1}{2} + \frac{7}{10}$

14. $5\frac{5}{9} - 2\frac{1}{3}$

15. $4\frac{5}{8} - 1\frac{3}{16}$

16. $9\frac{2}{5} + 3\frac{1}{3}$

Find the reciprocal of each number.

17. 7

18. $\frac{1}{14}$

19. $\frac{7}{12}$

20. $\frac{5}{8}$

21. $\frac{1}{20}$

22. 100

23. $\frac{5}{13}$

24. $\frac{6}{7}$

25. $1\frac{1}{5}$

26. $2\frac{3}{5}$

27. $\frac{3}{9}$

28. $\frac{12}{17}$

29. $6\frac{2}{5}$

30. $10\frac{1}{3}$

31. $\frac{2}{7}$

32. $4\frac{3}{4}$

Multiply or divide. Write the answer as a fraction or a mixed number in lowest terms.

33. $\frac{1}{2} \times \frac{1}{2}$

34. $\frac{2}{3} \times \frac{4}{5}$

35. $\frac{5}{8} \times \frac{4}{15}$

36. $\frac{3}{7} \times \frac{7}{9}$

37. $\frac{3}{4} \times \frac{8}{9}$

38. $1\frac{2}{3} \times \frac{3}{5}$

39. $3 \times 2\frac{5}{9}$

40. $5\frac{1}{4} \times 1\frac{1}{7}$

41. $\frac{7}{8} \div \frac{3}{4}$

42. $\frac{5}{12} \div \frac{1}{2}$

43. $\frac{4}{5} \div \frac{2}{3}$

44. $\frac{11}{16} \div 1\frac{1}{2}$

45. $4\frac{1}{2} \div \frac{3}{4}$

46. $2\frac{1}{4} \div 1\frac{1}{3}$

47. $3\frac{2}{5} \div 4$

48. $7\frac{1}{5} \div 2\frac{1}{4}$

Add, subtract, multiply, or divide. Write the answer as a fraction or a mixed number in lowest terms.

49. $\frac{15}{16} - \frac{1}{8}$

50. $\frac{5}{9} \times 1\frac{1}{2}$

51. $\frac{12}{13} \div \frac{12}{13}$

52. $\frac{24}{25} + \frac{1}{5}$

53. $5\frac{1}{2} - \frac{1}{8}$

54. $\frac{3}{10} \div \frac{1}{5}$

55. $\frac{7}{8} \times \frac{4}{9}$

56. $\frac{1}{3} + \frac{1}{6}$

57. $4\frac{1}{4} \times \frac{2}{3}$

58. $9\frac{2}{5} + 3\frac{1}{2}$

59. $\frac{4}{5} \div \frac{1}{2}$

60. $6\frac{5}{7} - 2\frac{1}{5}$

61. $\frac{9}{10} + \frac{3}{8}$

62. $8\frac{1}{2} \times \frac{1}{4}$

63. $\frac{11}{15} \times \frac{3}{8}$

64. $\frac{4}{7} \div \frac{4}{5}$

65. You went trout fishing. You caught trout with the lengths (in inches) of $8\frac{5}{8}$, $10\frac{1}{2}$, $9\frac{1}{4}$, $8\frac{3}{4}$, $10\frac{2}{3}$, and $9\frac{5}{6}$. Find the average length of the trout you caught.

FRACTIONS, DECIMALS, AND PERCENTS

Percent (%) means "divided by 100."

$53\% = 53$ divided by $100 = \dfrac{53}{100}$

The grid contains 100 squares.

53 of the 100 squares are shaded.

53% of the squares are shaded.

To write a percent as a decimal, move the decimal point two places to the *left* and remove the percent symbol.

EXAMPLES

a. $85\% = 85\% = 0.85$

b. $3\% = 03\% = 0.03$

c. $427\% = 427\% = 4.27$

d. $12.5\% = 12.5\% = 0.125$

To write a percent as a fraction in lowest terms, first write the percent as a fraction with a denominator of 100. Then simplify if possible.

EXAMPLES

a. $71\% = \dfrac{71}{100}$

b. $10\% = \dfrac{10}{100} = \dfrac{1}{10}$

c. $4\% = \dfrac{4}{100} = \dfrac{1}{25}$

d. $350\% = \dfrac{350}{100} = \dfrac{7}{2} = 3\dfrac{1}{2}$

To write a decimal as a percent, move the decimal point two places to the *right* and add a percent symbol.

EXAMPLES

a. $0.93 = 0.93 = 93\%$

b. $1.47 = 1.47 = 147\%$

c. $0.025 = 0.025 = 2.5\%$

d. $0.005 = 0.005 = 0.5\%$

To write a decimal as a fraction in lowest terms, first write the decimal as a fraction with a denominator of 100. Then simplify if possible.

EXAMPLES

a. $0.73 = \dfrac{73}{100}$

b. $0.25 = \dfrac{25}{100} = \dfrac{1}{4}$

c. $0.05 = \dfrac{5}{100} = \dfrac{1}{20}$

d. $2.75 = 2\dfrac{75}{100} = 2\dfrac{3}{4}$

It is simple to write a fraction as a percent if the denominator of the fraction is a factor of 100. If not, divide the numerator by the denominator.

EXAMPLES

a. $\frac{17}{25}$ ➤ 25 is a factor of 100, so write $\frac{17}{25} = \frac{17 \cdot 4}{25 \cdot 4} = \frac{68}{100} = 68\%$.

b. $\frac{1}{8}$ ➤ 8 is not a factor of 100, so divide: $1 \div 8 = 0.125 = 12.5\%$.

c. $\frac{1}{6}$ ➤ 6 is not a factor of 100, so divide: $1 \div 6 = 0.1666\ldots \approx 0.167 = 16.7\%$.

You should memorize the percent, decimal, and fraction relationships in this chart.

Equivalent percents, decimals, and fractions		
$1\% = 0.01 = \frac{1}{100}$	$33\frac{1}{3}\% = 0.\overline{3} = \frac{1}{3}$	$66\frac{2}{3}\% = 0.\overline{6} = \frac{2}{3}$
$10\% = 0.1 = \frac{1}{10}$	$40\% = 0.4 = \frac{2}{5}$	$75\% = 0.75 = \frac{3}{4}$
$20\% = 0.2 = \frac{1}{5}$	$50\% = 0.5 = \frac{1}{2}$	$80\% = 0.8 = \frac{4}{5}$
$25\% = 0.25 = \frac{1}{4}$	$60\% = 0.6 = \frac{3}{5}$	$100\% = 1$

PRACTICE

Write the percent as a decimal and as a fraction or a mixed number in lowest terms.

1. 63% **2.** 7% **3.** 24% **4.** 35% **5.** 17%

6. 125% **7.** 45% **8.** 250% **9.** $33\frac{1}{3}\%$ **10.** 96%

11. 62.5% **12.** 725% **13.** 5.2% **14.** 0.8% **15.** 0.12%

Write the decimal as a percent and as a fraction or a mixed number in lowest terms.

16. 0.39 **17.** 0.08 **18.** 0.12 **19.** 1.5 **20.** 0.72

21. 0.05 **22.** 2.08 **23.** 4.8 **24.** 0.02 **25.** 3.75

26. 0.85 **27.** 0.52 **28.** 0.9 **29.** 0.005 **30.** 2.01

Write the fraction or mixed number as a decimal and as a percent. Round decimals to the nearest thousandth. Round percents to the nearest tenth of a percent.

31. $\frac{7}{10}$ **32.** $\frac{13}{20}$ **33.** $\frac{11}{25}$ **34.** $\frac{3}{10}$ **35.** $\frac{3}{8}$

36. $2\frac{3}{4}$ **37.** $5\frac{1}{8}$ **38.** $\frac{19}{20}$ **39.** $\frac{7}{8}$ **40.** $3\frac{7}{25}$

41. $\frac{5}{6}$ **42.** $3\frac{3}{5}$ **43.** $\frac{8}{15}$ **44.** $8\frac{1}{5}$ **45.** $1\frac{5}{12}$

USING PERCENT

A fraction shows what part one number is of another. You can first write a fraction to determine what percent one number is of another.

EXAMPLE   What percent of 120 is 48?

SOLUTION   First write a fraction that compares 48 to 120: $\frac{48}{120}$.

$$\frac{48}{120} = 0.4 \qquad \text{Write the fraction as a decimal.}$$

$$= 40\% \qquad \text{Write the decimal as a percent.}$$

▶ 48 is 40% of 120.

To find a percent of a given number, first write the percent as a decimal or as a fraction. Then multiply.

EXAMPLE   What is 75% of 160?

SOLUTION $75\% = \frac{3}{4}$ Write 75% as a fraction.

$$\frac{3}{4} \times 160 = 120 \qquad \text{Multiply.}$$

▶ 75% of 160 is 120.

EXAMPLE   What is 6% of $29.95?

SOLUTION $6\% = 0.06$ Write 6% as a decimal.

$0.06 \times \$29.95 = \$1.797$ Multiply.

$$= \$1.80 \qquad \text{Round to the nearest cent.}$$

▶ To the nearest cent, 6% of $29.95 is $1.80.

PRACTICE

Find the answer.

1. What percent of 90 is 15?
2. 12 is what percent of 60?
3. What percent of 80 is 30?
4. What percent of 60 is 90?
5. What percent of 90 is 60?
6. 6 is what percent of 120?
7. 15 is what percent of 90?
8. What percent of 18 is 4.5?
9. 18 is what percent of 96?

Find the number. Round sums of money to the nearest cent.

10. 38% of 250
11. 12% of 75
12. 25% of 84
13. 50% of 96
14. 42% of 115
15. $33\frac{1}{3}\%$ of 114
16. 5.5% of $102.95
17. 70% of 60
18. $66\frac{2}{3}\%$ of 48
19. 8% of $12.99
20. 150% of 90
21. 4.5% of $75

22. You are charged 6.5% tax on a $42 purchase. Find the amount of the tax.

RATIO AND RATE

A ratio compares two numbers using division. If a and b are two quantities measured in the same units, then the **ratio of a to b** is $\frac{a}{b}$. The ratio of a to b can be written in three ways: a to b, $a : b$, and $\frac{a}{b}$.

EXAMPLE Write the ratio 7 to 15 in three ways.

SOLUTION   7 to 15   7 : 15 $\frac{7}{15}$

EXAMPLE Write the ratio 12 to 60 in lowest terms.

SOLUTION   12 to 60 $= \frac{12}{60}$ First write the ratio as a fraction.

$= \frac{1}{5}$ Then write the fraction in lowest terms.

If a and b are two quantities measured in different units, then the **rate of a per b** is $\frac{a}{b}$. A **unit rate** is a rate per one unit of a given quantity. To determine a unit rate, write the rate with a denominator of 1.

EXAMPLE   A car traveled 648 miles using 18 gallons of gas. Find the unit rate in miles per gallon.

SOLUTION $\dfrac{\text{miles}}{\text{gallons}} \longrightarrow \dfrac{648}{18} = \dfrac{36}{1}$

▶ The unit rate is 36 miles per gallon.

PRACTICE

Write each ratio in lowest terms.

1. 75 to 20

2. 162 : 36

3. $\frac{36}{60}$

4. 21 : 15

5. $\frac{60}{85}$

6. 42 to 72

7. 136 : 24

8. $\frac{216}{120}$

9. 24 cars to 36 cars

10. 39 students : 104 students

11. 75 hours to 35 hours

12. 8 hours : 2 hours

13. 9 inches to 36 inches

14. 48 hours to 10 hours

Find each unit rate.

15. $90 for 4 tickets

16. $51 for 6 hours

17. 208 miles in 4 hours

18. $1050 in 6 weeks

19. 476 miles for 17 gallons

20. 128 ounces for 16 people

21. $2.70 for 27 minutes

22. $8.67 for 3 notebooks

23. 65 meters in 3 seconds

24. 18 hours in 4 days

25. $476 for 425 miles

26. $50 for 5 hours

COUNTING METHODS

Suppose your family's favorite pizza toppings are hamburger, sausage, pepperoni, mushroom, onion, and pepper. You have to choose one meat topping and one vegetable topping. How many choices are possible?

There are many ways to answer that question, including **making a list**, drawing a **tree diagram**, and using the **counting principle**.

EXAMPLE   Make a list to determine the number of topping choices.

SOLUTION   Pair each meat topping with each vegetable topping.

hamburger, mushroom	**hamburger**, onion	**hamburger**, pepper
sausage, mushroom	**sausage**, onion	**sausage**, pepper
pepperoni, mushroom	**pepperoni**, onion	**pepperoni**, pepper

▶ There are nine possible choices.

EXAMPLE   Use a tree diagram to determine the number of topping choices.

SOLUTION   Draw a tree diagram and count the number of branches.

MEAT	VEGETABLE
hamburger	mushroom onion pepper
sausage	mushroom onion pepper
pepperoni	mushroom onion pepper

▶ The tree has nine branches. There are nine possible choices.

THE COUNTING PRINCIPLE   When one item is selected from each of two or more lists, the total number of possible combinations is the product of the number of items in each list.

EXAMPLE   Use the counting principle to determine the number of topping choices.

SOLUTION   Multiply the number of meat choices by the number of vegetable choices.

   3 meat choices $\times$ **3** vegetable choices = **9** possible topping choices

▶ There are nine possible choices.

In situations involving a greater number of items, it may not be practical to make a list or to draw a tree diagram. Use the counting principle instead.

EXAMPLE One state plans to issue a series of license plates using codes consisting of three letters followed by two digits. Letters and digits may both be repeated. How many different plates are possible?

SOLUTION Use the Counting Principle.

| 26 choices for first letter | × | 26 choices for second letter | × | 26 choices for third letter | × | 10 choices for first digit | × | 10 choices for second digit |

$$26 \times 26 \times 26 \times 10 \times 10 = 1,757,600$$

▶ There are 1,757,600 different license plates possible.

PRACTICE

Use the indicated method to answer each question.

1. Jacob is choosing an outfit from three pairs of jeans and three shirts. The jeans are blue, black, and gray. The shirts are white, blue, and yellow. How many such outfits are possible? (Make a list.)

2. The student council is selling sweatshirts with the school name and emblem. The shirts come in the colors, styles, and sizes shown at the right. How many different types of sweatshirt are available? (Make a tree diagram.)

   Sweatshirt Choices

   Colors: white, gray, black

   Styles: hooded, plain

   Sizes: small, medium, large

   Ex. 2

3. There are 270 girls and 210 boys enrolled in the Jefferson School. The cover of the yearbook will show a photograph of a pair of students, one girl and one boy. How many different pairs of students are possible? (Use the counting principle.)

Answer each question using any method you choose.

4. A student can choose one sandwich, one salad, and one piece of fruit in the cafeteria. The choices include the following: grilled cheese sandwich, hamburger, tuna sandwich, garden salad, fruit salad, apple, banana, and orange. How many different lunches are possible?

5. In a given calling area, telephone numbers have the same three first digits. The four-digit number that follows is different for each telephone number. How many numbers are possible?

6. A radio host plans to play one song from each of three CDs by a single artist. The first CD includes 12 songs. The second includes 14 songs, and the third includes 13 songs. How many different combinations are possible?

7. Members of a video club choose a personal identification number (PIN) consisting of two letters followed by two digits. How many PINs are possible if letters and digits may be repeated? How many are possible if neither letters nor digits may be repeated?

PERIMETER, AREA, AND VOLUME

The **perimeter** P of a figure is the distance around it.

EXAMPLES

$$P = 6 + 5 + 4$$
$$= 15$$

$$P = 4 + 2 + 4 + 5$$
$$= 15$$

$$P = l + w + l + w$$
$$= 2l + 2w$$

EXAMPLE   Find the perimeter of a rectangle with length 14 centimeters and width 6 centimeters.

SOLUTION $P = 2l + 2w = (2 \times 14) + (2 \times 6) = 28 + 12 = 40$

▶ The perimeter is 40 centimeters.

A **regular polygon** is a polygon in which all the angles have the same measure and all the sides have the same length. The perimeter of a regular polygon can be found by multiplying the length of a side by the number of sides.

EXAMPLES

regular (equilateral) triangle

square

regular pentagon

$$P = 3s$$

$$P = 4s$$

$$P = 5s$$

The **area** A of a figure is the number of square units enclosed by the figure.

EXAMPLES

$$A = 5 \times 3$$
$$= 15 \text{ square units}$$

$$A = \text{length} \times \text{width}$$
$$= l \times w$$
$$= lw$$

$$A = \text{side} \times \text{side}$$
$$= s \times s$$
$$= s^2$$

EXAMPLE   Find the area of a square with sides 15 inches long.

SOLUTION $A = s^2 = 15^2 = 225$

▶ The area is 225 square inches.

The **volume** of a space figure is the amount of space enclosed by the figure. Volume is measured in cubic units.

One such unit is the cubic centimeter (cm^3). It is the amount of space enclosed by a cube whose length, width, and height are each 1 cm.

EXAMPLES

$$V = 6 \times 2 \times 3$$
$$= 36 \text{ cubic units}$$

$$V = l \times w \times h$$

EXAMPLE Find the volume of a box with length 8 feet, width 5 feet, and height 9 feet.

SOLUTION $V = l \times w \times h = 8 \times 5 \times 9 = 360$

▶ The volume is 360 cubic feet (ft^3).

PRACTICE

Find the perimeter of each figure.

1.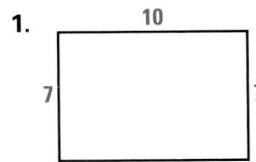

2.
0.5 in.
0.75 in.   0.75 in.
0.5 in.

3.

4.

5. a square with sides of length 18 ft

6. a rectangle with length 6 m and width 7 m

Find the area of each figure.

7. a square with sides of length 29 yd

8. a rectangle with length 7 km and width 4 km

9. a square with sides of length 3.5 in.

10. a rectangle with length 24 ft and width 6 ft

11. a square with sides of length 7.2 cm

12. a rectangle with length 7.5 in. and width 8 in.

13. a square with sides of length 45 km

14. a rectangle with length 5.3 m and width 4 m

Find the volume of each box.

15. a cube with sides of length 25 ft

16. a cube with sides of length 4.2 cm

17. a box with length 15 yd, width 7 yd, and height 4 yd

18. a box with length 7.3 cm, width 5 cm, and height 3.2 cm

19. a box with length 5.3 in., width 4 in., and height 10 in.

DATA DISPLAYS

A **bar graph** can be used to display data that fall into distinct categories. The bars in a bar graph are the same width. The height or length of each bar is determined by the data it represents and by the scale you choose.

EXAMPLE In 1998, baseball player Mark McGwire hit a record 70 home runs. The table shows the locations to which the home runs were hit. Draw a bar graph to display the data. ▶ Source: *The Boston Globe*

Field location	Number of home runs
left	31
left-center	21
center	15
right-center	3
right	0

SOLUTION

❶ First, choose a scale. Since the data range from 0 to 31, make the scale increase from 0 to 35 by fives.

❷ Draw and label the axes. Mark intervals on the vertical axis according to the scale you chose.

❸ Draw a bar for each category.

❹ Give the bar graph a title.

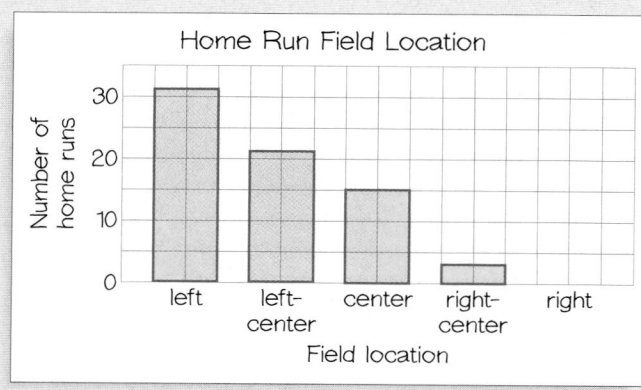

A **histogram** is a bar graph that shows how many data items occur within given intervals. The number of data items in an interval is the **frequency** for that interval.

EXAMPLE The table shows the distances of McGwire's home runs. Draw a histogram to display them.

Distance (ft)	Frequency
301–350	4
351–400	24
401–450	27
451–500	11
501–550	4

SOLUTION Use the same method you used for drawing the bar graph above. However, do not leave spaces between the bars.

Since the frequencies range from 4 to 27, make the scale increase from 0 to 30 by fives.

Draw and label the axes. Mark intervals on the vertical axis and draw a bar for each category. Do not leave spaces between the bars.

Give the histogram a title.

A **line graph** can be used to show how data change over time.

EXAMPLE   A science class recorded the highest temperature each day from December 1 to December 14. The temperatures are given in the table. Draw a line graph to display the data.

Date	1	2	3	4	5	6	7
Temperature (°F)	40	48	49	61	24	35	34

Date	8	9	10	11	12	13	14
Temperature (°F)	42	41	40	22	20	28	30

SOLUTION

❶ Choose a scale.

❷ Draw and label the axes. Mark evenly spaced intervals on both axes.

❸ Graph each data item as a point. Connect the points.

❹ Give the line graph a title.

A **circle graph** can be used to show how parts relate to a whole and to each other.

EXAMPLE   The table shows the number of sports-related injuries treated in a hospital emergency room in one year. Draw a circle graph to display the data.

Related sport	Number of injuries
basketball	56
football	34
skating/hockey	22
track and field	10
other	28

SOLUTION

❶ To begin, find the total number of injuries.

$$56 + 34 + 22 + 10 + 28 = \textbf{150}$$

To find the degree measure for each sector of the circle, write a fraction comparing the number of injuries to the total. Then multiply the fraction by 360°. For example:

Football: $\dfrac{34}{150} \cdot 360° = 81.6°$

❷ Next, draw a circle. Use a protractor to draw the angle for each sector.

❸ Label each sector.

❹ Give the circle graph a title.

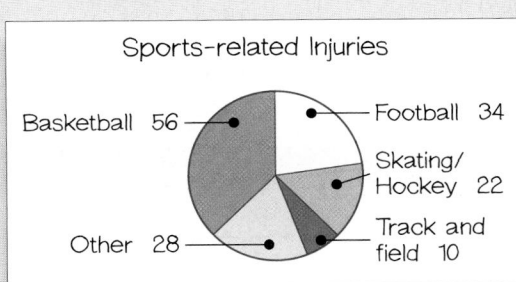

PRACTICE

In 1998, baseball player Sammy Sosa hit 66 home runs. The tables show the field locations and distances of his home runs. ▶ Source: *The Boston Globe*

1. The location data range from 10 to 22. The scale must start at 0. Choose a reasonable scale for a bar graph.

2. Draw a bar graph to display the field locations of Sosa's home runs.

3. The distance data range from 1 to 16. The scale must start at 0. Choose a reasonable scale for a histogram.

4. Draw a histogram to display the distances of Sosa's home runs.

Field location	Number of home runs
left	12
left-center	22
center	10
right-center	11
right	11

Exs. 1 and 2

Distance (ft)	Frequency
326–350	5
351–375	12
376–400	14
401–425	16
426–450	14
451–475	1
476–500	4

Exs. 3 and 4

5. There are 150 runs at the Mountain Mania ski resort, including 51 expert runs, 60 intermediate runs, and 39 beginner runs. Draw a circle graph to display the data.

6. A nurse recorded a patient's temperature (°F) every 3 hours from 9 A.M. until noon of the following day. The temperatures were 102°, 102°, 101.5°, 101.1°, 100°, 101°, 101.5°, 100°, 99.8°, and 99°. Draw a line graph to display the data.

Choose an appropriate graph to display the data. Draw the graph.

7.

Value of one share of Company Stock						
Year	1994	1995	1996	1997	1998	1999
Value ($)	15	18	16	12	10	15

8.

Passenger Car Stopping Distance (dry road)				
Speed (mi/h)	35	45	55	65
Distance (ft)	160	225	310	410

9.

Fat in One Tablespoon of Canola Oil	
Type of fat	Number of Grams
saturated	1
polyunsaturated	4
monounsaturated	8

▶ Source: U.S. Department of Agriculture

10.

Population of Meridian City by Age					
Age	Under 5	5–19	20–44	45–64	65 and older
Population	912	2556	4812	2232	1502

PROBLEM SOLVING

One of your primary goals in mathematics should be to become a good problem solver. It will help to approach every problem with an organized plan.

STEP ① UNDERSTAND THE PROBLEM.
Read the problem carefully. Organize the information you are given and decide what you need to find. Determine whether some of the information given is unnecessary, or whether enough information is given. Supply missing facts, if possible.

STEP ② MAKE A PLAN TO SOLVE THE PROBLEM.
Choose a strategy. (Get ideas from the list given on page 796.) Choose the correct operations. Decide if you will use a tool such as a calculator, a graph, or a spreadsheet.

STEP ③ CARRY OUT THE PLAN TO SOLVE THE PROBLEM.
Use the strategy and any tools you have chosen. Estimate before you calculate, if possible. Do any calculations that are needed. Answer the question that the problem asks.

STEP ④ CHECK TO SEE IF YOUR ANSWER IS REASONABLE.
Reread the problem and see if your answer agrees with the given information.

EXAMPLE   How many segments can be drawn between 7 points, no three of which lie on the same line?

❶ You are given a number of points, along with the information that no three points lie on the same line. You need to determine how many segments can be drawn between the points.

❷ Some strategies to consider are: draw a diagram, solve a simpler problem and look for a pattern.

❸ Consider the problem for fewer points.

| 2 points | 3 points | 4 points | 5 points |
| 1 segment | 3 segments | 6 segments | 10 segments |

Look for a pattern. Then continue the pattern to find the number of segments for 7 points.

Number of points	2	3	4	5	6	7
Number of segments	1	3	6	10	15	21

$\llcorner+2\lrcorner\llcorner+3\lrcorner\llcorner+4\lrcorner\llcorner+5\lrcorner\llcorner+6\lrcorner$

▶ Given 7 points, no three of which lie on the same line, 21 segments can be drawn between the points.

❹ You can check your solution by making a sketch.

In **Step 2** of the problem solving plan, you may want to consider the following strategies.

PROBLEM SOLVING STRATEGIES

- **Guess, check, and revise.**   When you do not seem to have enough information.

- **Draw a diagram or a graph.**   When words describe a picture.

- **Make a table or an organized list.**   When you have data or choices to organize.

- **Use an equation or a formula.**   When you know a relationship between quantities.

- **Use a proportion.**   When you know that two ratios are equal.

- **Look for a pattern.**   When you can examine several cases.

- **Break the problem into simpler parts.**   When you have a multi-step problem.

- **Solve a simpler problem.**   When easier numbers help you understand a problem.

- **Work backward.**   When you are looking for a fact leading to a known result.

PRACTICE

1. Tasha bought salads at $2.75 each and cartons of milk at $.80 each. The total cost was $16.15. How many of each did Tasha buy?

2. A rectangular garden is 45 feet long and has perimeter 150 feet. Rows of plants are planted 3 feet apart. Find the area of the garden.

3. If five turkey club sandwiches cost $18.75, how much would seven sandwiches cost?

4. How many diagonals can be drawn from one vertex of a 12-sided polygon?

5. Nguyen wants to arrive at school no later than 7:25 A.M. for his first class. It takes him 25 minutes to shower and dress, 15 minutes to eat breakfast, and at least 20 minutes to get to school. What time should he plan to get out of bed?

6. There are 32 players in a single-elimination chess tournament. That is, a player who loses once is eliminated. Assuming that no ties are allowed, how many games must be played to determine a champion?

7. Andrea, Betty, Joyce, Karen, and Paula are starters on their school basketball team. How many different groups of three can be chosen for a newspaper photo?

8. Carl has $135 in the bank and plans to save $5 per week. Jean has $90 in the bank and plans to save $10 per week. How many weeks will it be before Jean has at least as much in the bank as Carl?

9. The Peznolas are planning to use square tiles to tile a kitchen floor that is 18 feet long and 15 feet wide. Each tile covers one square foot. A carton of tiles costs $18. How much will it cost to cover the entire kitchen floor?

Extra Practice

CHAPTER 1

Evaluate the expression for the given value of the variable. (Lesson 1.1)

1. $15a$ when $a = 7$

2. $0.75 + x$ when $x = 2.25$

3. $y - 14$ when $y = 32$

4. $\dfrac{c}{23}$ when $c = 391$

5. $\dfrac{1578}{d}$ when $d = 3$

6. $\dfrac{3}{4} \cdot z$ when $z = \dfrac{2}{3}$

Evaluate the expression for the given value(s) of the variable(s). (Lesson 1.2)

7. $3y^2$ when $y = 5$

8. $(4x)^3$ when $x = 2$

9. $6x^4$ when $x = 4$

10. $a^4 - 5$ when $a = 3$

11. $(x + 2)^3$ when $x = 4$

12. $(c - d)^2$ when $c = 10$ and $d = 3$

Evaluate the expression for the given value of the variable. (Lesson 1.3)

13. $3a^2 + 8$ when $a = 5$

14. $44 - 4c$ when $c = 7$

15. $(d^4 - 6) \div 5$ when $d = 3$

Evaluate the expression. (Lesson 1.3)

16. $3^3 - 12 \div 4$

17. $10^2 \div 4 + 6$

18. $10^2 \div (4 + 6)$

19. $\dfrac{9 \cdot 7^2}{5 + 8^2 - 6}$

20. $3 + 7(3.5 \div 5)$

21. $2 + 21 \div 3 - 6$

22. $50 \div (6^2 - 11) - 2$

23. $\left[(5 \cdot 2^3) + 8\right] \div 16$

Use mental math to solve the equation. (Lesson 1.4)

24. $x + 7 = 13$

25. $3y = 21$

26. $8t - 1 = 23$

27. $\dfrac{m}{4} = 6$

Check whether the given number is a solution of the inequality. (Lesson 1.4)

28. $y + 10 < 22;\ 12$

29. $2n + 5 > 15;\ 8$

30. $7d > 15 - d;\ 2$

31. $\dfrac{c + 1}{2} \le 3;\ 5$

32. $b(2b - 5) < 40;\ 6$

33. $12x > x + 27;\ 3$

34. $17 - 3t \ge 3;\ 4$

35. $r(r - 7) \le 16;\ 9$

36. Your friend's score in a game is 225. This is 25 more than twice your score. Write an equation to model the situation. What is your score? (Lesson 1.5)

Write the verbal sentence as an equation or an inequality. (Lesson 1.5)

37. Thirteen less than the product of 25 and a number n is 37.

38. The sum of five and a number y is less than twelve.

39. WIRELESS INDUSTRY The table shows the estimated number of cellular telephone subscribers (in millions) in the United States. Make a bar graph and a line graph of the data. (Lesson 1.6)

Year	1993	1994	1995	1996	1997	1998
Subscribers (millions)	16	24	34	44	55	69

▶ Source: Cellular Telecommunications Industry Association

Make an input-output table for the function. Use 0, 1, 2, and 3 as the domain. Then draw a line graph to represent the data in the table. (Lesson 1.7)

40. $y = 8 - 2x$

41. $y = 4.5 + x$

42. $y = 7x + 1$

43. $y = x$

CHAPTER 2

Graph the numbers on a number line. Then write two inequalities that compare the two numbers. (Lesson 2.1)

1. -7 and 8 **2.** -5.2 and 3.6 **3.** -2.4 and -2.5 **4.** $1\frac{2}{3}$ and $1\frac{5}{6}$

Evaluate the expression. (Lesson 2.1)

5. $|8.5|$ **6.** $|-3|$ **7.** $|-4| + 3$ **8.** $7 - |-5|$

Find the sum. (Lesson 2.2)

9. $-3 + 8$ **10.** $18 + 27$ **11.** $5 + (-7)$ **12.** $-4 + (-11)$

13. $-4 + 13 + (-6)$ **14.** $15 + (-12) + (-4)$ **15.** $-2 + (-9) + 8$ **16.** $17 + (-5) + 15$

Evaluate the expression. (Lesson 2.3)

17. $-8 - 5$ **18.** $4.1 - 6.3$ **19.** $-3 - (-7)$ **20.** $-6 + (-3) - 4$

21. $3.6 - 2.4 - (-6.1)$ **22.** $-15 + 4 - 12$ **23.** $-11 - (-6) - 7$ **24.** $\frac{9}{10} - \frac{1}{2} + \left(-\frac{1}{5}\right)$

Find the sum or the difference of the matrices. (Lesson 2.4)

25. $\begin{bmatrix} 8 & -4 \\ 9 & 3 \end{bmatrix} + \begin{bmatrix} -2 & 6 \\ -1 & 5 \end{bmatrix}$ **26.** $\begin{bmatrix} 3 & -6 \\ 1 & 4 \end{bmatrix} - \begin{bmatrix} 5 & 9 \\ 2 & -2 \end{bmatrix}$ **27.** $\begin{bmatrix} -6 & 8 & 3 \\ 4 & 2 & 6 \end{bmatrix} + \begin{bmatrix} 3 & -6 & 7 \\ -4 & -5 & 8 \end{bmatrix}$

Simplify the expression. (Lesson 2.5)

28. $(-6)(-7)$ **29.** $(-5)(9)$ **30.** $(3)(-8)(-2)$ **31.** $(-8)(-4x)$

32. $-3(-y)(-y)$ **33.** $(-c)^3(c)$ **34.** $(-7)^2(b)(-b)$ **35.** $-4(-a^4)$

Use the distributive property to rewrite the expression without parentheses. (Lesson 2.6)

36. $6(y + 5)$ **37.** $4(a - 6)$ **38.** $(x + 3)(-5)$ **39.** $-r(r - 5)$

40. $-k(7 + k)$ **41.** $(x + 4)6x$ **42.** $s(s - s^2)$ **43.** $(0.5z - 1.4)6$

Simplify the expression. (Lesson 2.6)

44. $3x + 7x$ **45.** $5.4m - 2.3m$ **46.** $82p - (-29p)$ **47.** $6 - 4t - 4$

48. $5 + 4(x - 2)$ **49.** $8x^2 + 5 - 2x^2$ **50.** $2x(7 - x) + 3x^2$ **51.** $\frac{2}{3}x + \left(-\frac{1}{6}\right)x$

Simplify the expression. (Lesson 2.7)

52. $18 \div (-2)$ **53.** $-48 \div 12$ **54.** $16 \div \left(-\frac{4}{5}\right)$ **55.** $\frac{3x}{8} \div \frac{1}{2}$

56. $21x \div 7$ **57.** $8x \div \left(-\frac{1}{4}\right)$ **58.** $-24x \div \left(-\frac{2}{3}\right)$ **59.** $\dfrac{-22}{-\frac{1}{3}}$

60. PROBABILITY You randomly choose a button from a bag containing 9 yellow, 7 green, 11 blue, and 9 red buttons. What is the probability that you choose a red button? (Lesson 2.8)

Given the probability, find the odds. (Lesson 2.8)

61. The probability of scoring the basket is 0.20.   **62.** The probability of winning the election is $\frac{1}{3}$.

CHAPTER 3

Solve the equation. (Lesson 3.1)

1. $y - 6 = 8$ **2.** $n + 5 = -10$ **3.** $a - (-6) = 22$ **4.** $14 - r = 3$

5. $|-7| + k = 4$ **6.** $\frac{1}{5} + m = -\frac{2}{5}$ **7.** $-t - (-3) = 0$ **8.** $-b + 3 - 1 = 3 \cdot 4$

Solve the equation. (Lesson 3.2)

9. $7x = 35$ **10.** $6a = 3$ **11.** $\frac{x}{10} = -2$ **12.** $-\frac{3}{8}t = 0$

13. $|-5| = 15b$ **14.** $-\frac{7}{8}r = \frac{3}{4}$ **15.** $\frac{y}{10} = \frac{-2}{5}$ **16.** $-\frac{2}{3} = \frac{1}{9}k$

Solve the equation. (Lesson 3.3)

17. $6x + 8 = 32$ **18.** $2x - 1 = 11$ **19.** $-x - 5 + 3x = 1$ **20.** $4(x - 9) = 8$

21. $\frac{3}{5}x - 7 = 17$ **22.** $x = 2(x - 1) + 6$ **23.** $\frac{x}{4} = -\frac{x}{2} - 1$ **24.** $-5 = \frac{3}{8}(x - 1)$

Solve the equation if possible. (Lesson 3.4)

25. $-6 + 5x = 8x - 9$ **26.** $8x + 6 = 3(4 - x)$ **27.** $4\left(\frac{1}{2}x + \frac{1}{2}\right) = 2x + 2$

28. $-3(-x - 4) = 2x + 1$ **29.** $4x = -2(-2x + 3)$ **30.** $-4(x - 3) = 6(x + 5)$

31. PHOTO FRAMING A photo measuring 5 inches by 7 inches is placed in a frame that adds a 1-inch border around the photo. Sketch a diagram of the photo and frame. What is the total width and length of the frame? (Lesson 3.5)

Solve the equation. Round the result to the nearest hundredth. (Lesson 3.6)

32. $4x = 82.50$ **33.** $-26x - 59 = 135$ **34.** $2.3 - 4.8x = 8.2x + 5.6$

35. $18.25x - 4.15 = 2.75x$ **36.** $3(3.1x - 4.2) = 6.2x + 3.1$ **37.** $8.4x - 3.2 = 4.1(3.4 - 2.1x)$

38. BICYCLING If you ride your bike for 2.5 hours and travel 37.5 miles, what is your average speed? (*Hint*: Solve $d = rt$ for r.) (Lesson 3.7)

Rewrite the equation so that y is a function of x. Then use the result to find y when $x = -2, -1, 0,$ and 1. (Lesson 3.7)

39. $3 - y = x$ **40.** $6x - 2y = 10$ **41.** $-6x - 1 = -4y + 2$

42. $-2y - 3x - 16 = 0$ **43.** $\frac{1}{2}x - \frac{1}{2}y = 6$ **44.** $-2(x - 4) = 2(y + 5)$

Find the unit rate. (Lesson 3.8)

45. $3 for 5 yogurt snacks   **46.** $50.75 for working 7 hours   **47.** Drive 122 miles in 2.5 hours

Convert the measure. Round your answer to the nearest hundredth. (Lesson 3.8)

48. 24 miles to kilometers (1 mile = 1.609 km)   **49.** 6 fluid ounces to cups (1 cup = 8 fluid ounces)

Find the percent. Round to the nearest whole percent. (Lesson 3.8)

50. Tax of $1.00 on an item priced at $19.99   **51.** 9 field goals made out of 14 attempted

52. $4.50 tip on a restaurant bill of $22   **53.** 127 surveys returned out of 350

CHAPTER 4

Plot and label the ordered pairs in a coordinate plane. (Lesson 4.1)

1. $A(2, 4)$, $B(-2, 0)$, $C(5, -2)$ **2.** $A(4, 4)$, $B(0, -2)$, $C(-3, -3)$ **3.** $A(4, -4)$, $B(2.5, 5)$, $C(-3, 2)$

4. $A(0, -1)$, $B(1, -3)$, $C(3, 1)$ **5.** $A(-4, -2)$, $B(-2, 4)$, $C(4, 0)$ **6.** $A(-3, -4)$, $B(1, -1)$, $C(-1, 1)$

Use a table of values to graph the equation. (Lesson 4.2)

7. $y = 5x + 1$ **8.** $y = -2x + 4$ **9.** $y = -2$ **10.** $4x + y = -8$

11. $x = 3$ **12.** $y = -(6 + x)$ **13.** $y = \frac{1}{2}x - 1$ **14.** $y = -\frac{1}{3}x - 4$

Find the x-intercept and the y-intercept of the line. Graph the equation. Label the points where the line crosses the axes. (Lesson 4.3)

15. $5x + y = -5$ **16.** $2x - y = 6$ **17.** $y = 2x - 5$ **18.** $6y + 2x = 12$

19. $14 = y - 2x$ **20.** $8x + 2y = -16$ **21.** $y = 6 - 3x$ **22.** $1.5y = x - 3$

Find the slope of the line passing through the points. (Lesson 4.4)

23. $(6, 1)$, $(-4, 1)$ **24.** $(2, 2)$, $(-1, 4)$ **25.** $(0, 6)$, $(-3, 0)$ **26.** $(4, 5)$, $(2, 2)$

27. $(-4, 2)$, $(-3, -5)$ **28.** $(3, 6)$, $(3, -1)$ **29.** $(-1, 0)$, $(0, -1)$ **30.** $(-2, -3)$, $(1, -2)$

The variables x and y vary directly. Use the given values to write an equation that relates x and y. (Lesson 4.5)

31. $x = 6$, $y = 18$ **32.** $x = 4$, $y = 1$ **33.** $x = 8$, $y = -7$ **34.** $x = -\frac{1}{2}$, $y = -10$

35. $x = -2$, $y = -2$ **36.** $x = 8$, $y = -4$ **37.** $x = 2.5$, $y = 2$ **38.** $x = 2.1$, $y = -6.3$

39. EARNINGS Your earnings vary directly with the number of hours you work. If you earn \$60 for 4 hours of work, how much will you earn for working 35 hours? (Lesson 4.5)

Write the equation in slope-intercept form. Then graph the equation. (Lesson 4.6)

40. $x - y = 1$ **41.** $y = 3$ **42.** $-3x + 2y = 6$ **43.** $y + 4 = 0$

44. $x = 2y + 1$ **45.** $2(x + y + 1) = 4y$ **46.** $2x - 4y + 6 = 0$ **47.** $5x - 3y + 2 = 14 - 4x$

Solve the equation graphically. Check your solution algebraically. (Lesson 4.7)

48. $6 - 5x = 1$ **49.** $2x = -12$ **50.** $6x + 8 = 2x$ **51.** $8x + 3 = 19$

52. $\frac{4}{3}x - 2 = -6$ **53.** $15 - 2x = 3x$ **54.** $\frac{2}{3}x + 5 = -2$ **55.** $7x - 4 = -3 + 4x$

Decide whether the relation is a function. (Lesson 4.8)

56.

57.

Input	Output
4	−2
0	0
4	2
2	4

58.

59.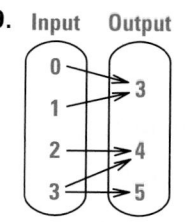

CHAPTER 5

Write an equation of the line in slope-intercept form. (Lesson 5.1)

1. The slope is 2; the y-intercept is 1.

2. The slope is -3; the y-intercept is -2.

3. The slope is 1; the y-intercept is -3.

4. The slope is -4; the y-intercept is 0.

Write an equation of the line that passes through the point and has the given slope. Write the equation in slope-intercept form. (Lesson 5.2)

5. $(-1, 0)$, $m = 3$ **6.** $(5, 2)$, $m = -2$ **7.** $(3, 6)$, $m = 0$ **8.** $(-2, 1)$, $m = -5$

9. $(-3, -1)$, $m = 4$ **10.** $(1, 5)$, $m = 8$ **11.** $(2, -1)$, $m = \frac{1}{2}$ **12.** $(-4, 3)$, $m = -\frac{1}{3}$

Write an equation in slope-intercept form of the line that passes through the points. (Lesson 5.3)

13. $(3, -2)$, $(5, 4)$ **14.** $(2, 17)$, $(-1, -1)$ **15.** $(5, 1)$, $(0, -6)$ **16.** $(-2, -1)$, $(4, -4)$

17. $(-1, 7)$, $(5, 7)$ **18.** $(0, 0)$, $(2, 3)$ **19.** $(-3, 5)$, $(-6, 8)$ **20.** $(5, 2)$, $(1, 14)$

Draw a scatter plot for the data. Draw a best-fitting line and write an equation of the line. (Lesson 5.4)

21.

x	−1	0	1	3	4	5
y	0	−1	1	3	2	4

22.

x	2	2.5	3	3	3.5	4
y	2	−1	1	−3	−2	−4

Write the point-slope form of the equation of the line that passes through the point and has the given slope. Then rewrite the equation in slope-intercept form. (Lesson 5.5)

23. $(5, 3)$, $m = -2$ **24.** $(3, 7)$, $m = -3$ **25.** $(5, 4)$, $m = 5$ **26.** $(-2, -4)$, $m = \frac{3}{4}$

27. $(-3, -5)$, $m = -\frac{5}{3}$ **28.** $(0, 8)$, $m = \frac{1}{4}$ **29.** $(2, 4)$, $m = -\frac{1}{2}$ **30.** $(-1, -7)$, $m = 4$

Write an equation in standard form of the line that passes through the given point and has the given slope, or that passes through the two points. (Lesson 5.6)

31. $(5, -2)$, $m = 3$ **32.** $(1, 2)$, $(3, 4)$ **33.** $(-1, 0)$, $(-5, -3)$ **34.** $(-4, 3)$, $m = -\frac{5}{6}$

35. $(-3, 7)$, $(1, 7)$ **36.** $(5, 7)$, $m = -\frac{3}{4}$ **37.** $(-2, -5)$, $m = 5$ **38.** $(4, -2)$, $(4, 5)$

WIND CHILL Wind chill is based on the combined effects of temperature and wind speed. The table shows the wind chill for various temperatures (in degrees Fahrenheit) when the wind speed is 5 miles per hour. (Lesson 5.7)

Temperature	35	30	25	20	15	10
Wind chill	32	27	22	16	11	6

39. Make a scatter plot of the data.

40. Write a linear model for the data.

41. Use the linear model to estimate the wind chill at $5°$ Fahrenheit.

CHAPTER 6

Solve the inequality and graph its solution. (Lesson 6.1)

1. $x + 5 > -4$ 2. $m - 4 < -20$ 3. $3 \geq y - 4$ 4. $9x \geq 36$

5. $\dfrac{k}{9} \leq 2$ 6. $-5a > 35$ 7. $-\dfrac{x}{10} < \dfrac{1}{5}$ 8. $0.5 \leq -\dfrac{b}{6}$

Solve the inequality. (Lesson 6.2)

9. $0 \leq \dfrac{1}{2}x + 6$ 10. $\dfrac{3}{4}x + 5 \leq 8$ 11. $3x + 8 \geq -2x + 3$

12. $-3x - 7 < 2$ 13. $-(x + 5) < -4x - 11$ 14. $-(4 + x) > 2(x - 5)$

Solve the inequality and graph the solution. (Lesson 6.3)

15. $8 \geq x + 4 > 3$ 16. $-36 \leq 6x < 12$ 17. $-15 < -3x < 18$

18. $2x + 1 > 9$ or $3x - 5 < 4$ 19. $x + 1 > 4$ or $2x + 3 \leq 5$ 20. $-4x + 1 \geq 17$ or $5x - 4 > 6$

Solve the equation or the inequality. (Lesson 6.4)

21. $|10 + x| = 4$ 22. $|2x + 3| = 9$ 23. $|x - 4| + 4 = 7$

24. $|6x - 5| + 1 < 8$ 25. $|3x + 4| - 6 \geq 14$ 26. $|10 - 4x| \leq 2$

Sketch the graph of the inequality. (Lesson 6.5)

27. $y \geq -2$ 28. $x - y \leq 0$ 29. $x + y \geq 5$ 30. $4y + x < 4$

31. $x - 3y \leq 0$ 32. $3y - 2x < 6$ 33. $5x - 3y > 9$ 34. $2y - x > 10$

35. **PURCHASING SNACKS** You have $20 to spend on snacks for your friends. Each juice drink costs $2 and each bag of popcorn costs $1.25. Let x represent the number of drinks. Let y represent the number of bags of popcorn. Write and graph an inequality to model the numbers of juice drinks and popcorn bags you can buy. (Lesson 6.5)

Make a stem-and-leaf plot for the data. (Lesson 6.6)

36. 18, 31, 98, 71, 22, 14, 20, 66, 18, 76, 33, 13

37. 13, 22, 40, 21, 45, 65, 66, 16, 31, 33, 41, 35, 51

38. 3, 22, 41, 5, 63, 8, 17, 24, 60, 64, 6, 55, 78, 91, 13, 32, 54, 72

39. 44, 19, 51, 2, 46, 8, 39, 41, 38, 39, 56, 27, 54, 43, 60, 62, 21, 49, 22, 63

Find the mean, the median, and the mode of the collection of numbers. (Lesson 6.6)

40. 8, 3, 2, 8, 1, 4, 8, 5, 6

41. 13, 15, 17, 13, 11, 13, 9, 17, 4, 8

42. 3.2, 5.4, 2.3, 1.2, 3.2, 5.1, 4.2

43. 123, 151, 121, 112, 146, 112, 138

Find the first, second, and third quartiles of the data. (Lesson 6.7)

44. 8, 6, 7, 4, 9, 7, 5

45. 16, 20, 76, 31, 14, 88, 54

46. 41, 45, 10, 11, 31, 15, 18, 25, 33, 32

47. 19, 72, 93, 82, 22, 21, 14, 31

Draw a box-and-whisker plot of the data. (Lesson 6.7)

48. 6, 14, 8, 13, 5, 11, 9, 18, 3

49. 2, 7, 8, 3, 5, 7, 9, 3

50. 18, 22, 13, 9, 4, 31, 52, 40

51. 1, 8, 21, 12, 5, 2, 9, 10, 4, 15, 3, 23, 31

CHAPTER 7

Graph and check to solve the linear system. (Lesson 7.1)

1. $y = 5$
$x = -2$

2. $x = 0$
$y = 3x + 7$

3. $y = \frac{1}{2}x + 5$
$y = -3x + 5$

4. $5x + 3y = 15$
$4x - 3y = 12$

5. $y = -2x - 6$
$y = -4$

6. $x + y = 10$
$x - y = -2$

7. $-2x + 4y = 12$
$5x - 2y = 10$

8. $\frac{1}{8}(x + y) = 1$
$x - y = 4$

Use the substitution method to solve the linear system. (Lesson 7.2)

9. $x = 5y$
$2x + 3y = -13$

10. $y = -2x$
$x + y = 7$

11. $x + y = 9$
$x - y = 3$

12. $2a + 3b = 3$
$a - 6b = -6$

13. $s - t = 5$
$3s + 4t = 16$

14. $5x - 8y = -17$
$3x = 5 + y$

15. $2m + n = 7$
$4m + 3n = -10$

16. $5a + b = 4$
$7a + 5b = 11$

Use linear combinations to solve the system of linear equations. (Lesson 7.3)

17. $3x + 3y = 6$
$2x - 3y = 4$

18. $3x + 7y = -1$
$7y = -6x$

19. $\frac{2}{5}x - \frac{1}{2}y = 1$
$\frac{1}{5}x + \frac{1}{2}y = -1$

20. $x + 4y = \frac{9}{2}$
$\frac{1}{2}(x - y) = 0$

21. $2x + y = 3(x - 5)$
$x + 5 = 4y + 2x$

22. $2x + 3y = 15$
$3y + 5x = 12$

23. $y = 2x - 36$
$3x - 0.5y = 26$

24. $-4x - 15 = 5y$
$2y = 11 - 5x$

25. CONCERT TICKETS You pay $105 for 8 tickets to attend a folk festival. Tickets for students cost $10 each and tickets for adults cost $15 each. How many of each type of ticket did you buy? (Lesson 7.4)

PRINTING T-SHIRTS The tennis team wants to purchase T-shirts for its members. Company A charges a $20 setup fee and $8 per shirt. Company B charges a $10 setup fee and $10 per shirt. (Lesson 7.4)

26. How many shirts would have to be purchased for the costs to be equal?

27. Which company offers a better price for 12 shirts?

Use any method to solve the linear system and tell how many solutions the system has. (Lesson 7.5)

28. $x + y = 4$
$2x + 3y = 9$

29. $x + y = 6$
$3x + 3y = 3$

30. $x + 2y = 5$
$3x - 15 = -6y$

31. $12x - y = 5$
$-8x + y = -5$

32. $y = -3x$
$6y - x = 38$

33. $2x - 3y = 3$
$6x - 9y = 9$

34. $3x + 6 = 7y$
$x + 2y = 11$

35. $3x - 8y = 4$
$6x - 42 = 16y$

Graph the system of linear inequalities. (Lesson 7.6)

36. $y \geq 0$
$x \leq 0$

37. $y > x + 1$
$y < x + 3$

38. $x \geq 1$
$y + x \leq 5$

39. $y + 2 < -x$
$2y - 4 > 3x$

40. $x < 5$
$x \geq 1$
$y \geq -2$
$y < 7$

41. $y > x - 4$
$y \geq -x - 1$
$y \leq 0$

42. $y > x - 3$
$x - y > -2$
$x \leq 3$

43. $3x - 1 < 5$
$-x + y \leq 10$
$-5x + 2 < 12$

CHAPTER 8

Simplify, if possible. Write your answer as a power or as a product of powers. (Lesson 8.1)

1. $(7^2)(7^3)$

2. $2^3 \cdot 2^4$

3. $(12x)^3$

4. $-(4x)^2 \cdot (5x^3)$

5. $(4r^2s)^2(-2s^2)^3$

6. $(7x^3y) \cdot (-2x^4)$

7. $(3x)^3(-5y)^2$

8. $(-x^3)^2(x)^2(-x^4)^3$

Rewrite the expression with positive exponents. (Lesson 8.2)

9. m^{-4}

10. $\left(\dfrac{x}{2}\right)^{-2}$

11. $\dfrac{y}{x^{-2}}$

12. $\dfrac{6}{(2a)^{-3}}$

13. $\dfrac{3}{3x^{-4}y^3}$

14. $(-3t)^0 \cdot \dfrac{2}{s^{-2}}$

15. $6x \cdot \dfrac{1}{x^{-3}}$

16. $\left(\dfrac{4b^{-1}}{2a^4}\right)^{-2}$

Graph the exponential function. (Lesson 8.2)

17. $y = 3^{-x}$

18. $y = -2^x$

19. $y = \dfrac{1}{4} \cdot 2^x$

20. $y = \left(\dfrac{1}{2}\right)^x$

Simplify the expression. The simplified expression should have no negative exponents. (Lesson 8.3)

21. $\dfrac{2^{11}}{2^8}$

22. $\dfrac{6^5}{6^7}$

23. $\left(\dfrac{3x^2z^4}{2xz}\right)^3$

24. $\dfrac{(a^3)^5}{(a^4)^5}$

25. $\dfrac{18b^2c}{4bc^3} \cdot \dfrac{(3ab)^{-2}}{5a^2c^3}$

26. $\dfrac{(rst)^{-2}}{rs} \cdot \dfrac{(t^2)^3}{(s^{-3})^4}$

27. $5^0 \cdot \dfrac{(5xy)^2}{(x^3y^{-5})^3}$

28. $\left(\dfrac{3}{8}\right)^{-1} \cdot \dfrac{(2a^3x^5)^2}{(8a^{-3}x^{-1})^{-3}}$

29. You roll a die three times. What is the probability that you would roll a two each time? (Lesson 8.3)

Rewrite in decimal form. (Lesson 8.4)

30. 4.813×10^{-6}

31. 3.11×10^4

32. 8.4162×10^{-2}

33. 9.43×10^0

34. 5.0645×10^{10}

35. 1.2468×10^{-3}

36. 2.34×10^{-8}

37. 6.09013×10^{10}

Rewrite in scientific notation. (Lesson 8.4)

38. 5280

39. 0.0378

40. 11.38

41. 33,000,000

42. 827.66

43. 0.208054

44. 16.354

45. 0.000891

INTEREST A principal of $1100 is deposited in an account that pays 5% interest compounded yearly. Find the balance after the given number of years. (Lesson 8.5)

46. 1 year

47. 10 years

48. 15 years

49. 25 years

Classify the model as *exponential growth* or *exponential decay*. Identify the growth or decay factor and the percent of increase or decrease per time period. (Lesson 8.6)

50. $y = 16(0.99)^t$

51. $y = 22(0.5)^t$

52. $y = 8(1.12)^t$

53. $y = 35(1.04)^t$

54. $y = 13\left(\dfrac{7}{6}\right)^t$

55. $y = 110\left(\dfrac{2}{3}\right)^t$

56. $y = 4(1.5)^t$

57. $y = 9(0.68)^t$

58. DEPRECIATION A piece of equipment originally costs $120,000. Its value decreases at a rate of 10% per year. Estimate its value after 6 years. (Lesson 8.6)

CHAPTER 9

Evaluate the expression. Give the exact value if possible. Otherwise, approximate to the nearest hundredth. (Lesson 9.1)

1. $-\sqrt{100}$
2. $\pm\sqrt{676}$
3. $-\sqrt{0.25}$
4. $\pm\sqrt{169}$
5. $\sqrt{379}$
6. $-\sqrt{36}$
7. $\sqrt{220}$
8. $\sqrt{0.01}$

Solve the equation or write *no solution*. Write the solutions as integers if possible. Otherwise, write them as radical expressions. (Lesson 9.1)

9. $x^2 = 25$
10. $4x^2 - 8 = 0$
11. $x^2 = -16$
12. $x^2 + 1 = 1$
13. $3x^2 - 48 = 0$
14. $6x^2 + 6 = 4$
15. $2x^2 - 6 = 0$
16. $x^2 - 4 = -3$

17. **FALLING OBJECT** A ball is dropped from a bridge 150 feet above a river. How long will it take for the ball to hit the surface of the water? (Lesson 9.1)

Simplify the expression. (Lesson 9.2)

18. $\sqrt{250}$
19. $6\sqrt{8} \cdot 7\sqrt{2}$
20. $\sqrt{4} \cdot 3\sqrt{2}$
21. $-2\sqrt{6} \cdot 7\sqrt{30}$
22. $\sqrt{\dfrac{11}{16}}$
23. $\dfrac{\sqrt{20}}{\sqrt{5}}$
24. $\dfrac{1}{2}\sqrt{\dfrac{8}{50}}$
25. $\sqrt{\dfrac{2}{3}} \cdot \sqrt{\dfrac{5}{3}}$

Sketch the graph of the function. Label the vertex. (Lesson 9.3)

26. $y = 3x^2$
27. $y = x^2 - 4$
28. $y = -x^2 - 2x$
29. $y = x^2 - 6x + 8$
30. $y = 4x^2 + 4x - 5$
31. $y = x^2 - 2x + 3$
32. $y = -x^2 + 3x + 2$
33. $y = -3x^2 + 12x - 1$

Represent the solution graphically. Check the solutions algebraically. (Lesson 9.4)

34. $x^2 - 6x = -5$
35. $x^2 + 5x = -6$
36. $x^2 - 3x = 4$
37. $\dfrac{1}{4}x^2 = 9$
38. $x^2 + 3x = 10$
39. $x^2 - 9 = 0$
40. $\dfrac{1}{2}x^2 + 2x = 6$
41. $-2x^2 + 4x + 6 = 0$

Write the quadratic equation in standard form. Solve using the quadratic formula. (Lesson 9.5)

42. $x^2 + x = 12$
43. $3r^2 + 2 = -8r$
44. $3k^2 + 11k = 4$
45. $-x^2 + 5x = 4$
46. $m^2 - 2m - 4 = -3$
47. $2x^2 - 6x = 5$
48. $b^2 - 8 = 7b$
49. $10 - 2x^2 = -x$

Find the discriminant for the equation. Then tell if the equation has *two solutions*, *one solution*, or *no real solution*. (Lesson 9.6)

50. $3x^2 + 14x - 5 = 0$
51. $4x^2 + 12x + 9 = 0$
52. $x^2 + 10x + 9 = 0$
53. $2x^2 + 8x + 8 = 0$
54. $5x^2 + 125 = 0$
55. $x^2 - 2x + 35 = 0$
56. $2x^2 - x - 3 = 0$
57. $-3x^2 + 5x - 6 = 0$

Sketch the graph of the inequality. (Lesson 9.7)

58. $y > -x^2 + 4$
59. $y \le 4x^2$
60. $y > 5x^2 + 10x$
61. $y < x^2 + 5x$
62. $y \ge -3x^2 - 6x + 4$
63. $y < x^2 - 4x + 3$
64. $y \le -x^2 + 4x + 5$
65. $y \ge -x^2 + 8x - 1$

Make a scatter plot of the data. Then name the type of model that best fits the data. (Lesson 9.8)

66. $(-1, -1.5), (2.5, 2), (0.5, 0), (-0.5, -1), (1.5, 1), (-2, -2.5), (0, -0.5)$

67. $(4, 6), (-2, 12), (3, 2), (2, 0), (1, 0), (0, 2), (5, 12), (-1, 6)$

CHAPTER 10

Use a vertical format or a horizontal format to find the sum or the difference. (Lesson 10.1)

1. $(7x^2 - 4) + (x^2 + 5)$ **2.** $(3x^2 - 2) - (2x - 6x^2)$ **3.** $(8x^2 - 3x + 7) + (6x^2 - 4x + 1)$

4. $(-z^3 + 3z) + (-z^2 - 4z - 6)$ **5.** $(5x^2 + 7x - 4) - (4x^2 - 2x)$ **6.** $(3a + 2a^4 - 5) - (a^3 + 2a^4 + 5a)$

Find the product. (Lesson 10.2)

7. $x(4x^2 - 8x + 7)$ **8.** $-3x(x^2 + 5x - 5)$ **9.** $5b^2(3b^3 - 2b^2 + 1)$ **10.** $(t + 9)(2t + 1)$

11. $(d - 1)(d + 5)$ **12.** $(3z + 4)(5z - 8)$ **13.** $(x + 3)(x^2 - 2x + 6)$ **14.** $(3 + 2s - s^2)(s - 1)$

Find the product. (Lesson 10.3)

15. $(x + 9)^2$ **16.** $(-c - d)^2$ **17.** $(a - 2)(a + 2)$ **18.** $(-7 + m)(-7 - m)$

19. $(4x + 5)^2$ **20.** $(5p - 6q)^2$ **21.** $(2a + 3b)(2a - 3b)$ **22.** $(10x - 5y)(10x + 5y)$

Solve the factored equation. (Lesson 10.4)

23. $(x + 3)(x + 6) = 0$ **24.** $(x - 11)^2 = 0$ **25.** $(z - 1)(z + 5) = 0$ **26.** $-8(5w - 2)(w + 4) = 0$

27. $(6n - 9)(n - 7) = 0$ **28.** $3(x + 2)^2 = 0$ **29.** $(2d - 2)(4d - 8) = 0$ **30.** $2(3x - 1)(2x + 5) = 0$

Find the x-intercepts and the vertex of the graph of the function. Then sketch the graph of the function. (Lesson 10.4)

31. $y = (x - 8)(x - 6)$ **32.** $y = (x + 4)(x - 4)$ **33.** $y = (x - 5)(x - 7)$ **34.** $y = (x + 1)(x + 6)$

35. $y = (-x + 5)(x - 9)$ **36.** $y = (-x + 1)(x + 5)$ **37.** $y = (x - 3)(x + 1)$ **38.** $y = (-x - 3)(x + 7)$

Solve the equation by factoring. (Lesson 10.5)

39. $x^2 + 6x + 9 = 0$ **40.** $x^2 + 2x - 35 = 0$ **41.** $x^2 - 12x = -36$ **42.** $-x^2 - 4x = 3$

43. $x^2 - 15x = -54$ **44.** $-x^2 + 14x = 48$ **45.** $x^2 - 2x = 24$ **46.** $x^2 - 5x + 4 = 0$

Solve the equation by factoring. (Lesson 10.6)

47. $2x^2 + x - 6 = 0$ **48.** $2x^2 + 7x = -3$ **49.** $9x^2 + 24x = -16$ **50.** $20x^2 + 23x + 6 = 0$

51. $4x^2 - 5x = 6$ **52.** $3x^2 - 5 = -14x$ **53.** $3x^2 - 17x = 56$ **54.** $12x^2 + 46x - 36 = 0$

Factor the expression. Tell which special product factoring pattern you used. (Lesson 10.7)

55. $x^2 - 1$ **56.** $9b^2 - 81$ **57.** $121 - x^2$ **58.** $12 - 27x^2$

59. $t^2 + 2t + 1$ **60.** $x^2 + 20x + 100$ **61.** $64y^2 + 48y + 9$ **62.** $20x^2 - 100x + 125$

Factor the expression completely. (Lesson 10.8)

63. $x^4 - 9x^2$ **64.** $m^3 + 11m^2 + 28m$ **65.** $x^4 + 4x^3 - 45x^2$ **66.** $x^3 + 2x^2 - 4x - 8$

67. $-3y^3 - 15y^2 - 12y$ **68.** $x^3 - x^2 + 4x - 4$ **69.** $7x^6 - 21x^4$ **70.** $8t^3 - 3t^2 + 16t - 6$

71. GEOMETRY The width of a box is 4 inches less than the length. The height is 9 inches greater than the length. The box has a volume of 180 cubic inches. What are the dimensions of the box? (Lesson 10.8)

CHAPTER 11

Solve the proportion. Check for extraneous solutions. (Lesson 11.1)

1. $\dfrac{x}{2} = \dfrac{8}{x}$

2. $\dfrac{9}{m} = \dfrac{15}{10}$

3. $\dfrac{c^2 - 16}{c + 4} = \dfrac{c - 4}{3}$

4. $\dfrac{3}{5} = \dfrac{x + 2}{6}$

5. $\dfrac{14}{2} = \dfrac{7}{n - 5}$

6. $\dfrac{12}{8} = \dfrac{5 + t}{t - 3}$

7. $\dfrac{x + 15}{16} = \dfrac{-9}{x - 10}$

8. $\dfrac{x + 30}{-4} = \dfrac{143}{x - 18}$

Solve the percent problem. (Lesson 11.2)

9. What number is 40% of 60?   **10.** 75 is what percent of 250?   **11.** How much is 4% of 525 pounds?

12. 8 is 20% of what number?   **13.** 35% of 720 is what number?   **14.** 12% of what amount is $1482?

Decide if the data in the table show *direct* or *inverse* variation. Write an equation that relates the variables. (Lesson 11.3)

15.

x	0.5	1	2	4
y	4	2	1	0.5

16.

x	0.5	1	2	2.5
y	1.5	3	6	7.5

Simplify the expression if possible. (Lesson 11.4)

17. $\dfrac{12x^4}{42x}$

18. $\dfrac{5x^2 - 15x^3}{10x}$

19. $\dfrac{x + 6}{x^2 + 7x + 6}$

20. $\dfrac{x^2 - 8x + 15}{x - 3}$

GEOMETRIC PROBABILITY **A coin is tossed onto the large square region shown. It is equally likely to land on any point in the region.** (Lesson 11.4)

21. Find the probability that the coin lands in the small square.

22. Find the probability that the coin lands in the circle.

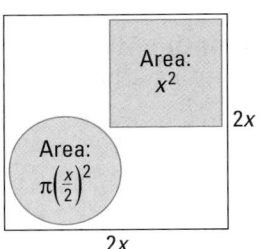

Simplify the expression. (Lesson 11.5)

23. $\dfrac{3x}{5} \cdot \dfrac{15}{18x}$

24. $\dfrac{4x^2}{7} \cdot \dfrac{14}{8x}$

25. $\dfrac{2x^2}{3x} \cdot \dfrac{6x^3}{20x^2}$

26. $\dfrac{x - 3}{5(x + 4)} \cdot \dfrac{4(x + 4)}{x - 3}$

27. $\dfrac{1}{4x} \div \dfrac{6x}{15}$

28. $\dfrac{10x^2}{x^2 - 25} \cdot (x - 5)$

29. $\dfrac{5x}{x - 3} \div \dfrac{x - 8}{x - 3}$

30. $\dfrac{x^2 + 5x - 36}{x^2 - 81} \div (x^2 - 16)$

Simplify the expression. (Lesson 11.6)

31. $\dfrac{20}{5x} - \dfrac{15}{5x}$

32. $\dfrac{4}{x + 2} + \dfrac{8}{x + 2}$

33. $\dfrac{3}{x + 7} - \dfrac{7}{x - 4}$

34. $\dfrac{5x + 3}{x^2 - 25} + \dfrac{5}{x - 5}$

35. $\dfrac{7}{2x} - \dfrac{1}{9x^2}$

36. $\dfrac{3x}{6x^2 + 13x + 2} + \dfrac{x + 1}{x^2 + 5x + 6}$

Divide. (Lesson 11.7)

37. Divide $14x^3 + 7x^2 + x$ by $7x$.

38. Divide $x^2 + 6x - 16$ by $x + 8$.

39. Divide $12x^2 - 2x - 2$ by $3x + 1$.

40. Divide $2x^3 + 9x^2 - 6x + 2$ by $2x + 1$.

Solve the equation. (Lesson 11.8)

41. $\dfrac{4}{x - 6} = \dfrac{x}{10}$

42. $\dfrac{-2}{3x} = \dfrac{4 + x}{6}$

43. $\dfrac{4}{x} + \dfrac{2}{3} = \dfrac{6}{x}$

44. $\dfrac{x}{x - 5} - \dfrac{11}{x - 5} = 7$

45. $\dfrac{1}{x - 3} = \dfrac{5}{x + 9}$

46. $\dfrac{5}{x - 1} + 1 = \dfrac{4}{x^2 + 3x - 4}$

CHAPTER 12

Find the domain and the range of the function. Then sketch its graph.
(Lesson 12.1)

1. $y = 8\sqrt{x}$

2. $y = \sqrt{x} - 5$

3. $y = \sqrt{x + 3}$

4. $y = 0.5\sqrt{x}$

5. $y = \sqrt{x - 2}$

6. $y = \sqrt{x} + 1$

7. $y = \sqrt{3x + 2}$

8. $y = \sqrt{4x - 3}$

Simplify the expression. (Lesson 12.2)

9. $3\sqrt{5} + 2\sqrt{5}$

10. $8\sqrt{7} - 15\sqrt{7}$

11. $2\sqrt{8} + 3\sqrt{32}$

12. $\sqrt{20} - \sqrt{45} + \sqrt{80}$

13. $\sqrt{3}\left(7 - \sqrt{6}\right)$

14. $\left(4 + \sqrt{10}\right)^2$

15. $\dfrac{4}{\sqrt{24}}$

16. $\dfrac{3}{5 - \sqrt{2}}$

Solve the equation. Check for extraneous solutions. (Lesson 12.3)

17. $\sqrt{x} - 11 = 0$

18. $\sqrt{2x - 1} + 4 = 7$

19. $\sqrt{x + 20} = x$

20. $12 = \sqrt{3x + 1} + 7$

21. $\dfrac{1}{2}x = \sqrt{2x - 3}$

22. $\sqrt{18 - 2x} + 5 = x$

Solve the equation by completing the square. (Lesson 12.4)

23. $x^2 + 10x = 56$

24. $x^2 - 6x + 4 = 20$

25. $x^2 - 7x = -10$

26. $x^2 + x = 3$

27. $5x^2 - 12x - 15 = 0$

28. $3x^2 - 10x - 29 = 0$

Find the missing length of the right triangle if a and b are the lengths of the legs and c is the length of the hypotenuse. (Lesson 12.5)

29. $a = 1, b = 1$

30. $a = 1, c = 2$

31. $b = 6, c = 10$

32. $a = 7, b = 10$

33. $b = 15, c = 25$

34. $a = 30, c = 50$

Find the distance and the midpoint between the two points. Round the distance to the nearest hundredth if necessary. (Lesson 12.6)

35. $(0, 4), (4, 5)$

36. $(-3, 3), (6, -1)$

37. $(1, 0), (4, -4)$

38. $(0, 0), (3, -2)$

39. $(7, -6), (-1, -6)$

40. $(5, 2), (5, -4)$

41. $(12, -7), (-4, 2)$

42. $(-4, -5), (-8, -9)$

Find the sine, the cosine, and the tangent of $\angle D$ and $\angle E$. (Lesson 12.7)

43.

44.

45.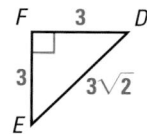

Find the lengths of the sides of the triangle. Round your answer to the nearest hundredth. (Lesson 12.7)

46.

47.

48.

49. Find a counterexample to show that the statement is not true.
   If a, b, and c are real numbers, then $a \cdot (b \cdot c) = (a \cdot b) \cdot (a \cdot c)$. (Lesson 12.8)

Table of Symbols

Symbol		Page
$\cdot$	multiplication, times ($\times$)	3
a^n	nth power of a	9
...	and so on	9
( )	parentheses	10
[ ]	brackets	10
=	equal sign, is equal to	24
$\overset{?}{=}$	is this statement true?	24
$\neq$	is not equal to	24
$<$	is less than	26
$\leq$	is less than or equal to	26
$>$	is greater than	26
$\geq$	is greater than or equal to	26
$\circ$	degree(s)	64
$-a$	the opposite of a	65
$|a|$	absolute value of a	65
$\begin{bmatrix} 1 & 0 \\ 0 & 1 \end{bmatrix}$	matrix	86
$\dfrac{1}{a}$	reciprocal of a, $a \neq 0$	108
P	probability of an event	114
$\dfrac{a}{b}$	ratio of a to b	140

Symbol		Page
$\overline{AB}$	segment AB	140
AB	the length of $\overline{AB}$	140
$\approx$	is approximately equal to	166
$\dfrac{a}{b}$	rate of a per b	180
(x, y)	ordered pair	203
m	slope	226
k	constant of variation	234
b	y-intercept	241
π	pi, an irrational number approximately equal to 3.14	452
a^{-n}	$\dfrac{1}{a^n}$, $a \neq 0$	456
$c \times 10^n$	scientific notation, where $1 \leq c < 10$ and n is an integer	470
$\sqrt{a}$	the nonnegative square root of a	503
$\pm$	plus or minus	503
$\triangle ABC$	triangle ABC	745
$\angle A$	angle A	752
$\sin A$	sine of $\angle A$	752
$\cos A$	cosine of $\angle A$	752
$\tan A$	tangent of $\angle A$	752

Table of Measures

Time	
60 seconds (sec) = 1 minute (min)	$\left.\begin{array}{l}365 \text{ days}\\52 \text{ weeks (approx.)}\\12 \text{ months}\end{array}\right\}$ = 1 year
60 minutes = 1 hour (h)	
24 hours = 1 day	10 years = 1 decade
7 days = 1 week	100 years = 1 century
4 weeks (approx.) = 1 month	

Metric

Length

10 millimeters (mm) = 1 centimeter (cm)

$\left.\begin{array}{l}100 \text{ cm}\\1000 \text{ mm}\end{array}\right\}$ = 1 meter (m)

1000 m = 1 kilometer (km)

Area

100 square millimeters = 1 square centimeter
$\left(\text{mm}^2\right)$ $\left(\text{cm}^2\right)$

10,000 cm^2 = 1 square meter $\left(\text{m}^2\right)$

10,000 m^2 = 1 hectare (ha)

Volume

1000 cubic millimeters = 1 cubic centimeter
$\left(\text{mm}^3\right)$ $\left(\text{cm}^3\right)$

1,000,000 cm^3 = 1 cubic meter $\left(\text{m}^3\right)$

Liquid Capacity

1000 milliliters (mL) = 1 liter (L)

1000 L = 1 kiloliter (kL)

Mass

1000 milligrams (mg) = 1 gram (g)

1000 g = 1 kilogram (kg)

1000 kg = 1 metric ton (t)

Temperature — Degrees Celsius (°C)

0°C = freezing point of water

37°C = normal body temperature

100°C = boiling point of water

United States Customary

Length

12 inches (in.) = 1 foot (ft)

$\left.\begin{array}{l}36 \text{ in.}\\3 \text{ ft}\end{array}\right\}$ = 1 yard (yd)

$\left.\begin{array}{l}5280 \text{ ft}\\1760 \text{ yd}\end{array}\right\}$ = 1 mile (mi)

Area

144 square inches $\left(\text{in.}^2\right)$ = 1 square foot $\left(\text{ft}^2\right)$

9 ft^2 = 1 square yard $\left(\text{yd}^2\right)$

$\left.\begin{array}{l}43{,}560 \text{ ft}^2\\4840 \text{ yd}^2\end{array}\right\}$ = 1 acre (A)

Volume

1728 cubic inches $\left(\text{in.}^3\right)$ = 1 cubic foot $\left(\text{ft}^3\right)$

27 ft^3 = 1 cubic yard $\left(\text{yd}^3\right)$

Liquid Capacity

8 fluid ounces (fl oz) = 1 cup (c)

2 c = 1 pint (pt)

2 pt = 1 quart (qt)

4 qt = 1 gallon (gal)

Weight

16 ounces (oz) = 1 pound (lb)

2000 lb = 1 ton (t)

Temperature — Degrees Fahrenheit (°F)

32°F = freezing point of water

98.6°F = normal body temperature

212°F = boiling point of water

Table of Squares and Square Roots

No.	Square	Sq. Root	No.	Square	Sq. Root	No.	Square	Sq. Root
1	1	1.000	51	2,601	7.141	101	10,201	10.050
2	4	1.414	52	2,704	7.211	102	10,404	10.100
3	9	1.732	53	2,809	7.280	103	10,609	10.149
4	16	2.000	54	2,916	7.348	104	10,816	10.198
5	25	2.236	55	3,025	7.416	105	11,025	10.247
6	36	2.449	56	3,136	7.483	106	11,236	10.296
7	49	2.646	57	3,249	7.550	107	11,449	10.344
8	64	2.828	58	3,364	7.616	108	11,664	10.392
9	81	3.000	59	3,481	7.681	109	11,881	10.440
10	100	3.162	60	3,600	7.746	110	12,100	10.488
11	121	3.317	61	3,721	7.810	111	12,321	10.536
12	144	3.464	62	3,844	7.874	112	12,544	10.583
13	169	3.606	63	3,969	7.937	113	12,769	10.630
14	196	3.742	64	4,096	8.000	114	12,996	10.677
15	225	3.873	65	4,225	8.062	115	13,225	10.724
16	256	4.000	66	4,356	8.124	116	13,456	10.770
17	289	4.123	67	4,489	8.185	117	13,689	10.817
18	324	4.243	68	4,624	8.246	118	13,924	10.863
19	361	4.359	69	4,761	8.307	119	14,161	10.909
20	400	4.472	70	4,900	8.367	120	14,400	10.954
21	441	4.583	71	5,041	8.426	121	14,641	11.000
22	484	4.690	72	5,184	8.485	122	14,884	11.045
23	529	4.796	73	5,329	8.544	123	15,129	11.091
24	576	4.899	74	5,476	8.602	124	15,376	11.136
25	625	5.000	75	5,625	8.660	125	15,625	11.180
26	676	5.099	76	5,776	8.718	126	15,876	11.225
27	729	5.196	77	5,929	8.775	127	16,129	11.269
28	784	5.292	78	6,084	8.832	128	16,384	11.314
29	841	5.385	79	6,241	8.888	129	16,641	11.358
30	900	5.477	80	6,400	8.944	130	16,900	11.402
31	961	5.568	81	6,561	9.000	131	17,161	11.446
32	1,024	5.657	82	6,724	9.055	132	17,424	11.489
33	1,089	5.745	83	6,889	9.110	133	17,689	11.533
34	1,156	5.831	84	7,056	9.165	134	17,956	11.576
35	1,225	5.916	85	7,225	9.220	135	18,225	11.619
36	1,296	6.000	86	7,396	9.274	136	18,496	11.662
37	1,369	6.083	87	7,569	9.327	137	18,769	11.705
38	1,444	6.164	88	7,744	9.381	138	19,044	11.747
39	1,521	6.245	89	7,921	9.434	139	19,321	11.790
40	1,600	6.325	90	8,100	9.487	140	19,600	11.832
41	1,681	6.403	91	8,281	9.539	141	19,881	11.874
42	1,764	6.481	92	8,464	9.592	142	20,164	11.916
43	1,849	6.557	93	8,649	9.644	143	20,449	11.958
44	1,936	6.633	94	8,836	9.695	144	20,736	12.000
45	2,025	6.708	95	9,025	9.747	145	21,025	12.042
46	2,116	6.782	96	9,216	9.798	146	21,316	12.083
47	2,209	6.856	97	9,409	9.849	147	21,609	12.124
48	2,304	6.928	98	9,604	9.899	148	21,904	12.166
49	2,401	7.000	99	9,801	9.950	149	22,201	12.207
50	2,500	7.071	100	10,000	10.000	150	22,500	12.247

Table of Trigonometric Ratios

Angle	Sine	Cosine	Tangent
1°	.0175	.9998	.0175
2°	.0349	.9994	.0349
3°	.0523	.9986	.0524
4°	.0698	.9976	.0699
5°	.0872	.9962	.0875
6°	.1045	.9945	.1051
7°	.1219	.9925	.1228
8°	.1392	.9903	.1405
9°	.1564	.9877	.1584
10°	.1736	.9848	.1763
11°	.1908	.9816	.1944
12°	.2079	.9781	.2126
13°	.2250	.9744	.2309
14°	.2419	.9703	.2493
15°	.2588	.9659	.2679
16°	.2756	.9613	.2867
17°	.2924	.9563	.3057
18°	.3090	.9511	.3249
19°	.3256	.9455	.3443
20°	.3420	.9397	.3640
21°	.3584	.9336	.3839
22°	.3746	.9272	.4040
23°	.3907	.9205	.4245
24°	.4067	.9135	.4452
25°	.4226	.9063	.4663
26°	.4384	.8988	.4877
27°	.4540	.8910	.5095
28°	.4695	.8829	.5317
29°	.4848	.8746	.5543
30°	.5000	.8660	.5774
31°	.5150	.8572	.6009
32°	.5299	.8480	.6249
33°	.5446	.8387	.6494
34°	.5592	.8290	.6745
35°	.5736	.8192	.7002
36°	.5878	.8090	.7265
37°	.6018	.7986	.7536
38°	.6157	.7880	.7813
39°	.6293	.7771	.8098
40°	.6428	.7660	.8391
41°	.6561	.7547	.8693
42°	.6691	.7431	.9004
43°	.6820	.7314	.9325
44°	.6947	.7193	.9657
45°	.7071	.7071	1.0000

Angle	Sine	Cosine	Tangent
46°	.7193	.6947	1.0355
47°	.7314	.6820	1.0724
48°	.7431	.6691	1.1106
49°	.7547	.6561	1.1504
50°	.7660	.6428	1.1918
51°	.7771	.6293	1.2349
52°	.7880	.6157	1.2799
53°	.7986	.6018	1.3270
54°	.8090	.5878	1.3764
55°	.8192	.5736	1.4281
56°	.8290	.5592	1.4826
57°	.8387	.5446	1.5399
58°	.8480	.5299	1.6003
59°	.8572	.5150	1.6643
60°	.8660	.5000	1.7321
61°	.8746	.4848	1.8040
62°	.8829	.4695	1.8807
63°	.8910	.4540	1.9626
64°	.8988	.4384	2.0503
65°	.9063	.4226	2.1445
66°	.9135	.4067	2.2460
67°	.9205	.3907	2.3559
68°	.9272	.3746	2.4751
69°	.9336	.3584	2.6051
70°	.9397	.3420	2.7475
71°	.9455	.3256	2.9042
72°	.9511	.3090	3.0777
73°	.9563	.2924	3.2709
74°	.9613	.2756	3.4874
75°	.9659	.2588	3.7321
76°	.9703	.2419	4.0108
77°	.9744	.2250	4.3315
78°	.9781	.2079	4.7046
79°	.9816	.1908	5.1446
80°	.9848	.1736	5.6713
81°	.9877	.1564	6.3138
82°	.9903	.1392	7.1154
83°	.9925	.1219	8.1443
84°	.9945	.1045	9.5144
85°	.9962	.0872	11.4301
86°	.9976	.0698	14.3007
87°	.9986	.0523	19.0811
88°	.9994	.0349	28.6363
89°	.9998	.0175	57.2900

Table of Formulas

Geometric Formulas

Perimeter of a polygon	$P = a + b + \ldots + z$ where $a, b, \ldots, z =$ side lengths
Area of a triangle	$A = \frac{1}{2}bh$ where $b =$ base and $h =$ height
Area of a square	$A = s^2$ where $s =$ side length
Area of a rectangle	$A = lw$ where $l =$ length and $w =$ width
Area of a trapezoid	$A = \frac{1}{2}h(b_1 + b_2)$ where $h =$ height and $b_1, b_2 =$ bases
Volume of a cube	$V = s^3$ where $s =$ edge length
Volume of a rectangular prism	$V = lwh$ where $l =$ length, $w =$ width, and $h =$ height
Circumference of a circle	$C = \pi d$ where $\pi \approx 3.14$ and $d =$ diameter $C = 2\pi r$ where $\pi \approx 3.14$ and $r =$ radius
Area of a circle	$A = \pi r^2$ where $\pi \approx 3.14$ and $r =$ radius
Surface area of a sphere	$S = 4\pi r^2$ where $\pi \approx 3.14$ and $r =$ radius
Volume of a sphere	$V = \frac{4}{3}\pi r^3$ where $\pi \approx 3.14$ and $r =$ radius

Other Formulas

Average speed	$r = \frac{d}{t}$ or $d = rt$ where $r =$ average rate or speed, $d =$ distance, and $t =$ time
Probability of an event	$P = \frac{\text{Number of favorable outcomes}}{\text{Total number of outcomes}}$ where $0 \leq P \leq 1$

Algebraic Formulas

Slope formula	$m = \frac{y_2 - y_1}{x_2 - x_1}$ where $m =$ slope and (x_1, y_1) and (x_2, y_2) are two points
Quadratic formula	The solutions of $ax^2 + bx + c = 0$ are $x = \frac{-b \pm \sqrt{b^2 - 4ac}}{2a}$ when $a \neq 0$ and $b^2 - 4ac \geq 0$.
Pythagorean theorem	$a^2 + b^2 = c^2$ where $a, b =$ length of the legs and $c =$ length of the hypotenuse of a right triangle
Distance formula	$d = \sqrt{(x_2 - x_1)^2 + (y_2 - y_1)^2}$ where $d =$ distance and (x_1, y_1) and (x_2, y_2) are coordinates of two points
Midpoint formula	The midpoint between (x_1, y_1) and (x_2, y_2) is $\left(\frac{x_1 + x_2}{2}, \frac{y_1 + y_2}{2}\right)$.

Table of Properties

Basic Properties

	Addition	Multiplication
Closure	$a + b$ is a real number.	ab is a real number.
Commutative	$a + b = b + a$	$ab = ba$
Associative	$(a + b) + c = a + (b + c)$	$(ab)c = a(bc)$
Identity	$a + 0 = a, 0 + a = a$	$a(1) = a, 1(a) = a$
Inverse Property	$a + (-a) = 0$	$a \cdot \dfrac{1}{a} = 1, a \neq 0$
Prop. of zero in mult.		$a(0) = 0$
Property of opposites		$(-1)a = -a$ or $a(-1) = -a$
Distributive	$a(b + c) = ab + ac$ or $(b + c)a = ba + ca$	

Properties of Equality

Addition	If $a = b$, then $a + c = b + c$.
Subtraction	If $a = b$, then $a - c = b - c$.
Multiplication	If $a = b$, then $ca = cb$.
Division	If $a = b$, and $c \neq 0$, then $\dfrac{a}{c} = \dfrac{b}{c}$.

Properties of Exponents

Product of Powers	$a^m \cdot a^n = a^{m+n}$
Power of a Power	$(a^m)^n = a^{m \cdot n}$
Power of a Product	$(a \cdot b)^m = a^m \cdot b^m$
Quotient of Powers	$\dfrac{a^m}{a^n} = a^{m-n}, a \neq 0$
Power of a Quotient	$\left(\dfrac{a}{b}\right)^m = \dfrac{a^m}{b^m}, b \neq 0$
Negative Exponent	$a^{-n} = \dfrac{1}{a^n}, a \neq 0$
Zero Exponent	$a^0 = 1, a \neq 0$

Properties of Radicals

Product Property	$\sqrt{ab} = \sqrt{a} \cdot \sqrt{b}$
Quotient Property	$\sqrt{\dfrac{a}{b}} = \dfrac{\sqrt{a}}{\sqrt{b}}$

Properties of Proportions

Reciprocal	If $\dfrac{a}{b} = \dfrac{c}{d}$, then $\dfrac{b}{a} = \dfrac{d}{c}$.
Cross-multiplying	If $\dfrac{a}{b} = \dfrac{c}{d}$, then $ad = bc$.

Special Products and Their Factors

Sum and Difference Pattern	$(a + b)(a - b) = a^2 - b^2$
Square of a Binomial Pattern	$(a + b)^2 = a^2 + 2ab + b^2$
	$(a - b)^2 = a^2 - 2ab + b^2$
FOIL	$(a + b)(c + d) = a \cdot c + a \cdot d + b \cdot c + b \cdot d$
	First $\quad$ Outer $\quad$ Inner $\quad$ Last

Properties of Rational Expressions

Multiplication	$\dfrac{a}{b} \cdot \dfrac{c}{d} = \dfrac{ac}{bd}$
Division	$\dfrac{a}{b} \div \dfrac{c}{d} = \dfrac{a}{b} \cdot \dfrac{d}{c}$
Addition	$\dfrac{a}{c} + \dfrac{b}{c} = \dfrac{a+b}{c}$
Subtraction	$\dfrac{a}{c} - \dfrac{b}{c} = \dfrac{a-b}{c}$

Mixed Problem Solving

CHAPTER 1

1. SOFTBALL A softball player's batting average is $\frac{h}{a}$, where h is the number of hits and a is the number of at bats. So far this season, Jessica has 8 hits in 17 at bats. Find Jessica's batting average. Round your answer to the nearest thousandth. **(Lesson 1.1)**

2. CANDLES A candle company makes candles shaped like pyramids. One of the molds for these candles has a height of 8 centimeters and a square base that measures 9 centimeters on each side. Find the amount of wax needed to fill the mold by finding the volume of the pyramid. (The formula for the volume of a pyramid is $\frac{1}{3}$ times the height times the area of the base.) **(Lesson 1.2)**

AMUSEMENT PARKS In Exercises 3–7, use the following information. **(Lesson 1.3)**
A family of six has coupons for discounted admission to an amusement park. The members of the family are the following ages: 67, 40, 39, 14, 8, and 4.

Amusement Park Admission Prices		
Age	Regular price	Discounted price
13–59	$10.00	$7.50
5–12 and 60+	$8.00	$6.00
under 5	free	free

3. Write an expression that represents the total cost of admission for the family at the regular price.

4. Evaluate the expression from Exercise 3.

5. Write an expression that represents the total cost of admission for the family at the discounted price.

6. Evaluate the expression from Exercise 5.

7. How much money did the family save by using the coupons?

8. TRAVEL While planning a vacation, your family budgets $1200 to spend on lodging. The hotel costs $129 per night. Will you have enough money in the budget to stay for 7 nights? You write the inequality $129h \leq 1200$ to model the situation. What do 129, h, and 1200 represent? **(Lesson 1.4)**

BULK FOODS In Exercises 9–11, use the following information. **(Lesson 1.5)**
The trail mix in the bulk foods section of a grocery store costs $1.90 per pound. Martin paid $5.70 for the bag that he filled with trail mix. Martin wants to know how many pounds of trail mix he bought.

9. Write a verbal model that relates the cost per pound of the trail mix, the pounds of trail mix, and the total cost of the trail mix.

10. Assign labels and write an algebraic model based on your verbal model in Exercise 9.

11. Use mental math to solve the equation in Exercise 10. How many pounds of trail mix did Martin buy?

12. CONCERT BAND The table below shows the number of students in the concert band at a school for the given years. Make a line graph of the data. Discuss what the line graph shows. **(Lesson 1.6)**

Year	1997	1999	2001	2003
Students	62	51	54	57

TELEPHONE CALLS In Exercises 13 and 14, use the following information. **(Lesson 1.7)**
The total cost C (in dollars) of a telephone call from the United States to Moscow, Russia is given by $C = 0.4t$, where t represents the length of the call in minutes.

13. Evaluate the equation for $t = 5, 10, 15, 20, 25$. Organize your results in an input-output table.

14. Describe the domain and range of the function whose values are shown in the table.

CHAPTER 2

TEMPERATURES In Exercises 1–3, use the table below, which shows the daily low temperatures in Petoskey, Michigan during a week in January. **(Lesson 2.1)**

Day	Temperature
Monday	7°F
Tuesday	−3°F
Wednesday	2°F
Thursday	−7°F
Friday	−5°F
Saturday	−2°F
Sunday	9°F

1. Which low temperature was the coldest?

2. Which days had low temperatures above −2°F?

3. What is the absolute value of the low temperature on Tuesday?

4. MONEY On a Saturday morning, your parents give you $15 for your allowance. You spend $18.50 at the mall. Then you make $20 baby-sitting that night. Do you end the day with more money than you started with? If so, how much more? **(Lesson 2.2)**

5. STOCK You purchase some shares of stock. The price of each share fell by $3.20 in the first month, rose by $5.45 in the second month, and fell by $1.12 in the third month. Did the price of a share increase or decrease over the three months? **(Lesson 2.2)**

WEATHER In Exercises 6 and 7, use the following information. **(Lesson 2.3)**
On Sunday, there were 14 inches of snow on the ground. About 1.5 inches of the snow melted on Monday, 2 inches melted on Tuesday, and 1.5 inches melted on Wednesday.

6. How much snow remained at the end of the day on Wednesday?

7. At the end of the day on Thursday, there were 8.5 inches of snow on the ground. How much snow melted on Thursday?

CONCESSION STAND In Exercises 8–10, use the table below, which shows the sales at a concession stand during two different events. **(Lesson 2.4)**

	Soccer Game		Football Game	
	Small	Large	Small	Large
Popcorn	24	13	62	55
Nachos	18	11	29	20
Soda	31	28	53	66

8. Write a matrix for the concession stand sales at the soccer game.

9. Write a matrix for the concession stand sales at the football game.

10. Find the sum of the matrices from Exercises 8 and 9. Explain what the resulting matrix represents.

11. HOT AIR BALLOON A hot air balloon descends with a velocity of −678 feet per minute. Find the vertical distance traveled in 3.5 minutes. **(Lesson 2.5)**

12. GEOMETRY Write and simplify an expression for the perimeter of the figure. **(Lesson 2.6)**

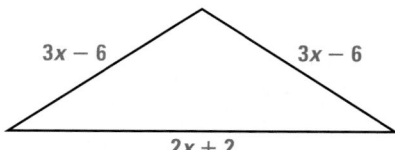

13. FOOD There are $19\frac{1}{2}$ ounces of pretzels in a bag. If a serving size is $\frac{3}{4}$ ounce, then how many servings are in the bag of pretzels? **(Lesson 2.7)**

14. MUSIC Your compact disc collection contains 27 rock discs, 15 country discs, 28 pop discs and 10 hip-hop discs. You randomly choose a compact disc from your collection. What is the probability that the disc is a pop disc? **(Lesson 2.8)**

CHAPTER 3

1. **CATS** A veterinary assistant steps on a scale while holding a cat. The scale reads 161 pounds. Alone the assistant weighs 147 pounds. Write and solve an equation to find the weight of the cat. **(Lesson 3.1)**

2. **SNOWFALL** The average snowfall in Alpena during the month of February is 3 times the average snowfall in Madison during the month of February. The average snowfall in Alpena during February is 15 inches. Write and solve an equation to find the average snowfall in Madison during the month of February. **(Lesson 3.2)**

3. **GEOMETRY** The triangles below are similar. Write and solve an equation to find the length of the side marked x. **(Lesson 3.2)**

4. **GARDENING** An online garden supply company offers daffodil bulbs for $.59 each plus $2.75 for shipping and handling for the entire order. You want to spend $15 on an order of daffodil bulbs. Write and solve an equation to find the number of daffodil bulbs you can purchase. **(Lesson 3.3)**

5. **BOOKS** You spend $13.25 to buy 6 books and a bookmark at a used book sale. You pay the same amount for each book you buy, and the bookmark costs $1.25. Write and solve an equation to find the cost of one book. **(Lesson 3.3)**

6. **EXERCISE** Each yoga class at a gym costs $10 for nonmembers. If you are a member of the gym, you pay a one-time joining fee of $45, and each yoga class costs $5. Write and solve an equation to find the number of yoga classes you must take to justify becoming a member. **(Lesson 3.4)**

TRANSPORTATION In Exercises 7 and 8, use the following information. **(Lesson 3.5)**
Two planes leave an airport at 1:00 P.M. One plane heads south and the second plane heads north. The plane heading north is traveling 150 miles per hour. At 3:00 P.M. the two planes are 650 miles apart.

7. At 3:00 P.M., how far has the plane heading north traveled?

8. At 3:00 P.M., how far has the plane heading south traveled?

9. **TELEPHONES** Your long-distance telephone company charges a monthly fee of $4.75 plus $.10 for each minute of long-distance telephone calls. Your bill for last month was $15.25. Write and solve an equation to find the number of minutes of long-distance telephone calls for last month. **(Lesson 3.6)**

ELECTRICAL POWER In Exercises 10 and 11, use the following information. **(Lesson 3.7)**
The electrical power rating P, in watts, of an electrical appliance is given by the formula $P = VI$, where V is the voltage and I is the current in amps.

10. Solve the formula for I.

11. Use the new formula to find the current running through the appliance given its power rating and voltage.

Appliance	Stereo	Coffeemaker
Power rating	30 watts	900 watts
Voltage	110 volts	110 volts

12. **FOOD** You spend $2.34 on 6 pounds of bananas. What is the cost per pound? **(Lesson 3.8)**

13. **JEWELRY** A craft store sells assorted collections of beads. One assortment contains 100 beads and costs $8.00. A larger assortment contains 250 beads and costs $12.50. Which assortment is the better buy? Explain how you decided. **(Lesson 3.8)**

CHAPTER 4

ICE HOCKEY **In Exercises 1 and 2, use the table below, which shows the number of shots on goal and the number of goals scored by players on an ice hockey team during one season.** (Lesson 4.1)

Shots	Goals
64	11
39	6
38	5
43	7
46	7
28	4
51	7
35	6
28	3

1. Make a scatter plot that shows the number of shots on goal and the number of goals scored for the players. Use the horizontal axis to represent the number of shots on goal.

2. What conclusions (if any) can you make from the scatter plot?

SUMMER JOBS **In Exercises 3 and 4, use the following information.** (Lesson 4.2)
You charge $50 for cleaning a large office and $25 for cleaning a small office. You want to make $500 in one week. An algebraic model for your earnings is $50x + 25y = 500$, where x is the number of large offices you clean per week, and y is the number of small offices you clean.

3. Write the algebraic model in function form. Then use a table of values to graph the equation.

4. If you do not clean any large offices during the week, how many small offices do you have to clean to earn $500?

5. **MUSEUMS** The cost of admission to a science museum is $18 for adults and $12 for students. The museum collected $2376 from admissions for one day. Make a graph that shows the possible numbers of adults and students admitted to the museum. (Lesson 4.3)

6. **BOWLING** In 1995, the cost of bowling one string at a bowling alley was $1.75. In 2000, the cost of one string was $2.25. If the cost of bowling one string increased the same amount each year, find the rate of change of the cost in dollars per year. (Lesson 4.4)

HEALTH CARE **In Exercises 7 and 8, use the information below.** (Lesson 4.5)
The dosage of a medication for a child is based on the child's weight. Examples of such recommendations are shown in the table below. The recommended dosage (in milligrams) varies directly with the weight (in pounds) of the child.

Weight (lb)	Dosage (mg)
20	125
28	175
32	200
40	250

7. Write a direct variation model that relates the weight w to the dosage d.

8. Estimate the dosage for a child who weighs 45 pounds.

9. **CLOTHING** A tailor charges a $15 fee plus $2.50 per letter to sew a name onto a jacket. The equation $y = 2.5x + 15$ models the total cost y of sewing a name with x letters. Find the slope and y-intercept of the equation. Explain what the slope and y-intercept mean in the cost model. (Lesson 4.6)

10. **CLUB MEMBERSHIP** The total cost y of a family membership to a health club for x months can be modeled by the equation $y = 30x + 75$. How many months of family membership do you have if your family pays $225? (Lesson 4.7)

11. **BICYCLES** You ride your bicycle from your house to school. Your average speed is 15 miles per hour. Write a linear function that models the distance you travel $d(t)$ as a function of t, the time spent traveling. Then use your model to estimate the distance traveled after you ride for 0.2 hours. (Lesson 4.8)

CHAPTER 5

DOGS In Exercises 1–3, use the following information. (Lesson 5.1)

A group of dogsledders set off on an expedition with 91 pounds of dog food for their dogs. The dogs eat 7 pounds of dog food each day.

1. Write an equation in slope-intercept form to model the total remaining dog food y (in pounds) in terms of x, the days on the expedition.

2. Copy and complete the table using your equation from Exercise 1.

Days (x)	3	5	7	9
Remaining dog food (y)	?	?	?	?

3. Find the number of days that the supply of dog food will last.

VINTAGE CARS In Exercises 4 and 5, use the following information. (Lesson 5.2)

You bought a vintage car for $4500 last year. You are told that the car is worth $600 more this year, and you should expect the value of the car to increase by $600 every year.

4. Write an equation that models the total value v of the car in terms of n, the number of years you have owned the car.

5. Calculate the value of the car after you have owned it for 7 years.

MOVING VANS In Exercises 6–8, use the following information. (Lesson 5.3)

The cost of renting a moving van for a 26 mile trip is $62.50. The cost of renting the same moving van for a 38 mile trip is $65.50.

6. Write a linear equation that models the cost c of renting the van in terms of m, the length (in miles) of the trip.

7. Use your equation from Exercise 6 to find the cost of renting the van for a 50 mile trip.

8. You have only $75 to spend on the moving van. What is the longest trip you can take?

BASKETBALL In Exercises 9 and 10, use the following information. (Lesson 5.4)

You stood in 6 locations on a basketball court and made 20 attempts at a basket from each location. The table shows the distance each location was from the basket and the number of shots made.

Distance from basket (feet)	Shots made
5	18
10	15
15	10
20	10
25	7
30	4

9. Make a scatter plot of the data. Let x equal the distance from the basket and let y equal the shots made.

10. Find an equation of the line that you think best fits the data.

11. **CANOEING** You are on an 18 mile long canoe trip and you are paddling at a constant rate. You started the trip at 9:00 A.M., and you traveled 6 miles by 10:30 A.M. Write an equation that gives the distance d (in miles) remaining in terms of the time t (in hours). What is the slope of the line? (Lesson 5.5)

12. **FUNDRAISING** Your scout troop holds a breakfast to raise money for a local charity. Your troop charges $8 for an adult and $4 for a child, and you raise a total of $1200. Write an equation that represents the different amounts of adults x and children y that could have attended the breakfast. (Lesson 5.6)

13. **WEB SITES** The table shows the hits received by a Web site each week after its launch. Write a linear model for the data. Then predict the number of hits the Web site will receive in week 7. (Lesson 5.7)

Week	Hits
1	57
2	76
3	107
4	236
5	367
6	499

CHAPTER 6

1. **MONEY** You want to purchase a bicycle that costs $165. You have already saved $118 for the bicycle. Let x represent the additional amount of money you need to purchase the bicycle. Write an inequality for x. What is the least additional amount of money that you need to purchase the bicycle? **(Lesson 6.1)**

2. **CATERING COSTS** Dave is planning the awards banquet for his bowling league. He has $1500 in the budget to spend on the catering for the 108 people that will be attending the banquet. The catering company charges a $150 for a setup fee plus a set amount per person. Dave needs to decide how much he can afford to spend per person. Write and solve an inequality to determine the maximum amount of money that he can spend per person. **(Lesson 6.2)**

3. **GEOMETRY** Write an inequality for the value of x. **(Lesson 6.2)**

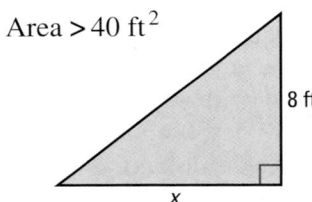

Area $> 40 \text{ ft}^2$

8 ft

x

4. **TEMPERATURE** The table shows the normal daily high temperatures for the month of January in four cities in California. Write a compound inequality that represents the different temperatures. **(Lesson 6.3)**

City	Temperature (°F)
Los Angeles	65.7
Sacramento	52.7
San Diego	65.9
San Francisco	55.6

5. **CALCIUM** The recommended daily intake of calcium for teenagers is estimated between 1200 milligrams and 1500 milligrams. Write an absolute-value inequality to represent the recommended daily intake of calcium for teenagers. **(Lesson 6.4)**

6. **QUALITY CONTROL** Dara works in the quality control department at a company that packages baking mixes. Each box of vanilla cake mix that she inspects must weigh between 509 grams and 525 grams. Write an absolute-value inequality to represent this situation. **(Lesson 6.4)**

7. **SEWING** You have $15 to spend on two different fabrics for a sewing project. The solid fabric that you want costs $2.50 per yard and the printed fabric that you want costs $4.99 per yard. Let x represent the number of yards of the solid fabric you can buy. Let y represent the number of yards of the printed fabric you can buy. Write and graph an inequality to model the amounts of each fabric you can buy. **(Lesson 6.5)**

TRAVEL TIME In Exercises 8–10, use the following information. (Lesson 6.6)
A survey asks 20 students the average time (in minutes) it takes them to get to school in the morning. The results are listed below.

18, 23, 17, 30, 13, 22, 20, 20, 7, 22,
25, 15, 13, 30, 15, 5, 30, 21, 30, 10

8. Use a stem-and-leaf plot to order the times from least to greatest.

9. Find the mean, median, and mode of the data.

10. Is one measure of central tendency most representative of a typical travel time? Explain your reasoning.

11. **AGES** The ages of the employees at a roller rink are listed below. Draw a box-and-whisker plot of the data. **(Lesson 6.7)**

24, 22, 30, 18, 29, 38, 33, 17, 22, 25, 16, 41

12. **TEST SCORES** Create a collection of 16 test scores that could be represented by the box-and-whisker plot shown below. **(Lesson 6.7)**

64   71   84   89   99

CHAPTER 7

1. **TENNIS** A tennis club charges $55 for a summer membership plus $12 for each hour of court use. A second club charges $20 for a summer membership plus $17 for each hour of court use. Use the graph below to determine the number of hours of court use for which the total cost of playing tennis at each club is the same. **(Lesson 7.1)**

Court use (hours)

2. **CARPETS** Store A charges $3 per square foot for a wall-to-wall carpet and charges $85 for installation. Store B charges $2 per square foot for the same carpet and charges $100 for installation. Use a graph to determine the square footage for which the total cost of the carpet and installation at each store is the same. **(Lesson 7.1)**

3. **MONEY** A bag contains quarters and dimes. There are 15 coins in the bag. The value of the coins is $2.70. Use substitution to determine the number of quarters and dimes in the bag. **(Lesson 7.2)**

4. **MOVIES** A movie rental store sells previously viewed movies. The movies in DVD format cost $10 each and the movies in VHS format cost $7 each. Jana bought 6 movies for $51, excluding tax. Use substitution to determine the number of DVDs that Jana bought. **(Lesson 7.2)**

5. **TELEPHONE RATES** A telephone company offers two long distance plans. One plan charges $4.95 per month and $.07 per minute. The other plan does not have a monthly fee and charges $.10 per minute. Use linear combinations to determine the number of minutes for which the cost of each plan is the same. **(Lesson 7.3)**

6. **AGES** Twice Mark's age minus Tom's age is equal to 9. Twice Tom's age minus 8 is equal to twice Mark's age. Use linear combinations to determine Mark's age and Tom's age. **(Lesson 7.3)**

7. **PLANETARIUM SHOWS** The prices for admission tickets to the planetarium shows at a science museum are listed in the table below. On Monday, 540 admission tickets for the planetarium shows are purchased. The museum collected $3257.50 in admission ticket sales for the planetarium shows. How many student admission tickets were sold? **(Lesson 7.4)**

Admission Ticket Prices	
Adult	$8
Student	$5.50

ART SUPPLIES In Exercises 8 and 9, use the following information. **(Lesson 7.5)**
At an art supply store, all of the tubes of oil paint cost the same, and all of the tubes of acrylic paint cost the same. An art teacher paid $43.71 for 3 tubes of oil paint and 6 tubes of acrylic paint. The next week he paid $14.57 for one tube of oil paint and 2 tubes of acrylic paint.

8. Can you determine how much the art teacher paid for one tube of oil paint? Explain.

9. The following week, the art teacher paid $39.89 for 3 tubes of oil paint and 5 tubes of acrylic paint. Can you determine how much he paid for one tube of oil paint? Explain.

JOBS In Exercises 10 and 11, use the following information. **(Lesson 7.6)**
During a summer, you can work a total of no more than 30 hours a week at your two jobs. Your camp counseling job pays $8 an hour, and your job at a retail store pays $10 an hour. You want to earn at least $250 a week.

10. Write a system of linear inequalities that shows the various number of hours you can work at each job.

11. Graph the system of linear inequalities.

CHAPTER 8

1. **GEOMETRY** The volume V of a cylinder is given by $V = \pi r^2 h$, where r is the radius of a base, h is the height, and $\pi \approx 3.14$. What is the volume of the cylinder in terms of t? **(Lesson 8.1)**

6t

9 cm

TESTS In Exercises 2 and 3, use the following information. (Lesson 8.1)
Part A of a test has 15 true-false questions. Part B has 5 multiple choice questions, each of which has 4 choices. There are 2^{15} ways to answer the questions in Part A. There are 4^5 ways to answer the questions in Part B.

2. How many ways are there to answer all 20 questions?

3. If you guess the answer to each question, what is the probability that you will get them all right?

4. **SAVINGS ACCOUNTS** You opened a savings account in 1994. The balance A is modeled by $A = 320(1.03)^t$, where $t = 0$ represents the year 2004. What is the account balance in 1994? in 2004? in 2014? **(Lesson 8.2)**

5. **SPORTS** The volume V of a ball is given by $V = \frac{4}{3}\pi r^3$, where r is the radius of the ball. The radius of a baseball is about $\frac{1}{3}$ the radius of a soccer ball. Find the ratio of the volume of the baseball to the volume of the soccer ball. Let r represent the radius of the soccer ball. **(Lesson 8.3)**

PROBABILITY In Exercises 6 and 7, you roll a number cube five times. (Lesson 8.3)

6. What is the probability that you roll a three each time?

7. What is the probability that you roll five odd numbers in a row?

ASTRONOMY In Exercises 8–11, write the mass (in kilograms) of the planet in scientific notation. (Lesson 8.4)

8. Mercury: 330,000,000,000,000,000,000,000

9. Venus: 4,900,000,000,000,000,000,000,000

10. Mars: 640,000,000,000,000,000,000,000

11. Pluto: 13,000,000,000,000,000,000,000

12. **HEARTBEATS** Consider a person whose heart beats 65 times per minute and who lives to be 90 years old. Estimate the number of times the person's heart beats during his or her life. Do not acknowledge leap years. Write your answer in decimal form and in scientific notation. **(Lesson 8.4)**

13. **INVESTING** Which description best represents the growth curve in the graph? **(Lesson 8.5)**

    A. Deposit = $150, annual rate = 5%

    B. Deposit = $350, annual rate = 11%

    C. Deposit = $150, annual rate = 18%

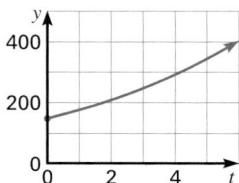

STEREOS In Exercises 14 and 15, use the following information. (Lesson 8.6)
You want to sell your old stereo system. You place an advertisement about your stereo system in the classified section of your local newspaper. The selling price listed in the advertisement is $80.50. You decide to decrease the price by 10% each week that you do not sell the stereo system.

14. Write an exponential decay model to represent the situation.

15. You sell your stereo system for the price listed in the advertisement for the third week. How much money did you get for your stereo system?

CHAPTER 9

1. **DIVING** You dive from a cliff that is 20 feet above the water. Your height h after t seconds can be modeled by $h = -16t^2 + 20$. How long will it take you to reach the water? **(Lesson 9.1)**

2. **GEOMETRY** Find the area of the rectangle below. Give both the exact answer in simplified form and the decimal approximation rounded to the nearest hundredth. **(Lesson 9.2)**

$\sqrt{30}$ cm

$\sqrt{50}$ cm

LAWN SPRINKLERS In Exercises 3–5, use the following information. **(Lesson 9.3)**
The arc of the water sprayed from a lawn sprinkler is given by the model

$$y = -0.04x^2 + 0.93x$$

where x is the distance (in feet) across the lawn and y is the height (in feet) of the arc.

3. Sketch the graph of the function. Label the vertex.

4. What is the maximum height of the water sprayed from the sprinkler?

5. The distance across the lawn from the sprinkler to where the arc lands is called the *distance of throw*. What is the distance of throw for the sprinkler?

SKI JUMPS In Exercises 6 and 7, use the following information. **(Lesson 9.4)**
The path of a ski jumper after takeoff can be modeled by the equation

$$y = -0.036x^2 + 1.38x + 20$$

where x is the horizontal distance (in feet) and y is the vertical distance (in feet).

6. Sketch a graph of the model for positive values of x and y.

7. Use the graph to estimate a positive root of the equation below.

$$0 = -0.036x^2 + 1.38x + 20$$

8. **SOFTBALL** You and a partner are practicing catching fly balls. When you throw the softball upward for your partner to catch, it leaves your hand when it is 5.5 feet off the ground. The softball has an initial velocity of 35 feet per second. Suppose that your partner misses the ball and it hits the ground. How long does it take for the softball to hit the ground? **(Lesson 9.5)**

9. **CHEERLEADING** A cheerleading squad does a stunt that has a flyer, who is thrown in the air and caught. The stunt works best when the flyer's feet reach a height of at least 30 feet off the ground. The flyer starts with her feet 4.5 feet off the ground and her initial velocity is 31 feet per second. Will the flyer's feet reach a height of at least 30 feet off the ground? Explain. **(Lesson 9.6)**

10. **BRIDGES** The parabolic opening in the bridge below can be modeled by $y = -0.04x^2 + 25$, where x is the distance (in feet) from the center of the opening and y is the height (in feet) above the road. Write a system of inequalities that describes the shaded region. **(Lesson 9.7)**

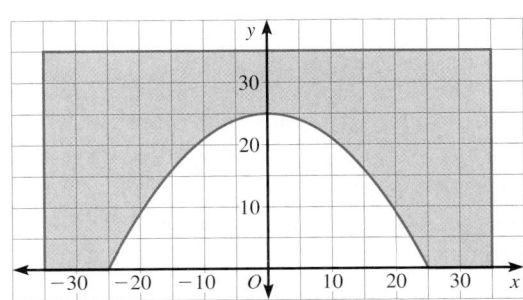

11. **AUTOMOBILES** The table below lists the value of an automobile over time. Which type of model best represents the data? Write a model. **(Lesson 9.8)**

Year	Value (dollars)
2002	12,500.00
2003	11,250.00
2004	10,125.00
2005	9112.50

CHAPTER 10

1. **GEOMETRY** Write an expression in standard form for the perimeter of the triangle shown below. (**Lesson 10.1**)

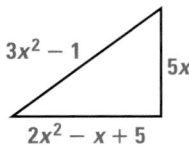

$3x^2 - 1$ $5x$

$2x^2 - x + 5$

QUILTS In Exercises 2 and 3, use the information below. (**Lesson 10.2**)
You are making the quilt shown below, which has 6 squares in the center. The border around the squares is 0.5 foot wide, and the border around the outside of the quilt is 1.5 feet wide.

0.5 ft

x
x

1.5 ft

2. Write a polynomial expression that represents the total area of the quilt. Give your answer as a quadratic trinomial.

3. Use the expression from Exercise 2 to find the area of the quilt when $x = 1.5$, 2, and 2.5.

4. **MICE** In mice, the black eye color gene E is dominant, and the red eye color gene e is recessive. A mouse whose eye color genes are EE or Ee will have black eyes. The Punnett square shows the possible results of crossing two mice that have recessive eye color genes. Write a polynomial model that can be used to represent the Punnett square. (**Lesson 10.3**)

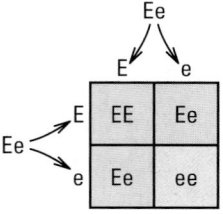

Ee

E e

E | EE | Ee
Ee
e | Ee | ee

ARCHITECTURE In Exercises 5 and 6, use the following information. (**Lesson 10.4**)
An architect designs a large arched doorway for the main entrance to an office building. The shape of the arch can be modeled by $y = -0.04(x + 22)(x - 22)$, where x and y are measured in feet.

5. How wide is the arch at the base?

6. How high is the arch?

7. **GARDENS** You decide to plant a bulb garden. You want the length of the rectangular garden to be 3 feet longer than its width. The bulbs that you have will cover 88 square feet. What should the length and the width be? (**Lesson 10.5**)

SPORTS In Exercises 8 and 9, use the following information. (**Lessons 10.6, 10.7**)
In the vertical motion model $h = -16t^2 + vt + s$, h is the height (in feet), t is the time in motion (in seconds), v is the initial velocity (in feet per second), and s is the initial height (in feet).

8. A quarterback releases a football when it is 6 feet off the ground, and the football has an initial upward velocity of 46 feet per second. The receiver misses the pass and the football hits the ground. How long does it take for the football to hit the ground?

9. A volleyball is hit when it is 4 feet off the ground. The volleyball has an initial upward velocity of 32 feet per second. Does the volleyball reach a height of 20 feet? If so, how long does it take to reach that height?

GEOMETRY In Exercises 10 and 11, the rectangle below has an area of 32 square meters. (**Lesson 10.8**)

x

$x^2 + 2x - 16$

10. Write a polynomial equation that you can solve to find the length and the width of the rectangle.

11. What are the dimensions of the rectangle?

CHAPTER 11

1. **SCALE DRAWINGS** You want to make a scale drawing of your classroom. The actual length of your classroom is 36 feet and the actual width is 32 feet. In your drawing, the length of your classroom is 9 inches. What should the width of your classroom in your drawing be? **(Lesson 11.1)**

MUSIC In Exercises 2 and 3, use the following information. (Lesson 11.2)
The graph shows the responses of 200 students when asked to name their favorite type of music.

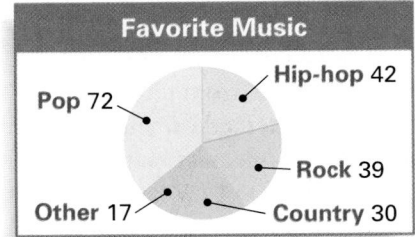

Favorite Music

Pop 72
Hip-hop 42
Rock 39
Country 30
Other 17

2. What percent of the students said that rock is their favorite type of music?

3. What percent of the students said that pop is their favorite type of music?

4. **BABY-SITTING** The table below lists the money you receive for baby-sitting. Decide if the data show *direct* or *inverse* variation. Then write an equation that relates the hours worked h and the total pay p. **(Lesson 11.3)**

Hours, h	2	3	5
Pay (dollars), p	17	25.50	42.50

5. **PROBABILITY** A coin is tossed onto the large rectangular region below. It is equally likely to land on any point in the region. Write a model that gives the probability that the coin will land in the small red rectangle. **(Lesson 11.4)**

$3x + 2$
x^2
$5x - 1$
$3x^2 + 2x$

REAL ESTATE In Exercises 6 and 7, use the following information. (Lesson 11.5)
The models show the total value (in millions of dollars) of homes sold each year and the number of real estate agents selling homes each year at a real estate agency. Let t represent the number of years since 2000.

Total value of homes sold: $V = \dfrac{1000 + 140t}{2 - 0.1t}$

Number of agents: $A = \dfrac{210 + 10t}{1 - 0.05t}$

6. Find a model for the average value of homes sold each year per agent.

7. Use your model from Exercise 6 to find the average value of homes sold per agent for 2005.

HIKING In Exercises 8–10, use the following information. (Lesson 11.6)
You are planning a 20-mile hiking trip. Some of the trails that you plan to hike are steep and some are relatively flat. You average 2 miles per hour on the steep trails and 4 miles per hour on the flat trails.

8. Write an expression for the total time of the hike. Let x represent the miles of steep trails.

9. Write your answer to Exercise 8 as a single rational expression.

10. Use your expression from Exercise 9 to determine the total time of the hike if you hike 5 miles of steep trails.

11. **GEOMETRY** The area of the rectangle below is $3x^2 + 3x - 6$. Find the length. **(Lesson 11.7)**

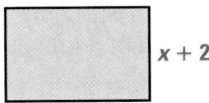

$x + 2$

12. **BASKETBALL** You have made 27 free-throws in 45 attempts. Your free-throw average is $\dfrac{27}{45} = 0.6$. How many consecutive free-throws must you make to increase your free-throw average to 0.75? **(Lesson 11.8)**

CHAPTER 12

1. **BASEBALL** The radius of a sphere can be found using the formula $r = \sqrt{\dfrac{S}{4\pi}}$, where S is the surface area and r is the radius of the sphere. Find the radius of a baseball that has a surface area of 168 square centimeters. Round your answer to the nearest hundredth. **(Lesson 12.1)**

PENDULUMS **In Exercises 2 and 3, use the following information.** **(Lesson 12.2)**
The *period* of a pendulum is the time it takes for the pendulum to swing back and forth. The model $T = 2\pi\sqrt{\dfrac{L}{981}}$ relates the period T (in seconds) of a pendulum to the length L (in centimeters) of the pendulum.

2. A pendulum has a length of 50 centimeters. A second pendulum has a length of 32 centimeters. Write an expression that can be used to find the difference of the periods of the pendulums.

3. Simplify your expression from Exercise 2. Round your answer to the nearest hundredth.

ROLLER COASTERS **In Exercises 4 and 5, use the following information.** **(Lesson 12.3)**
The model $v = 8\sqrt{h}$ relates the velocity v (in feet per second) of a roller coaster at the bottom of a drop to the height h (in feet) of the drop.

4. The velocity of a roller coaster at the bottom of a drop is 44 feet per second. Find the height of the drop.

5. The velocity of a roller coaster at the bottom of a drop is 68 feet per second. Find the height of the drop.

6. **FOOTBALL** The path of a kicked football can be modeled by
$$y = -0.012x^2 + 1.11x$$
where x is the horizontal distance (in feet) and y is the vertical distance (in feet). Suppose that the football is not caught and it hits the ground. Find the horizontal distance covered by the football. **(Lesson 12.4)**

7. **PARKS** The dimensions of a rectangular park are shown below. Find the length of the path that connects opposite corners of the park. **(Lesson 12.5)**

75 ft

100 ft

HELICOPTERS **In Exercises 8 and 9, use the following information.** **(Lesson 12.6)**
A helicopter is located 4 miles east and 2 miles north of a hospital. It travels to a destination 8 miles east and 12 miles north of the hospital.

8. What is the distance from the helicopter's original location to its destination? Round your answer to the nearest hundredth of a mile.

9. What is the distance from the helicopter's destination to the hospital? Round your answer to the nearest hundredth of a mile.

10. **SKATEBOARDING** You are building a skateboarding ramp. You want the angle of incline of the ramp to be $15°$, and you want the height to be 3 feet, as shown below. What is the horizontal distance x? Round your answer to the nearest tenth of a foot. **(Lesson 12.7)**

3 ft

15°

x

COUNTEREXAMPLES **In Exercises 11–13, find a counterexample to show that the statement is not true.** **(Lesson 12.8)**

11. If a and b are odd integers, then $a + b$ is an odd integer.

12. If a and b are nonzero real numbers and $a > b$, then $\dfrac{1}{a} > \dfrac{1}{b}$.

13. For any integer a, $a^3 > a^2$.

Appendix 1 — Samples and Surveys

GOAL *Recognize bias in samples and survey questions; analyze the results of surveys.*

Surveys are often conducted to gather data about a *population*. A **population** is the entire group of people or objects that you want information about. When it is difficult to survey an entire population, a **sample,** or a part of the group, is surveyed.

TYPES OF SAMPLES

SIMPLE RANDOM SAMPLE
Members are chosen using a method that gives everyone an equally likely chance of being selected.

SYSTEMATIC SAMPLE
Members are chosen using a pattern, such as selecting every other person.

STRATIFIED SAMPLE
The population is first divided into groups. Then members are randomly chosen from each group.

CONVENIENCE SAMPLE
Members are chosen because they are easily accessible.

SELF-SELECTED SAMPLE
Members volunteer to participate.

EXAMPLE 1 *Classifying a Sample*

A teacher wants to select a group of 5 students. Classify the sample.

a. The teacher selects the first 5 students who raise their hands.

b. The teacher draws the names of 5 students from a hat.

SOLUTION

a. This is a self-selected sample because the students volunteer.

b. This is a simple random sample because each student has an equally likely chance of being selected.

In a **random sample**, each person or object has an equally likely chance of being selected. A random sample is most likely to produce a representative sample of a population. A sample that is not representative of a population is a **biased sample**. In a biased sample, one or more of the parts of a population are overrepresented or underrepresented. A non-random sample can result in a biased sample.

Simple random, systematic, and stratified samples are preferred because the resulting samples are usually random. The results of convenience and self-selected samples are more likely to be biased.

EXAMPLE 2   *Identifying Potentially Biased Samples*

Administrators at your school are considering adding lacrosse as a school-sponsored sport. They decide to survey students to see if there is enough interest in the sport. Decide whether the sampling method could result in a biased sample. Explain your reasoning.

a. Survey students that currently participate in sports at your school.

b. Survey every tenth student who enters the school in the morning.

SOLUTION

a. This method could result in a biased sample because students who already participate in sports are more likely to favor the addition of a new sport than other students in the school.

b. This method is not likely to result in a biased sample because a wide range of students will be surveyed.

· · · · · · · · · ·

When conducting a survey, it is important that the survey questions are carefully written. If a question is poorly written, then the responses of the people surveyed may not accurately reflect their opinions or actions. These types of questions are called **biased questions**.

EXAMPLE 3   *Identifying Biased Questions*

Decide whether the survey question may be biased. Explain.

a. Do you agree with your school's attendance policy?

b. Due to the large number of accidents among drivers that are under the age of 18, do you support raising the minimum driving age to 18?

SOLUTION

a. This question may be biased. It assumes that the student being surveyed is familiar with the attendance policy.

b. This question may be biased. Respondents may think a "no" response means that they are in favor of drivers under 18 getting into accidents.

ANALYZING DATA To help you make conclusions about data collected from a survey, the data needs to be organized. Data displays are often used to organize and present data collected from a survey. However, the data should be accurately displayed so that it can be correctly interpreted.

EXAMPLE 4 *Making Conclusions About Data from a Survey*

You conduct a survey that asks 30 students the average number of minutes they spend talking on the phone each day. The information collected from the survey is shown at the right.

Minutes	Tally
0–14	卌 |||
15–29	卌 卌 ||
30–44	卌	
45–59	||||

a. Make a histogram of the data.

b. Make a conclusion about the data.

STUDENT HELP

Look Back
For help with making histograms, see p. 792.

SOLUTION

a. Draw and label the horizontal and vertical axes.

List each interval from the table on the horizontal axis.

The greatest frequency is 12. So, start the vertical axis at 0 and end at 14, using increments of 2.

Draw a bar for each interval. The bars should have the same width.

b. The histogram shows that the interval with greatest frequency is the 15–29 minute interval.

In general, more than half of the students spend less than 30 minutes talking on the phone each day.

· · · · · · · · · ·

ANALYZING SURVEYS The results of public opinion surveys often appear in newspapers and magazines. You should be critical of these surveys, especially if the results are meant to persuade you in some way. If you notice non-random sampling, biased questions, or poorly displayed data, then it is likely that the survey results are biased.

EXAMPLE 5 Analyzing the Results of a Survey

A survey asks shoppers whether they prefer to shop for clothes on-line or at a store. The results are shown at the right.

a. Tell why the results are biased.

b. Suggest a way to eliminate the bias.

SOLUTION

a. The results of the survey are biased because the sampling method is biased. The sample contains only on-line shoppers, so the group of people who prefer shopping for clothes at a store are underrepresented.

b. The survey should be conducted using a random sample. For example, conduct a telephone survey.

EXERCISES

In Exercises 1–4, classify the sample involving the following situation.
A fast-food restaurant decides to conduct a survey to find out if their customers are satisfied with the service at the restaurant.

1. Survey every twentieth customer.

2. Survey every tenth male customer and every tenth female customer.

3. Survey customers randomly chosen by the computer system.

4. Survey customers only when the restaurant is not busy.

In Exercises 5–8, classify the sample.

5. The staff at a town library want to know what new programs residents would be interested in. A computer generates a list of 100 randomly chosen town residents to be telephoned and surveyed.

6. The manager of a grocery store wants to know if shoppers are satisfied with the selection of items in the deli case. A deli customer is surveyed every 30 minutes.

7. The editor of a school newspaper wants to know how students feel about the extracurricular activities offered by the school. Twenty students from each class (freshman, sophomore, junior, and senior) are randomly chosen from the school directory and surveyed.

8. The manager of a hotel wants to know how guests rate the cleanliness of the rooms. Response cards are left in each room for guests to fill out during their stay.

Decide whether the sampling method could result in a random sample. Explain your reasoning.

9. A dentist wants to expand her office hours to better accommodate her patients. She decides to list her patients alphabetically and survey every tenth patient on the list about his or her time preferences.

10. The manager of a radio station wants to know the listeners' favorite songs. He decides to have listeners call the radio station and request their favorite songs.

Decide whether the sampling method could result in a biased sample. Explain your reasoning.

11. Administrators at your school want to know if more vegetarian items should be added to the lunch menu. They decide to survey every fifth student waiting in line to purchase lunch.

12. A Boston-based market research company wants to learn more about the television viewing habits of average teenagers. They decide to survey randomly chosen teenagers who live in Boston.

13. The editor of a snowboarding magazine wants to know the readers' favorite places to ride. The latest issue of the magazine includes a survey for readers to complete and return.

14. A restaurant critic wants to taste a variety of items at a restaurant. She randomly chooses two items from each of the following groups on the menu: appetizers, entrées, and desserts.

Decide whether the survey question may be biased. Explain.

15. Do you agree with the rules established for traveling on public transportation with a dog?

16. How often do you read the local newspaper?

17. Would you rather see an exciting laser show or visit a boring art museum?

18. The fewer trash cans that a community has, the more litter the community has. Should our community include more money in its budget for more trash cans and trash pick up?

In Exercises 19–21, use the following information.
Your class officers are planning a dance. They need to decide whether to have a disc jockey or a live band at the dance. They decide to survey a sample of students to determine their preference.

19. Describe a sampling method that can be used so that the sample will most likely be random.

20. Write a question to ask the members of the sample. The question should be carefully written so that it is not biased.

21. Which is more likely to give accurate results, 50 students randomly chosen from a class of 300, or 20 students randomly chosen from a class of 300? Explain your reasoning.

In Exercises 22 and 23, use the following information.
A sample of 100 students, 50 boys and 50 girls, are asked to name their favorite type of movie. The results are shown in the table below.

Group	Drama	Comedy	Action	Other
Boys	9	18	21	2
Girls	17	14	11	8

22. Make a double bar graph of the data.

23. Use your display from Exercise 22 to make a conclusion about the data.

In Exercises 24 and 25, use the following information.
A sample of 19 students enrolled in a swimming class are asked to hold their breath underwater for as long as possible. The results (in seconds) are listed below.

65, 29, 38, 50, 60, 43, 27, 48, 29, 79, 37, 45, 48, 32, 57, 35, 54, 53, 37

24. Make a histogram of the data using the following intervals: 20–29, 30–39, 40–49, 50–59, 60–69, 70–79.

25. Use your display from Exercise 24 to make a conclusion about the data.

In Exercises 26 and 27, tell why the results of the survey are biased. Then tell how to eliminate the bias.

26.

27.

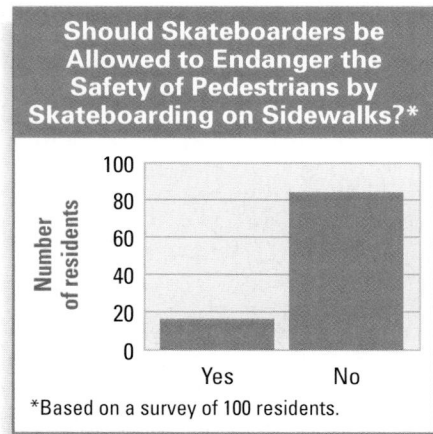

28. Find the results of a survey published in a magazine or newspaper. Do you think that the results of the survey are biased? Explain your reasoning.

In Exercises 29–32, you want to learn more about the music that students in your school listen to.

29. Describe how you would choose a sample of students to survey.

30. Write a survey that consists of 3 or 4 questions.

31. Give the survey to the sample and present your results.

32. Review your results. Would you change anything about the way the survey was designed or conducted? Explain.

Probability of Compound Events

GOAL *Find the probability of independent, dependent, mutually exclusive, and overlapping events.*

When you consider the probability of two events occurring, the events are called **compound events**. *Independent, dependent, mutually exclusive,* and *overlapping events* are examples of compound events.

Two events are **independent events** if the occurrence of one event does not affect the occurrence of the other. Two events are **dependent events** if the occurrence of one event *does* affect the occurrence of the other.

EXAMPLE 1 *Deciding Whether Events Are Independent or Dependent*

Decide whether the events are *independent* or *dependent*.

    a. Each whole number from 1 through 10 is written on a piece of paper and placed in a hat. You randomly choose a piece of paper, do not put it back, then randomly choose another piece of paper.
    Event *A*: Choose the 5 first.
    Event *B*: Choose an odd number second.

    b. You flip a coin and roll a number cube.
    Event *A*: Get tails when flipping the coin.
    Event *B*: Get a 2 when rolling the number cube.

SOLUTION

    a. The events are dependent. Choosing the 5 and not putting it back affects the outcomes of choosing an odd number second.

    b. The events are independent. Getting tails when flipping a coin does not affect the outcomes of rolling a number cube.

STUDENT HELP

▶ **Study Tip**
In the formula for the probability of dependent events, $P(B \mid A)$ represents the probability that B will occur given that A has occurred.

PROBABILITIES OF INDEPENDENT AND DEPENDENT EVENTS

For two independent events A and B, the probability that both events occur is the product of the probabilities of the events.

$$P(A \text{ and } B) = P(A) \bullet P(B) \qquad \text{Events } A \text{ and } B \text{ are independent.}$$

For two dependent events A and B, the probability that both occur is the product of the probability of the first event and the conditional probability of the second event given the first event.

$$P(A \text{ and } B) = P(A) \bullet P(B \mid A) \qquad \text{Events } A \text{ and } B \text{ are dependent.}$$

EXAMPLE 2 **Finding the Probability of Independent Events**

Of the 35 CDs in your collection, 21 are rock and 14 are hip-hop. You randomly choose a CD and put it back. Then you randomly choose another CD. Find the probability of choosing a rock CD first and choosing a hip-hop CD second.

SOLUTION

Let event A be "choose a rock CD first" and let event B be "choose a hip-hop CD second." Since the first CD chosen is replaced before the second CD is chosen, events A and B are independent. The probability of A and B is shown below.

$$P(A \text{ and } B) = \frac{21}{35} \cdot \frac{14}{35} = \frac{6}{25} = 0.24$$

▶ The probability is 0.24.

EXAMPLE 3 **Finding the Probability of Dependent Events**

A drawer contains 9 white socks, 7 black socks, and 5 blue socks. You randomly choose one sock from the drawer. Then you randomly choose another sock without replacing the first. Find the probability of events A and B.

a. Event A: Choose a white sock first.
Event B: Choose a black sock second.

b. Event A: Choose a blue sock first.
Event B: Choose a blue sock second.

SOLUTION

a. First, find the probability of each event.

$$P(A) = \frac{9}{21} \qquad \text{Of the 21 socks, 9 are white.}$$

$$P(B \mid A) = \frac{7}{20} \qquad \text{Of the remaining 20 socks, 7 are black.}$$

Then multiply the probabilities.

$$P(A \text{ and } B) = \frac{9}{21} \cdot \frac{7}{20} = \frac{3}{20} = 0.15$$

▶ The probability is 0.15.

b. First, find the probability of each event.

$$P(A) = \frac{5}{21} \qquad \text{Of the 21 socks, 5 are blue.}$$

$$P(B \mid A) = \frac{4}{20} \qquad \text{Of the remaining 20 socks, 4 are blue.}$$

Then multiply the probabilities.

$$P(A \text{ and } B) = \frac{5}{21} \cdot \frac{4}{20} = \frac{1}{21} \approx 0.048$$

▶ The probability is about 0.048.

Mutually exclusive events are events that have no outcomes in common.
Use the rule below to find the probability of mutually exclusive events.

PROBABILITY OF MUTUALLY EXCLUSIVE EVENTS

For two mutually exclusive events A and B, the probability that either of the
events occurs is the sum of the probabilities of the events.

$$P(A \text{ or } B) = P(A) + P(B) \qquad \text{Events } A \text{ and } B \text{ are mutually exclusive.}$$

EXAMPLE 4 *Finding the Probability of Mutually Exclusive Events*

You are playing a game using the spinner at the
right, which is divided into equal parts. On your
spin, what is the probability that the spinner
lands on an even number or a prime number?

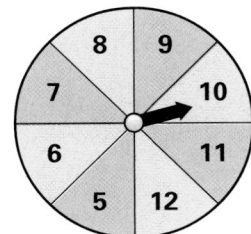

SOLUTION

First, find the probabilities of the events.
Let event A be getting an even number
and let event B be getting a prime number.

$$P(A) = \frac{4}{8} \qquad \text{Of the 8 numbers, 4 are even.}$$

$$P(B) = \frac{3}{8} \qquad \text{Of the 8 numbers, 3 are prime.}$$

Then find the sum of the probabilities.

$$P(A \text{ or } B) = \frac{4}{8} + \frac{3}{8} = \frac{7}{8} = 0.875$$

▶ The probability that the spinner lands on an even number or a prime number is
0.875, or 87.5%.

· · · · · · · · · ·

Overlapping events are events that have one or more outcomes in common.
Use the rule below to find the probability of overlapping events.

PROBABILITY OF OVERLAPPING EVENTS

For two overlapping events A and B, the probability that either of the events
occurs is the sum of the probabilities of the events, minus the probability
that both events occur.

$$P(A \text{ or } B) = P(A) + P(B) - P(A \text{ and } B) \quad \text{Events } A \text{ and } B \text{ are overlapping.}$$

EXAMPLE 5 *Finding the Probability of Overlapping Events*

You roll a number cube. What is the probability that you get an odd number or a number greater than 3?

SOLUTION

Find the probabilities of the events. Let event *A* be getting an odd number and let event *B* be getting a number greater than 3.

$$P(A) = \frac{3}{6}$$ Of the 6 numbers, 3 are odd (1, 3, 5).

$$P(B) = \frac{3}{6}$$ Of the 6 numbers, 3 are greater than 3 (4, 5, 6).

$$P(A \text{ and } B) = \frac{1}{6}$$ Of the 6 numbers, 1 is odd and greater than 3 (5).

Find the probability of the events.

$$P(A \text{ or } B) = \frac{3}{6} + \frac{3}{6} - \frac{1}{6} = \frac{5}{6} \approx 0.83$$

▶ The probability that the number is odd or greater than 3 is about 0.83.

EXERCISES

Decide whether the events are *independent* or *dependent*.

1. You toss a coin two times.
   Event *A*: Get tails on the first toss.
   Event *B*: Get tails on the second toss.

2. A box contains blue and yellow paper clips. You randomly choose a paper clip, then choose another without replacing the first paper clip.
   Event *A*: The first paper clip is blue.
   Event *B*: The second paper clip is yellow.

3. A bag contains tulip bulbs and daffodil bulbs. You randomly choose a bulb, plant it, and randomly choose another bulb.
   Event *A*: The first bulb is a daffodil bulb.
   Event *B*: The second bulb is a daffodil bulb.

4. You randomly choose a card from a standard deck of 52 cards. You put the card back in the deck and then your friend randomly chooses a card.
   Event *A*: You choose the queen of diamonds.
   Event *B*: Your friend chooses the six of clubs.

5. Each week you and your sister assign chores by writing the chores on pieces of paper and randomly choose them from a hat.
   Event *A*: You choose "rake the leaves" the first week of October.
   Event *B*: You choose "rake the leaves" the second week of October.

Events *A* and *B* are independent. Find the indicated probability.

6. $P(A) = 0.5$
$P(B) = 0.8$
$P(A \text{ and } B) = \underline{?}$

7. $P(A) = 0.6$
$P(B) = \underline{?}$
$P(A \text{ and } B) = 0.24$

8. $P(A) = \underline{?}$
$P(B) = 0.5$
$P(A \text{ and } B) = 0.055$

Events *A* and *B* are dependent. Find the indicated probability.

9. $P(A) = 0.9$
$P(B \mid A) = 0.7$
$P(A \text{ and } B) = \underline{?}$

10. $P(A) = 0.2$
$P(B \mid A) = \underline{?}$
$P(A \text{ and } B) = 0.042$

11. $P(A) = \underline{?}$
$P(B \mid A) = 0.4$
$P(A \text{ and } B) = 0.34$

Decide whether the situation describes *independent* or *dependent* events. Then answer the question.

12. You plant a fruit tree. The probability that the tree will survive its first winter is 0.8. If it survives the first winter, the probability that the tree will bear fruit by its fourth year is 0.6. What is the probability that the tree will bear fruit by its fourth year?

13. You toss a coin and roll a number cube. What is the probability that you get tails and a 3?

14. A bucket of tennis balls contains 12 yellow, 5 orange, and 3 pink tennis balls. You randomly choose a ball, put it back, and randomly choose another ball. What is the probability that the first ball is yellow and the second ball is orange?

15. A bowl contains 22 green grapes and 28 purple grapes. You randomly choose a grape, eat it, and randomly choose another grape. What is the probability that both grapes are green?

In Exercises 16 and 17, use the following information.
The formula for finding the probability of independent events can be extended to three or more events. This is also true for dependent events.

16. You are assigned a 4 digit personal identification number (PIN) for use with your bank card. Each of the digits can be a whole number from 0 to 9, and the digits can repeat. What is the probability that your PIN is 1234?

17. In Exercise 16, suppose that the digits cannot repeat. What is the probability that your PIN is 1234?

In Exercises 18 and 19, read the first 100 words of a book. Count the number of words that satisfy each of the events below, which are independent.

Event *A*: The word starts with a vowel.
Event *B*: The word has more than four letters.
Event *C*: The word has one letter.

18. You randomly choose a word from the first 100 words. What is the probability that the word starts with a vowel and has more than four letters?

19. You randomly choose a word from the first 100 words. What is the probability that the word starts with a vowel and has one letter?

Events A and B are mutually exclusive events. Find P(A or B).

20. $P(A) = 0.2$
$P(B) = 0.12$

21. $P(A) = 0.07$
$P(B) = 0.33$

22. $P(A) = 62\%$
$P(B) = 15\%$

Events A and B are mutually exclusive events that involve rolling a number cube. Find P(A or B).

23. **Event A:** Get a number greater than 4.
Event B: Get a number less than 4.

24. **Event A:** Get a 2.
Event B: Get an odd number.

In Exercises 25–27, you randomly choose a letter from the word INDIANA. Find the probability of choosing the given letters.

25. I or N

26. N or D

27. A or N

28. A wallet contains six \$1 bills, one \$5 bill, and three \$10 bills. A bill is randomly chosen from the wallet. What is the probability that the bill is a \$1 bill or a \$5 bill?

Events A and B are overlapping events. Find P(A or B).

29. $P(A) = 0.4$
$P(B) = 0.5$
$P(A \text{ and } B) = 0.2$

30. $P(A) = 0.5$
$P(B) = 0.5$
$P(A \text{ and } B) = 0.375$

31. $P(A) = 11\%$
$P(B) = 58\%$
$P(A \text{ and } B) = 23\%$

In Exercises 32–35, events A and B are overlapping events that involve spinning the spinner below. Find P(A or B).

32. **Event A:** Lands on an odd number.
Event B: Lands on green.

33. **Event A:** Lands on an even number.
Event B: Lands on yellow.

34. **Event A:** Lands on green.
Event B: Lands on a number divisible by 3.

35. **Event A:** Lands on a number greater than 4.
Event B: Lands on a number less than 11.

36. A standard deck of 52 playing cards contains 13 cards in each of the following four suits: hearts, diamonds, clubs, and spades. You randomly choose a card from the deck. What is the probability that the card is a 4 or a club?

Events A and B are *complementary*. Use the following information to find the indicated probability.

Two mutually exclusive events in which one or the other event must occur are called *complementary events*. The sum of the probabilities of two complementary events is 1. So, if A and B are complementary events, then $P(A) + P(B) = 1$.

37. $P(A) = \underline{\ ?\ }$
$P(B) = 0.6$

38. $P(A) = 0.14$
$P(B) = \underline{\ ?\ }$

39. $P(A) = \underline{\ ?\ }$
$P(B) = 28\%$

Estimation and Reasonableness

GOAL *Use estimation to solve problems and to determine whether answers are reasonable.*

Some real-world problems require only an estimate for an answer instead of an exact answer. Before using estimation, you need to decide whether estimation is appropriate.

EXAMPLE 1 *Deciding Whether Estimation is Appropriate*

A music store is having a sale on CDs. All of the new releases have a sale price of $10.88, which includes tax. Erik wants to buy 3 CDs that are new releases. Decide whether an *estimate* or an *exact answer* is appropriate. Then solve.

a. How much money should Erik take with him to pay for the CDs?

b. What is the total cost of the CDs?

SOLUTION

a. An estimate is appropriate. To be sure that Erik has enough money, he should round up: $11 • 3 = $33. So, Erik should bring $33.

b. An exact answer is appropriate.

$10.88 • 3 = $32.64

· · · · · · · · · ·

Estimation can often be used to check the reasonableness of an answer.

EXAMPLE 2 *Using Estimation to Check Reasonableness*

Determine whether the answers to the problem are reasonable.

Problem Use the formula $S = 2\pi r^2 + 2\pi rh$ to find the surface area S (in square meters) of the cylinder at the right.

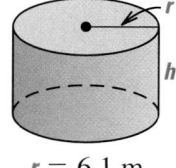

Susan's answer: about 324 m^2

Len's answer: about 525 m^2

$r = 6.1$ m
$h = 7.6$ m

STUDENT HELP

▶ **Study Tip**
The Greek letter π (pi) is often approximated by the number 3.14.

SOLUTION

To find an estimate of the surface area, round the radius, height, and pi to the nearest whole number: $S \approx 2(3)(6^2) + 2(3)(6)(8) = 504$ m^2.

The estimate of 504 square meters is not close to Susan's answer, but it is close to Len's answer. So, Susan's answer is not reasonable and Len's answer is reasonable.

ESTIMATION METHODS *Front-end estimation* can be used to estimate a sum when all the numbers have the same number of digits. When numbers being added have about the same value, *clustering* can be used to estimate their sum. Different types of estimation may yield different levels of accuracy.

EXAMPLE 3   *Comparing Estimation Methods*

You recently started working at a grocery store. The table below shows the amounts of your first 6 paychecks.

Week	1	2	3	4	5	6
Pay	$30.44	$31.62	$38.12	$40.01	$43.19	$46.88

a. Use front-end estimation to estimate your total pay for the 6 weeks.

b. Use clustering to estimate your total pay for the 6 weeks.

c. Find the actual total. Which method gives a closer estimate? Why?

SOLUTION

a. To use front-end estimation, add the values of the greatest digits to get a low estimate. Then use the remaining digits to adjust the sum and get a closer estimate.

❶ Add the values of the tens' digits.

```
  30.44
  31.62
  38.12
  40.01
  43.19
+ 46.88
  210
```

❷ Approximate the sum of the remaining digits.

```
  30.44 ↘
  31.62 →about 10 more
  38.12 ↗
  40.01 ↘
  43.19 →about 10 more
+ 46.88 ↗
        about 20 more
```

❸ Add the two sums.

```
  210
+  20
  230
```

▶ Your total pay for the first 6 weeks is about $230.

b. When a group of data are clustered, you can choose a convenient value near the center of the cluster to represent each data value in the group.

In the table, the amounts cluster around $40. An estimate of the sum is given by 6 • 40 = 240.

▶ Your total pay for the first 6 weeks is about $240.

c. The actual total is $230.26. The estimate obtained by front-end estimation is closer than the estimate obtained by clustering. The estimate obtained by clustering is greater than the estimate obtained by front-end estimation because the value chosen to represent the data in the cluster group is greater than the average data value in the cluster.

EXERCISES

Decide whether an *estimate* or an *exact answer* is appropriate.

1. the balance of a bank account on a bank statement

2. the number of hours spent doing homework during a week

3. the amount of money left as a tip for a waiter

4. a baseball player's batting average on a baseball card

Decide whether an *estimate* or an *exact answer* is appropriate. Then solve the problem.

5. You are helping prepare fundraising materials. It takes you 28 seconds to stuff an envelope and put an address label on the envelope. How many minutes should it take you to prepare 50 envelopes?

6. You have received the following scores on your science tests: 76, 82, 91, 87, 89. What is your average?

Determine whether the answer to the problem is reasonable. Explain your reasoning.

7. **Problem** Evaluate $5x - 5$ when $x = 6.1$.   **Answer** 25.5

8. **Problem** Evaluate $3z^2 + z$ when $z = -1.9$.   **Answer** -12.73

9. **Problem** Evaluate $2\pi r$ when $r = 4.8$ ft.   **Answer** 9.6 ft

10. **Problem** Solve $9.85x = 66.98$.   **Answer** $x = 6.8$

11. An airplane travels 1448 miles in 3 hours 20 minutes. A passenger calculates the average speed of the aircraft to be 580 miles per hour. Use an estimate to decide if the calculation is reasonable.

In Exercises 12–15, use the following information.
You are waiting in line to pay for several items at a grocery store. You want to be sure that you will have enough money for the items. The prices of the items are $5.89, $3.23, $1.79, $2.97, $6.78, $3.44, and $4.88.

12. Estimate the total price by adding the values of the ones' digits, ignoring the decimal parts.

13. Is your estimate in Exercise 12 high or low? Is your estimate appropriate for the situation? Explain.

14. Estimate the total price by rounding each dollar amount up to the next whole number and adding the rounded amounts.

15. Is your estimate in Exercise 14 high or low? Is your estimate appropriate for the situation? Explain.

16. The weights (in pounds) of the starting defensive players for a football team are listed below. Use clustering to estimate the total weight of the starting defensive players.

    216, 218, 220, 224, 230, 245, 251, 265, 268, 272, 278

In Exercises 17–19, use the following information.
You are mailing a box of items to a relative. The weights (in ounces) of the items are listed below.

12.5, 13.2, 13.6, 20.8, 21.9, 22.7, 22.9

17. Use front-end estimation to estimate the total weight of the items in the box.

18. Use clustering to estimate the total weight of the items in the box.

19. Find the actual weight of the items in the box. Which method gives a closer estimate? Explain.

In Exercises 20 and 21, use the cube at the right.

20. Estimate the volume of the cube. (The volume V of a cube is given by the formula $V = s^3$, where s is the length of a side of the cube.)

21. Use a calculator to compare the actual volume of the cube to your estimate from Exercise 20. By what percent does your estimate differ from the actual volume?

11.8 in.

In Exercises 22–25, use the following information.
Recall that if $a = b^2$, then $\sqrt{a} = b$. For example, because $9 = 3^2$, $\sqrt{9} = 3$.

22. Determine whether $\sqrt{21}$ is closer to 4 or 5. Explain your reasoning.

23. On a number line, between what two consecutive integers does $\sqrt{154}$ lie?

24. Find the value of $\sqrt{227}$ to the nearest whole number.

25. Estimate the value of $7.15 + 3.9\sqrt{89}$ by using whole number estimates.

In Exercises 26–28, use estimation to solve the problem.

26. The time it takes a pendulum to swing back and forth is called its *period*. The formula $T = 2\pi\sqrt{\dfrac{L}{384}}$ can be used to find the period T (in seconds) of a pendulum with a length of L inches. Estimate the period of a pendulum that is 90 inches long.

27. A sphere with radius r has a surface area S of 220 square centimeters. Use the formula $S = 4\pi r^2$ to estimate the length of the radius.

28. As Earth orbits the sun, the distance from Earth to the sun varies from about 9.14×10^7 to 9.45×10^7 miles. The speed of light is 186,282 miles per second. Estimate the time, in seconds, it takes for light from the sun to reach Earth when Earth is 9.1421555×10^7 miles from the sun.

Glossary

A

absolute value (p. 65) The distance between the origin and the point representing the real number. The symbol $|a|$ represents the absolute value of a number a.

algorithm (p. 39) A step-by-step process used to solve a problem.

asymptote (p. 692) A line that a graph approaches. The distance between the graph and the line approaches zero.

axioms (p. 758) A The basic properties of mathematics that mathematicians accept without proof.

axis of symmetry of a parabola (p. 518) The line passing through the vertex that divides the parabola into two symmetric parts. The two symmetric parts are mirror images of each other. *See also* parabola.

B

bar graph (p. 41) A graph that organizes a collection of data by using horizontal or vertical bars to display how many times each event or number occurs in the collection.

base number of a percent equation (p. 649) The number that is being compared *to* in any percent equation. The number b in the verbal model a is p percent of b.

base of a power (p. 9) The number or variable that is used as a factor in repeated multiplication. For example, in the expression 4^6, 4 is the base.

best-fitting line (p. 292) A line that best fits the data points on a scatter plot.

binomial (p. 576) A polynomial with two terms.

box-and-whisker plot (p. 375) A data display that divides a set of data into four parts. The box represents half of the data. The segments, or whiskers, extend to the least and greatest data items.

34	56	70	82	108
Least number	First quartile	Second quartile	Third quartile	Greatest number

C

center of a hyperbola (p. 692) The point (h, k) in the graph of the rational function $f(x) = \dfrac{a}{x - h} + k$.

closed set (p. 113) A set of numbers is closed under an operation if applying the operation to any two numbers in the set results in another number in that set. This set is said to have closure.

coefficient (p. 102) A number multiplied by a variable in a term. The number is the coefficient of the variable.

completing the square (p. 730) The process of rewriting a quadratic equation so that one side is a perfect square trinomial.

compound inequality (p. 346) Two inequalities connected by *and* or *or*.

conclusion (pp. 187, 739) The "then" part of an if-then statement. In the statement "If p, then q," q is the conclusion.

conjecture (p. 759) A statement that is thought to be true but is not yet proved. Often it is a statement based on observation.

conjugates (p. 717) The expressions $\left(a + \sqrt{b}\right)$ and $\left(a - \sqrt{b}\right)$ are conjugates of each other.

consecutive integers (p. 149) Integers that follow each other in order. For example, 4, 5, 6.

constant terms (p. 102) Terms with no variable factors. For example, in $x + 2 - 5x - 4$, the constant terms are 2 and -4.

constant of variation (p. 234) The constant in a variation model. Represented by the variable k. *See also* direct variation *and* inverse variation.

converse of a statement (p. 739) A related statement in which the hypothesis and conclusion are interchanged. The converse of the statement "If p, then q" is "If q, then p."

coordinate plane (p. 203) A plane formed by two real number lines that intersect at a right angle.

correlation (p. 295) The relationship between two data sets.

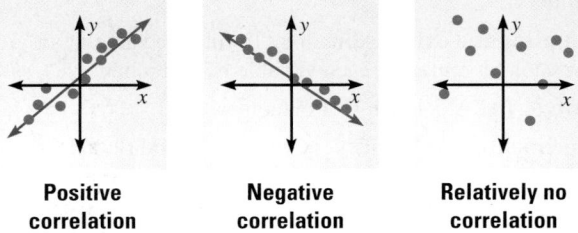

Positive correlation	Negative correlation	Relatively no correlation

cosine (p. 752) *See* trigonometric ratio.

counterexample (p. 66) An example used to show that a given statement is false.

D..

data (p. 40) Information, facts, or numbers used to describe something.

decay factor (p. 484) The expression $1 - r$ in the exponential decay model where r is the decay rate. *See also* exponential decay.

decay rate (p. 484) The variable r in the exponential decay model. *See also* exponential decay.

deductive reasoning (p. 187) Reasoning where a conclusion is reached based on facts, definitions, rules, or properties.

degree of a polynomial (p. 576) The largest degree of the terms of the polynomial.

degree of a term (p. 576) The exponent of the variable of the term.

direct variation (pp. 234, 656) The relationship of two variables x and y if there is a nonzero number k such that $y = kx$, or $\frac{y}{x} = k$. The variables x and y *vary directly.*

discriminant (p. 541) The expression $b^2 - 4ac$ where a, b, and c are coefficients of the quadratic equation $ax^2 + bx + c = 0$.

distance formula (p. 745) The distance d between the points (x_1, y_1) and (x_2, y_2) is
$$d = \sqrt{(x_2 - x_1)^2 + (y_2 - y_1)^2}.$$

distributive property (p. 100) The product of a and $(b + c)$: $a(b + c) = ab + ac$ or $(b + c)a = ba + ca$. The product of a and $(b - c)$: $a(b - c) = ab - ac$ or $(b - c)a = ba - ca$.

domain of a function (p. 47) The collection of all input values.

E..

entry or element of a matrix (p. 86) Each number in the matrix. *See also* matrix.

equation (p. 24) A statement formed when an equal sign is placed between two expressions.

equivalent equations (p. 132) Equations with the same solutions as the original equation.

equivalent inequalities (p. 335) Inequalities with the same solution(s).

evaluating the expression (p. 3) To find the value of an expression by replacing each variable by a number.

event (p. 114) A collection of outcomes.

experimental probability (p. 115) A probability that is based on repetitions of an actual experiment.

exponent (p. 9) The number or variable that represents the number of times the base is used as a factor. For example, in the expression 4^6, 6 is the exponent.

exponential decay (p. 484) A quantity that is decreasing by the same percent in each unit of time t where C is the initial amount.

Exponential decay model: $y = C(1 - r)^t$

exponential function (p. 458) A function of the form $y = ab^x$, where $b > 0$ and $b \neq 1$.

exponential growth (p. 477) A quantity that is increasing by the same percent in each unit of time t where C is the initial amount.

Exponential growth model: $y = C(1 + r)^t$

extraneous solution (pp. 644, 723) A trial solution that does not satisfy the original equation.

extremes of a proportion (p. 643) In the proportion $\frac{a}{b} = \frac{c}{d}$, a and d are the extremes.

F..

factor (p. 777) The numbers and variables that are multiplied in an expression. For example, 4 and 9 are factors of 36 and 6 and x are factors of $6x$.

factor a polynomial completely (p. 625) To write a polynomial as the product of:
• monomial factors
• prime factors with at least two terms

factor a quadratic expression (p. 604) To write a quadratic expression as the product of two linear expressions.

factored form of a polynomial (pp. 597, 625) A polynomial that is written as the product of two or more prime factors.

favorable outcomes (p. 114) The outcomes for a particular event that are being considered. *See also* outcomes.

FOIL pattern (p. 585) A pattern used to multiply two binomials. Multiply the First, Outer, Inner, and Last terms.

For example, $(x + 4)(2x + 3) = 2x^2 + 3x + 8x + 12$
$$= 2x^2 + 11x + 12$$

formula (p. 174) An algebraic equation that relates two or more real-life quantities.

function (p. 46) A rule that establishes a relationship between two quantities, called the input and the output. For each input, there is exactly one output.

function form (p. 176) A two-variable equation is written in function form if one of its variables is isolated on one side of the equation. The isolated variable is the output and is a function of the input.

function notation (p. 257) A way to name a function that is defined by an equation. For an equation in x and y, the symbol $f(x)$ replaces y and is read as "the value of f at x" or simply as "f of x."

G..

generalization (p. 187) A conclusion based on several observations.

geometric mean (p. 723) The geometric mean of a and b is $\sqrt{ab}$.

geometric probability (p. 666) The probability P that an object is tossed onto Region A and lands in Region B where Region B is contained in Region A is

$$P = \frac{\text{Area of Region } B}{\text{Area of Region } A}.$$

graph of an equation in two variables (p. 210) The set of *all* points (x, y) that are solutions of the equation.

graph of a function (p. 257) The set of all points $(x, f(x))$, where x is in the domain of the function.

graph of a linear inequality in one variable (p. 334) The set of points on a number line that represents all solutions of the inequality.

graph of a linear inequality in two variables (p. 360) The graph of all ordered pairs (x, y) that are solutions of the inequality.

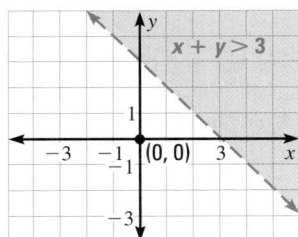

graph of a number (p. 63) The point that corresponds to a number.

graph of an ordered pair (p. 203) The point in the plane that corresponds to an ordered pair (x, y).

graph of a quadratic inequality (p. 548) The graph of all ordered pairs (x, y) that are solutions of the inequality.

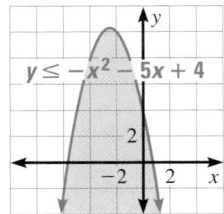

graph of a system of linear inequalities (p. 432) The graph of all solutions of the system.

grouping symbols (p. 10) Symbols such as parentheses ( ) or brackets [ ] that indicate the order in which operations should be performed. Operations within the innermost set of grouping symbols are done first.

growth factor (p. 477) The expression $1 + r$ in the exponential growth model where r is the growth rate.

growth rate (p. 477) The variable r in the exponential growth model. *See also* exponential growth.

half-plane (p. 360) In a coordinate plane, the region on either side of a boundary line.

hyperbola (p. 692) The graph of a rational function

$$f(x) = \frac{a}{x - h} + k,$$

whose center is (h, k).

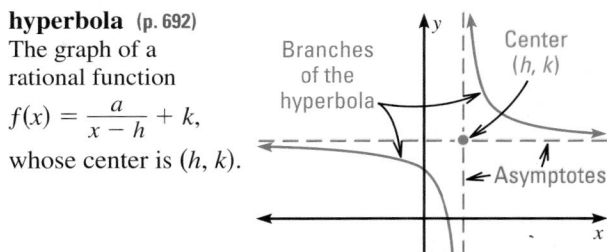

hypotenuse (p. 738) The side opposite the right angle in a right triangle.

hypothesis (pp. 187, 739) The "if" part of an if-then statement. In the statement "If p, then q," p is the hypothesis.

I

identity (p. 155) An equation that is true for all values of the variables.

if-then statement (p. 187) A statement of the form "If p, then q," where p is the *hypothesis* and q is the *conclusion*.

indirect proof (p. 760) A type of proof where it is first assumed that the statement is false. If this assumption leads to an impossibility, then the original statement has been proved to be true.

inductive reasoning (p. 187) A form of reasoning in which a conclusion is reached based on several observations.

inequality (p. 26) A sentence formed when an inequality symbol is placed between two expressions.

initial amount (pp. 477, 484) The variable C in the exponential growth or decay model. *See also* exponential growth *and* exponential decay.

input (p. 46) *See* function.

input-output table (p. 46) A table used to describe a function by listing the inputs and outputs.

integers (p. 63) Any of the numbers ... $-3, -2, -1, 0, 1, 2, 3, \ldots$.

intersecting lines (p. 426) Two lines that share exactly one point.

inverse operations (p. 132) Operations that undo each other, such as addition and subtraction.

inverse variation (p. 656) The relationship of two variables x and y if there is a nonzero number k such that $xy = k$, or $y = \frac{k}{x}$. The variables x and y *vary inversely*.

irrational number (p. 504) A number that cannot be written as the quotient of two integers.

leading coefficient (pp. 505, 576) The coefficient of the first term in a polynomial written in standard form.

least common denominator, LCD (p. 677) The least common multiple of the denominators of two or more fractions.

legs of a right triangle (p. 738) The two sides of a right triangle that are not opposite the right angle.

like terms (p. 102) Terms that have the same variable raised to the same power.

line graph (p. 42) A graph that uses line segments to connect data points. It is especially useful for showing changes in data over time.

linear combination (p. 411) An equation obtained by adding one of two equations (or a multiple of one of the equations) to the other equation in a linear system.

linear equation in one variable (p. 133) An equation in which the variable is raised to the first power and does not occur in a denominator, inside a square root symbol, or inside an absolute value symbol.

linear extrapolation (p. 318) A method of estimating the coordinates of a point that lies to the right or left of all of the given data points.

linear inequality in x and y (p. 360) An inequality that can be written as follows:
$$ax + by < c \qquad ax + by \leq c$$
$$ax + by > c \qquad ax + by \geq c$$

linear interpolation (p. 318) A method of estimating the coordinates of a point that lies between two given data points.

linear model (p. 274) A linear function that is used to model a real-life situation. In the linear model $y = mx + b$, m is the rate of change and b is the initial amount.

M..

mathematical model (p. 33) An expression, equation, or inequality that represents a real-life situation.

matrix (p. 86) A rectangular arrangement of numbers into horizontal rows and vertical columns. The plural of *matrix* is *matrices*.

mean or average (p. 369) The sum of n numbers divided by n.

means of a proportion (p. 643) In the proportion $\frac{a}{b} = \frac{c}{d}$, b and c are the means.

measure of central tendency (p. 369) A number that is used to represent a typical number in a data set. *See also* mean, median, *and* mode.

median (p. 369) The middle number of a collection of n numbers when the numbers are written in numerical order. If n is even, the median is taken to be the average of the two middle numbers.

midpoint between two points (p. 747) The midpoint of the line segment connecting them.

midpoint formula (p. 747) The midpoint between (x_1, y_1) and (x_2, y_2) is $\left(\frac{x_1 + x_2}{2}, \frac{y_1 + y_2}{2} \right)$.

mode (p. 369) The number that occurs most frequently in a collection of n numbers. A set of data can have more than one mode or no mode.

modeling (p. 33) Writing algebraic expressions, equations, or inequalities that represent real-life situations.

monomial (p. 576) A polynomial with only one term.

N..

negative numbers (p. 63) Any of the numbers less than zero. *See also* real number line.

negative square root (p. 503) One of two square roots of a positive real number.

O..

odds (p. 116) The ratio of the number of ways an event can occur to the number of ways the event cannot occur.

open sentence (p. 24) An equation that contains one or more variables.

opposites (p. 65) Two points on a number line that are the same distance from the origin but are on opposite sides of it.

order of operations (p. 16) The rules established to evaluate an expression involving more than one operation.

ordered pair (p. 203) A pair of numbers used to identify a point in a plane. *See also* coordinate plane.

origin of a coordinate plane (p. 203) The point (0, 0) in a coordinate plane at which the horizontal axis intersects the vertical axis. *See also* coordinate plane.

origin of a number line (p. 63) The point labeled zero on a number line.

outcomes (p. 114) The different possible results of a probability experiment.

output (p. 46) *See* function.

P..

parabola (p. 518) The U-shaped graph of a quadratic function.

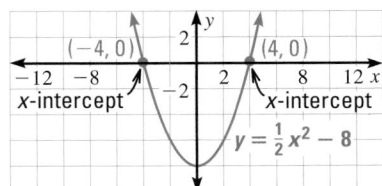

parallel lines (p. 242) Two different lines in the same plane that do not intersect.

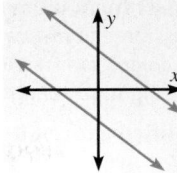

percent of decrease (p. 484) The expression $100r$ is the percent of decrease where r is the decay rate in the exponential decay model.

percent of increase (p. 477) The expression $100r$ is the percent of increase where r is the growth rate in the exponential growth model.

perfect square (p. 504) A number whose square roots are integers or quotients of integers.

perpendicular lines (p. 246) Two nonvertical lines in the same plane such that the slope of one line is the negative reciprocal of the slope of the other.

A vertical line and a horizontal line in the same plane are also perpendicular.

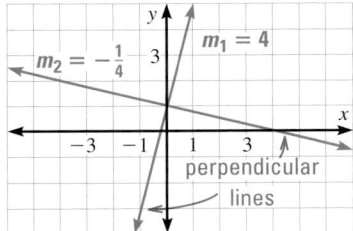

plotting a point (pp. 63, 203) Drawing the point on a number line that corresponds to a number. Drawing the point in a coordinate plane that corresponds to an ordered pair of numbers.

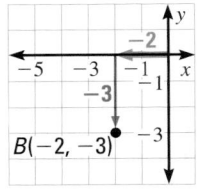

point-slope form (p. 300) The equation of a nonvertical line $y - y_1 = m(x - x_1)$ that passes through a given point (x_1, y_1) with a slope of m.

polynomial (p. 576) An expression which is the sum of terms of the form ax^k where k is a nonnegative integer.

positive numbers (p. 63) Any of the numbers greater than zero. *See also* real number line.

positive square root, or principal square root (p. 503) One of two square roots of a positive real number.

postulates (p. 758) The basic properties of mathematics that mathematicians accept without proof.

power (p. 9) The result of repeated multiplication. For example, in the expression $4^2 = 16$, 16 is the second power of 4.

prime factor (p. 625) A factor that is not the product of polynomials having integer coefficients.

probability of an event (p. 114) A measure of the likelihood that the event will occur due to chance. It is a number between 0 and 1, inclusive.

properties of equality (p. 139) The rules of algebra used to transform equations into equivalent equations.

proportion (p. 643) An equation that states that two ratios are equal. For example, $\frac{a}{b} = \frac{c}{d}$, where a, b, c, and d are nonzero real numbers.

Pythagorean theorem (p. 738) If a triangle is a right triangle, then the sum of the squares of the lengths of the legs a and b equals the square of the length of the hypotenuse c.

$$a^2 + b^2 = c^2$$

Q. . . . .

quadrant (p. 203) One of four parts into which the axes divide a coordinate plane. *See also* coordinate plane.

quadratic equation in standard form (p. 505) An equation written in the form $ax^2 + bx + c = 0$, where $a \neq 0$.

quadratic formula (p. 533) The formula used to find the solutions of the quadratic equation $ax^2 + bx + c = 0$, when $a \neq 0$ and $b^2 - 4ac \geq 0$.

$$x = \frac{-b \pm \sqrt{b^2 - 4ac}}{2a}$$

quadratic function in standard form (p. 518) A function written in the form $y = ax^2 + bx + c$, where $a \neq 0$.

quadratic inequality (p. 548) An inequality that can be written as follows:

$$y < ax^2 + bx + c \qquad y \leq ax^2 + bx + c$$
$$y > ax^2 + bx + c \qquad y \geq ax^2 + bx + c$$

quadratic model (p. 554) A function used to model a collection of data or a real-life situation.

Quadratic model: $y = ax^2 + bx + c$

quartiles (p. 375) Three numbers that separate a set of data into four parts.

• The *first quartile* is the median of the lower half of the data.
• The *second quartile* (or median) separates the data into two halves: the numbers that are below the median and the numbers that are above the median.
• The *third quartile* is the median of the upper half of the data.

R. . . . .

radicand (p. 503) The number or expression inside a radical symbol.

range of a function (p. 47) The collection of all output values.

rate of a per b (p. 180) The relationship $\frac{a}{b}$ of two quantities a and b that are measured in different units.

rate of change (p. 229) A comparison of two different quantities that are changing. Slope provides an important way of visualizing a rate of change.

ratio of *a* to *b* (p. 140) The relationship $\frac{a}{b}$ of two quantities a and b that are measured in the same unit.

rational equation (p. 690) An equation that contains rational expressions.

rational expression (p. 664) A fraction whose numerator, denominator, or both numerator and denominator are nonzero polynomials.

rational function (p. 692) A function of the form $f(x) = \frac{\text{polynomial}}{\text{polynomial}}$.

rational number (p. 664) A number that can be written as the quotient of two integers.

real number line (p. 63) A line that pictures real numbers as points.

real numbers (p. 63) The set of numbers consisting of the positive numbers, the negative numbers, and zero. *See also* real number line.

reciprocal (p. 108) If $\frac{a}{b}$ is a nonzero number, then its reciprocal is $\frac{b}{a}$. The product of a number and its reciprocal is 1.

relation (p. 256) Any set of ordered pairs (x, y).

roots of a quadratic equation (p. 526) The solutions of $ax^2 + bx + c = 0$.

round-off error (p. 166) The error produced when a decimal result is rounded in order to provide a meaningful answer.

scalar multiplication (p. 97) Multiplication of a matrix by a real number.

scatter plot (p. 204) A graph of pairs of numbers that represent real-life situations. It is a way to analyze the relationship between two quantities.

scientific notation (p. 470) A number expressed in the form $c \times 10^n$, where $1 \le c < 10$ and n is an integer.

similar triangles (p. 140) Two triangles are similar if they have equal corresponding angles. It can be shown that this is equivalent to the ratios of the lengths of the corresponding sides being equal.

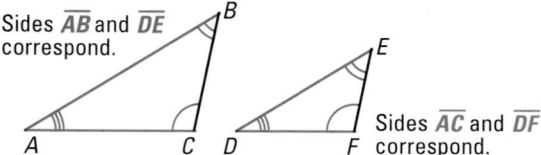

Sides $\overline{AB}$ and $\overline{DE}$ correspond.

Sides $\overline{AC}$ and $\overline{DF}$ correspond.

simplest form of a radical expression (p. 512) An expression that has no perfect square factors other than 1 in the radicand, no fractions in the radicand, and no radicals appearing in the denominator of a fraction.

simplified expression (p. 102) An expression is simplified if it has no symbols of grouping and if all the like terms have been combined.

simplified rational expression (p. 664) A rational expression is simplified if its numerator and denominator have no factors in common (other than ±1).

sine (p. 752) *See* trigonometric ratio.

slope (p. 226) The number of units a nonvertical line rises or falls for each unit of horizontal change from left to right. The slope m is $m = \frac{y_2 - y_1}{x_2 - x_1}$.

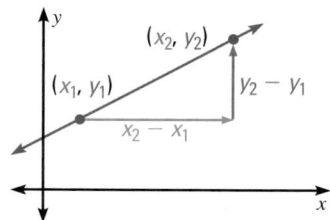

slope-intercept form (pp. 241, 273) A linear equation written in the form $y = mx + b$. The slope of the line is m. The y-intercept is b. *See also* slope *and* y-intercept.

$y = 2x + 3$
Slope is 2.
y-intercept is 3.

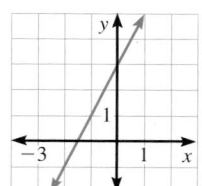

solution of an equation (p. 24) A number that, when substituted for the variable in an equation, results in a true statement.

solution of an inequality (p. 26) A number that, when substituted for the variable in an inequality, results in a true statement.

solution of a linear equation (p. 210) An ordered pair (x, y) is a solution of a linear equation if the equation is true when the values of x and y are substituted into the equation.

solution of a linear inequality (p. 360) An ordered pair (x, y) is a solution of a linear inequality if the inequality is true when the values of x and y are substituted into the inequality.

solution step (p. 133) The result of applying a transformation to an equation when solving the equation.

solution of a system of linear equations in two variables (p. 398) An ordered pair (x, y) that satisfies each equation in the system.

solution of a system of linear inequalities (p. 432) An ordered pair (x, y) that is a solution of each inequality in the system.

solving an equation (p. 25) Finding all the solutions of an equation.

solving a right triangle (p. 753) Finding the lengths of the other two sides of a right triangle, given the measure of one acute angle and the length of one side of the right triangle.

square root (p. 503) If $b^2 = a$, then b is a square root of a. Square roots are written with a radical symbol $\sqrt{}$.

square root function (p. 709) The function defined by $y = \sqrt{x}$.

standard form of an equation of a line (p. 308) A linear equation of the form $Ax + By = C$ where A, B, and C are real numbers and A and B are not both zero.

standard form of a polynomial (p. 576) A polynomial whose terms are placed in descending order, from largest degree to smallest degree.

stem-and-leaf plot (p. 368) An arrangement of digits that is used to display and order numerical data.

system of linear equations (p. 398) Two or more linear equations in the same variables. This is also called a linear system.

system of linear inequalities (p. 432) Two or more linear inequalities in the same variables. This is also called a system of inequalities.

tangent (p. 752) *See* trigonometric ratio.

terms of an expression (p. 80) The parts that are added in an expression. For example, in the expression $5 - x$, the terms are 5 and $-x$.

theorem (pp. 738, 759) A statement that can be proven to be true.

theoretical probability (p. 114) A type of probability that is based on the number of favorable outcomes divided by the total number of outcomes.

time period (p. 477) The variable t in the exponential growth and decay models. *See also* exponential growth *and* exponential decay.

transform an equation (p. 132) To change an equation into an equivalent equation.

trigonometric ratio (p. 752) The ratio of the lengths of two sides of a right triangle. For example:

$$\sin A = \frac{\text{side opposite } \angle A}{\text{hypotenuse}}$$

$$\cos A = \frac{\text{side adjacent to } \angle A}{\text{hypotenuse}}$$

$$\tan A = \frac{\text{side opposite } \angle A}{\text{side adjacent to } \angle A}$$

trinomial (p. 576) A polynomial with three terms.

unit analysis (p. 5) Writing the units of each variable in a real-life problem to help determine the units for the answer.

unit rate (p. 180) A rate per one given unit.

values (p. 3) The numbers represented by variables.

variable (p. 3) A letter that is used to represent one or more numbers.

variable expression (p. 3) A collection of numbers, variables, and operations.

velocity (p. 66) The speed and direction in which an object is traveling (up is positive and down is negative). The speed of an object is the absolute value of its velocity.

verbal model (p. 5) An expression that uses words to represent a real-life situation.

vertex of a parabola (p. 518) The lowest point of a parabola that opens up or the highest point of a parabola that opens down. *See also* parabola.

vertical motion models (p. 535) A model for the height of a falling object that is dropped and the model for an object thrown down or up.

x-axis (p. 203) The horizontal axis in a coordinate plane. *See also* coordinate plane.

x-coordinate (p. 203) The first number in an ordered pair. *See also* ordered pair *and* plotting a point.

x-intercept (p. 218) The x-coordinate of a point where a graph crosses the x-axis.

y-axis (p. 203) The vertical axis in a coordinate plane. *See also* coordinate plane.

y-coordinate (p. 203) The second number in an ordered pair. *See also* ordered pair *and* plotting a point.

y-intercept (p. 218) The y-coordinate of a point where a graph crosses the y-axis.

zero-product property (p. 597) If a and b are real numbers and $ab = 0$, then $a = 0$ or $b = 0$.

English-to-Spanish Glossary

A

absolute value (p. 65) **valor absoluto** La distancia entre el origen y el punto que representa el número real. El símbolo $|a|$ representa el valor absoluto de un número a.

algorithm (p. 39) **algoritmo** Un proceso para resolver un problema que se lleva a cabo paso a paso.

asymptote (p. 692) **asíntota** Una recta a la que se acerca una gráfica. La distancia entre la gráfica y la recta va acercándose a cero.

axioms (p. 758) **axiomas** Las propiedades fundamentales de las matemáticas que los matemáticos aceptan sin pruebas.

axis of symmetry of a parabola (p. 518) **eje de simetría de una parábola** La recta que al pasar por el vértice divide una parábola en dos partes simétricas. Las dos partes simétricas son imágenes especulares entre sí. *Ver también* parabola / parábola.

B

bar graph (p. 41) **gráfica de barras** Una gráfica que organiza un conjunto de datos mediante el uso de barras horizontales o verticales para mostrar cuántas veces cada suceso o número ocurre en el conjunto.

base number of a percent equation (p. 649) **número básico de una ecuación de porcentaje** El número *al que* se compara en una ecuación de porcentaje. El número b del modelo verbal: a es el porcentaje p de b.

base of a power (p. 9) **base de una potencia** El número o variable que se usa como factor en la multiplicación repetida. Por ejemplo, en la expresión 4^6, 4 es la base.

best-fitting line (p. 292) **recta que mejor se ajusta** La recta que se ajusta mejor a los puntos de datos de un diagrama de dispersión.

binomial (p. 576) **binomio** Un polinomio con dos términos.

box-and-whisker plot (p. 375) **gráfica de frecuencias acumuladas** Una manera de mostrar datos que divide un conjunto de datos en cuatro partes. La caja representa la mitad de los datos. Los segmentos se extienden hacia los datos mayor y menor.

C

center of a hyperbola (p. 692) **centro de una hipérbola** El punto (h, k) de la gráfica de la función racional $f(x) = \dfrac{a}{x - h} + k$.

closed set (p. 113) **conjunto cerrado** Un conjunto de números se cierra bajo una operación si al aplicar la operación a dos números cualesquiera en el conjunto resulta otro número contenido en el conjunto. Se dice que tal conjunto está cerrado.

coefficient (p. 102) **coeficiente** Un número multiplicado por una variable en un término. El número es el coeficiente de la variable.

completing the square (p. 730) **completar el cuadrado** El proceso de volver a escribir una ecuación cuadrática de manera que un lado sea un trinomio cuadrado perfecto.

compound inequality (p. 346) **desigualdad compuesta** Dos desigualdades conectadas por *y* u *o*.

conclusion (pp. 187, 739) **conclusión** La parte "entonces" de un enunciado "si…, entonces…" En el enunciado "si p, entonces q", q es la conclusión.

conjecture (p. 759) **conjetura** Un enunciado que se piensa es verdadero pero que todavía no ha sido probado. A menudo se trata de un enunciado basado en la observación.

conjugates (p. 717) **conjugados** Las expresiones $\left(a + \sqrt{b}\right)$ y $\left(a - \sqrt{b}\right)$ son conjugados entre sí.

consecutive integers (p. 149) **números enteros consecutivos** Números enteros que van seguidos. Por ejemplo, 4, 5, 6.

constant terms (p. 102) **términos constantes** Términos sin factores variables. Por ejemplo, en $x + 2 - 5x - 4$, los términos constantes son 2 y -4.

constant of variation (p. 234) **constante de variación** La constante de un modelo de variación. Se representa con la variable k. *Ver también* direct variation / variación directa *e* inverse variation / variación inversa.

converse of a statement (p. 739) **recíproco de un enunciado** Un enunciado relacionado en el que se intercambian la hipótesis y la conclusión. El recíproco del enunciado "Si p, entonces q", es "Si q, entonces p".

coordinate plane (p. 203) **plano de coordenadas** Un plano formado por dos rectas numéricas reales que se cortan en un ángulo recto.

correlation (p. 295) **correlación** La relación entre dos conjuntos de datos.

 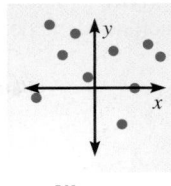

| Correlación positiva | Correlación negativa | Ninguna correlación |

cosine (p. 752) **coseno** *Ver* trigonometric ratio / razón trigonométrica

counterexample (p. 66) **contraejemplo** Un ejemplo que se usa para mostrar que un enunciado es falso.

data (p. 40) **datos** Información, hechos o números que se usan para describir algo.

decay factor (p. 484) **factor de decrecimiento** La expresión $1 - r$ del modelo de decrecimiento donde r es la tasa de decrecimiento. *Ver también* decay rate / tasa de decrecimiento.

decay rate (p. 484) **tasa de decrecimiento** La variable r del modelo de decrecimiento exponencial. *Ver también* exponential decay / decrecimiento exponencial.

deductive reasoning (p. 187) **razonamiento deductivo** Razonamiento mediante el que se llega a una conclusión basándose en datos, definiciones, reglas o propiedades.

degree of a polynomial (p. 576) **grado de un polinomio** El mayor grado de los términos del polinomio.

degree of a term (p. 576) **grado de un término** El exponente de la variable del término.

direct variation (pp. 234, 656) **variación directa** La relación entre dos variables x e y cuando hay un número k distinto a cero donde $y = kx$, o $\frac{y}{x} = k$. Las variables x e y varían directamente.

discriminant (p. 541) **discriminante** La expresión $b^2 - 4ac$ donde a, b y c son coeficientes de la ecuación cuadrática $ax^2 + bx + c = 0$.

distance formula (p. 745) **fórmula de la distancia** La distancia d entre los puntos (x_1, y_1) y (x_2, y_2) es
$$d = \sqrt{(x_2 - x_1)^2 + (y_2 - y_1)^2}.$$

distributive property (p. 100) **propiedad distributiva** El producto de a y $(b + c)$: $a(b + c) = ab + ac$ o $(b + c)a = ba + ca$. El producto de a y $(b - c)$: $a(b - c) = ab - ac$ o $(b - c)a = ba - ca$.

domain of a function (p. 47) **dominio de una función** El conjunto de todos los valores de entrada.

entry or element of a matrix (p. 86) **entrada o elemento de una matriz** Cada uno de los números de la matriz. *Ver también* matrix / matriz.

equation (p. 24) **ecuación** Un enunciado formado cuando un signo de igualdad se pone entre dos expresiones.

equivalent equations (p. 132) **ecuaciones equivalentes** Ecuaciones con la misma solución que la ecuación original.

equivalent inequalities (p. 335) **desigualdades equivalentes** Desigualdades con la misma solución o las mismas soluciones.

evaluating the expression (p. 3) **evaluar la expresión** Hallar el valor de una expresión mediante la sustitución de una variable por un número.

event (p. 114) **suceso** Un conjunto de casos.

experimental probability (p. 115) **probabilidad experimental** Una probabilidad que se basa en repeticiones de un experimento real.

exponent (p. 9) **exponente** El número o variable que representa el número de veces que la base se usa como factor. Por ejemplo, en la expresión 4^6, 6 es el exponente.

exponential decay (p. 484) **decrecimiento exponencial** Una cantidad que disminuye en el mismo porcentaje durante cada unidad de tiempo t donde C es la cantidad inicial.

Modelo de decrecimiento exponencial: $y = C(1 - r)^t$

exponential function (p. 458) **función exponencial** Una función que tiene la forma $y = ab^x$, donde $b > 0$ y $b \neq 1$.

exponential growth (p. 477) **crecimiento exponencial** Una cantidad que aumenta en el mismo porcentaje durante cada unidad de tiempo t donde C es la cantidad inicial.

Modelo de crecimiento exponencial: $y = C(1 + r)^t$

extraneous solution (pp. 644, 723) **solución extraña** Una solución tentativa que no satisface la ecuación original.

extremes of a proportion (p. 643) **extremos de una proporción** En la proporción $\frac{a}{b} = \frac{c}{d}$, a y d son los extremos.

factor (p. 777) **factor** Los números y las variables que se multiplican en una expresión. Por ejemplo, 4 y 9 son factores de 36 y 6 y x son factores de $6x$.

factor a polynomial completely (p. 625) **factorizar un polinomio completamente** Escribir un polinomio como el producto de:
• factores monomiales
• factores primos con por lo menos dos términos

factor a quadratic expression (p. 604) **factorizar una expresión cuadrática** Escribir una expresión cuadrática como el producto de dos expresiones lineales.

factored form of a polynomial (pp. 597, 625) **forma factorizada de un polinomio** Un polinomio que se escribe como el producto de dos o más factores primos.

favorable outcomes (p. 114) **casos favorables** Los casos de un suceso determinado que se están considerando. *Ver también* outcomes / casos.

FOIL pattern (p. 585) **patrón FOIL** Un patron que se usa para multiplicar dos binomios. Se multiplican los primeros términos (*First*), los términos exteriores (*Outer*), los interiores (*Inner*) y los últimos (*Last*).

Por ejemplo, $(x + 4)(2x + 3) = 2x^2 + 3x + 8x + 12$
$$= 2x^2 + 11x + 12$$

formula (p. 174) **fórmula** Una ecuación algebraica que relaciona dos o más cantidades de la vida real.

function (p. 46) **función** Una regla que establece la relación entre dos cantidades, llamadas entrada y salida. Para cada entrada, hay exactamente una salida.

function form (p. 176) **forma de función** Una ecuación de dos variables se escribe en forma de función si una de sus variables se aísla en un lado de la ecuación. La variable aislada es la salida y es una función de la entrada.

function notation (p. 257) **notación de función** Una manera de nombrar una función definida por una ecuación. Para una ecuación en *x* e *y*, el símbolo $f(x)$ reemplaza a *y* y se lee como "el valor de *f* en *x*", o simplemente como "*f* de *x*".

generalization (p. 187) **generalización** Una conclusión basada en varias observaciones.

geometric mean (p. 723) **media geométrica** La media geométrica de *a* y *b* es $\sqrt{ab}$.

geometric probability (p. 666) **probabilidad geométrica** La probabilidad *P* de que un objeto lanzado en la región *A* caiga en la región *B* cuando la región *B* se sitúa dentro de la región *A* es:

$$P = \frac{\text{Área de la región } B}{\text{Área de la región } A}$$

graph of an equation in two variables (p. 210) **gráfica de una ecuación de dos variables** El conjunto de todos los puntos (x, y) que sean soluciones de la ecuación.

graph of a function (p. 257) **gráfica de una función** El conjunto de todos los puntos $(x, f(x))$, donde *x* está en el dominio de la función.

graph of a linear inequality in one variable (p. 334) **gráfica de una desigualdad lineal de una variable** El conjunto de todos los puntos de una recta numérica que representen todas las soluciones de la desigualdad.

graph of a linear inequality in two variables (p. 360) **gráfica de una desigualdad lineal de dos variables** La gráfica de todos los pares ordenados (x, y) que sean soluciones de la desigualdad.

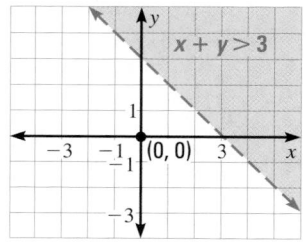

graph of a number (p. 63) **gráfica de un número** El punto que corresponde a un número.

graph of an ordered pair (p. 203) **gráfica de un par ordenado** El punto del plano que corresponde a un par ordenado (x, y).

graph of a quadratic inequality (p. 548) **gráfica de una desigualdad cuadrática** La gráfica de todos los pares ordenados (x, y) que sean soluciones de la desigualdad.

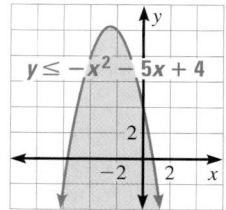

graph of a system of linear inequalities (p. 432) **gráfica de un sistema de desigualdades lineales** La gráfica de todas las soluciones del sistema.

grouping symbols (p. 10) **signos de agrupación** Signos tales como paréntesis ( ) o corchetes [ ] que indican el orden en que las operaciones deben realizarse. Se realizan primero las operaciones dentro de los signos más interiores.

growth factor (p. 477) **factor de crecimiento** La expresión $1 + r$ del modelo de crecimiento exponencial donde *r* es la tasa de crecimiento.

growth rate (p. 477) **tasa de crecimiento** La variable *r* del modelo de crecimiento exponencial. *Ver también* exponential growth / crecimiento exponencial.

half-plane (p. 360) **semiplano** En un plano de coordenadas, la región de un lado o del otro lado de una recta límite.

hyperbola (p. 692) **hipérbola** La gráfica de una función racional $f(x) = \frac{a}{x - h} + k$, cuyo centro es (h, k).

hypotenuse (p. 738) **hipotenusa** El lado opuesto al ángulo recto de un triángulo rectángulo.

hypothesis (pp. 187, 739) **hipótesis** La parte "si…," de un enunciado "si…, entonces…". En el enunciado "Si p, entonces q", p es la hipótesis.

identity (p. 155) **identidad** Una ecuación que es verdadera para todos los valores de las variables.

if-then statement (p. 187) **enunciado de "si…, entonces**…" Un enunciado de la forma "Si p, entonces q" donde p es la hipótesis y q es la conclusión.

indirect proof (p. 760) **prueba indirecta** Un tipo de prueba donde primero se asume que el enunciado es falso. Si esto lleva a una imposibilidad, entonces se ha probado que el enunciado original es verdadero.

inductive reasoning (p. 187) **razonamiento inductivo** Una forma de razonamiento en el que se llega a una conclusión basándose en varias observaciones.

inequality (p. 26) **desigualdad** Una oración formada al colocar un signo de desigualdad entre dos expresiones.

initial amount (pp. 477, 484) **cantidad inicial** La variable C del modelo de crecimiento o decrecimiento exponencial. *Ver también* exponential growth / crecimiento exponencial y exponential decay / decrecimiento exponencial.

input (p. 46) **entrada** *Ver* function / función.

input-output table (p. 46) **tabla de entradas y salidas** Una tabla usada para describir una función mediante una lista de las entradas y salidas.

integers (p. 63) **números enteros** Cualquiera de los números ... $-3, -2, -1, 0, 1, 2, 3, \dots$.

intersecting lines (p. 426) **rectas que se cortan, rectas secantes** Dos rectas que comparten exactamente un punto.

inverse operations (p. 132) **operaciones inversas** Operaciones que se anulan entre sí, como la suma y la resta.

inverse variation (p. 656) **variación inversa** La relación entre dos variables x e y si hay un número k distinto a cero tal que $xy = k$, o $y = \frac{k}{x}$. Las variables x e y varían inversamente.

irrational number (p. 504) **número irracional** Un número que no puede escribirse como el cociente de dos números enteros.

leading coefficient (pp. 505, 576) **coeficiente inicial** El coeficiente del primer término de un polinomio escrito en forma general.

least common denominator, LCD (p. 677) **mínimo común denominador, m.c.d.** El mínimo común múltiplo de los denominadores de dos o más fracciones.

legs of a right triangle (p. 738) **catetos de un triángulo rectángulo** Los dos lados de un triángulo rectángulo que no están opuestos al ángulo recto.

like terms (p. 102) **términos semejantes** Términos que tienen la misma variable elevada a la misma potencia.

line graph (p. 42) **gráfica lineal** Una gráfica que usa segmentos de recta para conectar puntos de datos. Sobre todo es útil para mostrar cambios en los datos a través del tiempo.

linear combination (p. 411) **combinación lineal** Una ecuación que se obtiene al sumar una de dos ecuaciones (o un múltiplo de una de dos ecuaciones) a la otra ecuación de un sistema lineal.

linear equation in one variable (p. 133) **ecuación lineal de una variable** Una ecuación en la que la variable se eleva a la primera potencia y que no se encuentra en un denominador, ni dentro del signo de raíz cuadrada, ni dentro de un símbolo de valor absoluto.

linear extrapolation (p. 318) **extrapolación lineal** Un método de estimar las coordenadas de un punto que está situado a la derecha o a la izquierda de todos los puntos de los datos mostrados.

linear inequality in x and y (p. 360) **desigualdad lineal con x e y** Una desigualdad que puede escribirse como sigue:
$$ax + by < c \qquad ax + by \le c$$
$$ax + by > c \qquad ax + by \ge c$$

linear interpolation (p. 318) **interpolación lineal** Un método de estimar las coordenadas de un punto que está situado entre dos puntos de los datos dados.

linear model (p. 274) **modelo lineal** Una función lineal que se usa para representar una situación de la vida real. En el modelo lineal $y = mx + b$, m es la razón de cambio y b es la cantidad inicial.

mathematical model (p. 33) **modelo matemático** Una expresión, ecuación o desigualdad que representa una situación de la vida real.

matrix (p. 86) **matriz** Un arreglo rectangular de números en filas horizontales y columnas verticales.

mean or average (p. 369) **media o promedio** La suma de n números dividida por n.

means of a proportion (p. 643) **medios de una proporción** En la proporción $\frac{a}{b} = \frac{c}{d}$, b y c son los medios.

measure of central tendency (p. 369) **medida de tendencia central** Un número que se usa para representar un número típico de un conjunto de datos. *Ver también* mean / media, median / mediana y mode / moda.

median (p. 369) **mediana** El número en el medio de un conjunto de *n* números cuando los números se escriben en orden numérico. Si *n* es par, es el promedio de los dos números en el medio del grupo.

midpoint between two points (p. 747) **punto medio entre dos puntos** El punto medio del segmento de recta que los conecta.

midpoint formula (p. 747) **fórmula del punto medio** El punto medio entre (x_1, y_1) y (x_2, y_2) es $\left(\frac{x_1 + x_2}{2}, \frac{y_1 + y_2}{2} \right)$.

mode (p. 369) **moda** El número que ocurre con más frecuencia en un conjunto de *n* números. Un conjunto de datos puede tener más de una moda o ninguna.

modeling (p. 33) **hacer un modelo, representar** Escribir expresiones algebraicas o desigualdades que representan situaciones de la vida real.

monomial (p. 576) **monomio** Un polinomio con un solo término.

negative numbers (p. 63) **números negativos** Cualquiera de los números menos de cero. *Ver también* real number line / recta numérica real.

negative square root (p. 503) **raíz cuadrada negativa** Una de las dos raíces cuadradas de un número positivo real.

odds (p. 116) **probabilidad de ocurrencia** La razón entre el número de maneras de que puede ocurrir un suceso y el número de maneras de que no puede ocurrir.

open sentence (p. 24) **expresión con variables** Una ecuación que contiene una o más variables.

opposites (p. 65) **opuestos** Dos puntos de una recta numérica que están a la misma distancia del origen pero situados en lados opuestos.

order of operations (p. 16) **orden de las operaciones** Las reglas establecidas para evaluar una expresión cuando hay que realizar más de una operación.

ordered pair (p. 203) **par ordenado** Un par de números que se usan para identificar un punto de un plano. *Ver también* coordinate plane / plano de coordenadas.

origin of a coordinate plane (p. 203) **origen de un plano de coordenadas** El punto (0, 0) de un plano de coordenadas donde el eje horizontal corta el eje vertical. *Ver también* coordinate plane / plano de coordenadas.

origin of a number line (p. 63) **origen de una recta numérica** El punto marcado cero de una recta numérica.

outcomes (p. 114) **casos** Los posibles resultados de un experimento de probabilidad.

output (p. 46) **salida** *Ver* function/función.

parabola (p. 518) **parábola** La gráfica con forma de U de una función cuadrática.

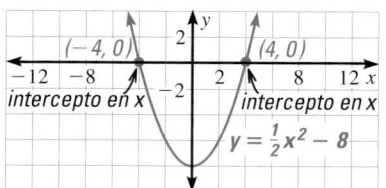

parallel lines (p. 242) **rectas paralelas** Dos rectas diferentes del mismo plano que no se cortan.

percent of decrease (p. 484) **porcentaje de disminución** La expresión $100r$ es el porcentaje de disminución donde *r* es la tasa de decrecimiento del modelo de decrecimiento exponencial.

percent of increase (p. 477) **porcentaje de aumento** La expresión $100r$ es el porcentaje de aumento donde *r* es la tasa de crecimiento del modelo de crecimiento exponencial.

perfect square (p. 504) **cuadrado perfecto** Un número cuyas raíces cuadradas son números enteros o cocientes de números enteros.

perpendicular lines (p. 246) **rectas perpendiculares** Dos rectas no verticales de un plano situadas de tal manera que la pendiente de una es el recíproco negativo de la otra.

Una recta vertical y una recta horizontal situadas en el mismo plano también son perpendiculares.

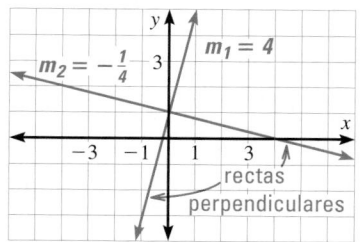

plotting a point (pp. 63, 203) **marcar un punto** Dibujar el punto en una recta numérica que corresponde a un número. Dibujar el punto en un plano de coordenadas que corresponde a un par ordenado de números.

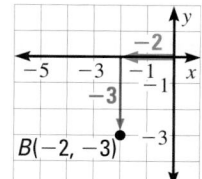

point-slope form (p. 300) **ecuación punto-pendiente** La ecuación de una recta no vertical $y - y_1 = m(x - x_1)$ que pasa por el punto dado (x_1, y_1) con una pendiente de *m*.

polynomial (p. 576) **polinomio** Una expresión que es la suma de los términos de la forma ax^k donde *k* es un número entero no negativo.

positive numbers (p. 63) **números positivos** Cualquiera de los números mayores que cero. *Ver también* real number line / recta numérica real.

positive square root, or principal square root (p. 503) **raíz cuadrada positiva o principal** Una de dos raíces cuadradas de un número real positivo.

postulates (p. 758) **postulados** Las propiedades básicas de las matemáticas que los matemáticos aceptan sin pruebas.

power (p. 9) **potencia** El resultado de la multiplicación repetida. Por ejemplo, en la expresión $4^2 = 16$, 16 es la segunda potencia de 4.

prime factor (p. 625) **factor primo** Un factor que no es el producto de polinomios con coeficientes que son enteros.

probability of an event (p. 114) **probabilidad de un suceso** Una medida de las probabilidades de que el suceso ocurra al azar. Es un número entre 0 y 1, inclusive.

properties of equality (p. 139) **propiedades de igualdad** Reglas de álgebra usadas para transformar ecuaciones en ecuaciones equivalentes.

proportion (p. 643) **proporción** Una ecuación que enuncia que dos razones son iguales. Por ejemplo, $\frac{a}{b} = \frac{c}{d}$, donde a, b, c y d son números reales distintos a cero.

Pythagorean theorem (p. 738) **teorema de Pitágoras** Si un triángulo es rectángulo, entonces la suma de los cuadrados de las longitudes de los catetos a y b es igual al cuadrado de la longitud de la hipotenusa c.

$$a^2 + b^2 = c^2$$

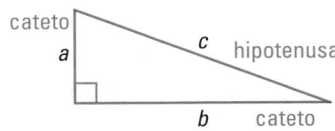

Q

quadrant (p. 203) **cuadrante** Una de las cuatro partes en las que los ejes dividen un plano de coordenadas. *Ver también* coordinate plane / plano de coordenadas.

quadratic equation in standard form (p. 505) **ecuación cuadrática en forma general** Una ecuación escrita en la forma $ax^2 + bx + c = 0$, donde $a \neq 0$.

quadratic formula (p. 533) **fórmula cuadrática** La fórmula que se usa para hallar las soluciones de la ecuación cuadrática $ax^2 + bx + c = 0$, donde $a \neq 0$ y $b^2 - 4ac \geq 0$.

$$x = \frac{-b \pm \sqrt{b^2 - 4ac}}{2a}$$

quadratic function in standard form (p. 518) **función cuadrática en forma general** Una función escrita en la forma $y = ax^2 + bx + c$, donde $a \neq 0$.

quadratic inequality (p. 548) **desigualdad cuadrática** Una desigualdad que puede escribirse así:

$$y < ax^2 + bx + c \qquad y \leq ax^2 + bx + c$$
$$y > ax^2 + bx + c \qquad y \geq ax^2 + bx + c$$

quadratic model (p. 554) **modelo cuadrático** Una función que se usa para representar un conjunto de datos o una situación de la vida real.

Modelo cuadrático: $y = ax^2 + bx + c$

quartiles (p. 375) **cuartiles** Tres números que separan un conjunto de datos en cuatro partes.

- El primer cuartil es la mediana de la mitad inferior de los datos.
- El segundo cuartil (o mediana) separa los datos en dos mitades: los números por debajo de la mediana y los números por encima de la mediana.
- El tercero es la mediana de la mitad superior de los datos.

R

radicand (p. 503) **radicando** El número o expresión dentro del símbolo radical.

range of a function (p. 47) **rango de una función** El conjunto de todos los valores de salida.

rate of *a* per *b* (p. 180) **relación de *a* por *b*** La relación $\frac{a}{b}$ entre dos cantidades a y b que se miden con unidades distintas.

rate of change (p. 229) **razón de cambio** Una comparación de dos cantidades diferentes que están cambiando. La pendiente sirve de modelo importante para visualizar la razón de cambio.

ratio of *a* to *b* (p. 140) **razón de *a* a *b*** La relación $\frac{a}{b}$ entre dos cantidades a y b que se miden con las mismas unidades.

rational equation (p. 690) **ecuación racional** Una ecuación que contiene expresiones racionales.

rational expression (p. 664) **expresión racional** Una fracción cuyo numerador, denominador o ambos son polinomios distintos a cero.

rational function (p. 692) **función racional** Una función de la forma $f(x) = \frac{\text{polinomio}}{\text{polinomio}}$.

rational number (p. 664) **número racional** Un número que puede escribirse como el cociente de dos números enteros.

real number line (p. 63) **recta numérica real** Una recta que representa números reales como puntos.

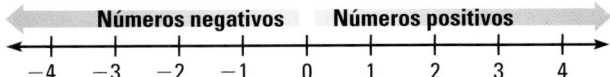

real numbers (p. 63) **números reales** El conjunto de números que consiste en los números positivos, los números negativos y cero. *Ver también* real number line / recta numérica real.

reciprocal (p. 108) **recíproco** Si $\frac{a}{b}$ es un número distinto a cero, entonces su recíproco es $\frac{b}{a}$. El producto de un número y su recíproco es 1.

relation (p. 256) **relación** Cualquier conjunto de pares ordenados (x, y).

roots of a quadratic equation (p. 526) **raíces de una ecuación cuadrática** Las soluciones de $ax^2 + bx + c = 0$.

round-off error (p. 166) **error de redondeo** El error que se produce cuando se redondea un resultado decimal para llegar a una respuesta significante.

scalar multiplication (p. 97) **multiplicación escalar** La multiplicación de una matriz por un número real.

scatter plot (p. 204) **diagrama de dispersión** Una gráfica de pares de números que representan situaciones de la vida real. Es una manera de analizar la relación entre dos cantidades.

scientific notation (p. 470) **notación científica** Un número expresado en la forma $c \times 10^n$, donde $1 \le c < 10$ y n es un número entero.

similar triangles (p. 140) **triángulos semejantes** Dos triángulos son semejantes si tienen ángulos correspondientes iguales. Puede mostrarse también que son semejantes si son iguales las razones de las longitudes de los lados correspondientes.

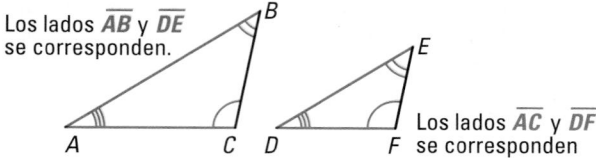

Los lados $\overline{AB}$ y $\overline{DE}$ se corresponden.
Los lados $\overline{AC}$ y $\overline{DF}$ se corresponden

simplest form of a radical expression (p. 512) **forma más simple de una expresión radical** Una expresión que no tiene factores cuadrados perfectos distintos de 1 en el radicando, ninguna fracción en el radicando y ningún radical en el denominador de una fracción.

simplified expression (p. 102) **expresión simplificada** Una expresión está simplificada si no tiene signos de agrupación y si todos los términos semejantes se han combinado.

simplified rational expression (p. 664) **expresión racional simplificada** Una expresión racional está simplificada si el numerador y denominador no tienen factores en común (distintos de ± 1).

sine (p. 752) **seno** *Ver* trigonometric ratio / razón trigonométrica.

slope (p. 226) **pendiente** El número de unidades que sube o baja una recta no vertical por cada unidad de cambio horizontal de izquierda a derecha. La pendiente de m es $m = \dfrac{y_2 - y_1}{x_2 - x_1}$.

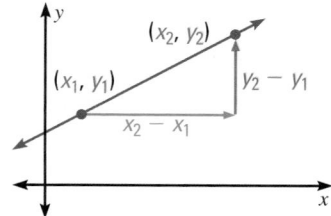

slope-intercept form (pp. 241, 273) **ecuación de pendiente-intercepto** Una ecuación lineal escrita en forma de $y = mx + b$. La pendiente de la recta es m. El intercepto en y es b. *Ver también* slope / pendiente y y-intercept / intercepto en y.

$y = 2x + 3$
La pendiente es 2.
El intercepto en y es 3.

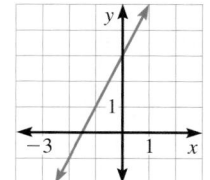

solution of an equation (p. 24) **solución de una ecuación** Un número que cuando se sustituye por la variable de una ecuación produce un enunciado verdadero.

solution of an inequality (p. 26) **solución de una desigualdad** Un número que cuando se sustituye por la variable de una desigualdad produce un enunciado verdadero.

solution of a linear equation (p. 210) **solución de una ecuación lineal** Un par ordenado (x, y) es una solución de una ecuación lineal si la ecuación es verdadera cuando se sustituyen los valores de x e y en la ecuación.

solution of a linear inequality (p. 360) **solución de una desigualdad lineal** Un par ordenado (x, y) es una solución de una desigualdad lineal si la desigualdad es verdadera cuando se sustituyen los valores de x e y en la desigualdad.

solution step (p. 133) **paso de una solución** El resultado de aplicar una transformación a una ecuación al resolverla.

solution of a system of linear equations in two variables (p. 398) **solución de un sistema de ecuaciones lineales de dos variables** Un par ordenado (x, y) que satisface cada ecuación del sistema.

solution of a system of linear inequalities (p. 432) **solución de un sistema de desigualdades lineales** Un par ordenado (x, y) que es una solución de todas las desigualdades del sistema.

solving an equation (p. 25) **resolver una ecuación** Hallar todas las soluciones de una ecuación.

solving a right triangle (p. 753) **resolver un triángulo rectángulo** Hallar las longitudes de los otros dos lados de un triángulo rectángulo, dadas la medida de uno de los ángulos agudos y la longitud de un lado del triángulo.

square root (p. 503) **raíz cuadrada** Si $b^2 = a$, entonces b es una raíz cuadrada de a. Las raíces cuadradas se escriben con un signo de radical $\sqrt{\ }$.

square root function (p. 709) **función con raíces cuadradas** La función definida por $y = \sqrt{x}$.

standard form of an equation of a line (p. 308) **forma general de la ecuación de una recta** Una ecuación lineal de la forma $Ax + By = C$ donde A, B y C son números reales y A y B no son ambos cero.

standard form of a polynomial (p. 576) **forma general de un polinomio** Un polinomio cuyos términos se sitúan en orden descendiente, de grado mayor a grado menor.

stem-and-leaf plot (p. 368) **tabla arborescente** Un arreglo de dígitos que se usa para mostrar y ordenar datos numéricos.

system of linear equations (p. 398) **sistema de ecuaciones lineales** Dos o más ecuaciones lineales con las mismas variables. También se llama sistema lineal.

system of linear inequalities (p. 432) **sistema de desigualdades lineales** Dos o más desigualdades lineales con las mismas variables. También se llama sistema de desigualdades.

 T

tangent (p. 752) **tangente** *Ver* trigonometric ratio / razón trigonométrica.

terms of an expression (p. 80) **términos de una expresión** Las partes de una expresión que se suman. Por ejemplo, en la expresión $5 - x$, los términos son 5 y $-x$.

theorem (pp. 738, 759) **teorema** Un enunciado que puede probarse verdadero.

theoretical probability (p. 114) **probabilidad teórica** Un tipo de probabilidad que se basa en el número de casos favorables dividido por el número total de casos.

time period (p. 477) **período de tiempo** La variable t en los modelos de crecimiento y decrecimiento exponencial. *Ver también* exponential growth / crecimiento exponencial y exponential decay / decrecimiento exponencial.

transform an equation (p. 132) **transformar una ecuación** Cambiar una ecuación en una ecuación equivalente.

trigonometric ratio (p. 752) **razón trigonométrica** La razón de las longitudes de dos lados de un triángulo rectángulo. Por ejemplo:

$$\operatorname{sen} A = \frac{\text{lado opuesto a } \angle A}{\text{hipotenusa}}$$

$$\cos A = \frac{\text{lado adyacente a } \angle A}{\text{hipotenusa}}$$

$$\tan A = \frac{\text{lado opuesto a } \angle A}{\text{lado adyacente a } \angle A}$$

trinomial (p. 576) **trinomio** Un polinomio con tres términos.

 U

unit analysis (p. 5) **análisis dimensional** Escribir las unidades de cada variable en un problema de la vida real para ayudar a determinar las unidades de la respuesta.

unit rate (p. 180) **relación unitaria** Una relación por una unidad dada.

 V

values (p. 3) **valores** Los números representados por variables.

variable (p. 3) **variable** Una letra que se usa para representar uno o más números.

variable expression (p. 3) **expresión algebraica** Un conjunto de números, variables y operaciones.

velocity (p. 66) **velocidad** La rapidez y dirección con las que se mueve un objeto (hacia arriba es positiva y hacia abajo es negativa.) La rapidez de un objeto es el valor absoluto de su velocidad.

verbal model (p. 5) **modelo verbal** Una expresión en la que se usan palabras para representar una situación de la vida real.

vertex of a parabola (p. 518) **vértice de una parábola** El punto más bajo de una parábola que abre hacia arriba o el punto más alto de una parábola que se abre hacia abajo. *Ver también* parabola / parábola.

vertical motion models (p. 535) **modelos del movimiento vertical** Un modelo para representar la altura de un objeto en movimiento que se ha dejado caer y para representar un objeto lanzado hacia abajo o hacia arrriba.

 X

x-axis (p. 203) **eje de x** El eje horizontal en un plano de coordenadas. *Ver también* plano de coordenadas / coordinate plane.

x-coordinate (p. 203) **coordenada x** El primer número en un par ordenado. *Ver también* ordered pair / par ordenado y plotting a point / marcar un punto.

x-intercept (p. 218) **intercepto en x** La coordenada x de un punto donde una gráfica cruza el eje de x.

 Y

y-axis (p. 203) **eje de y** El eje vertical en un plano de coordenadas. *Ver también* plano de coordenadas / coordinate plane.

y-coordinate (p. 203) **coordenada y** El segundo número de un par ordenado. *Ver también* ordered pair / par ordenado y plotting a point / marcar un punto.

y-intercept (p. 218) **intercepto en y** La coordenada y de un punto donde una gráfica cruza el eje de y.

 Z

zero-product property (p. 597) **propiedad del producto nulo** Si a y b son números reales y $ab = 0$, entonces $a = 0$ o $b = 0$.

Index

function notation, 257
inequality, 26
plus or minus, 503

T

Table(s)
graphing calculator, 15, 173
organizing data with, 11, 13, 23, 40–44, 56, 156, 211, 225, 310, 315, 483, 582, 589, 648, 662, 729
representing functions with, 46–51, 80, 458, 556, 709–711
using as a check, 156, 161
using to find patterns, 11, 13, 14, 23, 209, 310, 506, 555
of values, 210–217, 458, 479, 519, 520, 597, 663, 678, 692, 693
Tangent, 752–757
Technology, *See* **Calculator; Computer; Graphing calculator; Internet Connections; Technology Activities**
Technology Activities
Adding and Subtracting Matrices, 92
Box-and-Whisker Plots, 382
Families of Square-Root Functions, 715
Fitting Models, 299, 492, 525, 663
Graphing
Absolute-Value Equations, 359
Functions, 248–249, 367, 462, 583, 698
Scatter Plot, 209
Making a Table, 15
A Program for the Quadratic Formula, 539
Solving Linear Systems by Graphing, 404
Solving Quadratic Equations by Graphing, 532
Using a Table or a Spreadsheet to Solve Equations, 173
Temperature,
Centigrade/Fahrenheit formula for, 29, 30, 147, 174
Terms
of an expression, 80, 102
of a polynomial, 576
Test Preparation
multi-step problem, 14, 21, 45, 51, 84, 91, 106, 137, 151, 165,

171, 208, 223, 255, 269, 284, 298, 321, 339, 351, 380, 410, 431, 437, 455, 468, 523, 538, 546, 582, 589, 602, 648, 661, 669, 689, 714, 743, 757, 763
multiple choice, 8, 30, 38, 77, 98, 113, 119, 144, 159, 179, 217, 233, 239, 246, 268, 278, 290, 305, 313, 345, 358, 365, 403, 424, 461, 475, 482, 490, 516, 531, 553, 559, 609, 616, 624, 631, 675, 681, 696, 721, 736, 750
quantitative comparison, 70, 185, 261, 269, 374, 416, 461, 509, 595, 655, 727
Test-taking strategies, 58, 126, 194, 268, 328, 388, 444, 498, 566, 638, 704, 770
Theorem, 739, 759
proving, 759–763
Pythagorean, 737–745, 767
Theoretical probability, 114–115
Transformations, 132, 138, 145–146
Translating verbal statements, 134, 137, 168, 345
Tree diagram
as a counting method, 788–789
for prime factorization, 777
Trigonometric ratios, 751–757, 768
Trinomial, 576, *See also* **Polynomial**
factoring, 603–617, 635, 636
Trinomial denominators, 681

U

Undefined expression, 665
Unit analysis, 5, 6, 37, 95, 97, 150, 156, 163, 181, 183, 184, 229, 258, 274, 275, 277, 468, 472, 475, 711, 713
Unit rate, 181–184, 787

V

Values of a variable, 3
Variable expression, 3–8, 54, 94
Variable(s), 3
on both sides of an equation, 153–159, 190
coefficient of, 102
Variation
constant of, 234, 656
direct, 234–239, 265, 656–662, 701
inverse, 656–663, 701

Velocity, 66
Verbal model, 5, 28, 32–38, 48, 55, 95, 110, 134, 141, 147, 150, 156, 160, 161, 162, 168, 182, 216, 220, 229, 258, 274, 275, 307, 310, 334, 342, 362, 400, 407, 413, 418–420, 434, 578, 586, 592, 606, 627, 649–652, 672, 678, 691, 718
Vertex, of a parabola, 518
Vertical line
equation of, 213, 309
slope of, 227, 228, 242
Vertical line test, for functions, 256
Vertical motion model, 535–538, 543, 545, 613, 615, 621, 623, 630
Visual thinking, 215, 255, 298, 437, 460, 490, 538, 726, *See also* **Graphs; Manipulatives; Modeling; Multiple representations**
Volume, 11, 13, 29, 177, 192, 791, *See also* **Formulas**

X

x-**axis,** 203
x-**intercept(s),** 218
linear graphs and, 218–224
quadratic graphs and, 542

Y

y-**axis,** 203
y-**intercept(s),** 218
linear graphs and, 218–224, 242

Z

Zero
division by, 108, 109
as an exponent, 456–461, 494
Zero property, of addition, 73
Zero slope, 227
Zero-product property, 597–598, 635, 665

Credits

Cover Credits

Earth Imaging/Tony Stone Images (background); Dan Bosler/Tony Stone Images (t); T. Kevin Smyth/The Stock Market (r); courtesy, NASA (b); Don Mason/The Stock Market (l).

Text Credits

143 Adapted from *The Pleasures of Japanese Cooking* by Heihachi Tanaka with Betty Nicholas. Copyright © 1963 by Prentice-Hall, Inc., renewed in 1991 by Heihachi Tanaka and Betty Nicholas. Reprinted with the permission of Simon & Schuster, Inc.

Photography

i, ii Earth Imaging/Tony Stone Images (background); Dan Bosler/Tony Stone Images (t); T. Kevin Smyth/The Stock Market (r); courtesy, NASA (b); Don Mason/The Stock Market (l); **iv** Sovfoto/Eastfoto/PNI/PictureQuest (tl); Dean Siracusa/FPG International (tc); **v** RMIP/Richard Haynes (tc); CORBIS/Tim Mosenfelder (tr); **vi** Stuart Westmorland/Photo Researchers, Inc.; **vii** Baron Wolman/Tony Stone Images; **viii** Darrell Gulin/Tony Stone Images; **ix** Dennis Hallinan/FPG International; **x** Melissa Farlow/National Geographic Image Collection; **xi** Bob Daemmrich/The Image Works; **xii** Billy Hustace/Tony Stone Images; **xiii** Dean Abramson/Stock Boston/PNI/PictureQuest; **xiv** Vincent Laforet/Allsport; **xv** David Parker/Science Photo Library/Photo Researchers, Inc.; **xvi** CORBIS/Phillip Gould; **xvii** Rex A. Butcher/Tony Stone Images; **xix** Robert Rathe/Stock Boston (t); Keith Wood/Tony Stone Images (c); Rachel Epstein/PhotoEdit (cl); Chuck Savage/The Stock Market (cr); Roger Tully/Tony Stone Images (b); **xxii, 1** Stuart Westmorland/Photo Researchers, Inc.; **3** T. Kevin Smyth/The Stock Market; **5** Ken Biggs/Tony Stone Images; **7** courtesy, Heidi Zimmer; **9** Wolfgang Kaehler; **13** John Kuhn (l); Howell/Liaison Agency, Inc. (br); **16** Mark Gibson; **20** RMIP/Richard Haynes; **24** Don Smetzer/Tony Stone Images; **26** Ziggy Kaluzny/Tony Stone Images; **29** Hurlin-Saola/Liaison Agency; **32** Ted Streshinsky/Photo 20-20; **34** David H. Frazier/Tony Stone Images; **37** David Young-Wolff/PhotoEdit; **38** Robert Ginn/PhotoEdit; **39** Bibliothèque Nationale, Paris (bl); X512.Sch2. Rare Book and Manuscript Library, Columbia University (bcl); Stock Montage (bcr); courtesy, IBM Archives (br); **40** Mark Stouffer/Bruce Coleman Inc.; **42** Tom McHugh/Photo Researchers, Inc.; **46** Mark Wagner/Tony Stone Images; **48** Stephen Frink/The Stock Market; **60** Baron Wolman/Tony Stone Images; **61** George Hall/Woodfin Camp and Associates; **63** Everett Johnson/Tony Stone Images; **66** courtesy, NASA; **68** Jay M. Pasachoff/Visuals Unlimited; **69** AP Photo/Osamu Honda; **72** Eric Berndt/Unicorn Stock Photo; **74** Stephen Frisch/Stock Boston; **76** CC Lockwood/DRK Photo; **79** Marilyn "Angel" Wynn/Sun Valley Video and Photography; **81** Alan Schein/The Stock Market; **83** James Hazelwood; **86** AP/Wide World Photos; **87** UPI/CORBIS/Bettmann; **90** Jim Shippee/Unicorn Stock Photo; **95** Nick Bergkessel/Photo Researchers, Inc.; **97** MONKMEYER/Grantpix; **100** Carl J. Single/The Image Works; **102** MONKMEYER/Wyman; **104** Phil Degginger/Bruce Coleman Inc; **107** The Bodleian Library, University of Oxford, MS Sansk. d.14 folio 47r (cr); *The Emperor SiuenLi,* 17th century, Bibliothèque Nationale, Paris, France/Bridgeman Art Library (bl); Science & Society Picture Library (bc); Gail McCawn/Photo Researchers, Inc. (br); **108** Tony Freeman/PhotoEdit; **110** James Handkley/Tony Stone Images; **112** Stephen Dunn/Allsport; **114** Doug Perrine/DRK Photo; **115** Bob Daemmrich Photos, Inc.; **118** David Parker/Photo Researchers, Inc.; **128** Darrell Gulin/Tony Stone Images; **129** Tom & Pat Leeson/DRK Photo; **132** Peter Pearson/Tony Stone Images; **136** Robert Brenner/PhotoEdit; **138** Rob Matheson/The Stock Market; **140** Mel Traxel/Motion Picture & Television Photo Archive; **142** Antman/The Image Works; **143** A & J Verkaik/The Stock Market; **145** Bachmann/PhotoEdit; **147** Jackson Smith/Uniphoto; **149** Reproduced with permission of the Thornton Wilder Collection, and the Barbara Hogenson Agency/Yale Collection of American Literature, Beinecke Rare Book and Manuscript Library.; **150** J. F. Towers/The Stock Market; **152** CORBIS/Macduff Everton (bl); CORBIS/Bettmann (bc); CORBIS/Gail Mooney (br); **154** Don Mason/The Stock Market; **158** courtesy, Gary Scott, Callison Architecture (bl); courtesy, Callison Architecture (br); **160** Steve Woit/Stock Boston; **162** Ahup & Manoj Sham/Animals Animals; **164** Rick Edwards/Animals Animals; **166** Peter Menzel/Stock Boston; **170** Aaron Haupt/Photo Researchers, Inc.; **171** Flip Nicklin/Minden Pictures; **174** Mike Brown/Florida Today/Liaison Agency; **175** National Geographic Image Collection; **180** Chuck Savage/The Stock Market; **181** Wolfgang Kaehler; **182** Paolo Koch/Photo Researchers, Inc.; **185** David Young-Wolff/Tony Stone Images; **198** David Young-Wolff/PhotoEdit; **199** Bob Daemmrich/Tony Stone Images (bl); David Sutherland/Tony Stone Images (br); **200, 201** Dennis Hallinan/FPG International; **203** Duomo Photography, Inc.; **205** Eric Berndt/Unicorn Stock Photo; **207** CC Lockwood/Animals Animals; **210** Bongarts Photography/Sportschrome; **216** Thomas Zimmerman/Tony Stone Images; **218** Aaron Haupt/Stock Boston; **220** John Warden/Tony Stone Images; **222** Mark Harris/Tony Stone Images; **224** René Descartes/from a painting by Frans Hals. © North Wind Picture Archives (bl); Publication of Descartes text, *La Géométrie* (1637). Stock Montage, Inc. (bcl); courtesy, Casio, Inc. (bcr); Barbara Alper/Stock Boston/PNI/PictureQuest & Sovfoto/Eastfoto/PNI/PictureQuest (montage, br); **225** School Division, Houghton Mifflin Company (background, cl); RMIP/Richard Haynes (inset, cl); Alan Kearney/Viesti Associates, Inc. (tr); **226** Dean Siracusa/FPG International; **231** Robert Rathe/Stock Boston; **232** TriStar Pictures/Shooting Star; **234** Bob Daemmrich/Stock Boston; **235** courtesy, Zeppelin Library Archive; **236** Keith Wood/Tony Stone Images; **238** Sovfoto/Eastfoto (tl); Artville, LLC.(br); **240** RMIP/Richard Haynes (all); **241** Nathan Benn/Stock Boston; **243** Charles Gupton/Stock Boston; **245** Matthew J. Atanian/Tony Stone Images; **250** Tony Freeman/PhotoEdit; **252** Roger Tully/Tony Stone Images; **254** Charlie Westerman/Liaison Agency; **256** David Young-Wolff/PhotoEdit; **258** Ron Sanford/Tony Stone Images; **261** CORBIS/Tim Mosenfelder; **270** Melissa Farlow/National Geographic Image Collection; **271** Mastrorillo/The Stock Market (r); Werner Forman Archive, Maxwell Museum of Anthropology, Albuquerque, NM, USA/Art Resource (bc); **273** Eastcott/The Image Works; **274** Bill Aron/PhotoEdit; **279** David Sailors/The Stock Market; **281** Mark Burnett/Stock Boston; **285** Uniphoto; **287** Kenneth Garrett/National Geographic Image Collection; **292** RMIP/Richard Haynes; **294** Steven E. Sutton/Duomo; **295** Luis Bongarts/Allsport; **300** Tom Stewart/The Stock Market; **302** Matthew Stockman/Allsport; **306** Grant/Mesa Verde National Park, 09116.4 (bl); Special Collections, The University of Arizona Library (bc); CORBIS/Richard A. Cooke (br); **308** Len Rue Jr./Photo Researchers, Inc.; **310** courtesy, Texas Gas Transmission; **312** Wayne Lankinen/DRK Photo; **316** Kevin Horan/Stock Boston; **318** Dan Bosler/Tony Stone Images; **320** Matthew Borkoski/Stock Boston; **330, 331** Bob Daemmrich/The Image Works; **334** Tony Freeman/PhotoEdit; **337** Gunther/Motion Picture & Television Photo Archive; **338** James Sugar/Black Star/PNI (l); Frederica Georgia/Photo Researchers, Inc. (br); **340** Donald C. Johnson/The Stock Market; **342** David J. Sams/Stock Boston; **344** Tony

Freeman/PhotoEdit; **346** Chuck Pefley/Tony Stone Images (cl); Rich Iwaski/Tony Stone Images (br); **350** Erich Lessing/Art Resource; **352** The Granger Collection (cr); Stock Montage (bl, bcl, bcr); Superstock (br); **353** Ken Clark; **355** Kaluzny/Thatcher/Tony Stone Images; **360** Al Giddings Images, Inc.; **362** Al Giddings Images, Inc.; **365** Yoav Levy/Phototake; **368** Harry M. Walker; **375** Porter Gifford/Liaison Agency; **379** David Shopper/Stock Boston; **392** RMIP/Richard Haynes (all); **393** Jon Riley/Tony Stone Images; **394** Billy Hustace/Tony Stone Images; **395** Bob Daemmrich/Uniphoto; **398** Mark E. Gibson; **400** Chuck Savage/The Stock Market; **403** Monkmeyer/Goodwin; **405** David Young-Wolff/PhotoEdit; **407** AP Photo; **409** RMIP/Richard Haynes; **411** Uniphoto; **413** North Wind Picture Archives; **415** Tom Evans/Photo Researchers, Inc.; **417** Reproduced by Permission of the Commercial Press (Hong Kong) Limited from the publication of *Chinese Mathematics: A Concise History*. (cl); Michael W. Thomas/Stock South/PNI (bl); Artville, LLC. (bc); Chris Sorensen/The Stock Market & Artville, LLC. (montage, br); **422** CORBIS/Kevin R. Morris; **426** James Amos/National Geographic Image Collection; **428** Richard Harrington/FPG International (cl, mid-cr); James Amos/National Geographic Image Collection (mid-cl, cr) **430** Mark E. Gibson; **432** Lee Greenwood/Stock Boston; **434** MONKMEYER/Anderson; **436** M. Granitsas/The Image Works; **446** Dean Abramson/Stock Boston/PNI; **447** David Madison; **450** Peter Menzel/Stock Boston; **452** Mark Wagner/Tony Stone Images; **454** Keith Wood/Tony Stone Images; **456** Brian Drake/Sportschrome; **460** courtesy, Texas Historical Commission; **463** Duomo Photography, Inc.; **465** Tim Flach/Tony Stone Images; **467** John Eastcott/DRK Photo; **468** Randy Wells/Tony Stone Images; **470** Jacques Jangoux/Tony Stone Images; **474** North Wind Picture Archives; **477** Tom McHugh/Photo Researchers, Inc.; **481** Marcia Griffen/Animals Animals; **483** RMIP/Richard Haynes; **484** Sears Roebuck & Co./Brown Brothers; **489** Patrick Ramsey/International Stock Photo; **491** CORBIS/Bettmann (cr); Andrew Syred/Science Photo Library/Photo Researchers, Inc. & CORBIS/Bettmann (montage, bl); CORBIS (bc); Secchi-Lecaque/CNRI/Science Photo/Photo Researchers, Inc. (br); **492** Dr. David Jones/Science Photo Library/Photo Researchers, Inc.; **500, 501** Vincent Laforet/Allsport; **503** Richard B. Levine; **509** Ken M. Johns/Photo Researchers, Inc. (tl); Photo Researchers, Inc. (cl); Charles D. Winters/Photo Researchers, Inc.(tc); E.R. Degginger/Photo Researchers, Inc. (cr, bl); Tom McHugh/Photo Researchers, Inc. (bc); Biophoto Associates/Photo Researchers, Inc. (br); **511** Stephen Munday/Allsport; **513** Mike Hewitt/Allsport; **518** Tim Davis/Photo Researchers, Inc.; **520** Tony Duffy/Allsport; **522** Gordon R. Gainer/The Stock Market; **523** Michel Hans/Vandystadt/Allsport; **526** David Madison/Duomo; **530** Kevin Vandivier/Viesti Associates, Inc.; **533** Stephen Dunn/Allsport; **535** Ferne Saltzman/Albuquerque International Balloon Fiesta; **537** Gordon & Cathy Illg/Animals Animals; **541** Daniel D. Lamoreux/Visuals Unlimited; **545** Gary A. Conner/PhotoEdit; **546** Chad Slattery/Tony Stone Images; **547** Yale University Library, Babylonian Collection (bl); Stock Montage (bc); courtesy, NASA (br); **548** Susan Van Etten/PhotoEdit; **550** Fugifotos/The Image Works; **552** Dave Bartruff/Stock Boston; **554** Roger Klocek/Visuals Unlimited; **555** Kevin Schafer/Peter Arnold, Inc.; **556** Jonathan Nouros/PhotoEdit; **570** Christopher M. Schnurr; **571** RMIP/Richard Haynes (background); David Pollack/The Stock Market (inset); **572, 573** David Parker/Science Photo Library/Photo Researchers, Inc.; **576** Spencer Grant/PhotoEdit; **578** Elizabeth Tustian; **581** Rathe/Stock Boston; **584** David Young-Wolff/Tony Stone Images; **590** CORBIS/Tom Brakefield; **592** Mark E. Gibson/The Stock Market; **594** Michael Schimpf; **596** Amy Reichman/Envision (cr); Fred Hultstrand History in Picture Collection, NDSU, Fargo, N.D. (bl); CORBIS/Bettmann (bc); reproduced with permission from the Sweden Post (br); **597** Randy Wells/Tony Stone Images; **601** Allen E. Morton/Visuals Unlimited; **604** Orion Press/Tony Stone Images; **606** Rachel Epstein/PhotoEdit; **608** Richard Vogel/Liaison Agency; **611** CORBIS/Charles & Josette Lenars; **615** Vandystadt/Allsport; **619** Rob Tringali Jr./Sportschrome;

621 Tony Freeman/PhotoEdit; **623** Darren Carroll/Duomo (cr); Mike Powell/Allsport (bl); **625** courtesy, NASA; **630** Account Phototake/Phototake; **640, 641** CORBIS/Phillip Gould; **643** Cordelia Williams; **645** Louis Mazzatenta/National Geographic Image Collection; **647** Cordelia Williams (tr); Don Hamerman/New England Stock Photo (bl); **649** David Young-Wolff/PhotoEdit; **651** Burke/Triolo/Artville; **654** David Young-Wolff/PhotoEdit; **656** Karl Weatherly/Allstock/PNI; **660** Superstock; **662** CORBIS/Bettmann (bl); Artville, LLC. (bcl); CORBIS/Joseph Sohm/ChromoSohm Inc. (bcr); School Division/Houghton Mifflin Company (br); **664** Jonathan Blair/Woodfin Camp and Associates; **668** Bill Bachman/Photo Researchers, Inc.; **674** Tony Page/Tony Stone Images; **676** Ron Dorsey/Stock Boston; **680** Joseph Pobereskin/Tony Stone Images; **684** David Young-Wolff/PhotoEdit; **688** Frank Siteman/Stock Boston; **690** C.J. Allen/Stock Boston; **691** CORBIS/Neal Preston; **695** CORBIS/Keren Su (l); RMIP/Richard Haynes (cr); **706, 707** Rex A. Butcher/Tony Stone Images; **709** Louis Mazzatenta/National Geographic Image Collection; **711** Peter Menzel/Tony Stone Images; **713** Tony Freeman/PhotoEdit; **716** Chuck Fishman/Woodfin Camp and Associates; **720** John Bova/Photo Researchers, Inc.; **721** RMIP/Richard Haynes; **722** Art Montes De Oca/FPG International; **726** Jeff Persons/Stock Boston; **730** William Sallaz/Duomo; **733** Paolo Koch/Photo Researchers, Inc.; **735** Norbert Wu (all); **738** Elizabeth Tustian; **744** Rare Book and Manuscript Library, Columbia University. Cunieform, Plimpton 322 (cr, bl); SEF/Art Resource (bc); CORBIS/Joseph Sohm/Chromosohm Inc. (br); **745** Doug Pensinger/Allsport; **749** Bob Daemmrich/PNI/PictureQuest; **752** John Neubauer/PhotoEdit; **758** John Neubauer/PhotoEdit; **760** Dennis MacDonald/PhotoEdit; **775** RMIP/Richard Haynes (tl, br); CORBIS/Jim Winkley/Ecoscene (tr); CORBIS/Peter Harholdt (cr).

Illustration

Steve Cowden **658, 718, 735, 746**
Laurie O'Keefe **162, 236, 415, 537, 567**
School Division, Houghton Mifflin Company **397, 413, 501, 513, 515, 522, 550, 552, 556, 571, 581, 586, 592, 594, 606, 608, 616, 630, 641, 662, 668, 675, 678, 747, 754, 756**
Doug Stevens **357, 419, 543, 599, 573, 601, 613, 724**

Selected Answers

CHAPTER 1

SKILL REVIEW (p. 2) **1.** $0.6, \frac{3}{5}$ **2.** $0.33, \frac{33}{100}$

3. $0.0008, \frac{1}{1250}$ **4.** $1.5, 1\frac{1}{2}$ **5.** $<$ **6.** $>$ **7.** $>$ **8.** $>$
9. $12.25\ \text{cm}^2$, 14 cm **10.** $6\ \text{ft}^2$, 12 ft **11.** $8.32\ \text{mi}^2$, 13.6 mi

1.1 PRACTICE (pp. 6–8) **5.** 30 **7.** 25 **9.** 2 **11.** 15

13. 3 h; $\frac{\text{mi}}{\text{mi/h}} = \text{mi} \cdot \frac{\text{h}}{\text{mi}} = \text{h}$ **15.** 138 mi; $\frac{\text{mi}}{\text{h}} \cdot \text{h} = \text{mi}$

17. time $= \frac{\text{distance}}{\text{rate}}$; time $= t$ h, distance $= 10$ mi,

rate $= 1.25$ mi/h; $t = \frac{10}{1.25}$; 8 h **19.** 60 **21.** 0.25 **23.** 82

25. 2.1 **27.** 5 **29.** $\frac{7}{16}$ **31.** $2.40 **33.** She did not use the
correct decimal equivalent of 2.5%, 0.025.

35. $1\frac{4}{11}$ mi/min ≈ 1.36 mi/min **37.** $\frac{2}{15}$ km/min ≈ 0.13
km/min **39.** 3 h **41.** 4.3 cal/min **43.** Distances are given
to the nearest foot. Mt. McKinley: 20,322 ft and 8707 ft;
Mt. Elbrus: 18,481 ft and 10,548 ft; Mt. Kilimanjaro:
19,564 and 9465 ft; Mt. Aconcagua: 22,831 ft and 6198 ft

1.1 MIXED REVIEW (p. 8) **51.** $\frac{3}{10}$ **53.** $2\frac{3}{4}$ **55.** 4 **57.** $10\frac{1}{10}$
59. $70\ \text{in.}^2$ **61.** 4 **63.** 6 **65.** 8 **67.** 10

1.2 PRACTICE (pp. 12–14) **5.** D **7.** A **9.** 64 **11.** 216
13. 125 **15.** 1000 **17.** 2^3 **19.** 9^y **21.** $3^4 y$ **23.** c^6
25. $(4x)^3$ **27.** 25 **29.** 1296 **31.** 2401 **33.** 729 **35.** 1024
37. 1,000,000 **39.** 2197 **41.** 64 **43.** 16 **45.** 100
47. 59,049 **49.** 1,953,125 **51.** 262,144 **53.** 1,679,616
55. 15,625 **57.** 343 **59.** 4096 **61.** 1, 4, 9, 16, 25
63. $148.84\ \text{ft}^2$ **65.** $1728\ \text{in.}^3$ **67.** about $1,333,333\ \text{ft}^3$

1.2 MIXED REVIEW (p. 14) **73.** 10.2 **75.** 0.625, 62.5%
77. 0.55, 55% **79.** 21 **81.** 4 **83.** $2\frac{1}{4}$

TECHNOLOGY ACTIVITY 1.2 (p. 15)
1. 33,554,432; 1.13×10^{15}; 3.78×10^{22}; 1.27×10^{30}
3. 16; 64; 256; 1024; 4096 **5.** 36; 1296; 46,656;
1,679,616; 60,466,176

1.3 PRACTICE (pp. 19–21) **5.** 150 **7.** 2 **9.** 0 **11.** 3 **13.** 19
15. 300 **17.** 34 **19.** 18 **21.** 17 **23.** 12 **25.** 16 **27.** 8
29. 11 **31.** 27 **33.** 27 **35.** 27 **37.** 0.125 **39.** 3
43. Calculator B; $15 - [(6 \div 3) \times 4]$ **45.** Calculator A;
$15 + (10 \div 5) + 4$ **47.** $(2 \times $49.99) + (3 \times $44.10)$
49. $28,475 **51.** $30 **53.** $2\pi rh + 2\pi r^2$ or $2\pi r(h + r)$

1.3 MIXED REVIEW (p. 22) **59.** 8 **61.** $\frac{2}{9}$ **63.** $-\frac{1}{16}$ **65.** 108
67. 1280 **69.** 6144 **71.** $2\frac{1}{2}$ h

QUIZ 1 (p. 22) **1.** 18 **2.** 12 **3.** 32 **4.** 1 **5.** 1 **6.** 18 **7.** 13.5
8. 16.7 **9.** 40 mi/h **10.** 60 mi/h **11.** 60 mi/h **12.** 6^3
13. 4^5 **14.** $(5y)^3$ **15.** 5^2 **16.** $3^6 \cdot t$ **17.** $(7x)^2$ **18.** 7776
19. 432 **20.** 1728 **21.** 33 **22.** $1\frac{2}{7}$ **23.** $\frac{1}{2}$ **24.** $\frac{1}{3}$ **25.** 2
26. $1.728\ \text{ft}^3$

1.4 PRACTICE (pp. 27–29) **9.** B **11.** C **13.** B
15. not a solution **17.** solution **19.** not a solution
21. not a solution **23.** solution **25.** not a solution
27. What number can be added to 6 to get 11? 5
29. What number can be multiplied by 3 to get 12? 4
31. What number can be multiplied by 4 to get 36? 9
33. One less than two times what number is 9? 5
35. What number when divided by 7 gives 3? 21
37. What number cubed gives 125? 5 **39.** solution
41. not a solution **43.** not a solution **45.** not a solution
47. solution **49.** solution **51.** solution **53.** solution
55. not a solution **57.** G **59.** H **61.** B **63.** A
65. the number of ft^2 per station, the number of stations, the
total number of ft^2 available; 20 stations **67.** cost each
time you fill the tank, number of times you fill the tank,
total amount to be paid for gas; yes **69.** 400 m/min
71. 5 h **73.** 0°C **75.** 8 ft **77. a.** The length of the jet is
1.212 times the wingspan. **b.** It is longer than it is wide;
since $y > 0$, $1.212y > y$.

1.4 MIXED REVIEW (p. 30) **85.** $\frac{1}{4}$ **87.** $\frac{4}{25}$ **89.** y^2 **91.** c^4
93. $(5y)^4$ **95.** $(9a)^6$ **97.** 1^3 **99.** t^6

1.5 PRACTICE (pp. 35–38) **5.** C **7.** B **9.** $x + 10 = 24$
11. $\frac{20}{n} \leq 2$ **13.** $x + 9$ **15.** $\frac{1}{2}x + 3$ **17.** $\frac{x}{0.2}$ **19.** $\frac{2^3}{x}$
21. $5^2 - x$ **23.** $9 > 3s$ **25.** $14x = 1$ **27.** $3(x - 2) = 10$
29. $(38 - n) - 23 < 8$ **31.** $(20 - x) - 5 \geq 10$
33. $9 + \frac{b}{10} \geq 11$ **35.** $q \geq 100$ **37.** $\frac{35}{t} \leq 7$ **39.** $b = e - 1.50$
41. $c = 3r + 229$ **43.** $V \leq 30 - 3$ or $s^3 \leq 30 - 3$
45. $P = 4(s - 2)$ **47.** $A = \frac{1}{2}(7 + 9)(h + 7)$
49. The number of subscriptions times the cost of each
subscription equals the amount the club needs to raise.
51. 21 **53.** $21 \cdot 15 = 315$; the answer is reasonable.
55. $20m = 260$ **57.** $\frac{\text{dollars}}{\text{mi/h}} \cdot \text{mi/h} = \text{dollars}$
59. The number of weeks times the total of $20 plus the
additional amount saved per week equals the total saved; let
$x =$ the additional amount saved per week; $12(x + 20) = 480$.
61. Let $x =$ the total number of points the team must equal
or exceed; $x \geq 18\left(\frac{544}{17} + 5\right)$.

1.5 MIXED REVIEW (p. 38) **67.** = **69.** > **71.** <

73.

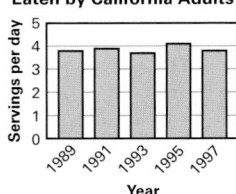
Fruits and Vegetables
Eaten by California Adults

75. 10 **77.** 360

QUIZ 2 (p. 39) **1.** $2\frac{3}{4}$ **2.** 21 **3.** 34 **4.** 12 **5.** 42 **6.** 54
7. not a solution **8.** solution **9.** solution **10.** not a solution
11. solution **12.** not a solution **13.** Let x = the total cost of
the pizza; $\frac{1}{4}x = 2.65$; $10.60.

1.6 PRACTICE (pp. 43–45) **5.** true **7.** false **9.** false

11.

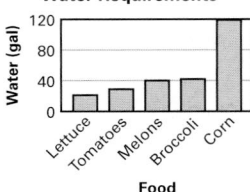
Water Requirements

13. paper; about 33 million tons **15.** 6 years **17.** 1991

19.

Passenger Car Fuel Efficiency

1.6 MIXED REVIEW (p. 45) **23.** not a solution **25.** solution
27. $12 = \frac{n}{3}$

1.7 PRACTICE (pp. 49–51)
7. 44.5; 89; 133.5; 178; 222.5; 267

9.

Daytona 500
Fastest Winning Speed

13. Output: 2, 5, 8, 11
15. Output: 0, 5, 10, 15
17. Output: 1, 3, 5, 7
19. Output: 6.5, 8.5, 14.5, 20.5,
26.5 **21.** Output: 19, 16, 13, 12,
11.5 **23.** Output: 0.5, 1.75, 8.5,
19.75, 35.5 **25.** 360 · 2, 720;
360 · 3, 1080; 360 · 4, 1440;
360 · 5; 1800

27.

Temperature

29. domain: 0, 5, 10, 15, 20, 25,
30, 35, 40; range: 32, 41, 50, 59,
68, 77, 86, 95, 104
31. domain: 1, 2, 3, 4, 5, 6, 7;
range: 6.25, 7.50, 8.75, 10.00,
11.25, 12.50, 13.75

33. $C = 0.375n$ **35.** Input values represent the number of
posters; corresponding output numbers represent the cost
of the posters. **37.** Let n = the number of days and a = the
amount in dollars that you earn; $a = 2n + 5$.

1.7 MIXED REVIEW (p. 52) **45.** x^6 **47.** y^7 **49.** 6
51. 219 **53.** solution **55.** solution **57.** not a solution
59. $250 million

QUIZ 3 (p. 52)
1.

Arts Activity Attendance

2. Conclusions may include the following:
• Nearly half of all 18-to-24-year-olds attended a historic
park.
• More of the 18-to-24-year-olds attended a musical play
than attended a non-musical play.
• The events in increasing order of popularity are jazz,
non-musical play, musical play, art museum, historic
park.
• More than three times as many 18-to-24-year-olds
attended a historic park as attended a jazz event.
• About twice as many 18-to-24-year-olds attended an
art museum as attended a non-musical play.
3. B **4.** Let t = the number of minutes after you turn on the
heat and a = your altitude; $a = 25t + 200$. **5.** Input: 0, 1, 2,
3, 4, 5, 6; Output: 200, 225, 250, 275, 300, 325, 350

CHAPTER 1 REVIEW (pp. 54–56) **1.** 37 **3.** 10 **5.** 10 **7.** 2 h
9. 3125 **11.** 33 **13.** 15,625 **15.** 9 **17.** 1.5 **19.** solution
21. solution **23.** *Sample answer:* The women have won
41 Wimbledon titles, while the men have won 30, so the
women have won 11 more Wimbledon titles than the men
have won.

25.

Percent of Voting-Age
Population That Voted
in Yearly Municipal
Referendum, 1976–1996

27. Perimeter = Length +
Width + Length + Width;
$P = 10w$

29. domain = 1, 2, 3, 4, 5; range = 10, 20, 30, 40, 50

CHAPTER 2

SKILL REVIEW (p. 62) **1.** 4.07, 4.6, 5.06, 5.46, 5.5, 6.1
2. $\frac{25}{11}, 2\frac{3}{5}, 2\frac{5}{8}, 2\frac{2}{3}, \frac{11}{4}, 2\frac{5}{6}$ **3.** $\frac{3}{14}$ **4.** $1\frac{1}{2}$ **5.** $3\frac{7}{8}$ **6.** $5\frac{2}{3}$

7. $2\frac{1}{2}$ 8. $\frac{1}{6}$ 9. 28 10. $6\frac{2}{3}$ 11. 5 12. 2 13. 19 14. 1
15. 0 16. 11

2.1 PRACTICE (pp. 67–70) 5. < 7. <

9.
−4, 2, 3

11.
−1.1, −1, −0.1

13. 4.1 15. 103 17. negative

19.
−6.4 < −6.3, −6.3 > −6.4

23.
−2.8 < 3.7, 3.7 > −2.8

25.
$-0.5 < -\frac{1}{3}, -\frac{1}{3} > -0.5$

27. −1.8, −0.66, 0.7, 3, 4.6, 4.66 29. $-3, -2.6, -\frac{1}{2}, 0, \frac{1}{2}, 4.8$

31. $-5.8, -\frac{3}{4}, -\frac{1}{2}, \frac{1}{3}, 2.4, 7$ 33. −8 35. −3.8 37. $\frac{5}{6}$

39. 2.01 41. 7 43. 4.5 45. $\frac{4}{5}$ 47. 4.3 49. 0.09 51. 0

53. −1, 1 55. False; 0 and all negative numbers are counterexamples. 57. False; all real numbers except 0 are counterexamples. 59. ≥ 61. ≤ 63. −8 65. 0 67. Regulus
69. Canopus, Vega, Sirius, and Arcturus 71. Kobayashi
73. Bemvenuti, Early, Kobayashi, Scranton 75. Sörenstam
77. 429 ft/min, 429 ft/min 79. 10°F, 25 mi/h
81. 10°F, 20 mi/h

2.1 MIXED REVIEW (p. 70) 89. $\frac{5}{6}$ 91. $\frac{23}{24}$ 93. $6\frac{13}{63}$ 95. 5

97. 53 99. $\frac{4}{5}$ 101. $r + 8 = 17$

2.2 PRACTICE (pp. 75–77) 5. −2 7. −5 9. 5 11. 118°F
13. −3 15. −10 17. −6 19. −4 21. 2 23. 19 25. −19
27. 2 29. −8.2 31. 6 33. identity property of addition
35. property of zero 37. −85.79 39. 126.04 41. 5304.128
43. −1 45. −10 47. 3 49. −24 51. no; 9 + (−5) + 4 + 5 = 13 53. F atom 1: 0, not an ion; F atom 2: −1, ion; F atom 2 55. No; the sum of the losses is greater than the sum of the profits by $1011.01. 57. 10:00 A.M.

2.2 MIXED REVIEW (p. 77) 63. $\frac{2}{9}$ 65. $\frac{5}{8}$ 67. $\frac{13}{18}$ 69. $\frac{11}{48}$
71. 15 73. 37 75. no 77. yes 79. yes 81. domain = 1, 2, 3, 4, 5; range = 6.85, 7.70, 8.55, 9.40, 10.25

2.3 PRACTICE (pp. 82–84) 5. 3 + 8; 11 7. 2 + 3 + (−6); −1
9. −3.6 + 6; 2.4 11. $\frac{2}{3} + \frac{1}{6} + \left(-\frac{1}{3}\right)$; $\frac{1}{2}$ 13. $-7y^2, 12y,$ and -6

15.

Input	Function	Output
−2	y = −(−2) − 3	−1
−1	y = −(−1) − 3	−2
0	y = −0 − 3	−3
1	y = −1 − 3	−4
2	y = −2 − 3	−5

Each time x increases by 1, y decreases by 1.

17. −7 19. 5 21. −15 23. −6 25. −4.9 27. 9.5 29. 3
31. $-1\frac{3}{20}$ 33. 9 35. −23.1 37. 3 39. 2 41. −28 43. 23
45. −8 47. −28.6 49. $-1\frac{17}{18}$ 51. −4 and −y 53. −3x and 6
55. −9 and 4b 57. x, −y, and −7

59.

Input	Function	Output
−2	y = −2 − 8	−10
−1	y = −1 − 8	−9
0	y = 0 − 8	−8
1	y = 1 − 8	−7

61.

Input	Function	Output
−2	y = −(−2) + 12.1	14.1
−1	y = −(−1) + 12.1	13.1
0	y = −0 + 12.1	12.1
1	y = −1 + 12.1	11.1

63.

Input	Function	Output
−2	y = 27 + (−2)	25
−1	y = 27 + (−1)	26
0	y = 27 + 0	27
1	y = 27 + 1	28

65. 3.1 67. 1.54 69. 5.8 71. 275 ft; up 73. −$.66/oz
75. −$.19/oz 77. from start of trail to cave: 410 ft; from cave to Oak Ridge: 1040 ft; from Oak Ridge to trail junction: −235 ft; from trail junction to Mt. Parker: 1110 ft
79. −7301 ft, −662 ft, −1883 ft, 77 ft, −1311 ft, 8021 ft

2.3 MIXED REVIEW (p. 85) 85. $5\frac{2}{3}$ 87. 16 89. 88 91. $1\frac{1}{2}$
93. false 95. Yes; the sum of the profits, $7932.18, exceeds the sum of the losses, $6934.36, by $997.82.

QUIZ 1 (p. 85) 1. −6.2, −5.32, 5.04, 5.3, 5.31, 6.3
2. −1.6, −1.07, −0.28, 0.18, 1.06, 1.16 3. $-7.5, -7\frac{1}{3}, 7.3,$ $7\frac{1}{3}, 7.5, 7\frac{2}{3}$ 4. $-\frac{33}{5}, -6\frac{2}{5}, -6.3, 6.05, 6.42, \frac{33}{5}$ 5. 3.76
6. 75 7. −345 8. 27.5 9. 7 10. 67.4 11. 24 12. −472
13. −3 14. −1 15. −14 16. 54 17. 3.8 18. −91 19. −0.4
20. 47.3 + (−2.1) + (−11.3) + 12.9; 46.8 in.

2.4 PRACTICE (pp. 89–90)

5. $\begin{bmatrix} -1 & -4 \\ -5 & 1 \\ 0 & 5 \end{bmatrix}; \begin{bmatrix} -5 & 4 \\ -7 & 7 \\ 2 & -13 \end{bmatrix}$ 7. yes 9. no 11. $\begin{bmatrix} 7 & -5 \\ -3 & -1 \end{bmatrix}$

13. $\begin{bmatrix} 4 & -6 & 7 \\ -8 & -2 & 10 \end{bmatrix}$ 15. $\begin{bmatrix} 7.7 & 8 \\ 4.1 & -6.6 \\ 9.1 & -12.9 \end{bmatrix}$ 17. $\begin{bmatrix} 1 & -10 \\ 6 & 4 \end{bmatrix}$

19. $\begin{bmatrix} 2 & -2 \\ 5 & -21 \\ 0 & -1 \end{bmatrix}$ 21. −4, −1, 7, −3 23.

	Sale	Reg.
CD	52	3300
Tape	28	1600

$$25. \begin{bmatrix} 76 & 59 \\ 50 & 46 \\ 97 & 66 \end{bmatrix} \quad 27. \begin{bmatrix} 0.20 & 0.20 & 0.20 \\ 0.35 & 0.35 & 0.35 \\ 0.45 & 0.45 & 0.45 \end{bmatrix}$$

2.4 MIXED REVIEW (p. 91) **33.** 5^2 **35.** $x^2 y^3$ **37.** $3t^4$
39. -43.7 **41.** 36 **43.** 15 **45.** -21 **47.** -3 **49.** -14 **51.** -3

TECHNOLOGY ACTIVITY 2.4 (p. 92)

$$1. \begin{bmatrix} 7 & -6 \\ 6 & -3 \\ -10 & -14 \end{bmatrix}; \begin{bmatrix} 7 & -4 \\ 4 & -3 \\ -8 & -2 \end{bmatrix} \quad 3. \begin{bmatrix} 10.7 & -1.9 \\ -3.8 & -1.9 \\ 1.7 & -11.1 \\ 7.2 & -8.4 \\ -4.4 & 13.2 \end{bmatrix}; \begin{bmatrix} 4.1 & -8.3 \\ 2.6 & -7.3 \\ 18.1 & -7.7 \\ -3 & 1.2 \\ 3.4 & 1 \end{bmatrix}$$

2.5 PRACTICE (pp. 96–98) **5.** -8 **7.** 35 **9.** 72 **11.** 70
13. 48 **15.** -47 ft **17.** -16 **19.** 5 **21.** $-\frac{11}{8}$ **23.** 24
25. 78 **27.** 12 **29.** 8 **31.** $-7x$ **33.** $-4x^3$ **35.** $-16y$
37. $-y^5$ **39.** x **41.** $3w^3$ **43.** -12 **45.** 21 **47.** -20
49. 76 **51.** -70.70 **53.** 1809.86 **55.** -89.04 **57.** 14.8
59. False; any nonpositive number a is a counterexample.
61. The total amount lost is the loss per pound times the
number of pounds of bananas sold. **63.** $248.56
65. $-$125; $50 **67.** 940,000 visitors **69.** $\begin{bmatrix} -42 & 28 & -21 \\ 7 & -28 & 63 \end{bmatrix}$
71. Sample answers are given. **a.** $\frac{1}{3}(x)(-24)$ **b.** $-\frac{1}{6}(x) + 3.5x$

2.5 MIXED REVIEW (p. 98) **77.** 10 **79.** 32 **81.** 11, -11
83.

$-4 < 9, 9 > -4$

85.

$-3.8 > -4.0, -4.0 < -3.8$

89. $-t$ and 5 **91.** 31 and $-15n$ **93.** m, $-2n$, and $-t^2$
95. y, 6, and $-8x$ **97.** $-$11.9 billion

2.6 PRACTICE (pp. 103–105) **5.** $5w - 40$ **7.** $12y - xy$
9. $-\frac{5}{6}b + 5$ **11.** 6.9 **13.** simplified **15.** simplified
17. $8t^2 + 3t - 4$ **19.** false; $3(2) + 3(7)$ **21.** true
23. true **25.** $3x + 12$ **27.** $5y - 10$ **29.** $-y + 9$
31. $-4t + 32$ **33.** $x^2 + x$ **35.** $-r^2 + 9r$ **37.** $6x - 2$
39. $-6x + 12$ **41.** $4x^2 + 32x$ **43.** $15y^2 - 10y$ **45.** $9t + 27$
47. $\frac{5}{2}x - \frac{10}{3}$ **49.** $11x$ **51.** $-17b$ **53.** $y + 4$ **55.** $-0.8t$
57. $-101a$ **59.** $5x^3 - 2$ **61.** $-5y - 2$ **63.** $10s + 14$
65. $4x - 3x^2$ **67.** $9t^2 - 15t$ **69.** $2w^2 + 3w$ **71.** no
73. 16,098 tons **75.** $T = 5000 + 0.02s + 0.06(5000 - s)$;
$T = 5300 - 0.04s$ **77.** $w = 45b + 240$ **79.** $4x - 14$
81. $(x + 5)11 = 11x + 55$; $11x + 55$
83. $T = 0.10C + 0.5(0.10C)$ **85.** Yes; the simplified version
of your friend's equation is identical to your equation.
87. $3150 **89.** no

2.6 MIXED REVIEW (p. 106) **95.** $\frac{11}{6}$ **97.** 1 **99.** $\frac{1}{435}$
101. $\frac{8}{27}$ **103.** 1 **105.** 3 **107.** 5 **109.** -7 **111.** -6 **113.** 8.8

QUIZ 2 (p. 107)
$$1. \begin{bmatrix} 5 & -13 \\ -4 & 9 \\ -9 & -8 \end{bmatrix}; \begin{bmatrix} -1 & 1 \\ -6 & 1 \\ -5 & 8 \end{bmatrix} \quad 2. -63 \quad 3. -21 \quad 4. 14$$
5. -2800 **6.** -3 **7.** 10.8 **8.** 110 **9.** 270 **10.** $7.1t$
11. $-13x$ **12.** $-10b^3$ **13.** $-\frac{1}{2}x^4$ **14.** $-43x$ **15.** $2y$
16. $-8t$ **17.** $-24 + 3b$ **18.** $20y + 10$

19.
	ft	m
Sears Tower	1454	443
Empire State Building	1250	381
Aon Center	1136	346

2.7 PRACTICE (pp. 111–112) **7.** $-\frac{1}{8}$ **9.** $-\frac{5}{11}$ **11.** -50
13. -72 **15.** $-$.17 **17.** -5 **19.** -7 **21.** -11 **23.** $-\frac{1}{3}$
25. $-21\frac{7}{9}$ **27.** $-43\frac{1}{5}$ **29.** -7 **31.** 145 **33.** $-12t$
35. $-\frac{x}{36}$ **37.** $\frac{3y}{2}$ **39.** $121x$ **41.** $-10x^2$ **43.** $30x^2$ **45.** x
47. $-2w$ **49.** $-11x - 5$ **51.** $9 - x$ **53.** 4 **55.** $217\frac{1}{2}$ **57.** 24
59. all real numbers except 2 **61.** all real numbers except 0
63. -2.5 ft/sec **65.** $100x$; $1000x$; 10,000x; 100,000x
67. 10,000,000x **69.** -11 ft/sec

2.7 MIXED REVIEW (p. 113) **75.** 0.75 **77.** 0.1 **79.** 0.17
81. 0.75 **83.** 147 **85.** -250 **87.** 20,736 **89.** 0.45 **91.** -27
93. 15 **95.** 12 **97.** -1 **99.** -8

2.8 PRACTICE (pp. 117–119)
5. Unlikely; the probability is 0.25. **7.** 0.2 **9.** 0.25
11. 0.65 **13.** 4 to 7 **15.** 1 to 3 **17.** 1 to 3 **19.** 0.5
21. a. 0.6 **b.** 3 to 2 **23.** 0.45 **25.** 690 to 298, or about 7 to 3
27. 1 to 19 **29.** $\frac{253}{1310} \approx 0.19$ **31.** 1 to 3

2.8 MIXED REVIEW (p. 120) **39.** 8 **41.** $5\frac{1}{2}$ **43.** 120
45. $z - 17 = 9$ **47.** $-3 = y + (-6)$ **49.** -13 **51.** -5
53. -11.7 **55.** -17.4 **57.** $-4\frac{1}{8}$

QUIZ 3 (p. 120) **1.** -49 **2.** 54 **3.** 128 **4.** -4 **5.** -5 **6.** -16
7. -320 **8.** $\frac{1}{3}$ **9.** $-7x$ **10.** $\frac{7}{x}$ **11.** $18x$ **12.** $5x$ **13.** $35x$
14. $-20t$ **15.** $-55y$ **16.** $\frac{x}{36}$ **17.** 0.32 **18.** Unlikely; the
probability is less than 0.25. **19.** Certain; the definition
of a certain event is an event with probability 1.
20. Unlikely; the probability is $\frac{1}{30,001}$, which is very
small but not equal to 0. **21.** Quite likely; the probability
is about 0.7.

CHAPTER 2 REVIEW (pp. 122–124)

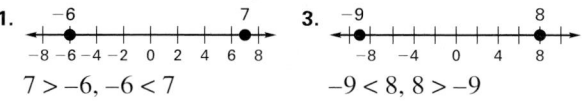

1.

$7 > -6, -6 < 7$

3.

$-9 < 8, 8 > -9$

5.

$13.9 > -14.9, -14.9 < 13.9$

7. 5 **9.** -0.7 **11.** -12 **13.** -1 **15.** -17 **17.** $-4\frac{1}{16}$

19. $\begin{bmatrix} 1 & -4 \\ 1 & 9 \end{bmatrix}$; $\begin{bmatrix} -7 & 0 \\ 15 & -1 \end{bmatrix}$ **21.** -36 **23.** 600 **25.** $-3\frac{7}{9}$

27. 49.5 **29.** -84 **31.** 14 **33.** $5x + 60$ **35.** $5.5b - 55$
37. $-3t - 33$ **39.** $-2.5z + 12.5$ **41.** -4 **43.** -3 **45.** -50
47. -64 **49.** 0.25, 1 to 3 **51.** 0.1, 1 to 9

CHAPTER 3

SKILL REVIEW (p. 130) **1.** 71.5 **2.** 29.315 **3.** 15 **4.** 2.52
5. no **6.** yes **7.** yes **8.** $12r + 18$ **9.** $-18 + 30z$
10. $3x - 21$ **11.** $-9 + 3x$ **12.** $3a + 2$ **13.** $1 + 4y$

3.1 PRACTICE (pp. 135–137) **5.** 13 **7.** 3 **9.** 3
11. Add 4.65 to both sides. **13.** Subtract 28. **15.** Add 15.
17. Subtract -3 (or add 3). **19.** Add -45 (or subtract 45).
21. -3 **23.** 8 **25.** -11 **27.** 10 **29.** $-\frac{3}{4}$ **31.** 5 **33.** 6
35. 29 **37.** -6 **39.** -16 **41.** -9 **43.** B; 8 members
45–49 odd: Sample equations are given. **45.** $x + 7 = 24$; \$17
47. $43,368 + x = 49,831$; 6463 seats **49.** $x - 732 = 645$;
1377 min **51.** 20 cm **53.** $c + 248 = 4218 + 3800 + 2764$;
10,534 acres

3.1 MIXED REVIEW (p. 137) **57.** $\frac{n}{6} = 32$ **59.** $\frac{2}{3}n = 8$ **61.** y
63. x **65.** y **67.** $-a$ **69.** $21 - 14y$ **71.** $-6x - 16$
73. $-5xy - 15x$ **75.** $18xy + 54y^2$

3.2 PRACTICE (pp. 141–144) **5.** 32 **7.** -12 **9.** $-\frac{5}{3}$ **11.** 5
13. Sample equation: $\frac{x}{3} = \frac{4}{6}$; 2 **15.** Divide by -2.
17. Divide by $\frac{2}{3}$ (or multiply by $\frac{3}{2}$). **19.** Multiply by $-\frac{4}{3}$.
21. no **23.** no **25.** -2 **27.** $\frac{1}{6}$ **29.** 18 **31.** $\frac{3}{8}$ **33.** 84
35. -40 **37.** 3 **39.** -90 **41.** -1 **43.** $-7\frac{1}{3}$ **45.** 20 **47.** $4\frac{1}{2}$
49–53 odd: Sample equations are given. **49.** $52x = 676$;
13 pieces **51.** $\frac{3}{8}x = 3.3$; \$8.80 **53.** $30,000x = 10,000$; $\frac{1}{3}$ ft^2
57. a. 12 min **b.** 36 sec **59.** $\frac{x}{12} = \frac{4}{8}$; 6 in. **61.** $\frac{5}{4} = \frac{x}{1}$; $1\frac{1}{4}$ c

3.2 MIXED REVIEW (p. 144) **67.** $9n - 12 = 60$
69. $11 = \frac{2}{5}(n - 13)$ **71.** $7y - 9$ **73.** $12y + 15$ **75.** $-19y + 54$
77. 3 **79.** 30 **81.** 7

3.3 PRACTICE (pp. 148–151) **3.** 2 **5.** 13 **7.** 10 **9.** 6 errands
11. yes **13.** no **15.** no **17.** 3 **19.** 14 **21.** 4 **23.** 12
25. 2 **27.** 1 **29.** 8 **31.** 3 **33.** 3 **35.** 8 **37.** -13 **39.** 2
41. The distributive property was applied incorrectly;
$2(x - 3) = 2x - 6$; $5\frac{1}{2}$. **43.** The left side was simplified
incorrectly; $4\left(\frac{1}{4}x - 2\right) = x - 8$; 36.

47, 49. Preferences may vary. **47.** -24 **49.** -1
51. 21, 33, and 69 **53.** Sample equation: $34x + 339 = 458$;
3.5 h **55.** 125 students **57.** 48 pounds per square inch
59. Let t = time to complete; $1800t + 2400t = 8400$; 2 h
61. Sample equation: $15x + 20x = 910$; 26 h
63. Sample equation: $25q + 10(q - 4) + 5(2q) = 500$;
12 quarters, 24 nickels, and 8 dimes

3.3 MIXED REVIEW (p. 151) **67.** 4^2 **69.** a^6 **71.** 2^4
73. 10 **75.** 13.9 **77.** -22 **79.** $\frac{1}{2}$ **81.** -3 **83.** hamburgers:
\$134 income, \$24 expense; hot dogs: \$137 income,
\$29 expense; tacos: \$118 income, \$45 expense **85.** tacos

QUIZ 1 (p. 152) **1.** 17 **2.** $4\frac{1}{2}$ **3.** -2 **4.** $\frac{5}{8}$ **5.** 32 **6.** 3
7. -46 **8.** 12 **9.** -5 **10.** Sample equation: $x + 4 = 91$; 87
11. $22\frac{2}{9}°C$

3.4 PRACTICE (pp. 157–158) **5.** -7; one solution
7. no solution **9.** 5; one solution **11.** 10 pies **13.** 1
15. $\frac{1}{4}$ **17.** 1 **19.** -7 **21.** $-\frac{3}{32}$ **23.** $\frac{1}{4}$ **25.** 2 **27.** $\frac{1}{2}$ **29.** 1
31. all real numbers **33.** 4 **35.** $-\frac{1}{2}$ **37.** no solution **39.** 1
41. 1 **43.** Since $-6 = -6$, you can conclude that the given
equation is true for all real numbers, not that $b = -6$.
45. Sample equation: $3x + 25 = 5x$; 12.5 sessions; it is
worthwhile to become a member if you expect to attend
13 or more sessions. **47.** The possible number is $3\frac{1}{2}$ more
than the actual number, 50. **49.** about 12 ft

3.4 MIXED REVIEW (p. 159) **55.** 0.28 **57.** 0.03 **59.** 37.8
61. 410.4 **63.** \$74.28 **65.** dollars **67.** hours **69.** 6 cm

3.5 PRACTICE (pp. 163–165) **3.** rate your friend is driving =
52 (mi/h); time after you start driving = t (h); friend's
distance when you leave = 32 (mi); rate you are driving =
60 (mi/h); $52t + 32 = 60t$.
5. Sample answer:

Hours	Your distance (mi)	Friend's distance (mi)
1	60	84
2	120	136
3	180	188
4	240	240

7. C; 18 in. **9.** hours **11.** ft **13.** No; according to the graph
the solution is 5 weeks, not 25 weeks.
15. Let x = the width in inches of the photos; $2x + 2 = 6\frac{1}{2}$.
17. Sample equation: $45 + 3x = 108 - 4x$; in 9 years
19. $\frac{1}{2}$ mi; $x + \frac{1}{2}$

3.5 MIXED REVIEW (p. 165) **27.** 0.27; 27% **29.** 0.81; 81%
31. -25 **33.** -1.5 **35.** -27 **37.** $1\frac{3}{4}$ **39.** $-\frac{1}{2}$

3.6 PRACTICE (pp. 169–171) **5.** 23.4 **7.** −13.9 **9.** 6.82
11. 3.17 **13.** $33.38 **15.** 36.3; 36.26 **17.** 7.3; 7.32
19. 34.7; 34.70 **21.** 4.33 **23.** 5.78 **25.** 1.71 **27.** −2.88
29. 0.11 **31.** 0.14 **33.** 1.60 **35.** 12.17 **37.** 2.75 **39.** 0.31
41. $-625y - 184 = 2506y$ **43.** $4500n - 375 = 750n + 2000$
49. $7.29 **51.** 0.24, or 24% **53.** *Sample equation:*
$500 + 440x = 2975$; 6 min **55.** 9.75 h; the total number of
hours that you used your Internet service last month
57. $(t - 10)°C$, $0.37(t - 10)$ mm, $[16.8 - 0.37(t - 10)]$ mm

3.6 MIXED REVIEW (p. 172)

61.

Input	Output
2	13
3	15.5
4	18
5	20.5
6	23

domain: 2, 3, 4, 5, 6;
range: 13, 15.5, 18, 20.5, 23

63. 3 **65.** −7.9 **67.** $\frac{8}{15} \approx 0.533$ **69.** It increased by $85.25.
71. −$234.87

QUIZ 2 (p. 172) **1.** $\frac{1}{2}$ **2.** $3\frac{1}{4}$ **3.** no solution **4.** $1\frac{2}{5}$
5. no solution **6.** $\frac{1}{4}$ **7.** 0.45 **8.** 1.29 **9.** −0.10 **10.** 0.41
11. C **12.** 10 dogs

TECHNOLOGY ACTIVITY 3.6 (p. 173) **1.** 12.3 **3.** 5.3

3.7 PRACTICE (pp. 177–179) **9.** $y = 5 - x$ **11.** $b = \frac{2A}{h}$
13. $h = \frac{V}{\pi r^2}$ **15.** $y = 5 - 2x$ **17.** $y = 6x - \frac{13}{2}$
19. $y = -1.5x + 9$ **21.** $y = -10x + 35$ **23.** $y = \frac{3}{4}x - \frac{9}{4}$
25. $y = 12x - 2$ **27.** $y = x - \frac{9}{4}$ **29.** $y = \frac{1}{2}x + 1$
31. $x = 3y - 12$; −18, −15, −12, −9 **33.** $x = \frac{5}{2}y - 3$; −8,
$-5\frac{1}{2}$, −3, $-\frac{1}{2}$ **35. a.** 0.2; 20% **b.** 0.4; 40% **c.** 0.5; 50%
37. $d = \frac{P - 2112}{64}$ **39.** P is a function of d; P is the
isolated variable. **41.** $2\pi X$ **43.** The first and third columns
are identical.

3.7 MIXED REVIEW (p. 179) **51.** no **53.** $-8b$ **55.** $-3x^3$
57. $16t^2$ **59.** pro sports **61.** 31

3.8 PRACTICE (pp. 183–185) **5.** $213 **7.** $0.45(280) = x$; 126
9. $0.2x = 15$; 75 **11.** $.40/can **13.** about $.93/qt
15. 300 mi/h **17.** 0.05 mi/min **21.** 21,000,000 mi/wk
23. $1\frac{1}{2}$ c, or 1.5 c **25.** 90.1 km **27.** about 300 mi
29. *Sample equation:* $50 \cdot 47 = x$; about 2350 more books
31. $5 **33.** 16% **35.** 65% **37.** about 28.9% **39.** about
1013 people **41.** *Sample estimate:* about 350 students

3.8 MIXED REVIEW (p. 186)

49.

$4 > -3$; $-3 < 4$

51.

$-0.2 > -0.21$; $-0.21 < -0.2$

53.

$\frac{3}{4} > -\frac{5}{6}$; $-\frac{5}{6} < \frac{3}{4}$

55. −1.91 **57.** 1.47 **59.**

Projected Number of People 85 Years and Older

QUIZ 3 (p. 186) **1.** $y = -\frac{3}{2}x + 6$; 9, 6, 3 **2.** $y = 3x + 12$; 6,
12, 18 **3.** $y = -\frac{1}{5}x + 1\frac{3}{5}$; 2, $1\frac{3}{5}$, $1\frac{1}{5}$ **4.** $w = \frac{V}{\ell h}$ **5.** $h = \frac{2A}{b}$
6. $r = \frac{P}{C} - 1$ **7.** $93 **8.** 20 in. **9–12.** Equations may vary.
9. $33 \cdot 12 = x$; 396 mi **10.** $0.03x = 42$; 1400 students
11. $900 \cdot \frac{210}{525} = x$; about 360 people **12.** 40%

CHAPTER 3 EXTENSION (p. 188) **1.** Inductive reasoning;
a conclusion is reached based on observation of a pattern.
3. Deductive reasoning; a conclusion is reached because the
hypothesis is true. **5.** *Sample counterexample:* The square
of 1 is equal to itself. **7.** 21, 24, 27 **9.** hypothesis: "you are
in Minnesota in January"; conclusion: "you will be cold"

CHAPTER 3 REVIEW (pp. 190–192) **1.** 11 **3.** −60 **5.** −432
7. −12 **9.** 3 **11.** −8 **13.** −1 **15.** $\frac{15}{2}$ **17.** −2
19. all real numbers **21.** −15 **23.** $12\left(\frac{5}{12}\right) = x\left(\frac{1}{2}\right)$; 10 km/h
25. 2.6 **27.** 0.4 **29.** $r = \frac{S}{\pi s} - R$
31. $y = -\frac{3}{4}x + \frac{7}{2}$; 5, $\frac{7}{2}$, $2\frac{3}{4}$, $-\frac{1}{4}$ **33.** $200

CUMULATIVE PRACTICE (pp. 196–197) **1.** 14 **3.** 81 **5.** 1.01
7. −3 **9.** 2 **11.** −20 **13.** 4 **15.** $\frac{5}{6}$ **17.** yes **19.** yes **21.** yes
23. $4n + 17$ **25.** $-3n > 12$ **27.** $\begin{bmatrix} 5 & 4 \\ -6 & -5 \end{bmatrix}$
29. $\begin{bmatrix} 26 & 14 & -6 \\ -54 & -3 & 35 \end{bmatrix}$ **31.** $\frac{2}{11} \approx 0.18$ **33.** $\frac{1}{6} \approx 0.17$ **35.** 8
37. 15 **39.** 16 **41.** −19 **43.** $-1\frac{4}{11}$ **45.** −2.30 **47.** 1.51
49. $x = \frac{3}{2}y - \frac{1}{2}$; $-3\frac{1}{2}$, $-\frac{1}{2}$, $1\frac{3}{4}$, 4 **51.** $27\frac{7}{9}°C$ **53.** 300 rolls
55. 3639 kronor **57.** 4852 kronor

CHAPTER 4

SKILL REVIEW (p. 202) **1.** $0.5, \frac{1}{2}$ **2.** $0.75, \frac{3}{4}$ **3.** $0.01, \frac{1}{100}$

4. $0.2, \frac{1}{5}$ **5–7.** Sample answers are given.

5.

x	y
0	70
1	75
2	80
5	95
10	120

6.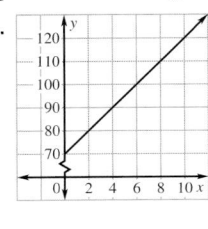

7. domain: $x \geq 0$; range: $y \geq 70$ **8.** -1 **9.** 2

4.1 PRACTICE (pp. 206–208) **3.** $A(1, 1), B(-2, 1), C(0, -2)$

5.   **7.**

9. *Sample answer:* Yes; The amount spent on snowmobiles increased but not rapidly. **11.** $A(2, 4), B(0, -1), C(-1, 0), D(-2, -1)$

13.   **17.**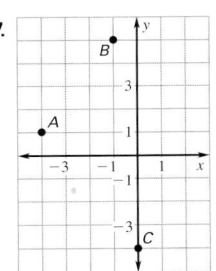

19. Quadrant IV **21.** Quadrant I **23.** Quadrant III
25. Quadrant III **27.** pounds; inches **29.** C
31. It decreases. **35.**

37. As wing length increases, wing-beat rate decreases.

4.1 MIXED REVIEW (p. 208) **43.** 7 **45.** 15 **47.** 39 **49.** 1.07
51. $\frac{2}{3}$

TECHNOLOGY ACTIVITY 4.1 (p. 209) **1.** As age increases, time decreases. **3.** From ages 10–14, as age increases, time decreases. From ages 14–16, time increases, then decreases at age 17.

4.2 PRACTICE (pp. 214–217)

5. 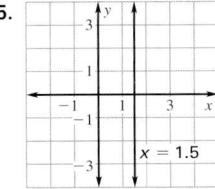 **7.** no **9.** no

11. about 35,180,000 households **13. a.** no; $y \neq 5$ **b.** yes; $y = 5$ **15.** no **17.** yes **19.** no **21–29 odd:** Sample answers are given. **21.** $(-1, -8), (0, -5), (1, -2)$

23. $(-1, -4), (0, -6), (1, -8)$ **25.** $\left(\frac{1}{2}, -1\right), \left(\frac{1}{2}, 0\right), \left(\frac{1}{2}, 1\right)$

27. $(-1, 3), (0, 2), (1, 1)$ **29.** $(-1, -6), (0, -4), (1, -2)$

31. $y = -\frac{2}{3}x + 2$ **33.** $y = -x + \frac{19}{5}$ **35.** $y = -x - 5$

37.   **39.**

41.   **45.**

49.   **51.**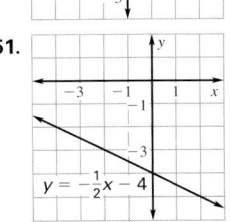

53. D **55.** C **57.**

59. $x = -1.6$; $2(-1.6) - 3 = -6.2$, but $y = -5.5$. **61.** $(-8, 11)$
63. $(4, -4)$ **65.** $(3, 0)$ **67.** $y = -2x + 30$ **69.** yes
71. Running time; Calories burned while swimming; 7.1; Calories burned while swimming; Swimming time; $7.1x + 10.1y = 800$ **73.** about 48 min **75.** Horizontal; the number of senators does not vary.

4.2 MIXED REVIEW (p. 217) **81.** 4 **83.** -29 **85.** 0

87. $\begin{bmatrix} 16 & 3 \\ -4 & 18 \end{bmatrix}$ **89.** $\begin{bmatrix} -16 & 50 \\ -9 & 19 \end{bmatrix}$ **91.** 13 **93.** -16 **95.** -15

97. 9

4.3 PRACTICE (pp. 221–223)

5. -3 **7.** $-2; 2$

9. $2; -4$

11. $-3; 3$

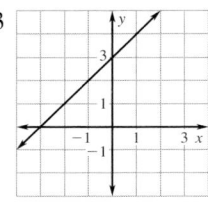

13. *Sample answer:* $8 for adult tickets and $4 for student tickets or $9 for adult tickets and $2 for student tickets
15. $-2; 4$ **17.** 5 **19.** -5 **21.** 9 **23.** -6 **25.** -5 **27.** -4
29. -15 **31.** -8 **33.** 3 **34.** 3

35.

37.

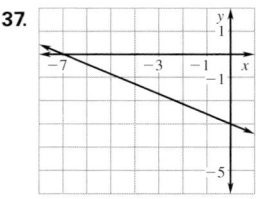

41. A **43.** B **45.** $3; -3$

47. $2; -6$

49. $8; 4$

53. $-18; -4$

55. $4; 16$

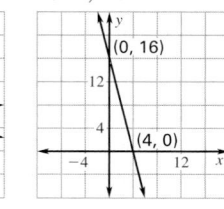

57. True; when $y = 0$, $3x = 30$ and $x = 10$. **59.** False; the graph is a vertical line. **61.** 75; the number of adult tickets that must be sold if no student tickets are sold
63. The possible pairs (x, y) are (0, 120), (5, 112), (10, 104), (15, 96), (20, 88), (25, 80), (30, 72), (35, 64), (40, 56), (45, 48), (50, 40), (55, 32), (60, 24), (65, 16), (70, 8), and (75, 0).

65. Running Time vs. Walking Time

67. Theater Attendance

Sample answers:
(1.5, 3.55), (2.25, 2.05),
(2.5, 1.55), (2.75, 1.05),
(3, 0.55)

4.3 MIXED REVIEW (p. 223) **71.** -4 **73.** -17 **75.** $\frac{5}{3}$ **77.** 6
79. 6 **81.** -60 **83.** -2 **85.** 8 **87.** B

QUIZ 1 (p. 224)

1.

2.

3.

4.

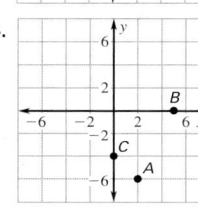

5–10. Sample answers are given.

5. $(0, -6), (3, 0), (2, -2)$ **6.** $(0, -1), \left(\frac{1}{2}, 1\right), \left(-\frac{1}{2}, -3\right)$

7. $(0, 2), (1, -4), (-1, 8)$ **8.** $(3, -1), (3, 0), (3, 1)$

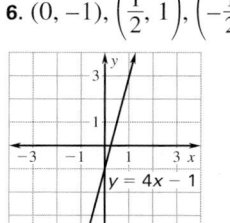

9. $(0, 12), (1, 9), (4, 0)$ **10.** $(-3, -5), (9, -5), (2, -5)$

11. 4; 4

12. $2\frac{1}{2}$; -5

13. -4; 12

14. 9; 9

15. $\frac{1}{2}$; -3

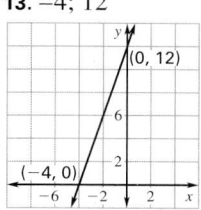

16. -5; 50

19. $\frac{5}{4}$; $\frac{5}{4}$ **21.** yes **23.** $y = 3x$ **25.** $y = \frac{2}{9}x$ **27.** $y = 0.2x$ **29.** $y = x$ **31.** $y = -\frac{1}{3}x$ **33.** 324 lb **35.** yes **37.** 45 in.; lower

4.5 MIXED REVIEW (p. 239) **45.** 2 **47.** -5 **49.** -3 **51.** $x = -\frac{5}{2}y + 6$ **53.**

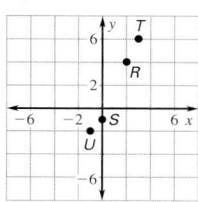

55. No; $3(-4) - 6(-2) =$ 0 and $0 \neq -2$ **57.** No; $-4(-4) - 3(2) =$ 10 and $10 \neq -8$

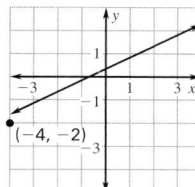

59. 10; $-9\frac{1}{11}$ **61.** 10; 2 **63.** 7; $-\frac{7}{3}$

4.6 PRACTICE (pp. 244–246) **5.** 2; 1 **7.** 1; 3 **9.** 5; -3 **11.** 30; 50 **13.** 6; 4 **15.** 2; -3 **17.** 0; -2 **19.** $\frac{1}{4}$; $\frac{1}{2}$ **21.** -3; $\frac{1}{2}$ **23.**

25.

29.

31.

33.

35. $y = \frac{1}{2}x - \frac{3}{2}$ **37.** $y = 4x - 3$

4.4 PRACTICE (pp. 230–233) **5.** 2 **7.** -1 **9.** 3 **11.** -9
13. Negative; the line falls from left to right. **15.** Negative; the line falls from left to right. **17.** Negative; the line falls from left to right. **19.** Undefined; the line is vertical.
21. $-\frac{3}{4}$ **23.** $\frac{3}{4}$ **25.** -4 **27.** $-\frac{5}{2}$ **29.** undefined **31.** $\frac{5}{2}$
33. $-\frac{3}{5}$ **35.** a: -1; b: 1 **37.** a: -2; b: undefined **39.** 4
41. 1 **43.** -3 **45.** 3 **47.** No matter which pairs of points are chosen, the slope is the same, $\frac{1}{2}$. **49.** No; the slope of the line that passes through $(-2, 4)$ and $(2, -2)$ is $-\frac{3}{2}$. The slope of the line that passes through $(2, -2)$ and $(6, 0)$ is $\frac{1}{2}$. The slope of the line that passes through $(-2, 4)$ and $(6, 0)$ is $-\frac{1}{2}$. Three distinct lines, each with a different slope, are determined by the three points. **51.** $\frac{3}{50}$; The road grade is the slope of the road expressed as a percent. **53.** $8/year
55. section 1: $-\frac{1}{20}$; section 2: $\frac{3}{20}$; section 3: $\frac{1}{6}$
57. $5,500,000/year **59.** about $.15/year **63.** 1960–1970; about 0.5 million people/year

4.4 MIXED REVIEW (p. 233) **73.** 12 **75.** 11 **77.** 8 **79.** x^2
81. $-2x^2$ **83.** $-\frac{1}{2}x^2$ **85.** $y = -\frac{5}{9}x + 2$ **87.** $y = \frac{1}{4}x + 9$
89. $y = -\frac{3}{5}x + \frac{17}{5}$ **91.** -6; 12 **93.** 3; -6 **95.** $-\frac{1}{2}$; 1

4.5 PRACTICE (pp. 237–238) **3.** yes; 1; 1 **5.** yes; $\frac{1}{2}$; $\frac{1}{2}$ **7.** no
9. 6; 6; 6; 6 **11.** $36 **13.** $-\frac{2}{5}$; $-\frac{2}{5}$ **15.** -3; -3 **17.** 0.4; 0.4

39. $y = -x$

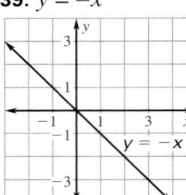

41. $y = -\frac{1}{3}x + 1$

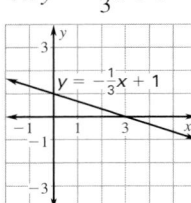

47. Yes; both have slope 2.   **49.** No; one has slope $\frac{4}{3}$, the other has slope $-\frac{4}{3}$.   **51.** Yes; both have slope 3.   **53.** C

55. B   **63.** A triangle; 9 square units; the base is 6 units long and the height is 3 units.

65.

67. 4 ft

4.6 MIXED REVIEW (p. 247)   **79.** 5   **81.** 12   **83.** 6   **85.** -1
87. A   **89.** from 2001 to 2002

QUIZ 2 (p. 247)   **1.** $\frac{2}{5}$ **2.** $\frac{2}{5}$ **3.** $\frac{7}{9}$ **4.** 2   **5.** 0   **6.** -1 **7.** $y = 5x$
8. $y = 8x$ **9.** $y = 6x$ **10.** $y = \frac{3}{4}x$ **11.** $y = 0.7x$ **12.** $y = \frac{4}{9}x$

13. $y = 2x - 4$

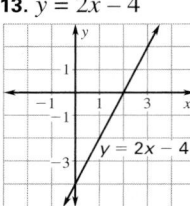

14. $y = -\frac{1}{2}x - \frac{1}{3}$

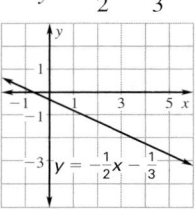

15. $y = \frac{1}{2}x - 6$

16. $y = x + 2$

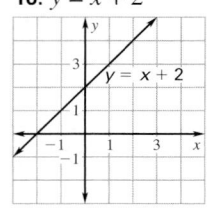

17. $y = -\frac{1}{2}x + 1$

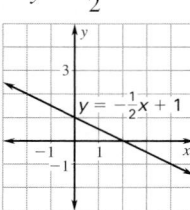

18. $y = -x + \frac{1}{2}$

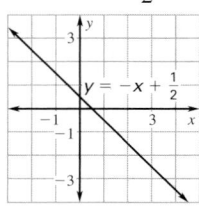

19. $-\$30,080$/month

TECHNOLOGY ACTIVITY 4.6 (p. 248–249)

1.

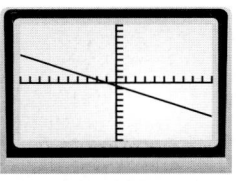

3.

5.

7.

9. *Sample answer:* standard viewing window
11. *Sample answer:* Xmin $= -10$, Xmax $= 30$, Xscl $= 5$, Ymin $= -10000$, Ymax $= 50000$, Yscl $= 5000$
13. about 662.5   **15.** about -1911

4.7 PRACTICE (pp. 253–254)   **7.** A   **9.** B   **11.** C   **13.** B
15. $-4x - 7 = 0$; $y = -4x - 7$ **17.** $4x + 5 = 0$; $y = 4x + 5$
19. $x + 7 = 0$; $y = x + 7$ **21.** 3   **23.** $1\frac{1}{2}$ **25.** -4 **27.** 1   **29.** 1
31. 3   **33.** 2   **35.** -4 **37.** -4 **39.** -5 **41.** 6   **43.** -2
45. 1999   **47.** 2001

4.7 MIXED REVIEW (p. 255)   **53.** no   **55.** no   **57.** no
59. $-64 + 8y$ **61.** $-3q^2 - 12q$ **63.** $-2d + 10$
65. $15w - 10w^2$

4.8 PRACTICE (pp. 259–261)   **3.** -10 **5.** -16
7. yes; 10, 20, 30, 40, 50; 100, 200, 300, 400, 500
9. no   **11.** Yes; no vertical line passes through two points on the graph.   **13.** No; there are vertical lines that pass through two or more points on the graph.
15. yes; 1, 2, 3, 4; 0   **17.** yes; 0, 1, 2, 3; 2, 4, 6, 8
19. yes; 1, 3, 5, 7; 1, 2, 3   **21.** 14; -2; -26 **23.** 2.5; 0; -3.75
25. -1.34; -2; -2.99 **27.** 7.8; 7; 5.8   **29.** C   **31.** B

33.

35.

37.

39.

43. -1 **45.** -3 **47.** 1.75   **49.** 0
51. about 16 million   **53.** Yes; each input is paired with exactly one output.   **55.** $f(t) = \frac{100}{17}t$, or $f(t) \approx 5.88t$

4.8 MIXED REVIEW (p. 262)

63. $\begin{bmatrix} 9 & -11 \\ 12 & 7 \end{bmatrix}$ **65.** $\begin{bmatrix} 9.8 & -17.9 \\ -12.3 & -0.1 \\ 12.4 & -13.2 \end{bmatrix}$ **67.** 4 **69.** -3 **71.** $2\frac{1}{2}$

73. $y = 2x + 3$

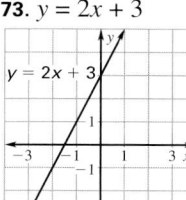

75. $y = 2x - 7$

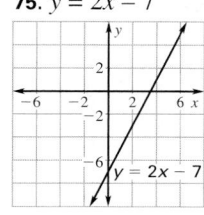

77. $y = \frac{1}{2}x + 1$

79.

QUIZ 3 (p. 262) **1.** -2 **2.** $\frac{1}{2}$ **3.** 1 **4.** $-\frac{1}{2}$ **5.** -13 **6.** $-5\frac{1}{3}$
7. $6; -9; -29$ **8.** $-9; 3; 19$ **9.** $3.25; -2; -9$ **10.** $-4.2; 0; 5.6$
11. $9\frac{3}{4}; 9; 8$ **12.** $2; \frac{2}{7}; -2$ **13.**

14.

15.

16.

17.

18.

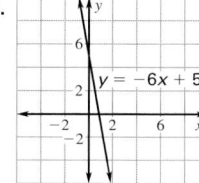

19. 250 lunches

CHAPTER 4 REVIEW (pp. 264–266)

1.

3, 5.

7.

9.

11.

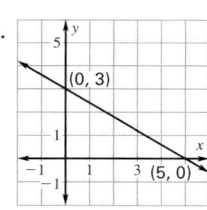

15. 6 **17.** 0 **19.** $y = -\frac{1}{3}x$

21. $y = 3.5x$ **23.**

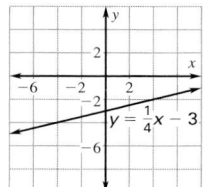

25. 2 **27.** 8

29. -9

31. 0

CHAPTER 5

SKILL REVIEW (p. 272) **1.** 2 **2.** 10 **3.** −6

4.

5.

6. 4.5, 2
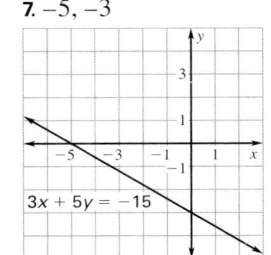

7. −5, −3

8. $-\frac{4}{3}$, −4
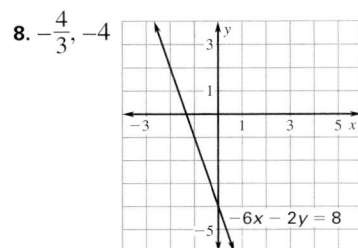

5.1 PRACTICE (pp. 276–277) **3.** $y = x$ **5.** $y = -x + 3$
7. $y = -3x + \frac{1}{2}$ **9.** $y = 1.5x + 4$ **11.** \$22 **13.** $y = x + 2$
15. $y = 2x - 1$ **17.** $y = -\frac{1}{4}x + 1$ **19.** $y = -3x - \frac{1}{2}$
21. $y = x - 3$ **23.** *a:* $y = 2x + 3$; *b:* $y = 2x$; *c:* $y = 2x - 4$
25. *a:* $y = 4$; *b:* $y = 1$; *c:* $y = -2$ **27.** about 3,710,400
29. \$36.25; \$42.50; \$48.75; \$55 **31.** Let y = your uncle's weight in lb and x = the number of months from the start of his weight loss; $y = 180 - 2x$; lb = lb − $\frac{\text{lb}}{\text{month}}$ · ~~months~~.
33. $y = 200 - 50t$; the distance from home decreases as time increases. **35.** $T = 5x$ **37.** *Sample answer:* If the club members can sell only 200 calendars, the fundraising project will not raise any money at all because the cost for producing 200 calendars will equal the money raised by selling 200 calendars. Therefore, it is not a very effective project.

5.1 MIXED REVIEW (p. 278) **41.** −3 **43.** −11
45. Let x = the width of each photograph; $3x + 3\frac{1}{2} = 13\frac{1}{4}$.

47. $y = 10x$

Sailboard Rental Cost

49. −2, 2

51. $\frac{3}{2}$, 3

53. −3, 4

55. $-\frac{1}{3}$, 5

57. 1, −10
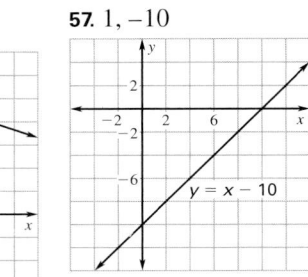

5.2 PRACTICE (pp. 282–283) **3.** $y = \frac{1}{2}x + \frac{5}{2}$ **5.** $y = \frac{2}{3}x - \frac{50}{3}$
7. $y = 5x - 12$ **9.** $y = \frac{1}{2}x + 7$ **11.** $y = -8.25x + 616.5$
13. $y = 2x - 7$ **15.** $y = -4x + 1$ **17.** $y = 4x - 1$
19. $y = \frac{1}{3}x + 3$ **21.** $y = 4x - 2$ **23.** $y = 4$ **25.** $y = \frac{1}{2}x + \frac{3}{2}$
27. $y = \frac{3}{5}x$ **29.** $x = 2$ **31.** $y = 3x - 12$ **33.** $y = x + 2$
35. $y = -3x + 14$ **37.** $y = -\frac{1}{3}x + \frac{7}{3}$ **39.** $y = 6x - 33$
41. $y = \frac{1}{2}x - 2$ **43.** about 162,000 **45.** \$21,750
47. \$39.80 **49.** \$2

5.2 MIXED REVIEW (p. 284) **53.** 32,768 **55.** 531,441
57. 64 **59.** 10,000 **61.** 10,077,696
63. about 2,541,865,828,000 **65.** $-\frac{1}{2}$ **67.** −11 **69.** −20
71. 14 **73.** $\frac{3}{4}$ **75.** $-\frac{2}{3}$

5.3 PRACTICE (pp. 288–290) **3.** $\frac{1}{4}$ **5.** −1 **7.** $y = \frac{4}{5}x - \frac{1}{5}$
9. $y = \frac{4}{5}x + \frac{9}{5}$ **11.** $y = -\frac{10}{3}x - \frac{31}{3}$ **13.** $y = \frac{1}{2}x$
15. $y = 6x - 27$ **17.** $y = 2$ **19.** $y = -3x - 3$ **21.** $y = \frac{8}{3}x + \frac{2}{3}$
23. $y = -2$ **25.** $y = -2x + 1$ **27.** $y = -\frac{6}{7}x + \frac{8}{7}$

29. $y = \frac{1}{2}x + \frac{1}{2}$ **31.** $x = 5$ **33.** $y = -\frac{1}{11}x + \frac{17}{11}$
35. $y = -\frac{14}{13}x + \frac{116}{13}$ **37.** $y = 3$ **39.** $y = -\frac{3}{5}x + \frac{27}{5}$
41. $y = -\frac{2}{3}x + \frac{11}{3}$ **43.** $y = -\frac{15}{7}x + \frac{4}{7}$ **45.** Lines p and r; their slopes are negative reciprocals. **47.** $y = -2x + 13$
49. $\overline{WX}$: $y = -\frac{4}{3}x + 4$; $\overline{XY}$: $y = \frac{3}{4}x - \frac{9}{4}$; $\overline{ZY}$: $y = -\frac{4}{3}x - \frac{13}{3}$
51. $y = -\frac{26}{3}x + 60$; $-\frac{26}{3}$ **53.** $s = \frac{3}{5}T + 331$ **55.** $25°C$ **57.** 686 m

5.3 MIXED REVIEW (p. 291) **67.** $\frac{6a - 7b}{2}$ **69.** -5 **71.** -35
73. $\frac{1}{3}$ **75.** positive

QUIZ 1 (p. 291) **1.** $y = \frac{4}{3}x + 4$ **2.** $y = -2x + 2$ **3.** $y = \frac{4}{3}x - 4$
4. $y = 2x + 14$ **5.** $y = -3x + 7$ **6.** $y = x - 3$ **7.** $y = x - 2$
8. $y = -\frac{1}{3}x - \frac{1}{3}$ **9.** $y = \frac{13}{3}x + \frac{44}{3}$ **10.** $y = 4$ **11.** $y = 28x + 10$
12.

Canoe Rental Cost

13. $94

5.4 PRACTICE (pp. 296–297) **7.** negative correlation; *Sample answer:* $y = -1.54x + 3.23$ **9.** positive correlation; *Sample answer:* $y = 1.16x - 6.22$ **11.** *Sample answer:* $y = 1.19x + 1.19$ **13.** *Sample answer:* $y = 1.64x + 2.57$ **15.** *Sample answer:* $y = -1.79x + 15.45$ **17.** positive correlation **19.** negative correlation **21.** positive correlation **23.** *Sample answer:* $y = 25x + 50$
25.

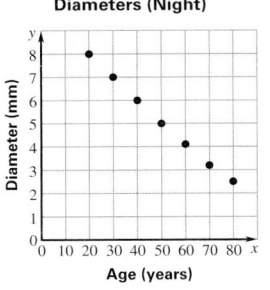
Sample Pupil Diameters (Daylight)   **Sample Pupil Diameters (Night)**

5.4 MIXED REVIEW (p. 298) **35.** horizontal
37. vertical **39.** positive **41.** zero **43.** $y = -\frac{1}{4}x + \frac{11}{2}$
45. $y = -x + 10$ **47.** $y = -\frac{3}{7}x - \frac{2}{7}$ **49.** $y = \frac{7}{2}x - \frac{33}{2}$

TECHNOLOGY ACTIVITY 5.4 (p. 299) **1.** $y = 0.47x + 2.01$
3. $y = 0.95x + 1.41$

5.5 PRACTICE (pp. 303–304) **3.** $y - 4 = \frac{1}{2}(x - 3)$ **5.** $y + 2 = 0$
7. $y - 4 = \frac{1}{2}(x - 3)$ **9.** $y - 10 = 4(x + 3)$ **11.** $y + 7 = -8(x - 7)$ **13.** $y + 1 = -\frac{3}{5}(x + 4)$ or $y - 2 = -\frac{3}{5}(x + 9)$

15. $y - 12 = -2(x - 2)$ or $y - 2 = -2(x - 7)$ **17.** $y + 7 = \frac{3}{2}(x + 4)$ or $y - 2 = \frac{3}{2}(x - 2)$ **19.** $y + 3 = -\frac{1}{2}(x + 1)$
21. $y - 5 = 5(x - 1)$ or $y + 5 = 5(x + 1)$
23. $y - 10 = -\frac{13}{5}(x + 9)$ or $y + 3 = -\frac{13}{5}(x + 4)$ **25.** $y - 10 = -12(x + 5)$ or $y + 2 = -12(x + 4)$ **27.** $y + 9 = -\frac{1}{3}(x + 3)$ or $y + 8 = -\frac{1}{3}(x + 6)$ **29.** $y + 7 = -(x - 1)$ or $y + 5 = -(x + 1)$
31. $y - 2 = -5(x + 6)$ **33.** $y + 2 = 2(x + 8)$ **35.** $y - 4 = 6(x + 3)$ **37.** $y + 1 = 0$ **39.** $y - 4 = 2(x - 1)$; $y = 2x + 2$
41. $y - 2 = \frac{1}{2}(x - 6)$; $y = \frac{1}{2}x - 1$ **43.** $y + 1 = -1(x - 5)$; $y = -x + 4$ **45.** $y - 1 = -\frac{1}{8}(x + 1)$; $y = -\frac{1}{8}x + \frac{7}{8}$ **47.** $y + 6 = -\frac{2}{3}(x + 9)$; $y = -\frac{2}{3}x - 12$ **49.** $y = -\frac{1}{3}x - \frac{4}{3}$ **51.** $y - 3 = 2(x - 1)$ or $y - 5 = 2(x - 2)$ **53.** $y + 10 = -\frac{3}{2}(x - 7)$ or $y + 22 = -\frac{3}{2}(x - 15)$ **55.** $y + 4 = \frac{3}{4}(x + 3)$ or $y + 1 = \frac{3}{4}(x - 1)$ **57.** $d = -0.76t + 120$ **59.** at about 11:38 A.M.
61. at about 11:49 A.M. **63.** at about 2:25 P.M.

5.5 MIXED REVIEW (p. 305) **71.** solution **73.** solution
75. solution **77.**

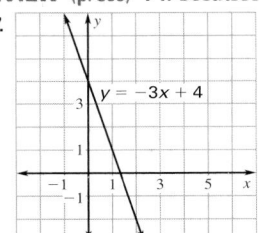
$y = -3x + 4$

79.

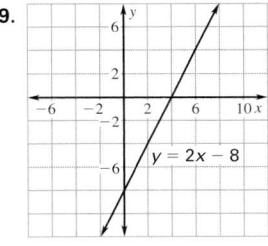
$y = 2x - 8$

81.

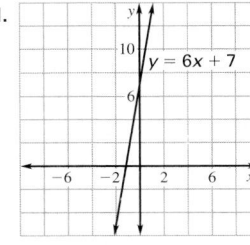
$y = 6x + 7$

83.

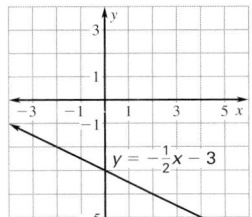
$y = -\frac{1}{2}x - 3$

85.

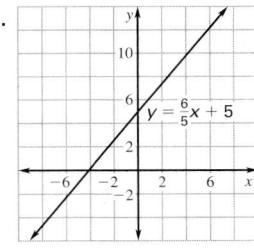
$y = \frac{6}{5}x + 5$

87. $33\frac{1}{3}\%$

QUIZ 2 (p. 306) **1.** *Sample equation:* $y = 0.82x - 2.78$; positive **2.** *Sample equation:* $y = -0.53x - 0.73$; negative **3.** *Sample equation:* $y = 1.38x + 0.99$; positive **4.** $y + 4 = -1(x - 1)$ **5.** $y - 5 = 2(x - 2)$ **6.** $y + 2 = -2(x + 3)$ **7.** $y + 3 = 0$ **8.** $y - 6 = \frac{1}{2}(x + 6)$

9. $y - 8 = 7(x - 3)$ **10.** $y = \frac{1}{3}x$ or $y + 1 = \frac{1}{3}(x + 3)$
11. $y + 2 = 0$ **12.** $y + 3 = \frac{3}{2}(x + 5)$ or $y - 6 = \frac{3}{2}(x - 1)$

5.6 PRACTICE (pp. 311–313) **5–15 odd:** Sample answers are given. **5.** $5x + y = 6$ **7.** $x - 2y = -16$ **9.** $3x - 2y = 4$
11. $5x - y = 7$ **13.** $x + y = -3$ **15.** $2x + y = 5$
17. 8; 6; 4; 2; 0 **19–53 odd:** Sample answers are given.
19. $x + 3y = 4$ **21.** $2x - 3y = 14$ **23.** $y = -3$ **25.** $3x - y = 8$
27. $6x - 7y = -18$ **29.** $5x - 2y = -18$ **31.** $x + 7y = 6$
33. $2x - y = -19$ **35.** $3x + y = 1$ **37.** $5x - y = 17$
39. $7x + y = 23$ **41.** $2x + y = 17$ **43.** $x - y = -3$
45. $3x - 4y = -13$ **47.** $x + y = -3$ **49.** $y = 0$ **51.** $y = -4$,
$x = 2$ **53.** $y = -3$, $x = 0$ **55.** $y = 4$, $x = -4$ **57.** $y = -1$, $x = 6$
59. $y = 0$, $x = -9$ **61.** $y = -3$, $x = 10$ **63.** The expression
inside the brackets was simplified incorrectly;
$x - (-6) = x + 6$. **65.**

67. *Sample answer:* $2x + 3y = 10$ **69.** 3 students
71. 0% blue, 60% red; 10% blue, 50% red; 20% blue,
40% red; 30% blue, 30% red; 40% blue, 20% red;
50% blue, 10% red; 60% blue, 0% red
73. 0% blue, 80% red; 10% blue, 70% red; 20% blue,
60% red; 30% blue, 50% red; 40% blue, 40% red;
50% blue, 30% red; 60% blue, 20% red; 70% blue,
10% red; 80% blue, 0% red

5.6 MIXED REVIEW (p. 314) **85.** 11 **87.** 4 **89.** $5\frac{1}{4}$

91.

93.

95.
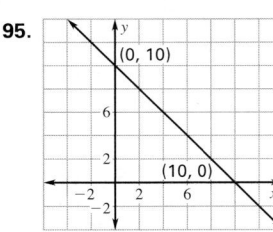
97. $y = \frac{15}{2}x - \frac{93}{2}$

99. $y = \frac{6}{11}x - \frac{58}{11}$ **101.** $y = -\frac{1}{15}x - \frac{11}{15}$ **103.** $y = -\frac{6}{19}x - \frac{87}{19}$
105. \$118.67 **107.** 25%

5.7 PRACTICE (pp. 319–321) **7.** *Sample answer:* $y = 0.62x +$
1.96 **9.** about 20.56 gal; extrapolation **11.** no **13.** yes

15. yes **17.**

Movie Theaters

19. indoor screens

21. about 35,000 theaters **23.** $y = 0.94x + 16.17$
25. $y = 2.24x + 30.91$ **27.** about \$64.51 billion;
linear extrapolation

5.7 MIXED REVIEW (p. 322)
39.
$-2 < -1, -1 > -2$
41.
$-\frac{1}{2} < \frac{3}{2}, \frac{3}{2} > -\frac{1}{2}$
43.
$-3 > -\frac{7}{2}, -\frac{7}{2} < -3$
45. $y = \frac{1}{2}x - 8$ **47.** $y = -2x - 6$ **49.** $y = 7x + 28$
51. $y = -5x + 44$ **53.** $y = 2x + 23$

QUIZ 3 (p. 322) **1–6.** Sample answers are given.
1. $x - 2y = -6$ **2.** $9x + 3y = 18$ **3.** $-2x + 6y = 8$
4. $9x - y = -12$ **5.** $2x - 3y = -18$ **6.** $14x - 16y = 1$
7. $2x + y = 4$ **8.** $x + 2y = 6$ **9.** $3x + y = 8$ **10.** $2x - y = -5$
11. $3x - y = -40$ **12.** $6x - y = -94$ **13.** Let $x =$ the number
of years since 1985; $y = 0.13x + 74.80$.
14. about 75.32 years **15.** about 78.7 years

CHAPTER 5 REVIEW (pp. 324–326) **1.** $y = 2x - 2$
3. $y = -8x - 3$ **5.** $y = 2x + 22$ **7.** $y = -\frac{11}{7}x - \frac{19}{7}$
9. $y = \frac{3}{10}x + \frac{22}{5}$ **11.** *Sample answer:* $y = 1.98x + 1.11$
13. $y - 4 = \frac{1}{6}(x + 4)$ or $y - 5 = \frac{1}{6}(x - 2)$; $y = \frac{1}{6}x + \frac{14}{3}$
15. $y + 2 = -5(x - 1)$ or $y - 8 = -5(x + 1)$; $y = -5x + 3$
17–21 odd: Sample answers are given. **17.** $8x + 3y = 2$
19. $x + 3y = 2$ **21.** $4x - 3y = 12$ **23.** about 242 million;
linear extrapolation **25.** about 178 million; linear
extrapolation

CHAPTER 6

SKILL REVIEW (p. 332) **1.** solution **2.** not a solution
3. solution **4.** not a solution **5.** not a solution **6.** solution
7. 10 **8.** 24 **9.** 9 **10.** 6 **11.** 7 **12.** 2
13.

14.

15.   **16.**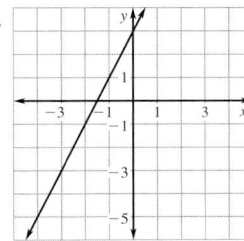

6.1 PRACTICE (pp. 337–338)   **9.** open dot   **11.** open dot
13. closed dot   **15.** $y \geq -5$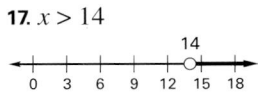

17. $x > 14$ **19.** $y \geq -6$

21. 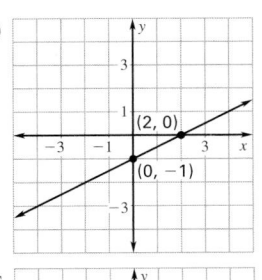   **23.**

25.   **27.**

29.

31. $x < 2$

33. $x < 24$ **35.** $p \geq 11$ **37.** $x > 5$

39. $c \geq 4$ **41.** $m \geq -17$ **43.** $x < 2$

45. $x \geq -10$ **47.** $a < -10$

49. $m \geq -5$ **51.** $x \leq -5$ **53.** $a \geq 20$ **55.** $x < 5$; E
57. $x > 5$; C   **59.** $x \geq 0$; A   **61.** $x < \dfrac{6}{55}$

63. $M < 1376$ **65.** $\ell < 1700$

67. $131 \leq f \leq 587$

6.1 MIXED REVIEW (p. 339)

71. $\dfrac{1}{9}$ **73.** 14   **75.** 56   **77.** 3   **79.** -4

81. $y = \dfrac{1}{2}x - 1$; $(0, -1)$ and $(2, 0)$
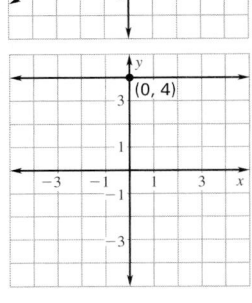

83. $y = 4$; the line does not cross the x-axis and crosses the y-axis at $(0, 4)$.

85. $x = 5$; the line crosses the x-axis at $(5, 0)$ and does not cross the y-axis.
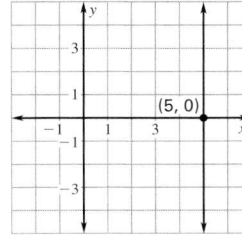

87. $d = 0.12t$

6.2 PRACTICE (pp. 343–344)   **5.** $y > -3$ **7.** $x \leq 3$ **9.** $x \leq 10$
11. $x < -4$ **13.** $x < -\dfrac{3}{4}$ **15.** $x > -18$ **17.** $x \geq \dfrac{7}{6}$ **19.** $x \geq -3$
21. $x < 3$ **23.** $x \leq -5$ **25.** $x > -9$ **27.** $x \geq 12$ **29.** $x > -8$
31. $x \geq 11$ **33.** $x > 6\dfrac{2}{3}$ **35.** $x > \dfrac{1}{6}$ **37.** $1.25r + 5 \leq 25$;
16 rides   **39.** $0.75t + 14 \leq 18.50$; 6 toppings   **41.** 2 years
43. $x > 4$ m   **45.** $x < 10$ ft   **47.** $x \leq 5$ in.

6.2 MIXED REVIEW (p. 345)   **55.** -10 **57.** 12   **59.** $\dfrac{16}{17}$
61. $t > 2\ell$ **63.** 3   **65.** 0.75

6.3 PRACTICE (pp. 349–350)
3. $2 < x < 5$ **5.** $3 < x < 4$

7. $2 < x \leq 4$ **9.** $x < -2$ or $x > 1$ **11.** $1 \leq d \leq 3$
13. $x > 7$ or $x < 5$ **15.** $-9 \leq x < 4$

17. $-6 < x < -1$

19. x is greater than -2 and less than 9.   **21.** x is greater than or equal to 1 and less than or equal to 6.   **23.** x is less than or equal to -5 or greater than or equal to 10.
25. x is greater than -2 and less than or equal to 9.

27. $-5 < x < -4$ **29.** $-\dfrac{1}{3} \leq x < \dfrac{2}{3}$

31. $x > 3$ or $x \leq 1$

33.   **35.**
$2 < x \leq 5$; solution $-5 < x \leq 7$; solution

37. $85{,}000 \leq x \leq 2{,}600{,}000$ **39.** *Sample answer:* A solution would be a number on the graph of both inequalities. Since the graphs do not overlap, there are no such numbers.
41. A   **43.** $10^8 < d < 10^9$

6.3 MIXED REVIEW (p. 351)   **49.** 7   **51.** 10   **53.** 16.5
55. -8 **57.** 16   **59.** -12 **61.** -7 **63.** 7.8   **65.** 3
67. at least 30 times   **69.** 4 mi

QUIZ 1 (p. 352)   **1.** $x < 5$

2. $x \leq -8$ **3.** $x \leq 4$

4. $x \leq -10$

5. $x \leq -4$

6. $3 < x < 12$

7. $x < 2$

8. $x \geq 17$

9. $-12 \leq x \leq -2$

10. $x > -9$ or $x < -12$

11. $x > 5$ or $x < -1$

12. $x < -1$ or $x > 5\frac{4}{5}$

13. $x > -\frac{5}{6}$ or $x < -4$

14. $x \geq 52$ **15.** $-128.6 < T < 136$

6.4 PRACTICE (pp. 356–357) **7.** 0 **9.** $-6, 14$ **11.** $\frac{1}{3}, -1\frac{2}{3}$

13. C **15.** $-10 < x < -2$ **17.** $-2 \leq x \leq 1\frac{1}{3}$ **19.** $-7, 7$

21. $-25, 25$ **23.** $-16, 6$ **25.** $3, 7$ **27.** $-12, 6$ **29.** $-3.8, 10.2$

31. $-5, 6$ **33.** $-9\frac{1}{3}, 6$ **35.** $-7, 11$ **37.** $-8.2, 1$ **39.** $-2, 3$

41. $-1 \leq x \leq 10$ **43.** $x < -0.8$ or $x > 5.2$ **45.** $x \leq -2$ or $x \geq 8$

47. $-1 < x < 9$ **49.** $-14 \leq x \leq 20$

51. $x \leq -11$ or $x \geq 5$ **53.** $x < -3\frac{1}{2}$ or $x > \frac{1}{2}$

55. $-6 < x < 0$ **57.** $-5 \leq x \leq 4\frac{3}{5}$

59. $-6 < x < 1$ **61.** $|x - 15| \leq 7$

63. $|x - 28| \leq 4$ **65.** orange or red **67.** green

6.4 MIXED REVIEW (p. 358) **75.** $\begin{bmatrix} 8 & -17 \\ 9 & 5 \end{bmatrix}$ **77.** $y = -\frac{2}{3}x + 4$

79.

81.

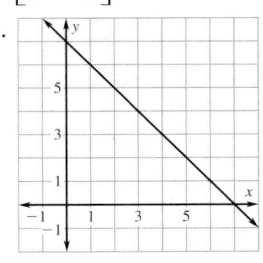

83. $y + 5 = -2(x - 2)$; $y = -2x - 1$ **85.** 57 mi/h

TECHNOLOGY ACTIVITY 6.4 (p. 359) **1.** $-7, 1$ **3.** $-10, 18$
5. $-4, 64$ **7.** $1.8, 6.8$ **9.** $-50, -22$

6.5 PRACTICE (pp. 363–365)

5. solution

7. not a solution

9. solution   **11.** solution

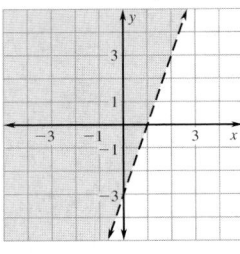

13. Let x = the number of 2-point shots and y = the number of 3-point shots; $2x + 3y \geq 12$.   **15.** solution, not a solution

17. solution, solution   **19.** not a solution, not a solution

21. solution, not a solution

31.

33.

35.

37.

43. D   **45.** E   **47.** C   **49.**

53.

59.

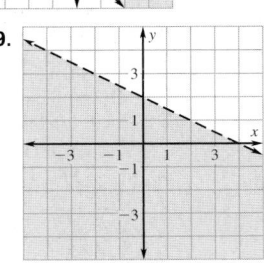

61. $y \geq -2x + 2$ or $2x + y \geq 2$ **63.** $y < 2x$ or $2x - y > 0$
65. a. $3x + 7y < 21$

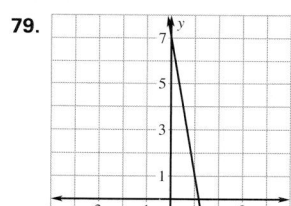

b. No; only points for which both coordinates are nonnegative integers represent solutions, since only a whole number of touchdowns or field goals can be scored. The real-life solutions are (0, 0), (0, 1), (0, 2), (1, 0), (1, 1), (1, 2), (2, 0), (2, 1), (2, 2), (3, 0), (3, 1), (4, 0), (4, 1), (5, 0), and (6, 0). **67. a.** Let (x, y) represent x cups of cereal and y cups of skim milk; the possible solutions are (1, 1), (1, 2), (1, 3), (1, 4), (2, 1), (2, 2), (2, 3), (3, 1), (3, 2), (4, 1).
b. *Sample answer:* 1 glass of tomato juice, 2 cups of cereal, and 2 or 3 cups of milk **c.** The possible solutions are all those in part (a) as well as (1, 5), (2, 4), (3, 3), (4, 2), and (5, 1). *Sample answer:* one glass of tomato juice, 3 cups of cereal, and 2 cups of milk

6.5 MIXED REVIEW (p. 366) **75.** 19 **77.** $r = \dfrac{d}{t}$

79.
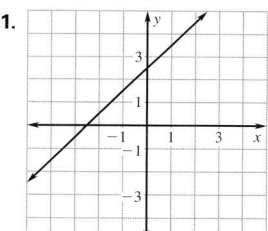

81.

83. $-5, 2$ **85.** $1, -\dfrac{1}{5}$ **87.** $0, -2$ **89.** $3, -6.5$ **91.** $-\dfrac{3}{2}, 5$

QUIZ 2 (p. 366) **1.** $-15, 15$ **2.** $-22, 22$ **3.** $-9, 3$
4. $-8, 12$ **5.** $-7, 0$ **6.** $-\dfrac{5}{3}, 3$

7. $x < 3$ or $x > 5$

8. $-9 < x < -5$

9. $3 \leq x \leq 21$

10. $x < -2$ or $x > \dfrac{5}{2}$

11. $-16 \leq x \leq 9$

12. $x < -6$ or $x > 5$

13. solution, solution **14.** not a solution, solution
15. not a solution, solution **16.** solution, not a solution

17.

18.

19.

20.

21.

22.

23. $|x - 104| \leq 39$

TECHNOLOGY ACTIVITY 6.5 (p. 367)
1, 5. The lines are not part of the solution.

1.

3.

5.

7.

13. $y > x$

6.6 PRACTICE (pp. 371–373) **5.** 3, 2, 2 **7.** $1, -\dfrac{1}{2}$, no mode
9. 11, 13, 13, 15, 16, 17, 18, 20, 20, 22, 25, 27, 27, 28, 31, 33, 34, 37, 38
11. 50, 52, 54, 60, 63, 65, 70, 74, 74, 74, 75, 78, 78

13.
```
0 | 1 2 3 4 5
1 |
2 | 0 0 2 4 6 8 8 8
3 | 0 1 7 9      Key: 2|0 = 20
```
1, 2, 3, 4, 5, 20, 20, 22, 24, 26, 28, 28, 28, 30, 31, 37, 39

15. 30, 33, 37, 39, 44, 48, 52, 54, 61, 61, 62, 68, 68, 76, 76, 76, 77, 79, 80, 81, 82, 84, 86, 87, 87 **17.** 7, 7, 10
19. 6, 6, 6 **21.** 8, 7.5, 5 and 10 **23.** 4.19, 3.98, 1.2
25. 72.8, 66 **27.** yes; 61

29. No; the mean salary of the other 99 adults is $25,000. The median and mode (both $25,000) are much more representative of the "average" salary.   **31.** *Sample answer:* The median (619) and the mode (619) are both slightly more representative than the mean (753) because they are closer to more scores in the lower three fourths of the data.

33.
```
 1 | 3 24 25
 2 | 3 20 22
 3 | 17
 4 | 1  8 14 17 30 30
 5 | 10
 6 | 3  5 13 24
 7 | 31
 8 | 21 26
 9 | 12
10 | 11 17
11 | 4 11 28
12 | 9 15 28    Key: 12 | 9 = 12–9 (Dec. 9)
```
1–3, 1–24, 1–25, 2–3, 2–20, 2–22, 3–17, 4–1, 4–8, 4–14, 4–17, 4–30, 4–30, 5–10, 6–3, 6–5, 6–13, 6–24, 7–31, 8–21, 8–26, 9–12, 10–11, 10–17, 11–4, 11–11, 11–28, 12–9, 12–15, 12–28

35.
```
20 | 44
21 | 93
22 | 14 17 26 52
23 | 93
24 | 78
25 | 70 74    Key: 25 | 70 = 257.0
```
204.4, 219.3, 221.4, 221.7, 222.6, 225.2, 239.3, 247.8, 257.0, 257.4

37. 300

39. *Sample answers:*
• About half of the 17 top male and female golfers had fewer than 40 tournament wins.
• For both males and females, by far the most common stem was 3, meaning between 30 and 39 tournament wins.
• There were 4 male and 2 female golfers with 60 or more tournament wins.

6.6 MIXED REVIEW (p. 374)

45. 358   **47.** not a solution   **49.** A   **51.** −1   **53.** $-\frac{1}{2}$

55. $x \geq 9$

57. $-8 \leq x < -2$

59. $x \leq -25$ or $x \geq -7$

6.7 PRACTICE (pp. 378–380)

5. 2, 4, 6   **7.** 6, 11, 16   **9.** C   **11.** 5, 6.5, 9   **13.** 4, 5, 7

15.

17.

19. Days of Rainfall

21. Movie Attendance

23. *Sample answer:* 10, 11, 11, 12, 14, 15, 16, 18, 20, 21, 25, 27, 27, 29, 30, 38

25. 3.6, 3.8, 4.8, 6.2, 6.7, 7.0, 7.1, 7.7, 8.4, 8.8
```
3 | 6 8
4 | 8
5 |
6 | 2 7
7 | 0 1 7
8 | 4 8    Key: 8 | 4 = 8.4 oz
```

27. 60, 70, 75, 80, 90, 90, 90, 135, 140, 260
```
 6 | 0
 7 | 0 5
 8 | 0
 9 | 0 0 0
10 |
11 |
12 |
13 | 5
14 | 0
 ⌇
26 | 0    Key: 14 | 0 = 140 min
```

31. 0.75 h   **33.** No. *Sample answer:* More people travel 0.5–1 hour; the box represents about 50% of the data, each whisker about 25%.

35.
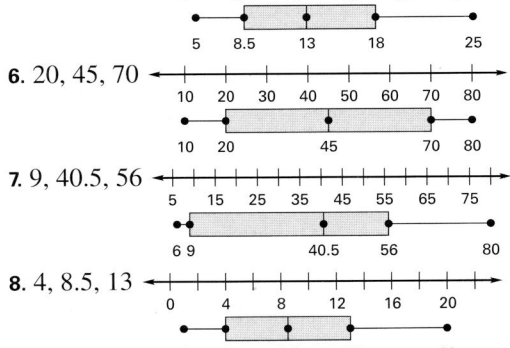

6.7 MIXED REVIEW (p. 381)   **39.** $x = \frac{1}{4}y + 1$; $\frac{1}{2}, \frac{3}{4}, 1, 1\frac{1}{4}$

41. $x = \frac{3}{2}y - \frac{5}{2}$; $-\frac{11}{2}, -4, -2\frac{1}{2}, -1$ **43.** $10.50/h

45. solution   **47.** not a solution

49. *Sample answer:* $y = 1430x + 64{,}500$ (in thousands)

QUIZ 3 (p. 381)   **1.**
```
0 | 5 7
1 | 0 6
2 | 0 3 4 5 9
3 | 1 2 7 8    Key: 3 | 1 = 31
```
5, 7, 10, 16, 20, 23, 24, 25, 29, 31, 32, 37, 38

2.
```
1 | 2 8
2 | 6 7
3 | 3 3
4 | 2 4 6 7
5 | 9
6 | 1    Key: 5 | 9 = 59
```
12, 18, 26, 27, 33, 33, 42, 44, 46, 47, 59, 61

3. 8, 9, 9 and 10   **4.** 37.5, 41, no mode

5. 8.5, 13, 18

6. 20, 45, 70

7. 9, 40.5, 56

8. 4, 8.5, 13

9. Mean: 39
Median: 40
Mode: 57

TECHNOLOGY ACTIVITY 6.7 (p. 382)

1. (least: 4; greatest: 19); **3.** (least: 20.1; greatest: 43.4); quartiles: 10, 13.5, 18   quartiles: 23.2, 25.7, 38.65

CHAPTER 6 REVIEW (pp. 384–386)

1. $x \le 2$ **3.** $x < -15$

5. $x > -\dfrac{2}{3}$ **7.** $x \le 5$ **9.** *Sample answer:* x is greater than 2 and less than 5.   **11.** x is less than or equal to $-1\dfrac{1}{4}$ or x is greater than 7.   **13.** $-6, 16$ **15.** $-11 \le x \le 1$

17. $-4\dfrac{2}{3} \le x \le 3\dfrac{1}{3}$

19.   **21.**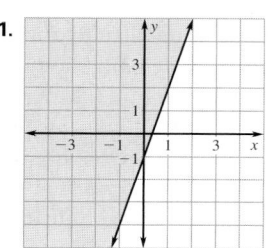

23. 72, 74.5, 58 and 78   **25.** *Sample answer:* The temperatures in Tokyo are much higher. The highest Paris temperature is only slightly higher than the median Tokyo temperature. Only 25% of the Paris temperatures are at least 15.3°, while half of the Tokyo temperatures are at least 15.85°.

CUMULATIVE PRACTICE (pp. 390–391) **1.** 7   **3.** 45   **5.** 6

7. -6 **9.** 14.5   **11.** $\begin{bmatrix} 6 & 7 & -6 \\ -5 & -1 & 5 \end{bmatrix}$ **13.** $18 + 3x$

15. $-15t + 5t^2$ **17.** $11b + 7$ **19.** $5.3y$ **21.** 12   **23.** 24

25. 12   **27.** $1\dfrac{11}{14}$ **29.** 4   **31.** 1   **33.** $y = \dfrac{4}{5}x - \dfrac{13}{5}$ **35.** \$.50/can

37.   **39.**

41. $\dfrac{1}{3}$

43. undefined

45.   **47.**

49. 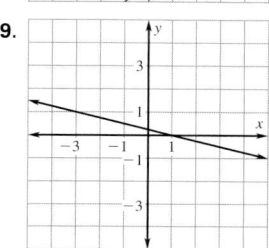   **51.** $y = x - 3$ **53.** $y = 2x + 3$

55. $y = -5x - 9$ **57.** $y = \dfrac{1}{2}x + 3$ **59.** $x < 2$ **61.** $x \le -48$

63. $x < 6$ **65.** $x \ge 10.1$ **67.** $4 < x < 6$ **69.** $x < -2$ or $x > 18$

71. 16, 12.5, 5   **73.** No. *Sample answer:* By estimation, you have about $\$25 - 2(\$10) = \$5$ left. The actual amount is $\$25 - 2(\$9.99) = \$5.02$, which is less than \$5.95.

75. -100 ft/min, 100 ft/min   **77.** \$9.90   **79.** *Sample answer:* $y = 365x + 4896$

CHAPTER 7

SKILL REVIEW (p. 396) **1.** $21x$ **2.** $-36r$ **3.** $-d$ **4.** $\dfrac{5}{4}w$

5. $-\dfrac{16}{21}g$ **6.** $\dfrac{23}{40}y$ **7.** -1 **8.** no solution   **9.** all real numbers

10. $\dfrac{1}{2}$ **11.** solution   **12.** not a solution   **13.** not a solution

14. not a solution

7.1 PRACTICE (pp. 401–403)   **3.** not a solution

5. not a solution   **7.** $-(-4) + (-2) = 2; \ 2(-4) + (-2) = -10;$ $(-4, -2)$ is not a solution of either equation.   **9.** $(2, -1)$

11. solution   **13.** not a solution   **15.** not a solution   **17.** $(4, 5)$

19. $(3, 0)$ **21.** $(6, -6)$ **23.** $(-3, -5)$ **25.** $(-4, -5)$

27. $(1, 4)$ **29.** $(-8, -4)$ **31.** $(8, 6)$ **33.** $\left(-1\dfrac{1}{2}, -2\dfrac{1}{2}\right)$

35. 125,000 mi   **37.** *Sample answer:* coastal: $y = 0.12t + 46$; inland: $y = -0.12t + 54$ **39.** *Sample answer:* 1973

7.1 MIXED REVIEW (p. 403) **47.** -3 **49.** 5 **51.** 9
53. $y = -4x + 12$ **55.** $y = 4x - 9$ **57.** $y = 2x - 1$
59. $x < 4260$

TECHNOLOGY ACTIVITY 7.1 (p. 404) **1.** $(-3.5, 2.5)$
3. $(-1, -2)$ **5.** The lines are parallel. Since the lines do not intersect, the system has no solution.

7.2 PRACTICE (pp. 408–410) **7.** $(-2, -3)$ **9.** $(1, 2)$ **11.** $(1, 0)$
13. $\left(1\frac{1}{2}, -\frac{1}{2}\right)$ **15.** *Sample answer:* I would isolate m in the second equation because it is easy to do so and the value is easy to substitute in the other equation. **17.** $(6, 2)$
19. $(3, 8)$ **21.** $(2, 9)$ **23.** $(5, 15)$ **25.** $(-3, -3)$ **27.** $(12, 17)$
29. $(-168, -108)$ **31.** $(4, 1)$ **33.** $\left(\frac{1}{3}, -4\frac{1}{3}\right)$

35. The variables are eliminated, leaving a statement that is always true. You solved for one variable in one equation and substituted for that variable in the same equation; Substitute $y = -3x + 9$ into Equation 2 to get $(1, 6)$ for the solution. **37.** $(100, 50)$ **39.** $(7, -6)$ **41.** $(24, -4)$ **43.** 30 11-in. softballs, 50 12-in. softballs
45. $3375 in company EFG, $1125 in company PQR
47. 882 m uphill, 675 m downhill

7.2 MIXED REVIEW (p. 410) **55.** $-2x$ **57.** $26y$

59. $y = 2x + 4$

61. $y = -\frac{5}{3}x + 1$

63. $y = -2$

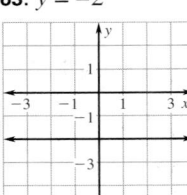

65. $-19 \leq x \leq 9$

67. $x < -\frac{1}{2}$ or $x > 5\frac{1}{2}$

7.3 PRACTICE (pp. 414–416) **5.** *Sample answer:* Multiply either equation by -1, solve for y, then substitute in either original equation to solve for x; $(3, 1)$. **7.** *Sample answer:* Subtract $2x$ from each side of the first equation, solve for y, then substitute in either original equation to solve for x; $(3, 2)$. **9.** $(14, 6)$ **11.** $(-1, 1)$ **13.** $(1, 1)$ **15.** $(1, 1)$
17. $(-2, 3)$ **19.** $(3, 2)$ **21.** $(2, 0)$ **23.** $\left(13, \frac{5}{8}\right)$ **25.** $(21, -3)$
27. $(8, -1)$ **29.** $(50, 50)$ **31.** $(1, 2)$ **33.** $(4, 3)$ **35.** $(2, 1)$

37. $(2, 0)$ **39.** $(3, 2)$ **41.** $(0, 4)$ **43.** 5 g **45.** Let $s =$ speed in still air and $w =$ wind speed; $s - w = 300$, $s + w = 450$.
47. 375 mi/h; 75 mi/h

7.3 MIXED REVIEW (p. 416) **57.** $y = \frac{1}{2}x$ **59.** $y = x - 1$
61. $y = -\frac{1}{3}x + 6$ **63.** solution; not a solution **65.** solution; not a solution **67.** $(-3, -2)$ **69.** $(10, -2)$ **71.** $(3, 5)$

QUIZ 1 (p. 417) **1.** $(3, -4)$ **2.** $(6, 8)$ **3.** $(0, 0)$ **4.** $(1, 9)$
5. $(-1, 3)$ **6.** $(10, -6)$ **7.** $(5, 1)$ **8.** $\left(-\frac{1}{2}, \frac{1}{2}\right)$ **9.** $\left(2\frac{2}{3}, -6\frac{2}{3}\right)$
10. 4 CDs; 6 CDs

7.4 PRACTICE (pp. 421–424) **3.** *Sample answer:* Substitution or linear combinations; it would be simple to write either variable in terms of the other or to eliminate x by multiplying either equation by -1.
5. *Sample answer:* Any of the three methods would be reasonable; it would be simple to write either variable in terms of the other, both would be simple to graph, and y could be eliminated by multiplying either equation by -1.
7. Let $x =$ price per gallon of regular and $y =$ price per gallon of premium. **9.** regular: $1.19; premium: $1.39
11. $(3, 2)$ **13.** *Sample answer:* Substitution or linear combinations; it would be simple to write y in terms of x, and y could be eliminated by adding the equations.
15. *Sample answer:* Substitution; either variable may be easily eliminated using one of the equations.
17. *Sample answer:* Linear combinations; no variable has a coefficient of 1 or -1. **19.** $(2, 1)$ **21.** $(2, -1)$ **23.** $(1, -1)$
25. $(2, -1)$ **27.** $\left(5\frac{5}{9}, 10\right)$ **29.** $(-4, 4)$ **31.** $(3, 0)$ **33.** $(4, 2)$
35. $\left(-\frac{3}{4}, 3\frac{1}{2}\right)$ **37.** $(6, 6)$ **39.** $(6, -5)$ **41.** $(-4, 5)$ **43.** $\left(\frac{1}{3}, 0\right)$
45. $(2, 6)$ **47.** 20 mL of the 5% solution, 40 mL of the 2% solution **49.** 4 children **51.** $y = 172x + 6200$ and $y = -16x + 6500$; $\left(1\frac{28}{47}, 6474\frac{22}{47}\right)$; the point of intersection represents the number of years after 1970 (about 1.6) when the demand for low-income housing and the availability were equal (about 6,474,500). **53.** $y = 7x + 50$ **55.** 1 h at 4 mi/h and $\frac{1}{2}$ h at 6 mi/h **57.** substitution, graphing, linear combinations **59.** No; solving the system involving any two of the equations will produce the desired solution.
61. $r + b = 12$; $r = 3b$ **63.** 0.75

7.4 MIXED REVIEW (p. 424) **67.** parallel **69.** not parallel
71.

73.

75. 70 out of 100 households

7.5 PRACTICE (pp. 429–431)

7. no solution **9.** no solution

11. exactly one solution, (5, 12) **13.** D; no solution
15. B; infinitely many solutions **17.** C; infinitely many
solutions **19.** infinitely many solutions **21.** infinitely many
solutions **23.** no solution **25.** infinitely many solutions
27. no solution **29.** no solution **31.** No; the system of
equations that describes the situation is $4x + 2y = 99.62$,
$12x + 6y = 298.86$, which has infinitely many solutions.

7.5 MIXED REVIEW (p. 431) **43.** A **45.** D **47.** 55 ft/h

7.6 PRACTICE (pp. 435–437)

5. **7.**

9. C **11.** B **13.** $y \le \frac{1}{2}x + 2$, $y \ge \frac{1}{2}x - 2$

15. **17.**

19. **21.**

23. **25.**

27. (0, −5), (0, 11), (6, 5) **29.** (0, 0), (−2, 1), (2, 5)
31. $1 \le x \le 7$, $1 \le y \le 6$

33. $y \le x + 2$, $y \le -x + 7$, $1 \le y \le 3$

35. 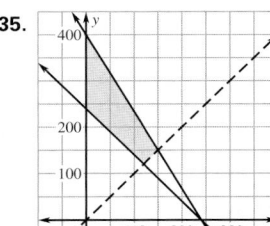 **37.** 8 square units

39. *Sample answers:* 4 h baby-sitting and 14 h as cashier,
12 h baby-sitting and 6 h as cashier **41. a.** (0, 0), (0, 2400),
(900, 600), (1050, 0) **b.** 0; 72,000; 27,000; 10,500
c. $72,000

7.6 MIXED REVIEW (p. 438) **45.** 243 **47.** 137 **49.** 33
51. 49 **53.** −60 **55.** 9 **57.** 47, 56, 57

QUIZ 2 (p. 438) **1.** length: 8 ft, width: 3 ft **2.** no solution
3. no solution **4.** infinitely many solutions **5.** exactly one
solution, (5, −6) **6.** exactly one solution, (0, 1)
7. infinitely many solutions **8.**

9. **10.**

11. **12.**

13. 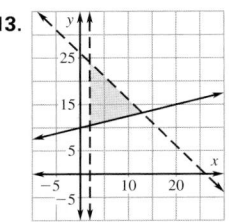 **14.** $10,000 at 5%, $6000 at 6%

CHAPTER 7 REVIEW (pp. 440–442)

1.   **3.**

5.

7. $(0, 3)$ **9.** $\left(\frac{5}{8}, 1\frac{1}{2}\right)$ **11.** $\left(\frac{1}{2}, 0\right)$

13. $\left(-5, 2\frac{3}{5}\right)$ **15.** $(3, -5)$

17. $(-1, 1)$ **19.** Ferris wheel: 5 times, roller coaster: 7 times

21. infinitely many solutions **23.** exactly one solution, $(2, 6)$

25. exactly one solution, $\left(-3\frac{1}{4}, 6\frac{1}{2}\right)$

27. 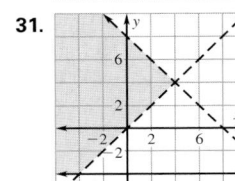 **29.**

31.

CHAPTER 8

SKILL REVIEW (p. 448) **1.** 6^2 **2.** 4^3 **3.** $(2y)^5$ **4.** $\frac{1}{4}$ **5.** $\frac{1}{9}$

6. $\frac{3}{4}$ **7.** $\frac{1}{2}$ **8.** \$8.25/h **9.** \$.79/cantaloupe **10.** \$.50/can **11.** 45 mi/gal

8.1 PRACTICE (pp. 453–455) **5.** m^3 **7.** 3^7, or 2187 **9.** x^9 **11.** 4

13. 4^9, or 262,144 **15.** m^{32} **17.** a^2b^4 **19.** $x^{12}y^{20}$

21. $(-2)^3x^9$, or $-8x^9$ **23.** 5^{11}, or 48,828,125 **25.** 7^8, or 5,764,801 **27.** $3^2 \cdot 7^2$, or 441 **29.** $(-5)^3a^3$, or $-125a^3$

31. $(-4)^6$, or 4096 **33.** $(5 + x)^{18}$ **35.** 3^3b^4, or $27b^4$ **37.** $4x^9$

39. $-3^2 \cdot 7^2 \cdot x^{10}$, or $-441x^{10}$ **41.** $3 \cdot 2^3 \cdot y^5$, or $24y^5$

43. $-r^3s^7$ **45.** $-(-3)^3c^3d^5$, or $27c^3d^5$ **47.** $6^2 \cdot \left(\frac{1}{4}\right)^2 \cdot a^{14}$, or $\frac{9}{4}a^{14}$ **49.** -3^2w^7, or $-9w^7$ **51.** $(-x)^9$, or $-x^9$

53. $-r^4s^{14}t^9$ **55.** a^5; 1 **57.** a^6; 1 **59.** a^2b^4; 16 **61.** $-(a^2b^6)$; -64

63. $>$ **65.** $<$ **67.** $>$ **69.** 788.9 **71.** 308.9 **73.** 333,446,267.9

75. approximately $113.04a^3$ **77.** 8 to 1 **79. a.** 2^{30} or 1,073,741,824 ways **b.** $\left(\frac{1}{2}\right)^{30}$, or about 0.0000000009

81. 3^{14}; $\frac{1}{3^{14}}$, or about 0.0000002

8.1 MIXED REVIEW (p. 455) **87.** 10,000 **89.** $\frac{1}{25}$ **91.** $\frac{45}{4}$

93.   **95.**

97.   **99.**

101.

103. $x \geq -\frac{10}{3}$

105. \$.07 $\leq p \leq$ \$.71, where p is the price of a quart of milk

8.2 PRACTICE (pp. 459–461) **3.** $\frac{1}{3}$ **5.** not defined **7.** $\frac{1}{m^2}$

9. $\frac{a^5}{b^8}$ **11.** yes **13.** about 26.9 points per game

15. $\frac{1}{81}$ **17.** 32 **19.** 100 **21.** $\frac{1}{2}$ **23.** 1 **25.** 1 **27.** -9

29. $\frac{1}{125}$ **31.** $\frac{3}{x^4}$ **33.** $\frac{y^4}{x^2}$ **35.** $\frac{8}{x^2y^6}$ **37.** $\frac{x^{10}}{4y^{14}}$ **39.** $-\frac{1}{64x^3}$

41. $\frac{1}{9x^2y^2}$ **43.** $8m^2$ **45.** $-\frac{1}{2x^3}$ **47.** C **49.** 0.03125

51. 0.00352 **53.** no **55.** no

57.   **59.**

61. 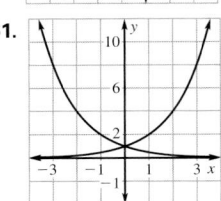 *Sample answer:* Both graphs are curves that pass through $(0, 1)$ and both increase without limit in one direction and get very close to the x-axis in the other.

63. $(0, 1)$; yes; $(0, 2)$

65. a. 117; 141; 203; 243; 292 **b.**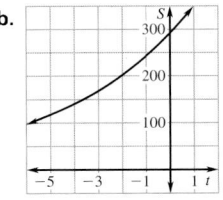

8.2 MIXED REVIEW (p. 461) **71.** $\frac{4}{25}$ **73.** $-\frac{729}{1000}$

75. $-12 \leq x \leq 2$ **77.** $-11 \leq x \leq 7$

79. $4 < x < 5$

81.

83. $\left(\dfrac{1}{2}, 3\right)$

85. $(100, 50)$ **87.** $(-129, 9)$

TECHNOLOGY ACTIVITY 8.2 (p. 462) **7.** *Sample answer:* The graph is close to the negative x-axis and curves upward to the right. **9.** *Sample answer:* The graph is close to the negative x-axis and curves downward to the right.

8.3 PRACTICE (pp. 466–468) **3.** 125 **5.** a^3 **7.** a^3 **9.** $\dfrac{1}{5}$

11. $\dfrac{1}{32}$ **13.** $\dfrac{25}{m^2}$ **15.** $\dfrac{64}{125}$ **17.** $\dfrac{x^{18}}{y^{30}}$ **19.** 125 **21.** -1

23. 2187 **25.** $\dfrac{1}{125}$ **27.** 27 **29.** $\dfrac{9}{25}$ **31.** $\dfrac{81}{x^4}$ **33.** $\dfrac{1}{x^5}$ **35.** $\dfrac{1}{x^3}$

37. y^2 **39.** $\dfrac{1}{r^{12}}$ **41.** $\dfrac{8x^6 y^9}{27}$ **43.** $5x^3 y^3$ **45.** $\dfrac{x^6}{256y^8}$

47. $\dfrac{5}{4x^{11} y^4}$ **49.** $\dfrac{6^3}{6} = 6^{3-1} = 6^2 = 36$ **51.** The volume of Earth is about 64 times the volume of the Moon.

53. $\dfrac{1}{1.2^6} \approx \dfrac{1}{3}$ **55.** about 3 times **57.** $\dfrac{1}{1.13^2}$ or about 0.8

59. a. 200; 160; 128; 102; 82; 66; 52 **61.** $\left(\dfrac{1}{2}\right)^6 \approx 0.02$

8.3 MIXED REVIEW (p. 469) **67.** 100,000 **69.** $\dfrac{1}{10,000}$

71.

73.

75.

77.

79. solution **81.** solution **83.** $(8, 4)$ **85.** $(4, 3)$

QUIZ 1 (p. 469) **1.** 2187 **2.** 256 **3.** 10,000 **4.** $\dfrac{1}{2401}$

5. $\dfrac{1}{16,384}$ **6.** $\dfrac{7}{6}$ **7.** $\dfrac{1}{3125}$ **8.** 2187 **9.** $\dfrac{64}{125}$ **10.** -128 **11.** 64

12. 4 **13.** x^9 **14.** $-32x^5$ **15.** $-3a^5$ **16.** c^5 **17.** x^2 **18.** x

19. $\dfrac{16m^4}{81n^4}$ **20.** x **21.** $-1728a^6$ **22.** $16m^{10}$ **23.** $30x^2$

24. $145.87; $214.33; $250

8.4 PRACTICE (pp. 473–475) **3.** 430 **5.** 0.245 **7.** 3.96×10 **9.** 1.2×10^3 **11.** 6.9×10^6 **13.** 7.2×10^7 **15.** approximately 1.97×10^4 sec, or about 5.5 h **17.** 0.98 **19.** 8652.1 **21.** 0.000006002 **23.** 100,012,000 **25.** 5×10^{-2} **27.** 4.22×10^{-2} **29.** 7×10^8 **31.** 8.551×10^{-3} **33.** 4.59×10^{-4} **35.** 8.8×10^7 **37.** 1.2×10^5; 120,000 **39.** 1.5×10^5; 150,000 **41.** 1.6×10^2; 160 **43.** 6.0×10^0; 6 **45.** 8.1×10^7; 81,000,000 **47.** 2.4×10^{10}; 24,000,000,000 **49.** 1.09926×10^6; 1,099,260 **51.** 5.76×10^{-8}; 0.0000000576 **53.** 1.2×10^8 **55.** 5.0819×10^{13} **57.** about 3.57×10^{14} mi^3 **59.** Louisiana Purchase: \$.03/acre; Gadsden Purchase: \$.53/acre **61.** 4.4064×10^{10} m^3 **63.** Answers are rounded to the nearest whole number; TX: 2167; MN: 1522; PA; 1583; VT: 810; CA: 1806

8.4 MIXED REVIEW (p. 475) **67.** 0.22 **69.** 0.0007 **71.** 0.005 **73.** 2.55 **75.** $(1, 4)$

77.

79.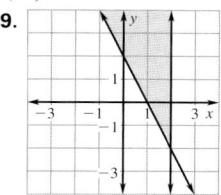

81. 1000 **83.** $\dfrac{1}{49}$

8.5 PRACTICE (pp. 480–482) **5.** B **7.** $2231.39 **9.** $4489.99 **11.** $379.25 **13.** $505.67 **15.** $325.40 **17.** about 46.3 L/min; about 86.5 L/min **19.** A **21.** $P = 10,000(1.25)^t$

23.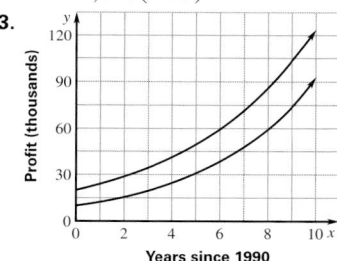

Sample answer: I would base my choice on how long I thought I would own the business (and how realistic I thought the continued annual increase was). The profits for the business in Ex. 22 started higher than those for the other business and would remain higher for 16 years. After that, the profits of the other business would increase more rapidly and be much higher. For example, after 20 years the profits would be more than $100,000 greater. **25.** B

8.5 MIXED REVIEW (p. 482) **33.** 176.25 **35.** 260 **37.** 0.96 **39.** $-\dfrac{16}{15}$ **41.** -0.29999952 **43.** 0.41405 **45.** 2.4 **47.** 3

8.6 PRACTICE (pp. 488–490) **5.** $5137 **7.** $3770 **9.** C **11.** $5450 **13.** $2845 **15.** B **17.** exponential growth; 1.18; 18% **19.** exponential growth; $\dfrac{5}{4}$; 25% **21.** exponential decay; $\dfrac{2}{5}$; 60% **23.** 160 mg **25.** 246 mg

27. $N = 64\left(\dfrac{1}{2}\right)^t$ **31.** $M = 302(0.9)^t$

33.

8.6 MIXED REVIEW (p. 490) **41.** 20 **43.** 7 **45.** −1.3 **47.** 2.4

QUIZ 2 (p. 491) **1.** 1.1205×10^{-2} **2.** 1.4×10^8
3. 6.7×10^{-8} **4.** 3.072×10^{10} **5.** 4820 **6.** 5,000,000,000
7. 0.00000704 **8.** 0.01112 **9.** $y = 50(1.05)^t$; about \$70
10. $y = 20,000(0.85)^t$; about \$8874

TECHNOLOGY ACTIVITY 8.6 (p. 492)
1. $y = 1.0339(1.6293)^x$

CHAPTER 8 REVIEW (pp. 494–496) **1.** 2^9, or 512
3. $3^3 \cdot 2^2 \cdot a^5$, or $108a^5$

5. s^7; 128 **7.** $s^6 t^2$; 576 **9.** $\dfrac{1}{125}$ **11.** 32 **13.** $\dfrac{x^6}{y^6}$ **15.** 1

17.

19.

21. $\dfrac{1}{27}$ **23.** $\dfrac{16}{81}$ **25.** $\dfrac{531,441}{b^6}$ **27.** m^6 **29.** $-27a^3b^3$

31. $-24a^2b^2$ **33.** $\dfrac{1}{1.17^5} \approx 0.46$ **35.** 768,000 **37.** 0.0002

39. 6.79×10^{-4} **41.** 7.52×10^7 **43.** $w = 2(1.05)^x$
45. $e = 125(0.97)^x$

CHAPTER 9

SKILL REVIEW (p. 502) **1.** −60 **2.** 12 **3.** 44 **4.** 2
5.

6.

7.

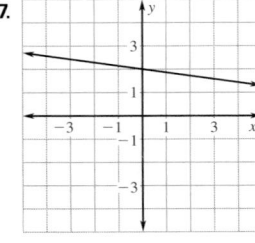

8. not a solution **9.** solution
10. solution

9.1 PRACTICE (pp. 507–509) **9.** 0.9 **11.** ±3 **13.** 3, 7
15. −2, 2 **17.** −1.2, 1.2 **19.** about 1.7 sec **21.** about 3.5 sec
23. −7, 7 **25.** no square roots **27.** 0 **29.** −0.3, 0.3
31. −13 **33.** 3.61 **35.** 0.2 **37.** −0.32 **39.** 3 **41.** undefined
43. $\sqrt{109}$ **45.** −2.27, 4.27 **47.** −1.33, 2.13 **49.** −11.24,
−2.76 **51.** −1.80, 5.13 **53.** −1.34, −0.99 **55.** −8, 8
57. −4, 4 **59.** no solution **61.** −3, 3 **63.** −4, 4
65. no solution **67.** −3, 3 **69.** −3.87, 3.87 **71.** −2.65, 2.65
73. no solution **75.** −2.83, 2.83 **77.** −1.41, 1.41
79. $h = -16t^2 + 60$ **81.** $\sqrt{3.75} \approx 1.94$ sec **83.** 3 sec
85. 5 sec **87.** 2003 **89.** 0.40 mm **91.** 0.15 mm
93. 0.12 mm

9.1 MIXED REVIEW (p. 510) **101.** 11 **103.** $2^3 \times 3^2$
105. $(-1, -2)$ **107.** $(-48, 14)$ **109.** $(-4, -19)$
111. 1225 student tickets, 1117 general admission tickets

9.2 PRACTICE (pp. 514–515) **5.** A **7.** C **9.** *Sample answer:*
The factor 5 cannot be taken outside the radicand. The first
step should be $\sqrt{50} = \sqrt{25 \cdot 2}$. Then, by the product
property, this equals $\sqrt{25} \cdot \sqrt{2}$, or $5\sqrt{2}$. **11.** $3\sqrt{3}$
13. $5\sqrt{3}$ **15.** $5\sqrt{5}$ **17.** $4\sqrt{5}$ **19.** $\sqrt{6}$ **21.** $4\sqrt{3}$ **23.** $\dfrac{\sqrt{11}}{4}$

25. $2\sqrt{5}$ **27.** $3\sqrt{3}$ **29.** $\dfrac{3\sqrt{2}}{4}$ **31.** $\dfrac{3\sqrt{3}}{4}$ **33.** $8\sqrt{5}$ **35.** $\dfrac{\sqrt{3}}{2}$

37. 2 **39.** $\dfrac{4\sqrt{3}}{9}$ **41.** $\sqrt{30}$ **43.** $18\sqrt{7}$ **45.** −18 **47.** −3

49. $\dfrac{-2\sqrt{5}}{5}$ **51.** $\dfrac{1}{4}$; 0.25 **53.** $\dfrac{\sqrt{15}}{2} \approx 1.94$ m² **55.** $70\sqrt{2}$ m/sec

9.2 MIXED REVIEW (p. 516)
65.

67.

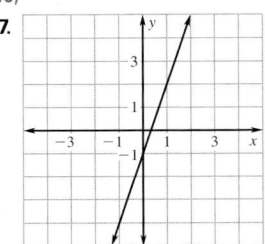

69. b^8; 256 **71.** $\dfrac{x^5}{2}$ **73.** $\dfrac{y^3}{x^4}$ **75.** $(1.3)^4 \approx 2.86$

9.3 PRACTICE (pp. 521–523) **5.** up; $x = -2$ **7.** up; $x = -\dfrac{7}{2}$

9. up; $x = \dfrac{1}{5}$ **11.** (0, 0)

13. (0, 10)

15. (3, −1)

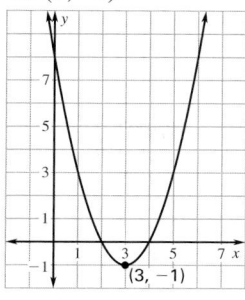

17. $\left(-\dfrac{1}{2}, 13\right)$ **19.** (2, −5)

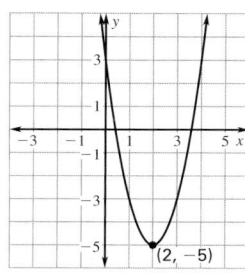

21. a. up **b.** (0, 0) **c.** $x = 0$ **23. a.** up **b.** (0, 0) **c.** $x = 0$
25. a. down **b.** (0, 0) **c.** $x = 0$ **27. a.** down **b.** (0, 0) **c.** $x = 0$
29. a. up **b.** $\left(2\dfrac{1}{2}, -12\dfrac{1}{2}\right)$ **c.** $x = 2\dfrac{1}{2}$ **31. a.** down

b. $\left(\dfrac{3}{5}, 3\dfrac{3}{5}\right)$ **c.** $x = \dfrac{3}{5}$ **33. a.** up **b.** (−1, 2) **c.** $x = -1$

35. a. up **b.** $\left(1\dfrac{3}{4}, -14\dfrac{1}{8}\right)$ **c.** $x = 1\dfrac{3}{4}$ **37. a.** down **b.** (4, 48)

c. $x = 4$ **39. a.** up **b.** $\left(-\dfrac{1}{32}, -8\dfrac{1}{256}\right)$ **c.** $x = -\dfrac{1}{23}$

41. a. up **b.** (2.56, −13.1) **c.** $x = 2.56$ **43. a.** down
b. (−0.35, 3.885) **c.** $x = -0.35$

45. (0, 0)

47. (−2, −5)

49. (−1, −7)

51. $\left(\dfrac{1}{3}, -\dfrac{2}{3}\right)$

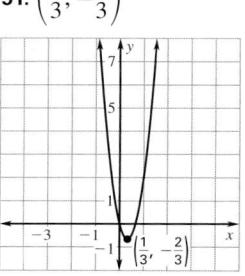

53. $\left(-\dfrac{1}{2}, \dfrac{15}{4}\right)$ **55.** $\left(\dfrac{1}{3}, -\dfrac{4}{3}\right)$ **57.** $\left(-\dfrac{1}{3}, -\dfrac{2}{3}\right)$ **59.** $\left(\dfrac{1}{2}, 8\right)$

61. $\left(\dfrac{3}{2}, -\dfrac{1}{2}\right)$

63. (−4, 14)

65. 5 ft **67.** 70 ft **69.** 1980 to 1984 **71.** The vertex is the
point at which the graph changes direction, that is, when
the values of G stop decreasing and begin increasing.
73. about 0.21 sec

9.3 MIXED REVIEW (p. 524)

81. $y = 3x - 6$

83. $y = -2x + 6$

85.

87.

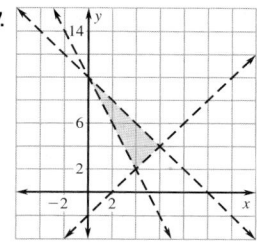

89. 3^6, or 729 **91.** a^6 **93.** $216x^3$ **95.** $-27a^6b^6$
97. 9.87×10^5 **99.** 1.229×10^9 **101.** 9.99×10^{-3}

QUIZ 1 (p. 524) **1.** 12 **2.** −14 **3.** −26 **4.** −5.20 **5.** 2.45
6. 1.22 **7.** 0.4 **8.** 1.5 **9.** −13, 13 **10.** −4, 4
11. $-\sqrt{10}$, $\sqrt{10}$ **12.** $-2\sqrt{2}$, $2\sqrt{2}$ **13.** $3\sqrt{2}$ **14.** 10 **15.** 11
16. $\dfrac{\sqrt{5}}{2}$ **17.** up; (−1, −12); $x = -1$ **18.** up; (2, −14); $x = 2$

19. up; (−1, −13); $x = -1$ **20.** up; $\left(-5, -15\dfrac{1}{2}\right)$; $x = -5$

21. up; $\left(\dfrac{1}{2}, 5\dfrac{1}{4}\right)$; $x = \dfrac{1}{2}$ **22.** up; $\left(-4\dfrac{1}{2}, -20\dfrac{1}{4}\right)$; $x = -4\dfrac{1}{2}$

23.

24.

25.

TECHNOLOGY ACTIVITY 9.3 (p. 525)

1. $y = 5.25x^2 + 67.21x - 81.46$

9.4 PRACTICE (pp. 529–530) **7.** $-2, 2$ **9.** $-3, 3$ **11.** $-3, 3$
13. $-3, 3$ **15.** $-2, -1$ **17.** $-4, 5$ **19.** $-4.2, 0.2$ **21.** $-4, 4$
23. $-5, 5$ **25.** $-12, 12$ **27.** $-5, 5$ **29.** $-4, 4$ **31.** $-9, 9$
33. $-2, 3$ **35.** $-1, 2$ **37.** $-3, 1$ **39.** $-1, 5$ **41.** $-7, 3$
43. $-2, -1$ **45.** $-1, 4$ **47.** $-1.17, 0.17$ **49.** $-8, 4$
51. 69.19 ft; the distance was greater than that for an initial
angle of 65°, but less than that for an initial angle of 35°.

53.

55. 1994

9.4 MIXED REVIEW (p. 531) **65.** $\left(-\dfrac{5}{2}, \dfrac{3}{4}\right)$; one solution

67. infinitely many solutions **69.** no solution
71. $-1.17, 6.17$ **73.** $-1.47, 7.47$ **75.** $2\sqrt{10}$ **77.** $2\sqrt{15}$
79. $2\sqrt{5}$ **81.** $\dfrac{1}{2}\sqrt{2}$ **83.** pasta dishes: \$5.95, salads: \$1.95

TECHNOLOGY ACTIVITY 9.4 (p. 532)
1. $0.26, 6.41$ **3.** $0.21, 4.79$ **5.** $1.71, 2$ **7.** $3.04, 6.40$

9.5 PRACTICE (pp. 536–537) **5.** $5, -3$ **7.** $0.5, 1.5$
9. $-3 + 2\sqrt{3}, -3 - 2\sqrt{3}$ **11.** $8x^2 + 6x - 2 = 0; -1, \dfrac{1}{4}$
13. $2x^2 - 14x - 36 = 0; -2, 9$ **15.** $4x^2 + 4x + 1 = 0; -0.5$
17. $-2, -8$ **19.** $\dfrac{-3 + 3\sqrt{3}}{2} \approx 1.10, \dfrac{-3 - 3\sqrt{3}}{2} \approx -4.10$
21. $\dfrac{-2 + \sqrt{5}}{2} \approx 0.12, \dfrac{-2 - \sqrt{5}}{2} \approx -2.12$ **23.** 25 **25.** 1 **27.** 1
29. 21 **31.** 39 **33.** $-10, -1$ **35.** $-\dfrac{4}{3}, 2$
37. $\dfrac{-7 + \sqrt{22}}{9} \approx -0.26, \dfrac{-7 - \sqrt{22}}{9} \approx -1.30$
39. $\dfrac{-1 + 2\sqrt{2}}{7} \approx 0.26, \dfrac{-1 - 2\sqrt{2}}{7} \approx -0.55$
41. $6 + \sqrt{62} \approx 13.87, 6 - \sqrt{62} \approx -1.87$
43. $\dfrac{5 + \sqrt{177}}{-4} \approx -4.58, \dfrac{5 - \sqrt{177}}{-4} \approx 2.08$

45. $x^2 - 3x + 2 = 0; 1, 2$ **47.** $6x^2 + 5x - 1 = 0; -1, \dfrac{1}{6}$
49. $2z^2 - 5z - 7 = 0; -1, \dfrac{7}{2}$ **51.** $5c^2 - 9c + 4 = 0; \dfrac{4}{5}, 1$
53. $4, -2$ **55.** $-2, 3$ **57.** $-2.56, 1.56$ **59.** $-1, \dfrac{1}{3}$
61. $-0.62, 1.62$ **63–69 odd:** Sample answers are given.
All the equations can be solved using the quadratic formula.
63. $4\sqrt{2} \approx 5.66, -4\sqrt{2} \approx -5.66$; finding square roots;
simplest method **65.** $-\dfrac{7}{2}, \dfrac{7}{2}$; finding square roots;
simplest method **67.** -9; finding square roots;
the expression on the left can be written $(h + 9)^2$.
69. $\dfrac{1 + \sqrt{5}}{6} \approx 0.54, \dfrac{1 - \sqrt{5}}{6} \approx -0.21$; quadratic formula;
when written in standard form, the expression cannot be
written as a perfect square. **71.** 2.30 sec **73.** 2.21 sec
75. 1.31 sec **77.** 1.37 sec **79.** 5.70 sec **81.** 0.44 sec
83. 0.79 sec

9.5 MIXED REVIEW (p. 538)
87. 25 **89.** -48 **91.**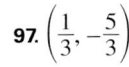

93. $-3 < x < 5$ **95.** $x \le -15$ or $x \ge 5$

97. $\left(\dfrac{1}{3}, -\dfrac{5}{3}\right)$ **99.** $\left(-\dfrac{3}{4}, \dfrac{25}{8}\right)$

101. $\left(\dfrac{1}{32}, 3\dfrac{255}{256}\right)$

103. about 3.84×10^4 people; about 1.17×10^6 people

TECHNOLOGY ACTIVITY 9.5 (p. 539) **1.** $-6, 5$ **3.** -2
5. no solution **7.** $-2.4, 1$ **9.** $-6.35, -2.16$

9.6 PRACTICE (pp. 544–545) **3.** -56; no real solution **5.** 65;
two solutions **7.** A **9.** two solutions **11.** two solutions
13. no real solution **15.** one x-intercept; B **17.** no
x-intercept; A **19.** two solutions **21.** The equation has two
solutions for all values of c less than 4, one solution for
$c = 4$, and no real solution for all values of c greater than 4.

23. The equation has two solutions for all values of c less than $1\frac{1}{8}$, one solution for $c = 1\frac{1}{8}$, and no real solution for all values of c greater than $1\frac{1}{8}$.

25. Yes; no; *Sample answer:* Because the discriminant for you is positive, your equation has two solutions; because the discriminant for your friend is negative, your friend's equation has no real solution. That is, there is no time when your friend's jump height will be 3.4 ft.

27. *Sample answer:* The payroll will reach $80 billion if the discriminant of the equation $26t^2 + 1629t - 60,042 = 0$ is nonnegative; since the discriminant is 8,898,009, the payroll will reach that amount.   **29.** yes

9.6 MIXED REVIEW (p. 546)

35.   **37.**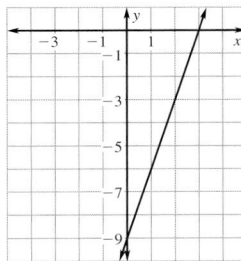

39. $x \le -45$ **41.** $x \le 12$

43.   **45.**

47.

Modem Prices

QUIZ 2 (p. 547) **1.** $-2, 5$ **2.** 6 **3.** $-3, -1$ **4.** -3
5. $-6, -0.5$ **6.** $-2, 8$ **7.** $1.5, 2$ **8.** $-3, 1\frac{1}{3}$ **9.** $-1, -0.6$

10. two solutions   **11.** one solution   **12.** no real solution
13. Yes; *Sample answer:* The discriminant of the equation $-16t^2 + 50t + 6 = 45$ is positive, so the equation has two real solutions, meaning that the ball would reach a height of 45 ft.

9.7 PRACTICE (pp. 551–552) **5.** $(1, -2)$ is not a solution; $(0, 0)$ is a solution. **7.**

9.   **11.**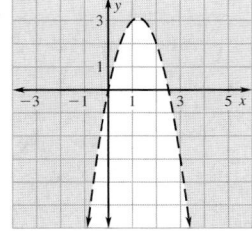

13. solution   **15.** not a solution   **17.** C   **19.** E   **21.** D

23.   **25.**

29.

33.

35. I3; for every value of x, the value of y (that is, the cost of the diamond) is lower for that grade than for either of the others.

37. A; VS2

9.7 MIXED REVIEW (p. 553)

45.   **47.**

49. 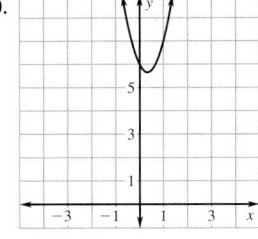   **51.** $y = -\frac{1}{6}x$ **53.** $y = 4x$

55. $y = \frac{6}{23}x$ **57.**

59.

61.

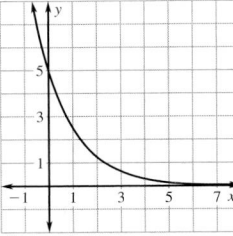

63. 1, 2 **65.** $\frac{9 + \sqrt{105}}{-4} \approx -4.81, \frac{9 - \sqrt{105}}{-4} \approx 0.31$

67. $\frac{-2 + \sqrt{10}}{2} \approx 0.58, \frac{-2 - \sqrt{10}}{2} \approx -2.58$

9.8 PRACTICE (pp. 557–559) **3.** quadratic **5.** linear
7. Quadratic; the graph is a curve but the ratios of consecutive y-coordinates are not the same.

9.

quadratic

11.

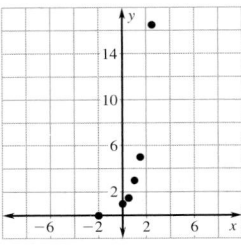

exponential

13. exponential **15.** quadratic

17.

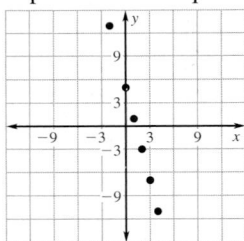

linear **19.** linear; $B = 0.43w$

21.

Year t	Attendance A	Change in A from previous year
0	12,580,660	—
1	12,338,980	−241,680
2	12,781,160	442,180
3	13,907,200	1,126,040
4	15,717,100	1,809,900

23. $y = -2x + 9; -2$ **25.** (4, 1)

9.8 MIXED REVIEW (p. 560) **33.** $-3, x$ **35.** $-5, -8x$
37. $-5y^2$ **39.** $2r^3$ **41.** $-y^3$ **43.** 0.73 **45.** -0.41
47. $y = 3x - 11$ **49.** $y = -\frac{1}{2}x + 4$

QUIZ 3 (p. 560) **1.** not a solution **2.** solution **3.** solution
4. solution **5.** B **6.** C **7.** A

8.

linear

9.

exponential

10.

quadratic

11.

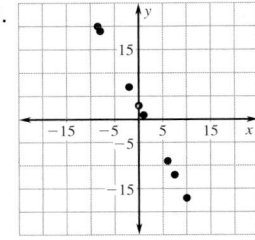

linear; $y = -2x + 3$

12.

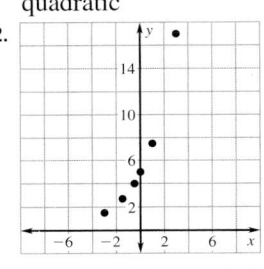

exponential; $y = 5(1.5)^x$

13.

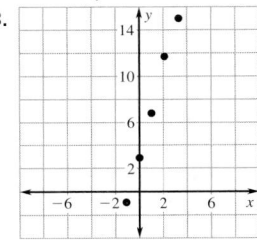

linear; $y = 3.72x + 3.16$

CHAPTER 9 REVIEW (pp. 562–564)
1. $-12, 12$ **3.** 0 **5.** $-5, 5$ **7.** $3\sqrt{5}$ **9.** $\frac{3}{4}$

11.

13.

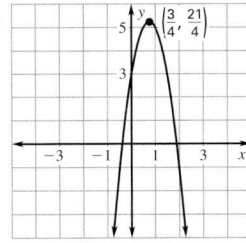

15. $-3, 5$ **17.** $-6, 4$ **19.** $-\frac{3}{2}, 2$ **21.** one solution

23. no real solution **25.**

27. **29.**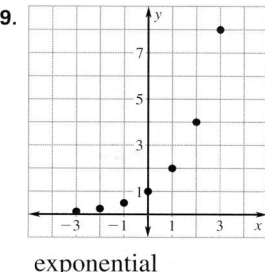

quadratic   exponential

CUMULATIVE PRACTICE (pp. 568–569) **1.** Yes; no input value has two different output values. **3.** Yes; no input value has two different output values. **5.** $\frac{2}{9} \approx 22\%$; 2 to 7 **7.** *Sample equation:* $\frac{x}{35} = \frac{6}{15}$; 14 in. **9.** 4 **11.** 2 **13.** 6 **15.** $2x - 6y = -4$ **17.** 5, 7, 8 **19.** 4, 4, 8 **21.** $\left(14, -3\frac{1}{2}\right)$ **23.** $(-5, -3)$ **25.** $(6.8, -3.7)$

27. **29.**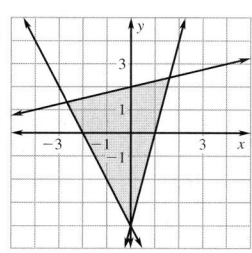

31. $\frac{1}{x^2}$ **33.** $\frac{4x^4}{y^{10}}$ **35.** $9a^{12}$ **37.** $5x^5y^4$ **39.** $4.2 \times 10^{-8} = 0.000000042$ **41.** $2.92 \times 10^{-12} = 0.00000000000292$ **43.** $2.1952 \times 10^{-5} = 0.000021952$ **45.** B **47.** A **49.** $\frac{\sqrt{7}}{3}$ **51.** $\frac{4\sqrt{7}}{7}$ **53.** $\sqrt{3}$ **55.** 15 **59.** $-9, -1$ **61.** $\frac{-4 - \sqrt{31}}{3} \approx -3.19, \frac{-4 + \sqrt{31}}{3} \approx 0.52$ **63.** 1, 5 **65.** \$10.31; \$26.28 **67.** No; the discriminant of the equation $-16t^2 + 100t = 180$ is negative, so the equation has no real solution. That is, there is no time t at which the flare will reach a height of 180 ft.

CHAPTER 10

SKILL REVIEW (p. 574) **1.** $3x^2 + 18x$ **2.** $14 - 28x$ **3.** $-4x - 20$ **4.** $-64 + 16x$ **5.** $3x - 6$ **6.** $2x + 3$ **7.** $-2x - 4$ **8.** $x^2 - x$ **9.** x^{10} **10.** x^{12} **11.** $-8a^3b^3$ **12.** $9x^4y^8$ **13.** -56; no real solution **14.** 196; two solutions **15.** 0; one solution

10.1 PRACTICE (pp. 579–581) **7.** linear, binomial **9.** cubic, trinomial **11.** constant, monomial **13.** $4x^2 - 7x - 2$ **15.** $-4x^2 + 9x + 4$ **17.** $-x^2 - x - 16$ **19.** -3; linear, binomial **21.** 1; cubic, polynomial **23.** -6; constant, monomial **25.** 5; quartic, trinomial **27.** -4; quartic, polynomial **29.** -16; cubic, monomial **31.** $-6x^3 + 3x^2 + 4$ **33.** $-7m^2 + 7m - 3$ **35.** -6 **37.** $8y^3 + 6y^2 - 3y - 3$ **39.** $3x^2 - 5$ **41.** $x^3 + 1$ **43.** $2n^3 + 3n - 5$ **45.** $10b^4 - 3b^3 - 13b^2 + 20b - 4$ **47.** $25x^3 - 4x + 14$ **49.** $x^2 + 2x + 2$ **51.** $-3x^2 + 6$ **53.** $-9z^3 - 8z^2 + 10z$ **55.** $-19t + 2$ **57.** $x^4 + x^3 + \frac{1}{12}x^2 - 9$

59. $9x^4 - 3x^3 - 7x^2 + 6x - 17$ **61.** $-0.7y^3 + 6.9y^2 - 3.9y + 10.4$ **63.** $1.5x^2 + 60x$ **65.** $F = 1223.58t + 79,589.03$ **67.** $A = 1.381t^2 + 3.494t + 235.325$ **69.** From top to bottom the models are A, E, and N.

10.1 MIXED REVIEW (p. 582) **73.** $-3x - 5$ **75.** $8x + 24$ **77.** $3 + 4x$ **79.** *Sample answer:* $y = -1.42x + 7.35$ **81.** 2^{16}; 65,536 **83.** $(1.1^3)(3.3^3)$; 47.83 **85.** 2.9^{15}; 8,629,188.75

TECHNOLOGY ACTIVITY 10.1 (p. 583) **1.** correct **3.** $3x^2 - 9x$ **5.** $-2x^2 + 14x + 4$ **7.** $6x^2 + 12x - 1$

10.2 PRACTICE (pp. 587–588) **5.** $8x^2 + 14x + 3$

7. $2x(4x) + 2x(1) + 3(4x) + 3(1) = 8x^2 + 2x + 12x + 3 = 8x^2 + 14x + 3$ **9.** $-8x^2 - 14x$ **11.** $-y^2 - 10y - 16$ **13.** $x^2 + 15x + 54$ **15.** $-2b^2 - 10b + 48$ **17.** $15w^3 - 3w^2 - 45w + 9$ **19.** $21t^3 - 3t^5 - 9t^2$ **21.** $-6y^3 - 5y^2$ **23.** $-6b^5 + 16b^3 - 11b^2$ **25.** $6d^2 + 11d + 3$ **27.** $3s^3 + 5s^2 - 3s - 2$ **29.** $x^3 - 38x - 12$ **31.** $6z^2 + 25z + 14$ **33.** $2w^2 + 5w - 25$ **35.** $10t^2 + 9t - 9$ **37.** $4x^2 - 31x - 8$ **39.** $99w^2 - 2w - 80$ **41.** $68.62y^2 - 151.91y + 62.22$ **43.** $4n^2 - \frac{26}{5}n - 12$ **45.** $2.5z^2 + 4.65z - 26.23$ **47.** $-4s^3 - 15s^2 + 3s - 4$ **49.** $2x^2 - 11x - 6$ **51.** $-x^3 - 13x^2 - 40x + 14$ **53.** $3x^2 + \frac{19}{2}x - 10$ **55.** 300 **57.** The revenue decreases from \$989.12 million to \$678.08 million. **59.** *Sample answer:* As time goes on, the revenue will increase because the value of the model $1.5125t^2 + 156.1846t + 3066.344$ will increase as t increases.

10.2 MIXED REVIEW (p. 589) **63.** $\frac{1}{9}m^2$ **65.** $0.25w^2$ **67.** 4^8, or 65,536 **69.** $256c^8$ **71.** $-w^{12}$ **73.** $512x^6y^{24}$ **75.** one solution **77.** two solutions **79.** two solutions

81. **83.**

85.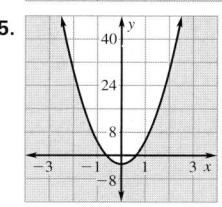

10.3 PRACTICE (pp. 593–594)

5. $x^2 + 4x + 4$ **7.** $w^2 - 121$ **9.** $4y^2 - 12y + 9$

11. $t^2 - 36$ **13.** $4y^2 - 25$ **15.** $x^2 - 9$ **17.** $4m^2 - 4$
19. $9 - 4x^2$ **21.** $x^2 + 10x + 25$ **23.** $9t^2 + 6t + 1$
25. $16b^2 - 24b + 9$ **27.** $x^2 - 16$ **29.** $9x^2 - 1$ **31.** $a^2 - 4b^2$
33. $9y^2 + 48y + 64$ **35.** $4x^2 - \frac{1}{4}$ **37.** $9s^2 - 16t^2$ **39.** true
41. true **43.** 884 **45.** 256 **47.** $(x + 3)^2$, $x^2 + 6x + 9$;
square of a binomial **49.** $(0.5C + 0.5c)^2 = $
$0.25C^2 + 0.5Cc + 0.25c^2$ **51.** $(0.5F + 0.5f)^2 = $
$0.25F^2 + 0.5Ff + 0.25f^2$ **53.** $P(1 - r)(1 + r) = P(1 - r^2)$
55. a decrease of Pr^2 dollars

10.3 MIXED REVIEW (p. 594) **63.** $\frac{x^3}{64}$ **65.** $\frac{64x^3}{y^9}$ **67.** $9x^2$

69. $\left(-\frac{3}{4}, 4\frac{7}{8}\right)$; $x = -\frac{3}{4}$ **71.** $(2, 20)$; $x = 2$ **73.** $(6, 14)$; $x = 6$
75. $-4, 4$ **77.** $-5, 5$ **79.** $-3, 3$ **81.** Yes; *Sample answer:* Let
x be the length of the rectangle and y be the width. Then
$2x + 2y = 52$ and $xy = 148.75$. Substituting, $x(26 - x) = $
148.75, which is equivalent to $x^2 - 26x + 148.75 = 0$. Since
the discriminant of the equation is 81, the equation has two
solutions. The rectangle is 17.5 by 8.5.

QUIZ 1 (p. 596) **1.** $3x^2 + 5x + 9$ **2.** $-6x^3 - 14x^2 + 2x - 2$
3. $3t^2 - 13t + 14$ **4.** $6x^3 - 5x^2 + 4x + 3$ **5.** $x^2 + 7x - 8$
6. $16n^2 - 49$ **7.** $-2x^3 + 5x^2 - 6x + 8$ **8.** $27m^2 - 3m - 4$
9. $\frac{1}{4}x^2 + x - 15$ **10.** $-12x^5 + 11x^4 - 3x^2$ **11.** $x^2 - 36$
12. $16x^2 - 9$ **13.** $25 - 9b^2$ **14.** $4x^2 - 49y^2$
15. $9x^2 + 36x + 36$ **16.** $36 + 96x + 64x^2$
17.

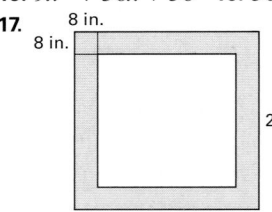

$(2x - 16)^2 = $
$(4x^2 - 64x + 256)$ in.^{2}

10.4 PRACTICE (pp. 600–601) **9.** no **11.** yes **13.** 3, 5
15. $-9, 2$ **17.** $-\frac{1}{4}$ **19.** $-4, -1$ **21.** $-8, 6$ **23.** $9, -8$
25. $2, -1$ **27.** $7, 5$ **29.** -9 **31.** 5.6 **33.** 5 **35.** -4
37. $-3, \frac{3}{2}$ **39.** $\frac{5}{4}, 3, \frac{4}{3}$ **41.** $1.9, -2.1$ **43.** $\frac{1}{8}, -\frac{3}{50}, \frac{2}{9}$ **45.** B
47.

49.

51.

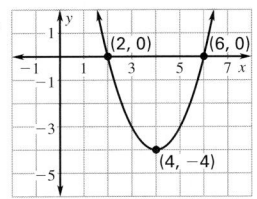

53. Use the distance between
the x-intercepts at $(-500, 0)$
and $(500, 0)$.

55. 600 ft **57.** 1200 m

10.4 MIXED REVIEW (p. 602)
61. 210,000 **63.** 857,000,000 **65.** 0.00371 **67.** 0.000722
69. $x^2 - 9x + 14$ **71.** $x^2 + x - 20$ **73.** $x^2 + \frac{1}{3}x - \frac{2}{9}$
75. $6x^2 + 19x - 7$ **77.** $24x^2 - x - 3$ **79.** $x^2 + 20x + 100$
81. Exponential decay; let P be the price in 1996, t the
number of years since 1996, and y the price after t years;
$y = P(0.84)^t$. **83.** Exponential decay; let n be the number
of members in 1996, t the number of years since 1996, and
y the number of members after t years; $y = n(0.97)^t$.

10.5 PRACTICE (pp. 607–608) **5.** D **7.** B **9.** The equation
can be solved by factoring because the discriminant, 0, is a
perfect square. **11.** The equation cannot be solved by
factoring because the discriminant, 40, is not a perfect
square. **13.** B **15.** $(x + 9)(x - 1)$ **17.** $(b + 8)(b - 3)$
19. $(y - 6)(y + 3)$ **21.** $(m - 10)(m + 3)$ **23.** $(11 - s)(4 - s)$
25. $(x - 15)(x - 30)$ **27.** $-2, -5$ **29.** $2, 7$ **31.** $-1, -15$
33. $-13, 5$ **35.** $3, 17$ **37.** $-7, 4$ **39.** $-9, 10$ **41.** $2, 9$
43. yes; $(y + 15)(y + 4)$ **45.** no **47.** no **49.** $-15, 7$
51. $-32, -20$ **53.** *Sample answer:* $x^2 + 11x + 30 = 0$
55. *Sample answer:* $x^2 - 427x = 0$ **57.** 18 or -1 **59.** $x - 9$
61. $x^2 - x \le 20$ **63.** platform: 95 m by 95 m; building:
57 m by 57 m

10.5 MIXED REVIEW (p. 609) **73.** 1 **75.** 7 **77.** 18
79. $y^2 + 5y - 36$ **81.** $60 + 3w - 3w^2$
83. $2b^4 + 4b^3 - 6b^2 - 20b$ **85.** $36z^2 + 4z + \frac{1}{9}$
87. $-12, -7$ **89.** 19 **91.** 9, 6 **93.** $1, -\frac{1}{2}$ **95.** $\frac{3}{2}$

10.6 PRACTICE (pp. 614–616) **5.** B **7.** A **9.** $(2x + 1)(x - 2)$
11. cannot be factored **13.** $-8, \frac{1}{2}$ **15.** A **17.** A
19. $(6b + 1)(b - 2)$ **21.** $(5w + 1)(w - 2)$ **23.** $(2y - 5)(3y + 2)$
25. $(3c - 4)(c - 11)$ **27.** $(7y - 4)(2y - 1)$ **29.** $(2t + 7)(3t - 10)$
31. $(z + 10)(2z - 1)$ **33.** $-2\frac{1}{2}, 7$ **35.** $-11, -\frac{1}{3}$ **37.** $-1, 9\frac{1}{2}$
39. $-8, -1\frac{1}{2}$ **41.** $-\frac{2}{3}, 4\frac{1}{2}$ **43.** $-1\frac{1}{2}, 1\frac{1}{5}$ **45.** $-1, -\frac{5}{8}$
47. $-1\frac{1}{9}, 6\frac{1}{2}$ **49.** 5 **51.** $-\frac{1}{2}, 0$ **53.** $\frac{3}{5}, 1\frac{1}{7}$ **55.** $-2, 2\frac{1}{2}$
57. $-\frac{2}{7}, 1\frac{3}{8}$ **59.** $\frac{-23 - \sqrt{2089}}{24}, \frac{-23 + \sqrt{2089}}{24}$ **61.** $\frac{8}{23}, 2$
63. $\frac{11}{17}, \frac{5}{7}$ **65.** 3 sec; $t = 0.125$ is not a reasonable solution
because at that time the acrobat is still rising.
67. $2.5x^2 = 9000$ **69.** $x^2 - x - 12 = 0$; explanations will vary.
71. $6x^2 + x - 1 = 0$; explanations will vary.

10.6 MIXED REVIEW (p. 617) **79.** $(-2, 3)$ **81.** $(40, 40)$
83. not a solution **85.** $b^2 - 81$ **87.** $4a^2 - 49$
89. $10{,}000 + 5400x + 729x^2$

QUIZ 2 (p. 617) **1.** -5 **2.** $\dfrac{3}{2}, 4$ **3.** $-\dfrac{7}{2}, 4$ **4.** $-\dfrac{1}{12}$ **5.** -4

6. $4, -7, -1$ **7.** $-2, \dfrac{1}{2}, \left(-\dfrac{3}{4}, -\dfrac{25}{16}\right)$

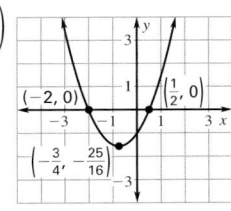

8. $-4, 4, (0, -16)$ **9.** $\dfrac{1}{3}, -2, \left(-\dfrac{5}{6}, -\dfrac{49}{12}\right)$

10. $(y + 4)(y - 1)$ **11.** $(w + 2)(w + 11)$ **12.** $(n + 19)(n - 3)$
13. $(x + 6)(x + 11)$ **14.** $(t - 43)(t + 2)$ **15.** $(9 - z)(-5 + z)$
16. $(4b + 9)(3b - 11)$ **17.** $(t + 29)(2t + 5)$
18. $2(3d - 2)(3d - 7)$ **19.** $-6, 1$ **20.** $-25, -1$ **21.** $2, 9$
22. $-5, 34$ **23.** $-37, 2$ **24.** $-\dfrac{17}{2}, -8$ **25.** $-\dfrac{7}{3}, -\dfrac{2}{5}$ **26.** $\dfrac{4}{9}, \dfrac{9}{2}$
27. $-\dfrac{11}{2}, \dfrac{16}{3}$

CONCEPT ACTIVITY 10.7 (p. 618)
1. $(x + 2)^2$ **3.** $(2x + 1)^2$ **5.** $a + b; a + b; (a + b)^2$
7. $(4x + 7)^2$ **9.** $(a - b); (a - b); (a - b)^2$

10.7 PRACTICE (pp. 622–623) **7.** $(t + 5)^2$ **9.** $(4 + t)(4 - t)$
11. $2(3 + z)(3 - z)$ **13.** $-12, 12$ **15.** $-5, 5$ **17.** 3
19. $(10x + 11)(10x - 11)$ **21.** $60(y + 3)(y - 3)$
23. $2(7 + t)(7 - t)$ **25.** $(3t - 2q)(3t + 2q)$ **27.** $(x + 4)^2$
29. $(y + 15)^2$ **31.** $(3x + 1)^2$ **33.** $(5n - 2)^2$ **35.** $2(3x + 1)^2$
37. $-4(2w + 5)^2$ **39.** $(z + 5)(z - 5)$; difference of two squares
41. $4(n + 3)(n - 3)$; difference of two squares
43. $4(b - 5)^2$; perfect square trinomial **45.** $-2(x - 13)^2$;
perfect square trinomial **47.** $(x + 100w)(x - 100w)$;
difference of two squares **49.** $\left(x + \dfrac{1}{3}\right)^2$; perfect square
trinomial **51.** $-6, 6$ **53.** $-\dfrac{2}{5}, \dfrac{2}{5}$ **55.** $-\dfrac{3}{2}, \dfrac{3}{2}$ **57.** 9 **59.** $\dfrac{5}{6}$
61. $\dfrac{7}{4}$ **63.** 1.5 in. **65.** $\dfrac{1}{2}$ sec **67.** yes; 7 sec **69.** 32 ft/sec

10.7 MIXED REVIEW (p. 624) **75.** 15 **77.** 2
79. not a solution **81.** solution **83.** $(-2, -6)$ **85.** $(-4, 1)$
87. $5\sqrt{3}$ **89.** 18 **91.** $4\sqrt{2}$ **93.** $-6\sqrt{3}$ **95.** $\dfrac{4}{9}, 6$

10.8 PRACTICE (pp. 629–631) **7.** $3x^2(2 + x^2)$ **9.** no;
$x(7x^2 - 11)$ **11.** no; $3w(3w + 4)(3w - 4)$ **13.** $-5, -6$;
Sample answer: factoring **15.** $6v(v^2 - 3)$ **17.** $3x(1 - 3x)$
19. $2a^2(2a^3 + 4a - 1)$ **21.** $6x^2(4x + 3)$ **23.** $2y(y - 6)(y + 1)$
25. $-7m(m - 3)(m - 1)$ **27.** $4t(t + 6)(t - 6)$
29. $(c^3 - 12)(c + 1)$ **31.** $(b^3 - 4)(6b + 5)$
33. $(a + 6)(a + 2)(a - 2)$ **35.** $3(m^2 - 2)(m - 5)$
37. $-3, -4$; *Sample answer:* factoring **39.** $-13, 9$; *Sample
answer:* factoring **41.** $-3, 9$; *Sample answer:* factoring
43. $0, -4, 4$; *Sample answer:* factoring **45.** $0, \dfrac{29 - \sqrt{593}}{2}$,
$\dfrac{29 + \sqrt{593}}{2}$; factoring and quadratic formula
47. $\dfrac{-9 - \sqrt{305}}{16}, \dfrac{-9 + \sqrt{305}}{16}$; quadratic formula
49. $0, \dfrac{-3 - \sqrt{457}}{8}, \dfrac{-3 + \sqrt{457}}{8}$; factoring and quadratic
formula **51.** 3 sec **55.** $L = h - 3, w = h - 9$ **57.** $L = 9$ in.,
$w = 3$ in., $h = 12$ in. **59.** $(3x + 7)(x + 2)$

10.8 MIXED REVIEW (p. 632)
69. $x \le -16$ **71.** $x \ge -7$

73. $-2, 12$ **75.** no solution **77.** $-3, \dfrac{3}{2}$
79.   **81.** $\dfrac{31}{23} \approx 134.78\%$

QUIZ 3 (p. 632) **1.** $(7x + 8)(7x - 8)$; difference of two squares
2. $(11 + 3x)(11 - 3x)$; difference of two squares
3. $(2t + 5)^2$; perfect square trinomial
4. $2(6 + 5y)(6 - 5y)$; difference of two squares
5. $(3y + 7)^2$; perfect square trinomial **6.** $3(n - 6)^2$; perfect
square trinomial **7.** $-8, 8$ **8.** -4 **9.** $-\dfrac{16}{3}$ **10.** 4 **11.** $-\dfrac{2}{3}, \dfrac{2}{3}$
12. $-\dfrac{1}{3}$ **13.** $3x^2(x + 4)$ **14.** $3x(2x + 1)$ **15.** $9x^3(2x - 1)$
16. $2x(4x^4 + 2x - 1)$ **17.** $2x(x - 1)(x - 2)$
18. $3x(4x - 5)(4x + 5)$ **19.** $(x^2 + 4)(x + 3)$ **20.** $0, -\dfrac{3}{2}, \dfrac{3}{2}$;
factoring special products **21.** $-3, \dfrac{5}{3}$; factoring $ax^2 + bx + c$
22. 2; graphing **23.** 0, about 0.77, about 2.26; quadratic
formula **24.** $0, -3, 4$; factoring **25.** 0, about -7.15,
about -0.35; quadratic formula

CHAPTER 10 REVIEW (pp. 634–636) **1.** $2x^2 + 5x + 7$
3. $x^3 + 2x^2 + 2x - 2$ **5.** $-8x^4 + 12x^3$ **7.** $x^2 + 14x + 33$
9. $2x^3 + 11x^2 - 5x - 50$ **11.** $x^2 - 225$ **13.** $x^2 + 4x + 4$
15. $-1, -10$ **17.** -9 **19.** $9, 12$ **21.** -13 **23.** $(2x - 3)(x + 4)$
25. $(2x - 3)(2x - 3)$ **27.** $-\dfrac{3}{4}$ **29.** $-2x^3(x + 2)(x - 1)$
31. $(x^2 + 5)(3x + 1)$

CHAPTER 11

SKILL REVIEW (p. 642) **1.** $\frac{1}{2}$ **2.** $1\frac{3}{10}$ **3.** $-\frac{3}{55}$ **4.** $1\frac{5}{18}$ **5.** $\frac{4x}{3}$
6. $-21x$ **7.** $3x + 5$ **8.** $\frac{4-x}{2}$ **9.** $-9, 9$ **10.** $1, 1\frac{1}{2}$ **11.** $-1, 4$

11.1 PRACTICE (pp. 646–647) **9.** $\frac{6}{7}$ **11.** $4\frac{1}{2}$ **13.** $-2, 3$
15. Other proportions include:
$$\frac{\text{height of actual statue}}{\text{height of model}} = \frac{\text{length of actual statue}}{\text{length of model}},$$
$$\frac{\text{height of model}}{\text{height of actual statue}} = \frac{\text{length of model}}{\text{length of actual statue}},$$
$$\frac{\text{length of actual statue}}{\text{height of actual statue}} = \frac{\text{length of model}}{\text{height of model}}.$$
17. 3 **19.** $5\frac{5}{8}$ **21.** $2\frac{1}{2}$ **23.** -10 **25.** $-1\frac{1}{2}$ **27.** 27 **29.** $2\frac{4}{5}$
31. 2, 5 **33.** 4 **35.** 6 **37.** $1\frac{2}{3}$ **39.** $-\frac{1}{3}$ **41.** 22 in.
43. *Sample answer:* By rewriting 1 ft as 12 in., you can set
up the proportion $\frac{\frac{1}{16}\text{ in.}}{12\text{ in.}} = \frac{1\text{ in.}}{192\text{ in.}}$. Now that all the units
are the same, you can use the cross product property. This
gives 12 in. = 12 in., which shows that the proportion is
correct. **45.** food: about 16; clothes, accessories: about 4;
books, magazines, comics: about 3; toys, stickers, games:
about 3; movie tickets: about 3; arcade games: about 3;
gifts: about 3; movie rentals: about 3; music: about 2;
footwear: about 2; grooming products: about 2
47. about 4771

11.1 MIXED REVIEW (p. 648) **51.** $-8, 8$ **53.** $-2\sqrt{3}, 2\sqrt{3}$
55. no square roots **57.** $-\frac{3}{5}, \frac{3}{5}$ **59.** $3\sqrt{2}$ **61.** $4\sqrt{5}$ **63.** 54
65. $\sqrt{7}$

11.2 PRACTICE (pp. 652–654) **5.** 175% **7.** 48 **9.** $.36$;
Sample answer: The equations for the two methods are
$a = 0.06(5.99)$ and $\frac{a}{5.99} = \frac{6}{100}$. Notice that the right side
of the second equation is the rate expressed as a fraction
instead of a decimal. Both methods involve multiplying the
base by the rate. **11.** A **13.** 20 **15.** 30% **17.** 30.8 ft
19. 84 ft **21.** 50 **23.** 150 g **25.** 65.6 tons **27.** $86\frac{1}{9}\%$, or
about 86.1% **29.** 480% **31.** $86\frac{2}{3}\%$, or about 86.7%;
$13\frac{1}{3}\%$, or about 13.3% **33.** about 248 people
35. about 1113 people **37.** 18% **39.** about 420 students
41. yes; no **43.** about 395 people **45.** No; the price is $56
at the first store and $57.60 at the second. **47.** $13.80; the
total cost of the ride

11.2 MIXED REVIEW (p. 655) **53.** $y = 2x$ **55.** $y = \frac{1}{2}x$
57. $y = \frac{3}{2}x$ **59.** solution **61.** solution **63.** $(x + 7)(x - 2)$
65. $(5x - 6)(x - 9)$ **67.** $2x(3x + 8)$ **69.** $3x(x + 2)(x + 5)$
71. $5x^2(3x + 2)(x - 4)$

11.3 PRACTICE (pp. 659–660) **7.** neither **9.** inverse variation
11. $y = \frac{24}{x}$; 3 **13.** $y = 4x$ **15.** $y = 3x$ **17.** $y = \frac{1}{9}x$ **19.** $y = \frac{9}{5}x$
21. $y = \frac{10}{x}$ **23.** $y = \frac{16}{x}$ **25.** $y = \frac{4}{x}$ **27.** $y = \frac{9}{x}$ **29.** $y = \frac{225}{x}$
31. $y = \frac{27}{x}$ **33.** 4, 2, $\frac{4}{3}$, 1 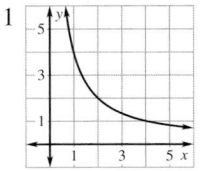 inversely

35. 3, 6, 9, 12 directly
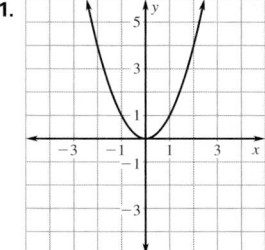

37. direct variation; $y = 5x$ **39.** inverse variation
41. neither **43.** 116 lb **45.** $T = \frac{4440}{d}$
47. $\frac{1}{26}$ gal/mi ≈ 0.04 gal/mi **49.** Neither; the equation
cannot be written either in the form $g = km$ or $g = \frac{k}{m}$ for
any constant k.

11.3 MIXED REVIEW (p. 661) **55.** $\frac{3}{4}$ **57.** $\frac{8}{15}$ **59.** $\frac{1}{6}$ **61.** y^6
63. $-\frac{y^2}{x^2}$ **65.** -5, linear, binomial **67.** -1, cubic, binomial

QUIZ 1 (p. 662) **1.** 8 **2.** $\frac{27}{7}$ **3.** 4 **4.** $-\frac{5}{3}, 1$ **5.** $y = \frac{12}{x}$
6. $y = \frac{12}{x}$ **7.** $y = \frac{18}{x}$ **8.** about 904 people
9. about 204 people

TECHNOLOGY ACTIVITY 11.3 (p. 663)
1. directly; 0.825; $y = 0.825x$

11.4 PRACTICE (pp. 667–668) **5.** 5 **7.** C **9.** $\frac{x}{5}$ **11.** $-\frac{3x}{2}$
13. $\frac{6-x}{3x}$ **15.** $\frac{7}{x+12}$ **17.** $-\frac{1}{2x}$ **19.** $\frac{1}{3-x}$ **21.** $\frac{x-4}{x-3}$
23. $\frac{x+1}{x+6}$ **25.** 8 **27.** $-3, 3$ **29.** $-6, 1$ **31.** $\frac{x}{5x+3}$; $\frac{1}{6}$
33. $\frac{x-y}{x}$ **37.** $\frac{1625}{R}$

11.4 MIXED REVIEW (p. 669) **43.** $\frac{25}{2}$ **45.** $-\frac{1}{81}$ **47.** $4m^3$
49. $-\frac{8c^2}{3}$ **51.**

53. **55.**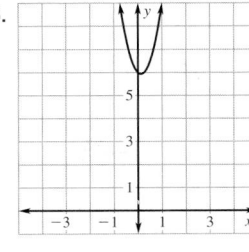

57. $y = 2500(0.92)^x$; 2116; 1947; 1791; 1648; 1516

11.5 PRACTICE (pp. 673–674) **5.** $\dfrac{2(x+1)}{3}$ **7.** $\dfrac{3x}{x-5}$ **9.** $\dfrac{2x+5}{4x}$

11. $x(3x+1)$ **13.** x **15.** 8 **17.** $13x$ **19.** $\dfrac{1}{(x+3)(2x+3)}$

21. $\dfrac{5}{6x}$ **23.** 15 **25.** $-\dfrac{x+6}{5x^2}$ **27.** $\dfrac{1}{(x+4)(2x+3)}$ **29.** $-\dfrac{x+1}{5x^2}$

31. $\dfrac{1}{3x}$ **33.** $3x(x+2)$ **35.** $A = \dfrac{(3150-400t)(10-t)}{(1-0.12t)(111-12t)}$

37. 258 mi **39.** $R = \dfrac{46+0.7t}{1055+23t}$; decreasing; *Sample answer:*
The ratios in order (rounded to the nearest hundred-thousandth) are 0.04360, 0.04332, 0.04305, 0.04279, 0.04255, 0.04231, 0.04208, and 0.04186.

43. $\dfrac{2x-4}{x^2-4} = \dfrac{2(x-2)}{(x+2)(x-2)} = \dfrac{2}{x+2} \cdot \dfrac{x-2}{x-2} = \dfrac{2}{x+2} \cdot 1 = \dfrac{2}{x+2}$

11.5 MIXED REVIEW (p. 675) **49.** 18 **51.** 162 **53.** $3-\sqrt{2}$, $3+\sqrt{2}$ **55.** $3t^2 + 8t + 10$ **57.** $a^4 + 4a^3 - a - 1$ **59.** $1000 + 2000r + 1000r^2$

11.6 PRACTICE (pp. 679–681) **5.** 5 **7.** $\dfrac{6x-5}{20x^2}$ **9.** $\dfrac{3x+4}{2(x-5)}$

11. 2 **13.** $\dfrac{2-5x}{3x-1}$ **15.** $\dfrac{1}{x^2}$ **17.** $\dfrac{155}{78x}$ **19.** $-\dfrac{3(x+12)}{(x+4)(x-2)}$

21. $\dfrac{3(x+3)}{x(x-3)}$ **23.** $\dfrac{2(x^2-20)}{(x-10)(x+6)}$ **25.** $\dfrac{4x^2+17x+5}{(3x-1)(x+1)}$

27. $-\dfrac{x^2+14x-2}{(3x-1)(x-2)}$ **29.** $\dfrac{x+5}{x+2}$ **31.** $\dfrac{2(4x^2+8x-5)}{(x+1)(x-2)(x+4)}$

33. $\dfrac{2(7x^2-8x-14)}{(2x-1)(x-3)}$ **35.** *Sample answer:* They get very large; they get very large; they get very close to 2; as x gets very large, the numbers subtracted in the numerator and the denominator become insignificantly small compared to $2x$ and x, so the rational expression gets closer and closer to $\dfrac{2x}{x} = 2$. **37.** $\dfrac{48x}{(x-2)(x+2)}$ **39.** $\dfrac{1}{x}; \dfrac{1}{35} + \dfrac{1}{x}$ **41. a.** A: $\dfrac{3}{56}$; B: $\dfrac{16}{315}$; C: $\dfrac{18}{385}$ **b.** A or B **43.** $\dfrac{3x}{7}$ **45.** $\dfrac{4(x-6)(x-8)}{(x+6)(x+8)}$

47. $\dfrac{5x+12}{(x-2)(x+2)(x+3)}$ **49.** $\dfrac{8x^2-15x+19}{(2x+3)(x-5)(x+1)}$

11.6 MIXED REVIEW (p. 682) **57.** $\dfrac{2m}{3}$ **59.** $\dfrac{7x}{y^6}$

61. $2x^2 + 6x - 9 = 0$ **63.** 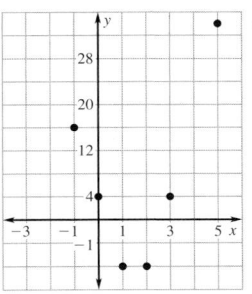 quadratic

65. $|x - 8500| \le 1000$

QUIZ 2 (p. 682) **1.** $\dfrac{3x}{2}$ **2.** $\dfrac{5}{11+x}$ **3.** $-\dfrac{1}{x-2}$ **4.** cannot be simplified **5.** $\dfrac{7x^2}{2}$ **6.** 10 **7.** $\dfrac{3}{2}$ **8.** $\dfrac{x-3}{x+2}$ **9.** $\dfrac{1}{x-7}$

10. $\dfrac{1}{x+1}$ **11.** $\dfrac{15}{x+2}; \dfrac{15}{x-2}$ **12.** $\dfrac{15}{x+2} + \dfrac{15}{x-2} = \dfrac{30x}{(x+2)(x-2)}$
13. 10 h

11.7 PRACTICE (pp. 687–688) **5.** $y+2\overline{)y^2+0y+8}$
7. $3y+5\overline{)8y^2-2y+0}$ **9.** $29\dfrac{15}{29}$ **11.** $x-5$

13. $-5b^2 + 4b + \dfrac{5}{2}$ **15.** $4x + \dfrac{13}{2}$ **17.** $9c+3$ **19.** $x+6$

21. $3a - 18 - \dfrac{12}{a}$ **23.** D **25.** B **27.** $a-2$

29. $2b + 1 - \dfrac{2}{b-2}$ **31.** $5g - 1 + \dfrac{1}{g+3}$ **33.** $x+6-\dfrac{5}{x-9}$

35. $-x - 4 - \dfrac{8}{x+2}$ **37.** $b - 10 + \dfrac{34}{b+3}$ **39.** $-x+4-\dfrac{25}{x+4}$

41. $-5m - 5 - \dfrac{3}{m-1}$ **43.** $-s + 5 - \dfrac{21}{s+5}$ **45.** $\dfrac{1}{2}c - 2 + \dfrac{9}{2c-6}$

47. $5x+3$ **49.** $3x+2$ **51.** $\dfrac{2}{9} - \dfrac{8}{9t+99}$ **53.** increasing

11.7 MIXED REVIEW (p. 689) **61.** 15 **63.** 3 **65.** $1\dfrac{3}{7}$
67. $-1\dfrac{1}{3}, 2\dfrac{1}{2}$ **69.** $-1\dfrac{1}{5}$ **71.** 12; 6; 4; 3; 2.4

11.8 PRACTICE (pp. 694–696) **7.** $\dfrac{1}{2}$, 1 **9.** 3 **11.** -3

13. (2, 3) 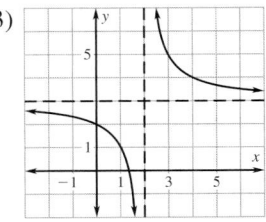 **15.** 28 **17.** $\dfrac{1}{2}$ **19.** 13

21. -27 **23.** 11 **25.** $1\dfrac{1}{2}$ **27.** $-\dfrac{1}{3}, 2$ **29.** $-8, 9$ **31.** $-8, 2$
33. $\dfrac{3}{5}$ **35.** $-8, 10$ **37.** -4 **39.** B **41.** A

43. domain: all real numbers except 3

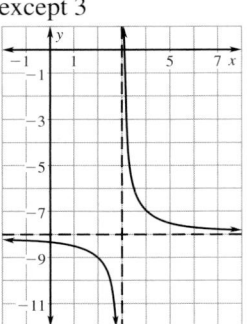

45. domain: all real numbers except −1

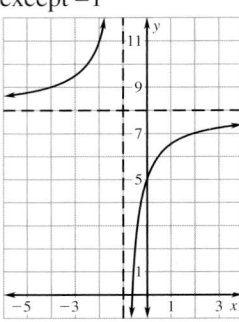

47. domain: all real numbers except −3

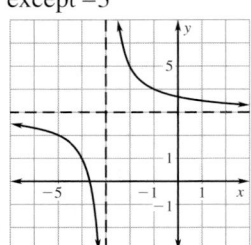

49. domain: all real numbers except 1

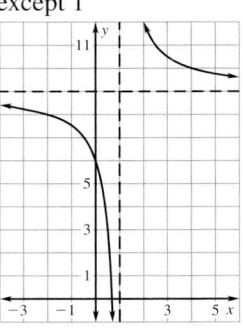

51. 6 hits   **53.** $y = \dfrac{5000 + 10x}{x + 1}$

55. $\dfrac{60}{2000} = \dfrac{3}{100}$ **57.** $\dfrac{3}{100} + \dfrac{3}{50x} = \dfrac{3x + 6}{100x}$

59.

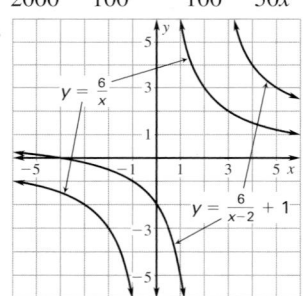

$y = \dfrac{6}{x}$

$y = \dfrac{6}{x-2} + 1$

61. *Sample answer:* For $a > 0$, as a increases, the branches of the hyperbola (which are in the first and third quadrants) become wider and more open. For $a < 0$, as $|a|$ increases, the branches of the hyperbola (which are in the second and fourth quadrants) become wider and more open.

11.8 MIXED REVIEW (p. 697) **69.** 9, 8, 7, 6, 5

71. 0, −1, −4, −9, −16   **73.** 0, $\dfrac{1}{2}$, 2, $4\dfrac{1}{2}$, 8   **75.** $6^2 = 36$

77. $-4^2 = -16$ **79.** $6\sqrt{2}$ **81.** $\sqrt{13}$ **83.** 16   **85.** $6\sqrt{11}$

QUIZ 3 (p. 697) **1.** $\dfrac{x}{6} - \dfrac{4}{3x}$ **2.** $\dfrac{3}{5}a + \dfrac{1}{2}$ **3.** $x - 4 + \dfrac{32}{x + 4}$

4. $y + 6.5 + \dfrac{27.5}{2y - 5}$ **5.** $\dfrac{1}{3}z + 2 + \dfrac{20}{3z - 6}$ **6.** $4x + 3 - \dfrac{11}{3x + 2}$

7. −2   **8.** 4   **9.** 3   **10.** 130   **11.**

12.

13.

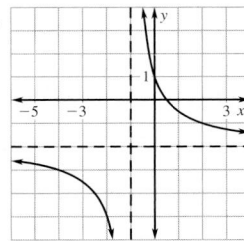

14. $\dfrac{7}{8} - \dfrac{103}{4t + 262}$

TECHNOLOGY ACTIVITY 11.8 (p. 698) **1.** $y = \dfrac{3x + 2}{x + 5}$; all real numbers except −5 and 5; all real numbers except −5 **3.** $y = \dfrac{2x + 1}{x - 3}$; all real numbers except −4 and 3; all real numbers except 3   **5.** $y = \dfrac{2x + 3}{x + 1}$; all real numbers except −1 and 3; all real numbers except −1 **7.** *Sample answer:* No; they do not have the same domain. The domain of the first is all real numbers except −3 and 1; the domain of the second is all real numbers except −3.

CHAPTER 11 REVIEW (pp. 700–702) **1.** $1\dfrac{1}{7}$ **3.** 4 **5.** \$76

7. \$120   **9.** $y = 3x$ **11.** $\dfrac{x}{3x^2 + 1}$ **13.** $\dfrac{-x^2 + 3}{2x}$ **15.** $20x^2$

17. $\dfrac{(x + 2)^2}{(x + 4)^2}$ **19.** $\dfrac{4x + 3}{24x}$ **21.** $\dfrac{4x - 5}{x - 2}$ **23.** $x - 6 + \dfrac{5}{6x}$

25. $x + 3$ **27.** −4, 2

CHAPTER 12

SKILL REVIEW (p. 708) **1.** 5.2   **2.** 3.9   **3.** $7\sqrt{2}$ **4.** $2\sqrt{35}$

5. $\dfrac{\sqrt{7}}{2}$ **6.** 3   **7.** $(x - 6)(x + 3)$ **8.** $(x + 4)(x - 2)$

9. $(2x + 5)^2$

12.1 PRACTICE (pp. 712–714) **3.** 0, 4, 5.7, 6.9, 8

5. 4, 7, 8.2, 9.2, 10   **7.** 1.4, 1.7, 2, 2.2, 2.4   **9.** Both the domain and range are all the nonnegative numbers.

11. domain: all nonnegative numbers; range: all numbers greater than or equal to −10   **13.** domain: all numbers greater than or equal to −5; range: all nonnegative numbers

15.

$y = 3\sqrt{x}$

17.

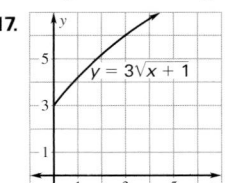

$y = 3\sqrt{x} + 1$

19. 100 lb/in.^{2} **21.** 1 **23.** 4 **25.** 5 **27.** about 1.4
29. 4 **31.** $x \geq 17$ **33.** $x \geq -5$ **35.** all nonnegative numbers
37. all nonnegative numbers **39.** all nonnegative numbers
41. $x \geq -9$ **43.** all nonnegative numbers
45. Both the domain and range are all the nonnegative numbers.

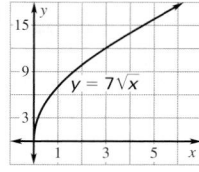

49. domain: all nonnegative numbers; range: all numbers greater than or equal to 4

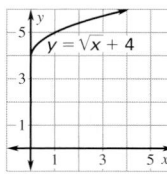

51. domain: all numbers greater than or equal to 4; range: all nonnegative numbers

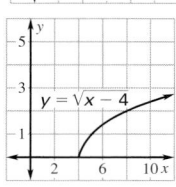

55. domain: all numbers greater than or or equal to −2.5; range: all nonnegative numbers

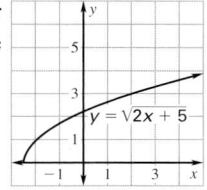

57. 1.41 m^2 **59. a.** cm^2 = cm · $\sqrt{\text{cm}^2 + \text{cm}^2}$ = cm · cm
b.

c. 1456 cm^2 (to the nearest cm^2)

12.1 MIXED REVIEW (p. 714) **65.** $2\sqrt{6}$ **67.** $5\sqrt{7}$ **69.** $\dfrac{2\sqrt{5}}{5}$
71. $\sqrt{7}$ **73.** $-2 - 2\sqrt{3}, -2 + 2\sqrt{3}$ **75.** $3 - 2\sqrt{2}, 3 + 2\sqrt{2}$
77. $-1\frac{1}{2}, 1$ **79.** $x^2 + 9x - 22$ **81.** $10x^2 - 33x + 27$
83. $6x^3 - 4x^2 - 8x - 2$ **85.** $\dfrac{8}{3}$ **87.** $\dfrac{x}{x+1}$

TECHNOLOGY ACTIVITY 12.1 (p. 715)
1. k moves the graph of $y = \sqrt{x}$ up k units if k is positive and down $|k|$ units if k is negative. **3.** −2 **5.** 3

12.2 PRACTICE (pp. 719–720) **5.** $\sqrt{7}$ **7.** $2\sqrt{6}$ **9.** $15 - 6\sqrt{2}$
11. $\dfrac{8 + \sqrt{10}}{18}$ **13.** $6\left(\sqrt{26}\right)^2 - 156 = 6(26) - 156 = 0$; solution
15. $\left(6 + \sqrt{31}\right)^2 - 12\left(6 + \sqrt{31}\right) + 5 = 67 + 12\sqrt{31} - 72 - 12\sqrt{31} + 5 = 0$; solution **17.** $6 - 3\sqrt{2} \approx 1.8$ mi **19.** $6\sqrt{3}$
21. $\sqrt{6}$ **23.** $6\sqrt{3}$ **25.** $3\sqrt{2}$ **27.** $12\sqrt{5}$ **29.** $-\sqrt{6}$ **31.** 6
33. −12 **35.** $21\sqrt{2} + 6\sqrt{6}$ **37.** $a - 2b\sqrt{a} + b^2$
39. $37 - 20\sqrt{3}$ **41.** $\sqrt{2}$ **43.** $\dfrac{\sqrt{3}}{4}$ **45.** $\dfrac{3 + \sqrt{3}}{2}$ **47.** $\dfrac{42 + 6\sqrt{3}}{23}$

49. $34 + 18\sqrt{17}$ **51.** $\dfrac{45\sqrt{3} + 90}{2}$ **53.** $2 - \sqrt{10}, 2 + \sqrt{10}$
55. $\dfrac{1 - \sqrt{5}}{4}, \dfrac{1 + \sqrt{5}}{4}$ **57.** $3 - \sqrt{22}, 3 + \sqrt{22}$ **59.** 0.35 sec
61. 80 ft/sec

12.2 MIXED REVIEW (p. 721) **69.** 48
71.   **73.**

75. domain: all numbers greater than or equal to 8; range: all nonnegative numbers **77.** domain: all nonnegative numbers; range: all numbers greater than or equal to 4 **79.** domain: all numbers greater than or equal to −3; range: all nonnegative numbers

12.3 PRACTICE (pp. 725–727) **5.** 3 **7.** no solution **9.** 3
11. 25 **13.** 3 **15.** 81 **17.** no solution **19.** 225 **21.** 216
23. −567 **25.** 17 **27.** 5 **29.** −9 **31.** $13\frac{1}{5}$ **33.** 272 **35.** 40
37. no solution **39.** 5 **41.** no solution **43.** 10 **45.** 9
47. 6, 48 **49.** 64 **51.** 49 **53.** 1352 **55.** $15^2 = 225$, not −225; $x = 225$ **57.** 11.85 **59.** 17 **61.** 3, 4 **63.** 2
65. *Sample answer:* The graphs do not intersect; the graph of $y = \sqrt{11x - 30}$ is entirely in the first quadrant, while the graph of $y = -x$ is entirely in the second and fourth quadrants. **67.** 113 **69.** 160 **71.** about 66.3 min
73. By the cross product property, $ad = b^2$, so $b = \sqrt{ad}$.
75. 4 and 25

12.3 MIXED REVIEW (p. 728) **83.** $-\sqrt{11}, \sqrt{11}$ **85.** $-\dfrac{2}{5}, \dfrac{2}{5}$
87. $-\sqrt{3}, \sqrt{3}$ **89.** $4x^2 - 12x + 9$ **91.** $36y^2 - 16$
93. $4a^2 - 36ab + 81b^2$ **95.** $(x - 6)^2$ **97.** 4 **99.** −3 and 2

QUIZ 1 (p. 728)
1. Both the domain and range are all nonnegative numbers.

2. domain: all numbers greater than or equal to 9; range: all nonnegative numbers

3. domain: all numbers greater than or equal to $\dfrac{1}{2}$; range: all nonnegative numbers

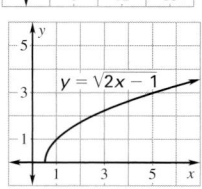

4. all nonnegative numbers, all numbers greater than or equal to $-\dfrac{2}{3}$

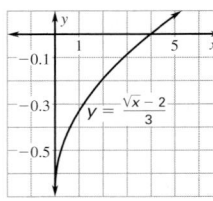

5. $18\sqrt{10}$ **6.** $-8\sqrt{7}$ **7.** $5\sqrt{5}$ **8.** $3\sqrt{6} + 3$ **9.** $32 + 10\sqrt{7}$
10. $\dfrac{40 - 5\sqrt{7}}{19}$ **11.** 144 **12.** 64 **13.** $-\dfrac{1}{3}$ **14.** 6 **15.** 7 **16.** 3
17. $1\dfrac{7}{9}$ lb/in.^{2}

12.4 PRACTICE (pp. 734–735) **3.** 100 **5.** 25 **7.** 121
9. $\dfrac{3 - \sqrt{41}}{2}, \dfrac{3 + \sqrt{41}}{2}$; choices may vary **11.** $-13, -1$
13. no solution **15.** $-\dfrac{2}{3}, -5$; factoring; the expression $3x^2 + 17x + 10$ can be factored $(3x + 2)(x + 5)$. **17.** $\dfrac{5 + \sqrt{85}}{6}$,
$\dfrac{5 - \sqrt{85}}{6}$; quadratic formula; the expression is not
factorable, and the coefficient of x is odd.
19. $\dfrac{\sqrt{6}}{3}, \dfrac{-\sqrt{6}}{3}$; finding square roots; the expression is
equivalent to $x^2 = \dfrac{2}{3}$. **21.** 16 **23.** 121 **25.** 400 **27.** $\dfrac{9}{64}$
29. 6.76 **31.** $\dfrac{1}{9}$ **33.** $-17, 1$ **35.** $2, 6$ **37.** $-\dfrac{21}{2}, -\dfrac{1}{2}$
39. $\dfrac{-3 - \sqrt{109}}{10}, \dfrac{-3 + \sqrt{109}}{10}$ **41.** $\dfrac{-1 - 2\sqrt{3}}{2}, \dfrac{-1 + 2\sqrt{3}}{2}$
43. $\dfrac{10 - \sqrt{107}}{2}, \dfrac{10 + \sqrt{107}}{2}$ **45.** $-1, 5$ **47.** $\dfrac{-3 - \sqrt{41}}{4}$,
$\dfrac{-3 + \sqrt{41}}{4}$ **49.** $\dfrac{30 - 17\sqrt{5}}{10}, \dfrac{30 + 17\sqrt{5}}{10}$ **51.** $-\sqrt{3}, \sqrt{3}$;
factoring or finding square roots; both methods are easily
applied. **53.** $\dfrac{5}{3}, -\dfrac{5}{3}$; factoring or finding square roots;
both methods are easily applied. **55.** $-11, 5$; completing
the square or factoring; $a = 1$ and b is an even number.
57. $-1 - 3\sqrt{3}, -1 + 3\sqrt{3}$ **59.** $-4, 4$
61. $\dfrac{12 - \sqrt{174}}{6}, \dfrac{12 + \sqrt{174}}{6}$ **63.** $0, 2$ **65.** $-\dfrac{3}{7}, 7$
67. $-10 - 3\sqrt{10}, -10 + 3\sqrt{10}$ **69.** $2x(x + 5) = 600$;
30 ft by 20 ft **71.** about 8.58 ft **73.** about 11.8 ft

12.4 MIXED REVIEW (p. 736) **81.** $3\dfrac{1}{7}, 3, 1$ **83.** $-\dfrac{2}{5}, -6$, none
85. $(2, 8)$ **87.** $(3, -2)$ **89.** $-3\sqrt{7}, 3\sqrt{7}$ **91.** $-6, 6$ **93.** $-\dfrac{3}{5}, \dfrac{3}{5}$
95.

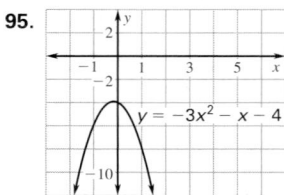

97. $-4, 8$ **99.** $-6, -5$
101. 3 **103.** $(x + 5)(x - 4)$
105. cannot be factored
107. $(2x - 3)(x + 1)$

12.5 PRACTICE (pp. 741–742) **5.** 12 **7.** 40 **9.** 37 **11.** 29
13. 5 **15.** $2\sqrt{10}$, or about 6.32 **17.** $5\sqrt{7}$, or about 13.23
19. 24, 18 **21.** 5, 10 **23.** 1, $\sqrt{2}$, or 1, about 1.41
25. Yes; $9^2 + 12^2 = 225 = 15^2$. **27.** No; $8^2 + 10^2 = 164$ and
$13^2 = 169$. **29.** Yes; $15^2 + 20^2 = 625 = 25^2$.
31. Yes; $11^2 + 60^2 = 3721 = 61^2$. **33.** Yes; $9.9^2 + 2^2 = 102.01 = 10.1^2$. **35.** hypothesis: a polygon is a square;
conclusion: it is a parallelogram **37.** hypothesis: the area
of a square is 25 sq. ft; conclusion: the length of a side is
5 ft **39.** about 116.6 ft **41.** 113.58 ft **43.** about 55.6 in.

12.5 MIXED REVIEW (p. 743)
51. **53.**

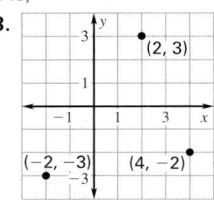

55. no x-intercepts **57.** $\dfrac{-1 - \sqrt{41}}{2}, \dfrac{-1 + \sqrt{41}}{2}$
59. $\dfrac{-3 - \sqrt{5}}{2}, \dfrac{-3 + \sqrt{5}}{2}$ **61.** $-4 - \sqrt{26}, -4 + \sqrt{26}$
63. $2 - \sqrt{5}, 2 + \sqrt{5}$ **65.** $(4x - 5)(4x + 5)$ **67.** $7(x - 2)^2$
69. $-3(4x - 9)^2$ **71.** $0.04 \le x \le 0.33$

QUIZ 2 (p. 744) **1.** $-2, 5$ **2.** $\dfrac{-1 - \sqrt{10}}{2}, \dfrac{-1 + \sqrt{10}}{2}$
3. $-1 - \sqrt{3}, -1 + \sqrt{3}$ **4.** no **5.** yes **6.** yes **7.** 13 **8.** 60
9. 16 **10.** 2000 ft

12.6 PRACTICE (pp. 748–749) **3.** Estimates may vary; 5.66
5. Estimates may vary; 6.71 **7.** yes **9.** no
11. $\left(4, -\dfrac{1}{2}\right)$ **13.** 25 yd **15.** 12.08 **17.** 8.60 **19.** 4.24
21. 9 **23.** 10.63 **25.** 2.69 **27.** no **29.** yes **31.** no
33. yes **35.** $(0, 4)$ **37.** $(3, 3)$ **39.** $(3, 5)$ **41.** $\left(-\dfrac{5}{2}, -\dfrac{5}{2}\right)$
43. $\left(-2, -\dfrac{1}{2}\right)$ **45.** $\left(-\dfrac{5}{2}, -4\right)$ **47.** Estimates may vary;
about 460 mi **51.** $(-1, 0), \left(1\dfrac{1}{2}, 0\right), \left(-\dfrac{1}{2}, -2\right)$
53. The perimeter of the original triangle, 14.78, is twice
that of the perimeter of the new triangle, 7.39.
55. You could meet at a point 1 mi east and 1 mi north of
the starting point. Both you and your friend would each
have to walk $\sqrt{13} \approx 3.6$ mi. **57.** Side $\overline{DC}$ is parallel to side
$\overline{AB}$ because both have slope 2. Sides $\overline{CB}$ and $\overline{DA}$ are not
parallel because $\overline{DA}$ has slope -3 and $\overline{CB}$ has slope $\dfrac{1}{3}$.

12.6 MIXED REVIEW (p. 750) **65.** $3x(x + 5)(x - 1)$
67. inverse variation **69.** neither **71.** $\dfrac{7x^2 - 2x}{14}$
73. $30(14) = 21x$; 20 in.

12.7 PRACTICE (pp. 755–757) **3.** $\frac{7}{25}$ **5.** $\frac{7}{24}$ **7.** $e \approx 27.16$, $f \approx 56.02$ **9.** about 459 ft; about 655 ft **11.** $\sin R = \frac{5}{13}$, $\cos R = \frac{12}{13}$, $\tan R = \frac{5}{12}$; $\sin S = \frac{12}{13}$, $\cos S = \frac{5}{13}$, $\tan S = \frac{12}{5}$ **13.** $b \approx 12.81$, $c \approx 21.29$ **15.** $x \approx 13.42$, $y \approx 19.90$ **17.** $v \approx 51.96$, $w = 60$ **19.** about 172 ft **21.** about 170 ft **23.** 11.56 km

12.7 MIXED REVIEW (p. 757) **29.** False; the opposite of a positive number is negative. **31.** $-p^2 - p$ **33.** $x^2 + 3x$ **35.** $-24x - 6x^2$ **37.** $2x^3 + 6x^2 + 15x + 6$ **39.** $5x^2 - 4x + 12$ **41.** $\frac{3}{4a + 1}$ **43.** $-\frac{13}{12x}$ **45.** $\frac{4(x-1)}{(x+1)}$

12.8 PRACTICE (pp. 761–763) **13.** Multiplication axiom of equality; Substitution property of equality
15. $a - b = a + (-b)$ Definition of subtraction
$a - b = -b + a$ Commutative property of addition
17. $a + (-1)(a) = 1(a) + (-1)(a)$ Identity property of
          multiplication
$= [1 + (-1)](a)$ Distributive property
$= (0)(a)$ Inverse property of
          addition
$= 0$ Multiplication property
          of 0
Since $a + (-1)(a) = 0$, $(-1)(a) = -a$ by definition.
19. *Sample answer*: $(1 + 2)^2 \neq 1^2 + 2^2$ **21.** *Sample answer*: 2 and 3 are integers, but $\frac{2}{3}$ is not an integer. **23.** Yes; this map shows that the proposal is false. **25.** Assume that p is an integer, p^2 is odd, and p is even. Let $p = 2n$. Then $p^2 = (2n)^2 = 4n^2 = 2(2n^2)$, an even number, which is impossible since p^2 is odd. Then p must be odd. **27.** Assume that $ac > bc$, $c > 0$, and $a \leq b$. By the multiplication property of inequality, $ac \leq bc$, which is impossible since it was given that $ac > bc$. Then $a > b$.

12.8 MIXED REVIEW (p. 764) **31.** no real solutions
33. one solution **35.** two solutions **37.** two solutions
39. two solutions **41.** not a solution **43.** not a solution
45. solution **47.** not a solution **49.** 82% **51.** 200%
53. $15.15

QUIZ 3 (p. 764) **1.** 13.42; $(4, -3)$ **2.** 10; $(2, -8)$ **3.** 16.12; $(4, -7)$ **4.** 16; $(-8, 0)$ **5.** 6; $(0, 4)$ **6.** 10.30; $\left(-\frac{3}{2}, \frac{5}{2}\right)$
7. 5; $\left(0, -\frac{3}{2}\right)$ **8.** 7.28; $\left(\frac{1}{2}, 2\right)$ **9.** 8.06; $\left(\frac{5}{2}, 0\right)$
10. $\sin A = \frac{3}{5}$, $\cos A = \frac{4}{5}$, $\tan A = \frac{3}{4}$; $\sin B = \frac{4}{5}$, $\cos B = \frac{3}{5}$, $\tan B = \frac{4}{3}$ **11.** $\sin A = \frac{15}{17}$, $\cos A = \frac{8}{17}$, $\tan A = \frac{15}{8}$; $\sin B = \frac{8}{17}$, $\cos B = \frac{15}{17}$, $\tan B = \frac{8}{15}$
12. $(a - b)c = [a + (-b)]c$ Definition of subtraction
$= a(c) + (-b)c$ Distributive property
$= ac + (-bc)$ $(-b)c = -bc$
$= ac - bc$ Definition of subtraction

13. Any real numbers a, b, and c with $a < b$ and $c \leq 0$. *Sample answer*: $a = 1$, $b = 2$, and $c = -1$: $1 < 2$, and $1(-1) > 2(-1)$. **14.** Accept any real numbers a and b with $b \neq 0$. *Sample answer*: $a = 1$ and $b = 2$; $-(1 + 2) \neq (-1) - (-2)$.

CHAPTER 12 REVIEW (pp. 766–768)
1. Both the domain and range are all nonnegative numbers.

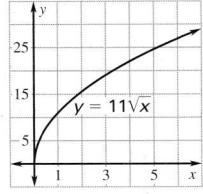

3. domain: all nonnegative numbers; range: all numbers greater than or equal to 3

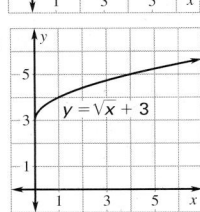

5. $6\sqrt{2} - 8\sqrt{3}$ **7.** $11 + 4\sqrt{6}$ **9.** 2 **11.** no solutions
13. $2 - 2\sqrt{3}$, $2 + 2\sqrt{3}$ **15.** $\frac{1 - \sqrt{113}}{4}$, $\frac{1 + \sqrt{113}}{4}$ **17.** 1
19. $3\sqrt{10}$, $\left(\frac{19}{2}, \frac{1}{2}\right)$ **21.** $2\sqrt{29}$, $(0, 3)$ **23.** commutative property of multiplication

CUMULATIVE PRACTICE (pp. 772–773) **1.** $\frac{m}{7} \geq 16$; $m \geq 112$
3. $t = 3\frac{2}{3}(3)$; 11 mi **5.** -2 **7.** -63 **9.** -15 **11.** $11\frac{1}{3}$
13. -49 **15.** $-1\frac{7}{11}$ **17.** -5.35 **19.** Accept any equation of the form $y = \frac{2}{3}x + b$ for any number b except -1.
21. function; domain: $-1, 1, 3, 5, 7$; range: $-1, 1, 3, 5$
23. function; domain: $-2, -1, 0, 1, 2$; range: $-2, -1, 0, 1$
25. $4x - 5y = 15$ **27.** $-\frac{5}{4} \leq x < 3$
29. $x > 3$ or $x < 2$ **31.** $(24, 21)$
33. b^6; 64 **35.** $-8a^3b^6$; -512 **37.** $\frac{4b^5}{a^4}$; 128
39. two solutions; $\frac{\sqrt{39}}{3}$, $-\frac{\sqrt{39}}{3}$ **41.** one solution; -1
43. $(x - 28)(x + 4)$ **45.** $(2x + 3)^2$ **47.** $(x - 7)^2$ **49.** $-1\frac{1}{2}$, $1\frac{2}{3}$
51. $-5, -2, 2$ **53.** $\frac{2}{3}$ **55.** $\frac{2}{x - 3}$ **57.** $\frac{1}{3x}$ **59.** $\frac{x(2x - 7)}{(x + 4)(x - 1)}$
61. $-15\sqrt{2}$ **63.** $\frac{77 + 11\sqrt{3}}{46}$ **65.** $b = 19.80$, $c = 21.36$
67. $13\frac{1}{3}$ months

SKILLS REVIEW HANDBOOK

FACTORS AND MULTIPLES (p. 778) **1.** 1, 2, 3, 6, 9, 18
3. 1, 7, 11, 77 **5.** 1, 3, 9, 27 **7.** 1, 2, 3, 6, 7, 14, 21, 42
9. 1, 2, 4, 13, 26, 52 **11.** 1, 11, 121 **13.** 3^3 **15.** 2^5
17. $5 \cdot 11$ **19.** $2^4 \cdot 3$ **21.** $2 \cdot 3^2 \cdot 5$ **23.** $3 \cdot 13$
25. $2^3 \cdot 7 \cdot 13$ **27.** 2^9 **29.** 1, 3, 5, 15 **31.** 1, 5 **33.** 1, 3, 9
35. 1, 5 **37.** 5 **39.** 1 **41.** 14 **43.** 51 **45.** 2 **47.** 29 **49.** 14
51. 1 **53.** 35 **55.** 48 **57.** 12 **59.** 420 **61.** 100 **63.** 51
65. 70 **67.** 330

COMPARING AND ORDERING NUMBERS (p. 780) **1.** <
3. > **5.** < **7.** < **9.** < **11.** > **13.** = **15.** > **17.** > **19.** >
21. > **23.** 40,071; 40,099; 45,242; 45,617 **25.** 9.003,
9.027, 9.10, 9.27, 9.3 **27.** $\frac{1}{3}, \frac{3}{8}, \frac{5}{6}, \frac{5}{4}$ **29.** $\frac{15}{16}, 1\frac{1}{8}, 1\frac{2}{5}, \frac{5}{3}, \frac{7}{4}$
31. $\frac{5}{12}, \frac{7}{8}, \frac{5}{4}, 1\frac{1}{3}$ **33.** Goran

FRACTION OPERATIONS (p. 783) **1.** $\frac{5}{6}$ **3.** $\frac{1}{3}$ **5.** $\frac{5}{8}$ **7.** $1\frac{1}{30}$
9. $2\frac{3}{8}$ **11.** $1\frac{13}{24}$ **13.** $8\frac{1}{5}$ **15.** $3\frac{7}{16}$ **17.** $\frac{1}{7}$ **19.** $1\frac{5}{7}$ **21.** 20
23. $2\frac{3}{5}$ **25.** $\frac{5}{6}$ **27.** 3 **29.** $\frac{5}{32}$ **31.** $3\frac{1}{2}$ **33.** $\frac{1}{4}$ **35.** $\frac{1}{6}$ **37.** $\frac{2}{3}$
39. $7\frac{2}{3}$ **41.** $1\frac{1}{6}$ **43.** $1\frac{1}{5}$ **45.** 6 **47.** $\frac{17}{20}$ **49.** $\frac{13}{16}$ **51.** 1 **53.** $5\frac{3}{8}$
55. $\frac{7}{18}$ **57.** $2\frac{5}{6}$ **59.** $1\frac{3}{5}$ **61.** $1\frac{11}{40}$ **63.** $\frac{11}{40}$ **65.** $9\frac{29}{48}$ in.

FRACTIONS, DECIMALS, AND PERCENTS (p. 785)
1. 0.63, $\frac{63}{100}$ **3.** 0.24, $\frac{6}{25}$ **5.** 0.17, $\frac{17}{100}$ **7.** 0.45, $\frac{9}{20}$
9. $0.\overline{3}, \frac{1}{3}$ **11.** 0.625, $\frac{5}{8}$ **13.** 0.052, $\frac{13}{250}$ **15.** 0.0012, $\frac{3}{2500}$
17. 8%, $\frac{2}{25}$ **19.** 150%, $1\frac{1}{2}$ **21.** 5%, $\frac{1}{20}$ **23.** 480%, $4\frac{4}{5}$
25. 375%, $3\frac{3}{4}$ **27.** 52%, $\frac{13}{25}$ **29.** 0.5%, $\frac{1}{200}$ **31.** 0.7, 70%
33. 0.44, 44% **35.** 0.375, 37.5% **37.** 5.125, 512.5%
39. 0.875, 87.5% **41.** 0.833, 83.3% **43.** 0.533, 53.3%
45. 1.417, 141.7%

USING PERCENT (p. 786) **1.** $16\frac{2}{3}$% **3.** 37.5% **5.** $66\frac{2}{3}$%
7. $16\frac{2}{3}$% **9.** 18.75% **11.** 9 **13.** 48 **15.** 38 **17.** 42
19. $1.04 **21.** $3.38

RATIO AND RATE (p. 787) **1.** 15 to 4 **3.** $\frac{3}{5}$ **5.** $\frac{12}{17}$ **7.** 17:3
9. 2 to 3 **11.** 15 to 7 **13.** 1 to 4 **15.** $22.50 per ticket
17. 52 miles per hour **19.** 28 miles per gallon **21.** $.10 per
minute **23.** $21.\overline{6}$ meters per second **25.** $1.12 per mile

COUNTING METHODS (p. 789) **1.** 9 outfits **3.** 56,700 pairs
5. 10,000 numbers **7.** 67,600 PINs; 58,500 PINs

PERIMETER, AREA, AND VOLUME (p. 791) **1.** 34 units
3. 84 ft **5.** 72 ft **7.** 841 yd^2 **9.** 12.25 in.^{2} **11.** 51.84 cm^2
13. 2025 km^2 **15.** 15,625 ft^3 **17.** 420 yd^3 **19.** 212 in.^{3}

DATA DISPLAYS (p. 794) **1–9 odd:** Sample answers are
given. **1.** 0–25 with increases of 5 **3.** 0–20 with increases
of 5

5. Ski Runs

7. Stock Prices
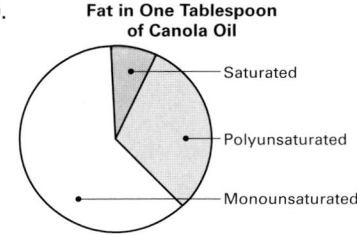

9. Fat in One Tablespoon of Canola Oil

PROBLEM SOLVING (p. 796) **1.** 5 sandwiches, 3 cartons of
milk **3.** $26.25 **5.** no later than 6:25 A.M. **7.** 10 groups
9. The problem cannot be solved; not enough information
is given.

EXTRA PRACTICE

CHAPTER 1 (p. 797) **1.** 105 **3.** 18 **5.** 526 **7.** 75 **9.** 1536
11. 216 **13.** 83 **15.** 15 **17.** 31 **19.** 7 **21.** 3 **23.** 3
25. 7 **27.** 24 **29.** solution **31.** solution **33.** solution
35. not a solution **37.** $25n - 13 = 37$

39.

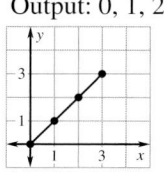

41. Input: 0, 1, 2, 3;
Output: 4.5, 5.5, 6.5, 7.5

43. Input: 0, 1, 2, 3;
Output: 0, 1, 2, 3
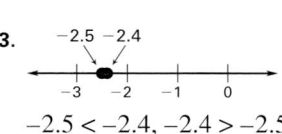

CHAPTER 2 (p. 798)
1.
$-7 < 8, 8 > -7$

3.
$-2.5 < -2.4, -2.4 > -2.5$

5. 8.5 **7.** 7 **9.** 5 **11.** -2 **13.** 3 **15.** -3 **17.** -13 **19.** 4
21. 7.3 **23.** -12 **25.** $\begin{bmatrix} 6 & 2 \\ 8 & 8 \end{bmatrix}$ **27.** $\begin{bmatrix} -3 & 2 & 10 \\ 0 & -3 & 14 \end{bmatrix}$ **29.** -45
31. $32x$ **33.** $-c^4$ **35.** $4a^4$ **37.** $4a - 24$ **39.** $-r^2 + 5r$

41. $6x^2 + 24x$ **43.** $3z - 8.4$ **45.** $3.1m$ **47.** $2 - 4t$ **49.** $6x^2 + 5$
51. $\frac{1}{2}x$ **53.** -4 **55.** $\frac{3x}{4}$ **57.** $-32x$ **59.** 66 **61.** 1 to 4

CHAPTER 3 (p. 799) **1.** 14 **3.** 16 **5.** -3 **7.** 3 **9.** 5
11. -20 **13.** $\frac{1}{3}$ **15.** -4 **17.** 4 **19.** 3 **21.** 40 **23.** $-\frac{4}{3}$
25. 1 **27.** all real numbers **29.** no solution
31. 7 in., 9 in. **33.** -7.46

35. 0.27 **37.** 1.01 **39.** $y = -x + 3$; 5, 4, 3, 2 **41.** $y = \frac{3}{2}x + \frac{3}{4}$;
$-2\frac{1}{4}, -\frac{3}{4}, \frac{3}{4}, 2\frac{1}{4}$ **43.** $y = x - 12$; $-14, -13, -12, -11$
45. \$.60 per yogurt snack **47.** 48.8 mi/h **49.** 0.75 cup
51. 64% **53.** 36%

CHAPTER 4 (p. 800)
1.   **7.**

15. $-1, -5$ **17.** $2\frac{1}{2}, -5$ **19.** $-7, 14$
21. 2, 6 **23.** 0
25. 2 **27.** -7
29. -1 **31.** $y = 3x$

33. $y = -\frac{7}{8}x$ **35.** $y = x$ **37.** $y = \frac{4}{5}x$ **39.** \$525 **41.** $y = 3$
43. $y = -4$ **45.** $y = x + 1$ **47.** $y = 3x - 4$
49. -6 **51.** 2 **53.** 3 **55.** $\frac{1}{3}$
57. not a function **59.** not a function

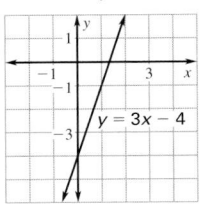

CHAPTER 5 (p. 801) **1.** $y = 2x + 1$ **3.** $y = x - 3$ **5.** $y = 3x + 3$
7. $y = 6$ **9.** $y = 4x + 11$ **11.** $y = \frac{1}{2}x - 2$ **13.** $y = 3x - 11$
15. $y = \frac{7}{5}x - 6$ **17.** $y = 7$ **19.** $y = -x + 2$
21. 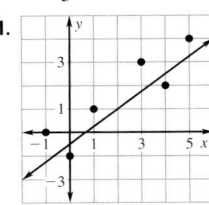 *Sample answer:* $y = \frac{3}{4}x - \frac{1}{2}$

23. $y - 3 = -2(x - 5)$; $y = -2x + 13$ **25.** $y - 4 = 5(x - 5)$;
$y = 5x - 21$ **27.** $y + 5 = -\frac{5}{3}(x + 3)$; $y = -\frac{5}{3}x - 10$

29. $y - 4 = -\frac{1}{2}(x - 2)$; $y = -\frac{1}{2}x + 5$ **31.** $3x - y = 17$
33. $3x - 4y = -3$ **35.** $y = 7$ **37.** $5x - y = -5$
39.

41. Solution may vary depending upon method used to derive the linear model; $-1°$F.

CHAPTER 6 (p. 802) **1.** $x > -9$
3. $y \le 7$ **5.** $k \le 18$ **7.** $x > -2$
9. $x \ge -12$ **11.** $x \ge -1$ **13.** $x < -2$
15. $4 \ge x > -1$ **17.** $-6 < x < 5$

19. $x > 3$ or $x \le 1$ **21.** $-14, -6$
23. 1, 7 **25.** $x \le -8$ or $x \ge 5\frac{1}{3}$ **27.**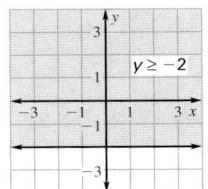

35. $2x + 1.25y \le 20$

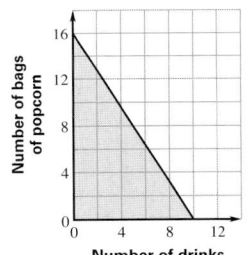

37.
1	3	6
2	1	2
3	1	3	5
4	0	1	5
5	1
6	5	6	Key: 6	5 = 65

39.
0	2	8
1	9
2	1	2	7
3	8	9	9
4	1	3	4	6	9
5	1	4	6
6	0	2	3	Key: 6	0 = 60

41. 12, 13, 13 **43.** 129, 123, 112 **45.** 16, 31, 76
47. 20, 26.5, 77 **49.**

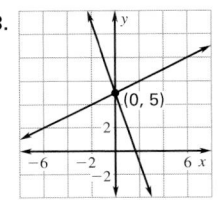

CHAPTER 7 (p. 803) **1.** $(-2, 5)$ **3.**

5. $(-1, -4)$ **7.** $(4, 5)$ **9.** $(-5, -1)$ **11.** $(6, 3)$ **13.** $\left(5\frac{1}{7}, \frac{1}{7}\right)$

15. $\left(15\frac{1}{2}, -24\right)$ **17.** $(2, 0)$ **19.** $(0, -2)$ **21.** $(13, -2)$

23. $(4, -28)$ **25.** 3 student, 5 adult **27.** Company A
29. no solution **31.** one solution, $(0, -5)$
33. infinitely many solutions **35.** no solution

37.   **41.**

CHAPTER 8 (p. 804) **1.** 7^5, or 16,807 **3.** $1728x^3$
5. $-128r^4s^8$ **7.** $675x^3y^2$ **9.** $\frac{1}{m^4}$ **11.** x^2y **13.** $\frac{x^4}{y^3}$ **15.** $6x^4$

17.   **19.** 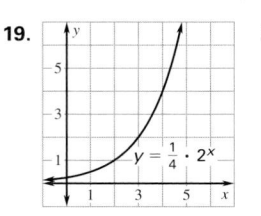 **21.** 8

23. $\frac{27x^3z^9}{8}$ **25.** $\frac{1}{10a^4bc^5}$ **27.** $\frac{25y^{17}}{x^7}$ **29.** $\frac{1}{216} \approx 0.005$

31. 31,100 **33.** 9.43 **35.** 0.0012468 **37.** 60,901,300,000
39. 3.78×10^{-2} **41.** 3.3×10^7 **43.** 2.08054×10^{-1}
45. 8.91×10^{-4} **47.** \$1791.78 **49.** \$3724.99
51. exponential decay; 0.5; 50% **53.** exponential growth;
1.04; 4% **55.** exponential decay; $\frac{2}{3}$; $33\frac{1}{3}$%
57. exponential decay; 0.68; 32%

CHAPTER 9 (p. 805) **1.** -10 **3.** -0.5 **5.** 19.47 **7.** 14.83
9. $-5, 5$ **11.** no solution **13.** $-4, 4$ **15.** $-\sqrt{3}, \sqrt{3}$

17. about 3.06 sec **19.** 168 **21.** $-84\sqrt{5}$ **23.** 2 **25.** $\frac{\sqrt{10}}{3}$

27.   **33.**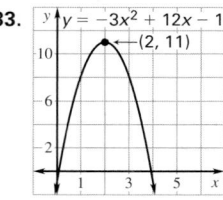

35. $-3, -2$ **37.** $-6, 6$ **39.** $-3, 3$ **41.** $-1, 3$
43. $3r^2 + 8r + 2 = 0$; $\frac{-4 - \sqrt{10}}{3}$, $\frac{-4 + \sqrt{10}}{3}$
45. $-x^2 + 5x - 4 = 0$; 1, 4
47. $2x^2 - 6x - 5 = 0$; $\frac{3 - \sqrt{19}}{2}$, $\frac{3 + \sqrt{19}}{2}$
49. $-2x^2 + x + 10 = 0$; $-2, \frac{5}{2}$ **51.** 0; one solution
53. 0; one solution **55.** -136; no real solution
57. -47; no real solution **67.** quadratic

CHAPTER 10 (p. 806) **1.** $8x^2 + 1$ **3.** $14x^2 - 7x + 8$
5. $x^2 + 9x - 4$ **7.** $4x^3 - 8x^2 + 7x$ **9.** $15b^5 - 10b^4 + 5b^2$
11. $d^2 + 4d - 5$ **13.** $x^3 + x^2 + 18$ **15.** $x^2 + 18x + 81$
17. $a^2 - 4$ **19.** $16x^2 + 40x + 25$ **21.** $4a^2 - 9b^2$
23. $-3, -6$ **25.** $1, -5$ **27.** $\frac{3}{2}, 7$ **29.** 1, 2

31. 6, 8; $(7, -1)$ 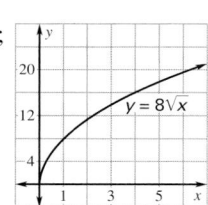 **33.** 5, 7; $(6, -1)$
35. 5, 9; $(7, 4)$
37. $-1, 3$; $(1, -4)$

39. -3 **41.** 6 **43.** 6, 9 **45.** $-4, 6$ **47.** $-2, 1\frac{1}{2}$ **49.** $-\frac{4}{3}$
51. $-\frac{3}{4}, 2$ **53.** $-2\frac{1}{3}, 8$ **55.** $(x + 1)(x - 1)$; difference of
two squares **57.** $(11 - x)(11 + x)$; difference of
two squares **59.** $(t + 1)^2$; perfect square trinomial
61. $(8y + 3)^2$; perfect square trinomial **63.** $x^2(x + 3)(x - 3)$
65. $x^2(x + 9)(x - 5)$ **67.** $-3y(y + 4)(y + 1)$ **69.** $7x^4(x^2 - 3)$
71. 2 in. by 6 in. by 15 in.

CHAPTER 11 (p. 807) **1.** $-4, 4$ **3.** 4 **5.** 6 **7.** $-6, 1$ **9.** 24
11. 21 lb **13.** 252 **15.** inverse variation; $xy = 2$

17. $\frac{2x^3}{7}$ **19.** $\frac{1}{x + 1}$ **21.** $\frac{1}{4}$ **23.** $\frac{1}{2}$ **25.** $\frac{x^2}{5}$ **27.** $\frac{5}{8x^2}$

29. $\frac{5x}{x - 8}$ **31.** $\frac{1}{x}$ **33.** $\frac{-4x - 61}{(x + 7)(x - 4)}$ **35.** $\frac{63x - 2}{18x^2}$

37. $2x^2 + x + \frac{1}{7}$ **39.** $2(2x - 1)$ **41.** $-4, 10$ **43.** 3 **45.** 6

CHAPTER 12 (p. 808)
1. all nonnegative numbers;
all nonnegative numbers
3. all numbers greater
than or equal to -3;
all nonnegative numbers

5. all numbers greater than or equal to 2; all nonnegative
numbers **7.** all numbers greater than or equal to $-\frac{2}{3}$;
all nonnegative numbers **9.** $5\sqrt{5}$ **11.** $16\sqrt{2}$
13. $7\sqrt{3} - 3\sqrt{2}$ **15.** $\frac{\sqrt{6}}{3}$ **17.** 121 **19.** 5 **21.** 2, 6

23. $-14, 4$ **25.** 2, 5 **27.** $\frac{6 - \sqrt{111}}{5}$, $\frac{6 + \sqrt{111}}{5}$ **29.** $c = \sqrt{2}$

31. $a = 8$ **33.** $a = 20$ **35.** 4.12; $\left(2, 4\frac{1}{2}\right)$ **37.** 5; $(2.5, -2)$

39. 8; $(3, -6)$ **41.** 18.36; $\left(4, -2\frac{1}{2}\right)$ **43.** $\sin D = \frac{4}{5}$, $\cos D = \frac{3}{5}$,
$\tan D = \frac{4}{3}$; $\sin E = \frac{3}{5}$, $\cos E = \frac{4}{5}$, $\tan E = \frac{3}{4}$ **45.** $\sin D = \frac{\sqrt{2}}{2}$,
$\cos D = \frac{\sqrt{2}}{2}$, $\tan D = 1$; $\sin E = \frac{\sqrt{2}}{2}$, $\cos E = \frac{\sqrt{2}}{2}$, $\tan E = 1$

47. $a = 25.37$, $b = 9.23$ **49.** any nonzero numbers b and c
and any nonzero number a except 1

MATHEMATICS REFERENCE SHEET

Area

 Triangle $A = \frac{1}{2}bh$

 Rectangle $A = lw$

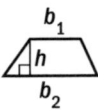 **Trapezoid** $A = \frac{1}{2}h(b_1 + b_2)$

 Parallelogram $A = bh$

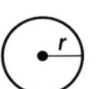 **Circle** $A = \pi r^2$

Key

b = base	d = diameter
h = height	r = radius
l = length	A = area
w = width	C = circumference
ℓ = slant height	V = volume
$S. A.$ = surface area	

Use 3.14 or $\frac{22}{7}$ for π.

Circumference

$$C = \pi d = 2\pi r$$

	Volume	**Total Surface Area**
Right Circular Cone	$V = \frac{1}{3}\pi r^2 h$	$S.A. = \frac{1}{2}(2\pi r)\ell + \pi r^2 = \pi r\ell + \pi r^2$
Square Pyramid	$V = \frac{1}{3}l^2 h$	$S.A. = 4\left(\frac{1}{2}l\ell\right) + l^2 = 2l\ell + l^2$
Sphere	$V = \frac{4}{3}\pi r^3$	$S.A. = 4\pi r^2$
Right Circular Cylinder	$V = \pi r^2 h$	$S.A. = 2\pi rh + 2\pi r^2$
Rectangular Solid	$V = lwh$	$S.A. = 2(lw) + 2(hw) + 2(lh)$

In the following formulas, n represents the number of sides:

In a polygon, the sum of the measures of the interior angles is equal to $180(n - 2)$.

In a regular polygon, the measure of an interior angle is equal to $\frac{180(n - 2)}{n}$.